Human Resource
Management
in a Business Context

3rd edition

Human Resource
Management
in a Business Context

3rd edition

ALAN PRICE

SOUTH-WESTERN
CENGAGE Learning™

Australia · Brazil · Japan · Korea · Mexico · Singapore · Spain · United Kingdom · United States

SOUTH-WESTERN
CENGAGE Learning

Human Resource Management in a Business Context, Third Edition
Alan Price

Publishing Director: John Yates

Publisher: Pat Bond

Edotorial Assistant: Leandra Paoli

Production Editor: Fiona Freel

Manufacturing Manager: Helen Mason

Senior Production Controller: Maeve Healy

Marketing Director: Rossella Proscia

Typesetter: Photoprint, Torquay, UK

Cover design: Keith Marsh, Fink Creative

Text design: Design Deluxe Ltd, Bath, UK

For product information and technology assistance, contact **emea.info@cengage.com**.

For permission to use material from this text or product, and for permission queries, email **clsuk.permissions@cengage.com**

British Library Cataloguing-in-Publication Data
A catalogue record for this book is available from the British Library.

ISBN: 978-1-84480-548-8

Cengage Learning EMEA
High Holborn House, 50-51 Bedford Row
London WC1R 4LR

Cengage Learning products are represented in Canada by Nelson Education Ltd.

For your lifelong learning solutions, visit
www.cengage.co.uk

Purchase e-books or e-chapters at:
http://estore.bized.co.uk

Printed by Seng Lee Press, Singapore
3 4 5 6 7 8 9 10 – 10 09

Brief **contents**

Contents

List of **figures**

List of **tables**

List of **case studies**

Acknowledgments

My thanks are due to past colleagues, students and website visitors from many countries who helped me develop and test the contents of this book. I am indebted to a number of people at Cengage Learning who have contributed to its production, especially Jennifer Pegg who commissioned this edition, and James Clark who saw it through to fruition. I am also grateful to Claire Martin of Photoprint for her highly professional management of the copy editing, typesetting, proofreading and other work needed to produce the final print files. Lastly, despite major changes and additions over the years, it must be stated that this book still benefits from the rigorous and supportive editorial advice provided for the first edition by Eugene McKenna and David Needle.

Reviewer acknowledgments

Dave Doughty, Nottingham Trent University
Margaret Heffernan, Dublin City University Business School
Nicolina Kamenou, Heriot-Watt University
Dr Louise Preget, University of Bournemouth
Aarti Vyas-Brannick, Manchester Metropolitan University

Preface

This book is intended to provide a comprehensive account of the critical issues in human resource management (HRM), taking the reader from an introductory level to a relatively sophisticated understanding of an increasingly important business topic.

We will see that there is no universal agreement on the meaning of HRM. In fact, there are varying and contradictory models. Yet they embody common elements that distinguish them from previous approaches to managing people – specifically, personnel management.

The book takes a distinctive approach, locating the subject of human resource management and its various perspectives within a business context. We recognize that readers will come from a variety of backgrounds, that some will become HR specialists, but that many are interested in the relationship between human resource management and other business functions. This is not a 'cookbook' of best practices: it is firmly focused on human resource management in the real world. Accordingly, we set out to understand the role and meaning of HRM from a number of practical and theoretical perspectives.

Framework for the book

The material in this text has a systematic framework with which we explore the complexities involved in managing people at work. There are four levels of discussion: environmental, organizational, strategic and operational. At the environmental level we see that the activities of people managers are constrained by a number of factors. For example:

- The economy, affecting business growth and, subsequently, the balance between demand and availability of employees.
- The actions of government and supranational structures such as the European Union (EU) and the North American Free Trade Agreement (NAFTA).
- Legislation on a wide range of employment issues, including hours, diversity, working conditions, minimum pay, redundancy rights, consultation, and so on.
- Competing demands from stakeholders such as customers, trade unions, shareholders and senior managers.

At the organizational level, the dimensions of size, structure and culture constrain and sometimes determine the way in which HRM takes place. Organizations range from one-person 'start-ups' to transnationals employing hundreds of thousands of people. As a consequence, HRM can vary from simply managing individuals at a very human level to the strategic and logistical issues involved in controlling vast numbers. Not surprisingly, HRM in small businesses tends to be commonsensical, with an emphasis on solving day-to-day problems. People management is a natural part of the owner–manager's role, along with finance, production, marketing, customer service and everything else.

By contrast, large organizations require a more sophisticated and structured human resource function. Even where the notion of HRM as an integrated approach has been adopted as a strategy, with operational responsibility delegated to line managers, there is likely to be a major role for a specialist HR function. Such a function may be focused on coordination with operational activities such as resourcing, counselling, employee relations, communications and training/development provided on an in-house or external consultancy basis.

The next level – strategic decisionmaking – is particularly relevant for this topic since HRM is often viewed as a strategic alternative to traditional personnel management. Employees are a major cost to organizations of any size. Hence decisions about employee requirements are strategic issues with important consequences for the profitability and growth of organizations.

The final (operational) level encompasses the activities of people managers, including recruitment and selection procedures, performance assessment, training and development, and employee relations. Increasingly, these aspects may be outsourced to external providers or delivered through modern web technologies. In this volume we see that they are individually important but also form part of a much wider approach to managing people.

Learning features

The book includes a number of features to help students make the most of this text as a key element in their learning experience:

- *Learning objectives* – the main learning outcomes that a student should aim to achieve from each chapter.
- *Key concepts* – highlighted concepts of considerable significance in understanding HRM and related topics.
- *HRM in reality* – boxed articles relating the topic under discussion to human resource management in the real world. This third edition includes over a hundred new articles, each with a discussion question.
- *Tables and figures* – providing detailed information and graphical representation of major concepts.
- *Chapter summaries* – brief outlines of the content and main points in each chapter.
- *Further reading* – suggested articles and books providing greater depth and alternative perspectives on chapter topics.
- *Review questions* – to check understanding of the principal issues raised in every chapter.
- *Case studies for discussion and analysis* – provided at the end of each chapter, designed to stimulate critical analysis, discussion and reflection on the issues raised.
- *Glossary* – alphabetical list of key terms used in the book with succinct explanations for easy reference.

Plan of the book

The book is divided into nine parts, each composed of a number of related chapters, and a conclusion. Part one addresses the development and scope of HRM as a philosophy of people management, critically examining the claim that it is a coherent and integrated approach to managing people. Part two also addresses the link between HRM and 'high-performance' or 'high-commitment' management, and the effects of new technology on its practice.

The chapters in Parts two to four take us through the environmental, organizational and strategic levels, also covering the employment market, human resource planning, organizational change and the nature of resourcing decisions in some detail. The remainder of the book, Parts five to nine, addresses the key activity areas, including recruitment and selection, the management of diversity, performance management, reward management, human resource development and employee relations. Finally, the conclusion evaluates the effectiveness of HRM in real organizations and its likely development in the future.

Each chapter includes a number of boxed articles designed to illustrate particular themes within a real-life context. The flavour of reality is emphasized throughout the book with references to contemporary issues in the media and debate in academic journals. HRM really happens out there – even if it is labelled as 'economics', 'labour' or 'industrial relations'.

Related websites

This text benefits from companion websites:

- www.cengage.co.uk/price3 includes additional questions and case studies for students and PowerPoint™ slides and an instructors' manual for lecturers.

- Sites in HRM Guide Network (http://www.hrmguide.net) – one of the largest and most comprehensive sources of human resource management information available on the Internet. HRM Guide is international in its scope with separate sections for a number of countries, including Australia, Canada, New Zealand, the United Kingdom and the United States of America. This is regularly updated with new articles and also provides direct links to human resource journals, societies, associations and business organizations throughout the world.

Alan Price, September 2006

Walk-through tour

Part one
Introduction to HRM

The first part of *Human Resource Management* introduces you to the essential elements of HRM, its origins and applications. HRM is viewed as an all-embracing term describing a number of distinctive approaches to people management. Part one helps you to understand and evaluate the different and sometimes ambiguous views of human resource management by investigating its origins, explanatory models, technology and practice.

The chapters in Part one address a number of specific issues:

- Where do the fundamental concepts of HRM come from?
- What distinguishes HRM from other approaches to managing people – particularly personnel management?
- Is HRM here to stay or is it just another management fad?
- Is HRM a coherent and integrated approach to managing people?
- How prevalent is HRM?
- What is the link between HRM and high performance?
- HRM and knowledge management.
- How has technology changed the practice and delivery of HRM?
- Does its use lead to greater organizational effectiveness?

Part opener Each part of the book has an opening section summarizing the content and structure of the following chapters, and also listing key issues addressed in the part.

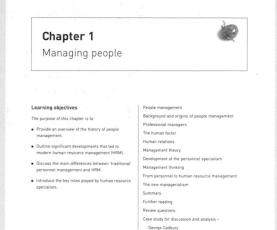

Chapter 1
Managing people

Learning objectives

The purpose of this chapter is to:

- Provide an overview of the history of people management.
- Outline significant developments that led to modern human resource management (HRM).
- Discuss the main differences between 'traditional' personnel management and HRM.
- Introduce the key roles played by human resource specialists.

People management
Background and origins of people management
Professional managers
The human factor
Human relations
Management theory
Development of the personnel specialism
Management thinking
From personnel to human resource management
The new managerialism
Summary
Further reading
Review questions
Case study for discussion and analysis – George Cadbury

Chapter opener Every chapter opens with a list of learning objectives that you should have acquired after studying the chapter, and also an outline of the chapter content.

---

have fax, e-mail and postal facilities to send information, confirmations, follow-up queries and printed brochures to users. They are also monitored in the same way as conventional call centres and can generate useful statistics on types and frequency of enquiries. Walker contends that most reports show that organizations find HR service centres to be highly cost-effective and provider faster and more consistent answers than traditional HR departments.

6 *Human resource information systems (HRIS) and databases.* According to Walker (2001, pp.8–9): 'The HRIS system is the primary transaction processor, editor, record-keeper, and functional application system which lies at the heart of all computerized HR work. It maintains employee, organizational and HR plan data sufficient to support most, if not all, of the HR functions depending on the modules installed.' It will also supply information to other systems and generate reports.

7 *Stand-alone HR systems.* A massive choice of applications are available from commercial vendors which can be linked to a HRIS. They include online application forms, tests, appraisal databases, 360-degree performance assessments and so on.

8 *Data-marts and data-warehouses.* Sources of information, usually held as relational databases which can be interrogated. Data-marts normally hold data from single sources, such as HR; data-warehouses amass information from multiple sources.

HRM in reality HR executives still not making the most of HR technology

Human resource self-service offers many advantages in terms of cost and efficiency but many HR executives are still concentrating on routine transactions and are not reaping the benefits of available technology, according to the findings of the HR service delivery survey by Towers Perrin, a global professional services firm.

Tom Keebler, principal and author of the study said:

With increased technological efficiencies and options in recent years, HR professionals have an opportunity to make greater gains and realize better results than they have in the past. But it takes more than good technology to optimize service delivery as a strategic management tool, as opposed to simply a basic HR transaction. Other requirements include effective long- and short-term planning, updated processes, and a focus on the larger workforce needs of the organization. Simply stated, implementing out of the box HR technologies just isn't enough.

HR technologies have developed beyond payroll and staffing rotas to the point where they can now support workforce effectiveness in new and increasingly efficient ways. Most growth areas in HR technology fall under the umbrella of talent management. Organizations can expand applications that help attract and hire employees, for example:

- recruiting
- job posting and 'onboarding' solutions
- employee retention
- career development and online learning

- rewarding staff via online performance management and reward portals
- engagement with recognition programmes and online training opportunities.

HR systems
Ninety per cent of the 244 large and mid-size organizations surveyed in 2005 used a vendor-purchased human resource system with Oracle/PeopleSoft continuing to be dominant. Just over a half (51 per cent) of organizations reported equal spending of HR technology in 2005 compared with 2004, while almost a quarter (24 per cent) had higher levels of spending and an additional 10 per cent said they had much higher spending on HR technology. The survey found that enterprise resource planning (ERP) applications most likely to be implemented in 2006 included:

- both employee and manager self-service in reward and compensation management
- learning applications (in SAP), and
- recruiting applications (in PeopleSoft).

Employee self-service
Employee self-service (ESS) is now a widely used and successful method of HR service delivery. At least 80 per cent of companies surveyed used self-service in 2006 to help employees enroll in annual benefits, view benefit plans and policies, access wellness information, view pension contributions, change personal data, view pay stubs and view job postings. Most of the larger

'HRM in reality' boxes HRM concepts are brought to life in every chapter with real recent examples of HRM practice from all around the world.

---

companies had these features in place in 2004 but smaller organizations have lagged behind although they are now catching up quickly.

Having reached the limit of benefits from simple transaction-based ESS, a number of organizations reported that they had moved on to the implementation of new, and largely unprecedented, ESS-based processes. They said these were complex and dealt with tasks previously handled by HR generalists with specific subject matter knowledge.

ESS promises to free up time that can be devoted to strategic, business objective-aligned pursuits. While employees gained an average of nearly 2 per cent less work, ESS reduced the workloads of HR generalists/specialists by an average of 15 per cent.

These results demonstrate the clear need for organizations to identify new roles, responsibilities and tasks for the HR function if they want to reap the rewards of HR technology, added Keebler. 'But equally important, the HR team has to be ready, willing and able to take on these new roles.'

Manager self-service
Manager self-service (MSS) has not taken off so quickly, but the momentum is accelerating. Three-fifths (60 per cent) of respondents said that their organizations would be providing self-service to managers in 2006, covering:

- planning annual merit and base salary changes
- viewing employee data history

- initiating and approving job requisitions
- posting jobs
- viewing applicant resumés.

Managers have found ESS relatively easy to use but they have had some difficulties in the areas of MSS. However, when MSSs are properly used, they can reduce the HR generalist/specialist workload for these activities by over 21 per cent. Managers were more concerned with factors such as level of data edits and validations required, usability of tools, improved processing time, and the level of change management and communication at rollout than with any reduction in their own workload. According to Tower Perrin's media release: 'The better the tools given to managers, and the more an organization helps them to embrace the tools, the more receptive they will be to them – regardless of the impact on their workload.'

Said Keebler:

It's not enough to 'plug and play'. HR leadership needs to carefully examine how employees and managers will use the system, what additional information will be needed, what checks and balances should be created and installed, and the role that HR itself will play in the new world of self-service – from running the system to leading users through the change.

What factors appear to be holding back the full implementation of human resource information systems?

Source: HRM Guide USA (http://www.hrmguide.com) 3 April, 2006.

HR professionals and the HR system

The pressure is on for proactive HR innovations that contribute directly to the bottom-line or improve employee morale and efficiency. Ajuwon (2002) points out that the typical HR professional gets involved with one step in many different flows of work. Very often the involvement of HR has no purpose except to validate the process in some way and acts as an interruption to the flow of work. In other words, the HR function is a 'gatekeeper for information that's been deemed too highly classified for the data owner'.

So HR is not actually making a measurable contribution – in fact, quite the opposite. HR involvement creates a queue or delay in the process. We should ask if the HR involvement is really necessary. Once upon a time the HR _____ – probably because it was paper-based. But now tec[**management**]us portions of the database. So an employee can sa _____nk account details, while the ability to change certain appraisal details might be confined to the line manager. In either case, there is no reason for HR to be involved. HR should move on from the role of intermediary.

Nor surprisingly, the use of employee self-service systems for records, information, payroll and other functions is becoming increasingly common. Libraries of forms can be kept online to be downloaded as and when required. Wiki technology, similar to that used for the online Wikipedia encyclopaedia, allows in-house 'experts' to collectively build a HR knowledge database or employee manual on an incremental basis as procedures change. Systems can be

Glossary terms are defined at the back of the book and highlighted where they first appear in the text.

Development of the personnel specialism

Personnel management has been a recognized function in the USA since NCR opened a personnel office in the 1890s. American personnel managers worked within a *unitarist* tradition, identifying closely with the objectives of their *organization* (Key concept 1.3). It was natural for HRM to emerge comparatively smoothly from this perspective.

In other countries, the personnel management function arrived more slowly and came via a number of routes. Moreover, its orientation was not entirely managerial. In the UK, for example, its origins can be traced to the 'welfare officers' employed by Quaker-owned companies such as Cadbury. At an early stage it became evident that there was an inherent conflict between their activities and those of line managers. They were not seen to have a philosophy compatible with the worldview of senior managers. The welfare officer orientation placed personnel management as a buffer between the business and its employees. In terms of 'organizational politics' this was not a politically viable position for individuals wishing to further their careers, increase their status and earn high salaries.

> **Key concept 1.3** Unitarism
>
> A managerialist stance which assumes that everyone in an organization is a member of a team with a common purpose. It embodies a central concern of HRM – that an organization's people, whether managers or lower-level employees, should share the same objectives and work together harmoniously. From this perspective, conflicting objectives are seen as negative and dysfunctional. By definition it is the opposite of pluralism (the acceptance of several alternative approaches, interests or goals within the same organization or society. Arguably, in the field of HRM, unitarism represents a US tradition, whereas pluralism is more typical of European attitudes towards people management.

Tyson (1989) distinguished between three 'types' of personnel management jobs:

- *'Clerk of works'*: The majority, involved in the routine of administration, record-keeping, letter-writing, setting up interviews and welfare matters. Reports to personnel or senior line manager.
- *'Contracts manager'*: Likely to be found in large organizations with formal industrial relations structures. Involved in detailed short-term policy-making and resolving problems. A 'fixer' with some degree of influence on trade unions and senior management.
- *'Architect'*: Probably highly qualified but not necessarily in 'personnel'. Broad portfolio with a significant strategic role. A business manager first and personnel manager second.

The second tradition – industrial relations – further compounded this distinction between personnel and other managers. In the acrimonious industrial relations climate prevailing in many developed countries throughout much of the 20th century, personnel/industrial relations managers played an intermediary role between unions and line management. Their function was legitimized by their role – or, at least, their own perception of that role – as 'honest brokers'.

But from the 1980s onwards governments with a neo-liberal or free market orientation, such as Mrs Thatcher's administration in the UK, reined in union freedom severely. Overall, there was a marked reduction in the importance of collective bargaining throughout any English-speaking countries. The perceived importance of collective bargaining reduced as managerial power increased. Trade union membership declined along with centralized pay bargaining and other forms of collective negotiation – and with them, the importance of the personnel manager with negotiating experience. The focus switched from the collective to

Key concepts  Essential HRM terminology is simply and concisely explained at relevant points in every chapter.

Summary

The meaning and prevalence of HRM are topics that continue to attract debate and disagreement. As a consequence, practitioners and textbook authors use a diverse and sometimes contradictory range of interpretations. We found that HRM has a variety of definitions but there is general agreement that it has a closer fit with business strategy than previous models. specifically personnel management. The early models of HRM take either a 'soft' or a 'hard' approach, but this may be a simplistic distinction as economic circumstances are more likely to drive the choice than any question of humanitarianism. The status of HRM is also problematic, with a range of views on the value and purpose of the profession.

Further reading

Human Resource Management: A Critical Text edited by John Storey (2nd edition, Thomson Learning, 2001) provides a wide-ranging and authoritative account of the origins and development of HRM. David Ulrich's *Human Resource Champions* Harvard Business Press (1997), has been a best-seller among practitioners and outlines much of his thinking on the key roles of the HR function. *The Future of Human Resource Management: 64 Thought Leaders Explore the Critical HR Issues of Today and Tomorrow*, edited by Michael R. Losey, Sue Meisinger and Dave Ulrich (2nd edition, Wiley, 2006) is a compilation of articles by an international panel of expert contributors who offer their views on the state of HR and what to expect in the future.

Review questions

1. Is HRM a fashion or is it here to stay? What is the probability that HRM will be the dominant framework for people management in the 21st century?
2. Compare and contrast the textbook and practitioner definitions of HRM. In what ways (if any) are they different?
3. Evaluate the following statement: 'HRM is in reality a symbolic label behind which lurk multifarious practices, many of which are not mutually dependent on one another' (Storey, 1992).
4. Is managing people just a matter of commonsense? If so, what value can we attach to theories and models?
5. What do you understand by the statement that 'functions should be managed as a whole, and not as stand-alone activities'?
6. Given Cakar and Bititci's criticism, how useful are 'typologies' of HRM such as Legge's?
7. Evaluate the contributions of Fitz-Enz, Pfeffer and Ulrich towards understanding the purpose of human resource management. Are they stating anything beyond the obvious?
8. Do you consider that the Harvard 4Cs model can give us a complete evaluation of HRM in a particular organization?
9. What do you understand by the concept of 'stakeholder'?
10. The Harvard model of HRM is an idealistic representation of people management. In the real world it is bound to be displaced by harder models of HRM. Do you agree or disagree with these statements?
11. HRM theorists argue that employees are assets and not just costs. What does this mean in practice?
12. What are the main differences between the Harvard and Michigan models?
13. Compare and contrast the 'hard' and 'soft' forms of HRM. Is this a useful distinction?

Case study for discussion and analysis

Read the following case study. Trace the main ways in which the management of people has changed during IBM's history.

Summary, further reading and review questions Each chapter concludes with a brief review of the chapter content, a list of related reading material, and a set of questions to test your understanding of the chapter.

Human resource management at IBM

Origins

IBM was originally formed as Computing Tabulating and Recording (CTR), a combination of three companies put together by Charles Flint, a former arms dealer. Flint recruited Thomas Watson, who became its chairman in 1924. Watson renamed the company International Business Machines in 1929. IBM had a long history of dominance: at this early stage it already had 95 per cent of the market in punched-card machines – a mechanical predecessor of the electronic computer.

Watson had previously worked for NCR and had a reputation for aggressive sales activity – to the extent that he had been indicted in an anti-trust suit. From these inauspicious beginnings, however, Watson modelled a sales force on a highly ethical basis. He required his staff to behave in an 'honest, fair and square way'. This sober behaviour was expected at home as well as work and included wearing the familiar dark suits and white shirts. The company benefits included lifetime employment and IBM country clubs which developed a collective feeling. Company songs and slogans (such as THINK) were encouraged and inculcated at company training schools.

This approach was eventually transmitted to Japan. In the 1950s, Japanese management style was deliberately modelled on IBM by the Ministry of International Trade and Industry (MITI) who found the IBM way eulogized in American business textbooks. Ironically, the company resembled civil service organizations more than other industrial corporations. Its style was paternalist and hierarchical, offering employment for life and excellent career paths for its brightest workers.

Computing began in Britain and the USA in the 1940s and the first significant commercial product, Remington Rand's UNIVAC, was launched in the early 1950s. IBM entered the market soon afterwards and used its powerful resources to take a leading position. Under Watson's son, Thomas J. Watson Jr., IBM and computing became virtually synonymous, controlling 70 per cent of the world market in the 1960s. Big Blue became one of the largest corporations in the world, its international workforce reaching a peak of 405 000 in 1985.

IBM's overwhelming control of the computing industry was symbolic of the USA's technological and economic dominance in the post-war world. The strength was based on an integrated product range of highly expensive mainframe computers, peripherals and software which locked users into IBM once they had made their initial purchase. Gradually, however, cracks

appeared in this dominance. Despite being an IBM invention, the personal computer liberated individual users from the mainframe. PC 'clones' were supplied more cheaply by competitors with much lower overheads. PCs became more powerful, not just because of increasingly faster processing chips but also from the software this speed allowed. Profitability moved from the mainframe sector to the PC, and particularly to software producers such as Microsoft.

People management

IBM was traditionally a non-unionized organization. In fact the corporation was accused of being anti-union – but most of its staff seemed to like it that way. An ACAS survey in 1977 showed that only 4.9 per cent of the company's British employees wanted a union, with 91 per cent saying they would refuse to join if there were one. For half a century its culture was strongly based on lifetime employment and excellent working conditions. The company did not possess a formal system of employee relations as such: the nature of the employment relationship was implicit in the corporation's human resource policies. Needle (1994: p.332) describes these as taking the form of:

- A sophisticated system of human resource planning, recruitment and training.
- A system of lifetime employment in which staff changed their jobs as and when required by the organization.
- Equal status for all IBM employees in terms of fringe benefits, staff restaurants and other facilities, although company cars were restricted to senior management and some sales staff.
- Centrally determined salaries, geared to bettering those of competitors and reviewed annually; increases based on a performance objective system.
- Considerable emphasis on training, particularly related to people management and averaging 40 days a year for managers.
- An audit of staff opinion held every year, focused on attitudes towards work methods, HR practices, pay and conditions.
- A model HRM approach with decisionmaking and people management delegated to line managers at the lowest possible level.
- Formal communication procedures designed to encourage debate at business problems and to allow aggrieved staff to appeal against local management decisions.

Case studies for discussion and analysis Case studies situated at the end of each chapter present realistic challenging HRM scenarios inviting you to analyze the situation and discuss potential solutions.

By the early 1990s, however, IBM was in serious trouble. The company had been cutting costs for six years under the chairmanship of John Akers, a lifelong IBM man in his late 50s. A former navy pilot, he joined IBM as a sales representative and was soon identified as senior management material. Silver-haired and youthful, he was the image of the IBM corporate employee. The severity of the problem and Akers' bleak assessment of sales performance and poor productivity came to light in 1991. A middle-manager who attended a confidential briefing inadvertently distributed his summary of the meeting through IBM's internal electronic mail network. This soon brought the media spotlight on the corporation, publicizing Akers' attempts to correct the situation. One failure was the recruitment of 5000 additional sales representatives, to boost the existing 20 000, which increased revenues by less than 4 per cent. He then announced 14 000 job cuts, increased to 17 000 shortly afterwards. In IBM-speak these were referred to as 'management-initiated-separation' (MIS). Some 47 000 IBM employees had already had an MIS experience over the previous five years but the latest announcement would still leave the company with a worldwide workforce of over 350 000.

The media and industry analysts increasingly criticized the momentum of change. Forecasts of reduced profits and drastic turnover led to calls for more radical action. IBM's strong points, its culture and structure, had apparently become its major weaknesses. The company was described as insular and complacent, slow to react to the move away from large expensive mainframe computers to powerful PCs and workstations.

IBM's bureaucratic decisionmaking structure dragged down its ability to react at a time when the industry was becoming increasingly fast moving. Whereas a local office in Europe, for example, had to refer to its regional head office and possibly to New York, competitors could take the initiative immediately. Procedures which functioned adequately when product development had a four-year cycle were hopelessly ineffective when the lead time had shrunk to a year. IBM had a tradition of producing virtually everything in-house, further increasing its insularity and inability to react quickly to market changes.

A loss of over US$4 billion in 1992 led to Akers' replacement by the first outsider, Louis Vincent Gestner, destined to take the serious decisions which Wall Street analysts had demanded. Despite making IBM's first-ever job cuts the conclusion had been that Akers was too imbued in the IBM culture to be able to take sufficiently drastic measures.

New broom sweeps . . .

Louis Vincent Gestner Jr, 51, was appointed chairman in April 1993 with no experience of running a computer business. Gestner, a devout Catholic, was the son of a truck dispatcher from Long Island. He started his career with management consultants McKinsey after Harvard Law School and later became head of RJR Nabisco. There will be no pussyfooting, no more salami-slicing,' he told shareholders a month later. He quickly hired two experienced cost-cutters as aides: Jerome York, former chief financial officer of Chrysler; and Gerald Czarnecki, who had implemented reductions in staff at Honolulu's HonFed bank. Gestner listed four immediate priorities:

- major staff reductions, reducing IBM's workforce worldwide to about 250 000 and including the first compulsory redundancies in the company's history
- defining IBM's core areas
- improving customer relations
- decentralization.

In 1993 Gestner announced a record quarterly loss of US$8 billion that included an US$8.9 billion charge for laying off 50 000 employees that year – double the previous estimates. Gestner said: 'Getting IBM's costs and expense structure in line with the revenue realities of our industry – right-sizing the company – is my highest near-term priority.' But he declined to break up IBM's eight product groups and disappointed stock market analysts, who were looking for more radical surgery.

One key element of cost was, of course, the company payroll. Gestner's team made significant changes to IBM's compensation (pay) plan:

- *Look to the marketplace.* The single salary structure (for non-sales employees) was changed to different salary structures with merit budgets for different job families. This allowed IBM to pay employees in different job families according to market-oriented rates.
- *Fewer, faster jobs in a flatter organization.* The traditional salary grades were scrapped in the USA, and the number of separate job titles cut from over 5000 to less than 1200.
- *Reward for performance.* The old compensation plan based pay raises on a complex formula linking performance assessments to salary increases measured in tenths of 1 per cent. Under the new system, managers were given a budget and told to differentiate between the pay given to 'stars' and 'acceptable performers' on the grounds that otherwise the stars would not stay too long.

About the website

Visit the *Human Resource Management in a Business Context* 3e companion website at **www.cengage.co.uk/price3** to find valuable teaching and learning material including:

For students

- Link to relevant websites related to chapter material
- Multiple-choice questions to test your understanding

For lecturers

- An Instructors' Manual including teaching material built around the textbook content
- Case study notes to complement each end of chapter case study
- PowerPoint™ slides to accompany each chapter of the book

Further resources

- ExamView® – This testbank and test generator provides a huge amount of different types of questions, allowing lecturers to create online, paper and local area network (LAN) tests. This CD-based product is available only from your Thomson sales representative.
- This textbook is also available in eBook format, please visit the companion website for further details.

Part one
Introduction to HRM

The first part of *Human Resource Management* introduces you to the essential elements of HRM, its origins and applications. HRM is viewed as an all-embracing term describing a number of distinctive approaches to people management. Part one helps you to understand and evaluate the different and sometimes ambiguous views of human resource management by investigating its origins, explanatory models, technology and practice.

The chapters in Part one address a number of specific issues:

- Where do the fundamental concepts of HRM come from?

- What distinguishes HRM from other approaches to managing people – particularly personnel management?

- Is HRM here to stay or is it just another management fad?

- Is HRM a coherent and integrated approach to managing people?

- How prevalent is HRM?

- What is the link between HRM and high performance?

- HRM and knowledge management.

- How has technology changed the practice and delivery of HRM?

- Does its use lead to greater organizational effectiveness?

Chapter 1
Managing people

Learning objectives

The purpose of this chapter is to:

- Provide an overview of the history of people management.

- Outline significant developments that led to modern human resource management (HRM).

- Discuss the main differences between 'traditional' personnel management and HRM.

- Introduce the key roles played by human resource specialists.

People management

In this chapter we set out to understand the purpose of **human resource management**, how it developed and the range of tasks covered by human resource specialists. Arguably, HRM has become the dominant approach to people management throughout much of the world. But it is important to stress that HRM has not 'come out of nowhere'. There is a long history of attempts to achieve an understanding of human behaviour in the workplace. For a century and more, practitioners and academics have developed theories and practices to explain and influence human behaviour at work. HRM has absorbed ideas and techniques from a wide range of these theories and practical tools. In effect, HRM is a synthesis of themes and concepts drawn from a long history of work, more recent management theories and social science research.

Over and over again, managers must deal with events that are clearly similar but also different enough to require fresh thinking. For example:

- businesses expand or fail
- they innovate or stagnate
- they may be exciting or unhappy organizations in which to work
- finance has to be obtained
- workers have to be recruited
- new equipment is purchased, eliminating old procedures and introducing new methods
- staff must be reorganized, retrained or dismissed.

Some items we have listed are clearly to do with people management (for example, recruiting or reorganizing staff). Others – such as innovation or stagnation – are less obviously so. However, they are likely to be affected by having trained, motivated people with suitable skills in place. Some seem irrelevant to HRM, and you might have identified 'raising finance' in this category. But compare two businesses: one has an excellent industrial relations record with no strikes or disputes, while another has many such problems that have been reported in the media. For which company would you find it easier to raise extra finance? Businesses are made up of people and there is no business activity that might not be touched on by HRM.

Human resource management draws on many sources for its theories and practices. Sociologists, psychologists and management theorists, especially, have contributed a constant stream of new and reworked ideas. They offer theoretical insights and practical assistance in areas of people management such as recruitment and selection, performance measurement, team composition and organizational design. Many of their concepts have been integrated into broader approaches that have contributed to management thinking in various periods and ultimately the development of HRM (see Figure 1.1).

Background and origins of people management

The roots of people management and, therefore, of HRM lie deep in the past. Just as the tasks that have to be done in modern organizations are allocated to different jobs and the people who perform those jobs, humans in ancient societies divided work between themselves. The **division of labour** (see Key concept 1.1) has been practised since prehistoric times: family groups shared the work of hunting and gathering; tasks were allocated according to skills such as ability to find food plants, track animals or cook; age, strength and health were taken into account and the oldest and youngest members were not expected to travel far from home or to be involved in the dangers of hunting.

Social customs determined separate roles and tasks for males and females. Traditional self-sufficient communities, dependent on agriculture or fishing, rarely had more than 20–30 categories of labour, in contrast to modern industrial states that have thousands of different job types. Some functions, such as religious and political leadership or medicine, were restricted to individuals with inherited or specialist knowledge. As civilization and technology evolved, however, specialization led to a proliferation of different forms of work, and farmers and fishermen were joined by skilled craftworkers using metal, pottery, and wood.

Key concept 1.1 Division of labour

The subdivision of work so that specific tasks or jobs are allocated to individuals deemed most suitable on the basis of skill, experience or cultural tradition. All societies practise division of labour. Some cultures traditionally allocated tasks to particular social groups, such as the caste system in India. In others, higher status jobs have been reserved for the members of a power elite such as the products of the British 'public school and Oxbridge' system or the French 'grandes écoles'. Modern HRM aims to identify and develop the best people for specific jobs, regardless of background, class or gender.

Every generation believes that its problems and achievements are greater than those of the past. Modern business is seen as being uniquely complex and on a larger scale than the enterprises of earlier times but, in the ancient world, large numbers of people were organized to build great pyramids, fortresses and irrigation systems; military leaders marshalled huge armies; slave owners operated massive plantations and mines. Leadership, power and organization, therefore, have been matters of study and debate for thousands of years. *The Farmer's Almanac*, a 5000-year-old Sumerian text, includes useful tips on the supervision of farm labourers – making it the oldest known HRM textbook (Kramer, 1963: p.105). The text advised the farmer to prepare a selection of whips and goads to keep men and beasts working hard. No idleness or interruptions were to be tolerated. Even planting barley seed had to be closely supervised as the unfortunate labourers were not trusted to do it properly.

This authoritarian approach has predominated throughout most of recorded history, but there has been a continuing and increasing search for less coercive ways of managing people.

Figure 1.1

Influences on the development of HRM

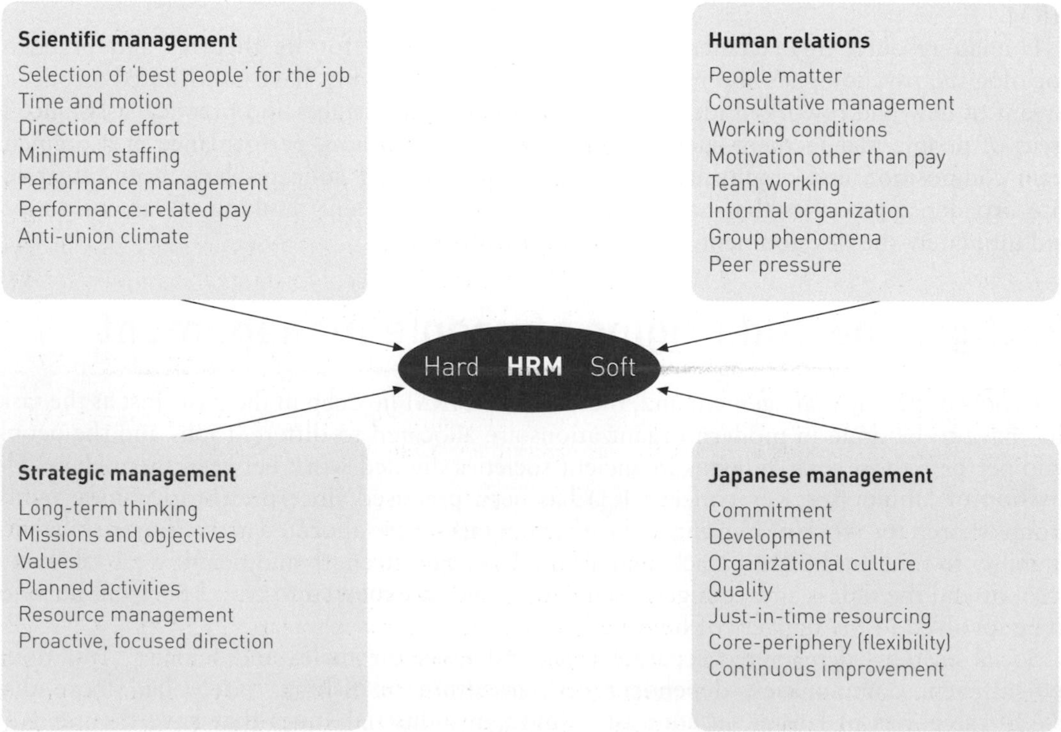

Scientific management
Selection of 'best people' for the job
Time and motion
Direction of effort
Minimum staffing
Performance management
Performance-related pay
Anti-union climate

Human relations
People matter
Consultative management
Working conditions
Motivation other than pay
Team working
Informal organization
Group phenomena
Peer pressure

Hard **HRM** Soft

Strategic management
Long-term thinking
Missions and objectives
Values
Planned activities
Resource management
Proactive, focused direction

Japanese management
Commitment
Development
Organizational culture
Quality
Just-in-time resourcing
Core-periphery (flexibility)
Continuous improvement

In 16th century Italy, for example, Niccolo Machiavelli (1469–1527) wrote *The Prince* (by which he meant a leader), detailing a wide range of strategies and tactics that continue to offer insights into the exercise of power. Although famous for advocating ruthlessness in the conduct of public (i.e. political) activities, Swain (2002) considers Machiavelli to be the originator of three themes more relevant to private management: modernity, publicness and the executive. According to Swain (2002, p.281) Machiavelli's modernity distinguished his world from that of antiquity:

> When Machiavelli jettisons the Christian religion and ancient philosophy as sources of guidance in the human condition, he may do so for the sake of politics, but the ramifications spill over into all other aspects of human life. The modern enterprise, simply put, is humankind taking care of itself as best it can in an otherwise pretty lonely universe. Science and technology are harnessed to make life more pleasant. Politics and political orders are mostly guided by the ends of political stability and serving humankind's needs.

According to Machiavelli, the ideal leader should have a degree of virtue and be regarded with both fear and love – although, if only one was possible, it was better to be feared than loved. Amongst his other prescriptions, the leader should be both a Fox and a Lion, able to exercise cunning and be a champion.

The division of labour required the most suitable people to perform skilled tasks, producing an early interest in the differences between individuals. According to Smith (1948, p.10):

> In the 16th century John Huarte wrote a book in Spanish concerning what we should now refer to as vocational guidance and selection. It was translated into Italian, and from this version an English translation was made under the title of 'The Tryal of Wits', which, translated into modern speech, means the testing of intelligence. He maintained that it is nature which enables a man of ability to learn, and that it is quite superfluous for good teachers to try to teach any particular subject to a child who has not the disposition or the ability required for it. Each person, unless he is a dolt, has some predominant quality which will enable him to excel in some way.

Huarte produced the following classification (Smith, 1948, p.11):

1 Some have a disposition for the clear and easy parts, but cannot understand the obscure and difficult.

2 Some are pliant and easy, able to learn all the rules, but no good at argument.

3 Some need no teachers, they take no pleasure in the plains but seek dangerous and high places and walk alone, follow no beaten track; these must fare forthwith, unquiet, seeking to know and understand new matters.

Individuals perform their jobs within a wide environmental context. In 1776, Adam Smith (1723–1790) published *An Inquiry into the Nature and Causes of the Wealth of Nations*. This foundation text for the science of economics began by emphasizing the importance of the division of labour in achieving increased productivity, thereby anticipating the Industrial Revolution. The UK is conventionally regarded as the first country to experience this process which then spread throughout Europe and North America and continues to transform developing countries. However, Cannadine (1992, p.18) observes that:

> The view that Britain was the first industrial nation, whose achievements all others consciously emulated, has also been severely undermined, especially in the case of France where, it is now argued, industrialization was taking place in a different way and where, in any case for much of the eighteenth century, its productivity was higher than Britain's.

'Revolution' implies a rapid transition from craft to industrial methods but British industrialization was a relatively slow process in comparison with the recent development of the 'tiger' economies of east Asia. At the end of the 18th, and the beginning of the 19th centuries, workers were gradually concentrated in factories and work centres, more or less under their own free will. This concentration was linked to increasing mechanization and the consequent need for machine-operating skills. Developing from older craft-based industries, work was divided between employees according to the nature of their skills. One worker would no longer be totally responsible for all stages of production, such as making a piece of furniture.

In the industrial system the task was subdivided into simpler, less skilful jobs. Different people would deal with parts of the process: one would turn chair legs, another would prepare seats, yet another would stain and polish, and so on.

By the late 19th century, the size and complexity of the new industries demanded more sophisticated methods of control and organization, eventually evolving into modern management. Until this time, workers were not directly employed by large capitalists: their employers were gang bosses, subcontracted to provide and organize labour. In the developed world, subcontractors of this kind continue to exist in the building sector and in fruit and vegetable-picking. In developing countries their power is even greater. Under autocratic but loose control, skilled or unskilled workers largely organized their own efforts, forming autonomous teams. However, as factories grew larger and people were concentrated in greater numbers in specific locations, this indirect approach became increasingly unworkable. People were needed to control permanent workforces, which were directly employed by factory owners.

Initially they took the form of overseers, foremen or supervisors; exercising 'coercion by means of observation' (Foucault, 1977, p.175). At first they were people promoted from the workforce: the concept of a distinct managerial class with separate recruitment paths evolved slowly. Jacques (1997) points out that 'the foreman was not in any sense a middle manager, but a key player in a form of control in the works radically different from and preceding *management*.'

In the 19th century industry was dominated by individual owners, family businesses and partnerships. The principals of these companies managed their businesses in a direct, personal way, partly because the numbers of people involved were small enough to be within the span of control of a few individuals. Family-controlled businesses became a major economic force and many achieved considerable importance. Some of the most successful were happy to publicize their methods and were featured in the media of the time. Biographies were written glorifying their achievements and presenting their ideas in largely uncritical terms. George Cadbury is one such example and he is featured in the case study at the end of this chapter. Along with explorers, scientists and colonial adventurers, business heroes were presented as role models for the masses. Such books met the demands of a reading population who preferred to perceive the world in terms of good and bad, heroes and villains, and required a presentation of success in simplistic terms. Examination of modern 'pop management' books suggest that little has changed.

Key concept 1.2 Alienation

A state of estrangement, or a feeling of being an outsider from society. Karl Marx observed that although work in a traditional, agricultural or craft-based society had been exhausting, workers had control over their own jobs. Their work required considerable knowledge and skill that had been removed from many factory jobs. Dull, boring and repetitive work induces a feeling of **alienation**. Assembly line workers are involved with a small part of the final product, have little control over the rhythm of their work and may have no idea of the significance of their contribution. Their work can appear to be alien with no relationship or meaning to their lives other than to produce income. As a consequence they may feel little enthusiasm and, often, active hostility towards what seems like forced labour.

Professional managers

The literature on organization is both extensive and old, but organization is not the same as management. Much of the literature on management history is American in origin and, not surprisingly, attributes most of the credit for the development of management to US originators. Jacques (1997) comments:

Moderns appear to be superior to other people because we see clearly what has hitherto been seen through the eyes of bias and superstition; English are superior among Moderns because they are the ones who produced the entire body of early work; Americans are superior to British because they have superior character. That this hierarchy of ethnocentrism is commonplace in American writing makes it no less worthy of comment.

One of the principal originators of modern management highlighted in the US literature was, in fact, neither English nor (born) an American. The Scot, Daniel McCallum, was general superintendent of the Eric Railroad in the USA. This railroad, in common with other large rail companies, was finding it difficult to operate profitably, unlike smaller local railroads. He wrote (see Chandler, 1962) that:

A superintendent of a road fifty miles in length can give its business his professional attention and may be constantly on the line engaged in the direction of its details; each person is personally known to him, and all questions in relation to its business are at once presented and acted upon; and any system however imperfect may under such circumstances prove comparatively successful.

However, McCallum contended, when the railroad is 'five hundred miles in length a very different state exists. Any system which might be applicable to the business and extent of a short road would be found entirely inadequate to the wants of a long one.'

He set about creating a management system in which responsibility for the railroad was split into geographical divisions, each of manageable size. Superintendents were given responsibility for operations within their respective divisions but had to provide detailed reports to the central headquarters. There McCallum and his assistants were able to coordinate the whole operation. McCallum advocated a number of management principles:

- good discipline
- specific and detailed job descriptions
- frequent and accurate reporting of performance
- pay and promotion based on merit
- clearly defined hierarchy of superiors and subordinates
- enforcement of personal responsibility and accountability
- the search for and correction of errors.

The lines of authority from headquarters to superintendents and then to their subordinates were laid out clearly on paper – effectively on an organizational chart. Other railroads copied this system and were able to become effective and profitable. In turn, these ideas spread to other US businesses.

By 1900 the USA had undergone several decades of rapid, large-scale industrialization. Large American companies such as Heinz and Singer Sewing Machines had the characteristics of modern, highly-structured organizations. They produced standardized consumer durables for the mass market. These organizations required a supply of trained managers. Notionally selected on the basis of ability and expertise – rather than family connections – they needed to know how to organize, reward and motivate their staff. In the USA, state and private universities were opened to cater for this new professional need.

The first companies of equivalent size and organization did not arise in Britain and the Commonwealth until the 1920s and management education was similarly late in developing. Like most European or Asian companies they still tended to employ relatives or to promote long-standing workers to management roles. Reliability and ability to impose discipline were held to be more important than technical knowledge. Increasingly, however, managers (especially those at a senior level) developed vested interests incompatible with those of the working-classes (labour) and shareholders (capital).

A distinctive form of scientific management was taken up in the new high-volume production industries. This came to be known as **Fordism** after the mass production methods used by Henry Ford for automobile manufacturing. Jelinek (quoted in Mintzberg, 1994, p.21) considers that Taylor 'for the first time made possible the large-scale coordination of details – planning and policy-level thinking, above and beyond the details of the task itself'. This

Scientific management

In 1903, F.W.Taylor – an American engineer – published *Shop Management*, outlining a system for extracting maximum output from workers. Later, his methods were presented as *The Principles of Scientific Management* (1911). Controversial at the time, and still the subject of debate, Taylor is quoted frequently as the inspiration for many modern industrial practices – including Japanese production methods. He outlined a systematic but controversial programme based on:

● rudimentary time and motion studies
● selection of 'first-class men' for the job
● premium pay for a 'fair day's work'.

Taylor's ideas were not original. They embodied attitudes of the time, including strict discipline to control soldiering ('slacking' or 'skiving'). Taylor saw two forms: (a) 'individual' soldiering where workers' were naturally lazy; and (b) 'systematic' soldiering where workers conspired to maintain a comfortable work rate. Activities were timed to prevent employees from taking it easy. As chief engineer at the Midvale Steel Company, Taylor sacked slow workers, cut piece-rates, and brought in non-union workers. Productivity was raised by standardizing and simplifying procedures into specified and unvarying jobs. Employees were not allowed to think about their jobs, bring in new ideas, or vary tasks to alleviate boredom. Broad craft knowledge was no longer required – knowledge was transferred to the manager.

Taylor's basic concept was the 'task idea': planning out every job in minute detail; giving precise instructions on what to do, in what order, at what speed; and eliminating wasteful or unnecessary actions. This produced 'one best way' for any task. At the Bethlehem Steel Company he applied his principles to shovelling and handling pig iron (Taylor, 1947, p.43) :

> Now, gentlemen, shovelling is a great science compared with pig-iron handling. I dare say that most of you gentlemen know that a good many pig-iron handlers can never learn to shovel right; the ordinary pig-iron handler is not the type of man well suited to shovelling. He is too stupid; there is too much mental strain, too much knack required of a shoveler for the pig-iron handler to take kindly to shovelling.

The plant employed 400–600 men to move several million tons of material each year. Taylor found the optimum load for shovelling, designed better shovels and scheduled carefully timed rest-pauses. He was able to achieve the same output from 140 men with an average 60 per cent bonus, virtually halving costs. He argued that the men were not being overworked but simply doing their jobs more sensibly.

Taylor used Henry Knolle –a 'first-class' labourer immortalized in management literature as 'Schmidt' –to demonstrate the motivating effect of premium pay. Knolle's pig-iron handling increased four-fold to 50 tons a day, for a bonus equivalent to half his normal pay. Only one in eight workers could match this performance, the remainder being given lower-paid work. Many employers used Taylor's system to increase productivity, but without extra pay. In fact, wages were often reduced on the grounds that the rationalized jobs could be classified as unskilled. The work was given to people, such as new immigrants, who would accept lower pay.

In his writings, Taylor presented his work at Bethlehem Steel as a success. In fact, there were angry reactions from workers, managers and others. Press publicity on likely redundancies, threats of industrial action, and management resentment led to Taylor's dismissal. He spent the rest of his life publicizing his theories. He believed that he had developed a science that would legitimize the professional status of managers. Rose (1975, p.32) describes Taylorism as 'an instructive reminder of how "scientific" theories of workers' behaviour which fail when actually applied in industry can none the less acquire a substitute vitality as managerial ideologies'. In other words, ideas which do not work in practice can still be sold to other managers!

As an early management guru, Taylor used recognizable tactics:

● he developed a relatively simple set of principles
● took personal credit for devising them
● gave them a pretentious name – scientific management
● and publicized them extensively.

What relevance do Taylor's methods have for modern human resource management?

produced a new division of labour, splitting tasks and their coordination into different roles. So management had become 'abstracted' from day-to-day activities, allowing it to 'concentrate on exceptions'.

Taylor's ideas were developed further by Frank and Lilian Gilbreth who made valiant efforts to turn human beings into automatons. Their bizarre concepts included the 'therblig' (Gilbreth backwards) as a measure of work (Rose, 1975, p.84). Frank Gilbreth became famous for his study of bricklaying in which he reduced the movements involved from 15 to eight, and increased the number of bricks laid from 120 an hour to 350. Smith (1948, p.144) gave an example of a simple motion study using the Gilbreths' terminology, a bottle of gum and a brush:

Actual movements	Generalized description
1 Reach for the gum bottle	Transport empty
2 Grasp the brush	Grasp
3 Carry the brush to the paper	Transport loaded
4 Position for gumming	Position
5 Gum the paper	Use
6 Return the brush to bottle	Transport loaded
7 Insert the brush	Pre-position
8 Release the brush	Release
9 Move the hand back	Transport empty

What was the point of such a motion study? Smith quoted a paper by H.G. Maule from the *Journal of the Institution of British Launderers*, May 1935, which reported on use of the methodology to investigate the process of folding sheets:

The sequence of movements was: collect a sheet as it came from the calendar, fold it, place the folded article on a table. In the course of timing he noticed that a disproportionate amount of time was taken in the last movement owing to the position of a table on which the folded articles were placed. By calculating the time taken and multiplying it by the number of sheets folded in a week he found that 20 miles a week were walked unnecessarily. ... By a slight rearrangement of the table this was altered, and yet no one had noticed it before this.

Huczynski and Buchanan (2000) argue that **Taylorism** and related techniques are more prevalent today than ever. Japanese just-in-time techniques bear a number of similarities to some aspects of scientific management. **Scientific management** was one of the first of the 'one best way' methodologies of dealing with people management.

The human factor

The 'science' in scientific management was doubtful. At the same point in time, however, academic researchers had begun to take an interest in the practical aspects of work. Work psychology was pioneered by the German psychologist Hugo Munsterberg (1863–1916) who

Henry Ford

Ford made his first car in 1893 and formed the Ford Motor Company in 1903. He started the company with 11 other men, together putting up US$28 000. Eventually he bought out his associates and Henry Ford became the company. According to Beynon, (1973, p.18):

> He was The Man. And he was to remain The Man until his death. Throughout his life he maintained a single-minded, autocratic hold over his company, entirely convinced of his right to run it as he thought fit.

Ford standardized products ('any colour as long as its black'), applied modern technology to a flowing production line and allocated workers' jobs according to Taylorist principles. Ford's plant at Highland Park, Michigan, was dedicated to a single mass-market car – the Model T. The main building at Highland Park was four storeys high, 865ft long and 75ft wide – a staggering 260 000 square feet – and was the largest building in the state of Michigan (McIntyre, 2000, p.271).

His major innovation, the moving assembly line, was inspired by Chicago slaughterhouses where vast numbers of cattle were 'disassembled' on a moving line. At Ford every worker had one task such as fitting a door to each car as they moved up the line. This development was given considerable publicity and Ford made every effort to present himself as a great engineer. In fact, there was nothing new about the equipment. The distinctive feature of the assembly line was the organization of human resources. Assembly workers were allowed a minimum time to complete an operation before the car continued to the next stage. 'The idea is that the man ... must have every second necessary but not a single unnecessary second' (Ford, 1922, quoted in Beynon, 1973, p.19).

A harsh attitude permeated the company. Employees were watched closely and were regarded as objects rather than human beings. They were to do as they were told – to be hired and fired arbitrarily. Whilst maximizing production efficiency, assembly-line manufacturing led to high rates of absenteeism and employee turnover. In 1913 Ford needed 13 000–14 000 workers but over 50 000 came and went in that year. Something had to be done. In 1914 Ford announced a package deal for his workers: the 'Five Dollar Day', presented as a profit-sharing system that more than doubled workers' wage rates. However, it included a number of changes which benefited the company. Ford did not agree with Taylor's simplistic incentive system. He never paid on a 'piece-work' basis, believing that it led to rushed or 'botched' work. Instead his new scheme increased management control of workers' performance through a combination of:

- Job evaluation, leading to a thorough rationalization of workflow.
- Pay grades, matched to the 'value' or difficulty of jobs.
- Disqualifying clauses, which prevented workers with less than six months' service, men under 21 and all women from receiving US$5 a day. 'Young ladies' were expected to get married and leave the company.

Finally, eligible workers only received the full pay rate if their behaviour and personal habits at work and home were deemed to be satisfactory. Alcohol and tobacco were frowned upon; gambling or taking in boarders were unacceptable. Ford believed that high wages should be paid only to the morally deserving, since the others would spend it unwisely. A Sociological Department was established with 30 investigators checking workers domestic circumstances and spending habits. Within two years, 90 per cent of Ford workers were thought good enough to receive US$5 a day, but investigators could recommend the loss of six months' bonus at any time if their lifestyles were not acceptable. Ford believed in the virtue of hard work but did not value charity – the poor deserved their fate. He never expressed any concern about the drudgery and boredom of the assembly line, considering most people to be incapable of any better.

Ford's conditions were more attractive than the alternatives open to immigrants in Detroit. Some 10 000 unemployed people mobbed the factory looking for jobs. Absenteeism and employee turnover dropped dramatically: in 1914 only 2000 workers left their jobs. The assembly line speeded up and the average cost of a car actually dropped, despite the wage increases. A reduction of working hours from nine to eight hours a day was easily absorbed. Ford's approach offered an unstoppable competitive advantage over more humane, craft-based companies. By 1923 Ford produced two million cars a year, with a new Model T produced every 40 seconds. Mass production dominated the world economy.

The American car industry gradually consolidated into General Motors, Ford and Chrysler. They dominated the US automobile market until the coming of the Japanese in the 1980s. After the initial success of the Model T, Ford lost market share to General Motors. At first, he tried to compete by cutting costs and producing a cheaper product, achieved by relentlessly speeding up the assembly line. Eventually he recognized the need for a new model. He began construction of a new plant to manufacture the Model A. Using more extensive technology it needed far fewer men than the Model T assembly line. In its last year (1927) he drove the Model T line flat out until he had sufficient stocks of the car. Then he shut the plant and laid off 60 000 employees for six months – without pay. He considered this to be a useful lesson to the workers who would appreciate that 'things are not going along too even always'.

Ford became increasingly dictatorial and suspicious. He avoided technical experts – for a long time he did not hire college graduates. As ambitious employees rose in the hierarchy, he found reasons to sack them when their authority threatened his. His cars became technically obsolescent. His marketing and planning were poorly organized – he banned advertising for several years. By the 1930s the company was losing money heavily and was only to be saved by his death and new management.

What distinguishes the Fordist approach from older methods of manufacturing?

Sources: Beynon (1973) and Galbraith (1967).

moved to the USA and became responsible for a research laboratory at Harvard. Between 1900 and 1914, he applied the techniques of the young science of psychology to issues such as the selection of engineers to operate new machines, and the efficiency of various industrial practices (Thomson, 1968, p.133). Work psychology is deemed to have taken off after the publication of his *Psychology and Industrial Efficiency* in 1913. In Germany and the UK the demands of war boosted further research. In Britain, the Health of Munition Workers Committee (1915–17) was required to: '. . . consider and investigate the relation of hours of labour and other conditions of employment, including methods of work, to the production of fatigue, having regard both to industrial efficiency and to the preservation of health amongst the workers' (quoted in Thomson, 1968, p.345).

In 1919, the researchers involved formed the UK National Institute of Industrial Psychology (NIIP), a body similar to the Australian Institute of Industrial Psychology founded in 1917. These organizations investigated and researched working conditions, and developed vocational guidance and selection techniques. In New Zealand, vocational guidance dates from 1913 where it was offered by the Christchurch branch of the YMCA. Initially the work of occupational psychologists bordered on physiology as they investigated fatigue and monotony. It had been believed that fatigue was caused by a build-up of toxins in the blood. It was even thought that an elixir could be found which would neutralize these chemicals; when injected into exhausted workers this could allow them to work indefinitely! The researchers proved conclusively that fatigue was not purely physiological – it was also psychological (Rose, 1975, p.70).

Their work directly countered the myth that working longer hours produced greater output. In their research on monotony the NIIP psychologists took a deliberately anti-Taylorist perspective. They confirmed Taylor's views on the value of rest pauses but argued against the notion of 'one best way by a first-class man'. The simple truth was that individual tasks could be done equally effectively in a variety of ways by a diverse range of people. Different people had their own ways of performing effectively: they worked more efficiently when allowed to vary their own working methods. It became clear also that money was not the sole motivator for working people: the social relations between workers influenced their attitude to the job and their productivity. Workers were human beings and should be treated as such: the researchers had identified the importance of human factors.

In effect they had anticipated the conclusions of the more famous 'Hawthorne studies', but their reports – expressed in dry scientific language – made for dull reading, and were not accessible to a wide audience. Moreover, their income came from industrial commissions which were expected to be confidential. The most positive response came from the chocolate makers, Cadbury and Rowntree, which were Quaker-owned and humanitarian in attitude. They were receptive to ideas about training, vocational guidance, staff welfare, and joint worker–management councils. Many, if not all, employers were not like-minded. The soft approach of the NIIP also had a hard centre, in the shape of efficiency measures such as selection tests to identify suitable workers for specific jobs.

Psychological tests for selection, or 'psychometric tests', were extensively developed in the USA and the UK from World War I through to World War II. Some two million Americans were tested during World War I alone. Their particular priority was the identification of 'sub-normals' at one extreme and officer material at the other. After the war, testing became a lucrative commercial activity in the USA but introduced a worrying element of 'scientific' racism which has not been entirely eliminated.

The Union Bank of Australia: HR 100 years ago

Personnel, payroll and other records from the Union Bank of Australia were examined for employees who joined between 1888 and 1900. The researchers found that employment was characterized by limited ports of entry, impersonal rules for pay and promotion, well-defined career ladders, shielding from the external labour market, and a long-term employment relationship. Additionally tenure within the bank was rewarded considerably more than experience elsewhere, and pay increased significantly after 25–30 years' service.

Source: Seltzer and Merrett (2000).

Human relations

The US **human relations** movement dominated management thinking until the 1950s and was a significant influence on the development of modern HRM. The movement gained most of its inspiration from the famous Hawthorne studies at the Western Electric Company plant of that name in Chicago from the 1920s to the early 1940s. The plant employed 40 000 people and was regarded as progressive. The studies were organized by the company, with some assistance from the Harvard Business School. The intention was to find out how productivity might be affected if working conditions such as lighting, heating and rest pauses were varied. Elton Mayo, an Australian professor at Harvard, picked up these studies and publicized a new approach in American management philosophy which spread to many other countries.

Mayo is credited often with the Hawthorne research. In fact, as Rose (1975) points out, there is no evidence that Mayo did any 'leg-work' at the plant. Different accounts of the research provide contradictory descriptions. It seems that early research at Hawthorne was conducted using Taylorist 'time and motion' and industrial psychology techniques. The latter were similar to the methods of the 'human factors' researchers in the UK.

In early experiments on changed lighting conditions, the researchers observed two groups. In one group, regardless of whether lighting was worsened or improved, output increased. The other group was used as a control, with no variation in lighting, yet output also increased.

The Relay Assembly Test Room was set up in April 1927 to investigate this phenomenon. Six cooperative women were selected to work in an area partitioned from the main workroom. Relay assembly was their normal work and their output had been measured secretly before the experiment began. They had regular briefing meetings and their comments were taken into account. Also, they were given periodic medical examinations. An observer was stationed in the room to ensure that the women paid full attention to the test. The experiment continued for five years, but the significant findings came from the first two years.

During this period, systematic changes were made in the women's working conditions. They were put on a group incentive scheme. Frequency and duration of rest-pauses, free meals, and shorter working days and working week were introduced. In general, the improvements were incremental. Output increased with virtually every change. This has been called the 'Hawthorne effect'. Even when – for a period – conditions were returned to their original levels, output did not drop significantly. After two years, output stood at around 30 per cent higher than at the start of the experiments.

The group became cohesive, helped by the replacement of two uncooperative women. Other workers envied their conditions. Gradually the observer developed a friendly relationship with the women, shielding them from their official supervisors. Mayo described the situation in his book on the Hawthorne studies, *The Human Problems of an Industrial Civilization* (1933):

> It was also noticed that there was a marked improvement in their attitude towards their work and working environment. This simultaneous improvement in attitude and effectiveness indicated that . . . we could more logically attribute the increase in efficiency to a betterment of morale than to any of the alterations made in the course of the experiments.

Mayo argued that the women were responding to the interest shown in them and their work. The experiment was presented as evidence of the importance of human relations. However, from 1929 to 1932 morale and performance steadily deteriorated. In particular, the women became anxious about their security as the economy slumped. Eventually there was so much bitterness and hostility that the experiment was concluded.

Among many other studies at Hawthorne, the 'Bank-wiring Room' is most significant. It led to an appreciation of group norms and conformity. It appeared from this study of 14 men that they had determined the level of 'a fair day's work' between themselves. Anyone doing too much ('rate-busters'), or too little ('chisellers'), or who 'squealed' to management, was picked on and pressurized to conform. Strangely, these group effects were played down by the researchers because most recommendations from the human relations school were geared towards individual worker satisfaction.

The human relations movement shifted management thinking towards 'soft' people management – away from the 'hard' approaches of Taylor and Ford. According to Holloway (1991, p.71), the Hawthorne studies caused:

1 A shift from a psycho-physiological model of the worker to a socio-emotional one.

2 An appreciation of the fundamental importance of the worker's attitude to the job in determining performance.

Later Hawthorne studies depended on interviews. Sympathetic interviewing produced valuable information for management, and interviews could also change workers' **attitudes**. In the 1930s, companies such as Kimberley-Clarke introduced attitude surveys among their workers. Questioning gave workers extra insight into the nature of their jobs and feelings about work. This was a major discovery in a country dominated by gigantic factories, where managers did not know individual workers. What was unthought of before was now a part of commonsense: workers have feelings!

Management theory

The human relations and human factors approaches were absorbed into a broad behavioural science movement in the 1950s and 1960s. This period produced some influential theories on the motivation of human performance. For example, Maslow's hierarchy of needs provided an individual focus on the reasons why people work. He argued that people satisfied an ascending series of needs from survival, through security to eventual 'self-actualization'.

In the same period, concepts of job design such as job enrichment and job enlargement were investigated. It was felt that people would give more to an organization if they gained satisfaction from their jobs. Jobs should be designed to be interesting and challenging to gain the commitment of workers – a central theme of HRM.

By the 1970s most managers participating in formal management training were aware of: Theory X and Theory Y (McGregor, 1960); of Maslow and Herzberg's motivation theories; and knew where they should be in terms of the managerial grid (Blake and Mouton, 1964). These theorists advocated participative, 'soft' approaches to management. However, only a minority of managers in the USA received such training, with even fewer in other countries. Most operational managers concerned with production, engineering, or distribution, had worked their way up from low-level jobs: they were probably closer in spirit to F.W. Taylor than the theorists of the 1950s and 1960s. This contrasted with personnel departments with a higher proportion of people who had received academic training; additionally, 'personnel' was an area where women were prevalent – as opposed to production which was male dominated. Were women naturally more open to human relations concepts than men?

In the UK, the influence of industrial psychology persisted in Alec Rodger's slogan 'fitting the man to the job and the job to the man'. Holloway (1991) quotes from a student handout issued by Rodger in the 1970s (which appears to ignore the concept of the working woman):

Fitting the man to the job

- through occupational guidance
- personnel selection
- training and development.

Fitting the job to the man

- through methods design
- equipment design
- design and negotiation of working conditions and
- (physical and social) rewards.

Key management theories

Management by objectives
Based on work by Drucker in the 1950s, and further developed by McGregor, **management by objectives (MBO)** linked achievement to competence and job performance. MBO primarily focused on the individual, tying rewards and promotion opportunities to specific agreed objectives, measured by feedback from performance assessment. Individual managers were given the opportunity to clarify the purposes of their jobs and set their own targets. MBO developed into modern performance management schemes and performance-related pay.

Contingency
Many researchers found difficulty in applying academic theories to real organizations. The socio-technical school developed models of behaviour and performance which took

into account **contingency** variables, or 'it depends' circumstances, found in particular work situations (Burns and Stalker, 1961; Woodward, 1980). They argued that employees were part of a system that also included the equipment and other resources utilized by an organization. The system could not function optimally unless all its components – human and non-human – had been considered. The HRM concepts of coherence and integration derive, in part, from this line of thought.

Organizational development

Also drawn from the long tradition of organizational theory, **organizational development (OD)** offered a pragmatic approach to change. Theory and practice were mixed in a tentative process called '**action research**'. Organizational development familiarized managers with the idea that changes in processes, attitudes and behaviour were possible and that organizations should be thought of as whole entities.

Strategic management

Directing people to achieve strategic objectives so that individual goals are tied to the business needs of the whole organization, strategic management has become a dominant framework for organizational thinking since World War II. It is based on concepts first used for large-scale military and space programmes in the USA. Frequently, it employs project and team-based methods for planning and implementation. Lately, internal (including human) resources and key competencies have been identified as crucial elements of long-term competitive success. Strategic management has become the major unifying theme of undergraduate and (especially) postgraduate business courses. The concern with strategy is said to distinguish HRM from personnel management.

Leadership

Many writers have concluded that a visionary leader is essential, particularly in developing and inspiring teams. McGregor's (1960) *The Human Side of Enterprise* linked leadership and management style to motivation. McGregor expressed the contrast between authoritarian people management ('Theory X') and a modern form based on human relations ideas ('Theory Y'). His ideas parallel **'hard' and 'soft' HRM**. Effective managers do not need to give orders and discipline staff, they draw the best from their people through encouragement, support and personal charisma. Later authors (such as Peters and Waterman, 1982) featured the leader's vision and mission as a quasi-religious means of galvanizing worker commitment and enthusiasm.

Corporate culture

Deal and Kennedy (1982) popularized the belief that organizational effectiveness depends on a strong, positive **corporate culture**. They combined ideas from leadership theory and strategic management with prevailing beliefs about Japanese business success. Managers were exhorted to examine their existing organizational climates critically and work to change them into dynamic and creative cultures. The excellence movement inspired by Peters and Waterman (*In Search of Excellence*, 1982, and others) has been particularly influential with practising managers, despite criticisms of the research on which it was based.

Some people believe that managing people is just a matter of commonsense. What benefits can human resource specialists gain from the concepts and theories described here?

Development of the personnel specialism

Personnel management has been a recognized function in the USA since NCR opened a personnel office in the 1890s. American personnel managers worked within a **unitarist** tradition, identifying closely with the objectives of their **organization** (Key concept 1.3). It was natural for HRM to emerge comparatively smoothly from this perspective.

In other countries, the personnel management function arrived more slowly and came via a number of routes. Moreover, its orientation was not entirely managerial. In the UK, for example, its origins can be traced to the 'welfare officers' employed by Quaker-owned companies such as Cadbury. At an early stage it became evident that there was an inherent conflict between their activities and those of line managers. They were not seen to have a philosophy compatible with the worldview of senior managers. The welfare officer orientation placed personnel management as a buffer between the business and its employees. In terms of 'organizational politics' this was not a politically viable position for individuals wishing to further their careers, increase their status and earn high salaries.

Key concept 1.3 Unitarism

A managerialist stance which assumes that everyone in an organization is a member of a team with a common purpose. It embodies a central concern of HRM – that an organization's people, whether managers or lower-level employees, should share the same objectives and work together harmoniously. From this perspective, conflicting objectives are seen as negative and dysfunctional. By definition it is the opposite of pluralism: the acceptance of several alternative approaches, interests or goals within the same organization or society. Arguably, in the field of HRM, unitarism represents a US tradition, whereas pluralism is more typical of European attitudes towards people management.

Tyson (1989) distinguished between three 'types' of personnel management jobs:

- *'Clerk of works'*: The majority, involved in the routine of administration, record-keeping, letter-writing, setting up interviews and welfare matters. Reports to personnel or senior line manager.
- *'Contracts manager'*: Likely to be found in large organizations with formal industrial relations structures. Involved in detailed short-term policy-making and resolving problems. A 'fixer' with some degree of influence on trade unions and senior management.
- *'Architect'*: Probably highly qualified but not necessarily in 'personnel'. Broad portfolio with a significant strategic role. A business manager first and personnel manager second.

The second tradition – industrial relations – further compounded this distinction between personnel and other managers. In the acrimonious industrial relations climate prevailing in many developed countries throughout much of the 20th century, personnel/industrial relations managers played an intermediary role between unions and line management. Their function was legitimized by their role – or, at least, their own perception of that role – as 'honest brokers'.

But from the 1980s onwards governments with a neo-liberal or free market orientation, such as Mrs Thatcher's administration in the UK, reined in union freedom severely. Overall, there was a marked reduction in the importance of collective worker representation in many English-speaking countries. The perceived importance of collective bargaining reduced as managerial power increased. Trade union membership declined along with centralized pay bargaining and other forms of collective negotiation – and with them, the importance of the personnel manager with negotiating experience. The focus switched from the collective to the relationship between employer and individual employee. To support this change, a variety of essentially individualistic personnel techniques were applied to achieve business goals. These included performance measurement, objective setting, and skills development related to personal reward.

As we can see from the list of functions in Table 1.1, personnel had become a well defined but low status area of management by the 1980s. Practitioner Associations in industrialized countries recruited members in increasing numbers, developed qualification structures and attempted to define 'best practice'. Although they drew on psychology and sociology, the knowledge and practices they encouraged were largely pragmatic and commonsensical and did not present a particularly coherent approach to people management. Moreover, in some instances training and industrial relations were considered to be specialist fields outside mainstream personnel management. Traditional personnel managers were accused of having a

Traditional personnel departments typically encompass functions such as:	
Recruitment	Advertising for new employees and liaising with employment agencies.
Selection	Determining the best candidates from those who apply, arranging interviews, tests, references and so on.
Promotion	Running similar selection procedures to determine progression within the organization.
Pay	A minor or major role in pay negotiation, determination and administration.
Performance assessment	Coordinating staff appraisal and counselling systems to evaluate individual employee performance.
Grading structures	Comparing the relative difficulty and importance of functions as a basis for pay or development.
Training and development	Coordinating or delivering programmes to fit people for the roles required by the organization now and in the future.
Welfare	Providing or liaising with specialists in a staff-care or counselling role for people with personal or domestic problems affecting their work.
Communication	Providing an internal information service, perhaps in the form of a staff newspaper or magazine, handouts, booklets and videos.
Employee relations	Handling disputes, grievances and industrial action, often dealing with unions or staff representatives.
Dismissal	On an individual basis as a result of failure to meet requirements or as part of a redundancy or closure exercise, perhaps involving large numbers of people.
Personnel administration	Record-keeping and monitoring legislative requirements, for example related to equal opportunities.

Table 1.1

Specialist personnel functions

Using Tyson's classification of personnel work into 'clerk of works', 'contracts manager', and 'architect', what role would each of these three types play in the functions listed in Table 1.1?

narrow, functional outlook. For example, Storey (1989, p.5) commented that personnel management '. . . has long been dogged by problems of credibility, marginality, ambiguity and a "trash-can" labelling which has relegated it to a relatively disconnected set of duties – many of them tainted with a low-status "welfare" connotation.'

In practice, the background and training of many personnel managers left them speaking a different language from other managers and unable to comprehend wider business issues such as business strategy, market competition, labour economics, and the roles of other organizational functions – let alone balance sheets (Giles and Williams, 1991). The scene was set for a reintegration of personnel management with wider trends in management thinking.

Management thinking

Like fashions in hairstyle and clothing, management ideas come and go. One year's best-selling management concept is soon overtaken by the next 'big idea'. Significantly, however, a consistent theme has prevailed for more than two decades: the most successful organizations make the most effective use of their people – their human resources.

The emergence of HRM was part of a major shift in the nature and meaning of management towards the end of the 20th century. This happened for a number of reasons. Perhaps most significantly, as we will see in Part two of this book, major developments in the structure and intensity of international competition forced companies to make radical changes in their working practices (Goss 1994, p.1).

From the 1970s onwards, managers in the industrialized countries felt themselves to be on a roller coaster of change, expected to deliver improved business performance by whatever means they could muster. Their own careers and rewards were increasingly tied to those improvements and many were despatched to the ranks of the unemployed for not acting quickly and imaginatively enough. Caught between the need to manage decisively and fear of failure, managers sought credible new ideas as a potential route for survival.

The development of dynamic new economies in the Asia–Pacific region emphasized the weakness in traditional Western – specifically, American – management methods. To meet competition from East Asia, industries and organizations in older, developed countries were forced to restructure. The Japanese, in particular, provided both a threat and a role model that Eastern and Western companies tried to copy. Frequently, reorganized businesses in Australasia, Europe, North America and South Africa adopted Japanese techniques in an attempt to regain competitiveness. The term '**Japanization**' came into vogue in the mid-1980s to describe attempts in other countries to make practical use of 'Japanese' ideas and practices, reinforced by the impact of Japanese subsidiaries overseas. Initially, the main interest lay in forms of technical innovation and manufacturing methods such as 'continuous improvement' and 'just-in-time'. And their ways of managing people also attracted attention.

Key concept 1.4 Stakeholders

Employees have rights and interests beyond pay. They are stakeholders along with members of other recognizably separate groups or institutions with a special interest in an organization. These include shareholders, managers, customers, suppliers, lenders and government. Each group has its own priorities and demands and fits into the power structure controlling the organization. Employees have limited importance in free market countries such as the USA, UK, Ireland, Australia or Canada, in comparison with most European and many Asian–Pacific countries. Notionally, shareholders are paramount in English-speaking countries. In reality, top managers normally have effective control and pursue their own interests – often at the expense of their staff. (This topic is dealt with at some length in Chapter 2.)

The Japanese role model

Until 1868 Japan had been sealed from the outside world for 300 years. The sense of being 'different' remains. Kobayashi (1992: p.18) comments that Japan has never set out to be integrated into the international community. Rather, the country adapted selective aspects of foreign cultures which seemed useful to its development. The Japanese borrowed freely from Western ideas, both at the turn of the century, and again during the period of reconstruction after World War II. However, Japanese industrialists did not simply copy American management methods; they revitalized Asian values (Chung, 1991).

A key to Japanese industrial progress was the development of 'Japan Incorporated': the close-knit cooperation between government and business. Specific industrial sectors were targeted for long-term market penetration and dominance. Supposedly competing businesses acted cooperatively at the expense of foreign firms, sacrificing immediate profits for later success.

Economic problems hit the West increasingly from the 1970s onwards and Japan's growing industrial dominance became obvious. This stimulated a flow of influential writing (for example, Ouchi, 1981; Pascale and Athos, 1981), leading to a continuing debate on the applicability of Japanese management methods to other countries. Ironically, Western managers have examined Japanese techniques just as intently as the Japanese studied the West half a century ago. Developing countries in East Asia took Japan rather than the USA as their model.

The term 'Japanization' came into vogue in the mid-1980s to describe attempts in other countries to make practical use of 'Japanese' ideas and practices as well as the impact of Japanese subsidiaries overseas. Japanese practice emphasized human resources as an organization's key asset. A key feature of Japanese businesses in the 1970s and 1980s was the emphasis on worker commitment, flexibility and development. Books such as Pascale and Athos' (1981) *The Art of Japanese Management*, highlighted the competitive advantage which the Japanese gained through effective people management. The message came through that 'essentially, it is the human resource among all the factors of production which really makes the difference' (Storey, 2001: p.6).

Initially, the main interest lay in forms of technical innovation and manufacturing methods such as 'continuous improvement' and 'just-in-time'. More recently their ways of managing people have attracted attention. People management became a central strategic issue rather than a 'necessary inconvenience' (Goss 1994, p.4). The early component ideas of HRM theory parallel elements of Japanese people management in that period. But, whereas HRM is still a matter of rhetoric for most Western managers, the Japanese viewed it as a way of life: an instrumental approach to ever-increasing efficiency focused on employee commitment and skill. Traditionally, Japanese companies placed the interests of their employees first amongst their **stakeholders** (see Key concept 1.4), followed by customers and lastly the shareholders. This is virtually the opposite situation to that found in free market Western countries such as Australia, Canada, the UK or the USA. But the recession of the 1990s forced a number of Japanese companies to adopt Western ways.

The Japanese role model is a mixture of racial stereotyping, myth and reality. It is difficult to tell when truth ends and myth begins. Foreign commentators encountering a radically different culture tend to emphasize the points of difference rather than the similarities. The Japanese were seen as workaholics, rarely taking holidays and eager to work every available hour. They were conformists with a distinctive form of decision-making based on consensus. They worked in teams and hated to be seen as individuals. They searched for continuous improvement and were proud to be identified with their employing organization. Large businesses offered slow but steady promotion paths and life-long careers in return for total commitment.

▶

▶

However, Japan is constantly changing. Most accounts of Japanese business practice refer to the behaviour and beliefs of a generation who had to work hard to restore the economy after World War II. The younger generation do not necessarily share their view of life.

Japanese companies first drew on their profits in lean times in order to keep their workforce. Companies in English-speaking countries would have been unable to withstand the wrath of shareholders demanding dividend payments. Responsibility for the security of their workforce was not simply a matter of goodwill or obligation but the necessary price for commitment from employees. This was difficult for companies operating in a global environment, exposed to fluctuations in the value of the yen or overseas economic demand. These companies made considerable use of peripheral workforces – primarily their suppliers' employees – who took the brunt whenever demand fell. These peripheral workers faced little or no income for prolonged periods while favoured employees in multinational organizations maintained their privileges. But as recession deepened at the end of the 20th century closures and retrenchments became a new feature of the Japanese industrial scene.

What were the most significant influences of Japanese people management on the development of HRM?

From personnel to human resource management

Human resource management-type themes, including 'human capital theory' (discussed in Part two) and 'human asset accounting' can be found in literature dating as far back as the 1970s. But the modern view of HRM first gained prominence in 1981 with its introduction on the prestigious MBA course at Harvard Business School. The Harvard MBA provided a blueprint for many other courses throughout North America and the rest of the world, making its interpretation of HRM particularly influential (Beer, Walton and Spector, 1984; Guest, 1987; Poole, 1990). Simultaneously, other interpretations were being developed in Michigan and New York.

These ideas spread to other countries in the 1980s and 1990s, particularly Australia, New Zealand, parts of northern Europe – especially the UK, Ireland and Scandinavia – and also South and South-East Asia and South Africa. Today, the HRM approach is influential in many parts of the world. Typically, in this period HRM was presented in four distinct ways.

First, as a radically new approach to managing people, demarcated sharply from traditional personnel management (Storey, 1989, p.4). Personnel management was commonly viewed as having an operational focus, emphasizing technical skills and day-to-day functions such as recruitment and selection, training, salary administration, and employee relations. 'Personnel' was a detached and neutral approach to staff. By contrast, HRM was often portrayed as being proactive – looking at people in economic terms as either assets or costs to be actively managed. HRM was seen to be strategic, tying people management to business objectives. It was an attempt to manage people – not necessarily employees – in the long-term interests of the business.

Secondly, HRM was seen as an integrated approach which provided a coherent programme, linking all aspects of people management. Whereas personnel managers employed a piecemeal range of sophisticated techniques for assessment or selection, HRM integrated these within a meaningful and organized framework. Each element needed to fit into a pattern that ultimately met business needs. Additionally, HRM was seen to be holistic: in other words, it was concerned with the overall people requirements of an organization. It implied a significant shift towards more conceptual, higher-level concerns such as the structure and culture of the organization and the provision of necessary competences.

Thirdly, HRM represented a consistent view of people management in which employees were treated as valuable assets. An organization's reward systems, performance measures, promotion and learning opportunities were to be used to maximize the utilization of its human resources. In particular, they were focused on the attitudes, beliefs and commitment of employees to achieve behavioural consistency and a culture of commitment.

Finally, HRM was presented as a general management function. Personnel management was often viewed as the work of specialists, whereas HRM was the responsibility of all managers. In some organizations human resource experts provided an internal consultancy service to line managers. There was a particular stress on the role of top management and an overall increase in the status of people management. Traditional personnel managers had little power or prestige.

Why should HRM have attracted such attention, particularly from senior managers? From a strategic viewpoint, Lengnick-Hall and Lengnick-Hall (1988) identify a clear rationale for adopting the HRM approach:

- HRM offers a broader range of solutions for complex organizational problems.

- It ensures that an organization's people are considered as well as its financial and technological resources when objectives are set or capabilities assessed.

- It forces the explicit consideration of the individuals who implement and comprise the strategy.

- Two-way links are encouraged between the formulation of strategy and its human resource implications, avoiding problems which might arise from: (a) subordinating strategic considerations to HR preferences; and (b) neglecting an organization's people as a potential source of organizational competence and competitive advantage.

The renewed emphasis on the importance of human resources drew attention to the practice of people management. Conventionally, this had been divided between line and personnel managers, now frequently called human resource managers. For some, HRM was simply a matter of relabelling 'personnel' to redress the criticisms made about traditional personnel management and sceptics have argued that familiar personnel functions were repackaged and given a more up-market image – 'old wine in new bottles' (Armstrong, 1987). Indeed, until the early 1990s, 'Human Resource Management' textbooks tended to be slightly revised 'Personnel Management' texts covering familiar topics in a prescriptive manner.

Writing at that time, Torrington and Hall (1991, p.15) concurred that the term was adopted in order to get away from the ineffectual image of previous eras: '. . . personnel managers seem constantly to suffer from paranoia about their lack of influence and are ready to snatch at anything – like a change in title – that might enhance their status.' It was also fuelled by long-standing criticisms from other managers. This includes a general prejudice that is often expressed within organizations and sometimes finds its way into print. Thus the following from an article entitled 'Support for an old-fashioned view', *The Independent*, 12 May, 1994):

> Many of us have long held the view that personnel management, or human resource management as companies sometimes insist on calling it, is a uniquely irrelevant executive function fulfilling no obvious purpose other than to stifle initiative, flair and creativity.

Similarly, Kellaway (2001) revisited an article about 'a piece of incomprehensible HR waffle that purported to lay out the future of HR' about which she had made 'a few averagely derogative remarks'. She cited 120 responses she had received of which 115 'referred to the HR profession with scepticism, sarcasm, rudeness or obscenity'. According to Kellaway, no one had a good word to say for HR. 'So demoralised are HR people that they churn out junk and when you attack it they do not even have the spirit to get angry'.

Where does this prejudice come from? Some critics have argued that personnel people should relinquish their ambiguous roles and adopt unashamedly managerialist positions. Others concluded that if human resources were fundamental to business success they were too important to be left to operational personnel managers. One of Lucy Kellaway's e-mailers stated: 'For HR to work it should (a) rename itself personnel and (b) stick to the basics, e.g. payroll, healthcare, training – of other people, not themselves – and pensions.'

But many commentators in the HR and management literature contend that major human resource decisions should be made by top managers and the consequences of those decisions should be carried through by line management. These considerations place HRM on a strategic rather an operational footing and therefore make HRM a concept of greater interest than personnel management to senior executives. However, in an article from the US business magazine *Fast Company* entitled 'Why We Hate HR', Hammonds (2005) repeats some familiar criticisms, stating:

> ... let's face it: After close to 20 years of hopeful rhetoric about becoming 'strategic partners' with a 'seat at the table' where the business decisions that matter are made, most human resources professionals aren't nearly there. They have no seat, and the table is locked inside a conference room to which they have no key. HR people are, for most practical purposes, neither strategic nor leaders.

Hammonds goes on to describe HR as 'at best, a necessary evil – and at worst, a dark bureaucratic force that blindly enforces nonsensical rules, resists creativity, and impedes constructive change.' While conceding that HR is 'the corporate function with the greatest potential' and, theoretically, the key driver of business performance, he also considers it to be 'the one that most consistently underdelivers.'

Whatever the underlying level of hostility, or press disdain, it remains the case that, in larger organizations, there has been a reappraisal of the previously unfashionable and low-status personnel department. 'Personnel' cannot be regarded as peripheral if it controls an organization's people since the rhetoric states that they are its greatest resources. Many businesses have adopted some form of HRM in recognition of this importance. As Fowler (1987) famously stated, 'HRM represents the discovery of personnel management by chief executives'.

HRM in reality Laughing gurus

The use of humour is one key to the success of management gurus. Researchers Dr Tim Clark and Dr David Greatbatch, authors of *Management Speak: Why We Listen to What Management Gurus Tell Us*, analysed the techniques used by world-famous gurus such as Tom Peters, Rosabeth Moss Kanter and Gary Hamel. They found that successful gurus employ skilful communication techniques, especially humour, to promote their sometimes uncomfortable messages. Filling a lecture theatre or conference venue with laughter avoids alienating their audiences and brings people 'on-side.'

'Examining live and video-recorded performances of leading international gurus enabled us to analyse the presentational techniques they use to disseminate their ideas during live presentations,' said Dr Greatbatch.

Gurus are faced with the problem of advocating unorthodox organizational practices that their audiences are probably not using, and disparaging the practices they are using. This is a delicate task with an inherent risk of alienating their audience members. So how do they do it? Dr Clark argues: 'These gurus remain highly regarded on the world-speaking stage and we wanted to discover their grammar of persuasion – in other words the communication techniques which underpin their frequently charismatic and persuasive public speaking performances.'

The study shows that gurus avoid offence by evoking laughter and telling stories. 'Basically, whenever the guru says anything potentially uncomfortable to audiences of managers they use humour and wrap it up as a joke,' said Dr Greatbatch. The researchers found that gurus used a number of specific techniques to 'invite' laughter. 'Collective audience laughter is not simply a spontaneous reaction to humour or jokes,' argued David Greatbatch. 'Rather, the gurus invite laughter by indicating when it is appropriate for the audience members to do so.'

Gurus used verbal and non-verbal actions to invite laughter, including:

- laughing themselves
- using exaggerated, ironic or comedic gestures
- showing their teeth in a 'laughing' smile.

Having achieved laughter from the audience, the gurus played on this bonding to encourage the audience to feel part of an 'in group' sharing a common viewpoint with the gurus. The audience then began to turn against the management practice(s) being criticised by the guru.

Storytelling seemed to be particularly important in the two processes of evoking laughter and deflecting criticism. The researchers found that more than two-thirds of audience laughter studied occurred within the context of stories. Stories make the gurus' messages more entertaining and memorable and also reinforce the authority of the gurus' knowledge. So their stories make constant references to famous and respected managers and organizations, personally known to the gurus. Audience research confirms that those speakers who use funny stories to develop their arguments are those who are most remembered.

'Our research clearly shows that gurus deploy humour at those points in their presentation where they face possible dissent,' asserts Dr Greatbatch. 'Because they package their ideas in a non-offensive way, the world's leading gurus are never booed from the stage and typically generate very positive audience reaction and a high feel-good factor. Anyone can learn the techniques which they use and public speakers ranging from politicians to trainers could benefit from having a greater range of presentation techniques to deploy when necessary.'

Management gurus have had a significant influence on the practice of management. Are their ideas brought into question by the use of the theatrical techniques described in this article?

Source: *HRM Guide UK* (http://www.hrmguide.co.uk), amended 29 April, 2006.

Function	Roles	
1 Planning and organizing for work, people and HRM	Strategic perspective	**Table 1.2**
	Organization design	Core roles in human resource management
	Change management	**Source** Plenary group of the Steering Committee for HRM Standards & Qualifications, South Africa, 1999.
	Corporate 'wellness' management	
2 People acquisition and development	Staffing the organization	
	Training and development	
	Career management	
	Performance management	
	Industrial relations	
3 Administration of policies, programmes and practices	Compensation management	
	Information management	
	Administrative management	
	Financial management	

Does this list of core HR roles differ in any significant way from the list of personnel functions given in Table 1.1?

The new managerialism

Schuler (1990) emphasized that the HR function had an opportunity to shift from being an 'employee advocate' (associated with personnel management) to a 'member of the management team'. Schuler's view was that this required HR professionals to be concerned with the bottom line, profits, organizational effectiveness and business survival. In other words, human resource issues should be addressed as business issues.

In fact, line and general managers have been instrumental in the adoption of HRM, often pushing changes through despite the resistance of personnel specialists (Storey, 2001, p.7). Radical changes in business structures and supportive, largely right-wing, governments encouraged a renewed confidence in the power of managers to manage. The balance of power moved away from workers and their representatives with the collapse of traditional heavy industries in Western countries. High levels of unemployment allowed managers to pick and choose new recruits. Existing employees felt pressurized to be more flexible under the threat of losing their jobs. As a result, managers were able to design more competitive organizations with new forms of employment relationships.

Encouraged by the writing of management gurus and, more recently, by the burgeoning legions of consultants (Legge, 2004, p.2), managers eagerly adopted new management fads and fashions. Businesses moved away from multi-layered, rigid hierarchies and long-term career paths. Instead we saw an increase in flatter, project-oriented forms of organizations resourced in a flexible way – including short-term, part-time and contract workers. People managers found themselves needing a framework within which to comprehend and justify these innovative practices. The stage was set for HRM, which was presented as a coherent and integrated philosophy by its originators, covering every aspect of people management (Beer *et al*, 1984, p.1).

Summary

In this chapter we introduced the concept of HRM. Human resource management has evolved from a number of different strands of thought and is best described as a loose philosophy of people management rather than a focused methodology. It derives largely from the last century but incorporates older notions about the management of people at work. These ideas have many different roots and they do not fit comfortably within one coherent and self-consistent body of knowledge. One major point of debate has been the difference, if any, between HRM and 'traditional' personnel management. As we shall see in later chapters, the development of HRM continues today as new management theories, fashions and fads emerge.

Further reading

There are many introductory texts on human resource management, several with an orientation towards a single country. The following texts are of more general use. Wendy Holloway's *Work Psychology and Organizational Behaviour* (Sage, 1991) remains one of the best overviews of scientific management, human factors, human relations and other early approaches. The various editions of *Organizational Behaviour* by David Buchanan and Andrzej Huczynski (FT Prentice Hall) also contain useful discussions of these early movements, complete with illustrations. For more on Henry Ford see: *The People's Tycoon: Henry Ford and the American Century* by Steven Watts (Alfred A. Knopf, 2005) and *My Life and Work* by Henry Ford (R.A. Kessinger Publishing Co., 2004). Issues involved in the development of personnel management and HRM are best covered in texts edited by John Storey, including the second edition of *Human Resource Management: A Critical Text* (Thomson Learning, 2001).

Review questions

1 How would you explain the difference between 'organizing' and 'managing' people?

2 The world in which writers such as Huarte and Machiavelli expressed their opinions was very different from ours. Their views would not be regarded as 'politically correct' today. What value can we attach to their views on dealing with working people?

3 What problems would have resulted from personal control of businesses when they began to develop into large work organizations employing hundreds, and sometimes thousands of workers?

4 How would you describe the main differences between the 'scientific management', 'human factors' and 'human relations' approaches?

5 What is HRM? Is it really different from personnel management? Summarize the main differences between personnel management and HRM as you see them.

6 Is 'relabeling' personnel as HRM anything more than a makeover or a cosmetic change?

7 How much does the concept of HRM owe to Japanese management practices?

8 Which theoretical developments do you consider to have contributed most to modern people management?

9 What is meant by 'management gurus'? What value can be placed on the ideas they have popularized?

Case study for discussion and analysis

Read the following case study which is largely based on a 'eulogy' of George Cadbury, designed to present both the man and the company in a good light. How many of today's methods of people management can you identify?

George Cadbury (1839–1922)

George Cadbury took on people management without the benefit of a business education or the advice of management gurus. Together with other Quaker manufacturers, Cadbury was eulogized as a hero of Victorian industry. A champion of paternalist management, he exemplified the virtues of thrift and hard work, tempered with a concern for the welfare of his workers.

Virtuous hard work

His father, John Cadbury, started a tea and coffee business in Birmingham, England, in 1824. Forty years later, aged 22, George Cadbury took on the ailing company with his brother Richard. Brought up with stern discipline, self denial was their way of life, believing in hard work and a frugal lifestyle.

George removed every distraction, even a morning paper. He abstained from tobacco and alcohol, and later tea and coffee. This was reflected in the business, which concentrated on cocoa and chocolate. He loved sport, especially cricket and boating, but these were largely sacrificed for work. Each day was planned for maximum effectiveness. In winter he started work by 7.00 am – earlier in summer – rising at 5.15 am. Frequently, he worked until 9.00 pm. Breaks consisted of a walk home for lunch, and a later meal at work: bread and butter and water. George Cadbury followed Emerson's maxim that 'the one prudence in life is concentration; the one evil dissipation'.

Total quality

The business became profitable and expanded. As with other manufacturers in an age of low standards, Cadburys' products contained only one-fifth cocoa, the rest being potato starch, sago flour and treacle. In 1861, for example, Cadburys were manufacturing 'Iceland Moss', containing 10 per cent 'Icelandic moss gelatine'. A 'comforting gruel', it probably tasted medicinal and was marketed as having healing properties. Unhappy with such poor products, Cadburys became the first UK firm to make pure cocoa for drinking. They imported Dutch machinery that pressed out some of the cocoa butter, making it unnecessary to add starchy material to counter the natural fat.

▶

The medical press was drawing attention to the danger of food additives and Cadburys new product received favourable mentions in the *British Medical Journal* and *The Lancet*. The Adulteration of Food Act in 1872 required manufacturers to state clearly the nature of any additives to their products. Cadburys gradually abandoned inferior products and adopted the motto 'absolutely pure', eventually becoming the leading producers in the UK.

The greenfield site and the all-embracing company

In 1879 development began on a new factory and workers' housing at a greenfield site outside Birmingham. The development was presented as a rare appreciation, for the time, that industrial success depended on people more than machines. There were two motives: business efficiency and staff welfare. As 'our people spend the greater part of their lives at their work ... we wish to make it less irksome by environing them with pleasant and wholesome sights, sounds and conditions'. At the same time, having new, efficient premises had considerable marketing value. The British chocolate industry was keen to emulate the French, regarded as the best producers. The French Menier company advertised extensively in the UK, featuring model premises and employee welfare. They had started to build workers' accommodation in 1870. Cadburys chose the French-sounding name of Bournville and set about constructing a village for their key employees. The village and 370 houses were handed over to an independent Bournville Village Trust in 1900 to avoid the accusation of using tied housing.

Employee relations

Unions barely existed at the time. Employers and workers were normally hostile, but the Cadburys had a close, sympathetic relationship with their workers. They believed that business success lay in cooperation rather than friction. Despite initial heavy losses, they gradually pushed workers' pay above the wretched levels normal at that time. They used incentives to encourage punctuality and other improvements but loyalty and commitment were largely won through positive personal relations. Cadbury was the first company in Birmingham to adopt a Saturday half-holiday. The brothers addressed everyone by their first names and played cricket with the workers on spare afternoons.

Between 1879 and 1899, the workforce increased from 230 to 2685, including 1885 women production workers. Cadburys' business methods were relatively gentle but they were frequently accused of being autocratic. They were deeply concerned with workers' welfare and standards of morality, watching over them keenly. Their own code of business ethics removed many of the evils of the factory system. For them the factory was a centre of learning, fostering good hygiene and intellectual development.

The brothers required female employees to wear company dresses at work. The firm provided the material, free for the first dress and subsidized thereafter. Female workers were asked to put on a clean frock every Monday morning. This gave them a clean appearance and encouraged self-respect, making a favourable impression on visitors. Until the 1940s, Cadburys did not employ married women. As explained by Dean Kitchin (1910), quoted in Gardiner (1923):

> ... In this vast multitude, all dressed in pure white and ready for a day's active work, there was not a single married woman. For Mr Cadbury will never take the mothers away from their homes and children; he told me, with a grave smile, that when he had allowed married women to work with him, he found that their husbands were quite content to loaf about doing nothing, living on the wages of their wives; and, he added, that the poor things invariably came back after child-bearing to work, long before they were fit to work.

Cadbury reintroduced the practice of a brief daily service with the workpeople. This was also a custom followed by the chocolate firm of Fry at Bristol. According to Joseph Fry:

> In addition to the religious benefit which may be looked for, I think that there is a great advantage in bringing the workpeople once a day under review. It is often a means of observing their conduct and checking any tendency to impropriety.

Valuing the human resource

Traditionally, it was believed that labour should be bought in the cheapest market like any other commodity. Improved pay or conditions were undesirable expenses. George Cadbury believed that economizing on labour was unethical and also bad business. He considered employees' safety, health, and even pleasure to be positive investments. Commonly thought optional, Cadbury regarded them as essential for efficient management.

Cadbury considered that people were infinitely valuable and should be used effectively. Work should be well paid but directed to make best use of expensive labour: using low-paid workers to compete with automation was foolish. New technology and efficiency went along with high pay. Inevitably, new machinery displaced workers and, if required, he did not shirk at dismissal. However, the business was always growing so redundant workers from one department could transfer to another.

Sources: Gardiner (1923); Smith, Child and Rowlinson (1990).

Chapter 2
The concept of HRM

Learning objectives

The purpose of this chapter is to:

- Outline the variety of ways in which HRM is defined.

- Offer a working definition for the purposes of this book.

- Discuss the most influential early models of HRM.

- Review some of the evidence for the adoption of HRM.

Defining human resource management

In the previous chapter we introduced the concept of human resource management and outlined the territory of people management covered by specialists in personnel or HRM. But what exactly is 'human resource management'? In Chapter 1 we discussed some of the theoretical and other developments which led to HRM being distinguished to some extent from 'traditional' personnel management. In this chapter we will examine the concept in greater detail.

Human resource management can seem to be a vague and elusive concept, not least because it has a variety of definitions (see Table 2.1). In fact, pinning down an acceptable definition can seem like trying to hit a moving target in a fog. This confusion reflects the different interpretations found in articles and books about human resource management. HRM is an elastic term (Storey, 1989, p.8). It covers a range of applications that vary from book to book and organization to organization.

Simple reflection on the three words 'human resource management' does not provide much enlightenment. 'Human' implies it has something to do with people; 'management' places it in the domain of business and organization; but 'resource' is a highly ambiguous concept which many people find difficult to relate to.

In fact, much of the academic literature suffers from forgetting the human element in HRM. Most of us would not take kindly to being classified as a 'resource', along with our desks and computers. It seems that there is a fundamental difficulty in considering a person's worth or value to an organization. This arises from that person's humanity. People are different from other resources and cannot be discussed in exactly the same way as equipment or finances. This difference lies at the heart of the antagonism and ambiguity that surrounds HRM in practice.

From an organizational perspective human resources encompass the people in an organization – its employees – and the human potential available to a business. The people in an organization offer different skills, abilities and knowledge that may or may not be appropriate to the needs of the business. Additionally, their commitment and motivation vary. Some people identify with an organization and are motivated to help achieve its objectives. Others regard their employing firm as a vehicle for their personal goals. Some may be overworked while others are under-utilized. Invariably, there is a gap or mismatch between the actual performance of employees and the ideal requirements of a business. Human resource management focuses on closing this gap to achieve greater organizational effectiveness. As we shall see later, this has been referred to as the 'matching model'.

The human potential available to a business includes the recognition and development of unrealized skills and knowledge. Ingenuity and creativity can be tapped to develop innovative services and products. This also extends to people outside an organization – contractors, consultants, freelancers, temporary and part-time workers – who can add expertise, deal with unusual problems and provide the flexibility to give a competitive advantage.

HRM in reality Human resources

'Sir, – While visiting a patient in Edinburgh's Western General hospital, I was shocked to see a six-foot-long board with large letters proclaiming: HUMAN RESOURCES. This distinguishes people who work in the hospital – doctors, nurses, porters, office workers, painters, managers – from other resources such as computers, laser beams, toilet rolls, refuse bins, beds, etc.

If these human resources are ill, are they labelled "out of order" or "broken down" and when being treated, are they being repaired? Are babies listed as "in process of being manufactured" with an expected date when they will be "operational"? Are old and dead people "non-usable human resources" or can they be listed as "replacement parts"?

When we define humans as resources, we are in danger of forgetting that we are dealing with people!'

Source: Cited in Price (1997).

Storey (2001) introduces *Human Resource Management: A Critical Text* by saying:

It is hard to imagine that it is scarcely much more than a decade since the time when the term 'human resource management' (HRM) was rarely used – at least outside the USA. Yet nowadays the term is utterly familiar around the globe and hardly a week goes by without the publication of another book on the subject.

But he observes that despite the proliferation of books, journals, conferences, academic sub-groups, etc., the subject remains 'and always has been from its earliest inception, highly controversial.' Specifically, he highlights questions about the nature of HRM, the domain it covers, the characteristics of HR practice, the reach of the subject and its antecedents, outcomes and impact.

Along with management writers (primarily American) on HRM, Storey pinpoints inputs from a wider field that have supported the increased importance of HRM:

- the resource-based theory of the firm
- the '**learning organization**'
- **Knowledge management.**

We will discuss these inputs further in later sections of this book.

Table 2.1 gives a selection of definitions taken from various books and articles published over the past 20 years. Generally they come from an academic view of HRM. Would the defi-

---

HRM in reality UK workers have little trust in bosses

The attitudes of British employees towards senior managers are significantly more negative than those of their counterparts in the USA, with fewer than a third expressing trust and confidence in their leaders, according to a Watson Wyatt study.

Watson Wyatt's WorkUK and WorkUSA surveys – involving a representative sample of more than 15 000 private sector workers in the USA and UK – showed that while approx. one half (51 per cent) of workers in the USA had trust and confidence in the job being done by their organization's leaders, just under a third (31 per cent) of UK employees felt the same. The surveys are part of Watson Wyatt's global benchmarking studies of employee opinions, communications, pay and benefits, performance management, HR effectiveness and work–life balance.

'Clearly there may be cultural factors at play here when we compare the UK and USA', said Andrew Cocks, European head of employee research at Watson Wyatt. 'But nevertheless, UK business leaders can take little comfort from these results. There is a clear need for a better dialogue between management and employees and the development of a real climate of openness and trust, especially if we are going to compete effectively with the USA in the new "cheap dollar" world.'

The study found that workers' ratings of senior managers in the USA had risen from a low of 44 per cent in 2002 (following Enron and other high profile corporate scandals) whereas there was no evidence for a similar upward trend in the UK survey.

'Lack of confidence in senior management does not just make for a difficult atmosphere at work,' said Andrew Cocks. 'Our research shows that it can hit the bottom line hard. In an employee survey we recently conducted for a major European company, belief in senior management proved to be the strongest leading indicator of new product sales and was their top business performance indicator.'

According to Watson Wyatt, effective communication is a key way in which leaders can build trust with employees. But months before the implementation of the new EU Directive on Informing and Consulting Employees, a mere 30 per cent of British employees believe that management explains the reasons behind major decisions and just 18 per cent feel that management successfully involves employees in decisionmaking.

'Greater mutual understanding has to be key to the future success of business in the UK,' said Andrew Cocks. 'In order to play an active part in taking any organization forward, employees need to understand and support any vision leaders have for the future and know how they can contribute to the process in their day-to-day work. Our research has consistently shown a link between factors such as employee alignment and commitment and enhanced business and financial performance.'

What methods can managers use to gain the trust of their employees?

Source: *HRM Guide UK* (http://www.hrmguide.co.uk), 2 March, 2005.

nitions be any different if decided by practitioners who were actively involved in human resource management? A plenary group – including practitioners – of the Steering Committee for HRM Standards & Qualifications in South Africa produced the following working definition in 1999:

It is proposed that we take *human resource management* to be that part of management concerned with:

● all the decisions, strategies, factors, principles, operations, practices, functions, activities and methods related to the management of people as employees in any type of organization (including small and micro enterprises and virtual organizations);

Table 2.1 Definitions of HRM	Definition	Source
	Human resource management involves all management decisions and actions that affect the relationship between the organization and employees – its human resources.	Beer *et al.*, 1984, p.1
	A method of maximizing economic return from labour resource by integrating HRM into business strategy.	Keenoy, 1990, p.3
	A strategic, coherent and comprehensive approach to the management and development of the organization's human resources in which every aspect of that process is wholly integrated within the overall management of the organization. HRM is essentially an ideology.	Armstrong, 1992, p.9
	Perhaps it is best to regard HRM as simply a notion of how people can best be managed *in the interests of the organization.*	Armstrong, 1994
	A diverse body of thought and practice, loosely unified by a concern to integrate the management of personnel more closely with the core management activity of organizations.	Goss, 1994, p. 1
	HRM is a discourse and technology of power that aims to resolve the gap inherent in the contract of employment between the capacity to work and its exercise and, thereby, organize individual workers into a collective, productive power or force.	Townley, 1994, p.138
	Human resource management is a distinctive approach to employment management which seeks to achieve competitive advantage through the strategic development of a highly committed and capable workforce, using an integrated array of cultural, structural and personnel techniques.	Storey, 2001, p.6
	Human resource management is the attraction, selection, retention, development and use of human resources in order to achieve both individual and organizational objectives.	Cascio, 1998, p.2
	Human resources can be described as the organizational function accountable for obtaining and maintaining qualified employees. In today's complex environment, fulfilling that mission is a major contributor to an organization's success.	American Management Association, 2000, p.xvii
	… The element of managerial work which is concerned with acquiring, developing and dispensing with the efforts, skills and capabilities of an organization's workforce and maintaining organizational relationships within which these human resources can be utilized to enable the organization to continue into the future within the social, political and economic context in which it exists.	Watson, 2003, p.1

- all the dimensions related to people in their employment relationships, and all the dynamics that flow from it (including the realization of the potential of individual employees in terms of their aspirations);
- all aimed at adding value to the delivery of goods and services, as well as to the quality of work life for employees, and hence helping to ensure continuous organizational success in transformative environments.

We will see that the variety, scope and intention found in definitions of HRM can be explained, in part, by some of the theories and models of human resource management to be explored in the next section.

We conclude this section by reflecting on Storey's (2001) comment that HRM is 'an amalgam of description, prescription and logical deduction' and that it is an 'historically-situated phenomenon.' Moreover, for Storey, HRM reflects the beliefs and assumptions of influential 'leading-edge' practitioners. As we shall see in the next section, there are grounds also to believe that it arose when confidence had been lost in more traditional approaches to people management because of new levels and types of competition.

Human resource management has often been presented as a proactive approach to managing people (Storey, 2001). This entails an emphasis on long-term thinking, anticipating changes and requirements before they become critical. But, in reality, HRM is a mixture of anticipation and reaction (Price, 2000). Tamkin, Barber and Dench (1997) pointed out that human resource managers may have to deal with unexpected problems and radical changes in employer policy – for example, site closures and redundancies because of market changes. To do so, they must react quickly and competently within the bounds of employment law and contractual agreements. This requires that HRM should be both pragmatic and eclectic (Price, 2000): pragmatic because it aims to achieve practical solutions to real work problems; and eclectic because those solutions can be drawn from a variety of theoretical and managerial traditions as we saw in Chapter 1.

Before we finish this section we need to determine our working definition of HRM for the purposes of this book. This is shown in Key concept 2.1.

Key concept 2.1 Human resource management

A philosophy of people management based on the belief that human resources are uniquely important to sustained business success. An organization gains competitive advantage by using its people effectively, drawing on their expertise and ingenuity to meet clearly defined objectives. Human resource management is aimed at recruiting capable, flexible and committed people, managing and rewarding their performance and developing key competencies.

Maps and models of HRM

Keenoy (1999) compares HRM with a hologram:

As with a hologram, HRM changes its appearance as we move around its image. Each shift of stance reveals another facet, a darker depth, a different contour. As a fluid entity of apparently multiple identities and forms, it is not surprising that every time we look at it, it is slightly different. This is why, conceptually, HRMism appears to be a moving target, and why, empirically, it has no fixed (fixable) forms.

Keenoy's comparison is helpful in explaining why there are so many divergent definitions of HRM. There are numerous, widely-different interpretations, some in the shape of formal models. The two most influential are the **Harvard** and **Michigan** models from the 1980s which we will consider later in this chapter. Consistent with the confusion over the definition of HRM, the major models are to some extent contradictory but also have common elements. Partly this is because some of the key concepts have arisen several times in different contexts.

Sisson (1990) contends that there are four major features that appear to some degree in all HRM models and theories:

- Integration of human resource policies with each other and with the organization's business plan. HRM is a key instrument of business strategy, viewing employees as important assets.
- Responsibility for managing people moves from personnel specialists to senior (line) managers. Specialists provide a consultancy service for line managers.
- **Employee relations** shift away from **collective bargaining** – dialogue between management and unions. Instead, direct discussion between management and individual employees is encouraged.
- A stress on commitment to the organization and personal initiative.

Key concept 2.2 Hard and soft HRM

Storey (1989) has distinguished between hard and soft forms of HRM, typified by the Michigan and Harvard models respectively. 'Hard' HRM focuses on the resource side of human resources. It emphasizes costs in the form of 'headcounts' and places control firmly in the hands of management. Their role is to manage numbers effectively, keeping the workforce closely matched with requirements in terms of both bodies and behaviour. 'Soft' HRM, on the other hand, stresses the 'human' aspects of HRM. Its concerns are with communication and motivation. People are led rather than managed. They are involved in determining and realizing strategic objectives.

Softer models of HRM typically suggest that HR managers should become:

- *Enablers*: structuring organizations to allow employees to achieve objectives.
- *Empowerers*: devolving decisionmaking to the lowest level.
- *Facilitators*: encouraging and assisting employees.

From this perspective, managers are no longer supervisors. The organizations move away from rigid hierarchies and power distinctions towards people taking responsibility for their own work. Guest (1987) provides a fusion of various HRM approaches into a theory of HRM which incorporates a number of policy goals:

- Aim for a high level of commitment from employees, so that workers identify with the organization's goals and contribute actively to its improvement and success.
- This enables the organization to obtain a high quality output from workers who want to continually improve standards.
- An expectation of **flexibility** from workers – willingness to depart from fixed job definitions, working practices and conditions.
- Strategic integration – all these strands link the organization's strategy. They are directed towards agreed objectives and interact with each other in a cohesive way.

These goals require support from top managers and integration of human resource strategy with business policy. The activities we outlined in Table 1.1 in the first chapter of this book are linked and overlaid by HR staff so as to improve communication and increase involvement, commitment and productivity. They are integrated and match the requirements of the organization's strategic plans. We cannot take a decision or make a change in one without having repercussions in at least some of the other areas.

The central aim of the HRM approach is to combine all personnel or human resource activities into an organized and integrated programme to meet the strategic objectives of an enterprise. It moves us away from commonsense solutions for day-to-day problems, such as 'get someone to fill that job', towards a conscious attempt to think through the consequences of hiring that 'someone'. Do we want a recruit who is perfect for that particular position right now, or an individual who might require considerable training but shows great adaptability? Do we hire someone for an overworked production department, knowing that the sales department are forecasting a drop in orders later in the year? The essential point of HRM is that the functions should be managed as a whole, and not as stand alone activities.

Legge (1989, 1995, 2001, 2004), for example, has been a steadfast critic of simplistic or evangelistic interpretations of HRM. The rhetoric of HRM claims that personnel and human resource management are distinctively different forms of people management. She demonstrates some flaws in this argument (Legge, 1989: p.20; 1995: p.36). First, we have seen that 'hard' and 'soft' models of HRM themselves describe very different approaches. The 'soft' model can be identified readily with the welfarist tradition in personnel management in countries such as the UK and Ireland, Australia, New Zealand, and South Africa. Secondly, most texts do not actually compare like with like:

- Accounts of HRM are normative – they are theoretical models of how human resource management could or should take place. That is to say, they express an 'ideal' or set of intentions for HRM. They do not tell us how human resource management actually happens in the real world. Moreover, the intentions of soft HRM are often pious and contradictory. We saw earlier that they are derived from much older concepts and techniques. What makes them 'HRM' is that their components are welded together into expressions of a particular, if divergent, philosophy of people management.

- In contrast, accounts of personnel management are generally descriptive of personnel practice. Models of personnel are grounded in decades of activity whereas HRM is still comparatively new, and empirical evidence of its conduct is only beginning to emerge.

In short, we are comparing the theory of a young form of people management (HRM) with the practice of an old form (personnel management). If we seek out normative models of personnel management, Legge concludes that there is not much difference from normative models of HRM. We can do so by examining textbook accounts of personnel management in the 1980s which used the same terminology of 'integrating with **organizational goals**' and 'vesting control in the line' as newer HRM literature of the 'soft' variety. However, she finds differences in emphasis:

- Personnel management focuses on the non-managerial workforce. HRM concentrates on managers and the 'core workforce'.

- HRM is vested in line managers in their role as business managers not people managers. The focus is on managing all resources to maximize profit.

- HRM models feature the role of senior managers in managing the culture of organizations.

Watson (2003) finds the use of 'hard' and 'soft' distinctions 'utterly unhelpful as an analytical tool', arguing that 'it confuses variations in intellectual or academic emphasis with variations in managerial practice.' More importantly, Watson considers that 'it ignores the

Storey (1994a)	Legge (1995)	Tyson (1995)	**Table 2.2**
Conceptual	Normative	Normative	Classifications of HRM models
Descriptive	Descriptive-functional	Descriptive	
Prescriptive	Descriptive-behavioural	Analytical	
	Critical evaluative		

political–economic context of managerial practices.' For Watson, the 'hard–soft' distinction is meaningless in a world where managers may choose either approach (or a mixture) on purely business grounds. Watson is equally unhappy with the use of the term 'rhetoric' (as opposed to reality) which he considers should be restricted to 'conceptualize the *linguistic techniques used by social actors to persuade others of the validity of their arguments* (Watson's emphasis).' Tellingly, he argues that:

> To criticize managers for talking rhetorically is like criticizing birds for singing or dogs for barking. It is a manager's job to persuade people to think and work in particular ways.

From an entirely different perspective, Cakar and Bititci (2001) argue that whereas a number of authors, including Legge, have attempted to classify the various models of HRM using terms such as 'descriptive', 'normative' and 'prescriptive' (see Table 2.2), they do not offer precise definitions of these terms. Cakar and Bititci identify two sources of confusion: (a) confusion over the different types of classification, e.g. is there a difference between 'normative' (Legge, 1995) and 'prescriptive' (Storey, 1994a); and (b) lack of clear definitions for each classification.

Cakar and Bititci (2001) state that:

> HRM (people management) is a critical input enhancing the business results. . . . HRM criteria covers planning, managing and improving the human resources; identifying, developing and sustaining people's knowledge and competencies; involving and empowering people. All these things have an effect on business results, because human resources are key assets. HRM has a significant impact on the performance of the manufacturing business.

Cakar and Bititci locate HRM within business process architecture, a classification of business processes into three groupings: manage processes, operate processes and support processes. They classify HRM as a support process together with finance and IT, arguing that HRM needs to be understood as a business process in order to improve manufacturing performance.

The same argument can apply to service, non-profit and public organizations. Fitz-Enz (1994) argues that businesses can adopt one of three approaches to HRM, offering the practitioner one of three career choices:

- *Zombies*: Those which take the traditional 'staff as expense' approach to people management. Estimating that 30–50 per cent of companies take this approach, especially small–medium, family-owned enterprises described as the 'living dead' with no real professionalism in any of their managerial activities.

- *Reactors*: Where line managers have grabbed back HR responsibilities as they have (probably) never seen a professional HR function. Fitz-Enz describes this as the 'outsource–decentralize' model. Line managers don't really want some of the HR responsibilities but think they have no alternative. Perhaps 20–30 per cent of organizations follow this approach.

- *Confidants*: A small, trusted group of HR talents are in place as trusted experts, consultants and brokers of external services. Fitz-Enz regards this as the most desirable, again perhaps found in 20–30 per cent of organizations.

More recently, '**best practice**' approaches have featured, the best known of which are those presented by Jeffrey Pfeffer and David Ulrich.

Pfeffer (1998) stresses, in a series of books, that the greatest competitive advantage is to be obtained from people rather than technology. He contends that investment in technology is not enough, because that technology is (or soon will be) available to competitors. And the more complex the technology, the more it requires people skills anyway. Instead we need that variant of HRM described as 'high-performance management' (US) or 'high-commitment management' (elsewhere). This topic will be discussed in Chapter 3.

Ulrich (1997) argues that:

> HR professionals must focus more on the deliverables of their work than on doing their work better. They must articulate their role in terms of value created. They must create mechanisms to

deliver HR so that business results quickly follow. They must learn to measure results in terms of business competitiveness rather than employee comfort and lead cultural transformation rather than to consolidate, re-engineer, or downsize when a company needs a turnaround.

Ulrich contends that modern HR professionals should have four roles: strategic partner, agent of change, administrative expert and employee champion. Each role furthers the goals of both the business and its employees. As strategic partner, the HR function must make sure that its practices, processes, and policies complement the overall organizational strategy. It must also develop the capacity to execute that strategy in the minimum amount of time.

As we shall see in later sections of this book, organizational change has become a major issue due to speedier communication and global communication. The HR role as change agent, according to Ulrich, is that of a facilitator, involving modelling change to other departments, being a positive advocate of change across the entire organization, resolving employee issues arising from change, and embedding change by implementing efficient and flexible processes.

The HR function spends most of its time as administrative expert, and rightfully so, according to Ulrich. This role covers the infrastructure of people management: recruiting, hiring, compensating, rewarding and disciplining, training, record keeping, and terminating – and all of the other processes that involve people. HR's focus should be on ensuring that these processes are both efficient and optimized. The HR function must track, monitor and continuously improve on these basic processes to give credibility to its own existence.

The final role, 'employee champion', draws on the welfare manager roots of the personnel profession. This requires the HR function to know the concerns of employees and spend time talking to them and listening to their concerns. Moreover, according to Ulrich, the HR function should promote all possible methods of communication, including employee surveys, suggestion programmes, team meetings, and any other means of sharing information and views. A key element of this role is ensuring that employees receive a fair hearing.

The Harvard map of human resource management

We noted earlier that the Harvard Business School generated one of the most influential models of HRM. The Harvard interpretation sees employees as resources. However, they are viewed as being fundamentally different from other resources – they cannot be managed in the same way. The stress is on people as *human* resources. The Harvard approach recognizes an element of mutuality in all businesses, a concept with parallels in Japanese people management, as we observed earlier. Employees are significant stakeholders in an organization. They have their own needs and concerns along with other groups such as shareholders and customers.

The Harvard view acknowledges that management has the greatest degree of power. Nevertheless there must be scope for accommodation of the interests of the various stakeholders in the form of trade-offs, particularly between owners, employees and different employee groups. The model also acknowledges the need for mechanisms to reconcile the inevitable tension between employee expectations and management objectives.

Beer *et al.* (1984) argue that when general managers determine the appropriate human resource policies and practices for their organizations, they require some method of assessing the appropriateness or effectiveness of those policies. Beer *et al.* devised the famous Harvard 'map' (sometimes referred to as the Harvard model) of HRM shown in Figure 2.1. This map is based on an analytical approach and provides a broad causal depiction of the 'determinants and consequences of HRM policies'. It shows human resource policies to be influenced by two significant considerations:

- *Situational factors* in the outside business environment or within the firm such as laws and societal values, labour market conditions, unions, workforce characteristics, business strategies, management philosophy, and task technology. According to Beer *et al.*

these factors may constrain the formation of HRM policies but (to varying degrees) they may also be influenced by human resource policies.

- *Stakeholder interests*, including those of shareholders, management employees, unions, community and government. Beer *et al.* argue that human resource policies should be influenced by all stakeholders. If not, 'the enterprise will fail to meet the needs of these stakeholders in the long run and it will fail as an institution.'

The emphasis is on psychological objectives: the 'human' side of human resource management, including:

- motivating people by involving them in decisionmaking
- developing an organizational culture based on trust and teamwork.

Within the Harvard 'map' four strategic policy areas are addressed: **human resource flows,** reward systems, employee influence and work systems.

1 *Human resource flows*: managing the movement (flow) and performance of people:
   - Into the organization, by means of effective recruitment programmes and selection techniques which result in the most suitable people.
   - Through the organization, by placing them in the most appropriate jobs, appraising their performance, and promoting the better employees.
   - Out of the organization, terminating the employment of those no longer required, deemed unsuitable or achieving retirement age.

   Human resource policies must ensure the right mix and number of staff in the organization. This is achieved by the processes of resourcing and development of employee competences.

2 *Reward systems*: including pay and benefits designed to attract, motivate and keep employees.

3 *Employee influence*: controlling levels of authority, power and decisionmaking.

4 *Work systems*: defining and designing jobs, so that the arrangement of people, information and technology provide the most productive and efficient results.

Figure 2.1

The Harvard interpretation of HRM

Source: Beer *et al.* (1984: p.16). Reproduced by permission of The Free Press, a division of Simon & Schuster from *Managing Human Assets* by Beer, M., Spector, B., Lawrence, P.R., Mills, D.Q. and Walton, R.E. Copyright © 1984 by The Free Press.

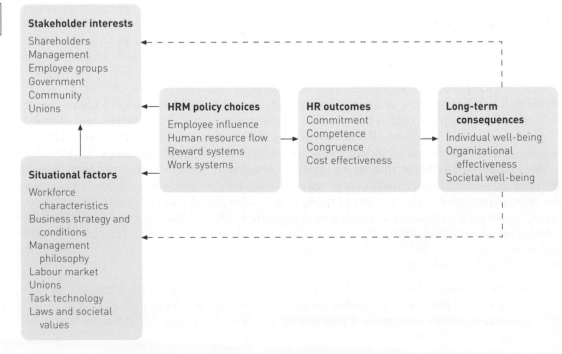

These policies result in the 'four Cs':

Commitment of employees to the organization's mission and values in a way thought to be typical of Japanese workers.

Congruence, linking human resource objectives with the organization's goals.

Competence, developing an appropriate mixture of skills, abilities and knowledge.

Cost-effectiveness, delivering performance in a competitive manner.

The Harvard model is strongly influenced by behavioural research and theory and stands in the tradition of 'human relations'. This is a humanistic and anti-authoritarian viewpoint which holds that employees will only adopt an organization's objectives if they wish to. They will not demonstrate enthusiasm and commitment if they are forced to comply. Accordingly, although strategic decisionmaking is channelled through top managers there is an emphasis on participation throughout the organization.

A further key point is that HRM is the responsibility of all managers – not just human resource specialists. Delivery of HRM initiatives is pushed down to line managers wherever possible. The Harvard model applies HRM to any manager with staff responsibilities. It should consider issues such as delegation, leadership, participation, team-building and organization from a non-specialist perspective. This will be further explored in Chapter 4 in our discussion of organizational HRM. Taken to its extreme, it can be argued that if managers are sufficiently competent in handling people then personnel or human resource specialists are unnecessary.

Beer *et al.* (1984) argue that:

> In the long run, striving to enhance all four Cs will lead to favourable consequences for individual wellbeing, societal wellbeing, and organizational effectiveness (i.e., long-term consequences, the last box in Figure 2.1). By organizational effectiveness we mean the capacity of the organization to be responsive and adaptive to its environment. We are suggesting, then, that human resource management has much broader consequences than simply last quarter's profits or last year's return on equity. Indeed, such short-term measures are relatively unaffected by HRM policies. Thus HRM policy formulation must incorporate this long-term perspective.

Beer *et al.* state that these 'four Cs' do not represent all the criteria that human resource policymakers can use to evaluate the effectiveness of human resource management, but consider them to be 'reasonably comprehensive' although they suggest that readers may add additional factors depending on circumstances.

HRM policies and their consequences

Beer *et al.* (1984) propose that long-term consequences (both benefits and costs) of human resource policies should be evaluated at three levels:

Individual. They argue that the wellbeing of employees must be considered separately and distinctly from that of the organization. Employees can be affected economically, physically or psychologically by HRM policies. But managers have different values and will weight those consequences differently according to those values. Some will focus on the organization at the expense of workers whereas others will regard employees as having legitimate claims to fair treatment.

Organizational. Human resource policies have to be evaluated in terms of their contribution to business goals and organizational survival. Specifically, HRM policies can increase an organization's:
- efficiency
- adaptability
- service performance
- price performance
- short-term results
- long-term results

Societal. HR practices can have wide consequences on society. For example, Beer *et al.* ask: 'What are the societal costs of a strike or a layoff?' They point out that 'alienated and laid-off workers may develop both psychological and physical health problems that make them burdens to community agencies funded by the local, state, or federal government. Today employers pass on many of the costs of their management practices to society.'

Beer *et al.* suggest that managers use their 4 Cs to analyze the questions raised above.

1 *Commitment*: do HRM policies enhance the **commitment** of employees to their work and their organization – and to what extent? Improved commitment may lead to more loyalty and better performance for the business. It can also benefit the individual through enhanced self-worth, dignity, psychological involvement and identity. And there is a societal spin-off because of these psychological benefits.

2 *Competence*: do HRM policies serve to attract, keep, or develop employees who have valuable skills and knowledge – **competence** – both now and in the future? Again there are benefits at all three levels. If skills and knowledge are there when required, the organization benefits, and its employees experience an increased sense of self-worth and economic wellbeing.

3 *Cost-effectiveness*: the **cost-effectiveness** of particular HRM policies can be evaluated in terms of wages, benefits, turnover, absenteeism, strikes, etc. The costs can be judged for organizations, individuals, and society as a whole.

4 *Congruence*: the question can be raised about the level of **congruence** in HRM policies between, for example:
   - management and employees
   - different employee groups
   - the organization and the community
   - employees and their families, and
   - within the individual?

Stakeholder theory

'We must commit ourselves to "wrestling" with this stakeholder stuff.' say Steven F. Walker and Jeffrey W. Marr in *Stakeholder Power: A Winning Plan for Building Stakeholder Commitment and Driving Corporate Growth* (2001):

> Only a brave leader explores what the troops really think. . . . But to be a true leader in the new economy, we must earn the trust of all our key stakeholders by learning to place faith in people and by weighing their needs and opinions into our business decisions. If we as managers use tools to listen to them, then collaborate with them fairly and intelligently, we will take care of the business and its constituents and, as a result, take care of ourselves as well.

It is a fairly obvious truism that a wide range of people and interest groups have an involvement with any organization – including stock/shareholders, customers, suppliers, employees, the local community, government and others. Clearly, they also have different and varying degrees of influence on the conduct and progress of the organization. There is a cultural context: the American stockholder approach contrasts strongly with the continental European or Japanese.

The US approach (mirrored to some extent in countries like Australia, Canada, New Zealand, South Africa and the UK) places power (and reward) in the hands of the stockholder. According to Windsor (1998):

> Stakeholder theory is a critique of the strong stockholder doctrine in US corporation law and financial–economics theory positing that management's clear fiduciary responsibility is to maximize economic rents on behalf of the firm's legal owners (the residual claimants).

Strong stockholder doctrine was articulated in *Dodge Brothers v. Ford* (1919), in which the Michigan Supreme Court ordered Ford Motor Co. to pay a special dividend.

In the stockholder model, other stakeholders – particularly employees – do not count. But Walker and Marr (2001) contend that:

It is always a mistake to operate as if employees are dispensable or easily interchangeable, because they are not. By definition, we cannot have an organization without the right employees – people who fit our cultures, who bring the right combination of talent, experience and personality to our organizations. These people are never easily replaced. Further, how humanely they are treated when they leave has a lasting impact on those who stay. It certainly sends a clear message about the company's commitment to workers.

You might think that stakeholder theory has its origins in HRM. Certainly Beer *et al.*'s (1984) Harvard map of HRM makes considerable use of the concept. But the main protagonist is regarded as being R. Edward Freeman, Olsson Professor of Applied Ethics at the University of Virginia's Darden School. He argued that managers should serve the interests of everyone with a 'stake' in (that is, affect or are affected by) the firm.

Stakeholders include shareholders, employees, suppliers, customers and the communities in which the firm operates – termed by Freeman the 'big five.' According to Freeman the purpose of the firm is to serve and coordinate the interests of its various stakeholders. The firm's managers are morally obliged to strike an appropriate balance among the big five interests when directing the firm's activities.

The influence of business ethics as an increasingly influential discipline is indicated by the following comment (Marcoux, 2000, p.1):

. . . among business ethicists there is a consensus favouring the stakeholder theory of the firm – a theory that seeks to redefine and reorient the purpose and the activities of the firm. Far from providing an ethical foundation for capitalism, these business ethicists seek to change it dramatically.

Windsor (1998) points out that stakeholder theory is arguably at an early stage of intellectual development, identifying Donaldson and Preston (1995) as having 'only recently revolutionized our conception of stakeholder theory by delineating nested descriptive, instrumental,and normative dimensions with the latter at the core'. Windsor also notes that Donaldson and Preston (1995: p.66) characterize 'the bulk of earlier stakeholder literature as blurred theorizing.

Windsor (1998) states that:

The lack of an explicit specification of the relationship between stakeholder and economic reasoning is a major lacuna. While stakeholder theory has achieved a degree of acceptance in the strategic management literature, now being commonly noted in new textbooks as a tool of strategic analysis, there is substantial resistance to stakeholder reasoning in the financial–economics literature. There is a counter-movement favouring stronger stockholders' rights and corporate-governance standards; shareholder value and economic value-added notions are gaining currency.

Shareholder theorists such as Milton Friedman argue that managers should serve the interests of a firm's owners – the shareholders. They contend that the social obligations of the firm are limited to:

- making good on contracts
- obeying the law
- adhering to ordinary moral expectations.

Briefly, 'obligations to nonshareholders stand as sideconstraints in the pursuit of shareholder interests' (Marcoux, 2000).

▶

Marcoux (2000, p.1) asks, in the Friedman vein:

. . . why firms are obligated to give something back to those to whom they routinely give so much already. Rather than enslave their employees, firms typically pay them wages and benefits in return for their labor. Rather than steal from their customers, firms typically deliver goods and services in return for the revenues that customers provide. Rather than free ride on public provisions, firms typically pay taxes and obey the law. Moreover, these compensations are ones to which the affected parties or (in the case of communities and unionized employees) their agents freely agree. For what reasons, then, is one to conclude that those compensations are inadequate or unjust, necessitating that firms give something more to those whom they have already compensated?

Even if one accepts the validity of stakeholder theory as a general approach, there remains a dispute over the meaning of 'stakeholder'. For example, Windsor (1998) considers that: 'who is logically a stakeholder is in fact an unresolved matter in the literature . . .' whereas Freeman's seminal conception was that the stakeholder community should include everyone who affected or was affected by an organization, a widely accepted definition.

Donaldson and Preston (1995: p.86) distinguished between non-stakeholder *influencers* and 'true' stakeholders. They argued that stakeholdership as a concept is more than just a union of influence and impact. Windsor (1998) describes this restricted class of stakeholders as 'contributing beneficiaries'.

A harder approach – people as human *resources*

A different view of HRM is associated with the Michigan Business School (Tichy *et al.*, 1982). There are many similarities with the Harvard 'map' but the Michigan model has a harder, less humanistic edge, holding that employees are resources in the same way as any other business resource. People have to be managed in a similar manner to equipment and raw materials. They must be:

- obtained as cheaply as possibly
- used sparingly
- developed and exploited as much as possible.

Moreover, the same approach should be applied to all people who resource an organization – not just its employees. Human beings are 'matched' to business needs. They are recruited selectively and trained to perform required tasks. Whereas the Harvard approach was inspired by the behavioural sciences, the Michigan view was strongly influenced by strategic management literature. HRM is seen as a strategic process, making the most effective use of an organization's human resources. Hence there must be coherent human resource policies which 'fit' closely with overall business strategies.

In fact, HRM is seen as a secondary product of strategy and planning rather than a primary influence. Within this model, the purpose of human resource strategy is to assist in the achievement of an organization's goals. This requires an alignment of all HR systems with the formal organization. Since the nature of HRM is determined largely by the situation and the environmental context, there is little freedom of operation for human resource managers. At best, human resource managers can only choose from a menu of possible initiatives which fit business strategy. The Michigan School identified the following key areas for the development of appropriate HR policies and systems:

Selection of the most suitable people to meet business needs.

Performance in the pursuit of business objectives.

Appraisal, monitoring performance and providing feedback to the organization and its employees.

Rewards for appropriate performance.

Development of the skills and knowledge required to meet business objectives.

The Michigan model (see Figure 2.2) takes a top-down approach. In contrast with the Harvard viewpoint, control of human resources lies firmly in the hands of senior management. People are selected and trained to meet the performance needs of the organization. However, this is not sufficient. Their attitudes and behaviour must also fit the strategic requirements of the business. The Michigan model advocates that HRM requires that employees show **behavioural consistency** with the ways of thinking and operating necessary to achieve business goals. For example, if strategy focuses on sales, employees will be expected to be extrovert, responsive and attentive to customer needs. On the other hand, an innovative strategy based on research and development will emphasise creativity, technical skill and long-term diligence. Behavioural consistency is an objective of change management, discussed in Chapter 6.

Adopting HRM

So far, we have tried to establish a reasonably clear concept of HRM, despite the different emphases between the two major early models. At this point, however, we must inject a necessary element of caution. Human resource management has been presented as a radical alternative to personnel management: so much so that it has been regarded as a new paradigm (Kuhn, 1962) – a framework of thinking – consisting of exciting, modern ideas which would replace the stale and ineffective prescriptions of personnel management. Enthusiasts saw the transition from 'personnel' to 'human resources' as an inevitable and unstoppable process – a paradigm shift. In fact, the process has proven to be somewhat slow.

The HR function can be organized in a variety of ways. Adams (1991) identifies five main types of HR service:

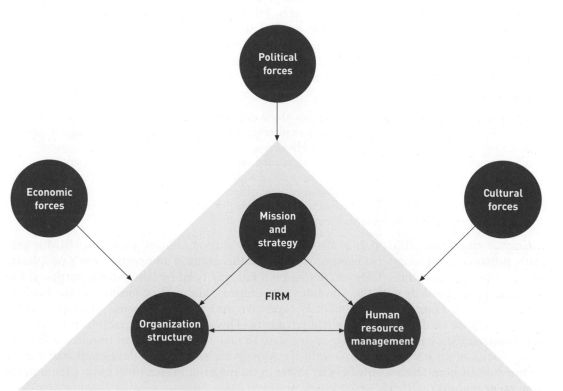

Figure 2.2

The Michigan model of HRM

Source: Devanna *et al.* (1984) in Fombrun *et al.*, *Strategic Human Resource Management*
© 1984 John Wiley & Sons Inc. Reproduced by permission of John Wiley & Sons Inc.

1 The traditional personnel department with a range of specialist human resource services.

2 In-house HR agencies which act as cost-centres, charging client departments for activities, e.g. recruitment.

3 Internal HR consultancies, selling their activities to the organization – possibly competing with outside agencies.

4 Business-within-business HR consultancy, selling services within and outside the company.

5 Outsourcing human resource services to an external provider.

Different interpretations of HRM

As we have seen, HRM is primarily North American in origin but in the USA, far from causing a revolution in people management techniques, acceptance of the new interpretation has not been universal. Kochan and Dyer (2001, pp. 272–3) comment that, despite an explosion of interest in human resource management:

> . . . even today we find that the human resource function within many American corporations remains weak and relatively low in influence, relative to other functions such as finance, marketing and manufacturing . . . little progress has been made in developing systematic theory or empirical evidence on the conditions under which human resources are elevated to a position where the firm sees and treats these issues as a source of competitive advantage. Nor is there much research that actually tests the effects of different strategies on the competitive position of the firm.

Why is this so? A number of explanations can be considered. First, there is the issue of perception: many US businesses fail to see the difference between HRM and earlier forms of people management. We observed at the beginning of this chapter that the term 'human resource management' had been used interchangeably with 'personnel management' in the USA. This continues to be the case. For example, many American 'HRM' texts are concerned with the functional activities of personnel specialists – their philosophy is little different from 1970s texts. In part, this is due to the managerialist and anti-union tradition of personnel management in the USA. For US practitioners, HRM was not such a radical departure from previous practice as it seemed to be for welfare-orientated personnel managers and industrial relations specialists in other countries. Legge (2004: p.3) has changed her position or, perhaps more fairly, moved with the times, in concluding that the preoccupation with supposed differences between 'personnel management' and HRM is now a moribund, indeed meaningless, debate:

> There is little point in discussing the niceties of the differences between personnel management and HRM when, in the USA, HRM is just another term for personnel management. In any case it was a bit of a straw man debate. Whether HRM was considered to be different from personnel management – in the UK at least – largely depended on the point of comparison. Sharp distinctions and contrasts emerged if the normative aspirations of HRM were compared with the descriptive practices of personnel management, but otherwise faded into several different emphases, all of which, though, pointed to HRM, in theory at least, being an essentially more central, strategic task than personnel management.

Kochan and Dyer (2001, p.282) also point to the 'market failures' problem. HRM is generally portrayed as a long-term perspective. Within this context an organization's people are investments for the future. They are not to be hired and fired for short-term purposes. But this concept sits uneasily with the prevailing short-termist ideology of business in the English-speaking world. Long-term investment is expensive and requires the use of money which might otherwise be diverted to dividend payments. This draws unfavourable comment from shareholders. If all businesses in an industry were to take the same human resource initiatives there would be no problem. This is unlikely. Moreover, expensively developed staff can be creamed off by competitors unwilling to invest in training but prepared to pay a premium for competent recruits.

In the case study at the end of this chapter we see how the difficulties associated with long-term, soft HRM are reflected in the history of IBM. As one of the world's major businesses, IBM was used as an example of excellence by Peters and Waterman (1982). It hit its high point in 1984 with profits of over US$6 billion – a sensational 25 per cent return on equity for shareholders. At that time it was the dominant force in world computing with 37 per cent of the total market. IBM was also featured by Beer and his colleagues as an example of a corporation which utilized the Harvard form of HRM. However, recent years have seen a significant shift towards a harder model as IBM encountered serious problems in the 1990s. Despite increases in overall revenues, the company was forced into major restructuring and job losses.

The IBM case study emphasises a number of difficulties associated with the adoption of 'soft' HRM. When business is good and continued growth seems probable, a company can afford to manage its people in a humane and considerate way. However, when the going gets tough and significant change is demanded, profitability becomes the prime consideration. The pressure for action from other stakeholders becomes overwhelming. It appears that, in such circumstances, managers have no alternative to adopting a 'hard' approach. The choice between hard and soft models is governed as much (if not more) by the prevailing market situation as it is by any question of managerial humanitarianism (Watson, 2003).

According to Weiss (1999, p.3):

> In the past the HR department attempted to meet the company's needs without actively focusing on the company's direction and the return on investment. Today, however, the conditions under which HR needs to operate have changed . . . Just as the finance department is responsible for overseeing the financial assets of the business, human resources' role is to oversee and be accountable for the investment in human capital (the money it takes to cultivate people and their talents). The company will maximize its return on this investment in human capital when HR maximizes the contribution people make to the company's strategic direction.

HRM in reality The fourth best job in America

That's 'human resources manager', in case you're wondering, according to the *Money* magazine and Salary.com list of 50 Best Jobs in America.

The survey of about 250 of the best-paid jobs in 19 industries, mostly requiring higher education, found that software engineers have the best jobs in the USA, with college professors second and (the much better compensated) financial advisors placed third. Online surveys were completed by 26 000 people to rank the best jobs.

The HR profession is rated well on:

- flexibility
- overall compensation
- opportunity for growth
- level of stress

Additionally, the survey highlights a trend toward outsourcing operational and administrative tasks, freeing HR to concentrate on a strategic role and adding to the challenge and interest in the profession.

'We're not surprised to see HR rank so highly. We couldn't agree more that HR is a great profession,' said Susan R. Meisinger, SPHR, President and CEO of the Society for Human Resource Management (SHRM). 'The profession is rapidly evolving where HR executives are playing a much larger role in determining the overall direction of their organization. These developments add to the vibrancy of the profession as more organizations look to HR for strategies to align their workforce with the goals of the business.'

'HR is an exciting profession, and with the projected growth and competitive salaries, there will be many opportunities available for bright new HR professionals who want to play a critical role in shaping the success of organizations,' added Meisinger.

Following HR came physician's assistant, market research analyst, computer/information technology analyst, real estate appraiser, pharmacist and psychologist.

To what extent does this survey indicate that HR is a prestigious occupation?

Source: *HRM Guide USA* (http://www.hrmguide.com), 4 April, 2006.

Weiss argues for the transformation of the human resource function in terms of its priorities, accountabilities, roles and organizational design. He emphasizes:

Strategic value: ensuring that HR focuses on transforming organizational processes and people management practices in order to achieve competitive advantage.

A *competitive mindset*: awareness that people management processes can be supplied by an outside specialist provider if the HR department is not efficient and proactive.

Process outcomes: achieving a balance between the need for measurable outcomes from HR initiatives and practices and 'excellence in process', i.e. doing it well. In the past human resource departments could have been accused of an obsession with the quality of practices, and showing little concern for the value of their outcomes.

Weiss (1999) contends that some companies have transformed their HR function, giving it due importance in their corporate strategies – but most have not. Also, the meaning of 'strategy' has changed in recent years. In the past it meant a fairly relaxed 'high-level game plan' played over a long period of, say, five to seven years. But in today's unstable and unpredictable business environment such a strategy would be indulgent if not impossible. Modern strategy is rather more immediate and Weiss offers an operational definition for strategy as 'a plan to achieve relative advantage against the competition'.

Kochan and Dyer (2001) could find no evidence that American businesses (in general) had taken the value of HRM seriously. They argued that there was little in US management history – or in the behaviour of present-day American managers – 'to suggest that management alone, left to its own devices, will produce the transformation in organizational principles needed to sustain and diffuse the delineated human resource principles'. Accepting that some senior executives may share general values such as those outlined by Weiss, Kochan and Dyer contend that other pressures tend to force them into short-term actions (such as firing people) in order to placate major shareholders.

Professionalization

Human resource specialists have found it difficult to achieve the same esteem and influence as their colleagues in other business functions such as finance and marketing, although their status is probably higher in the USA than most other countries. There have been some attempts at a professionalization of HR practice through certification programmes and encouragement of wider-ranging business knowledge within HR qualifications.

Sunoo (1999) argues that to be taken seriously, HR professionals need to understand the work of other business specialists, particularly in finance and strategy. The increasing need to quantify the costs of HR activities such as recruitment and the benefits from new initiatives require human resource practitioners to be comfortable with budgets and plans. Weiss (1999) agrees, concluding that human resource practitioners can only be taken seriously at a senior level (in other words, as 'strategic partners') if they have the following:

- A broad understanding of the business.
- A knowledge of how all the activities need to align.
- A professionalism in investing in human capital and HR processes.
- A unique perspective – one not provided by any other business specialist.

How do HR professionals obtain and demonstrate these qualities? A number of organizations provide certification with the aim of increasing credibility and career opportunities for newcomers and experienced HR practitioners. Certification is intended to demonstrate an understanding of human resource practices and their link to wider business issues. Observing that advertisements for human resource practitioner jobs increasingly require business qualifications and HR certification, Sunnoo (1999) considers that:

Clearly, today's business world demands a higher level of HR and business competency than ever before. Without advancing your career in HRM through certification and eventually even a master's degree in business administration, organisational development, human resources management or leadership, your chances of being taken seriously as a business partner are nil.

Other commentators are not so sure that certification is necessary. Aguinis, Michaelis and Jones (2005) analyzed 1873 HR job announcements available over a one-week period on four employment websites. Results showed that only nine (0.48 per cent) stated that there was a requirement for a certified HR professional, and only 70 (3.73 per cent) stated that this was a preference. In spite of low overall demand for certified HR professionals, results indicated that demand is slightly higher for: jobs posted on a specialist website; certain job titles (e.g. HR director, HR generalist); HR specialty areas (e.g. employee relations, general HR); industries (e.g. manufacturing); and for jobs requiring more years of HR experience.

The spread of HRM

When HRM was imported into other countries, it arrived with many of the contradictions inherent in American practice. Further confusion was created as its principles were considered in the light of local people management traditions. As many commentators have been quick to point out, there is a 'central uncertainty' as to exactly what HRM is (Blyton and Turnbull, 1992: p.2). The nature of HRM has been the focus of a particularly vigorous debate in the UK. Its meaning and distinctiveness from personnel management have been the topic of numerous articles, texts and conference papers. For example, Guest (1989, 1997) has developed a particularly influential model of HRM with six dimensions of analysis:

- HRM strategy
- HRM practices
- HRM outcomes
- Behaviour outcomes
- Performance outcomes
- Financial outcomes.

The model is prescriptive in the sense that it is based on the assumption that HRM is distinctively different from traditional personnel management (rooted in strategic management, etc.). Additionally, it is idealistic, implicitly embodying the belief that fundamental elements of the HRM approach (essentially those of the Harvard map) such as commitment, have a direct relationship with valued business consequences. However, Guest has acknowledged that the concept of commitment is 'messy' and that the relationship between commitment and high performance is difficult to establish. It also employs a 'flow' approach, seeing strategy underpinning practice, leading to a variety of desired outcomes.

Like its American predecessors, this British model is unitarist (tying employee behaviour and commitment into the goals of strategic management) and lukewarm on the value of trade unions. Guest views the employee relationship as one between the individual and the organization.

Paradoxically, attempts to define HRM too precisely seemed to have resulted in confusion and contradiction rather than clarity. Already there are different variations on the terminology such as human capital management and **talent management** and jobs at the 'C' level occur with titles such as chief people officer as well as chief human resource officer. Nevertheless, personnel departments have refused to go away. A casual examination of job advertisements in the press will reveal that applications are sometimes still to be sent to 'personnel managers', 'personnel departments', and even 'staffing officers'. At the same time, advertisements for 'human resource' jobs are common – particularly at a senior level – even if applications are to be sent to the personnel office! Indeed, as we can see in the 'HRM in reality' box, the lead representative body in the UK continues to use the word 'Personnel' in its title, unlike its equivalents in the USA (SHRM – Society for Human Resource Management) and Australia (AHRI – Australian Human Resource Institute).

It is evident, therefore, that defining and accepting HRM comes down to a matter of opinion – or vested interest. Indeed, some interpretations have a strong constituency. It can

HRM in reality The myths about HR careers

A new Chartered Institute of Personnel and Development (CIPD) survey finds most HR professionals are happy with their career choice and 81 per cent would make the same choice if they started all over again.

The CIPD report looks at the career experiences of over 1800 HR professionals and challenges many of the negative myths about human resource specialists. According to Jessica Jarvis, CIPD Learning, Training and Development Adviser and author of the report:

> It sometimes seems that it is fashionable for the HR profession to indulge in doom, gloom and self-loathing. But this survey turns some of the myths on their heads. A profession where the vast majority would pick the same career path if they could start over again is a confident one that is happy with itself.

Main findings:

- Contrary to the common belief that the most senior people in HR have little background in human resources and are parachuted into their jobs, the average HR director has 20 years' HR experience, has worked in four different organizations, and taken five major career steps to their present jobs.

- Human resource professionals are (mostly) not serial career changers. They average 15 years' service within the HR profession.

- HR professionals do not lack experience elsewhere in the world of work. Just 26 per cent of those surveyed began their careers in human resources. Eighty-three per cent of respondents had worked outside HR at some point in their careers – typically, sales/marketing/retail, or possibly general business/management and finance.

- Survey respondents rated the most important factors in a HR career as personal drive, business/industry awareness and generalist experience.

- Moving between organizations is seen as important to career progression. On average, respondents had taken four major career steps and worked for an average of three organizations.

Staying in one organization, over-specializing and call centres/shared service centres were highlighted as significant barriers to career progression. Forty per cent of respondents felt outsourcing was having a negative impact on HR careers.

Apart from age, there were few reliable indicators of the chances of reaching senior levels in HR. These were: being a generalist rather than a specialist; having a degree; having worked for a number of different organizations and having had a number of significant career steps. But many other factors – including qualifications, experience and competencies – had an influential role in reaching senior ranks.

Jessica Jarvis commented:

> It seems that this voicing of more positive beliefs about HR from those we surveyed signals a change in attitude within the profession, with people gaining more belief in the function's ability to become a more credible and respected business player. Certainly it seems that the time is now ripe for this to happen. Several factors are coming together to improve the standing of HR in the business community – the rise of business partnering is making HR more integral to the business, and prominent issues such as human capital reporting and corporate social responsibility are carrying HR up the corporate ladder. HR must step up to the challenge and demonstrate how their strategic activities can impact in business terms.

The CIPD report also highlighted some other myths and realities:

- 'Nobody applies for top jobs any more – it's all done by head hunting'. Not true according to the survey. Job applications were the most likely way to senior HR positions. Only 26 per cent of directors and 17 per cent of senior/group executives were headhunted.

- 'Consultants are too young to know much about HR'. Not according to the survey, the independent consultant group had an average age of 51. They had also, on average, been in HR for 22 years – longer than the average HR Director.

- 'People in HR don't understand the business'. A mere 17 per cent of respondents had no experience of working outside the HR function. 'Business awareness/sense' was the second most important factor in getting to the top in HR, and three-quarters agreed that 'Experience in another function (outside HR) furthers HR careers'.

How would you explain the stereotypical views about human resource specialists given the findings in this report?

Source: *HRM Guide UK* (http://www.hrmguide.co.uk), 28 October, 2005.

be seen from Table 2.3 that each of these views has a natural audience able to identify their own interests with a particular interpretation. Hence it is possible to find accounts stressing one of the following:

- *HRM is really personnel management*. Human resource management is a modernized form of 'personnel', repackaged to enhance the status of personnel managers. It has a hard edge, entitling HR managers to the same respect as finance professionals. HRM is based on integrated and coherent recruitment, assessment and development programmes. It is sophisticated, requiring rigorous training under the auspices of a professional body or university.

- *HRM is a strategic model*. It employs the techniques of strategic management for the utilization of human resources. It focuses on senior managers' concern with achieving objectives and containing costs. HRM aims for a seamless link between business policy and recruitment, performance assessment, reward management, development and dismissal. HRM is a mechanism for control and the exercise of power by top management. It encourages employee attitudes and behaviour which are consistent with business goals. HRM is just one aspect of a senior manager's strategic repertoire. It requires a wide appreciation of the industry and the organization and fits resource-based theories which are familiar from business strategy literature. This interpretation owes its inspiration largely to the Michigan model.

HRM in reality Chartered Institute of Personnel and Development

'HRM' has never been a favoured title amongst HR practitioners in the UK. In fact the HR community seems to have gone out of its way to avoid using the term. Currently the lead body in the UK calls itself the 'Chartered Institute of Personnel and Development' but this is just the latest in a long list of titles.

It originated as the 'Welfare Workers' Association' in 1913, changed to 'Industrial Welfare Workers' in 1924, changed again to the 'Institute of Labour Management' in 1931 and then the 'Institute of Personnel Management (IPM)' in 1946. The IPM label lasted for almost half a century.

Then in 1994 the 'Institute of Personnel Management' merged with the 'Institute of Training and Development' to become (very imaginatively) the 'Institute of Personnel and Development' (IPD). This was a time when management fashion dictated that basic human resource management should be conducted by line managers and it seemed that the old personnel profession might soon dwindle to a small number of recruitment, development and other specialists. Mike Bett, IPD president, argued that: 'There should be a professional personnel and development specialist on all top management teams: in the boardroom and on the executive committees.' The role of the IPD was to be 'the pre-eminent professional body influencing and improving the quality, thinking and practice of people management and development.' But there

was little evidence that the influence and authority of personnel specialists increased during the late 1990s.

From 1 July 2000 the Chartered Institute of Personnel and Development replaced the IPD. Geoff Armstrong, Director-General of the CIPD said that: 'To all intents and purposes, the two organizations are the same.' In terms of staff, organization and mission that is. But he identified three benefits from proclaiming the chartership:

- A recognition of professionalism, a body of knowledge and the practical competence of the membership.
- It emphasizes the 'must belong' status of the organization for anyone involved in people management and development.
- A recognition in the charter that this is a body that government and other influential bodies should consult.

Technology, globalization and competition are making renewed demands on the way people are managed. According to Geoff Armstrong: '. . . we are the specialists, the experts in the field. As the knowledge economy gathers pace, our colleagues increasingly look to us to deliver the strategies that make the winning difference.' Time will tell!

Source: *HRM Guide UK* (http://www.hrmguide.co.uk)

● *HRM is people management*. It covers all aspects of managing employees in its widest sense and emphasizes the role of line managers in overseeing their own staff. From this perspective, HRM is a new generic label for all the techniques and tactics available to manage people. It concentrates on translating organizational objectives into operational achievement by winning employee commitment and gaining high-quality performance. HRM is practical and pragmatic. This interpretation derives from the Harvard model. With some reservations, this is the approach taken in this book.

The value and popularity of HRM may derive from its openness to varied interpretations. It is possible to argue that the term is a useful, 'catch-all phrase, reflecting general intentions but devoid of specific meaning' (Guest, 1989). This allows it to be applied in a variety of circumstances. Individual authors and practitioners interpret HRM according to their own background, interests and intended audiences. Applying the principle from *Alice in Wonderland*, 'it is almost as if HRM is whatever you want it to be' (Armstrong, 1989: p.60). Indeed, Keenoy and Anthony (1992: p.238) consider that we should not look too closely:

> . . . once we seek to explain HRM, to subject it to any analysis or criticism, it ceases to function as intended. Its purpose is to transform, to inspire, to motivate and, above all, to create a new 'reality' which is freely available to those who choose or are persuaded to believe. To explain it is to destroy it.

Table 2.3	Perspective	Audience	Focus	Interest
Perceptions of HRM	HRM as people management	General/line managers	Managing people as a direct, inter-personal activity	Commitment Performance Leadership Team-building
	HRM as personnel management	Personnel specialists	Technical skills for assessment, selection, training, etc.	Appraisals Recruitment Selection methods Development
	HRM as strategic management	Senior managers	People as assets (and liabilities)	Strategic planning Performance management Development Managing change

HRM in reality The 21st century chief human resources officer

Senior HR leaders have a changing role to play with the rise in prominence of issues such as:

● workforce demographics and global talent trends
● corporate scandals and intensifying regulatory challenges
● rising costs of health care and pensions
● technology innovations enabling new ways of working
● increasing globalization

● endless pressures to boost workforce profitability and performance.

Meet a developing 21st century professional: the Chief Human Resources Officer (CHRO).

A new report from Deloitte Consulting, 'Strategist & Steward: The Evolving Role of the Chief Human Resources Officer', outlines the challenges, processes and performance measures facing today's CHRO. According to the report, the modern CHRO is required increasingly to act as both strategist and steward. To quote Deloitte's media release, they are 'leaders who not only manage the HR function and operations team, but also collaborate directly with the CEO and board of directors on a range of critical business issues.'

Jeff Schwartz, principal and national co-leader of Deloitte Consulting's CHRO Services said:

> The requirements and perception of HR are changing dramatically as this function's leadership is now expected to play a central role in building and shaping – not just staffing – the enterprise strategy.
>
> This is an environment that HR leaders have longed for – where their executive peers would view HR as a business partner, rather than as a back-office administrator. Now CHROs must make sure that they are up to the task. The central challenge for CHROs is to view themselves as business leaders first, i.e., senior business executives responsible for the HR portfolio.

Deloitte Consulting's framework categorizes the CHRO's roles and responsibilities in four major ways:

Workforce strategist. Integrating business strategy and overall performance are increasingly important tasks. As well as supporting and implementing overall workforce strategy, CHROs also have a significant role to perform in developing and informing HR strategy – helping the CEO and other senior managers design strategies that are consistent with global labour trends, available talent and next-generation leadership and employees.

Organizational and performance conductor. How do businesses get the best performance from their employees? Organizations are increasingly complex and performance improvements can be required from departments involving:

– operations across geographic boundaries
– virtual teams
– contingent workforces
– telecommuting
– job-sharing
– flexible hours
– workforce diversity.

Modern CHROs need to be able to navigate all such options, acting as change masters and architects of organizational structures and rewards programmes.

HR service delivery owner. Despite the increasing focus on wider business issues, CHROs must still provide cost-effective, day-to-day HR administration and operations. But they need to devote less time to overseeing their own HR systems and processes and spend more time managing a complex mix of in-house, self-service and external resources. Internal and external services must be blended into a cohesive and seamless working operation.

Compliance and governance regulator. CHROs must work directly with their boards on employee issues directly related to the critical areas of:

– risk management
– regulatory compliance
– ethics
– integrity.

Additionally, they are expected also to assist with a wide range of board-related issues, such as board member selection and orientation, executive compensation and succession planning.

William Chafetz, principal and national co-leader of Deloitte Consulting's CHRO Services said:

> The role of the CHRO as an enterprise business leader is still evolving – but this transformation has never been more timely or relevant. As human capital-related issues, such as baby boomer retirement, generational differences, skills gaps and workforce globalization continue to challenge a company's overall strategy and bottom line, the CHRO must become an increasingly familiar face and, in many companies, a potent force in the boardroom and executive suite, paving the way toward change, performance and new ways of working.

Is this a realistic or an idealistic portrayal of a senior HR job?

Source: *HRM Guide USA* (http://www.hrmguide.com), 4 April, 2006.

Summary

The meaning and prevalence of HRM are topics that continue to attract debate and disagreement. As a consequence, practitioners and textbook authors use a diverse and sometimes contradictory range of interpretations. We found that HRM has a variety of definitions but there is general agreement that it has a closer fit with business strategy than previous models, specifically personnel management. The early models of HRM take either a 'soft' or a 'hard' approach, but this may be a simplistic distinction as economic circumstances are more likely to drive the choice than any question of humanitarianism. The status of HRM is also problematic, with a range of views on the value and purpose of the profession.

Further reading

Human Resource Management: A Critical Text edited by John Storey (2nd edition, Thomson Learning, 2001) provides a wide-ranging and authoritative account of the origins and development of HRM. David Ulrich's *Human Resource Champions* Harvard Business Press (1997), has been a best-seller among practitioners and outlines much of his thinking on the key roles of the HR function. *The Future of Human Resource Management: 64 Thought Leaders Explore the Critical HR Issues of Today and Tomorrow*, edited by Michael R. Losey, Sue Meisinger and Dave Ulrich (2nd edition, Wiley, 2006) is a compilation of articles by an international panel of expert contributors who offer their views on the state of HR and what to expect in the future.

Review questions

1 Is HRM a fashion or is it here to stay? What is the probability that HRM will be the dominant framework for people management in the 21st century?

2 Compare and contrast the textbook and practitioner definitions of HRM. In what ways (if any) are they different?

3 Evaluate the following statement: 'HRM is in reality a symbolic label behind which lurk multifarious practices, many of which are not mutually dependent on one another' (Storey, 1992).

4 Is managing people just a matter of commonsense? If so, what value can we attach to theories and models?

5 What do you understand by the statement that 'functions should be managed as a whole, and not as stand-alone activities'?

6 Given Cakar and Bititci's criticism, how useful are 'typologies' of HRM such as Legge's?

7 Evaluate the contributions of Fitz-Enz, Pfeffer and Ulrich towards understanding the purpose of human resource management. Are they stating anything beyond the obvious?

8 Do you consider that the Harvard 4Cs model can give us a complete evaluation of HRM in a particular organization?

9 What do you understand by the concept of 'stakeholder'?

10 The Harvard model of HRM is an idealistic representation of people management. In the real world it is bound to be displaced by harder models of HRM. Do you agree or disagree with these statements?

11 HRM theorists argue that employees are assets and not just costs. What does this mean in practice?

12 What are the main differences between the Harvard and Michigan models?

13 Compare and contrast the 'hard' and 'soft' forms of HRM. Is this a useful distinction?

Case study for discussion and analysis

Read the following case study. Trace the main ways in which the management of people has changed during IBM's history.

Human resource management at IBM

Origins

IBM was originally formed as Computing Tabulating and Recording (CTR), a combination of three companies put together by Charles Flint, a former arms dealer. Flint recruited Thomas Watson, who became its chairman in 1924. Watson renamed the company International Business Machines in 1929. IBM has a long history of dominance: at this early stage it already had 95 per cent of the market in punched-card machines – a mechanical predecessor of the electronic computer.

Watson had previously worked for NCR and had a reputation for aggressive sales activity – to the extent that he had been indicted in an anti-trust suit. From these inauspicious beginnings, however, Watson modelled a sales force on a highly ethical basis. He required his staff to behave in an 'honest, fair and square way'. This sober behaviour was expected at home as well as work and included wearing the familiar dark suits and white shirts. The company benefits included lifetime employment and IBM country clubs which developed a collective feeling. Company songs and slogans (such as THINK) were encouraged and inculcated at company training schools.

This approach was eventually transmitted to Japan. In the 1950s, Japanese management style was deliberately modelled on IBM by the Ministry of International Trade and Industry (MITI) who found the IBM way eulogized in American business textbooks. Ironically, the company resembled civil service organizations more than other industrial corporations. Its style was paternalist and hierarchical, offering employment for life and excellent career paths for its brightest workers.

Computing began in Britain and the USA in the 1940s and the first significant commercial product, Remington Rand's UNIVAC, was launched in the early 1950s. IBM entered the market soon afterwards and used its powerful resources to take a leading position. Under Watson's son, Thomas J. Watson Jr., IBM and computing became virtually synonymous, controlling 70 per cent of the world market in the 1960s. 'Big Blue' became one of the largest corporations in the world, its international workforce reaching a peak of 405 000 in 1985.

IBM's overwhelming control of the computing industry was symbolic of the USA's technological and economic dominance in the post-war world. This strength was based on an integrated product range of highly expensive mainframe computers, peripherals and software which locked users into IBM once they had made their initial purchase. Gradually, however, cracks appeared in this dominance. Despite being an IBM invention, the personal computer liberated individual users from the mainframe. PC 'clones' were supplied more cheaply by competitors with much lower overheads. PC's became more powerful, not just because of increasingly faster processing chips but also from the software this speed allowed. Profitability moved from the mainframe sector to the PC, and particularly to software producers such as Microsoft.

People management

IBM was traditionally a non-unionized organization. In fact the corporation was accused of being anti-union – but most of its staff seemed to like it that way. An ACAS survey in 1977 showed that only 4.9 per cent of the company's British employees wanted a union, with 91 per cent saying they would refuse to join if there were one. For half a century its culture was strongly based on lifetime employment and excellent working conditions. The company did not possess a formal system of employee relations as such: the nature of the employment relationship was implicit in the corporation's human resource policies. Needle (1994: p.332) describes these as taking the form of:

- A sophisticated system of human resource planning, recruitment and training.
- A system of lifetime employment in which staff changed their jobs as and when required by the organization.
- Equal status for all IBM employees in terms of fringe benefits, staff restaurants and other facilities, although company cars were restricted to senior management and some sales staff.
- Centrally determined salaries, geared to bettering those of competitors and reviewed annually; increases based on a performance objective system.
- Considerable emphasis on training, particularly related to people management and averaging 40 days a year for managers.
- An audit of staff opinion held every two years, focused on attitudes towards work methods, HR practices, pay and conditions.
- A model HRM approach with decisionmaking and people management delegated to line managers at the lowest possible level.
- Formal communication procedures designed to encourage debate of business problems and to allow aggrieved staff to appeal against local management decisions.

▶

By the early 1990s, however, IBM was in serious trouble. The company had been cutting costs for six years under the chairmanship of John Akers, a life-long IBM man in his late 50s. A former navy pilot, he joined IBM as a sales representative and was soon identified as senior management material. Silver-haired and youthful, he was the image of the IBM corporate employee. The severity of the problem and Akers' bleak assessment of sales performance and poor productivity came to light in 1991. A middle-manager who attended a confidential briefing inadvertently distributed his summary of the meeting through IBM's internal electronic mail network. This soon brought the media spotlight on the corporation, publicizing Akers' attempts to correct the situation. One failure was the recruitment of 5000 additional sales representatives, to boost the existing 20 000, which increased revenues by less than 4 per cent. He then announced 14 000 job cuts, increased to 17 000 shortly afterwards. In IBM-speak these were referred to as 'management-initiated-separation' (MIS). Some 47 000 IBM employees had already had an MIS experience over the previous five years but the latest announcements would still leave the company with a worldwide workforce of over 350 000.

The media and industry analysts increasingly criticized the momentum of change. Forecasts of reduced profits and static turnover led to calls for more radical action. IBM's strong points, its culture and structure, had apparently become its major weaknesses. The company was described as insular and complacent, slow to react to the move away from large expensive mainframe computers to powerful PCs and workstations.

IBM's bureaucratic decisionmaking structure dragged down its ability to react at a time when the industry was becoming increasingly fast moving. Whereas a local office in Europe, for example, had to refer to its regional head office and possibly to New York, competitors could take the initiative immediately. Procedures which functioned adequately when product development had a four-year cycle were hopelessly ineffective when the lead time had shrunk to a year. IBM had a tradition of producing virtually everything in-house, further increasing its insularity and inability to react quickly to market changes.

A loss of over US$4 billion in 1992 led to Akers' replacement by the first outsider, Louis Vincent Gestner, destined to take the serious decisions which Wall Street analysts had demanded. Despite making IBM's first-ever job cuts the conclusion had been that Akers was too imbued in the IBM culture to be able to take sufficiently drastic measures.

New broom sweeps . . .

Louis Vincent Gestner Jr, 51, was appointed chairman in April 1993 with no experience of running a computer business. Gestner, a devout Catholic, was the son of a truck dispatcher from Long Island. He started his career with management consultants McKinsey after Harvard Law School and later became head of RJR Nabisco. 'There will be no pussyfooting, no more salami-slicing,' he told shareholders a month later. He quickly hired two experienced cost-cutters as aides: Jerome York, former chief financial officer of Chrysler; and Gerald Czarnecki, who had implemented reductions in staff at Honolulu's HonFed bank. Gestner listed four immediate priorities:

- major staff reductions, reducing IBM's workforce worldwide to about 250 000 and including the first compulsory redundancies in the company's history
- defining IBM's core areas
- improving customer relations
- decentralization.

In 1993 Gestner announced a record quarterly loss of US$8 billion that included an US$8.9 billion charge for laying off 50 000 employees that year – double the previous estimates. Gestner said: 'Getting IBM's costs and expense structure in line with the revenue realities of our industry – right-sizing the company – is my highest near-term priority'. But he declined to break up IBM's eight product groups and disappointed stock market analysts who were looking for more radical surgery.

One key element of cost was, of course, the company payroll. Gerstner's team made significant changes to IBM's compensation (pay) plan:

- *Look to the marketplace*. The single salary structure (for non-sales employees) was changed to different salary structures with merit budgets for different job families. This allowed IBM to pay employees in different job families according to market-oriented rates.
- *Fewer, faster jobs in a flatter organization*. The traditional salary grades were scrapped in the USA, and the number of separate job titles cut from over 5000 to less than 1200.
- *Reward for performance*. The old compensation plan based pay raises on a complex formula linking performance assessments to salary increases measured in tenths of 1 per cent. Under the new system, managers were given a budget and told to differentiate between the pay given to 'stars' and 'acceptable performers' on the grounds that otherwise the stars would not stay too long.

According to Czarnecki: 'IBM *did* deliberately foster paternalism, with a social contract between employer and employee. But economic realities forced us to rethink the relationship. Now we're no longer asking people for total commitment to us. They're eager to stay but prepared to leave' (Sampson, 1995: p.228).

The company still refrained from using terms such as 'layoff', but employees soon got the message. At the original IBM site, Endicott in New York State, the process was called ETOP – the Endicott Transition Opportunity Program. Cynical staff translated this as 'Eliminate the Older People'. Local mental health services reported a massive increase in requests for stress counselling. 'Surplused' staff felt stigmatized and rejected by the firm. For the company itself, however, the picture was looking better. By 1995 the corporation returned to profitability.

Restructuring HR

When the business units were given autonomy in the early 1990s, the HR department had to react without an expansion of staff (Shugrue, Berland, Gonzales and Duke, 1997). HR was turned into a separate business with a national benefits call centre. Separate human resource functions were consolidated into a number of geographical regions where experts were relocated. Their expertise was offered to other companies on a commercial basis. Small teams of HR advisers were left at individual IBM locations. The business made a saving of more than US$100 million from these changes in just 2 years.

Following this event, IBM's new CEO re-centralized the autonomous business units and indicated to the HR department that its costs should be cut by 50 per cent. Taking the national benefits centre as its model, the company then consolidated the remaining regional HR units within the National Human Resource Service Centre in Raleigh, North Carolina, so that all human resource functions were under one roof.

In recent years IBM's 2500 HR specialists around the world have focused on reducing the paper load of dealing with the company's huge workforce, with some 500 pieces of data on each employee. Much of this information is required by other departments, making fast and accurate communication a priority. A number of electronic HR initiatives have transferred paper-driven processes on to human resource management systems accessible through web technology.

Chapter 3
HRM and business effectiveness

Learning objectives

The purpose of this chapter is to:

- Introduce the concept of high commitment/performance work systems.

- Investigate the relationship between HRM and knowledge management.

- Provide an overview of human resource systems.

- Evaluate the contribution of HRM and HR technology to business effectiveness.

- Provide a checklist of HRM principles.

High performance organizations

Knowledge management

Knowledge management practice

Knowledge management, knowledge sharing – or sheer bunkum?

HRM and business effectiveness

HR professionals and the HR system

Measuring the impact of HRM

Major findings

A 10-C checklist for effective HRM

Summary

Further reading

Review questions

Case study for discussion and analysis – Accenture

High performance organizations

In all the debates about the meaning, significance and practice of HRM, nothing *seems* so certain than the link between HRM and performance. But is it? Legge (2001), one of the most respected and astute commentators on human resource management states:

> And what, might it be asked, are the present-day concerns of HRM researchers, who . . . are of a modernist, positivist persuasion? In a word, their project is the search for the Holy Grail of establishing a causal relationship between HRM and performance. And in this search some success is claimed, in particular that the more the so-called 'high commitment/performance' HRM practices are adopted, the better the performance

Legge argues that in order to examine the relationship between performance and HRM we need to address three fundamental questions:

1 How are we to conceptualize HRM?
2 How are we to conceptualize performance?
3 How are we to conceptualize the relationship between the two?

The theoretical meaning of HRM was addressed in the previous chapter. Here we will look at HRM operationalized (according to Legge's approach) in terms of high commitment or high performance work practices. In practice, unpicking the meaning of 'high performance management' from wider notions of management can be difficult. For example, the US Department of Labor (1998) defines high performance as: 'A comprehensive customer-driven system that aligns all of the activities in an organization with the common focus of customer satisfaction through continuous improvement in the quality of goods and services.'

You will probably have recognized that the roots of this definition lie in **total quality management**. In the past, the practice of TQM has often been procedural and bureaucratic but the high-performance approach has brought in elements of human relations or 'soft' HRM such as commitment and empowerment. The term was publicized by Nadler *et al.* (1992) within his 'organizational architecture' approach, focusing on 'autonomous work teams' and '**high performance work systems**'. Lawler III (1991) used the term 'high performance involvement' as an alternative to **empowerment**, advocating the use of small teams of highly committed employees.

Is 'high performance management' just another management fad or fashion? Holbeche (2005, p.10) ventures the opinion that 'while some guru-led management fashions may have come and gone over the last 20 years or so, the aspiration towards more sustainable high performance is a more enduring theme, underpinning much of what has gone before . . .'

The Institute of Work Psychology (2001) at the University of Sheffield states that high performance work systems usually involve three main sets of management practices designed to enhance employee involvement, commitment and competencies. They describe these as:

1 Changing the design and conduct of jobs through flexible working (especially functional flexibility – broadening the pool of 'who does what' through training), team work, quality circles, suggestion schemes.
2 Ensuring that employees are given the knowledge and competences to handle high performance work through teamwork training, team briefings, inter-personal skills, appraisal, information-sharing.
3 Resourcing and development practices designed to attract and keep the right people with the right motivation. These include some guarantee of job security, an emphasis on internal selection, sophisticated selection techniques, and employee attitude surveys with feedback to the workers involved. Here there are further indications of an integration of 1970s and 1980s management techniques together with a certain amount of repackaging for the 21st century.

Pfeffer (1998) acknowledges that building a high-commitment organization is not easy and that CEOs are often too busy or distracted to focus on the people. However, he advocates the following as key elements of high-commitment management:

- *Building trust* so that everyone in the organization can share knowledge.
- *Encouraging change.*
- *Measuring what matters*, arguing that financial data tends to be historical rather than what matters now. He advocates use of the '**balanced scorecard**' a technique that also weighs non-financial criteria in the equation.

> ### Key concept 3.1 Balanced scorecard
>
> A conceptual framework used to translate an organization's vision into a set of performance indicators, including measures of: financial performance, customer satisfaction, internal business processes, and learning and growth. Both current performance and efforts to learn and improve can be monitored using these measures.

Pfeffer (1998) presents his model of the high performance work system, including seven key factors:

1 *Employment security.* This is fundamental to gaining employee commitment. If employees are not in fear of working themselves out of their jobs, they will contribute freely to improved productivity. When employees are secure they are prepared to think and act with the long term in mind.

2 *Selective hiring.* Employment resourcing has to be disciplined to ensure that the right people are in the right places. Pfeffer advocates competency based selection aimed at identifying critical skills and job-related attributes. The quality of employees has a direct impact on organizational effectiveness and market success.

3 *Self-managed teams and decentralization of decisionmaking.* Traditional supervision should be replaced by peer control, allowing a large proportion of the workforce to accept accountability and responsibility for company performance. They are more likely to understand how their work affects the work of other employees. Ideas can be pooled and layers of unnecessary hierarchy disposed of.

4 *High compensation contingent on organizational performance.* Profits can still be made with higher pay rates if the right pay format is used, such as gain sharing, stock options and pay for skill. When employees feel that they are fairly rewarded they are more likely to show commitment .

5 *Training.* Employees possessed of up-to-date skills and knowledge are more flexible and prepared to initiate change, predict and solve problems, and take responsibility for product and service quality.

6 *Reduction of status differences.* Creating a more egalitarian workplace encourages open lines of communication. Employees have a greater sense of common purpose.

7 *Sharing information.* Making financial information available to employees encourages trust and commitment to the company. Employees can also prioritize multiple and conflicting goals.

In the public sector, the US Department of Labor (1998) sees high performance revolving around three main principles:

1 An organizational focus on achieving customer satisfaction.

2 A constant search for continuous, long-term improvement in all organizational processes and outputs.

3 Taking steps to ensure the full involvement of the entire workforce in achieving quality.

So what are the key operating practices of such a high performance system? According to the US Department of Labor they are:

Leadership and support from top levels of management: the most critical element of the process. Top managers must develop a climate of trust where risk-taking and innovation are encouraged and rewarded. This means that workers and managers must together develop a shared vision of where they want the organization to go. It also means that there must be tolerance shown towards the inevitable setbacks and mistakes along the way. And managers must be open to suggestions and requests from workers for the removal of barriers to good customer service. This implies a considerable change from the top-down 'I'm in charge and all mistakes will be punished' attitude prevalent among higher management.

Strategic planning: mapping out how the organization will achieve its strategic objectives. But such a plan must be constantly reviewed.

Ongoing commitment to training and development for all employees: not just top–middle ranking staff where organizations concentrate their funds too often. Neglecting the training and development of customer-facing staff is potentially damaging in terms of its consequences. Somehow, an organization must also withstand the pressure from budget-cutters to reduce training levels as an easy (and stupid) way of reducing costs.

A focus on the customer: not just meeting customer expectations but exceeding them, and devoting considerable energy into finding out the changing expectations of customers through surveys, feedback and other mechanisms. This applies to internal as well as external customers.

A focus on quality: advocating a TQM approach to dealing with problems as they occur and providing a perfect end product. This differs from the traditional 'inspect, reject or deal with complaint' approach.

Empowering frontline employees and an emphasis on teamwork: the buzzwords empowerment, employee involvement and teamwork come in here. Harness the intelligence and energies of your employees 'the potential for successful and quality results is virtually limitless'.

Developing measures of progress: data collection mechanisms to ensure that customers are receiving reliable and satisfactory service and that internal processes are functioning properly.

The US Department of Labor (1998) identified the following problems which also apply in most cases to all non-manufacturing sectors:

1 High performance is conceptually easier to understand in a manufacturing rather than a service context.

2 Competitiveness is a main motivating factor in the private sector, but scarcely a consideration in the public sector. 'Government is mission-driven rather than profit-driven'.

3 'Government is viewed by many as the archetypal, inflexible, hierarchical structure, and, therefore, incapable of change.'

4 The traditional measurable outcomes of the manufacturing sector – reduced production costs, improved market share, increased profitability – are not so easy to measure in the service sector.

In recent years, increasing scepticism has been shown towards the apparent link between HRM and various interpretations of high performance. Gardner, Wright and Gerhart (2000) queried the nature of the evidence supporting the supposed value of HR initiatives in improving performance:

> While extremely promising, this research, with few exceptions, has relied on the survey responses from one knowledgeable informant per company to measure the quantity and quality of firms' human resource management systems. Reliance on just one informant makes the measurement of the human resource management construct susceptible to excessive random (i.e. unreliability) and systematic (i.e. bias) measurement error . . .

As they point out, this threatens the validity of the construct that HR practices are directly related to high performance. Paradoxically, however, the two types of error may be having opposite effects. Citing earlier statistical work by Gerhart, they argue that random errors from single-informant surveys may be obscuring and therefore undervaluing the financial benefit of HR practices. Conversely, there is likely to be an over-estimate from systematic errors.

Where do these systematic errors come from? Gardner *et al.* (2000) argue that:

> This type of error will occur if respondents report HR practices based not on accurate valid estimates, but rather based on an implicit theory that high performing firms must be engaged in progressive HR practices while low performing firms must not be engaged in such practices.

They cite the example of a large diversified, perhaps multinational, company. If a senior HR person is asked to state the percentage of employees covered by a 'progressive' human resource practice, where does the HR person get the information from? Hopefully from a sophisticated human resource management system, but probably not. Instead, they contend, the respondent will provide an answer based on their own **implicit theory** (see Key concept 3.2) of what is happening in the firm.

Key concept 3.2 Implicit theory

An internal or mental model of how and why a set of events or behaviours takes place. A belief system developed by individuals to explain part of their world or organization based on their own interpretations and experiences.

Discussing coverage of this issue in research literature they point out that surveys typically ask for the views of senior managers who, to paraphrase, are likely to believe in their own upbeat propaganda aimed at shareholders and employees. In more academic terms, they say that, surveying the literature, 'there is general consensus that executives' descriptions of past events suffer from low reliability'. They also point to studies which show that outsiders' judgements of a firm are based on financial performance and conclude that it is reasonable to assume that insiders are also likely to be influenced in the same way.

They formulated two hypotheses:

1 The estimated extent of the usage of human resource practices for high-performing firms will be greater than for low-performing firms.

2 The evaluation of the effectiveness of the HR function for high-performing firms will be higher than for low-performing firms.

These hypotheses were tested on line managers, HR executives, MBAs and HR masters students who were given scenarios of high- and low-performing companies and asked to rate a range of HR practices. The scenarios did not provide any information on HR practices, so their judgements were based entirely on implicit theories. The conclusion was that the hypotheses were confirmed to some extent in all four groups. This places a question mark on the supposed evidence from much of the survey research on the relationship between HR practices and high performance.

Wall and Wood (2005) critically evaluated 25 studies, including 'highly cited milestone studies of the mid- to late-1990s, and a selection of more recent ones (whose citation rate is yet to be determined)' and concluded that the evidence was 'promising but circumstantial'. They argue that consultants and researchers should temper the language they use, particularly the term 'high-performance' itself because it 'clearly presupposes the very effects researchers should be investigating, and should be avoided.' Also, they contend that terms such as 'impact', 'determinant' and 'effect' should be replaced by more modest terminology such as 'associated with' or 'related to', given the relatively weak relationships found.

Methodologically, Wall and Wood propose that researchers should aim to compare competing hypotheses rather than set out to prove or (notionally) disprove what is essentially a pet theory. Finally, they state that there is a need for research designs that counter the weaknesses of existing studies, specifically to overcome:

Reliance on a single-source measure of HRM practices such as a CEO or HR manager. These are often of unknown reliability, sensitivity and validity and typically are also the source of the measure of performance. Wall and Wood support the use of independent but suitably experienced auditors, external to the organization and unaware of its performance, drawing on multiple sources of information within the organization. Moreover, they should examine also other 'comparator practices' such as R&D or total quality to highlight the relative importance of HR practices.

Use of small samples coupled with low response rates. Larger sample sizes are essential to reveal the effects of complex interactions predicted from theory.

Lack of sophisticated longitudinal studies. In particular, studies to examine how changes in HR practices relate to subsequent changes in performance. These could be retrospective or prospective – in other words, looking backwards or forwards.

We will return to the topic of high performance in our discussion of strategic HRM in a later chapter. In the next section we consider knowledge management, another highly fashionable topic that has exercised the minds of theorists and practitioners over the past decade or so.

Knowledge management

The knowledge economy stands on three pillars. The first: knowledge has become what we buy, sell, and do. It is the most important factor of production. The second pillar is a mate, a corollary to the first: knowledge assets – that is, intellectual capital – have become more important to companies than physical or financial assets. The third pillar is this: to prosper in this new economy and exploit these newly vital assets, we need new vocabularies, new management techniques, new technologies, and new strategies. On these three pillars rest all the new economy's laws and its profits. (Stewart, 2001, p.5)

Storey (2001) states that knowledge management has become one of the most significant developments in management and organization theory in recent years. It seems to give fresh insights into the theory of the firm and it is also the subject of claims about a completely new kind of economy – the 'knowledge economy.'

Knowledge is scarcely as novel a concept as many protagonists of knowledge management claim, but it has only become a management topic relatively recently. Moreover, a large number of organizations are attempting knowledge management projects – not always successfully.

O'Dell and Essaides (1998) argue that knowledge management is not a fad because:

● The power of learning will never be obsolete.

● Some people may treat knowledge management as a religion but real knowledge management is practical rather than theoretical and should have bottom-line results.

● Technology is not relied upon to make processes efficient, instead, technology is used to facilitate the sharing of knowledge in people's heads.

● It is consistent with modern team- and process-based approaches to management.

We will see later that there are criticisms of the way that information technology has come to dominate conferences and publications on knowledge management and, in doing so, often lost the point. In fact, if you think that buying (or rather, *being sold*) a software package to collect information is 'knowledge management' you are probably wasting your money. Knowledge is more than technology.

> **Key concept 3.3** Knowledge management
>
> 'Knowledge management caters to the critical issues of organizational adaption, survival and competence in face of increasingly discontinuous environmental change. ... Essentially, it embodies organizational processes that seek synergistic combination of data and information processing capacity of information technologies, and the creative and innovative capacity of human beings.' (Malhotra, 1998, p.59)

> **What knowledge management is not**
>
> - 'Knowledge management (KM) is *not* a new religion or spiritual calling.
> - 'It is *not* an attempt to rally disgruntled employees around an appealing physical concept.
> - 'It is *not* an existential search for the truth. (Actually, it's about the entirely worldly task of making money.)
> - 'It is *not* a science or a discipline – yet.
> - 'It is *not* the latest management fad.'
>
> Source: O'Dell and Essaides, (1998).
> Note: Authors' emphases.

Knowledge management: a big idea

According to Stewart (2001), three big ideas have been fundamental in the past decade or so in changing the ways in which organizations are run:

Total quality management. O'Dell and Essaides (1998) say that this 'may not have yielded big-time change, but it laid the foundation for a corporate-wide systematic initiative for measurement and change and cross-functional teaming, all of which . . . are critical to the successful management of knowledge'.

Business process re-engineering. O'Dell and Essaides (1998) comment that **BPR** 'may not have delivered sustainable success but it has "delivered" the mind-set of the process-oriented organization. Processes can be made explicit, and knowledge about how to make them work can be transferred.'

Intellectual capital. Stewart divides intellectual capital or knowledge assets into two main forms: 'hard' assets such as patents, copyrights, software and databases; and, most importantly, 'soft' employee-focused assets including skills, capabilities, expertise, culture and loyalty.

Information is already a major component of economic activity. Stewart points to the scale of the knowledge economy:

- Worldwide we produce between 700 and 2400 terabytes of information annually. One terabyte is equivalent to a million bytes.
- This estimate does not include the services provided by the likes of accountants, lawyers, doctors, psychologists and consultants – information that is not necessarily provided in documentary form.
- Knowledge was the USA's most valuable export in 1999, accounting for $37 billion in licensing fees and royalties. By comparison, aircraft exports amounted to $29 billion.

Wolff (2005, p.38) calculates that the percentage of employees in the USA who could be described as information workers has increased from 37 per cent of the workforce in 1950 to

59 per cent in 2000. These include employees who produce knowledge as well as those who handle data. Wolff (*ibid.*, p.42) concludes that much of the increase in the 1990s was driven by investment in computers and that the 21st century may not see the same rate of growth as data jobs are outsourced overseas.

Knowledge management has been approached from a number of perspectives, with information management and organizational approaches being two of the most important. In fact, within organizations and especially in conferences and journals, information technology and human resources have competed for the lead role. Information technology has tended to be the dominant force but not always beneficially (Storey and Quintas, 2001).

Tacit and explicit knowledge

Knowledge management owes its inspiration to the work of the philosopher Michael Polanyi and the Japanese organization learning 'guru' Ikijuro Nonaka. Both of these theorists argued that knowledge has two forms: **explicit** and **tacit**, which has some similarity to Stewart's hard and soft knowledge assets.

Key concept 3.4 Explicit versus implicit knowledge

Explicit knowledge is the obvious knowledge found in manuals, documentation, files and other accessible sources.

Implicit, or tacit knowledge are found in the heads of an organization's employees and are more difficult to access and use, for obvious reasons. Typically, an organization does not even know what this knowledge is. Worse, the knee-jerk reaction of top managers who fire employees at the first sign of any downturn means that the knowledge is often lost.

Grant (1997) argues that HRM can improve an organization's competitiveness through its impact on the 'knowledge base' of a business: the skills and expertise of its employees. Management of human resources can provide a competitive advantage through a knowledge management perspective. One strategy is to encourage replication of tacit knowledge within an organization without allowing it to replicate outside. From this perspective, organizations should:

1 Accept that knowledge is a vital source for value to be added to business products and services and a key to gaining competitive advantage.

2 Distinguish clearly between explicit and tacit knowledge.

3 Accept that tacit knowledge rests inside individuals and is learned in an unstructured and informal way.

4 Identify and tap this tacit knowledge and make it part of the 'structural capital' of the business, so that it can be made available to others.

Drucker (1998) contends that knowledge management will have a major impact on the structure of future organizations. He predicts that knowledge-based organizations will have half the number of management layers found in businesses today – and the number of managers will be cut by two-thirds. Drucker considers that the organizational structures featured in current textbooks are still those of 1950s manufacturing industries. In the future, businesses will come to resemble organizations that today's managers and students would not pay any attention to: hospitals, universities, and symphony orchestras. In other words, knowledge-based organizations 'composed largely of specialists who direct and discipline their own performance through organized feedback from colleagues, customers and headquarters.'

In the 20th century information was collected in order to monitor and control workers. 'Knowledge' was held at the top of the organization where strategies were determined and decisions made. But this Tayloristic view of the organizations ignored the wealth of knowledge held by ordinary workers. In Drucker's opinion, specialist knowledge workers will resist the primitive 'command and control' model of people management in the same way as professionals such as doctors and university teachers do already.

Oliver and Kandadi (2006) identified ten major factors affecting knowledge management practices and associated organizational culture. These include leadership, organizational structure, evangelization, communities of practice, reward systems, time allocation, business processes, recruitment, infrastructure and physical attributes.

Davenport and Prusak, in *Working Knowledge* (2000) say that **knowledge, data** and information are not identical concepts. They point out that confusion between the three has resulted in many organizations investing large amounts of money in the technology of knowledge management without achieving any useful results. They consider that understanding the difference between the three concepts is crucial:

> Organizational success and failure can often depend on which one of them you need, which you have, and what you can and can't do with each. Understanding what these three things are and how you get from one to another is essential to doing knowledge work successfully.

Data is hard, factual information often in numerical form – it can tell you when, and how often something happened, how much it cost and so on, but it does not say why it happened. Organizations love accumulating vast quantities of data – the sheer bulk of which serves to confuse and obscure any value.

Information for Davenport and Prusak comes in the form of a message – and it is the receiver rather than the sender of the message who determines that it is information – through some communication channel whether voice, e-mail, letter, etc. It is different from data in that it has meaning or shape. In fact, data can be transformed into information with the addition of meaning and they list a number of ways, each beginning with C:

> *Contextualized*: the purpose of the data is known.
>
> *Categorized*: the unit of analysis or key component is known.
>
> *Calculated*: perhaps through a statistical or mathematical analysis.
>
> *Corrected*: through the removal of errors.
>
> *Condensed*: by being summarized or tabulated.

Knowledge transcends both data and information in a number of ways. Davenport and Prusak define it as follows:

> Knowledge is a fluid mix of framed expertise, values, contextual information and expert insight that provides a framework for evaluating and incorporating new experiences and information. It originates from and is applied in the minds of knowers. In organizations it often becomes embedded not only in documents or repositories but also in organizational routines, processes, practices and norms.

Knowledge management practice

Proponents of knowledge management argue that long-term competitive advantage can come from mapping and tapping tacit knowledge. But simply agreeing with this principle on the grounds of commonsense does not tell us how to do it. And many accounts of knowledge management fall down on this issue. One notable exception is Tiwana (1999) who points out that:

> In the technology industry, companies that have prospered are not the companies that have invented new technology, but those that have applied it. Microsoft is perhaps a good example of a company that had first relied on good marketing, then on its market share, and now on its innovative knowledge – mostly external.

Tiwana considers that Microsoft has also learned a great deal from its past failures, describing its founder Bill Gates as 'the richest man in the world: a fierce, tireless competitor who hires people with the same qualities'. Microsoft uses knowledge management without a specific knowledge management agenda and gains by applying knowledge rather than creating it. In fact, according to Tiwana, tangible business assets such as technology, patents or market share can only provide a business with a temporary advantage. Eventually, a particular market-leading technology, for example, becomes the staple of every business in the same industry.

Often organizations do not know what they know. And if they do know what they *did* know:

- That knowledge can be out of date.
- The person(s) who possessed it may have gone – perhaps to a competitor.
- The knowledge has been replaced or updated.
- The location or possessor of the new knowledge is not known.

Schack (2004, p.2) highlights the confusion about knowledge, even for people who can be described as 'experts':

> Performance seems to accompany knowledge, and experts clearly know more about the fields in which they are active. However, closer inspection . . . reveals a frequent failure to distinguish between knowledge that is functionally relevant for the control and organization of actions, and knowledge that merely accompanies actions or justifies them in retrospect. As a result, we cannot assume that the knowledge high performers (experts) report is the same as the knowledge responsible for their performance.

Corrall (1999) gives examples of how knowledge can be stored and accessed:

Knowledge databases and repositories (explicit knowledge): Storing information and documents that can be shared and re-used, for example, client presentations, competitor intelligence, customer data, marketing materials, meeting minutes, policy documents, price lists, product specifications, project proposals, research reports, training packs.

Knowledge route maps and directories (tacit and explicit knowledge): Pointing to people, document collections and datasets that can be consulted, for example, 'yellow pages'/'expert locators' containing CVs, competency profiles, research interests.

Knowledge networks and discussions (tacit knowledge): Providing opportunities for face-to-face contacts and electronic interaction, for example, establishing chat facilities/'talk rooms', fostering learning groups and holding 'best practice' sessions.

Knowledge management, knowledge sharing – or sheer bunkum?

In a scathing attack on the concept of knowledge management, Wilson (2002) concludes that the 'knowledge management idea' is '. . . in large part, a management fad, promulgated mainly by certain consultancy companies, and the probability is that it will fade away like previous fads.' In his opinion, the concept rests on two foundations:

The management of information: Wilson finds much of the topic to be no more than the relabeling of 'information management'.

The effective management of work practices: based on a Utopian vision of business organization where everyone benefits from information exchange, individuals are free to develop their own expertise and organizational 'communities' determine how that expertise is used.

According to Wilson, we are some distance from that Utopia: 'Whatever businesses claim about people being their most important resource, they are never reluctant to rid themselves of that resource (and the knowledge it possesses) when market conditions decline.' He instances British Airways, which dispensed with 7 000 of its 'knowledge resources' after the 9/11 terrorist attack in 2001, and Barclays Bank, which reduced its worldwide workforce by

10 per cent in the same year despite profits of £2 billion. Wilson passes judgement on these actions: 'No imagination appears to have been used by either of these companies to determine ways in which their "most important resource" might be more effectively employed to increase turnover and profits.' He asks: 'If getting promotion, or holding your job, or finding a new one, is based on the knowledge you possess – what incentive is there to reveal that knowledge and share it?'

HRM in reality Knowledge management gives Canadian businesses a competitive edge

A study by Ipsos-Reid for Microsoft Canada Co. showed that 91 per cent of Canadian business leaders believe knowledge management practices have a direct impact on organizational effectiveness. Knowledge management may be defined as a formal, directed process of determining what information an organization has which could benefit other people in the business – and then devising ways of making this information easily available.

This is one of the first studies on the prevalence of knowledge management. It was designed to investigate the specific knowledge management practices used by Canadian organizations and to measure the success and impact of those KM practices. The study indicates that the top three knowledge management processes in place are:

- Development of an intranet.
- Holding events to share knowledge throughout an organization.
- Using software to encourage sharing and collaboration.

The study indicates that 65 per cent of Canadian businesses practising knowledge management believe that it has given their organization a competitive advantage. It also shows that despite recent criticisms, knowledge management has been a considerable success in most Canadian organizations that have implemented KM practices:

- Ninety-one per cent of respondents agree that knowledge management practices have been successful in creating value in improving organizational effectiveness.
- Eighty-eight per cent agree that KM practices have succeeded in delivering customer value.
- Eighty-nine per cent of respondents felt that the positive impact of KM practices also extended to employee satisfaction.
- The average return to date is 41 per cent among those organizations able to calculate a return on

investment, the average dollar value being CDN$41 278.

- Eighty-nine per cent of respondents considered that their organization has a culture that encourages and provides opportunities for communicating ideas, knowledge and experience internally.
- One-third of organizations without KM practices in place have plans to implement one in the next 12 months.

'The results indicate that the positive impact of knowledge management processes in Canadian companies extends throughout all different departments, creating value in customer service, product development, human resources, sales and marketing,' said Chris Ferneyhough, vice president, technology research, Ipsos-Reid Canada. 'We see the implementation of KM practices expanding over the next few years, helping to make even more Canadian companies competitive in the global marketplace.'

The Ipsos-Reid knowledge management study was sponsored by Microsoft Canada. It was based on survey responses from 402 Canadian organizations with no fewer than 50 PCs. The survey targeted senior business and information technology decisionmakers.

'The primary goal of knowledge management is to deliver the intellectual capacity of a firm to the employees who make the day-to-day decisions that in turn determine the success or failure of a business,' according to Anne McKeon, product manager, Microsoft Canada. 'The Ipsos-Reid knowledge management study results support Microsoft's view that knowledge management should be a priority for Canadian business leaders because it shows there is competitive advantage and return on investment gains to be made when a knowledge management solution is implemented.'

Can these conclusions be applied outside Canada?

Source: *HRM Guide Canada* (http://www.hrmguide.net/canada/) 14 March, 2001.

HRM and business effectiveness

One of the most significant issues faced by modern organizations is the use of technology to streamline activities, cut costs and increase business effectiveness. Perhaps later than many other business functions, technology has recently come into human resource management in a major way. There is still a considerable debate on its cost effectiveness and ability to provide what is required. Walker (2001) states that if HR technology is to be considered successful, it must achieve the following objectives:

Strategic alignment: it must help users in a way that supports the users.

Business intelligence: it must provide the user with relevant information and data, answer questions, and inspire new insights and learning.

Efficiency and effectiveness: it must change the work performed by the HR personnel by dramatically improving their level of service, allowing more time for work of higher value, and reducing their costs.

But, despite extensive implementation of enterprise resource planning (ERP) projects, **human resource information systems (HRIS)**, and **HR service centres** costing millions of dollars,

---

HRM in reality Hoarding knowledge

Forget knowledge sharing – colleagues hide their best ideas

Has a colleague ever ignored you when you asked for information? Did you have the feeling that they were deliberately avoiding you or were only pretending to be ignorant? Recent research suggests that you may have been right.

Catherine Connelly, assistant professor of HR and management at McMaster University's DeGroote School of Business, has found that workers often protect their knowledge, even taking steps to hide it from colleagues. Catherine Connelly and colleagues David Zweig of the University of Toronto and Jane Webster of Queen's University presented their findings at the annual conference of The Society for Industrial and Organizational Psychology in Dallas.

Connelly considers that companies regard knowledge acquired on the job as proprietary and implement expensive knowledge management systems to ensure that those in the know share their knowledge with others. Hoarding knowledge is bad for business.

Catherine Connelly says that the reluctance to share produces a contagious tendency to hide important knowledge and as a result productivity suffers.

Connelly's research indicates that employees are more likely to share with people they trust and who treat them fairly. 'When organizations emphasize positive relationships and trust among employees, knowledge sharing will become part of the culture', she explained.

Clues that show you've been a victim of knowledge hiding:

- You ask a colleague for help, and they say: 'I'm sorry. My boss doesn't want this to be public right now.'
- Nothing. They ignore your request.
- 'I don't know. Maybe someone else can help you out.'

Why people engage in knowledge hiding:

- They feel that an injustice has been done to them.
- They are distrustful of co-workers or management.
- They are retaliating against someone else's behaviour toward them.
- The organizational climate encourages secrecy, not sharing.
- They can get away with it.

How to encourage knowledge sharing:

- Emphasize positive relationships and trust among employees.
- Explain the mutual benefits of having colleagues share their knowledge.
- Treat all workers fairly and respectfully.
- Make knowledge sharing part of the culture.

Is the concept of knowledge sharing against human nature?

Source: *HRM Guide Canada* (http:www.hrmguide.net/canada) 2 May, 2006.

Walker concludes that few organizations have been entirely happy with the results. Why is this?

Many systems have been implemented by cutting HR staff, outsourcing and imposing technology on what was left. Arguably this approach should, at least, have cut costs. But Walker (2001) argues that survey results demonstrate that overall HR departments have actually *increased* their staffing levels over the past decade to do the same work. Moreover he considers that:

> Most of the work that the HR staff does on a day-to-day basis, such as staffing, employee relations, compensation, training, employee development, and benefits, unfortunately, remains relatively untouched and unimproved from a delivery standpoint.

Walker advocates business process re-engineering the HR function first, then re-engineering the HR work. He suggests the formation of re-engineering teams of providers, customers and

---

HR systems

Human resource systems can differ widely. They may be:

- Intranets using web-type methods but operating purely within one organization or location.
- Extranets encompassing two or more organizations.
- Portals offering links to internal information and services but also accessing the worldwide web.

Advantages

- Familiarity (looking like web pages).
- Attractiveness (colourful, clearly laid out, graphics).
- Integration (linking different HR systems such as basic personnel records, employee handbooks, terms and conditions, contracts, various entitlements and payroll).
- Allowing employees and managers to enter, check and amend controlled ranges of personal and other information.
- Eliminating printing, enveloping and mailing of personnel and other employee information.
- Reducing need for telephone handling of routine enquiries by HR staff.

Basic system requirements

1 Desktop PCs for accessing and inputting information locally. Standard browsers are used to access information, e.g. Firefox or Internet Explorer.
2 Organization-wide server. In a small company this need be nothing more than an additional PC. The server must have an intranet server software package installed .
3 Server-side software such as HTML, Java, Javascript, Perl.
4 Intranet communications protocol running on both PCs and the server.
5 Relational database/information processing software for records, payroll, etc. If data is to be accessed then the procedure is made slightly more complicated with the need for CGI scripts and database server software on the server.
6 Basic documents such as policy manuals typically loaded in HTML or a more advanced web coding language, but formats such as Adobe Acrobat PDF are also an alternative.

Source: *HRM Guide UK* (http://www.hrmguide.co.uk)

users to examine the whole range of HR activities – including those which are not being done at present. The end product is a set of processes organized into broad groupings such as resourcing, compensation or training and development. These processes should then be examined by the re-engineering team and redesigned to: (a) be better aligned with organizational goals; (b) streamlined so as to be cost-effective in comparison with the 'best in class'; and (c) have a better integration with other processes.

From this redesign comes the picture of a new HR function. What next? The organization could be restructured and the tasks handed out to existing or new staff. But Walker argues that the most effective approach is to introduce new technology to deal with the redesigned processes.

Walker also discusses a range of technologies available for re-engineered HR processes, contending that they are all capable of dealing with HR activities in a secure and confidential manner.

1 *Workflow*. Walker describes this as being like 'e-mail with a database and built-in intelligence'. Essentially, a user accesses a range of employee records (perhaps their own) through a computer terminal, keys in data such as a change of address and submits the data electronically to the next person in the chain. The system is configured so that only certain individuals are authorized for a specific range of access or actions. The workflow chain is organized to ensure that the most suitable person approves an action. For example, a bonus payment would be authorized by a line manager's own manager. Also, the system can be structured so that bonuses over a certain level can be monitored by a HR specialist. The paths and actions are all specified in accordance with company rules.

2 *Manager self-service*. Managers can have access to 'front-end' applications on their desk tops in the form of HR portals. Typically, they are able to view a range of personal details and aggregate information. They are also allowed to change and input certain details and model the consequences on their budgets of salary increases or bonus payments. More generally, policy manuals, plans and strategies can be made available. Walker highlights the facility to 'push' information requiring attention to managers – including those dreaded employee performance appraisals.

3 *Employee self-service*. Similarly, employees can view company information, change selected personal details, make benefit enquiries (pension plans, sick pay entitlement), book leave and apply for training programmes. Walker makes the point that 'portal technology will personalize this data further and "push" relevant data to them as well'.

4 *Interactive voice response (IVR)*. A low-tech method, using the push-button control facility found in most modern telephones. Most of us are familiar with automatic responses such as: 'If your call is about vacancies in the accounts department, press 3 followed by #' when we dial large organizations. The system is restricted but easy to use and inexpensive in comparison to web-based methods. It is suitable for job openings and training course details where straightforward information can be recorded as simple scripts.

5 *HR service centres*. Walker notes that this has become one of the most widely used solutions to re-engineered HR in large organizations. Such centres centralize a number of HR processes and may deal with geographically widespread users. For example, the Raleigh, North Carolina, service centre can deal with all of IBM's North American current and former staff. Operators or 'agents' take enquiries by phone, e-mail or online that may already have been filtered through interactive voice response scripts or desktop HR systems. In effect, they deal with the relatively non-routine issues that cannot be handled by basic technology. However, they do use recognizable call centre techniques such as scripted protocols. The agent can enter keywords or a question into a knowledge database and bring up relevant information with which to answer the caller's query. If that query is not covered by information in the knowledge database it can be referred to a supervisor using workflow. HR service centres also

have fax, e-mail and postal facilities to send information, confirmations, follow-up queries and printed brochures to users. They are also monitored in the same way as conventional call centres and can generate useful statistics on types and frequency of enquiries. Walker contends that most reports show that organizations find HR service centres to be highly cost-effective and provider faster and more consistent answers than traditional HR departments.

6 *Human resource information systems (HRIS) and databases.* According to Walker (2001, pp.8–9): 'The HRIS system is the primary transaction processor, editor, record-keeper, and functional application system which lies at the heart of all computerized HR work. It maintains employee, organizational and HR plan data sufficient to support most, if not all, of the HR functions depending on the modules installed.' It will also supply information to other systems and generate reports.

7 *Stand-alone HR systems.* A massive choice of applications are available from commercial vendors which can be linked to a HRIS. They include online application forms, tests, appraisal databases, 360-degree performance assessments and so on.

8 *Data-marts and data-warehouses.* Sources of information, usually held as relational databases which can be interrogated. Data-marts normally hold data from single sources, such as HR; data-warehouses amass information from multiple sources.

HRM in reality HR executives still not making the most of HR technology

Human resource self-service offers many advantages in terms of cost and efficiency but many HR executives are still concentrating on routine transactions and are not reaping the benefits of available technology, according to the findings of the HR service delivery survey by Towers Perrin, a global professional services firm.

Tom Keebler, principal and author of the study said:

With increased technological efficiencies and options in recent years, HR professionals have an opportunity to make greater gains and realize better results than they have in the past. But it takes more than good technology to optimize service delivery as a strategic management tool, as opposed to simply a basic HR transaction. Other requirements include effective long- and short-term planning, updated processes, and a focus on the larger workforce needs of the organization. Simply stated, implementing 'out of the box' HR technologies just isn't enough.

HR technologies have developed beyond payroll and staffing rotas to the point where they can now support workforce effectiveness in new and increasingly efficient ways. Most growth areas in HR technology fall under the umbrella of talent management. Organizations can expand applications that help attract and hire employees, for example:

- recruiting
- job posting and 'onboarding' solutions
- employee retention
- career development and online learning

- rewarding staff via online performance management and reward portals
- engagement with recognition programmes and online training opportunities.

HR systems

Ninety per cent of the 244 large and mid-size organizations surveyed in 2005 used a vendor-purchased human resource system with Oracle/PeopleSoft continuing to be dominant. Just over a half (51 per cent) of organizations reported equal spending of HR technology in 2005 compared with 2004, while almost a quarter (24 per cent) had higher levels of spending and an additional 10 per cent said they had much higher spending on HR technology. The survey found that enterprise resource planning (ERP) applications most likely to be implemented in 2006 included:

- both employee and manager self-service in reward and compensation management
- learning applications (in SAP), and
- recruiting applications (in PeopleSoft).

Employee self-service

Employee self-service (ESS) is now a widely used and successful method of HR service delivery. At least 80 per cent of companies surveyed used self-service in 2006 to help employees enroll in annual benefits, view benefit plans and policies, access wellness information, view pension contributions, change personal data, view pay stubs and view job postings. Most of the larger companies had these features in place in 2004 but smaller organizations have lagged behind although they are now catching up quickly.

Having reached the limit of benefits from simple transaction-based ESS, a number of organizations reported that they had moved on to the implementation of new, and largely unprecedented, ESS-based processes. They said these were complex and dealt with tasks previously handled by HR generalists with specific subject matter knowledge.

ESS promises to free up time that can be devoted to strategic, business objective-aligned pursuits. While employees gained an average of nearly 2 per cent less work, ESS reduced the workloads of HR generalist/specialists by an average of 15 per cent.

'These results demonstrate the clear need for organizations to identify new roles, responsibilities and tasks for the HR function if they want to reap the rewards of HR technology,' added Keebler. 'But equally important, the HR team has to be ready, willing and able to take on these new roles.'

Manager self-service

Manager self-service (MSS) has not taken off so quickly, but the momentum is accelerating. Three-fifths (60 per cent) of respondents said that their organizations would be providing self-service to managers in 2006, covering:

- planning annual merit and base salary changes
- viewing employee data history
- initiating and approving job requisitions
- posting jobs
- viewing applicant resumés.

Managers have found ESS relatively easy to use but they have had some difficulties in the areas of MSS. However, when MSSs are properly used, they can reduce the HR generalist/specialist workload for these activities by over 21 per cent. Managers were more concerned with factors such as level of data edits and validations required, usability of tools, improved processing time, and the level of change management and communication at rollout than with any reduction in their own workload. According to Tower Perrin's media release: 'The better the tools given to managers, and the more an organization helps them to embrace the tools, the more receptive they will be to them – regardless of the impact on their workload.'

Said Keebler:

It's not enough to 'plug and play'. HR leadership needs to carefully examine how employees and managers will use the system, what additional information will be needed, what checks and balances should be created and installed, and the role that HR itself will play in the new world of self-service – from running the system to leading users through the change.

What factors appear to be holding back the full implementation of human resource information systems?

Source: *HRM Guide USA* (http://www.hrmguide.com) 3 April, 2006.

HR professionals and the HR system

The pressure is on for proactive HR innovations that contribute directly to the bottom-line or improve employee morale and efficiency. Ajuwon (2002) points out that the typical HR professional gets involved with one step in many different flows of work. Very often the involvement of HR has no purpose except to validate the process in some way and acts as an interruption to the flow of work. In other words, the HR function is a 'gatekeeper for information that's been deemed too highly classified for the data owner'.

So HR is not actually making a measurable contribution – in fact, quite the opposite. HR involvement creates a queue or delay in the process. We should ask if the HR involvement is really necessary. Once upon a time the HR database had an 'all-or-nothing' quality – probably because it was paper-based. But now technology allows controlled access to various portions of the database. So an employee can safely amend his or her own address or bank account details, while the ability to change certain appraisal details might be confined to the line manager. In either case, there is no reason for HR to be involved. HR should move on from the role of intermediary.

Not surprisingly, the use of employee self-service systems for records, information, payroll and other functions is becoming increasingly common. Libraries of forms can be kept online to be downloaded as and when required. Wiki technology, similar to that used for the online Wikipedia encyclopaedia, allows in-house 'experts' to collectively build a HR knowledge database or employee manual on an incremental basis as procedures change. Systems can be enhanced to include streaming video, podcasts and other new software, providing wide access to corporate videos, training, etc. E-mail announcements, newsletters and corporate blogs can be used to alert employees to new developments or urgent requests. Calls to HR service centres can be reduced by adding answers to common queries to wiki-based databases and blogs.

Ajuwon (2002) argues that HR should be proactive in the process and highlights three different perspectives for action:

> *The process perspective*: getting the fundamental building blocks (people processes) right and ensuring their relevance at all times. This demands close and detailed knowledge of HR processes and a commitment to improvement and efficiency. HR professionals need to understand their own objectives and the relationship with business strategy.

> *The event perspective*: a focus on providing a framework for knowledge management. In other words, capturing the experience and information available in the organization and making it available to individuals.

> *The cultural perspective*: acknowledging that HR has a 'pivotal role in the proactive engagement of the entire organisation in a changing climate'.

HRM in reality HR poorly supported by IT systems

Results from 'The gap between IT and strategic HR in the UK', a study by talent management solutions company, Taleo, show a significant disconnect between HR's strategic functions, including talent acquisition and workforce planning, and IT's ability to support these business initiatives.

The survey of 100 senior HR managers, all in organizations employing more than a thousand people, found that only a quarter thought that strategic functions such as workforce planning, leadership development and performance management were well supported by their IT systems. Only a third felt confident in systems support for recruitment and employee progression. Other findings included:

- Current technology systems were out-of-date. Over half the respondents (55 per cent) felt that more sophisticated technology systems and processes were needed to support recruitment and development.

- IT focused on lower-level, administrative functions. Respondents said that payroll and employee administration (68 per cent) and evaluation and management reporting (53 per cent) were adequately supported by IT. However, more strategic HR initiatives such as performance management (28 per cent), leadership development and planning (25 per cent) and strategic workforce planning (25 per cent) were not well supported.

- Inadequate data and technology systems obstructed workforce management. Just 29 per cent of respondents felt that they had sufficient systems in place to gain a clear picture of existing employee skills.

- The HR function was striving to become more strategic. 63 per cent of respondents cited talent management (including recruitment) as a significant priority in the year ahead.

Taleo research vice president, Alice Snell, said:

The gap between the support of administrative functions and strategic HR responsibilities needs to be addressed in order for HR directors to deliver results to the board. When HR directors can assess the workforce changes needed by the business, acquire and develop the talent needed to optimize the workforce, and then measure the results, their true value can be realized.

Neil Hudspith, senior vice president, international operations, Taleo, added:

Findings of this study clearly show that HR is evolving to play a more strategic role in supporting fundamental business objectives, but the systems being used by HR functions are not keeping up. It's clear that talent management and other strategic initiatives are being recognized as essential functions by ambitious companies that want to retain and recruit the best people, but organizations need to arm their HR directors with the tools and technology needed to support this strategy. The right HR technology is a critical element of any HR strategy moving forward.

What reasons can you suggest to explain the inadequacy of IT support for higher level and strategic HRM?

Source: *HRM Guide UK* (http://www.hrmguide.co.uk), 22 June, 2006.

During the 1990s the business process re-engineering approach resulted in many organizations taking a 'root and branch' look at HR and other processes. Subsequent re-organizations may have produced fresh, streamlined processes but often they became inappropriate or inefficient as circumstances changed. It is not enough to design a corporate human resource strategy or acquire a piece of technology. There has to be some way of ensuring effective operational delivery. A more fluid, constantly changing methodology is required. Ajuwon contends that we have the means:

> It's more than innovating and/or streamlining your HR processes; or building an HR portal; or introducing a culture change programme. It's about weaving together all three in a way that sustains change, engages the entire organization and deploys the organization's knowledge assets to gain competitive advantage and deliver profitability, even in times of economic downturn.

So-called 'Web 2.0' technologies such as wikis, blogs and podcasts allow a degree of inter-action so that anyone with expert knowledge, or even an opinion, can contribute to the HR function's evolving knowledge database.

Measuring the impact of HRM

Human resource departments are often targeted by senior managers wanting to cut budget costs. So it makes sense for HR managers to know how to optimize their practices within tight financial constraints. A study by US **benchmarking** specialists, Best Practices, LLC, explored how businesses focus their limited HR assets into critical areas.

They found that most of the 'benchmark partners' they examined (companies identified as using best practices), outsourced a number of HR tasks in order to release staffing resources for more important functions. The most commonly outsourced functions were benefits and compensations.

Benchmark partners also tracked their HR metrics (measurements) carefully in order to determine return on investment and to evaluate performance. One company used a balanced scorecard, measuring a wide range of financial, quality, operational and strategic metrics to determine the HR department's performance and contribution to business profitability.

Key concept 3.5 Benchmarking

Direct comparisons of different measures between an organization and 'best practice' competitors in the same business sector. This indicates the gap in performance, costs, morale, etc., between that organization and industry best practice.

Major findings

The following data analysis and best practice lessons were identified through quantitative surveys and executive interviews:

Coordinate HR roles and responsibilities. Most benchmark companies – whether centralized or decentralized – assigned corporate human resource functions the following responsibilities: managing benefits; compensation; leadership development/management; and human resource information systems and other HR technologies.

They also found that few business units had sole responsibility for any specific HR activity. In decentralized companies, business unit HR groups were also responsible for: staffing and recruiting; employee communications; and generalist functions.

Centralize HR performance measurement. Every benchmark company monitored their competitiveness for compensation/benefits, and over half tracked their overall headcount, employee turnover rates and safety incidents. But monitoring methods varied considerably. Decentralized companies gave responsibility for HR performance measurement decisions to individual business units or locations, letting each decide which metrics to track and how to collect them.

Maximize use of staffing and budgeting resources. The ratio of employees to HR generalists among the companies surveyed ranged from 141:1 to 318:1. But the researchers pointed out that companies at the high end of this spectrum ran the risk of short-changing some of the tasks assigned to generalists.

Self-service technologies. Companies were increasingly creating HR call centres and incorporating self-service HR software programs within company websites in order to: reduce administrative costs and time; increase information access to employees and managers; enable strategic HR; reduce overall HR headcount; improve information accuracy.

In fact these companies regarded their HR call centres as valuable entry points and training grounds for future full-time HR employees. HR assistance offered through self-service software and call centres included: clarifications on benefits plans; performance management worksheets and monitoring; questions about company policies; incentive compensation allocations; monitoring employee training administration.

HRM in reality   Using HR metrics

A report by The Conference Board suggests that while few (12 per cent) of the surveyed organizations make significant use of HR measures to meet strategic targets, 84 per cent of 104 HR executives interviewed in the survey say that they will increase their use of people metrics over the next three years.

Stephen Gates, principal researcher at The Conference Board and report author, said:

> When determining how best to demonstrate achievement, human resource managers must choose from the hundreds of metrics that are currently available to track every aspect of an HR department's endeavours to recruit, develop, and retain employees. What's imperative for the health of their businesses, however, is that these HR professionals tie these people measures more closely into their efforts to meet their companies' overall strategic targets.

Lisa Hartley, director HCM Marketing, PeopleSoft, which supported the research said:

> Though widespread adoption has been slow, we all see that our best practice customers are beginning to use people metrics to understand and drive business decisions. We've had great people data for a long time. It's just that it hasn't been presented in a relevant way. That is finally changing. We believe that the use of analytics is nothing less than transformational to making HR relevant to the strategic needs of the business.

Is HR up to the task?
According to the survey, a mere 31 per cent of respondents felt that HR executives in their organizations had

a strong understanding of strategic key performance indicators. Even fewer (25 per cent) surveyed considered their HR leaders capable of linking people measures to such indicators or (16 per cent) believed that HR professionals received extensive training to connect people measures to strategy.

Fifty-one per cent of participants in the survey said that HR professionals in their organizations were partially capable of identifying talent critical for implementing strategy but only 22 per cent said that those executives were fully able to identify strategic talent pools.

Effective people metrics
HR professionals have tended to use metrics to study the time and cost of utilizing people, but they are more likely to:

- provoke discussions with managers that lead to action plans;

- serve as educational tools that help bring implicit ideas about the value of human capital to the surface; and

- improve the HR decisionmaking process when they are used to evaluate the effectiveness and impact of people investments and HR activities.

Correlating popular individual measures with important perceived benefits can lead to a successful linking of certain people measures to specific strategies. The Conference Board report cites the following examples:

- employee satisfaction and competencies/training metrics were found to match a policy of customer responsiveness;
- leadership and competencies/training measures were found to have solid connections to innovation strategies;
- remuneration and leadership measures can help boost revenue growth.

But most of the organizations surveyed only partially tied their people measures and targets to strategic plans (52 per cent) or annual budgets (46 per cent). Half of the survey participants reported that their people metrics were fully or partially linked to customer data.

Making the case for people measures

Many respondents reported difficulties in implementing HR metrics with only 19 per cent rating their IT systems highly for HR data gathering. There is also an issue of organizational politics since HR metrics have implications on performance ratings, prestige, power, and resource allocation. Many organizations were trying to build support for their HR metrics efforts through collaboration with colleagues from finance (54 per cent) and strategy (45 per cent) and employing business managers as champions for HR measures (43 per cent).

According to Stephen Gates:

If people metrics highlight a problem that could be interpreted as critical of a business manager's performance, then the manager could be tempted to distort or suppress the negative data. When they point to a problem with HR's functional activities, then HR could also be motivated to hide negative data. In both instances, manipulating people data destroys the diagnostic power of the people metrics effort.

In 78 per cent of surveyed organizations, people measure reports are delivered to senior management. In a few companies, business managers – rather than HR representatives – present information back to business divisions directly, greatly enhancing the credibility of the process with those divisions.

'However, the finding that only 19 per cent of companies distribute briefings on people measurement to all of their business managers indicates that many companies do not view these reports as decision making tools for managers,' said Gates.

Summarize the main reasons for using HR metrics.

Source: *HRM Guide USA* (http://www.hrmguide.com), 24 January, 2005 based on 'Measuring More Than Efficiency: The New Role of Human Capital Metrics Report #1356', The Conference Board.

A 10-C checklist for effective HRM

Conscious of the risk of 'destroying it' (HRM), we will conclude the first part of this book with a discussion of the principles which appear to be essential to understanding HRM. First, why do we need a concept such as HRM? Surely, people management is a matter of commonsense. Certainly, some good people managers have – from many years of experience – developed an internal model which guides them well in the way they deal with their employees. However, there are many indifferent managers who appear to have learned little from their careers. In any case, students need to acquire a comprehensible and communicable framework without the benefit of years of experience. Second, if HRM has been in existence for at least two decades, has it not fulfilled its role? Unfortunately not. Comparing the early 1980s, the birth period of the subject, with the situation in the early 21st century, the need for a coherent approach to people management continues to be justified by some obvious deficiencies:

- In the 1980s, personnel management had its own agenda: its priorities were not necessarily matched to those of the organization, and its professional training and structure focused on a narrow range of techniques at the practitioner level rather than emphasizing a global view of business needs. It is arguable that the 'personnel profession' has become aware of these criticisms and has gone some way towards addressing them. However, there is still room for improvement.
- Other managers practised people management through a ragbag of often dubious and counter-productive methods, usually developed from intuition and experience. This continues to be largely the case.

● In the 1980s, theories of strategic management concentrated on areas such as finance and marketing, tending to ignore human resources. Since then, theoretical accounts have become much more people-conscious, but there is still a gap between theory and practice.

As a consequence, the people in many organizations were, and are, dealt with in a largely inconsistent and parochial manner. The 'You are our most valuable asset and, by the way, you're fired' approach describes people management in so many organizations. As we shall see in later chapters, the evidence shows that a meaningful form of HRM still does not prevail in many organizations. Little has changed.

So how should we practice meaningful HRM? At this point we introduce a systematic framework incorporating ten principles, each conveniently beginning with 'C' – in the best management guru style – for use as a checklist as we go through the various aspects of HRM discussed in this book. In fact, terms beginning with 'C' have a considerable track record in HRM and, therefore, the principles are not intended to be novel or surprising. The Harvard

Table 3.1	Principle	Purpose	Action
10-C checklist of HRM	**1** Comprehensiveness	Includes all aspects of people management	People management must be organized, rather than left to ad-hoc decisions at local level
	2 Coherence	HR management activities and initiatives form a meaningful whole	Clear link between individual performance/reward and business needs
	3 Control	Ensures performance is consistent with business objectives	Participative management, with delegation of *how* an objective is achieved
	4 Communication	Objectives understood and accepted by all employees; open culture with no barriers	Clear, simple and justified strategies; cascading process of communication with feedback to the top
	5 Credibility	Staff trust top management and believe in their strategies	Top managers are sincere, honest and consistent
	6 Commitment	Employees motivated to achieve organizational goals	Top managers are committed to their staff
	7 Change	Continuous improvement and development essential for survival	Flexible people and working systems; culture of innovation; skills training
	8 Competence	Organization competent to achieve its objectives – dependent on individual competencies	Resourcing strategies, selection techniques and human resource systems in place
	9 Creativity	Competitive advantage comes from unique strategies	System for encouraging and tapping employee ideas
	10 Cost-effectiveness	Competitive, fair reward and promotion systems	Top managers pay themselves on equivalent basis to staff

model has its central four Cs – commitment, congruence, competence, cost-effectiveness – three of which have been incorporated in our checklist. These and the other principles have been chosen because they are measurable in some way and are sufficiently broad in their totality to reveal the tension and balance that is the essential feature of effective HRM within the 'high commitment' or 'high performance' approach.

There is a risk of venturing into the 'prescriptive' but HRM is not simply a subject for academics who can afford to dissect ideas and argue over interpretations without worrying too much about their usefulness in real life. As with medicine and engineering, HRM is a practical subject with a foundation in theory, previous experience and forward thinking, based on a carefully assessed degree of risk. Real people managers have to deal with real situations, often with major cost implications. There is no time for sterile debate – they have to deliver – and it is not surprising that many and, perhaps most, pay little attention to academic theory.

Comprehensiveness

All people management activities should be part of a single, comprehensive system. This implies that the attitudes, behaviour and culture of every individual in an organization – especially those with people management responsibilities – should be integrated within a deliberate framework. This approach ensures that HRM is holistic and systematic, with every aspect – together with their interrelationships – brought into consideration. It reflects the perspective that business problems, especially those involving people management, are highly complex. The relevant variables are densely interconnected (Checkland, 1981). In other words, simple solutions are rarely possible.

Coherence

The second principle of coherence addresses the internal balance and integration of the people management system. Strategies and actions must be consistent with each other. For example, if a business has a strategy of increasing sales of high-profit-margin products, rewards in the sales department should be focused on these products rather than less profitable items. Similarly, if the organization has chosen to take a team-based approach, recruitment and training should emphasize team skills rather than strong individualism.

Control

As with any other form of management, HRM is aimed at directing and coordinating employees to meet an organization's objectives. As such, it cannot be anarchic nor totally democratic in its approach. However, the nature of control must be consistent with the remaining principles. Human resource literature mostly advocates a participative approach with a high degree of empowerment and delegation. An autocratic approach is unlikely to encourage good communication and employee commitment.

Communication

Effective communication facilitates coherence. Serious attention must be given to communicating the organization's strategic objectives, together with the parameters – acceptable behaviour, cost and time – within which they can be achieved. Good communication is essential to the smooth running of the people management system. It must be a two-way process, made easier by new interactive technologies such as the corporate blog. This can involve a cascaded flow of information from the top and also feedback from lower levels through surveys, performance measures, open meetings and blog feedback. An open culture should be encouraged: employees need to feel confident that they can express their opinions and concerns without fear of retribution.

Credibility

Many organizations spend a great deal of money and effort in their attempts to communicate with their employees. Often, however, employees dismiss glossy brochures and websites or time-consuming team briefings as so much management propaganda. A degree of healthy cynicism is unavoidable, but in today's down-sized workplaces this frequently extends into mistrust of and contempt for senior management. This feeling reflects the way many staff feel they are themselves regarded by management. Regaining trust depends on personal **credibility** which, in turn, can only come from honesty and sincerity.

Commitment

Earlier, we noted that the Harvard model of HRM places a strong emphasis on the notion of commitment. It embodies a 'can-do' approach, going further than is normally asked. Committed employees can give that competitive edge – the extra something which distinguishes a successful company from its lesser rivals. However, commitment is difficult to achieve. As we will find in our discussion in Chapter 10, it is dependent on confidence in the organization, the people who lead it, the reward mechanism and the opportunity for staff to develop themselves. More than anything, it depends on the degree of commitment which managers show to their own people. As we saw in the IBM case study in Chapter 2, economic realities can jeopardize this commitment.

Change

Businesses must **change** to survive. However, change is a difficult management task. Effective change requires sure-footed, considerate people managers who can take employees through the process with minimum anxiety and maximum enthusiasm. It requires the recognition that an organization's people should not be the pawns of strategy but active participants in change. In Chapter 12, we will see that their detailed job knowledge, customer contact and ingenuity can be harnessed to provide ideas for improvement.

Competence

Organizations must have the capability to meet changing needs. In current parlance this is often expressed in terms of competences – skills, knowledge and abilities. These are qualities possessed by the people who work for those organizations. Competences can be brought into businesses through the recruitment of skilled individuals. They can also be developed within existing people by investing in training, **education** and experiential programmes. The establishment and cultivation of a high level of relevant competences leads to a distinct competitive advantage.

Creativity

Advantages can also come from the ingenuity of staff. **Creativity** is under-emphasized in management training but it can lead to new products and services, novel applications and cost-savings. Competences such as detailed knowledge of products and procedures are required before innovation can occur. A creative environment develops from a trusting, open culture with good communication and a blame-free atmosphere. Conversely, creativity is inhibited by lack of trust or commitment and fear of the consequences of change.

Cost-effectiveness

One of the original Harvard 'four Cs', it provides the hard kernel of an otherwise 'soft' model of HRM. Expressed in terms of profitability, it has been extensively used as the justification for large-scale job cuts. This aspect has attracted considerable criticism, primarily because of the obsessive way in which many senior managers have pursued 'down-sizing' at the expense of commitment to their staff. However, as a reflection of the value of its human assets, an organization has a duty to use its people wisely and cost-effectively. In itself, there is nothing wrong with an attention to cost – provided that it does not become the one and only management criterion.

These checklist principles are developed further in later chapters. It can be seen that they are interlocked – failure to observe any one of them can lead to the breakdown of the people management system. Throughout the remainder of the book we will find illustrations of such failure, usually attributable to management belief that HRM initiatives and practices can be adopted on a 'pick and mix' basis.

Summary

In this chapter we discussed recent and ongoing ways in which the human resource management function is changing – perhaps more radically than ever before. The HR function and its activities are being examined in microscopic detail in many large organizations. Human resource processes, especially those involving the collection and dissemination of information, are being computerized and automated, potentially eliminating routine clerical activities. HR information and knowledge is being linked and integrated with other information systems, breaking down departmental barriers.

As HR processes become more easily measurable, the need for justification and the means to do so become more obvious. Many consultants have advocated the concepts of high performance organization and knowledge management, suggesting that they offer HR specialists the chance to push HRM to the fore. HR processes and their outcomes are central to these concepts and the introduction of technology allows more exact methods of determining whether or not human resource initiatives do affect the 'bottom line' and shareholder value.

Yet there is some cynical scepticism and contradictory research findings coming from HR practitioners and academics, some of it associated with dogged technophobia, together with justifiable questioning of the methodology, rationale and, not least, the capabilities of the systems and concepts we have discussed.

Further reading

Karen Legge provides a carefully reasoned critique of the high commitment/performance concept and its links to HRM in a chapter of Storey (ed.) *Human Resource Management: A Critical Text* (2nd edn, Thomson Learning, 2001). In the same book, John Storey and Paul Quintas provide an overview of knowledge management and its implications on HR in their chapter on the topic. Linda Holbeche's *High Performance Organisation* (Butterworth-Heinemann, 2005) sets out to provide information and practical tools for people engaged in leading organizational change. *How to Measure Human Resource Management* (3rd edn, 2001) by Jac Fitz-Enz and Barbara Davison, published by McGraw-Hill, contains practical information on measuring elements of HR. There is a vast selection of books about knowledge management, few questioning the entire concept and many having an IT orientation. *If Only We Knew What We Know: The Transfer of Internal Knowledge and Best Practice* by Carla S. O'Dell and Nilly Essaides (The Free Press, 1998) remains a good exposition of how applying the ideas of knowledge management can help employers identify their own internal best practices and share this intellectual capital throughout their organizations. *Managing for Knowledge: HR's Strategic Role* by Christina Evans (Butterworth-Heinemann, 2003) is one of the few with a human resource perspective. *The Future of Knowledge Management*, edited by Birgit Renzl, Kurt Matzler and Hans H. Hinterhuber (Palgrave Macmillan, 2005) is unusual in its critical and analytic scope.

Keep an eye on further developments in these areas as new articles and updates appear on the HRM Guide Network of websites (http://www.hrmguide.net).

Review questions

1 How would you define the following terms?
   - High performance work system
   - Knowledge
   - Knowledge management
   - Human resource information system
   - Human resource service centre.

2 Is the concept of high performance management fundamentally different from HRM?

3 'High performance' and 'high commitment' are terms used to describe the same or a similar concept. What are the implications of the different terms on the management of staff?

4 What differences would you see in using the high performance approach for private and public sector employees?

5 Does current research show a clear link between HR procedures and high performance?

6 What do you consider to be the main benefits to an organization from the ability to manage knowledge?

7 How can organizations capture knowledge? What are the main obstacles?

8 To what extent are HR processes and outcomes measurable?

9 What positive outcomes have been attributed to human resource systems? What are the disadvantages of such systems?

10 In what circumstances would you *not* introduce HR technology into an organization?

Case study for discussion and analysis

Read the following case study. What is the likelihood of achieving a high-performance work system in the circumstances described?

Accenture

HR and training not delivering skilled workforces

Recent international research conducted for Accenture shows that most senior executives surveyed consider that their workforces lack the skills needed by their companies to achieve market leadership, and even critical functions are not performing as well as they should. Moreover, only 11 per cent of respondents said they were very satisfied with the performance of their human resource function with marginally fewer (10 per cent) rating their training function very highly.

Just 14 per cent of executives surveyed believed that the overall skill level of their organization's entire workforce was industry-leading. And only 20 per cent felt that the vast majority of their employees understood their companies' strategy and what was required to be successful in their industry.

Peter Cheese, global managing partner in Accenture's human performance practice, commented:

The lack of essential skills is a vital issue for senior managers. As the competitive environment grows more demanding and as markets become increasingly commoditized, the need to cultivate these skills – particularly in the critical functions – should be at the top of every corporate to-do list. Those companies that fail to develop their workforces risk losing their competitive edge.

Accenture attributes these shortcomings, in part, to a number of HR and training issues, including:

Lack of connection to business drivers. A mere 36 per cent of survey respondents said that their organizations tailored HR and training support to each function's needs and contributions to the business.

Failure to measure the business impact of HR and training efforts. Two-fifths (40 per cent) did not evaluate the impact of human resource and training efforts against profitability. 50 per cent did not evaluate those efforts against revenues and sales.

Inadequate knowledge capture and sharing capabilities. Some 42 per cent of respondents said that the process of capturing and sharing knowledge was a challenge or a severe challenge for their organizations. The following reasons were most commonly cited: lack of a common business culture across different locations (38 per cent); no knowledge support infrastructure with dedicated people (37 per cent); knowledge sharing typically not rewarded in the organization (32 per cent).

The talent time bomb. Sixty per cent of respondents expected to begin feeling the impact of the ageing workforce and impending retirement of baby boomers within the next five years. 28 per cent of these were already feeling the impact. 43 per cent of all survey participants said that talent sourcing was a challenge or a severe challenge, primarily because the talent pool was shrinking.

Lack of functional leaders' involvement in people issues. Few of the survey respondents said their heads of functions were highly involved in human capital management initiatives. Specific percentages were: customer service (29 per cent), finance (31 per cent), sales (34 per cent) and strategic planning (37 per cent).

Human performance leaders

A number of companies were identified that Accenture refers to as 'human performance leaders'. These were defined as organizations in which the three functions their executives deemed to be most important performed at the highest levels. Compared to the 'laggards' in which none of the top three functions were high performers, performance leaders were more likely to succeed in addressing organizational issues that contributed to strong financial performance. The following were identified as high performing areas:

- Acquiring new customers and increasing market share (43 per cent of 'human performance leaders' compared with 14 per cent of 'laggards').

- Encouraging strong customer loyalty and retention (52 per cent against 17 per cent).

- Responding to changing market conditions (52 per cent against 14 per cent).

- Finding and developing talented leaders (39 per cent against 7 per cent).

- Attracting and retaining skilled staff (30 per cent against 12per cent).

- Generating superior business value from technology investments (35 per cent against 15 per cent).

The findings show that 'human performance leaders' possess more effective HR and training support. The practices that help them excel include:

- Formal measures to measure the impact of all HR and training support activities on their top functions.

- Tailored HR and training support to match the contribution of specific functions.

- A more strategic approach to HR and training, including viewing the HR function leader as a strategic business partner to the executive suite.

'A company's ability to manage its workforce strategically and develop its capabilities will set it apart from its competitors,' said Peter Cheese. 'Some companies focus well on one or two aspects of human capital management, such as learning or internal communications, but the best take a broad view of managing their workforce. These are the companies that vastly increase their chances of being industry leaders.'

The study was conducted by GfK NOP Limited on behalf of Accenture between February and April 2006. It included telephone surveys with 251 senior executives – chief executive officers, chief operating officers, chief financial officers and chief information officers, human resource leaders, chief learning officers – in the United States of America, United Kingdom, Australia, France, Germany, and Spain. Respondents' companies came from seven broad industry sectors: retail, travel and transportation, financial services, electronics and high tech, communications, energy and utilities.

Source: *HRM Guide USA* (http://www.hrmguide.com) 23 June, 2006.

Part two
HRM and the business environment

At first sight it may seem strange to devote a large and early part of this book to the relationship between HRM and the business environment. But people management within individual organizations cannot take place in isolation from the rest of the world: 'HRM does not exist within a vacuum' (Hollinsead and Leat, 1995: p.7). As we saw in Part one, this is reflected by the somewhat understressed inclusion of outside stakeholders in the Harvard model of HRM.

Many practitioners and academics have neglected HRM's environmental context, preferring to concentrate on technical detail. This is consistent with criticisms of traditional personnel management for its narrow focus on functional or 'micro' matters such as recruitment. In fairness, however, it must be recognized that personnel or HR managers have always required a detailed knowledge of employment legislation, together with an understanding of industrial tribunals and trade union organization. Nevertheless, this represents a restricted selection from the wide range of environmental factors impacting on people management.

The chapters in Part two address a wider perspective and introduce a number of fundamental issues which are developed further in later chapters in the book.

For example:

- Is there a clear link between human capital and national success?
- What is the effect of globalization on the practice of HRM?
- How do multinational companies manage their people?
- Do governments determine the effectiveness of HRM?
- What is the employment market?
- Have traditional 9-to-5 jobs been replaced by more flexible work patterns?

Chapter 4
International HRM and the global economy

Learning objectives

The purpose of this chapter is to:

- Outline positive and negative aspects of the globalization of trade and production that affect human resource management.

- Provide an overview of the HR implications of economic growth and stagnation.

- Critically evaluate the importance of regional trading blocs and multinational companies in the process of globalization.

- Highlight human resource issues specific to developing countries.

- Investigate the roles of supranational organizations such as the International Labour Organization and the European Union regarding the management of people.

Globalization

'The modern business has no place to hide. It has no place to go but everywhere' (Lane, Distefano and Maznevski, 1997).

We concluded the previous chapter by considering HRM as a people management system, acknowledging its intricate and interdependent principles. However, HRM is a system within other systems. The most complex of these is the international **business environment** (see Key concept 4.1). The forces that act on people management are not purely internal to an organization. They encompass innumerable active players in the world economy, including international agencies, governments, competitors, unions, speculators and consumers – each pursuing their own goals.

Key concept 4.1 The business environment

'All factors which exist outside the business enterprise, but which interact with it' (Needle,1994, p.26). Traditionally, human resource managers have been closely involved with employment legislation, industrial tribunals and trade unions at a functional level. HRM's strategic emphasis requires a focus on other environmental variables. Government economic, social security, education and training policies affect the supply, cost and quality of available employees. International competition, strategic alliances and supranational organizations such as the European Union are exercising increasing influence on people management.

Changes in the business environment have major consequences for people managers. As we saw in the IBM case study (Chapter 2), these forces may be so powerful that an individual organization loses the discretion to pursue its own strategies (Kochan and Dyer, 2001, p.282). In essence this means that factors outside a company's control will affect its requirements for human resources and the way they are managed. For example, unexpected changes in competitor technology or currency exchange rates may compel a business to abandon long-term human resource plans and shed staff in order to survive. **Globalization** is frequently cited as the most significant factor affecting the deployment of human resources worldwide.

Why is globalization (Key concept 4.2) important to our understanding of human resource management? Examine the business pages of any national newspaper and you are almost certain to find examples of businesses engaged in cross-border mergers, takeovers or expansion overseas. Moreover, domestic mergers of banks, airline companies and even retailers are often explained as defensive moves by national organizations attempting to build sufficient critical mass to withstand competition from giant multinationals. Businesses simply cannot ignore the global dimension, and neither can human resource managers.

Key concept 4.2 Globalization

A systematic trend towards integration of production and marketing with brand-named goods and virtually identical 'badge-engineered' products such as cars being made available throughout the world. This process has been fostered by 'transnational' or 'multinational' companies operating in more than one country. Such companies are relatively free to switch resources and production from one country to another. Typically this is done in order to maximize the benefit (to the corporation) of greater skills availability and lower employee costs. This has been described as the new international division of labour.

Scholte (2000) argues that globalization involves 'the growth of "supraterritorial relations" among people'. Physical location is becoming steadily less relevant as new technology and increasingly complex international supply links are developed. This has a considerable impact on culture, language and working practices throughout the world. Globalization is driven by marketing to a considerable extent. Large corporations are attempting to achieve global recognition in their particular market sectors. Brands such as Coca-Cola, Mcdonald's, BP and Shell are internationally recognized and have become drivers for growth and market dominance. The implications for the nature and availability of work and its management are profound.

Branded products are becoming less diverse. Consequently employees in one country increasingly use the same manufacturing processes as any other and are expected to achieve equivalent standards of productivity. As a result, the costs and skills of human resources have become a matter of competition between countries. And giant corporations can take advantage of this competition. The car industry is a clear example in which a few major players, especially Ford, Toyota and General Motors, manufacture specific models (or basic 'platforms') in a number of global locations with parts coming from competing sources. Ford, for example, ceased car production in Dagenham, England in 2002, following unfavourable comparison with sites in Belgium, Germany and Spain.

Will standardized products and production techniques lead to virtually identical human resource practices throughout the world? We will see later in this book that significant cultural and linguistic differences between and within countries provide major obstacles to a 'homogenized' global HRM. But some degree of standardization is inevitable. This issue has been the subject of debate for some time. In the 1980s it was discussed under the heading of the 'internationalization of labour'. Some commentators considered that different regions or countries should specialize in specific industries depending on the factors that gave them a competitive advantage (Legge, 1995). Two main types of economy were envisaged:

1 Countries that had cheap, low-skilled labour focusing on assembling low-cost, high-volume products or producing agricultural or mineral commodities. This was typical of 'third-world' countries in an early stage of development.

2 Countries with well-paid, skilled 'knowledge workers' who concentrated on the provision of goods and services with a high value-added component.

In reality, economies are more complex and most countries demonstrate characteristics that are between these two extremes (Dicken, 1998; Fishlow and Parker, 1999). But this kind of analysis led some economists in developed countries into discounting the importance of mass production. Instead they advocated that advanced countries should concentrate on high-value sectors such as financial services and information technology. Similar ideas today are addressed in the concept of the 'knowledge economy'.

The International Labour Organization (ILO) (2000) concluded that globalization intensified in the latter years of the 20th century, especially in terms of trade, investment, financial liberalization and technological change. Despite some fluctuations, growth in world trade has continued into the 21st century. In 2005, for example, the value of world merchandise exports increased by 13 per cent to US$10.1 trillion, while the value of world commercial services exports rose by 11 per cent to US$2.4 trillion (WTO, 2006).

The ILO (2000, p.vii) states that:

The benefits of globalization have been very unevenly distributed both between and within nations. At the same time a host of social problems have emerged or intensified, creating increased hardship, insecurity, and anxiety for many across the world, fuelling a strong backlash. As a result, the present form of globalization is facing a crisis of legitimacy resulting from the erosion of popular support.

Some of the main factors identified as being at the root of widespread public disquiet are:

● Reduction in job security because work (and therefore jobs) can be moved from one country to another.

● Undercutting of one country's wages by another, leading to erosion of wage rates.

- Exceeding generally accepted working hours and exposure to health and safety risks in order to cut costs.

The 1995 Social Summit of the United Nations highlighted the positive and negative consequences of globalization, concluding that 'globalization ... opens new opportunities for sustained economic growth and development of the world economy, particularly in developing countries'. It also recognized that rapid changes and adjustments 'have been accompanied by intensified poverty, unemployment and social disintegration'. Overall, the Summit identified that the key challenge was 'to manage these processes and threats so as to enhance their benefits and mitigate their negative effects upon people' (United Nations, 1995).

Weisbrot (2002, pp.10–12) makes the following observation:

Consider this: In Latin America and the Caribbean, where gross domestic product grew by 75 per cent per person from 1960 to 1980, it grew by only 7 per cent per person from 1980 to 2000. The collapse of the African economies is more well known, although still ignored: GDP in sub-Saharan Africa grew by about 34 per cent per person from 1960 to 1980; in the past two decades, per capita income actually fell by about 15 per cent. Even if we include the fast-growing economies of East Asia and South Asia, the past two decades fare miserably. For the entire set of low- and middle-income countries, per capita GDP growth was less than half of its average for the previous 20 years. Also, as might be expected in a time of bad economic performance, the past two decades have brought significantly reduced progress according to such major social indicators as life expectancy, infant and child mortality, literacy, and education – again, for the vast majority of low- and middle-income countries.

In total contrast, Kostas Karamanlis (2006), prime minister of Greece and chair of the 2006 OECD Ministerial Council holds a strongly positive view of globalization:

... fostering trade can lead to a new era of prosperity for the world. Trade and globalization should not be seen as a threat to job security but rather as a challenge for a more prosperous world. Maintaining living standards in our societies cannot be achieved by protecting jobs in uncompetitive industries, but by investing in knowledge, innovation and well-targeted social

---

HRM in reality Commonwealth games souvenirs possibly breach labour standards

Unions have expressed concern about souvenirs produced for the Melbourne Commonwealth Games. They claim that souvenirs may have been manufactured in breach of the international labour standards previously agreed upon by the Games authority and unions.

Yesterday, Steven Lew, the chief executive of Playcorp, the Games' key apparel licensee, said in the federal court that he had not made any effort to ensure that Chinese workers making T-shirts, polo shorts and other clothing for the Commonwealth Games had access to free trade unions.

ACTU President Sharan Burrow said:

It is not good enough for the Games organizers to agree to adopt internationally accepted labour standards and then fail to ensure the rights of workers making souvenirs and clothing for the Games are protected.

What is the point of entering into an agreement with Victorian unions unless you are going to adhere to it?

Unions entered into an agreement with the Commonwealth Games organizers that would protect local jobs as well as ensure that the rights of overseas workers involved in producing Games clothing and souvenirs would be protected.

Now we find that a key licensee of Games clothing made no effort to check whether workers at the Chinese clothing factory in Ningbo had a right to collectively bargain and access to a trade union.

Textile Clothing and Footwear Union Secretary Michele O'Neil commented:

As part of the agreement with Games officials, Victorian unions were able to achieve a commitment that 75 per cent of the uniforms for the Games workforce would be made in Australia – ensuring the products were made ethically by Australian workers.

It is very disappointing that the Games organizers have clearly paid only lip service to the licensees meeting their obligations and have made no effort to monitor the working conditions of the overseas manufacturers.

Is international trade an opportunity for unscrupulous businesses to ignore civilized labour standards?

Source: *HRM Guide Australia* (http://www.hrmguide.net/australia/), 3 March, 2006.

welfare systems. Also, training, re-training and life-long learning systems have a crucial role to play. There are several examples of countries demonstrating that open, competitive economies can achieve prosperity, without sacrificing social cohesion, especially when assistance for adjustment during transition facilitates the introduction of reforms.

Sen (2002) tries to balance positive and negative views of globalization. He notes that proponents and opponents of globalization tend to perceive it as global Westernization. Those who have a positive view of globalization consider it to be a 'marvellous contribution of Western civilization to the world'. Many see a stylized sequence of history in which everything important happened in Europe: the Renaissance, the Enlightenment and the Industrial Revolution. These led to improved living standards in the West that are now being spread to the rest of the world. From this perspective, 'globalization is not only good, it is also a gift from the West to the world'.

But those with the opposite point of view see globalization as an extension of Western imperialism. They see contemporary capitalism as being 'driven and led by greedy and grabby Western countries in Europe and North America' using 'rules of trade and business relations that do not serve the interests of the poorer people in the world'.

On the other hand, Jackson (1998) argues that the concept of globalization has been demonized by opponents of the free market, contending that 'they have shamelessly used it to exploit fear and ignorance'. He considers that claims that globalization leads to lowered real wages and 'destroys jobs, causes financial crises, creates social tension and undermines national sovereignty' are false. Jackson refutes such claims despite a prevailing but naive public belief in their status as 'self-evident truths'. He considers that globalization is not a new phenomenon. On the contrary, it is just an alternative name for free trade and an ongoing process of the internationalization of trade and capital, concluding that: 'What many fear today was commonplace a hundred years ago. Globalization is no more damaging or de-stabilizing now than it was in the 1890s'.

Similarly, Sen (2002) points to the longer-term nature of globalization:

> Is globalization really a new Western curse? It is, in fact, neither new nor necessarily Western; and it is not a curse. Over thousands of years, globalization has contributed to the progress of the world through travel, trade, migration, spread of cultural influences, and dissemination of knowledge and understanding (including that of science and technology). These global interrelations have often been very productive in the advancement of different countries. They have not necessarily taken the form of increased Western influence. Indeed, the active agents of globalization have often been located far from the West.

The degree of perceived job insecurity is highlighted in the OECD survey shown in Table 4.1.

Key concept 4.3 The insecurity thesis

Heery and Salmon (2000) identify a connection between globalization and the 'insecurity thesis', a belief that: 'Employment in the developed economies has become more insecure or unstable in the sense that both continued employment and the level of remuneration have become less predictable and contingent on factors which lie beyond the employee's control.'

Perception of the effects of globalization is coloured by such views. One consequence is that the media take a keen interest in human resource practices throughout the world – no matter how remote the location. The coverage inevitably increases public awareness and hostility towards practices that may be viewed as unfair or exploitative. This creates pressures to bring such practices within the remit of international bodies.

The World Economic Forum commissioned a survey of 25 000 people in 25 countries during the last few months of 2001. Contrary to some of the opinions we have discussed, the attitude towards globalization was broadly favourable. They found that:

- The majority of people in most countries surveyed expected that more economic globalization would be positive for themselves and their families.
- Globally, more than six in ten citizens see globalization as beneficial, with just one in five seeing it as negative.
- Positive views of globalization had grown over the previous year, especially in North America and Europe.
- People (especially citizens of poorer countries) had high expectations that globalization would deliver benefits in a number of economic and non-economic areas. But, on average, people also believed that globalization would worsen environmental problems and poverty in the world, and reduce the number of jobs in their country.

Table 4.1	**Country**
Job insecurity across the OECD in 2000	Korea
Source International Survey Research, OECD, 2001.	United Kingdom

Country	Unsure of a job even if they perform well (%)
Korea	46
United Kingdom	41
Japan	38
United States of America	37
Australia	37
France	37
Sweden	36
Czech Republic	35
New Zealand	34
Germany	34
Italy	32
Finland	31
Unweighted average	**30**
Greece	29
Spain	27
Canada	27
Hungary	26
Switzerland	26
Belgium	26
Austria	23
Ireland	23
Netherlands	22
Denmark	20
Portugal	21
Norway	17

- Most citizens of the richest countries (G-7) did not believe that poor countries benefited as much as rich countries from free trade and globalization. But the opposite was true in low GDP countries.

Table 4.2 shows a breakdown of opinions solicited by the survey.

The complexity of globalization and its effects reduces the ability of national governments to deal with social and economic problems, for example by means of employment legislation. According to Sen (quoted in ILO, 2000): 'The market economy itself is not merely an international system. Its global connections run beyond the relation between nations: it is very often relations between individuals in different countries, between different parties in a business transaction.' Such interconnections have significant consequences for the ways in which employees are organized and managed in multinational businesses.

International human resource management

Globalization has been driven largely by issues of marketing, cost and competition. International HRM is a subject that has developed in the wake of these driving forces. Consequently, people management on the international scale has often lagged behind other management functions (such as production and finance) at both practical and theoretical levels. Adler (1997, p.xiii) argues that:

> Although the other functional areas increasingly use strategies that were largely unheard of or that would have been inappropriate only one and two decades ago, many firms still conduct the worldwide management of people as if neither the external economic and technological environment, nor the internal structure and organization of the firm, had changed.

Growth in international business has led to massive interest in the ways people are best and, perhaps, differently managed in various countries. Yet American business school models of management have been assumed to be normal – the 'best practice' methods to be applied

	Better (%)	Worse (%)
Access to foreign markets	66	22
Availability of foreign products	63	25
National culture	60	28
Family's quality of life	60	23
Human rights, freedom/democracy	57	28
National economy	56	33
Income and buying power	54	27
Economic development in poor countries	51	36
Quality of jobs	48	39
Workers' rights	47	40
Peace and stability	47	38
Economic equality	45	40
Number of jobs available	42	46
Poverty and homelessness	41	45
Environmental quality	41	47

Table 4.2

Perception of the effects of globalization across 25 countries

Source: Adapted from World Economic Forum media release 1 February, 2002.

universally, regardless of local tradition, culture or business history. Throughout much of the 20th century and into the 21st century, US corporations have dominated world trade and it is not surprising that North American business methods – focused on tight financial controls and marketing – have been widely copied. But there have been occasions when the universality of these methods has been questioned. For example, Brewster (2002, p.5) observes that '… in Europe HRM is less dependent, companies have less autonomy and freedom of action, trade unionism is more important, the social partners have more influence, legal regulations are more important and there is a stronger tradition of employee involvement.'

The US Human Resource Planning Society conducted a state of the art/practice survey among HR practitioners in several countries (Tebbel, 2000). Survey questions focused on key issues facing human resource managers in the following three to five years. The key environmental trend identified as having the greatest effect on organizations (and, therefore, the HR function) in the near future was 'the increasingly dynamic and unpredictable nature of globalization'. Intriguingly, however, one of the authors of this study (cited in Tebbel, 2000) commented that: 'Globalization will continue to have a great impact on human resource management. But whenever the Human Resource Planning Society offers seminars [on the subject] they barely fill up.'

The short-term attitudes of senior American executives have been much criticized. Managers with financial or legal backgrounds have gravitated to the top at the expense of those with technical or scientific expertise. This has led to a prevailing management style emphasizing cash management with fast measurable returns. Mergers and takeovers, disposals and closures fit neatly into this mindset whereas long-term research, product development and people management have been neglected. Senior managers elsewhere in the English-speaking world have followed the US lead. American practice was enthusiastically copied in

---

HRM in reality   Singapore – The world's most globalized economy

The 2005 A.T. Kearney/Foreign Policy Globalization Index™ records Singapore's rise to the top ranking based on the strength of its increased political engagement and foreign trade ties. Singapore edged out Ireland, the most globalized country in the previous three annual surveys.

The USA joined the top five for the first time. Despite its weaker political and economic connections with the rest of the world, the USA increased its globalization ranking due to its technological strength. The USA holds first place for both the number of Internet users and secure servers. Canada's rating on the index also reflected its technological sophistication.

The A.T. Kearney/Foreign Policy Globalization Index™ is claimed to be the first comprehensive empirical measure of globalization and its impact. The index measures economic, person-to-person, political and technological integration in a total of 62 countries. These countries account for 96 per cent of world GDP and 85 per cent of the globe's population.

Global Top 20

1 Singapore	4 United States of America
2 Ireland	5 Netherlands
3 Switzerland	6 Canada
7 Denmark	14 Norway
8 Sweden	15 Czech Republic
9 Austria	16 Croatia
10 Finland	17 Israel
11 New Zealand	18 France
12 United Kingdom	19 Malaysia
13 Australia	20 Slovenia

The 2005 survey looked at wider aspects of globalization and found that:

- Globally integrated countries, particularly those that could be classified as 'developing' tended to spend more than the average on public education.

- Citizens of globally integrated countries typically had greater political rights and civil liberties. Politicians in these countries were more likely to be honest and adhere to international standards of governance.

- Having fewer international barriers did not lead to increased vulnerability to terrorism.

What factors might be responsible for the relative rankings of the countries listed here and in Table 4.1?

Source: *HRM Guide* (http://www.hrmguide.net), 30 April, 2005.

HRM in reality UK business vulnerable to globalization

A new TUC report acknowledges that UK employees undoubtedly benefit from cheap goods and greater prosperity resulting from globalization, but are more vulnerable to its negative effects than others in Europe. In a submission to the government's 2007 comprehensive spending review, the TUC says that priorities for funding should include support for workers who are adversely affected and for British companies to increase their competitiveness on the global market.

The TUC report says that UK employees are more vulnerable to negative effects of globalization than their European counterparts for three main reasons:

- Britain buys more than it sells on the global market.
- The UK is home to more multinational companies who can easily relocate overseas.
- UK business strategy typically keeps down costs in areas such as wages and investment in skills and training, which risks work being outsourced to countries where it can be done more cheaply.

TUC general secretary Brendan Barber said:

Globalization has made a real difference to the quality of life of working people in the UK and across the world but there are victims as well as winners. Too many British workers are losing their jobs when companies move abroad or fail to compete. Cheap DVD players and clothes are scant compensation if you are being downgraded to poor quality, insecure, low-paid work.

Of course we can't say 'stop the world I want to get off' and turn back the tide of globalization by erecting barriers to try and protect industries and jobs. But that does not mean we are powerless in shaping its impact. The government must provide support to older and unskilled individuals to help them adapt to the opening up of world markets and ensure that all UK workers benefit.

But the UK also has a responsibility, mainly through international trade agreements, to make sure that workers in developing countries have access to decent work.

The TUC report highlights economic trends that may adversely affect UK workers. While the EU as a whole has a trade balance, Britain imports 25 per cent more than it exports. Germany accounts for 27 per cent of EU exports compared with 12 per cent from the UK. UK trade in services as a percentage of gross domestic product (GDP) has grown in line with EU figures. However, trade in goods has fallen in the UK while increasing across the EU, reflecting the decline in UK manufacturing and growth in GDP. UK companies are more vulnerable to international variations such as price changes, and are failing to capitalize on growing world markets. Only the USA is more popular for foreign direct investment than the UK. Such investment is good for jobs and economic growth, but multinational companies can easily move jobs overseas.

The TUC argues that fewer UK jobs are at risk from globalization than is often assumed, but 'displaced' employees earn less in future work – if they can find it. They are also more affected if they are older, have been in their jobs a long time or have had to change industries. Eight months after being laid off, only half the former MG Rover workers were in full-time work and on average were earning £3523 less a year.

Reducing taxation, regulation and public spending are not the most important factors in managing the effects of globalization. Only Germany and some Canadian provinces have lower business taxes than the UK and the UK labour market is one of the least regulated. The biggest global traders among OECD nations have large public sectors and high government spending.

The TUC argues that government could balance the costs and benefits of globalization if they prioritized:

- increasing skills levels to raise productivity
- developing a modern industrial strategy for the global market
- securing UK energy supply and investing in environmental technology
- improving transport links in growth areas of the country
- promoting lifelong health to increase employment chances for older workers.

The TUC makes the following specific proposals:

- Establish a UK fund to provide training and job search support administered at regional level, to partner the EU Globalization Adjustment Fund set up in 2005.
- Develop a 'responsible restructuring' model that would require companies moving jobs abroad to insure redundant UK workers for 70 per cent of any fall in earnings for up to two years. It would include consultation with trade unions and help employees find work or set up their own businesses.
- Invest in the employability of workers in industries threatened by global competition. This would include various measures to improve UK skills levels across the workforce and to keep older and disabled workers in employment.

▶

▶

● Promote industrial and service sectors that employ highly-skilled, well-paid workers to improve international competitiveness.

● Extend government support for science and industry.

Critically review the TUC's proposals. Are they realistic and practical?

Source: *HRM Guide UK* (http://www.hrmguide.co.uk) 29 August, 2006.

the UK, for example, where it fitted a long-standing class prejudice against 'dirty hands' and 'trade'. 'New Right' policies ensured government support for such attitudes, defended within the mythology of 'market forces'.

In Part one of this book we saw that Japan served as a role model for Western businesses in the 1980s. HRM owes much of its inspiration to the long-term and people-orientation, rather than cash-orientation, of Japanese business. For some time it was believed that the Japanese had 'magic answers' for people management and that these could be identified and translated into Western businesses. Teamworking, quality circles and continuous improvement produced discernible benefits in car manufacturing in the UK, for example. However, in the 1990s the Japanese role model lost some of its mystique. Despite a record trade surplus of US$145.8 billion (£93.5 billion) in 1994, Japanese industrial dominance had peaked – for the time being at least – with the next decade being a period of stagnation. Ironically, given the previous influence of Japanese manufacturing practices on North American, European and Australasian management thought, major Japanese companies began to introduce Western methods of people management.

In fact, no single approach to people management can ever be guaranteed to be more effective than any other. Different business environments generate different forms of managerial structures that can be equally successful in world markets. Different approaches develop because organizations are dependent on the social, political and financial institutions of the countries in which they operate. Hegewisch and Brewster (1993) found that the country involved was much more significant in the way people management is handled than business size or commercial sector. Contrary to former UK prime minister Margaret Thatcher's confident ideological statement that 'there is no society' it is evident that societies determine what organizational structures and managerial practices are acceptable and 'normal' (Tyson, 1995). The perception of normality varies widely from country to country and is attributable to the business cultures of those countries. As we will see in later chapters, the concept of culture features prominently in human resource literature, both at a corporate and national level.

Torrington (1994, pp. 5–6) goes as far as denying that many of the most familiar topics in HRM such as recruitment and selection are within the scope of international HRM:

> Employees are selected in one country or another, and wherever the selection is undertaken there are a range of conventions and legal requirements that have to be met. The person appointed will usually have a contract of employment that will fit within the legal framework of one country but probably not another. Recruitment and selection is therefore a national activity, not an international activity. Similarly, negotiation with trade unions and the nature of agreements vary markedly between countries, so industrial relations is a national rather than an international activity.

Brewster (2002, pp.14–17) highlights the complexity of integration and differentiation that international HRM encompasses and the tension between global and local practices. He considers that the pat phrase 'think global, act local' used by many consultants is meaningless in practice. Even greater complexity is revealed when we consider that many organizations are divisionalized, such that one part may be operating in a 'global' fashion and another may be 'local'. These issues will be further examined in later chapters on culture and organization.

Brewster, Sparrow and Harris (2005) argue that rapid development of international HRM is underpinned by five organizational drivers: efficiency orientation; global service provision; information exchange; core business processes and localization of decisionmaking. These factors are creating new pressures for HRM specialists. Three enablers of high-performance international HRM are being developed by multinational enterprises: HR affordability; central HR philosophy; and HR excellence and knowledge transfer. Different strategic recipes combining these drivers and enablers are delivered through a series of important HR processes: talent management and employer branding; global leadership through international assignments; managing an international workforce; and evaluation of HR contribution.

Trading blocs

Partly due to the activities of multinational firms, international trade has grown to colossal proportions in recent decades. The bulk of this trade is concentrated in three major trading blocs:

1 The North American Free Trade Area (NAFTA) – essentially Canada, Mexico and the USA.

2 The European Union (EU) with 27 member states at the time of writing and a number of additional applicant countries.

3 The Asian–Pacific region with various trading arrangements and including Australia, China, India, Japan, New Zealand, Singapore and many developing states.

Other trading arrangements include: the Andean Community, the Caribbean Community and Common Market (CARICOM), LAIA, formerly the Latin American Free Trade Area, MERCOSUR, the South American Common Market, the Economic Community of West African States (ECOWAS) and the Arab Common Market (United Nations, 2005, pp.63–64).

Individual countries may belong to a number of trading blocs. The 25 OECD countries (plus Lichtenstein) average 11 trading arrangements per country; Latin American and Caribbean countries average 8 schemes; East Asia, 2 schemes; and the Pacific, 7 arrangements (*ibid*). Globalization and the consolidation of trade within such regional trading blocs are leading to a shift from trade between countries with distinct economic boundaries, to a world economy where national boundaries are not so significant. Instead cross-border manufacturing and trade in goods, services and financial products are now commonplace (ILO, 2000).

The boundaries of the trading blocs are shifting and generally expanding. The most obvious example is the European Union which has absorbed countries in central and eastern Europe that were formerly beyond the Iron Curtain. Integration of former communist countries into the free world brings different philosophies and practices of management into focus and possible conflict. Currently the central and eastern European countries have a much lower standard of living than most of the EU's long-standing members. The Czech Republic is closest to the western European norm with tourism booming and exports to the EU replacing business lost in the former communist countries. It seems reasonable to assume that inequalities between eastern and western Europe will gradually even out as businesses move to the regions with lower costs. However, the evidence of recent economic history indicates that this may not happen quickly – if at all. The reality has been that whereas poorer areas have cut employee costs to maintain their competitiveness, more affluent regions have been unwilling to consider this tactic and have turned to more upmarket quality products instead.

Countries such as South Korea, Taiwan and Singapore and, more recently, China and India, have shown much faster rates of economic growth than those of the West. Competitive labour costs and strong adherence to the work ethic have appeared highly attractive to foreign investors. Chung's (1991, p.419) remarks remain true:

> Business people from and in the Asian–Pacific area have become more self-confident, and they are demanding respect for Asian culture if European or American business people want to cooperate with them. The one-way street is a thing of the past, and what is needed now is the ability to engage in culture-specific dialogue. The ability to communicate interculturally has become a crucial factor for success in the global business of the future.

Within the trading blocs, there is increasing scope for integration and rationalization. This is exemplified by the defence and aerospace industries in the EU. Cuts in defence expenditure following the end of the Cold War, together with ever-escalating costs for the development of new planes and other equipment, have encouraged a consolidation between the former national defence specialists. Closer working arrangements such as those employed by Airbus Industrie will replace joint development and marketing agreements. The consequences on employment will probably include overall staff reductions within the sector, increased specialization and a demand for higher language and technology skills.

Productivity comparisons

Productivity has a direct relationship with the wealth of any country (see Key concept 4.4). A study by the Conference Board (2006) shows that US productivity has outpaced most developed countries in recent decades and that information and communication technologies have been the major drivers of US productivity growth. For example, in 2005, although sharply reduced from the previous year's 3.0 per cent, the USA's productivity growth of 1.8 per cent compared with Japan at 1.9 per cent and markedly outperformed an average of 0.5 per cent in the 15 older members of the EU. Productivity growth in the EU-15 ranged from 1.5 per cent in Ireland to −1.3 per cent in Spain.

Key concept 4.4 Productivity

Productivity may be defined as the amount of output (what is produced) per unit of input used. Labour is one input amongst many. Total productivity is dependent upon a variety of diverse and hard-to-measure inputs. One simple measure of productivity is the gross domestic product (GDP) per person-hour worked. But it is also a simplistic measure of productivity because it neglects a number of factors such as capital investment.

In total contrast, most of the new European member states showed 'a spectacular acceleration' in their productivity growth in 2005. The Conference Board report indicates that, on average, the 10 new member states raised their labour productivity growth rate from 4.1 per cent in 2004 to 6.3 per cent in 2005. Poland increased its rate of productivity growth by 7.7 per cent, a rate comparable with rapidly developing countries in other parts of the world.

China has had remarkable rates of productivity growth in recent years, averaging 8.7 per cent a year since 2000. India has achieved more modest rates, averaging 4.1 per cent in that period, but this reflects around double the increase in employment levels compared with China.

Economic growth and employment

The growth of the economy is the most significant overriding variable for people management because it determines overall demand for products and services and hence employment. Table 4.3 shows a ranking of the world's largest economies in terms of gross domestic product adjusted to reflect market exchange rates of their currencies. From this it is clear that the European Union and the United States of America account for well over one half of the world's economy.

The British economy has the longest industrial history but UK growth has been consistently slow, rarely exceeding 3 per cent per annum. There is a tendency for countries that are lower in the GDP league to have higher rates of growth in a 'catching-up' process. Consequently, high rates of growth in the People's Republic of China and India have accompanied medium growth in the developed countries. However, this is not universal – there has been consistently low growth in Africa, for example.

The reasons for differing rates of growth have been endlessly debated but the effective exploitation of human resources appears to be a crucial factor. The nature of the link between human resources and economic success is not simple. This is illustrated by attempts to provide an index of international competitiveness. For some years the World Economic Forum (WEF), an international business organization, and the Institute for International Management Development (IMD), a Swiss business school, cooperated in the production of such an index. Since 1996, however, they have produced independent league tables. We can see in Table 4.4 that their conclusions differ markedly.

Both organizations calculate their competitiveness indices by combining hundreds of different measures. These range from GDP per head to estimates of the competence of a country's managers. The main difference lies in the relative weightings given to the measures. The WEF regards government regulation and welfare provision as negative factors for national growth, whereas openness to international trade and investment are viewed favourably. Hence, for example, the UK's comparatively low pension burdens and flexible employment market are seen as strengths. The IMD, on the other hand, emphasizes investment in higher education and vocational skills – areas of weakness in the UK. Significantly, both organizations rate the quality of British management as low. These ratings reflect two important perspectives of the role of human resources in the competitiveness debate. We can regard them as the 'hard' and 'soft' versions of macro HRM.

Country	GDP (US$)
World economy	44 433 002
European Union	13 446 050
1 United States of America	12 485 725
2 Japan	4 571 314
3 Germany	2 797 343
4 People's Republic of China	2 224 811
5 United Kingdom	2 201 473
6 France	2 105 864
7 Italy	1 766 160
8 Canada	1 130 208
9 Spain	1 126 565
10 South Korea	793 070
11 Brazil	792 683
12 India	775 410
13 Mexico	768 437
14 Russia	766 180
15 Australia	707 992
16 Netherlands	625 271
17 Belgium	372 091
18 Switzerland	367 513
19 Turkey	362 461
20 Sweden	358 819

Table 4.3

Top 20 economies 2005 by GDP (at market exchange rates)

Source: Adapted from International Monetary Fund World Economic Outlook Database April, 2006.

Multinationals and global competition

Businesses are not entirely passive or helpless. They are also active players in their environment. They can influence and, sometimes, control their markets. Effectively, major industrial sectors such as petroleum, information technology, aerospace and automobile manufacture are dominated by a small number of multinational corporations. At a local level, strategic alliances between small companies can have the same effect: establishing a degree of control and predictability on the market.

HRM in reality China, India and the USA will drive growth

Report predicts world growth to 2020

A new research report from the Economist Intelligence Unit predicts that more than half the growth in the world's GDP over the next 15 years will come from China (27 per cent), the USA (16 per cent) and India (12 per cent).

The Foresight 2020 research report, sponsored by Cisco Systems, bases its predictions on new long-term economic forecasts, a survey of more than 1650 executives and in-depth interviews with senior business leaders. Other predictions in the study include:

- The USA will average close to 3 per cent growth a year between now and 2020.

- In comparison, the 25 European Union countries will average 2.1 per cent.

- Japan's growth will average less than 1 per cent a year as its population shrinks.

- The EU will compensate for the slower growth rate by territorial expansion, increasing to a union of more than 30 countries.

- Average income of the enlarged EU will be just 56 per cent of the US average in 2020.

- China will close the gap in economic size with the USA by 2020.

- In terms of purchasing power parity (PPP), Asia will increase its share of world GDP from its current 35 per cent to 43 per cent in 2020.

Laza Kekic, director of forecasting services at the Economist Intelligence Unit, considers talk of the 'Asian century' to be premature: 'On a per-capita basis, China and India will remain far poorer than Western markets and the region faces a host of downside risks,' he says, 'Asia will narrow the gap in wealth, power and influence, but will not close it.'

The report assumes that world economic growth depends on the pace of globalization. If global trade continues to be gradually liberalized, the global economy will be two-thirds larger in 2020 than in 2005. But if globalization reverses or unravels, annual rates of

Real GDP growth in selected countries – 2006–20 (annual average %)	
World	3.5
EU25	2.1
EU15	2.0
Asia	4.9
Latin America	3.2
Middle East and North Africa	4.0
Sub-Saharan Africa	2.8
United States of America	2.9
France	1.9
Germany	1.9
Italy	1.0
United Kingdom	2.3
Russia	3.3
Japan	0.7
China	6.0
India	5.9
Brazil	3.2

global economic growth would be two percentage points lower. On the other hand, faster liberalization could boost annual global growth by a further percentage point.

Labour-intensive production will continue to shift to lower-cost countries but the report concludes that fears of the death of Western manufacturing are premature. Workers in the low-cost economies will benefit but Chinese average wages, for example, will rise only to about 15 per cent of the developed-country average in 2020 compared with today's 5 per cent.

What are the implications of rapid growth in developing countries such as China on other economies around the world?

Source: *HRM Guide* (http://www.hrmguide.net), 1 April, 2006.

It has been estimated that some large corporations operating internationally, described as multinationals, are responsible for a greater proportion of international trade than most independent states. At one time, companies such as IBM in the USA, ICI in the UK, Volkswagen in West Germany and Toyota in Japan were viewed as national champions. They were key players in those countries' economic activities. Their senior managers influenced governments. As long as profits flowed, shareholders, banks and employees were relatively content. In recent decades, however, industrial competition has become global. National champions have become multinational corporations moving functions around the world without loyalty to any nation. Research and development takes place in one country, manufacturing in a second, with sales in different continents.

This importance has given them the power to play one country against another and to take actions that would be unacceptable for companies operating within single states. Their ability to switch investment from one country to another has been a significant cause for concern. Multinationals are major determiners of action on the world scene, able to move their operations from country to country in defiance of government attempts to maintain minimum wages or workers' consultation. Private capital is being moved around the world in search of profit from flexible and open economies. Complex factors attract this capital: it is not simply a case of the cheapest employees. Japanese manufacturers have opened factories in the UK and other parts of Europe where employee costs are high in comparison with developing countries. They have done so in order to avoid EU import restrictions and cut transport costs.

1995	IMD 2006	WEF 2005
1 USA	**1** USA	**1** USA
2 Singapore	**2** Hong Kong	**2** Singapore
3 Hong Kong	**3** Singapore	**3** Denmark
4 Japan	**4** Iceland	**4** Iceland
5 Switzerland	**5** Denmark	**5** Finland
6 Germany	**6** Australia	**6** Canada
7 Denmark	**7** Canada	**7** Taiwan
8 Netherlands	**8** Switzerland	**8** Sweden
9 New Zealand	**9** Luxembourg	**9** Switzerland
10 Norway	**10** Finland	**10** UK
11 Austria	**11** Ireland	**11** Canada
12 Sweden	**12** Norway	**12** France
13 Canada	**13** Austria	**13** Austria
14 Taiwan	**14** Sweden	**14** Belgium
15 UK	**15** Netherlands	**15** Japan
16 Australia	**16** Bavaria	**16** Iceland
17 Luxembourg	**17** Japan	**17** Israel
18 Finland	**18** Taiwan	**18** Hong Kong
19 France	**19** China	**19** Norway
20 Chile	**20** Estonia	**20** New Zealand

Table 4.4

Relative competitiveness

Source: Adapted from International Institute for Management Development, World Economic Forum.

But they have also created jobs in developed rather than developing countries in order to make use of better skills and education.

Uncontrolled globalization has not gone unquestioned. The possibility of **social dumping** puts societies and national economies under intense pressure and is generally destabilizing (see Key concept 4.5).

Key concept 4.5 Social dumping

The concept of social dumping describes the practice of switching production from countries with relatively high employee costs to those with cheap labour. It is an accusation made against large multinational corporations. Social dumping has led to long-term structural changes including the closure of older, heavy manufacturing industries such as steel and shipbuilding in established industrial countries.

Initially, corporations such as Ford adopted a policy of dual-sourcing, in which two or more plants in a regional trading bloc such as Europe or North America had the same function, for example building engines. If there were engineering or industrial relations problems in one plant, the other could supply the required components. This insurance policy became less necessary as quality control improved but afforded the opportunity of shifting production, and hence employment, from the country with the greater labour costs to the cheaper. Potentially, this had the effect of driving down employee costs. Deliberate government policy has made dismissal cheaper and easier in the UK than in other European countries, thereby encouraging manufacturers in volatile industries to consider the UK for inward investment. However, this policy has its drawbacks. Short-term expediency induced corporations to close UK plants because this was effectively easier than tackling less competitive European plants protected by social legislation.

Another feature of multinational activity has been the sourcing of components of manufactured products in different countries. Low skill items were the first affected, but more sophisticated items have followed. Wage levels and required skills are not constant factors and it can be argued that this form of sourcing is a natural and progressive feature of industrial growth. Alternatively, it could be described in terms of unscrupulous corporations chasing low wages around the world with the connivance of desperate and sometimes corrupt politicians. A number of countries have tried to attract foreign direct investment by creating special economic zones, free of the usual taxation arrangements. The most famous of these – maquiladoras – are concentrated on the Mexican–US border.

The maquiladoras programme

Maquilas or maquiladoras are assembly plants that import parts and export the finished products. Initially developed under the auspices of the Mexican government in the 1960s, they have mushroomed in Mexico and other Latin American countries. They produce manufacturing exports geared to the US market. The Mexican government copied similar plants in the 'tiger' economies of South-East Asia, almost all owned by US multinationals. The term has its derivation in *maquila* – the fee collected by a miller for processing grain in Mexico's colonial period (Teagarden, Butler and Von Glinow, 1992).

In Mexico, the programme is restricted to Mexican-registered companies formed with the purpose of manufacturing, assembling, repairing, or other processing of goods destined mainly for the export market – but they can be wholly owned by partner operations in other countries. They were introduced as part of a Mexican government human resource strategy described as the 'Border Industrialization Programme'. According to Teagarden, Butler and Von Glinow (1992), the aims of this programme were to:

- increase the level of industrial activity in Mexico, particularly in the border area;
- create new jobs;

- increase the domestic income level;
- facilitate technology transfer into Mexico and encourage absorption of relevant skills;
- attract foreign exchange.

Foreign multinationals benefited from significantly lower costs than similar operations in the USA – especially wages, energy and rent. Creating jobs is a key part of maquiladora operations. According to Mexican law, maquiladora companies must create a minimum of 25 jobs. But the Ministry of Commerce and Industrial Development can authorize an operation to begin with fewer than 25 jobs – as long as the number increases from year to year.

According to Mexican employment law, nine out of ten workers taken on by an employer must be Mexican nationals. But this rule has been enforced flexibly for management and technical personnel in the case of maquiladora companies. Moreover, the rule does not apply to

---

HRM in reality CBI says benefits of offshoring outweigh drawbacks

A survey released at the 2004 CBI Annual Conference shows that 51 per cent of responding companies say that the pressure to offshore has increased over the past two years. Twenty-one per cent described these pressures as 'very great' and 30 per cent said they had already taken some activities abroad with almost one in four considering doing so in future.

The CBI argues that the benefits of offshoring outweigh the drawbacks, saying the process will increase productivity, profitability and economic growth. The main drawbacks to offshoring are the difficulties of exercising managerial control and the risk of supply disruption. Smaller companies are less likely to offshore than larger businesses but there is no sign of a reversal in the trend as 87 per cent of respondents are satisfied with the offshoring experience.

The MORI survey on the topic was sponsored by the CBI (the employers' organization) and Alba, the electronic goods and power tool specialist. The survey was based on responses from 150 CBI member companies employing three-quarters of a million people in the UK and 2.2 million globally. The survey shows the trend increasingly extending beyond manufacturing to areas such as information technology, financial services, design, research and development.

Digby Jones, CBI director-general, said:

Offshoring is now part-and-parcel of doing business in the global economy. Make no mistake, this is a survival issue. Anyone who believes that firms have a great deal of choice is naive. Companies know if they don't do it, somebody else will. If competitors act and they don't respond, they may put their business at risk. It is short-sighted simply to see all this as a bad thing. Globalization was made for Britain. Offshoring means greater productivity and more efficient goods and services. It also means UK jobs will be of higher quality, more skilled and in many cases more secure.

Globalization means that jobs will come, jobs will go and nothing remains the same forever. The challenge is to create more jobs than we lose – which we are doing – and to ensure people have the skills to take advantage of them, which remains a problem. But the government must avoid forcing firms to offshore through an increase in policies unfriendly to business. The rising cost of compliance with regulation is now starting to drive firms abroad.

The main reason to go offshore is to cut costs but improving the speed and quality of services are also important justifications. Twenty-six per cent of respondents said they were currently considering a move because of restrictive regulations. The choice of country is governed by low employment costs and the availability of a skilled workforce, according to the survey. China and India are the most popular offshore locations, each cited by around half of the respondents. However, eastern Europe is viewed as an increasingly attractive alternative, particularly Poland and the Czech Republic.

The survey found that, on average, offshoring firms send the equivalent of about 4 per cent of their UK jobs overseas. The West Midlands has been most affected, while South-East and North-West England have also been hit. However, the CBI points out that just over half of responding firms have continued creating jobs in the UK since they began offshoring.

Meanwhile, UK jobs have risen in quality with firms saying they are creating mostly skilled and graduate jobs in the UK, with semi-skilled and unskilled jobs moving offshore.

What factors help or hinder the transfer of jobs to the most competitive country?

Source: *HRM Guide UK* (http://www.hrmguide.co.uk/), 8 November, 2004.

foreign workers who are not employed by the Mexican maquiladora company but rather by a foreign partner company.

Maquiladora employment reached 1.3 million in October 2000, and then fell to 1.1 million, with about 400 of the 3700 maquiladoras closing during 2001. By 2004, however, maquiladora employment had begun to rise again and the number of plants rose to 4700. The emphasis switched to a more balanced workforce making technologically advanced parts for major US companies in the automobile, electronics and textile industries. The companies that have made use of maquiladoras include General Motors, Ford, General Electric, Honeywell, Fisher Price, Mattell, Sony, Sanyo, Matsushita, Hitachi and Lucky Goldstar.

Working and living conditions in the maquiladora regions have been heavily criticized. Employers have resisted unionization, frequently ignored Mexican employment legislation and paid low wages to employees living in squalid shanty towns. US labour activists have been particularly critical as up to 800 000 relatively well-paid manufacturing jobs have disappeared across the border. But average rates of pay have moved upwards in recent years and the Mexican government has indicated its intention to follow the path of countries such as Malaysia into higher-skilled jobs. Higher wage rates have already led to the departure of many sweatshop textile manufacturers for more vulnerable countries in central America such as Guatemala and Honduras.

International outsourcing and subcontracting

The marriage of global telecommunications and advanced information technology has resulted in a phenomenon known as 'teletrading'. Initially, teletrading focused on low-skill work being handled by low-wage workers, but the trend is towards transferring more skilled programming and query handling.

HRM in reality Outsourcing medical records threatens lives

Thousands of lives are being threatened because of the 'dangerous practice' of sending medical notes overseas for typing, according to speakers at the UNISON annual conference.

Speaking anonymously, one medical secretary said that mistakes had 'undoubtedly increased' since notes dictated by NHS doctors were being transcribed in South Africa, the Philippines and India. The transcribers do not have medical records, prescriptions or letters to compare for accuracy.

Condemning the practice as dangerous, UNISON general secretary Dave Prentis said:

> It's beyond belief. It does not improve the service and the health and welfare of patients is being put at risk. Look what happened to hospital cleaning when it was privatised – a 50 per cent increase in infections. The government needs to rethink this off-the-wall idea.

The union also says that outsourcing is risking patient confidentiality and leading to job losses among local staff. For example, they cite East and North Herts NHS Trust which has issued redundancy notices to 160 medical secretaries and asked for 58 volunteers.

According to Dave Prentis: 'Medical secretaries in the NHS work to 99.8 per cent accuracy targets and once "phased out" their knowledge and expertise will be lost forever.'

Some of the mistakes collected by UNISON include confusing:

- 'hypertension' (high blood pressure) with 'hypotension' (low blood pressure)
- 'a septic' (infected) with 'aseptic' (not infected)
- '15mg' and '50mg' drug dosages.

'With more staff and an unknown technology there is greater scope for error,' said UNISON head of health Karen Jennings. 'All the government is doing is looking for a cheaper workforce – yet it's doctors and medical students in these other countries that are being used to do the transcriptions.'

Are UNISON's criticisms of offshoring valid or blown out of proportion?

Source: *HRM Guide UK* (http://www.hrmguide.co.uk), 22 June, 2006.

Heeks (1996) identified five main factors to explain the massive growth in software sub-contracting to Indian suppliers:

1 Indian software programmers were paid substantially less than their counterparts in the West. According to Heeks this meant that Indian subcontractors were typically charging about 70 per cent of Western contract rates and 40 per cent for work carried out offshore.

2 The Indian education system was producing a huge pool of software workers who were highly educated and fluent in English. Conversely, most Western countries had skill shortages in this sector.

3 The Indian software market was itself growing so that use of Indian subcontractors laid the ground for future strategic penetration of Indian markets.

4 Indian companies were enthusiastic about cooperating with foreign high-tech organizations in order to gain access to new markets and technology.

5 The Indian government had become more open towards inward foreign investment and collaboration.

Despite the criticisms of multinationals, many governments – including those of developed countries such as the UK and those of underdeveloped economies – have devoted much energy and money into attracting overseas investment. In the 1980s and 1990s, the British focused on American and Japanese manufacturers of computers and electronic equipment, many of which left for the attractions of cheaper workforces in eastern Europe and South America in the 21st century.

Lasserre and Schutte (1999) argue that outside investment depends upon the level of economic development. Looking at East Asia, for example, they identify five levels:

1 *Platform countries*, such as Singapore and Hong Kong, which can be used for regional coordination, initiating new contacts and gathering intelligence.

2 *Emerging countries*, for example Vietnam.

3 *Growth countries*, particularly China.

4 *Maturing economies*, as in South Korea and Taiwan.

5 *Established economies*, such as Japan.

Multinationals have ruthlessly played one country or region against another, accepting the highest subsidies and lowest controls over pollution and workers' welfare. Environmental and employee legislation in their 'home' countries has been cynically avoided by transferring production overseas. Trade unions have been slow and largely ineffective in providing employee protection to match global managers.

Admittedly, however, despite the bad press multinationals also produce clearly positive benefits. Multinationals have introduced innovative human resource practices including: mobility packages; cross-cultural and language training; greater sensitivity to national management practices; recruitment and development of local employees; and some exciting international careers.

Even in such quasi-monopolistic sectors, however, management is constrained by a range of environmental factors. Western economies have experienced alternating periods of global recession and recovery. Spurts of growth have been followed by cuts in both production and employment. In a dynamic economy, businesses expect growth in sales, production and ultimately in employee numbers. Conversely, companies experiencing recession or intense competition may have to **retrench** – 'downsize' in modern management-speak. For instance, in the mid-1990s air travel recovered slowly from recession. Airlines struggled to meet competition and cut costs to remain in existence. Orders for new aeroplanes were deferred or cancelled. The consequences for aeroplane manufacturers were severe. The world's largest aircraft manufacturer, Boeing, was forced to cut production, leading to thousands of job losses. Similarly, losses at the Dutch company Fokker, leading producer of medium-sized aircraft, impacted heavily on its major German shareholder Daimler-Benz. By the year 2000 production of aircraft was brisk once more as the world economy recovered its momentum.

Then, on 11 September 2001, the sudden impact of terrorism at the World Trade Center in New York brought airlines to their knees and returned the aircraft production industry to the doldrums. Employment in tourism, airlines and aircraft production was dramatically affected throughout the world by the events of one day. No human resource strategist could have forecast such sudden changes in employment needs.

Supranational organizations

The International Labour Organization

The International Labour Organization (ILO) is the highest international authority responsible for the conduct and development of human resources. It has a global programme on decent work (ILO, 2000) with the overall goal for the global economy of providing 'oppor-

---

HRM in reality Offshoring worries but does not demotivate employees

A fifth of employees in the UK worry about their jobs because of the risk of 'offshoring' to low-cost countries such as India or China, according to new research from consultants Watson Wyatt.

'Offshoring jobs can reduce costs and enhance service. But it can also unnerve and demotivate home country employees,' said Jonathan Gardner, an economist at Watson Wyatt. 'We wanted to know how much of a concern to employers this should be.'

Watson Wyatt researched employees' feelings about job security in UK-based companies that have offshored work, compared with their counterparts in organizations that had not shifted jobs overseas. 5000 people were sampled:

- 37 per cent worked for companies that offshored work for the UK market, either directly or had suppliers that had done so
- 52 per cent had not had this experience
- 'Don't knows' – 11 per cent were unable to answer.

36 per cent of those with experience of offshoring said they felt less secure in their job as a result of the trend to offshoring, compared with 11 per cent of employees in the second group. And 1 per cent of the first group felt that there was a large risk of their own job being offshored within the next 12 months, compared with 2 per cent in the second group. In fact, 13 per cent of the first group were prepared to admit that their job could be done equally as well offshore as in the UK, compared with 5 per cent of those with no experience of offshoring.

Differences between the two groups were less pronounced when motivation was considered:

- Around 30 per cent of those with experience of offshoring said they were less motivated at work,

compared with 19 per cent in the group without such experiences.

- 21 per cent of the first group said they were less willing to take risks and share new ideas at work. This compared with 15 per cent in the second group.
- 58 per cent of those with offshoring experience thought that perceived stress at work was manageable, compared with 66 per cent of the second group.

'The impact on motivation seems to be fairly small,' said Jonathan Gardner. 'Perhaps most telling is the result of the question as to whether or not they were considering finding a new job in the next year.'

36 per cent of people who had already experienced offshoring said they would be looking for a new job in the next 12 months. But this was little different to the 37 per cent of those who had not had the experience. Employees may feel less secure and a little less motivated because of offshoring but this does not increase the likelihood that they will start hunting for a new job. Watson Wyatt argue that this may be because they are working in industry sectors where competing employers are also engaged in offshoring.

'While the majority of employers may consider the short-term demotivational – and consequent productivity – impact of offshoring acceptable, they cannot afford to be complacent,' said Jonathan Gardner. 'It should be of great concern if otherwise committed and high performing employees, for whose roles their employer has no plans to shift overseas, are being demotivated by fears of offshoring.'

Are employees in developed countries such as the UK right to be worried by the consequences of offshoring?

Source: *HRM Guide UK* (http://www.hrmguide.co.uk), 22 June, 2006.

tunities for all men and women to obtain decent and productive work in conditions of freedom, equity, security and human dignity'. It outlines four objectives:

Creation of employment. Developing a positive environment in which investment and enterprise creation can take place both nationally and internationally with due regard to good practice. Specifically, the ILO considers that there should be worldwide recognition of 'the interdependence between respect for freedom of enterprise for investors and freedom of association for workers'. It calls for a particular focus on stimulating creativity, innovation and entrepreneurship and promoting small enterprises.

Promotion of human rights at work. With a special focus on the rights of women, the ILO highlights freedom of association, collective bargaining, non-discrimination, forced labour and child labour. The ILO measures annual progress in these areas.

Improvements in **social protection**. These include legislation governing dismissal and redundancies.

Promotion of strong institutions. To improve social dialogue between business and labour. Such institutions may include works councils, arbitration systems, joint consultative committees and a variety of other institutions.

World Trade Organization

According to the World Trade Organization website (www.wto.org):

> The World Trade Organization (WTO) is the only international organization dealing with the global rules of trade between nations. Its main function is to ensure that trade flows as smoothly, predictably and freely as possible.

The WTO came into existence in 1995 as successor to the General Agreement on Tariffs and Trade (GATT) established after World War II. It began as a result of the tariff reduction negotiations known as the Uruguay Round. It is not designed to deal with employment regulation but, by its actions, it has a major influence on human resources around the world. Its member states account for 97 per cent of world trade.

It has been severely criticized by environmentalists, union activists and others. For example, the International Forum on Globalization (IFG) describes the WTO as follows (see http://ifg.org/wto.htlm):

> ... among the most powerful, and one of the most secretive international bodies on earth. It is rapidly assuming the role of global government, as 134 nation-states, including the US, have ceded to its vast authority and powers. The WTO represents the rules-based regime of the policy of economic globalization. The central operating principal of the WTO is that commercial interests should supersede all others. Any obstacles in the path of operations and expansion of global business enterprise must be subordinated. In practice these 'obstacles' are usually policies or democratic processes that act on behalf of working people, labour rights, environmental protection, human rights, consumer rights, social justice, local culture, and national sovereignty.

The WTO has also been accused of not addressing the impact of unfettered free trade on employment rights, although countries that enforce employment rights are at a disadvantage compared with countries that consistently violate employment conventions promulgated by the International Labour Organization.

HRM in reality World Bank accused of promoting the elimination of worker protection

The International Confederation of Free Trade Unions (ICFTU) has strongly criticized the 2007 edition of the World Bank publication, *Doing Business*, prepared by the private sector development department. This declares the Marshall Islands to be the world's 'best performer', displacing last year's winner, Palau. Both are tiny Pacific island nations that are not among the 179 member countries of the International Labour Organization (ILO). As such they are not obliged to abide by the organization's core labour standards: elimination of forced labour, child labour and discrimination; and respect for freedom of association and right to collective bargaining.

Guy Ryder, general secretary of ICFTU, commented that World Bank presidents have expressed support for ILO core labour standards as being consistent with the Bank's development mission. He therefore finds it ironic that *Doing Business* is promoting countries that offer almost no protection for their workers. ICFTU claims that both nations 'allow workers to be forced to work up to 24 hours per day and up to seven days per week and require no vacations or advance notice for dismissal'.

Another division of the World Bank, the International Finance Corporation, stipulates that it will not lend to firms not applying the core labour standards. However, Ryder noted that earlier editions of *Doing Business* have been used in World Bank and International Monetary Fund (IMF) strategy documents to force countries to abolish various kinds of protection for their workers. For example, a recent World Bank economic memorandum to Colombia made it a condition for loans that the government make hiring and firing decisions more flexible. This was to improve its *Doing Business* indicators, even though the economic impact of the strategy is uncertain.

Similarly, the IMF recently recommended that the South African government should improve its *Doing Business* indicators by 'streamlining' its hiring and dismissal procedures. These changes would have required doing away with affirmative action policies implemented by post-apartheid governments to correct the legacy of decades of racial discrimination.

Guy Ryder said:

> The World Bank should get its message straight. If the Bank truly believes that the ILO's core labour standards are good for development, it can't turn around and praise countries that don't join the ILO and don't respect the core standards as the world's 'best performer' for their labour standards. The Bank should remove the mandate of labour market regulation from the department that prepares *Doing Business* and stop using *Doing Business* as the basis for its labour market reform proposals.

Is this a fair criticism of the WTO?

Source: *HRM Guide* (http://www.hrmguide.net) 6 September, 2006.

Summary

Human resource management takes place within a business environment that is increasingly global in its reach. Globalization is a hotly debated subject with many implications for the practice of HRM, both within and between countries. The allocation of human resources depends on comparative issues such as international competitiveness and productivity, factors that are themselves dependent upon a wide range of variables. Foreign inward investment and subcontracting can bring benefits in terms of increased employment opportunities, earnings and economic development but this may be at the expense of comparatively low pay, poor working conditions and denial of employment rights. However, along with a trend towards reduction of trading barriers and encouragement of international trade, there is an increasing call for worldwide regulation of labour issues.

Further reading

There are numerous books on globalization, many with a markedly political agenda. *The Silent Takeover: Global Capitalism and the Death of Democracy* by Noreena Hertz (published under the Heinemann, Arrow and Free Press imprints, 2001, 2002) takes a highly critical view of the uncontrolled behaviour of multinationals in the globalization process. *Globalization and Its Discontents* by Joseph E. Stiglitz (W.W. Norton, 2002) adopts an all-round view of the process of globalization. For a positive view see *In Defense of Globalization* by Jagdish Bhagwati (Oxford University Press, 2004). *The Maquiladora Reader: Cross-Border Organizing Since NAFTA* edited by Rachael Kamel and Anya Hoffman (American Friends Service Committee, 1999) is a union-minded text. *Smart Sourcing: International Best Practice* by Andrew Kakabadse and Nada Kakabadse (St. Martin's Press, 2002) takes a managerial perspective on wider subcontracting issues. *What's This India Business? Offshoring, Outsourcing and the Global Services Revolution* by Paul Davies (Nicholas Brealey, 2004) is a practical guide on offshoring.

Review questions

1 What is globalization? Why should globalization concern human resource managers?

2 Outline the positive and negative attributes of globalization for:

(a) employees in the developed world;

(b) employees in the developing world.

Given the evidence provided, are you for or against globalization?

3 What are the main reasons for distinguishing 'international HRM' from mainstream human resource management?

4 What is the relationship between a country's international competitiveness rating and employment prospects in that country?

5 What do you understand by 'labour productivity'? How is it measured?

6 Summarize the relationship between labour productivity and the economic wellbeing of a country. What other factors are involved?

7 What are the job creation strategies open to developing countries that need to provide employment for growing populations?

8 As an international HR consultant you have been asked to consider the merits of introducing a 'maquiladora' programme for a Caribbean country. What would you advise?

9 Outline the factors to be evaluated before a major computer supplier outsources software development to a developing country.

10 What is the role of the International Labour Organization in the growth of global employment?

Case study for discussion and analysis

Read the following case study and answer the questions that follow.

Change in Japan

The recession of the 1990s and early 2000s seemed to be of a different order from those of the past. In just one year – from October 2000 to October 2001 – the number of people with jobs fell to 64.05 million, a drop of 1.03 million. The Labour Ministry estimated that for every 100 people seeking work, only 55 jobs were available. At the end of October 2001, 49.3 per cent of high school students who had graduated in June and looking for jobs were still unemployed – the worst level ever recorded. Overall, unemployment reached 5.4 per cent in May 2002, the highest for 50 years.

Smaller Japanese companies without financial muscle suffered badly. In October 2001, 1804 businesses employing 19 550 workers went bankrupt. This was the 32nd consecutive month in which more than 10 000 people lost their jobs due to bankruptcy.

At the start of the recession in the 1990s, the larger companies tried to avoid compulsory redundancies through redistributing human resources, freezing recruitment and early retirement. Major companies also laid off 'temporary' workers, typically comprising 10 per cent of the staff. This was followed by reduction in overtime – possibly 20 per cent of an average worker's pay packet. Then came the first announcements of redundancies in core workforces.

Nissan, the country's second-largest car maker, announced heavy losses and began a restructuring involving 5000 fewer staff (9 per cent of its employees). The most dramatic part of the announcement was the closure of the Zama plant employing 2500 workers. This was a showcase factory capable of making 260 000 cars a year, using the most advanced technology, including extensive employment of robots. However, Nissan did not anticipate any job losses at all from this move, offering transfers to other Nissan plants. Then Nissan received an injection of cash and an equity investment from Renault on condition that Western management techniques were introduced. By 2002 profitability was soaring – at the expense of traditional Japanese employment practices and job levels.

During much of the recession the rising value of the yen made overseas production cheaper than domestic manufacturing for Japanese multinationals. This had the effect of exporting jobs. After a period of huge investment in Japan and overseas, much of the domestic production capacity was standing idle. Initially the overcapacity was not tackled by sacking workers. Redundant executives were left within organizations as *Madogiwazoku*, the 'window-gazing tribe' with nothing to do but stare out of their windows. Western managers would not have hesitated to close surplus factories and make large numbers of workers redundant. Japanese businesses had to overturn their basic philosophy in order to come to terms with firing their people.

At first, many Japanese companies exerted pressure on higher-paid salarymen to leave of their own accord. Managers over 45 earning 10 million yen or more were the main target. Ironically, this generation had been accustomed to doing what their employers asked them to do. Now they were asked to leave and found it difficult to say no. Companies exerted psychological pressures on them, for example appealing to their sense of duty by leaving and helping the company's financial situation.

In general, Japanese manufacturing companies employed large numbers of people they did not need. More critically, overstaffing in the Japanese retail and distribution system was remarkably high in comparison with manufacturing and with retailers in the West. One estimate put the surplus at 1.5 million people in manufacturing alone, with around 4 million overall. If these workers were dismissed, the true level of unemployment would be 11–12 per cent.

Japanese attitudes towards workers in overseas operations were less sympathetic. American employees of Japanese subsidiaries falsely assumed that, if not having a job for life, their employment was virtually secure. Instead, American employees were shed quickly when orders fell. Americans were not the only people to lose their jobs: hundreds of Japanese executives were sent home to lower-status positions.

Underlying the reaction to the recession is a change in Japanese beliefs. The attitudes of the workaholic senior executives of the post-war era are not shared by their middle-aged successors and even less by young graduates. They have different values and are prepared to take on some of the risks of the Western way of business. Whether or not the recession is quickly overcome, a falling birth rate and increasing independence for young people require long-term changes. Excellence in manufacturing has disguised organizational inefficiency. The commitment expected from employees can no longer be guaranteed. Younger men and women with career aspirations are not prepared to work 'long hours for little money while waiting to fill dead men's shoes'. For the first time, there is a debate about fast-track career paths, appointment on merit and performance pay.

By 2002 a survey of companies listed on Section 1 of the Tokyo Stock Exchange showed that the lifetime employment and seniority systems considered typical of Japanese companies were being severely questioned. Just 19.5 per cent of the companies that responded said that they would continue the lifetime employment systems into the future – 53.9 per cent said that they were considering re-examining them. However, Rebick (2005) argues that, although there has been an increase in 'involuntary separations', Japanese firms have continued to engage in labour hoarding and the increase in unemployment has come mostly from a slowdown in hiring. In practice, he contends, job guarantees for 'regular' employees have not gone away. The poorly educated have suffered the most as the opportunities for regular employment have diminished. Rebick (*ibid*) agrees that graduates have also turned to less traditional forms of work as the restrictions of regular employment have become less attractive.

Why were Japanese people management practices questioned during the recession of the 1990s and early years of this century?

Should Japanese multinationals treat Japanese and foreign employees in different ways?

Chapter 5
HRM and the state

Learning objectives

The purpose of this chapter is to:

- Provide an overview of the role played by governments in creating the context for human resource management.

- Outline the concept of human capital and its implications for development throughout the world.

- Introduce the legal frameworks that regulate employment in the major economies.

- Describe initiatives taken by the European Union as examples of governmental initiatives with a human resource focus.

> ### Key concept 5.1 Labour market
>
> The meeting point between suppliers and providers of labour. Labour markets can be internal or external to an organization. 'Labour market' is a somewhat old-fashioned term that implies physical work as opposed to the time, knowledge and intellectual effort required in many modern jobs. 'Job market' or 'employment market' is more meaningful in today's context.

The state and intervention

'Losses of work or assets providing subsistence are often the first shocks that lead to poverty and destitution. Hence, labour markets are central mechanisms for rehabilitation programs when adversities occur, to reverse the spiral of poverty.' (Abrahart and Verme, 2001).

National and regional (state or province) governments have a powerful influence on the practice of HRM because they set the legislative, regulatory and economic contexts in which people work. Economists typically describe the political and regulatory initiatives taken by governments as '**labour market** policies'. Abrahart and Verme distinguish three broad types of labour market policies adopted by governments around the world: the Japanese, European and American models.

The Japanese model relied (at least, until the early 1990s) on full employment as one basic principle of a stable society. The emphasis was on the 'internal labour market' rather than the external job market. In other words, firms were hierarchical and protected their own workers from the consequences of economic fluctuations. In turn, employees were expected to be fully committed to their employing organizations. The role of government was to support firms through skills upgrading and training or finding production alternatives for changing markets. Labour market policies were seen to be part of economic and industrial strategies managed by relevant government departments. Abrahart and Verme describe this as an 'enterprise-centred and industry-driven form of labour market management'. The Japanese model was the main frame of reference for many Asian governments until relatively recently.

Abrahart and Verme perceive the European model as one that accepts market laws and the existence of unemployment – but only as a 'necessary temporary condition to facilitate and maximize the allocation of labour'. There is limited government intervention in support of firms. Instead, governments support the unemployed by maintaining their income and providing training schemes to help them find jobs. The European model accepts that the market will fail to protect the public interest from time to time and that governments need to step in to mitigate the short-term economic and social consequences. Unemployment support tends to be generous and is meant to provide a basic standard of living. Responsibility for labour market policies lies with ministries of employment. Abrahart and Verme describe this as a 'mediating, public-interest driven labour market management style'.

The American model limits government intervention to a considerable extent. Firms can dispense with employees to match economic fluctuations. The role of government is to 'maximize mobility of workers and minimize labour market rigidities such as hiring costs and mismatching of the supply and demand of labour'. Unemployment benefits are provided in the short-term but the unemployed are expected to be very active in seeking jobs. Abrahart and Verme perceive this as an individualistic model. For example, in the area of employee relations:

- Employment conflicts have been rare in Japan as workers expected to be protected by their enterprises and the government.

- In the European model the government is seen as a mediator that can protect the interests of both employees and enterprises.

- In the American model, however, labour disputes are viewed as civil disputes between individuals for the courts to settle with an army of lawyers available to service them.

Abrahart and Verme describe the American model as a 'liberal market-driven labour management system'.

The USA is an exception among developed countries, having generated more new jobs than any other country through flexible job markets, minimal welfare benefits and comparatively low wages for unskilled work. However, the cost has been considerable social inequality and a high crime rate. In most other developed countries the employment market is subject to a greater level of governmental control as a result of traditionally greater concerns for the welfare of the whole population, not just the economically successful. Governments attempt to exercise a major influence on the quantity and quality of workers in their employment markets by means of economic, social and employment legislation, and investment in human capital through education and training programmes.

Underlying beliefs regarding the degree of employment protection, unemployment benefits, and acceptable wages have become tougher throughout developed countries indicating a general swing towards the 'American model'. Against an agenda primarily set by 1980s right-of-centre leaders, especially Ronald Reagan in the USA and Margaret Thatcher in the UK, even left-wing parties have adjusted their views to fit what is now termed a 'neo-liberal' perspective. Hence, parties supposedly at opposite ends of the political spectrum such as 'New Labour' in the UK and the Liberals in Australia have adopted policies advocating:

- restrained and affordable public sector spending (fiscal prudence)
- control of inflation
- encouragement of inward investment
- tax rates that compare favourably with those of international competitors
- employment protection that does not cause rigidity or inflexibility in the job market
- maintenance (in the case of the UK Labour Party) of some of the 1980s Conservative government legislation restricting the scope of trade union activities
- partnership between public and private sectors to revitalize investment-starved infrastructure – for example, railways and roads
- the reform of education to boost the nation's skill base.

In the European Union, the pursuit of a single market has led increasingly to measures allowing free circulation of employees and freedom of residence in any EU country. Other barriers to job mobility are being removed with recognition of different educational qualifications and further social and economic cohesion. There are increasing moves towards standardization of employment regulation and protection measures to further promote a single European job market with the goal of full employment. The result is an apparent hybrid between a US-style, 'free for all' employment market and the more rigid, social protectionism of mainland western Europe between the 1950s and 1980s.

Outside these comparatively rich areas of the world, governments have an uphill battle to achieve high growth and reduced unemployment in the face of rapidly increasing populations and low levels of industrialization. In the Middle East and North Africa, for example, the International Labour Organization projects an annual increase of more than 3 per cent between the year 2000 and 2015. In total, these countries will need to provide more than 5 million new jobs each year, rising to 6.18 million in 2015. But, according to World Bank estimates, the region already has 20 million unemployed. Unemployment rates are estimated to be between 10 per cent and 19 per cent in Oman, Egypt, Syria, Jordan, Tunisia, Bahrain, Morocco and Lebanon. The unemployment level reaches between 25 and 30 per cent in Libya, Algeria, Iran and Yemen.

One of the major contributing causes is the population explosion in the region during the 1970s and 1980s when the birth rate was among the highest in the world. Population growth has slowed considerably since that time but it will take at least 20 years for this to be translated into slower growth in the labour force. On a more optimistic note it may be that the rapid growth in available workers will fuel high economic growth as happened in East Asia during the 1980s.

Analysis of statistics from the 1990s suggests that there are additional problems to be overcome, with a reduction of productivity and a decline in real wages being seen in Kuwait, Algeria and Jordan, for example. Whereas the rate of GDP growth was double the growth rate of the labour force in East Asia between 1970–1980, GDP growth and labour force growth were more or less the same in the Middle East and North Africa during the 1990s.

The Economic Research Forum (2000) suggests that almost all countries in the region should focus on:

1 macroeconomic stability

2 human resource development

3 promotion of exports

4 reforming the state and empowering the private sector.

Dicken (1998) concludes that successfully developing economies have one thing in common:

> Despite many popular misconceptions, none of today's NIEs (newly industrializing economies) is a free-wheeling market economy in which market forces have been allowed to run their unfettered course. They are, virtually without exception, *developmental* states: market economies in which the state performs a highly interventionist role.

The Economic Research Forum (2000) also takes a neo-liberal stance on the purpose of the state, arguing that most governments in the region still perceive their role as employers

---

HRM in reality Boost For New Brunswick contact-centre industry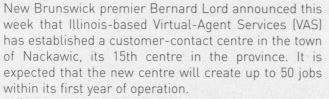

New Brunswick premier Bernard Lord announced this week that Illinois-based Virtual-Agent Services (VAS) has established a customer-contact centre in the town of Nackawic, its 15th centre in the province. It is expected that the new centre will create up to 50 jobs within its first year of operation.

'This is another great day for Nackawic, coming less than a week after the official opening of the AV Nackawic mill,' Lord said. 'Government has pledged to help diversify the economy of this community, and that commitment is being honoured. New Brunswick has enjoyed an extraordinary partnership with VAS, an award-winning international operation. We are proud to support this next step in its growth, and I know that it will be welcomed warmly into Nackawic's business community.'

The premier said that the New Brunswick government wants the province to be known as the 'investment province by having the lowest tax burden east of Alberta and the biggest decrease in the unemployment rate in Canada.' He said that efforts to foster a competitive business environment in New Brunswick are delivering more jobs.

The provincial government is providing VAS with CDN$7 500 per job created in the form of a forgivable loan to assist the company with: training new employees; implementation, and administration costs

The province will also directly fund the Town of Nackawic with up to CDN$100 000 for site renovations where the new customer contact centre will be located.

VAS has now officially opened centres in Doaktown, Minto, Saint-Louis-de-Kent, St Andrews, St George, Neguac, Petitcodiac, Chipman, Norton, Rogersville, Hillsborough, Bouctouche and Sussex (two operations). They are linked by a single telephone system to form an integrated virtual operation. The company's clients include hospitality and travel, catalogue and retail sales, utility, financial, insurance and roadside assistance.

'VAS now employs more than 800 people across the province, and is an outstanding example of an innovative, committed corporate citizen,' Business New Brunswick Minister Kirk MacDonald said. 'It is one of many success stories in New Brunswick's customer-contact-centre industry, which contributes in excess of CDN$1 billion to the economy every year, and employs more than 20 000 New Brunswickers. We look forward to future partnerships with VAS, and the creation of more centres across New Brunswick.'

What are the advantages and disadvantages of government assistance for attracting and keeping employment?

Source: *HRM Guide Canada* (http://www.hrmguide.net/canada/) 22 June, 2006.

and producers of public goods. They contrast this with the growth model of the newly industrialized countries (NICs) which they see as 'a deliberately selective approach to intervention by the state to provide an optimal institutional environment'.

This selective approach is made up of a number of elements:

- Maximizing the flow of knowledge to all market players (market information, technology, quality education and training) through the establishment of a modern information infrastructure connecting them with knowledge networks.

- Transforming government bureaucracy from being a passive or even obstructive element in the economy into an active agent of development. This requires creation of an elite technocracy recruited on the basis of merit and operating in a transparent environment with clear objectives, rewards and penalties; grounded in an effective system of monitoring and performance evaluation.

HRM in reality A world of work

A report from the International Labour Organization (ILO 2006) says today's labour market is characterized by a widening gap between unprecedented opportunity for some and growing uncertainty for many.

The report, entitled *Changing patterns in the world of work* describes recent trends and future prospects in an emerging global labour market. The report says: 'Change provides welcome opportunities for more rewarding and satisfying work and a better life. For others, change is worrisome, closing off rather than opening up chances for improving living and working conditions.'

According to ILO director-general Juan Somavia:

There is a growing feeling that the dignity of work has been devalued; that it is seen by prevailing economic thinking as simply a factor of production – a commodity – forgetting the individual, family, community and national significance of human work. People are reacting in conversations at home, in the secrecy of the voting booth and, when necessary, by forcefully voicing their complaints in the streets.

The report's key findings include:

- The global workforce is growing rapidly. Over 3 billion are either working or looking for work. This is expected to increase by over 430 million by 2015, almost all coming from developing countries.

- 'Hundreds of millions of new jobs will be needed over the next decade.' Economies will have to create an average of more than 43 million new jobs annually to reduce global unemployment, which increased to 192 million in 2005, up from 157 million in 1995.

- 'The impact of HIV/AIDS will be increasingly decisive in many countries.' The epidemic, which

has the greatest impact on people of working age, is expected to cause an estimated total loss of some US$270 billion by 2020 in 41 countries hardest hit by the disease.

- Women constitute 40 per cent of the labour force. From 1991 to 2005 the global female workforce increased from under 1 billion to 1.22 billion, 'but women still face many obstacles to equal integration in the labour market'.

- During the last decade, global youth employment rates increased from 12.1 to 13.7 per cent. In 2005, young people in developing regions were 3.3 times more likely, and in the developed world 2.3 times more likely to be unemployed compared with adult workers.

- In 2004, there were 218 million children trapped in child labour, representing a decrease of 11 per cent over the last four years.

- The number of people aged 60 years and over is growing faster than all other age groups. Labour force participation rates for women and men above 50 years of age have increased worldwide.

- The services sector increased from 34.4 per cent in 1995 to nearly 39 per cent of global employment in 2005. The agricultural sector represents 40 per cent and the industrial sector 21 per cent.

Juan Somavia says:

A major effort is needed to improve productivity, earnings and working conditions in order to reduce working poverty that affects nearly half of all the workers in the world. We live in a time of opportunity and uncertainty in which some of the barriers that have prevented women and men from fully realizing their capabilities are coming

▶

down, but in which good jobs that provide the foundation of security to build better lives are increasingly difficult to find.

The report identifies four major forces interacting to drive change in global workplaces and labour markets:

1 The development imperative, stemming from urgent need to reduce poverty and inequality.
2 A technological transformation resulting from developments in information processing and communications.
3 An intensification of competition following trade and financial liberalization and a dramatic reduction in transport and communication costs.
4 A shift in political thinking regarding labour markets.

'If we want to achieve the goal of decent work for all, it is vital to understand what is driving the process of change so that it can be shaped to yield more and better jobs for working women and men everywhere,' the report says.

Trends in the global labour market identified by the report include:

● changes in the world labour force
● shifts in employment due to evolution of global production systems
● skills shortages emerging worldwide
● increasing international labour migration
● growth of the informal economy
● discrimination in employment and occupation
● growing pressures for flexibility and security in labour markets.

The report stresses that there is a major transformation in the world of work with the potential for creating opportunities for all working men and women to have a decent job.

The report says: 'Technological progress, if applied in ways that promote inclusion rather than exclusion, could increase productivity and make material poverty history within a generation. The main means for ensuring an inclusive character to the growth of the global economy is the way in which work and labour markets are organized and governed. Recent history is however disturbing, the employment intensity of growth has slipped back globally.'

It adds that there are three components of a strategy to reduce the world's 'decent work deficits':

1 a more employment-intensive form of growth especially in countries with large-scale underemployment and working poverty;
2 an increase in the productivity of poorest workers to enable improvement in earnings and working conditions; and
3 a faster rate of overall growth increasing demand for labour and the movement of poorest workers into more productive jobs.

The report cautions that the ratio of dependents to those of working age is beginning to rise in some developed countries and will start to increase rapidly in a number of developing countries including China over the next 25 years.

'The economic reality is that the current working population essentially pays from their earnings for retirees' pensions and health care, whether through taxes on wages and a state transfer mechanism or through the dividends paid on investments in the companies for which they work.'

The report identifies common patterns in current developments in labour market governance. It suggests that the enormous variety of work demands diverse governance mechanisms. Formulation of laws, regulations and contracts should be based on broadly accepted principles. Some countries focus on evaluating existing systems built up over many years. Most face the challenge of extending labour legislation to cover the informal economy. The report suggests that the ILO's International Labour Standards have an important continuing influence on legislation worldwide.

What factors are likely to constrain the achievement of decent jobs for all working men and women?

Source: *HRM Guide* (http://www.hrmguide.net) 1 August, 2006.

● Aiming for rapid insertion into the global market and opting for openness and flexibility in their political and economic institutions so as to realize the potential productivity gains of the second economic revolution.

It should be noted that changes in economic or political circumstances can lead to decline as well as growth in employment opportunities and living standards.

Human capital

Personal and national success is increasingly correlated with the possession of skills. Skilled individuals can command a premium salary in periods of high economic activity. Worldwide, unemployment levels remain high, while organizations have difficulty filling vacancies that require specific expertise. A shortage of skilled people can act as a limiting factor on individual organizations and on the economy as a whole. For example, in Canada and the UK small businesses report an inability to expand because of the difficulty in finding people with the right skills. Small firms are also vulnerable because their owners do not possess basic marketing and finance skills. It is in the interest of any country to maximize its human resources by investing in the skills of its workforce: its **human capital** (see Key concept 5.2). Human capital is a crucial component of a country's overall competitiveness.

Key concept 5.2 Human capital

It can be argued that economic growth, employment levels and the availability of a skilled workforce are interrelated. Economic growth creates employment, but economic growth partly depends on skilled human resources – a country's human capital. The concept encompasses investment in the skills of the labour force, including education and vocational training to develop specific skills.

Clarke (2006b) compares attitudes to construction industry labour in the UK and other leading European countries. The UK industry is characterized by casual self-employment, output-based pay, rigid trade divisions, low levels of training and a sharp division between operative and professional/technical skills. Skill shortages beset the industry and the solution focuses not on employment regulation and a comprehensive industry-wide training scheme, but on importing the necessary skilled labour. Other leading European countries rely on higher skill levels, based on knowledge gained through the training process and on a more stable and collectively negotiated structure of training provision and employment.

Countries that have shown some of the highest rates of growth, for example Singapore and Malaysia, have invested heavily in the education and technical skills of their population. Similarly, South Korea aimed for 90 per cent of its young people to have an 18-plus qualification with 60 per cent undertaking higher education. Britain, conversely, was only able to provide 28 per cent of its youth with higher education at the beginning of the 1990s. Yet industry recognized the value of human capital – unskilled people were paid at just 40 per cent of the graduate rate. Belatedly, the UK government set targets for higher levels of achievement in the 21st century. Migration is also increasingly a factor in the retention of human capital as can be seen in the HRM in reality article on p.114.

Skill requirements are particularly critical at the managerial level. For example, the arrival of multinational corporations in China has led to an increased demand for professional managers. In the past, Chinese colleges have produced large numbers of technicians but few accountants, lawyers or marketing specialists.

Competition is not restricted to marketing and product development. It also entails competition for staff. Availability of skilled employees in the external job market may constrain growth. Additional expensive advertising may be required, together with the offer of enhanced salaries to attract suitable applicants. We saw in Part one that businesses are inhibited from investing in training by the non-activity of other businesses in the same sector. Companies like Motorola and IBM, which invest heavily in training and development, are at risk of losing their investments (Kochan and Dyer, 2001, p.282). Their staff can be poached for higher wages by businesses that spend little on training. In turn, this may lead good trainers to conclude that training is not worthwhile.

Human capital theory also deals with personal investment in self-development, such as enrolling on a degree course. It presupposes that individuals balance the cost of education and training (time, loss of income, fees) against the benefits of a higher income in the future. As such it predicts that the young are more likely to invest in training because their losses are relatively less – and the potential gains greater – than for older people. In general, the income of employees with degrees and other higher education qualifications is significantly higher than that of people who ceased education at an earlier stage.

It has been suggested that the value of education may lie not in any real investment in skills but in its 'screening' power (Sapsford and Tzannatos, 1993, p.89). Recruiters assume that individuals with 'pieces of paper' are better candidates than those without. Qualifications are used as a cheap and easy selection filter. However, a survey designed by the US National

---

HRM in reality Canadian brains on the move

A study published by the C.D. Howe Institute shows that the slowdown of Canada's productivity growth and the widening gap between Canadian and US per capita incomes in recent years has led to fresh concerns about a brain drain of highly qualified individuals and entrepreneurs.

The study takes the form of a collection of essays entitled *Brains on the Move* and focuses on the importance of labour mobility to a nation's economy.

While concerns about a brain drain from Canada to the USA have been around for decades, the study highlights a subtle shift in the kinds of brains emigrating in recent years. There is vigorous competition between developed countries to acquire knowledge and develop leading-edge technology by attracting highly skilled professionals and technical workers. In one essay, Stephen Easton examines trends in the flows of scientists and economists from Canada to the United States. His findings reveal that Canadian scientists are now more than twice as likely to move to the USA as they were in the 1960s. There has also been a significant increase in the likelihood that Canadian-trained economists will work outside Canada.

In his essay, William Gibson looks at Canadians who choose to obtain at least some of their education in the USA. Canadians are much more likely to study in the United States than citizens of other countries – and the trend is growing. And students who are educated in the USA are more likely to look for subsequent employment there.

In another essay, Richard Harris focuses on what he calls the 'Wayne Gretzky model' of the brain drain. This model proposes that, whereas the number of talented people moving south of the border might be small, they include 'superstars' whose emigration has a disproportionate effect on Canada's economy. Moreover, while knowledge spillovers increasingly drive economic growth, emigration of highly trained and talented people from Canada to the USA creates a permanent knowledge gap and sustains an increasing per capita income gap between the two countries.

Elsewhere in the book attention is paid to:

● the effect of government policies on the quality of entrepreneurs a country may attract;

● the effect of 'cultural clustering' in attracting talented individuals, particularly those from less-developed countries, to join their ethnic compatriots in a specific location; and

● the effect of immigration policies on flows of increasingly globally mobile and highly talented individuals.

Increasing economic integration between Canada and the USA, as a result of the North American Free Trade Agreement, has stalled since 9/11, but there are calls for the freer movement of labour between the two countries. If this happens there may be one of two effects:

1 The flow of labour out of Canada could produce a growing skills shortage in Canada, leading to a reduction in the wage gap between the two countries.

2 Investment and jobs could move to Canada to meet the supply of Canadian-grown brains.

Either way, the concept of an integrated labour market in North America will become a matter of active debate – one, the study concludes, that will rival in intensity the free-trade debate of the 1980s.

What can such governments do to retain talent?

Source: *HRM Guide Canada* (http://www.hrmguide.net/canada), 25 February, 2006.

Center on the Educational Quality of the Workforce at the University of Pennsylvania produced evidence to show that improved workers' education directly increased productivity
(*The Times Higher*, 26 May, 1995). The survey of owners and managers in 3000 businesses
showed that whereas a 10 per cent increase in capital investment (machinery, tools, buildings,
etc.) produced a 3.4 per cent increase in productivity, a 10 per cent improvement in education attainment increased productivity by 8.4 per cent.

The survey found that organizations that used education grades as selection criteria and
were linked to schools through work placement arrangements or training schemes also
showed higher levels of productivity and innovation. However, most employers disregarded
school grades and reports in favour of 'attitude', communication skills and previous work
experience.

We can see from Figure 5.1 that human capital is a significant unifying concept in HRM.
It links four major people management activities – resourcing, assessment, development and
reward – with an environmental variable which is a key to both organizational and national
success. Each of these areas is further explored in later chapters in this book. Table 5.1
locates macro HRM in the context of a changing world and a background of economic
uncertainty.

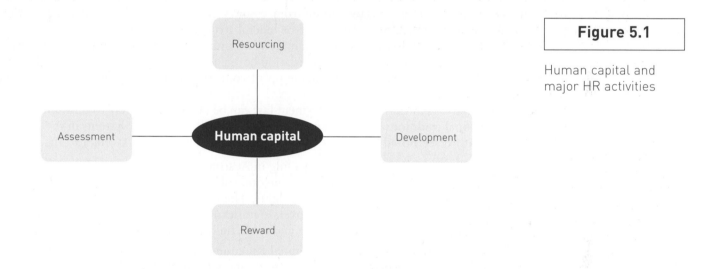

Figure 5.1

Human capital and
major HR activities

Table 5.1

Macro HRM in context

| | Levels of analysis | | | |
	Environment	Organization	Strategy	Activities
HRM type	Macro HRM	Organizational HRM	Strategic HRM	Operational HRM
Features	Economy Labour market Culture Political climate	Structure Culture Power Functions	Mission Objectives Policy Planning	Recruitment Development Reward Dismissal
Traditional responsibility	State	Senior management	Senior management	Personnel
Modern responsibility	Supranational National Multinationals	Managers Employees	Senior-middle management	Line managers HR specialists

Legislative frameworks

One of the most important environmental constraints on the job market and the activities of people managers comes from the law. Employment law changes continuously and varies extensively in different parts of the world. Much of the legislation relating to business derives from custom or precedent. Precedents are also decided by judges working to the system that 'like cases be decided alike'. Within the Anglo-Celtic countries these have been systematized into a common law framework. Many of these countries, such as the USA, also have a written constitution which provides a further code. Most European countries employ an entirely code-based system called civil law descended from the law code of the Roman Empire. A further element is that of 'equity', which is discretionary and has relevance to cases involving non-monetary actions or injunctions, for example against an illegal strike.

In the 21st century, national governments have become law-making machines, creating a complex legal environment for businesses. Governments implement statutes for strategic reasons, ensuring, for example, that employees who are disciplined or dismissed are dealt with in a particular manner. Organizations that fail to meet their legal obligations must compensate aggrieved individuals appropriately. Not only does this apply to current employees but also ex-employees and job applicants. One of the major complications for human resource managers is that relevant laws differ from country to country, and also between different states within countries with a devolved or federal structure.

The European Union is a useful example to examine in greater detail since there are still marked differences in employment legislation covering operating units in different locations. Unlike the USA, for example, it is made up of countries with widely different employment laws, traditions and practices.

The variations in European employment law can be attributed largely to different legal systems, national traditions and accidents of history. The different legal systems in the EU can be divided into three broad groupings (Due, Madsen and Jense, 1991; Gold, 1993):

1 The Roman-German system prevailing in Austria, Belgium, France, Germany, Italy and the Netherlands. Government has a pivotal role in employee relations, guaranteeing a fundamental core of constitutional rights. These provide the foundation for national industrial relations. Legislation covers significant aspects of employment market conditions such as working hours and trade union representation.

2 The Anglo-Celtic system in the United Kingdom and the Irish Republic. This promotes a minimalist approach to the role of the state with limited legislative protection.

3 The Nordic system, covering Denmark, Finland, Norway and Sweden. The 'basic agreement' between employers and unions forms the foundation of employee relations. The state plays a limited role, intervening only at the request of these two parties.

The central and dominant group of the EU follows the Roman-German model. Not surprisingly, their way of thinking has shaped many proposals to the European Commission. The European Court of Justice has also contributed to harmonization with an increasing body of case law (Gold, 1993, p.16). However, debate on employee relations reflects changing business practices and a shifting balance of attitudes within an enlarging EU.

In our earlier discussion of globalization we observed that the EU is not sealed off from other trading areas such as East Asia and North America – its industries are often in direct competition. We also noted that the process of social dumping (see Key concept 4.5) has led to a questioning of the fitness of traditional methods of industrial relations within the EU. Institutionalized worker participation can function smoothly in a growing company but what happens when employees are asked to participate in determining their own redundancies?

Many governments and employee groups have been concerned that social dumping can also take place from one country to another within the EU. They have proposed improvements in employment rights for all workers across the Union. Gold (1993, p.17) has described this approach as 'social protectionist' (Key concept 5.3) in contrast to the largely deregulatory views of the UK Conservative government and, to a considerable extent, its Labour successor. Indeed, the Conservative UK government refused to sign the 'Social Chapter' of the Maastricht Treaty in 1991 arguing that it would lead to higher employee costs and a reduction in the country's competitive position. It was agreed that the other 11 members at the time would implement a common social and employee policy whether or not the UK acquiesced. Later in the decade an incoming Labour government accepted this policy.

Key concept 5.3 Social protection

According to the World Bank, social protection measures improve or protect human capital, ranging from labour market interventions, unemployment or old-age insurance, to income support, for individuals, households and communities.

Whereas HRM in the USA has been predominantly within non-unionized firms, this has not been the case in Europe. In Britain and Ireland, where HRM has had its earliest and greatest impact, there is a longstanding pluralist tradition of collective bargaining. In the pre-Thatcher era, the industrial relations scene in the UK, especially, could be described as confrontational and competitive. Unions and management were in a state of frequent disagreement, with strikes or other forms of industrial action being commonplace.

During the Thatcher period, the UK witnessed a massive reduction in union power: a phenomenon associated with large-scale redundancies and restructuring within the British economy. The old labour-intensive industries, where the major union power lay, were particularly affected by these processes. By the mid-1990s fewer than half of Britain's commercial sector employees were covered by collective bargaining arrangements. UK-wide agreements were being eroded in the public sector, with government pursuing a policy of breaking up structures such as the National Health Service into local trusts with separate bargaining powers. There was a marked move towards authoritarian styles of management in this period with the right of unions to take industrial action considerably reduced. This was partly a result of government legislation but also reflected awareness of economic reality among the workforce and a reluctance to risk further job losses. This has been described as the 'new industrial relations' within which: 'management has seized the initiative to change working practices and unions have become less confrontational, more flexible, more accommodating to "local" conditions, and generally more "realistic" ' (Goss, 1994, p.140).

This new realism was reinforced by a succession of changes in legislation with four main consequences:

1 *Making it easier for people not to join a union.* For example, this was achieved by strengthening rights for non-union workers when a 'closed shop' agreement between union and employer prevailed. It included protection for workers who lost their jobs, and those who were victimized for not being members, or chose not to join a trade union because of personal conviction. In effect, closed shops became unworkable.

2 *Making unions financially liable for their members' actions.* A union could be held responsible for any damage caused by an individual member to property during a strike.

3 *Curtailing the power of solidarity.* For instance, through the restriction of picketing: a maximum of six at any one entrance and only at an employee's own place of work. Secondary industrial action had to be directly related to the dispute and required a contractual relationship with the employer, preventing sympathetic action by other union members. This was further reinforced by sharpening the definition of a trade dispute. This now applied to a dispute between workers and *their* employer (the previous definition had been 'employers and workers' generally). The dispute had to be 'wholly or mainly' related to (rather than 'connected' with) one or more specific issues – such as terms and conditions, recruitment or dismissal, duty allocation, discipline and negotiation.

4 *Increasing the accountability of union leaders.* A secret postal ballot was required before any industrial action, including strikes, overtime bans and working-to-rule. Similarly, senior union officials were required to offer themselves for re-election every five years by secret ballot.

This approach contrasts markedly with the so-called 'Rhineland' model – the form of **social market** (see Key concept 5.4) developed in Germany and adjacent countries. According to Bolkestein (2000):

> The Rhineland model may be seen as a regulated market economy with a comprehensive system of social security. Government, employers' organizations and labour unions consult each other on economic goals and on the policy instruments to be used. In the Rhineland, therefore, the welfare state is combined with a so-called 'consultation economy'.
>
> Rhineland participants in the economic process (widely known as stakeholders) try to achieve a harmony of interests. In such a stakeholder economy the primary goal, it is said, is not the maximization of short-term profits for the benefit of the shareholders. The main concern is a sustainable, stable and continuous economic growth and a high level of employment.

HRM in reality Governments should be more dynamic

New reports from the Organization of Economic Cooperation and Development (OECD) say that if countries want to improve living standards and keep welfare systems functioning they urgently need to get more people into paid employment. This means rejecting policies that discourage people from working and companies from hiring, and by doing more to increase skill levels. The reports find that many people on welfare gain little financial advantage from going into employment. Those who want to work often find their chances hampered by constrictive regulations, lack of support in the job search, or their own lack of skills. The result is to restrict economic growth and prosperity as well as individual wellbeing.

The report entitled *Boosting Jobs and Incomes*, is an assessment of employment policies in the OECD's 30 member countries. Also new is a review by Sveinbjörn Blöndal and Raymond Torres of the OECD Jobs Strategy launched in 1994 when high unemployment was a persistent problem. Rapid technological advances and globalization require workers in OECD countries to be able to adapt quickly to new challenges and increased competition.

Overall unemployment in OECD countries has fallen since 1994. Rates of participation of women in the workforce have generally increased and the decline in participation of older workers (aged 55–64) appears to have been reversed in some countries. The OECD argues that most economies remain unprepared for the imminent challenge of ageing populations, although some countries (the USA, Canada, some of the Nordics, Australia and New Zealand) will be affected less than others. Young workers are over-represented among the unemployed. This is only partly explained by longer periods in education.

The OECD argues that some characteristics of strong labour markets are timeless:

> High employment, low unemployment and high productivity, with ease of movement of skilled, confident workers from all backgrounds among dynamic, high valued-added sectors and the capacity to absorb and adjust to shocks. Add to the package an ongoing ability to attract and retain fixed investment, whether domestic or foreign, and broadly speaking this is how most governments would like their labour markets to function.

The OECD acknowledges that very few member countries can claim to fulfil this broad characterization, and even the best have weaknesses that need addressing.

OECD secretary-general Angel Gurría said:

> Getting people who want to work into jobs is one of the biggest challenges facing many OECD governments. Systems that exclude people from employment are unfair and need to be changed. The key is to ensure that all economic policies are in line with and supportive of measures to boost employment and incomes. We believe that countries that take action along the lines we are recommending will be rewarded by a stronger labour market and, most importantly, improved living standards.

The OECD makes it clear that no single set of economic policies can solve employment problems. Some countries achieve low unemployment by maintaining comparatively low welfare benefits and minimal regulations, but at the expense of relatively wide inequality in earnings. Others obtain similar results with generous welfare benefits and a proactive approach to job seekers, but at high cost in terms of public spending on labour market policies.

The OECD notes that countries successfully boosting employment have in common an emphasis on macroeconomic stability and strong product market competition. In addition, most provide strong job-search support combined with obligations placed on those looking for work, including the threat of benefit sanctions. Some have introduced reforms that supplement welfare benefits with measures to ensure recipients look for work and have a financial incentive to take a job.

The OECD finds that some social benefits can prove a disincentive to work. 'Too many people in some countries are on sickness, disability and lone-parent benefits, for instance, and pension and other benefits tend to encourage early retirement. Yet, many of these people could and often want to work. Governments should tighten up entry to these schemes and develop ways of activating people on such inactive benefits.'

Review of the 1994 Jobs Strategy recommendations includes the following themes:

- High payroll taxes and social charges impede job creation for low-productivity workers.

- Escalating costs of private healthcare in some countries is an inhibiting factor.

- Several countries have cut employers' social security contributions on low-wage employment and some have reported more hiring of such workers.

- Decentralized and centralized wage bargaining offer greater flexibility than sectoral agreements, but change in this area has been slow.

- Anti-competitive regulations have a negative effect on employment.

- Policies need to be supported by sound macroeconomic policy that encourages investment and growth, and reduces cyclical fluctuations in the economy.

- Better skills will help workers adjust to change. Policy should help promote investment in human capital, while also addressing existing learning inequalities.

The OECD argues that countries following the recommendations of the 1994 Jobs Strategy have succeeded in reducing persistently high unemployment, as have those adopting Nordic-type approaches such as Denmark's 'flexicurity' hybrid. This combines relatively easy hire–fire with strong support for, and obligations on, jobseekers. Countries that have not reformed enough, including France, Germany and Italy, as well as some central and East European countries, continue to experience high unemployment despite strong global growth.

In its revised Jobs Strategy, the OECD urges governments to:

- Set macroeconomic policies aimed at maintaining price stability and sustainable public finances.

- Ensure that recessions do not lead to permanent falls in employment.

- Make it more attractive for people to work than to stay on benefits.

- Make sure that benefit recipients receive high-quality services, and that there is close monitoring of job search processes, backed up by possible benefit sanctions.

- Adapt regulations and tax policies to encourage companies to recruit new staff.

- Strengthen competition in product markets.

- Ensure that legislation to protect job security does not undermine the dynamism of the labour market or lead to discrimination in hiring and firing.

- Provide people of working age with education and training opportunities needed to get jobs and raise incomes.

The OECD acknowledges that suggested reforms mainly relate to rich countries, but argues that issues relevant for the newest members of OECD are also addressed, such as how to promote the transition from undeclared work to formal employment. Reform needs political will and among the toughest tasks facing governments are likely to be winning public support for necessary changes and implementing them effectively. The OECD argues that countries that fail to reform face continued weak employment performance.

Should governments follow the OECD recommendations?

Source: *HRM Guide* (http://www.hrmguide.net), 1 July, 2006.

Europe-wide initiatives

The European Union has created a new dimension for people management in its member states. The European Commission has undertaken a number of initiatives aimed at improving economic conditions in less privileged regions. The differences in income between the EU's richest and poorest regions are dramatic, ranging between 30 per cent and 209 per cent of the average. It was once believed that the division between rich and poor could be described simply in terms of location. The rich were concentrated in a belt from south-east England, through northern France, Belgium, and the Netherlands into northern Germany. The peripheral areas along the Mediterranean and Atlantic seaboard were thought to be poorer. Today, the situation has become far more complex. For a variety of reasons, rich and poor regions are found next to each other in a patchwork throughout the EU.

In particular, there was pressure from the then president of the European Commission, Jacques Delors (1985–1995), for the EU to take a unified and strongly interventionist approach to the problem of 17 million people without work. This was an area of conflict between the majority social market (Key concept 5.4) position in Europe and the UK's free market stance. Both Conservative and Labour governments in the UK advocated a 'hands-off' approach to the issue, arguing that the 'market' would take care of the problem if employment laws were loosened and 'flexibility' encouraged. However, it is clear that having a pool of unskilled people in rundown industrial or mining areas is not sufficient to attract industry. Companies need to be able to draw on an infrastructure of transport facilities, service companies and highly trained potential employees.

Key concept 5.4 Social market

A term coined by Alfred Müller-Armack, Secretary of State at the Economics Ministry in Bonn, Federal Republic of Germany between 1958 and 1963. He defined the social market as an economic system that combined market freedom with social equilibrium. In this kind of economic system the government plays a regulating role and creates the framework for market processes, going beyond securing competition to ensure social equity.

Worries about job losses in the EU led to a decision at the Essen summit of 1994 to adopt a monitoring procedure based on five recommendations:

- improving employment opportunities
- increasing the intensity of employment growth
- reducing non-wage employment costs
- developing active labour market polices
- targeting measures on the long-term unemployed.

Member states were required to produce annual reports and money was made available from the European Social Fund.

A few years later, the European Council meeting in Lisbon, March 2000, formulated new strategic goals for the first decade of the 21st century. The strategic goals demand an ambitious programme through which the EU aims to 'become the most competitive and dynamic knowledge-based economy in the world, capable of sustainable economic growth, with more and better jobs and greater social cohesion (Bolkestein, 2000). The goals are based on the assumption that the EU can reach an average annual economic growth of around 3 per cent and a labour participation rate rising from 61 per cent in 2000 to 70 per cent in 2010.

The Europeanization of employment policies has already aroused academic debate within the European Union. Bertozzi and Bonoli (2002) point to a new policy instrument adopted by the EU to bring governments to heel. This is described as the 'open method of coordination'. Used first for the European Employment Strategy, it involves a complex framework beginning with adoption by the Council of the European Union of common objectives and agreed targets. Member states are then required to submit reports to the European Commission detailing their efforts and progress towards meeting those objectives and targets. Recommendations for the Employment Strategy were first issued in 1999. The process is repeated each year and culminates in an assessment by the Commission of the progress made by each country.

Bertozzi and Bonoli assume that this process will have the most impact on the countries that show the greatest 'misfit' between their current employment practices and those put forward in the European Strategy, stating that: 'we assume that the EU develops a European model of employment policy and that the OMC will be applied most forcefully on those countries that are furthest from this model, whereas it will just mildly try to reorient policies in countries that are closest to the model.'

Further pressures on member states come via three routes (Leibfried and Pearson, 2000):

Direct positive pressures of integration. Actions taken directly by the European Commission to create a social dimension.

Direct negative pressures of integration. Through the market-building process that encourages labour mobility and freedom of provision of services.

Indirect pressures of integration. Stemming from factors such as tax harmonization, common European currency (with implications for setting a unified interest policy), and other economic initiatives.

As regards the Employment Strategy, Bertozzi and Bonoli (2002) distinguish between four different European traditions: the English-speaking countries, continental and southern European countries, and the Nordic countries. This classification is broadly similar to the different legal traditions we identified earlier.

English-speaking countries – specifically the UK. Here, employment markets have been left to themselves to survive the changes of the 1980s and 1990s. Redundancies in the old heavy industries such as coal, steel and shipbuilding have not been accompanied

---

1999 European Union employment guidelines

Pillar 1: *Employability*
- Tackling youth unemployment and preventing long-term unemployment.
- Transition from passive measures to active measures for benefit and training systems.
- Encouraging a partnership approach for training, work experience, traineeships and other employability measures.
- Easing the transition from school to work.

Pillar 2: *Entrepreneurship*
- Making it easier to start up and run businesses.
- Exploiting the opportunities for job creation.
- Making the taxation system more employment-friendly.

Pillar 3: *Adaptability*
- Modernizing work organization.
- Support adaptability in enterprises.

Pillar 4: *Equal opportunities*
- Tackling gender gaps.
- Reconciling work and family life.
- Facilitating reintegration into the labour market.
- Promoting the integration of people with disabilities into working life.

Source: The European Commission.

by major changes in employment policy. Benefits have been kept to subsistence level 'so that people are prepared to accept low-paid jobs in the service sector'. Women have been modestly encouraged to join the employment market through tax changes but nothing more radical. Bertozzi and Bonoli conclude that: 'The road followed by the UK, that can be characterized as liberal, has been relatively successful in terms of job creation in the service sector (although not as successful as in the USA), but has resulted in growing wage inequality and social problems of poverty and exclusion.'

Continental and southern Europe. High levels of social protection but relatively low levels of **childcare** and tax arrangements that are based on household income predominate in a number of northern countries such as the Netherlands and Germany. France has attempted to absorb job losses by severely curtailing working hours. Other countries have offered generous benefits for early retirement. In southern Europe the 'black economy' accounts for a great deal of untaxed economic activity.

Nordic countries. These are characterized by relatively weak employment protection but generous unemployment benefits. They also have a tradition of active labour market policies, including retraining, childcare and generous parental care. These policies, together with a relatively large public sector have encouraged a high level of female participation in the job market. They have produced high levels of employment and low wage equality at the cost of expensive state intervention in the job market.

HRM in reality Red tape deters recruitment

Between them, small businesses in the UK are spending half a billion (500 000 000) hours each year meeting the demands of government regulations and paperwork, according to the latest NatWest/SERTeam Quarterly Survey of Small Business in Britain.

On average, each small business currently spends 26.7 hours a month filling in government forms and other paperwork. Sole traders suffer the most, spending an average of 8 hours per month (down from 8.5 hours in 2005) per individual trader compared with the 1.5 hours per employee (1.8 hours in 2005) in larger companies.

Thankfully, the overall trend has been for a reduction in the average time estimated to be spent on compliance and red tape by small businesses over recent years:

- 1999 – 4.2 hours per person per month
- 2003/2004 – 3.8 hours
- Currently – 3.7.

Respondents cite dealing with VAT as the most time-consuming for mid-sized businesses, but aspects of payroll, particularly taxation and National Insurance, follow close behind.

NatWest's media release states that employment laws, especially health and safety regulations, are continuing to have a detrimental effect on the growth of small businesses in the UK with 44 per cent of small firms reporting that at least one aspect of employee health and safety regulations has a significant impact on their business because of the time, cost or inconvenience involved. This compares with 39 per cent in 2003 and 2004.

Over a half of small businesses said that the burden of red tape has affected their employment levels:

- 37 per cent reported that they have avoided employing more people.
- A further 19 per cent said that they reduced the numbers they employed because of the burden of employee regulation and paperwork.
- 45 per cent of businesses without employees had made a conscious decision not to be employers in order to avoid this type of regulation completely.

Pete Ferns, Director of NatWest Business Banking, said: 'The government constantly needs to look closely at what it can do to encourage growth in the small business community, and cutting the amount of red tape could be the way forward. Small businesses are the engine room of our economy and their success is paramount for the overall economic prospects of the UK.'

Are you convinced that red tape inhibits business growth?

Source: *HRM Guide UK* (http://www.hrmguide.co.uk), 5 April, 2006.

Bolkestein (2000) draws attention to the particular success of the Netherlands economy in achieving an average of 1.6 per cent growth in the number of jobs over the past 15 years. This equals the USA job gain and is four times the European average. This job growth is attributed to wage moderation, itself encouraged by tax cuts. But he also points to the fact that this success is 'merely relative to a worse past'. Bolkestein quotes a 1997 McKinsey report on the Dutch economy. Four key barriers were identified as having a significant role in holding the Netherlands back:

1 *Lack of competition*. In the past, Dutch legislation on competition has been relatively lax. Stricter rules are now in place that will have to be enforced vigorously.

2 *Inflexible labour-market rules*, including those on working hours, on hiring and firing, and stringent collective bargaining agreements.

3 An *unattractive climate for starting new companies* in fast-growing sectors. Strict regulation drives up employee costs, especially for small businesses.

4 *Lack of incentives* for the low skilled to find jobs. Social security benefits in the Netherlands are among the most generous in the world, so that many unemployed are stuck in a poverty trap. If everyone able to work but receiving social benefits were included in the official jobless statistics, the unemployment rate would rise to over 20 per cent of the labour force.

Bolkestein does not agree that the Netherlands should follow the so-called 'Anglo-Saxon' model, but concludes that:

If the Netherlands still have a long way to go, that goes even more for those European countries which are still firmly stuck in the Rhineland rut. European unemployment is a man-made disaster. Policy harmonization may cause this blight to spread. According to conventional wisdom the coordination of economic policies is considered the key to creating employment. This belief is often professed by governments, which espouse unsuccessful policies. They say they fear that tax rates will suffer a race to the bottom. Harmonization, though, is more likely to result in a race to the top. High tax rates will undermine economic incentives and thus be inimical to investments, growth and employment. Altogether, harmonization would lessen the pressure to carry out necessary but unpopular structural adjustments to the welfare state.

Instead he advocates:

- Wage moderation and differentiation.
- Liberalization of legislation on job security.
- Less generous and more strictly administered unemployment and other welfare-state benefits.
- A policy that would reduce the market power of established parties.

Summary

In this chapter we examined the role played by governments in creating the context for human resource management through labour market policies, regulation and legal frameworks. We emphasized the particular influence of state intervention in developing human capital and growth of the employment market. Employment legislation sets a framework for the practice of human resource management but these frameworks vary widely and embody different traditions and views on the nature of the employment market. We took the European Union as an example and highlighted a number of initiatives with a human resource focus which were interpreted differently in member states.

Further reading

Texts on labour market policies include: *Why Deregulate Labour Markets?* edited by Gosta Esping-Andersen and Marino Regini (Oxford University Press, 2000); *The European Employment Strategy: Labour Market Regulation and New Governance* by Diamond Ashiagbor (Oxford University Press, 2005); *Innovations in Labour Market Policies: The Australian Way* by D. Grubb, Douglas Lippoldt and Peter Tergeist (OECD, 2001); *Labor Movement: How Migration Regulates Labor Markets* by Harald Bauder (Oxford University Press, 2000).

Most books about human capital are focused on the firm, but more generally *Rethinking Development Theory and Policy: A Human Factor Critique* by Senyo B.S.K. Adjibolosoo (Praeger Publications, 1999) looks at failure within the context of development. There is a huge selection of books available on employment policies in the European Union. *EC Employment Law* by Catherine Barnard (Oxford University Press, 2006) is a detailed review of employment legislation in the EU. More generally, *Taxation, Wage Bargaining, and Unemployment* by Isabela Mares (Cambridge University Press, 2006) looks at European employment strategies over the last few decades.

Review questions

1 If businesses have little control over economic growth or recession, is there any value in attempting to follow long-term organizational human resource strategies for employee development?

2 How much power do governments have to influence employment and development of their human resources? What factors can you identify that would act as obstacles to government initiatives?

3 Define the concept of human capital in your own words. What are the most effective measures open to a government for improving a country's human capital?

4 Is it possible to quantify a nation/company's human capital?

5 It has been said that a successful multinational must have a strong presence in each of the three main trading blocs. What are the human resource implications for an organization undertaking this strategy?

6 In what ways do approaches to people management differ between 'social market' and 'free market' countries. Relate these differences to hard and soft models of HRM.

7 What can be gained from comparing people management practices in different countries?

8 To what extent are the policies of the European Union encouraging identical employment legislation in member countries of the EU?

Case studies for discussion and analysis

Location choice/Graduate development/South Africa

1 You have been appointed general manager at a new European subsidiary of a Japanese television manufacturer. The subsidiary is controlled by three senior Japanese managers who have been seconded from the parent company for a five-year period. Your first task is to identify and shortlist suitable locations for production and then participate in choosing suppliers and staff.

What elements of employment legislation, government support and industrial relations would encourage you to locate in a particular country? Describe the likely decision processes and contrast with the way a typical local company would have dealt with the same problem.

2 Leyanne has recently graduated with a degree in business studies, specializing in finance. She has been recruited as a trainee by a large conglomerate involved in airport management and cargo distribution. The company operates in Australia, Singapore, Europe and the Caribbean. Corporate

headquarters are in Sydney, Australia but the largest operational units are in Singapore and Germany. The organization prefers to develop its own management and expects a broad range of

experience and grasp of different cultural traditions. Leyanne is ambitious and wants to become a senior manager in the company.

Outline a possible career plan for Leyanne, including aspects that the company should take responsibility for and issues for her own self-development.

3 With the demise of apartheid, President Nelson Mandela's government of national unity faced a formidable challenge. Some 4.7 million South Africans were unemployed, or 32 per cent of the available workforce. Half of them were under 30, with a further 400 000 school-leavers joining the queue for jobs each year. In 2002, according to the *Economist* country briefing, under President Mbeki the official unemployment rate was 26.7 per cent but estimates range up to 40 per cent depending on the definition used. The annual growth rate has averaged around 3.0 per cent in GDP – nowhere near the level required to reduce unemployment significantly. Inequality in income is considerable and the informal economy has grown at the expense of formal employment.

Reforming the economy

The strategy for reforming the moribund economy included:

- the partial privatization of South African Airways
- partial sale of the telecommunications utility, Telekom
- encouragement of tourism; and
- an unbundling of private conglomerates.

Government policy did not include large-scale privatization along New Zealand or British lines. Politicians were unlikely to accept the image of closures, heavy redundancies and large capital gains for a few shareholders. The intention of privatization – where it happened – was to empower the disadvantaged and spread wealth more widely.

Foreign businesses began to renew investment. Ford and IBM bought back into former subsidiaries that had been sold off in the 1980s. Microsoft, Apple, Pepsi and Proctor and Gamble were new investors. Pepsi made a point of putting black managers in charge of their operation. Rover said it would make South Africa its major production hub for Land Rovers in Africa. Other investors were holding back because of a perception of relatively high wage levels and low productivity, inflexible working practices and poor management (Horwitz and Smith, 1998).

Productivity levels

A *Monitor* company report commissioned by the then National Economic Forum found that – in almost every industrial sector examined – identical products were being made at much lower cost or to a higher standard of quality in other countries. Many industries could only survive through protectionism and subsidy. The *Monitor* report demonstrated how South Africa lost its international competitiveness because of low levels of productivity. They compared South African vehicle assembly with Mexico and the USA:

	Employee cost per hour (US$)	Employee hours per car	Employee cost per car (US$)
South Africa	5.6	63.5	355
Mexico	6.0	24.3	145
USA	38.0	18.56	705

The same pattern was found in the textile industry. Paradoxically, a long-term cure for unemployment requires short-term job losses in order to increase productivity. Both the public and private sectors were regarded as inefficient and overstaffed. Rising expectations among workers, however, meant a likely clash with trade unions.

Affirmative action

Around 75 per cent of South Africa's population is black, but only a minority of its managers are black. Under apartheid, Blacks had been prevented from having business accommodation in many city sites. They had been denied skills training and access to capital. Black empowerment required a nurturing of small businesses, backed by extra training and finance. Franchising and joint ventures with overseas companies offered considerable possibilities. Kentucky Fried Chicken and Mcdonald's actively sought black franchisees.

Many firms used affirmative action programmes to recruit black professionals, partly in an attempt to appease the government and public opinion. Job-hopping – the 'pinball syndrome' – became normal, with educated black employees moving from one job to another every six to eight months. People have attempted to climb up the status and responsibility ladder much faster than their experience and training will allow. Skilled, experienced black professionals remain such a valued resource that they have been offered salaries 20–50 per cent higher than their white counterparts. Jobs have imposing titles and may be accompanied by cars and cellular telephones. In practice, these positions often turned out to be disappointing, the responsibilities bearing no comparison to the titles. Black professionals became frustrated as high salaries were not matched withthe opportunity to develop self-esteem.

Officially, according to South African Department of Labour figures (1999) the proportion of non-white managers had increased to junior 39 per cent, middle 25 per cent, senior 22 per cent and executive director 7 per cent. Many employers were seen as cynical, hiring black faces for 'soft' jobs such as human resources but not for financial and line management positions. Support in the form of training, development or mentoring was frequently absent. The process was usually initiated by the board of directors without consulting existing managers who subsequently did little to help the new appointees.

From your reading of this case study, outline a programme of possible government initiatives that could lead to improved and real employment in South Africa.

Chapter 6
The employment market

Learning objectives

- Outline some of the major theories about why people work.

- Develop an understanding of the conditions and salaries for which people work and the expectations they have of employers.

- Explore the relationship between human capital and national employment levels.

- Determine some of the effects of competitor activities on employee availability.

- Investigate the patterns of work that are replacing 'nine-to-five' jobs.

Why do people work?

Social preferences

Individual preferences

Participating in the employment market

Employee supply and demand

Active labour market programmes

Part-time and temporary working

Summary

Further reading

Review questions

Case studies for discussion and analysis –

    Rob's career/Jefford trading

The **employment or job market** (see Key concept 6.1) is the ultimate source of all new recruits. The dynamics of this market affect human resource managers directly when they deal with employee resourcing or set competitive reward packages. To do so effectively, they need to understand the expectations of prospective employees and have an insight into their decisionmaking process when applying for, or accepting jobs.

Key concept 6.1 The employment market

The employment market comprises all those people who are available for work. Neo-classical economics views this potential workforce as forming a labour market. The market is affected by national or regional supply and demand for appropriately skilled employees. It is constrained by demographic factors such as the number of young people leaving schools and universities and by cultural norms such as expectations for mothers to stay at home looking after children.

We begin this chapter by exploring the reasons why people seek employment. These are evaluated first from an economic perspective, introducing competitive market and institutional theories, and from social and individual viewpoints. The chapter moves on to consider the issue of unemployment. Finally, the characteristics of the flexible job market are debated, including new forms of part-time working and the effects of greater female participation in the working economy.

Why do people work?

The simple answer in most cases is that they have to. Few of us have the private resources needed to maintain a satisfactory lifestyle without an income from employment. This seems obvious but the issue becomes much more complex on examination. For example, many wealthy people (or lottery winners) continue to work even though they do not 'need' to. Moreover, unless they are in a desperate financial state, people pick and choose the type of work they are prepared to do. Professions such as nursing and social work attract large numbers of people despite relatively low rates of pay in many countries. Clearly, there are many other factors, other than money, that have to be taken into account in understanding people's motives in the employment market.

The issue has been made all the more complicated because economists have provided several different and contradictory theories in this area. They can be divided broadly into two main approaches: competitive and institutional.

Competitive market theories

These are derived from the neo-classical economic concepts of rational choice and maximization of utility. The assumption here is that individuals choose jobs that offer them maximum benefits. The utility or value of these benefits – money, vacation time, pension entitlement and so on – varies for different individuals according to their personal preferences. People move from one organization to another if improved benefits are available. At the same time, employing organizations attempt to get the most from their employees for the lowest possible cost. It can be argued that pure competitive theories of the employment market have little to do with HRM since they are not 'concerned with what goes on inside organizations' (Claydon, 2001, p.70). It can also be argued that employment markets are never truly competitive because of various 'rigidities' such as union intervention, minimum-wage laws or social protection rights that are not found in other markets.

In the purest form of competitive employment market (remembering that this is likely to be more theoretical than real) the outcome is a dynamic and shifting equilibrium in which both employees and organizations compete to maximize benefits for themselves. Within a specific region or industry there is a balance between supply and demand for human resources. Pay and conditions for employees – the theory goes – are determined by the relative scarcity or abundance of their skills and abilities in the employment market. Competitive forces push wages up when demand for products, and hence employees, increases, and downwards when the economy is in recession. In the latter case a 'market clearing wage' is arrived at eventually which is sufficiently low to encourage employers to increase recruitment and eliminate unemployment. This discourse reinforces the view that employees are objects to be traded like any other commodities in the market – human resources in the hardest possible sense. Supposedly, they offer themselves – their skills and human qualities – for sale to the highest bidders. Within this mindset they could just as well be vegetables on a market stall.

According to Claydon (2001, p.74) 'this model is a heroic simplification of the real world. It has nothing to say about the internal processes of managing people at work.' In reality, it is obvious that the job market does not work in such a simple fashion: people do not move readily between organizations in search of higher wages; most firms do not cut benefits when unemployment levels are high and cheaper workers are available. Indeed, in the 1980s wages soared for those in work at the same time as unemployment levels increased. Such contradictions are partly explained by the omission of HR development issues such as training and career structures in competition theories. More generally, they assume that employment markets are purely external when, in fact, large organizations have internal job markets operating through promotion and transfer of existing employees.

Competition theories assume that jobseekers have perfect knowledge of available jobs and benefits. Job-searching is an expensive and time-consuming business. The unemployed do not have money and those in work do not have time. The result is that few people conduct the extensive searches required to find jobs that meet their preferences perfectly. In practice, most individuals settle for employment which is quickly obtained and which exceeds the 'reserve minimum wage' they have in mind. There is a considerable element of luck involved. Moreover, the jobseeker does not make the choice: in most cases the decision is in the hands of the employer.

In a test of competitive labour market theory, Machin and Manning (2004) selected a situation that would come within most economists' definition of a competitive labour market (elder care assistants working for competing firms in the South of England) and found that the distribution of wage rates deviated markedly from that predicted by competitive market theories. They concluded that (p.383):

> ... it is hard to avoid the conclusion that there are very serious limitations to the usefulness of the competitive model in explaining the data. In particular, we feel that the competitive model cannot explain one of the most striking patterns our evidence reveals – the presence of very little wage dispersion within firms, and of high wage dispersion between firms. Moreover, what wage dispersion there is does not seem to be closely related to the characteristics of workers that seem to be associated with high productivity.

Entry barriers to skilled jobs provide a further constraint on the competitive job market. Many jobs are restricted to people possessing key skills – often specific to a particular firm or industrial sector. In fact, the external job market is made up of many sub-markets with widely different circumstances and constraints.

Institutional theories

An alternative approach places its main focus within the firm rather than the external job market. Institutionalists do not accept the principle of individual maximization of utility, arguing that both individuals and organizations cooperate to some extent and take account of the preferences of others in similar situations. Individual workers are less concerned with maximum benefits than achieving a fair rate compared to their peers. But this comparison may be restricted to employees within the same organization: most people appear indifferent (much of the time, at least) to benefits offered by other employers and large variations occur between firms in the same sector. Employers set wages for a variety of reasons ranging from profitability to tradition – competition with other firms is a relatively minor consideration. As a result, remuneration levels within many firms are relatively rigid. Wage rates are more likely to go up than down and are largely immune to influence from the external job market.

Competition theories assume that hiring and firing in reaction to changing market conditions is good practice. There are close parallels between this way of thinking and 'hard' HRM. In fact, most firms take active steps to avoid **employee turnover**. This is because turnover is disruptive and costs money. Recruitment advertising and redundancy payments are expensive and training new employees represents a considerable investment in time and effort. Organizations may encourage workers to remain with them by means of HR policies that increase benefits such as annual leave and pensions in line with length of service.

Key concept 6.2 Insiders and outsiders

Employers know that replacing existing workers with others from the outside world has inherent costs. This inhibits recruitment from the external employment market. Also, to some extent, there are costs or risks that inhibit employees from looking for work outside the organization. Consequently, there is rarely a free flow of workers in and out of a business. This disconnection is reflected in the pay and conditions of established employees ('insiders') which may deviate considerably from the 'market rate' in the wider world. Insiders will tend to push for a premium rate of pay, regardless of more competitive rates acceptable to outsiders, because of their perceived power to retain their jobs.

HRM in reality Graduates at home

Experience, Inc. has announced the findings of its 2006 Life After College online survey of recent American graduates on the growing 'boomerang kids' trend towards returning to live in the family home, career paths and the overall reality of life after college.

The majority of respondents (58 per cent) returned to live with parents after college, three-quarters did so immediately on graduating and one-third stayed more than 12 months. Almost half (48 per cent) of those who returned home did so to save money; 37 per cent were unemployed. Returning home was financially advantageous with no contributions paid towards utilities (92 per cent), rent (85 per cent) or groceries (74 per cent). Attitudes to returning to the family home varied: 59 per cent reported feeling 'indifferent or neutral'; 31 per cent 'embarrassed'; and 10 per cent 'proud and happy'.

Jobhopping has become customary for today's graduates; the average tenure at a first full-time job is 1.6 years. Three-quarters had changed jobs in the five years following graduation:

- up to one year (36 per cent)
- one to two years (51 per cent)
- three to five years (77 per cent)

Only 23 per cent had remained with the same employer since graduating. Seventy-five per cent chose to stay within their home state when changing jobs. Respondents cited various reasons for changing jobs, the most common being:

- salary increase (18 per cent)
- unhappy with existing employer (17 per cent)
- to try a new profession, department or company (13 per cent)
- move home (9 per cent)
- promotion (3 per cent)

Why are graduates keener to change jobs than they are to leave the parental home?

Source: *HRM Guide USA* (http://www.hrmguide.com), 17 August, 2006.

Reflecting on our discussion in Part one, we can conclude that institutional approaches to the job market have a greater affinity with 'soft' HRM. They recognize that group effects underlie notions of fairness and loyalty, fundamental to the notion of employee commitment. They are consistent with the stakeholder concept, recognizing the important roles played by government and trade unions. For example, the 'insider–outsider' model offers an explanation for simultaneously high wages and high levels of unemployment (Lindbeck and Snower, 1988). Insiders have stakeholder status whereas outsiders do not (see Key concept 6.2). Outsider status particularly affects immigrants. Frijters, Shields and Price (2005) found that immigrants to the UK do not compete effectively for employment. Job search methods are less successful; they are as likely to gain employment through informal routes; and the probability of success increases with years since immigration. This may partially explain why immigration has little impact on the job market.

At the organizational level, human resource managers also affect the nature of the market as a result of their recruitment and redundancy strategies. When business is optimistic recruitment numbers increase; if conditions are bad, employees may be shed. Technological change is a further complicating factor, leading to fewer but more highly skilled employees.

Figure 6.1 demonstrates some of the forces that shape the employment market, including elements discussed in Chapter 5, such as the major role played by government, particularly in the shape of legislation. The interactions between organizations and the job market are debated again later in the book when we consider human resource strategy. At this stage it is appropriate to note some omissions from most accounts of this subject such as the influence of social class, age, status, gender and ethnic origin in the job expectations of employees and the attitudes of employers towards these characteristics. As we shall see in later discussions on equal opportunities, suitable people can appear invisible to managers who associate competence for high-level jobs with a particular age, accent, sex or colour.

Social preferences

Participating in employment is not an 'all-or-nothing' decision: individuals also determine the amount of time they are prepared to devote to paid work. The allocation of time is affected by 'expected market earnings', taking travel, clothing and taxation into account. Traditionally,

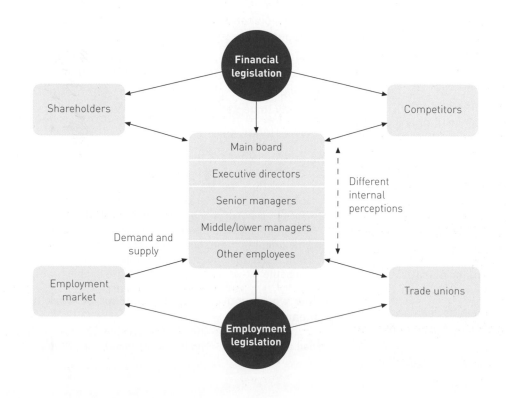

Figure 6.1

Competing influences on job creation within an organization

time given to 'market work' is distinguished from that devoted to any other activity – described as 'leisure'. However, it is recognized that time outside paid work is not necessarily devoted to pleasure. Far from lying on a beach, sipping a cool drink, people spend much of their 'leisure' time on some form of work without pay. This could be housework, maintenance, looking after children, cooking or providing a voluntary service.

Deciding to take a job, or not, involves a trade-off between family members. If an additional member works, there should be a reduction or reallocation of that person's unpaid activities. Employment may change lifestyle significantly. In developed countries this can result in the purchase of labour-saving devices such as a dishwasher, changing from fresh to ready-prepared food and hiring a cleaner or child-minder.

The decision to seek employment can be complex and is likely to be taken in conjunction with other members of the household. The household is viewed as the 'decisionmaking unit'. The household chooses how to allocate its members' time, evaluating the comparative advantages of working as against not working. For example, where the possibility of choice exists, the emphasis can be on working for money in order to buy the largest possible house, a brand new car, expensive holidays and consumer goods such as convenience foods. Alternatively, the

---

HRM in reality Job satisfaction in the UK

Results from a new survey of over 1000 workers for The Work Foundation reveals strikingly positive attitudes towards work but also confirms that work remains simply a way of making a living for many people. Commissioned as part of The Work Foundation's campaign for 'good work' the study found most people feel their work has got better since the beginning of their working lives.

The survey found:

- 60 per cent said their satisfaction with work had increased, 31 per cent felt it had gone down, and 8 per cent said it had stayed the same.

- 78 per cent said they found their work 'stimulating and challenging' (55 per cent agreeing strongly with this statement) and 69 per cent said their work was a 'source of personal fulfilment'.

- 86 per cent did not agree with the statement 'I regard my work as meaningless' with only 9 per cent saying they agreed (the remainder did not express a view).

- Just over half (51 per cent) said their work was 'a means to an end'. People with lower pay and lower skills tended to be less satisfied with their jobs.

- Over three-quarters of respondents described themselves as 'very satisfied' (35 per cent) or 'quite satisfied' (43 per cent) with their current jobs; 10 per cent were neither satisfied nor dissatisfied; 6 per cent were 'quite dissatisfied'; and 5 per cent very dissatisfied.

Will Hutton, chief executive of The Work Foundation, said:

Traditionally, work has been seen as purely a grim economic necessity, which there is no getting out of, and little more to be said about. Our survey indicates that that view is no longer a fair reflection of how people feel. Today, work is increasingly thought of as a source of fulfilment, an important aspect of life that matters to people in a very personal way.

Other key findings in the survey included:

- Women are slightly more likely to be satisfied with their job compared with men.

- The over-55s are more likely to be satisfied with their job compared with younger workers, especially those aged 16–34 years.

- Managers and professionals are more likely to be satisfied compared with other occupational groups.

- People earning over £50 000 per year are more likely to be satisfied than those who earn less.

Will Hutton said:

Employers and organizations are going to have to think much harder about the jobs they offer. The wage packet still matters, but there are crucially important psychological, social and personal dividends from work, too – it is about money and meaning. Well over two-thirds of workers regard work as a source of personal fulfilment to them, but only a very few employers ever succeed in making the most of this huge personal appetite for work that more and more people have.

How would you explain the concept of work having 'meaning'?

Source: *HRM Guide UK* (http://www.hrmguide.co.uk), 29 July, 2006.

household can minimize working time and maximize leisure, making do with a more modest home and car, spending effort on home-grown and prepared food. In a fluid and global economy there are decisions to be made also about relocation. For example, in two French studies Challiol and Mignonac (2005) found strong evidence for decisionmaking based on compromise when dual-earning couples were faced with career opportunities that required one partner to change geographical location.

HRM in reality When work and family conflict, men are more likely than women to leave their jobs

---

Male and female employees are confronted with conflicts between work and family, but men who believe they have a heavy workload are more likely to leave their jobs than their female counterparts. This is the conclusion of a Texas A&M University study, conducted by Ann Huffman, a doctoral student in psychology; Dr Stephanie Payne, a Texas A&M professor of psychology; and Carl Castro of Walter Reed Army Research Institute. Their study examined whether the time demands of a job and perception of workload affected male workers more than women – and if the differences were enough to make male, more than female employees, want to leave their jobs.

'The short answer is "yes," gender does make a difference,' Huffman says.

Their finding was presented at the recent Society for Industrial and Organizational Psychology's annual conference in Orlando.

'I think a lot of the time when people think about work–family conflict, they immediately think of female employees – that they would be the ones to experience the conflict more so than men, but that was not what we found,' Payne says.

According to the researchers, men have significantly higher levels of 'work–family angst' than women. Also men, more than women, believe that long working hours are detrimental to their personal time, are too time-consuming and greater numbers would consider leaving their jobs, in comparison to women.

A partial explanation is that the two sexes have traditionally played different roles. Stephanie Payne says that women are traditionally committed to roles that support the family and although they may be expending a lot of time at work, they can still find the energy for family responsibilities.

Men, on the other hand, are more accustomed to the role of breadwinner and can find it difficult to adapt to increased demands of taking care of family and home, Payne explains.

Nevertheless, more men are being called upon to handle more family responsibilities, whether they are married with a working spouse and have children or they are single dads with child-care concerns, she notes.

'In terms of the way we think of men and women, and the roles they play, we're really not as far along as we would like to think we are when it comes to attitudes about gender. I think when women first started entering the workplace, they probably experienced work–family conflict during this transition, but now with things changing, men are going through this transition and experiencing the same type of conflict,' Huffman says.

She notes that the workplace is changing in increasing magnitude, with men assuming more family responsibilities while women are taking a more active role in the workplace. The potential impact of this one trend alone, she says, is something that more and more organizations are paying attention to. Forward-thinking organizations know employees facing serious work–family conflicts are likely to leave their jobs if the demands interfere too much with their family responsibilities.

Therefore, organizations are working to provide a healthy balance between work and personal life. In fact, one national study found 70 per cent of workers are not satisfied with their work–family balance, and half of those people are considering looking for new jobs because of problems of coping with both personal life and work.

'It seems that organizations will have to take this changing demographic into consideration if they are going to keep their employees productive and happy,' Huffman says.

'In this day and age, the boundaries between work and home are less defined,' Payne says. 'With beepers, cell phones and email people are expected to respond to work demands even when they are physically some place else. The boundaries of "when am I at home and when am I at work" are less clear.'

Why do men seem to have greater difficulties than women in balancing jobs and domestic life?

Source: *HRM Guide USA* (http://www.hrmguide.com), 24 May, 2003.

Doing without paid work in order to maximize free time is an opportunity cost. In other words, if paid work is available, not working has a cost for the household. There may be preferences for particular family members to stay at home – typically mothers – whereas others (fathers) are expected to earn a wage. As we will see later in this chapter, this pattern has changed radically in most industrialized countries in recent years.

Recognition of household preferences is important to people managers because there are strong cultural differences between one region and another. There are considerable pressures on potential and actual workers to behave in the way perceived as normal for their particular society. However, most organizations pay little attention to the domestic influences on an employee's motivation and performance. Employees are recruited and their performance assessed as if they were entirely free agents with no domestic responsibilities or interests outside work.

When is it worthwhile going to work? The total available resources of the household unit may be weighed up in the equation, including the time available for all its members, other income and total wealth. The financial benefit of work can only be gauged when tax, social security deductions, travelling, child-minding costs and so on have been calculated. This benefit may prove insignificant.

Mathematical models have been developed to predict the hours that people are prepared to work. They take into account factors such as the availability of overtime work, the effects of taxation, opportunities for self-employment and payment by results (Sapsford and Tzannatos, 1993, p.27). Empirical studies do not necessarily support this approach – unemployment is an experience that can arrive like a tidal wave. There may be no opportunity to make a free decision on whether or not to work. During a recession, for example, it can be common for both partners in a relationship to lose their jobs in quick succession (Morris, 1987). Women tend to be in highly vulnerable part-time jobs. Morris argues that his research contradicts the notion of the household decisionmaking model. He concludes that such models take no account of the local social network that influences beliefs and expectations of employment. Neither do they accommodate local differences in employment opportunities and cultural ideas of gender behaviour. Job choices also reflect individual career plans and preferences.

Individual preferences

We have seen that people do not behave as mere commodities. Human behaviour involves deep complexities that bring unpredictability and apparent contrariness into the employment market. Most people's motives and ambitions involve much more than seeking the highest salary. Money is important but to a degree that varies between individuals. People will remain in comparatively lowly-paid jobs such as nursing because the satisfaction that comes from helping other people can be valued above a high salary. There has been much criticism of the quality of work offered by the fast-food industry, a major area of youth employment. However, Allan, Bamber and Timo (2006) concluded that employee attitudes towards 'McJobs' were not entirely negative after studying students' perceptions of work in the fast-food sector in Australia. Fast-food workers were generally dissatisfied with industrial relations and work organization, and much more satisfied with human resource management and social relations aspects of their jobs.

An economic model based purely on income will go some way to explain employment behaviour on the large scale but it will not explain *individual* human behaviour. Other motivations come into play in determining people's approach to work. As we can see from Table 6.1, psychologists have attempted to provide explanations at the individual level.

It is common to ask the question: 'What do you do?' For many of us, self-identity is provided by a job. The psychological benefits obtained from work include the fulfilment of social needs such as companionship, group cohesion and a sense of belonging. Kidder (2006) points to the limitations of an economic model to explain employment behaviour using bike messengers as an example. Bike messengers work in a dirty and dangerous occupation with low pay and no benefits. Nevertheless, many messengers consider their occupation to be their primary source of identity. The creativity and spontaneity of courier work allows messengers to become emotionally attached to their job. It brings the thrill-seeking of leisure pursuits into the workplace, which creates an authentic self intimately tied to the occupation, a rare achievement in an increasingly rationalized employment system.

Participating in the employment market

Who is involved in the job market? We have seen that the resourcing of organizations is affected by national or regional availability (supply) and demand for appropriately skilled employees. On the supply side of this balance, people can be divided into three groups, the first two of which are described as '**economically active**' (Key concept 6.3).

Economically inactive people are neither in paid work nor seeking jobs, including people in education, with medical conditions, looking after dependants and the retired. Proportions of these categories vary from country to country, depending on economic conditions and custom. Accurate figures for each group are not easily calculated as our 'HRM in reality'

Factor	Characteristics
Opportunities for control	Limited control over work, or no job at all, leads to higher levels of anxiety, depression, tiredness and psychosomatic symptoms. Also lower general life-satisfaction and self-esteem.
Opportunities for skill use	People benefit from stretching jobs. Morale, self-esteem, sociability and life satisfaction are reduced when a worker's job is de-skilled or lost. Some people can compensate through hobbies or voluntary work, but many are unable to fill the gap.
Goal and task demands	Jobs set demands on our lives in general. Many unemployed people find it hard to fill their time, often spending a high proportion sleeping, sitting around or watching TV, further contributing to lowered morale.
Variety	Work can increase variety, providing a contrast with home life. It also provides the income to pay for experiences such as cinema, music, sporting activities and holidays.
Environmental clarity	Work helps us understand and predict the world around us. Mental health is better if we are clear about our roles and purpose in life. Conversely, uncertainty is detrimental, especially over a lengthy period.
Availability of money	The unemployed have a lower income level (40–60 per cent on average) than those in work. This can make it difficult to repay credit and keeping up mortgage payments, adding further stress. Expensive activities are curtailed, contributing to feelings of isolation and boredom.
Physical security	In western cultures people are brought up to value personal and private space. To provide feelings of personal security, self-worth and well-being they need a home to call their own. This requires an income.
Opportunity for interpersonal contact	Interaction with other people reduces feelings of loneliness and provides emotional support.
Valued social position	Work provides a self-identity and a feeling of worth.

Table 6.1

Psychological benefits of work

Source: Adapted from Warr (1987).

Key concept 6.3 Economically active

The economically active comprise two groups: (a) *the employed* – those in paid work; and (b) *the unemployed* – those who are looking for paid work but are unable to find it.

example on hidden unemployment in Australia shows. In particular, it is difficult to estimate true unemployment because the unemployed are identified on the basis of registration with state agencies. As an illustration, Table 6.2 shows official figures for a number of OECD countries in 2006. Often the registration of individuals as unemployed is linked to the payment of unemployment relief or other social security benefit. If the benefit system is generous, people are more likely to register. Conversely, if benefits are restricted, the registered unemployment figure decreases.

Developed countries have experienced considerable variations in unemployment levels. This is reflected in changes in public expectations and concern over the level of unemployment. It can be argued that more people would work if jobs were easy to find – but they do not search when work is scarce. This has been called the '**discouraged worker hypothesis**' (see Key concept 6.4). Workers calculate the probability of finding a job in relation to the wage they are likely to get and conclude that the effort is not worthwhile. This hypothesis suggests that the number of active jobseekers decreases in times of high unemployment, leaving an unmeasurable hidden unemployment rate behind the official statistics.

Table 6.2		
Country	**Unemployment (%)**	
Australia	5.2	
Belgium	8.2	
Canada	5.7	
Denmark	4.4	
Finland	8.1	
France	9.4	
Germany	9.1	
Ireland	4.2	
Italy	7.7 (Dec 2005)	
Japan	4.2	
Netherlands	4.2	
New Zealand	3.9 (March)	
Norway	3.9	
Poland	16.9	
Portugal	7.7	
Spain	8.2	
Sweden	5.3	
United Kingdom	5.2	
United States of America	4.8	

Comparative levels of unemployment (February 2006)

Sources: OECD, US Dept of Labor, 2006.

> **Key concept 6.4** Discouraged worker hypothesis
>
> Workers calculate the probability of finding a job in relation to the wage they are likely to get and conclude that the effort is not worthwhile.

Organizations in free market countries focus on the external employment market, seeking new staff from outside the business. This is compatible with a competitive market approach in which employees are recruited when needed and dispensed with when no longer required. This view also provides a clear rationale for the 'hard' HRM form of employee planning that we will discuss in a later chapter. In the first chapter of this book we observed that the softer Harvard model of HRM emphasizes commitment between organizations and their employees. The latter approach is more consistent with social market and East Asian capitalist models. In Germany and Japan – together with the ideal organizations of 'soft' HRM rhetoric – the traditional focus has been on the internal employment market with:

- Recruitment taking place almost entirely at the lower levels from the pool of available school-leavers and graduates.
- Organizations offering a structured career on a lifetime basis.
- Little movement, or labour turnover, between organizations.

You will remember from earlier discussions on Japan that, until recently, major Japanese companies offered life-long employment and career development. German organizations emphasize the recruitment of apprentices who will eventually fill middle and senior posts, whereas in free market countries companies advertise vacancies externally at all levels. This has implications on the average job tenure in different countries. An ILO Report (ILO, 2004, p.188), using data from a variety of sources between 1998 and 2004, found that people

> **HRM in reality** Hidden unemployment
>
> Today's official unemployment figures continue to hide the real number of people who want to work in Australia, according to the Brotherhood of St Laurence.
>
> 'The current definition that "one hour's work a week" equals employment produced today's official jobless rate of 5.1 per cent,' Tony Nicholson, Executive Director of the Brotherhood said today. 'At the risk of being predictable, we are compelled to say that this figure paints a misleading picture. Many Australians believe low unemployment means overall prosperity and financial security but today's figure fails to acknowledge the Australian battlers who are struggling against underemployment or those who have given up hope of finding a job.
>
> 'Based on the latest ABS (Australian Bureau of Statistics) figures . . . we believe the real jobless rate is more than twice the size of the official figure when you include those who want more work and those who've given up looking for work altogether.'
>
> UnitingCare Australia National Director, Lin Hatfield Dodds said Australian government figures show 3.6 million Australians live on a household income of less than $400 a week but many of these people are not counted in jobless figures.
>
> 'These people find themselves in low paid, part-time and casual jobs that don't provide enough money each week to cover the basics of food, utilities, medical bills and a roof over their heads," Ms Hatfield Dodds said. 'We want to send a message to our political leaders that for more and more Australians, a decent life is a pipe dream because they are caught in jobs that do not provide them with the means to offer a decent life for them and their families.
>
> 'With welfare reform on the National Agenda, we call on the Australian government to engage with those of us who work daily with Australia's forgotten jobless.'
>
> **Are official unemployment figures misleading?**
>
> Source: *HRM Guide Australia* (http://www.hrmguide.net/australia/), 10 March, 2005.

stayed with one employer for an average of 12.2 years in Japan, 11.2 years in France and 10.6 years in Germany. This compared with 8.2 years in the UK and 6.6 years in the USA.

Trends and levels vary significantly between public and private sectors. At the end of the 20th century, public sector tenure levels were over twice those of the private sector. This may be partly explained by the tendency of government workers to be older than their counterparts in private industry. Also, there is less likelihood of public sector employees being laid off or being affected by cyclical factors to the degree experienced by private sector workers – for example those in construction or wholesale and retail trade.

Intriguingly, the archetypal East Asian economy, Singapore, has seen high rates of employee turnover to match its remarkable growth rate due to competition for scarce skills. Similarly, Japanese companies have changed their traditional practices to attract electronics experts with premium technological skills.

Projections of the future size of the employment market are critical to planned economic development. On a local basis, individual companies need to anticipate the availability of suitable recruits to meet business planning needs. These are normally calculated from:

- **Demographic trends** (Key concept 6.5), including the birth rate at least 16 years previously.

- Retirement rates (in the last few decades there has been a pronounced trend towards earlier retirement in developed countries – see Table 6.3).

- Numbers of people in higher education.

Reductions in demand for manual work have seen many unskilled workers leaving the employment market. In the UK, the Institute of Public Policy Research found that the

---

HRM in reality London worst region in the UK for unemployment

The rate of unemployment in London is 7.6 per cent (January to March) according to the Labour Force Survey. This is almost 1 percentage point higher than the next region, the North East of England which has a rate of 6.7 per cent for the same period. The UK national average for January–March is 5.2 per cent. London's total of 301 000 unemployed is more than the totals for Wales, Scotland and Northern Ireland added together, more than the entire English Midlands and more than the North West and North East of England combined.

There are enormous variations between the different boroughs in London, however. A letter from Karen Dunnell, national statistician, dated January 18, 2006, gave a response to a parliamentary question. She listed the numbers of claimants for Jobseekers allowance who had been out of work for two years or more in the London boroughs. They ranged from 5 in the city of London, 60 in Kingston-upon-Thames, 65 in Hounslow and 80 in Richmond to 710 in Brent, 740 in Haringey, 805 in Tower Hamlets and a whopping 1160 in Southwark.

Unemployment in the UK, January–March 2006, by country/region

Country/region	LFS unemployed (1000's)	Rate of unemployment (%)
N. Ireland	35	4.4
London	301	7.6
Scotland	139	5.3
West Midlands	137	5.1
North East	82	6.7
North West	163	4.9
Yorks/Humberside	134	5.3
Wales	65	4.7
East Midlands	111	4.9
South East	191	4.4
South West	92	3.6
East	138	4.8

Source: Adapted from ONS Labour Market Statistics, June 2006 (seasonally adjusted).

What explanations can you suggest for the differences in regional unemployment?

Source: *HRM Guide UK* (http://www.hrmguide.co.uk), 19 June, 2006.

Country	1960–61	1994	% decrease
Australia	79.6	48.7	39
Austria	66.0	12.7	81
Finland	79.1	23.9	69
France	71.1	18.2	74
Germany	72.5	34.9	51
Italy	70.1	37.2	46
Japan	81.9	75.6	8
Netherlands	80.8	18.0	88
Sweden	82.5	57.8	29
United Kingdom	87.4 (est.)	52.2	40
United States of America	77.1	54.9	29

Table 6.3

Percentage of older males in the workforce (aged 60–64)

Source: 1994 figures copyright © 1995 International Labour Organization.

HRM in reality Living longer, working longer

People in developed countries are living longer and many are working well past traditional retirement age. Some are even returning to work after 'retiring' and/or opting for 'portfolios' of paid and volunteer positions, according to a recent MetLife Mature Market Institute® study, *Living Longer, Working Longer: The Changing Landscape of the Aging Workforce*, conducted by David DeLong & Associates, Inc. and Zogby International.

'Today, older workers view retirement as a desirable state, not a particular date,' said Dr David DeLong, author of *Lost Knowledge: Confronting the Threat of an Aging Workforce* and a research fellow at the MIT AgeLab. 'When we conducted the study, we found that mature workers are struggling to balance the conflicting pressures of income security, post-retirement-age employment and, often, age discrimination – perceived or real – as they look for a sense of security and meaning during their "retirement" years.'

This study is unusual in that it examines the actual work experiences of 2719 employees aged 55–70 whereas most other studies offer predictions of ageing baby boomers' retirement expectations. The MetLife study shows that the following percentages of respondents are working or looking for work:

- 78 per cent of respondents age 55–59
- 60 per cent of 60–65 year-olds, and
- 37 per cent of 66–70 year-olds.

Around 15 per cent of employees across all three age groups have accepted retirement benefits from previous employers, but have chosen to return to work (or are looking for work). These 'working retired', represent:

- 11 per cent of 55–59 year-olds
- 16 per cent of 60–65 year-olds
- 19 per cent of 66–70 year-olds.

Motivations to Work
There are significant differences between age groups when it comes to the motivation to work. Employees aged 55–59 cited economic incentives as the major motive, with 72 per cent of this group saying that 'need income to live on' was their primary reason for working. Sixty per cent of 60–65 year-olds also cited this as their main motivation, followed by a desire to 'stay active and engaged' (54 per cent) and 'do meaningful work' (43 per cent). However, 72 per cent of 66–70 year-olds cited the desire to 'stay active and engaged' as their primary reason to work, followed by 'the opportunity to do meaningful work' (47 per cent) and 'social interaction with colleagues' (42 per cent).

What does 'retirement' mean?
Respondents in the MetLife study cited the following definitions of retirement:

▶

- 'freedom from the demands of work' (26 per cent)
- 'more control over one's personal time' (24 per cent)
- 'limited financial concerns' (21 per cent)
- 'the ability to pursue other opportunities'

'As organizations seek to attract and retain older workers, they must be careful not to lump all "older workers" into the same category – it's important to differentiate the work experiences and motivations of these employees. While some may be working for financial reasons, others place a special premium on feeling engaged and doing work that means something,' says Sandra Timmermann, Ed.D., gerontologist and director of the MetLife Mature Market Institute. 'Recruiting and retaining older workers requires careful consideration of job design, work environment, and creating new and challenging opportunities.'

What motivates the 'working retired'?

Twenty per cent of working retireds age 60–65 said they 'wanted to try something new and different'. However, this option was cited by only 12 per cent of 55–59 year-olds and 7 per cent of 66–70 year-olds. 19 per cent of 66–70 year-olds cited 'becoming self-employed or starting a business' compared with 7 per cent of 60–65 year-olds and 8 per cent of 55–59 year-olds.

Twenty-eight per cent of respondents aged 55–59 said they were 'self-employed or business owner.' This increased to 36 per cent of 60–65 year-olds and 42 per cent of 66–70 year-olds.

'Clearly, these findings suggest there are conditions in the job market and in older workers' desire for autonomy and flexibility that make self-employment an attractive option for those in their late sixties,' said Dr DeLong. 'As the oldest boomers turn 60 in 2006, their desire for autonomy and trying new things could portend a significant wave of departures in the next five years. Employers will need to identify ways to retain the valuable knowledge of these workers.'

Financial reality

Financial necessity underlies the need to work for many older employees. Eighteen per cent of baby boom workers aged 55–59 said that they expected to have no access to retirement benefits (e.g., pension, 401(k), SEP) and are likely to feel compelled to work beyond traditional retirement age. Fourteen per cent of those aged 60–65 and 10 per cent aged 66–70 expected to receive nothing but Social Security when they finally cease working.

'Retirement experts have been predicting for years the serious repercussions that will arise as baby boomers' lack of retirement assets collides with their increased longevity to create widespread economic hardship. The rational solution – to continue working full-time beyond traditional retirement age – is at odds with many boomers' interests, values and priorities for their retirement,' notes Dr Timmermann.

Some other survey findings

Age discrimination. Older workers frequently cited 'age bias' as a reason for unsuccessful job searches, including:

- 39 per cent of 55–59 year-olds
- 42 per cent of 60–65 year-olds
- 60 per cent of 66–70 year-olds

Preference for part-time work. Of those still in employment, 76 per cent of 55–59 year-olds worked more than 35 hours a week, compared with only 39 per cent of 66–70 year-olds.

Portfolio work. Interviews were also conducted for the study, in which some older employees said their lives had taken on a 'portfolio quality' – mixing part-time paid work, volunteer work, and travel, together with more time for hobbies and family. In fact, 25 per cent of survey respondents across all age groups had more than one paid job with about 20 per cent of those working having two jobs, and another 4 per cent having three jobs.

Why are some older people keen to work while others are not?

Source: *HRM Guide USA* (http://www.hrmguide.com/), 16 April, 2006.

proportion of men of working age in employment fell from 91 per cent in 1977 to 80 per cent in 1992. But 10 years later there had been little change with 79.3 per cent in employment during April–June 2002. Ranzijn *et al.* (2006) studied the impact of mature-aged unemployment on individuals in Adelaide, South Australia and suggest that their quality of life is substantially impaired. Frustration at being unable to contribute to society, support adult children, and use skills can lead to the 'peg-down' phenomenon, described as an intermediate step between becoming unemployed and premature exit from the workforce.

Key concept 6.5 Demographic trends

Long-term changes in the overall population level and age distribution in countries, regions and localities due to variations in birth, death and migration. These changes affect the availability of employable people.

Employee supply and demand

Individuals determine how much time they will devote to paid work for a variety of reasons. The proportion of people of working age in work, or seeking jobs, is described as the labour force participation rate. In the year 2000, for example, 64.7 per cent of the working-age population of Australia were in work or seeking jobs. This compared with 65.9 per cent in Canada, 62.0 per cent in Japan, 63.5 per cent in the Netherlands, 63.3 per cent in the United Kingdom and 67.2 per cent in the United States of America.

The flow of young people into the workforce is fundamental to the employment market. The underlying demographic pattern is changing throughout the world. Whereas most developing countries have seen an explosion of growth in the youngest age groups, the developed world is experiencing a reduction in birth rate. This follows a baby boom after World War II which produced a wave of people who will mostly retire in the first quarter of the 21st century. In western Europe and North America, numbers of people entering the employment market have been falling. This will reduce the overall size of their workforces, shifting the age balance towards older employees. This has been compensated by a massive increase in working women, especially in part-time jobs.

HRM in reality Migrants boost labour market

In the period from May 2004 to June 2006, 447 000 people from EU accession states applied to the Worker Registration Scheme and just over 427 000 were approved. Including freelance workers, such as builders, the total number from accession states is believed to be around 600 000. Few brought families with them, an estimated 36 000 dependants are believed to have accompanied migrant workers. Home Office minister Tony McNulty said these new workers were filling a gap in the labour market that could not be met from those born in the UK.

A total of 137 000 work permit holders and their families were admitted to the UK in 2005, an increase of 10 per cent over the previous year. The number of foreign nationals settling in the UK increased by 29 per cent to 179 210. During the same period, 58 215 people were removed from the UK, a decrease of 5 per cent over 2004. Tony McNulty stated that the government is committed to ensuring that those entering the UK will benefit the economy. He pointed out that the government's recently announced points-based immigration system will help control migration more effectively. 'It will allow only those people with the skills the UK needs to come to this country, while preventing those without skills applying' he said.

John Philpott, chief economist at the CIPD, argued that today's Home Office figures reinforce the need for a clear restatement of government policy on mass economic migration, and a thorough independent cost/benefit analysis. He argued that this is the 'only way to restore public confidence and bring a much needed sense of balance to a debate on immigration policy which tends to swing from one extreme ("the open door") to another ("the raised drawbridge")'.

John Philpott continued:

Since EU enlargement in 2004 the CIPD has been one of the few organizations to highlight that large scale migration from the new member states of central and eastern Europe imposes costs on the UK as well as bringing benefits. Employers, consumers and migrants are the main beneficiaries with less skilled workers, the core jobless and poorer communities – often themselves with high concentrations of disadvantaged ethnic minorities – bearing the brunt of the cost. This is because, contrary to common perception, the vast majority of migrants enter low skilled low paid

▶

employment. The CIPD has in turn drawn attention to the significant, though limited, role recent EU migration has played in the overall rise in UK unemployment since the end of 2004, contrary to the conclusion of government economists that there has been no identifiable impact.

John Philpott said the CIPD believed that on balance the benefits of mass economic migration from accession states have outweighed the cost. It has helped keep wage inflation under control and enabled a faster rate of economic growth than would otherwise have occurred. CIPD research shows that one-third of UK organizations employ workers from accession countries. Key reasons for hiring them are their willingness to work and skill levels. The CIPD remains concerned about mitigating the costs, for example, by improved education and welfare to work measures for unemployed UK nationals.

Tony McNulty confirmed that the government is 'yet to take a decision as to what access Bulgarian and Romanian nationals will have to our labour market when they join the EU'. Any decision on that issue will be based on objective factors, including an evaluation of the UK labour market and the position of other EU member states.

John Philpott said it should not be a forgone conclusion that restrictions should be placed on further migration from new EU countries. He continued:

If restrictions on migrants are deemed necessary for labour market or other reasons these should be imposed on less skilled migrants from outside the EU, which would demonstrate that the UK remains at the forefront of promoting the wider economic objective of a single European labour market and increased labour mobility within the EU (matching that found in the United States of America).

But in making any policy decision it is vital that the government conducts and publishes a – preferably fully independent – analysis of the total costs and benefits of overall migration to the UK. This would not only inform and instil a sense of balance in public debate but also improve the chances of achieving a much needed cross party political consensus on immigration policy in an increasingly global economy.

Is immigration always beneficial to a country's job market?

Source: *HRMGuide.co.uk* (http://www.hrmguide.co.uk) 23 August, 2006.

Key demographic trends include the following:

- Populations in developed countries are stabilizing or declining. Birth rates are tending to fall below replenishment rates.

- Ageing populations in 'first world' countries may be counterbalanced by immigration.

- Developing countries experience a period of rapid population growth as infant mortality rates are reduced – well in advance of birth control measures being adopted.

- Most developing countries experience population pressure for decades until stability is achieved.

- The population balance will change markedly between the developed and developing world. Eventually the developed world will decline in importance, in line with their reduced working population.

Employee demand

Employee demand is linked to the economic cycle, increasing in boom times and decreasing in recession. Other factors include the adoption of new technology, productivity improvements and changing skill requirements. Superficially, calculating employment supply and demand seems easy. In practice, the combination of variable consumer demand, development of new products and technology, and **economic turbulence** make it extremely problematic. In the last decade, for example, commentators have confidently predicted both permanently high levels of unemployment *and* shortages of labour.

As we observed in the last chapter, the role of the state is important in this respect: through fiscal or monetary policy, governments can directly increase or diminish consumption and economic activity. Such actions lead quickly to changes in demand for human resources as firms relate their requirements to production or provision of services. Activity in service and manufacturing services may follow different patterns. The decline in manufacturing in the UK, for example, has been dismissed as unimportant by some commentators who believed that production jobs would be replaced by new work in financial and other services. The reality is that these sectors have proven incapable of generating enough employment to compensate for the loss of full-time jobs in manufacturing. As we shall see shortly, there has been a widespread trend for well-paid jobs to be replaced with low-paid, part-time work.

Active labour market programmes

Active labour market programmes (ALMPs) are government initiatives to reduce unemployment and increase participation in the employment market. They include public works, training and retraining, job search assistance, support for self-employment or new enterprises, and wage subsidies (Dar and Tzannatos, 1999). Such programmes are justified in a variety of

---

HRM in reality Employers struggling to find and keep employees

A survey by Hewitt Associates, a global HR services company, has found that big and small organizations in all industries throughout Canada are finding it challenging to attract and retain workers. Most of the 232 employers in the survey are focusing on flexibility as a means of addressing the problem.

While three-quarters of Canadian companies are finding difficulties in attracting or retaining employees, 44 per cent have problems with both. The situation is worst in Alberta where 97 per cent of respondents were having difficulties and almost two-thirds reported that both attraction and retention were challenging. With an ageing workforce – half are over 40 – the problem can only get worse.

According to Cathy Course, a senior benefits consultant in Hewitt's Calgary office: 'Canadian employers understand that they will all soon be facing the labour shortages companies in Alberta are already experiencing. As a result, we're working with HR professionals across the country to look at new ways to adapt workplace policies and practices to appeal to workers in a competitive environment.'

Flexibility offers a solution, according to the survey. More than half (52 per cent) of respondents said that flexible hours and benefits will help attract and keep the best employees.

John Tompkins, a principal in Hewitt's Toronto benefits consulting group says that: 'Organizations are beginning to realize the need to convince older workers to stay on the job longer. At the same time, they want to convince Generation X and Y employees – those under age 40 – to join them. With an employee population so diverse in terms of age, a "one size fits all" approach is no longer effective. Employers who can identify and meet the different needs of their employees will be most successful in the current labour market.'

Hewitt's survey indicates that 55 per cent of organizations are intending to introduce formal phased retirement programmes, offering shorter working weeks for older employees near retirement, by 2009. This compares with the 26 per cent that have such schemes at present. Additionally, there is increasing interest in offering other flexible arrangements such as:

- Job sharing
- Flexible hours
- Compressed work schedules
- Vacation buying and selling
- Working from home
- Elder care support
- Wellness accounts
- Unpaid time off for charitable work
- Assistance with home technology purchases.

Hewitt advises employers to take a disciplined approach to such working arrangements. 'Employers need to balance their need to have the right talent with the reality of their financial situation. We recommend organizations undergo a process to audit their current talent pool, assess their future workforce needs, and then determine what they want to change and how that fits within their budget,' said Cathy Course.

'Workers need to really understand the value of what employers are providing over and above wages and salary,' she said. 'With the labour shortage, organizations can't afford to lose employees because they don't know the extent of their full compensation package.'

Can retaining older employees in work solve the skills crisis?

Source: *HRM Guide Canada* (http://www.hrmguide.net/canada/), 20 June, 2006.

ways. For example, the provision of public works is a demand side intervention, whereas training is intended to have an effect on supply side skills availability. However, all such interventions are based on the assumption that the employment market is failing in some way or that the social outcomes (particularly unemployment) are unacceptable.

Dar and Tzannatos (1999) review 100 evaluations of such programmes undertaken in OECD and developing countries (including Turkey, Hungary, Poland, the Czech Republic and Mexico) and draw some general conclusions:

- Public works may help the most disadvantaged groups such as older workers, the long-term unemployed, and people in distressed regions by acting as a poverty/safety net. However, they are ineffective in providing a channel into permanent employment.

- Job search assistance programmes have a greater positive impact and are more cost-effective than other ALMPs. They are most effective when the general economic climate is favourable. However, they do not appear to significantly improve either the employment prospects or wages of young jobseekers.

- Training for the long-term unemployed is useful when the economy is improving. The best returns are offered by small-scale, tightly targeted on-the-job training programmes, especially those aimed at women and older groups. In general, however, they are rarely cost-effective and no more successful than job search assistance programmes in terms of post-programme placement and wages.

- Mass retraining for redundant workers is usually ineffective and, as in the case of the long-term unemployed, is also more expensive and no more effective than job-search assistance.

HRM in reality Toronto surveys people who left Ontario Works

In May 2002, a Toronto City survey of people leaving social assistance shows that they still face a poverty trap from which it is difficult to escape.

Toronto's Social Services Division commissioned the random telephone survey of more than 800 people who left Ontario Works (OW) in the first quarter of 2001 to find out how they fared, and whether they were better off after leaving. The survey indicates that people were not significantly better off than they were while on OW, or than they were five years ago. The survey data revealed three key findings: 77 per cent of survey respondents worked at some point after leaving OW; just 43 per cent said their finances had improved; and 17 per cent returned to OW in 2001 (a third of these were ill or disabled).

'Having a skilled workforce is vital to Toronto's economic health and development,' said Councillor Brad Duguid, Ward 38 Scarborough Centre, Chair of the Community Services Committee. 'We encourage senior levels of government to re-invest in strategies that recognize education, supports and skills upgrading for people on social assistance. Not only do people need to connect to the labour market, they need to secure stable jobs and increase their earning potential over time.'

Education is a key factor in determining who is likely to return to OW – returners in 2001 were more likely to have less than a high school education. And 38 per cent of survey respondents said they required access to education and skills upgrading to help them keep their current job or find a better one. Unfortunately, funding cuts at both federal and provincial levels over the last five years have substantially reduced access to education and training.

'Many people can't break the cycle of moving back and forth between social assistance and marginal employment,' said Heather MacVicar, general manager of Social Services. 'While our clients obtain jobs, they are typically unstable and low paying with few benefits. Our survey finds that our clients want to work, and most of them use at least one job-related service that the City provides.'

What factors limit the success of welfare-to-work initiatives?

Source: *HRM Guide Canada* (http://www.hrmguide.net/canada/), 29 May, 2002.

- Training for young people has no positive impact on either their employment prospects or post-training earnings. Such programmes generally offer a negative return on the investment.

- Start-up assistance for small businesses is usually taken up by a small proportion of the unemployed and the failure rate of these businesses is high. Targeting at women and older individuals increases the likelihood of success.

- Wage subsidy programmes are unlikely to be effective and may be exploited by unscrupulous employers.

Part-time and temporary working

Part-time employees contract to work for anything less than normal full-time basic hours. Advantages to employers can include: more intensive work with less time used for breaks; lower absenteeism; enthusiasm and commitment can be higher (less opportunity for boredom); and less unionization among part-time staff.

The main forms of part-time work include:

- *Classical.* Work that does not require full-time cover, typically restricted to a few hours each day. For example, cleaning offices, or staffing a canteen.

- *Supplementary.* Where a part-time worker replaces overtime and for example, performs an evening shift, or works short days to cover peak periods.

- *Substitution.* In which part-timers replace full-timers through job-splitting. It is common for older workers to be retained as part-timers before full retirement.

More recent types of part-time work include key working and job sharing. Key working is typically found in service industries such as retailing. Service work differs from 'traditional' work. Peak activity occurs on days and at times when other workers are at leisure. Peak times may be so short that it is impossible for an employer to use full-time workers effectively. In these circumstances few 'core' full-timers are required. Correspondingly, a large number of 'peripheral' part-timers work at busy periods. Peripheral numbers can be shrunk or expanded as required. This allows greater flexibility than would be possible for a completely full-time workforce.

Job sharing is where two people are responsible for one full-time job, dividing pay and benefits in proportion to the hours worked. Days or weeks may be split or alternate weeks worked. An advantage for some employees, job sharing can also benefit employers. For example:

- Sharers can overlap hours so that busy periods receive double cover.

- Jobs are at least partly covered when one person is away through illness or annual leave.

- Two individuals can bring greater experience and a broader range of views to a job than a single employee.

Job sharing allows skilled people to be retained if they give up full-time employment. However, there are some disadvantages such as:

- Training, induction and administration overheads for two people.

- Finding a suitable partner with matching skills and availability if one sharer leaves.

- Communication on tasks that cannot be dealt with quickly ('hand-over' problems).

- Responsibility for staff can be problematic; people may find difficulty in working for two supervisors.

- Fair allocation of work.

Part-time workers come especially from specific groups, including:

Female parents with children. The largest group, typically working when children are at school.

Retired or semi-retired. Supplementing pensions, filling time and using their skills. Again, they tend to work during the day.

Moonlighters. With full-time jobs elsewhere, supplementing income in the evening or at weekends. For instance, driving mini-cabs, delivering free newspapers or bar work.

Students. Supplementing grants or servicing loans by delivering papers, pizzas, serving in fast-food outlets. They may also work in vacation periods or undertake seasonal work, for example, in the tourist industry.

Paradoxically, many managers question part-timers' commitment, seeing them as being primarily home-oriented. They are often excluded from interesting and senior positions. Part-time workers tend to get fewer training and promotion opportunities. Some managers have contradictory beliefs about women part-timers. On the one hand they believe them to be reliable, loyal and flexible. At the same time, they consider that they take time off to be with children and give precedence to partners' careers.

Temporary workers

It is frequently assumed that temporary job contracts are increasing but this statement 'needs to be heavily qualified' (Martin and Stancanelli, 2002). An analysis of 1985–2000 data from 13 OECD countries shows that the proportion of temporary employment in total salaried employment has risen (on average) by less than 3 per cent. France, Italy, the Netherlands and Spain are responsible for much of this less-than-massive increase. In five other countries, the proportion actually decreased. Countries in this category include the USA. Martin and Stancanelli (*ibid.*) suggest that 'one reason for the low recourse to temporary work in the United States may be that US permanent positions are less rigidly protected than in Europe, for instance, so there is less incentive for employers to offer temporary contracts.' On the other side of the Atlantic, Biggs (2006) analyzed data from the employment agency industry plus Labour Force Surveys from 1997–2004 to reveal a reduction of over 250 000 temporary workers in the UK over a six-year period. Regional variations were apparent, with increases in Northern Ireland and Wales. This was thought to reflect the impact of new legislation and a stable economy.

The largest temporary staff agency, Manpower Inc. places 2 million people in jobs in a year, over 40 per cent of whom go on to permanent employment. More than 10 per cent of workers in the EU have temporary jobs, with the highest level (30 per cent) in Spain. A UK Labour Force Survey found that 1.6 million British workers were employed on a temporary basis.

Forde and Slater (2006) examined Labour Force Survey data on agency workers in the UK and found no evidence of a relationship between the use of agency workers and the growth of the 'knowledge economy'. Instead, their use seems to be governed by short-term issues and the need to keep labour costs down – although the long-term costs may be higher than using permanent staff. Forde and Slater's analysis of occupations found that people in managerial occupations were significantly less likely to be in agency employment and there was only an insignificant positive relationship between professional and associate professional occupations with agency employment. This contrasted with data for clerical, personal and protective, operative and other occupations where there was a significant relationship with agency working suggesting that agency work was most closely related to low-paying entry-jobs in the service sector.

Additionally, there are commitment issues to consider: 50 per cent of agency workers were found to be involuntary, i.e. they could not find a permanent job. Only 30 per cent were agency workers because they did not want permanent employment. Druker and Stanworth (2004) found that employers expected agency workers to show loyalty, commitment and high levels of motivation but the employers gave little in return. Forde and Slater's (*ibid.*) data indicate agency workers' comparatively high levels of dissatisfaction about the content of their work and opportunities for using their initiative. Longer-term contracts and the possibility that permanent jobs might improve levels of commitment, they conclude. Hall (2006) comes to similar conclusions in a study of agency workers in Australia. Comparing attitudes and preferences of agency workers with permanent employees, he found agency workers to be no more satisfied with their level of flexibility than direct workers. Moreover, agency workers were less satisfied with their pay, job security, use and development of skills, autonomy and influence at work. Hall concludes that, in fact, the use of agency workers may be incompatible with human resource strategies based on high performance work practices.

Apart from the familiar 'temps' obtained from specialist agencies, two other groups of temporary workers can be highlighted; **contingent employees** and seasonal employees:

Contingent employees. In the UK there are 500 000 professional and highly-skilled people working on temporary contracts. For example, 'interim managers'. These are generally freelance executives aged over 40. Most assignments last for 40–80 days, allowing for short-term problems to be handled without long-term commitment to expensive staff. Specialist expertise can be bought in for specific tasks or projects. Contingent managers have been rated highly in functions such as human resources, finance, information technology, marketing, operations and property.

Seasonal employment. Seasonal workers are hired to cope with fluctuations in demand – to keep down stock volumes, and hence cost. For example, the chocolate industry has especially high periods of demand at times when gifts are commonly given, such as Christmas.

From the employee's point of view, part-time or temporary work may be both convenient and attractive to many people. McDonald, Bradley and Guthrie (2006) studied a group of 275 working mothers and found that nearly two-thirds of those working full time would prefer to work part time. The major reasons for not acting on this preference were the nature of the job and lack of available career opportunities for part-time employees.

For most people, however, part-time jobs are no substitute for the loss of full-time jobs but the 20th century concept of the nine-to-five job and a lifetime career may be disintegrating in favour of much more flexible arrangements. Levels of insecurity and stress are rising as people have increasingly uncertain working lives. It has become a truism that most people will experience at least two or three careers in their lifetime. Handy (1989, p.46) sees work becoming part of a portfolio of activities. At any one time, individuals may have a number of part-time jobs, together with leisure or study periods. Flexibility and career development will be further explored in Chapter 7.

Summary

In this chapter we discussed some important features of the employment market. We considered factors which lead to people seeking work and joining that market. We examined key economic and psychological concepts and identified a number of links with fundamental elements of HRM. Participation in the job market was investigated, comparing rates in different countries. Different working patterns were described as a prelude for later discussion of flexibility.

Further reading

The range of books on the employment market is vast but tends towards political or economic analysis. The following books are of particular interest. *Unemployment: Macroeconomic Performance and the Labour Market* by Richard Layard (Oxford University Press, 2005) takes a broad view of unemployment and looks at the lessons of experience and theory.

The End of Work: The Decline of the Global Labor Force and the Dawn of the Post-market Era by Jeremy Rifkin (Jeremy P. Tarcher, 2004) is an updated American classic presenting a critique of the way employment figures are calculated. *Employment and the Family: The Reconfiguration of Work and Family Life in Contemporary Societies* by Rosemary Crompton (Cambridge University Press, 2006) takes a gender and comparative perspective on the way employment has changed in recent years.

Review questions

1 How is it possible to regard jobs as being in a market? Discuss the usefulness of the competitive market model in describing the ways in which the employment market functions in the real world.

2 Summarize the main differences between competitive market and institutional models of the employment market. How do competitive and institutional models of the job market relate to 'hard' and 'soft' versions of HRM?

3 Describe in your own words what is meant by the 'labour force participation rate'.

4 To what extent do people behave as individuals – as opposed to households – when they seek work? Consider your family, relatives or friends as examples.

5 Is full employment a practical goal for every country?

6 What is the relationship between levels of welfare payment or unemployment benefit and the level of employment?

7 How will demographic trends affect employment in your country in the 21st century?

8 Outline the advantages and disadvantages of part-time jobs for employers and employees.

9 Why has the introduction of new technology not led to a 'leisure revolution'?

10 Summarize the advantages and disadvantages of 'active labour market programmes'.

Case studies for discussion and analysis

Rob's career/Jefford Trading

1 Rob is a student on placement with a thriving media marketing company. As an intern, he enjoys the challenges of dealing with customers and other staff. He prefers work to university where, academically, he is an average performer. Rob enjoys some parts of his course but dreads other aspects – particularly the end of semester assessments. He was pushed into higher education by an ambitious father whose own career was limited by his lack of qualifications. Personally, Rob cannot wait to complete the course and get on with his career.

Rob's placement company has lost a number of key staff to a competitor. Senior managers have looked at the younger staff and highlighted Rob as a potential high-flyer. He has the energy and the enthusiasm to cope with the long hours and the considerable travelling required. They have offered Rob a higher level position which is now vacant. The rewards are high and the prospects for the next few years are excellent. However, Rob has been told that he cannot accept this position and return to full-time education to complete his final year.

Rob has to make a choice quickly. What factors should he take into account in making his decision?

2 Jefford Trading is a medium-sized business selling high quality designer furnishings. Originally started 20 years ago from one small shop, Jan and Keith Jefford have built the company into a multi-shop retailer with ventures around the country. In the last three years business has become a struggle: other firms have entered the same market and rental and other costs have risen sharply. The company continues to make a profit but further expansion will be hard work.

There are 57 employees. Apart from the founders there is one other director, Paul Stevens the company secretary (49), who looks after major contracts and personnel. He is competent but not ambitious. There are five middle managers, all graduates under 35 picked by Paul, with responsibilities for buying, logistics, finance, marketing and retailing respectively. The logistics and retail managers are responsible for most of the staff. Junior managers run the shops, all without higher education qualifications but keen. The other head office staff are of mixed ages with little potential for advancement.

The Jeffords have worked long hours developing the company, taking few holidays and little money out of the company. Keith is 48, looks much older and has some health problems. Jan is 43, more determined, but worried about her husband. The managers have suggested that they take over the running of the company, allowing the owners to sit back and enjoy life.

The Jeffords' accountants have little faith in the managers: they believe them to be too young and inexperienced. The accountants have advised the sale of the company and investment of the proceeds. The Jeffords accept this is sensible advice but would prefer to keep the company going.

You have been brought in as a consultant to advise them. What would you do?

Activity brief

How would you conduct your investigation?

What are the options?

What do you anticipate your recommendations to be?

How are the Jeffords likely to react?

Part three
Organizational HRM

This part of the book examines HRM within the organization. Human resource practices are enabled and constrained by a variety of organizational factors, including organizational size, structure, culture and employee commitment.

The chapters in Part three address a number of specific issues:

- What are the different structures found within organizations and what effect do they have on human resource management practices?

- Are there any significant differences between people management practices in small and large organizations?

- What are entrepreneurs like as people managers?

- How do organizations grow and what are the implications on HRM?

- How do national business cultures impact on international HRM?

- What is the relationship between corporate culture and human resource management?

- What is employee commitment and how is it achieved?

- Is employee branding a road to commitment or a method of brainwashing employees?

- How do we manage professionals without losing their trust and commitment?

Chapter 7
HRM in large organizations

Learning objectives

The purpose of this chapter is to:

- Investigate why organizations structure their people management systems in different ways.

- Determine the influence of organizational goals on the management of human resources.

- Outline the advantages and disadvantages of alternative organizational structures.

- Compare and contrast the work of human resource specialists in different forms of organization.

Introduction

This is a world of organizations: more and more elements of life that were once matters of personal action are now integrated into organizational frameworks. Modern society depends on people working together effectively to solve problems and achieve objectives that are beyond the scope of individuals. It is a truism to say, therefore, that all people management takes place within organizations. But what are they? We talk about familiar corporations such as Microsoft, the BBC and Sony as if they were objects. Yet we cannot see them in their totality. We recognize them as entities but they are also intangible: 'Although organizations are real in their consequences, both for their participants and for their environments, they are essentially abstractions. They cannot be picked up and dropped, felt, or fulfil any of the other tests that we apply to physical things' (Butler, 1991, p.1).

The very idea of something, which everyone is aware of but no-one can fully grasp, is fascinating in itself. It has spawned an entire field of academic enquiry – organization theory. Whitley (2003, p.483) states that:

> From being a collection of rather uncoordinated research areas within sociology, psychology and other academic disciplines, the study of organizations became a distinct intellectual endeavour with its own journals, training programmes and teaching positions in major US universities in the 1960s and 1970s.

Initially it focused on formal structures, developing early work by Weber and others on the notion of 'bureaucracy', but the field has since diversified considerably. Where books on organization used to focus inwardly on structured – almost mechanical – management systems, seemingly ignoring environmental pressures, modern approaches are more likely to consider social networking, telecommunications and **outsourcing** as major features of business organization. Key concept 7.1 outlines some of the main characteristics identified by organization theorists. In this chapter we focus on how they can be understood in terms that have meaning for people managers.

Key concept 7.1 Organizations

Organizations are the means by which human and other resources are deployed so that work gets done. They can be defined by a number of characteristics:

- They are social entities created by humans.
- They have purpose expressed in the form of common goals.
- They are unrestricted in range – from corner shops to multinational corporations.
- Each organization has a boundary – but not necessarily a geographical or physical boundary – that leads to inclusion of some people and exclusion of others.
- Within this boundary, people are patterned into a structure composed of formal and informal relationships.

First, we must recognize that the term 'organization' is wide-ranging: it can be used to describe bodies as disparate as Toyota and scout troops. For our purposes, the concept has to be defined more narrowly. The key lies with the nature of control within organizations functioning on business lines, exercised through the employment relationship between staff and management and integration with internal and external parties. Business organizations such as Volvo or News International are set apart from 'social arrangements' – for example lunch clubs or photographic societies – by a preoccupation with controlled performance (Huczynski and Buchanan, 2000, p.10). They are set financial, service or production targets that determine the activities of their employees and external providers. People managers have a critical role in monitoring and controlling performance in order to achieve these targets. In the first part of this book we stressed that HRM is a 'holistic' approach to people management. To make the best use of an organization's human resources, it is necessary to manage not only its people but also its corporate structure and culture.

Organizations are highly complex, and not amenable to simple analysis, but managers must attempt to predict and control their activities in order to conduct business. Stewart (1993, p.3) explains the value of theoretical understanding to practising managers:

> . . . even the most practical managers can think about a problem more easily if they have some frame of reference that will help them to decide what kind of problem it is. . . . Organizations are highly complex. We do not understand enough about how they work to have developed comprehensive theories. Instead we have a number of partial explanations which have been put forward by writers from different backgrounds. Each represents a different way of looking at organizations. An understanding of these different viewpoints can help managers to identify what kind of problem they are worrying about.

The formal allocation of people management responsibilities is fundamental to the process. Businesses vary considerably in this respect: small firms tend to incorporate people management within line or general management; larger organizations are likely to have specialist functional roles. We noted that these roles might have titles such as 'human resource manager', 'personnel officer', or 'staff administrator'. These titles do not give much indication of the activities undertaken or the power vested in the jobs. In fact, they differ significantly from one firm to another. This chapter explains some of the major reasons for these variations. We begin by placing organizations in their environmental context: the competitive business world. We go on to discuss how and why organizations are formed and their implications for the nature of the people function.

Organizations and the business environment

Competitive pressures on businesses and national economies have increased markedly in recent decades. As a consequence, the organizations that impact on our lives are constantly changing. Powerful entities have arisen at the international level – the European Union being a prime example – and multinational corporations increasingly dominate particular sectors such as cars and aerospace. New competitors are emerging and forcing older organizations to adapt and reform themselves in order to survive.

Like Russian dolls, most organizations are parts of larger entities with one business unit fitting within another, larger structure or network. They are the complex products of a world subject to the international division of labour, geographic rationalization, product differentiation and the revolution in business and personal communications brought about by the humble microchip. There is nothing unusual in a business section in Cork reporting to a Dublin-based department within the Irish operating division of the European subsidiary of a US multinational. Theoretically, this reporting may be instantaneous and seamless – it does not matter where in the world it takes place. For marketing purposes some firms deliberately obscure these relationships. Walking through a typical high street or shopping mall in a developed country, we find an apparent diversity of retail traders. In fact, many are brand names controlled by just a few conglomerates.

In Part two we saw that organizations also interact with their environment through the regulatory, economic and cultural framework in which they operate. Different levels and types of organization supervise, support and impede each other's operations with contradictory demands. External stakeholders such as governments, financiers, customers and shareholders exercise their influence through legislation, tax benefits, interest rates, consumer demand and the purchase and sale of shares.

Organizations reflect the values and norms of society, supplying products and services that meet the needs of the culture in which they function. They structure and manage themselves in ways that are acceptable to those societies. Inevitably, therefore, there are differences in the nature of organizations between one country and another with some more likely to adopt bureaucratic, hierarchical organizations while others tend towards flatter, less rigidly differentiated structures.

Different structures affect the way people are managed. HRM is intimately bound up with the way firms are organized. Businesses throughout the world require the same basic human resource activities: they recruit new employees; they develop and train their staff; they have reward systems; they have control and feedback mechanisms; and people must interrelate and make decisions (Brewster and Tyson, 1991, p.9). But these issues are handled in different ways, reflecting the expectations and acceptable behaviour patterns within national business cultures. Similarly, employee values and attitudes are shaped to a considerable extent by people's native culture. Since national cultures are so pervasive, we will see in Chapter 9 that they strongly influence the cultures within organizations.

This chapter focuses on organizational structure but we must be aware that structures are influenced by culture. People have strong feelings towards the organization in which they work. Siemens, Saab and Qantas are psychological entities to which employees react positively or negatively, a perspective that underpins the concept of employer branding. Internal stakeholders – employees, managers and owners – expect organizations to operate in an acceptable manner but the notion of acceptability is culturally determined and varies from one country to another. For example, Korean employees expect and accept more authoritarian management than their Japanese neighbours. Expectation and acceptability are important factors in determining the range of possible organizational structures that can operate successfully in a particular country.

To a considerable extent, therefore, environmental factors constrain the operations of commercial enterprises; but, conversely, businesses must control elements of the environment to ensure their own survival. Organizations are not passive – they can take a number of actions that increase their freedom in meeting environmental demands. Managers do so by devising strategies for survival and growth that can prove to be beneficial or counter-productive. They can influence public perception through advertising, or achieve competitive advantage by developing new products.

Equally, an organization's prospects can be improved by deploying its human resources in a novel and effective way, drawing on their competences and creativity. Throughout the world, the use of human resources is moving away from the employment of inflexible, full-time workers with expectations of lifelong careers in a single organization. Businesses can make strategic choices between a range of alternatives: part-timers, contingent workers, outsourcing, franchises and so on, as we shall see in our discussion of flexibility later in this chapter.

Some organizational strategies have been misguided. In the 1980s and 1990s most large corporations indulged in tumultuous restructurings, variously described as 'downsizing', 'rightsizing', de-layering', and 'focusing on core areas'. These dramatic disruptions were justified largely on financial grounds. Often the consequences for employees – including those remaining – were negative. Older redundant workers had to accept early retirement. Others faced long periods of unemployment. Morale then slumped and stress increased amongst surviving employees who were expected to work harder in a climate of uncertainty.

In many organizations blind pursuit of cost-effectiveness destroyed the credibility of senior managers in the eyes of their staff, leading to a marked reduction in employee commitment. In this chapter we seek to pinpoint more positive approaches in the organization of people management.

Dimensions of organization

How can we differentiate one organization from another? Large companies spend considerable amounts of money on developing strong images for themselves. Corporate logos, decoration schemes, uniforms, marketing literature and advertisements are all designed to create a favourable impression with customers and share analysts. But public image tells us little about an organization as an employer. In fact, it obscures the nature of people management.

From our perspective the first question to ask in any organization is: who manages the people? In Part one we noted that early HRM models placed the responsibility for people management with line managers. This is a debate in itself: should the management of people be part of the function of every manager in an organization; or does it demand an expertise which can be expected only from trained specialists? Opinions have changed markedly, sometimes due to fickle fashion and sometimes to the idiosyncratic opinions of senior managers. One view is that managing people is what business is all about and, therefore, every manager and supervisor should deal with the individuals within their area of responsibility. Conversely, it can be argued that the detailed aspects of people management such as resourcing and reward management are too complex for the average sales manager, accountant or engineer – untrained in the behavioural sciences – to handle satisfactorily.

In reality examples are found along the entire length of the dimension from specialist to non-specialist. The decision to manage people in a particular way depends on a number of factors, including the basic organizational dimensions we shall consider next: goals, size and structure.

Organizational goals

According to Simon (1955, p.30):

> Organizations are formed with the intention and design of accomplishing goals; and the people who work in organizations believe, at least part of the time, that they are striving towards these same goals. We must not lose sight of the fact that, however far organizations may depart from the traditional description . . . most behaviour in organizations is *intendedly rational behaviour*.

As we have seen, the rhetoric of HRM attaches great importance to strategy and the linking of employee performance to organizational goals (Key concept 7.2). What are these goals? They are expressions of a company's purpose and long-term objectives. Often written in the form of a mission or values statement, they give purpose or direction to an organization. They are intended to influence the behaviour of employees but few small companies have a written statement and many larger companies provide woolly verbiage without clear meaning. We will discuss mission statements in more detail later in this book when we consider HR strategy.

Key concept 7.2 Organizational goals

The logical starting point for human resource management lies in an organization's goals – the reasons for its existence. Most modern businesses express these goals in the form of a mission statement. The allocation and control of human resources serves to assist or constrain the achievement of these objectives.

Taken at face value, mission statements appear to show that businesses have clear objectives. Traditionally, competitive market models portray the firm as a single decision unit engaged in maximizing profits. This approach ignores the possibility of **conflict** between owners, managers and employees. Organizations are political structures – usually surface unity is purely cosmetic. Needle (1994, p.99) observes that, as abstract entities, organizations do not have goals – their public objectives are those of some dominant person or group. Hidden behind the published goals of a business we find a series of conflicting agendas held by various individuals or work units. So, for example, the human resources or personnel department may have its own priorities, inconsistent with those of senior management. The HR department may be concerned with being 'professional', using the best selection techniques and careful job evaluation, whereas senior executives may be more concerned with short-term employee costs.

Size

Organizations can range from single-person businesses to multinational corporations employing hundreds of thousands of people. Generally, the sophistication and importance of people management is greater in larger organizations. However, sophistication does not lead necessarily to effective people management. In small companies all management functions – including human resources – are dealt with by the owners. By 'professional' standards these activities – especially selection and training – often are inadequately handled, yet the quality of the employment relationship can be high. Owners and employees work on a down-to-earth, personal level. Some are genuine friends and there may be mutual trust and confidence.

Conversely, larger organizations employ highly trained human resource practitioners using advanced selection, assessment and reward techniques. But size also brings problems in meeting the need for comprehensiveness, coherence, control and communication, resulting in the possibility of remote and conflict-ridden relationships between people at the top and bottom of the firm. Analysis of data from the UK 1998 Workplace Employee Relations Survey (WERS) shows that large workplaces (over 500 employees) are five times more likely to have a HR specialist than workplaces with 25–49 employees (Cully *et al.*, 1999, p.50). Similarly, titles including the words 'human resource' were more likely to be used in larger workplaces, although a greater proportion of personnel specialists in workplaces with fewer than 50 employees (40 per cent) were using such titles than in any other size group (Sisson, 2001). Also, the HR practices we identified as 'high commitment or high performance' in Chapter 3 were more common in larger workplaces.

HRM in reality   British Airways cuts management jobs

British Airways has announced plans to restructure the business and cut 35 per cent of its 1715 management jobs by March 2008.

This includes:

- A 50 per cent reduction in senior managers – from 414 jobs to 207.

- A proposed 30 per cent reduction in middle management jobs – from 1301 to 911.

According to Willie Walsh, BA's new chief executive: 'I said when we reported our second quarter financial results last month that our costs were up in most areas and that, as a result, we need to re-energise our efforts to deliver a competitive cost base.

'We must lower our costs so that we can fund future investment in our business. Today marks the start of a renewed effort to deliver our goal of a 10 per cent operating margin. I am confident that these measures, however difficult, will help to build a robust British Airways and one that will benefit from sustained profitability. This action will enable us to carry out the investment we need to make in our business in the coming years in order to deliver a more competitive and efficient airline.'

The proposed management job reductions are intended to reduce BA's costs by £50 million as part of its £300 million cost reduction programme by March 2007. The reduction in the number of senior managers will be phased:

- 94 of the top executives (23 per cent) will leave the business by March 31, 2006.

- More jobs will go in the next two years with the 50 per cent target to be achieved by March 2008.

- Full proposals and a timetable for achieving the planned 30 per cent reduction in middle managers will be developed and communicated by March 2006.

Willie Walsh added: 'We are restructuring the airline to remove duplication, simplify our core business and provide clearer accountability. Managers will have greater accountability for making decisions, delivering results and leading the business.

'The decision to embark on a major reduction in management numbers is not one I have taken lightly. We have extremely talented managers and they have led the way in transforming our company during the last four years since the tragic events of 9/11.

'But it is essential that we streamline our business further and I believe it is right that we have started by looking closely at the number of senior managers we need to deliver a sustainable, profitable future.'

Why is it 'essential' for BA to streamline the business further?

Source: *HRM Guide UK* (http://www.hrmguide.co.uk), 30 November, 2005.

To make sense of size differentials, it is useful to divide business enterprises into three categories (Curran and Stanworth, 1988):

1 Small-to-medium enterprises (SMEs), further subdivided by the European Commission into: micro-enterprises, with less than ten employees; small enterprises, with 10–99 employees; and medium enterprises, employing 100–499 people.

2 Large commercial enterprises with over 500 people.

3 Organizations within the public or state sector. These continue to have distinctive characteristics despite government attempts to place them on a business-like footing.

Cooperatives

The origins of this form of organization are lost in history. The first successful **cooperative** in North America was initiated by Benjamin Franklin in 1752. The Philadelphia Contributionship for the Insurance of Houses from Loss by Fire provided fire insurance for its members in Pennsylvania – and has continued to do so into the 21st century. In fact, the 'Contributionship' was the first mutual in the USA and is now the third oldest corporation in the country. But Benjamin Franklin probably copied a model of fire insurance pioneered in Britain in the 17th century.

Other ventures in Britain included a corn cooperative formed by workers in the Chatham and Woolwich areas of south London in the 18th century. Most significantly, the 19th century development of retail and wholesale cooperative societies pioneered in Rochdale in the north of England brought fair-priced groceries to the working classes. By the 1970s, however, the number of cooperatives in the UK had dwindled to around 20. Elsewhere, however, the concept took root throughout the world. According to the International Cooperative Alliance (http://www.coop.org) 800 million people are involved with cooperatives globally with 100 million being employed by them – 20 per cent more than multinational enterprises.

The work team became a fashionable obsession amongst human resource theorists and consultants in the 1990s. In the small cooperative the work team *is* the organization. This offers us an opportunity to examine the supposed benefits of teamworking in a relatively pure form. According to the International Cooperative Alliance, cooperative relationships are based on seven principles:

1 Voluntary and open membership.

2 Democratic member control, usually based on 'one-member, one-vote'.

3 Member economic participation, with 'surpluses' allocated to further investment or dividends.

4 Autonomy and independence.

5 Education, training and information for all participants and the general public.

6 Cooperation among cooperatives.

7 Concern for community.

Cooperatives arise in three ways:

● as new business start-ups, deliberately created in this fashion
● as buy-outs of existing factories or companies by the workforce
● conversion of existing enterprises into cooperatives.

Of these, the first has been the most common. They tend to be providers of services, usually benefiting from the different skills of the participants, rather than manufacturers, although farming cooperatives have become common. Most start-ups of this nature have been established with groups of fewer than five people who feel that the cooperative relationship fits their social values and need to structure their own work. But some are larger – 30 cooperative organizations in the United States of America have an annual turnover of over 1 billion US dollars. However, there are many instances of cooperatives failing. An examination of such organizations can tell us a great deal about the advantages and disadvantages of the 'softer' aspects of HRM such as participative management, commitment and the functioning of self-organized teams. Table 7.1 summarizes the nature of people management in smaller cooperatives, using our familiar 10-C checklist for HRM.

Larger cooperatives such as mutuals and agricultural cooperatives may employ managers but ultimate power lies in the democratic voting system. Similar structures are found in legal and medical practices, where specialists are independent but obtain administrative support and accommodation from the practice in which they operate. Success in such a system requires much tolerance and goodwill. Many cooperatives have failed because of a lack of clear strategy and leadership; often the maintenance of a harmonious relationship has obscured the need for financial viability. However, some have expanded to a considerable size; for instance the John Lewis Partnership is a major retailing force in the UK and over 100 million Americans invest with mutuals and other cooperatives. But even large cooperatives face structural problems that impact on people management because of their size.

Managerial structures

As organizations grow larger and technology becomes more complex, it becomes increasingly difficult to coordinate the people involved in an enterprise (see Key concept 7.3). Beyond a certain size it is impossible for one person to know what people are doing or even what their

Principle	Range	Comment
1 *Comprehensiveness*	Cooperatives are uniquely focused on their working members	People systems such as resourcing and training are not necessarily sophisticated
2 *Coherence*	Medium–good, depending on mutual understanding between members	Where specific aspects have not been discussed and agreed, members may 'do their own thing'
3 *Control*	Generally decentralized	Assertive members can have undue influence
4 *Communication*	Tends to be fairly good with shared and well-understood objectives	Generally open with intermittent conflict and possible political factions
5 *Credibility*	Strategies have to be discussed and agreed (or accepted) by all	Management and staff are the same in smaller cooperatives
6 *Commitment*	Belonging implies commitment	People vary and there are committed activists and less committed 'passengers'
7 *Change*	May be slow because of the need for consensus agreement	A sensitive and highly political subject and may be the major cause of conflict
8 *Competence*	Competent initially but needing to bring new partners in as requirements change	What happens to the partners whose skills are no longer appropriate?
9 *Creativity*	Can be high	Where members are free to deal with own areas of work
10 *Cost-effectiveness*	Depends on realism of the partners	Transparent and equitable as pay is agreed among members

Table 7.1

HRM in cooperative businesses

> ### Key concept 7.3 Coordination
>
> Tasks divided among a group of individuals must be synchronized and integrated in some way so as to achieve the overall objectives of the group. Jobs must fit into a coherent flow of work. Coordination involves the distribution of decisionmaking. This can be formal, with rigid rules and regulations, or informal, giving freedom for local decisions. Coordination may be routine, because of structure and control mechanisms, including a performance management system or direct, by management action.

names are. It is necessary to introduce some form of managerial structure as a framework for control and **coordination**. Large businesses – including sizeable cooperatives – have to be organized in a deliberate, formal way, probably with groups of workers reporting to individual managers or supervisors.

Along with a formal structure there is likely to be a clearer division between specialist functions, including that designated to look after aspects of people management – usually labelled 'Personnel' or 'Human Resources'. Someone, at least, has to keep basic records. Typically HR managers are closely involved in the effective distribution of people and the development of management structures. The focus is on matching human resources to strategic objectives. Larger organizations display some degree of **specialization, centralization** and **hierarchy** (see Key concepts 7.4, 7.5 and 7.6). This applies to people management as much as to any other activity.

> ### Key concept 7.4 Specialization
>
> The division of work between individuals or departments, allocating responsibilities for specific activities or functions to people who can achieve a high standard of work in a relatively narrow range of activities. They may require specific training or expertise. For example, HR managers are concerned with organization of the HR function and resourcing of all other functions.

> ### Key concept 7.5 Centralization–decentralization
>
> This depends on where decisions are taken. The human resource function may be held within a separate headquarters department or devolved to local sections. Alternatively, it may be allocated to line managers, with an in-house 'consultancy' provided by specialists for procedures such as selection, development and performance measurement.

> ### Key concept 7.6 Hierarchy
>
> The structure by which individual responsibility and authority is divided in an organization, usually represented by a tree and branch chart and reflecting the perception of senior managers. 'Vertical complexity' is indicated by a tall or flat hierarchy. 'Taller' organizations tend to be bureaucratic but have clear lines of command. Each individual has one boss. 'Flatter' organizations are increasingly common. They demand more responsibility and self-control from staff, but decisionmaking and authority are less clear.

For a long time, large organizations were bureaucratic – typified by precise job titles, grading structures and segregated departmental activities. Status and responsibility were matched accordingly. We noted earlier that French organizations have continued to follow this pattern. The 'people function' was identified with the personnel department, which primarily had a supportive, maintenance role in a comparatively rigid framework. This department held an intermediate position – part of the 'glue' which held the balance between differentiation (allowing specialist tasks to be fulfilled by relatively expert people) and integration (combining all those tasks into a coordinated whole).

Nowadays organizations are structured more diversely and the people function has taken on a variety of forms. The diffusion of HRM ideas on the one hand and simple cost-cutting on the other have led to a move away from 'all-embracing' personnel departments in many companies, particularly in Scandinavia and the UK. Line managers have become more involved in activities such as selection, recruitment and performance appraisal. Typically, there is a division of work between various aspects of people management. Senior management may take responsibility for human resource strategy; line managers assume operational responsibility for their people; human resource specialists provide specific services ranging from administration to selection programmes and counselling.

In line with the fundamental HRM principles of comprehensiveness and coherence, the basic elements of people management must be interdependent. Supervision, recruitment and selection, training and development, reward systems and performance management cannot be considered in isolation. Each activity has implications for a number of other functions and subtly influences many more. Interactions throughout an organization's systems have to be assessed before making changes in any one function. The move away from permanent, nine-to-five jobs towards short-term contracts, part-timers and subcontracting offers a particular opportunity for human resource specialists with expertise in training, contracting and controlling workers in these categories.

Large organizations cannot be discussed as a homogeneous group. Their human resource and other management functions are dependent on the nature of their structures.

Organizational structures

Organizations can be regarded as people management systems. They range from simple hierarchies along traditional lines to complex networks dependent on computer systems and telecommunications. Structures may be relatively formal, following strict reporting lines; alternatively, they may be based on informal working relationships. Structures are power and control systems which constrain or facilitate the freedom of employees to act and make decisions.

Chandler (1962) argued that structure follows on from strategy. Human resource managers can encourage strategies that foster both cost-effectiveness and employee commitment. Whether as line managers or specialist practitioners, they are able to use employee information and assessments to gauge the effectiveness of a particular structure. As managers they can influence or determine changes leading to improved employee performance and productivity. Organizational structures can be classified into a number of types, including **functional**, divisional, federations, matrix and networks.

Functional structures

Early **organizational design** divided enterprises into relatively simple parts, splitting them into defined activities such as production, marketing or personnel. This is still a common structure in medium-sized companies but it has become unusual in large (particularly multi-national) organizations. Such a design normally divides human resource management between specialized activities dealt with by a designated department (Figure 7.1) and day-to-day aspects handled by the operational functions.

As we can see from Table 7.2, there are both advantages and disadvantages to such an arrangement. On the one hand, functional organizations are simple to understand with clear

Figure 7.1

Functional structures
in HR

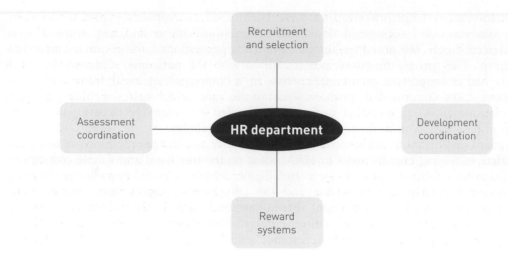

Table 7.2

HRM in functionally
structured
organizations

Role	Activity	
1 *Comprehensiveness*	Different functions are likely to be treated differently	Specific people systems such as resourcing and training may be sophisticated
2 *Coherence*	Low–medium, as functional managers block or value different aspects, e.g. performance-related pay	Organization is divided into separate camps
3 *Control*	Split between functions	Some functions are more powerful than others
4 *Communication*	Good vertically within a function but dreadful horizontally between functions	Prone to 'us and them' misunderstanding and warfare between departments
5 *Credibility*	Promotion and reward policies not understood if they do not fit functional needs	Parochial view restricts comprehension of overall business objectives
6 *Commitment*	Focused on functional department, not whole organization	People march in different directions
7 *Change*	Structural change regarded as threatening	Managers fight to preserve departmental power
8 *Competence*	High at functional and individual levels	Limitations on developing generalists with all-round abilities
9 *Creativity*	Limited	Little cross-fertilization between functions
10 *Cost-effectiveness*	Can be good if management kept to minimal levels	Specialist managers expect professional rates: jealousy between functions.

lines of command, specified tasks and responsibilities. Staff can specialize in a particular business area such as production or marketing and follow well-defined career paths. This is equally true of human resource specialists who can develop expertise in specific areas such as employee relations or reward management. Table 7.3 details a number of specialist roles performed by human resource specialists in functional and other large organizations.

However, there are also major disadvantages to functional structures. People managers have to tread carefully because this form of organization is prone to interdepartmental conflict, often degenerating into 'them and us' tribal warfare. Coherence and good communication are particularly hard to achieve between virtually independent functions. Moreover, HR development is complicated as it is difficult for individuals to gain a broad range of experience and an overview of the organization as a whole. Additionally, functional organizations have a tendency towards rigidity and ever-increasing layers of management. Since the 1980s, however, larger organizations of this type with tall and bureaucratic hierarchies have suffered the brunt of reorganization and **de-layering**. Our 'HRM in reality' case study on the Home Products company provides a simple illustration of de-layering. Restructuring is further considered in Chapter 12.

Divisional structures

Divisions may be based on specific products or product ranges, as in the pharmaceutical industry, or alternatively on a territorial basis.

Role	Activity
Chief human resource officer	Human resource director/manager. Head of specialist people management function
Personnel administrator	Formerly a clerical function concerned with maintaining paper records. Latterly requires expertise in creating and developing computer databases of human resource information
Employee relations manager	A long-standing specialist role with responsibility for collective bargaining and liaison with trade union officials. Now extends to employee involvement and communication
Recruitment specialist	Less common than previously. Trained in interviewing techniques and psychometric testing. May be occupational psychologist in larger organizations. This activity is often outsourced to specialist firms
Training and development specialist	Previously concerned with direct training. Now becoming an internal consultancy role. Often possessing a psychology qualification
Human resource planner	Statistical and planning expert providing projections of human resource requirements for strategists
Employee counsellor	Comparatively new but increasingly common role. May be part-time or outsourced. Requires counselling qualification and knowledge of stress reduction techniques. Typically replaces the welfare role of personnel management
Health and safety officer	Ensures that legislation on workplace health and safety is complied with. Liaises with local authority and other enforcement officials

Table 7.3

Specialist HR roles in large organizations

HRM in reality Home Products

Home Products came into existence in the UK in 1975 and grew to be a medium-sized importer and distributor of plastic and wood domestic goods. Spreading over the entire country, a network of distribution points and sales offices was gradually built up employing 80 staff. By the early 1990s, however, the company began making heavy losses. Eventually, the managing director was replaced and management consultants brought in to recommend changes in the structure of the organization.

The consultants examined the operation of the company in detail. They found a traditional, functionally-split company with a low level of computerization and a high level of middle management for its size. They recommended the streamlining of the company, development of a team-based structure and investment in networked personal computers. Over a period of two years the company was transformed by eliminating expensive layers of management. Apart from financial savings, the improved communication and devolved decisionmaking produced a higher quality of service to customers. Before and after organization charts are set out in Figure 7:2.

Summarize the advantages and disadvantages of both structures in your own words.

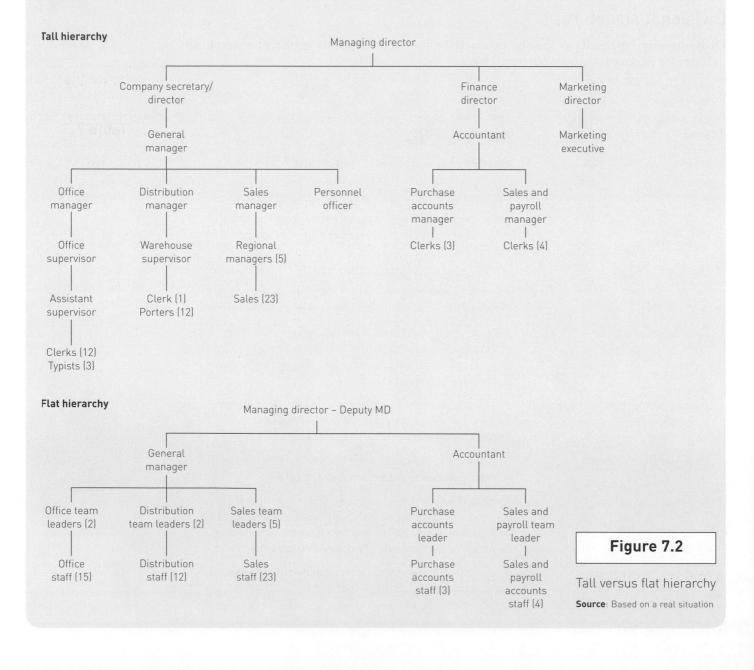

Figure 7.2

Tall versus flat hierarchy

Source: Based on a real situation

Divisions encourage team spirit and identification with a product or region. Managers can develop broad skills as they have control of all basic functions. Performance of business units and their employees can be readily monitored because costs and productivity are tied to product or territory. This allows organizations to:

- increase investment with certainty
- introduce new divisions for additional products
- dispose of ineffective or unwanted divisions without repercussions on the remainder.

Each division is likely to have a devolved human resource function. There is a risk, however, of duplicating activities between head office and divisional human resource departments and of conflict between staff in successful and unsuccessful divisions. The divisional level may be intermediate between corporate headquarters and individual business units. As a result, the division plays a coordinating role, reconciling decisions taken at the corporate and business unit levels. This results in a complex picture of people management, outlined in Table 7.4.

The key issue for people managers is the relationship between division and corporate head office. A few large organizations do without HR specialists at this level but most assign a role, usually of a policy nature, to the centre. Hence central HR departments in companies such as Ford, Barclays and Sainsbury are comparatively large. This makes sense where the activities

Principle	Range	Comment	
1 *Comprehensiveness*	Successful and unsuccessful divisions are likely to be treated differently	Centrally provided people systems such as performance management may be sophisticated	**Table 7.4**
2 *Coherence*	Corporate HR strategies may be neutralized at divisional level	Divisional people managers behave independently	HRM in divisional organizations
3 *Control*	Divided between divisions and head office	Scope for conflict and confusion	
4 *Communication*	Can be good within divisions but more problematic between divisions and head office, and poor between divisions	Prone to resentments and misunderstandings between head office and divisions	
5 *Credibility*	Corporate HR strategies not understood if they do not fit divisional needs	Parochial view restricts comprehension of overall business objectives	
6 *Commitment*	Focused on division – not whole organization	Divisions quasi-independent	
7 *Change*	Emphasis on acquisition and de-merger	Managers fight to preserve integrity of division	
8 *Competence*	High at functional and individual levels	Limitations on developing generalists with all-round abilities	
9 *Creativity*	Scope for considerable creativity in suitable divisions	Small firm climate encourages cooperation between functions	
10 *Cost-effectiveness*	Tendency for managerial/ administrative jobs to be duplicated	Little consistency between divisions	

in different locations or divisions are closely related. In practice, the more diversified and unrelated the divisions, the more likely it becomes that HRM is fully devolved to divisional level. In very diverse conglomerates, even senior managers are recruited and developed locally.

Federations

One variant of the divisional form which has a particular relevance because of its human resource implications is the '**federation**', a loosely connected arrangement of businesses with a single holding company or separate firms in alliance. For example, a decade ago the Cable & Wireless group functioned as a worldwide federation of equals with a small corporate centre. HRM operated on a partly formal, partly informal basis. The central human resource function offered an extensive support facility for international managers. This form of organization attracted criticism from stock market analysts who found difficulty in comprehending its subtle informality.

Matrix structures

As we have seen, both functional and divisional forms suffer from the 'them and us' problem between different parts of the organization. A number of large businesses have experimented with **matrix structures** to try and overcome these difficulties. Matrix structures focus on project teams, bringing skilled individuals together from different parts of the organization. Individuals are responsible to their line manager and to the project manager for different aspects of their jobs.

Their effectiveness is dependent not only on the provision of skilled people but also clear information on location and activities. This is difficult to achieve and many matrix experiments have resulted in failure, largely due to the 'matrix muddle': a general confusion of roles and responsibilities. Some activities may be duplicated because no-one understands the structure, and others may be neglected because it is assumed that someone else is responsible. Some of these difficulties have been overcome in more recent 'network' structures.

New structures

Older accounts of people management within organizations propose a highly structured, directive role for managers. This kind of management style and the rigid organizational context which it requires is inconsistent with the 'tight–loose' frameworks advocated by gurus such as Peters and Kanter. They propose new relationships which offer the flexibility to respond quickly to changing market demands but also allow retention of effective managerial control. Such organizations require a fine balance between centralization and decentralization. The key lies in organization design (see Key concept 7.7).

Key concept 7.7 Organization design

The design of an organization patterns its formal structure and culture. It allocates purpose and power to departments and individuals. It lays down guidelines for authoritarian or participative management by its rigidity or flexibility, its hierarchical or non-hierarchical structure. Appropriate design is crucial to effective use of resources and long-term success and survival.

In recent years the emphasis has been towards differentiated but integrated organizations. This paradoxical view stresses that individuals work for the business rather than for specific departments which might compete rather than cooperate with each other. Communication and information distribution systems in earlier days were based on paper memos and reports. Paper-based systems could only work if functional activities were broken down into defined, quasi-independent sections.

Today, developments in telecommunications and computing allow raw or analysed data to be collected electronically and distributed to any point in the organization. This makes it easier for an organization to be managed as a whole. As we have seen, such an organization is likely to be slimmed-down, 'de-layered' and focused on core activities. Non-core functions, including HR activities such as recruitment and training, can be outsourced. Integrated information technology allows previously unimagined control mechanisms and organizational forms. The boundaries between organizations become increasingly blurred and the nature of people management takes on a new and complex level of intricacy. For example, we can ask how we manage 'employees' who have no employment contract with our own organization?

Managers, including human resource specialists and others, must play a new role. They cease to be checkers and order-givers. Instead they are more likely to become:

- enablers, structuring organizations to allow employees to achieve objectives
- empowerers, devolving decisionmaking to the lowest level
- facilitators encouraging and assisting employees.

In such a context, people managers are no longer supervisors. Their organizations move from rigid hierarchies and power distinctions towards an environment where people take responsibility for their own work. Various forms of integrated structure are technically and ideologically feasible within relatively loose arrangements that encompass different organizations, agencies and specialist contractors.

Principle	Range	Comment
1 *Comprehensiveness*	Dependent on design of organizational structure – is it formalized or ad hoc?	Flexibility of the organization allows expertise to be bought in for any need
2 *Coherence*	Amorphous nature of organization can lead to incoherence	Reward, performance and development systems apply to some, but not to others
3 *Control*	Project or customer-driven	Dependent on software systems
4 *Communication*	Tends to consist of informal connections forged to solve problems and achieve task goals	Self-managed and problem-solving approach leads to direct communication
5 *Credibility*	Evident that organization is there to meet project or customer needs	Emphasis on performance gives high credibility to the network
6 *Commitment*	Focused on project, not whole organization	No long-term commitment to the organization required
7 *Change*	Organization changes continuously	Structure and processes driven by customer needs
8 *Competence*	Focus on skilled knowledge workers	Dependent on identification and availability of most suitable people
9 *Creativity*	Emphasis on people devising their own approach to work	Freedom for creativity comes from self-management
10 *Cost-effectiveness*	Theoretically, human resources are perfectly matched to work	Minimal supervision requirement

Table 7.5

HRM in networked organizations

Networks

In the context of organizational design, networks extend firms beyond their own boundaries. Focused organizations concentrate on core activities – those areas in which they believe they have particular strengths. Other functions are provided by subcontractors, which may be different business units within the firm or entirely independent providers. For example, one organization manufactures and sells its products but purchases its research, design and computing functions from other firms within the network. Snow, Miles and Coleman (1992) distinguish a number of network types:

Internal networks. Comprised of business units, mostly owned by the parent organization, each specializing in one function. These units network with other internal units and also interact with external suppliers and customers. This is a development of the divisional system.

Stable networks. Basically working to the core-periphery model of flexibility which we will consider later in this chapter. A small core of professional and managerial staff subcontracts most of its activities to external providers. Television stations frequently work on this basis.

Dynamic networks. A further extension where the core acts as a broker for independent suppliers, producers and distributors.

HRM in reality   Who telecommutes?

Rising oil prices have resulted in many professionals considering telecommuting as an economical work option, but spending too much time working from home can mean saying goodbye to promotion prospects.

Recent surveys developed by OfficeTeam, a leading staffing service specializing in placement of administrative professionals, were conducted by an independent research firm and included responses from 100 senior executives in Canada and 150 in the USA.

They found 32 per cent of Canadian respondents and 43 per cent of US respondents said telecommuting was best suited for staff-level employees, compared with 28 per cent and 18 per cent respectively who felt telecommuting was most beneficial for managers.

In addition, more than half of Canadian respondents and more than two-thirds of US respondents said senior executives at their firms rarely or never telecommute.

When asked, 'At which level do you think telecommuting programmes are most beneficial?' participants responded:

Level	Canada (%)	USA (%)
Staff	32	43
Manager	28	18
Executive	16	14
Administrative support	15	11
Don't know/no answer	9	14

When asked, 'Overall, how frequently do senior executives at your firm telecommute?' participants responded:

Frequency	Canada (%)	USA (%)
Very frequently	18	5
Somewhat frequently	21	23
Rarely	38	55
Never	20	12
Don't know/no answer	3	5

According to Diane Domeyer, executive director of OfficeTeam, it is often easier for staff-level employees to telecommute because their work can be performed autonomously. However, even those people who work from home need to spend time in the office.

Diane Domeyer added:

Effective management requires plenty of 'face time' with employees. Supervisors should have an open-door policy, and that means being available to staff who need guidance with projects. Employees who work from home must ensure that being out of sight doesn't also mean being out of mind for promotions, team projects and plum assignments.

What jobs are unsuitable for teleworking?

Source: *HRM Guide* (http://www.hrmguide.com/) 14 September, 2006.

In general, networking takes some familiar producer-wholesaler-distributor concepts, extends them into new industrial sectors and binds them into a seamless structure with no visible boundaries between individual parts of the network.

Human resource management takes on issues in networked structures that are outside the familiar boundaries of the employee–employer relationship. Traditional personnel management is replaced by operational managers with strengths in people management – true 'human resource managers'. People managers in networked structures are diplomats, encouragers and resource-allocators. Table 7.5 outlines the main characteristics of HRM in network structures.

Virtual organizations

Advancing technology allows firms to extend the network concept to form enterprises with no permanent structures. These **virtual organizations** bring people together for specific projects. Teams dissolve on completion, to reappear in new combinations for other tasks. The network is composed of expert nodes. These are people who add value through their knowledge. Traditional hierarchical structures have no role in this model. Departments, divisions and offices disappear leaving an amorphous mass of people connected electronically and meeting only when required. Through web-based technology and teleworking, there is scope for considerable change in the nature of work.

Organizational strategies

If the purpose of organizations is to coordinate people's activities to achieve certain objectives, why do they go about it in such different ways and why are some organizations spectacularly poor at achieving their goals? A partial explanation comes from organizational design. This may be strategic or unplanned. Some organizations have come into being almost through accidents of history. Perhaps they started as small enterprises with individuals taking on regular or specialist roles, looking after stock, keeping financial records, going out to meet customers and so on. As the business expanded individual jobs grew into departments, following the same division of work; eventually, the original job-holders moved on but their functions remained to be done by other people. A mature organization is still shaped according to the skills and personalities of people who are no longer there.

Other organizations are designed in a particular way from their inception. Government departments may be set up to achieve a particular social purpose. Their objectives, form and operation will be determined by conscious thought. To some degree, organizing (patterning) of all enterprises is deliberate. Even the 'accidental organization' will be remodelled and reshaped at some time.

Some enterprises contain the remnants of a succession of reorganizations. Most large organizations are diversified. They operate in different product areas. In the free market model prevalent in English-speaking countries, this has happened mainly by acquisition of other firms. This has a number of implications for the overall organization of such firms. In many cases they will display 'hybrid' characteristics, preserving much of the character and structure of the original businesses. Such organizations are prone to inconsistencies and misunderstandings on people management issues.

Some strategists have insisted on the 'one best way' approach to organizational design, advocating a specific method. Conversely, others have elected the contingency view which adopts the line of: 'it depends. . . .' Contingent strategies can range between two extremes: determinism and strategic choice.

Determinism holds that critical variables are decisive. Woodward (1980) pointed to the importance of technology in determining the span of managerial control – how many staff one person can manage realistically – and therefore the organizational structure. The span of control is highest in mass production where activities are relatively predictable and low numbers of managers are required. Another example is where environmental factors such as market or economic conditions determine which form of organization is most appropriate. Burns and Stalker (1961) advocated organic (flexible and adaptive) forms of organization for periods of technological change; and mechanistic (rigid) structures for stable, long-term processes.

At the other extreme is strategic choice. Essentially it is 'up to you!' based on your perception of the situation with no necessary constraints from external conditions.

Peters and Waterman (1982) shifted the emphasis to people. Their concept of 'simultaneous loose and tight controls' advocated fuzzy (loose) controls over employee decision-making, requiring tight adherence to the central mission of the enterprise. Mintzberg (1983) used the term 'adhocracy' to describe a flexible, fuzzy structure able to adapt its form continuously to meet changing circumstances. Three factors are particularly relevant:

Uniformity of organization. A firm with one product range or branded outlet is likely to have a centralized human resource function to preserve a common approach.

Attenuation. De-layered and otherwise slimmed-down companies have a limited number of specialist roles. Probably, there is a senior HR figure and administrators at clerical

Table 7.6 Summary of organizational structures	Type	Focus	Benefits	Disadvantages
	Functional	Department e.g. sales, accounts, personnel	Simple to understand Clear lines of command Specialist expertise Career structures	Slow to react 'Us and them' Hierarchies tend to grow into vast pyramids Managers have difficulty in gaining organization-wide perspective
	Divisional	Product or market, e.g. pharmaceuticals	Self-contained units Can be evaluated separately	Conflict between divisional and organizational objectives
		Geographical territory, e.g. brewing region	Can be added to, closed or sold as wholes Team-based, loyalty to division and product Managers obtain overall experience	Morale difficulties in unsuccessful divisions Duplication of functional activities, e.g. marketing, human resources
	Federations	Loose relationship	Informal, flexible	Disliked by stock exchange commentators
	Matrix	Project or team	Strong focus on project, client objectives	Complex Conflict between reporting lines Conflict over allocation of resources
	Networks	Nodes Individuals as resources	Talents focused on tasks Seamless organization – no departmental boundaries Open to external contributors	No job security Potentially anarchic

level but no specialist support in between. Line management has been given the bulk of people management activity.

Decisionmaking. Each organization has a decisionmaking style. This varies from democratic – as in cooperative organizations – to the autocratic where decisions are taken by the powerful or self-elected. Autocratic (centralized) decisionmaking is common in small firms but it is seen also in large businesses where delegation (decentralized) is the more usual style.

Butler (1991) considers that decisionmaking is the driving force of an organization. Its structure is the decision framework: the enduring set of decision rules which allow or constrain uncertainty. The elasticity of the rules produces a fuzzy (organic) or a crisp (mechanistic) structure so that fuzziness indicates the flexibility of the rules. Butler argues that every organization or part-organization should be designed to optimize the quality of managerial decisionmaking. This can be done by selecting the appropriate degree of fuzziness or crispness, based on the uncertainty of the decisions involved.

A fuzzy structure eases decisionmaking in conditions of high uncertainty. Correspondingly, decisions with relatively certain outcomes should be given comparatively crisp, if not rigid organizational structures. Further, an individual organization can have zones of relative fuzziness or crispness to reflect the differing functional decisions.

Crisp structures restrict the level of individual decisionmaking. Fuzzy structures give a high degree of decision freedom, loosely determining:

- who can do what
- who is involved in decisions
- how operating procedures can vary
- who reports to whom
- how they are rewarded
- how much analysis is required for a decision.

As a consequence of such thinking, large firms may take on a variety of forms. An organization does not have to be homogeneous, with identical structures and processes throughout. It can take on varied characteristics to suit its activities in different parts of the firm. These activities can be classified into (Handy, 1993, p.201):

Steady-state. Routine, programmed activities typically making up 80 per cent of work in the average organization.

Innovation. Researching and developing new products and methods or opening new markets.

Crisis. The branch of management known as 'fire-fighting' or dealing with the unexpected, emergencies and industrial disputes.

Policy. Identifying goals, setting standards, allocating scarce resources and generally getting people to do things.

This implies also that: different people need to be employed to fit the requirements of specific activities; these workers should be motivated in diverse ways; and management style needs to be tailored to the jobs and the personal characteristics of individual employees.

What does this mean for ordinary workers? Effectively, job satisfaction and personal challenge depend on specific situations within the organization. One finance clerk may have a domineering boss who does not allow her to make any decisions, whereas another will be given a considerable amount of discretion by a more trusting supervisor. However, the first clerk may have access to a powerful computer information system, allowing her to handle much greater sums of money. Overall, the first employee may feel the greater sense of personal responsibility and self-importance.

As with any theoretical model, individual organizational theories simplify reality to an excessive degree. They miss out many of the intricacies that we experience in real organizations. From our discussion it has already become clear that organizations are not simply formal structures – they also consist of informal relationships, cultures, power allocations and political intrigues. People managers have to be aware of all these varied aspects at one and the same time.

Morgan (1986) offers an alternative way of conceptualizing these complexities by providing us with the eight different metaphors described in Table 7.7. The metaphors reflect the essentially human and changing nature of organizations and can be used to provide an insight into organizational dynamics. Any business can be examined from a number of perspectives because any one organization can be a mix of two or three dominant metaphors.

The HR role in large organizations

People management functions are themselves affected by organizational strategies. Moves to restructure large organizations and reduce the number of managers have affected HR specialists as much as anyone else. The activities of the HR function have been 'balkanized' or parcelled-up into discrete areas (Sisson, 1995, p.96), mirroring 'developments in management more generally' (Sisson, 2001, p.78).

HRM may be organized in a number of ways (Adams, 1991):

- Traditional 'personnel'-type departments providing a full range of HR services.
- In-house agencies, or cost centres, performing one or more activities such as recruitment. Their costs are automatically charged to client divisions or departments.

Table 7.7	Metaphor	Perspective
Organizational metaphors **Source**: Based on Morgan (1986).	*Organizations as machines*	Working machines with visible structures, levels and routines. Typical of bureaucracies, providing continuity and security but limiting people's capacities to by prescriptive regulations
	Organizations as organisms	Responsive, dynamic living things. As the environment changes the organization adapts to fit the new circumstances. Best for a fast-moving industry in uncertain market conditions
	Organizations as brains	An organization does more than respond, it appears to be inventive and rational, self-changing, an innovative learning system that is open to self-criticism. Akin to the 'learning organization' concept
	Organizations as cultures	The Deal and Kennedy definition of shared meanings, values and customs outlined in Chapter 9. Cultures make each organization unique.
	Organizations as political systems	Each organization has its own equivalent to a governmental ethos which might be comparatively authoritarian or democratic. A recognition that it functions through processes of power and patronage, bargaining and negotiation, alliances and control of information
	Organizations as psychic prisons	Based on Plato's allegory of the people tied in a cave and ascribing meaning to shadows on the wall thrown by the fire. Similarly, people live with the organization's myths and believe in the representation they provide to the world. They are therefore constrained by the image that they have created
	Organizations as flux and transformation	Organizations are constantly in a process of change, the logic and conduct of which has to be understood
	Organizations as vehicles for domination	The recognition that organizations are coercive places

- Internal consultancies that 'sell' their activities to other parts of the organization, perhaps in competition with external services.

- Business-within-a-business arrangements that provide both internal and external services to clients inside and outside the organization.

- Outsourcing, sub-contracting HR activities to external agencies.

By the late 1990s, based on the UK 1998 WERS data, Millward, Forth and Bryson (2000, p.80) could state that: 'One of the most significant changes is that the people responsible for managing employee relations in 1998 were quite different from those who were managing it at the beginning of the 1980s.' Specifically, responsibility for HRM had shifted away from general managers to HR specialists and line managers and HR specialists were better qualified.

Turning the developments of recent decades on their head, Coggburn (2005) examined views on the possible merits of centralizing HR in Texas, a US state where public HR functions had always been decentralized. Traditional justifications for centralized HR included:

- Employees were afforded better protection from political coercion.

- Standardization of HR processes led to more equitable conditions (such as equal pay for equal work).

- Consistency of HR service delivery.

- Efficiency gains because of economy of scale.

- More professional HR service leading to better employee selection and assessment.

In practice, however, a centralized HR function can be perceived as being:

- Too rigid, more interested in enforcing rules than in responding to individual HR needs.

- Slow, with time-consuming procedures, losing some of the best applicants because of the time taken to process the paperwork.

- Complex, with labyrinthine grievance procedures that make it impossible to sack poorly performing employees.

Conversely, Coggburn argues, today's orthodox thinking is that decentralized HR has the benefit of speed, local discretion and autonomy, and, therefore is more efficient, effective and responsive. Moreover, it is more appropriate for modern, flexible working arrangements. Coggburn asserts that, ironically, efforts to outsource the HR function to a single outside provider will lead to a new version of centralization.

Flexibility

Quoting Wood (1989, p.1):

> In Japan . . . it began after the 1973 oil shock . . . [and] has recently concentrated on how to handle reductions in labour demand, whereas in the USA attention has especially centred on changing work rules which are thought to inhibit intra-organizational job mobility. In Britain . . . much of the concern has been with the balance between non-standard and regular contracts.

Sociologists have long perceived industrialization as a process leading through a sequence from agriculture, to heavy industry to service economies. In Chapter 2, we noted that the process is particularly visible in older industrial countries such as the UK and the USA. These countries are described sometimes as 'post-industrial' in that the service element of their economies is a bigger proportion than manufacturing. This is reflected in the nature of employment which has changed from predominantly manual and blue-collar jobs to white-collar. Work has been revolutionized by the introduction of information technology which puts a premium on skilled, competent 'knowledge workers'.

We have already observed that one of the most pronounced trends in recent years has been the replacement of full-time, long-term jobs with other types of positions. These include part-timers, 'temps', consultants, franchisees and so on. Business strategies have focused increasingly on flexible working in order to reduce employee costs of products and services (see Key concept 7.8). As we saw, this is exemplified in the concept of the virtual organization.

Key concept 7.8 Flexibility

The concept covers a combination of practices that enable organizations to react quickly and cheaply to environmental changes. In essence, flexibility is demanded from the workforce in terms of pay, contractual rights, hours and conditions, and working practices. This extends to the employment market, requiring jobseekers to show a willingness to move location, change occupation and accept radically different terms of employment.

Flexibility has become a much-quoted term. Neo-liberal politicians argue that, at the environmental level, competitiveness comes from the reduction of perceived 'rigidities' in the employment market. Rigidities in the job market have been pinpointed as causes of industrial decline and flexibility has become an unquestioned 'good'. Rigidity includes lack of mobility, refusal to accept new conditions, unorthodox working hours and so on. By scrapping minimum pay rates, removing legislation which limits employers' rights to hire and fire, and generally deregulating the job market, they believe that businesses will achieve the maximum degree of competitiveness.

Simplistically, it can be argued that the terms have an implicit political agenda: rigidity equates with worker protection and therefore left-wing, socialist attitudes; flexibility matches with 'hard' HRM, exploitation of workers and hence a right-wing, capitalist approach.

Flexibility takes a number of forms, **numerical**, functional and pay:

Numerical flexibility. Matching employee numbers to fluctuating production levels. This is difficult to achieve with 'regular' workers on full-time, long-term contracts.

Functional flexibility. Abolishing demarcation rules and skill barriers so that workers can take on a variety of jobs.

Pay flexibility. Offering different rates of pay for the same work – depending on geographical location and skills availability.

HRM in reality Give us a 6.00am start

Many British workers would welcome the introduction of a 6.00am start, if they could go home earlier in exchange, according to research by business communications firm Your Communications.

The survey of over 2000 employees found that a majority believed they work most efficiently between 6.00am and 3.00pm.

A mere one in 20 said they were most productive between 3.00pm and 6.00pm and almost half the respondents said they could do their job as effectively from home.

Your Communications argued that this could spell the death of the traditional 9 to 5 working day. In particular, allowing employees to work flexibly from home at times best-suited to them meant that businesses could dramatically boost their productivity.

The report also concluded that employers should consider the 'obvious benefits' that flexible working schemes bring, including: strengthening staff loyalty, and improving employees' work–life balance.

'Most workers believe they work more effectively at different times of the day,' said Paul Lawton, from Your Communications. 'Flexible work arrangements, which allow them to work from home, at their clients' offices, or for that matter at airport lounges, may help them to work more productively and vary their working hours.'

What is your ideal pattern of working hours?

Source: *HRM Guide UK* (http://www.hrmguide.co.uk), 1 August, 2005.

A further requirement is 'flexible specialization' . Consumer demand increasingly reflects individual tastes. Purchasers want an ever-wider choice of goods, making it difficult, if not impossible, for mass production techniques to satisfy the market. The Fordist assembly-line is outmoded – even if it does offer cars in colours other than black. Producers must switch equipment and employees from one product to another in a flexible but economic way. Staff must have versatile skills. Proponents of flexible specialization hold that mass production, the dominant industrial force of the 20th century, is obsolete, along with Taylorism and Fordism. Organizations in developed countries will only survive by employing a multi-skilled, highly flexible core workforce able to turn their hands to a wide variety of tasks.

Atkinson's (1984) 'flexible firm' model combines flexibility with Japanese concepts of 'core' and 'peripheral' workforces (see Figure 7.3). Core workers are employed on standard contracts. Peripheral workers are employed by subcontractors, or on short-term contracts. However, Atkinson's model does without mutual obligations essential to the Japanese system: core workers provide functional flexibility – but without lifelong employment; peripheral workers and subcontractors are not rewarded with close, long-term relationships.

Against a background of globalization, workers have been forced to accept a reduction in employment rights, unsociable working hours, short-term contracts and lower pay rates. This

---

HRM in reality Flexible working may hamper careers

A recent study by business communications provider Inter-Tel questioned over 100 office-based workers about attitudes to flexible working. This identified positive reasons for applying to work flexibly but significant doubts about the likely response of employers.

Significant findings included:

- 90 per cent of respondents agreed that all employees should have the same right to request more flexible work patterns, irrespective of domestic circumstances.

- 30 per cent felt their organization did not respond equitably to such requests and 54 per cent were unsure about this issue.

- 60 per cent believed requesting greater flexibility could have a negative impact on the careers of people without children.

- 82 per cent considered flexible working a privilege; only 18 per cent felt it should be a right.

- 40 per cent felt their employer would not trust them to work from home.

Duncan Miller of Inter-Tel EMEA said:

The trend for home working continues to grow. Data from the UK Office of National Statistics confirms that there are now more than two million people working from home and a further eight million opting to spend at least part of their working week outside the office. Clearly, there are still issues to be overcome and an education process needs to take place so that everyone knows what their rights are and ways in which they can improve their work/life balance.

Over two-thirds of respondents identified 'a better quality of life' as the most important reason for applying to work flexibly. Other factors centred on more time for family (22 per cent), non-work activities such as courses (6 per cent), and travel (3 per cent).

Duncan Miller concluded:

We are now at a stage of technological development where people can work as effectively from their home or on the move, as they can at a desk in their company's office. Of course, flexible or home working is not feasible or suitable for all organizations, but employers should be looking at ways to address the work/life balance of their staff and be very clear on their policy in this area. A happier, healthier workforce can lead to greater productivity in the long term and increase staff retention.

New rights to flexibility may be leading to a reversal of the trend seen over the last decade. A 2001 Industrial Society (now the Work Foundation) survey of 516 human resource specialists found that 91 per cent of respondents' organizations used some form of flexible working. This compared with 84 per cent in 1998. Seventy-five per cent of respondents said that flexible working made good business sense for the organization, with almost two-thirds (63 per cent) saying that it built trust, loyalty and commitment.

Summarize the advantages and disadvantages of flexibility to employees and employing organizations?

Source: *HRM Guide UK* (http://www.hrmguide.co.uk) 16 August, 2006.

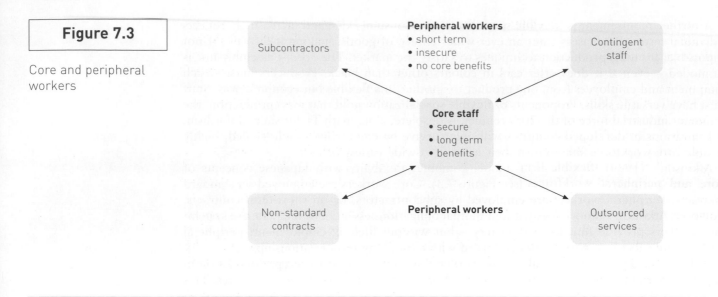

Figure 7.3

Core and peripheral workers

HRM in reality More Work/Life programmes provided

Employers are increasing provision of Work/Life programmes, according to results from recent Mellon research. Mellon Financial Corporation's Human Resources & Investor Solutions (HR&IS) study, *Work/Life – A delicate balance*, surveyed policies and practices in more than 600 organizations. Selected results were compared with its 1996 survey. The new survey found that:

- 81 per cent of employers offer employee assistance programmes – compared with 70 per cent in 1996
- 54 per cent now provide family sick days – up from 42 per cent
- 35 per cent of employers now offer domestic partner benefit – compared with a mere 6 per cent in 1996.

Additionally, the new survey results show that:

- 88 per cent of employers offer work-related tuition reimbursement.
- 55 per cent provide general resource and referral services.
- 47 per cent provide unpaid family leave beyond the requirements of the Family and Medical League Act (FMLA).

'Work/Life programmes help employees manage the broader and more complex challenges and responsibilities they now face on the job and at home' said Mellon HR&IS principal, Allison Levin. 'And for employers, they usually provide a cost-effective way to energize and support key performers, especially during periods of economic uncertainty. Our survey found the most commonly cited reasons for offering work/

life programmes are to enhance recruitment efforts (73 per cent), raise morale (74 per cent), and remain competitive (72 per cent).'

About one-half of respondents had increased the number of work/life programmes over the past two years, with only 5 per cent reducing the number. Other significant findings from Mellon's HR&IS survey include:

- 71 per cent of businesses surveyed offer flex-time – up from 32 per cent in 1996.
- 50 per cent of respondents offer telecommuting and work-at-home arrangements – compared with 9 per cent in 1996.
- 44 per cent of businesses offer compressed work weeks – up from 16 per cent in 1996.
- 86 per cent have part-time employees (who work fewer than 1000 hours per year) – compared with 50 per cent in 1996.

The Mellon study also measured the popularity of work/life programmes with employees. The most frequently used programmes included:

- family sick days
- paid family leave
- on- or near-site child care centres
- on-site vaccinations, and
- credit unions.

Why should organizations involve themselves with non-work issues?

Source: *HRM Guide USA* (http://www.hrmguide.com) 10 February, 2004.

development has occurred throughout the industrialized world. It has been driven by competition, primarily from Asia. It is also a development that has attracted a considerable degree of theoretical and ideological debate. Flexibility enables organizations to react quickly and cheaply to environmental changes. In free market countries there is a trend towards replacing full-time, long-term jobs with other employment relationships. Nevertheless, this is still a minority situation. For example, 70 per cent of workers in the UK have been employed by the same organization for over 20 years.

The idea of flexibility has definitely taken root but its theoretical basis has weaknesses. On the one hand, it is consistent with the concept of the 'virtual organization' discussed earlier, forming and re-forming to meet particular demands. Conversely, it is doubtful that we are really moving to a 'world of quasi-bespoke production concerned with gratifying fleeting market whims' (Hyman, 1988). Rather, niche marketing is concerned with defined 'varieties' of mass produced products. Consumers are not purchasing unique cars made to their specific requirements, but red 2.3 litre high-specification models, or white 1.0 litre basic models from a controlled choice – built in factories that Henry Ford would find recognizable. The availability of such varieties has more to do with computer-controlled robots, switchable from one program to another, than with a flexible, multi-skilled workforce.

Further problems arise in practice. Where are the necessary skilled people supposed to come from? A true transition to total flexibility requires a system for training non-permanent workers. Most employers are not equipped to provide this. Companies in countries such as Australia and the UK have been heavily criticized for under-investing in training their permanent employees. Ironically, the same countries have a weak record of providing such training on a national basis as well. We will return to this issue in our discussion of training and development.

Employees have their own views on flexibility. Hall and Atkinson (2006) investigated employee perceptions of flexibility utilized or available to them in an NHS Trust. They found that informal rather than formal flexibility was more widely used and valued, generating an increased sense of employee responsibility. Staff needed to be proactive to access formal flexibility but some did not see it as relevant to themselves.

Summary

Organizations are taking increasingly divergent forms but the key dimensions of size and structure still constrain the people function. HRM is conducted in a variety of ways, partly due to these constraints but also because of strategic decisions taken to meet organizational goals. Businesses can choose to vary their structures and their people management systems for a number of reasons. Increasingly, flexibility is required from employees and managers to meet new circumstances. Centralized personnel departments have been largely replaced with more specialized units, some of which may be outsourced. Nevertheless there are opportunities for human resource specialists dealing with complex issues arising from new organizational structures and flexible working patterns. These include contract arrangements, selection, control, assessment and training.

Further reading

The literature on large organizations is vast. *Organization Theory and Design* by Richard L. Daft (South-Western College Publishing, 2006) is a classic in its field. *Organization Theory: Modern, Symbolic, and Postmodern Perspectives* by Mary Jo Hatch (Oxford University Press, 2006) provides a good overview of organizational theory. *Levers of Organization Design* by Robert Simon (Harvard Business School Press, 2005) looks at how organizations can be designed to maximize performance. *Understanding Organizations* by Charles Handy, Oxford University Press, 4th edition (1993) remains the most user-friendly introduction.

Review questions

1 Think of situations where human beings are collected together. List five that can be described as organizations and five that cannot. What are the main reasons for classifying some as organizations and some not?

2 Summarize the significance of decisionmaking as a factor in organizational design.

3 What are the principal dimensions by which organizations vary? What are the implications for the management of their human resources?

4 How would the management of people differ between small and large organizations?

5 What are the major differences between the following types of organization: (a) functional structures; (b) divisional structures; and (c) networked organizations? How is people management likely to be organized in each of these? What priorities and constraints will human resource specialists experience within each type of structure?

6 What HRM issues might be problematic for larger cooperatives?

7 Discuss the consequences of advances in information technology on business organization and the work of employees. In what ways would the activities of human resource specialists differ between networked or virtual organizations and more traditional organizational structures?

8 How would you implement a major reorganization in a large company involving a change from a tall, hierarchical structure to a flatter organization based on self-managing teams?

9 What do you understand by 'flexibility'? Is total flexibility possible?

10 Distinguish between numerical and functional flexibility. How would demands for flexibility differ between organizations in the following sectors: (a) public service, e.g. local government; (b) production; (c) retailing; (d) the hotel industry.

11 How has the organization of the human resource function changed over the last few decades? What opportunities are there for human resource specialists in diversified, flexible organizations?

Case study for discussion and analysis

Rapid Supply Company

The Rapid Supply Company is a large electronic and mechanical parts wholesaler, supplying independent outlets throughout the country. The company purchases and distributes items from global manufacturers, supplying many specialist orders. The progress department monitors orders from placement to delivery. Dealing with customers, warehouse and manufacturers, the department has to maintain a careful and diplomatic relationship with both suppliers and customers.

Rapid Supply credits its success to the ability to efficiently obtain and deliver a wide range of parts. Five years ago the company was purchased by its managers from a large multinational conglomerate. Its market share has increased by 30 per cent in the last two years. The catalogue range has grown extensively with an additional 53 listed manufacturers.

The owners and the venture capital company supporting the organization have decided to float the business on the stock market next year. This will allow them to realize a proportion of their investment and will make millionaires of the senior executives. To maximize the potential share value of the company, their advisers have recommended a number of cost-cutting efficiency exercises. These include a reduction in warehouse stocks, increasing the proportion of items supplied to special order.

The progress department is divided into two sections: record clerks update files with changes and information from manufacturers and lead a comparatively peaceful life. Order-chasing clerks deal with e-mail, telephone and postal enquiries from customers and have a hectic existence, frequently experiencing verbal abuse. The department's work has increased considerably over the last two years but staff levels have remained the same. The progress department is managed by Julie Dee, a tough, resilient and detached person. She is adept at dealing with confrontation and seems to have an impenetrable shell. More junior employees wilt under the onslaught of enquiries. The average length of employment is three to four months but there are a few experienced people who have worked in the department for several years.

Most enquiries are from customers chasing orders. If clerks confirm items have arrived, customers are referred to the despatch section to arrange delivery. More often, parts have not arrived, requiring e-mails or phone calls to manufacturers and return contact with customers. At its simplest, a progress enquiry can be dealt with during the customer's first contact; at its worst, a succession of communications might be required over several days. Matters are complicated by inefficiencies elsewhere in the system. Goods might be in the warehouse even if shown as 'not arrived' on the computer screen. Equally, they might not have left the manufacturer or may be in transit.

Order-chasing irritates other staff and the suppliers. There have been complaints from manufacturers about progress requests from Rapid Supply regarding parts that were delivered to the warehouse days ago. An instruction has been circulated stating that progress clerks must check with the warehouse first, before contacting manufacturers. This has caused considerable friction between the progress department and the warehouse. Progress staff complain about the apparent slowness of recording receipt of goods; the warehouse complains of being pestered about parts which sometimes are not yet due. There is a further conflict with the despatch clerk who cannot be contacted for lengthy periods. Similar difficulties are experienced with suppliers, often needing several e-mails, etc. in order to obtain a response. Frequent errors by recording clerks compound the problems.

Progress clerks have a difficult role to play and risk upsetting everyone they deal with. Customers became irate if they do not get an immediate positive response.

Clerks become stressed with the pressure of work, colleagues' absenteeism, time limits on dealing with individual customers, being unable to deal with queries properly, and an escalating backlog. The manager now spends much of her time dealing with complaints about the service.

The marketing department has completed a customer survey which shows high levels of dissatisfaction with the progress department. Senior managers are furious and have seconded you to work alongside Julie and 'sort things out'.

What will you do?

Chapter 8

HRM in small and medium-sized organizations

Learning objectives

The purpose of this chapter is to:

- Outline the nature of entrepreneurship.

- Evaluate the consequences of business growth on human resource practice.

- Discuss research findings on human resource management in small and medium-sized businesses.

- Consider the consultancy as a special instance of the small business.

HRM in smaller organizations

Business start-ups and entrepreneurship

Collaborative entrepreneurship

Small firm growth

The growth process

HRM practices in the small business

Entrepreneurship and business growth research

Working in small businesses

Consultancies

Summary

Further reading

Case studies for discussion and analysis –
New Age Finance/The Craft Partnership/
Royal Ocean

HRM in smaller organizations

Serious appreciation of HRM in small to medium-sized enterprises (SMEs) is a comparatively recent phenomenon. HRM researchers have largely ignored the SME sector, preferring to concentrate on large organizations with recognisable 'personnel' structures (Hendry, 1994, p.106). The complexity and wide-ranging sizes and structures of SMEs is ignored and 'management training and advice to SMEs is based largely on textbook prescriptions that require the adoption of formal management procedures more suited to large firms' (Kotey and Slade, 2005, p.16). Yet the SME sector is an important aspect of any country's economy, already employing large numbers of people and embodying future growth potential. But the information available on people management in these organizations is sparse. Researchers attempting to investigate the topic have found access difficult, largely because small business owners are often busy entrepreneurs and perhaps regard academics with some suspicion. However, smaller companies should be fruitful subjects for study because many conduct people management in the direct fashion advocated by HRM models.

Business start-ups and entrepreneurship

'It's important to understand that the rewards of small business ownership are not instantaneous. You must be ready to defer gratification and make sacrifices to ensure the rewards eventually do come' (Lesonsky, 2001, p.14).

One in ten adults in the USA has started a business. Australia is not far behind with one in twelve, and Brazil is ahead with one in eight according to the *Global Entrepreneurship Monitor, 2000*. By contrast, older established countries are less entrepreneurial: for example, Germany (one in 25), the UK (one in 33), Finland and Sweden (one in 50) and Ireland and Japan (fewer than one in 100).

Why do people start businesses and what is an **entrepreneur**? (see Key concept 8.1).

HRM in reality Around 40 per cent of new jobs created by small businesses

Small businesses hired twice as many people as large companies during the first six months of 2002, according to CIBC World Markets. And, over 12 months to July 2002, 40 per cent of all new jobs in Canada were generated by small businesses.

The study released by Benjamin Tal, senior economist of CIBC, indicated that firms with fewer than 20 employees increased their labour forces by 2.8 per cent compared with the first six months of 2001. This compares with an increase of just 1.2 per cent in employment in companies with more than 500 employees.

Tal's study seems to explain reports of strong growth in the Canadian employment market despite massive lay-offs after the bursting of the 'tech bubble'. 'Downsizing in large firms has given small business owners a golden opportunity to tap into a new pool of workers,' says Tal. 'And small business owners are capitalizing on it, especially in the case of highly skilled workers.'

In fact, growth in the number of professional employees in small businesses was dramatic, showing an increase of 9 per cent during the first six months of 2002. This was three times the rate of growth in total small business hiring.

Rob Paterson, a senior vice-president working in CIBC's small business group, argued that small business is often the bell-weather of changes in the overall economy: 'Small business tends to be the first to experience the effect of an economic downturn, and the first to respond positively to a pick-up in economic recovery. Therefore, the fact that small business activity is accelerating is good news for all of us.'

Why are small businesses better at creating jobs than their larger counterparts?

Source: *HRM Guide Canada* (http://www.hrmguide.net/canada/), 10 July, 2002.

Key concept 8.1 Entrepreneurship

A classic definition of entrepreneurship is provided by Timmons (1994, p.7): 'Entrepreneurship is the process of creating or seizing an opportunity and pursuing it regardless of the resources currently controlled.'

According to Stolze (1999, p.13):

Long ago I read one author's comment that, 'Entrepreneurship is a profession for which there is no apprenticeship.' No matter how many books you have read, no matter how many courses or seminars you attend, no matter how much advice you get from 'experts', no matter how many small companies you work for, there is no substitute for the actual experience of doing it yourself.

Catlin and Matthews (2001, p.6) list the following classic entrepreneurial strengths:

- vision and a pioneering spirit
- being able to see possibilities where others do not

HRM in reality Would-be entrepreneurs

Forty per cent of Australians would like to be self-employed and/or their own boss, according to a survey by global recruitment agency, Kelly Services.

A total of 3000 people were surveyed in four countries – Australia, New Zealand, Malaysia and Singapore. New Zealanders were most enthusiastic about becoming entrepreneurs with 50 per cent stating they would like to be self-employed and/or their own boss; followed by Malaysia (48 per cent), Singapore (42 per cent), and Australia (40 per cent).

Among the Australian respondents, men wanted to be their own boss more than women – 44 per cent against 38 per cent. People in the 25–34 age range were most attracted to self-employment with 42 per cent wanting to become their own boss/self-employed.

According to managing director of Kelly Services, Garie Dooley, the findings point to a trend of increasing entrepreneurialism from people who would once have been happy to remain employees.

'New technology and the internet have opened up a host of opportunities which would previously have been unattainable without the significant resources of a large firm. It is possible for many people to set up a business with little more than a mobile phone and an internet connection. They are able to operate with a minimum of overheads and resources; they can stay in touch with their customers; and even promote themselves globally at relatively low cost.'

Employees were asked how long they would commit themselves for if they were to receive the offer of a very attractive job with the security of a contract. Around 67 per cent of Australian respondents said they would sign it for five years or less. Just 12 per cent would sign it for 10 years or longer. Women were less likely than men to commit to a long-term contract.

The youngest respondents were the least willing to commit themselves, even for an attractive job. A mere 5 per cent of 15–19 year olds, 7 per cent of 20–24 year olds, and 6 per cent of 25–34 year olds were willing to sign a contract for 10 years or more for an attractive job. This compared with 19 per cent for 35–44 year olds and 40 per cent for those aged 55 and older.

'We are seeing employees much more prepared to change their careers and their jobs and this appears to be the result of personal choice, not because it will be forced upon them,' Garie Dooley said. 'Employees seem to have embraced the end of the job for life and they are certainly not prepared to give their undying loyalty to one employer, even where the job package is considered very attractive.'

Australian respondents were also asked to rate their chances of becoming unemployed at some time in the future. Those from Queensland were most concerned about their futures (13 per cent), followed by New South Wales (12 per cent), Victoria (11 per cent), South Australia (10 per cent), and Western Australia (8 per cent). Those aged over 55 were the most uncertain, almost 20 per cent convinced of facing unemployment in the near future.

Why does the likelihood of being an entrepreneur vary between countries and regions?

Source: *HRM Guide Australia* (http://www.hrmguide.net/australia/), May 17, 2002.

- always searching for new opportunities and challenges
- possessing energy and passion
- having a drive to succeed and achieve results with high standards of excellence
- being creative – idea generators, able to 'think out of the box'
- constantly striving to do things better
- proactive and focused on the future
- intelligent, capable and decisive
- having a strong sense of urgency
- confident about taking risks
- problem solvers seeking new challenges and believing that nothing is impossible
- a determination to succeed, be wealthy or 'make a difference'.

Stolze (1999, p.16) divides the reasons why entrepreneurs start businesses into two categories: reactive and active. Reactive reasons are negatives that push people out of working for other people; active reasons are the positives that pull people towards the idea of working for themselves.

Reactive reasons include:

1 *Inequity between contribution and reward*. People who are high achievers tend not to enjoy working in large organizations. According to Stolze: 'They want rewards based on accomplishment – not on seniority, conforming to the corporate culture, or political clout.'

2 *Promotion and salary policy*. Large organizations tend to categorize people and mavericks do not fit the conventional promotional paths and salary bands.

3 *Adversity*. One of the commonest reasons – basically, job insecurity. When the job is not safe, people tend to think about alternatives. According to Stolze: 'I get very upset when a young college graduate seems unduly concerned about a retirement plan, fringe benefits and so forth. Long ago, I concluded that there is only one kind of job security that means anything – your ability to get another job fast.' Redundancies may also mean severance packages, allowing people to fund their own businesses.

4 *Red tape and politics*. Stolze says they are 'shortcomings of all large organizations that drive the entrepreneurial type bananas. Politicians and bureaucrats are rarely entrepreneurs.'

5 *Champion of orphan products*. Those of us who have cared about products or services outside the mainstream can understand how negative a large organization can be about 'orphan products'. This can be a first step towards the entrepreneurial leap.

Active reasons include:

1 *Wanting to be one's own boss*. According to Stolze: 'Many entrepreneurs have personality traits that make it difficult (if not impossible) for them to work for others.' Running their own business is the only solution. But also, there is the opportunity of professional satisfaction, seeing a job through, using time more flexibly, and so on.

2 *Fame and recognition*. Stolze does not consider this to be a common reason for starting a business, considering that there are 'more extrovert egotists' in established large organizations. In fact, he believes that starting one's own business is often a lesson in humility.

3 *Participation in all aspects of a business*. The all-round experience is elating and challenging. Being able to see the whole picture is more interesting than being one 'cog in the wheel'.

4 *Personal financial gain*. This can be important for some people, but not all. Potentially, the gains are much greater than normal wages.

Entrepreneurship offers a way through employment barriers for certain groups, such as immigrants. Using data from the German Socioeconomic Panel, Constant and Shachmurove (2006) examined entrepreneurial differences between different groups in Germany: West Germans, East Germans, guestworkers and other immigrants. They found that while the probability of self-employment increased significantly with age for all these groups, greater levels of education and having a self-employed father were important influences on the choice of self-employment for West Germans only. Immigrants were pushed into self-employment to avoid being unemployed but this often proved to be a way of achieving considerable economic success. Apart from East Germans, self-employed people in all groups earned more than those on a salary with immigrants having the highest earnings of all.

Lesonsky (2001) considers that, according to surveys and research, entrepreneurs share some common personality traits – confidence being the most important. They have confidence in themselves, in their ability to sell their ideas, set up their own businesses, and trust in their intuition. Confidence is essential in the fiercely competitive world of small business. The value of confidence is shown in a commonly held belief that the critical determinant of

---

HRM in reality Entrepreneurship in the UK

The London Business School has released findings from its 2005 Global Entrepreneurship Monitor United Kingdom (GEM UK) survey of 32 500 adults across the country on their views about entrepreneurship and whether they were involved in any entrepreneurial activity.

The 18–24 age group were the most positive in their attitudes towards entrepreneurs with 69.7 per cent considering it to be a good career choice and 13.4 per cent expecting to be their own boss within three years.

GEM UK examined the effect of enterprise training on levels of entrepreneurial activity for the first time. This is a major feature of the British government's policy of fostering more entrepreneurship in the UK. The survey shows that enterprise training doubles the likelihood of setting up a business for most age and gender groups. For example, women who have had some enterprise training were twice as likely to be involved in an entrepreneurial activity (6.9 per cent compared to 3.3 per cent) than those who had not.

In 2005, 12.4 per cent of the US adult working population and 9.3 per cent in Canada were involved in some form of entrepreneurship. The UK came in third of the G7 economies with 6.2 per cent. The Total Early Stage Entrepreneurial Activity (TEA) index used by the survey identifies the proportion of adults of working age who are either setting up or have been running a business for 2005 for less than 42 months.

There is a substantial difference between male and female entrepreneurship levels in the UK – 8.2 per cent of males are entrepreneurs, compared with 3.9 per cent of females. Entrepreneurship also varies across the country, from 8.3 per cent in London to 3.8 per cent in the North-East of England. Generally, however, rural areas have higher levels (8.2 per cent) of entrepreneurship than urban ones (6 per cent).

Ethnic minority groups are considerably more entrepreneurial than their white neighbours with non-white ethnic minority groups being 40 per cent more likely to be entrepreneurs. Black Africans are the most entrepreneurial. They are over three times more likely to be entrepreneurs than the white British while people of Indian and Pakistani origin are twice as likely as white British people to be entrepreneurs.

According to Rebecca Harding, GEM Global chief executive, London Business School, a cultural change is evident in the UK. 'Since 2002, there does appear to be a step change in attitudes towards entrepreneurship, especially among the young. Fear of failure, however, remains a challenge since, over the period as a whole, there has been little change in this attitudinal indicator. If the government is to close the gap between the UK and the USA in entrepreneurial activity, then this is a key feature which should be addressed with some urgency.'

There has been a striking change in the proportions of necessity and opportunity entrepreneurship in the UK. Necessity entrepreneurship fell from 1.4 per cent of the adult working age population to a mere 0.7 per cent between 2001 and 2005. Opportunity entrepreneurship increased slightly (from 5.1 to 5.2 per cent) over the same period. The UK is the only country in the G7 to have shown this pattern of change.

How would you distinguish between 'necessity entrepreneurship' and 'opportunity entrepreneurship'?

Source: *HRM Guide UK* (http://www.hrmguide.co.uk) 1 March, 2006.

entrepreneurship is the ability to raise significant amounts of money from investors: 'If you can make people believe in your dreams and share your goals so that they are willing to invest hard-earned cash in your venture, chances are you have what it takes' (Lesonsky, 2002, p.14). Greenbank (2006) examined the decisionmaking process leading to small business start-ups and classified potential owners as 'dissatisfiers' or 'motivators'. Uncertainty arises because the motivation to become self-employed is often based on beliefs rather than actual experience. This increases the perceived level of risk attached to self-employment as a career option.

Key concept 8.2 Collaborative entrepreneurship

Cooperation between two or more individuals in order to found or acquire a business. The degree and nature of collaboration may vary from one company to another in terms of financial input, time devoted, skills and knowledge.

Collaborative entrepreneurship

There has been extensive research on collaboration between enterprises (to be considered later) but little on the relationship between entrepreneurs within an organization. This is despite the fact that it has been well-known for decades that 40–60 per cent of small businesses have been collaboratively funded or acquired (see Key concept 8.2).

Evidence is limited but Quince (2001, p.3) suggests that 'collaboratively funded firms are more likely to survive and achieve faster growth' and 'there is evidence from the USA in particular that collaborative entrepreneurship is a feature of high-technology firms'. Whittaker (1999) also cites a study of over 500 high-technology entrepreneurs in the UK which found that over two-thirds (68 per cent) had been collaboratively funded.

Quince (2001, p.5) identifies three types of relationship within **collaborative entrepreneurship**:

1 The enterprise is an economic entity, having economic relations with other organizations and individuals. Moreover, there is an economic relationship between the co-founders or acquirers. Co-owners both provide and *are* resources: their own human capital in terms of skill, knowledge and experience, labour and often finance. In return, they are entitled to a share in the profits of the firm.

2 The co-owners or co-founders have an organizational relationship in which roles, responsibilities and accountability have been allocated.

3 An interpersonal relationship exists, typically embedded in a pre-existing social or personal friendship with friends, work colleagues, family or life partners.

How do SMEs fit into the knowledge economy? Nunes *et al.* (2006) investigated knowledge management understanding and usage in small and medium knowledge-intensive enterprises. Organizations studied acknowledged that adequately capturing, storing, sharing and disseminating knowledge can lead to greater innovation and productivity, but managers were not prepared to invest the relatively high effort on long-term knowledge management goals for which they had difficulty establishing added value. Knowledge management activities within SMEs tend to happen in an informal way, rarely supported by purposely designed ICT systems.

Most of the research into small businesses has focused on the economic dimension. But there are also issues of self-identity and notions of possession. As Quince points out, the 'I am the business' and 'My baby' elements of possession are 'common, if potentially psychologically damaging, entrepreneurial perspectives'. The business is perceived as an extension of the self.

Quince (2001, p.7) reports on a study of almost 500 East Anglian businesses in the manufacturing and business services sectors, each employing between 15 and 250 workers. A high incidence of collaborative entrepreneurship was found with 238 (60 per cent) of the 395 first generation independent firms having been founded or acquired collaboratively. Of these, 50 were family firms. Intriguingly, of the other 188 (non-family) firms that had been founded or acquired collaboratively, almost a half (43 per cent) were now owned by just one of the collaborators. According to Quince:

> Follow up telephone conversations with 47 remaining owners suggested that in 60 per cent of these cases the break-up of the team had been acrimonious. These conversations indicated the level of personal trauma associated with such conflict, including one case of attempted murder, several cases of serious assault and fraud, attempted suicides, depressions, and mental or family break-ups.

Small firm growth

Most small businesses never become large, and many are unsuccessful. Some of the reasons for this can be traced back to the start-up. Goltz (1998) describes a number of the common-sense elements of starting a business, for example:

1 Going into business for yourself is more responsibility than you can possibly imagine. You may start off thinking that when you go into business for yourself, you do not have to answer to anyone. In fact, the list is endless: your bank, your customers, your spouse, the Revenue people and so on.

2 Behind every failed business are a dozen friends who said it was a great idea. And they did – enthusiastically – along with your life partner. It is always best to get an expert opinion and not to rely on people who want to be supportive and not hurt your feelings.

3 If you've got it, use it. Even if it's a great smile. Hard work is not enough – you need to leverage the assets you have. And assets could be just about anything.

4 It is easier to steal a share of the market than create a market. Remember that Bill Gates was not the first in the computer software market. You might believe that a totally original idea is the key to success but if you have no competition you cannot be sure that there is a market out there.

HRM in reality High-potential entrepreneurs

US entrepreneurs are streets ahead of their counterparts in other countries when it comes to developing innovative businesses that keep the economy dynamic and productive, according to the latest US Global Entrepreneurship Monitor (GEM) directed by Babson College and the London Business School.

Entrepreneurs in the USA are more likely than any others to be motivated by opportunities in 'high-potential entrepreneurship' – the term GEM researchers use to describe fast-growing, new ventures involving the latest technologies and knowledge-transfer businesses. In nine cases out of ten US entrepreneurs are 'opportunity entrepreneurs'. A mere one in ten are self-employed because they have no choice.

Early-stage entrepreneurship is robust in the USA, having maintained greater stability than the other G7 economies (Canada, France, Germany, Italy, Japan and the UK) after the economic downturn in 2000.

US entrepreneurs have an excellent record of developing early-stage entrepreneurship (startups) into established business ownership. Compared with other countries, the USA has:

● more early-stage and high-expectation entrepreneurship

● greater investment rates, and

● a healthier economy overall.

According to the GEM report, high potential entrepreneurs (HPE) have increased US productivity levels more than 100 per cent in recent years.

High-potential entrepreneurs tend to be:

● young and male

● come from the upper income groups

● are motivated by opportunity

- don't suffer from fear of failure
- social networkers, benefiting from relationships with other entrepreneurs and 'business angel' investors
- skillfully choose opportunities from the business, rather than the consumer sector – with 60 per cent of those opportunities being in the innovative technology sectors
- believe that there is no competition
- have different ways of thinking than the general population.

Much of the startup activity involving high-potential entrepreneurs has been internet-related. The USA dominates internet-related products and services. In 2004, for example, US venture capital firms invested US$21 billion in this sector, compared with US$4.2 billion in 1994. In the same period the number of companies increased from 961 to 2399. However, informal investing fuels most startup and early-stage companies. US entrepreneurs average US$70 200 to start a new business and contribute 67.9 per cent of that amount themselves.

Stephen Spinelli, Jr, vice provost for Entrepreneurship and Global Management at Babson College, is confident that there is a healthy entrepreneurial investment environment in the USA. 'For US entrepreneurs great and small, there is more than sufficient external financing for them to start and grow their ventures. This is because there is much more equity capital available than before the internet bubble, and there are almost twice as many venture capitalists looking for good companies,' said Spinelli.

What reasons can you suggest for the high level of entrepreneurship in the USA?

Source: *HRM Guide USA* (http://www.hrmguide.com/) 31 August, 2006.

Until the late 1970s and early 1980s it was assumed that small businesses were a thing of the past: 'big is beautiful' was the prevailing view. Since then it has become clear in countries such as Hong Kong, Singapore and latterly the UK and the USA, that small firms are the basic seeds of a successful economy. They are a dynamic force for growth in comparison with the relatively slow movement of large and bureaucratic organizations. For example, in a number of East Asian countries the Chinese family-owned business is a key economic unit. Few of these businesses are large as younger members tend to spin off their own enterprises.

Type	Characteristics
1 *Craftsmen*	Self-employed in order to spend as much time as possible expressing their creativity. This freedom would not be possible in a large organization. They would prefer to make the product or provide the service personally and are reluctant employers. They probably experience difficulties in marketing or sales, and resent spending time on paperwork and administration. Many are 'hobbyists' and fail to create a viable business.
2 *Promoters (opportunists)*	With the ambition of creating personal wealth through 'deals'. Many have a succession of different businesses with varying degrees of success. They are not committed to a specific product or service. Proactive individuals, they are focused on marketing and finance and capable of rapid rates of growth in the right circumstances.
3 *Professional managers*	Aim to develop businesses with the hierarchical characteristics of larger organizations. They aim for controlled and sustained growth and take a long-term view of their businesses.

Table 8.1

Types of business owner

Source: Based on Hornaday (1990, p.29).

The growth process

Flamholtz and Randle (2000, p.9) state that:

> The first challenge entrepreneurs face is that of establishing a successful new venture. If they have the ability to recognize a market need and to develop (or to hire other people to develop) a product or service appropriate to satisfy that need, their fledgling enterprise is likely to experience rapid growth. It is at this point, whether the entrepreneur recognizes it or not, that the game begins to change. The firm's success creates its next set of problems and challenges to survival.

Entrepreneurs such as Richard Branson of Virgin, Bill Gates of Microsoft and Michael Dell are unusual. Rarely do the founders of start-up businesses remain in charge as their businesses become large organizations. Catlin and Matthews (2001, p.4) point out that: 'The irony of entrepreneurial leaders is that the very behaviours and habit patterns that lead to success at one stage of growth can contribute to failure at the next stage. It seems that just when you get good at something, you discover it's the wrong thing to be doing!'

There are several models of business growth ranging from three to ten stages (Rutherford, Buller and McMullen, 2003). For example, Flamholtz and Randle (2000) identify the following stages of successful business growth:

1 new venture
2 expansion
3 professionalization
4 consolidation
5 diversification
6 integration
7 decline and revitalization.

Catlin and Matthews consider that entrepreneurs begin with an intuitive leadership style. In the start-up phase they can make decisions 'on the fly', improvise when required and manage everything on a day-to-day basis. As the business expands, this approach results in more and more frenzied activity, less time to think and a gradual feeling of being overwhelmed. Flamholtz and Randle point to characteristic organizational growing pains such as:

- feeling that there are not enough hours in the day
- spending too much time 'fire-fighting'
- not knowing what other staff are doing
- a failure to understand the organization's goals
- not enough good managers
- an attitude of 'I have to do it myself if I want it done properly'
- meetings are generally felt to be a waste of time
- plans are rarely made and where they exist they are seldom followed, so that things are often not done
- some people do not feel secure about their positions
- sales may be increasing, but profits are not.

These problems are symptomatic of a lack of organizational and managerial infrastructure that can support a larger and more complex operation. The original leadership style has become inappropriate and inadequate. Now there is a need for leadership to be more deliberate and for growth to be designed rather than accidental. Nevertheless, a successful owner needs to combine this approach with the best of their entrepreneurial characteristics to achieve consistent growth.

Flamholtz and Randle consider that the firm (and therefore the entrepreneur) has to go through 'a fundamental transformation or metamorphosis from the spontaneous *ad hoc*, free-spirited enterprise that it has been to a more formally planned, organized and disciplined entity'. Catlin and Matthews contend that if the founder is to remain in charge of the expanding business, he or she has to:

- Develop strategies, products/services, customers and markets.
- Develop organizational processes for planning, management and work flow – and also the infrastructure to accommodate growth and expansion.
- Recruit new people and develop teams to handle growth.
- Create a business culture to align people and teams so that they work together effectively.
- Monitor the evolution of the business and adapt their own leadership style as the business expands and changes.

But what if the owner-entrepreneur is unable to meet these requirements? Flamholtz and Randle contend that there are four alternatives:

1 Resign and let someone else be brought in to run the organization.
2 Move up to chairperson, allowing a new manager to run day-to-day operations.
3 Carry on as before and hope the problems will go away.
4 Sell out and start a new entrepreneurial venture.

In general, they conclude that: 'Founder-entrepreneurs typically experience great difficulty in relinquishing control of their businesses. Some try to change their skills and behaviour but fail. Others merely give the illusion of turning the organization over to professional managers.'

Few researchers have considered the value of learning in helping business growth. Friedrich *et al.* (2006) designed a 3-day action learning programme to improve the skills of entrepreneurs in South Africa in relation to personal initiative, planning, goal setting and innovation. They divided a sample of 84 entrepreneurs into an experimental group who took the training course, and a control group who did not. They compared the two groups after six months. The training group showed much greater progress in their business performance than the control group.

HRM practices in the small business

Defining the role of HRM in small organizations is problematic because of the limited research findings available: 'Given the importance of SME employees to the US economy, it is disheartening to note that scant attention in the SME research literature is given to the study of human resource management practices. No matter where you look . . . scholars are lamenting the dearth of information about human resource management practices in SMEs' (Heneman, Tansky and Camp, 2000).

Heneman *et al.* reasonably ask how useful or valid HR theory can be if it is based almost entirely on research conducted in large organizations. Is it relevant to the needs of practitioners or general managers in small or medium-sized enterprises? And the bulk of businesses fall into the SME category. The authors point also to the mismatch between the concerns of SME owners and the focus of HR researchers, quoting recent surveys results on the importance of labour shortages and the 'handful' of research studies on SME recruitment practices compared with hundreds of studies on recruitment in large organizations.

Aldrich (2000) summarizes the position: entrepreneurship research, while improving, is still of limited topical concern and value to entrepreneurs. There has been a focus on established businesses to the neglect of the start-up and growth phases. Research on entrepreneurship and organizations in Europe and North America has developed separately to a considerable extent. Surprisingly, government and foundation support has been greater in Europe.

Researchers on both sides of the Atlantic have a strong normative and prescriptive orientation and have kept in close touch with practitioners and policymakers. European researchers focus on fieldwork while North American researchers prefer survey methods. But

North American researchers tend to assume that their findings have universal applicability whereas European researchers show an awareness of national differences.

Entrepreneurship as a research field includes scholars of many different disciplines viewing the topic from their own academic perspective. Aldrich observes that by the 1990s organization studies in North America had moved from sociology and psychology departments into business schools. The same trend appears to be developing in Europe.

Table 8.2 summarizes the position of SMEs in relation to the 10 principles of HRM outlined in Chapter 3. It is obvious that the nature of people management varies widely in small businesses but they tend to be characterized by a number of factors illustrated in Figure 8.1.

Centralized control. A spider's web, with the owner at the centre. Limited financial and organizational resources ensure that people management is a non-specialist activity. The small business tends to be direct and informal. The character of the principal determines the climate, the morale of the workforce, and whether it is a friendly or unfriendly place to work. Employees have poorly defined responsibilities and little authority. The principal normally controls all major functions. Job tasks, pay rates and benefits are negotiated with the owner. The boss hires and fires, determines pay and conditions and requires considerable flexibility from the workers.

Table 8.2

HRM in small and medium-sized organizations

Principle	Range	Comment
1 *Comprehensiveness*	All people management handled by owner/small executive team	Tends to the extreme: comprehensively good, or totally ineffective
2 *Coherence*	Dependent on owner's personality	May be haphazard and idiosyncratic
3 *Control*	Often completely centralized	Can be either autocratic or 'clubby'
4 *Communication*	Highly variable: objectives may be a mystery to staff	Dependent on owner: often an open culture with direct communication
5 *Credibility*	Highly variable: employees tend to develop a fixed opinion of the owner	Owner's personality is visible to all
6 *Commitment*	Can be exciting and challenging for people of the right type	People who relate to the owner will stay – others will quickly leave
7 *Change*	Varies between static and growth businesses	Change usually reactive rather than strategic
8 *Competence*	Dangerously dependent on the abilities and knowledge of the owner and core staff	Often erratic and personalised resourcing: 'development' unsystematic and restricted to the chosen few
9 *Creativity*	Most SMEs do the same as their competitors: the few exceptions are destined for success	Creative owners generally make use of their own ideas
10 *Cost-effectiveness*	Often run on a shoe-string: minimal staffing and low pay	Most owners do not reward themselves and their staff on the same criteria

Strategy. There is little forward planning. Decisions are taken when problems are encountered. Staff development and training are often neglected. Succession and career planning are rare. Performance assessment is rudimentary and arbitrary.

Fire-fighting or crisis management. Employees are expected to be totally flexible, prepared to work long or irregular hours. They must perform a variety of tasks without necessarily having appropriate skills or training.

People function. Companies with fewer than 50 employees are unlikely to have an identified human resource function.

Wilkinson (2000) provides an analysis of responses to questions about the practice of HRM in the 1997 CBR survey of 2520 small and medium-sized, independent, manufacturing and business service firms. This revealed that: 35 per cent of respondents used job rotation/multi-skilling; 31.9 per cent used performance-related pay; 29.6 per cent used total quality management; and 13.1 per cent used quality circles. Grouping the last two procedures together as 'quality management', 39 per cent of firms used none of these categories, 30 per cent used one only, 23 per cent used two and just 9 per cent used all three.

Firms that used HRM-type procedures were more growth-oriented than those that did not. But these companies also saw the greatest obstacles to growth, identifying shortages of skilled labour and marketing, sales and management skills as significant constraints. HRM-users rated these limitations 10 per cent higher in significance than non-users. The most marked difference was between firms that used performance-related pay and those that did not. According to Wilkinson (2000, p.9):

> The positive associations between the growth and related business objectives, and HRM, and between HRM and non-price competitive strategies, are not difficult to explain. Firms looking to grow, expand their market share and increase the return on assets in highly competitive conditions, can be expected to adopt non-price competitive policies, and to support these by HRM strategies geared to: involving employees more in reducing costs, improving quality and productive performance; increasing their skill and flexibility to make this possible; and linking their pay to performance to reward their effort. In this sense, product market and HRM strategies are complementary and proactive means of securing the firms' objectives in a hard competitive environment.

HRM-using firms were found to be dedicating a greater proportion of total employee costs to formal training than non-HRM-using firms. In fact, roughly twice as many firms using quality management procedures had formal training than did companies not using quality

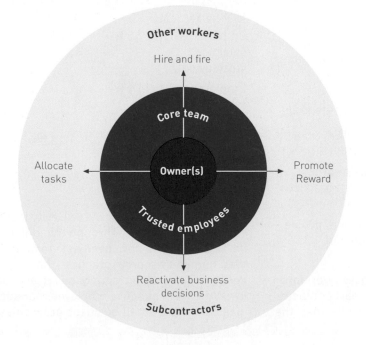

Figure 8.1

HRM in the small firm

management. HRM-using companies were also more innovative than non-users, citing an extension of their product range, improving product quality and gaining market share as the main reasons for innovation.

A further means of improving performance is to network with other companies. A third of the firms surveyed had some form of formal, informal or partnership arrangements with other businesses. Most commonly these were suppliers, customers or other companies in the same business sector. A few SMEs had developed links with colleges or universities. The reasons given by firms involved in some form of external collaboration were to: expand the range of expertise (75 per cent); assist in development of specialist services or services required by customers (70 per cent); provide access to UK markets (54 per cent); and provide access to overseas markets (45 per cent).

HRM-using businesses were significantly more like to collaborate with other firms than non-users. HRM-using firms were also more likely to use services or advice from outside agencies, contractors and consultants. Another striking finding was that companies that used 'bundles' of HRM practices fared better than those using a more restricted range. Firms that used all three HRM practices did better than those that used none by the following percentages: innovation (+80 per cent), exporting (+124 per cent) and increased employment (77 per cent).

HRM in reality Small businesses benefit from effective employee management strategies

Effective HR practices can directly affect business results for small enterprises, according to a four-phase landmark study, conducted by Cornell University associate professor Christopher Collins, PhD. Sponsored by the Gevity Institute, Collins' study shows that small businesses implementing 'effective employee management strategies' can experience:

- 22.1 per cent higher revenue growth
- 23.3 per cent higher profit growth
- 66.8 per cent reduction in employee turnover

In comparison to companies that do not.

The fourth stage of the Gevity/Cornell research looked at 323 businesses with between eight and 600 employees (average = 53) across a wide range of industries. Manager/owners and employees were both surveyed to minimize bias.

The study divides HR practices into three categories:

1 Administrative relief – processing payroll, taxes and insurance premiums and keeping records.

2 Business protection – maintaining up-to-date regulatory compliance, risk management practices and access to insurance programmes.

3 Workforce alignment – employee selection, people management and employee motivation and retention practices.

This study focuses on the third category. Workforce alignment practices have been shown in earlier studies to have a greater effect on business results than the other two categories combined. Businesses with aligned workforces can produce results that are 39 per cent better than those that do not have optimal people management strategies. The gap is only 8 per cent for the other two categories of HR practices.

Effect of strategies

Strategy implementation type	Revenue growth improvement	Profit growth improvement	Employee turnover reduction
All effective strategies	22.1%	23.3%	66.8%
Employee selection strategy only	7.5%	6.1%	17.1%
Employee management strategy only	11.5%	3.9%	15.1%
Employee motivation and retention strategy only	3.8%	13.3%	19.1%

David Sikora, director of the Gevity Institute, says the results are definitive. 'Through this unique and first-of-its-kind study, we have been able to quantify the impact that human resource practices have on small businesses. Rather than simply being an additional cost, investments in effective employee management strategies can help a small business grow sales and profits.'

What are the most effective employee management strategies for small businesses? The study identified the most effective selection, people management and employee motivation and retention strategies:

1 Base recruitment on person–organizational fit rather than person–job fit. Hiring candidates who fit the organization's culture is more effective than recruiting solely on the basis of skills that fit a particular job.

2 Use self-management rather a controlling management strategy. When employees are empowered with greater discretion and trust they perform better than people who are tightly controlled and closely monitored.

3 Create a family-like environment/community to motivate and retain employees rather than focus on pay as a motivator.

The research also looked at the effect of different business environments on results and identified the conditions where HR practices can be most effective. The greatest business impact is experienced by companies that are in highly competitive markets; have high-growth goals; and employ more than 50 people. Sample findings:

Person–organizational fit	No growth goal	High growth goal
One-year revenue growth	7.1%	14.7%

Self-management	Under 50 employees	Over 50 employees
One-year profit growth	8.4%	15.8%

High competition	Individual monetary incentives	Family-like community
One-year employee turnover	27.8%	7.9%

'The study is groundbreaking because we've proven that specific human resources strategies have a meaningful, and statistically significant impact to small business financial performance', said Christopher Collins. 'So much of existing research concerns large companies. However, the relative impact of a single person leaving a small business can be an even greater setback. Our research clearly supports the importance of having a formal employee management strategy as part of any small business plan – either in-house or outsourced to a professional like Gevity.'

'The results are encouraging to Gevity as one of the only human resource services providers that includes workforce alignment support in its offerings,' said Erik Vonk, Gevity's chairman and chief executive officer. 'Our unique ability to implement effective employee management practices enables us to assist our clients drive revenue and profit growth, while reducing employee turnover.'

Summarize the HR strategies that appear to have the greatest benefits for small businesses.

Source: *HRM Guide* (http://www.hrmguide.net/), 31 August, 2006.

Kotey and Slade (2005) reported on a survey of 371 micro, small and medium-sized firms on the Sunshine Coast of Queensland, Australia. They found that the adoption of formal HR practices increased with organizational size but there was a substantial move towards formal HRM quite early in the growth process. Some of the major trends that occurred with growth were:

● Use of a greater range of recruitment sources such as newspapers and government agencies and a wider range of selection techniques. However, these were used more extensively at the operational level in micro and small firms, with the recruitment process for managers lagging behind in terms of sophistication. This tended to be corrected in medium-sized firms. Word-of-mouth recommendations prevailed in the smaller firms but this approach did not produce applicants with the levels of skill required by medium-sized firms.

● On-the-job training prevails in all SMEs but other training methods were used as firms grew in size. Delegation of training to supervisors and middle-managers increased in larger SMEs but, even there, more on-the-job training came from owner-managers than delegated staff. External training for operational staff decreased as firms grew, presumably because of better in-house training capabilities, but external training for managers increased. Medium-sized firms became more formal in their training procedures. For example, orientation was check-listed in half the firms of that size surveyed.

- While micro firms could monitor employee performance on an observational basis, increasing size required some degree of formal appraisal. Small and medium-sized firms did this extensively for operational staff but formal appraisal of managers tended to be restricted to medium-sized businesses. Rating scales were the most common method for operational staff.

- HR policies and documentation appeared very early in the growth process, reflecting legislative requirements, for example on health and safety, and the need for individual records and control as the number of staff grew beyond the point where the owner-manager knew all the employees. While application forms were extensively used, job descriptions were not always provided in small and medium-sized firms, reflecting the inherent flexibility of employment in SMEs.

Entrepreneurship and business growth research

Howard E. Aldrich has been a considerable influence on the topic of entrepreneurship. In his *Organizations Evolving* (1999) he makes the point that:

> Organizational scholars have done an excellent job in explaining how things work in organizations that have been around for a while, but not how they came to be that way. In contrast, I am interested in the genesis of organizations, organizational populations, and communities. Even really large organizations started small, usually, but the absolute miracle of their creation does not seem to interest most organization theorists. It should.

He advocates an evolutionary approach to the emergence and change of organizations. Using Darwinian language he describes the creation of new organizational structures as 'variation', the way in which entrepreneurs modify those structures and use resources to meet changing circumstances as 'adaptation', the circumstances leading to survival or extinction as 'selection', and imitation of successful concepts by other entrepreneurs as 'retention'.

Aldrich points to the weakness of traditional (romantic) views of the entrepreneur, when most are only modestly successful and that success is often dependent on others. He

---

HRM in reality Small firms lose staff to large companies

The belief that small companies poach trained staff from large businesses is a myth, it seems. A NatWest Small Business Research Trust (SBRT) Quarterly Survey of Small Businesses suggests the opposite: small firms lose more staff to large organizations than they gain from bigger companies.

Most small firms get new employees from other small firms and the pool of unemployed. Just 20 per cent of their new recruits come from large organizations, whereas more than 40 per cent of full-time workers recruited by small firms in the survey over the 12 months to April 2001 came from businesses with fewer than 100 employees. Around 20 per cent of recruits were unemployed and another 13 per cent were students. This finding is all the more remarkable given that more people work in large than small firms across the economy as a whole. The survey also shows that more people leave small firms to set up their own businesses than to become small firm employees.

According to Peter Ibbetson, Head of NatWest Business Banking:

> These findings yet again underline the considerable contribution small firms make to the UK economy in terms of employment. Overall, small firms appear to recruit from the unemployed and students and then lose them, probably after providing much valuable training and experience, to large firms.

Suggest some actions that small businesses can use to retain key employees.

Source: *HRM Guide UK* (http://www.hrmguide.co.uk) 17 April, 2001.

draws attention to the issue of the 'nascent entrepreneur', someone who initiates a series of activities that are intended to result in a business start-up but often do not end up doing so (Reynolds, 1994). Every year, between four and six per cent of working Americans embark on actions aimed at a business venture – 40 per cent of Americans do so at some point in their adult lives, according to Reynolds and White (1997).

Working in small businesses

Entrepreneurs start small businesses in order to obtain freedom, challenge and personal income. Starting one's own business offers a way around the lack of equal opportunities. Women are strongly represented in the SME sector. Immigrants often overcome prejudice, language difficulties and barriers in the employment market by starting their own businesses.

The picture is different for employees, however. Staff in small businesses can feel insecure because of the lack of structure and planning. Career aspirations are frustrated as most owners either do not wish the business to expand beyond their personal span of control or do not have the management skills necessary for effective delegation. Few corner shop owners have the skills or inclination to develop large businesses and many of their children are disinclined to carry on with the family firm. In contrast, the best entrepreneurs have a range of general business skills – including people management – or have the good sense to obtain specialist assistance from:

- *Consultants*. Providing advice on recruitment, pay and benefits, management structures and organizational change associated with growth.
- *Training agencies*. Providing skills training on a local or regional basis.
- *Networks*. Small businesses can link together to pay for resourcing and development assistance, possibly through chambers of commerce and business clubs.

Entrepreneurial structures can only function up to a certain size. When they become too large for personal relationships they must evolve into a more clearly defined organization. The nature of people management must change fundamentally when this occurs. However, it is possible to preserve some of the informal and non-hierarchical characteristics of the small business by forming a formal cooperative or, informally, a team-based organization.

The problems and concerns of small and medium-sized businesses are also seen in other organizations: schools, colleges, religious institutions, charities, trusts – and ships. Abrashoff (2002, p.13) describes taking command of a US Navy ship:

> . . . as the new captain of *Benfold*, I read some exit surveys, interviews conducted by the military to find out why they are leaving. I assumed that low pay would be the first reason, but in fact it was fifth. The top reason was not being treated with respect or dignity; second was being prevented from making an impact on the organization; third, not being listened to; and fourth, not being rewarded with more responsibility. Talk about an eye opener.

Abrashoff observes that the same findings appear in exit surveys from the civilian sector and concludes that leaders all make the same mistakes. As a naval captain there was little he could do about the pay scales, so he concentrated on the other four 'gripes'. He advocates a simple organizational approach: 'The key to being a successful skipper is to see the ship through the eyes of the crew. Only then can you find out what's really wrong and, in so doing, help the sailors empower themselves to fix it.'

But he also observes that while the Navy applauds this approach in principle, it negates it in practice because officers are taught never to say the words 'I don't know'. Many entrepreneurs have worked themselves into the same psychological position – an unwillingness to admit that they do not know everything about their business. Abrashoff describes their behaviour as being 'on constant alert, riding herd on every detail'. They micromanage everything and thereby disempower their employees. He concludes that: 'A ship commanded by a micromanager and his or her hierarchy of sub-micromanagers is no breeding ground for initiative.'

Consultancies

Business organizations rarely have the expertise or spare resources to conduct large-scale change initiatives without outside assistance. What options do they have? They may turn to the academic world that contains a large number of 'experts' who research and theorize in this area. Alternatively – and far more likely – they use business consultants (Key concept 8.3). Whereas academics appear to have played a major role in the appearance of HRM, consultants have taken the lead in the wider area of change management.

Key concept 8.3 Consultants

Biech (2001, p.1) describes a consultant as someone who 'provides unique assistance or advice to someone else, usually known as the "client". The work is defined by the consultant's expertise, the structure in which the consultant works, and the process the consultant uses.'

Astute consultants understand how important packaging is in marketing their services. More than anything, they sell themselves. As we have noted in earlier chapters, image plays a disproportionate role in business credibility. Academics appear to believe that the quality of the ideas is what matters. In fact, sound methodology and process value are virtually irrelevant when it comes to client acceptability. The average academic is not as adept at the self-marketing and impression management necessary to win over top managers. Consultants play the business game, dress and behave appropriately knowing that 'their clients will be acutely aware of the messages that are sent by such small things as the type of watch, size of briefcase and elegance of technology used' (Furnham, 1992, p.xix).

According to Furnham, academics look for puzzles, consultants are given problems; the researchers are 'satisfied to know and understand, while the latter want to use the knowledge and sell it'. The former veer towards 'pure' understanding for its own sake; consultants focus on the 'applied'. University researchers tend to be overcautious, taking a considerable time to develop ideas and theories. Their detached, independent view does not fit business managers' expectations of enthusiastic commitment to 'owning the problem'. Unlike academics brought up in the dense waffle school of explanation, the most successful consultants are polished presenters. They have a considerable store of supportive anecdotes and make a point of expressing ideas clearly and simply. Consultants are aware of managers' urgent timescales; of the requirement to provide 'solutions'; of a need for face-to-face reassurance.

Furnham finds different personality traits in academics and consultants, outlined in Table 8.3, describing successful consultants as 'time-conscious, high-urgency people, driven by deadlines'. Their use of time is quite different from that of academics who appear sluggish and hesitant by comparison. Given that most businesses turn to established consultancies, what services do they provide?

According to Wood (1983), reasons for using consultants include:

1 Specialist knowledge and expertise. For instance, a venture in a new country is made easier by using consultants familiar with the local language and business practices.

2 An independent perspective on the organization's problems. This requires mutual trust and respect between client and consultant.

3 Acting as a catalyst for change. Consultants can provide cautious managers with reassurance, having been through similar circumstances before. By reducing the level of anxiety, decisions can be taken more swiftly and risks accepted with greater confidence.

4 Provision of additional resources for temporary needs. Within the context of flexibility, this is a form of outsourcing or subcontracting of management tasks.

5 To help develop a consensus when views are divided.

Table 8.3

Characteristcs of
academics and
consultants

Source: Based on Furnham
(1992).

	Academics	Consultants
Major aims	Insight and knowledge	Action and operation
Speed of solution	Low urgency	High urgency
Type of solution valued	Elegant and critical	Applicable and comprehensible
Source of data	Direct empirical base	Second-hand empirical base
Level of complexity	Frequently complex	Frequently simple
Dealing with uncertainty	Dealt with statistically	Dealt with personally
Preferred medium or presentation	Written documents/tables	Face to face
Self-presentation	Irrelevant, often shabby	Crucial, fashionably smart
Means of persuasion	Empirical data	Rhetorical
Cost–benefit analysis	Irrelevant	Crucial
Type of personality valued	Introvert	Extrovert

6 Demonstrating impartiality and objectivity about changes to the organization's employees.

7 To provide the justification for unpleasant decisions.

We can distinguish between: (a) resource consultancy, transferring knowledge or understanding from consultant to client; and (b) process consultancy, in which the consultant helps the client organization to develop new skills of analysis and diagnosis for themselves (Torrington, 1994).

Of course, consultants are not without their critics. According to Townsend (1970, p.97):

> The effective ones are the one-man shows. The institutional ones are disastrous. They waste time, cost money, demoralize and distract your best people, and don't solve problems. They are people who borrow your watch to tell you what time it is and then walk off with it. Don't use them under any circumstances. Not even to keep your stockholders and directors quiet. It isn't worth it.

Ironically, the many consultant-inspired de-layering and downsizing programmes have unleashed a mass of redundant managers who have elected to become consultants themselves! Faced with an employment market saturated with middle-aged, middle managers, consultancy may be seen as the only way of generating income. However, consultancy and the practice of management require different skills. Many would-be consultants do not have the appropriate qualities; others can put on an impressive performance of impression management but have little specialist knowledge or ability in diagnosis and facilitation.

Summary

This chapter introduced entrepreneurship and people management issues in small and medium-sized enterprises. This remains an inadequately researched area in HRM terms despite its importance to job creation and national economies. There is a fair amount of knowledge about individual entrepreneurs and their aspirations but comparatively little 'hard evidence' about many other aspects of the small firm. SMEs come in a wide range of sizes and structures. These differences introduce complexities into any understanding of their HR procedures. However, recent research supports the view that introduction of formal human resource processes increases with organizational size.

Further reading

International differences and similarities in small business research are outlined by Howard Aldrich in 'Learning together: national differences in entrepreneurship research' in D.L. Sexton and H. Landstrom (eds) *The Blackwell Handbook of Entrepreneurship* (Blackwell Handbooks in Management), published by Blackwell (2000). Books on HR in small businesses are few and far between. *The Human Resource Function in Emerging Enterprises* by Jeffrey S. Hornsby (Brooks Cole, 2001) and *Human Resource Development in Small Organizations: Research and Practice* by Jim Stewart (Routledge, 2003) are worth consulting. Good texts on the growth process in SMEs include: Catlin and Matthews' *Leading at the Speed of Growth: Journey from Entrepreneur to CEO*, published by John Wiley & Sons (2001); and Flamholtz and Randle's *Growing Pains: Transitioning from an Entrepreneurship to a Professionally Managed Firm*, published by Jossey-Bass (2000).

Huge numbers of 'how-to' and 'real life problem-solving' books exist, including: Cheryl D. Rickman's *The Small Business Start-up Workbook: A Step-by-step Guide to Starting the Business You've Dreamed of* (How To Books, Ltd., 2005); Alan Le Marinel's *Start and Run Your Own Business: The Complete Guide to Setting Up and Managing a Small Business* (How To Books, Ltd. 2004); and D. Michael Abrashoff's engaging *It's Your Ship: Management Techniques from the Best Damn Ship in the Navy*, Warner Books (2002).

Review questions

1. Outline some of the ways in which people management skills could be made available to entrepreneurs.

2. Are entrepreneurs special people? How would you explain the difference between a 'nascent entrepreneur' and an entrepreneur who succeeds in starting a business?

3. Why does the level of entrepreneurship vary between countries?

4. How does the size of a small business limit the practice of human resource management? What difficulties are human resource specialists likely to experience in dealing with a founding entrepreneur as a business grows?

5. What do you consider to be the main advantages and disadvantages of collaborative entrepreneurship? Why do collaborative ventures often end as single-owner companies?

6. Few small companies become major corporations. In terms of people management, why do you think this is so?

7. What is 'micro-management' and what is its significance to a growing business?

8. How can knowledge about effective people management aboard a ship be regarded as relevant to small business management?

9. Summarize the advantages and disadvantages of the use of consultants by small and medium-sized enterprises. What are the key issues to take into account when commissioning consultants and evaluating results?

10. Is it the case that: (a) firms using HRM procedures benefit because of those procedures? or (b) firms that are forward-looking and growing are more likely to use HRM procedures because they are forward-looking and growing?

Case studies for discussion and analysis

New Age Finance/The Craft Partnership/Royal Ocean

1 New Age Finance is a venture recently started by two experienced graduates. They have launched a range of financial services geared towards middle-aged suburban house owners. The products have proved very successful and have attracted the interest of a large insurance company that has agreed to fund a major expansion through internet sales. Their forecast suggests that around 40 sales and administration staff need to be in place by the end of the year. The business plan envisages regionally grouped sales staff with administrative functions located centrally.

What are the possible organizational structures for this company? On what basis should the decision be made for the chosen structure?

2 The Craft Partnership is a cooperative of twenty independent producers. They are based at an old factory site on the outskirts of town that is divided into small workshops. HR, marketing and finance services are provided by an office manager and two staff. The cooperative has grown successfully over the last five years. Now they have the opportunity of taking on a much larger site adjacent to the tourist centre.

Opinion is divided among the partners on the way forward. Some are content to stay as they are. A few have said that they will leave and set up on their own if the cooperative gets much larger. Others are excited by the prospect of better facilities, room for growth, and space for new members in the cooperative. They also see big advantages in being accessible to tourists.

The office manager sees this as the opportunity to make more radical changes. She is concerned that the partnership is unwieldy and makes external finance difficult. She spends much of her time sorting out squabbles between partners and trying to get them to share resources sensibly. Some partners are overworked and others do not have enough to do. She can see many ways of increasing efficiency if the partnership becomes a conventional business. This could be done by creating a holding company, making the existing partners both shareholders and employees. A local venture company is prepared to make a substantial investment for a 50 per cent share in the new organization. However, they would require a formal structure with defined management roles. They feel that the office manager would make a suitable managing director.

She has arranged a meeting with the partners and the venture company. (a) How should she proceed? (b) What is the reaction likely to be? (c) What is the way forward?

3 The Royal Ocean is a well-established resort hotel. Its clients are in the middle to upper income bracket and many return year after year. It has developed a reputation for attentive service and is regarded as expensive but good value. In recent years, however, a new marina development further down the coast has provided extra competition. The new hotels are larger and more modern, boasting a choice of restaurants, bars and leisure facilities. They have seriously affected the Royal Ocean's profitability.

The hotel is on a restricted site and the owners, a small regional chain, cannot afford substantial capital investment. Like most hotels it has a highly seasonal pattern of business. Despite the competition, the Royal Ocean has no difficulty in filling rooms during peak periods. Occupancy rates have been mainly affected during quieter periods. The company has decided to encourage more business out of season through selective promotions to group travel organizers. During the low season, the country has a national holiday when, traditionally, the hotel has allowed most of its staff to take two days off. The small number of remaining employees has been sufficient to cater for the few guests. In the past, visitors at this time of year have tended to be middle-aged people seeking quiet relaxation. They have been happy to tolerate restricted service in the restaurant, bar and pool area.

▶

This year, the hotel has achieved 80 per cent occupancy over the holiday period. The regular clients have been vastly outnumbered by families with young children.

Rooms have been sold cheaply to low-income groups who are not expected to spend heavily on the more profitable services. Accordingly, the hotel general manager decided not to increase staffing to normal weekly levels. He felt that the low return would not justify upsetting employee morale.

However, the consequences have proven to be unfortunate. The regular clients have been angered by the inability of the hotel to provide even the basic service experienced in previous years.

Most shops, restaurants and visitor facilities in the area are closed because of the holiday. The clients are forced to remain within the hotel. The restaurant has been besieged by noisy family groups. The pool area has become a playground. Clients are waiting for up to 20 minutes for an elevator because children are continuously going up and down in them. The quiet middle-aged regulars are complaining vociferously to any member of staff they can find. It seems that they are largely affluent professionals who are accustomed to having their way. They are becoming increasingly demanding and are threatening never to come back.

What can be done (a) now and (b) in the future?

Chapter 9
Organizational culture

Learning objectives

The purpose of this chapter is to:

● Introduce the concept of culture at international, national and organizational levels.

● Describe and evaluate theoretical approaches to culture, especially that of Hofstede.

● Evaluate the contribution of Deal and Kennedy to the debate on corporate culture.

● Discuss how cultures may be managed.

Culture and international HRM

Management practices vary throughout the world. **Culture**, history, language and beliefs obviously underlie much of this variation. More than any other business function, the practice of people management has been closely linked to national culture.

To quote Bunge and Ardila (1987, p.225):

> Culture is the great social matrix within which we are born, we grow, and we die. It gives meaning to human action, and we transmit it to our biological and spiritual descendants (our children and our students). It has many philosophical, political, and practical implications: it tells what is good and bad; how to live and die; how to talk, dress, and love; things to eat and when to eat them; how to express happiness and sadness; what to consider desirable and what to detest.

Comparing one country with another we find components of people management are accorded different degrees of importance and are carried out differently. The activities undertaken by HR managers vary as a consequence. However, there has also been recent consideration of the extent to which globalization, the internationalization of business and consolidation of legal systems dilute the impact of national identity. It is increasingly possible to distinguish practices that are universally applicable from those based on a particular national culture.

Key concept 9.1 Culture

The anthropologist Edward Tylor (1871) defined culture as 'knowledge, belief, art, morals, law, custom and any other capabilities and habits' acquired through membership of society. In a narrower sense the term is used to describe the differences between one society and another. In this context, a culture is an all-pervasive system of beliefs and behaviours transmitted socially. Specifically it consists of the set of values – abstract ideals – and norms or rules held by a society, together with its material expressions (Giddens, 1989, p.30).

Cultural differences are seen also at the organizational level. Human resource literature places considerable emphasis on corporate culture. We saw in Chapter 2 that the classic Harvard model of HRM emphasizes the link between a culture that fosters appropriate employee attitudes, behaviour and commitment in order to achieve competitive performance. This requires sophisticated people management systems allowing careful selection and development of people with suitable characteristics, plus accurate performance assessment and reward packages to encourage desirable behaviour.

International comparisons

International comparisons of HRM focus on similarities and differences between people management practices in different countries. A number of fundamental questions can be raised (Pieper, 1990):

- How is HRM structured in individual countries?
- What strategies are discussed?
- What is put into practice?
- What are the main differences and similarities?
- To what extent are corporate policies and strategies influenced by national factors such as culture, government policy and educational systems?

The answers to these questions are not simply of theoretical interest. They provide lessons that we can learn from other cultures and, for the international manager operating in more than one country, they define the cultural elements and behaviours that must be learned in order to be effective.

We noted in Part two that the market place is global and the key players are multinational or transnational organizations. Consequently, HR managers cannot confine themselves to an understanding of people management in their own countries. An awareness of international HRM is essential.

Torrington (1994, p.5) argues that international HRM has the same basic dimensions as HRM in a national context, but with added features:

- it operates on a greater scale
- strategic considerations are more complex
- operational units vary more widely and require coordination across more barriers.

Torrington considers that we all operate within the 'learned frameworks' of our own cultures. People managers need to transcend these frameworks. Human resource managers often have responsibility for developing and training staff for subsidiaries in several countries and cultural issues are particularly significant for any international joint venture where a merger of cultures takes place (Lu, 2006). Training programmes to meet the needs of international managers include:

- language training
- cultural awareness
- economic and political understanding
- appreciation of different legal systems
- awareness of management style and conventions.

HRM in reality Asian businesses prefer locals to expats

Conference Board report finds 'problems with expatriates'

A report from The Conference Board finds that major Asia–Pacific companies are searching more intensively for executives living in the region, rather than relying on expatriate executives brought in from other parts of the world.

Fifty-five organizations based in the Asia–Pacific region were surveyed for the report. Almost four-fifths (79 per cent) are seeking to develop leadership talent within the region and equal percentages are either maintaining (47 per cent) or increasing (47 per cent) the financial resources devoted to leadership development initiatives despite widespread budget cuts elsewhere.

Respondents to the survey identified the following actions being taken to develop a stronger leadership supply:

- Identifying talent gaps and company requirements (92 per cent).
- Improving talent assessment (91 per cent).
- Involving the CEO in talent development (91 per cent).

- Placing priority on developing and retaining high potentials (90 per cent).
- Reinforcing accountability of leaders for development (84 per cent).
- Developing specific Asia–Pacific development programmes (76 per cent).

Survey participants cited the following methods as those being used in their organizations to develop business leaders:

- Internal management development programmes (44 per cent).
- Company training programmes (40 per cent).
- International assignments greater than two years (36 per cent).
- Mentoring and/or coaching (33 per cent).
- Participation in cross-functional international teams (33 per cent).
- Action learning assignments (26 per cent).

The report also shows that many international businesses are trying to cut the number of expatriates and

▶

international assignees occupying longer term (in contrast to developmental) leadership roles. Companies in the region are coming to the conclusion that home-grown executives impact more effectively on company performance than expatriates and cost less. In fact, with salary supplements and additional benefits, such as home leave, school tuition and accommodation subsidies, expatriates can cost at least twice as much as a local executive.

Andrew N. Bell, Program Director for the Asia–Pacific HR Council and author of the report said:

> One reason for reducing expatriates and international assignees is based on the premise that in the lifecycle of most businesses, the localization of leadership has a positive impact on performance. This positive impact results from a range of factors in which local leadership is more likely to have a deeper understanding and familiarity with the needs and expectations of local consumers and clients, local business infrastructure such as distribution channels and external relations, including with the government and media. Also, language may be a critical factor. An inability to work in the local language can be a serious impediment in some aspects of business operations.

Asia–Pacific businesses face two challenges:

Local supply limitations. There is intense competition for the limited supply of local leadership talent. For example, in some sectors, turnover rates in Shanghai and Bangalore are greater than 40 per cent per year. Salary levels can also be high. Some talented executives in Shanghai may receive absolute salary levels that are equal to or greater than their counterparts in Singapore or London.

Expatriate proliferation. Leadership competence and technical expertise may have to be imported during initial investments in a new market or periods of significant expansion and large-scale capital investments. The process of developing local replacements often takes longer than planned.

Survey participants identified the following competencies as being relevant to success in the Asia–Pacific region:

- cultural understanding
- adaptation
- collaboration
- teamwork
- communication
- alignment across borders
- people development
- coaching.

Barriers to developing leaders in the Asia–Pacific region mentioned by companies included:

- the capabilities of HR professionals in some locations;
- mismatches between location of talent and business opportunities;
- preservation of established company cultures, networks, and behaviours;
- low mobility within region for some; and
- competition for talent leading to high turnover and escalating salaries.

The report is titled *Leadership Development in Asia–Pacific: Identifying and Developing Leaders for Growth Report #1387-06-WG*, The Conference Board (2006).

Is the trend towards employing more local and fewer expatriate employees good for businesses in the Asia–Pacific region?

Source: *HRM Guide* (http://www.hrmguide.net), 13 April, 2006.

Ethnocentrism and cultural differences

According to Taylor (2006, p.12):

> Ethnocentric people tend to form pre-conceived judgements of different cultures based on one experience, or based on limited evidence. Perhaps they tend to take stereotyping a little too far and don't keep an open mind, so they cannot move beyond a certain stage. Therefore, despite the fact that a person from a different culture may have many unique personal qualities, the ethnocentric person cannot see beyond their fixed ideas, even when those ideas are wrong, so their mind remains closed.

There is a misleading assumption that the social, class and cultural values underlying management ideas are – or should be – 'normal' for every country. The following list (based on the work of Campbell and associates, cited in Triandis, 1990, p.35) highlights key conclusions from studies of ethnocentrism. Characteristics of the 'in-group' are that everyone tends to:

- Define their own culture as 'natural' and 'correct' and other cultures as 'unnatural' and 'incorrect'.

- Perceive in-group customs as universally valid – 'what is good for us is good for everybody'.

- Think that in-group norms, rules, and values are obviously correct.

- Consider it natural to help and cooperate with members of one's in-group.

- Act in ways which favour the in-group.

- Feel proud of the in-group.

- Feel hostility towards out-groups.

Scientifically-based management methods are regarded as culturally neutral and universal (Chung, 1991). In fact, they are mostly North American and based on that particular culture but Western managers have regarded factors such as performance-related pay and particular selection techniques as best practice everywhere.

English is the major business language, allowing the spread of largely American business concepts via colonial/post-colonial routes and multinational corporations (Brewster and Tyson, 1991). These methodologies were accepted as 'received wisdom' in large areas of the world, including Africa, the Middle East and India. They were also adopted by countries in Europe and Asia that had been brought within the American orbit after World War II. North American business ideas continue to flourish in both these continents as a managerial 'lingua franca' in highly diverse markets where no single local culture dominates. However, eastern countries can be just as ethnocentric. Lee (2006), for example, states that the Chinese are '. . . a very nationalistic race, they have continued to preserve ethnic practices and traditional customs and characteristics in modern business negotiations.'

Shih, Chiang and Kim (2005) interviewed expatriate employees and human resource managers of five multinational enterprise subsidiaries in the information technology industry: Applied Material (American); Philips (Dutch); Hitachi (Japanese); Samsung (Korean); and Winbond (Taiwan). All used standardized performance forms set by headquarters and not tailored to local operating environments. Lack of on-the-job training for expatriates was found to be prevalent. Divergent practices in goal setting, performance appraisal and performance-related pay were largely attributed to the parent company's culture.

Walton (1999) distinguishes between a global mindset and an international mindset. Managers in an internationally minded company are 'more one-directional, ethnocentric, outward-looking from the country in which they are based'. Whereas a true global organization will feature highly adaptable managers, and an organizational value structure that allows managers to detach themselves from their original national roots and thereby shed their ethno-centric outlook (Rhinesmith, 1996).

This global-oriented mindset suggests that multinationals should become 'free-floating' – not tied to any specific country. Instead, the location of their operations should take into account a balance of factors including:

- Differing national employment legislation, ways of doing business, customs, national investment policies, fiscal incentives, attitudes to foreign investment, and other competitors.

- Issues related to physical location, including local market potential, geographical and cultural distance from the company's base, transport logistics and communications.

- Employee costs including wages, training needs, skills availability, social and industrial infrastructure.

- Fit of new locations with existing customers, management and production.

- The organizational structure of the firm.

It is worth noting, however, that few transnational companies are truly global multinationals, most having strong ties to one or more countries.

Cultures and standards

Cultures are human creations but, unlike bridges, buildings, roads and other material objects of our making, cultures are subjective (Triandis, 1990, p.36). They are made up of elements such as attitudes, beliefs, norms, roles and values (see Key concept 9.1). We take our own culture for granted. In fact, we are scarcely aware of it until we interact with another. Each culture has a '**world view**' – a set of values and beliefs. This is meaningful to its members but alien to others. As a consequence, we look at people from other cultures, see that their ways are different and often dislike these ways. It is normal to 'use our own culture as the standard and judge other cultures by the extent they meet the standard' (Triandis, 1990, p.34). As we have seen, this ethnocentrism can be related to the concept of the '**in-group**' – those people we identify with. It can be argued that the export of Western (American) management methods by multinationals and business schools – including HRM and its associated paraphernalia of assessment, performance-related pay and related ideas – is an example of ethnocentrism on a massive scale. Trompenaars and Hampden-Turner (1997, p.2) consider that:

> Even with experienced international companies, many well-intended 'universal' applications of management theory have turned out badly. For example, pay for performance has in many instances been a failure on the African continent because there are particular, though unspoken, rules about the sequence and timing of reward and promotions. Similarly, management-by-objectives schemes have generally failed within subsidiaries of multinationals in southern Europe, because managers have not wanted to conform to the abstract nature of preconceived policy guidelines.

Trompenaars and Hampden-Turner (*ibid.*) point out that international HR (and other) managers have a particularly difficult task. They have to operate in three different cultures at the same time: their culture of origin; the culture within which they are currently working; and the corporate culture of the organization. The training they are offered does not necessarily help. For example, Shen and Darby (2006) used semi-structured interviews to examine international training and development policies and practices in ten Chinese multinational enterprises (MNEs). They found that these organizations provided limited training to expatriates and other nationals and lacked any systematic international management development system. They describe the MNEs as having an essentially ethnocentric approach to international training and development, providing different levels of training and development for host-country nationals and others.

Culture is important also when employees in different countries operate as a 'virtual team'. Horwitz, Bravington and Silvis (2006) identified cross-cultural communication improvement, managerial and leadership communication, goal and role clarification, and relationship building as the most important factors leading to effective virtual team performance.

Cultural variety

Cultures should not be confused with countries or so-called 'nation states'. There is a danger in examining cultures as 'wholes': there are not only differences between cultures but also within cultures (Brewster and Tyson, 1991). For example, Australian culture can be identified with that of the majority Anglo-Celtic population but the nation's culture also encompasses a number of distinctive sub-cultures. These include that of the indigenous Aboriginal population and a number of significant immigrant groups, such as Italian, Greek and Vietnamese communities. More accurately, Aboriginal culture is itself plural, composed of hundreds of different cultural and linguistic groups. Hofstede (1994 [1991], p.10) argues that an individual's culture has several levels:

- National – according to country (or countries for migrants).
- Regional and/or ethnic and/or religious and/or linguistic.
- Gender – different assumptions and expectations of females and males.

- Generation – differences between age groups.
- Social class – linked to educational opportunities and occupations.
- Organizational – different organizations have their individual cultures.

We can see readily that this mixture provides an intriguing cocktail for a selector to attempt to disentangle; for a performance assessor to misunderstand; a management developer to 'correct'. All in all, there is massive scope for a clash of cultures – and prejudices. As we shall see in Part six on the management of diversity, there is a major issue about the real meaning of 'equal opportunities' in this context.

The perception of time

Managing people depends a great deal on our perceptions and expectations of others. We assess, we select, we reward according to our own criteria. We have our inbuilt standards, the origins of which we rarely question and which, as we have seen, we interpret as 'normal'. Given that this is the case, can we identify firm dimensions of difference that people managers can be taught to recognize and respect?

Triandis (1990) identifies a number of such dimensions, or cultural syndromes. One example is 'cultural complexity', which particularly affects the perception of time. Think about time for a moment and consider how many basic business activities depend on people 'doing something within three hours', 'arriving for an interview at 10am', 'achieving an objective in six months' and so on. In fact, our judgement of other people depends heavily on our conception of time. How do we feel about people who do not turn up to an interview on time, or fail to complete a task within the agreed period? If we live in an industrial culture we will regard them unfavourably.

But what if their concept of time is not the same as ours? Of course, an hour, a day, or a month is the same for everyone, but we vary in our beliefs about the significance of these periods. Albert Einstein showed that time is relative and this notion is as significant for human resource management as it is for space travel.

Triandis (*ibid.*) argues that different cultures have different attitudes towards time. Time-keeping is treated tolerantly in undeveloped societies – with less complex things to do, they can be done in any order. However, as societies become industrial and technological, people must pay increased attention to time. In industrialized countries, there are many things to do and they must be coordinated with other people. Hence, time becomes more important. Time is regarded as something precise and highly significant. So, if a manager moves to a less-developed country, what standard is it fair for that person to expect?

Another significant time characteristic is that of short or long-term orientation (Hofstede and Bond, 1988). East Asians tend to have a much longer time perspective than, for example, nationals in Australasia, Nigeria, North America, Pakistan and the UK. In Part one we identified HRM as a philosophy of people management that is long term in its intent. The root of this orientation lies in comparisons of US and Japanese management and criticism of the former's short-term attitudes towards human resources. In effect, the adoption of HRM requires short-termist cultures to take on Japanese attitudes towards time. As we saw in earlier chapters, this does not come naturally and provides a partial explanation for the failure of many organisations to take on true HRM.

Confucianism

Hofstede and Bond (*ibid.*) attribute the long-term orientation in East Asians to '**Confucian Dynamism**'. It embodies values from the teaching of Confucius such as perseverance, a need to order relationships by status, a sense of shame and a habit of thrifty saving. Kahn (1979, p.121) also saw the rise of the East Asian 'tiger' economies as due to the Confucian ethic, including factors such as sobriety; placing a high value on education; a need for accomplishment in various skills; seriousness about job, family and obligations; and a sense of hierarchy. Yang (2005) points to the different emphases between various Confucian cultures In Korea, for example, there is an emphasis on emotion and feelings ('jeong'). This is an extension of family ties that now has a similar role in management systems to the Western concept of emotional intelligence.

More generally, Tan and Chee (2005) found several factors unique to a Confucian context that facilitated the development of trust: diligence, perseverance, filial piety, thriftiness, respect for authority, a shared value of collective effort, harmonious relationship in the office, humbleness and magnanimous behaviour.

Roles

Triandis (1990) relates cultural complexity to the way we define our working and other roles. In complex societies roles become increasingly specific – compartmentalized into separate mental boxes. We can be finance managers, parents, social club officials and behave differently in each role. In less complex societies, on the other hand, roles are diffuse, affecting every aspect of people's lives. Religion, politics and matters of taste are important in diffuse cultures. They are less important in role-specific cultures. Developed countries tend to be role-specific, avoiding role confusion. Theory and best practise in key HRM areas such as selection, performance measurement and development assume an equal opportunities approach in which people are dealt with without favour or prejudice. However, this notion is alien to diffuse-role cultures in which it is natural to favour members of one's own family or community.

Diffuse-role cultures value politeness and courtesy – even towards people who are disliked – something that would be regarded as hypocrisy in specific cultures. Again human resource texts assume that outright, if tactful, honesty is required in rejecting job applicants, counselling for performance weaknesses and dismissal. In short, if we feel that someone is not up to the job – we more or less say so. This approach can appear arrogant and aggressive to people from diffuse societies.

Related cultures

In a classic study Haire, Ghiselli and Porter (1966) surveyed 3500 managers in 14 different countries and estimated that 28 per cent of discernible differences in management attitudes were culturally based, identifying four main cultural groups: Nordic-European, Latin-European, Anglo-American and developing nations. This started a trend to try and divide the world's complex pattern of cultures into neat, analytical groupings – with all the attendant risks of historical inaccuracy and gross insensitivity. Take for example, an attempt by Leeds, Kirkbride and Duncan (1994): '. . . we can distinguish a number of reasonably clear country clusters . . . which parallel the work of other commentators . . . These would include:

1 Scandinavia: Denmark, Finland, Norway and Sweden.
2 Anglo: Ireland and the UK in Europe but also other English-speaking countries including Australia, New Zealand and Canada (excluding Quebec), and the United States of America.
3 Germanic: Austria, Germany and Switzerland.
4 Latin and Mediterranean: Italy, Portugal and Spain.
5 Near Eastern: Greece and Turkey. The Turks and Greeks are close culturally, and both are proud of their European and Oriental associations. However, the Greeks have also been considered very close to the Italians culturally.
6 Northern (quasi) Latin: France and Belgium have frequently been placed in a separate cluster of two. However, France is often also put in the Latin and Mediterranean group.
7 Miscellaneous: regions such as Alsace (France), the Flemish and German-speaking Belgium and countries such as Luxembourg are difficult to categorize. They possess their own special identity as well as cultural traits based on national identity, and are also influenced by values from neighbouring countries such as Holland and Germany. Holland . . . has been placed in the Nordic group . . . but shares many of the traits associated with the Anglo group.'

The authors speculate on the historical origins of these patterns and qualify this classification with the caveat that reality is much more complex. However, they do not accept the Thurley and Wirdenius (1990, p.33) criticism of 'the tendency to over simplify national culture and make comparisons based on exaggerated cultural stereotypes'.

Psychology and culture

Classification difficulties aside, there is no denying that cultural differences can be deeply imbedded. Chung (1991), for example, draws on the psychology of thinking styles to explain differences between business cultures, arguing that Europeans are taught to think in a linear way, whereas Asians see things as a whole (see Table 9.1).

We can see from the table that, according to Chung, Europeans value rational logic while Asians think intuitively in circles and leaps. Whereas Europeans are individualistic and dependent on legalistic controls, Asians are community-minded and prepared to build and work on the basis of trust. European thinking is comparatively short term whereas Asians look further ahead. This model provides a cultural explanation of the different forms of people management: contract-based in the West; commitment-based in the East. Despite the additional insight this model provides again, however, we have a case of two groups of very diverse cultures being 'lumped together' to suit an argument.

Culture and business behaviour

Western observers recently have come to appreciate the **diversity** of cultures in Asia. Religions go beyond Confucianism to include Buddhism, Islam, Christianity and others, with wide-ranging effects on people management. In Malaysia and Indonesia, for example, a predominantly Moslem culture has produced distinctive role differences between men and women at work. There can be restrictions on employment of female workers in 'male' areas of a factory and in promoting women to be in charge of men. For Western people managers this can cause conflict between moral commitment to equal opportunities and respect for local traditions, an issue we will develop further in Part six on the management of diversity.

The constitutional context and role of the state also varies considerably throughout the region with political arrangements ranging from democracy to one-party rule. At the level of individual behaviour, we can also see that variations in rules on politeness and directness produce contrasting ways of conducting business:

- National cultures vary widely within the region.
- Courtesy and politeness are valued highly in all these cultures.

	European	Asian
Thinking styles	Causal, clear-cut, single-track thinking – one thing follows another	Network, whole vision, complex, taking in different perspectives
Decision styles	To suit controls Individual, free To suit the majority	Based on trust Group solidarity Reaching consensus
Behaviour	True to principles Based on legal principles Dynamic, facing conflict Open, direct, self-confident, extrovert	To suit a situation To suit a community Harmonious, conservative Restrained, indirect, with self-assurance, introvert

Table 9.1

Ways of thinking

Source: Adapted from Chung (1991).

- Business structure is family-based in some, but not all, of these countries.
- There is widespread contact and cooperation between Chinese communities throughout the region.
- Business practices are changing because younger people are being trained in Western-style business schools.

Cultural training

Human resource managers have a considerable role to play in preparing staff for work overseas. Given the range and sensitivity of cultural differences, it is clear that people working in an international context can benefit from tuition in the business customs and social manners of the countries they will work in. Human resource managers can play a major part in developing programmes for sales and other staff whose behaviour must be fully acceptable in target countries. For example, it is evident that export managers travelling to other countries in east Asia need to have considerable awareness of cultural differences. Consultants from the West have even greater hurdles of understanding to overcome.

What kind of training can HR managers arrange for travelling staff? We provide an answer to this question in Chapter 20 when we examine development programmes for international managers. At this stage, it is sufficient to say that training can encompass language, social

---

Diversity in Asia

Western observers have tended to regard Asian countries as one business culture, primarily based on the Japanese model. In fact the region contains a wide diversity of cultures, including several large countries such as Bangladesh, China, India and Pakistan – some of which are not homogeneous in themselves – and a number of smaller countries with very different traditions and economic problems. Failure to appreciate the contrasts between cultures is not confined to Westerners: the variations in business practices in these countries are just as surprising to the Japanese.

Perhaps the only issue they have in common is a keen attention to etiquette and politeness. Rudeness and over-eagerness can be the downfall of visiting executives who must expect some obligatory courtesies. Thereafter, however, diversity begins. In Singapore and Malaysia, long accustomed to Western business, negotiations can be relatively direct, whereas in Indonesia and Thailand the participants must engage in further elaborate ritual. Sensitivity to these variations is essential for negotiations to succeed.

As a relatively recent creation, Singapore pays less attention to tradition than countries such as Thailand and business is less dependent on family or clan connections. In a region where corruption is still not uncommon, Singapore's stringent legislative system encourages transparent honesty in business activities. Familiarity with Western ways and a good command of English also lead to a greater readiness amongst Singaporeans and Filipinos to ask questions or challenge instructions than, for example, Thais and Malays.

Chinese minorities are widespread throughout South-East Asia and have their own ways of conducting business, sharing a similar management philosophy. In many countries they dominate business but in Malaysia and Indonesia they are constrained by nationalist sensitivities. Throughout the region, and especially among the Chinese communities, there is a gradual trend away from family-owned business towards free market joint-stock arrangements. In conjunction with this development, and partly due to contrasting business traditions, it is becoming common for younger managers to be trained according to American principles.

Source: based on Luce (1995)

behaviour, local business structure and practice, and table etiquette. However, the most critical area is that of non-verbal behaviour. Stories abound of contracts being lost because of inappropriate expressions, overeagerness, unacceptable familiarity and general insensitivity. Argyle (1991) details a number of key behavioural features that differ from one culture to another.

Non-verbal behaviour

Proximity, touch and gaze. Cultures can be classified as contact or non-contact. For example, Arabs and Latin Americans stand much closer to each other than East Asians and northern Europeans. In Greece, staring is regarded as an expression of interest and politeness, even at a complete stranger in the street. Conversely, a Caribbean employee may avoid eye-to-eye contact with a manager during a conversation, having been taught to regard this as discourteous. Opportunities for misunderstanding here are boundless.

Expressiveness. The Japanese are reluctant to be too expressive for fear of causing offence. Many northern Europeans are also reticent in showing emotion. By contrast, African-Caribbean people are more likely to be open about expressing opinions, including negative emotions and attitudes.

Gestures. It is dangerous to make use of one's own familiar gestures in another country. In all innocence you may indicate a threat or pornographic meaning.

Accompaniments of speech. People often expect listeners to show obvious attention while they are talking. Failure to do so can be interpreted as lack of interest or boredom. This feedback is not expected in all cultures. According to Argyle 'black Americans often annoy white interviewers by their apparent lack of response while listening'.

Symbolic self-presentation. Appearance, dress, badges and uniforms have significance for individuals in a particular culture but may mean nothing to outsiders.

Rituals. Seating positions at a dining or conference table may be highly significant to one culture – for example Japan – and virtually irrelevant to another.

Customs or rules

Bribery. A bribe in one culture is a gift in another. In many cultures it is normal to pay a commission to people involved in a transaction. People such as civil servants, managers and sales representatives expect a percentage of the contract value. Western European and North American tradition regards this as unethical if not illegal.

Nepotism. Cultures that feature personal obligations to large extended families expect powerful individuals to look after relatives; for example, by giving jobs or contracts. This 'social welfare' system is normally governed by codes of conduct that regulate its abuse.

Gifts. Every culture expects its members to give presents in certain circumstances such as weddings or birthdays. Some cultures extend gift-giving to everyday business meetings. For example, the Japanese spend a great deal of money on standard presents from special gift shops.

Buying and selling. The importance of bargaining varies from 'fixed price' cultures where haggling is regarded with distaste, to others where negotiation is expected in any transaction.

Eating and drinking. Each culture has taboos on various foods. For example the eating of pork is unacceptable in religious Jewish and Moslem communities. Alcohol is particularly problematic. It is a feature of business transactions in parts of Europe, but drinking is increasingly frowned upon in North America and abhorred in many Arab countries. The ritual of eating, commonly described as 'table manners' also varies considerably. The international manager risks causing offence and prejudicing business if local eating customs are not observed.

Rules about time. Being on time is regarded as polite and a demonstration of business efficiency in Western countries. Conversely, lateness is taken as normal in other cultures – the more powerful the individual, the later that person will appear.

Language

The use of language has critical implications. For example, in appraisal feedback meetings or interviews people managers must be aware of cultural differences covering directness and politeness.

As regards directness, Westerners often begin an informal meeting with a joke, but at this stage in a Japanese relationship such familiarity would be regarded as extremely offensive. The Japanese expect formality until each other's status and authority are clearly understood. People of different status would not expect to conduct discussions at an informal level. Americans discuss business in a direct way.

Northern Europeans, being sometimes reserved and formal, are closer to East Asians – but only slightly. According to Chung: 'Asians prefer indirect communication, they want the correct form, they esteem absolute politeness and reserve, with self-control.' The Japanese, for example, may leave sentences unfinished to allow listeners to draw their own conclusions. Westerners live with confrontation and conflict, but this would cause considerable loss of face in Japan. Losing face (*mianxi*) is also highly significant in China where, according to Lee (2006, p.95) 'A person without "face" is considered dishonourable and will not be given a lot of respect from others. They are considered not to be trustworthy and people avoid them. In patching up conflicts and correcting mistakes, it is important that a Westerner does not embarrass the Chinese in front of many people. Confrontation should be avoided to avoid losing face. Negotiations, concessions and compromises are preferred more.'

As regards politeness, all cultures employ polite forms of address that are expected in particular circumstances. For instance, senior staff expect to be addressed more formally by juniors than by colleagues at the same level. In several languages the word for 'you' has to be used carefully. In French, for example, respect is shown to individuals by using the plural '*vous*', rather than the singular '*tu*'.

Politeness is socially supportive behaviour that maintains harmony and respect between individuals. It varies considerably both in importance and practice. Politeness is so important in Japan that it is even regarded as rude to say 'no'. Foreign business visitors are famously advised that 'yes' does not mean agreement but 'yes, I have heard you'.

Torrington (1994, p.19) describes the end-product as 'inter-cultural self-confidence'.

Key concept 9.2 Attitudes

Attitudes are dispositions held by people, towards or against people, things and ideas. They have individual components based on factors such as personality and understanding, and social elements derived from shared experiences and cultural history. Attitudes are complex systems of belief, evaluation, emotion and behaviour (Eiser, 1994; McKenna, 1994, p.251).

National and organizational cultures

We have identified some of the broader implications of culture on people management. In this section we examine some specific contributions to cross-cultural understanding, including the classic research conducted by Hofstede (1980). In our earlier discussion we touched on the dangers of stereotyping. Cultural stereotypes are composed of a few accurate notions mixed with generalizations, misconceptions and prejudice. Some elements are historical and take no account of change in a modern, technologically advanced country that also has distinctive regional cultures. Is it possible to define real differences between countries, avoiding the trap of stereotyping?

Organizations are microcosms of national cultures, reflecting crucial differences. Hofstede (1980; 1994) compared several thousand IBM employees in over 50 countries using attitude questionnaires (see Key concept 9.2). He found significant differences between employees in different countries, despite similar jobs and membership of an organization which, as we saw in Chapter 2, is renowned for its strong corporate culture.

Using factor analysis, a sophisticated statistical method, Hofstede analysed the employees' responses and attributed the variation to four main dimensions: **power distance**; **collectivism** versus **individualism**; masculinity versus femininity; and uncertainty avoidance.

Power distance

How marked are the status differences between people with high and low degrees of power? Questions tested whether:

- people were afraid of expressing disagreement with their managers
- management style was perceived as paternalistic, autocratic, participative and so on
- employees preferred a particular management style.

Table 9.2 shows ratings on power distance and other dimensions. Individuals in countries with autocratic management styles preferred their own bosses to have that style. Individuals in countries with low power distance scores preferred consultation. Consistent with our discussion on diversity in Asia, it is not surprising to find that the highest score was found in Malaysia where workers have been known to ask Western managers to be more 'bossy'. In a culture where respect for authority is a valued quality, participative management can make people feel uncomfortable.

Collectivism versus individualism

Is a culture focused on individuals or groups? Hofstede describes most societies as 'collectivist' in a non-political sense. In these cultures people obtain their identity from an extended family or a work organization. This is particularly relevant to people management, and HRM in particular, since most of its concepts come from the USA – a strongly individualistic country. Indeed, Hofstede found the highest scores for individualism in the USA, followed by Australia and the UK (both countries that have followed US management developments keenly). Individualistic cultures are characterized by:

- An emphasis on care for self and immediate family – if necessary, at the expense of others.
- 'I' consciousness – heightened awareness of the distinction between oneself and other people.
- Self-orientation – looking for advantage and career progression for the individual.
- Keen defence of the right to a private life and personal opinions.
- Emphasis on decisions being made individually.
- Emotional independence from the work organization.
- Autonomy and individual financial security.

The least individualistic scores came from Latin America and East Asia. High power distance and collectivism usually go together. France and Belgium are exceptional, combining medium power distance with high individualism. In collective cultures such as Taiwan, socially respected jobs are valued highly. In contrast, individualistic cultures value personal success, responsibility, and self-respect. Triandis (1995, p.33) points to key differences leading to reward and promotion: 'People in individualistic countries have the tendency to emphasize *ability* more than is necessary, and to underemphasize *effort*. In collectivist cultures, the reverse is true.'

Hui (1990, p.193) argues that Hofstede's notion of the collective is too vague: people in collective cultures relate to particular in-groups, not to everybody. For example, the Japanese identify with the organization in which they work. The important difference is a sharper distinction between 'in' and 'out' groups in collectivist cultures, compared with individualistic cultures where boundaries tend to blur. Hence, recruitment may be restricted to members of a particular in-group, especially the extended family. Collectivist cultures emphasize harmony, and avoidance of shame or loss of face. These are social elements of culture emphasizing obligations to others within the in-group. This point is further developed later in this chapter in our discussion of commitment in Japanese organizations.

Further contradictory evidence was provided by Ramamoorthy *et al.* (2005) who analyzed 180 MBA students from the USA, Ireland and India on their individualism/collectivism (IC) orientations and their preferences for HRM practices. Contrary to expectations, the Indian sample tended to be more individualistic than the American or Irish sample. There were no differences in preferences for progressive HRM practices, but the Americans showed the greatest preference for paternalistic practices. The Americans also showed a greater preference for equality in rewards than the Irish, and procedural fairness in appraisals/rewards than did the Indians. At the individual level, controlling for nationality, age and gender, higher individualism scores on the supremacy of individual goals and self-reliance dimensions were positively related to progressive HRM practices and procedural fairness in appraisals/rewards, and negatively related to paternalistic HRM practices. A higher preference for working alone was negatively related to progressive HRM practices. Higher individualism scores on the

Table 9.2	Dimension	High	Medium	Low
Cultural dimensions (after Hofstede, 1980, and others)	Individualism (versus collectivism)	Argentina, Australia, Belgium, Brazil, Canada, France, Ireland, New Zealand, Spain, UK, USA	Austria, Germany, Israel, Italy, Japan, Netherlands, Scandinavia, Switzerland, South Africa	Chile, Greece, Hong Kong, India, Iran, Mexico, Pakistan, Peru, Portugal, Taiwan, Singapore, Turkey
	Power distance (inequality between levels in organizations)	Belgium, France, Iran, Hong Kong, Nigeria, Philippines, Singapore, South America, Spain, Taiwan, Thailand	Japan	Australia, Germany, Italy, UK, USA
	Uncertainty avoidance (intolerance of ambiguity)	Austria, Argentina, Belgium, France, Germany, Greece, Iran, Israel, Italy, Japan, Spain, Turkey, South Africa, Switzerland		Australia, Canada, Ireland, Netherlands, New Zealand, Scandinavia, UK, USA.
	Masculinity (competitiveness)	Japan, Austria, Venezuela, Italy, Switzerland	Canada, Jamaica, Greece, India, Hong Kong, Pakistan, South Africa, UK, USA	Chile Netherlands, Scandinavia, Costa Rica
	Work centrality	Japan	Belgium Israel, USA	Germany, Netherlands, UK
	Job satisfaction	Canada, UK, Germany, Netherlands, Scandinavia		Greece, Spain, Italy, Portugal, Japan

supremacy of individual interest dimension was negatively related to progressive HRM practices and positively related to paternalistic HRM practices.

Masculinity versus femininity

Hofstede rates the aggressiveness of a culture as masculinity – its level of individual assertiveness and competition. Positive responses to questions relating to high earnings, recognition, advancement and challenging work rated highly on masculinity. Good working relationships, cooperation, living in a desirable area and employment security were scored at the 'feminine' end of the dimension. Japan scored highest on this dimension with the lowest levels in Scandinavia and the Netherlands.

The dimension has practical consequences on people management:

Recruitment. Applications in 'masculine' cultures are expected to be couched in positive, achievement-orientated language. Interviews are searching and sometimes aggressive. In contrast, applicants from 'feminine' cultures are expected to be modest about their achievements, giving the opportunity for interviewers to 'discover' undeclared talents. Thus Americans applying for jobs in the Netherlands can appear brash and boastful, whereas Dutch people may appear soft and unassertive to American interviewers.

Meetings. In Scandinavia and the Netherlands, meetings are held to achieve cooperation, exchange ideas and solve problems. The intention is positive and participative. In masculine cultures, such as Australia and the UK, meetings are more competitive and are used for displays of power, posturing and political point-making.

The masculine–feminine dimension helps to explain the different forms of market found in Part two, and the styles of management and employee relations prevalent in those markets. The welfare-focused social markets in Scandinavia and the Netherlands emphasize mutual respect and care for all members of the community at the expense of individual wealth. Employee relations take place within a context of extensive worker participation and protection. The 'masculine' countries, on the other hand, feature highly competitive free markets, an imbalance of power and income between management and workers, and comparatively low levels of social security. There are exceptions, of course, since Japan and Germany are high on masculinity but do not show the same range of characteristics.

Uncertainty avoidance

How do people deal with conflict, particularly aggression and the expression of feelings? Hofstede's fourth dimension measures people's reactions to unusual situations. High **uncertainty avoidance** favours precise rules, teachers who are always right and superiors who should be obeyed without question. Low uncertainty avoidance leads to flexibility. Arguing with superiors is acceptable and students are happy with teachers who do not claim to know everything. According to Hofstede, 1994, p.145):

In weak uncertainty avoidance cultures, like the USA and even more in the UK and, for example, Sweden, managers and non-managers alike feel definitely uncomfortable with systems of rigid rules, especially if it is evident that many of these were never followed. In strong uncertainty avoidance cultures, like most of the Latin world, people feel equally uncomfortable without the structure of a system of rules, even if many of these are impractical and impracticable.

Dimension mix

The characteristics of national business cultures are further defined by the particular mix of these four dimensions. In the last chapter we outlined a range of organization structures. Hofstede argues that the choice of structure is strongly influenced by the prevalent culture. For example, matrix structures have never been popular in France because the idea of having more than one boss to report to does not meet the French need for clearly defined authority. A culture with high power distance and strong uncertainty avoidance prefers a functional 'pyramid of people' hierarchy. Lower power distance but high uncertainty avoidance, as in Austria, Germany and Israel, encourages a 'well-oiled machine': an organization with a clear structure, rules and procedures. Anglo-Celtic and Scandinavian cultures, with low power distance and uncertainty avoidance favour a flexible structure focused on human relations: a 'village market'. Finally, the large power distance and low uncertainty avoidance typical in East Asia features a strong boss, equivalent to the father, and hence an organizational model based on the family.

Hofstede's statistics have been questioned but the thesis remains popular. It fits conventional wisdom and common stereotypes. Such research has relevance to HRM in cross-border mergers and acquisitions. Olie (1990) found that British–Dutch mergers were more successful than German–Dutch mergers. Netherlands and UK cultures had greater synergy than those of the Netherlands and Germany. Similarly, Olie observed the difficulties of American managers in the US subsidiary of a Japanese bank. Americans expected firm performance targets from head office. Japanese managers could not understand why the Americans could not identify their own objectives, based on the parent company's philosophy. Olie found differences between British and American directors about information required for decision-making, the Americans wanting far more data than the British.

A study by Pheng and Yuquan (2002) used Hofstede's dimensions to compare construction workers in Singapore and two cities in China. Although apparently from related cultures, their different histories seemed to result in some interesting variations:

Power distance. Singapore workers showed a higher power distance than their Chinese counterparts. In Singapore, superiors and subordinates were more likely to consider each other as unequal. Pheng and Yuquan (2002, p.7) state that 'the hierarchical system is felt to be based on some existential inequality; power is the basic fact of society that antedates good or evil and where its legitimacy is irrelevant. Indigenous organizations centralize power more and subordinates are expected to be told what to do. Superiors are believed to be entitled to privileges.'

Construction employees in China felt themselves to be more equal, whether they were subordinates or superiors. They were likely to regard the hierarchical system as an inequality of roles, established for convenience, which could change in different circumstances. This attitude leads to more decentralized organizations with flatter hierarchies and fewer supervisors.

Uncertainty avoidance. Singapore respondents had a low index value for uncertainty, in contrast with Chinese respondents who had a high index value. According to Pheng and Yuquan: 'In Singapore, people feel less threatened by ambiguous situations. Emotions are shown less in public. Younger people are trustworthy. People are willing to take risks in life. The authorities are there to serve the citizens. Conflicts and competition can be contained on the level of fair play and are used constructively.'

In China, on the other hand, 'people tend to establish more formal rules, reject deviant ideas and behaviour, accept the possibility of absolute truths and the attainment of unchallengeable expertise. Younger people are looked upon suspiciously. People are concerned with security in life. Ordinary citizens are incompetent, unlike the authorities. Conflict and competition can unleash aggression and should therefore be avoided.'

Individualism/collectivism. Singapore workers are more individualistic than their counterparts in China, tending to think of themselves as 'I' and also tending to classify people by individual characteristics, rather than by group membership. Employees in China are less inclined to differentiate an individual from the group and put a lower emphasis on self-actualization.

Masculinity/femininity. The masculinity score in the Singapore construction industry is lower than that for respondents in China, meaning that Chinese employees tend to place a greater emphasis on work goals such as earnings and advancement and also on assertiveness. In Singapore, by contrast, respondents showed a greater concern with personal goals, a friendly atmosphere, getting along well with the boss and others, etc.

Converging cultures?

The accelerating trend towards the internationalization of business is eroding these cultural differences. For example, the development of business within the European Union has led to talk of 'Euromanagers' (Tyson *et al.*, 1993). But attempts to create pan-European businesses can still founder due to national differences. Throughout the world, younger and more travelled managers are more alike in attitudes and practices than colleagues less open to foreign influences. They prefer to associate with people who have similar ideologies and personalities – even if they come from different cultures. Additionally, technological development is leading to an increasing convergence of business methods.

Corporate culture

As Deal and Kennedy (1982, p.15) propose: '. . . people are a company's greatest resource, and the way to manage them is not directly by computer reports, but by the subtle cues of a culture.' In this section we turn to the cultures that distinguish one organization from another, whether or not they are in different countries. It has been long recognized that the organization cannot simply be described in terms of its formal structure (Bakke, 1950). Often this is no more than window dressing: the illusion of order that senior management believe they have created.

Key concept 9.3 The informal organization

An organization is both a formal and informal entity. The formal aspect of an organization is its official structure and public image visible in organization charts and annual reports. The informal organization is a more elusive concept, describing the complex network of psychological and social relationships between its people. The informal organization is an unrecognized world of cliques and politics, friendships and enmities, gossip and affairs.

Behind and in parallel with the 'official' system there is the reality of action and power commonly described as the **'informal' organization**: 'those patterns of coordination that arise among members of a formal organization which are not called for by the blueprint' (Schein, 1988, p.16).

Formal organization design is concerned with only certain activities that are felt important to the organization. All other aspects of working life, from gossip on the line to complaining about management, are the territory of the informal organization (see Key concept 9.3). Real action depends on this informal structure of opinion leaders and power-brokers (Brunsson, 1989, p.7). The formal organization is there for 'demonstration and display to the outside world . . . defined as rituals'. Management literature earlier in the 20th century frequently regarded informal behaviour as undesirable: 'Basing their actions on the logic of formal organization, they try to neutralize or do away with the informal behaviour through directive leadership, management controls, and pseudo human relations programmes' (Argyris, 1957, p.231).

This was typical of the North American business schools that tended to view organization structure as a prescriptive matter of 'one best way' with scant regard for functional purpose or cultural location. This form of management served to increase feelings of dependence, submissiveness and subordination amongst employees. Ironically, workers coped by increasing the scope of the informal organization, using it as a mechanism to counter management initiatives.

By the 1980s, however, the informal organization was regarded in a new and more favourable light. From being perceived as something to be ignored or bludgeoned out of existence, it was realized that features of the informal organization could be harnessed for competitive advantage. This notion developed along with the concept of corporate culture – a central theme of the 'excellence' literature (Peters and Waterman, 1982) as well as HRM and total quality management (see Key concept 9.4). Its major exponents presented a 'strong' corporate culture as a key factor in enhancing competitive performance through greater employee commitment and flexibility (Deal and Kennedy, 1982). Employees in strong cultures know what is expected of them. Conversely, staff in weak cultures waste time trying to discover what is required. Employees identify with a strong culture and take pride in their organization.

Key concept 9.4 Corporate culture

The simplest – and probably most often – quoted definition is Bower's (1966) 'the way we do things around here'. Trice and Beyer (1984) elaborated this as: 'the system of . . . publicly and collectively accepted meanings operating for a given group at a given time'. Hofstede (1994 [1991]) describes corporate culture as 'the psychological assets of an organization, which can be used to predict what will happen to its financial assets in five years time'.

The creation – or even the definition – of such a culture is not easy. In managing people to achieve organizational goals, organizations prefer clarity, certainty and perfection (Pascale and Athos, 1981, p.105). However, those same organizations have people as their basic building bricks. Their human relationships involve ambiguity, uncertainty and imperfection. The trick of good management is to honour, balance and integrate these. One way to do so is somehow to use the information channels of the informal organization to transmit and re-inforce messages of commitment to management goals. Jones (2006) undertook a cultural analysis of organizational energy and commitment in a family business in the American south and found a 'mutual confirmation' between southern cultural values and those in the organizational history of the firm. The company, Omega Coffee and Tea, provides its employees with a powerful affirmation of cultural identity, which is then transformed into commitment, energy and effectiveness.

Unlike many other 'new' management ideas, corporate culture has endured and appears to have had a 'material effect upon the politics of work' (Willmott, 1993, p.515). We will see in Chapter 12 that a whole industry has arisen to supply management of change programmes, much of it devoted to changing and strengthening corporate cultures. However, it is worth noting that although a wealth of literature exists publicizing the importance of culture change, most of this is relatively uncritical.

The Deal and Kennedy model of corporate culture

We have noted that, together with Peters and Waterman's *In Search of Excellence* (1982), Deal and Kennedy's *Corporate Cultures* (1982) was inspirational in this area. As a prelude to discussion of the role of corporate culture in people management, it is appropriate to outline Deal and Kennedy's model. It incorporates five critical elements: the business environment; values; heroes; rites and rituals; and the cultural network.

The business environment

In line with our discussion in Part two, Deal and Kennedy argued that the activities of governments and competitors, changes in technology, customer demand and general economic conditions are instrumental in shaping the cultures of organizations with survival potential. The orientation of organizations within this environment – for example a focus on sales or concentration on research and development – develops specific cultural styles.

HRM in reality Meetings, meetings

Meetings are depressing for most people – but not everyone

Meetings, don't we hate them? Apparently, there was a doubling (at least) of meetings at work in the second half of the 20th century. The implications have been little studied but recent research on the link between the experience of meetings and the effects on worker wellbeing has shown some surprising findings.

Written by a team of psychologists, led by Steven G. Rogelberg from the University of North Carolina at Charlotte, the research* is reported in the March issue of the *Journal of Applied Psychology*. It is claimed to be the first international scientific study ever conducted on the effects of meeting time on employee wellbeing and is based on responses from 980 employees to two work surveys.

One significant finding is that more people actually believe that meetings are a positive part of the workday than they will admit publicly. 'When speaking publicly, people generally claim that they hate meetings,' said Rogelberg, 'but in the surveys you see a different story – some people's private sentiments are much more positive.

'It's an interesting finding because it really helps to explain why we have all these meetings. And, though they are typically publicly negative, overwhelmingly people say that they want the day to have at least one meeting. They have to feel like they are accomplishing something positive in their meetings to produce this response,' he said.

The two surveys tested the impact of meetings on employees in two different contexts – at the end of a specific day and in general, by examining the number of meetings employees had in a typical week.

It appears that some individuals see meetings as interruptions while others regard them as welcome events. The study finds that the effects of meetings on worker wellbeing is 'moderated' by three different factors:

1 by whether jobs specifically require group work
2 by whether the meetings were efficiently run; and perhaps most importantly,
3 by where the worker falls on the personality scale of her/his 'accomplishment striving'.

'People differ on this accomplishment striving personality scale,' Rogelberg explained. 'In general, you can think of people who are high in accomplishment striving as those individuals who are very task-focused, who are very goal-focused, who have goals and objectives for the day that they want to get accomplished. People who have low accomplishment striving are not slackers, though – they are just individuals with a much more flexible orientation to work and like to allow the agenda for the day to emerge much more naturally.'

According to this research, individuals high in accomplishment striving are predictably and negatively affected by meetings – particularly if they are frequent. A large number of short meetings affect their wellbeing more than a few long meetings – even if they take the same overall amount of time.

But meetings had a positive impact on respondents with low scores on accomplishment striving. They seemed to welcome meetings and the more time they spent in meetings, the greater their sense of well-being.

'People who are high in accomplishment striving look at meetings more from the perspective of seeing them as barriers to getting real work done,' Rogelberg said. 'But the others may view meetings as a way to structure their day or a way to network and socialize. As a result, these people see meetings as a good thing.'

Steven Rogelberg observes that there are some intriguing social paradigms operating that disguise the dynamic. 'It is socially unacceptable to talk about liking meetings, unless someone else starts talking about it,' he said, explaining why the low accomplishment striving folks do not go public with their preference for meetings. 'And it is also interesting that the people who are high on accomplishment striving are not complaining more than the others. The toll that meetings take seems to be much more subtle. If you ask these individuals if they are more dissatisfied with the meetings, they don't report anything different from those who enjoy meetings,' he said.

How do meetings contribute to the development and maintenance of a company culture?

Source: *HRM Guide USA* (http://www.hrmguide.com), 27 February, 2006.

Note: *'Not another meeting': Are meeting time demands related to employee wellbeing?, by S.G. Rogelberg and D.J. Leach from the University of Sheffield and J.L. Burnfield from Bowling Green State University, Ohio. *Journal of Applied Psychology*, 91(2), 2006.

Values

Values are at the heart of corporate culture. They are made up of the key beliefs and concepts shared by an organization's employees. Successful companies are clear about these values and their managers publicly reinforce them. Often values are unwritten and operate at a subconscious level.

Heroes

Personifications of the organization's values: achievers who provide role models for success within the company. Heroism is an element of leadership that has been virtually forgotten by modern managers: 'Since the 1920s, the corporate world has been powered by managers who are rationalists, who do strategic planning, write memos, and devise flow charts' (Deal and Kennedy, 1982, p.37). Heroes, on the other hand, create rather than run organizations; are intuitive rather than decisive; have all the time in the world because they make time; are experimenters rather than routinizers; are playful; get things 'just right'. Heroes have vision and break the existing order if necessary in order to achieve that vision. Deal and Kennedy describe this process in terms of 'making success attainable and human'.

A figurehead such as Sir Richard Branson, is presented as being the Virgin group, serving the purpose of 'symbolizing the company to the outside world' (Deal and Kennedy, 1982, p.40).

Rites and rituals

Ceremonies and routine behavioural rituals reinforce the culture. Examples include product launches, sales conferences, away days or the Friday afternoon 'beer-bust'.

The cultural network

The carrier of stories and gossip that spreads information about valued behaviour and 'heroic myths' around the organization. The degree of factual content involved is questionable. Michelson and Mouly (2000, p.339) attempt to draw a distinction between rumour and gossip:

> While the basis of rumour is information that is unsubstantiated, gossip may or may not be a known fact. . . . This distinction is more a matter of degree than substance and the issue becomes problematic in the context of celebrity or political gossip. In such cases the 'facts' or 'truth' are likely to be highly elusive. It is also conceivable that the initiation of rumour may be underpinned by some element of 'truth', no matter how obscure or circumstantial the evidence. The extent of factuality or truth is hard to determine any way, and one can never know if something is a 'white lie' or 'half truth'.

Table 9.3 outlines an anthropological classification of the elements of corporate cultures.

Key concept 9.5 Rumour and gossip

Rumour is typically regarded as unsubstantiated talk that is not supported by evidence or authority. Gossip is commonly held to have a factual basis of some kind.

Deal and Kennedy produced a framework with two key dimensions: the 'risk' attached to the company's activities and the speed of 'feedback' to employees. Taking the extreme combinations of these two dimensions they described four types of culture:

1 *Tough guy culture*: characterized by entrepreneurial, high-risk-taking individuals, receiving quick feedback, but with a low level of teamwork. Such companies tend to follow a cycle of boom and bust, with the possibility of high earnings during the successful period.

2 *Work hard, play hard*: where work is fun and there is plenty of action with low risk and quick feedback on success. A high volume sales company is a typical example. The individual works alone but has a supportive team.

3 *Bet-your-company*: high-risk, long-term industries usually requiring significant technical expertise, such as the oil and aerospace businesses.

4 *Process culture*: low-risk, low-feedback organizations, typical of traditional models of public institutions, banks, civil service, etc., where the focus is on the actual conduct of the work. In this kind of culture, status issues such as the right to sign-off memos and use of graded titles are of paramount importance.

Different kinds of people have varying degrees of success in these cultures. Someone who reacts well to a high-pressure, fast-moving 'work-hard, play-hard' culture will be unhappy and unsuccessful in a process culture. With the wrong cultural style an individual can lose self-esteem and confidence. Deal and Kennedy (1982, p.17) reasoned that 'culture shock may be one of the major reasons why people supposedly "fail" when they leave one organization for

---

HRM in reality New code of conduct for NHS managers

A code of conduct published for consultation by then National Health Service chief executive Nigel Crisp set out the ethics and standards of behaviour expected of managers. A breach of the code would be regarded as gross misconduct, leading in many cases to dismissal. If the breaches were serious – for example, financial fraud, providing false information or negligence in providing for the safety of patients – then managers responsible were unlikely to be employed again in the NHS.

The code would cover all NHS managers and was developed following investigations into medical scandals, including practices at Bristol Royal Infirmary and Alder Hey in Liverpool, and also the inappropriate manipulation of waiting lists. The code stated NHS managers must:

- make the care and safety of patients their first concern
- respect the public, patients, relatives, carers, NHS staff and partners in other agencies
- be honest and act with integrity
- accept accountability for their work, the performance of those they manage and their own organization
- cooperate with colleagues in the NHS and the community.

Nigel Crisp said:

This code of practice is about the values we as NHS managers stand for. We decided to introduce this code in order to have a means for holding managers to account for their own professional behaviour. It will be used in that way and breaches of this code will be taken very seriously indeed.

The vast majority of managers in the NHS are highly principled and value-driven people who will welcome the code. But we must deal with failure. We simply must not repeat the mistakes of the past. We cannot have people re-employed in positions of trust if they have betrayed that trust in other parts of the NHS. We must have national standards applied nationally. This is about trust and about trust in us all as the NHS. It is corrosive if not handled well. We must be firm and fair.

However, the code is also a set of values and should inform development programmes and training for managers. It should make us all think exactly how we are going to work, how we make the care and safety of patients our first concern and how we respect the public, patients, relatives and carers.

But breaches of the code must be investigated fairly. Just as the code sets out how managers should behave and their responsibilities, they also have rights. They have the right to be treated with respect, judged consistently and fairly, encouraged to maintain and improve their knowledge and skills and to be helped to balance their work and home lives properly.

I am delighted with the work put in to this code by Ken Jarrold, chief executive of County Durham and Tees Valley Health Authority, in partnership with the NHS Confederation, the Institute of Health Management, the British Association of Medical Managers, the Health Financial Management Association and the NHS Modernisation Centre.

Is a code of practice a method of managing the culture of an organization?

Source: *HRM Guide UK* (http://www.hrmguide.co.uk), 23 May, 2002.

another.' Cultural fit is often ignored in selection procedures, leading to unhappy and non-productive experiences for some.

Corporate culture and people management

The concept of corporate culture continues the tradition of human relations and 'Theory Y' (McGregor, 1960). It fuses the two and moves further away from the logic of scientific management and Fordism towards a view of self-motivated employees who have internalized the values of the business (Wilmott, 1993, p.524).

For example, Hartmann (2006) identified a culture of innovation and creativity in a Swiss construction company fostered by immediate feedback, the existence of communication channels for implicit knowledge, the capacity for employees to be granted autonomous work and task identity, specifically identified innovation projects and a comprehensive reward and incentive system. If the culture is strong, people do not need orders or directives. Social norms constrain individual discretion so that employee values are those of the organization. In HRM terms the focus on values and norms is important to achieve behavioural consistency and commitment to the objectives of the business. The key point is that corporate culturalism requires the management of culture so that the 'correct' values are acquired. In effect 'normal', rational techniques of management are applied to the affective (emotional)

Table 9.3	Element	Ingredients
Elements of corporate culture **Source**: Adapted from Trice and Beyer (1984).	*Company practices*	*Rites*: planned, dramatic events in the life of the organization. *Ceremonial*: a series of rites such as the launch of a product, a graduation ceremony, the annual shareholders' meeting. *Ritual*: standardized, unimportant activities such as the Friday afternoon pub session that used to be a common place.
	Company communication	*Stories*: based on true events. *Myths*: untrue stories, old-timers stories. *Sagas*: heroic company histories. *Legends*: involving heroes and heroines in the organization's history. *Folk tales*: fiction with a message indicating successful behaviours that led to promotion or reward. *Symbols and slogans*: powerful components of a corporate identity, serving to create a recognizable image for people inside and outside the organization. They include colour schemes, letterheads, logos and uniforms.
	Physical cultural forms	*Artefacts*: tools, furniture styles, appliances and other equipment used in a factory or office. Some companies collect these in a haphazard way over time, others have central purchasing policies which ensure harmonization. *Physical layout*: offices, production areas and canteens may be laid out in an *ad hoc* manner or planned to follow an organizational theme.
	Common language	*Organizations* develop their own terminology and ways of expression. In Disneyland theme parks, staff are not employees but 'cast members' who wear 'costumes' (uniforms) 'onstage' (at work). 'Guests' (customers) use the 'attractions' (rides). Use of such terminology helps employees slip into role. At Land Rover, employees were called 'associates' and all wore company overalls (including the managing director).

domain (Wilmott, 1993, p.532). In other words, culture management is a 'hard' approach in thoroughly 'soft' territory.

Based on Handy (1993), corporate culture and organization types can be classified as follows:

1 *The club culture*. Typical of a small company; a personal, informal culture focused on the owner. The leader is all. This form of culture is suitable for new ventures needing strong personalities and fast responses.

2 *Role culture*. Hierarchical with an organizational chart portraying an orderly set of job boxes (roles). Individuals are less important than the roles they fill. A role culture is managed not led, with a formal communication system. Such a culture is best for stable, unchanging organizations with routine tasks. There is a strong tendency to adopt the role culture with increasing size, leading to a mechanistic, bureaucratic organization.

HRM in reality Retail employees not entirely happy

New Hay Group Insight Research Report shows that product and service quality are significant areas of concern for retail employees

Workers in the retail industry provided one of the lowest ratings of their company as a place to work compared to other industries, according to a recent Hay Group Insight Employee Survey Benchmark Report. Retail employees also gave lower ratings for product and service quality with just over a half (53 per cent) responding favourably on whether their company adapted well to changing market conditions. This compared to almost 60 per cent as a general industry average.

'As retail becomes more and more competitive, stores are open longer hours, staffing is stretched and associates have to work harder and more varied schedules — mandatory weekends, late hours, and split schedules,' said Craig Rowley, vice president and head of Hay Group's retail consulting practice. 'This clearly has an impact on working conditions and climate.'

Despite these relatively negative views, however, employees in retail also reported job satisfaction that was clearly favourable and slightly above the general industry norm. Contributing to this (contradictory) feeling was a strong understanding of how their jobs related to their companies' overall direction. They also gave high ratings for the interesting and challenging work provided by their jobs.

Retail respondents gave higher rankings than the general norm in two key areas: that they had a clear idea of expected results (88 per cent); that poor performance was not usually tolerated (53 per cent).

'Retail is one of the few industries that can and does measure performance down to the store level (even down to the department level) on an hourly basis and takes action based on this information daily,' continued Rowley. 'And because of this ability to monitor and track performance so closely, it's not uncommon to see a "two bad seasons and you're out" culture in retail.'

But the lowest scores in the retail industry were given for the competitiveness of their salaries, with fewer than 20 per cent responding favourably. This was approximately half the general industry norm.

'This is not surprising,' said Rowley, 'given retail's focus on cost control, and the heavy use of part-time employees in the industry. Best practices retailers deal with this by having very effective career progression programmes that rapidly promote the best performers to higher paying jobs.'

Career counselling excepted, retail supervisors are rated on a par with the norm. But the esteem with which employees hold other members of their work group, especially regarding cooperation received, is rated lower than the average across all industries.

'Human resource executives should take a look at compensation, turnover, tenure, and career advancement opportunities in their organizations and analyze how they compare to their competitors and top performing companies,' said Tom Agnew, a senior consultant with Hay Group Insight. 'This was not a one or two question "quick poll". In these employee surveys, we ask a broad set of questions, helping companies better understand what drives their performance and results.'

To what extent does a culture of performance monitoring contribute to employee dissatisfaction?

Source: *HRM Guide USA* (http://www.hrmguide.com), 21 February, 2006.

3 *Task culture*. The main focus is on groups such as project teams. Organization is based on trust and respect and geared to plans not procedures. This is a problem-solving environment – exciting and challenging but expensive to run. Work is based on projects. There is little job security: staff leave when tasks are finished.

4 *The person culture*. This is radically different and suited to professionals who are self-managing and require minimal structure or supervision. The focus is on talent and professional expertise – management has low status. This is reflected in non-managerial titles such as 'Dean'. Such a culture is best suited for professional practices and educational establishments.

However, there is an underlying tension between the 'humanizing' and the 'control' aspects of people management that is evident in this process. Whereas Theory Y was unashamedly humanistic, delegating discretion and freedom of choice to individual workers, corporate culturalism advocates: 'a *systematic* approach to creating and strengthening core organizational values in a way that *excludes* (through attention to recruitment) *and eliminates* (through training) *all other values*' (Willmott, 1993, p.524, original emphases). However, Appelbaum and Shapiro (2006) argue that remodelling an organization's norms, attitudes and social values in

---

HRM in reality   Gulf between HR and marketing

A survey by Corporate Project Resources, Inc. (CPRi), an interim marketing source for Fortune 500 companies, found that quality rather than quantity of communication between HR and marketing departments is an ongoing problem. The survey showed that:

- 81 per cent of HR and marketing departments communicate on a daily/weekly basis.

- 58 per cent of marketers do not feel that HR understands what the marketing department does on a daily basis.

- 36 per cent of marketers believe HR could work more effectively with marketing if they took the time to understand marketing's role within the organization.

'When it comes to finding the right skills and experience, marketing might be one of the most challenging to master,' said Sean Bisceglia, CEO of CPRi. 'Roles within marketing have been quickly evolving since the inception of the internet. As the economic pendulum swings back and companies are looking to rebuild their marketing departments, HR executives will be tasked with understanding their marketing department's needs.'

CPRi surveyed over 500 HR executives and over 1000 marketing executives within Fortune 500 companies. They found that over 45 per cent of marketing executives said that their biggest challenge was having HR provide qualified candidates for open marketing positions. Another 31 per cent of marketing executives said their biggest challenge was having HR understand the urgency of filling gaps within the marketing department. CPRi says that it aims to help bridge the communication gap by:

- being a strategic partner to the HR department

- helping them understand what marketing is looking for

- quickly helping fill the gaps with quality marketing professionals on an interim or temp-to-perm basis.

Using contingent marketers

The survey found another disconnect over the use of contingent (temporary/agency) employees to fill gaps within marketing departments. While 71 per cent of marketing executives said they would consider using contingent workers to fill gaps, only 45 per cent of HR executives agreed.

'Since most marketing departments go through certain spikes throughout the year, whether it's the launch of a new product or an event, interim marketers are a great way for marketing departments to fill gaps that are only needed for a certain period of time,' stated Bisceglia. 'In order to be a strategic partner to marketing, HR must understand the marketing department's workflow. CPRi helps provide insight to the ebb and flow of marketing departments and can be a resource to quickly fill needs with interim marketing professionals.'

Is there a cultural difference between HR and marketing?

Source: *HRM Guide USA* (http://www.hrmguide.com/) 15 June, 2005.

order to achieve a culture based on core ethical values is a worthy objective. Zablow (2006) also supports the notion of creating an ethical workplace by remodelling corporate culture.

People are promoted, appraised and rewarded according to management perception of their acceptance of core values. Hence the view in the Deal and Kennedy approach and much other corporate culture literature is that culture can be created and managed from the top. In this respect it is a departure from older ideas about informal organizations which are more closely aligned to the view that an organizational culture emerges from social interaction (Meek, 1988, p.293). In fact, the literature appears to transfer culture from the informal to the formal organization. As such it becomes the property of management and open to manipulation on their part. This has become the underlying logic for major change initiatives in many large organizations.

Furthermore, there is a common assumption that a unified culture – a 'monoculture' – exists to which all members of the organization belong. Earlier, we saw that narrow, simplified stereotypes of national cultures are misleading: most countries are pluralities with different regional, ethnic and class cultures. In the same way every organization has different cliques and minority groups with varying perspectives of culture. Far from being a management tool, culture can be regarded as a form of collective consciousness, reflecting the diversity of opinion, politics and ambition to be found in any organization. Indeed, as a product of the great mass of employees interacting with each other, it is often anti-managerial.

Legge (1995, p.185) asks 'If senior managers seek to manage "organizational culture", what exactly is it they are seeking to manage?' We can distinguish, therefore, between corporate culture as it is presented in most of the literature, and organizational culture. The former reflects the view that culture is something which an organization 'has', the latter that an organization 'is' (Smircich, 1983). Corporate culture is portrayed as something created by management that employees must accept. If we choose the organization culture view, however, we must acknowledge its long-term interactionist basis. From this perspective, it is difficult to see how senior management can control the culture of a firm – it is too diffuse, embedded and ever-changing. Indeed Legge (1995, p.186) suggests:

> Corporate culture – that shared by senior management and presented as the 'official' culture of the organization – may be only one of several sub-cultures within any organization, and may be actively resisted by groups who do not share or empathize with its values. If the corporate culture makes no sense of the organizational realities experienced by the employees other than senior management, it will not become internalized outside that small sub-group.

This idea of a small 'official' corporate culture floating on top of a multicultural informal organization is mirrored earlier in Handy's classification of cultures. Senior managers typically form a dynamic club culture that they believe to be universal in the organization whereas, in reality, it sits uncomfortably on top of a depressed and antipathetic role culture. From the managerial point of view, therefore, culture is a major variable to be influenced rather than a creation to be managed.

The concept of organizational climate, the prevailing 'atmosphere' in an organization, has been highlighted as an important mediating element in the transmission of culture. For example, Aarons and Sawitzky (2006) found that organizational climate partially mediated the effect of culture in mental health services where staff retention is an ongoing problem. Both elements impacted on job satisfaction and commitment and work attitudes significantly predicted one-year staff turnover rates.

Summary

We commenced this chapter by recognizing that international HRM can be considered analytically and that differences between national cultures are important to that analysis. However, descriptions of cultural differences tend to be stereotypical and do not pay sufficient attention to the diversity found in regions such as Asia.

We discussed the work of Hofstede (1994 [1991]) on dimensions such as cultural complexity, power distance, individualism, assertiveness and uncertainty avoidance. We extended our discussion to cover corporate culture with an account of Deal and Kennedy's (1982) model and more recent debates on the subject.

Further reading

Mind Your Manners: Managing Business Culture in a Global Europe by John Mole (3rd edn, Nicholas Brealey, 2003) is a good cross-cultural business guide. *When Cultures Collide: Leading, Teamworking and Managing Across the Globe* by Richard D. Lewis (Nicholas Brealey, 2005) is an enlightening account of national cultural differences across the world. Geert Hofstede's *Culture's Consequence: Comparing Values, Behaviours, Institutions and Organizations Across Nations* (Sage, 2003) provides a stimulating account of his research and ideas. Deal and Kennedy's (1992) *Corporate Cultures* is one of the classic texts on culture within organizations.

Review questions

1 Summarize the main benefits from gaining an understanding of international HRM. What are the arguments against employing the same human resource practices throughout the world?

2 What is 'culture'? Do attempts to classify cultures into groups or types enhance our understanding of international HRM?

3 To what extent do national cultures determine corporate cultures? How many different cultures can you identify in your own country? What are the implications of the differences between these cultures for human resource managers?

4 How can the concept of 'in-groups' help to explain the inadequacies of equal opportunities policies?

5 Is it possible to describe national business cultures without resorting to stereotypes? Does the analysis provided by Argyle go beyond cultural stereotyping?

6 Explain the following terms in your own words: power distance; avoidance; role specificity.

7 How does the notion of time vary around the world?

8 Explain the difference between organizational 'culture' and 'structure'. Is there a difference between the two concepts?

9 In what ways are the informal organization and the corporate culture of that organization (a) the same; (b) different?

10 What insights have Deal and Kennedy provided to further our understanding of corporate culture?

Case study for discussion and analysis

Volvo

In the 1970s Volvo was a model for the future of work: a partnership between management and employees. The company's policies recognized workers as human beings and moved manufacturing away from the production line towards team-based methods. Volvo's long-term commitment to its workforce placed it – together with many other Swedish companies – in the 'social market' or 'soft-HRM' model of capitalism (see Chapter 2). Workers were offered job security, high wages and comparatively short working hours. By the late 1980s, competition was severe and the company struggled to maintain its generous policies in a worsening financial situation.

In the 1990s a relationship developed between Volvo and the French car manufacturer Renault. It began with a cooperation agreement. This involved Volvo taking a 20 per cent shareholding in Renault and Renault taking 10 per cent of Volvo shares. Then, in September 1993, Pehr Gyllenhammer, Volvo's chairman, and Louis Schweitzer, his Renault equivalent, signed a deal in Paris which announced their intention to merge on 1 January 1994. Both groups had shed thousands of workers in previous years and there were immediate fears that the merger would lead to further job losses.

According to Louis Schweitzer, designated chief executive of the new Renault-Volvo Automobile (RVA), they would expect savings of Ffr30 billion (£3.3 billion) within the car and truck operations. RVA would maintain two distinct ranges of vehicles and separate dealerships. These savings would come from rationalizing research and development, lower investment costs and joint purchasing. They would also be able to launch new cars more quickly using common components. Pehr Gyllenhammer presented the deal as a large French investment in Sweden. The remainder of Volvo would be concentrating on other core activities such as Branded Consumer Products which had a leading share of the Scandinavian food, drinks and tobacco market.

The merger would have produced the world's sixth largest vehicle manufacturer with over 200 000 employees and sales of 2.4 million cars and small commercial vehicles a year. Despite the high-quality market served by Volvo it was the junior partner, with a total production of 300 000 vehicles in 1992 leading to a loss of Skr1.8 billion. The Volvo directors felt that this was too small a company to support the ever-increasing development costs of launching new models. There was never any doubt that Renault would be in charge, with a holding of 65 per cent of the joint company. Renault was still in French government ownership with an intention to privatize it by the end of 1994. The deal was supported initially by the major institutional shareholders such as insurance companies. However, it enraged private Swedish shareholders who could not accept the effective takeover of Sweden's largest company and industrial flagship. The media took a keen interest and the Volvo share price dropped immediately.

The Volvo shareholders' meeting to vote on the merger was postponed from 9 November to 2 December. This was because top managers felt they were unlikely to be able to muster sufficient support. On 2 December – virtually at the last minute – the Volvo board decided not to proceed with the merger. Pehr Gyllenhammer, the Volvo chairman for 22 years, resigned immediately along with three other directors, including Raymond Levy the former Renault chairman who had been instrumental in setting up the link. The reason for not proceeding was a revolt among the top managers. The managing director, Soren Gyll, said that the necessary support had not been available to proceed with the plan, either from within the company or among the shareholders. Soren Gyll had consistently backed Pehr Gyllenhammer in public but had become disenchanted with the latter's handling of the issue and had held secret meetings to discuss his misgivings with other managers.

1 Why do you think the negotiations fell through?

2 If shareholders had not objected too, would the views of the workforce have been sufficient to prevent it going through?

Chapter 10
Commitment and employer branding

Learning objectives

The purpose of this chapter is to:

● Define the concept of employee commitment.

● Examine the practice of employer branding as a form of commitment management.

● Relate commitment to culture.

● Evaluate the true nature of commitment.

Commitment and brand values

Organizational commitment is a central concept in HRM (see Key concept 10.1). It is one of the 4 'Cs' featured in the seminal Harvard model discussed in Chapter 1 and one of the measurable criteria in our 10-Cs checklist of HRM effectiveness (see Part one). Rhetorical accounts of human resource management have claimed that organizations that adopt the philosophy of HRM gain integration and coherence in their people management processes and systems. Integration is dependent on a strong and binding link between employee behaviour and the goals of the organization. According to this viewpoint, commitment to the mission and values of the organization is a fundamental principle. As a concept it is clearly related to that of 'strong' corporate culture. Commitment goes further than simple compliance: it is an emotional attachment to the organization. For example, Osborne and Cowen (2002, p.227) makes the claim that:

> A 'true believer' mentality pervades high-performing organizations. Everyone believes in the vision of the business and that it will bring certain success. People believe that they are involved in something bigger than simply their own self-interest. They have a strong sense of identity with the organization and act as if they were owners.

In particular, the Harvard approach views employee commitment as the key determiner of competitive performance. In Chapter 3 we observed that people working within a culture of commitment are prepared to work longer, apply greater ingenuity to resolve a problem, try that much harder to win an order. In effect they are in a high-commitment culture.

From this perspective, commitment comes within a climate of trust. It requires a shared understanding between employees at all levels as mutual stakeholders in the future of an enterprise. It emphasizes the employment relationship between worker and employer and raises questions about the mutual obligations of both parties. Is it reasonable, for example, to expect employees to volunteer suggestions that could produce reductions in the time and effort required to perform a task if there is a risk of job losses as a result?

It is easy to see how commitment can arise in a high-trust culture such as that which prevailed in Japan until the 1990s. It can be understood also within the context of the consensus social market in parts of Europe where jobs have a considerable degree of protection, employees are consulted through works councils and there is generous social security provision for people without jobs. But how can commitment arise in businesses operating in the free markets of most English-speaking countries where there is an imbalance of power between different stakeholders?

Key concept 10.1 Commitment

Commitment is defined as the degree of identification and involvement that individuals have with their organization's mission, values and goals (Mowday, Steers and Porter, 1979). This translates into: their desire to stay with the organization; belief in its objectives and values; and the strength of employee effort in the pursuit of business objectives (Griffin and Bateman, 1986).

Commitment has been the subject of research for some time because of its strong psychological connotations. Initially, attention was paid to commitment as behaviour. For example, Salancik (1977) identified four behavioural elements:

- *Explicitness.* Is it clear that an act of commitment took place? Can it be denied? Was it consciously determined?
- *Revocability.* Can we change our minds? Can the act be undone?
- *Volition.* Is an act performed under our own volition or under the control of someone else?
- *Publicity.* Has an expression or act of commitment been made in public?

Commitment arises as individuals perform acts such as joining a firm, working long hours and speaking well of the organization to customers or friends. Employees reflect on their own behaviour and conclude that because they have done something which is favourable towards their own organization, and done so in front of others, apparently of their own free will, they must have a commitment to that organization. In other words, free choice and public behaviour reinforce a feeling of commitment. This has been described as a 'neat theory' and there is some evidence in support (Arnold, Robertson and Cooper, 1991, p.147).

In recent years the emphasis has shifted towards a significant framework in social psychology that revolves around the concept of 'attitudes'. Attitudes are seen to have three components (McKenna, 2000, p.248). These are: belief (cognitive), feeling (affective), and action (behavioural or conative). Each can be positive or negative. The emotional (affective) component seems to be of greatest significance, able to influence or override the other two. From this viewpoint, commitment is seen as having three key elements (Allen and Meyer, 1990):

- *Affective*: the individual's emotional attachment to an organization.
- *Continuance*: an individual's perception of the costs and risks associated with leaving the organization (equivalent to the behavioural component).
- *Normative*: the obligation and responsibility a person feels towards the organization (equating to the cognitive component).

Research on attitudes indicates that these components usually show a considerable degree of consistency with each other. But this is not always the case. For instance, employees can feel proud of a company and believe that they owe an obligation for past good treatment, training or promotion. However, they may be aware that pay is relatively low and other organizations offer more attractive prospects. Lee and Gao (2005) studied organizational commitment among Korean retail employees by analyzing relationships among two facets of commitment (affective and continuance), three facets of job satisfaction (pay, co-worker, and supervisor), and two work outcomes (effort and propensity to leave). In the Korean retail setting they found:

1 satisfaction with pay and satisfaction with supervisor significantly increase both affective and continuance commitment;

2 satisfaction with co-workers positively influences affective commitment but has no significant effect on continuance commitment; and

3 affective commitment increases job effort but decreases the employees' propensity to leave the firm, while continuance commitment reduces propensity to leave but does not increase job effort.

It is clear, therefore, that commitment is not as simple a concept as some HR theorists maintain. In practice, many of us hold ambivalent attitudes towards our employing organizations, perhaps enjoying our own jobs and the company of our fellow employees but wary of the intentions of senior executives. Nevertheless, committed employees are crucial to high performance, not least because (Gotsi and Wilson, 2001, p.102):

> . . . staff and their behaviour represent the reality of the organization to the customers and therefore, if their behaviour does not live up to the expectations created through the organization's external communication campaigns, the organization's overall reputation will be damaged. Consultants argued that visionary organizations realize that front line personnel are the company. 'Because they know that when you walk into a store it doesn't matter about the big corporation, what matters is that moment of transaction, it's just you and that 19-year-old person, and so that person has to deliver the reputation. And if they don't, millions of pounds on advertising and products are lost' (Consultant A).

Employer branding

'Your **employer brand** can be a magical combination of what your business values, offers and rewards – marrying what your brand promises outside with what your experience demands inside; what your business believes in and how you fundamentally respect the people who deliver your brand' (Sartain and Schumann, 2006, p. 24).

Many commercial organizations are well experienced at promoting and cultivating a relationship between themselves and their clients through their brand image. Coca-Cola, BMW, Mcdonalds, Sony and BP are just some of the organizations whose brands are recognized throughout the world. Brands are not simply logos or names: by their existence they encourage people to develop a faith in the products or services provided by an organization and a belief in the integrity and reliability of its staff. Well-regarded brands are valuable in themselves and companies work hard at maintaining their brand images. Recently, the concept of branding has been extended from the organization as supplier of goods and services to the organization as an employer (see Key concept 10.2).

Key concept 10.2 Employer branding

The practice of developing, differentiating and leveraging an organization's brand message to its current and future workforce in a manner meaningful to them. Using the methodology of corporate brand-building strategy to attract and keep quality employees. Employer branding is aimed at motivating and securing employees' alignment with the vision and values of the company. From a HR perspective, the concept has subsumed the older term 'internal branding' that was essentially the process of communicating an organization's brand values to its employees.

The basis of employer branding is the application of the same marketing and branding practices to a company's human resource activities (specifically, recruitment and retention) as it uses for consumer-targeted marketing and branding efforts. In other words, the business markets its brand image to its staff. And just as customers will cease buying a company's products or services when a promise is unfulfilled, its employees will also leave if the company fails to live up to its employer brand promises. Sartain and Schuman (2006, p. 22) believe that 'your employer brand is shorthand for the emotional connection with employees. It frames how you motivate employees to deliver what your business promises to customers and how you nurture an environment that prospective employees will want to join.'

The concept of employer branding draws on the notion that employees who fully understand and embrace an organization's culture, values and business objectives are more likely to share

---

HRM in reality Employer branding

A study from The Conference Board (*Engaging Your Employees Through Your Brand, Report no. 1288*) found that many large organizations were using the methodology of corporate brand-building strategy to attract and keep quality employees. Their survey found that 'employer branding' was being used by 40 per cent of respondents in a survey of 138 leading companies to increase their attractiveness to potential and current employees. Yet most of these initiatives were relatively new, and many started in the year 2000. However, funding and awareness of 'employer branding' seems to be increasing, particularly in companies whose corporate brand image is not strong among the general public because, for example, they are suppliers to businesses rather than consumers. In other words, prospective employees are not so likely to have heard of them.

The report was sponsored by Charles Schwab and examined these businesses in relation to their branding experiences and practices. Two broad categories of managers were interviewed: communications/ marketing and human resources.

'The challenge to employers is not only to make potential employees aware of the company as a good place to work and bring the best applicants successfully through the recruitment and hiring process, but to retain them and ensure their understanding of the company's goals and commitment to them,' said David Dell, research director of The Conference Board's capabilities management and human resources strategies area. 'Companies have found employer branding programmes provide a real edge in competing for talent.'

'The findings suggest the amplification of a trend we noted in our 1998 research on corporate branding,' commented Kathryn Troy, director, The Conference Board's performance excellence and operations management research. 'Executives told us that their brand was being used as a rallying point for employees in a time of extensive change. Moreover, they expected employees to exemplify the promises the brand makes to the firm's customers.'

Some businesses were using separate, dedicated employer branding efforts aimed at aligning employees with their organizations' vision and values whereas others were pursuing this goal as one element of broader corporate branding strategies.

Comparing corporate branding and employer branding

For the corporate brand, the communications/marketing executives identified four goals as being most important:

- delivering the brand promise to customers (through employees)
- helping employees to internalize company values
- recruiting and retaining customers
- instilling brand values into key processes (e.g. customer service).

The HR executives gave a very similar response with their highest priorities for the corporate brand being:

- delivering the brand promise to customers
- helping employees to internalize the company values
- recruiting customers
- achieving a reputation as an employer of choice.

For the employer brand, the two sets of responses were more different. The communications/marketing executives identified the following as their top goals:

- helping employees internalize the company's values
- achieving a reputation as an employer of choice
- recruiting and retaining employees
- instilling brand values into key processes.

Priorities for HR executives were:

- helping employees to internalize the company's values
- recruiting employees
- retaining employees
- achieving a reputation as an employer of choice.

These findings show considerable overlap and muddling of the two concepts. Differences seem to be a matter of emphasis. And only 20 per cent of organizations seemed to have metrics to measure the consequences of employer branding initiatives. Elsewhere in the study they also report that senior managers are most concerned with corporate branding at the strategic level. But it is realized at a senior level that 'mergers, acquisitions, spinoffs, and other forces of change increasingly blur company identity, with adverse impact on the effectiveness of the workforce.'

The report notes that the 'employer of choice' concept emphasizes improvement of recruitment and retention, but indicates that true employer branding goes further. Employer branding is aimed at motivating and securing employees' alignment with the vision and values of the company. The authors argue that employer branding can be a stimulus to the improvement of all of those people-related processes that create organizational excellence.

How would you distinguish between corporate branding and employer branding?

Source: *HRM Guide USA* (http://www.hrmguide.net/usa/), 1 March, 2002.

---

common goals with the organization, work for those goals and share information with other people. Employer branding reinforces perception of the organization's culture (as top managers perceive it) through a variety of messages, behaviours and other forms of communication.

Employer branding begins with the **recruitment** process because this offers a number of tools that can be used to create perceptions of an employing organization, including:

- job advertisements and descriptions
- the interview process
- offer letters
- information packs for new recruits
- employee handbooks
- induction and training.

Effectively managed, and this should be comparatively simple for professional marketers, the recruitment process can be used to create a positive relationship between candidates and the organization. It depends on relatively simple, thought-through procedures that consistently project a company's image and values in order to create strong, positive views of the organization. This can even extend to unsuccessful candidates.

Gotsi and Wilson (2001) found that PR consultants considered it essential to have an alignment between employee behaviour and the values that an organization's brand stands for. They quote one consultant who stated that: 'aligning brand actions with brand promises is a critical test for managers'. The consultants they investigated highlighted the need to ensure that there was no gap between what an organization was saying in the outside world and what people believed inside that business. Employees were perceived as 'brand ambassadors' and brand marketing would only be successful if they 'lived the brand'. From this perspective, organizations have to: (a) encourage employees to 'buy in' to the business vision and values; and (b) ensure that everyone within the organization clearly understands the purpose of the common set of values.

It is necessary for these conditions to be realized for employees to be able to reflect them through their own behaviour. There has to be an understanding of the brand, if staff are to 'live the brand' and its values (see Key concept 10.3). One of their interviewees observed that for this to happen 'reputation has to be based on reality in order to be credible'.

It is worth observing that, while it may be comparatively easy to convince a new recruit of the positive nature of a company's culture, employer branding can be quickly undone if the organization turns out to be rather different from the recruit's initial perceptions. In fact, an employer brand that departs considerably from reality can be counter-productive, leading to rapid disillusionment rather than sustained commitment.

Key concept 10.3 Living the brand

Identifying with an organization's brand values to such an extent that employees' behaviours fit exactly with the image that the business is trying to portray to its customers.

Gotsi and Wilson (*ibid.*) indicate that the twin tasks of aligning staff behaviour with brand values and getting employees to 'live the brand' are very difficult – far more difficult than other aspects of conventional brand marketing such as creating a visual identity for an organization. They quote a consultant as saying: 'it's much harder to get people's behaviour and culture aligned with a brand, because people are much more unpredictable than graphics. People talk, walk, think, do things; graphics just stay there.'

To achieve these goals it is necessary to treat employees as an audience for corporate communications to ensure that all stakeholders receive the same message. The aim of internal communications, according to Gotsi and Wilson's respondents, is to encourage employees to believe that they can live up to projected brand values. This is done by talking and listening to staff and being aware of their need to believe in the organization's vision and values. But, whereas most consultants proposed a top-down communication exercise from senior managers to lower levels of employees, Gotsi and Wilson are more impressed by a minority view that communication should be two-way. They argue that communication should be a learning exercise in which ideas are shared and feedback obtained from the 'front line'.

Specifically, they contend that for employees' behaviour to reflect brand values organizations must align human resource management practices with their brand values. Recruitment policies, performance appraisal, training and reward systems must fit with brand values, otherwise conflicting messages will be sent about the behaviours that are really important for the business. Recruitment policies must be aimed at attracting the type of people who can fit the desired culture; performance management must identify and encourage behaviours that relate to brand values; reward systems should benefit people who live the brand.

Blumenthal (2001, p.37), using the term 'internal branding' (IB), concludes that:

While searching for meaning is uncomfortable and putting power in the hands of frontline employees is risky, it may also be the only way to actually find the kind of meaning that transforms employees' lives. If employees 'can live with it or without it', then the brand is not living up to its potential. As Bergstrom points out, people are looking to be a part of something special, something connected, something that they can be proud of building. Brand, and its particular application internally, has the potential to be wielded in that way. Although at its worst, IB can prove a cynical exercise, at its best there is potential for more than just profit. IB can provide a basis for mutual respect, community, and honest win–win relationships that profit the organization precisely because it improves the quality of people's lives.

HRM in reality Employers in fantasy land

Eighty per cent of Australian businesses believe they are seen as great employers offering positive and rewarding workplace environments. But 63 per cent of jobseekers say that employers are 'not delivering' on expectations.

Staff are likely to leave in droves from employers who do not deliver on original employment promises, according to a recent Hudson Report. The Hudson national survey of over 8000 Australian employers, found a significant disconnect between how Australian businesses think they are viewed as a workplace, by current and prospective employees, and reality. Hudson conclude that this could be costing Australian businesses millions in staff turnover at a time when they cannot afford to lose people.

The report found that 80 per cent of Australian managers believe that their company's workplace reputation is clearly understood, proactively managed and aligned with what employees expect of them. But only half of these employers actually have a system in place to measure this so-called 'great' reputation! Moreover, a Hudson survey of more than 2500 jobseekers has revealed that 63 per cent of them believe their current employer is not delivering the employment experience that was promised to them.

Matt Dale, Hudson's National Practice Manager for Talent Management, said, 'These results sound a clear warning to Australian businesses who believe they are getting it right and living up to their employees' expectations.

'In many cases, companies are operating under a misguided impression and believe their workers are happy in the workplace, when the truth is that they're not. Their employment promise may be working extremely well in luring employees into the company, but fails miserably when it comes to retaining them in the long-term.

'Disillusioned employees will simply leave if they feel the organization has not delivered on the employment experience that was originally promised to them. In a market where skills shortages are rife and candidates are in the driving seat, employers simply cannot afford to let this happen,' he added.

Matt Dale also commented that unfortunately, many businesses invest heavily in communicating an employment brand promise but fail to align this with actual employment experience.

'In many cases, a company's employment brand may work extremely well in attracting employees, but fails miserably when it comes to retaining them in the long-term,' Mr Dale said. 'In order to get an employment brand right, it means understanding what current and prospective employees want and defining a clear and compelling value proposition. Most critically, all of the organization's current human resources programmes, policies and practices must be aligned with the brand so that it has substance and integrity with employees across the whole organisation,' he concluded.

Hudson recommends the following for businesses wishing to develop their employer branding:

- Focus the employment brand on retention not just attraction.

- Systematically measure workplace reputation.

- Develop a clear and sustainable brand promise and align it with the employment experience.

- Leverage the power of the company's existing market brand.

- Ensure close interaction between the HR function and the company's marketing team.

Why do businesses appear to have a distorted view of the way they are perceived by their employees?

Source: *HRM Guide Australia* (http://www.hrmguide.net/australia/), 27 April, 2005.

Commitment and culture

Western companies have long striven to obtain the degree of commitment shown by Japanese workers. However, Japanese organizations have a significant and possibly insurmountable advantage: Japanese culture. The traditional Japanese managerial scale of values is different from those of Western cultures (Whitehill, 1991). Most crucially, commitment is a two way process – managers are committed to their people (Pascal and Athos, 1981, p.191). Physical status symbols that are so important to Western managers – such as named car parking spaces, large personal offices and executive dining areas – have little value for the Japanese. In contrast, traditionally minded Japanese managers and workers share fundamental values that lie at the heart of their commitment – a **work ethic**, conformity and avoidance of shame.

First, the work ethic centres on being seen to work hard and typically being in the office for long hours. Key to this culture is the belief that 'duty – in the form of work – must come first' (Briggs, 1991, p.41). Dissatisfaction, boredom and exhaustion are brushed aside in the commitment to duty. Indeed, surveys show poor job satisfaction in many Japanese companies. Commitment, therefore, is not to specific corporations so much as to 'duty' in general. Because of this cultural underpinning, it may be that Western managers are pursuing a futile goal in copying Japanese 'commitment'. If the national culture does not feature a similar pressure – for example the Protestant work ethic – then organizations may never achieve the same levels of employee commitment.

Secondly, on **conformity**, as we observed in earlier chapters, individuals have little importance in comparison with the in-group. There is a psychological need to belong and not to be isolated from one's community. The high degree of interdependence leads to the 'high trust' characteristics of Japanese business culture. Western companies are far more individualistic. As we shall see in Chapter 18 on performance management, conformity comes from external control rather than deep compulsion. The result is that workers often conform only when the boss is watching. The unpredictability of individualists also leads to an inevitable reduction in mutual trust.

Thirdly, as regards avoidance of shame, the Japanese manager has obligations and responsibilities derived from traditional culture rather than an employment contract or job description. Failure to discharge these according to the normal social rules can bring isolation and shame – loss of face – on managers and their families. This may be brought about, for example, by a breach of obligation (**psychological contract**) such as the guarantee of continued employment for one's staff. In the past this has reinforced a high-trust relationship and mutual commitment. However, as we observed in Chapter 2, the 1990s brought economic reality to bear on traditional values and large organizations in Japan have been forced to shed people, albeit by oblique methods such as early retirement and coerced resignations. Many Western managers have no concept of shame. Any obligation to staff is tempered by the need to maintain their own careers.

Commitment also depends on organizational culture. Indeed a 'culture of commitment' is frequently cited as a goal for organizational change. Paradoxically, however, change programmes designed to instil modern business methods and 'lean-mean' management structures can rebound, leading to a reduction in employee commitment.

Osborne and Cowen (2002) see a culture of commitment as a crucial basis for high-performance. They identify a number of characteristics of such a culture:

Emotion-packed vision. A simple, compelling vision for the future that resonates with employees. It must be easy to understand and visualize and go 'beyond simply making money'.

'True believer' mentality. Every employee having a belief in the vision of the business and convinced that it will bring certain success. The key is a strong sense of identity with the organization so that ordinary employees act as if they are owners.

Plain vanilla values. Three or four essential and basic values that may be formally expressed or implicit in the way the business is conducted. They need to be simple and have some emotional appeal. For instance, Jack Welch, formerly of General Electric, who highlighted self-confidence as the core of employee success, and also added speed and simplicity as basic values. Fair treatment is another typical 'high commitment' value.

HRM in reality   Overworked Americans can't use up their vacations

Americans have the least annual vacation entitlement (13 days) in the industrialized world. This compares with Italy 42; France 37; Germany 35; Brazil 34; Britain 28; Canada 26; South Korea 25; and Japan 25.* But one in six US employees are unable to use up their entitlement because of overwork. This is the conclusion of a landmark national survey released in February 2001. 'If you take off a week, you've got three times as much work to do when you get back,' said Bob Boudreau, 42, a computer analyst in Poughkeepsie, NY, who has gone without a vacation in two of the last four years.

Sheri Hinshaw, 31, of Seattle, Washington, quit her job, partly because she hasn't been able to take a vacation in five years. She remembers thinking, 'I can't go – I've got too many things to do.' She recently left her job as a program manager at Microsoft and took a less demanding position overseeing computers for the Seattle Opera in order to 'have a life' and possibly take a vacation next summer.

'This survey is a wake-up call for Americans to realize that taking a vacation is not frivolous behaviour. It's essential to staying healthy,' said Alan Muney, MD, chief medical officer and executive vice-president at Oxford Health Plans, Inc., which sponsored the national survey. 'Regular vacations are preventive medicine – they cut down on stress-related illness and save health care dollars.'

The survey of 632 men and women shows that workers often endure a high level of stress on the job:

- 34 per cent of respondents said their jobs were so pressing that they had no down time at work
- 32 per cent work and eat lunch at the same time
- 32 per cent do not leave the building during the working day
- 19 per cent said that their job makes them feel older than they are
- 17 per cent said work caused them to lose sleep at home.

The survey also showed that:

- Most employers make it easy to keep medical appointments (70 per cent) and return to work after illness (68 per cent) – but some have a corporate culture that discourages healthy behaviour.

- 19 per cent said workplace pressures make them feel they must attend work even when injured or sick.
- 17 per cent said it is difficult to take time off or leave work in an emergency.
- 8 per cent believe that if they were to become seriously ill they would be fired or demoted.
- 14 per cent believe their employer makes it difficult to maintain a healthy diet.
- 14 per cent felt that company management only promotes people who habitually work late.

Stress may be relieved by taking a vacation but there is another motivating factor – medical research linking vacation to a lowered risk of death, commented Dr Muney. 'Taking a vacation is a serious health issue that should not be ignored. It could save your life,' he said. In fact researchers at the State University of New York at Oswego published a study in September 2000 based on 12 866 men, aged 35 to 57, that found regular vacations lowered risk of death by almost 20 per cent. The random telephone survey of New York City, with a margin of error of plus or minus 4 per cent, was conducted from 17 August to 1 September 2000 by Central Marketing Inc.

A survey conducted for Expedia.com® found an average of 1.8 unused vacation days per employee each year in the USA. They calculate this to be worth US$19.3 billion a year to their employers. Yet 71 per cent of workers surveyed wished that their employers gave an extra week's paid vacation each year. And 53 per cent of respondents did not know that US employees receive considerably less annual vacation time than their counterparts in other industrialized countries.

Is the fact that Americans do not use their (low) vacation entitlement an illustration of national culture or commitment to their organizations?

Source: *HRM Guide USA* (http://www.hrmguide.net/usa/), May 31, 2001.

Note: *These figures come from a World Tourism Organization study and appear to refer to average vacation days taken by nationals from those countries, including public holidays.

Pride and dissatisfaction. An apparently contradictory mix of intense employee pride in the company combined with a dissatisfaction with their current performance. According to Osborne and Cowen (*ibid.*): 'Edgy ideas and attitudes are pervasive. High performers have a commitment to learning from every mistake and every success.'

Peer respect. From Osborne and Cowen's observations, high-performing organizations rarely rely on fear to motivate employees. Instead, an urge to earn and maintain mutual respect appears to govern the behaviour of senior managers. Respect for oneself comes as a result of respect from others. According to Osborne and Cowen: 'Cynicism is regarded as weakness, an excuse for not getting the job done.'

Long-term relationships. Instead of switching jobs frequently, from one company to another, long-term relationships are seen as the path to personal success. Employees expect to work for their company and with each other for a long time. This is related to peer respect since short-term 'one-upmanship' is not seen as a positive way forward in a high-performance organization.

Fun. Success is celebrated publicly and loudly.

HRM in reality TUC's campaign on call centre working

A total of 397 call handlers contacted a TUC hotline in the first week of its 2001 campaign on call centre working, complaining about issues such as:

- bullying
- being set impossible sales targets
- not getting their wages on time
- hostility towards union representation.

Although calls came from all over the UK, almost a third were from people working in South Wales (15 per cent) and Scottish (14 per cent) call centres. Just 30 per cent of calls were from men, indicating that this is a female-dominated industry. And 68 per cent of callers were non-union members.

Specific complaints included:

- being made to go into work to report in sick rather than make a simple phone call
- being required to put their hands up when they wanted to go to the toilet
- then having the length of time they were there monitored
- being allowed just three seconds' break between calls
- being restricted to no more than 3 days leave in one go – making it impossible to book a proper holiday.

According to the TUC General Secretary at the time, John Monks:

Many call centres already treat their staff with respect and others are making a real effort to clean up their act.

But these figures show there are still too many centres using bullying tactics to pressurize and intimidate employees. According to reports on our hotline, some call centres seem to be openly flouting the law.

The TUC cite a number of particularly bizarre instances:

- One call-handler was disciplined for being idle – after leaving a six-second gap between calls.
- Refusal to allow Christmas decorations in one office because (bosses claimed) it was a health and safety hazard. But the mice in the office were not, the staff were told.
- A claim that one call centre manager took disposable nappies into work and said that staff using the toilet the most would be told to wear one.
- The same call centre was said to have a 'shame' board to monitor staff progress. Anyone on the board for 3 weeks would be dismissed.

The facts about call centres

Call centres currently employ more than 400 000 people – more than the coal, steel and vehicle manufacturing industries put together. It is predicted that there will be more than 665 000 full-time equivalent jobs in the call centre industry by 2008. But staff turnover is a significant problem, with turnover rates of 20–30 per cent a year – although the TUC claims that these are 'public' figures. In reality, they say that turnover may be double the admitted figures.

Low pay is typical, according to the TUC report on call centres (*It's your call*) with average earnings of less

	Source of calls	
Region	Per cent of calls to hotline	Per cent call centre employment
North-west	9.0	17.1
South-east	12.0	15.8
Scotland	14.0	12.0
Yorkshire and Humberside	7.0	8.5
East Anglia	3.0	8.1
West Midlands	7.0	8.0
South-west	8.0	6.9
North-east	8.0	6.8
Greater London	9.0	6.6
East Midlands	5.0	4.7
South Wales	15.0	4.7
North Wales	2.0	n/a
Northern Ireland	0.5	0.8

than £8000 per annum. In general, salaries amount to only 60 per cent of average earnings in a specific region. But standards and pay are being driven up by concentration in some areas such as Glasgow and South Wales where it is possible to earn in excess of £20 000 as employers compete with each other to keep staff. About 44 per cent of call centres are unionized – mainly in the public sectors, privatized utilities and finance, which also tend to pay better.

As well as the incidents detailed by recent callers to the TUC hotline, the report also highlights:

- being listened to on the phone when discussing union business
- having pay withheld while serving probationary periods
- being expected to pay for their own headsets
- suffering 'acoustic shock' that can result in short-term memory loss and an inability to bear loud noises.

Case studies

The report includes a number of illustrative cases. For example, that of Jayne (not her real name), a student employed by a call centre in South Wales for three months. Anonymity is required because she (and her colleagues) signed a contract stipulating that she could not speak to the media about her working conditions.

When she started work, Jayne signed up to a 'training loyalty bond' and was told to go through one-month's training – but she would be paid for only two

weeks. The other two weeks' pay was held until she completed a three-month probationary period which started when her training finished. She considers that her pay isn't bad – £4.50 an hour – but Jayne was required to buy her own headset.

Another case highlights Anthony Samaroo. He had been working for BT for four years when he suffered two acoustic shocks in his left ear. He felt these like a high-pitched sound from a fax machine, but ten times worse:

> The shocks made me feel dizzy and disoriented and now, eighteen months later, I'm still suffering from tinnitus. I find it difficult to concentrate on conversations with several people at a time. I can't go to the theatre or to concerts any more and even squeaky brakes on a bus can leave me with terrible migraine-like pains.

He now wears cotton wool in his ears most of the time, which can cause ear infections. Nevertheless, the London BT centre where he works will not recognize his problem.

> I've taken myself off any duties involving a headset. BT aren't happy about it, but I can't work any other way. I'm frustrated they won't take responsibility for what's happened. Just because you can't see the effects of acoustic shock, doesn't mean it's not real.

Good practice

The report is not all bad. Some call centres are trying to be models of best practice. And some employers operate ethical policies and use good employee relations to achieve deals with new clients. They can offer flexible working patterns, including term-time working. They may also get rid of targets such as call-handling times and offer training and personal development to staff. BT has agreed a 'blueprint' for best practice including such features, agreed with the Communication Workers Union.

TUC General Secretary John Monks concluded:

> As the positive stories in our report show, many call centres don't deserve the sweatshop image they're tainted with. The good call centres we highlight prove the industry can offer good working conditions and still be profitable. But there are still too many call centres exploiting their staff. That's why we're running this campaign – to make sure call handlers know their rights and to raise the status of call centres by encouraging shoddy employers to improve their standards.

What are the shortcomings of the call centres highlighted in this report in achieving employee commitment?

Source: *HRM Guide UK* (http://www.hrmguide.co.uk), 20 February, 2001.

O'Malley (2000, p.7) considers that commitment is not easy to obtain:

Companies that are able to create commitment realize that commitment ultimately is personal. This is the hard part of commitment that has profound implications for corporate conduct. It requires being consistent in what one does even though there may be short-term costs attached; it requires being flexible and making exceptions; and it requires making choices about what employees are prepared and unprepared to do – and providing reasons. Commitment is not created through a grab bag of trendy corporate goodies. It requires the patient and concerted attention of the whole organization.

O'Malley lists a number of reasons why companies feel they cannot create a culture of commitment:

Too hard. The process is perceived as being too difficult. In essence, the company has decided that its management is not good enough to obtain commitment.

Too costly. When changes are considered to improve conditions for employees, the immediate focus is on the costs involved rather than the ultimate benefits: 'If it costs money and is not related to physical or financial capital, the answer is *no*' (O'Malley, 2000, p.7).

Too different. Business is supposed to be hard-nosed whereas treating employees in a way that will foster their commitment is seen as 'soft'. HR professionals worry about their soft image in the company, especially if a commitment programme fails.

Too hopeless. Companies may assume that they are in a competitive industry where staff are constantly being poached from other organizations. They conclude that there is nothing that can be done – unaware that other businesses *are* doing something.

Commitment strategies

According to Smither (1994) there are five barriers that are commonly encountered in changing organizations: disruption of personal relationships; the perceived threat to status; a preference for the status quo; economic factors; and problems arising from the use of consultants. If there is a risk that commitment may be a casualty of change initiatives, how is it best protected and developed? The answer seems to be that it must be regarded as a specific strategic objective in itself. This is best achieved by giving it a clear focus (Armstrong, 1992, p.102). In addition, it must be remembered that 'hearts and minds' commitment cannot be gained by top-down imposition of changes that run counter to the beliefs of employees.

Total quality management (TQM) programmes have been shown to be particularly effective in obtaining commitment. This may be due to their systematic and apparent objectivity, employing project management and other documentation to verify quality standards. These standards are externally justified: they are required to satisfy customers and are not seen as a local management invention. Commitment is reinforced by inbuilt feedback mechanisms that inform staff and management of quality levels.

A more sinister implication is the extension of this mechanism within Japanese production techniques into insidious forms of control: 'management by shame' and 'management by blame' (Garrahan and Stewart, 1992). Social pressure and individual feelings of guilt help to pressurize workers into meeting ever-increasing performance standards.

More positively, a commitment programme should involve a thought-through package of measures that addresses:

Communication. Outlining the direction that the organization's strategy is taking and the purpose of any changes. Staff need to understand why decisions have been taken before they will cooperate in their implementation. Additionally, they must be encouraged to contribute to the process from their experience and ideas.

Education. Where change involves new technology, systems or procedures there must be a suitable training package available to provide confidence in their use. Training also builds commitment and respect through direct contact with managers involved in planning developments.

Ownership. Commitment is encouraged by involving people in decisions and making them responsible for implementing specific actions.

Emotional identification is more likely in an atmosphere of enthusiasm. This can be created by acknowledging and encouraging responsibility and recognizing hard work and results.

Performance assessment and reward structures should be focused on commitment.

Rewards in the form of pay, bonuses and prizes can be linked to visible commitment behaviour. The introduction of performance-related pay has been extensive in recent years. Normally this has been justified as a method of increasing commitment. However, as we shall see in Chapter 19, evidence shows that performance-related pay can encourage a small proportion of good performers at the expense of demotivating the majority. In practice it reduces morale and leads to accusations of unfairness.

Employment contracts can include clauses to prevent employees from publicizing information or opinions that might disadvantage the organization. Regrettably, such 'gagging' clauses have been used by management in public sector organizations, where staff feel themselves committed to public service rather than a particular hospital trust, for example.

HRM in reality   Actively disengaged workers cost USA hundreds of billions a year

A 2001 Gallup study indicates that 'actively disengaged' employees – workers who are fundamentally disconnected from their jobs – are costing the US economy between US$292 billion and US$355 billion a year. This finding appeared in the inaugural issue of the *Gallup Management Journal* (*GMJ*).

These estimates are based on a Gallup 'Q12' employee engagement survey of the US workforce, which calculates that 24.7 million workers (19 per cent) are actively disengaged. The survey found that actively disengaged workers are absent from work 3.5 more days a year than other workers – or 86.5 million days in all.

Gallup research consistently shows a tendency for actively disengaged workers to be (in comparison with colleagues):

- significantly less productive
- report being less loyal to their companies
- less satisfied with their personal lives
- more stressed and insecure about their work.

Gallup has developed a proprietary formula to measure levels of employee engagement based on worldwide survey results and performance data in its database. In fact, over the past three years, Gallup's employee engagement consulting practice has surveyed more than 1.5 million employees at more than 87 000 divisions or work units.

The Q12 survey takes its name from 12 core questions (see below) that Gallup asks the employees at its clients' work units. The results allow Gallup clients to see and understand links between levels of employee engagement and productivity, growth and profitability.

Q12 survey

1 Do I know what is expected of me at work?

2 Do I have the materials and equipment I need to do my work right?

3 At work, do I have the opportunity to do what I do best every day?

4 In the last seven days, have I received recognition — or praise for doing good work?

5 Does my supervisor, or someone at work, seem to care about me as a person?

6 Is there someone at work who encourages my development?

7 At work, do my opinions seem to count?

8 Does the mission or purpose of my company make me feel my job is important?

9 Are my co-workers committed to doing quality work?

10 Do I have a best friend at work?

11 In the last six months, has someone at work talked to me about my progress?

12 This last year, have I had opportunities at work to learn and grow?

Cost calculations

The US$292 billion estimate of the annual cost of actively disengaged employees was derived through a three-step process:

1   The proprietary formula was applied to the Q12 survey results in order to calculate the number of actively disengaged employees in the USA.

2   Standard utility analysis methods (statistical guides) were applied to the US$30 000 per year US average salary, yielding US$2246.

3   This was multiplied by 130 million US workers who are 18 years old or older, resulting in the US$292 billion estimate.

Gallup's US$355 billion estimate had its basis in a different economic measure – the USA's US$10 trillion Gross Domestic Product in the year 2000.

●   The GDP figure was divided by the total number of US workers, yielding US$73 870 worth of goods or services per worker last year.

●   Also using standard utility analysis methods, Gallup statisticians found that a 3.7 per cent increase in output for each employee would be attributable to eliminating active disengagement from the workforce.

●   The 3.7 per cent increase, applied against the US$73 870 average output figure amounts to US$2733 per person in the workforce, or US$355 billion overall.

Suggest reasons why so many US workers are actively disengaged.

Source: *HRM Guide USA* (http://www.hrmguide.net/usa/) 23 March, 2001.

Note: 'Gallup', 'Q12 Advantage', 'The Gallup Poll,' and 'The Gallup Poll Monthly' are trademarks of The Gallup Organization.

Justifying commitment

In practice, Western managers have often imported the concept of commitment without a supporting framework which parallels that provided by Japanese culture. Some have appealed to the good sense of employees – a management rhetoric that presents commitment as voluntary. Supposedly, people are won over by the sound sense of strategic objectives and the 'obvious' view that commitment produces positive benefits for both staff and management. What are these benefits? First, management is made easier. A committed workforce consists of self-motivated staff who can function without the need for orders or managerial control. Left to themselves, they will work in a manner consistent with business objectives. Secondly, employees gain from management trust. They are empowered to make decisions and are rewarded through achievement. But what if the rhetoric is not matched by reality?

There are a number of contradictions inherent in the notion of commitment. Earlier, we discussed commitment in terms of three elements: emotion, belief and behaviour. As a combination of these, commitment can range between 'affective identification' and mere 'behavioural compliance' (see Key concepts 10.4 and 10.5) (Legge, 1995, p.44). For instance, it can be confused with the phenomenon of 'presentism' – the idea that putting in long, and perhaps ineffectual, hours is a demonstration of commitment to the organization.

Key concept 10.4 Affective identification

A real intellectual and emotional identification with the organization.

Key concept 10.5 Behavioural compliance

Appearing to have attitudes and behaviours expected by senior managers without any real commitment.

Kunda (1991, cited in Willmott, 1993, p.538) found evidence of 'distancing' in a study of middle managers in a company where the rhetoric of commitment and corporate culturism was strong. Managers deftly played the game of appearing to be committed to the organization's culture while, in reality, maintaining a sense of detachment from the process. In fact, many Western organizations have a prevailing climate of cynicism, with employees and managers alike acting out their roles with little faith in the outcome of their actions. Watson (1994, p.74), questioned managers in one organization and obtained the following response from one participant: 'We are a pretty committed bunch but I don't think ZTC knows what to with that commitment.'

Yaniv and Farkas (2005) show that person–organization fit (POF) – the fit between organizational values and the individual values of employees – can play a significant role in closing the gap between corporate brand values as perceived by customers and those declared by management. If companies transfer corporate brand values to customers that appear to differ from reality, employees may perceive this as a lie resulting in a lack of identification with the corporate brand and an unwillingness to support it adequately. As a consequence customers feel mistrust towards the corporate brand. Person–organization fit has usually been studied in relation to internal organizational aspects such as commitment, identification, job satisfaction, intention to leave, and willingness to do extra work. Yaniv and Farkas argue that HR managers should also regard the POF as a means of improving the organization's external

---

HRM in reality   Showing up for the paycheck?

A report by The Conference Board shows that job satisfaction is declining among workers of all ages and across all income brackets.

Half of all Americans today say they are satisfied with their jobs, but this is down from nearly 60 per cent 10 years ago. Moreover, among the 50 per cent who say they are content, a mere 14 per cent say they are 'very satisfied'.

The representative sample of 5000 US households, conducted for The Conference Board by TNS, a leading market information company, also includes information collected independently by TNS. This information shows that approximately one-quarter of the American workforce is simply 'showing up to collect a paycheck'.

'Rapid technological changes, rising productivity demands and changing employee expectations have all contributed to the decline in job satisfaction,' says Lynn Franco, Director of The Conference Board's Consumer Research Center. 'As large numbers of baby boomers prepare to leave the workforce, they will be increasingly replaced by younger workers, who tend to be as dissatisfied with their jobs, but have different attitudes and expectations about the role of work in their lives. This transition will present a new challenge for employers.'

Money can't buy me love
The survey finds a decline in job satisfaction across all income brackets in the last nine years. Fifty-five per cent of workers earning more than US$50 000 are satisfied with their jobs, but only 14% claim they are very satisfied. At the other end of the pay scale (employees earning less than US$15 000), about 45 per cent of workers are satisfied, with only 17 per cent expressing a strong level of satisfaction.

The survey also finds that employees are least satisfied with their companies' bonus plans, promotion policies, health plans and pensions. The majority are most satisfied with their commutes to work and their relationships with colleagues.

'Less than one-third of all supervisors and managers are perceived to be strong leaders,' says Shubhra Ramchandani, North American stakeholder management practice leader at TNS. 'The Enron/Worldcom era of corporate scandals and the outsourcing of jobs have increased the level of employee discontent. Shrugging off employee disengagement would be a disastrous, short-sighted view creating lasting global repercussions for American business.'

Job satisfaction – by age, income and region
The survey's findings showed that:

- The largest decline in overall job satisfaction, from 60.9 per cent to 49.2 per cent, occurred among workers aged 35–44.
- The second largest decline took place among workers aged 45–54, with the satisfaction level dropping from 57.3 per cent to 47.7 per cent.

- The smallest decline occurred among workers aged 65 and over. Overall job satisfaction declined from 60.8 per cent to 58.0 per cent, making this group the most satisfied with their jobs.

- The largest decline in job satisfaction took place among householders earning US$25 000 to US$35 000, with satisfaction falling from 55.7 per cent to 41.4 per cent. This income group expressed the second lowest level of overall satisfaction.

- The second largest decline was posted by householders earning US$35 000– $50 000. This group experienced a decline from 59.7 per cent to 46.7 per cent.

- With less than 47 per cent of householders claiming to be satisfied with their current job, workers in the middle atlantic and mountain states are the least satisfied workers in the USA

- The east south central region has the most content workers. Close to 59% of residents in these states claim they are satisfied with their jobs.

- Company promotion policies and bonus plans tended to be the lowest on the satisfaction scale.

- Educational and job training programmes did not fare well either. Only 30 per cent of workers claimed to be satisfied with these types of company programmes.

- Workers also rated their wages poorly, with only 33.5 per cent of householders expressing satisfaction with their pay.

Additional results from the supplemental survey conducted by TNS in August 2004 include:

- 40 per cent of workers feel disconnected from their employers.

- Two out of every three workers do not identify with or feel motivated to drive their employer's business goals and objectives.

- 25 per cent of employees are just 'showing up to collect a paycheck'.

How would you explain the variation in job satisfaction ratings between different age groups?

Source: *HRM Guide USA* (http://www.hrmguide.com/) 5 March, 2005.

---

performance. They caution that a strong corporate culture associated with a high POF might lead to inflexibility and inability to see the need for change.

Committed to what?

Individuals may identify with their work at a variety of levels: their job, profession, department, boss, or organization. Realistically, commitment may be diverse and divided between any or all of these. For example, there may be a significant conflict between commitment to the organization and commitment to a trade union. Multi-union situations diffuse commitment even further: they encourage identification with themselves and their own sectional interests; they become combatants in a power game and compete with each other for management attention. Single-union agreements and healthy consultation arrangements help to unify and refocus commitment to the strategic objectives of the company. Japanese 'enterprise unions', linked to and funded by individual organizations, further enhance a unified focus. Abolition of union representation removes the alternative focus completely, at the expense of a useful mechanism for developing a cohesive workforce.

Commitment conflicts with the notion of flexibility. Numerical flexibility has been a predominant feature of recent years, with 'downsizing' and 'de-layering' being an obsession for many large companies. A climate of fear has been created for those people remaining. Staff keep a wary eye on senior managers who have demonstrated a ruthless ability to cut employee costs. The workload has not been diminished in equal measure to the reduction in staff, imposing extra burdens on remaining staff.

Extra work, longer hours and fear of redundancy have increased stress and reduced commitment to employing organizations. Peak performance in the short term requires a significant level of commitment but this can only occur if managers 'ensure that a perception of healthy longevity is achieved' (Watson, 1994, p.111). In other words, insecurity does not lead to motivated employees.

This is so obvious that one is hesitant to make the point. Nevertheless many people in charge of organizations behave in a way that suggests it is beyond their awareness. Employees are far more likely to be committed to their employing organization if they can feel confidence in their employers' commitment to them. Recent evidence shows that such confidence is misplaced in many free market companies which, seemingly, are controlled by people concerned largely with furthering their own careers. There is no possibility of achieving real commitment without mutual trust.

HRM in reality Managing workplace negativity

One of the easiest ways for disgruntled employees to turn negativity into a dangerous weapon is to create a weblog or 'blog'. Blogs can be created without any need for technical ability and there are several free providers. Bloggers do not need to understand website coding, register their own domains or pay for hosting. In essence, blogs are personal online journals that are sometimes turned into 'electronic soapboxes' with the option of inviting comments from viewers to whip up more discord. This offers an easy opportunity for causing mischief, if not mayhem.

A survey by the Employment Law Alliance earlier this year found that 5 per cent of American workers maintain a blog – and 16 per cent of bloggers admitted to having posted something negative about an employer, supervisor or colleague. The Employment Law Alliance calculated that in a company with 120 employees, there is likely to be at least one employee making negative blog comments about the organization or its employees.

Despite the potentially harmful effect on employee morale and an organization's reputation, the survey found that only 15 per cent of employers had specific policies about work-related blogging. The Employment Law Alliance considers that employers should have rules on blogging in their employee handbooks, just as most have addressed e-mail and internet use. Employers cannot prevent workers from blogging in their own time, but they can attempt to restrict work-related content and blogging activity during working hours.

The survey found that 62 per cent of US employers with blogging policies prohibited any employer-related information – good or bad – being posted on a blog. Sixty per cent of surveyed employees believed that employers should have the right to discipline or dismiss employees who posted confidential, damaging or embarrassing information about their employer on their personal blog.

What factors contribute to lack of trust and employee negativity?

Source: *HRM Guide USA* (http://www.hrmguide.net/usa/) 27 June, 2006.

HRM in reality Psychopathic organizations

Corporate responsibility researchers have found that many large organizations display the criteria psychiatrists use to classify people as psychopaths. New research from the Turku School of Economics in Finland (Ketola, 2006) suggests that organizations showing evidence of psychopathic behaviour would benefit from a 'prince of virtues' approach to awake them from a '100-year sleep'.

Psychopathic characteristics in organizations
The article matches the personality characteristics of psychopaths (shown in bold) with some examples of organizational behaviour:

● **Unconcern for others' feelings**: harsh treatment of employees, customers and partners – sudden terminations of employment contracts and business contracts.

● **Inability to maintain human relations**: transferring business operations from country to country in order to minimize production expenses – constant change of employees and partners.

● **Disregard for others' safety**: products and production methods endangering human health and the environment – dangerous working conditions.

● **Dishonesty and lying to one's own advantage**: keeping silent about the risks of hazardous products and production methods, covering them up and denying their existence – deceiving employees, customers and partners.

- **Inability to feel guilt**: when exposed for wrongdoing, asserting innocence (denial), blaming others (projection) and justifying one's action (rationalization).

- **Inability to observe the laws and norms of society**: breaking human rights, labour, contract and environmental laws and agreements when it is economically more beneficial than observing them.

The author of the report, Dr Tarja Ketola, considers that managers and employees working in large companies that employ psychopathic practices which breach people's basic values carry a huge mental burden. However, she argues a solution can come from using ethical principles employed by individuals in their personal lives.

'According to the natural law (*lex naturae*) people all over the world share the same sense of morality, irrespective of their religion and background,' says Dr. Ketola. 'Why then, should people keep their personal values separate from their work values? If key individuals or the majority of personnel within psychopathic companies realize that the same ethical principles they use in their personal life also apply in business life, the "spell" will be broken and they will overcome organizational resistance to genuine corporate responsibility.'

She believes that these results suggest that 'psychopathic' organizations can move towards ideal responsibility by developing their economic, social and ecological responsibilities in harmony on the basis of virtue ethical values.

Dr Tarja Ketola notes: 'If these companies can stop schizophrenically separating their staff's personal values from their professional values, allowing people in organizations to integrate them into a natural harmonic unity, the corporate responsibility "100-year sleep" could be over.'

Should people keep their personal values separate from their work values?

Source: *HRM Guide UK* (http://www.hrmguide.co.uk), 27 February, 2006.

Managing professionals

Employee commitment faces one of its most difficult challenges in the management of people who regard themselves as professionals – for example, accountants, artists, designers, doctors, engineers, lawyers, scientists and teachers. Strictly speaking, they are salaried professionals in that they conduct their craft within the organization rather than in private practice (Raelin, 1991). The tendency has been to superimpose conventional management practices on these individuals despite several important differences affecting status, power, motivation, etc. According to Raelin: 'There is a natural conflict between management and professionals because of their differences in educational background, socialization, values, vocational interests, work habits and outlook.' He encapsulates the essential problem in the following way:

> As a manager of professionals, how often in your career have you had to confront attempts by your professional associates or subordinates to challenge your authority? As a salaried professional, how much longer can you put up with managers who interfere with your right to work autonomously on the problems to which you have been assigned?

Conventionally, professionals will have been trained and socialized in their professions outside the organization in which they are now working. Managers, on the other hand, will have had a comparatively short and non-specialized training and will probably gain much of their expertise on the job. The organization expects professionals, as employees, to obey its rules and procedures. Professionals may feel that these procedures conflict with the ethics or practices of their profession.

Their commitment and loyalty may take a number of forms: to their profession, to the organization or both. Sociologically, individuals primarily committed to the former are regarded as 'cosmopolitan', those to the organization as 'local'. This commitment may vary at different stages in a career and with different circumstances. There are also clear cultural tendencies: in Japan, commitment is overwhelmingly to the organization whereas the Anglo-Celtic economies such as the UK and the USA have encouraged a cosmopolitan attitude. This tendency matches prevailing attitudes towards job-change between organizations.

Professional status

To be classified as a professional, an individual needs to satisfy such criteria as the following:

1 Possession of expertise or detailed grasp of a recognized body of knowledge, usually after a prolonged period of formal training.
2 Autonomy: freedom to choose the methods by which they conduct their profession.
3 Commitment to a specific profession.
4 Identification with a group of like-minded professionals – e.g. an association.
5 Ethics: a recognised code of conduct.
6 Standards, the maintenance of which requires the policing of colleagues' activities and being policed in return.

Conflict factors

The interaction of professionals and their managers involves conflict between the aspirations and attitudes of the two. Systematic factors are likely to be responsible.

Overspecialization. There are forces both from within management and the profession that lead towards overspecialization of the individual. From the organization's viewpoint, greater efficiency is obtained by only using the professional for tasks where the specialization is specifically required. The professional is treated like a tool. Very often, professionals are happy to fit in with this process since it provides recognition of their expertise. However, the end result of this practice is to produce an individual lacking in the general experience and integrative skills required for senior levels within the organization.

Employment a loose attachment. The professional may tend to regard management as being unnecessary: self-management is the ideal. Obviously, this view is not shared by the manager who will regard such an attitude as disrespectful and obstructive. Furthermore, professionals may readily share opinions and information with their network outside the organization thereby revealing information that the manager could regard as being commercially sensitive. This process is further encouraged by the pressure on professionals to enhance their status through publication of papers in journals and attendance at conferences. Local commitment will operate against the perceived professional status of individuals who are more likely to gain respect among colleagues by frequently moving between jobs. Their reputation is reduced by staying with one organization.

Demand for autonomy. The organization holds the view that professional employees are 'hired to do the job' for which they have been taken on: the task requiring trained expertise. Management sets this agenda and normally finds little resistance from the professional who tends to be happy to fit in with it. The ends may not be as important to the professional as the means by which the job is done. Bad managers will exacerbate the situation by getting involved in the details of job methodology and demand constant reports.

Conflict situations

The conflict between manager and professional can be brought to a head in a number of specific circumstances: project termination; close supervision; and management by non-professionals.

Project termination. Professionals are often employed as members of project teams. Inevitably, a high proportion of projects fail to achieve their objectives. Many organizations deliberately start a large number of projects knowing that only a small proportion will produce marketable products or services. In these circumstances, the management decision to close a project will be clinical and unemotive. However, the staff involved will probably have invested a great deal of emotional commitment to the project and are unlikely to want to abandon it.

Close supervision. As we discussed earlier, professionals tend to be ready to accept the specification of ends and allow managers to determine what tasks the organization will undertake. However, they will not be ready to accept close managerial supervision of the means by which these tasks are completed. Professional work inevitably requires the flexibility to interpret rules and determine which techniques should apply. In these circumstances, self-supervision and peer control should replace traditional supervision.

Management by non-professionals. In many organizations, the overriding respect for technical competence has traditionally allowed professionals to manage their own institutions. Since the advent of neo-liberal agendas, the trend (e.g. in hospitals) has been to promote administrators as a separate cadre of professional managers. Achieving the correct balance of management between close or laissez-faire supervision has tended to be problematic.

HRM in reality   Employees and employers: 'A marriage breakdown in progress?'

A survey of 2000 UK employees commissioned by the Chartered Institute of Personnel and Development (CIPD) has found that relationships between employers and employees in many workplaces are characterized by poor communication and low levels of trust resulting in underperformance, low productivity and high staff turnover.

'Working Life: Employee Attitudes and Engagement 2006' is written by Catherine Truss, Emma Soane and Christine Edwards from the School of Human Resource Management at Kingston University and Karen Wisdom, Andrew Croll and Jamie Burnett from Ipsos MORI.

Comparing the situation to a marriage under stress, the authors highlight some of the survey findings relating to communication and trust:

- *We just don't talk anymore*: Around one-third of employees (30 per cent) say they rarely or never get performance feedback; 42 per cent feel they are not kept well informed about organizational developments; only 37 per cent are satisfied with opportunities to communicate views and opinions to management.

- *You just take me for granted*: One-quarter (25 per cent) of employees rarely or never feel their work counts; only 38 per cent feel they are treated with respect by directors and senior managers.

- *You really get me down*: Some 44 per cent of employees feel under excessive pressure at least once or twice a week; 22 per cent overall and 32 per cent of managers experience high levels of stress.

- *The magic is gone*: Almost half of employees (43 per cent) are dissatisfied with their relationship with

their manager; 26 per cent rarely or never look forward to going to work.

- *I just can't trust you*: One-third of employees (32 per cent) are dissatisfied with the management of their organization; only 37 per cent have confidence in their senior management team and 34 per cent trust their senior managers.

- *I want out*: About one-quarter of employees (26 per cent) are dissatisfied in their job; 47 per cent are looking for another job or in the process of leaving their current job.

Mike Emmott, CIPD employee relations adviser, said:

> As in any marriage, good relationships need work and commitment. But with only three in ten employees engaged, the findings suggest many managers just aren't doing enough to keep their staff interested. Lack of communication means many employees feel unsupported and don't feel their hard work is recognized.

Catherine Truss said:

> There is so much that managers can do to make their staff feel valued and improve levels of engagement that will benefit both employers and employees. We found that people who are engaged with their work perform better, are more likely to act as advocates for their employer and experience more job satisfaction. So it is in the interests of everyone to find ways of addressing low levels of engagement in the workplace.

Why are employers often reluctant to communicate honestly with their employees?

Source: *HRM Guide UK* (http://www.hrmguide.co.uk), 5 December, 2006.

Summary

In this chapter we examined the concept of commitment, particularly in relation to the concept of employer branding. Commitment has been a particular feature of human resource literature since the 1980s as a result of its inclusion in the influential Harvard map of HRM and the apparent advantage it gave Japanese firms over their Western counterparts. In recent years, internal brand management has been subsumed by the process of 'employer branding' – an attempt to build organizations that embody brand values by attracting, keeping and developing employees who 'live the brand' through the alignment of marketing communications and HR practices. We reconsidered the link between commitment and culture questioning its true justification and meaning and addressed the issue of commitment in the management of professionals.

Further reading

Karen Legge provides a powerful analysis of commitment in *Human Resource Management: Rhetorics and Realities* (1995), published by Macmillan Business. Michael O'Malley's *Creating Commitment: How to Attract and Retain Talented Employees by Building Relationships That Last* (2000), published by John Wiley is a highly readable practitioner account of developing commitment and identifying employees who 'fit'. There are hundreds of brand management books in print, but few go into employer branding in detail. *Brand From the Inside: Eight Essentials to Emotionally Connect Your Employees to Your Business,* by Libby Sartain and Mark Schumann (2006), published by Jossey-Bass, takes an enthusiastic practitioner approach to the subject. *Brand Manners: How to Create the Self Confident Organization to Live the Brand,* by Hamish Pringle and William Gordon (2001), published by John Wiley and *The Brand Mindset: Five Essential Strategies for Building Brand Advantage Throughout Your Company* by Duane E. Knapp and Christopher W. Hart (1999), published by McGraw-Hill, also contain some material on employees and branding.

Review questions

1 What do you understand by 'commitment'? To what extent are you committed to the organization in which you work or study?

2 Why is commitment significant in human resource literature?

3 What is the relationship between brand management, employer branding and commitment?

4 Take a well-known brand name as an example. What are its values and how should HR practices be aligned to fit?

5 Is employer branding an ethical form of 'internal marketing' or an attempt at brainwashing staff? How can individuals retain their individuality and freedom of expression in an organization that emphasizes employer branding?

6 Would you classify Osborne and Cowen's description of a high-commitment organization as idealistic or realistic? How would you design a commitment programme for an organization you know well?

7 To what extent is true commitment attainable? Is it just an example of management rhetoric? How easy is it to identify real commitment?

8 If Japanese commitment is dependent on Japanese culture, how useful is the concept likely to be in other parts of the world?

9 Outline some of the principal drivers and barriers to effective employee commitment.

10 What is the relationship between the concepts of 'strong culture' and 'commitment'?

11 Is it possible to obtain commitment in a situation where redundancies are inevitable?

12 What are the main points of friction between professionals and managers?

Case study for discussion and analysis

Ark Nurseries

Ark Nurseries is a specialist wholesaler of fresh and freeze-dried herbs and vegetables. These are grown within the country or brought in from other parts of the world and packaged in a small, chaotic factory. Most of the sales are to small retailers and restaurants in middle-class areas. The company was founded 10 years ago and has prospered as its products have become familiar and customers have been increasingly interested in a more varied range of foods. The managing director founded the company with her late husband and has taken complete control since his death three years ago. She was always accustomed to working hard and now spends virtually all her waking hours on company business. Her main interest is selecting and marketing new products and she is happy to spend a lot of her time travelling to meet growers and attending trade fairs and exhibitions. She is frequently away from the office for weeks at a time.

Employee numbers have gradually increased and most of the more senior managers have been with her for several years. She deals directly with her managers, usually on a one-to-one basis as problems come up, and dislikes committee-type meetings. An outgoing and energetic person, she takes decisions quickly, based on intuition and her experience of the market. She takes advice from her staff but does not feel obliged to follow it. Generally, she is a talker rather than a listener and is accustomed to having her way. She insists on vetting all staff recruitment, promotion and pay increases and takes all equipment-purchasing decisions herself. There is no one specifically in charge of human resources, each functional manager being responsible for their own staff. Pay is good for the area and employees are generally pleased to work for the company. The factory has a five-day week and is open for ten hours a day. There is no appraisal or performance management system, with senior staff being paid salaries and factory workers receiving wages based on a piece-rate system.

The sales manager has just clinched a deal with a major supermarket group which has agreed to take Ark produce for its 60 stores. The managing director was surprised by his success but is delighted that it has finally been achieved. The contract was announced last week but reactions within the company have been mixed. The managing director has spent years trying to break into this market and is astonished by the attitude of most of her senior staff. They have been accustomed to steady but undramatic growth and are now faced with tripling sales over the next three years. They argue that their regular growers could not meet the demand at the right level of quality, especially as the supermarket group will expect stringent standards and exact financial penalties for late delivery.

Over the last few days, fierce arguments have broken out between the managing director and her staff and there have been threats of resignation. However, she is convinced that the contract is feasible and that resignations will not happen because of the unemployment situation.

As a human resources consultant how would you analyse the situation and how could you help?

Part four
Strategic HRM

This part of the book discusses the basis, preparation and implementation of strategic HRM. Human resource management is closely identified with business strategy by many authors. In fact, HRM is typically distinguished from traditional personnel management by its concern with meeting business objectives in a strategic fashion.

The chapters in Part four address a number of specific issues:

- What is strategy?

- What is the role of HRM in the strategic process?

- How are human resource strategies prepared and implemented?

- What is the relationship between strategic HRM and human resource planning?

- How does HRM impact on the process of organizational change?

- What is the role of HR practitioners in outsourcing, mergers and acquisitions?

- How can behavioural change be achieved?

- What strategies are available for recruitment and retention?

- How are resourcing strategies prepared?

Chapter 11
People strategies

Learning objectives

The purpose of this chapter is to:

- Determine the nature and prevalence of strategic HRM.

- Evaluate the influence and involvement of people managers in high-level decisionmaking.

- Identify different approaches to strategic HRM, and outline their strengths and weaknesses.

- Consider how people strategies and practices can be adapted to meet perceived threats and opportunities in a changing business environment.

Strategy and HRM

Armstrong (1994) posed the question:

What *is* this thing called strategic HRM? It seems to be part of the brave new worlds of strategic management and human resource management. But have these terms any real meaning? How many people actually put either strategic management or human resource management into practice? And if they do, what do they look like and what impact, if any, do they make on organizational performance?

In Part one we saw that many theorists consider a strong link with strategy to be the key difference between HRM and earlier philosophies of people management. Exponents of HRM emphasize the importance of an organization's people in achieving its overall business objectives. Typically, it is claimed that **human resource strategies** combine all people management activities into an organized and integrated programme to meet the strategic objectives of an enterprise. It is claimed also that HRM is different from personnel management primarily because of its supposed emphasis on the link between people policies and overall business strategy. For example, Guest (1993, p.213) distinguishes traditional personnel management from HRM 'by virtue of the way in which the former ignored, but the latter embraces strategy'. This contrasts with the 'technical-piecemeal' approach of personnel management.

Purcell (2001, p.59) concludes that 'the integration with strategy is central to all models of HRM and virtually all authors are agreed that this is *the* distinctive feature of HRM, compared with personnel.' Personnel management, we are told, is essentially reactive whereas HRM, exemplified by HR strategy, is proactive. The personnel model focused on short-term, largely operational matters of little interest to strategists. HRM, by contrast, takes a longer perspective and is closer to the heart of the organization. HRM is portrayed as 'having come out of the shadows to claim a rightful place alongside other core management roles' (Beardwell, 2001, p.13). It takes a proactive stance towards the competitiveness and efficiency of the organization, unlike the mundane and reactive, day-to-day orientation of personnel management. However, this distinction is by no means accepted unanimously: 'HRM's claim to take a strategic approach to employment touches a particularly raw nerve among personnel managers. "*Of course*" personnel management has "*always*" advocated a strategic approach' (Hendry, 1995, p.12).

Moreover, human resource strategies are not easy to identify. For example, Marginson *et al.* (1988) found that 80 per cent of senior people managers claimed to have overall HR strategies – but few could describe what those strategies were! In fact, both academics and practitioners have found it difficult to understand what HR strategy means in practice. Hendry (1994), for example, acknowledges that strategy is the dominant theme in HRM but it is also a misunderstood concept. He concludes that 'the perspective writers on HRM offer on strategy is often glib and lacking in sophistication'. Hendry attributes this to HR theorists being 'strategically illiterate'. They use strategic concepts that are outmoded and defective. The problem is compounded by the lack of case studies to give us insight into the way strategies arise in practice.

We can compare these comments from the UK, where (as in Australia, India, Ireland, Malaysia, New Zealand, Singapore and South Africa) there is a perceived dichotomy between 'personnel management' and HRM, with the situation in North America where Rothwell, Prescott and Taylor (1998, p.5) compare 'traditional HR' and its more modern (and dynamic) form, 'strategic HR':

1 Traditional HR practitioners do not have enough 'working knowledge of what business is all about or of the strategic goals of the organizations they serve'. Instead they present what appears to be a social (i.e. dangerously liberal) agenda without explaining the organizational benefits. As a result the impression is created that they have little concern for business results.

2 They lack leadership ability, especially if they have no line management experience and are viewed as having less interest in helping line managers solve their problems

than they have in meeting HR objectives, such as complying with employment legislation.

3 HR practitioners are viewed as reactive. For example, insisting on individual pay scales when the organization has otherwise decided on a team-based approach. 'They appear unresponsive – and even resistant – to line management needs, interests and business pressures.'

4 They sometimes seem unable to take on 'the lead in establishing a vision for change and garnering the support necessary to lead the change'. The result is that they lose credibility and respect.

5 They are seen as 'fad-chasers' who try to use solutions for problems in other workplaces and 'drop them in place without taking into account the unique business objectives, corporate culture, organization-specific politics, and individual personalities of key decisionmakers found in their own organizational settings'.

Such criticisms of 'personnel management' or old-school HR are common and strategic HRM is seen as a possible solution. For example, Beardwell (2001, p.13) states:

In this respect one of the traditional stances of the personnel practitioner – that of the 'liberal' conception of personnel management as standing between employer and employee, moderating and smoothing the interchange between them – is viewed as untenable: HRM is about shaping and delivering corporate strategies with commitment and results.

HR and that elusive strategic role

It seems that finally senior managers – some of them, at least – are willing to give HR managers a significant role in strategic decisions. But how many human resource managers know how to fulfil that role? Kearns (2003: p.4) tells the tale of a workshop exercise for senior human resource managers when participants were given a military scenario. Briefly, they were asked to envisage that they, and a thousand soldiers under their command, had been dropped behind enemy lines – with no information about their opposition. What would they do? The first response he received was 'I'd retreat'. Kearns comments: 'Why does this response from an HR person not surprise me?' Perhaps because so many HR managers are used to operating someone else's strategy, rather than participating vigorously in their organization's strategic decisions.

Noting that 'business partner' and 'strategic thinker' have featured as the most important roles in some recent surveys of human resource management, Jamroq and Overhot (2004) observe that 'there's something elusive and ambiguous about this widely touted goal of becoming a strategic business partner'. They cite a recent conference on the future of HR where a panel of human resource experts came out with the statement that 'I can't define it, but I know it when I see it' when asked to define the term 'strategic business partner'.

Measuring the effectiveness of HRM
Is measurement at the root of the problem? Are HR managers measuring the wrong things? One common approach is to use a 'balanced scorecard' which includes a range of HR measures as well as the more traditional financial and other metrics. Gubman (2004) feels that:

Too many HR scorecards focused on operational metrics: time to hire, cost per hire, percentage of appraisals completed, etc. While important to track, these kinds of measures will not get HR to the strategic partner role. They only reinforce the view of HR as an administrative function. Key HR measures need to be central to business success.

More beneficially, according to Gubman, HR managers should focus instead on the same two major issues as their financial colleagues: return and growth. 'HR things' can only create economic value from three sources:

- employee turnover and retention
- productivity – revenue against employee costs
- expenditure on the HR function and related activities.

Providing measures for these three elements does not require any 'rocket science' because they relate to three familiar HR goals:

1 attracting, developing and retaining staff

2 aligning, engaging, measuring and rewarding performance

3 controlling or reducing HR costs.

HR-relevant measures for growth are trickier and need to be tailored to the organization's individual situation. Gubman believes that HR measures can be devised that, like market share, can indicate trends and forecasts for improved revenue in the future. He argues that the following are the most significant growth-related human resource measures at present:

- Leadership development, to be measured in terms of unique candidates ready to assume executive and other major roles.
- Engagement – levels of employees' intellectual and emotional commitment to their work.
- Diversity, particularly the number of women and ethnic minority employees coming through the system or 'talent pipeline'.

Behaving proactively

Weiss (1999) argues that HR managers must demonstrate the ability to provide stimulating ideas and challenge decisions that do not have business value. To do this, they need to perform at the same intellectual level as their colleagues in an executive meeting. Most importantly, they need to wear a 'business hat' rather than a 'HR hat' otherwise they will be relegated to the traditional administrative or tactical (second-level) role that has bedevilled the human resource function for decades. Weiss considers that HR managers need to demonstrate the following to show their ability to add value:

- Broad understanding of the business, thus helping the human resource function to contribute to the overall direction of the company.
- Knowledge of how all activities need to align, enabling the company to maximize the success of its strategic initiatives.
- Professionalism in investing in human capital and HR processes, allowing HR to help guide employees and the organization's decisionmaking.
- A unique perspective, allowing the HR function to become an 'ideas merchant' so that people and the outcomes of organizational processes can be made into strategic advantages.

Finally, we can consider Gubman's belief that:

HR needs to keep moving itself forward, toward the strategic partner role, by becoming better profit-and-loss business leaders. Be the ones to lead companies back into thinking externally, about customers and markets, and how to create unique value for them. What a surprising and powerful role that would be for HR leaders! Start measuring HR impacts on real business results, not HR activities. Instead of measuring time to hire, measure the people aspects of opening up a new market and the returns they generate.

Source: *HRM Guide UK* (http://www.hrmguide.co.uk) 6 May, 2005.

Strategic management

Strategy is about choice. The underlying assumption is that firms can make deliberate decisions about their markets, the products or services they provide, prices, quality standards and the deployment of human and other resources. According to most discussions of the subject, strategic thinking is based on rational decisionmaking, taking into account the competitive and financial pressures on an organization and the resources available to it, including its people. It imposes orderly, logical thinking on a messy real world, modelling the present situation and predicting the consequences of specific actions (see Key concept 11.1). In order to evaluate these outcomes there is an emphasis on quantitative statements – such as the number of people needed – based on an explicit set of objectives. But we will see that this approach has been questioned and alternative approaches have been proposed for strategic human resource management.

Under the influence of the Harvard MBA, business strategy has become an influential and integrative discipline at the organizational level. The emphasis on a planned approach to development and growth brings together the functional elements of operations management, marketing, finance and human resource management into a cohesive whole. Strategic management is a process by which organizations determine their objectives, decide on actions and suitable timescales, implement those actions and then assess progress and results. Fundamentally, it is the task of senior managers, although more junior employees contribute to the process and the implementation of strategy.

Key concept 11.1 Strategy

A strategy is the means by which an organization seeks to meet its objectives. It is a deliberate choice, a decision to take a course of action rather than reacting to circumstances. It focuses on significant, long-term goals rather than day-to-day operating matters.

As we observed in Part one, rhetorical accounts paint a picture of HRM as being focused and managerial, unified and holistic, and driven by strategy. According to Armstrong (1992, p.47):

> A strategic orientation is a vital ingredient in human resource management. It provides the framework within which a coherent approach can be developed to the creation and installation of HRM policies, systems and practices. . . . The aim of strategic human resource management is to ensure that the culture, style and structure of the organization, and the quality, commitment and motivation of its employees, contribute fully to the achievement of business objectives.

But there is a considerable debate about what '**strategic human resource management**' (SHRM) actually means (Key concept 11.2). There are many definitions, including:

- 'A human resource system that is tailored to the demands of the business strategy' (Miles and Snow, 1984).
- 'The pattern of planned human resource activities intended to enable an organization to achieve its goals' (Wright and McMahan, 1992).
- 'By *strategic* we mean that HR activities should be systematically designed and intentionally linked to an analysis of the business and its context' (Schuler, Jackson and Storey, 2001, p.127).

Such definitions range from a portrayal of SHRM as a 'reactive' management field where human resource management is a tool with which to implement strategy, to a more proactive function in which HR activities can actually create and shape the business strategy (Sanz-Valle, Sabatar-Sanchez and Aragon-Sanchez, 1998).

Key concept 11.2 Strategic HRM

Strategic HRM takes a long-term perspective and is concerned with issues such as corporate culture and individual career development as well as the availability of people with the right skills. It incorporates redundancy and recruitment planning and is increasingly focused on decisions about maintaining the internal capability of an organization's workforce to perform specific functions or to contract out (outsource) an activity to an external provider.

The range of activities and themes encompassed by SHRM is complex and goes beyond the responsibilities of personnel or HR managers into all aspects of managing people. It focuses on 'management decisions and behaviours used, consciously or unconsciously, to control, influence and motivate those who work for the organizations – the human resources' (Purcell, 2001, p.64). For example, Mabey, Salaman and Storey (1998) look at the subject from four perspectives:

1 The social and economic context of SHRM – including the internal (corporate) and external environments that influence the development and implementation of HR strategies.
2 The relationship between SHRM and business performance, emphasizing the measurement of performance.
3 Management style and the development of new forms of organization.
4 The relationship between SHRM and the development of organizational capability, including knowledge management.

Other authors have attempted to provide more analytical frameworks for SHRM. Delery and Doty (1996), for example, make distinctions between three different theoretical frameworks:

1 *Universalistic*: where some HR practices are believed to be universally effective.
2 *Contingent*: the effectiveness of HR practices are supposed to be dependent on an organization's strategy.
3 *Configurational*: where there are believed to be synergistic effects between HR practices and strategy crucial for enhanced performance.

Wright and Snell's (1998) model of SHRM aims to achieve both fit and flexibility. They emphasize a distinction between HRM practices, skills and behaviour in their relation to strategy on the one hand, and the issue of tight and loose coupling of HR practices and strategy on the other.

Strategic HRM: theory and practice

Why do management theorists stress the importance of strategy? A number of reasons are apparent:

- Strategic literature largely emphasizes the internal resources of a business as the source of competitive advantage. This 'resource-based' perspective (Boxall, 1996) views a firm as a bundle of resources. Such resources must possess four qualities for advantage to be maintained:
  - *Value*. They must add value to the organization's activities.
  - *Rarity*. They must be rare and (preferably) unique.
  - *Inimitability*. Competitors should have difficulty in copying them.
  - *Non-substitutability*. They cannot be replaced by technology.

Although the resource-based view originally came from economics, commentators such as Boxall have argued that it is particularly applicable in the case of human resources. The resources embodied in an organization's people are found in the form of skills, expertise and experience (Storey, 1995, p.4). Knowledge management (discussed in Chapter 3) can be viewed as a development of the resource-based view of the firm but focused on one particular aspect – tacit knowledge.

- HRM models focus strongly on strategy. Certainly, this is the case. However, models of human resource management largely derive from American business schools. The prevailing philosophy in these schools has been analytic, and strategic. This line of reasoning offers an explanation but not a justification. In fact, it is circular because if one asks why they devised strategic models for HRM, the answer might simply be that 'they would, wouldn't they'.

- Strategy is intellectual and, therefore, interesting – to management theorists. It is analytical and can be conceptualized in terms of models, abstractions and even numbers. In other words, it deals with a business subject within an orthodox academic framework. This contrasts with forms of operational management that deal with 'boring admin'. Day-to-day management tends to be commonsensical, uses ragbags of techniques that – from experience – have been found to work, and deals with messy problems. It is unteachable and difficult to intellectualize. Students without business experience find discussion of real-life people management hard to relate to. It does not have the tidiness and coherence of a proper subject with 'right' answers. Far easier to regard it with contempt!

- Degree courses major on strategy. Since the advent of the Harvard MBA, there has been a steady trend towards a final year focus on 'business policy' for undergraduate business studies degrees. The underlying rationale is the provision of an integrative subject that prepares students for high-level business jobs. It is taught by looking backwards – retrospective examination of case studies that are prepared within recognized frameworks. Essentially, it is a case of 'where did they go wrong' and, occasionally, right. Intriguingly, however, employers consistently ask for practical business skills such as presentation and teamwork – not strategic thinking. Essentially, strategy is for senior managers. In a time of mass higher education few students will ever become senior managers, and those who do will not achieve such jobs for at least a decade.

- Strategy is important. It deals with high-level decisions, concerning itself with the 'big agenda'.

Strategy and planning

Planning and strategy have a long history (Mintzberg, 1994, p.6). Writing in 1916, Henri Fayol (1916/1949) described having ten-yearly forecasts, revised every five years. Fayol supported the maxim that 'managing means looking ahead', regarding foresight as an essential part of management. Strategic thinking can occur at a number of levels. We have seen already that governments and multinational organizations can shape the future of whole economies and engage in strategic human resource planning at a macro level.

Mintzberg observes that, ironically, planning achieved its greatest importance in two of the most divergent societies on earth: the command economies of the communist world and in corporate America. However, many observers have argued that the Japanese economy is the best illustration of integrated government and corporate strategic planning (Whitehill, 1991, p.256). Japan has targeted and supported successful industries but that success has not just been a matter of good fortune. 'Winners' have been created by means of strategic thinking and careful planning at a joint national and organizational level.

If strategy is deemed so important by theorists, how much impact has strategic thinking had on practitioners? First, the emphasis given to strategy by HRM theorists has led to significant interest from senior managers. For example, there is a stress on the importance of maximizing the performance and potential of an organization's people. This does not come necessarily from an altruistic and soft-hearted interest in their welfare. More likely, it derives from a hard-headed appreciation of the long-term contribution they can provide to the business. 'Soft' HRM focuses on an organization's people as assets so that time spent on training and development is an investment in human capital (see Part two). But the organization's strategy for HRM may not see the HR function as a core part of the business, resulting in an outsourcing contract.

Hence strategic HRM can fit the interests of senior executives and there is evidence, for example from Australia (Sheehan, Holland and Cieri, 2006), of increasing involvement of senior human resource managers in strategic decisionmaking and implementation. But what of lower-level managers? There are two major difficulties for HR practitioners brought up in the personnel tradition. First, as we have noted, knowledge of wider business functions has not been a strength of the personnel profession. There is a gulf in personality between those attracted to strategy and the people actually dealing with human resources at company level. Differing interests and outlooks on life can lead to a serious failure of communication.

HRM in reality BT and Accenture sign 10-year HR outsourcing contract

BT and Accenture have signed a 10-year, £306 million (US$575 million) business process outsourcing (BPO) and transformation contract for human resource administration services. The contract significantly expands the geographic reach of services that Accenture has been providing to BT under a previous five-year contract.

According to the joint media release, the new contract is one of the largest renewals of an HR BPO contract in the world. It is designed to provide BT with higher levels of workforce management and performance services in 38 countries around the globe, along with further cost savings in addition to those already realized under the current contract. The services will continue to be delivered through Accenture HR Services, an Accenture business that provides people management services on an outsourced basis, via its global delivery network.

Accenture currently provides HR services to BT's 87 000 employees and 180 000 pensioners in the United Kingdom. Under the new contract, Accenture will provide services to those BT employees and pensioners plus another 10 000 BT employees in 37 countries around the world who were not covered in the previous contract.

Services to be provided under the new contract include:

- customer contact/call centre
- recruitment
- pension administration
- payroll and benefits administration
- performance management administration
- health and safety
- HR advisory and information services.

The new contract took effect on 1 August, 2005, preceded by a jointly developed transition programme to define the service delivery framework and develop new ways of working to ensure a consistent and standardized service for BT employees throughout the world.

Alex Wilson, BT group human resource director, said: 'Accenture HR Services has a proven track record of consistently high quality service and a true partnership approach. These were key factors in its selection, along with its unmatched ability to deliver HR services on a global basis. This agreement will allow our staff to concentrate even more on the strategic role of HR management to our growing global business.'

David Clinton, president of Accenture HR Services, said: 'BT's bold decision in August 2000 to undertake large-scale HR outsourcing has been validated with this new agreement. This is a tremendous vote of confidence in the industry, in the business value of outsourcing, and in Accenture's ability to deliver a consistent level of global support to multinational clients aiming to achieve high performance in their businesses.'

What consequences will the move to outsourcing have on existing staff?

Source: *HRM Guide UK* (http://www.hrmguide.co.uk), 2 February, 2005.

On the one hand, business school strategists have tended to minimize human resource considerations because of the ambiguity and uncertainty attached to human behaviour. Humans are the most unpredictable of strategic resources. Michael Porter, the doyen of strategic management, virtually discounted the HR aspects of strategy. On the other hand, personnel departments generally employed practitioners who viewed themselves as pragmatists dealing with practical issues such as recruitment, pay and discipline 'on the ground', remote from the grand theories of strategists (Beardwell and Holden, 1994, p.7).

The second difficulty comes from their historic role of independent arbitrators between staff and management. As conciliators and apologists personnel managers depended on the ability to find compromises and reconcile the two sides rather than developing a clear agenda of their own. As a result, they make uncomfortable stakeholders, unable to fight their corner. Instead they are forced to react to the decisions of more powerful stakeholders. In practice then (Giles and Williams, 1991, p.31):

> . . . personnel specialists find strategy difficult. Personnel specialists have not developed the strategic skills needed to contribute to their organization's effectiveness. Current education and training programmes give them little insight into how to link business, technical and human resource management skills in times of great uncertainty. Personnel specialists do not speak the language of top management in marketing and manufacturing and often seem to clam up when confronted with all the noughts on a company balance sheet.

Herein lies the source of difficulty between the planning mentality and human resource management. Good people managers, through intuition or experience, are profoundly aware of their lack of control over people. In a high proportion of situations, the most carefully constructed and devious tactics will fail to get people to behave in a desired way. Experienced managers will regard this as normal and inescapable. People are not puppets and it is not surprising that they do not behave as such. Coming to terms with this is very much a matter of personality. Managers with a high tolerance of ambiguity, able to operate in fluid, uncertain situations, gravitate towards jobs with a considerable people element.

In contrast, human quirkiness and unpredictability do not fit the planning mindset that demands ordered, rational and entirely predictable behaviour. Communication between dedicated planners and people managers can be a painful business. To the HR manager a plan can seem to be a statement of intentions, an attempt to forecast an ideal world – but not to be stuck to rigidly. If circumstances change, surely the plan can be bent to accommodate this? To the planner, human resource thinking seems woolly and vague. HR managers do not convey a feeling of confidence: they are far too tolerant of deviant behaviour and seem incapable of *making* employees toe the line. They are incorrigible 'firefighters' and hence likely to be perceived as unsuitable for senior, strategic roles. Not surprisingly, HR managers with a background or experience in other business functions are more likely to be accepted as authoritative by strategists.

Michael Porter and business strategy

Michael E. Porter is the world's most influential business thinker, according to an Accenture study conducted in 2002. His book, *Competitive Strategy: Techniques for Analyzing Industries and Competitors* (1980) has been required reading on numerous business strategy courses ever since it was published over two decades ago. His notion of strategy has been debated and criticized in academic circles but Porter's ideas have often been adopted uncritically (and, perhaps, misunderstood) by business leaders throughout the world (Hammond, 2001).

According to Harfield (1998):

> The question, 'what is strategic management?' often leads to the work of Porter. Strategic management texts inevitably contain his models, theories and frameworks which imply that they are 'fundamental' to the field. An historical journey through six prominent

management/organization journals, *Strategic Management Journal*, *Academy of Management Journal*, *Academy of Management Review*, *Journal of Management Studies*, *Organization Studies*, *Advances in Strategic Management*, shows that Michael E. Porter was not a constant contributor, in fact he is almost absent from the journals, but his work is often the study of empirical testing or theoretical debate.

In fact, Harfield argues that 'strategic management' is a myth with Michael E. Porter as its principal myth-maker.

Porter spent most of the 1990s concentrating on the competitive advantage of nations. Recently he has returned to look at corporate strategy and comments, according to Hammond (2001, p.150):

It's been a bad decade for strategy. Companies have bought into an extraordinary number of flawed or simplistic ideas about competition – what I call 'intellectual potholes'. As a result, many have abandoned strategy almost completely. Executives won't say that, of course. They say, 'We have a strategy'. But typically, their 'strategy' is to produce the highest-quality products at the lowest cost or to consolidate their industry. They're just trying to improve on best practices. That's not a strategy.

He argues that this course has been adopted for three main reasons:

1 That people simply found strategy too difficult in the 1970s and 1980s – they had problems with it and it seemed artificial.

2 They were distracted by the pre-eminence of Japanese production techniques. This seemed to be about implementation rather than strategy: produce higher quality products at lower prices than your rivals and keep refining the process of production continuously.

3 More recently it was believed by many that change was happening too quickly for strategies to be of any value. Strategy was seen as rigid and inflexible in a world of speed and dynamic reinvention.

Porter argues that strategy and operational effectiveness need to be distinguished from each other. According to Hammond (2001, p.150):

There's a fundamental distinction between strategy and operational effectiveness. Strategy is about making choices, trade-offs; it's about deliberately choosing to be different. Operational effectiveness is about things that you really shouldn't have to make choices on; it's about what's good for everybody and about what every business should be doing.

He contends that business leaders have concentrated too much on operational effectiveness rather than strategy. He points to the popular managerial enthusiasms of the late 20th century – total quality, just-in-time, business process re-engineering – as examples of this. In his view, they were driven by the incredible competitiveness of the Japanese up to the 1990s when some companies 'turned the nitty-gritty into an art form'.

Source: Bestbooks.biz (2003)

Forming HR strategies

Identifying the relationship between HRM and strategy, it seems, is simpler in theory than it is in practice. Frequently, strategic HRM is a matter of rhetoric. Organizations can usefully be grouped into five alternative categories on the basis of their approach towards human resource strategy (Torrington and Hall, 1995, p.47):

1 Businesses in which there is no consideration whatsoever of human resource issues in the preparation of organizational strategy. Typical of firms 20 years ago and still found in many small companies.

2 Organizations in which there is a growing understanding of the role of human resources in implementing corporate strategy. Human resource strategy cascades on from organizational strategy, very much along the lines of the Michigan model described in Chapter 1. The purpose of HR strategy is to match the requirements of organizational strategy, ensuring the closest possible fit in terms of employee numbers, skills and so on.

3 Businesses in which the relationship becomes two-way with some ideas initiated by HR managers. There is an element of debate about the people management consequences of particular strategies before they are implemented.

4 Organizations in which the HRM concept has been accepted and people are seen as the key to competitive advantage. Corporate and human resource strategies are developed simultaneously. They are coherent and comprehensive.

5 Companies where human resources become the driving force in the development of strategy. There is an overriding emphasis on developing their skills and capitalizing on their competences.

In practice, organizations may adopt any of these approaches although, at present, the first and last are rarely encountered in large businesses.

Strategies can encompass many issues. Whether or not a business gives prominence to its human resource strategies, when the organization takes decisions on its intended market and product or service range, it also determines the types of job and skills required (Purcell, 1995, p.63). Where organizations are genuinely concerned with their people, HRM normally focuses on certain strategic sub-goals, or second-order strategies in Purcell's terminology, as shown in Table 11.1. For example:

- Resourcing an organization with the most suitable people at the right time, in the right place. We will consider this issue in depth later in the book but for the moment we will note that, from a strategic viewpoint, there are two important elements:
(a) knowledge of and participation in the formulation of 'official' strategy; and
(b) awareness of underlying developments that will produce 'surprises' that lead to about-turns in the official policy, typically with little or no notice.

- Planning the redeployment or dismissal of staff who are no longer required for specific tasks. The emphasis varies between free market and social market companies with the former taking a hard-HRM line and the latter being committed to a softer approach.

- Determining the cultural characteristics appropriate to an organization's business objectives. Implementation requires us to plan the socialization, performance assessment, development and change programmes needed to realize that culture.

	Level	Organizational focus	Environmental constraints
Table 11.1 Levels of strategy affecting HRM **Source** Adapted from Purcell (1989)	First-order strategies	Long-term objectives Range of activities, markets, locations	Supranational authorities Government Culture and tradition
	Second-order strategies	Internal operating procedures, organizational structure	Capital market Product market Consumers
	Third-order strategies	Strategic choice in HRM	Job market Workforce Law
	Outcomes	Style, structure, conduct of HRM	

- Developing key skills for new products or equipment. This includes consideration of external and internal resourcing, training programmes, formal education, and job rotation.

Examining HR strategy within our 10-Cs checklist of HRM we can see in Table 11.2 how each element, or combination of elements, can be made the focus of strategy. Guest (1987), for instance, identifies a circular relationship between a number of strategic goals:

- As we have seen, HRM aims for a high level of commitment from employees, so that they identify with the organization's goals and contribute actively to its improvement and success.

- In turn, this enables the organization to obtain a high-quality output from workers who want to continually improve standards.

- Within this environment, there is an expectation of flexibility from workers: a willingness to depart from fixed job definitions, working practices and conditions.

- Strategic integration – all these strands link the organization's strategy. They are directed towards agreed objectives and interact with each other in a cohesive way.

Principle	Definition	Action
1 *Control*	Effective organizations require a control system for cohesion and direction	Clear, unambiguous mission statement supported by strategies and organization able to meet objectives
2 *Contiguity*	Human resource management should be closely matched to business objectives	HR strategies developed at board level and integrated with all other strategies
3 *Coherence*	Allocation and activities of human resources integrated into a meaningful whole	People management must be organized, rather than left to *ad hoc* decisions at local level
4 *Communication*	Strategies understood and accepted by all employees. Open culture with no barriers	Clear, simple and justified strategies: cascading process of communication with feedback to the top
5 *Credibility*	Staff trust top management and believe in their strategies	Top managers are sincere, honest and consistent
6 *Commitment*	Employees motivated to achieve organizational goals	Top managers show the same commitment to staff
7 *Competence*	Organization competent to achieve its objectives – dependent on individual competences	Resourcing strategies, selection techniques and human resource development systems in place
8 *Compensation*	Competitive, fair reward and promotion systems.	Top managers pay themselves on equivalent basis to staff
9 *Creativity*	Competitive advantage comes from unique strategies	System for encouraging and tapping employee ideas
10 *Change*	Continuous improvement and development essential for survival	Flexible people and working systems; culture of innovation; skills training

Table 11.2

Checklist for strategic HRM

> ### Key concept 11.3 Mission statement
>
> A mission statement should convey the essence of what an organization is about: why it exists, what kind of business it intends to be, and who its intended customers are. The mission is translated into objectives or goals within the strategic management process.

Business goals

Organizations are formed to achieve certain **goals**. Strategic thinking focuses on these long-term objectives. Thompson and Strickland (1998) provide a framework for strategic management based on five major activities that incorporate objective-setting:

- Deciding the type of business in which the business will operate, developing a strategic vision and producing a set of values together with a general strategy.
- Identifying the strategic issues for the business and setting strategic objectives.
- Developing strategic action plans.
- Creating and implementing strategic action plans for units within the business.
- Evaluating, revising and refocusing strategy for the future.

Human resource strategies are derived from overall business objectives in the same way as investment or marketing strategies. We noted also in Chapter 10 that commitment is seen to be particularly crucial for competitive advantage. For true commitment to occur, conventional management wisdom sees the need for employees to accept and believe in an organization's goals.

A **mission statement** communicates these goals to everyone in a company (Key concept 11.3). Mission statements have a particular significance in large companies where communication can be difficult and, as we have seen, departments and 'political' groups frequently focus on their own sectional interests. A small business may not need such a statement since its employees and owners have a clear understanding of its reasons for existence. Mission statements can be wide-ranging. For example, the Ford Motor Company states:

Our vision. Our vision is to become the world's leading consumer company for automotive products and services.

Our mission. We are a global family with a proud heritage, passionately committed to providing personal mobility for people around the world. We anticipate consumer needs and deliver outstanding products and services that improve people's lives.

Our values. The customer is Job 1. We do the right thing for our customers, our people, our environment and our society. By improving everything we do, we provide superior returns to our shareholders.

What prevents such a statement from being no more than a set of banal platitudes? It can be tied to some form of performance measure, perhaps in the form of detailed objectives. The mission statement is locked into the company's first-order strategies (see Table 11.2). These are major decisions on its long-term aims and the scope of its activities (Purcell, 1995, p.67). As we can see in the 'HRM in reality' article, outsourcing has been claimed to achieve major cost savings but the truth is more complex. Elliott (2006) views outsourcing as the latest in a series of cost-cutting approaches after downsizing and de-layering. He notes:

> In most cases the objective of outsourcing is a targeted 20 per cent cost reduction, with actual savings coming from direct labour and variable costs.
>
> Fully loaded (direct and fringe) unskilled labour costs in Vietnam, Thailand and some parts of India can run as low as $1.50 to $3 an hour against a US average that ranges between $23 and $25 an hour. While wages in some parts of China are still between $3 and $7 an hour, they are growing quickly and are already directing new sourcing decisions beyond China's borders to other lower cost countries, such as Vietnam.

The human resource implications on existing employees are evident in terms of job loss, industrial relations and, for remaining staff, their job security, career expectations and human resource development.

It has to be conceded that many businesses have a mission statement simply because it is the done thing to have one. Often they serve no clear purpose. As Whitehill (1991, p.123) points out, this has not been the case in large Japanese firms:

> A statement of mission, or overall philosophy, is particularly significant within the Japanese management system. It is this broad policy declaration which establishes the corporate culture within which regular employees will spend their working lives. Becoming 'socialized' within the

---

HRM in reality Outsourcing saves 15 per cent

Claims of 60 per cent savings through outsourcing are massively exaggerated according to a study by TPI, a leading sourcing advisory firm.

TPI's study examined outsourcing contracts awarded between 2003 and 2005 and found that savings net of severance pay, professional fees and governance costs averaged 15 per cent. The savings ranged between 39 per cent at the top end and 10 per cent at the bottom. 15 per cent was also the average level of savings anticipated when contracts were first let.

According to Duncan Aitchison, Managing Director of TPI:

> Opinions vary widely about the cost savings to be gained from outsourcing. This research proves that the promise of massive operational savings is unrealistic when you take into account the costs of procurement and ongoing contract management. In our experience, outsourcing arrangements which focus solely on delivering huge savings often fail to meet client expectations. 15 per cent is not only a realistic saving, but also a significant one.

Cost is the main driver

Cost reduction is still the primary motivation for current outsourcing contracts but the number of businesses outsourcing primarily in order to improve quality, has risen from 11 per cent in 2004 to 21 per cent in the recent study.

Duncan Aitchison said:

> Although clients continue to view outsourcing as a means of achieving cost savings, they are also increasingly concerned with improving the quality of their services. We are seeing an ever-growing number of clients using outsourcing as a way of introducing innovation into their business and the number of TPI-led deals with a 'transformational element' has never been higher.

Strongest first quarter ever

The first quarter of 2006 saw the largest ever number of outsourcing contracts for a first quarter with 83 signed contracts at a value of over €18 billion. This compares with 76 deals valued at just over €13 billion at the same point in 2005.

Duncan Aitchison added:

> This strong quarter is due in part to the rise in the number of contracts being restructured. However, even when we exclude restructurings, the number of contracts signed so far this year is still a first quarter record.

IBM (€3.7 billion), EDS (€3.6 billion) and T-Systems (€1.1 billion) were the chief beneficiaries of these contracts. TPI is currently advising on deals being competed for by EDS (€6.4 billion), IBM (€6 billion) and CSC (€4 billion).

A third (19) of the total value of contracts signed so far this year were restructuring contracts totalling €6 billion. This compares with a historical average of 15 per cent. A further 141 contracts totalling almost €33 billion appear to be due for restructuring later in 2006. TPI research shows that two-thirds (66 per cent) of restructurings were due to the first generation of contracts coming to the end of their term, rather than any complaint with the providers. In fact, most (86 per cent) incumbent providers were retained when contracts were restructured.

According to Duncan Aitchison:

> Although historically, most outsourcing restructurings have been renegotiated with the incumbent service provider, it can no longer be taken as read that the existing provider will retain all or even part of the original deal through a restructuring. Client retention will increasingly depend on an incumbent's ability to offer a competitive proposition for every facet of the service and this will often require significant changes in price, contractual terms, scope and delivery approach from the original agreement.

What are the human resource implications in terms of job loss, industrial relations and, for remaining staff, job security, career expectations and human resource development?

Source: *HRM Guide UK* (http://www.hrmguide.co.uk/), 15 April, 2006.

corporate culture, and internalizing the company spirit (*shafu*), are important foundations for building the Japanese employee's remarkable loyalty and dedication to the company.

Hence the mission statement plays a crucial role in developing the uniquely Japanese forms of organizational culture and commitment discussed in Part three.

Strategy formation

Strategic management takes into account all the complexities of the business environment, the pressures that prevail upon an organization, and the resources available to it. Despite a concentration on objective planning, it remains essentially an art rather than a science and draws on a range of theories, models and practical techniques. There is no single approach that guarantees formulation of a successful strategy. Business strategy draws heavily on management theory and is sometimes criticized for employing 'psycho-babble' or 'management speak'. Good strategies should be simple to understand. Sensible plans and changes can be obscured and discredited by excessive use of terminology which conveys little meaning to employees who do not have management literature as their favourite bedtime reading.

Several distinctive approaches to strategic management have arisen. Ansoff (1968) provided some classic principles:

1 Strategy formation should be a controlled, conscious process of thought. In other words it should not be the result of intuition or accident – it should be as 'deliberate as possible'.

2 Responsibility for the process must rest with the chief executive officer. This fits the 'leader is all' mentality that sees the top person as being the major influence on the organization.

3 The model of strategy formation must be kept simple and informal.

4 Strategies should be unique. The best result from a process of creative design. They should build on the particular 'core competencies' of the organization.

5 Strategies must come out of the design process fully developed.

6 Strategies should be made explicit and, therefore, have to be kept simple.

7 Finally, once these unique, full-blown, explicit and simple strategies are fully formulated, they must then be implemented.

More or less at the same time as this approach was developed a significant variant emerged from Harvard. It emphasized strategic planning as a process and played down the role of the chief executive. Its basic premises were that (Mintzberg, 1994, p.42):

1 Strategy formation should be controlled and conscious as well as a formalized and elaborated process, decomposed into distinct steps, each delineated by checklists and supported by techniques.

2 Responsibility for the overall process rests with the chief executive in principle; responsibility for its execution rests with the staff planners in practice.

3 Strategies come out of this process fully developed, typically as generic positions, to be explicated so that they can then be implemented through detailed attention to objectives, budgets, programmes and operating plans of various kinds.

Both models view strategy as encompassing all aspects of a business, including its people. Thus strategic thinkers envisaged a major role for human resource planning before HRM was conceived as a separate philosophy of people management. For example, Steiner (1969, p.34) wrote:

> The model that may be covered in strategic planning includes every type of activity of concern to an enterprise. Among the areas are profits, capital expenditures, organization, pricing, labour relations, production, marketing, finance, personnel, public relations, advertising, technological capabilities, product improvement, research and development, legal matters, management selection and training, political activities and so on.

Steiner presented strategic planning as an orderly sequence of steps:

1 Objectives-setting develops and quantifies the organization's purposes and goals. This takes a variety of forms, the most sophisticated of which is the Delphi technique. Integral to this step is a determination of the enterprise's fundamental values.

2 External audit for gaining information about the firm's position in the environment. Intricate techniques have been developed to provide exhaustive measures of virtually every external factor that has ever been thought of. Similarly, elaborate forecasting techniques can be employed including scenario building, exploring alternative views of the enterprise's future.

3 A similar internal audit examines the internal, organizational and functional factors that produce the 'competence profile' of the firm.

4 Strategy evaluation taking the above into account within a framework such as SWOT, outlining strengths, weaknesses, opportunities and threats and comparing the consequences of a variety of strategic options.

5 The strategy operationalization phase that produces a hierarchy of objectives and actions, cascaded down throughout the organization.

The orthodox view of strategy is that it is a deliberate, conscious process coming from the top of the organization (Ansoff, 1968). Figure 11.1 outlines a sequence of activities from this perspective.

However, this model cannot explain organizational strategies and the means of evaluating their relative usefulness. A business can choose between recruiting and training its own direct sales people or subcontracting the function to outside agents. It has to be recognized that all options may not be apparent and that trial and error may be the only practical method of evaluation. Other factors such as competition, organizational politics or the absence of resources may limit the choice. As we saw earlier, in order to reduce costs and improve quality Ford outlined plans in 2002 to reduce its workforce worldwide, partly by outsourcing component manufacture to subcontractors located alongside its car assembly plants.

Moreover, this model cannot explain the strategic process entirely. As the future is not perfectly predictable, a feedback mechanism must be built into the process to correct for

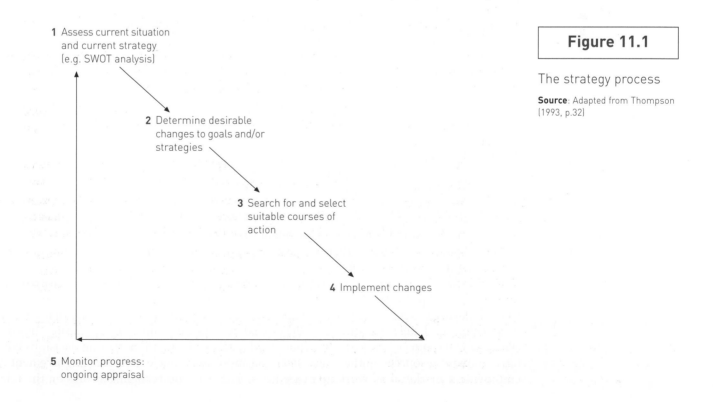

Figure 11.1

The strategy process

Source: Adapted from Thompson (1993, p.32)

unexpected developments. An alternative approach is that of Johnson and Scholes (1984), which divides the process into three components:

Strategic analysis. A successful organization is one that understands its market and is sensitive to changes in the business environment. It must be able to analyze its current position, the strengths and weaknesses of its current resources – for example, the skill and flexibility of its human resources – and assess the opportunities and threats present (and likely) to its continuing success.

Strategic choice. Determining all the courses of action open to the organization, and the means of evaluating their relative usefulness.

Strategic implementation. Senior managers may believe that by determining strategy they have decided the future of the organization. In fact, as we have seen in previous chapters, the structure and culture of the organization and the commitment of lower-level managers can influence or hinder the implementation of strategy. This is particularly evident in decentralized and loosely controlled organizations that require higher levels of consultation and communication to ensure cooperation. Later in this chapter we will consider these issues in relation to organizational change.

Coherent strategies and integrated practices sound fine in theory but how are they to be translated into action? This 'surface neatness' hides an organizational reality that is far from simple (Blyton and Turnbull, 1992, p.2). Mintzberg (1994, p.26) argues that the strategies that are actually carried through into practice include an unintended element which he terms 'emergent strategies'. This might result from poor strategic thinking, poor implementation or a sound state of realism. It reflects the view that strategic management should not be confined to the top layers in an organization. Emergent strategy rarely comes from the centre but rather from bright ideas and initiatives at a local level, which were not predicted but were found to work and then adopted more widely: '. . . big strategies can grow from little ideas (initiatives), and in strange places, not to mention at unexpected times, almost anyone in the organization can prove to be a strategist. All he or she needs is a good idea and the freedom and resources required to pursue it' (Mintzberg, 1994, p.26).

Orthodox strategic thinking tends to underestimate the limitations of people – their 'bounded rationality' (Simon, 1960). It supposes also that responsibility for strategy lies firmly in the hands of senior managers, whereas empirical evidence shows that strategy often 'emerges' as a consequence of low-level decisions (Mintzberg and Waters, 1985). In practice, we can distinguish between intended strategy and realized strategy. Intended strategy is planned or 'linear' strategy (see Table 11.3). Realized strategy is that which actually takes place. It consists of elements of intended strategy, found to be practical, together with 'emergent' strategy – that which was not intended. The latter results from poor strategic thinking, poor implementation, or simply being realistic. Chaffee's classification (Table 11.3) describes this as adaptive.

Chaffee (1985) considers the academic division of strategy into three distinct but sometimes conflicting models: linear strategy, adaptive strategy, and interpretive strategy. The linear model has been used by most researchers and focuses on planning and forecasting. The adaptive model is most closely associated with 'strategic management'. It 'tends to focus the manager's attention on means' and is largely concerned with 'fit'. The third, interpretative model, is a minority view that sees strategy as a metaphor and, therefore, not something that can be measured but viewed in qualitative terms. Mintzberg, Ahlstrand and Lampel (1998) distinguish no fewer than ten distinct 'schools' of strategic thought that have developed since the 1960s (see Table 11.4).

Further complications arise from the way firms are structured. In Chapter 7 we noted that divisional organizations have decisionmaking capabilities at a number of levels. It is possible to distinguish between corporate strategies (global, company-wide initiatives) that come from head office and business strategies developed by business units or operating subsidiaries (Purcell, 1995, p.67). The latter are concerned with product and marketing decisions but also have human resource implications since business units have a closer involvement with employment markets and working procedures. There are no recognized rules on the relation between corporate and business strategies, but it has been argued that strategic HRM should be focused at the business unit level. Nevertheless, business units cannot operate in isolation from the rest of the firm. Overriding issues such as succession planning and media comment on industrial relations demand corporate people strategies.

Management theory normally stresses order and control. Recently, however, chaos theory has been applied to business. In contrast to strategic thinking, which attempts to plan and predict, chaos theory states that much of the future is unknowable. Planning assumes straightforward relationships with a few measurable variables. In fact, most business problems – particularly those involving people – are highly complex. Often it is impossible to connect events to any individual actions which have been taken deliberately.

Peters (1987, p.510) argues that organizations become too safe and predictable. Managers should destabilize their business structures so that new, competitive relationships and

Strategy	Interpretation
Linear strategy	A planning process which determines basic long-term goals for an organization and then uses strategic decisionmaking to determine appropriate courses of action and allocate resources to achieve those goals.
Adaptive strategy	Matching process, continuously aligning an organization to a changing environment. Incremental or iterative, attaching more importance to the means by which this alignment can take place. This model views the involvement of operational managers as being important in the strategic process.
Interpretive strategy	A more thoughtful development of the adaptive model, it bears some resemblance to the approach advocated by Peters. Managers are expected to have a 'cognitive map' of the environment and its interactions with the organization and its resources. An understanding of these relationships allows the strategist to anticipate developments and plan accordingly. This model emphasizes the culture of the organization and the motivation and values of its members.

Table 11.3

Interpretations of strategy

Source: Based on Chaffee (1985).

Title	Concept
1 The Design School	Strategy as a process of conception
2 The Planning School	Strategy as a formal process
3 The Positioning School	Strategy as an analytical process
4 The Entrepreneurial School	Strategy as a visionary process
5 The Cognitive School	Strategy as a mental process
6 The Learning School	Strategy as an emergent process
7 The Power School	Strategy as a process of negotiation
8 The Cultural School	Strategy as a collective process
9 The Environmental School	Strategy as a reactive process
10 The Configuration School	Strategy as a process of transformation

Table 11.4

Ten 'schools' of strategy research developed since the 1960s

Source: Adapted from Mintzberg, Ahlstrand and Lampel (1998).

activities can emerge. He considers that strategic planning is 'irrelevant, or worse, damaging'. In his view, formal plans should be replaced by adding value to human capital. There are no good strategic plans but there is a good process which:

- gains commitment by getting everyone involved – it is not left to professional planners
- is open to radical ideas
- encourages creativity by asking new questions
- is considered and debated.

For Peters (1987, p.511), the plan should be short, have an emphasis on strategic skills, and should not be regarded as an icon. Its value lies in the thinking process, not in slavish implementation:

> The plan, whose development involves everyone, should be shared with everyone after completion. At that point, there is a serious case to be made for destroying it – if not in practice, at least in spirit. Its value is as an assemblage of thoughts, not constraints. The process of developing it is close to 100 per cent of its value – or perhaps more than 100 per cent of its value. Slavishly following the plan despite changing conditions (now the norm), because of the time and political capital spent in assembling it, is counterproductive.

This form of strategic planning is a 'bottom-up' rather than the traditional centralized, 'top-down' process. It is focused on front-line employees, their skills, creativity and commitment – although senior managers are involved in the debate. Its function is in attuning employees to be able to react quickly to opportunities – 'environmental scanning'. Peters' conception is similar to Chaffee's interpretive strategy (described in Table 11.3).

Mintzberg (1994, p.268) agrees with Peters that strategic planning should not be left to full-time planners on the grounds that they are likely to be out of touch with the front line. Strategic planning posts are often resourced with young graduates, MBAs and finance experts in the belief that planning is an abstract and theoretical exercise. It is scarcely surprising if plans emerging from such a department turn out to be unrealistic and impractical. More intriguingly, Mintzberg also draws attention to the 'tacit' knowledge that line managers use to make judgements. This non-verbalized and often subconscious knowledge is the stuff of the informal organization, being political and based on unofficial opinions and personal relationships. It is not passed on to planners but is crucial to the operation of the company.

Other aspects of strategy involve people making decisions about capital equipment, finance or marketing; HR strategy requires people to make decisions about themselves. It is, according to Stacey (1993, p.2):

> important . . . to think of strategy as a game that people play, because when it is discussed more seriously there is a strong tendency to slip into talking about it as a response that 'the organization' makes to an 'environment'. . . . The inevitable result is a lack of insight into the real complexities of strategic management because in reality organizations and their environments are not things, one adapting to the other, but groupings of people interacting one with another.

However, it is a deadly serious game with people's careers and livelihoods at stake (Stacey, 1993, p.9). The reality is that faced with a choice between profit and the wellbeing of employees, most commercial organizations will select the former. 'Softer' human resource issues continue to be secondary and subordinate to financial matters. Regardless of well-meaning statements to the contrary, within the free market capitalist model there is an emphasis on short-term improvement in financial performance. In Western organizations, financially knowledgeable managers have taken the lead as the 'bottom line' of profit or loss drives business. Strategic actions derived from technological or financial considerations can have direct and relatively immediate effect on an organization's people. Human resource initiatives are accommodated within a broad financial picture in which benefits or changes to people management compete with other resources. In reality, long-term HRM goals such as training and developing skills for the future are rarely considered. If employee commitment, flexibility and product quality are valued, they are sought for profit and not pursued as beneficial for workers.

Strategy, thinking and decisionmaking

According to Haslam and Baron (1994, p.33):

> Decisionmaking is the thinking, or lack of thinking, that determines what to do when we are faced with more than one option about what to do and when we have time to think. In general, thinking consists of some sort of search process plus some inference that we draw from what the search has found. In decisionmaking, the search is for alternative options, evidence bearing on the advantages and disadvantages of each option, and goals, which are criteria by which we evaluate the options in the light of the evidence. Decisions are typically made according to rules or habits, without much thinking. But the creation of these rules and habits results from earlier decisions, and thinking can come into play at several points in the formation of these rules and habits.

In recent years, a new approach to strategic management has developed based on cognitive science – the study of thinking and decisionmaking (Hodgkinson and Sparrow, 2002). This approach takes issue with the rationalist view of strategy presented by Michael Porter and others. Cognitive science can trace its origins to Craik's 1940s concept of the 'mental model'. This is an elegantly simple concept. Craik argued that through life the brain builds and maintains an internal, simplified model of the world on which it conducts mental operations before we take any action. He states, 'thought models, or parallels, reality in some form of symbolism'. In modern technical terminology this is described as mental representation.

Craik postulated that this involved three processes of reasoning:

1 A 'translation' of external process into an internal representation in the form of words, numbers, or other symbols.

2 The derivation of other symbols from them by means of an inference process. Ideas are tested against the mental model so that dangerous or unsuitable options are discarded before being tried in the real world.

3 'Retranslation' back into actions.

Mental representations take a variety of forms, including imagery (visual, sounds, etc.), analogies and symbols such as words and numbers. There are contradictory theories on the structure of representations. Some writers identify a single mental model. Others consider that we have mental maps, schemata (mini-models) or 'scripts' for familiar activities. Whatever rationale is employed, this approach indicates that strategic thinking is not the simple, rational activity portrayed in 'classical' accounts. Instead, it involves assumptions, intuition, simplification, 'rules-of-thumb' and emotion. It is just like every other kind of thinking or decisionmaking activity engaged in by human beings.

Translating strategy into action

At this point we turn to the issue of implementing human resource strategies. The classic approach follows the 'matching' process described in the Michigan model of HRM outlined in Chapter 1. The goal is a realization of the organization's strategic human resource requirements in terms of numbers and, more importantly; attitudes, behaviour and commitment. According to Miller (1989), the key lies with 'the concept of "fit": the fit of human resource management with the thrust of the organization'.

Truss (1999, p.44), reviewing a number of authors, finds that 'there is no evidence that a tight fit leads to positive outcomes and the concept of fit implies inflexibility and rigidity which could, in themselves, be detrimental to organizational outcomes.'

She also notes the underlying assumption of some 'matching models' of hard HRM which contend that every business strategy has one appropriate human resource strategy. This implies a 'simple, linear relationship between strategy and human resource strategy' that does not exist. Such models fail to acknowledge the complex relationship between strategy and HRM and they ignore issues of power politics and culture. She concludes that: 'The matching model is based on a narrow classical view of strategy formulation which assumes

Thought and logic

How rational is normal thinking? Naturally, our thinking is influenced by both cold logic and emotion. Rationality does not mean the denial of emotion. Basic rational thinking can be described in terms of a search–inference framework. Within this framework, thinking is a form of exploration or search for choice alternatives. We search for three types of information:

- Possibilities, which can be solutions to a problem or resolutions of doubt.

- Goals are your personal objectives and provide the criteria by which you judge the possibilities. Goals may be present at the beginning of your thinking or they may emerge during your search.

- Evidence is used to help make the judgement, taking the form of information or opinion.

Search makes use of observation, memory, knowledge and external aids – books, computer files, balance sheets, and so on. Together with these search processes we employ inference: using the evidence to evaluate the possibilities against our goals. Search and inference go on together – they do not have to be placed in any particular order. When we are solving a problem, the search–inference framework can be represented diagrammatically – for instance, in the form of a decision tree. Positive or negative evidence could be represented in terms of probabilities. The calculation could also be described in terms of subjective expected utility. The search–inference framework provides us with the basis for decision modelling.

This approach gives us some insight into the process of trial and error, which is the simplest form of decisionmaking. Trial and error can be active – for example, when we try to get out of a maze. Alternatively, it can be mental: working through the possibilities in our heads, using our mental models of the problem situation. This can be partly unconscious, leading to an apparently spontaneous answer popping into your head. This is called insight. It is a process similar to remembering a name some time after you tried to recall it. It also plays a role in creativity. An early group of psychologists called the Gestalt movement described it as a process of closure. Gestalt means 'form' or 'shape' in German. The Gestaltists argued that the brain constantly tries to form tidy 'wholes' out of the untidy or incomplete information it receives. The brain attempts to create rational forms or shapes and fills in any gaps in the information it has. Often this takes the form of a relationship between one thing and another.

As we develop through childhood we move away from inventing fresh solutions for every problem. More and more, we rely on stock solutions from memory and rules for thinking. There is a danger of becoming mechanical in our thinking and of ignoring novel solutions. One set of rules we acquire is that of formal logic. Logic and rationality are frequently assumed to be the same. Many prescriptive (do it like this) approaches to decisionmaking emphasize logical analysis of a problem. There is plenty of evidence that formal logic is not a natural method of thinking for humans. For example, the following is an example of a totally logical statement taken from instructions on UK National Insurance contributions:

> A Class 1 contribution is not payable for employment by any one employer for not more than 8 hours in any week – but if you normally work for more than 8 hours in any week for any employer, a Class 1 contribution is payable except for any week when you do not do more than 4 hours work for any employer.

Most people lose the thread of logic half-way through the paragraph. Logic suffers the same defects as utility. Logic can only work when the problem is relatively simple, self-contained and with complete information (evidence) on goals and possibilities. Most real-life problems do not come in such a neat package.

that formulation and implementation are separate activities and, consequently, that strategies in the HR area can simply be "matched" to business strategies at the formulation stage.'

Khilji and Wang (2006) argue that much of the apparent confusion about the effectiveness of strategic HRM results from a failure by researchers to distinguish between 'intended' and 'implemented' strategies. They contend that researchers often depend on single respondents from each organization in industry-wide surveys. Khilji and Wang questioned managers and non-managers from inside and outside HR departments to highlight the differences between the HR practices intended by their company's strategies and those that actually were implemented. They found that the two may be substantially different while consistent implementation leads to higher employee satisfaction with HRM, which is positively related to organizational performance.

Armstrong (1992, p.53) argues that the significant issue in HR strategy is that of integration with overall business strategy. In practice, this integration is difficult to achieve. Armstrong outlines some crucial difficulties:

Diversity of strategic processes, levels and styles. As we have seen, many organizations do not use neat, traditional approaches to business strategy based on rational planning. In line with the criticisms of Mintzberg and others, it may be more sensible to be open-minded and intuitive. However, from the perspective of people management it becomes difficult to discern appropriate HR strategies and the corporate strategies they are supposed to match. Further, in a diversified organization composed of strategic business units (SBUs), each unit may have its own idiosyncratic strategies. Consequently it becomes difficult to provide corporate HR strategies – such as management development – that can be reconciled with the different needs of individual SBUs.

The evolutionary nature of business strategy. It is not possible to provide a rational HR strategy if corporate strategy is evolving quickly and in a piecemeal way. In fact, the concept of 'rational' strategic planning is culture-bound: it is a product of free market economies. Other cultures naturally employ a more diffuse, emergent or evolving method of business planning (Legge, 1995, p.104).

The absence of written business strategies. This is particularly the case in smaller companies and overwhelmingly in cultural contexts where evolutionary planning is the rule. This does not help to clarify those corporate strategic issues with which HR strategy is expected to fit.

The qualitative nature of HR issues. Business plans have tended to be expressed in numerical terms, such as financial data, sales forecasts and competitive position. As we shall see later, traditional 'manpower planning' fitted this mould. Equally, human resource strategy has been identified with the 'hard' rationalist model of HRM. However, 'soft' or qualitative issues such as culture, motivation and employee relations have become increasingly important – even in free market countries.

Armstrong's solution to these problems is to emphasize the need for human resource practitioners to achieve an understanding of how business strategies are formed. They should adopt a wider point of view and an understanding of key business issues such as:

- Corporate intentions for growth or retrenchment, including strategic alliances (mergers, acquisitions, joint ventures, discussed earlier), product and market development, disposals.
- Methods of increasing competitiveness such as improvements in productivity, quality and service, reducing costs.
- A perceived need for a more positive, performance culture.
- Other cultural consequences of the organization's mission such as 'commitment, mutuality, communications, involvement, devolution and teamworking'.

Organizations vary considerably in the formality of their strategic planning, ranging from detailed 200-page documents to unwritten 'orientations'. Neat theoretical approaches with successive stages of analysis, choice and implementation are rarely seen in practice. The organizational characteristics of a firm, and the environmental constraints upon it, affect and sometimes transform the process. As Whipp (1992, p.33) explains:

> Seldom is there an easily isolated logic to strategic change. Instead that process may derive its motive force from an amalgam of economic, personal and political imperatives. . . . The application of over-rational, linear programmes of HRM as a means of securing competitive success is shown to be at odds with experience both in the UK and elsewhere.

Whipp concludes that control of the environmental, organizational and strategic aspects of both competition and human resources is so problematic that the relationship between the two can only be indirect and fragile. Another critical factor is that the human resource is but one of the resources of the firm. Strengths and weaknesses in other areas, such as marketing and finance, may obscure the best people management.

Whipp also points to the environmental context within which HR strategy is implemented. We have discussed cultural influences already. Individual companies also have their own control and industrial relations traditions. Attempts to import HRM into companies outside North America and link it to business strategy have foundered because many organizations have no tradition of strategy.

The greatest difficulties are experienced in large, diversified organizations with a wide range of interests. They are highlighted in recession when the business needs do not fit with 'soft' HR values. HR strategies may focus on redundancies and sacking employees inevitably damages or destroys a caring corporate image. Legge (1995) outlines a strategy described as 'tough love' – being cruel to be kind – in which employees are expected to be both dedicated and disposable. In fact, human resource strategy may only be unproblematic in the ideal circumstances described by Guest (1987):

1 It should take place within a purpose-built modern location, a greenfield site employing carefully selected 'green' labour. Such staff would have no previous experience of the industry in which the company operates and therefore would be untarnished by an 'undesirable' industrial sub-culture. They would not be hidebound by traditional but outmoded ways of doing things.

2 The organization requires highly professional management, preferably Japanese or American.

3 Employees should be given intrinsically rewarding work rather than uninteresting functions for which pay is the sole motivation.

4 Workers should have security of employment and not be constantly in fear of losing their jobs.

Guest acknowledges that these conditions are difficult to achieve in practice since most organizations – Japanese transplant factories excepted – have pre-existing staff, buildings and equipment that cannot be discarded. They bring with them patterns of power and behaviour that may be contrary to the HR philosophy.

More positively, human resource strategies can be aimed at improving an organization's competitiveness by increasing its 'knowledge base' or competence. This includes shedding old values and techniques in favour of new ones. It requires a collective change of the organization's shared world view – including perceptions of the company and the market. Pro-active SHRM is particularly important in highly competitive conditions where decisions about outsourcing parts of the organization, such as the HR function itself, are key elements of strategic decisionmaking.

HRM in reality HR outsourcing

Outsourcing basic human resource services can be the key to achieving a more influential and strategic role for the HR function. However, a new executive briefing from the Chartered Institute of Personnel and Development (CIPD) also concludes that:

- the decision to outsource needs to be carefully considered
- it will not be right for all, and
- considerable effort needs to be devoted to ensuring a smooth transfer of responsibilities.

Written by Professor William Scott-Jackson, Tim Newham and Melanie Gurney of the Centre for Applied HR Research, Oxford Brookes University, the report – *HR Outsourcing: the key decisions* – draws on the experiences of 17 organizations that are either outsourcing HR services or have considered the possibility and rejected it. The report is intended to offer practical guidance to HR and non-HR professionals responsible for developing and improving the delivery of HR services in their organizations.

Vanessa Robinson, organization and resourcing adviser at the CIPD, said:

People management plays a crucial role in delivering organizational performance. In today's modern, knowledge economy this is more true than ever before. The decision to outsource HR services is therefore not to be taken lightly.

However, there are many circumstances in which outsourcing HR services can deliver tangible benefits to the organization, for example freeing HR professionals to devote more time to a strategic role in supporting organizational performance.

Advantages and disadvantages of outsourcing

The report identifies a number of 'strategic drivers' for outsourcing HR services:

- *Reducing costs*: Key determinator in many outsourcing decisions, but should not be considered in isolation from other costs/benefits.
- *Increasing effectiveness of HR delivery*: Experienced outsourcing providers can often deal with HR processes more effectively. For example, recruitment may be undertaken more quickly, reducing employee turnover costs and speeding up the pace of growth.
- *Providing greater expertise*: External providers may offer greater levels of specialist knowledge or experience than affordably available in-house.
- *Moving HR up the value chain*: Outsourcing human resource administration can lead to a shift in HR focus towards policy and decisionmaking.

- *To aid organizational growth*: Fast-growing organizations can lack the HR capacity to deliver business objectives, making HR outsourcing an attractive solution.

The report warns against regarding HR outsourcing as a panacea for organizational problems. The potential pitfalls include:

- According to the report, handing over unnecessarily complex or badly understood systems to to an external provider can be like 'picking up spaghetti'. This limits potential benefits from outsourcing. If processes cannot be improved before a move, the organization may have to accept off-the-shelf replacements that are not specifically geared to their needs.
- The greatest financial benefits of outsourcing often come from using sophisticated software. If effective IT systems already exist in-house, cost savings may not be achieved from an external provider.
- Good employee management practices remain essential, and the key relationship between staff and their line managers remains in-house, leaving plenty of work on manager/staff relationships that still has to be handled despite the outsourcing relationship.
- Local knowledge and ownership of human resource processes could be lost.

Vanessa Robinson continued:

The decision to outsource HR services is a complicated one. Cost reasons alone are not sufficient to drive the decision. Decisionmakers need to ask whether there is a need to change the way the HR department operates and review existing provision. This review needs to consider cost, administrative efficiency and HR policy strategy and expertise. Where gaps are identified, organizations need to consider whether these are best solved by minor tinkering or major transformation.

It must also not be forgotten that a transition from in-house HR provision to the use of an outsourced provider is a significant change for the organization, and must be managed accordingly. If significant time is not devoted to the process of change, with unequivocal top-level support, there is a danger that staff/line manager relationships and other aspects of people management policy may be neglected.

Overall, is outsourcing the HR function likely to benefit an organization?

Source: *HRM Guide UK* (http://www.hrmguide.co.uk), 26 May, 2005.

Summary

Strategic thinking has its basis in rational thinking. In practice, strategists have accepted that there must be a place for the unexpected. Strategy and planning provide a framework for human resource requirements over a defined period but traditional personnel managers have experienced difficulty in understanding and implementing strategy. Human resource strategies tend to focus on numbers and also attitudes, behaviour and commitment in line with harder 'matching' models of HRM but their implementation is problematic. Recent thinking has accommodated the notion that HR strategy is not as simple as some rationalist accounts imply and that strategy itself has the same emotional, irrational and intuitive components as any other form of thinking or decisionmaking.

Organizational competencies are the sum product of the competencies of the workforce. This suggests that people management should drive rather than follow business strategy, by building employee competencies through selection, assessment, reward and development. In the next chapter, we elaborate further on the building of organizational competence with an examination of a fundamental aspect of people management – resourcing.

Further reading

Mintzberg, Ahlsrand and Lampel (1998), *Strategy Safari: A Guided Tour Through the Wilds of Strategic Management*, published by The Free Press provides an interesting excursion through the different types or 'schools' of strategic management. Mintzberg's *Strategy Bites Back* (Financial Times, 2004) provides a newer treatment of a range of strategic approaches. Good reviews of strategic human resource management are found in the articles by Purcell and by Schuler *et al.* in J. Storey (ed.) *Human Resource Management: A Critical Text*, 2nd edn, published by Thomson Learning (2001). *Strategic Human Resource Management: Theory and Practice* (2nd edn, Sage, 2005) edited by Graeme Salaman, John Storey and Jon Billsberry is a useful reader.

Review questions

1 What is a strategy? What is meant by first, second and third-order strategies?

2 Is HRM really 'strategic'? How does human resource strategy fit into the business planning process?

3 What is 'strategic human resource management'? Summarize the main goals of strategic human resource management and identify some of the key differences between strategic and operational HRM.

4 When is outsourcing a suitable strategy for the HR function?

5 To what extent is it possible to demonstrate that human resource strategies are vital for business success?

6 Within any organization, how are management styles and corporate culture likely to influence human resource strategy?

7 What are the ideal conditions for the implementation of a human resource strategy? What deficiencies are commonly found in strategic human resource plans?

8 Is strategic human resource management more important in some countries/industries than others?

9 What do you see as the main barriers to successful implementation of strategic HRM?

Case study for discussion and analysis

Supreme Sportscars

Supreme Sportscars makes high-powered luxury cars. With a deliberately limited manufacturing capacity, sales have been steady at 190 vehicles a month, with a two-year waiting list. The factory is poorly equipped with a large proportion of the work being done by traditional hand methods. However, the company has always been profitable at this level. The employees are loyal but modestly paid. They take pride in their craftsmanship and the reputation of the cars. They have close relationships with the lower-level managers, most of whom were promoted from the ranks.

Five years ago, the company was acquired by a major US manufacturer. Initially, the American company had significant expansion plans based on a small and cheaper sports car but nothing came of those plans. Under a new chief executive, the corporate strategy has changed and now the parent company is looking to dispose of Supreme Sportscars, possibly in the form of a management buy-out. Design of the new car is virtually complete but nothing has been done to increase production capacity. There are two key executives in the current company.

The managing director is Arnold Davies, a 45-year-old marketing man. He was recruited by the parent company last year after a career spent mainly in promoting and advertising washing machines and refrigerators. He has few academic or technical qualifications but is an intelligent, decisive man with a reputation for getting things done. A flamboyant character, he drives a bright red Supreme car from the top-end of the range. The workforce have accepted him but have no great respect for his managerial qualities. He believes in leading from the front and has asked your management consultancy to advise him on the merits of a management buy-out.

You are aware that a large multinational car manufacturer is interested in acquiring Supreme Sportscars and badging its own cars under this name. They would establish a new production facility. They would not consider a joint venture but might be prepared to take some of the management team and the design unit. The parent company is wary of selling to the multinational in case this encourages further competition for their other products.

The divisional accountant, Jeff Mathias, is an important figure in any decision. He is a long-term staff member of the US company, well-qualified and experienced. He is a quiet but firm person, known to be open to new ideas but also very loyal to his employers. He is respected by the other managers, although the nature of his work isolates him from the day-to-day running of the factory. He is well paid but is conscious that he will never become rich working for the US company. Mathias is also aware that the parent company is about to announce major job cuts worldwide because of heavy losses in the USA and declining sales in Europe.

This is your first impression of the problem. How would you proceed with collecting relevant information, determining the crucial issues and devising the decision strategy?

Chapter 12
Change strategies

Learning objectives

The purpose of this chapter is to:

- Introduce the concept of transformational human resource strategies.

- Compare incremental and packaged change programmes.

- Discuss the HR role in mergers and acquisitions.

- Consider the issue of behavioural transformation and negative change.

Transformational HR strategies

Enthusiasts have seen a transformational power in HRM, quoting major corporations such as IBM and Marks & Spencer that emphasize HRM-type values in their mission statements (Tyson, 1995, p.28). In fact transformation, or change, is an inevitable consequence of many human resource strategies. In this chapter we will consider various kinds of change initiatives from both a strategic and implementational perspective. **Change strategies** fall into one of two categories: turnaround change and organizational transformation (Bertsch and Williams, 1994):

1 *Turnaround change.* This is financially driven, often to ensure corporate survival by cutting unprofitable products and services. It involves the redesign of organizational structures, disposal of non-core activities and large-scale redundancies. This kind of change is painful but straightforward since existing hierarchical control systems can administer the process.

2 *Behavioural transformations.* This involves changing behaviour patterns throughout the company. Hierarchical control is inadequate because different power centres are likely to conflict and differences between business units make behavioural consistency a difficult objective to achieve.

Whatever the strategic purpose and product of change, its organization is likely to take the form of one of three models (Buchanan and Boddy, 1992):

Project management. This adopts a rational, linear problem-solving approach, very much in the tradition of classical business strategy. Decisions are generated at the top and orchestrated by a project manager who assigns objectives, allocates budgets and responsibilities and sets deadlines. The project management model embodies a control mechanism which monitors progress in the determined direction.

Participative management. This model takes more account of the skills and concerns of people affected by the change at lower levels of the organization. It involves a degree of emergent strategy. This approach is more time-consuming for managers and runs the risk of deviating into side issues. Participative management may lead to changes being blocked by inflexible interest groups. In general, however, it is more compatible with concepts of empowerment, commitment and team management.

A political perspective. This framework goes further in accepting and dealing with interpersonal and cultural aspects of change. It reflects awareness of power distribution within an organization and reasons for resistance. It is most useful when there is a lack of clarity or agreement over the objectives of the firm, or the need for strategic change. This approach has particular relevance in comprehending the effects of mergers and takeovers. It requires front stage political 'performances' from senior managers, together with Machiavellian intrigue in building behind-the-scenes power blocks and undermining resistance.

Each model has its merits and disadvantages. Individual organizations may also employ combinations of more than one approach.

Restructuring

Restructuring is the most common form of major organizational change (Key concept 12.1). According to its protagonists, restructuring should not be a defensive cost-cutting process but rather a proactive attempt to achieve innovative products and services: 'focus without fat' (Kanter, 1989, p.58). The goal should be **synergy** (Key concept 12.2).

Restructuring usually involves **reorganization** – a move from one form of organization to another. For example, a business may change from a divisional to a network structure. This requires breaking up the previous hierarchy or departmental structure. Some organizations are notoriously prone to reorganizations at intervals of two to three years or less, with the consequences of the last restructuring not being fully absorbed and analysed before being swept up in the next.

> **Key concept 12.1** Restructuring
>
> Breaking up and recombining organizational structures. Advantages include: reduced costs, eliminating duplication; and greater efficiency. Disadvantages include: disorder; interfering with normal activities; destruction of long-term commitment; loss of direction, especially in careers; and overwork from excessive cost-cutting. Recent strategic thinking has also emphasized the importance of relating business objectives to core organizational competencies. In other words, organizations should do what they are good at, leading to a new trend for companies to demerge, splitting into focused activity areas on which separate management teams can concentrate.

Restructuring can affect the HR function directly. Pollitt (2005b) describes how pharmaceutical giant AstraZeneca changed from site and functionally based human resources teams offering a full range of generalist support, to a 'one team' approach. Use of HR metrics helped to demonstrate the value of HR to the AstraZeneca businesses. The rationale was to create a more efficient and customer-oriented delivery of HR services and to ensure smooth implementation by communicating the new mindset to HR staff, combined with specific skills training to manage customer interactions both at strategic and transformational levels. The 'one team' approach has brought together everyone involved in HR delivery and it is claimed that there is a greater sense of team working, improved communication, a much more consultative approach and a customer-focused culture. HR is now in line with organizational strategy and is a value-adding part of the business.

Change and organization structures

According to Fritz (1996, p.4):

> Structure is an entity (such as an organization) made up of elements or parts (such as people, resources, aspirations, market trends, levels of competence, reward systems, departmental mandates, and so on) that impact each other by the relationship they form. A structural relationship is one in which the various parts act upon each other, and consequently generate particular types of behaviour.

Fritz points out that organizational structures are rarely designed in a deliberate manner. Small structures grow into larger ones and individual units become the focus of managerial power. Fritz (1996, p.5) says that: 'Departments and divisions become entrenched as power systems.' Any structural change is likely to meet resistance from these power systems.

Fritz also argues that organizations are structured either to 'advance' or to 'oscillate'. Advancement is a positive move from one state to another that acts as a foundation for further advances. Fundamental to structural advancement is the concept of 'resolution' when an outcome is achieved and a particular problem is resolved. According to Fritz (*ibid.*, p.6), management in an organization that is structured in advance coordinates 'individual acts into an organizational tapestry of effective strategy'. When all the individuals in this utopian organization are acting together, the result is synergy, allowing the achievement of 'enormous feats'.

The alternative is structural oscillation. Fritz (*ibid.*, p.6) explains this: 'Oscillating behaviour is that which moves from one place to another, but then moves back towards its original position.' So many organizations set out on some change programme, full of enthusiasm and energy. But, six months later, the enthusiasm has evaporated and the programme peters out leaving very little changed.

Melé (2005) studied the conversion of a medium-sized bureaucratic organization with highly specialized jobs into one in which employees were much more autonomous in managing their own work. Bureaucratic rules were reduced, but not eliminated completely, and management became less authoritarian. Employees could therefore apply greater entrepreneurial spirit, developing their talents in pursuit of company goals. It is argued that the new organizational form is ethically superior and reflects the basic requirements of the principle of subsidiarity. This holds that a larger and higher-ranking body should not exercise functions which could be efficiently carried out by a smaller and lesser body. The former should support the latter by aiding it in the coordination of its activities with those of the greater community. While usually applied in a political context, Melé explores the principle as a moral base for organizational forms within business, arguing that it would help to mitigate the effects of those bureaucracies in which individuals are often not fully appreciated.

Labovitz and Rosansky (1997, p.7) consider that senior managers can achieve alignment to ensure advancement through:

- Carefully crafting and articulating the essence of their business and determining the 'main thing'.
- Defining a few critical strategic goals and imperatives and deploying them throughout their organizations.
- Tying performance measures and metrics to those goals.
- Linking those measures to a system of rewards and recognition.
- Personally reviewing the performance of their people to ensure the goals are met.

Labovitz and Rosansky criticize traditional structures of organization that are based on the notion of breaking up a managerial problem into pieces: departments and divisions. As they point out (1997, p.8):

> Psychologists have long recognized that human beings like people who are like themselves and tend to reject people who are different from them. Yet organizations continue to create differences between people in the interest of efficiency. Line versus staff, management versus labour, field versus corporate, international versus domestic, East versus West, accounting versus sales – the list goes on. No wonder it's so hard to focus people around common goals when they are so different from each other simply by virtue of what they do and where they do it. Specialization and expertise can be a wedge that drives people further apart and makes it difficult for them to work together.

Key concept 12.2 Synergy

Making the new whole worth more than its old parts, sometimes described as '2 + 2 = 5'. Synergies involve economies from integrating activities, horizontally or vertically; but also unrealized potential for new ideas, products or processes by melding expertise from the different sources into centres of excellence.

The difficulty for corporate management comes in the attempt to achieve both synergy and workable new diversified or decentralized structures at one and the same time (Marginson *et al.*, 1993a, p.7). Public statements through the media and shareholder information normally present such changes as deliberate and thought-through, the implication being that restructuring would be dealt with by means of a project management approach. However, the notion that restructuring is usually decided at the most senior level on the grounds of balance sheet rationality is often illusory (Purcell, 1995, p.70). As we observed in earlier discussions on strategy and management, when faced with uncertainty, complex situations and conflict within the organization, managers typically resort to 'political' decisionmaking.

Unfortunately, as we concluded earlier, employees are a secondary consideration of change in free market organizations (Wilmott, 1995, p.313). Participative management is squeezed out in favour of the project management or political approach. Developing Wilmott's remark that 'the turkeys are unlikely to vote for Christmas', it is evident that they are generally kept in the dark until it is too late. Hence, little account is taken of the people who will be disrupted by the process and those who have to maintain quality and value during a period of major upheaval. Often the principal role of people managers is to sort out the resulting mess and smooth ruffled feathers.

Shrinkage

As we observed earlier, focusing on core activities and disposing of others has become particularly fashionable. In some cases, businesses have decided that management control and shareholder value are best served by a demerger, for example the hiving off of Zeneca from ICI, or the split of British Gas into distribution and retailing companies. More commonly, shrinkage involves **downsizing** – reducing the number of employees. In either case, HR managers are involved with communicating the change, conducting union negotiations and arranging redundancies or redeployment.

A particular concern is the cost-effectiveness of individual employees and departments. The more expensive, the greater the degree of justification required to retain them. For example, the 'de-layering' initiatives of the 1980s and 1990s focused on expensive middle-managers. Kanter (1989, p.94) suggests that 'overhead' functions such as divisional head-quarters have a duty to justify themselves to the business units they are meant to support. Approval and checking may delay decisionmaking, hindering the ability to compete. Wherever possible, these should be eliminated completely or transferred to the business units whose activities are involved. Decentralization is a dominant force, leaving small, slimmed-down central functions. Restructuring can be dangerous when companies treat people purely as costs rather than as assets. Kanter points to the inevitable 'discontinuity, disorder and distraction' that interfere with people's normal activities. She concludes that 'top management typically *overestimates* the degree of cooperation it will get and *underestimates* the integration costs'.

Cowboy management in these circumstances can destroy long-term commitment since restructuring removes many of life's certainties. Most of us try to create a state of order and predictability around our jobs. Restructuring can destroy this. No longer can we count on a job for life with any one company, but some sense of direction is essential to preserve motivation and obtain the best performance. Neither can people be expected to cope with overwork caused by excessive cost-cutting. According to American experience, much downsizing is really 'dumb-sizing', since two-thirds of the companies who have slashed workforces in recent years report no increase in efficiency. Often the principal role of human resource specialists is in rescuing the situation after the change has happened. Motivation and commitment must be rebuilt and skills training made available for staff involved in new tasks.

HRM in reality How CEOs can make the most of their top teams

The most powerful CEOs often fail to create and manage the right environment in which top executive teams can be effective. This is the conclusion of research by Hay Group, the global professional services firm, published in the Hay Group Working Paper, *Top Teams – Why Some Work and Some Don't: Five Things the Best CEOs Do to Create Outstanding Executive Teams.*

The research was based on a four-year study of executive-level teams at leading global corporations in the telecommunications, airlines, beverages, computer software and manufacturing sectors. In each case, the team was led by a CEO or other executive decision-maker and was made up of top business unit or geographic area leaders.

CEOs are under pressure to make teams deliver – quickly

The study began in 1998 and was coordinated by Hay Group senior vice-president, Debra Nunes, in conjunction with researchers from Harvard University and Dartmouth College. She said:

Average tenures of CEOs today are only about 18 months. As a result, they're under tremendous pressure to deliver results quickly. Assembling, managing and leading a top executive team is increasingly seen as critical to both the CEO's success, and the organization's. Given the increasingly important role of top teams, it's striking how many fall short of being truly effective. In our study, two-thirds of the teams failed to excel according to our criteria, and we discovered this was substantially tied to the team leader, usually the CEO, who often lacked an understanding of the dynamics of top teams. Because executive teams are generally charged with issues central to the company's future, the cost of an underperforming team is great – both in terms of unrealized opportunity and in the loss of executives' commitment to the strategic agenda of the organization. On the other hand, truly effective teams can have a tremendously positive influence on the performance of the organization, and can be a critical driver of shareholder value.

Corporate success is dependent on top teams

The Hay Group study suggests that:

- effective top teams can help advance the CEO's strategy and agenda more quickly
- make the organization more nimble and responsive to market changes
- lead to higher perceived valuations from institutional investors.

According to Debra Nunes:

Institutional investors are increasingly aware of the importance of top teams in executing a company's 'big picture' strategy. In fact, a recent study of institutional portfolio managers suggests that 35 per cent of an investment decision is driven by non-financial data, primarily 'execution of corporate strategy' and 'management credibility'. Since top teams exist primarily for these reasons, they are fast becoming a key component of a company's shareholder value proposition. And over time, we believe the role of top teams will only increase in importance. In fact, Gillette's bond rating was recently upgraded by agencies which cited the top executive team created by the new CEO.

What constitutes a 'real team'?

It seems that many CEOs hold the (mistaken) belief that their 12–15 key 'reports' are the top team. Probably this is not the case. These people exist in order to share information from each 'silo' of the business – they are not there to address the organization's biggest challenges and opportunities. And, significantly, they do not have a team dynamic.

Conversely, a real top team has 'collective tasks and challenges that demand a high level of interdependency among its members'. Also they have clear and stable boundaries so that membership is not constantly changing. The most effective top teams were found to have only six to eight members, handpicked by the CEO. Larger teams are likely to lack interdependence, have an unfocused agenda and unclear boundaries. And there is no need for a representative from every business unit as long as someone represents their interests.

The most effective teams tend to focus on the most consequential issues facing the business. They tend to stay away from operational matters and concentrate on big-picture mandates, including:

- mergers
- expansion into new markets
- sweeping reorganizations
- e-business strategy.

Debra Nunes argues that: 'Top executive teams have the potential to become entities that are smarter, more effective and more productive than the sum of their parts. In fact, resilient companies depend on top teams. But for those that are falling short, and risk becoming also-rans, there are steps that can maximize top team performance.'

CEOs need to be democratic but retain control

CEOs and other top executives have a variety of leadership styles – for example, coercion (expecting employees to comply with orders without question) or pacesetting (demonstrating performance standards by personally modelling the way). But the Hay Group research suggests that these styles are often ineffective, serving to alienate team members and retard the collaborative process. Debra Nunes explains:

One of the most interesting anecdotal findings of our research is that the most charismatic CEOs make some of the worst team leaders. In a sense, their mythologies precede them, and their strong, forceful presences simply suck the air out of the room, creating an environment of worship rather than teamwork. The challenge for these types of leaders, and others, is to turn off some of the skills and behaviours that have served them so well in their rise to the top, and turn on the listening and social skills that are not always reinforced in a hierarchical corporate culture.

Strong leaders were authoritative, gave strong direction, communicated the big picture and clearly articulated goals and behaviours expected of the team. But they were also democratic, allowing the team be a team and encouraging members to believe their voice would be heard, and that what they say matters.

Debra Nunes added: 'The most successful team leaders have a spectrum of managerial styles that they deploy based on the situation. In general, they create the right conditions for teamwork and then step into the background to act as moderator and guide.'

CEOs should provide more direction – even to the most insightful members of their team

There is an assumption that team members are powerful and committed and have the same core agenda. Not

▶

▶ necessarily so. Team leaders need to be forceful and provide direction. According to Debra Nunes:

> One leader of an oil refining business gave his team a quick quiz asking each member to write down the team's number-one priority. When the ten team members listed several different priorities related to safety, cost-cutting, environmental compliance and new markets, the leader was shocked. 'Don't you guys realize that if we can't cut our refining costs by three cents a gallon, they're going to shut us down?' The team members were equally stunned by the simplicity of the mission. In fact, over the following year, the team took steps that reduced costs by five cents per gallon. The lesson here: You can never be too clear, or overstate the team's primary goal.

Top teams need members with empathy and integrity

The members of the most successful top teams are neither brighter and more driven, nor more committed than people in less successful teams. But the members of the most successful teams excelled at working with others, bringing a high degree of emotional intelligence to the 'team dynamic'. Emotionally intelligent team members:

● have self-control

● are adaptable

● exude self-confidence and self-awareness

● display high levels of empathy and integrity.

In fact, empathy and integrity are particularly significant. Hay Group research shows members of outstanding teams to be far more empathetic, having an understanding of the emotional make-up of others, than team members of less successful teams. In fact, on high-performing teams, the research showed that 71 per cent of participants said their team peers were sensitive to the unspoken emotions of their fellow members. On average-performing teams, only 44 per cent showed this characteristic.

According to Debra Nunes: 'Empathy is incredibly important to the successful team's dynamic. This is because members of a team will only "buy in" to the team process if they feel they are being heard and understood. Resentment and withdrawal are the inevitable result if people feel their ideas and input are not being fairly evaluated.'

The research also identified perception of integrity among and between team members as being essential for team success. A team member with 'integrity' was defined as one who 'behaves consistently with the organization's or the team's values – even when it is personally risky to do so.' The researchers justified the importance of integrity through the trust it fosters among team members.

Just 3 per cent of team members in average-performing teams had taken the personal risk of challenging the team to live up to its values – compared with 44 per cent of the members of high-performing teams. As Debra Nunes explains:

> No one wants to commit professional suicide by challenging his or her peers, especially the CEO. But if the team dynamic is healthy enough, members should feel comfortable about raising an opposing point of view. In fact, productive conflict is desired as long as it's about ideas, not personalities. Top teams must be comprised of people who not only have the courage to identify, even create, conflict over ideas, but also the social skills to resolve friction constructively.

Necessary support and development

The research identifies strong operational support as a necessity if a top team is to be successful. This support must include sound data and forecasts; teamwork training; and appropriate compensation tied to its ability to meet its goals.

Debra Nunes concluded that:

> Outstanding team leaders also periodically review the team's performance, providing helpful feedback, encouragement and continuous reinforcement and refinement of the team's goals. Some effective team leaders even provide individual coaching, taking aside a team member who's not contributing enough, or speaking privately with someone who's personality may be getting in the way. Again, the team leader must learn to wear several hats to make the team function as smoothly and effectively as possible.

How might empathy and integrity act as positive factors in the process of change?

Source: *HRM Guide USA* (http://www.hrmguide.net/usa/), 2 October, 2001.

Incremental change

In the 1960s and 1970s, change often came under the label of organizational development (OD). This is an undramatic – but effective – long-term change process based on incremental improvements, essentially a continuous flow of emergent strategies. With the advent of modern change programmes such as 'business process re-engineering', this low-risk and long-term approach has gone out of fashion to a considerable extent. As we can see from Table 12.1, its underlying principles are similar to Japanese methods of continuous improvement and the methodology has considerable parallels with radical change initiatives described later in this chapter.

Action learning

What is **action learning**? Rothwell (1999, p.5) states that it is a 'real-time learning experience that is carried out with two equally important purposes in mind: meeting an organizational need and developing individuals or groups'. Rothwell notes that Reg Revans, the originator of action learning, avoided defining the term, preferring to say what it was not. But there are many formal definitions including the following by Dean (1998, p.3): '. . . a voluntary, participant-centred, evolutionary process to solve real, systemic, and so-far-up-till-now-unresolved organizational work-cum-learning problems in the workplace as it applies the principle of democratic values and team learning.'

Marquardt and Revans (1999, p.4) feel that 'Perhaps action learning's greatest value is its capacity for equipping individuals, teams and organizations to more effectively respond to change.' They go on to contend that action learning has a 'unique and inherent capacity' to deal simultaneously with five pressing organizational needs:

1 *Problem solving*. The more difficult the problem, the better suited is action learning to meet the challenge.
2 *Organizational learning*. Action learning provides a valuable focus for company-wide learning.
3 *Team building*. Helps build teams and team skills for future team building.
4 *Leadership development*. Prepares leaders to deal with future problems.
5 *Professional growth and career development*. Action learning facilitates high levels of self-awareness, self-development and continuous learning.

Theme	Features
1 Top management support	Initiatives will not succeed unless higher management levels are fully committed to the change process and its maintenance.
2 Problem-solving and renewal process	Allows adaptability and viability to be generated in an organization that may be living in the past. This should allow the organization continually to redefine its purpose.
3 Collaborative diagnosis and management of culture	The process of change must involve all levels within the organization in a search for ideas that will lead to improvement. This is a non-hierarchical, shared evaluation of the culture and long-term goals of the organization.
4 Formal work team	Focusing on work groups, group dynamics and team development.
5 Consultant facilitator	Bringing in an external change agent or catalyst, experienced in the mechanics of change, able to spot resistance and unbiased by any prevailing agenda.
6 Action research	A primary feature of classic organization development that is absent in many modern packaged initiatives.

Table 12.1

Themes of organization development

Source Adapted from French and Bell (1990).

The whole process revolves around a real-life problem that needs to be important to the organization. Marquardt and Revans (1999, p.5) say that:

> The problem should be significant, be within the responsibility of the team, and provide opportunity for learning. Selection of the problem is fundamental to action learning because we learn best when undertaking some action, which can then be reflected upon. The problem gives the group something to focus on that is real and important, that is relevant, and that means something to them.

This democratic – or, at least, participatory – process may follow a sequence such as (Rothwell, 1999, p.5):

- pinpoint the cause(s) of problems
- solve the problems
- formulate goals
- work toward achieving goals
- establish a shared vision of the future.

People are chosen for an action learning team (composed of four to eight members) for their experience and ability to contribute to the learning process – and also for the developmental benefit to them. So they must already possess relevant knowledge or skills for the particular issue they are working on. It is beneficial to have participants from a wide range of departments or functions, representing a number of views. They need to be positive and open-minded about the issue and possible solutions. It is also customary to appoint a team facilitator who is not a leader but helps the team work together effectively. Stark (2006) gives examples of effective action learning for different professional groups in the UK (nurses and educators) but argues that there are tensions and challenges in organizations such as political agendas that discourage learning and favour the status quo.

There are times when action learning is not appropriate according to Rothwell (*ibid.*, p.18):

- When the issue or need to be addressed is simple or straightforward.
- It is pressing or urgent, such as an emergency or catastrophe.
- The organization does not have the expertise to deal with the problem.
- Managers do not value their employees or see merit in the developmental benefits.

Competitive pressures often demand a faster, more dramatic process than that provided by organizational development or action learning. Many modern managers would question whether their organization had the time required. More pertinently, we can ask if ambitious executives on short-term contracts have enough time to make their mark with such a slow methodology. It is likely that a glossier and more public method will be better appreciated. This is provided by 'packaged', or 'off-the-shelf' approaches, which begin with top management and are cascaded down the organization. They are normally dramatized with considerable emphasis on communication and a spotlight placed on the lead personality.

In the 1980s most large organizations engaged in 'total quality management' (TQM) programmes, focusing on continuous improvement, quality assurance and zero faults. TQM programmes are geared to organizational processes such as production. HR involvement includes the selection of flexible people who are amenable to increasingly demanding levels of quality.

Business process re-engineering

Re-engineering is a methodology of the 1990s (see Key concept 12.3) that inspired many change strategies. The technique was first publicized by Hammer (1990) in a *Harvard Business Review* article with the somewhat dramatic title of 'Re-engineering Work: Don't Automate, Obliterate'. In typical guru fashion he outlined amazing benefits in a range of companies, proclaiming the existence of seven fundamental principles of re-engineering:

HRM in reality Offshoring could save US$58 billion a year

New research from The Hackett Group, a strategic advisory firm and an Answerthink company, estimates that Fortune 500 companies could potentially save US$58 billion annually, or over US$116 million on average, by offshoring many of their back office activities. Advances in technology, along with increasingly educated global workforces, enable the portability of business support activities across information technology (IT), finance, human resources (HR) and procurement, to take advantage of labour arbitrage. Increased use of offshore resources may impact up to 1.47 million general and administrative jobs, or nearly 3000 at a typical Fortune 500 company.

The report concludes that globalization has created an environment where executives must constantly re-evaluate their cost structures for general and administrative operations against a host of emerging global resources. The best companies are strategically improving performance in finance, IT, HR, procurement, working capital and other areas in ways that help them respond to the pressures of globalization.

However, the report argues that many companies are relying on outdated sourcing analysis techniques resulting in an underestimation of potential benefits of offshoring back office operations. With labour arbitrage savings approaching 60 per cent, executives should analyse their process optimization opportunities to capture the potential value of centralization. Failure to do so risks allowing activities that provide no competitive advantage to remain decentralized in industrialized countries with associated higher costs. Distributed activities are generally not portable, and therefore not included within the scope of a globalization initiative. The education base and skill sets available in India, China, the Philippines, Pakistan, Eastern Europe, Brazil and other emerging countries continue to expand, offering a new level of savings combined with improved quality and talent, significantly strengthening the business case for globalization.

Hackett director, Julio Ramirez, said:

Companies have long been aware that they can take out cost and improve back office efficiency by streamlining businesses processes, improving the way they use technology and centralizing operations, either in a shared service centre or with an outsourcer. But over the past few years, the resources available offshore have matured rapidly, creating immediate opportunities to materially reduce companies' cost structures.

Hackett director, Michel Janssen, added:

Today, companies can turn to established offshore resources that deliver labour costs reductions while maintaining or even improving the skill level of staff. The potential savings of up to US$116 million annually for a company are simply too compelling to ignore. Yet most executives will miss the potential impact of service globalization due to the under-scoping of initiatives. Taking full advantage of service globalization requires a deep understanding of the nature of business processes and how they can be optimally organized and delivered.

The report recommends use of a well-balanced assessment methodology that fully considers the business' strategy, culture, transactional characteristics and readiness for change. By taking the broadest logical view of relevant processes, combined with a holistic evaluation methodology, firms can ensure that they are maximizing the benefit opportunities available through global markets while managing the risk associated with these progressive transformation initiatives.

Current analysis of the Fortune 500 draws upon ongoing benchmark studies that have captured outsourcing costs since 1992. While information technology represents the largest functional opportunity, significant savings can be generated in other general and administrative areas, including finance, human resources, and procurement.

Annual savings (millions)

- Information technology US$58.5
- Finance US$32.1
- Human resources US$15.6
- Procurement US$9.9.

Analysis of the savings opportunity breakdown for a typical Fortune 500 company is based upon the median number of full-time employees (FTEs) per process group, labour arbitrage cost differential, and the potential degree for offshoring by process group.

What are the human resource management advantages and disadvantages of offshoring back office activities?

Source: *HRM Guide USA* (http://www.hrmguide.com), 28 November, 2006.

- Organize around outcomes, not tasks.
- Those who use the output should perform the process.
- Information processing work should be subsumed into the real work that produces the information.
- Geographically dispersed resources should be used as though they were centralized.
- Link parallel activities instead of integrating tasks.
- Decisions should be taken where work is performed and control built into the process.
- Information should only be captured once – at source.

Business process re-engineering (BPR) appears under the guise of a number of similar terms and a variety of definitions. Depending on the definition used, re-engineering can involve: change in individual work tasks; in interpersonal work processes within a department; between sections of a business; or beyond the boundaries of a firm in a networked or virtual organization. Critics argue that perhaps it is no more than organization and methods (O&M), TQM and just-in-time 'dusted down and repackaged' (Burke and Peppard, 1995, p.28).

Nevertheless, BPR swept the Western business world. Companies such as AT&T, BT, Ford, Mercury and Rank Xerox have used the methodology. Why was it apparently so popular? Instead of 5–10 per cent improvements from other methods, the proponents of re-engineering promised 30 per cent, 50 per cent or even more. But BPR requires total rethinking of the organization from the bottom up, rather than tinkering with an existing situation.

> **Key concept 12.3** Business process re-engineering
>
> A 'fundamental rethinking and radical redesign of business processes to achieve dramatic improvements in critical contemporary measures of performance, such as cost, quality, service and speed' (Hammer and Champy, 1993).

Hammer and Champy presented a process perspective in contrast to the functional basis of most businesses. Hence, organizations and departments are not re-engineered but processes are. For instance the process of order fulfilment is everything from an order request to its delivery to the customer, regardless of department or level. Hammer and Champy argue that traditional hierarchical structures 'stifle innovation and creativity'. Instead, new technology should be introduced to cut out stages and people in a process. Moreover, a multi-skilled team should be employed, able to deal with a process as a whole. In all, they describe 10 interrelated changes that Grint (1995, p.83) traces to much earlier origins (see Table 12.2). In fact, an examination of these change principles reveals some strong links between BPR and concepts, such as empowerment and facilitatory management, associated with HRM elsewhere in this book.

Business process re-engineering also has close parallels with the notion of a 'learning organization' discussed in Chapter 21. BPR works on the principle that an organization cannot learn before it has first unlearned. BPR does this by starting with a 'blank piece of paper' approach using techniques such as cognitive mapping and soft systems methodology. These are diagrammatic methods aimed at tapping creativity and ensuring that a holistic approach is taken. Four stages are identified:

1 Have a vision
2 Identify and understand the current processes
3 Redesign the processes
4 Implement the redesigned processes.

Matters become even more confusing when one asks 'who does it?' It is simultaneously presented as an empowering programme, with fine rhetoric about teamworking, multi-skilling and flattened hierarchies, and as a top-down exercise demanding (as ever) commitment from senior executives! Of course, consultants have to remember who pays the bill. Perhaps the true emphasis is reflected in the key roles required for re-engineering as presented by Hammer and Champy (1993):

- Leader – a visionary and motivator.
- Process owner – sufficiently senior to oversee the entire process to be re-engineered.
- Re-engineering team – composed of insiders who understand present activities; and outsiders to question assumptions.
- An optional steering committee to oversee the organization's re-engineering as a whole.
- 'Re-engineering czar' – the operational head of the organization's re-engineering activities.

Clearly, this is a directed process. Employees may be 'permitted and required to think, interact, use judgement, and make decisions' but this only applies to the workers who are allocated jobs after the process has been re-engineered – eliminating one or two departments along the way. The attractiveness to senior executives is evident in the promise of redundancy; the benefits to employees are somewhat less obvious. Conceivably, Willmott's 'turkeys' may be less than keen to cooperate, but this appears not to be a problem to the proponents of BPR (Wilmott, 1995, pp.311–12):

> . . . any employee hostility to BPR is interpreted not as warrantable resistance but as irrationality or inertia which can be overcome by effective leadership and commitment from top management. Hammer notes that the disruption and confusion generated by re-engineering can make it unpopular. But he is equally confident that any opposition can be effectively surmounted by top-level managers.

Principle	Origins
1 Switch from functional departments to processes	Principle of 1950s socio-technical systems and Volvo Kalmar experiment
2 Move from simple tasks to multi-dimensional work	1970s quality of working life and job enrichment
3 Reversal of power relationship from superordinate to subordinate empowerment	Seen in both above
4 Shift from training to education	A criticism of British 'education' since the 19th century
5 From payment for attendance to payment for value added	Common in Ancient Greece
6 Bifurcation of link between reward for current performance and advancement through assessment of ability	The 'Peter Principle' - every employee tends to rise to his (or her) level of incompetence
7 From concern for boss to concern for customer	See modern Japan
8 Managers become coaches rather than supervisors	Hawthorne experiments – USA 1930s
9 Flattening of hierarchies	Kalmar experiments
10 Executives move from scorekeepers to leaders	Human relations

Table 12.2

Origins of change principles in business process re-engineering

Source Adapted from Grint (1995, p.85).

Burke and Peppard (1995, p.34) identify a number of further barriers to implementing BPR:

- There is a paradox in that people with knowledge of a particular process are unlikely to have the authority to redesign it, and vice versa.

- Redesign disturbs existing patterns of power in an organization. The power base may not coincide with senior management but with a 'dominant coalition' with a vested interest in frustrating BPR.

- The firm's culture may work against a process-based organization and consequent changes in work practices, job content and relationships.

- Within multinational companies, processes may cross national boundaries, bringing in further difficulties.

Given the importance of employees in implementing BPR, and the embodiment of strong ideas about people management in its basic texts, it is surprising to find that human resource issues have scarcely been addressed (Wilmott, 1995, p.306). Tinaikar, Hartman and Nath (1995, p.109) in a survey of 248 articles on BPR found that:

> Almost all of the articles (95.9 per cent) portray BPR as being concerned with only technical issues. The few articles discussing social issues such as empowerment of the lower levels, resistance to change, etc, focused primarily on the managerially relevant benefits of BPR. Cost-cutting through technology and downsizing, or the politically correct 'rightsizing', were some of the most common themes. However, the implications of this potential job loss through BPR were singularly neglected.

They conclude that the human aspect has been trivialized in the BPR literature. However, it is not unreasonable to wonder if this lack of concern for people may be partly responsible for the high failure rate of re-engineering initiatives. Pink (2001, p.108) considers that: 'In the beginning [of the new economy] there was re-engineering. And it was good. Then it was big. Then it got scary'. Pink goes on:

> Re-engineering corporations quickly became a $50 billion industry. The craze turned Hammer, a former MIT computer-science professor, into a rock star of the then-fledgling new economy. His bearded face began appearing at corporate conferences, inside boardrooms, and on lists of America's most influential people. He scolded CEOs for not zeroing in on first principles. He exhorted them to repent. Some of his warnings verged on the apocalyptic: 'Re-engineering,' he wrote, 'is the only thing that stands between many US corporations – indeed, the US economy – and disaster.'

It seemed at one stage that BPR could be regarded as the answer to everything. But business process re-engineering is just one more set of practices in a long list of methodologies that have been in and out of fashion over recent decades. Perhaps it is not too surprising to read in Hammer (2001, p.5), a decade further on from his seminal paper:

> It is told that Albert Einstein once handed his secretary an exam to be distributed to his graduate students. The secretary scanned the paper and objected, 'But Professor Einstein, these are the same questions you used last year. Won't the students already know the answers?' 'It's all right, you see,' replied Einstein, 'the questions are the same, but the answers are different.' What is true of physics is true of business. Today's business world is not that of Drucker or of Peters and Waterman, and it calls for a new edition of the management agenda.

Of course, Hammer argues that a new agenda is required because circumstances have changed. 'Executives of the most powerful companies now tremble before their independent and demanding customers.' This implies that customers were somehow not independent or demanding in the past. An alternative explanation is that the last agenda (for which you can read 'fashion') did not work all that well. Amongst the recent innovations, he lists:

- just-in-time inventory management
- total quality management and its avatar 'six sigma quality'
- cross-functional teams

- portfolio management and stage gates (in product development)
- supply chain integration, including vendor-managed inventories and collaborative planning and forecasting
- performance-linked compensation
- competency profiling in human resources
- measurement systems based on EVA (economic value added) or balanced scorecards
- customer–supplier relationships
- business process re-engineering.

But Hammer (2001, p.8) regards these as being no more than the first phase in dealing with customer expectations. In fact, innovative as they were, 'yesterday's innovation is baseline today and obsolete tomorrow.'

Strategic alliances

Redesign or restructuring may take place within one organization, or go beyond its boundaries, perhaps resulting from the combination of one firm with another. There are several relevant variables to consider at the strategic stage:

Strategic intent. Regardless of negotiated positions and public positions of the partner companies, what are their long-term intentions? Are they committed to a joint venture? Does one partner intend to achieve control? Managers will be wary of losing their power.

Consolidation. How much autonomy and organizational independence is to be allowed? Mergers and acquisitions tend towards much greater consolidation than joint ventures and consortia. Employees feel threatened by obvious opportunities for staff reduction.

Cultural integration. Is cultural plurality to be respected? Does the alliance intend a common culture? If so, will it be based on the culture of the dominant partner or a negotiated hybrid? Being forced to change familiar ways is threatening.

Key concept 12.4 Mergers and acquisitions

'A merger occurs when one corporation is combined with and disappears into another corporation. For instance, the Missouri Corporation, just like the river, merges and disappears corporately into the Mississippi Corporation. Missouri Corporation stock certificates are turned in and exchanged for Mississippi Corporation stock certificates. Holes are punched in the Missouri certificates, and they are all stuck in the vault. The Missouri Corporation has ceased to exist. Missouri is referred to as the *decedent*, while the Mississippi Corporation is referred to as the *survivor*' (Reed and Lajoux, 1998, p.7). Acquisition, on the other hand is a generic term used to describe a transfer of ownership. Here, the two parties in the transaction may continue as entities in some form or other after the acquisition.

Alliances and mergers draw on the capacity and potential of participants but they have a poor history of success. Surveys show that over 50 per cent of mergers and acquisitions fail to achieve strategic objectives – often disastrously. An often-quoted McKinsey and Company study of mergers between 1972 and 1982 (involving 200 of the largest US corporations) found increased value to shareholders in just 23 per cent. The greatest proportion, 33 per cent, was seen in relatively small takeovers of closely related businesses. The explanation seems to have attracted yet another analogy with poultry, although the meaning is quite different: 'You don't put two turkeys together and make an eagle!' (unnamed economist quoted in Peters, 1987). Often the advantages are outweighed by (Porter, 1990; Buono, 1991):

- Restructuring costs: including redundancy payments, consultancy and legal fees, accommodation transfer.
- Strategic difficulties: harmonization of goals and objectives.
- Organizational problems: difficulties in coordinating two different structures; overloading the parent organization's management systems; reorganization taking attention away from day-to-day activities.
- Behavioural problems and barriers: managers fight to preserve their territories or take over others; motivation falls when staff feel they have been taken over by remote managers.

According to Mackay (1992, p.10):

> Most of the evidence suggests that a failure to acknowledge the human dimension undermines many potentially successful ventures. . . . There is a feeling that if 'the figures are right' all else will follow smoothly. Wrong! It is precisely 'all else' that can frustrate the best laid plans of marketing men and accountants as cultures fail to gel and key executives engage in destructive battles for dominance.

D'Annunzio-Green and Francis (2005) studied pressures faced by managers in a contract catering firm involved in an organizational change initiative that encouraged them to become self-sufficient and display entrepreneurial behaviours in an environment where they were also expected to comply with new operating procedures aimed at strengthening central control and cutting costs. They highlight the duality between the quantitative need for discipline in managerial procedures, while at the same time paying attention to the qualitative need for investment in human resources.

The nature of the power relationship is particularly significant. Many studies show that acquisitions are notoriously unsuccessful because of the manner of the takeover. Specifically, the benefits of an acquisition or merger can be destroyed by the way in which the merger process is handled. Staff working for new owners tend to feel defensive and threatened. It is almost as if they have been colonized. Similar feelings are experienced when internal restructuring results in merged departments or the absorption of one section by another. Frequently, takeovers are handled insensitively. Acquisitions and mergers bring power differences into sharp and highly visible focus. There is a temptation to charge into the acquired firm or department or to take a condescending attitude. Many takeovers have parallels with the sacking of Rome. The new managers are inclined to feel superior and to regard methods which are different from their own as inefficient or second-rate. Arrogance and organizational chauvinism on the 'conqueror's' part lead to defensiveness and concern on the other side. People sense a loss of power to determine their own fate (Kanter, 1989, p.65):

> Arrogance can destroy the essence of the company. Strangers in suits wander about the organization, misunderstanding what they see. Observation is accompanied by sniggers and sneering comments, serving to boost the acquiring management team's egos and sense of superiority. Mackay describes this as 'tribal warfare' – one culture trying to assert pre-eminence over the other.

The consequences are serious. This is not simply a matter of upsetting workers, important though that may be in terms of its consequences on morale and cooperation. There is a considerable risk of throwing the baby out with the bathwater by obliterating the victim's processes before their consequences and rationale are fully understood.

Employee fears and anxieties can be minimized but research shows that people who have been 'taken over' continue to be suspicious and uncomfortable in the new organization for some time. Maurer (1996, p.11) notes that:

> Change is unsettling. It disrupts our world. Some fear they will lose status, control, even their jobs. The larger the change, the stronger the resistance. Successful change requires vision, persistence, courage, an ability to thrive on ambiguity, and a willingness to engage those who have a stake in the outcome.

Kavanagh and Ashkanasy (2006) examined mergers between three large public sector organizations and found that resulting changes are often imposed on the leaders themselves. Pace of change frequently inhibits successful re-engineering of the culture. A successful merger hinges on individual perceptions about the manner in which the process is handled and the direction of change. Communication and a transparent change process are important, as this will often determine who is regarded as a leader post-merger. Leaders need to be competent and trained in the process of transformation to ensure that individuals within the organization accept changes prompted by a merger.

HRM in reality Mergers and acquisitions failing to achieve value

Mergers and acquisitions (M&As) continue apace but many deals fail to create expected value, according to a recent survey by Accenture and the Economist Intelligence Unit. The survey of 420 corporate executives from the United States of America, Germany, the United Kingdom, Sweden, Norway and Finland conducted in March 2006 also found that over half of recent deals in which respondents had been involved were cross-border transactions.

Less than half (45 per cent) of respondents thought that their most recent M&As achieved expected cost-saving synergies, while even fewer (30 per cent) said they had been able to successfully integrate IT systems in their most recent cross-border deal. Also, almost a half (49 per cent) said their deals did not achieve expected revenue synergies.

'Missing synergy goals by even a small percentage can mean losing hundreds of millions of dollars of shareholder value,' said Art Bert, a senior executive in Accenture's strategy practice. 'The most successful deals are approached with a comprehensive integration plan, with core team continuity through most of the transaction life cycle, from target identification, valuation, due diligence, deal execution, pre-close planning, and post-closing integration.'

Fifty-eight per cent of executives involved in a recent deal said their company's latest acquisition was a cross-border transaction. Around one half of respondents to the survey expected businesses in their industries to make cross-border acquisitions over the next five years. The following reasons were given:

- to guarantee profitability (55 per cent)
- to hit strategic corporate targets (49 per cent)
- just to survive (26 per cent).

Almost three-quarters (70 per cent +) of senior executives considered that the identification and execution of cross-border M&As was more difficult than domestic transactions.

According to Art Bert:

There is a growing body of evidence that most large transactions fail to create shareholder value for acquirers. But what makes M&A so alluring is the less common, successfully executed deal that allows an acquirer to create shareholder value far beyond what its peers and competitors can achieve. This is why we see most high-performing companies undertaking a disproportionate number of deals relative to their industry peers.

Almost a third (31 per cent) of respondents attributed 20 per cent or more of their companies' total revenue growth over the previous three years to acquisitions and 83 per cent thought that at least some growth came from deals. Similar responses were given for anticipated revenue over the next three years with 30 per cent expecting M&As to fuel growth of 20 per cent or more and 88 per cent expecting at least some growth from acquisitions.

'M&A remains a vital strategic tool for corporate executives worldwide,' Bert said. "Yet management teams must not be misled into thinking that deal closing is a prize, in and of itself. 'Rather, evaluating and integrating an acquired business in a manner that delivers a superior return on investment, demonstrating that a transaction is really the best use of shareholders' money, is what sets a good deal apart from a bad one.'

Respondents identified the following as some of the critical factors for M&A success:

- Orchestrating and executing the integration process (56 per cent for domestic and 47 per cent for cross-border deals)
- Conducting due diligence (42 per cent for domestic and 43 per cent for cross-border deals)
- Achieving an optimal price for a deal (20 per cent for domestic and 19 per cent for cross-border deals)

Most corporate executives thought that their firms were successful at retaining valuable employees from both the target business (72 per cent) and the acquiring company (77 per cent). Similarly, most also agreed or strongly agreed that their transactions did not have a negative impact on customers of the target business (67 per cent) or the acquirer (73 per cent).

What factors make cross-border M&As more difficult than domestic transactions?

Source: *HRM Guide USA* (http://www.hrmguide.com) 23 June, 2006.

Mergers and the HR function

Clemente and Greenspan (1999, p.1) point out that:

> There are literally hundreds of reasons why the M&A failure rate is so high. But many can be traced to the exclusion of human resource professionals in the pre-deal planning phase and the function's last-minute inclusion after the transaction has closed. It's a classic case of 'too little, too late'.

Clemente and Greenspan (1999) present a description of the typical merger or acquisition. The focus is on 'making the numbers work' and the sequence begins with an investment banker or equivalent presenting an apparently suitable candidate company to management. If this makes 'financial sense' the process is launched.

The 'due diligence' phase then begins, involving a detailed examination of financial, legal and regulatory, accounting and tax issues. If these check out, the merger partners 'plunge forward', assuming that all the strategic aspects will somehow fall in line. As the authors point out, the statistics on failure suggest that this is often highly erroneous thinking. Clearly, the 'ledgers and liability' aspects of the process are extremely important but the all-consuming focus on these matters ignores people issues. Clemente and Greenspan ask: 'If people issues are so important to the success of the deal, how can such little focus be paid to those issues in the strategy development, target company screening and due diligence phases?'

They answer their own question by stating that in most cases the merger partners have not looked closely enough at the 'people component' – strategic variables at the very heart of the deal. Most mergers and acquisitions are driven by apparent cost-cutting synergies and stock prices. But if they were driven by true strategic vision instead, HR professionals would need to be involved from the beginning to assess the people implications that do not feature in balance sheets or income statements. The authors conclude that:

> . . . identifying key human assets in a target company and quickly taking steps to prevent them from walking out the door on announcement of the deal is an HR-related imperative every company must take. Yet, historically, HR comes into the M&A process too late to make this vital contribution.

In most cases, the deal-making is more or less complete by the time that HR gets involved. HR specialists are left with the difficult role of developing communication strategies; aligning payroll, benefits and compensation systems; and melding different and possibly incompatible processes and cultures. But by this time a number of key personnel may have gone and those remaining may be confused or hostile.

Instead, Clemente and Greenspan argue, HR professionals should be involved in the earliest stage of any acquisition involving people. HR managers have the demanding task of integrating HR practices and performing two other roles simultaneously: a strategic role for company-wide integration and also a support role for business unit transactions (Antila, 2006). This means that human resource specialists must be familiar with the organization's strategic objectives, and its business and marketing plans. HR professionals must contribute to 'target screening' to identify and evaluate the worth and 'integrate-ability' of the proposed merger partner's human assets. This includes an evaluation of the two cultures and their potential compatibility.

Hanson (2001) observes that early coordination between HR specialists in both companies is ideal but due to the 'sensitive nature of many organization transactions, it is possible that the HR team on the receiving side of the transaction will be notified before the team on the sending side, or vice versa.' Tellingly, as someone writing from experience, she concurs with Clemente and Greenspan, noting that: 'The deal negotiators and attorneys will usually dictate when the intercompany communications can begin in the HR planning process.' Antila (*ibid.*) concludes that HR is important in the merger and acquisition process but is not always self-evident.

Mergers and acquisitions: project planning

Hanson (2001) advocates the use of a project plan as an organizational tool to schedule necessary actions and set deadlines. A simple plan document would have columns for the following:

1 major steps in the process
2 a breakdown of specific tasks within each step
3 ownership of each step/task, i.e. who is responsible
4 completion date for each task
5 comments/state of progress.

A wide variety of project and spreadsheet software can be used with the updated project plan being made available to the integration team through web technology. In Hanson's opinion the project plan is a mechanism for communication and control of the integration process. But the project manager, she argues, must be tenacious in the following respects:

- documenting necessary actions as they surface
- assigning them to a reliable owner
- determining appropriate deadlines that are compatible with other deliverables
- communicating with applicable parties
- following up to ensure that progress is on track
- escalating problems
- closing actions as they are completed.

HR due diligence

Hanson highlights the importance of HR due diligence as an early stage in the project plan. A due diligence investigation is designed to establish liabilities and vulnerabilities *before* signing the final agreement. According to Hanson the HR review offers the following possibilities:

1 Discovery of liabilities that could impact on the financial viability of the transaction.
2 Discovery of discrepancies that might be addressable in the agreement to both parties' satisfaction.
3 Discovery of variations in policy and practice that will be essential when integrating and communicating with employees.

The investigation may have to take place in two stages: a preliminary overview before the letter of intent is signed; and a more thorough investigation thereafter when confidentiality can be guaranteed, but before the final agreement. According to Hanson, the investigation involves a number of data-gathering components that divide into hard and soft. Hard facts are those that can be found in written records, reports, surveys, documented policies and statistics. They include information on pay, benefits, bonuses, employment regulations, third-party claims, employee relations, safety, and so on. Soft data are less easily established but can be critical, including key employee losses, management style, CEO reputation and senior management integrity. Hanson points to the particular importance of compensation and benefits plan information, not only in the due diligence stage but also later when close comparison is required. Issues of long-term liability are critical as regards pension plans and medical benefits.

In later stages of the integration plan, pay and other benefits have implications for the cost of 'golden parachutes' for people no longer required. Serious differences between salary structures, overtime, and 'perks' may also have significant consequences on morale and retention. Inevitably the question arises as to whether the more generous schemes are to be pushed down or the less generous increased in the future.

HRM in reality 5000 Managers surveyed on change

Contrary to some beliefs, a survey of 5000 mid-to-upper level managers shows that most are very open to change.

Discovery Learning, a developer of training products also used its *Change Styles Survey* to identify strategies for successful change management, placing respondents on a continuum between 'conserver' and 'originator,' with 'pragmatist' in between. Not surprisingly, most individuals are a blend of conserver-pragmatist or pragmatist-originator. Of the entire population surveyed between 1996 and 2001, 52 per cent of managers (57 per cent men/43 per cent women) scored in the pragmatist range, 26 per cent in the originator range and 22 per cent in the conserver range.

Survey developer Dr Chris Musselwhite characterizes the types as:

● *originators*: people who welcome dramatic change

● *conservers*: more comfortable with gradual change

● *pragmatists*: most enthusiastic about change that will address current circumstances.

'Americans are attracted to innovation, so we think being an originator is best,' says Musselwhite (president and CEO of Discovery Learning). 'But it takes all of these personality types to build a successful business.' Taking Enron as an example, he says: 'Conservers at Enron tried to warn of problems, but the leadership culture was apparently skewed so much toward originators charged with "reinventing business" that conservers were viewed as resisters and were either silenced or ignored.'

What can we learn from the survey? First, it is clear that a specific change will not meet with universal approval. Managers would benefit from knowing the change styles of staff and colleagues. 'You have to be gradual and clear with conservers, who are most concerned with the details of implementing the change,' says Musselwhite. 'You win the pragmatists over when they can see how the change will positively address current circumstances. And you may have to reel in the originators, who welcome dramatic change and sometimes move too fast for other team members' comfort.'

Musselwhite has an interesting perspective on the people who appear to resist change. He says that there are two kinds of resisters in the world. The most devoted staff sometimes voice the biggest objections to change and listening to them gives managers the opportunity to head off unanticipated problems. But some people are 'hard core' resisters. 'You want to be able to tell the difference,' explains Musselwhite. 'If someone's simply a conserver who's seeing red flags, you can benefit from their insights. They'll feel heard and will be more ready to move forward. But hard core resisters will fight the change no matter what.' Managers need to be careful not to treat every sceptic as a hard core resister – there is a risk of breeding dangerous alliances between the two groups. 'People may resist change on an emotional level,' says Musselwhite. 'It might have nothing to do with the change itself, but with territorial issues, problems at home, etc.' He also says that originators can cause problems at the other extreme – wanting to move too fast or in too many directions. In some cases, he argues, there's no way to get these people to work at a pace that's best for the organization, and you have to let them go.

Other findings of the survey include:

● Men (28 per cent) are more likely than women (23 per cent) to be originators, with women (27 per cent) being much more likely to be conservers than men (17 per cent). 'This may be due to women being more mindful of the implications of change, rather than being less open to change in general,' says Musselwhite.

● Among industries surveyed, communications had the highest percentage of pragmatists (71 per cent) and the lowest percentage of conservers (11 per cent). Petroleum had the lowest number of originators (4 per cent).

● Among professions, soldiers (46 per cent), school principals (42 per cent) and business consultants (40 per cent) had the highest percentage of originators. The lowest percentage of originators was security/police (3 per cent), support staff (8 per cent) and bankers (12 per cent).

● Among age groups, there are a substantially higher percentage of originators among 'baby boomers' (born 1946–65) than among earlier 'post war and depression' generations (born 1928–40) or the later 'generation X' (born 1966–81). Over 33 per cent of boomers were originators, compared with 26 per cent of generation X and 26 per cent of post-war/depression generations.

'The bottom line: the more aware people are of their co-workers' change styles, the better they work together, which improves business performance,' says Musselwhite.

What can be done about 'hard core' resistance to change?

Source: *HRM Guide USA* (http://www.hrmguide.net/usa/), 20 June, 2002.

Behavioural transformation

> If you ask people to brainstorm words to describe change, they come up with a mixture of negative and positive terms. On the one side, *fear, anxiety, loss, danger, panic*; on the other, *exhilaration, risk-taking, excitement, improvements*; *energizing*. For better or worse, change arouses emotions, and when emotions intensify, leadership is key. (Fullan, 2001, p.1, original emphases)

We noted earlier that the most difficult form of change involves modifying employees' attitudes, behaviour and commitment. Initiatives may come about as a result of deliberate strategic planning. Frequently, however, the process begins with a vague feeling among board members that there is 'something wrong' within the organization even though they are uncertain as to what it might be. The feeling may be fuelled by customer dissatisfaction, failure of innovation, conflict between departments or financial difficulties. The popularity of guru ideas and the spread of HRM have encouraged many senior executives to look to their people in order to improve overall organizational performance, quality of service and productivity. Black and Gregerson (2002, p.20) describe the realization of a need for change in the following way:

> Clearly, if you do not see a truck racing toward you, you are unlikely to jump out of the way. Likewise, if you do not realize that you are standing on a treasure of gold, you are unlikely to bend down and pick it up. It is no brilliant observation to say that if people fail to see the need for change (whether threat or opportunity driving it), they will not change.

It is impossible to plan an effective change programme without first defining what cultural change aims to achieve and how this differs from the existing situation. The objective of many organizations in managing cultural change is to move from a static or rigid culture to one that is flexible and adaptable (Fowler, 1993).

Fowler suggests that the process could begin with a theoretical comparison of static and adaptable cultures. Such a scale might include 30 items and would focus on the nature of the initiative – for example, quality or customer care. The current organization is then scored on this scale. Frequently, detailed and accurate information does not exist in a form that allows this to be done. This can be gathered from a 'where are we now' exercise, normally taking the form of survey research and feedback. Typically this involves the use of questionnaires and structured interviews at all levels of the organization. Research can focus on employee attitudes towards:

- the organization
- its methods
- communication channels
- company culture
- customers
- mechanisms for initiating and sustaining innovation and change.

Data is collated and a preliminary analysis fed back to the 'top team' and other interested parties, such as trade unions. After discussion – possibly involving a reappraisal of the company's mission and core values – action is agreed with the consultancy. To gain full cooperation it is best to discuss and agree the programme with employees and their representatives. Conventionally, the purpose and manner of any change is introduced to staff through presentations, discussions, videos, staff magazines and newspapers.

Action to improve such a situation could involve a cascading process in which groups of interested employees are asked to consider the data in relation to the company's core values. Staff could then be encouraged to suggest improvements and innovations and to take responsibility for seeing them through. There are instances of successful behavioural transformations of existing businesses, using a culture-change approach.

HRM in reality New views on mergers and acquisitions

Contrasting strongly with findings from the past 20 years, the current round of merger and acquisition deals tend to be financially successful and generate more shareholder value, according to a study by London's Cass Business School, in conjunction with Towers Perrin, a global professional services firm.

The Cass-Towers Perrin research looked at 218 international deals worth between US$400 million and US$1.5 billion (inflation-adjusted) concluded in 1988, 1998 and 2004. Company performance was analyzed for a one-year period – six months before and six months after each deal was closed – to evaluate the relative degree of financial success.

The study found that, in 2004, businesses involved in M&A deals worth over US$400 million (but excluding the biggest mega deals), outperformed the market by 7 per cent. This compared with an underperformance of approximately 3 per cent and 6 per cent, respectively, for companies involved in similar deals in the M&A cycles of 1998 and 1988.

Marco Boschetti, principal and leader of Towers Perrin's M&A consulting practice said:

> A paradox exists in the world of mergers and acquisitions. Other studies that have looked at M&A deals in the past 20 years have found that deals in earlier M&A cycles destroyed, rather than created, shareholder value. Yet to grow to be an organization operating on a global scale, it is almost impossible to do so quickly enough through organic growth alone. Mergers and acquisitions have in many ways become necessary. Interestingly, evidence is now mounting that the deals conducted in the current merger wave may be different. Across a broad range of industries throughout the world, lessons learned are being applied.

According to Tower Perrins' media release, deal success has been better in the current wave of mergers (those closed since 2003) on every single financial and share performance factor analyzed by Cass Business School, compared with the two major waves of the late 1980s and 1990s.

'We believe this success is a direct consequence of companies' improved management of the M&A process, from target selection and pricing, to due diligence to implementation,' said Boschetti. 'In the future, this learning curve will certainly continue. So, while gaining competitive advantage through M&As is now a legitimate business strategy for growth, long-term success will depend on increasingly sophisticated M&A capability.'

According to the Towers Perrin media release, the improved financial success of recent M&As comes from improvements in three areas of corporate behaviour:

1 *Better deal governance.* Senior business management has a much closer alignment with shareholders on the aims and objectives of corporate transactions. Today's managers are more likely to approach a deal rationally and focus on financial objectives. This implies that mergers in earlier cycles may have been more influenced by emotional factors.

2 *Better deal selection.* Due diligence processes have become more rigorous for M&A deals. For many businesses, due diligence currently includes financial assessment and quantification of factors such as corporate benefit programmes, e.g. pensions and their financial liabilities. These may not have been considered in earlier deals.

3 *Better focus on integration.* Improved corporate behaviour and strategies for post-deal implementation also produced stronger financial performance for M&A transactions during 2004. Specifically, businesses focused more on the implementation phase as a time to identify the merged companies' financial synergies and deliver results. In post-deal integration, retention and engagement of employees at all levels of the organization is increasingly acknowledged as having a direct impact on the operational success of M&As. This, in turn, is a key driver of M&A financial success.

'If M&As are now a successful business strategy for achieving above-average share performance, then ignoring M&A opportunities might place companies at risk of underperformance,' Boschetti added. 'But if M&A activity is becoming a competitive necessity, it is still a risky one, and companies engaging in this growth strategy would do well to ensure they understand the importance of deal management and governance, deal selection and integration. If they do not, they risk becoming one of the few cautionary tales of this wave or the next.'

Why were mergers and acquisitions more successful in the period 2003–2006?

Source: *HRM Guide UK* (http://www.hrmguide.co.uk) 4 April, 2006.

Negative change

To quote Maurer (1996, p.11):

> If the cost of failed change is high for organizations, the cost is equally dear for people. The first casualty is trust: people start to blame one another. Too many botched plans, and people become afraid to try again. Even so-called 'successful' efforts often leave a bitter taste in the mouths of those who were forced to change. The toll on individuals is enormous.

Implicitly, anyone opposing change is viewed as negative. Often, however, change is a destructive process and the end-product inferior to the original. This may be disguised by redefining quality requirements so that the lowering of standards becomes invisible or obscured. Newcomers to the situation know no better. Many may be involved in the change process and have a commitment to perceiving it as being necessary.

A redefinition of quality coincides inevitably with a change in the nature and flow of information, making a true 'before and after' comparison impossible. The proponents of change are unlikely to present their initiatives as failures; antagonists will never be happy with modifications in methods they have cherished. In the absence of objective evidence, debate is reduced to political confrontation with opponents of organizational change labelling new approaches as 'change for change's sake'. In fact, this is rarely the case. Change is difficult and disruptive and is not lightly entered into, but the true reasons for change may differ from its public justifications.

For example, we noted earlier that change is commonly associated with new management. This is not a coincidence. New managers have to work hard if the status quo is left alone. They are forever at the mercy of old networks and power balances. Far easier to highlight deficiencies in the current situation, pronounce it to be lacking in quality, and sweep it away to be replaced with another of their own making. Power-holders in the old networks can be eliminated or sidelined; there are always ambitious replacements available who are willing to become loyalists of the new regime. Young, or formerly disaffected, staff will show a naive enthusiasm for their new-found opportunities. Even better – from this somewhat cynical perspective – people can be imported from outside the organization who will be anxious to perform as required.

Summary

In this chapter we investigated transformational or change management. Nowadays, change initiatives are common elements of human resource strategies as companies and public sector organizations struggle to achieve their objectives in a competitive environment. Frequently these involve some form of organizational restructuring using a change programme such as business process re-engineering. Change programmes are fashion-driven and quickly become obsolete, to be replaced by the next heavily touted set of magic solutions. Some of the most difficult aspects of change management for human resource practitioners come from mergers and acquisitions where their involvement is often late – if not too late to rescue a disastrous situation. Finally we looked at behavioural transformation, involving attempts to change corporate culture and recognized that negative attitudes to change are to be expected and are not necessarily unhealthy.

Further reading

Bernard Burnes's *Managing Change: A Strategic Approach to Organisational Dynamics* (FT Prentice Hall, 2004) places change in a broader context of management theory. Esther Cameron provides a practical guide for managers in *Making Sense of Change Management: A Complete Guide to the Models, Tools and Techniques of Organizational Change* (Kogan Page, 2004). Hammer and Champy's *Re-engineering the Corporation: A Manifesto for Business Revolution* (Harper

Business, 1993) was probably the best-selling business book of the 1990s. Black and Gregersen's *Leading Strategic Change*, FT Prentice Hall (2002) is focused on the leadership of change but pays particular attention to resistance and harnessing negative attitudes.

Review questions

1 List as many possible organizational changes you can think of that would involve human resource specialists in their planning or implementation.

2 How important is leadership in achieving permanent change within an organization?

3 What is a transformational HR strategy?

4 Define: (a) synergy; (b) restructuring; (c) business process re-engineering. Has business process re-engineering been no more than a passing fad or is it a significant breakthrough in change management practice?

5 How would you distinguish between incremental and programmed methods of change management?

6 What is action learning? Is action learning most effective for change management or developing employees?

7 Why do people resist change? Is it possible for negative attitudes towards change to have positive benefits for an organization?

8 What role should human resource practitioners play ideally in a merger or acquisition? How does this differ from reality?

9 Why do so many mergers and acquisitions fail?

10 Summarize the concept of HR due diligence in your own words. Why is it important in increasing the probability of successful mergers and acquisitions?

Case study for discussion and analysis

West Five Care Trust

The West Five Care Trust controls four hospitals in a suburban area. Two of the hospitals are modern and have extra accommodation space. The other two are old but prestigious specialist units located in expensive areas. The Trust considers that it would make considerable financial sense to close the older hospitals and transfer their functions to the modern sites. Several senior physicians are extremely unhappy about the consequences and have launched a public campaign to save the specialist units. This has angered the general manager who has only just presented the plan as a proposal to the management committee. He considers the physicians to be disloyal as they have taken a confidential business matter to the press. He is also baffled since the new hospitals would offer them far better facilities.

The general manager was recently recruited from industry and has been keen to exercise his right to manage. In his first six months, he successfully outsourced cleaning and catering, brushing aside union opposition. He has also instituted stringent cost-control measures and now vets all budget requests personally, including expenses for attending conferences.

As human resources manager how would you analyse the situation and how could you help?

Chapter 13
Resourcing strategies

Learning objectives

The purpose of this chapter is to:

- Provide an overview of employee resourcing strategies.

- Discuss the purposes and methods of human resource planning.

- Outline the process of job analysis.

- Debate resourcing strategy in the context of staff retention and redundancy.

Resourcing

The basis of people management lies in how work gets done and who does it. Therefore, the rationale behind *why* we should decide on one solution rather than another is fundamental to HRM. There are important issues involved at all levels of analysis. At the environmental level, employee resourcing takes place against a background of:

- fluctuating economic conditions and global competition
- choice and availability within the local job market
- competition for scarce skills.

At the organizational level, the structure and functions of an enterprise are composed of the tasks that people perform. Allocating work to unsuitable or inadequately skilled people reduces the effectiveness of the whole organization. The consequences can be significant and – particularly with high-level or specialized work – may be critical to its future performance. Employee resourcing is no longer a matter of recruiting and selecting new people to fit existing posts. As we saw in earlier chapters, organizations have a range of 'flexible' alternatives.

At the strategic level, **employee resourcing** involves decisions on:

- subcontracting or creating vacancies
- allocating tasks
- choice of selection methods.

As an activity, it is a major element of the work of human resource specialists, involving considerable technical expertise. Employee resourcing can involve sophisticated methods intended to realize long-term objectives and balancing considerations such as: (a) satisfying the immediate need to minimize employee costs while maximizing worker contribution to the organization; and (b) fulfilling a longer-term aim of obtaining the optimal mix of skills and commitment in the workforce (Price, 2000).

Employee resourcing is also a subject of vital importance at a personal level because most of us have to apply for a job: probably the first practical aspect of human resource management we encounter. In many cases it is a frustrating and sometimes baffling process of rejection. Readers in employment may well participate on both sides of the issue – as selectors or as applicants. Inevitably, therefore, resourcing deserves serious discussion. In this chapter we focus initially on *why* resourcing decisions are taken.

The first section of the chapter begins with a consideration of the environmental constraints on resourcing and discusses the implications of the move towards flexible organizations. Next we determine the nature of resourcing strategy and consider various types.

In the second section we discuss human resource planning, examining the hard or 'people as numbers' approach – involving forecasting methods – and soft planning which takes commitment and culture into account.

Next we consider the use made of information gained from job analyses. We discuss the role of the job description and person specification in resourcing decisions. The chapter moves on to a debate on the merits of the 'best practice' approach in flexible organizations. Finally we discuss strategy and planning in relation to redundancies.

Employee resourcing is a fundamental aspect of people management (see Key concept 13.1). We can define four key stages:

Strategy and planning. Determining future human resources needs in terms of availability, expertise and location. We observed in Part one that HRM literature stresses the integration of resourcing activities with other people processes, such as performance management and human resource development, as well as the overall objectives of the enterprise.

Research and data collection. Determining the nature of work to be done and the criteria or competencies necessary to perform them. Additionally, obtaining adequate information about the people who possess these competencies, whether as employees, consultants or subcontractors.

> **Key concept 13.1** Employee resourcing
>
> Resourcing is the process by which people are identified and allocated to perform necessary work. Resourcing has two strategic imperatives: first, minimizing employee costs and maximizing employee value to the organization; second, obtaining the correct behavioural mix of attitude and commitment in the workforce. Employees are expensive assets. They must be allocated carefully and sparingly. In terms of costs and efficiency, effective resourcing depends on the care taken in deciding which tasks are worthwhile and the levels of skill and ability required to perform them.

Marketing. Making the work known – and attractive – to potential applicants in the internal and external job markets. Conventionally this function is contained within the term 'recruitment'.

Decisionmaking. Selection or allocation: choosing individuals to perform the work.

Marketing and decisionmaking are discussed in Chapters 14 and 15 on recruitment and selection. In this chapter we will concentrate on strategy and planning and the research necessary to establish the need for particular jobs.

Environmental constraints on resourcing

Unlike many other aspects of people management, employee resourcing involves direct interaction between organizations and their environment. In Part two we observed that, ultimately, businesses are dependent on the external job market for the supply of suitable staff. It is the source of school-leavers and university graduates for junior posts and experienced people for senior or specialized positions. Even in conditions of high unemployment there are shortages of people with skills that are in demand.

Countries such as Australia and Britain, for example, have a long record of failure in providing their young people with appropriate vocational training. If companies are unable to find staff or subcontractors with appropriate skills, their growth prospects and competitiveness are constrained. This may be so severe that companies are forced to relocate. Some multinationals have been forced to transfer operations from low-cost economies to high-wage countries, such as Germany, where skilled workers are available. Alternatively, businesses may compete for scarce skills through increased remuneration packages and benefits. Purcell (1989), for instance, sees star companies identified by the Boston Consulting matrix (discussed later in this chapter) as being prepared to pay above market rates to recruit and retain the best employees.

Economic changes over the last two decades have led to systematic responses in the attitudes and practices of employers. In his discussion of the flexible firm, Atkinson (1984) identifies a number of themes which underpin the employment plans of businesses in free market countries:

Market stagnation. Prolonged periods of recession and the increased competitiveness of world markets have produced a managerial obsession with the permanent reduction of unit employee costs.

Job loss. Most large firms have undergone dramatic reductions in levels of employment. These reductions have been expensive in redundancy costs and have had significant negative effects on relations with remaining employees.

Uncertainty. Despite continuous announcements of recovery, firms have been cautious about preparing for growth. In particular, they have been wary of a commitment to more full-time employees.

Technological change. This is happening at increasing pace and reducing cost, requiring organizations, and their employees, to respond quickly by changing products, manufacturing methods and ways of working.

Working time. Employers have maximized the value of employee time through restructuring work patterns to match periods of demand. This has led to a preference for part-time workers.

These factors have encouraged a move towards flexible jobs in flexible organizations.

HRM in reality Ageing workforces

More than one-third (34 per cent) of all American employers, and nearly half (46 per cent) with 25 000 or more workers, agree that the ageing workforce will have a significant impact on their company. However, more than three-quarters (79 per cent) have not taken any steps to accommodate older workers, according to the 2005/2006 MetLife Employee Benefits Trend Study.

The study, based on separate surveys of employees and HR/benefits executives, found that 33 per cent of baby boomers (aged 41–60) have not yet decided when they plan to retire. More than half (58 per cent) of young baby boomers (aged 41–50) are worried that they will have to continue to work either full- or part-time to live comfortably during retirement and 61 per cent say that 'outliving retirement money' is their number one retirement-related fear. Fuelling these concerns is the fact that 27 per cent of baby boomers admit to being 'significantly behind' in their savings, and one in 10 hasn't even started saving.

The MetLife study found that older workers are generally more satisfied with their jobs and more loyal to employers; 67 per cent of pre-retirees (aged 61–69) reported high levels of job satisfaction and 75 per cent indicated that they were very loyal to their employers. Comparative figures for all employees were 44 per cent and 46 per cent respectively. Pre-retirees are also more likely to report that benefits are an important reason for remaining with their employer.

The study argues that companies must grapple with a host of benefits-related issues specific to ageing employees. Senior management ranked 'health-care costs' as their top benefits-related concern (81 per cent). The impact of the ageing workforce is especially significant for the largest companies. Roughly one-third of employers with 25 000 or more workers cited 'long-term care issues' (35 per cent) and 'benefits for retired employees' (44 per cent) as a key concern in 2006. Companies with fewer than 50 employees rated these as key concerns in only 14 per cent and 18 per cent of cases.

The study found that, in addition to protection products such as disability and long-term care insurance, older employees are increasingly turning to the workplace for financial planning advice. Currently over half (56 per cent) of pre-retirees are interested in having access to financial planners to help them make decisions about 401(k) money (tax-free savings within a prescribed plan). In order to help employees address the needs of guaranteed income in retirement, nearly half (46 per cent) of the largest companies – and 31 per cent of companies with 500 or more employees – currently offer annuities through the workplace as an employee benefit.

Other key survey findings include:

- Longevity is a significant, but overlooked retirement risk. Many people will live up to 40 years in retirement, so ensuring a steady stream of income is crucial. While most (72 per cent) pre-retirees have tried to calculate how long their savings will need to last, only half (50 per cent) of baby boomers have taken steps to factor longevity into their retirement plans.

- The oldest baby boomers will reach traditional retirement age in five years time. Approximately one-quarter (26 per cent) of all baby boomers do not allocate any of their monthly household income to retirement savings vehicles. As a result, 38 per cent expect to remain behind in their retirement savings five years from now. Equally concerning is the fact that employees aged 51–60, who only have a few years left to accumulate savings, are allocating, on average, only 10 per cent of their monthly household income to retirement savings products.

- Nearly half of all employees are worried about providing for their own (47 per cent) and their spouses' (49 per cent) long-term care needs. Long-term care insurance was ranked as their most valued benefit by 16 per cent of employees, doubling from 8 per cent in 2004. Long-term care insurance is offered by nearly half (46 per cent) of all companies and 81 per cent of companies with 25 000 or more employees.

Maria R. Morris, executive vice president, Institutional Business said:

Over the next decade, the ageing workforce will transform the way that both employers and employees think about work and retirement. With increases in longevity, many workers recognize that they may need to stay in the workforce longer to fund their retirement, which could last 30 years or more.

Employers that make a long-term commitment to accommodate their older workers, not just through the physical environment or flexible work schedules, but by providing access to critical employee benefits that can protect an individual throughout their lifetime, will reap the benefits. Many older workers feel a strong sense of loyalty to their companies and expect the same in return. At a time when baby boomers are nearing retirement – and increased longevity is enabling many of them to work productively well into their 70s and 80s – older workers may prove to be the solution to the impending talent shortage. It's crucial for companies to identify a strategy for retaining trained, experienced workers and keeping them satisfied and engaged.

What changes should businesses make in their resourcing strategies to attract and retain older workers?

Source: *HRM Guide USA* (http://www.hrmguide.com/), 14 September, 2006.

Resourcing and the flexible organization

According to Blau and Schoenherr (1971, p.347): 'The recruitment of employees with the required skills becomes a crucial responsibility and a major mechanism of control.' During periods of relatively high unemployment in the 1980s and 1990s, organizations in many countries felt able to dictate the terms of employment they were prepared to offer new recruits, often moving away from traditional nine-to-five working days. As we have previously observed, there is a pronounced trend away from full-time work towards other job patterns. For example, in the late 1990s, nine out of ten posts created in the UK were part-time. We also noted earlier that many businesses have distanced non-core activities – such as catering and cleaning – allocating them to external contractors. Similarly, technically specialized functions, such as the management of computer and telecommunications networks, have been subcontracted to specialist firms.

A modern flexible organization may adopt a structure along the lines of Handy's three-leaf 'shamrock' model (Handy, 1989, p.70):

- A professional core made up of managers, technicians, and qualified specialists.
- Contractors providing non-core activities, who are not direct employees of the organization.
- The flexible labour force composed of part-timers, temporary staff, consultants and contract staff performing tasks as and when required.

The allocation of work between the 'leaves' of the shamrock organization is generally decided upon at a senior level. The implications are considerable, often requiring main board approval, particularly for the employment of subcontractors. The decision to 'outsource' activities is usually taken on purely financial grounds, leaving people managers to clear up the resulting employee relations mess.

Key concept 13.2 Grow or buy?

Organizations can focus on internal or external job markets, or draw from both. Firms with an internal focus recruit at junior levels and 'grow' their employees into valuable assets through training, development and experience in the organization. Alternatively, companies can buy talent at a variety of levels from the external employment market. A mixed strategy offers a balance of continuity and commitment from long-term staff together with fresh ideas from imported 'new blood'.

Resourcing strategies

Most large organizations employ human resource or personnel specialists to conduct or, at least, coordinate employee resourcing. This is a role that has long been regarded as part of the domain of personnel management (Iles and Mabey, 1992, p.255) and personnel textbooks conventionally describe resourcing as a passive, technical procedure – a matching of available candidates to the requirements of the organization. In fact, successful recruitment must be proactive. Organizations can take one of three actions to fulfil their employee resourcing needs:

1 *Reallocate tasks* between employees, so that existing staff take on more or different work. This may be part of an organizational change programme, such as restructuring or reorganization. The emphasis is on flexible working practices, requiring multi-skilled workers and sophisticated assessment and development programmes.

2 *Reallocate people* from the internal employment market, through promotion or transfer between different departments. Traditionally, German and Japanese organizations have filled their supervisory and management posts from existing staff. Large Japanese organizations expect their potential managers to move between different functions during their careers. Japanese human resource managers, for instance, are likely to have worked in finance, production and marketing rather than specializing in 'personnel'.

3 *Recruit* new staff from the external job market. Countries in the free market tradition have focused most of their resourcing activities on bringing in people from outside the organization. Employers have a choice between:

   – *Recruiting anybody and everybody.* Until comparatively recently, many workers in heavy industry were employed casually at the factory gate. In many parts of the world construction labourers and seasonal agricultural workers continue to be taken on in a casual fashion. With no commitment on either side, a rigid chain of command then rules. This approach predominates for employment at low skill and wage levels. It is especially common in small low-technology companies.
   – *Recruiting selectively.* Skilled and motivated workers are selected. These employees can be allowed to get on with the job with only broad guidelines or a policy framework to observe. This approach predominates in large organizations. The result has been the creation of an internal and external recruitment industry, including selection experts, recruitment consultants and headhunters.

External recruitment has the virtue of bringing in a wider range of experience but limits career opportunities for existing employees. It is predominantly a free market approach to resourcing but even Japanese businesses have begun to recruit externally, particularly for scarce technological skills such as computer programming. *Heddo-hantas* have become common in Japan, recruiting for small- to medium-sized enterprises and foreign companies (Whitehill, 1991, p.129).

Types of resourcing strategy

Resourcing is a dynamic process: the movement of human resources through an organization. In terms of systems theory this can be represented as input; throughput; and output.

Businesses can assign people largely from existing staff or from the external job market. Companies that focus on internal supply are likely to view people as assets, carrying long-term value, rather than as costs. This is in line with practice in social market and Japanese organizations. It also reflects the spirit of the Harvard model of HRM discussed in Chapter 2. In essence the choice is between 'growing' or 'buying' (see Key concept 13.2). 'Growing' is the central theme of human resource development discussed in Chapter 20. Needless to say, firms in free markets such as the UK and the USA have a tendency to 'buy' – and dispose – of employees as required.

Choices between 'growing' or 'buying' can be related to environmental conditions and organizational culture. In an early discussion of human resource strategy, Miles and Snow (1978) devised a typology based on the degree of risk taken by businesses in stable or unstable environments. They classified organizations as defenders, prospectors, analysers and reactors. A similar typology by Sonnenfeld, Peiperl and Kotter (1988) shown in Table 13.1 uses slightly more dramatic terminology: clubs, baseball teams, fortresses and academies.

Defenders. These are firms with small niche markets or narrow product ranges. As organizations they have an equally narrow focus, requiring stability and reliability. They need loyal employees with a long-term commitment. Staff enter at junior levels and are 'made' into worthwhile employees through extensive training and career development along largely functional routes. Incremental growth allows for new career opportunities within an internal job market grounded in a strong culture. Loyalty and commitment are encouraged through performance assessment based on behavioural compliance characteristics. Staff turnover is low, partly because employees are chained by organization-specific skills and a degree of institutionalization. This strategy is employed by 'clubs' in Sonnenfeld *et al.*'s (1988) classification.

Prospectors. Innovative firms, moving in and out of markets to capitalize on opportunities and avoid competition. Top management consider themselves to be dynamic. Equating to Sonnenfeld *et al.*'s 'baseball teams', they are typical of sports and entertainment businesses. The instability of their market-place requires constant flexibility and environmental scanning. In the eyes of 1970s and 1980s theorists, locked into the 'right person' recruitment models that we will discuss shortly, this could only be met by buying rather than making talent. Uncertainty does not allow for career systems, the focus being on recruitment from the external job market. New recruits have to be able to 'hit the ground running' (Rousseau, 1995, p.188). Rewards are high and geared to immediate results. However, commitment is low on both sides of the employment relationship: recruits are seen as 'passing through'. Learning is personal rather than organizational and knowledge leaves with the employee.

Analysers. These firms are cautious innovators, waiting for prospectors to open up new markets before entering themselves. Analyser organizations are structured into stable and efficient production units with highly flexible and responsive marketing or service

Type	Characteristics	Key HR function	Sectors	
1 Academies	Active growers Low staff turnover Long-term service	Development	Office products Pharmaceuticals Electronics	**Table 13.1**
2 Clubs	Passive growers Seniority Commitment Status Equal treatment	Retention or 'maintenance'	Public utilities Government Insurance Military	Resourcing strategies **Source** Based on Sonnenfeld *et al.* (1988).
3 Baseball teams	Active buyers Staff identify with profession more than firm	Recruitment of star performers	Accounting Law Consulting Software Advertising	
4 Fortresses	Cautious buyers Survival Cost-cutting	Recruitment of generalists Redundancies	Publishing Textiles Retailing Hotels	

units. They emphasize quality and skill and equate to Sonnenfeld *et al.*'s 'academies'. As hybrids they take a mixed approach to making and buying employees: stable business units rely on internal promotion and development; flexible units buy in expertise as and when required.

Reactors. These are 'fortresses' in Sonnenfeld *et al.*'s classification: failed defenders, analysers or prospectors, desperately attempting to survive. Their strategies are often incoherent, unable to 'make' employees but often 'buying' and selling. In their attempts to recover or instigate the 'turnaround' changes discussed in Chapter 12, the emphasis is likely to be on redundancies.

Human resource planning

For resourcing strategies to be implemented they must be translated into practical action. The strategic process can be organized logically – for example, following the decision sequence shown in Figure 13.1. For these decisions to be taken, information must be obtained, consequences gauged, political soundings taken and preferences assessed.

It is clear that many of these decisions are fundamental to an organization. If the implications are major, strategic decisions are taken at the centre of the business. The role of the human resource function is two-fold:

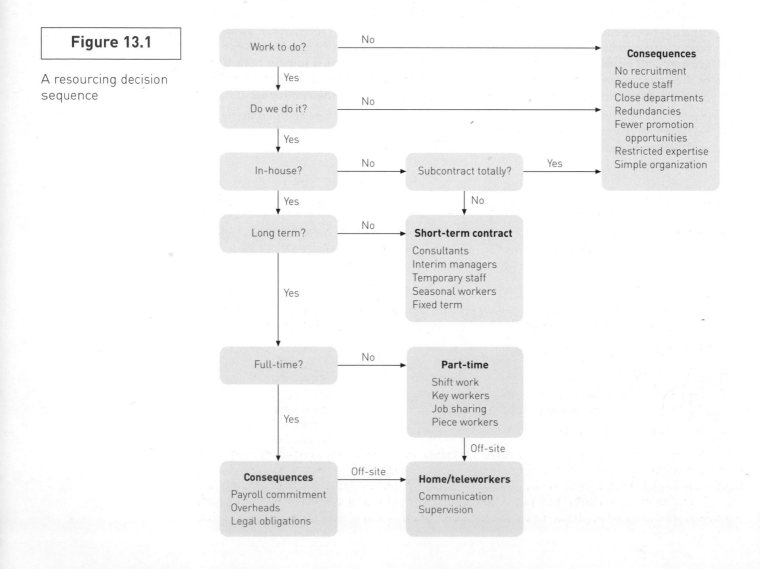

Figure 13.1

A resourcing decision sequence

1 To participate in the decision process by providing information and opinion on each option, including:

   – redundancy or recruitment costs
   – consequences on morale
   – redeployment/outplacement opportunities
   – availability of skilled staff within the organization
   – availability of suitable people in the job market
   – time constraints
   – development/training needs/schedules
   – management requirements.

   This forms part of the information collated from the organization as a whole.

2 To support line managers dealing with the people consequences of implementing the decision. Information already gathered provides the basis for a human resource plan.

In other instances, decisionmaking has consequences of lesser significance to the business. Resourcing decisions taken at an operational level may lead from departmental expansion or cost-saving, transfer of activities, new product ranges and comparatively small changes in function. In practice, therefore, **human resource planning** has short, medium, and long-term aspects (see Key concept 13.3).

Older texts refer to this topic as '**manpower planning**'. (Presumably 'womanpower planning' was not much different!) Use of this quaint term has declined – but not disappeared – in favour of human resource planning (HRP). Some authors distinguish between manpower planning and HRP as distinct approaches (Hendry, 1995, p.190).

Key concept 13.3 Human resource planning

A process that anticipates and maps out the consequences of business strategy on an organization's human resource requirements. This is reflected in planning of skill and competence needs as well as total headcounts.

Key concept 13.4 Manpower planning

'A strategy for the acquisition, utilization, improvement and retention of an enterprise's human resources.' Anonymous government publication cited in Pratt and Bennett (1989, p. 101).

Primarily a 'numbers game', manpower planning emphasized accurate personnel records and forecasting techniques (see Key concept 13.4). It focused on questions such as:

- How many staff do we have/need?
- How are they distributed?
- What is the age profile?
- How many will leave in each of the next five years?
- How many will be required in one, five, ten years?

O'Doherty (1997) argues that although simple workforce headcount predictions may have been undertaken by most companies, the use of detailed manpower forecasts was confined to large-scale organizations such as the public services, the armed forces, postal services and major banking groups. Corbridge and Pilbeam (1998) note that specialist planners in such organizations devised complex mathematical models but this was often an unreal process that attracted criticism.

Some authors see little difference between HRP and manpower planning. For example Graham and Bennett (1992, p.172) define human resource planning as:

... an attempt to forecast how many and what kind of employees will be required in the future, and to what extent this demand is likely to be met. It involves the comparison of an organization's current human resources with likely future needs and, consequently, the establishment of programmes for hiring, training, redeploying and possibly discarding employees. Effective HRP should result in the right people doing the right things in the right place at precisely the right time.

The manpower planning approach regards the human resource manager as a personnel technician. Within this framework, the function of the human resource planner is to provide 'management' with the necessary advice to make decisions on issues such as:

- recruitment
- avoiding redundancies
- training – numbers and categories
- management development
- estimates of 'labour' costs
- productivity bargaining
- accommodation requirements.

In this tradition, Graham and Bennett (1992, p.175) envisage a long-term human resource plan as a detailed specification, by location, function and job category of the number of employees 'it is practicable to employ at various stages in the future' (see Table 13.2). A plan should include:

- jobs that will come into being, be ceased, or changed
- possibilities for redeployment and retraining
- changes in management and supervision
- training requirements
- programmes for recruitment, redundancy and early retirement
- implications for employee relations
- a feedback mechanism to company objectives
- methods for dealing with HR problems such as inability to obtain sufficient technically skilled workers.

Such a plan requires organization, belief in the process and detailed information. Not surprisingly, many organizations cannot meet these criteria. Tyson (1995, p.77), reporting on a study of 30 large UK-based organizations, found that most had plans of three to five years' duration. Shorter-term plans were used by some retail firms that kept detail down to a year or so, whereas capital-intensive firms were more likely to favour long-term planning. Generally, managers were unhappy about five-year plans, regarding them as 'a constraint on business'. Tyson (1995, p.80) identifies three distinct approaches to planning:

Formal, long-range planning. Creating a planning framework, usually expressed in financial terms with verbal commentaries. Notably, all the companies studied that used this approach consulted widely with interest groups.

Flexible strategies. Covering most of the organizations studied. Plans changed frequently in response to market changes. Plans were intentionally short-term, often with minimal written detail.

Attributional strategies. 'One step at a time'. Previous actions can be rationalized but, in truth, organizations using this approach are cautious and are not really committed to any specific strategy. This can be compared with Mintzberg's concept of 'emergent strategies' discussed in the previous chapter.

In general it is worth observing (Price, 2000) that:

Modern human resource planners have tended to move away from predicting headcounts towards building 'what if' models or scenarios which allow the implications of different strategies to be debated. However, traditional HR planning techniques have become considerably easier to implement with the spread of Human Resource Information Systems which trap key employee information and generate reports and analyses as a matter of course.

People as numbers

Generally, it is accepted that modern human resource planning should have a wider perspective, in tune with the philosophy of HRM, including 'softer' issues such as competence, commitment and career development. Modern human resource planning continues to use the 'hard' techniques of manpower planning but also includes a new focus on shaping values, beliefs and culture, anticipating strategy, market conditions and demographic change.

Nevertheless, in line with the tradition of formal, observable and 'objective' planning, numerical measurement and forecasting have been favoured over qualitative studies of

Step	Aspects
1 Create a company HRP group	This should include the main functional managers of the company, together with human resource specialists.
2 State the organization's human resource objectives	Within the context of the overall business objectives and considering: – capital equipment plans – reorganization such as centralization or decentralization – changes in products or in output – marketing plans – financial limitations
3 Audit present utilization of human resources	Sometimes described as the 'internal manpower audit', detailing: – number of employees in various categories – an estimate of employee turnover for each grade, analysing the effects of high or low turnover on performance – amount of overtime worked – assessment of performance and potential of current employees – comparison of payment levels with local firms.
4 Assess the external environment	Placing the organization in its business context in terms of: – the recruitment position – population trends – local housing and transport plans – national agreements dealing with conditions of work – government policies in education, retirement, regional subsidies, and so on.
5 Assess potential supply of labour ('external manpower audit')	Including: – local population movements (emigration and immigration) – recruitment and redundancy by other firms – employing new work categories – e.g. part-time workers – productivity improvements, working hours and practices.

Table 13.2

Steps for long-term human resource planning

Source Based on Graham and Bennett (1992, p.174).

opinion, attitude and motivation. 'Hard' data allows managers and planners to sit in their offices and wait for information. 'No need to go out and meet the troops, or the customers, to find out how the products get bought ... all that just wastes valuable time'

HRM in reality Employee retention problems in China

Companies in China are struggling to retain their professional and support staff, and face having to pay higher salaries or excessive recruitment costs, according to research by Mercer Human Resource Consulting, a global leader for HR and related financial advice and services.

The China Employee Attraction and Retention Survey 2006 covered 114 organizations in Greater China, many of which are multinationals. About one-quarter (24 per cent) were from the high-tech industry. Other major industries included were consumer (19 per cent), chemical (14 per cent), pharmaceutical (11 per cent), automotive (8 per cent), and service (6 per cent).

The survey found that 54 per cent of organizations have experienced an increase in turnover for professional staff since the previous year, while 42 per cent have reported higher turnover for support staff. The survey also reveals that the average tenure for the age group most targeted by multinational companies (25–35 year-olds) fell from an average of 3–5 years in 2004 to just 1–2 years in 2005.

Fermin Diez, national business leader of human capital at Mercer Aus/NZ, said:

> The employment market in China has ignited in recent years, as more multinational organizations set up operations there and local companies expand. Individuals with transferable skills have become a valuable commodity, and companies are battling to keep hold of them. When employees threaten to walk out of the door, many companies respond by throwing more money at them. While this can sometimes work in the short term, more often than not a competitor is willing to pay just as much. Companies are starting to realize they need to be more sophisticated in their approach to employee attraction and retention. Those that offer variable pay, promote 'softer' benefits like flexible working and provide meaningful career opportunities, are most likely to keep hold of their best employees.

The survey found that 83 per cent of organizations offer healthcare and related insurance, while 41 per cent provide health and fitness plans and 24 per cent offer flexible working. Just 21 per cent offer supplementary pension plans and 10 per cent provide subsidized loans. Results also show that 44 per cent of organizations believe their employees are dissatisfied with the benefits offered.

Overseas assignments are felt to be the most effective tool for career development, although only 42 per cent of organizations offer such opportunities. Individual career development plans, offered by 51 per cent of companies, are also believed to be effective. In contrast, mentorship programmes are considered relatively ineffective and are offered by just one-quarter (26 per cent) of companies.

Fermin Diez said:

> Attractive pay and benefits and opportunities for career development are rated as the most important factors for attracting and retaining employees. Companies that offer structured overseas assignment programmes and individual career development plans demonstrate a willingness to invest in staff, and this can pay dividends.

He added:

> High-profile multinational organizations with strong employment brands typically provide more career opportunities and better training and mentoring programmes than many domestic companies in China. Employees tend to be attracted to these organizations because of the prospects they offer and the kudos associated with working for them.

According to the survey, the top five methods for attracting and retaining staff in China are: attractive salary and benefits package (23 per cent); opportunities for career development (19 per cent); meaningful and creative work (7 per cent); unique organizational culture (7 per cent); and company location (3 per cent). Organizations report that the average cost of replacing staff at any level is around 25–50 per cent of annual salary.

Fermin Diez commented:

> Many organizations in China underestimate the true cost of replacing staff, particularly at more senior levels. Taking account of all the elements that contribute to turnover cost, like recruitment agency fees, interviewing time, and loss of sales while positions remain unfilled, employers can face bills of over 200 per cent of salary for senior staff.

Companies in China need to be more sophisticated in their approach to employee attraction and retention. What factors should they focus on?

Source: *HRM Guide* (http://www.hrmguide.net/), 5 September, 2006.

(Mintzberg, 1994, p.258). The growth of information technology and management information systems has made numerical data readily available and possibly further discouraged collection of qualitative information. Numbers give a comforting feeling of unarguable objectivity and allow managers to detach themselves from shopfloor emotions. It is much easier to sack a number than a real human being.

Forecasting methods

Human resource planners have a choice of techniques available to them, for example:

Extrapolation. This method assumes that the past is a reliable guide to the future. Various techniques are suitable for short- and medium-term forecasting, such as time series, trend analysis and measures of cyclical requirements. Since they rely on present knowledge and cannot take the unpredictable into account, forecasts are best in a stable environment. They tend to do little harm if kept pessimistic, but enthusiasm and political considerations often lead to overestimation. This can have expensive consequences.

Projected production/sales information. As a normal part of the planning process, production, sales and marketing departments will prepare their own forecasts. Intelligent use of this data, taking the introduction of new technology and quality improvements into account, will provide an estimate of the quantity and nature of the human resources needed. Work study, managerial judgement and a certain amount of scepticism – particularly regarding sales forecasts – can be used to transform this information into employee requirements.

Employee analysis. Modern computer packages offer extensive possibilities for **employee analysis;** modelling the total profile of an organization's human resources. Employees can be classified in a variety of ways, such as function, department or grade. Age and length of service are important predictors of future availability. Skills levels and training or development needs can be compared with annual performance assessments.

Scenario building. Scenarios are not strictly forecasts but speculations on the future. It is impossible to predict what will happen in 20 – or even five – years' time, but it is possible to describe some alternatives. Working through a variety of possible states can identify the uncertainties, help us gain an understanding of the main driving factors and produce a range of options. Given the dramatic changes and discontinuities experienced today, scenario building seems to be one of the most realistic and useful forms of planning. Instead of prescribing detailed plans, the process allows strategists to work through the consequences for resources and costs of different courses of action.

Employee turnover

In recent years managers have been preoccupied with reducing the size of the workforce, closing plants and encouraging people to leave. In times of economic growth the emphasis changes to retaining the people with required skills. Human resource planning has a role in anticipating wastage. In its 'manpower planning' days, it received considerable attention from planners for whom 'the statistical possibilities' were enormous (Pratt and Bennett, 1989, p.106). **Turnover** covers the whole input-output process from recruitment to dismissal or retirement and takes the consequences of promotion and transfer into account. Wastage deals only with leavers. Its importance lies in the freedom of employees to leave when they choose and hence its relatively uncontrollable nature for employers.

Control of staff turnover or wastage is critical when there is a general skills shortage. Ahlrichs (2000, p.2) comments that:

> Employers have not ignored the hiring and retention crisis, but their choice of responses has been inadequate at best and off-target at worst. Misled by memories of applicants lined up outside the door, they have focused on the recruiting portion of the problem and largely ignored retention.

They have regarded employees as mere lists of hard skills, as plug-in parts who are interchangeable as long as the resumé matches the job description. They continue to hound their HR departments for more and better candidates while ignoring the cost of turnover and HR's strategies to bond with, develop, and retain existing employees.

Early work by Rice, Hull and Trist (1950) identified three main phases of turnover:

1 *Induction crisis*. Individuals who leave shortly after joining an organization: uncommitted employees tend to leave in the first few months. Recent research appears to show that there are several kinds of induction crisis experienced in different ways in different organizations.

Forecasting and reality

> Instruments may be made by which the largest ships, with only one man guiding them, will be carried with greater velocity than if they were full of sailors. Chariots . . . will move with incredible rapidity without the help of animals. Instruments of flying may be formed in which a man, sitting at his ease . . . may beat the air with his artificial wings after the manner of birds . . . also machines . . . will enable men to walk at the bottom of the seas. (Roger Bacon c.1214–92)

Planners attempt to anticipate future events but few strategists are likely to equal Bacon's powerful imagination. For most of us crystal-ball gazing or prediction is fraught with difficulty. Arthur C. Clarke (1973), a noted science fiction writer who invented the concept of satellite communications, concluded that 'it is impossible to predict the future . . . all attempts to do so in any detail appear ludicrous within a few years'. In the table we can see that many of today's major industrial products were not expected. Nevertheless, many management texts insist that the future should be anticipated and planned for: it is assumed that we have a good appreciation of what the next few years will bring us. This means that the training and development of tomorrow's managers is geared to the requirements of the future as we see them now.

Normative models tend to suggest that strategic decisionmaking is an entirely rational and orderly process: what *ought* to happen. Usually, of course, events get in the way and there will be some variation from intended strategy. As we saw in Part two, the business environment is complex and uncertain. It is impossible to predict the future with any degree of precision. Prediction is a dangerous business because it relies mainly on what has already happened. It depends on information that might be incomplete or inaccurate. Circumstances can change quickly. For example, it is probably just as well that the renowned Dr R. Woolley, space 'expert' and Astronomer Royal, was not employed as a strategist at NASA. In 1956 he confidently announced that 'Space travel is utter bilge' – the first satellite, Sputnik 1 was launched in the following year!

The expected and the unexpected

Unexpected	Expected	Still expected?
X-rays	Cars	Teleportation
Nuclear energy	Flying machines	Invisibility
Relativity	Robots	Time travel
Radio, TV	Telephones	Telepathy
Photography	Steam engines	
Sound recording	Submarines	
Electronics	Spaceships	

Source: Adapted from Clarke (1973, p.38).

2 *Differential transit.* During the first year or so, when some employees conclude that the organization is an unsuitable career vehicle or source of income.

3 *Settled connection.* Becoming a long-term 'stayer'.

Despite the increase in flexible approaches to employment and the demise of the 'job for life' this pattern remains common. Dibble (1999, p.19) suggests a working assumption that a company's employee population follows a normal distribution:

- Crucial to the organization's success, so we want to do everything we can to keep them (3 per cent).

- Very important and we are willing to do a lot to keep them (15 per cent).

- Employees we are happy to have and whose requests we will try hard to accommodate (68 per cent).

- Need to improve or leave (13 per cent).

- In a process leading to termination of employment (3 per cent).

HRM in reality Attracting and keeping top employees is still difficult

Most HR executives find attracting and retaining talent to be a big problem, according to a study, *Sustaining The Talent Quest: Getting and Keeping the Best People in Volatile Times* from The Conference Board. Some 90 per cent of the 109 surveyed executives said that they were finding it difficult to attract and keep the best people for their organization.

Respondents cited corporate turmoil and limited career opportunities as the key reasons for unwanted turnover. Non-competitive pay and benefits are also barriers.

David Dell of The Conference Board, co-author of the report with Jack Hickey, Research Consultant, The Conference Board said:

> While labour shortages in the 1990s were driven by technology skills and initiatives, employers are currently putting a high premium on general leadership competency.
>
> For this reason, the quest for top-flight talent has to be the job of everyone within an organization from CEO to junior employee. Even with unlimited funding and resources and the best intentions and programs, HR cannot conquer a turnover problem alone. Success requires a corporate-wide integrated recruitment and retention strategy that can respond quickly to change. Most companies still take a shotgun approach to keeping employees happy, and most still consider their efforts too reactive, especially in regard to retention.

Behaviours that can drive away talent
These include:

Failure to make talent supply a long-term strategic priority. New technology and tools are now available to address getting and keeping talent, but if HR is not actively engaged in the planning process and does not receive corporate commitment from the top, the supply of talented employees will almost certainly be limited to *ad hoc* clusters of programmes and boom-and-bust cycles of hiring and reductions that waste talent and inevitably cost more.

Not making the business case on turnover. Senior managers are not likely to recognize and treat employee turnover as a problem if they do not understand how it affects their business. HR executives need to quantify relevant costs and benefits in clear, concrete terms.

Just throw money at the problem. Pay and benefits are not the only reasons why employees leave their jobs. But companies frequently raise or sweeten the compensation package when valued employees look like leaving, even when compensation is not ranked among the most important staff turnover factors. This response is likely to be inadequate.

Organizational denial. Employers should acknowledge that employees' first loyalty is to themselves, followed by their craft or professional skills. Companies have to be aware that people make decisions to leave or stay not only on their career prospects with their current employers but also on how it might prepare them to move on elsewhere.

Translating turnover into numbers that executives understand is not only essential because they need to appreciate the true costs, but also because they have the solutions within their spheres of control. Individual managers control skills, behaviour and job design and are 'fairly inaccessible to HR's intervention'. But, although HR may take the lead on attacking turnover,

▶

responsibility for their own turnover numbers and any behaviours that may cause employees to leave the firm have to be delegated to line managers.

The HR executives surveyed cite five major objectives for their staffing management activities:

- organizational stability
- opportunities for career and personal development
- multi-level involvement and accountability for talent
- integrated talent strategies
- emphasis on employer brand and reputation.

Keeping the best talent

Companies are increasingly using the internet and intranets/enterprise portals to manage part, at least, of the recruitment and retention process. Web-based HR systems have often become the key to broader outreach strategies – they are especially cost-effective in accessing passive jobseekers, college students, and minorities.

E-recruiting is particularly efficient in cost and time, eliminating expensive headhunters and agencies and may significantly reduce the duration of the recruiting cycle. Speed matters, with each day of delay in hiring meaning a loss of potential revenue from a new employee. Online recruiting also vastly expands employers' access to some of the most desirable segments of the talent market – even high-level executives.

E-recruiting gathers more candidate information and makes it easier and cheaper to gather, track, organize and store applicant data. It is especially valuable for highly competitive campus recruiting, appealing to college students as leading-edge and dynamic.

Why is it becoming increasingly difficult to attract and retain talent?

Source: *HRM Guide USA* (http://www.hrmguide.net/usa/), 15 September, 2002.

The degree of wastage can be determined by a variety of turnover indices of varying sophistication. Three examples are:

1 The British Institute of Management (BIM) Index (annual labour turnover)

$$\frac{\text{Leavers in year}}{\text{Average number of staff in post that year}} \times 100 = \% \text{ wastage}$$

2 Cohort analysis – a survival curve is drawn of employees taken on at the same time to determine what happens to a group.

3 Census method – for example, providing a histogram of the length of employee service.

An annual survey conducted by the Chartered Institute of Personnel and Development (CIPD, 2006) found that turnover increased from 16 to 18 per cent in 2005. Losing staff, whatever the cause, is expensive. Overall, the average cost of turnover per employee (including any redundancy cost) was £8200, rising to £12 000 for managers and professionals.

'Soft' planning

HRM implies that planning has to go beyond the 'numbers game' into the softer areas of employee attitudes, behaviour and commitment. These aspects are critical to HR development, performance assessment and the management of change which are considered in some depth in Chapters 20, 18 and 12, respectively. At this point, we can consider an outline of the 'soft' planning process:

1 *Where are we now?* Information needs to be gathered through some form of human resource audit. This can be linked to a conventional SWOT analysis of the organization's human capital:
   - *strengths* such as existing skills, individual expertise and unused talents
   - *weaknesses*, including inadequate skills, talents that are missing in the workforce because they are too expensive, inflexible people and 'dead wood'
   - *opportunities*, such as experience that can be developed in existing staff and talent that can be bought from the external job market
   - *threats*, including the risk of talent being lost to competitors.

2 *Where do we want to be?* Essentially, a clear strategic vision and a set of objectives.

3 *What do we need to do?* For example, following the logical sequence in Figure 13.1 decisions must be made on the use of in-house or external staff (see Table 13.3).

4 *Devise an action plan.* Some kind of resource planning is used by as many as 60 per cent of large organizations but it has to be conceded that it is often done poorly. Ideally, it should be linked to corporate strategy but corporate planners tend to ignore the human dimension.

Iles (2001, p.139) argues that the extension of human resource planning to include 'soft' issues such as motivation, commitment and culture has its dangers since it:

... tends to conflate HRP with HRM as a whole, and takes the specificity away from HRP as a discrete dimension of employee resourcing concerned with forecasting and assessing the extent to

In-house resources	Outsourcing	**Table 13.3**
Management control	Legal contract	In-house and external human resources
Long-term people (can be developed; build experience; understand organization)	Focus on paying only for work you need	
	No extra pay/commitment	
People are hassle		
Contractual arrangements (talent expensive; overheads; large structure; hierarchy; support systems)	Range of options, e.g. consultants (variable expertise; expensive) or contingent workers (usually ex-managers; best for operational work) or homeworkers (lower level/specialist; low overheads; supervision issues) or sub-contracting	
People are ambitious (require advancement; can go elsewhere – taking knowledge)		

HRM in reality Holding on to talent 'top of mind' for Australian employers in 2006: Hudson Report

Holding on to existing employees is the highest priority for Australian organizations in 2006, according to the latest results from the Hudson Report, released by Hudson, a leading recruitment, outsourcing and human resource consulting firm. The Hudson Report found that 39 per cent of Australian employers identified 'staff development and retention' as their organization's leading priority for the year as the battle for suitably qualified workers intensifies.

Based on a survey of 8693 employers across Australia, the report indicates that a further 23 per cent considered 'attracting suitable staff' as their highest HR priority for this year. This was followed by 'enhancing performance and productivity', highlighted by 21 per cent of respondents.

Anne Hatton, CEO of Hudson Australia/New Zealand, said that as the talent pool in Australia continues to shrink, there is more pressure than ever to hold on to strong performers. 'Organizations need to get on the front foot and look at more sophisticated ways to track, manage and develop their existing talent.

They could otherwise face significant costs in staff losses at a time when they just cannot afford to let this happen,' Anne Hatton said.

The results also show that 'attracting suitable staff' has overtaken 'enhancing performance and productivity' as the second highest priority for employers this year, when compared with 2005 priorities.

'As the skills shortage gets worse, and businesses undertake more proactive employee retention strategies, sourcing suitably qualified and experienced staff will be more challenging,' said Hatton. 'Smart employers will reap the benefits of a diverse workforce, including part-time workers, return-to-work parents or the mature age population, but will need to ensure the right policies and practices are in place to accommodate these workers,' she added.

What would you consider to be a 'proactive' HR planning policy?

Source: *HRM Guide Australia* (http://www.hrmguide.net/australia), 3 February, 2006.

which the organization will meet its labour requirements (or perhaps increasingly its knowledge requirements, which may take the focus of HRP away from labour supply concerns to an interest in knowledge supply, and away from focusing on employees alone to emphasizing knowledge resources, chains and intermediaries).

HRM in reality Strategic workforce planning

A study from The Conference Board reports that the ageing workforce and an emerging retirement wave among 'baby boomers' are driving more businesses toward 'strategic workforce planning'.

Strategic workforce planning is a new approach to traditional human resource planning that involves analyzing and forecasting the talent required by organizations to meet the objectives of their business strategies. It helps:

- control employee costs
- assess talent needs
- make informed business decisions such as whether it's more cost effective to outsource an activity or add full-time employees
- assess human-capital needs and risks.

In short, according to the study, *Strategic Workforce Planning: Forecasting Human Capital Needs to Execute Business Strategy*, strategic workforce planning is aimed at helping businesses ensure they have the right people in the right place at the right time and at the right price.

'In many companies, traditional workforce planning was an onerous process that HR imposed on management,' said Mary B. Young, senior research associate, The Conference Board and author of the report. 'Too often, the net result was a humongous report, blinding spreadsheets, and a dizzying amount of data that provided very little value to the business.'

Methodology has moved on to meet changing business needs, new tools and technology. The study shows that some businesses have enhanced the simple gap analysis (workforce demand versus supply) used for traditional 'manpower' planning by adopting the logic and analytical tools of other management functions, including finance, strategic planning, risk management and marketing.

Rather than focusing on spreadsheets, the planning process needs to concentrate on the business plan and its implications for the workforce. Consistent, organization-wide data is essential. Other critical areas identified in the study include:

- making the process and tools simple and efficient
- developing HR's capabilities and comfort level

- establishing a common language to describe jobs and required competencies
- integrating workforce planning with business and budget planning
- driving the plan deep into the organization.

While most companies in the study are finding their way in the process, strategic human resource planning can deliver value already through:

- generating insights and knowledge to help managers make business decisions
- providing a deeper and more subtle understanding of workforce dynamics than was previously available
- enabling more efficient human capital management, for example by evaluating different staffing options for their long-term impacts or creating a stronger internal job market
- enabling the HR function to achieve a long-held desire to become a player and a valued contributor at a higher level of strategic management.

'Strategic workforce planning enables the organization to slice-and-dice its workforce data to discover critical issues, compare different groups, understand patterns and trends, home in on critical segments of the workforce such as mature workers and top performers, and customize its approach to managing different segments of its workforce,' said Mary Young. 'By enabling leaders to see across lines of business, workforce planning can leverage talent within a company. Ultimately, the same workforce planning database tools will enable employees to shop for new jobs, assess their own developmental needs, and prepare for career moves inside the organization.'

Some of the techniques adopted by companies exampled in the study include:

A workforce analytics approach: mining both current and historical workforce data to identify the key relationships among the variables and between employee and business data. Dow Chemical has used this approach throughout a 10-year evolution of its workforce planning process.

Forecasting and scenario modeling: using data to create forecasts that incorporate multiple what-if scenarios. These enable executives to evaluate strategic options. The study describes how a 'major bank' decides where to locate a new call centre based partly on this approach.

Human capital planning: used by Corning and others to segment jobs on a basis of their 'mission-criticality', making different levels of workforce investment in each segment. This approach focuses on broad 3–4 year trends, rather than precise headcounts and short-term plans.

Hewlett-Packard and IBM are cited as being committed to strategic workforce planning, customizing the process to address each company's specific conditions and needs. IBM's HR and finance departments help senior business leaders prepare realistic plans to execute their business strategy and manage drivers of employee costs. At HP, the study states that high-level discussions and a two-way educational process between business leaders and HR emphasizes qualitative over quantitative factors.

'While no organization claims to have achieved it yet, many believe that the ultimate payoff from strategic workforce planning will be a vibrant, internal job market that transcends the boundaries between business units and geographies,' concluded Young. 'The company will be able to mine employee data to locate talent anywhere in the organization, woo passive job candidates, and find the best use for each employee.'

How would you distinguish strategic workforce planning from traditional HR planning?

Source: *HRM Guide USA* (http://www.hrmguide.com), 8 August, 2006.

Resourcing information

Effective in-house resourcing requires accurate and comprehensive information. Strategies and human resource plans must be translated into actual jobs and people found or developed to perform them. Some basic questions can be asked:

- What tasks are involved?
- What skills or competencies are required to do the work?
- Are they to be found within the organization?
- If not, should extra people be recruited?

Researching the job

Conventionally, the first question is answered by a **job analysis** (Key concept 13.5). Reminiscent of Taylor's techniques of 'scientific management', discussed in Part one, it is a more-or-less detailed examination of the sub-tasks within an identified job. Jobs vary between the 'crystallized', such as manufacturing assembly where the job is precisely defined, to managerial and professional jobs in which individuals have considerable freedom to vary their work (McCormick and Ilgen, 1987, p.38). The degree of freedom is determined partly by technology or personal expertise and partly by the organization. Job analysis is geared towards tasks that are already being done in some form or can be easily extrapolated from current activities.

Key concept 13.5 Job analysis

The process of job analysis is that of gathering and analysing job-related information. This includes details about tasks to be performed as part of a job and the personal qualities required to do them. Job analysis can provide information for a variety of purposes including: determining training needs, development criteria, and appropriate pay and productivity improvements. For resourcing purposes, job analysis can generate job and personnel specifications.

Job analysis techniques vary from the rudimentary to the sophisticated. The latter require specialist skills and are more commonly used in the USA where equal opportunities legislation is more stringent than in most countries. Long-regarded as a somewhat tedious aspect of the personnel or work study function, job analysis has been highlighted as a valuable technique in ensuring compliance with anti-discrimination legislation in the USA. Conversely, the move towards flexible working has deterred many organizations in other countries from closely defining jobs.

The simplest forms of job analysis are conducted by observing or interviewing existing jobholders and supervisors. Alternatively, the same people can produce a self-report according to an agreed format. Information is also available from records, 'experts', training materials, equipment descriptions and manuals. A basic six-step approach could be conducted as follows (Smith and Robertson, 1993, p.15):

1 Make use of relevant existing documents such as training manuals.
2 Ask the line manager responsible about the main purposes of the job, the tasks involved and the links with other people.
3 Ask the same questions of jobholders, preferably backed by a detailed activity record over a week or two.
4 Where possible, sit in and observe jobholders at work – preferably on more than one day and at different times.
5 Try to do the job yourself. (This is not possible if specialist machinery or training are required.)
6 Write the job description.

The job-related information produced by job analysis can be arranged according to a number of headings (see Table 13.4) to ensure that all relevant details are covered.

This method is cheap and relatively easy. However, more complex methods may be justified, such as:

1 Questionnaires, generally purchased 'off-the-shelf' from specialist companies. Questionnaire techniques can provide a wealth of information but are often expensive and time-consuming. Examples include:
   – McCormick's position analysis questionnaire (PAQ). Worldwide, probably the best known. It includes 150 scales with benchmarks covering a variety of jobs (McCormick and Ilgen, 1987, p.44).
   – The work profiling system (WPS) is a modern, computerized and professionally packaged questionnaire system produced by Saville and Holdsworth. This is made up of three overlapping tests, each of 300–400 items. The package is analysed by computer to give a detailed job description and a profile of the ideal recruit.
2 The **critical incidents technique** can provide a rich, qualitative perspective on a job. Incumbents are asked to describe a number of specific real-life incidents in which they participated. The most effective incidents are those which detail qualities required to do the job well.

Job analysis is not a value-free source of information. Employees are prone to:

Exaggeration. Making jobs seem more demanding or complex than they really are.

Omission. Humdrum tasks are forgotten in favour of less frequent but more interesting activities.

In contrast, information given by supervisors may lead to:

Understatement. Jobs are portrayed as being easier and less complex than they are in reality.

Misunderstanding. Frequently bosses do not know workers' jobs in any detail.

The various systems of job analysis also differ in the kind of information collected:

Job-oriented methods. Detailed specifications of the tasks involved in specific jobs, for example 'spray chassis with anti-corrosive'. This approach produces accurate descriptions of individual tasks but it is difficult to extrapolate these to other jobs.

Worker-oriented methods. More generalized accounts of required behaviour that can be compared with those employed in other jobs. Both the PAQ and WPS systems use this approach.

Competence-oriented methods. Sometimes termed 'attribute' or 'trait'-oriented approaches. Highly descriptive in terms of the skills, experience and personal qualities required. Require considerable skill on the part of the analyst in translating job content into competencies.

The job description

Whatever the degree of sophistication, the common outcome of job analysis is the job definition or description. In the past, **job descriptions** have been used as quasi-legal documents, with employees declaring their contents to be a definitive list of the tasks they were expected to perform. Uncooperative employees would refuse to do anything that was not on the list and unions and employers would enter into trench warfare over any changes. Today, in a climate of change and flexibility, employers are reluctant to agree to a rigid list of tasks, preferring the employee to be ready to take on any required function. Job descriptions are out of date almost as soon as they are written and cannot be seen as documents to be adhered to rigidly.

Conventionally, job descriptions detail information such as job titles, summaries of main functions and more detailed lists of activities within each job. We will see later in the chapter that the 'flexible job description' has a significant role in modern selection strategies.

Researching people

Depending on the method used, job analysis provides a detailed description of the work to be performed but may not indicate the knowledge, skills or abilities needed to do so. The 'right person' model of resourcing advocates a **personnel specification** for this purpose. Personnel specifications represent 'the demands of the job translated into human terms' (Arnold,

Heading	Subject matter
Job identification	Job title, department, grade or level.
Relationships	Name or title of immediate boss; number and type(s) of staff jobholder is responsible for; links with other departments.
Outputs	What are the end-products or results of the job.
Activities	The behaviours or actions of the worker in achieving these outputs.
Performance	Required standards, agreed objectives.
Individual requirements	Abilities, skills, experience, temperament, training, languages, etc.
Working conditions	The physical and social surroundings of the job such as workspace, working hours, leave entitlement.
Equipment	Computers, machine tools, vehicles etc. used as an essential part of the job.
Other information	Promotion outlets, training available, transfer opportunities.

Table 13.4

A basic job analysis checklist

Robertson and Cooper,1991, p.95). Personnel specifications list 'essential' criteria that must be satisfied, and other criteria that rule out certain people from being able to do the job. Competence analyses and sophisticated forms of worker-oriented job analysis, such as WPS, generate personnel specifications as part of the package. The step from job to person specification never is entirely objective, requiring inference or intuition. In fact, it is a wonderful opportunity to introduce discriminatory criteria which rule out particular groups (Ross and Schneider, 1992, p.150). Personnel specifications may be no more than blueprints for clones, a matter that will be explored further later in this chapter.

Checklists such as Rodger's Seven-Point Plan (Rodger, 1952) have been commonly used for preparing personnel specifications. The desired qualities are categorized under seven headings:

1 physical qualities, including speech and appearance
2 attainments – qualifications, membership of professional associations
3 general intelligence
4 specific aptitudes, such as numerical ability
5 interests and hobbies
6 personality
7 domestic circumstances.

Slavish use of such a plan leads to evident danger. Items 1 and 7 could easily cause discriminatory choices and require rigorous and critical examination. As we shall see in the next chapter, further information is obtained by using selection techniques including formal interviews, psychometric tests, assessment centres and biodata.

Strategies for redundancy

Most of the discussion so far in this chapter has addressed human resource strategies relating to successful, growing companies. As we noted with reactor strategies, managers are also expected to implement redundancies and closures as a result of strategic decisions. Sir John Harvey Jones once observed that most companies refer to their workers as 'our greatest resource' but, in practice, do little to make them feel that way. We have observed in earlier chapters that the workforce is one group of stakeholders among many and within the free market model of capitalism they are probably the weakest. Presenting a caring image to staff and the consuming public may have advantages but greater attention is paid to more powerful voices when action is required. Directors and financiers ensure that their interests are satisfied first – well before those of the employees. This reflects a 'people as objects' rather than 'people as people' approach.

Handy (1993, p.222) argues that the concept of employees as assets is rarely treated with the same seriousness as football teams regard their players:

> . . . in a football club, the players truthfully are human assets. They have a productive capacity, an earning power, that is potentially far greater than their cost. That cost has both a capital and a maintenance element. Rewards are proportionate to group performance, the asset has a finite life. There is no question of the organization assuming responsibility for the asset beyond the limits of its useful life, nor is there any stigma in the declaration that the asset has grown too old to be worth maintaining. The care and attention and protection given to key assets by leading clubs is of a different order of people maintenance than any known in industry. Training and development become vital, for if you can increase the productive potential of the asset, in a short time you not only have greater productivity, but also an appreciated asset in terms of capital value.

He speculates whimsically that one day all businesses will require transfer fees for their best performers but concedes that this is unlikely.

Most job losses are due to age-old causes: business failures and cutting back on capacity in response to lower sales levels. Generally, the term 'redundancy' is losing its old stigma.

Planning for redundancies

There are some new features to job cutting which are indicative of systematic changes in the way that human resource strategists view the process. Despite the emphasis on job security as a prerequisite for an effective human resource strategy, reality in free market economies demands planning for redundancies. These may result from company failure, rationalization or reduction in demand for products and people. There are several terms for the process of losing a job, all with different connotations and nuances: being made redundant, 'letting you go', 'getting the sack' and so on. One currently fashionable euphemism is 'deselection'. This implies that some form of systematic or thought-out procedure has been used to decide who will lose their jobs.

Hendry (1995, p.202) details a number of key issues:

- To what extent can over-staffing be corrected through natural wastage or redeployment?
- What agreements constrain the redundancy process. For example, 'last in, first out'?
- When should a redundancy programme be announced? How much consultation is required?
- How are redundancy entitlements to be calculated?
- Is it possible to have an entirely voluntary process? What restrictions should be placed on key staff leaving?
- Should the organization play an active role in outplacement?
- When will savings in salary and related items pay for the redundancy costs?

Large companies often employ portfolio management systems that view business units as growth, closure or disposal prospects. A classic, if simple, portfolio planning model is based on the Boston Consulting matrix shown in Figure 13.2. This offers a further typology for resourcing strategy:

Stars. Profitable business units with a dominant market position. Good prospects for employees with promotion opportunities and competitive salaries.

Cash cows. Mature companies with a high market share but low growth rate. They produce a cash surplus as investment costs are low but profits are good. Secure but unchallenging for employees – promotions are only possible when staff leave or retire. The focus may be on managing a steady decline, squeezing as much profit out of the enterprise as possible. Comfortable salaries until later stages when hard cost-cutting is required.

Wild cats. New ventures with low market share but high growth rates. A risky environment for employees. If lucky, the group will invest and there will be considerable career opportunities and rapid promotion – provided they work for potential stars. Employees are expected to be flexible and the work can be exciting

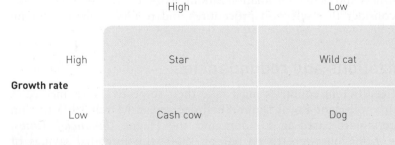

Figure 13.2

Boston Consuting Group portfolio planning matrix

and fast-moving. If unlucky, they face closure or disposal to another organization. This type closely parallels the 'prospector' strategy discussed earlier.

Dogs. Certain failures. Low growth, low share of market and no strategic potential. The only hope for employees is sale to a more positive owner. Essentially, these are 'reactor' companies.

Companies using portfolio planning are likely to take decisions on purely financial criteria without regard to the welfare of employees. HRM in such organizations tends to be tough-minded, favouring employees in profitable business units. Those in less successful areas are likely to be disposed of unceremoniously.

Redundancy and retention

Managers in charge of redundancy programmes typically focus on target numbers, with little or no thought about the quality of the staff leaving the business. Retention strategies for key staff are even more important during periods of redundancy. As Thomson and Mabey (1994, p.11) point out:

> It is the quality of the staff . . . not the quantity, which is the essential factor in downsizing. As we all know from experience, where there are programmes of voluntary redundancy, it is often the most skilled employees who go first because they are more marketable outside.

An obsession with numbers leads to a haemorrhaging of valuable skills: years of work on building a strong competence base can be undone in a matter of weeks.

The inspiration for many of the redundancy strategies of the 1980s and 1990s can be attributed to Tom Peters, the US management guru. In *Thriving on Chaos* (1987, p.355), Peters argues that most large companies are hopelessly over-managed. Specifically, he considers that there are too many managers in too many layers – not that there are not enough Indians but there are certainly too many chiefs. This over-management leads to inefficiency. He quotes a study by McKinsey and Company into 38 advanced manufacturing technology systems. The study concludes that:

> The first step in accomplishing successful plant floor implementation of new manufacturing approaches is the clearing out of all the middle managers and support service layers that clog the wheels of change. These salaried people are often the real barriers to productivity improvement, not the hourly workers on the floor.

The changes advocated by Peters – specifically de-layering – imply that companies are 'getting rid of dead wood' or 'winnowing out the poorer performers'. Current redundancy strategies have increasingly followed Peters' lines, aiming at keeping key skills and people with 'personal chemistry'. However, this approach is unlikely to gain favour amongst employees.

'Last in, first out', remains a common rule. Lee (2004) investigated the reasons why seniority rules are applied so widely to layoffs and promotion decisions in the USA. Under certain circumstances, he acknowledges, there may be economic benefits from the use of seniority rules but the evidence shows a greater popularity than economic explanations would account for. Lee notes that they have often arisen from employees' demands for fair and objective decisions. Lee concludes that seniority rules have procedural merits as they can reduce the likelihood of conflicts and help coordination among workers and employers, particularly when employees consider that selection procedures and results might be lacking objectivity or unfair.

International organizations and redundancies

Businesses with operations in different countries must take their respective severance rules into account. For example, the oil giant Royal Dutch Shell decided in March 1995 to slim down corporate headquarters staff based in London and the Hague (*Financial Times*, 14 November 1995). Some 1200 jobs were to go out of 3900 with intended savings of £190 million a year.

The costs involved in redundancies in the two countries varied sharply, reflecting the marked difference between UK and Netherlands legislation on redundancies. The Netherlands was committed to the EU's Social Chapter and enforced significantly higher entitlements for both voluntary and compulsory redundancy. Accordingly redundancies in the two capitals had widely different consequences. Whereas staff taking voluntary redundancy in the UK were given a lump sum based on years worked and final salary, Netherlands staff received a further year's salary with a minimum of £60 000 (US$90 000). People made redundant compulsorily in the Hague were entitled to 12 months' full salary, 85 per cent of eight months' salary, and 70 per cent of a further four months. This was equivalent to 21 months' salary in contrast to the six to nine months to which London staff were entitled.

Although Shell cannot be accused of doing so, other, less scrupulous, organizations may well concentrate their redundancies in the country where severance costs are lowest.

HRM in reality Tips for handling lay-offs

Consulting firm Drake Beam Morin (DBM) warned employers against short-sighted workforce decisions and badly handled employee terminations. Lay-offs may be necessary at times, but they can have a negative impact on an organization's productivity levels and affect their ability to retain and attract talented employees in the future.

'From a company's standpoint, the decision to terminate a group of employees is fraught with potential legal, financial and public relations consequences,' said Thomas Silveri, president and chief executive officer of DBM. 'It is critical that managers communicate the news of lay-offs in a professional, legal and humane way in order to treat the departing employees with sensitivity and to maintain a respectful corporate image.'

DBM conducted a global study revealing that one out of every ten individuals who lost their jobs involuntarily in 2000 told a colleague first of their job loss. So the manner in which employees are laid off can have a direct impact on the morale, commitment and retention of remaining staff.

Based on extensive experience, DBM recommends a five-step process for managers involved in laying off staff:

1 *Prepare the materials.* Explain the rationale and prepare all severance information in writing (notification letter; salary continuation/severance period; benefits; outplacement, etc.).

2 *Prepare the message.* Write the script you will use during the meeting and the key information you will convey to remaining employees. Keep it short and to the point.

3 *Arrange the next steps.* Schedule meetings with your organization's human resources and outplacement professionals. Review what should be done with the departing employees' personal belongings and specify when the employees should leave the organization.

4 *Prepare yourself emotionally.* Don't assume personal responsibility for the termination. Remember it is a business decision based on business needs. Acknowledge your anxiety, prepare your approach and talk about your feelings with the human resource and outplacement professionals.

5 *Anticipate employee reactions.* There are typically five reactions to termination: anticipation, disbelief, escape, euphoria, or violence. By acknowledging these various reactions and learning to recognize them, you will ensure that no matter what the reaction, you will be prepared to handle it in the best way.

DBM recommends that the following 'Dos and Don'ts' should be followed when conducting a termination meeting:

Do

- invite the employee in to sit down
- get right to the point
- explain the actions taken and the reasons for them
- listen to the employee and wait for a response
- restate the message if necessary
- use your prepared notes/guidelines
- clarify the separation date
- give an overview of the separation package
- explain the logistics for leaving the company
- provide appropriate written materials
- close the meeting within 15 minutes
- escort the employee to the next appointment.

▶

Don't

- say 'Good morning,' 'Good to see you', or 'How are you?'
- engage in small talk
- use humour
- be apologetic
- defend, justify or argue
- threaten
- discuss other employees
- sympathize
- try to minimize the situation

- make promises
- personalize the anger
- use platitudes like 'I know how you feel,' or 'You will be just fine,' etc.

'Managers need to learn how to manage this process in a way that preserves the current productivity levels and the company's ability to attract top talent in the future,' said Silveri.

What are the consequences of bad feeling when employees leave an organization?

Source: *HRM Guide USA* (http://www.hrmguide.net/usa/), 2 February, 2001.

Since the late 1990s, critics have argued that the cutting process has gone too far: as we have noted before, de-layering or downsizing have led to 'dumbsizing' – a condition described by Hamer as 'corporate anorexia' (*Financial Times*, 22 November 1995). Organizations have slimmed down to the point where they are denuded of the skills needed to grasp new opportunities and remaining staff are demoralized and overworked. With skilled staff in demand and often difficult to find, there is a greater focus on active retention. Moore, Cruickshank and Haas (2006) investigated the role of occupational therapy managers in influencing the job satisfaction of their staff. Those who showed care and support, while at the same time demonstrating strong advocacy and the ability to make decisions for the good of the department rather than for the benefit of the individual, influenced job satisfaction positively. Job dissatisfaction was strongest when managers were seen to treat staff differently, construed as a demonstration of favouritism. Results suggest that access to benefits, such as flexible working conditions and educational funding, should be transparent and guided by clear policies.

Summary

Employee resourcing is a wider issue than recruitment and selection. In this chapter we discussed strategies for determining resourcing from either the internal or external employment markets. We considered a variety of models for resourcing strategies. We also discussed some approaches to human resource planning and the use made of information collected during the resourcing process. We reviewed the issue of retention, staff turnover and wastage in terms of measurement, forecasting and action. Some of the limitations of job descriptions and personnel specifications were identified. Finally, we considered redundancies as an aspect of resourcing strategy.

Further reading

Ahlrichs' (2000) *Competing for Talent: Key Recruitment and Retention Strategies for Becoming an Employer of Choice*, Davies-Black Publishing, examines the topic of employee resourcing in a practitioner context. The planning process is discussed in *Strategic Human Resource Management: Theory and Practice* (2nd edn, Sage, 2005) edited by Graeme Salaman, John Storey and Jon Billsberry. Rothwell, 'Human resource planning' in J. Storey (ed.) 1995, *Human Resource Management: A Critical Text* takes a fairly technical overview of the subject and also provides a useful attempt at explaining why HRP is a 'textbook' topic rather than widespread practice. Iles' article on 'Employee resourcing' in the second (2001) edition of the same book places human resource planning in its context. The Harvard Business Review's *Finding and Keeping the Best People* (2001) provides some excellent material on employee retention.

Review questions

1   Why is employee resourcing a core activity for human resource staff?

2   How does employee resourcing relate to organizational strategy? Summarize the main resourcing strategy options open to modern organizations.

3   Consider an organization of your choice. (a) Does it obtain its human resource requirements from existing staff where possible? (b) At what levels are people brought in from the external employment market? (c) Would it be beneficial to change these practices?

4   Distinguish between 'hard' and 'soft' human resource planning. Which is of greatest value to modern businesses?

5   Are resourcing decisions normally taken on a short-term operational basis or at a strategic level?

6   Are long-term resourcing strategies realistic?

7   To what degree are resourcing strategies constrained by the nature of the external employment market?

8   How has the concept of flexibility affected resource decisions?

9   What is the relationship between resourcing strategy, HR planning and job analysis? Compare and contrast the classification systems proposed by Miles and Snow and Sonnenfeld, Peiperl and Kotter.

10   Is human resource planning a worthwhile activity?

11   Why is it important to measure and forecast staff turnover? Is there merit in the claim that resourcing strategies should focus on employee retention rather than recruitment?

12   When and why would you conduct a job analysis? What is the difference between a job description and personnel specification?

13   Are redundancies inevitably a matter of cynical expediency?

Case study for discussion and analysis

Pribake

Pribake manufactures biscuits ('cookies'). The company requires a steady stream of new product ideas, a small proportion of which will form a permanent element of its range. The board are considering a new appointment but cannot agree on the nature of the post. The production director feels that there is a need for an operational manager to look after chocolate-coated products. Conversely, the marketing director wants an 'ideas' person to devise new products and enliven the company's range. The two cannot agree and the managing director has imposed a compromise. She has asked the human resource manager to find an individual who can meet both requirements. After some dispute they have produced a basic job definition along the following lines:

Job title. New Products Production Manager.

Job summary. Reporting at a high level with responsibility for development team and – possibly – maintenance staff. Overseeing manufacture of chocolate-coated range. Developing new product ideas and progressing through from trial to production stages.

Desirable qualities. General management skills. Able to manipulate technology effectively and realistically. If the successful candidate does not have direct knowledge of the actual machinery and techniques used in the company's factories, then he/she must have the ability to appraise systems and technology quickly.

▶

After much discussion the HR manager has produced a list of additional competencies which seem to meet the requirements of the post:

- Creativity – to develop marketable products which can be produced at a reasonable cost.

- Experience of, or familiarity with market research techniques and able to formulate research programmes and evaluate results.

- Ability to design and test product manufacturing processes.

- Familiarity with the properties and possibilities of available materials: for example what can and cannot be done with different kinds of chocolate.

- Familiarity with production line equipment including ability to appraise production line speeds, error factors and quality improvements. New products must not pose insurmountable problems for production machinery or workforce.

- Versatility – the fewest development problems arise when products can be manufactured on existing equipment and made from simple and easily obtainable raw ingredients.

- Managerial skills to motivate and control the development team and ensure its effectiveness. A solitary genius will not work well in this environment.

- Ability to communicate persuasively with management and workforce, especially when products are trialled and inevitable teething problems occur. Also to communicate with senior management and marketing staff in promoting products within the company and in the market-place.

The directors have also agreed on the following criteria:

- Academic qualifications: likely to be a graduate with a production or engineering speciality.

- Ability: above average. Strong in mechanical aptitude. High on creativity scores. High on verbal fluency. A flair for design.

- Personality: neither highly introverted nor extroverted. Good leadership and persuasion skills.

- Experience: there are significant elements of the job which seem to demand familiarity with this particular industry.

What deficiencies are apparent in the job description, competence list and additional selection criteria? How would you conduct the recruitment and selection exercise for this vacancy? What is the likelihood of finding a suitable candidate?

Part five
The employee resourcing process

This part of the book addresses one of the core areas of human resource practice: recruitment and selection. These areas of employee resourcing are extensively covered in critical academic literature and prescriptive ('how to') books for people involved in hiring or being hired. Our discussion attempts to strike a balance between these two approaches, allowing you to gain an understanding of the wide range of practical techniques in use as well as an appreciation of some of the weaknesses and inconsistencies in the methodology and underlying theory.

The chapters in Part five address some key issues, including:

- Why are some recruitment channels more popular than others?

- What are the most cost-effective recruitment and selection methods?

- How is candidate information collected?

- What use is made of that information?

- Are interviews an effective method of determining the 'best' candidates?

- How prevalent are more sophisticated or non-traditional selection techniques such as psychometric tests, biodata and assessment centres?

- How valid are these selection techniques?

Chapter 14

Recruitment and preliminary candidate information

Learning objectives

The purpose of this chapter is to:

- Discuss the meaning and significance of recruitment in its organizational context.

- Provide a typology of recruitment strategies.

- Critically review preliminary information-gathering techniques.

- Discuss the merits of references and biodata.

Recruitment as a textbook subject

Matching people and jobs

Selectors and strategies

Marketing the job

Informal recruiting

Web-based recruitment

Formal recruiting

Targeting and diversity

Researching candidates

Applications

Qualifications

Biodata

References

Summary

Further reading

Review questions

Case studies for discussion and analysis –
   Saveplenty stores/Recruiting in Paris

Recruitment as a textbook subject

In Chapter 13 we discussed the 'why' of resourcing, evaluating strategies and plans that guide the process. We considered also the initial information gathering from job analysis and the – sometimes unwise – strategies employed by selectors. This chapter and the next follow on with an examination of the operational elements of resourcing, commonly termed recruitment and selection.

Recruitment and selection are major issues for human resource specialists. HRM and other management literature puts great emphasis on the process of selecting and orienting new recruits. There is no shortage of material on these topics and, together with performance assessment, they are critical elements of effective people management. Not surprisingly, therefore, these aspects of employee resourcing have attracted a great deal of attention from human resource practitioners and occupational psychologists. But, as Murphy (1994, p.58) observes: 'The very substantial volume of research in the areas of selection and appraisal is both a blessing and a curse.'

Textbooks in the personnel management tradition devote considerable space to *how* recruitment and selection are best conducted. As we will see in Chapter 15, the topic range has a well-rehearsed familiarity because selection methods are regarded as basic tools for human resource managers. Indeed, the underlying 'best practice' model has achieved the status of holy writ in certain quarters, with any deviation regarded as heresy.

Many HRM texts have followed this line. Others, particularly those written by commentators with a firmly academic background, have gone to the opposite extreme, sniffily avoiding discussion of mere 'tools'. Instead the subject is skirted or else discussed at a high – and somewhat unreal – socio-political level. We can take our choice, it seems, between superficial accounts of selection techniques and incomprehensible debates about post-modernist resourcing. Neither approach seems satisfactory.

There has been a pronounced tendency for textbook accounts to be prescriptive, dealing with the subject in a 'do it like this' fashion, almost invariably using an underlying 'right-person for the job' resourcing model. However, since the early 1990s this approach has been challenged (Sparrow, 1994, p.15; Iles and Salaman, 1995, p.203). For example, Iles and Salaman (*ibid.*, p.203) argue that: 'The limitation of the psychological and personnel-driven approaches to selection is that they are entirely, if understandably, concerned with improving the efficiency of the processes, and not with understanding their wider provenance and significance.' And again (Iles, 2001, p.134): '. . . despite the need for a fuller understanding of these processes, the bulk of existing social science and HR literature is concerned primarily and solely with assessing the efficiency of these processes, often in rather descriptive, prescriptive and atheoretical ways.'

As we noted in the last chapter, we cannot discuss how recruitment and selection take place without asking why certain techniques are used in preference to others. Iles (2001) sees much deeper consequences, meaning and significance in the exercise and justification of recruitment and selection processes. Within the HRM paradigm, they are not simply mechanisms for filling vacancies. Recruitment and redundancy can be viewed as key 'push' and 'pull' levers for organizational change. Recruitment and selection allow management to determine and gradually modify the behavioural characteristics and competencies of the workforce. The fashion for teamworking, for example, has focused on people with a preference for working with others as opposed to the individualist 'stars' preferred by recruiters in the 1980s. Attention has switched from rigid lists of skills and abilities to broader-based competencies. In general, as we noted in Chapter 13, there is a greater regard for personal flexibility and adaptability: a reorientation from present to future suitability.

Iles (2001) contends that the issue of resourcing is not 'simply, or even perhaps primarily, one of efficiency or rationality but of power: the capacity of, and the forms of knowledge and associated technologies through which organizations identify, define and assess individuals against structures of necessary competences or similar behavioural frameworks.'

Matching people and jobs

Focusing on in-house resourcing, how can we make the best use of people? In practice, it is rarely possible to match perfectly the requirements of an individual job with the skills and abilities of the people available. Square pegs in round holes are not only bad for the organization: wrongly placed workers are often unhappy and bored, or anxious about being out of their depth. In line with the three basic recruitment strategies outlined in Table 14.1, any mismatch between person and job can be resolved in one of the following ways (Drenth and Algera, 1987):

- Select the best qualified person for the job ('right person' approach).
- Change job characteristics to fit the abilities of the people employed ('culture-fit' model).
- Train people to perform more effectively (flexible person approach).

An organization may choose any one or a combination of these methods. However, all depend on the ability to identify and measure the characteristics necessary for successful job performance. At first sight this seems simple and obvious but a close examination reveals how complex it can be. People can perform a particular job successfully for varied and sometimes contrasting reasons. For example, a good manager may be personally well-organized and able to clear mountains of paperwork quickly. Another manager may deal with similar tasks

---

HRM in reality What hiring managers want

Hiring managers value teamwork more highly than other personal qualities such as ambition and the ability to think on their feet, according to a new study from Development Dimensions International (DDI), a global human resource consulting firm.

The survey of 1515 hiring managers investigated their experiences when interviewing, evaluating and hiring employees. Seventy-five per cent of hiring managers in the study were looking for employees who were compatible in a team setting but only 20 per cent looked for employees with ambition.

'In today's working environment, very little is accomplished without strong collaboration,' said Scott Erker, DDI's vice president of selection solutions. 'Overly ambitious hires will often only look out for themselves, which can harm team productivity and morale.'

Other findings included:

In an interview, clear communication can outweigh tardiness. Fifty-seven per cent of respondents would be turned off by inarticulate candidates or those who were vague about previous experience, compared with the 15 per cent of hiring managers turned off by candidates who were late to the interview or lacked knowledge about the company. 'Hiring managers don't want to train people to communicate,' Erker said. '"If candidates are vague communicators in the interview, chances are they

will be vague communicators in their jobs as well. It also indicates that they may be trying to hide something about past performance.'

Hiring managers are still interested in employees who have been out of work for more than a year – but with reservations. Eighty-five percent of respondents said they would hire a candidate who had been out of work but most noted that they would find out why the person had been out of work and how they had been spending their time off.

According to Erker, 'No one wants to hire a lemon.' Hiring managers need to ask more questions to determine the candidate's motivation or to detect indications that the candidate is counterproductive.

Internal pressure can leads to hiring mistakes. Just over a third (34 per cent) of respondents said they made a bad hiring decision because of pressure to fill the position. 'The cost of a bad hire is much higher than the cost of leaving the role open for a few more weeks,' according to Erker. 'Develop and follow a consistent hiring procedure. Don't rely solely on your gut, which hiring managers often do when they are in a hurry. You can accelerate the process to save time, but don't skip steps.'

Are hiring managers making appropriate decisions?

Source: *HRM Guide USA* (http://www.hrmguide.com) 18 August, 2004.

equally efficiently through skilful delegation. As such, it is the *totality of effectiveness* of the individual that matters rather than specific skills and abilities. Effectiveness also depends on context. Most jobs require an individual to work within a team where required skills or qualities can be spread between its members. In such a case it may not be necessary for every team member to possess all qualities needed for effective performance.

Companies may be forced to review their strategies to take account of new market conditions or technological changes. After several years of sustained growth the British supermarket group Sainsbury's faced competition from discounters. With 120 000 employees and a salary bill of over £1 billion a year, the company decided to examine its human resource requirements. With the maxim of 'retail is detail' Sainsbury's had achieved a reputation for high quality by ensuring that goods and procedures were extensively checked by staff. Management consultants were brought in to investigate the use of information technology in eliminating clerical and management tasks. Head office functions were subjected to a 'business process re-engineering review'. Automatic reordering linked to electronic point of sale (EPOS) terminals eliminated the need for several management layers in stores and offices. This programme produced a need to reduce staff numbers overall, changed the roles of remaining staff and required a major revision in human resource planning.

The right person?

Resourcing strategies should maintain the required number and quality of staff within an organization. They should also ensure suitability for its future development. There are two underlying and apparently contradictory approaches in common use (Haire, 1959). The first methodology emphasises the right (or best) person for the job. The individual is the variable element in the search; the job is fixed. This approach is associated with traditional Western personnel management. People are sought with appropriate abilities and experience to perform the job with minimal training. It implies that individual jobs are relatively long term and unchanging and that people can be 'bought in' at any stage in their careers. Vacancies are filled from the internal or external employment market. When the job is no longer required, the incumbent is disposed of.

This model is conventionally described as 'best practice' in the UK and other free market countries. Accordingly, most personnel or human resource management textbooks traditionally outline a 'prescriptive approach to recruitment based on a systematic analysis of the requirements of an individual job' (Wright and Storey, 1994, p.192). Almost invariably the account focuses on a series of selection techniques with limited discussion of the logic behind the resourcing process. There is rarely a suggestion that any other approach may be worth considering, although there may be references to the exotic practices of the Japanese in the obligatory 'international' section. Wright and Storey also rightly point out that 'best practice' only takes place in the largest organizations. Small and medium-sized enterprises generally recruit in an informal manner and rarely use sophisticated selection methods.

Approach	Objective	Organization	HR emphasis	**Table 14.1**
1 *Suitability – right person for the job*	Get the job done	Traditional Hierarchical Fixed job categories	Job analysis HR planning Selection	Recruitment strategies
2 *Malleability – fit the culture*	Fit in with today's organization	Small core Strong culture Variable periphery	Appraisal Job training Development	
3 *Flexibility – employee for tomorrow*	Build a competitive organization	Flexible Lean Virtual	Performance Skills training Talent management	

The 'right person' approach attempts to be 'objective'. It requires clear answers to questions such as:

- Is there a job to fill?
- If so, what tasks and responsibilities are involved?
- What qualities, skills or experience are required to perform the tasks?
- What process will best identify these criteria?

In essence, it is an attempt to find a seven-sided object to fit a seven-sided hole. It is a *discrimination* rather than a selection process: a matching technique that attempts to pin down the 'right' or 'best' applicant. By definition it excludes those people who are believed not to fit – a view of people as objects (Townley, 1994, p.94). Townley perceives an underlying belief that 'employees who are carefully and appropriately matched to their jobs are satisfied and productive'. Matching involves generating a taxonomy of qualities and skills (criteria) that are believed to be essential or desirable – including qualifications and experience. In turn a matrix is constructed that ranks candidates in relation to the job criteria and imposes a decision point at which some people are accepted and others rejected. In the simplest case, this process can take place inside a selector's head. In the most complex, it involves elaborate selection techniques, multiple dimensions and rating scales and requires a computer to calculate the resulting matrix. The 'right person' approach functions well when:

- It is possible to define a job tightly.
- The job is discrete and separable from other functions.
- The job is best done by an individual with a specific range of skills.

Frequently, however, these criteria do not apply and jobs are identified for less rational reasons such as:

- we have *always* had a 'major accounts manager'
- department 'x' *must* handle the task
- people *like* it done in a particular way.

The 'right person' model is geared to static, self-satisfied organizations. It meets the needs of the 'job box' model of organizational structure discussed in Chapter 7, where people come and go but the job continues indefinitely. It leads to positions being offered to people who match traditional criteria – the kind of people we have always had. It closes the appointments process to people who traditionally have been unsuccessful. In terms of equal opportunities this approach continues to disadvantage people from 'different' backgrounds and alternative outlooks. In essence it is a **cloning** process: resourcing a firm with more of the same people (see Key concept 14.1). It eliminates any opportunity for the organization to be creative or experimental.

Fit with the organization

The second approach described by Haire focuses on fitting the person to the organization. Jobs are changed and reshaped to make the best use of individuals' skills within the organization. People are permanent but jobs can be varied. If more employees are required, a search

---

Key concept 14.1 Cloning

Cloning, or 'elective homogeneity' is the tendency for selectors to pick people like themselves, thereby reducing the breadth of skills and personalities in an organization. Simply matching the set of characteristics possessed by previous successful post holders, it is a safe, conservative way to fill jobs. As a low-risk, but backward-looking approach, it is unlikely to meet the future needs of the organization.

is made for individuals who appear to have the personal qualities necessary to 'fit in' with the organization's culture. Personality is more important than technical skills in this context.

Culture fit predominates in the traditional large Japanese company. The emphasis is on matching individuals to organizational culture rather than to organizational structure. Recruitment focuses on young people who can be socialized into the company's way of working. Western managers have taken an interest in this approach in recent decades. It has been justified in terms of attracting creative and innovative employees. However, there is a distinction between creative and plastic minds. In reality, it is a means of hiring more potential clones who have the further 'advantages' of being young, cheap and easy to manage.

HRM in reality   Cultural fit and web-based recruiting

Around 90 per cent of large US businesses use the web in some form for recruiting, making access to the application process easier for jobseekers and cutting the time employers take to fill jobs. Web-based recruiting can also reduce recruitment costs by as much as 95 per cent compared with more traditional methods. But are these businesses attracting applicants who fit their company cultures?

'Companies are not only interested in skills and abilities; they want to know if an applicant will fit in their culture,' said Raymond A. Noe, Robert and Anne Hoyt designated professor of management at The Ohio State University's Fisher College of Business. Raymond Noe argues that a clearly defined culture can 'help with employee commitment, allow the employees to understand what the company stands for, and provide growth opportunities for those who match well.' It follows that enabling potential recruits to understand a company's culture should be a key part of its efforts to attract and retain high performers.

A study by Dineen, Ash and Noe, published in the August 2002 issue of the *Journal of Applied Psychology* found that feedback concerning cultural fit can affect a web-based applicant's attraction to an organization. Dineen, Ash and Noe conducted an experiment using a fictitious company website to examine person–organization fit and how feedback influenced jobseekers. Applicants completed a preliminary screening regarding their values preferences and were then given feedback about their likely fit with the organization's culture. Perhaps not surprisingly, those who did not seem to have a good match were less attracted to the company. But the results were more complex when looked at in detail.

As part of the study, student participants were asked to review background information about the business, what it did and how it had grown. They completed a 'tool' designed to collect their values preferences; and then received random, predetermined feedback about their fit with the business. Participants then viewed values information about the organization. Finally they were asked if they were interested in and attracted to the company.

Findings

- Feedback from a preliminary cultural screening can have an influence on the participant's level of attraction to the organization. But study participants did not just rely on this feedback. Instead, they acted as 'somewhat discerning consumers of the feedback, evaluating their fit based on their inferences about material on the website, as well as integrating the feedback into their assessment of fit.'

- The self-esteem of individual participants played a role in how the feedback was received. Students with high self-esteem were more likely to trust their own judgment above a low cultural fit score. Random test scores more easily swayed participants with low self-esteem even if they were a good match.

- Organizations can influence potential applicants by providing feedback about their cultural fit. The interactive capability of web-based recruitment makes this a significant feature compared with other forms of recruitment such as newspapers and recruitment brochures.

According to the authors, the research findings point to significant benefits of web-based recruiting that incorporates an organizational fit component, providing a win–win situation for both the jobseeker and the organization. 'Specifically, it helps jobseekers more accurately decide up front whether or not they would be a good fit with a company. If they decide they would not be a good fit, they can elect to forgo the application process, saving themselves and the organization time and administrative resources.' They conclude:

- When jobs are plentiful, the culture fit tool allows jobseekers to 'deselect' themselves, by reducing their options to those companies they believe would match well with their values.

▶

- When the job market is less favourable to jobseekers and businesses are swamped with applications, the inclusion of a culture fit tool can help to narrow applicant pools by giving jobseekers with a poor match the encouragement to opt out of the application process.

- This type of organizational feedback could help companies of various sizes, including the smaller ones.

While large organizations may have very public cultures, 'jobseekers don't have a preconceived notion of fit with smaller organizations,' the authors say. Including the feedback tool in their web-based application process may help smaller organizations publicize their culture. That, in turn, would help jobseekers make better choices about pursuing employment with small companies.

The researchers suggest future areas of study, including the financial outcomes of using tailored feedback and evaluating the applicant pool before and after implementation of a cultural fit assessment tool.

The use of web technology has just begun to reshape the recruiting process for companies, they say. The person–organizational culture fit tool has the potential to make jobseekers more savvy while also providing a smaller, 'better fitting' applicant pool for organizations.

'There is so much traffic on the internet, people need ways to filter through all the information. The culture fit tool can serve as an accurate shortcut that benefits both organizations and jobseekers.'

Points to consider when developing a web-based cultural fit tool

1 Consult with professionals in organizational culture measurement and use established methods to help ensure that you are accurately measuring the nature of your company's culture and providing accurate feedback to jobseekers.

2 Design your culture fit feedback tool so that it is anonymous, and let jobseekers know this up front. Otherwise, jobseekers may attempt to put their 'best foot forward' and not gain an accurate assessment of their culture fit.

3 Provide the culture fit tool before describing the culture of the organization, to avoid influencing the jobseekers' responses.

Does recruitment using web technology make culture fit easier or more difficult to achieve?

Source: *HRM Guide USA* (http://www.hrmguide.net/usa/), 24 September, 2002.

Flexibility

A third, more demanding, approach can provide a significant competitive advantage for organizations: recruiting 'flexible employees', prepared for future change and able to contribute rather than conform. Rather than aiming for rigid skills and ability profiles or malleable and gullible personalities, recruit people who are versatile and adaptable. This reflects a long-term strategy, geared towards realizing talent for tomorrow's requirements. It is not simply meeting current needs or filling the organization with compliant clones. The emphasis is on diversity. Organizations should identify a range of individuals required for the future – including 'mavericks to buck the system' and not just 'conformist clones' (Armstrong, 1992, p.135). They will require training and development; they will not be docile and managing them may be difficult; but their potential is massively greater than any clone.

Taking this approach, some of the rhetoric of HRM must become reality. Instead of viewing resourcing as a matter of recruiting individuals, it is seen as a means of adding to the total pool of competencies in an organization's human capital (Sparrow, 1994, p.13). There is a genuine need for integration and coordination between resourcing strategies and people management processes such as assessment, development and reward. Creative people must be freed from overbearing control. They cannot be managed through compliance: commitment is the only 'glue' that can bind individual talents and innovation to organizational objectives. Fine words have to be translated into sincere action.

All options, including subcontracting, must be considered carefully before hiring new people. This form of flexibility offers long-term benefits but needs people ready for new demands and hence a need for a detailed knowledge of individual jobs, people's capabilities and the range of work to be performed now and in the future.

Selectors and strategies

The 'right person' approach is entirely concerned with the individual, whereas the 'cultural fit' model is consistent with a focus on teamworking. In practice, the models are easily confused with each other and many selectors apply a mixture of both. Frequently, selectors believe they are using 'best practice' to find the person who meets the specified criteria. In fact, the person chosen is the one whose face fits. All too often resourcing emphasizes the selection of people who fit existing culture and practice at the expense of future needs.

Why does this occur? Employee resourcing involves risk and uncertainty. Above all, assessors want to avoid the consequences of picking the 'wrong' person. This may be for the valid reason that an unsuitable person will not perform to required standards. However, selectors are also aware of the consequences of an unfortunate choice rebounding directly on themselves (and their reputations). This encourages selectors to take 'safe' decisions minimizing risk of error. The individual clearly identified as a 'good bloke' by the organization and its senior managers becomes an attractive choice (Townley, 1989).

The in-breeding found at higher levels of management has been described as 'organizational dry rot' (Smith, 1991, p.29). Poverty of ideas, stultified thinking and blinkered behaviour can be due to a narrow range of experience. It is imperative, therefore, that resourcing activities should increase the breadth of experience within an organization. To do this the interests of the organization should be divorced from those of any specific stakeholders, including those of its senior managers. However, resourcing costs money directly (e.g. advertising) and indirectly (the time occupied by comparatively well-paid people). As a consequence many organizations avoid the hassle and expense by taking a casual approach to one of the most critical aspects of people management.

HRM in reality Jobhoppers worry potential employers

There are signs that potential employers are becoming cautious about hiring jobhoppers – those with a pattern of changing jobs every year or so.

Jerry Weinger, chairman of Bernard Haldane Associates, says that jobseekers need to be able to demonstrate a strong record of success in the down economy. Weinger points to a number of signals that are especially worrying to potential employers, including résumés listing positions that indicate backwards career steps, repeated lateral moves, or changes that look like a digression.

'Our booming economy enticed many people into jobhopping,' says Weinger. 'But as the job market tightens, they will be forced to justify the high turnover on their résumés.' Weinger advises jobseekers to look for signs of concern from the interviewer. For example, watch out for questions such as: 'Why didn't you pursue that project for longer?' or 'I see you earned your degree in a different field; why didn't you go into that?' Weinger lists the following tips:

- Put together an accomplishment-oriented résumé with your qualifications highlighted on the first page. Save your work history for the second page.
- Don't list positions older than 10 to 15 years – they are out of date.

- Short assignments with various companies should be listed under one job title such as 'consultant' or 'programmer'. Then give dates for the entire time you worked in that capacity.
- Plan to discuss the actual dates you spent at each company during the interview. Explaining turnover is easier in person than on paper, if you are mentally prepared to address the issue.
- Avoid stating that you left jobs for 'a better opportunity'. Instead demonstrate that the changes were strategic moves to acquire new skills and experiences.
- Prepare 30-second examples of how experience in one area led to success in another.
- Communicate why you expect to stay in your next position for an extended period of time.
- Always be honest about your career history, but don't volunteer damaging information.

How are jobhoppers regarded by prospective employers?

Source: *HRM Guide USA* (http://www.hrmguide.net/usa/), 29 March, 2001.

Geerlings and Veen (2006) argue that there is little material in the HR literature on the long-term consequences of selection policies. They simulated job-mobility patterns over time to show how different policies affected different situations. There is a common tendency to take on less capable recruits when there is a shortage of well-qualified people in order to deal with short-term problems. Geerlings and Veen found that this was counter-productive in the long-term with even a brief deviation from a resourcing strategy inhibiting the achievement of organizational goals for many years thereafter.

Marketing the job

Following on from our discussion in Chapter 13, if resourcing strategy and planning have identified the need for new or additional work to be performed in-house, it is obviously necessary to make potential applicants aware of any vacancy. Essentially, this is a marketing process conventionally termed 'recruitment' which Lewis (1985, p.29) defines as: 'the activity that generates a pool of applicants, who have the desire to be employed by an organization, from which those suitable can be selected.'

Potential candidates may come from an internal trawl of the organization, or from the external job market. The latter are reached through channels such as recruitment advertising, employment agencies, professional associations or word of mouth. We saw in Chapter 9 that organizations with a strong culture are likely to seek malleable new employees at school-leaving or graduate levels. More senior jobs are filled from the internal job market. When companies look for the 'right person', however, detailed personnel specifications may rule out internal candidates. In each case, the recruitment phase is critical because it determines the range of choice available to the selectors: 'The more effectively this stage is carried out the less important the actual selection of candidates becomes: if a firm can attract 20 high

---

HRM in reality Project work valuable for evaluating prospective hires

Enterprising job hunters have long sought to get a foot in the door as a way into their next job. A new survey for Robert Half Technology shows employers also embrace this approach. Sixty-three per cent of chief information officers (CIOs) polled said that it is beneficial for potential new hires to work on a project or contract basis before being offered a full-time position. And one-in-five CIOs said this strategy was very valuable. The nationwide survey includes responses from over 1400 CIOs taken from a stratified random sample of US companies with one hundred or more employees. The exercise was conducted by an independent research firm and developed by Robert Half Technology, a major provider of information technology professionals on a project and full-time basis.

CIOs in the survey were asked, 'How valuable is it to have a prospective employee work on a project or contract basis as a means of evaluation for full-time employment within your IT department?' Responses were:

Very valuable	16%
Somewhat valuable	47%
Not at all valuable	35%
Don't know/no answer	2%

'Interviews and reference checks alone don't always provide a complete picture of an individual's on-the-job performance,' said Katherine Spencer Lee, executive director of Robert Half Technology. 'Project assignments allow managers to make a first-hand assessment of not only technology expertise but also the individual's interpersonal skills, which aren't always evident from his or her work history.'

Lee added that by evaluating prospective employees on a contract or short-term basis first, firms can minimize the productivity losses and costs associated with poor hiring decisions. "Companies often use this approach to determine if they have a full-time staffing need or if the work can be handled by a combination of project professionals and existing employees."

Is it practical to offer all prospective employees a trial?

Source: *HRM Guide USA* (http://www.hrmguide.com/), 7 January, 2004

flyers for a job it hardly matters whether they choose amongst these high flyers with a pin, an interview or tests' (Smith, Gregg and Andrews, 1989, p.24).

Internal recruitment marketing can take place by word of mouth, staff notices, newsletters and vacancy journals. Recruiting may be on a 'one-off' basis or linked to a development programme as discussed in Chapter 20. External recruitment marketing can include media advertisements, various public and private employment agencies and headhunting. The role of the state varies, with some countries such as Italy requiring official notification to state employment agencies. As with other marketing campaigns the selection of appropriate channels, creativity of vacancy presentation and size of budget will determine success.

HRM in reality Childhood aspirations may be key

Children in the UK dream of becoming a teacher, footballer or police officer, according to new research for Jobcentre Plus, part of the Department for Work and Pensions. The poll of 397 children aged 5–11, conducted by LVQ Research, revealed that boys are most likely to aspire to sporting careers or working for emergency services and girls to caring or nurturing professions. One in ten boys (10 per cent) dream of being a footballer and 7 per cent a police officer or fireman; 13 per cent of girls would like to become a teacher and 9 per cent a nurse.

Overall the 10 most popular jobs children wanted to do when they grew up were:

- teacher (8 per cent)
- footballer (6 per cent)
- police officer (5 per cent)
- vet (5 per cent)
- fireman (5 per cent)
- hairdresser (4 per cent)
- nurse (4 per cent)
- dancer (3 per cent)
- doctor (2 per cent)
- driver (2 per cent).

Jobcentre Plus adviser, Jenni Vardy said:

When looking for work it is often worth considering hobbies and interests, as we are more likely to be good at something which we enjoy and which comes naturally. And there are often lots of opportunities which can incorporate hobbies or interests.

Many of us have childhood dreams of what we want to be when we grow up, often related to our interests, hobbies or natural skills. However, as we reach adulthood these aspirations often get forgotten or appear unattainable.

Jobcentre Plus incorporates employment and benefit services for people of working age in around 1000 locations and works with over 275 000 employers to place 17 000 people in work each week. Over 400 000 vacancies are listed weekly on its website and more than 4 million job search requests are received, making it the number one UK recruitment website. It is a key element in the government's objectives to help people based on 'Work for those who can, support for those who cannot'.

Jobcentre Plus provides personal advisers to offer practical support and advice to help those in need find and keep work, including training provision and benefits guidance. Specialist advisers support people in particularly difficult circumstances, for example lone parents or those who have left work because of ill-health or disability. Advisers can enable people to take a fresh look at how childhood dreams could become reality, by helping them assess their interests and look at relevant job opportunities.

Jobcentre Plus helped Ruth Jordan, aged 62, turn her love of cross-stitching and *decoupage* into a successful business. Ruth Jordan said:

When my arthritic condition worsened, I took up cross-stitching and *decoupage* as a hobby. Then I started to make greeting cards, which were very popular locally. My daughter, Catherine, suggested I could develop my interest into a small business, and that's when I contacted personal adviser, Ivan Wright, at Broker North East, part of Jobcentre Plus, who helped me turn my hobby into a really successful business.

According to Jenni Vardy, someone thinking of turning their hobby into a job should consider the following factors:

- Does a job already exist which involves your hobby or would it require you to start your own business?
- Does the job or career sector you are thinking of require specific qualifications?
- If you don't have a specific hobby, think about what you enjoy doing in your spare time. Do you enjoy being around people or do you prefer spending time alone?

▶

- Talk your thoughts through with a friend or an adviser to sound out different ideas and work out how a new job would fit in with your life and best suit your requirements.

Jenni Vardy continued:

If football is your passion, coaching training courses can be available at local football clubs, in particular for jobseekers aged 18–24, or opportunities working as a groundsperson or in hospitality at a football club. If you're interested in getting into teaching, one way might be to offer to help out at your children's school or look into becoming a classroom assistant, which can lead to a qualification. Those who aspire to be vets could start by trying voluntary work at their local RSPCA or animal sanctuary to see what it's like before looking for a job working with animals. Jobs could range from an administrator at a veterinary surgery to being a stable-hand. There are lots of different options available; it's just a question of thinking laterally around where your interests lie.

Is it realistic to base a career on childhood aspirations?

Source: *HRM Guide UK* (http://www.hrmguide.co.uk/), 14 September, 2006.

Informal recruiting

Cultural factors are important in determining the orientation between internal and external job markets. They also influence the nature of recruitment. Papalexandris (1991) compared multinational corporations operating in Greece and Greek-owned companies. She found that Greek employers preferred to recruit from among relatives, and friends of the owners or existing employees. Advertisements and agencies were used only when this failed to produce suitable candidates. Greek employers paid more attention to recommendations and previous experience than to qualifications such as degrees. In contrast, foreign-owned companies followed 'best practice' and focused on younger, inexperienced graduates attracted through agencies and advertisements. Acknowledging the usefulness of personal acquaintance and experience in providing information for the selection process, Papalexandris considers that Greek firms risk nepotism and depriving themselves of competent younger staff.

Formalized introduction schemes along similar lines occur in other countries, serving to perpetuate recruitment from pools of like-minded people. However, they have the benefit of supplying candidates who have a more realistic view of the organization, compared with people attracted by recruitment advertising. The former have gained their knowledge from the informal network, the latter from PR information. As a result, word-of-mouth applicants

Table 14.2	Recruitment method	2000	2006	
Percentage of firms using selected recruitment methods	Ads in specialist/trade press	86	66	
	Local newspaper ads	81	79	
	National newspaper ads	68	45	
	Jobcentre Plus	68	51	
	Employment agencies	66	76	
	Speculative/word of mouth	53+	49	
	Internet	47		
	Company website	–	75	
	Commercial job board	–	16	
	Links with education	44	37	
	Radio/TV	12	7	

are likely to stay longer and be more suitable than recruits obtained by advertising. Word of mouth is discriminatory since it restricts applications to established communities and excludes minority groups who are not part of informal networks (Smith, 1991, p.31). Inevitably, people will recommend others from their own in-group even if they have no intention of discriminating.

Informal recruitment is common. More widely, Table 14.2 shows a comparison of UK recruitment methods in 2000 and 2006 (CIPD, 2000, 2006).

At a senior level, **headhunting** has become a common, if not predominant, method of recruitment. Otherwise known as executive search, consultancies are used to locate supposedly 'outstanding' people. The marked absence of women and ethnic minorities in senior positions reveals this to be a further mechanism for cloning.

HRM in reality   Any jobs going for astronauts?

Superhero, trapeze artist, goddess, astronaut and slave are just some of the jobs people have looked for online, according to an analysis of six million career searches made on Fish4jobs. 'The vast majority of searches done on our site every month are serious ones,' says Fish4jobs publisher Ian Sprackling. However, he continues:

> A lot of workers seem to fantasize about a completely new career as a 'superhero' for example, or hope to see a position open as an 'astronaut'. Though we unfortunately can't claim to hold current vacancies for 'billionaires', we do have an enormous range of dream jobs available. For example, the people who thought it would be a laugh to type in 'tree surgeon', 'tarot card reader', 'wine taster' and 'lap dancer' will have been in for a surprise as positions for all four were advertised on the Fish4jobs website over the past month!

The research found that more than 1000 people could not spell common job titles correctly, including 15 different misspellings for 'secretary':

sercretary	sacratary	secreatarie
secrretary	scretary	secutery
secetary	secretie	secitery
sectary	secraterie	secreatire
sacretery	secritarie	secrectree.

Apart from 110 people spelling 'secretary' wrongly, 51 people replaced receptionist with anything from 'recepshionist' to 'receiptionist'. Manager became 'meneger', 'managar' and 'manger' for 34 applicants.
According to Ian Sprackling:

> Though it's easy to miss out the odd letter here or there when doing a search on a PC, attention to detail is one of the most important things employers look for. Therefore let's hope that the person wanting to become a 'manger' hasn't made the same mistake on his/her CV. However, the people who got it completely wrong and decided they

want to become a 'recepshionists' or 'secreties' should maybe consider a career change!

Top ten searches for jobs that don't exist comprised:

1	mover and shaker	6	slave
2	billionaire	7	astronaut
3	superhero	8	layabout
4	nun	9	male porn star
5	busy bee	10	trapeze artist.

Top ten unusual searches – where there have been vacancies on Fish4jobs – comprised:

1 lap dancer (posted for a club in Blackpool)

2 'car jockey' (an excusive hotel in Scotland wanted 'car jockeys' to park guests' cars)

3 tarot card reader (two vacancies available, one working from a call centre)

4 trainee forensic psychiatrist (postgraduate post in Newcastle)

5 tree surgeon (several vacancies)

6 footwear designer (design company in West Yorkshire)

7 drag racer (company in Basingstoke has sought professional drag car drivers)

8 rectal surgeon (a vacancy was posted for a health professional specializing in 'colorectal surgery')

9 reporter for the local paper (several positions nationwide)

10 'lollipop' lady (over the summer, several councils were seeking school road-crossing attendants).

How would you recruit an astronaut?

Source: *HRM Guide UK* (http://www.hrmguide.co.uk), 5 September, 2001.

Web-based recruitment

The internet has become a mainstream recruitment medium in recent years. It has become normal for jobseekers to scan employment sites on the web for opportunities; so much so that many organizations block access to job sites from their workstations to prevent employees from job hunting during working hours.

Most large organizations, and many smaller ones, make extensive use of corporate websites in their recruitment programmes. Typically, general career information is presented in an engaging manner to promote the employer brand and gain interest from prospective applicants. It has become common for the early stages of the selection process to be made accessible online, allowing résumés and CVs to be uploaded, application forms to be completed and preselection tests to be conducted.

HRM in reality Switch to online graduate recruitment

More and more of Australia's largest employers are moving to online graduate recruitment and away from slow and costly 'traditional' methods. This reflects market demand as recent surveys show that as many as 94 per cent of undergraduate and MBA jobseekers visit corporate websites to gather information and evaluate prospects before they make their applications.

Shell, Orica, Arthur Andersen, Ford Australia, MIM Holdings, Cap Gemini, Ernst & Young, and Westpac are just a few top businesses that are adding recruitment functionality to their websites with products such as GradManager from nga.net in Melbourne. GradManager was designed specifically for large organizations needing to collect and process applications at a fraction of normal recruiting costs.

Richard Ogier-Herbert, general manager of nga.net in Melbourne, claims administrative cost savings in the region of 70 per cent from the use of GradManager as a recruitment tool. 'The ease of access, centralized location, automated processing and communication and its position at the leading edge make GradManager ideal for large organizations to manage their volume recruitment,' he said. He expects up to 95 per cent of Australia's top 500 companies to adopt this type of technology to meet volume recruitment needs.

Shell Australia takes on about 30 graduates a year in engineering, business and IT. From this year all graduate applications will be handled online. Candice Topp, who deals with graduate applications for Shell Australia comments that the group had switched to online graduate recruiting because 'it is the way the market is heading.'

She added that: 'With more and more students using the internet, we saw significant benefits in encouraging online applications for our annual placement of graduates.'

With a turnaround time of just 24 to 48 hours, compared with a week or more for paper-based applications, there is a major benefit for applicants. According to Candice Topp:

> If you regard graduate applicants as customers, as we do, then it is in their best interests to have their interest and our determination acknowledged as quickly as possible. We can avoid so much time-consuming manual processing by capturing data electronically, uploading it into information systems and doing all sorts of tracking.

Natalie Rice, graduate programme coordinator for Orica, considers that online graduate recruiting indicates a more professional approach and improves organizational efficiency. Orica has 1500 graduate applications each year for around 20 places on the Graduate Leadership Programme in engineering, science, IT and marketing. As she explained:

> The paper-based system was becoming more and more demanding on us. The online application system will streamline the process, increasing our internal efficiencies and allowing us to screen and respond to applicants in a timely manner. It's a two-way thing: we need to be quick off the mark to ensure we get the right people and the applicants themselves deserve a timely response.

What are the benefits of online recruitment in comparison to more traditional methods?

Source: *HRM Guide Australia* (http://www.hrmguide.net/australia/), 19 February, 2001.

Formal recruiting

The effectiveness of recruitment is usually measured in terms of expediency: 'whether vacancies are filled with minimally qualified people at acceptable cost' or a sufficient number of applicants are attracted (Iles and Salaman, 1995, p.213). Rarely are the long-term consequences to the organization of cloned and barely adequate employees or the costs of recruitment taken into account. Doubts have also been expressed about the quality of people who are engaged in recruiting. Remarkably, the advertisements placed by recruitment agencies for their own staffing vacancies rarely ask for any knowledge of people management or selection techniques. Almost invariably they emphasize selling skills such as communication, dynamism and youth.

The likelihood of attracting 'suitable' applicants depends on the detail and specificity of the recruitment advertisement or literature. Key factors such as salary, job title, career and travel opportunities obviously influence response rates. As examples of marketing, considerable effort and money can be invested in the effectiveness of recruitment advertisements. However, employers do not wish to be swamped with applications from clearly unsuitable people. In some instances, honest job descriptions are designed to put off unwelcome applicants.

HRM in reality Jobseekers want traditional employer characteristics

Interesting work, recognition and reward for good performance and opportunities for promotion attract jobseekers the most, according to an Accenture global recruitment survey.

The survey also shows that fashionable offerings such as corporate citizenship and diversity programmes are not as attractive to jobseekers as 'traditional' benefits such as robust rewards programmes and personal development opportunities.

4100 entry-level and experienced jobseekers in 21 countries in the Asia–Pacific region, North and South America, and Europe were surveyed online to identify the career goals they valued most. Accenture carried out the research between November 2005 and March 2006 as part of the company's efforts to make sure that it remains competitive, relevant and attractive to the most talented applicants.

'Challenging and interesting work' was selected as a priority employer characteristic by 60 per cent of all respondents with the potential for accomplishments to be recognized and rewarded coming a close second (58 per cent of respondents).

The others in the top five characteristics of greatest interest to jobseekers were:

- opportunities for fast career growth (44 per cent);

- indications that an employer was well-established and likely to prosper in the long term (42 per cent); and

- indications that an organization has a particular focus on its employees (42 per cent).

Main findings of the survey:

Percentage of jobseekers selecting priority employer characteristic

1 Challenging and interesting work (60 per cent)
2 Recognizes and rewards accomplishments (58 per cent)
3 Provides an opportunity for fast career growth and advancement (44 per cent)
4 Financially strong/will prosper in the long run (42 per cent)
5 People-oriented (42 per cent)
6 Offers flexible work arrangements (41 per cent)
7 Innovative (33 per cent)
8 Approachable (27 per cent)
9 Team-oriented environment (27 per cent)
10 Global company (26 per cent)
11 Offers a variety of work (26 per cent)
12 Smart (21 per cent)
13 Collaborative environment (17 per cent)
14 Committed to the community/corporate citizenship (16 per cent)
15 Diverse workforce (16 per cent)

'Interestingly, we found that what is considered important to potential recruits was remarkably consistent across geographies,' said John Campagnino, Accenture's global director of recruitment. 'Also

The approach to recruitment reflects cultural priorities. Recruitment marketing in English-speaking countries normally features salaries and benefits but French equivalents are vague in this respect, reflecting different approaches to rewards (Barsoux and Lawrence, 1990, p.47). Base pay in English-speaking countries depends on job requirements; in France it depends on the candidate's qualifications. French advertisements define educational requirements in detail, sometimes indicating the number of years of study after the baccalaureat as the main heading. Specific *grandes ecoles* may be requested. Management in France is regarded as an intellectual rather than an interpersonal matter. Hence recruitment is geared towards cleverness (Barsoux and Lawrence, 1990, p.47). Instead of the managerial buzzwords, such as 'dynamic', 'energetic', 'high calibre' and 'outstanding' found in British advertisements, French equivalents seek out *'les elements les plus brilliants'*. The nuance is telling.

Targeting and diversity

In the UK, the recent massive increase in higher education has produced a consequent increase in the number of new graduates. British employers have begun to copy US organizations in **targeting** specific universities, courses and even lecturers. As we observed in Chapter 2, the pecking order favours 'old' universities, reflecting the prejudices of employers. A Glasgow consultancy, Yellowbrick Training and Development, indicated five 'insights' into targeting (*Financial Times*, 25 October, 1995; *Guardian*, 26 October, 1995):

- Competition for the 'best' graduates requires employers to have a clear idea of what they mean by 'best'. Recruitment needs to send a strong, distinctive message to these people.
- There must be a move away from junior staff indiscriminately attracting as many applicants as possible to a more selective process involving senior management.
- Target key institutions and specific courses.
- Recruit whenever the needs of the business dictate, rather than to a fixed 'milkround' calendar.
- There will be a diminished role for glossy brochures. Instead, vacation and placement jobs will be used to provide 'two-way interviews'.

It is clear that many employers are likely to use this form of targeting to ring-fence jobs so that only specific groups are considered. Essentially, they discriminate against institutions where ethnic minorities and working-class people are more heavily represented.

The choice and variety of new graduates has extended considerably in the UK during recent years as the result of government initiatives to widen access to higher education. A number of institutions have achieved university status, largely catering for students with a lower economic status, ethnic minorities and adult learners. But the people who were intended to gain the most benefit of this expansion in higher education actually 'gain somewhat less than their middle-class peers from achievement of a degree' (Purcell, 2002). And they earn less, on average, than people with similar qualifications who enter the job market with a 'traditional' graduate background.

The UK has moved from an elite to a mass market system of university education but recruiters have not changed their practices in line with this development. On the contrary, a significant number have introduced or emphasized recruitment practices that act against graduates from non-traditional backgrounds. This is a matter of critical concern to people considering an investment in time and money in order to gain a degree.

Purcell (2002) points to a situation where:

- graduates with non-traditional backgrounds complain that they are finding it difficult to access jobs that offer them the fullest range of opportunities and make the most of their skills; while
- companies appear to find difficulty in understanding the diversity of higher education courses and say that they cannot fill jobs with the right *calibre* of graduates.

Purcell (2002) contends that many of these problems result from the conservative recruitment strategies adopted by many organizations. Additionally, there is evidence to show that such strategies impact more on some groups of 'non-traditional' graduates than others – specifically those in older age groups. They appear to show the highest degree of dissatisfaction with the quality of their subsequent jobs and the value of having a degree. Also, the social background of graduates, regardless of age has a correlation with their levels of pay and job satisfaction after graduation. The lower their economic status before they embarked on higher education, the lower the consequent pay and job satisfaction.

Recruitment can be used to present a more positive, welcoming image to groups which are under-represented but, to be successful, this must be reinforced by similar initiatives further on in selection, induction and development mechanisms. Purcell (2002) identifies a number of key characteristics of 'leading practice employers', a similar concept to that of 'employers of choice' in North America:

- In line with the concept of employer branding, they understand that recruitment is intimately connected with marketing. This means that they have to actively sell their organizations as equal opportunity employers.
- They are clear about the skills and competencies they need for specific jobs and do not confuse these with (irrelevant) attributes. They target sources of these skills and competencies and design their recruitment and selection processes to identify them.
- Where skills shortages exist they work with regional bodies and higher education institutes to draw attention to vacancies and opportunities, so that under-represented groups are positively encouraged to apply.
- Expectations of recruits (internal and external) are managed to ensure that they understand the nature of the work, the culture of the organization and the career opportunities available.
- Work experience and placement opportunities are offered through higher education institutes, to encourage students to gain employment skills and experience and to allow them to make sensible career choices.
- They provide training and development programmes, plus assessment of progress, making internal progression possible.
- They recognize the diversity and changing needs of their staff through work–life balance, flexibility and people-friendly working policies.

Ming Chia (2005) looked at the effects of academic performance, extracurricular activities and emotional intelligence (EI) on initial and subsequent interviews and on job offers. The applications of graduates with accounting majors to major public accounting firms were investigated. Ming Chia found that academic performance and extracurricular activities influenced the number of initial interviews offered. The number of subsequent interviews depended on the number of initial job interviews and also the applicant's level of emotional intelligence. Job offers were again affected by the candidate's level of emotional intelligence and the numbers of initial and subsequent job interviews.

Researching candidates

Recruitment attracts a pool of applicants from whom successful candidates may be chosen. We now move on to the selection stages of the employee resourcing process. If a job analysis has been conducted, the criteria or competencies that are deemed necessary have been identified. These may be well-defined and focused on experience and skills, as in the 'right person' approach; or general and related to education, intellect and personality for the 'cultural fit' and 'flexible person' models. Since decisionmaking is based on these criteria, relevant information must be obtained from applicants. The initial response to a vacancy announcement can take a number of forms but each offers the opportunity for: (a) recruiters to obtain information on applicants; and (b) applicants to gain an understanding of the job and the organization.

The commonest responses requested are by telephone or letter. Telephone responses may be used for an exchange of information or as a means of eliciting an application form and literature describing the job and organization.

Applications

Application letters, CVs and résumés

Application or **cover letters** and résumés or CVs (*curriculum vitae*) are typically used initially. There is some variation between cultures. North American résumés are intended to present career objectives and history (usually in reverse chronological order, starting with the present) on one tightly written typed page. CVs in the British tradition are typically more detailed, running into two and sometimes more typed pages. The latter approach is also used by professionals in North America. In France, by contrast, advertisements often request a handwritten application letter, CV and photograph. (Many French companies use graphologists in

---

HRM in reality Is it racism or something else?

Are you looking for a white-collar technical job on the web? If so, you should make sure your name sounds Japanese, Jewish or 'White'. That will increase the likelihood of an interview by a factor of seven to eight times compared with your chances if your name sounds African-American, Greek, Hispanic or Italian, according to a recent CNW survey.

And if you are searching for a white-collar position at a Fortune 500 company, a Japanese, Jewish or Irish surname is three times as effective in landing an interview as a surname which sounds African-American, Italian, Greek or Hispanic.

But favouritism also works in other ways. People with African-American or Irish-sounding names seeking work at one of the top 25 Black Enterprise companies are more likely to get an interview call than Greek, Hispanic or Jewish applicants. Want to apply for one of the top 25 Hispanic businesses in the USA? Hispanic, Irish and Italians are more likely to land an interview than others. A similar pattern was observed when job searches were for blue-collar positions.

What about newspapers looking for entry level reporters? It's best to be Jewish, Irish or African-American. Your odds are two to three times better of getting an interview than if your name is 'White' and 10 times better than if it's Greek.

'While there is likely some racism involved, a large component may be one of association,' says Art Spinella, CNW president. 'NASCAR drivers typically don't hang out with kayakers and NBA players aren't seen clubbing with Little People. Is it racism or a comfort level with people presumed to have similar job and social experiences?'

The survey was conducted between October 2002 and January 2003. 8,500 applications and/or résumés were sent to more than 150 companies.

Can you suggest ways in which prejudice based on names may be avoided?

Source: *HRM Guide USA* (http://www.hrmguide.com), 25 April, 2003.

the selection process.) French CVs are shorter and more factual than the British model and include little or no personal information such as hobbies or sporting interests. Japanese recruiters expect an official family registry record, a physical examination report and letters of recommendation in addition to CV and photographs. The use of photographs arouses disquiet in countries where equal opportunities are a major issue since they imply that selection will be influenced by appearance and colour.

Watkins and Johnston (2000) investigated the effect of physical attractiveness and résumé quality on how job applicants were evaluated during the screening phase of the selection process. A total of 180 participants read a job advertisement and one of two differing quality versions of a *curriculum vitae*. Each CV had a passport-sized head-and-shoulders photograph of either an average or an attractive female attached. A control study was also conducted where a photograph was not attached. Participants were asked to state how likely they were to offer an interview to the applicant, rate the quality of the application and state the likely starting salary to be offered to the applicant. Overall, attractiveness had no impact with high-quality applications but was an advantage when the application was mediocre. For example, average quality résumés were evaluated more positively when a photograph was attached and attractive photographs increased the rating of a mediocre application.

Job clubs and career advisers spend a great deal of time coaching jobseekers on the preparation of polished application letters, résumés and *curriculum vitae*. Paradoxically, however, coaching often results in a bland, standardized application that does not stand out among hundreds of others. Applicants might be best advised to try some cautious experimenting in layout, paper quality and typeface to achieve a more distinctive product.

A survey by online recruiter, reed.co.uk, found that employers now prefer electronic résumés/CVs over paper versions (AGR online, 26 April, 2002). Of the 400 firms surveyed, almost 80 per cent said that given two equal candidates, they would favour a candidate who had supplied them with an electronic résumé or CV.

Nearly two-thirds said they would favour candidates with electronic versions when selecting for interviews. Not only are they quicker and easier to process, they also give a favourable impresion of candidates' computer literacy levels. Around 40 per cent of recruiters surveyed said that they currently receive more than 90 per cent of résumés or CVs electronically, but 15 per cent did not receive any electronic versions at all.

Such applications are often scanned into computers and screened by proprietary software which may use a simple keyword rating system or more intelligent 'knowledge-based' rating systems. Many people are worried by the implications of this process but hiring staff in large organizations typically give no more than 30–40 seconds to review CVs and résumés. Machines are more likely to be consistent in dealing with large numbers of such applications. The privacy and data protection issues arising from this practice are complex. The European Union has attempted to control the use of automated selection processes through a directive that forms the basis, for example, of the UK's Data Protection Act 1998 (PPRU, 1999). The code of practice for this act states in respect of shortlisting:

1 Be consistent in the way personal data are used in the process of shortlisting candidates for a particular position.

2 Inform applicants if an automated shortlisting system will be used as the sole basis for making a decision. Make provisions to consider representations from applicants about this and to take these into account before making the final decision.

3 Ensure that tests based on the interpretation of scientific evidence, such as psychological tests and handwriting analysis, are only used and interpreted by those who have received appropriate training.

Application forms/blanks

Both letters and CVs/résumés present a problem in a large recruitment programme: applicants may not provide all the relevant information and what there is will be presented in different ways. Comparison of applicants is easier if data is supplied in a standard form. Therefore, applicants replying to a job advertisement typically receive an **application form** (usually termed an application blank in North America), often asking for information already supplied. Stone-Romero, Stone and Hyatt (2003) found that completing an application blank was regarded as the least invasive of privacy out of 12 selection procedures.

Candidates face a paradox with application forms. Because information is regimented into a particular order and restricted space, jobseekers may present very similar applications. As with application letters, if candidates do not include details that distinguish them from (sometimes hundreds) of others they stand little chance of being shortlisted. Conversely, if their responses are too unorthodox, the form immediately becomes a test of conventionality:

> Application forms are of doubtful benefit; they torment applicants rather than motivate them. They blunt any initiative in presentation. . . . inane questions such as: 'Describe yourself in one hundred words' or: 'What are your greatest achievements and failures?' . . . create sarcastic answers in the mind and false answers on paper. The *curriculum vitae* is a better tool; it is a chance for the applicant to sell him or her self. Its presentation and its content are also more useful and less boring to the member of staff who has to scrutinize them (*Sunday Times*, 8 August, 1993).

HRM in reality Discrepancies in applications

A recent survey checked 2487 job applications for the financial services industry for discrepancies, embellishments and false information. Conducted by Powerchex, a pre-employment screening firm, the research looked at applications from a total of 1029 women and 1458 men over a six-month period. Employment histories, dates, university degrees, professional qualifications and criminal records were verified and checked against information provided by job applicants. With results compiled by the Shell Technology and Enterprise Program, the research was undertaken to discover any trends in discrepancies and the most common embellishments in job applications.

The survey found that 25 per cent of applications had at least one major discrepancy. While the majority of applicants falsifying information did so only once, some submitted forms with up to four major discrepancies. There is no significant difference between men and women in this respect.

The most common discrepancies overall relate to:

- employment titles or duties (12 per cent)
- employment dates
- bankruptcy or county court judgments
- academic qualifications
- reasons for leaving previous employment
- compensation received
- directorships held
- criminal record (less than 1 per cent).

The authors found that 37 per cent of applicants had gaps in their employment history and suggest that giving false information about dates (9.5 per cent of discrepancies) is probably intended to conceal this. The least common discrepancy identified related to criminal records which the authors link to applicants being aware that this can easily be checked against an existing database.

The survey found that the tendency to have discrepancies on applications increased with age, possibly suggesting that older workers feel the need to embellish in order to compete. Discrepancies were found in 28 per cent of applications from those aged 51–60, compared with 22 per cent of those aged 21–30. An alternative explanation might be difficulty in remembering the details of a complex employment history. British applicants gave false information in 32 per cent of cases overall (38 per cent of men and 26 per cent of women), compared with 25 per cent of their non-British counterparts.

The trend towards jobhopping is reflected in the survey, with 72.5 per cent having held at least two jobs in the last five years. Income had an interesting effect with people earning between £80 001 and £90 000 most likely to give false information (40 per cent) and those earning between £60 001 and £70 000 least likely to do so (9 per cent).

If the authors are correct in the assumption that all discrepancies identified are deliberate – and that is surely questionable – this survey indicates that one in four job applicants to the financial services sector are prepared to falsify information on their job applications in order to gain employment.

Is it reasonable to assume that all discrepancies are likely to be deliberate falsifications ?

Source: *HRM Guide UK* (http://www.hrmguide.co.uk), 22 August, 2006.

An applicant's heart sinks when a carefully crafted résumé or CV appears to be ignored and a standard form arrives in the post. Hours are wasted completing forms that are not read because applicants are rejected on decision criteria, such as qualifications, not mentioned in the marketing process. However, an organization that does not use application forms has a major problem dealing with hundreds of applications. How are they to be analysed and compared? How is the choice of a shortlist to be made? Applicants will leave out crucial items of information, particularly when they are likely to have a negative impact. When and how is this information to be acquired? Interviews are expensive methods for filling in the gaps in a CV or résumé. Moreover, it is unfair to raise hopes, cause inconvenience and possibly expense for interviewees who are disqualified on the basis of information that could be picked up from an application form.

Provided that they are not devised as mediaeval instruments of torture, short and pertinent application forms will continue to have a major role in recruitment. Purcell (2002) found that employers were increasingly tailoring application forms to identify specific competencies required for individual jobs.

Qualifications

We noted that educational qualifications are of major importance in some cultures, for example France and Japan. In other countries their value varies, depending on the level and nature of the vacancy. Purcell (2002) found that employers tended to use degrees as thresholds for considering applicants in order to guarantee minimum potential and ability. Also, with the massive increase in degree-qualified candidates in the UK, many employers were questioning the need for a degree as a basic qualification for a wide range of jobs. Many had moved, or were in the process of moving away from qualifications as a key element in the selection process. Instead they were looking for evidence of competencies, particularly generic competencies such as communication and teamworking or personal attributes such as resilience and commitment. In particular, they were increasingly valuing experience.

Purcell (2002) noted a clear difference between employers seeking to fill professional and technical jobs and those looking for general management or administration candidates. The former emphasized degrees as a qualification, particularly in subjects that featured numeracy, whereas degrees were often thought unnecessary for entry jobs in more generalized fields. Purcell quotes the instance of one high-street bank that sought to obtain A-level (high-school graduate) candidates for a five-year management programme rather than university graduates. They targeted working-class applicants who might consider the programme more attractive than a debt-incurring degree course.

Biodata

Application forms and model CVs invariably include **biodata**; sections on experience, hobbies and other spare-time activities. Applicants frequently have serious difficulties in providing answers if they have fairly mundane interests. Does a passing interest in stamps and a small collection of DVDs allow us to describe our hobbies as philately and music? Do holiday snapshots justify 'photography'?

Key concept 14.2 Biodata

Roberts (1997, p.10) describes biodata as a 'set of questions framed around "coincidences" in the lives of good performers'. People who are good at a particular job are likely to be more similar to each other than to individuals selected at random from the general population. Such similarities extend beyond work-related factors into hobbies, sports and social activities.

Traditionally, little use was made of this type of information. But it can be useful in discriminating (and that word is used advisedly) between applicants who are similar in most other respects. In fact, as we have already mentioned, an increase in coaching, books and professional writers aimed at preparing CVs or résumés and answering conventional forms, has resulted in applications becoming more and more similar. Supposing an employer advertises for trainee customer service assistants. The response is likely to include numerous applications from school-leavers with insufficient qualifications to proceed into higher education. These applicants may seem much the same on paper, but some have greater initiative or people skills than others. Biodata (biographical data) forms have been developed to identify non-academic qualities such as these. Biodata consists of systematic information about hobbies, interests and life history. The underlying rationale is described by Smith, Gregg and Andrews (1989, p.54):

> Biodata methods are based on the assumption that *either* our characteristics are formed by the experiences we are subjected to in the course of our lives *or* our abilities cause us to select or become involved in certain types of life event. In either case, it follows that if we can accurately assess the events of a person's life, we can deduce something about their skills and abilities.

Biodata forms request detailed information of this kind, normally in the form of a multiple-choice questionnaire, covering:

- age, sex, place of birth, residence
- family background, number of brothers and sisters, parental history
- education, work experience
- marital status, number of children
- physical characteristics (weight, height) and medical history
- hobbies and leisure interests
- reading habits: newspapers, magazines, type and frequency of books read.

Question items are largely factual or 'hard' and could be checked with other sources if necessary. Other items are 'soft' and include opinions, attitudes and feelings. It is also possible to collect the same data in a structured interview. Biodata is an expensive procedure to set up but cheap to administer, especially if the data can be entered on computer by optical scanning.

A typical biodata exercise follows an established sequence (Smith, Gregg and Andrews, 1989):

1 Job analysis identifies criteria for good performance.
2 A 'brainstorming' exercise generates relevant biodata items, such as 'interest in people', 'stability', 'imagination'.
3 Draft questionnaires are given to a large number – ideally over 300 – existing employees.
4 Replies are correlated with job performance. Items which correlate poorly or discriminate against particular groups should be discarded.
5 The revised questionnaire is then given to applicants.
6 Biodata items become out of date quickly. They should be rechecked every two years.

Biodata cannot be used in small organizations or for a 'one-off' job. A simplified version could be provided as a decision aid in such circumstances. This would entail interviewers collecting narrative personal histories and scoring the information against a previously determined scale. The main use of biodata is in pre-selection of basic or entry-level jobs such as apprenticeships or posts for trainees. The logic is that if candidates are matched with existing staff, people with similar interests can be found who are likely to be suitable for the job. The greatest value of the technique is its ability to reduce staff turnover.

Biodata is specifically used to select people who are similar to those already employed. Although designed to eliminate unfairness, in a less obvious way it consolidates and makes 'scientific' an embedded practice that is prejudicial to the disadvantaged. Furnham (1992, p.231) reviews a number of studies comparing biodata with job performance and finds strong supporting evidence for its usefulness. He instances Russell *et al.* (1990) who examined the life details of 900 naval recruits and measured five biographical features:

- life problems and difficulties
- aspects of task performance
- work ethic/self-discipline
- assistance from others
- extraordinary goals or effort.

These were found to relate to other measures such as military performance rating. Furnham notes that factor analyses of biodata information relate to well-attested personality dimensions. Roberts (1997) observes that we do not need to know why biodata items are significant in order to use them. In many respects it is similar to the actuarial techniques used by insurance companies to quote for car insurance cover. Clearly, however, there are distinct implications for equal opportunities in a technique which, it could be argued, is designed not to promote diversity and that raises a possibility of breaching anti-discrimination laws unless the biodata items are carefully assessed. There is also the issue of faking to consider (Lautenschlager, 1994). The 'correct' (expected) answers to questions on non-cognitive tests such as biodata questionnaires are often easy to guess. In fact present-day biodata questions may be indistinguishable from items on personality tests and may attract the same problems of impression management and dishonesty. The consequent uncertainty about the effect of distorted responses on selection decisions and validity is a matter for concern (Snell, Sydell and Lueke, 1999).

References

Virtually all employers request references as a matter of course, usually without any thought as to their purpose and value. Where a purpose is expressed, they tend to serve one or both of the following functions: (a) a factual check to maximize the probability of a truthful application; and (b) to provide evidence of character or ability.

The latter assumes that the referee is disinterested and capable of making a valid judgement and is frequently misused. Candidates are most unlikely to offer referees who will write unfavourably. A classic study is frequently quoted to demonstrate the dubious value of the reference (Mosel and Goheen, 1958). In the study 1000 applications for the US civil service were examined and it was found that:

- less than 1 per cent had poor references for ability or character
- approximately 50 per cent were described as outstanding by the referees
- the remaining references were at least satisfactory.

Moreover, when the work performance of successful candidates described by referees as being particularly suitable for the job were compared with those that were not, no difference was found between the two groups.

There is a growing and welcome trend for references to be simple factual checks rather than a source of 'evidence' for the selection process. There is also an issue regarding a referee's liability for the consequences of their comments. This is dependent upon employment law within specific countries.

HRM in reality Rising demand for top executives

A new report by Rick Slayton from Chicago-based Slayton Search Partners examines factors that have created a sellers' market in the executive search game. Slayton analyzes both sides of the recruiting equation and offers insights into strategies that are working both for companies and executives in transition. Slayton Search Partners has a 20-year track record of helping key industries fill crucial positions across all management disciplines.

Rick Slayton said:

The supply and demand dynamics have given high performing executives more career options than they've had in years, and from that perspective, it's beginning to smack of 1999 all over again. The A Players are much more selective about pursuing transition options, but they're also pouncing on the opportunity to get what they want.

Slayton points to recent studies documenting an increase in executive job transitions and moves by employers to change their pay practices to match a more competitive job market. For example, a study from Liberum Research found a nearly 60 per cent increase in executive turnover in 2006. ExecuNet reports a surge in hiring at executive search firms, and a Mercer Human Resources Consulting report reveals companies' plans to boost executive compensation.

Rick Slayton comments:

Candidates, as a general rule, have more power today. For much of the past five years, employers were holding the cards in the executive employment market, because new opportunities were scarce. But today, it's clear that the pendulum of the executive employment market has moved way over to the candidate or seller side. The bargaining advantage has shifted substantially beyond equilibrium in favor of the top candidates.

The author predicts no foreseeable downturn in the current situation and suggests that the 2006 recruiting season will keep corporate recruiters and executive search firms extremely busy trying to market compelling opportunities to top management talent. He expects corporate employers will continue to place a premium on the right mix of professional experience, advanced education, a track record of consistent performance and successive promotions, and intangibles he describes as 'executive presence'. Slayton also believes leading employers will continue to create more opportunities for women and minority executives.

Slayton notes an increasing number of executive job candidates are rejecting any company rumoured to have a tyrannical CEO, high executive turnover, and/or business practices that might remotely evolve into corporate scandal. He advises employers not to underestimate the importance of their reputation, their brand, and their overall workplace experience and corporate mission, because top calibre management candidates are usually motivated by the challenge of a new job with a growth-oriented employer.

Rick Slayton says:

Any company that can't effectively articulate its vision for the future and a compelling employment proposition for world-class management executives will find its ability to recruit diminished or hampered until that changes.

What would you consider to be an effective recruitment strategy to attract top executives?

Source: *HRM Guide USA* (http://www.hrmguide.com/), 14 September, 2006.

Summary

Recruitment and selection are core areas of human resource management but are frequently discussed in a prescriptive manner. They are not simply techniques for filling jobs – they are also levers for organizational change, sustaining employee commitment and achieving high performance. In free market countries, the personnel profession has adopted a 'best practice' model which fits the prevailing business ideology. This model prescribes a quest for the 'right (best) person for the job'. The 'best-person' or psychometric model has achieved the status of orthodoxy in free market countries. But different models of resourcing have been developed with a greater concern for personality and attitude than presumed ability. Recruits may be sought who will 'fit in' with the culture of the corporation; who will be content to build a career within the organization; who will absorb the goals of the organization.

Further reading

There are many titles available covering the topic of recruitment, usually in conjunction with selection. Some of the best include: *Competency-Based Recruitment and Selection* by Robert Wood and Tim Payne (John Wiley & Son, 1998); *Recruitment and Selection* by Gareth Roberts (CIPD, 2005); *A Manager's Guide to Recruitment and Selection* by Margaret Dale (Kogan Page, 2003).

Review questions

1 Distinguish between recruitment and selection. What is the purpose of recruitment?

2 Why is employee resourcing more than a matter of filling jobs?

3 What do you see as the main advantages and disadavantages of the 'right-person', 'culture fit' and 'flexibility' models of recruitment?

4 What are the critical characteristics of leading practice employers or employers of choice?

5 Write a covering letter and a résumé or CV that would be suitable for an application to a HR department in a large multinational company.

6 What are the best ways of obtaining basic candidate information? What types of information can be gleaned from application forms?

7 Review the positive and negative aspects of using biodata questionnaires.

8 What roles do the internet and company websites have in recruitment? How do they compare with other recruitment marketing channels?

9 Evaluate the role of the line manager in resourcing.

10 What are the legal pitfalls in the recruitment process?

Case studies for discussion and analysis

Saveplenty Stores/Recruiting in Paris

1 The general manager of Saveplenty Stores has been interviewing applicants for sales and management jobs for 23 years. She believes that she can identify good and bad candidates by chatting to them for 10 minutes. You have been placed in her department as a graduate trainee and have been given the task of organizing recruitment for a new superstore.

How would you do this and what role should the general manager play?

2 You are a human resource specialist with Online Solutions, a large software company. The company has agreed to set up a joint venture in Paris with a major French computer manufacturer. The venture will adapt and distribute software in French-speaking countries. Being fluent in French, you have been chosen as HR manager. Most of the other senior staff are longstanding managers from the French company. Your first task is to recruit approximately 60 junior managers and technical staff. The procedures and choices have to involve your French colleagues.

How would you conduct the exercise and what difficulties would you expect?

Chapter 15

Employee selection

Learning objectives

The purpose of this chapter is to:

- Evaluate the screening or pre-selection stage of employee resourcing.

- Introduce the concepts of validity and reliability in relation to different selection methods.

- Provide a critical overview of selection methods.

- Investigate the frequency of use of different selection methods.

Resourcing decisions

According to *The Dictionary of Daily Wants* (1859):

> In seeking employment, much depends upon the applicant's manner and dress; if he is rude and ungainly, and expresses himself in an awkward manner, an employer will at once conceive a prejudice against him, and curtly decline the proffer of his services. But if, on the other hand, he is pleasing in his manners and dress, he will not only be engaged to fill a vacancy, but will sometimes be taken into the establishment, although no vacancy exists. Applicants for employment should also be scrupulously neat in their attire, and clean in their persons; for an employer naturally argues that a person who is careless of himself will be equally so about about his business.

Selection is a decisionmaking activity: 'the psychological calculation of suitability' (Townley, 1994, p.94). If the recruitment process is open, selection decisionmaking normally takes place in a series of stages. Recruitment marketing may attract hundreds – sometimes thousands – of responses. The first decision stage is termed pre-selection. Its purpose is to reduce applications to a manageable number with the emphasis on rejection rather than selection. Evidence is gathered from letters, résumés/CVs, application forms, and possibly biodata or screening tests. Preselection increasingly involves telephone screening interviews, ranging from basic checking of information supplied in the application process to a 20-minute

---

HRM in reality Manpower introduces web-based employment prescreening tool

Manpower has added NetSelect^SM, a web-based employment prescreening tool, to its range of North American human resources services. The company considers that NetSelect is able to efficiently prescreen thousands of job candidates, thereby significantly reducing the amount of time hiring managers need to spend reviewing résumés and identifying the most suitable candidates.

'Manpower designed NetSelect in response to customer demand for new technology that facilitates faster hiring while improving quality,' said Barbara J. Beck, executive vice president of US and Canadian operations for Manpower Inc. 'This tool strengthens Manpower's line-up of staffing and HR services, creating added convenience for customers seeking a single partner who can bring a range of services to the table.'

NetSelect's web-based prescreening ability is achieved by means of an online questionnaire. A customized questionnaire is developed by Manpower in consultation with the hiring client. This determines if candidates possess the desired prerequisites for a position. When candidates express an interest in that open position, they are directed to the questionnaire that is posted at a unique web address. Employers can establish a link within an online job posting leading directly to the custom-built questionnaire. NetSelect is completely web-enabled – it requires no downloads, network configuration or IT integration.

Candidates can access the questionnaire when it suits – it is available 24 hours a day, 7 days a week.

When a candidate has completed the questionnaire, NetSelect assigns a score based on how closely that person's background and preferences match the job profile. NetSelect then organizes the results in a database. This allows employers to:

- see at a glance how many people completed the questionnaire;
- view their scores;
- determine who will move on to the next step in the hiring process.

Additionally, hirers can send e-mail messages to applicants directly through NetSelect, which keeps a record of correspondence.

'NetSelect brings unprecedented efficiency to the hiring process, and employers will appreciate the impact this tool has on the bottom line,' said Mark Gambill, vice president of marketing for Manpower North America.

Manpower considers that employers will save time and money because only candidates with the highest scores proceed to the more time- and cost-intensive screening procedures.

With fewer candidates to evaluate, the time-to-hire process is shortened and new hires are on the job faster than before.

Are there any disadvantages to web-based preselection?

Source: *HRM Guide USA* (http://www.hrmguide.com), 16 July, 2003.

question and answer sequence not unlike the formal interview. Regardless of the methods used, the intention is to arrive at a comparatively small number – the shortlist of apparently well-suited applicants.

Pre-selection is open to considerable abuse and plays a major role in the cloning process. Frequently decisions are made on arbitrary grounds, ranging from the absurd – use of the 'wrong' colour of ink, for example – to the discriminatory, excluding particular groups such as women, ethnic minorities and graduates from other than specific schools or universities. Pre-selection offers those so inclined an ideal opportunity to reject unwanted candidates without having to give detailed reasons. Unless the organization has an applicant tracking system, with each application logged, categorized and tracked throughout the selection procedure, pre-selection can be a glaring loophole, allowing hidden and illegal discrimination to take place. It is common for two identical applications to be treated differently if one is sent with an obvious ethnic minority name and the other is evidently from the majority population. Herriot and Fletcher (1990) note the irony that pre-selection and initial interview result in rejection of the largest proportion of candidates and yet these stages are the least valid and reliable.

After pre-selection screening, surviving applicants meet the formal decisionmaking procedure termed 'selection'. Biased selection processes can result in hiring unsuitable people (false positives); or may lead to a failure to hire applicants who would have been suitable for the job (false negatives). In the 'best person' model, selection is a matching process, where:

- an applicant's qualities are compared with criteria deemed necessary for the job;
- when the measurement of the former is extremely difficult; and
- evidence for the latter is a matter of opinion.

In contrast, 'culture fit' focuses on personality and compatibility with existing staff. In Japan, the traditional approach paid attention to such matters as political views, family background and personal finances – irrelevant to the average Western company (Whitehill, 1991). We have noted that these two models are frequently confused and decisionmaking is a matter of identifying the 'ideal' or clone candidate, a process rationalized by talk of 'fitting in'.

An alternative explanation comes from the cognitive process interpretation of selection (Vandenberghe, 1999). For whatever reason, selectors develop a cognitive schema (mental picture) of the 'ideal' candidate for a specific job or more generally as a recruit for their particular organization. The cognitive schema may be a complicated mental network of beliefs and attitudes shared by a group of selectors against which prospective candidates are assessed.

How consistent are selectors when it comes to looking for the qualities they consider important? In a study of selection decisions in Hong Kong, Moy (2006) compared recruiters' judgment on the qualities deemed to be necessary for effective performance and the qualities they actually looked for in their selection processes. She found that conscientiousness was thought to be the most important quality for effective performance whereas the quality that they spent most time assessing during interviews was extroversion.

Sophisticated selection methods are not common in small companies, most of which continue to depend on informal methods for selection decisions – typically references and one or two interviews. In contrast, large organizations have adopted a range of methods to aid decisionmaking. This is especially true for employment categories such as blue-collar workers where it had not previously applied (Townley, 1989). The trend is most obvious in Japanese and US-owned firms but it is also apparent in UK and other European companies. Regardless of the resourcing model employed, procedures have become more elaborate. At Mazda in Michigan, USA, for example, the process involved several weeks' assessment and included application forms, aptitude tests, personal interviews, group problem-solving and simulated work exercises. These were designed to weed out 'druggies, rowdies, unionists'. Selection emphasized teamworking behavioural traits rather than technical skills and successful candidates had an average age of 31, little or no factory experience and were overwhelmingly (70 per cent) male.

Townley argues that this has not resulted from the increasing professionalization of human resource specialists. Neither is it a reaction to the difficult task of selecting from the large number of applicants attracted by any job advertisement during an economic recession. She attributes the trend to the increasing prevalence of HRM with its emphasis on the 'attitudinal and behavioural characteristics of employees'. Guest (1992) observes that the 'excellence literature', authored by Tom Peters and others, together with accounts of Japanese management methods focused the minds of many Western managers on the importance of recruitment, selection and socialization of employees. This leads to an interest in factors that can be assessed by a range of technical methods such as psychometric tests. In recent years their use has increased in Europe, particularly in the UK, whereas equal opportunities legislation has forced a different approach in the USA.

HRM in reality Aesthetic labour: looking good, sounding right

'Aesthetic labour' is a concept based on the notion that employers in parts of the service industries described as the 'style labour market' (Nickson, Warhurst and Dutton, 2004, p.3), such as boutique hotels, designer retailers and style cafes, bars and restaurants, require 'aesthetic skills' in addition to social and technical skills from their workers. Dennis Nickson, Chris Warhurst and Eli Dutton of Strathclyde University, authors of *Aesthetic Labour and the Policy-Making Agenda: Time for a Reappraisal of Skills*, have examined the trend for recruiters to select staff with self-presentation skills in preference to experience or technical skills. These skills allow the chosen staff to 'look good' and 'sound right' to customers. They encompass body language, dress sense and style, personal grooming and voice and accents.

Nickson *et al.* (2004) argue that aesthetic skills are becoming key requirements in interactive service work but this trend has not been appreciated or analyzed by policymakers. Their study focused on Glasgow, which is reinventing itself as a post-industrial city where tourism and retail jobs are replacing those lost in manufacturing. Services now account for 80 per cent of the city's jobs. This is a change seen in many other formerly industrial cities throughout the developed world.

The authors highlight the differences between services, particularly those that are style-conscious, and manufacturing:

- services are produced and consumed simultaneously
- service workers and customers interact directly
- service employees are 'part of the product'
- service encounters between workers and customers are 'intangible, continent, spontaneous and variable'.

This means that effectiveness of service transactions depend to some extent on how employees 'come across': on how their moods, appearance, demeanour and personality are perceived by customers. While some employers have tried to replace this uncertainty through the use of technology (e.g. scripted call-centre encounters, automated systems, etc.), with somewhat mixed results, others have focused on training employees to deliver the employer brand image. The latter process requires the tight management and monitoring of employees' behaviour and responses or 'emotional labour'. The third alternative is to recruit and select 'oven-ready' employees, those with the right skills and attitudes to do the job almost immediately, through competency-based selection procedures.

This assumption that 'looking good' and 'sounding right' are skills that cannot easily be trained into people challenges the conventional understanding of 'soft skills'. Recruitment strategies based on this notion could lead to an increase in potential discrimination, but the authors believe that it would be more effective to create impression management training programmes than to ignore or condemn the trend. They argue that 'aesthetic labour' is here to stay. They conclude that other businesses, outside the 'style labour market', also see that recruiting staff with aesthetic skills leads to a competitive advantage.

Amongst relevant findings in this and an earlier report from the same team are:

- A survey of skills needs in hotels, restaurant, pubs and bars, indicated that 85% of employers ranked personal presentation and appearance in third place – above initiative, communication skills or even ability to follow instructions.
- Glasgow employers rated technical skills twenty-third out of twenty-four as criteria for recruitment and selection.
- In January 2000, the government announced that all New Dealers would be offered personal presentation skills.
- Job advertisements for the hospitality and retail sectors frequently ask for people who are 'stylish', 'outgoing', 'attractive' or 'trendy' and 'well-spoken and of smart appearance'.

- A 1996 survey of recruitment consultants indicated that strong regional accents – particularly those of Liverpool and Birmingham – were viewed negatively.
- Research in Glasgow shows that employers are, to a considerable extent, recruiting on the basis of physical appearance or accent.

Chris Warhurst said: 'Aesthetics have always been important to companies and to certain groups of employees. Politicians, managers, professionals and city types recognize the career benefits of dressing for success. And the name and visual style of an organization are sometimes the most important factors in making it appear unique.

'What is startling is the application of highly prescriptive aesthetic values in the wider job market. The danger is that many people in deprived areas are being denied work because of a lack of cultural capital. Take Glasgow as an example, 50 per cent of jobs are now filled by commuters from the middle-class suburbs. This situation is likely to be repeated in similar urban restructuring economies, such as Liverpool, Manchester and Newcastle.'

Examples of this kind of discrimination highlighted by the authors' include:

- A supermarket check-out girl sent home by her boss to shave her legs so she wouldn't 'put customers off'.

- A pregnant sales assistant who was sacked for becoming 'too fat and ugly'.
- A male off-shore oil worker who was dismissed for being too fat.

Richard Reeves, director of Futures at The Industrial Society (now the Work Foundation) said: 'In the service-crazy US, the reality of aesthetics has been accepted for decades. Charities exist to take cast-off clothes from professional women to help their jobless counterparts get work. We Brits are traditionally more squeamish about admitting that how you look, dress, talk – or even smell – might be as important as your GCSE results.

'Not everyone can enter the style labour market and, of course, not everyone would want to. But as the economy shifts towards "high touch" jobs, the premium on presentation is rising. A key task for government is to reconcile these commercial imperatives with those of fairness and social justice. Employers need to tread carefully too. Aesthetic labour should be about great service, not great teeth.'

To what extent could this approach be described as a new form of discrimination sometimes described as 'lookism'?

Source: *HRM Guide UK* (http://www.hrmguide.co.uk), updated 2 August, 2006.

So, confining our discussion to 'best-person' and 'culture-fit' models for the moment, is selection best conducted subjectively or objectively? Smith and Robertson (1993, p.255) compare the two approaches:

Clinical, or subjective. Just as a doctor diagnoses a medical condition on the basis of perceived sympoms, an 'expert' or experienced person reviews information on candidates. Choice is based on the expert's experience and expertise.

Actuarial. Comparable to calculating an insurance premium. Various factors are quantified and put into a weighted equation. For example, experience may be given twice the value of educational qualifications. The candidate scoring the highest number of points is selected.

They conclude that the actuarial approach is better than the clinical method, but not to a very major extent. But what happens in practice? Nowicki and Rosse (2002) note that the state of practice in employee selection differs markedly from the state of research. They conducted interviews with 166 line managers and asked them to describe their own successes and failures in hiring. The managers attributed successful hiring largely to luck and intuition, but they also acknowledged the value of more systematic and rigorous approaches to selection. From their comments it seemed that they simply lacked awareness of research on selection such as comparative validities, rather than choosing to ignore this information.

From a diversity perspective, Peppas (2006) compared Hispanic and non-Hispanic hirers in the USA on the importance they attached to 26 different selection criteria. Peppas found that there were significant differences on 13 of the criteria with Hispanics tending to favour more subjective criteria while non-Hispanics preferred objective criteria.

Psychometric tests

Psychological tests have become commonplace. Psychometric means 'measurement of the mind'. Psychometric tests purport to measure psychological characteristics including **personality**, motivation, career interests, competencies and intellectual abilities. Traditionally they take the form of pen and paper multiple-choice questionnaires but modern forms can also be presented on computer screens. Most tests require applicants to work through a large number of items in a given amount of time. Some ask candidates to choose between various alternatives, as in the following example:

'Which of the following best describes you?'

1 I never take time off from work because of illness.

2 Sometimes I take time off work if I am very ill.

3 I believe in taking care of myself. If I am ill, I stay at home.

This kind of item is typical of personality and motivation tests. Other tests use pictures and geometrical shapes. Tests of number ability might offer a series of numbers and ask for the next two:

2 4 8 16 ? ?

This is a simple illustration – tests normally include items of increasing difficulty. The limited amount of time allowed ensures that few people can complete all items correctly.

Users argue that they provide valuable evidence that is not revealed by other methods. Additionally, there is a widespread belief that they are somehow objective, contrasting strongly with the subjectivity of interviewing. Candidates often feel that they may justifiably 'sell' themselves in an interview, creating an excessively favourable impression, whereas tests will magically reveal the truth. They give resourcing the semblance of scientific professionalism (Townley, 1989).

Tests are based on the **psychometric model** (Key concept 15.1) which: '. . . assumes that there is an optimal set . . . of psychological characteristics for success at any human activity (in this instance, success at a particular job)' (Kline, 1993, p.374). Kline states that this is so obvious as to be banal. However, in our discussion of human resource planning we have seen that identifying such optimal sets is extremely difficult in practice. Specifically, job or personal specifications derived from traditional job analysis are backward-looking – they do not describe requirements for the future (Iles and Salaman, 1995, p.219). As we have seen, the traditional tightly prescribed 'job' is disappearing in favour of a more fluid, flexible role. Consequently, older notions of psychological 'dimensions' by which jobs and people are matched are being replaced by the more complex multi-dimensional concept of competencies.

Key concept 15.1 The psychometric model

The dominant approach to selection in British and US textbooks. In its traditional form, it grounds the 'best-person' model in psychological theory and testing. It embodies the use of refined techniques to achieve the best 'match' between job characteristics identified by formal job analysis and individual characteristics measured by psychological tests, structured interviews and other assessment methods.

Psychological testing has been used for different purposes in mainland Europe and North America, with the UK taking an intermediate view (Drenth, 1978). The reasons for this are complex and reflect different traditions. The 'softer' European approach has relied on more descriptive, observational methods such as projective techniques and qualitative performance tests that draw on psychoanalytic theory. Conversely, the American approach was dominated by behaviourist attitudes, emphasizing 'objectivity' and the quantitative use of data. This led to the development of a massive range of 'paper and pencil' tests, suitable for individual or group use. Many European selection theorists have never been convinced of their merits. However, in recent years, growth of a more systematic methodology has meant that the two approaches have converged to a considerable extent.

Jenkins (2001) reviewed 17 surveys of psychometric test usage published between the early 1970s and 2000. The wide variation in methodology, sampling sizes and sample frames made it difficult to provide precise estimates of test usage for specific periods. However, a clear growth in use was seen from the 1980s onwards, with evidence of widespread adoption by large organizations in particular. Wolf and Jenkins (2006) used case studies of organizations to identify the factors behind this and checked their consistency with Workplace Employee Relations Survey (WERS) data to see if these were national trends in the UK. The regulatory environment was found to be the most important factor: organizations were using tests as a precaution to protect their selection decisions from any challenge.

Jenkins (2001) considers that large organizations are more likely to use tests because they have a greater number of vacancies across which to spread the fixed costs associated with testing, and they are more likely to have specialized human resource specialists who are familiar with and trained for psychometric testing. Wolf and Jenkins (2006) also found the growing formal professionalization of HR departments to be a significant factor.

HRM in reality Making the most of psychometrics

Change management and training consultancy, cda, believes that too many companies are failing to maximize on the benefits of using psychometrics as an integral part of their recruitment policy. This is restricting return on investment and development of staff potential.

They quote the CIPD Recruitment, Retention and Development Survey 2006 indicating that 60 per cent of organizations are now using psychometrics as part of the recruitment process. Costs are significant, typically averaging up to several thousand pounds including training and licences. Nevertheless, it is said to represent a worthwhile investment. Comprehensive use of psychometrics is thought to result in a 'better-fit' recruit who is more likely to meet an employer's requirements, stay longer, contribute more and generally provide a better return on investment.

However, a significant percentage of firms using psychometrics only do so in the initial recruitment process and are not continuing to apply the approach as part of ongoing development.

Lisa Michelangeli, psychologist at cda said:

We encounter too many instances of what we call 'Silver Bullet' mentality. While there has been an increased recognition of the value of psychometrics, there can be an assumption that its integration into the recruitment process is a guarantee that it will result in a calibre of recruit who will have a long-term positive impact on the organization.

Some firms are not achieving full-value realization of their investment because they do not use the outputs of the psychometrics to inform development beyond the recruitment stage. For example, if a group of individuals is recruited, the outputs of the personality assessment can inform the development of the team and how they interact with each other. This is an example of the invaluable opportunities that we encounter organizations not always making the most of. Psychometrics are not a one-fix cure-all but have to be an integral part of the ongoing development process.

Consultants with cda report that this situation can be exacerbated by discontinuity between HR and line management. Often the HR function is involved only in the hiring (and firing) process and not in employee development, which can be regarded by line managers as their territory.

Lisa Michelangeli continues:

Given the sums of money companies are investing, we believe that it is essential for business leaders to ensure that their HR experts are educating and then supporting line management in incorporating the output of psychometrics into the various stages of the employee lifecycle.

For example, when line managers are trained in benefits such as the objective basis for performance management that psychometrics can provide, they embrace the practice wholeheartedly. However, it does need the business leaders to instigate clear policy to ensure that the essential instruction and ongoing support is properly implemented by HR and incorporated by line management. Leaving it to chance is not good enough.

Why do many organizations fail to make use of psychometric results after recruitment and selection?

Source: *HRM Guide UK* (http://www.hrmguide.co.uk), 24 August, 2006.

Key concept 15.2 Personality

Many lay people and psychologists believe that personality is a definite 'something' with a continuing existence at all stages of an individual's life, manifesting itself in every situation that person encounters. Generally expressed in terms of types or traits, the latter form the basis of most personality tests used for resourcing and the documentation employed for many performance appraisal systems. An alternative approach is to regard personality as an artefact of a particular set of circumstances. In other words, apparent personality depends on the meaning individuals give to a particular situation.

Table 15.1

Advantages and disadvantages of tests

Source: Adapted from Furnham (1992, p.39).

Advantages	Disadvantages
• Test results are numerical – allowing direct comparison of applicants on the same criteria.	• Responses can be faked on many tests to give a 'desirable' score. Some include 'lie detectors' to overcome this.
• Tests provide 'hard' data that can be evaluated for their predictive usefulness in later years – i.e. compare predicted with actual performance.	• Some people lack sufficient self-insight to give accurate responses.
• Tests provide explicit and specific results unlike interviews and references that can be vague or 'coded'.	• Tests are unreliable – temporary factors such as anxiety, headaches, illness can lead to variable results.
• Tests measure substance rather than image.	• Tests are invalid – many tests do not measure what they say they measure.
• A battery of tests can cover a comprehensive range of abilities and personal qualities.	• Tests are irrelevant – many tests do not measure qualities that are relevant to a specific organization, such as honesty and punctuality.
• Tests are 'scientific' – empirically based with a grounding in theory. They are reliable, valid and discriminate between good, average and mediocre.	• Tests require minimum literacy and a grasp of American jargon.
• Tests provide a conceptual language to users, enhancing understanding of behaviour.	• Good norms do not exist for most populations – comparison with white, middle-class, male US students has little practical value.
• Empirical data from tests provide objective evidence to justify decisions.	• Tests are unfair to anyone who is not a white, middle-class, male American because most have been constructed using them as a reference population.
• Tests provide insights and explanations for behaviour. They can be used to justify individual rejections.	• Freedom of information legislation opens 'objective' data to greater scope for challenge than vague, unrecorded interview data.
	• Firms tend to use the same tests so that practice effects and knowledge of desirable answers can destroy their value.

Criticism of psychological testing

Increasing use of psychological testing has caused some disquiet among psychologists, particularly the proliferation of personality assessments (Bartram, 1991). There are many available on the market promoted by people without adequate training and making extravagant claims about their value and effectiveness. Many employers, including those with human resource specialists, do not have the ability to identify good and bad products. In an attempt to distinguish the trained from the untrained, the British Psychological Society has introduced a Certificate in Occupation Testing Competence.

Furnham (1992, p.5) criticizes the underlying research which 'justifies' specific personality measures on a number of grounds:

- The personality characteristics chosen are often arbitrary and uninformed. Often they are historical relics, long-abandoned and condemned by psychologists but still exploited as commercial products.

- Statistical analyses tend to be simple and naive, leading to more findings of significant differences than there are in reality (Type II errors). Usually, simple correlations are used – rather than 'robust and sensitive' multivariate statistics – when all the variables involved are multi-factorial.

- Most studies are exploratory, with no theoretical basis and are not part of systematic programmes. As a result, they tend to be 'one-off', sometimes with interesting implications but no particular consequence.

- Organizational and social factors are often ignored – personality may not be the only relevant factor.

Blinkhorn and Johnson (1990) criticize personality tests as predictors of job performance when compared with ability and aptitude tests. They argue that their validity coefficients are often no better than chance. However, other specialists consider that personality tests are still valuable if they are used carefully and are not taken to be the main predictors. For example, 'conscientiousness' is linked to job performance and 'extroversion' scores are useful predictors for sales ability.

The greatest difficulty with personality tests is that candidates can lie. Moreover, they can fake results in different ways and to a varying extent (Zickar, Gibby and Robie, 2004). Individuals may score highly on extroversion because they are extroverts. Alternatively they can present themselves as outgoing because it is clear from the job description that selectors are seeking extroverts. In a **meta-analysis**, Li and Bagger (2006) looked at the effects of impression management and self-deception on the criterion validity of personality constructs. They used the balanced inventory of desirable responding (BIDR) and failed to find any evidence that impression management and self-deception created spurious effects on the relationship between personality measures and performance. They also found that removing the influence of these two dimensions from measures of personality did not significantly attenuate the criterion validity of personality variables.

	Table 15.2	Reason	% citing as a reason	% citing as main reason
		To predict job performance	76.1	39.4
	Reasons for using selection tests	To provide additional information before interview	73.5	27.9
		To assess ability of applicants to 'fit into' organizational culture	67.3	25.0
	Source: Adapted from IRS (1997).	To screen people for emotional stability	20.4	1.0
		Other	12.4	6.7

It has also been argued that, since tests are based on personality theory, they cannot be interpreted without knowledge of the theory in which most selectors are untrained. Another contentious issue is the effect of practice. If applicants are exposed to the same test on more than one occasion, they gain from the previous experience, often remembering answers. The doubts about personality tests have become well-known. Lievens, Highhouse and De Corte (2005) asked experienced retail store supervisors to rate job applicant profiles described on two dimensions including General Mental Ability (GMA). Unlike previous research, supervisors were also informed about the method of assessment used. The importance attached to extroversion and GMA decreased when store supervisors knew that scores were derived from a paper-and-pencil test rather than an unstructured interview. Store supervisors with more selection-related experience also attached more importance to GMA.

Wood and Baron (1992, p.34) consider the effect of psychological tests in terms of 'adverse impact' on ethnic minority groups: ' "Adverse impact" occurs when there is a significant disparity in test scores between ethnic groups, resulting in one group being disproportionately preferred over the other. The test is then said to have an adverse impact on the lower-scoring group.' They argue that the greater the degree of adverse impact, the more this has to be justified. Employers must be careful to test strictly for qualities that can be proven to be required for the job. Even when this can be demonstrated it remains important to find the method of measurement with the least adverse impact. A common problem is the effect of language proficiency on test performance. Typically, ethnic minority candidates are undergoing a selection procedure in the dominant community language, such as English, when they are stronger linguistically in another, such as Hindi or Italian. Their performance is masked by their comprehension of the questions and their ability to express their answers in a manner that is meaningful to the testers. Often, tests are time-limited. This is a reasonable gauge of mental speed for native speakers because their use of language is automatic. However, it is detrimental to people answering out of their native languages, since they need to translate at a conscious mental level. In effect the test becomes an assessment of 'proficiency in English' rather than a measure of its true objectives such as 'problem-solving ability' or 'motivation'. The test has become unfair for anyone whose first language is not English.

In a case involving British Rail (BR), it was shown that, in an analysis of 4000 tests taken by potential drivers, white people were twice as successful as ethnic minority candidates. Eight guards of Asian origin took BR to an industrial tribunal on the grounds that the tests were discriminatory. The verbal reasoning tests employed were not directly related to the job and were particularly difficult for people who spoke English as a second language. BR admitted that the tests had adverse impact on Asian workers and undertook to seek the advice of the Commission for Racial Equality in developing revised selection techniques.

Similarly, the Council for Legal Education (CLE) introduced a critical reasoning test for around 2300 applicants to the English Bar's training school. The CLE had attempted to provide a test that was as fair as possible, involving two firms of occupational psychologists and Birkbeck College of the University of London. However, the test was trialled on a group of existing students that included very few from ethnic minority groups. According to Makbool Javaid, chair of the Society of Black Lawyers, it was felt that 'some of the questions would be difficult to answer for anyone who was not from a middle-class public school kind of background' (*Times Higher*, 18 March, 1994). The results produced a storm of protest and the tests were soon reconsidered. These reservations are widely known among human resource specialists and may explain Storey's (1994a) report of a reduction in use of personality tests around that time.

Interviewing

The interview is a social ritual which is expected by all participants, including applicants. It is such a 'normal' feature of filling vacancies that candidates for a job would be extremely surprised not to be interviewed at least once.

Informal interviews

Many employers invite applicants for informal interviews prior to the main selection procedure. These interviews are useful for information exchange, particularly in the case of professionals (Breakwell, 1990, p.10). They provide the opportunity to discuss the full nature of the job, the working environment, prospects for further development and promotion. Candidates who decide that the job is not for them can elect to go no further. To avoid interviews degenerating into pointless chats, Breakwell emphasizes that both interviewer and applicant need to have checklists of essential points to cover. Interviewers should:

- Give a balanced picture of the job, including an honest account of its disadvantages together with a (larger) number of positive aspects. Honesty might seem dangerous but is best in the long run.
- A description of the organization in the same terms.
- Introduce the interviewee to other people in the department. This also allows interested parties to vet the applicant.

Blackman (2002a) investigated the common practice of informal telephone interviews. The study was aimed at determining if impoverished personality judgements of job applicants would come from telephone interviews in comparison to face-to-face interviews, given the lack of crucial non-verbal communication. Mock job interviews were used in both face-to-face format and telephone format. A significantly higher correlation was found between personality ratings of face-to-face interviewers and other sources of an applicant's personality ratings. Not surprisingly, face-to-face interviewers also rated applicants significantly higher or more favourably on personality traits that are normally best-revealed by non-verbal communication.

There seems to be some ambiguity as to whether informal interviews should be used as part of the pre-selection process by the employer rather than self-selection by the candidate. The crux of the issue depends on what interviewees have been told. If they have been led to believe that it is a truly informal information session they will not consider the process to be fair if they are subsequently told that they have not been shortlisted as a result.

Formal interviews

A selection interview can be defined neatly as 'a conversation with a purpose' but not infrequently the purpose is obscure to the point of invisibility. More often than not 'purposeless chat' would be nearer the mark. It is a form of social interaction in which the interviewer is engaged in active **person perception** of the interviewee (see Key concept 15.3). From the

---

Key concept 15.3 Person perception

The perception of other people. Cues such as facial expression, posture, gesture, body movement, tone of voice, etc., are used to evaluate their current mood and overall personalities (McKenna, 1994, p.144). Each one of us has an 'implicit personality theory' based on our experience, assumptions about people, beliefs and prejudices. The evidence of our senses is used to collect data about the perceived person and attribute characteristics to them according to our implicit theory. This is a simplification process and leads to a number of well-known errors of judgement, including:

- *Logical error*: assuming that certain traits are always found together – e.g. if a person is described as 'objective' we tend to perceive them as 'cold'.
- *Halo effect*: the tendency to perceive people as all 'good' or all 'bad'.
- *Stereotyping*: seeing all members of a particular group – e.g. Africans, Scots – to have the same characteristics. Stereotyping leads to prejudice.

interviewee's perspective 'one is managing a demonstration of knowledge or ability through a social vehicle, and one inevitably needs to attend to the social as well as the cognitive aspect of the interview' (Sternberg, 1994, p.181). In other words, the impression created depends as much on social factors as any demonstration of experience or expertise.

For many unskilled or semi-skilled jobs, the formal interview tends to be perfunctory and can be over in a few sentences. This is not necessarily a bad thing. For decades, the evidence has been that the more sophisticated and lengthy proceedings entered into by major organizations often have been no better in terms of outcome. According to Sternberg (1994, p.182): 'Interviewers tend to prefer interviewees who are relaxed, who put the interviewers at ease, who are socially as well as verbally facile, and who have some degree of interpersonal sparkle.'

In fact, the interview has attracted severe criticism for a very long time. W.D. Scott is quoted as having said in 1915 that the selection interview is not a dependable selection method (Lewis, 1985, p.150). Since then the interview has been attacked on the grounds of its subjective nature, questionable validity and unreliability. Webster (1964) noted some significant findings:

- First impressions count. Interviewers make their minds up in the first few minutes, then seek evidence to support their opinion.

HRM in reality   Snap judgements about faces

Recent research indicates that when we see an unfamiliar face, our brains decide intuitively whether a person is attractive and trustworthy within a tenth of a second – so quickly that reason may play no part in the process.

The study by Princeton University assistant professor of psychology, Alex Todorov, and research student, Janine Willis, published in the July 2006 issue of *Psychological Science* asked about 200 observers to look at 66 different faces flashed onto a screen for one of three time durations: 100 milliseconds, 500 milliseconds or a full second.

The observers recorded whether they found the face to be trustworthy or not, and also how confident they were in their analysis. Similar experiments tested for other traits, such as likeability, competence, and aggressiveness. Judgements made after the shortest exposure time correlated highly with those made without time constraints. With more time to decide, observers' judgements did not change, but their confidence in them increased.

Alex Todorov said:

The link between facial features and character may be tenuous at best, but that doesn't stop our minds from sizing other people up at a glance. We decide very quickly whether a person possesses many of the traits we feel are important, such as likeability and competence, even though we have not exchanged a single word with them. It appears that we are hard-wired to draw these inferences in a fast, unreflective way.

Todorov said that it is not yet clear why the brain makes such snap judgements. However, functional magnetic resonance imaging of brain activity suggests that the part of the brain that responds directly to fear may be involved in judgements of trustworthiness.

'The fear response involves the amygdala, a part of the brain that existed in animals for millions of years before the development of the prefrontal cortex, where rational thoughts come from. We imagine trust to be a rather sophisticated response, but our observations indicate that trust might be a case of a high-level judgement being made by a low-level brain structure. Perhaps the signal bypasses the cortex altogether,' Alex Todorov continued.

He cautioned that the findings do not imply that quick first impressions cannot be overcome by the rational mind:

As time passes and you get to know people, you, of course, develop a more rounded conception of them. But because we make these judgements without conscious thought, we should be aware of what is happening when we look at a person's face.

If our brains are 'hard-wired' to make snap judgements on faces, what are the likely consequences for fair selection?

Source: *HRM Guide USA* (http://www.hrmguide.com), 24 August, 2006.

- The candidate's appearance is the most significant factor, followed by information on the application form.
- Unfavourable evidence is valued more strongly than favourable evidence.
- The interviewer's opinion 'comes over' to the candidate during the interview and influences the candidate's further performance in an unfavourable or favourable direction.

Nevertheless, in a survey of 60 interviewers and 90 candidates in a 'milkround' exercise, 95 per cent of interviewers and 85 per cent of candidates considered interviews to be fair (*Personnel Management*, March 1992). Comparing panel with one-to-one interviews, 52 per cent of the interviewers said panel interviews were fairer, 35 per cent were unsure, and 13 per cent preferred one-to-one interviews. In contrast, nearly two-thirds of the candidates preferred one-to-one interviews, with only 13 per cent indicating a positive preference for the panel approach.

Hebl and Skorinko (2005) investigated the significance of acknowledgments made by physically disabled individuals in an interview setting, and looked at timing of an acknowledgment in relation to impressions formed by evaluators. 137 participants observed

---

HRM in reality Interview mistakes

A recent Canadian survey finds that how much applicants know about prospective employers plays a crucial role in successful jobseeking. Thirty-four per cent of executives polled said that having little or no knowledge of the company is the most common mistake made during interviews.

The survey was conducted by an independent research firm and developed by Accountemps, the world's largest specialized staffing service for temporary professionals in the financial sector. It included responses from 100 senior Canadian executives including those from human resources, finance and marketing departments.

Asked 'What do you think is the most common mistake candidates make during job interviews?' executives responded:

- little or no knowledge of the company (34 per cent)
- unprepared to discuss skills and experience (26 per cent)
- limited enthusiasm (11 per cent)
- late arrival (8 per cent)
- unprepared to discuss career plans and goals (7 per cent)
- lack of eye contact (5 per cent)
- monopolize interview (2 per cent)
- inappropriate dress (1 per cent)
- don't know/other (6 per cent).

Max Messmer, chairman of Accountemps and author of *Managing Your Career For Dummies®* said:

Candidates should learn as much as they can about a company before meeting a prospective employer. The most successful applicants will have a beyond-the-basics understanding of the firm, including its history, chief competitors and business objectives. Armed with this knowledge, job hopefuls should be able to describe how their skills and experience can help the business reach its goals.

Accountemps offers the following tips for researching potential employers:

Find information at your fingertips. Visiting the company's website can locate a wealth of information, such as the firm's mission and values, what products and services it provides, recent press releases etc. If it's a publicly traded company, call the investor relations department to request an annual report.

Research the industry. In addition to learning about the company, research the industry in which it competes to gain a better understanding of the market and specific issues and trends that may affect the organization.

Check your network. Ask your colleagues, friends and others for information about your prospective employer. Your contacts may have worked for or with the organization and could provide insight that may prove valuable during a job interview.

What are the best ways for a candidate to find information about a small company?

Source: *HRM Guide Canada* (http://www.hrmguide.net/canada/), 14 September, 2006.

interviews of disabled applicants who acknowledged their disability at the beginning, middle, or end of a job interview or made no acknowledgement at all. Applicants who acknowledged their disability early in the interview were perceived more favourably than those who acknowledged at the end of the interview or not at all.

In a Canadian study, Chapman and Webster (2006) also found that signal and expectancy mechanisms influenced candidate intentions and job choice. These effects appeared to be most important for applicants who had multiple job opportunities and less pre-interview knowledge of an organization.

Evaluating methods

How do we judge the value or effectiveness of interviewing – or any other method of selection? Before going further it is useful to consider the four basic requirements (Smith, 1991, p.32):

1 *Practicality*. Selection methods must be practical in a given situation – for example, cost, convenience and time available. Attitudes of employers and candidates to the methods are also relevant.

2 *Sensitivity*. The ability of a method to distinguish one candidate from another. Interviews may rank a number of candidates fairly closely, whereas tests may give a wide range of scores.

3 *Reliability*. How consistent are the results? Conventionally, there are three forms of reliability measure:
   – Comparison over time. If a method is used on the same group of candidates on different days, are the scores likely to be similar? This is sometimes called test-retest or intra-rater reliability.
   – Inter-rater reliability. If two or more assessors are involved, how much agreement is there between them?
   – Internal consistency. If several items in a test or procedure are meant to measure the same characteristic, such as sociability, how close are the ratings?

4 *Validity*. Does the method achieve its purpose in distinguishing the most suitable applicants from the others? Three measures of validity are available:
   – Face validity. Does the method appear to be measuring what it is supposed to measure? This is important because it is essential that candidates believe that they have been fairly treated. Disappointed applicants frequently complain about apparently irrelevant interview questions or test items. For example, one selection

Validity range	Methods	Rating	
0.5 to 0.6	Cognitive ability tests	Good to excellent	**Table 15.3**
0.3 to 0.39	Work sample tests Biodata Assessment centres Structured interviews	Acceptable	Comparative validities **Source**: Based on Bertua (2005), Smith (1991) and Roth (2005).
Less than 0.3	Personality tests Typical interviews References Graphology	Poor	
Chance (0)	Astrology		

test includes the question: 'Do you like tall women?' Whether or not this has deep psychological significance, its appearance is enough to bring derision on the test.

– Construct validity. To what extent does the method measure a particular construct or human quality such as commitment?
– Predictive validity. How well does the method predict the suitability of a successful candidate?

Reliability and validity are expressed as correlational coefficients where perfection is represented by 1.0 and pure chance is shown by zero. Establishing the validity of a particular procedure logically requires the employer to take on a large number of applicants, good and bad, and then compare their job performance with that predicted by the selection method. This kind of predictive validity study is impractical in most circumstances. Sometimes termed 'the one that got away' problem, we never know how the people we did not select might have performed.

Research shows that similar results can be obtained by a method termed 'concurrent study' where selection methods are employed on existing employees at the same time as the selection procedure is taking place. Performance of existing employees is then correlated with prediction scores of the selection method. Again, however, this is rarely done, partly because accurate performance measures are difficult to obtain for many jobs.

In a meta-analysis on the validity of over 500 tests of general mental ability and specific cognitive abilities, Bertua, Anderson and Salgado (2005) found that both types of tests are valid predictors of job performance and training success. They calculated that operational validities were in the magnitude of 0.5 to 0.6, in line with previous meta-analyses in the USA.

Fairness is a further requirement: specifically, candidates' perceptions of the equity of the process. Good candidates are more likely to accept an offer if they consider that the procedure has been fair, effective and considerate while rejected applicants will continue to have a positive view of an organization's employer brand if they feel they have been fairly treated. Schleicher et al. (2006) looked at a sample of 754 applicants to a US government agency. They found evidence that candidates' perception of their 'opportunity to perform' was an important predictor of their overall feelings about the fairness of the selection process, and was the single most important procedural rule after receiving negative feedback. Intriguingly, in a simulated exercise, Schinkel, van Dierendonck and Anderson (2004) found that rejected candidates who were given performance feedback were more likely to show negative effects on core self-evaluations and affective well-being than those who were simply given rejection messages.

People have different perceptions of fairness. Truxillo et al. (2006) related the 'Big Five' personality measures (neuroticism, extroversion, agreeableness, conscientiousness and openness to experience) to candidates' perceptions of post-test fairness, themselves, and the hiring organization. After controlling for gender and test score, they found that personality accounted for significant variance in all three, although the relationship with fairness was weakest. Neuroticism and agreeableness were the personality factors that most consistently predicted candidate perceptions.

Moscoso and Salgado (2004) examined students' reactions to selection methods in Spain and Portugal. They found similar results in both countries with interviews, résumés and work sample tests being rated most highly and contacts, integrity tests and graphology being judged least favourably. Face validity and opportunity to perform were the most important bases for a favourable judgment.

Interviews revisited

Since the late 1980s there has been a revision of opinion concerning the value of interviews (Smith, 1991; Eder and Harris, 1999). Earlier research findings were based on small samples. The use of meta-analytic techniques allows the combination of statistics from a number of small studies to give much larger samples. For example, Weisner and Cronshaw (1988) combined validity coefficients from 150 studies and conclude that interviews can be more valid than suspected. In fact, their validity depends on the type of interview. Traditional, or unstructured interviews comprise the vast majority and are generally no more than cosy chats. Their validity was found to be 0.2 (very poor) whereas structured interviews, especially those based on job analysis, were found to be significantly better with a validity of 0.63.

Structured interviews are conducted to a format, rather than a script, and focus questioning on the job rather than irrelevant incidentals such as holidays and golf. Two standard methods are:

- Criterion referenced interviews, based on job analysis with a set of questions geared to experience and skill for interviewers to choose from.

- Situational interviews, based on the 'critical incidents' technique. A reasonable number (typically 20) of real-life work incidents are obtained from jobholders or their supervisors. Possible ways of dealing with these situations are outlined and rated as

---

Crédit Suisse

Crédit Suisse provides financial and banking services to private clients and small and medium-sized companies in more than 50 countries. It employs over 20 000 people from more than 100 nationalities and receives large numbers of applications from potential recruits.

In May 2005 Crédit Suisse completed implementation of a structured recruiting process (SRP) that aims to make recruitment more efficient by focusing on pre-selection of candidates. This reduces the emphasis on unstructured interviews that frequently introduce bias and subjectivity. It is also intended to improve cost-effectiveness by accurately matching applicants to vacancies, and reducing the likelihood of wrong hires.

After dossier analysis, all applicants are asked to complete an internet-based personality test, lasting between 30 and 40 minutes. Selected candidates are informed immediately and proceed to a telephone interview. Successful applicants then attend a 'multimodal' face-to-face interview with relevant managers.

The questioning method used in the multimodal interview is highly structured and is applied to each candidate. Questions are designed by the line manager rather than by HR specialists. Responses are rated one to five in accordance with predetermined 'ideal' answers. The intention is to ensure that successful candidates not only have appropriate qualifications and experience, but also demonstrate qualities that are consonant with the organization's objectives.

Initially, a large number of line managers were sent questionnaires asking them to define the requirements for specific jobs. The organization then conducted 'critical incident workshops', involving a representative sample of managers. This led to formulation of interview questions that could be incorporated into either the telephone or multimodal stages of the process. Questions were translated into four languages. Web-based training courses were devised to provide recruiting managers, HR business partners and line managers with skills to implement the SRP effectively.

SRP was first introduced for newly graduated applicants in September 2002. A pilot project was conducted in the information technology and operations division in January 2004, and implementation was completed in May 2005.

The organization acknowledges considerable initial resistance, especially from HR. The process seemed excessively rigid but is now seen to require considerable interviewing skills. SRP also created extra work at first until the techniques became more familiar. Candidates appeared to accept the process without difficulty. On-line assessment is increasingly common and interview questions have greater relevance. The structured recruiting process is seen to be succeeding in improving recruitment efficiency.

Source: based on Pollitt (2005a).

suitable or unsuitable, frequently on a points system. These situations are presented to candidates as hypothetical problems and responses evaluated against predetermined ratings.

Peeters and Lievens (2006) investigated how structured interview formats, instructions to convey favourable impressions, and applicants' individual differences influenced the use and effectiveness of verbal and nonverbal impression management (IM) tactics. They found that interview format affected the kind of tactics used, which in turn positively influenced interviewer evaluations. Behaviour description interviews triggered self-focused defensive tactics, whereas situational interviews triggered other-focused tactics. Instructions to convey a desirable impression also enhanced the use of specific tactics (self-focused and other-focused verbal IM) and moderated the effects of individual differences on IM use. They suggest that nonverbal behaviour might be less intentionally controllable in selection situations.

Moscoso (2000) reviewed evidence on the criterion and construct validity of the interview. Based on the content of questions included in selection interviews, Moscoso identified two types of structured interview: the conventional structured interview and the behavioural structured interview. Criterion validity studies generally support the view that behavioural structured interviews show the highest validity coefficients. Moscoso found a lower level of investigation into construct validity but concluded from studies available that conventional structured interviews and behavioural structured interviews were clearly measuring different constructs. Also, behavioural structured interviews seemed to produce more frequent negative applicant reactions than conventional structured interviews.

A further study by Salgado and Moscoso (2002) included a series of meta-analyses on the construct validity of conventional interviews and behavioural interviews. Conventional interviews typically include questions aimed at checking credentials, description of experience, and self-evaluative information. Behavioural interviews consist mainly of questions regarding job knowledge, job experience, and behaviour descriptions. They found that conventional interviews assessed general mental ability, job experience, the 'Big Five' personality dimensions and social skills. Behavioural interviews, on the other hand, mainly assessed job knowledge, job experience, situational judgement and social skills. Although there was some overlap, the two main forms of interview seemed to be different.

In a more recent study, Krajewski *et al.* (2006) analyzed data from 157 applicants to managerial positions and found a significant correlation between predictions from past-behaviour structured interviews and subsequent job performance. Situational interview formats did not produce a significant correlation. They also found a closer relationship between past-behaviour structured interviews and relevant cognitive ability measures, assessment centre exercises and personality traits.

Van Iddekinge *et al.* (2006) examined differences in criterion-related validity estimates among ratings from individual interviewers and interview panels in the US army. They found considerable variation in interviewer validity coefficients in relation to multiple performance criteria. Results also indicated the importance of adopting a multivariate perspective when evaluating interviewer validity differences. Similar findings emerged for ratings averaged within interview panels. However, most or all of the variance for some interview-criterion combinations appeared to be due to statistical artefacts.

To be effective, an interview must be more than a friendly chat. The greater the degree of planning beforehand, the greater the likelihood of a higher degree of validity as a selection tool. The function of the interview is to obtain predictive evidence regarding a candidate's likely performance on specific criteria. The questioning style can be linked to the kind of evidence required and may take one of three principal routes:

(Hypothetical) problem-solving questioning in which the candidate is presented with situations to evaluate or solve and which can be expected to test the candidate's abilities in a number of respects – e.g. intellect, grasp of information, problem-solving ability, lateral thinking, practicality, creativity, etc.

Behavioural (past) event questioning, which assumes that previous handling of situations and problems predicts an individual's future performance in similar circumstances.

Patterned behavioural event (life) questioning, which attempts to identify an individual's career or life strategy, establishing how rational and sensible changes in that person's life have been and drawing conclusions about stability, seriousness of application and likely motivation. The 'culture fit' approach emphasizes this perspective. For example, Japanese companies such as Toyota are more interested in personality than technical skill. They look for a personal philosophy that fits the corporate culture. Modern call centres similarly seek a range of competencies from customer care through to commitment-related qualities (Callaghan and Thompson, 2002).

Kutcher and Bragger (2004) investigated the potential of structured interviews for mitigating biases. They asked 133 participants to observe videotaped interviews, varying between structured or unstructured interview scripts and average weight or overweight job applicants. The results confirmed a bias against overweight interviewees which was moderated by the use of structured interviews. A further study with a greater level of structure in the interviews appeared to increase the moderating effect.

Blackman (2002b) investigated structured and unstructured employment interviews in relation to the assessment of applicants' job-related personality traits. The hypothesis was that unstructured interviews would lead to more accurate personality assessments since interviewees would feel less constrained by a script and more readily manifest their true selves. Behaviour in mock job interviews (structured and unstructured) was coded by an independent rater. Self-ratings of job-related personality traits on the California Q-set were obtained for each interviewee, together with ratings of their personality from the interviewer and a peer of the interviewee. A correlation analysis supported the original hypothesis, showing that average self-interviewer and peer-interviewer agreement was significantly greater when interviews had used the unstructured method.

Barclay (2001), however, comes out in favour of the behavioural structured interview. A survey of the use of behavioural interviewing in selection for UK organizations showed that both interviewers and applicants were positive about the method. Barclay identifies the following as key benefits:

- better quality information-gathering leading to improved selection decisions
- more consistency and improved skills of interviewers
- better opportunities for applicants to explain their skills.

But Barclay also recognizes limitations in respect to training, practice and time required and scoring.

Other approaches that have ethical considerations to take into account include stress interviewing and 'sweet and sour'. Stress interviewing, where the candidate is pressurized, sometimes aggressively, is justified on the basis that the job is pressurized and, therefore, it is important to establish how the candidate is likely to perform under stressful circumstances. One study asked interviewers if they ever deliberately put candidates under stress in interviews to see how they would cope (*Personnel Management*, March 1992). The findings were disturbing with 13 per cent saying they often did, 27 per cent saying sometimes, and 27 per cent rarely.

'Sweet and sour' interviews are those where interviewers take completely different approaches, one pleasant, one unpleasant in an attempt to gain a wider range of responses from the candidate.

Preparation for interviews

Training for interviewers stresses a number of factors conducive to making a good impression on the candidate. The interviewer should ensure that relevant information (application form, etc.) is read beforehand – it is surprising how many interviewers are found to be reading such material for the first time *during* the interview. The interview should take place in an appropriate environment – a quiet room without interruptions, with comfortable but business-like furniture and so on. The candidate should be put at ease as much as possible.

Table 15.4	Method	%
	Interviews	
	Structured panel	88
	Structured one-to-one	81
	Biographical	85
	Competency-based	85
	Telephone	56
	Tests	
	Specific skills	82
	General ability	75
	Literacy/numeracy	72
	Personality/aptitude	60
	Online selection	25
	References (pre-interview)	
	Employment	50
	Academic	37
	Assessment centres	48
	Group exercises	48
	Other	6

Selection methods used by large organizations in the UK, 2006

Source: Based on CIPD (2006).

HRM in reality Candidates who perform last finish first

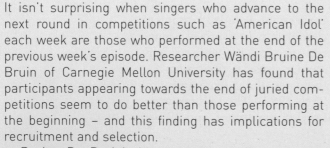

It isn't surprising when singers who advance to the next round in competitions such as 'American Idol' each week are those who performed at the end of the previous week's episode. Researcher Wändi Bruine De Bruin of Carnegie Mellon University has found that participants appearing towards the end of juried competitions seem to do better than those performing at the beginning – and this finding has implications for recruitment and selection.

Bruine De Bruin's latest paper, published in the journal *Acta Psychologica* (2005), describes her studies on European figure-skating competitions and the Eurovision Song Contest, a pop song competition that has taken place in Europe since 1956 (and which, like 'American Idol', includes voting by fans watching at home). Bruine De Bruin found that participants appearing near the end of the contests received higher marks from judges than those who performed earlier. This phenomenon, known as the serial position effect, doesn't just affect would-be pop idols; it is possible

that the effect may occur in other situations such as job interviews and student exams.

Bruine De Bruin found that the effect was progressive, with scores increasing throughout the competitions, not just when judges evaluated all candidates at the end of each contest, but also when they were asked to rate each individual performance after it had been completed. Bruine De Bruin conducted some of her research at Eindhoven University of Technology in The Netherlands.

'A friend of mine asked to go last in a series of job interviews, after hearing about my research. She got the job. I like to think that she got the job because she has great skills, but order effects may have tipped the balance for her,' Bruine De Bruin said.

Can you suggest any ways to minimize order effects in selection procedures?

Source: *HRM Guide USA* (http://www.hrmguide.com), 1 March, 2005.

A major change in recent years has been the improvement in applicants' interview techniques. Redundant staff are commonly given the opportunity of outplacement counselling, which normally includes advice on CV preparation and coaching in interview technique. Managers who are rarely involved in selection, perhaps only conducting interviews once or twice a year, are at a disadvantage against trained applicants. Interview coaching is similar in principle to training politicians for television appearances. Astute trainees can learn how to mask insincerity and to promise the earth with apparent conviction.

Against trained interviewers, the most useful tactic for applicants is to become familiar with the company they are applying to join. This requires research on the company's history, products or services and its reported strategy. Knowledge of the industry or sector in which it operates is also valuable. This information should not be acquired by pestering the recruitment section on the telephone. Given the number of applications to advertised vacancies at present, this is likely to be unwise. Whether or not any direct questions are asked on these subjects, applicants who have researched the territory will be able to form their responses in a way which makes it clear that they have done so.

Interviewing techniques

There are significant variations in the way employers conduct interviews. The most common method is the 'singleton' interview when the candidate's fate is determined by one session with a single interviewer. For obvious reasons, this method is likely to be regarded as unfair by interviewees who are not selected. There is no check or record of bias on the part of the interviewer who may have made a judgement on a complete whim.

A long-standing method which attempts to overcome this problem is the panel or board interview, involving a number of interviewers. Typically, two or three people ask questions in turn. A classic format involves an 'operational' interviewer, usually a line manager from the department offering the job and a personnel interviewer, normally from the HR department. There may be an additional chairperson. Each asks questions appropriate to their areas of expertise, the operational assessor asking task-related questions and the personnel assessor investigating career aspiration and motivation. The board is sometimes much larger: there are instances of seven or nine interviewers.

Superficially, the panel interview is judged to be fairer since all questioning takes place in a public arena and candidates' responses are heard by all parties. It also offers the candidate a more varied range of questions, expanding the evidence available to the assessors. As a consequence, personal bias should have less effect. However, the situation is likely to be more stressful for candidates. There are also opportunities for organizational politics to enter the situation, especially when the procedure is an internal selection.

Dipboye *et al.* (2001) looked at unstructured panel interviews for corrections officers and found a weak aggregate level of validity in the prediction of job performance and training success. Aggregate analyses also showed only a small incremental contribution to the prediction of job performance from panel judgements relative to paper credentials, and found the two sources of information to be only weakly related. But there was a considerable variation in simple and incremental validity at the level of individual panel members and among subgroups of panels. They conclude that aggregate analyses underestimate the validity of the typical unstructured panel interview.

A further variant is the 'sequential' method, with two or more interviews but with the candidate only being expected to face one interviewer at a time. This method carries most of the advantages of singleton and panel interviews with fewer of the disadvantages.

It is possible to use group interviews in certain circumstances. We will see later in this chapter that they are useful within assessment centre programmes as information sessions.

As with many other aspects of selection, interviewing has been formalized and packaged into training programmes available for both selectors and candidates. Untrained assessors are likely to conduct interviews in an unstructured way. Interview training is a useful component of management training. The best training programmes encourage people to become aware of their body language and questioning styles, helping them to develop interview techniques that open up fresh areas of evidence. Many junior managers and job club participants have had the opportunity to see themselves 'in action' on video, taking part in mock interviews. Initially demoralizing (for most), it is an invaluable method of feedback.

Packaged training methods have led to a certain sameness, however, and seasoned job applicants and interviewers now enter into formalized duals where each participant is aware of the underlying dynamics. Typically, interviewers are taught to:

- Ask open, not closed, questions to elicit the maximum information. Questions beginning with how, what, why, when, reduce the frequency of yes/no answers and force candidates to think about their replies.

- Provide supportive body language that suggests interest in what the candidate is saying without indicating approval or disapproval.

- Employ questioning styles such as the use of funnelling. Here the interviewer asks a succession of how, what, why, questions on the same subject in an attempt to achieve a depth of evidence.

- Consider factual or hypothetical questions, such as 'How would you go about setting up a telephone system for a remote island in the Pacific?' Provided that the interviewee is not a qualified telecommunications engineer, an applicant for a totally unconnected job will have to think hard to provide a full, imaginative but practical answer.

Tom Peters dismissed this 'quick analysis' technique as honouring glibness (*Independent on Sunday*, syndicated article 8 May 1994). Many interviewers have strong opinions on what they are looking for and how they should set about it. Peters held that 'interviews should be the centrepiece of a respectful courting process' foregoing 'pop quizzes and sadistic questioning rituals'. Arguing that the past was the only guide to future performance he set out an interviewing programme in typical guru style.

1 *Put the candidate's résumé under a microscope.* Pull an applicant's CV apart, following up experiences and achievements, including:
   - 'the kid who went through college without participating in extra-curricular activities – without *leading* those activities – is not likely to be a tiger on the job'
   - scrutinize college grades
   - an extensive check of references, previous work samples and work commendations ('employee of the month certificates or their equivalents').

2 *Look for a legacy.* Good performance in the past is not enough – how did they make their previous jobs better and different?

3 *Examine their turn-ons.* Talk about the applicant's 'peak experiences at work or school'. Apparently 'what a person brags about is a key to future job performance'. Essentially, is the candidate a solo performer or a teamworker?

4 *Seek deviance, defiance and adventure.* Has the applicant broken with convention and done something in an unusual way? For example, by taking time out from education and travelling the world. 'Curiosity and productive kinkiness in the past will raise the odds of getting more of the same in the future.'

5 *Pursue animal energy.* If the 'spirit and zest' of the candidate exhaust you by the end of the interview, 'hire that one on the spot'.

6 *Trust your gut.* Ignoring interview nervousness, is the applicant 'the kind of person you would like to hang around with?'

Work samples

Interviews suffer from a basic problem: they obtain answers from candidates which, in effect, are unverifiable claims. When asked what they would do in a particular situation it is only natural for candidates to give the answer which they feel the interviewer wants to hear. There is no guarantee that a candidate would actually behave in that way in a real situation. In addition, it is common for candidates to exaggerate their abilities or experience and play down their inadequacies.

The work sample technique attempts to overcome this problem by asking candidates to take on 'mini jobs' in a selection situation. Properly designed work samples capture key elements of a real job. As such, they are realistic rather than hypothetical or abstract and should include features of the context in which the job functions. Work samples have shown some of the highest validity scores compared with other selection methods (Smith, Gregg and Andrews, 1989, p.70). Roth, Bobko and Mcfarland (2005) re-examined classic literature supporting work sample tests as among the most valid predictors of job performance and suggest that the level of the validity may be approximately one-third less than previously thought. They also found that work sample tests were associated with an observed correlation of 0.32 with tests of general cognitive ability.

Work samples are comparatively easy to organize and even the smallest of companies could employ the simpler forms such as:

- a typing test for jobs requiring keyboard skills
- bricklaying
- role playing
- group decisions
- presentations
- reports.

The most sophisticated of work sample procedures include in-basket tests, sometimes called in-tray exercises. Normally used for managerial jobs, candidates are given a typical in-tray containing a selection of material such as letters to be answered, reports to be analysed, items to be prioritized, etc. They are given instructions on what to do and a time limit. Standard scoring methods are available. Work samples are often used as part of an assessment centre programme.

Assessment centres

Recent surveys indicate increasing use of **assessment centres**, especially by large companies. They have been heavily researched in recent years, with the emphasis on their reliability and predictive validity. They show up well in comparison with most other forms of selection or assessment such as interviews and personality tests. Meta-analyses indicate respectable validity coefficients for assessment centres in predicting managerial success. However, as we will discuss shortly, their use is not entirely without difficulties.

Assessment centres are procedures and not necessarily places. They function on the principle that no individual method of selection is particularly good and no individual assessor is infallible. Accordingly, they use multiple methods and several assessors in structured programmes that attempt to minimize the inadequacies of each method and cancel out the prejudices of individual selectors. Inevitably, assessment centres are very expensive methods of selection. However, cheaper methods are focused towards past or present performance. This may be adequate where applicants are being assessed for jobs that are broadly similar to their current or previous work. When this is not the case, and applicants are being considered for more stretching tasks, they fail to provide the evidence as to how candidates are likely to perform. Most management promotions come into this category. Good managers need to demonstrate knowledge, skills and abilities that may not have been required at lower levels. How can we identify these characteristics? Assessment centres are particularly useful in this respect because they are focused on potential. They bring taxing problems and challenges to candidates in a situation that allows systematic observation and measurement of their performance.

The origins of the assessment centre lie in the violent history of the 20th century and the need for officer selection. Originally devised by the German army in the 1930s, assessment centre techniques were soon taken up in other countries. The British War Office Selection Board subjected candidates to a three- to four-day assessment, geared to evaluate leadership and organizational abilities. This included exercises in which intending officers had to negotiate obstacles such as rivers with a motley collection of squaddies and an assortment of ropes, planks and oil drums. They also included lengthy interviews and long written reports.

Some modern assessment centres with an 'outward bound' inclination continue to include such exercises, but most consist of group discussions, psychometric tests, interviews and exercises such as 'in-basket' work samples and presentations. The underlying intention is to measure applicants on the competencies deemed to be appropriate to the job. Simulations in the assessment centre are designed to bring out the behaviour which demonstrates possession of these competencies. The intention is not to estimate current ability but to predict future performance, possibly at higher management levels.

After World War II the method spread to the public sector and then to industry. The first industrial application was at the American Telephone and Telegraph Company (AT&T). Their experience had a major influence on subsequent use elsewhere, following a number of studies in which employees were compared with initial assessment centre evaluations. These studies showed a significant correlation between the evaluations and subsequent work performance (Smith, Gregg and Andrews, 1989).

The model form of assessment centre is an expensive process (Byham, 1984). A typical assessment centre involves six participants and lasts from one to three days. As participants go through the simulations they are observed by assessors (usually three) who are specially trained in observing and evaluating behaviour. Assessors observe different participants in each simulation and take notes on special observation forms. Then, after the simulations are completed, assessors spend one or more days sharing their observations and reaching agreement on evaluations of participants. Their final assessment, contained in a summary report for each participant, gives a detailed account of participants' strengths and development needs as well as an evaluation of overall potential for success in the 'target' position. Based on Blanksby and Iles (1990), the following list sets out the seven conditions that classically characterize assessment centres.

1 A number of assessment techniques must be used, of which at least one must be a simulation. Simulations could take the form of work samples, group exercises and in-baskets. Simulations are designed to bring out behaviours that are related to dimensions of performance on the actual job in question.

2 There must be multiple trained assessors.

3 Ratings must be pooled between assessors and assessment techniques in order to provide a judgement on selection, training or development programme.

4 Overall assessment of behaviour has to take place at a different time from the observation of behaviour.

5 Simulation exercises must be pre-developed to elicit a number of desired behaviours. They must be tested in advance to ensure that the results are relevant to the organization and that they are reliable and objective.

6 All dimensions, qualities, attributes or characteristics to be measured by the assessment centre must be determined by some form of job analysis.

7 The assessment techniques used must be designed to provide evidence for the evaluation of these dimensions.

Problems with assessment centres

Whether or not it is costed in financial terms, the impact of assessment centres on management time is considerable. Managers may appreciate the value of high-quality selection procedures, but will be reluctant to devote so much time unless all other parts of the selection process have been thorough. For example, Hilton Hotels International conducted a one-day assessment centre as a final stage in a selection process for general managers. They contracted an outside provider to conduct exhaustive online tests to ensure that candidates who got that far deserved their place (Beal, 2004).

The effectiveness of an assessment centre depends upon its design and the anticipation of problems. Additionally, the traditional process is group-based and is unusable in situations where only one or two candidates are being considered. Common design faults have been well documented (Dulewicz, 1991):

- The criteria for measurement are too woolly. Often, the competencies on which candidates are being assessed are very poorly defined and not expressed in behavioural terms that can be measured.

- The competencies are not mutually exclusive and overlap each other. Candidates are rewarded or penalized twice, depending on their strength in a particular area.

- Criteria are tied to the past, rather than being forward-looking.

- Exercises are badly designed and do not relate to experiences that are likely to occur within the organization. Alternatively, and perhaps because of this, they do not relate to the assessment criteria.

- Assessment centres contain a wide range of procedures, from group exercises to psychometric tests. Results from these procedures take a variety of forms. Integrating the results is complex, particularly when combining evidence on single competencies from a number of procedures. Poor technical design at this stage will lead to misleading findings.

- Poor assessor training. Line managers are unlikely to be good assessors unless they have been trained to avoid pitfalls such as 'halos and horns'. Also they require guidance on the range and skew of their assessments. Assessors need to be consistent in how they pitch their ratings, avoiding over-leniency or severity.

- Poor pre-selection and briefing of candidates. The consequence is that some candidates flounder from the beginning of the programme. Others become hostile towards a procedure that appears to them to be unfair or disorganized.

- Poor programming, leaving both assessors and candidates unsure of what they are supposed to be doing. They may be allotted too little or too much time at different points in the assessment.

- Inadequate handling of the programme events due to lack of coordination or commitment.

- Inadequate (or non-existent) follow-up. This may occur in the form of badly handled feedback counselling or inaction on assessors' recommendations.

- Poor evaluation of candidates' experience and assessors' performance on the programme.

Dulewicz (*ibid*.) considered that there were three broad phases that accounted for most of these difficulties:

1 programme design
2 selection and training of assessors
3 effective follow-up action.

He attributed many of the shortcomings to inexperience. Assessment centres are involved and complex. Good design is dependent on the knowledge and skills to design and develop what is a 'highly precise and sophisticated tool'.

Graphology

Graphology, or handwriting analysis, has a long history on the mainland of Europe dating back to to the Ancient Greeks and Romans (Thomas and Vaught, 2001). Its modern form originated in Italy in the 17th century and was further refined in France and Germany where it is used widely. The essence of graphology is that analysts claim to be able to describe an individual's personality from a sample of their handwriting. Their theoretical base is that of trait psychology which holds that personality has a number of fixed dimensions that are relatively unchangeable and do not depend on the situation. This is not to say that people do not change, indeed many graphologists believe their strongest asset to be the identification of neurotic or stress-related conditions that may be transient. Some graphologists also claim to be able to detect such characteristics as alcohol problems, homosexuality and dishonesty.

For example, the following excerpt from a press report stated that the British company S.G. Warburg accepted a graphologist's opinion that 'cramped' handwriting indicated drug addiction:

> The recent candidate interviewed for a junior job in Warburg's computer department provided an excellent CV, and seemed able and confident in the course of two interviews. His handwriting sample, however, was abnormally cramped. The lines were crooked and the letters spidery and badly squashed. At best, it seemed the writing of an ill-educated child. But Mrs Nezos [graphologist] thought otherwise. For an employer like Warburg, the prospect of hiring a drug addict is too frightening to contemplate. The man was turned down for the job. (*Independent on Sunday*, 20 October, 1991)

Handwriting analysis is routine and highly regarded in many continental European countries but is generally regarded with disdain in most English-speaking countries. However, there are signs of increasing acceptability in countries such as the USA: In the trade journal *Pest Control*, a contributor lauded the services of a handwriting analyst (Tennenbaum, 2005):

> … Heidi mentioned that she could do analysis for potential employees. 'I can tell you everything about them, whether they'd be better in sales, for example,' she said. All she would need is a page-long essay from each candidate … the content doesn't matter as much as the handwriting itself.

The contributor was so impressed, it seems, that he no longer takes on new employees for his US$2 million company without her verbal approval (at less than US$75 a time) or a more expensive typed report. 'With that report in hand, I can decide whether I still want the person based on résumé, references and overall "gut feeling". [. . .] Nothing else work this consistently well. It's amazing.'

In a similar pitch at a trade audience in New Zealand (Hogenesch, 2004, p.10) another graphologist acknowledged that handwriting analysis has not yet caught on in that country, but that it is 'a science' and 'recognized as an authentic tool': 'Handwriting . . . is like body language. It is virtually impossible to hide or disguise personality characteristics by altering one's handwriting. In the eyes of a skilled handwriting analyst the true personality is unfailingly revealed.'

The evidence is not so flattering. Cox and Tapsell (1991) compared analyses by graphologists and non-graphologists of 50 handwriting samples provided by managers on a training course. When assessment centre results were compared with the handwriting analyses, they found that the graphologists did slightly worse than the non-graphologists in rating the candidates. Moreover, the two graphologists failed to agree with each other! Thomas and Vaught (2001) surveyed the available literature on graphology and concluded that there was no evidence that handwriting analysis was a valid method of predicting job performance (p.35):

> … there is virtually no research that supports the use of graphology as an effective selection technique. At its best, it has only moderate reliability. There is little evidence that graphology is accurate in predicting personality traits, or that the narrow traits that many analysts infer from handwriting samples correlate with job performance. Finally, there is no evidence of a direct link between handwriting analysis and various measures of job performance.

Some critics are even more damning, for example Dr Barry Beyerstein, professor of biological psychology at Simon Fraser University in British Columbia (Ellin, 2004, p.10). Dr. Beyerstein said:

> Graphology is a pseudoscience that claims to be a quick and easy way of saying how someone's wired, but there's no evidence that this is encoded in handwriting.

> In these litigious times, you can't ask people about their sexual orientation or previous run-ins with the law or their home life or marital status. But graphologists make statements that no

legitimate personnel person could make with such a degree of certainty and you can find a lot of gullible people who'll sign on. You'd think hard-nosed business people would be the last to be taken in, but they lap it up.

Why is graphology so popular in continental Europe and apparently increasingly used in the USA and the UK (Ellin, 2004)? Thomas and Vaught (2001) speculate that one reason may be that it has an apparent face validity that people can relate to: it looks like it 'should' work as a method.

Summary

In free market countries, the personnel profession has adopted a 'best practice' model that fits the prevailing business ideology. This model prescribes a quest for the 'right (best) person for the job'. To achieve this goal, criteria are used to rate prospective applicants by means of selection techniques, including biographical data, interviews, psychometric tests, group exercises, simulated work samples and even handwriting analysis. The most definitive form of selection is likely to take place within the context of assessment centres, involving several assessors and a variety of selection techniques. The 'best-person' or psychometric model has achieved the status of orthodoxy in free market countries. Elsewhere different models of resourcing apply. For example, in Japan there is a greater concern with personality and background than presumed ability. Recruits are sought who will 'fit in' with the culture of the corporation; who will be content to build a career within the organization; who will absorb the goals of the organization.

Further reading

Competency-based Recruitment and Selection by Robert Wood and Tim Payne (1998), published by John Wiley & Sons takes a 'best practice' approach to the selection process. *Human Resource Selection* by Robert Gatewood and Hubert Field (5th edn, Thomson Learning, 2000) has a more technical approach. Books on interviewing include: *The Selection Interview* by Penny Hackett (CIPD, 1998); and *Effective Interviewing* by Robert Edenborough, (Kogan Page, 2002). Robert Edenborough has also written *Assessment Methods in Recruitment, Selection and Performance: A Manager's Guide to Psychometric Testing, Interviews and Assessment Centres* (Kogan Page, 2005).

Review questions

1 Are selection methods objective?

2 When and why would you conduct an informal interview?

3 Discuss the merits and disadvantages of unstructured, structured and behaviourally structured interview methods. Evaluate Peters' approach against our discussion on the various types of interview.

4 Review the advantages and disadvantages of using psychometric tests for small and large organizations. Are psychometric tests fair?

5 What criteria can be used to judge the effectiveness of selection methods?

6 Define 'validity' and 'reliability' in your own words.

7 Why are some selection methods used more often than others?

8 What are the arguments for and against the use of assessment centres for employee selection?

9 Explain why hiring managers do not necessarily use the best decisionmaking practices in employee selection.

10 Is it possible to guarantee equality of opportunity in a resourcing process?

Case study for discussion and analysis

Everylang

Everylang is a small, fast-growing translation bureau. It needs to keep tight control of its costs in a very competitive market. The owner considers that its success depends on quality, presentation, speed of work and the ability to provide translations to and from any language. Most of the work is from the main European languages and into English. The company employs 12 staff, while the remaining work (over half) is farmed out to freelance translators who are only paid for the work they do. They communicate with the office by a variety of means, including courier, post, fax and e-mail. It is sometimes difficult to get and maintain relationships with top-quality freelancers.

Situation

Everylang has now grown to the point where the owner-manager is too busy with marketing, finance and developing new customers to be able to cope with the day-to-day operations. You have been invited as an external consultant to advise on selecting an office manager for Everylang. It is apparent that the owner knows a great deal about the translation market but is inexpert in managing people. The owner is keen to promote a member of the existing staff, partly in order to improve motivation but mainly in order to keep costs down. Five have applied and you have been provided with the following job summary on which to base your initial thoughts.

Title:	Office manager.
Pay:	Translator salary + 30 per cent + profit-related bonus and benefits.
Main purpose of job:	Day-to-day running of Everylang office, ensuring that incoming work is dealt with and returned to agreed standard of quality and delivery time.
Functions:	Providing quotations for customers; dealing with enquiries; allocating work to full-time staff or freelancers; recording and progressing all incoming work, delivery on time and to the agreed quality; dealing with complaints; finding and monitoring new freelancers; completing computer records for billing and administration; and dealing with any personal problems among staff.
Personnel specification:	None existing.

Applicants

Helen. Age 42. Five years with Everylang. No formal qualifications. Translates French and Spanish. Ex-secretary. Has been translating for almost 20 years and knows a large number of other translators. Very efficient, quick and accurate. She is keen on long legal translations and has developed a considerable knowledge of business law in French-speaking countries. Pleasant personality but a little short-tempered. She has a good working relationship with other staff members but tends to keep her distance and does not socialize with them. Likes to take a six-week holiday at her parents' home in France every summer. She has an arrangement with the owner to take this partly as unpaid leave.

John. Age 36. Has been 12 years with Everylang. High school qualifications in French and Italian. Also has a diploma in translating and interpreting in the same languages. A great language enthusiast, he is proud of his standard of work. He translates mostly from French, specializing in letters and product information. Takes a keen interest in the welfare of the other staff. They have a considerable regard for him, respecting his professionalism and his interest in them. Over the last year he has had arguments with the owner over policy and thinks the company is growing too fast. He believes that the ever-increasing pressure of work is leading to inadequate checking of translations. Personally, he is quite efficient but pays too much attention to small details. Has been thinking of going self-employed.

Jill. Age 32. Three years with Everylang. Left school at 16. Took evening classes in French for several years. Cheerful, chatty person who gets on well with customers. Not a particularly good translator but useful for short French translations needed quickly. Can understand Scandinavian languages quite well, particularly Norwegian – she worked in Norway as a managing director's personal secretary for two years. The other staff do not respect her as a translator and often patronize her. She copes well, brushing off their remarks and getting on with her job. She has applied for a number of other jobs recently – without success.

Francesca. Age 26. Graduate in Spanish and Italian. Diploma in Translating. Also speaks Portuguese. Has 18 months' service. Undoubtedly the best translator in the office. She had considered becoming a language teacher but dropped out of the training programme after a year and joined Everylang. She is younger than the other staff and relations are not particularly good. Gets on extremely well with major clients who find her vivacious personality attractive to deal with. She gives customers a feeling of confidence in her abilities. Francesca sees Everylang as a long-term career job, is ambitious and enthusiastic about major expansion. At the moment, she is having major problems with her pre-school age child who suffers from asthma. Sometimes she takes time off with little notice. She has promised the boss that her difficulties will be sorted out soon.

David. Age 55. Three years with company. BA and MA in German Literature. Former export manager, made redundant from a major company. He translated on a freelance basis before joining Everylang. He is the only full-time German translator. A workaholic – he never seems to leave the office and is always ready to work overtime to complete a piece of work. He is regarded as bookish by the other staff. Sometimes David is extremely critical of other people's standard of work.

He considers the qualifications of some of the other translators to be inadequate for the jobs they are doing. In general, he thinks that the owner is unimaginative and has failed to capitalize on non-European languages. He is very unhappy about his salary which is much lower than his pay as export manager. However, he knows that he cannot cope with the uncertainties of being a freelancer.

The company does not have a performance assessment system.

Activity brief

1 What criteria would you apply in seeking the most suitable applicant?

2 What methods would you use to obtain further information about these candidates?

3 What are the likely advantages and disadvantages of promoting any one of these individuals?

Part six
Managing diversity

This part of the book discusses the subject of equal opportunity in the workplace. We consider the prevalence of discrimination on the grounds of gender, race, religion, disability and age and discuss the use of anti-discriminatory legislation. Also we evaluate the effectiveness of proactive policies and initiatives aimed at the management of diversity within organizations.

The chapters in Part six address questions such as:

- Why should we encourage diversity in human resources?

- What is the purpose of anti-discriminatory legislation and why have some countries adopted different approaches?

- Why do people from certain backgrounds figure so prominently at the upper levels of virtually all professions?

- What is the empirical evidence for various types of discrimination?

- Is there any evidence for the effectiveness of legislation or management of diversity initiatives?

Chapter 16
Equality of opportunity

Learning objectives

The purpose of this chapter is to:

- Define and distinguish between the concepts of equal opportunity and the management of diversity.

- Assess the scope and effectiveness of legislation and other anti-discriminatory initiatives.

- Identify the significant barriers to equality and diversity in employing organizations.

- Outline the nature and extent of discrimination on the basis of sex and gender.

The meaning of diversity

Society and opportunity

Examples of national anti-discrimination legislation

The emphasis of anti-discrimination legislation

Diversity and the organization

Strategies for diversity

Gender and sexual discrimination

Summary

Further reading

Review questions

Case studies for discussion and analysis –

    Frank and Margaret/White male culture and

    disadvantage

The meaning of diversity

People are different. They vary in gender, culture, race, social, physical and psychological characteristics. But our attitudes towards these differences can be negative or positive, depending upon individual perspectives and prejudices. Bassett-Jones (2005) argues that diversity is a recognizable source of creativity and innovation that can provide a basis for competitive advantage. Diversity is also a cause of misunderstanding, suspicion and conflict in the workplace that can result in absenteeism, poor quality, low morale and loss of competitiveness. Organizations have to manage the resulting paradox.

In earlier chapters we identified the tendency to form like-minded 'in-groups', to favour members of one's own group and for those in authority to recruit people like themselves. This may seem natural or normal and often goes unquestioned – but it is unfair. The consequences can be seen in a lack of opportunity for women, ethnic minorities, the disabled, the middle-aged and other disadvantaged sections of the community as the best jobs are ring-fenced and barriers are placed to prevent their progress.

As members of organizations, it is difficult to challenge the often subconscious actions and elaborately entrenched justifications for unfairness. Not least, because discrimination and prejudice are expressions of power entailing the ability to prevent, inhibit or punish critical comment. Yet, if people are the key assets of a business it is important to realize the maximum benefit from their human capital. True competitive advantage requires the best from everyone – without restrictions; it demands a prejudice-free and inclusive attitude towards actual and potential employees. It requires diversity (see Key concept 16.1).

Key concept 16.1 Diversity

'Diversity is the variation of social and cultural identities among people existing together in a defined employment or marketing system' (Cox, O'Neill and Quinn, 2001, p.3).

In reality, this has to be viewed as an ideal since discriminatory and non-inclusive behaviours have a deep psychological basis. Research shows that prejudice is difficult to remove. For example, if someone is prejudiced against a particular group, meeting someone with positive qualities from that group does not dispel the prejudice. As McKenna (1994, p.260) states:

> . . . the prejudiced person is capable of rationalizing the situation in such a way as to conclude that the person he or she met is unique in some respects, and is unlike the stereotype. . . . For example, an anti-Semite will not be swayed in his or her view of Jews by evidence of their charitable behaviour, nor will those who have a deep prejudice against black people be persuaded by coming in contact with intelligent and industrious people in this group.

Nevertheless, equality of opportunity is an objective worth striving for. It can be addressed at all levels: governments have a role to play through legislation to prevent discrimination; organizations need to focus on the management of diversity, making the most of a wide pool of talent; strategists should consider equal opportunity policies, targeting and positive development of under-represented groups; people managers can monitor their activities and increase awareness to minimize discrimination.

Society and opportunity

Anthony Jay is reputed to have said that 'success is when preparation meets opportunity'. Preparation depends on personal effort but opportunity is linked to social factors such as economic conditions, education and other people. Effectively, society determines who is given opportunity and who is not through the process of discrimination. Overt prejudice is comparatively easy to observe but the true nature of unfairness lies in the way opportunity has been institutionalized within society. The status quo is constructed to benefit certain types of individual from particular backgrounds or those who are able to adapt most easily to its requirements. Typically this has denied opportunity to women and minority groups.

Most countries have a concentration of particular social groups at the top of their institutions. Others are found further down. As a consequence, skills and abilities are not used to the full – a situation that is detrimental to society as a whole. However, the advantaged are unlikely to admit that their positions come from privilege rather than competence. For them, change is not a priority. An example can be seen in India where government attempts to assist disadvantaged castes have met with violent protests by the privileged. Other instances are readily found in developing African states where paid employment is scarce. Managers are under pressure to offer jobs to people from their family or tribe (Akinnusi, 1991) and this has extended to politicians and civil servants to the extent of threatening the economic development of sub-Saharan Africa. This is a form of '**particularism**' (see Key concept 16.2) that is important still in South Africa, although the influence of convergent forces such as globalization, information technology and increased competition is becoming much more prominent (Horwitz *et al.*, 2002).

Key concept 16.2 Particularism

Discrimination favouring particular groups and individuals over others. It derives from a reliance on personal relationships such as ethnic origin, religion or tribal community. It contrasts with 'universalism' in which personal relationships are ignored and emphasis is on other criteria such as qualifications, expertise and ability to do the job.

Particularism leads to discrimination. Worldwide, this mechanism can be extended to include a number of forms, including discrimination on the grounds of:

Age. Arbitrary age boundaries excluding younger and older workers.

Appearance. Preferring people of a certain height or weight, for example.

Disability. Discriminating against people with special needs.

Gender. Limiting certain types of jobs to either males or females.

Ethnic origin. Preference for particular racial or linguistic communities.

Nationality.

Religion.

Background. Often seen as cliques – networks of people from similar backgrounds reserving the best jobs for themselves. In addition, people with socially undesirable backgrounds, such as ex-offenders, are actively discriminated against.

Nepotism. Common in small companies that rely heavily on family members.

Marti, Bobier and Baron (2000) found that some forms of discrimination, specifically gender and race, are more easily observed and recognized than others, such as age and weight. Participants in their studies were more likely to label actions of gender or racial discrimination as prejudice and also tended to rate such prejudice as more severe than in cases of prejudice on the grounds of age or weight. Harper (2000) reports on a study of longitudinal cohort data covering 11 407 individuals born in Britain in 1958. The results showed that physical appearance had a significant effect on earnings and employment patterns for both men and women. Regardless of gender, people assessed as unattractive or short were penalized. At the extremes, taller men tended to receive higher pay than average, while obese women were paid less than average women. The researchers attributed the bulk of the pay differential for appearance to employer discrimination.

Discrimination can be **direct** (Key concept 16.3) or **indirect** (Key concept 16.4). It can also extend into victimization when employers or their agents treat employees less favourably as a result of actions taken by those employees to assert their non-discriminatory rights. Many countries use legislation to reduce such discrimination, for example, in areas such as equal pay, selection and promotion. The effectiveness of such legislation is seen in the proportion of disadvantaged groups achieving responsible positions. Often this has been disappointing. We will see that, in most parts of the world, the presence of women and people from ethnic minority groups becomes increasingly rare towards the top of most organizations and some groups, such as the disabled and the over-50s, are conspicuously absent from many firms.

Key concept 16.3 Direct discrimination

Treating an individual or group less favourably on grounds such as disability, race, religion, age, gender or sexual orientation. Direct discrimination is fairly obvious because of its explicit nature (Corbridge and Pilbeam, 1998). The use of different criteria for promoting or paying male or female employees is an example of direct discrimination.

Key concept 16.4 Indirect discrimination

A less obvious form of discrimination than direct discrimination. This may take the form of applying certain conditions or requirements that are more easily satisfied by one group than another (Corbridge and Pilbeam, 1998). One example would be to specify a fixed minimum height requirement for entry into a police force. This is a requirement that would be more easily met by male than female applicants. Another example would be a requirement for an unnecessarily high standard of spoken or written English, that would favour people with a particular educational background.

Examples of national anti-discrimination legislation

Lappalainen (2001) observes that different countries have essentially chosen one of two paths for laws dealing with discrimination. Some have focused on a single law covering all the grounds of discrimination, while others have issued separate laws for each type of discrimination. Legislation has been in place in the USA since the 1960s with separate laws and programmes designed to protect women, individuals aged over 40, people with disabilities, war veterans and racial minorities (see the 'HRM in reality' box – New approach needed for equality).

Federal anti-discrimination laws in the USA

A number of federal laws prohibit discrimination in the workplace.

Title VII of the Civil Rights Act 1964
Title VII prohibits employers from discriminating against applicants and employees on the basis of race or colour, religion, sex, pregnancy, childbirth and national origin (including membership of a Native American tribe). It encompasses all terms, conditions and privileges of employment, including hiring, firing, compensation, benefits, job

▶

assignments, shift assignments, promotions and discipline. There are limited exceptions, termed bona fide occupational qualification (BFOQ) exceptions, covering sex, religion and national origin, but not race. Title VII also prohibits employers from retaliating against any applicants or employees who assert their rights under the law (e.g. firing someone who has complained about race discrimination). Title VII is restricted to the following types of organization:

- private employers with 15 or more employees
- state governments and their political subdivisions and agencies
- the federal government
- employment agencies
- labour organizations, and
- joint labour-management committees and other training programmes.

It is enforced by the US Equal Employment Opportunity Commission (EEOC). Title VII makes it illegal for employers to use apparently neutral practices that have a disproportionate impact on a protected group of people. There has to be a valid reason for using any such practice. Height and weight requirements are typical examples. Title VII also prohibits the harassment of someone because of their race or colour, religion, sex, pregnancy, childbirth or national origin (including membership of a Native American tribe). Sexual harassment is the most common form of harassment covered by Title VII.

The Age Discrimination in Employment Act (ADEA) 1967

The ADEA prohibits discrimination against employees who are age 40 or older. It also covers all aspects of employment and makes it illegal to retaliate against anyone exercising their legal rights. The range of employers covered by the ADEA is slightly different to Title VII. It does not apply to state governments or their agencies and private employers with fewer than 20 employees. However, it does apply to the federal government and its agencies, private employers with 20 or more employees, interstate agencies, employment agencies and labour unions. The ADEA is also enforced by the EEOC.

The Equal Pay Act 1963

The Equal Pay Act requires that employers give men and women equal pay for equal work. Equal work is defined as work done under similar working conditions or requiring equal skill, effort and responsibility. The job titles used have no bearing on whether two jobs are equal. However, employers can pay men and women different salaries for equal work if the difference is based on a seniority, merit or incentive system, or if the difference is based on factors other than gender. The Equal Pay Act applies to virtually all employers. Again, the Equal Pay Act is enforced by the EEOC.

The Americans with Disabilities Act (ADA) 1990

The Americans with Disabilities Act prohibits discrimination against people with disabilities in employment, transportation, public accommodation, communications, and activities of state and local government. The Act was signed into law in 1990 but its various elements came into force on different dates including: state and local government activities (January 1992); employers with 25 or more workers (July 1992); employers with 15 or more workers (July 1994).

The Act requires that employers, employment agencies, labour organizations and joint labour-management committees must:

- Have non-discriminatory application procedures, qualification standards and selection criteria in all other terms and conditions of employment.

- Make reasonable accommodation to the known limitations of a qualified applicant or employee unless to do so would cause undue hardship.

    The Act makes exceptions regarding the employment of a person with a contagious disease, a person who illegally uses drugs or alcohol, employment of someone by a religious entity, and private membership clubs.

    The ADA does not apply to the federal government and its agencies. The EEOC and the US Department of Justice oversee the Americans with Disabilities Act. Other federal laws that encompass discrimination include: Sections 501 and 505 of the Rehabilitation Act of 1973, which prohibit discrimination against qualified individuals with disabilities who work in the federal government; and the Civil Rights Act of 1991, which, among other things, provides monetary damages in cases of intentional employment discrimination.

New Zealand

New Zealand passed a Race Relations Act in 1971 and an Equal Pay Act in 1972. The Race Relations Act was passed primarily in order to allow the government to ratify the International Convention for the Elimination of All Forms of Racial Discrimination in the following year. Intriguingly, many people felt at the time that race relations in New Zealand were so good that such an Act was unnecessary!

Unlike the US court-based system of enforcement, the New Zealand Act created the Office of the Race Relations Conciliator with the aim of resolving incidents of discrimination, although the Conciliator could recommend to the Attorney-General that proceedings be taken against an offender in extreme cases.

The Human Rights Commission Act (1977) introduced a new element, the Equal Opportunities Tribunal, to which the Conciliator could take civil proceedings. That Act also outlawed discrimination on the grounds of sex, marital status and religious or ethical belief. The Human Rights Act (1993) consolidated earlier legislation and the Human Rights Amendment Act (2001) amalgamated the Race Relations Office with the Human Rights Commission.

Australia

The Australian Commonwealth Government passed its Racial Discrimination Act in 1975. The Sex Discrimination Act (1984), Human Rights and Equal Opportunity Commission Act (1988), **Disability Discrimination Act (1992)** and the Age Discrimination Act 2004 followed. However, individual Australian states inclined towards comprehensive anti-discriminatory laws, as in the New South Wales Anti-Discrimination Act (1977). The trend to comprehensiveness continued such that Tasmania's Anti-Discrimination Act (1998) encompassed the following:

Age, breastfeeding, carer status, disability, family responsibilities, gender/sex identity, industrial activity, irrelevant criminal activity, irrelevant medical record, lawful sexual activity, marital status, parental status, physical status, political activity, political belief or affiliation, pregnancy, race, religious activity, religious beliefs or affiliation, sexual orientation, personal association with a person who has, or is believed to have any of these attitudes or identities, sexual/sexist harassment, victimization, inciting hatred, publishing displaying or advertising matter that promotes, expresses or depicts discrimination or prohibited conduct.

The **Australian Human Rights and Equal Opportunity Commission** is led by a single Commissioner with some overall responsibility but there are separate Commissioners for each of the nationally recognized discrimination grounds (gender, race and disability). This approach retains a broad human rights focus but also pays attention to the separate issues involved in each form of discrimination.

United Kingdom

For many years the UK was the only country in Europe with comparatively comprehensive civil legislation on workplace discrimination, having had anti-discriminatory laws covering race and ethnicity since the 1970s. The main pieces of legislation covering equal opportunities were: the **Equal Pay Act (1970)**, providing for equal pay for comparable work; the Sex Discrimination Act (1975), which makes discrimination against women or men (including discrimination on the grounds of marital status) illegal in the working situation; the Race Relations Act (1976) with subsequent amendments; and the Disability Discrimination Act (1995). Subsequent UK and EU legislation has generally improved women's rights in the area of pregnancy and maternity. These Acts were supported by a Commission assigned to each piece of legislation. The **Commission for Racial Equality (CRE)** oversees the Race Relations Acts. The **Equal Opportunities Commission (EOC)** was established under the Sex Discrimination Act of 1975 with powers to monitor implementation of both the Sex Discrimination and Equal Pay Acts. The Disability Rights Commission was set up in 2000 in line with the Disability Rights Commission Act (1999) .

The equality guarantee contained in Article 14 of the European Convention of Human Rights also came into effect in October 2000 with the implementation of the Human Rights Act 1998 (Fredman, 2001). A single Commission for Equality and Human Rights will replace the EOC, CRE and DRC from October 2007.

HRM in reality   New approach needed for equality

A report from the Equal Opportunities Commission (EOC) shows there have been 250 000 employment tribunal cases of sex discrimination and 67 000 related to equal pay in the 30 years since the Sex Discrimination and Equal Pay Acts came into force, with record numbers filed over the last five years. Yet the EOC states that many of the problems of gender equality remain stubbornly persistent. The Commission cites as examples:

● Women working part-time earn nearly 40 per cent less per hour than men working full-time and this has barely changed over the last 30 years.

● Four out of five part-time workers, mostly women, find themselves stuck in jobs below their potential, partly due to the lack of flexible working at more senior levels.

● Nearly half of pregnant women experience some form of pregnancy discrimination at work, and 30 000 are forced out of their jobs.

The government is conducting a review of anti-discrimination laws as it works towards a Single Equality Bill. The Gender Duty, the biggest change to gender discrimination legislation in 30 years, will come into force in April 2007. It places a positive duty on public sector employers to actively promote equality in employment practices and the delivery of goods and services.

The EOC argues that laws to combat discrimination, until now based largely on people bringing individual tribunal cases when they experience inequality, are not delivering change fast enough. According to the EOC, there will always be a need for some legal redress for individuals but an approach that reduces the number of cases necessary in the first place would bring benefits to both employers and employees. The average cost of legal advice and representation for individuals is £4400, while employers spend an average of £5800 on legal costs for their defence, not including staff time.

Many individuals are deterred from pursuing cases and discrimination goes unchecked as a result. An EOC investigation found that seven in ten pregnant women treated unfairly by their employer do not take any further action. Ethnic minority women are more vulnerable to sex discrimination. Pakistani women, for example, face a pay gap 10 per cent higher than white women. Young ethnic minority women are twice as likely as white women to face questions at job interview about their plans for marriage and children.

Changes called for by the EOC include:

1 A debate about the role of the private sector in preventing discrimination. The EOC favours an approach that places a requirement on private and voluntary sector employers to address all three causes of the pay gap in a proactive way, following on from new legislation for the public sector. Action

could start with an equality check to see whether there is a pay gap, and help for employers to understand the nature of the problem at their particular organization. Further options could include a review of pay systems or extension of more flexible work opportunities to help employees better balance work and family.

2 Discrimination on the grounds of caring status to be explicitly recognized within the law. Many parents are now working and as the population ages, more people will face the additional responsibilities of caring for an older relative. Currently, 3 million people combine work with unpaid caring responsibilities, and 320 000 people with paid jobs do more than 50 hours of unpaid caring work each week. The unpaid caring work done by parents and carers in the UK is estimated to be worth £277 billion.

3 To achieve detailed, practical and in many cases long overdue changes to the law to make it more efficient and less complex.

Jenny Watson, chair of the Equal Opportunities Commission, commented:

Thousands of tribunal cases later, the reality of sex equality is still far from our grasp. Both individuals and employers rely on a costly tribunal system that delivers conflict better than change. We need to look afresh at equality law in today's modern context. Thirty years on from the Sex Discrimination Act, most mothers now work, fathers too want to be more involved at home and many more of us have caring responsibilities for parents or relatives. Many thousands of forward-looking employers are already creating a more welcoming environment through good policies and are reaping the business benefits. They find that preventing problems before they start works much better than tackling them after they arise.

The government is now undertaking a welcome review of discrimination laws to create a single Equality Act – a once-in-a-generation opportunity to establish laws that work better for both individuals and employers. We would like to see the widest possible debate about how best to achieve that outcome, including whether we should take the opportunity to build on recent changes in the public sector by asking private and voluntary sector employers to take active steps to promote sex equality. Prevention is always better than cure, and when it delivers business benefits too, it should be considered as an approach.

What benefits can be expected from a single Equality Act?

Source: *HRM Guide UK* (http://www.hrmguide.co.uk), 20 May, 2006.

Ireland (Republic)

Ireland introduced an Anti-Discrimination (Pay) Act in 1974 that established the right to equal pay for 'like work', defined in terms of skill, physical or mental requirements, responsibility and working conditions. This was followed in 1977 by the Employment Equality Act prohibiting discrimination in recruitment, training, conditions of employment and promotion opportunities on the grounds of sex or marital status. The Employment Equality Act (1998) combined the earlier Acts and prohibited discrimination in respect of all aspects of employment. It extended the grounds for discrimination to cover gender, marital status, family status, sexual orientation, religion, age, disability, race and membership of the Traveller community. Irish legislation is also affected by the EU anti-discrimination Directives discussed later in this chapter.

Canada

Canada's approach to anti-discrimination has long been distinctive, especially in comparison with its southern neighbour. Canadian legislation is grounded in human rights. The Canadian government signed the Universal Declaration of Human Rights in 1948 and has made universal human rights a key part of Canadian law. Four principal mechanisms are designed to protect human rights: the Canadian Charter of Rights and Freedoms (1982), the Canadian Human Rights Act (1977), Human Rights Commissions, and provincial human rights laws and legislation.

The Canadian Human Rights Act (1977) prohibits discrimination in federal or federally regulated organizations on grounds of race, colour, national or ethnic origin, religion, age, sex (including pregnancy and child-bearing), marital status, family status, physical or mental disability (including dependency on alcohol or drugs), pardoned criminal conviction, and sexual orientation. Similar laws have been enacted in the provinces and territories banning discrimination in their areas of jurisdiction. The Act is enforced by the Canadian Human Rights Commission.

By the 1980s there was an awareness that despite this legislation there was a need for a more proactive approach and, following the report of a Royal Commission, the first Employment Equity Act was passed in 1986. The Royal Commission had been asked to 'explore the most efficient, effective and equitable means of promoting equality in employment for four groups: women, native people, disabled persons, and visible minorities.' The term 'employment equity' was chosen to distinguish the Canadian approach from American affirmative action programmes associated with quotas.

The 1986 Employment Equity Act covered federally regulated companies with 100 or more employees, operating primarily in the banking, transportation and communications industries. These employers were required to identify workplace barriers and to develop and implement equity plans for the four designated groups. Employers were also required to report annually to the minister responsible but the Act had no enforcement mechanisms, other than for failure to report.

Over the next few years it was recognized that the Act had to be toughened and extended. A new Employment Equity Act came into effect in 1996 that also covered the federal public service and mandated the Canadian Human Rights Commission to conduct on-site compliance reviews. It also provided for final enforcement by an Employment Equity Review Tribunal that had the power to hear disputes and issue orders.

South Africa

The Canadian approach had a major influence on South Africa's Employment Equity Act that came into force in 1999 and bans direct or indirect unfair discrimination in employment policy or practice, on the grounds of: 'race, gender, sex, pregnancy, marital status, family responsibility, ethnic or social origin, colour, sexual orientation, age, disability, religion, HIV status, conscience, belief, political opinion, culture, language and birth.' Fair discrimination includes affirmative action that is designed to redress previous exclusion from education and employment of black people, women and those with disabilities. The Employment Equity Act is regulated by the Commission for Employment Equity.

The emphasis of anti-discrimination legislation

Countries with legal systems based on common law, including Australia, Canada, Ireland, New Zealand, the UK and the USA, have used civil rather than criminal law as the main method of counteracting discrimination. Government bodies may assist but, in essence, it is up to individuals to pursue their case. Possible costs are a negative aspect of this approach but there is a benefit in the lower burden of proof required in civil law (Lappalainen, 2001). There is also room for compromise and conciliation, possibilities not usually available in criminal law. The Netherlands had a tradition of using the European criminal law model. However, it was determined that this approach was not working and, in 1994, the Equal Treatment Act was introduced based on civil law, substantially influenced by Canada's Human Rights Act (Lappalainen, 2001).

Legislation can take a number of forms:

Positive action. Measures to prevent discrimination and remove inequalities by insisting, for example, on non-discriminatory recruitment procedures, training programmes and pay rates. **Positive action** does not include any preferential treatment for disadvantaged groups. UK and Irish legislation takes this approach.

Affirmative action or positive discrimination. A long-standing approach in the USA, designed to advantage the disadvantaged, including women, African-Americans and Hispanics. Laws only applied to the public sector and its suppliers. **Affirmative action** came under severe criticism in the 1990s from white, middle-class males who argued that laws intended to encourage equality were unfair to them.

Targeting. Quotas for the employment of particular groups have been enforced in the USA. In Europe quota systems existed for some time in respect of disability and, in a few countries, other groups such as ex-servicemen, but enforcement was not usually strict.

The European Union adopted two new directives in 2000: the first concerned discrimination on grounds of racial or ethnic origin; and the second extended the principle of equal treatment to prevent discrimination on the grounds of age, disability, religion and sexual orientation. The directives form the basis for national legislation on these matters, which member states such as the UK and Ireland are obliged to implement. By 2003 laws had to be in place preventing employers from discriminating against workers because of their sexual orientation or religion. By 2006 unequal treatment on the grounds of age or disability (the latter already covered by legislation in the UK for organizations employing 15 or more staff) was also made unlawful. Belatedly, the EU has taken responsibility for anti-discrimination on a par with developments in North America and Australasia and introduced a positive duty to promote equality, albeit in a somewhat vague fashion (Fredman, 2001).

More widely, it should be emphasized that legislation is only effective if institutions and individuals charged with its implementation are themselves committed to the concept of equal opportunity. Barnard, Deakin and Kilpatrick (2002) point to the fact that English law (which also provides the foundation for law in many other countries) lacks a general principle of equality of the kind found in constitutional texts in some European countries. They argue that anti-discriminatory legislation not founded on such a principle stresses formal rather than substantive equality, so that discrimination is described in terms of unequal treatment of individuals and ignores the structural sources of group disadvantage. They believe that this provides a partial explanation for the relatively limited impact of legislation, in the UK at least.

In practice, the number and range of disadvantaged groups is so huge that true fairness is a difficult objective to achieve. Well-meaning advocates can find themselves embroiled in endless verbal battles over the subtle nuances and implications of the concept. We turn next to its practical consequences on people management at the organizational level.

Diversity and the organization

'Fairness, justice, or whatever you call it – it's essential and most companies don't have it. Everybody must be judged on his performance, not on his looks or his manners or his personality or who he knows or is related to' (Townsend, 1970, p.59). Why should business organizations and their managers offer equal opportunities to a diverse range of employees? Two fundamental perspectives are identifiable that can be related to different models of HRM (Goss, 1994, p.156):

Human capital. 'Artificially' blocking the progress of any group results in less than optimal use of an organization's human capital. Discrimination is irrational since it limits the resource value of employees. This view is compatible with 'hard', or free market HRM discussed in Part one of this book.

Social justice. A moral or ethical interest in social equality, compatible with 'soft' or social market HRM. Economic benefits are secondary to this social duty.

Goss sees the human capital perspective as fluctuating and opportunistic: a shallow commitment '. . . capable of being adopted or abandoned, in line with legal or economic expediency'. It is also narrow, restricted to legal requirements and short-term employment market conditions. This contrasts with the more principled social justice viewpoint, that embodies a deeper and wider commitment, extending beyond minimum legal requirements.

According to Ross and Schneider (1992) organizations benefit from a deep, principled commitment to equality of opportunity because it leads to:

- A diverse workforce that enriches ideas and perspectives within an organization.
- Imaginative ideas to assist total quality management.
- Recruitment or promotion of the most talented people.
- An environment that encourages them to stay.
- Improved motivation and commitment that raises productivity.
- Reduced wastage and recruitment costs that increase profitability.

In recent years, the UK Equal Opportunities Commission has argued strongly for the human capital approach pointing, in particular, to the waste of women's abilities. However, some commentators contend that, whereas this is valid for the economy as a whole, equal opportunity practices may be a significant expense rather than a benefit for individual firms.

All businesses operate within the national or supranational legislation governing equal opportunities in a specific country. As we noted earlier, the USA and South Africa have required a number of employers to take measures of positive discrimination, typically requiring them to fill quotas from under-represented sections of the community. To do so,

HRM in reality Women directors 'own worst enemy'

A survey of over 100 female directors in the UK has found that many believe women may be their own worst enemies when it comes to success in the boardroom.

The survey of 105 women directors at companies across the UK, conducted by executive recruitment specialist, Praxis Executive Resourcing, showed that, while 66 per cent of them believed women enjoyed equal opportunities across the whole workplace, only 32 per cent believed that women had the same chance as men of becoming a board director.

However, the reasons why the majority felt that women had a harder time in reaching the boardroom made interesting reading:

- 44 per cent of this group believed that the reason was the current dominance by men of senior management positions.

- 64 per cent thought that breaking their careers to have a family put them at a disadvantage, while 48 per cent believed that putting family before career did the same.

- 58 per cent of the group blamed the shortage of female directors on a presumption that they would not reach the boardroom, while a massive 68 per cent also believe that it was down to a lack of networking skills in comparison to their male counterparts.

As one female director of a large plc put it, 'It doesn't matter whether you are a man or a woman – getting a meaningful board position isn't easy. It takes total commitment and a willingness to make a lot of sacrifices, particularly in your personal life. A lot of my female friends and colleagues just aren't willing to do that. Rightly or wrongly, they're more interested in achieving a balance between work and the rest of their lives and that's why I'm where I am and they're not.'

Despite their general negativity about the current situation, 68 per cent of the female directors questioned were optimistic about the prospects of women aiming for the boardroom in the future. Forty-six per cent of the optimists cited the increasing number of role models for ambitious younger women, 32 per cent the changing attitudes of society as a whole and 44 per cent the need for companies to recruit and retain the best talent irrespective of gender or ethnic background.

'Women are still very much in the minority in UK boardrooms and our record is comparatively poor compared with some of our European neighbours,' says Kate Mason, head of Praxis Executive Resourcing. 'A recent survey by the European Professional Women's Network, for example, found that only 10 per cent of UK directorships are held by women as opposed to 22 per cent in Sweden and 28 per cent in Norway. However it's encouraging that the increasing number of female role models such as Indra Nooyi, the new head of PepsiCo, is inspiring more women to break the glass ceiling into the boardroom.'

Why are the rates of female participation at board level so low?

Source: *HRM Guide UK* (http://www.hrmguide.co.uk), 14 September, 2006.

recruitment criteria such as qualification or skill requirements may be relaxed for members of those groups. This is an attempt to achieve the **equal share** level of opportunity outlined in Straw's model that also considers **equal chance** and **equal access** (detailed in Table 16.1).

Alternatively, positive action may be required or undertaken voluntarily by governments or employers. Under-represented groups are assisted and encouraged to participate in training and development initiatives, support groups and mentoring schemes. This requires that organizations are aware of their disadvantaged employees and the jobs they are doing, so that the problem of **occupational segregation** can be tackled (see Key concept 16.5).

Key concept 16.5 Occupational segregation

Disproportionate representation of particular groups in specific sectors, job types or levels of responsibility. Horizontal segregation places men and women, for example, in different jobs, such as chambermaids (women) and porters (men). Vertical segregation places one group in better-paid positions than another group, so that men are better represented at managerial levels while women are concentrated in lower, adminstrative jobs.

Turnasella (1999) suggests that the employment process is itself responsible for the persistent pay gap between men and women and between ethnic minorities and non-minorities. Specifically, employers usually require a salary history from job applicants and frequently ask questions about salary expectations during their selection procedures. If the applicant has a history of relatively low pay, employers tend to give lower offers of remuneration. Intriguingly, in an experimental study involving 100 participants (50 men and 50 women), Blanton, George and Crocker (2001) found that women compared themselves with other women to gauge satisfaction with a pay rate when it was framed as compensation for past work, but compared themselves with the men when framed as part of an offer for future employment. Drawing on police work as an example, Dick and Nadin (2006) argue that personnel selection alone can make little difference to the unequal position of women given the complex causes of social occupational discrimination and segregation along gendered lines.

Corbridge and Pilbeam (1998) also point out that networking and headhunting are inevitably discriminatory because they involve recruitment from a restricted pool of friends, social acquaintances and school or university peers. People from disadvantaged groups, if they

Level	Opportunities	Barriers
1 Equal chance	Everyone has same chance, e.g. right to apply for vacancies; be considered for a position.	Formal or informal barriers, e.g. employers may ignore applications from people living in ethnic minority areas.
2 Equal access	Disadvantaged groups not barred from entry into organizations but may be confined to lower levels of work.	Institutional barriers, e.g. appraisal methods that favour certain groups, or promotion requirements – such as mobility – that effectively bar many married women.
3 Equal share	Access is free. Representation achieved at all levels. Legislation may require quotas for disadvantaged groups, e.g. disabled.	Only those lawful, justifiable and necessary, e.g. specific language speakers to work with ethnic groups.

Table 16.1

Levels of opportunity

Source Based on Straw (1989).

are employed at all, tend to be confined to 'boring jobs with no prospects' in the secondary sector (Molander and Winterton, 1994, p.96).

The impact of discrimination on equality of pay is less in a unionized environment than in a non-union environment (Metcalf, Hansen and Charlwood, 2001). The authors attribute this to two factors:

- Union members and jobs are more homogeneous than their non-union counterparts.
- Union wage policies narrow the range of pay rates within and across firms and bring up the lowest wage rates.

Strategies for diversity

Many organizations have adopted **equal opportunities policies** – statements of commitment to fair human resource management. However, equal opportunities policies are notoriously ineffective, often no more than fine words decorating office walls, designed to appease politically vociferous activists and soothe consciences. They disturb vested interests too rarely. The obstacles to creating a diversified workforce are embedded in organizational culture – particularly the sub-culture at the top. According to Molander and Winterton (1994, p.102) serious equal opportunity policy requires:

- Allocation of overall responsibility to a specific senior executive.
- Agreement of the policy with employee representatives.
- Effective communication of the policy to all employees.

HRM in reality Stereotype of engineers puts women off the job

Classic stereotypes of engineers as men who are brilliant at and passionate about technology, but not very good at dealing with people, do not reflect real engineers and their work, according to Dr Wendy Faulkner from the University of Edinburgh. Moreover, such stereotypes are hampering efforts to recruit women into the engineering profession.

According to Dr Faulkner, who interviewed and observed 66 male and female engineers from a range of industries: 'Women and men engineers alike get excited about technology – even though fewer of the women have a "tinkerer" background. There are "gadget girls" as well as "boys and their toys" in engineering. At the same time, many different types of men and women enjoy engineering work – very few fit the classic stereotype.'

Wendy Faulkner adds: 'In practice, engineering encompasses a wide variety of jobs and roles. It is a "broad church" with room for a diverse range of people. Yet the image of engineering – and often the culture – remains a narrowly technical, "nuts and bolts" one.

'Retention is as important as recruitment – many of those women who do complete engineering degrees don't go on to engineering jobs or leave the industry after only a few years,' says Dr Faulkner. 'Part of the issue is that women who enter engineering have to become "one of the lads" in order to fit in. Many subtle aspects of the culture, which may appear trivial individually, when taken as a whole have a "dripping tap" effect – making it harder for women to belong, and get on in engineering.'

Her study details how the topics engineers talk about, as well as their style of humour and the social activities they engage in, reflect men's interests and ways of bonding. Women are left on the margins of this male society, finding it difficult to break into the 'inner circles' that carry influence on how the job gets done and who gets promoted.

'By contrast, engineering workplace cultures accommodate a range of men – laddish blokes, family men, pranksters, macho men, nerdy men, urbane men, genteel men – and so they are likely to feel comfortable to the great majority of men,' says Wendy Faulkner.

'If more women are to stay and progress in engineering workplaces, there is a strong business case for employers to introduce sustained and sensitive diversity training, to raise awareness of these kind of issues and to nurture more "inclusive" workplace cultures in which everyone is comfortable,' says Dr Faulkner.

Are the barriers to women taking up engineering as a profession due mainly to stereotyping or culture?

Source: *HRM Guide UK* (http://www.hrmguide.co.uk), 10 March, 2006

- An accurate survey of existing employees in terms of gender, ethnic origin, disability, etc. and the nature and status of their jobs.
- An audit of human resource practices and their implications for equal opportunities.
- Setting equal opportunity objectives within the human resource strategy.
- Resources, such as training and development capabilities, to back up these objectives.

Key concept 16.6 Management of diversity

The management of diversity goes beyond equal opportunity. Instead of merely allowing a greater range of people the opportunity to 'fit in', or be an honorary 'large, white male', the concept of diversity embodies the belief that people should be valued for their differences and variety. Diversity is perceived to enrich an organization's human capital. Whereas equal opportunity focuses on various disadvantaged groups, the management of diversity is about individuals. It entails a minimization of cloning in selection and promotion procedures and a model of resourcing aimed at finding flexible employees.

This approach can be incorporated within an integrated framework termed the 'management of diversity' (outlined in Key concept 16.6). The pitfalls in the process are evident. A 1995 report, 'Targeting Potential Discrimination' produced by the UK Equal Opportunities Commission detailed findings from 2000 companies that showed over two-thirds did not collect information about the gender and ethnicity of their employees. Auditing HR systems is also problematic.

However, the main difficulties arise from cost and lack of commitment, exemplified by 'tokenism' – the employment or promotion of isolated individuals to represent their gender or colour. This is no more than an inadequate sop to equal opportunities: 'We have done as much as we need to – we have a disabled person in the office.' 'Paternalism' is a related attitude, where discriminatory decisions are taken for the 'benefit' of particular groups, as illustrated in the case of American Cyanamid.

American Cyanamid

In an attempt to eliminate any liability for toxic damage to unborn children, American Cyanamid decided in January 1978 to remove all women of child-bearing age from contact with any chemical which, in the company's opinion, carried a risk. In effect, the company banned all women aged between 16 and 50 from production areas at its Willow Island, West Virginia plant. The only exception was for women who could prove they had been surgically sterilized or accepted such a sterilization at the company's expense. Five women accepted this offer.

The other women in the plant were only offered lower-paid jobs. Thirteen women and a union representative took legal action that was eventually settled out of court. In addition, the Occupational Safety and Health Administration (OSHA) cited American Cyanamid for violating a clause in the OSHA Act of 1970 that required employers to provide employees with a place of work that was free from recognized hazards. However, this was defeated by a summary legal judgement. This decision was confirmed by the OSHA's Health Safety Review Commission, which considered that the hazards that required sterilization for foetal protection were not cognizable under the OSHA Act. A further appeal by the Oil, Chemical and Atomic Workers Union to the District of Columbia Circuit Court of Appeals failed to overturn the judgment.

Source: Based on Nelkin and Tancredi (1989).

The case of American Cyanamid is a rather horrific example of heavy-handed action to 'protect' staff but it illustrates how people strategies can sometimes lose any sense of humanity.

HRM in reality Gender inequality begins at 16

A report by the Equal Opportunities Commission (EOC) shows that gender inequality in education and work begins at 16. Girls and boys study most subjects in roughly equal numbers for GCSE. Girls do very well but once their examinations are over the genders rapidly move towards traditionally 'male' or 'female' subjects.

The EOC's earlier investigation into occupational segregation at work, 'Free to choose – tackling gender barriers to better jobs' reported in March 2005 that many girls and boys were interested in non-traditional choices but were not supported by information and help. The EOC describes this as the start of a gender split that widens throughout their lives, with women often ending up in lower paid work at lower levels. The EOC cites as examples:

- Just under 50 per cent of students taking design and technology at GCSE are girls, but they represent only 1 per cent of electro-technical or construction apprentices, and 3 per cent of engineering apprentices. In engineering and technology subjects 87 per cent of students in further education and 86 per cent in higher education are male.

- Just over 40 per cent of students taking information technology at GCSE are girls. In computer studies at A-level 27 per cent are girls. Around 20 per cent of higher education computer studies students are female, and they make up the same proportion of ICT managers.

- In maths GCSE the gender split is exactly 50/50, which tips to 60/40 in favour of male students at A-level and university.

- The subject of social studies is taken by 69 per cent girls at A-level, and 59 per cent of women at degree level. Girls make up 87 per cent of health and social care apprentices, and 79 per cent of workers in the health and social work sector are women. Despite this huge majority, women in full-time work in this sector are paid on average 32 per cent less per hour than men.

Occupational segregation begins at 16, but the gap widens later in life. Thirty years after the Sex Discrimination Act came into force, the EOC's annual statistical review 'Facts About Women and Men in Great Britain, 2006' provides a snapshot of a workforce divided by gender:

- 66 per cent of managers and senior officials are men, while women hold 81 per cent of administrative and secretarial jobs.

- 83 per cent of directors and chief executives of major organizations are men, while 95 per cent of receptionists are women.

- In the finance sector women are just over 50 per cent of the workforce, yet the average hourly pay for a woman working full-time in finance is 41 per cent lower than for a man.

Jenny Watson, chair of the Equal Opportunities Commission, said: 'We run the risk of short-changing the next generation by failing to tackle the inequality that takes root after GCSE. The EOC's investigation into occupational segregation found that 80 per cent of girls and 55 per cent of boys said that they were or might be interested in pursuing a non-traditional career, but without the right information and support they will never get the chance.

'Although women have made great strides in education, from making up a third of higher education students 35 years ago to nearly two-thirds today, this doesn't tell the whole story. Jobs traditionally seen as "women's work", such as early years' care and education, are undervalued and underpaid, and later in life many women are forced to take a pay cut for the flexibility they need to raise their own children.

'Tackling the challenge posed by occupational segregation will provide huge economic gains, helping us meet skills shortages in highly-segregated areas such as construction and childcare. It will also go a long way to closing the gender pay gap, which the Women and Work Commission estimates could add as much as £23 billion to the UK economy.

'The Gender Equality Duty, which comes into force in April 2007, will give a major boost to the Women and Work Commission's recommendations by placing a requirement on all public bodies to promote gender equality. By taking action now we can transform the workplace into somewhere that the young people taking their exams today can fulfil their potential.'

Ruth Kelly, the then Secretary of State for Communities and Local Government and Minister for Women, said: 'This informative and helpful report highlights yet again that occupational segregation begins early.

'The Women and Work Commission suggested improvements to careers advice and work experience to ensure all pupils have the necessary information to make informed choices about their education and ultimately their careers. We've started to tackle this; while I was at the DfES we announced important changes to the careers advice and guidance pupils receive. We must avoid lazy stereotypes, particularly as pupils enter the crucial 14–19 phase.

'But if women are to have the same opportunity as men to have a satisfying and well-paid career, then we must do much more. In my new role as Minister for Women I'm determined to help make this happen. We will be producing an exciting action plan to ensure a cross-government approach tackling this major issue.'

Is the Gender Equality Duty likely to be effective?

Source: *HRM Guide UK* (http://www.hrmguide.co.uk), 15 May, 2006.

The monitoring of potential discrimination seems to be a variable commodity. It is most common in the recruitment stage, followed by promotion and then at exit stage. In contrast, training does not seem to be monitored closely for potential discrimination.

The management of diversity is a natural consequence of human resource strategies that focus on flexible working arrangements. Part-time work and, especially, homeworking are particularly attractive to some women and disabled employees. But fathers also may have reasons for more flexible working arrangements (see the 'HRM in reality' section – Has life improved for working fathers?).

HRM in reality   Has life improved for working fathers?

'Dad's Army', a 2002 report by Richard Reeves for The Work Foundation indicated that responsibilities affecting working fathers had not yet registered on the corporate radar. Men were nervous about taking paternity leave and asking for flexible working patterns or time off to help them manage childcare responsibilities. The report found that working fathers believed bosses discriminated against men who are fathers. The report also argued that real equality of opportunity for women would not be achieved until this situation changed.

The report highlighted some of the advantages of father-friendly working environments. Involved fathers tend to be happier at work and are more likely to have the 'emotional intelligence' considered essential for modern management.

The Work Foundation's director of research, John Knell said:

Rather than women conforming to a male model of work, men and women need to join forces to overthrow it. The focus should no longer be on the dual-career couple but the dual-carer couple with both taking on the rearing of their children without either suffering a setback to their careers.

The report's author Richard Reeves added:

Paternity leave is a great start but does not in itself constitute a 'father-friendly' approach to work.

Workplace culture is hugely important and this is not just created by Dinosaur Dads at the top. Men's lack of participation to date in companies' work–family programmes perpetuates an environment where both men and women unwittingly allow childcare to become sidelined as a mothers-only issue, rather than a parenting issue.

There are five recommendations in the 'Dad's Army' report for companies wanting to think more creatively about employees who are parents:

- *Daddy diagnostic*: find out what men want; it may not be paternity leave but leaving early on a Friday to pick up their kids for the weekend.

- *Paternity leave*: the necessary starting point but companies must think beyond it; children will need two parents throughout their lives.

- *Time sovereignty*: grant employees more control of their working hours and provide a range of options: flexi-time, compressed hours, term-time working etc.

- *Culture shift*: this has to come from the top but also requires staff changing their behaviour and assumptions.

- *Good work*: improving the quality of the job and the working environment, as opposed to reducing

▶

▶

hours, will have positive effects at home that will be reflected back at work.

However, being a father in 2006 has little effect on men's overall working patterns, despite reducing their working hours for a short time after the birth of a child, according to Economic and Social Research Council funded research by sociologist Dr Esther Dermott at the University of Bristol.

A new report 'The Effect of Fatherhood on Men's Patterns of Employment' finds that fathers neither work fewer hours than non-fathers, nor see this as a problem. Current policies encouraging a better work–life balance still don't take account of how fathers would like to accommodate family life. Greater use of employee-controlled forms of flexibility and pay-related paternity leave is indicated.

Esther Dermott said: 'Fatherhood is not a good pre-dictor of the number of hours men work once other variables are taken into account. Hours of work are significantly related to age, form of economic activity, occupation, earnings and partner's working-time.'

Statistical analysis of data for men living with their dependent children contained in the British Household Panel Study and the National Child Development Survey showed that around a quarter wanted to work fewer hours; less than one per cent wanted to increase their hours and the remainder wished to maintain existing hours. These preferences did not change when the men became fathers.

Esther Dermott said:

There is no evidence that 'new', involved fathers are adopting a 'female model' of parenthood, with part-time work and high levels of childcare. It seems that fathers don't want to work fewer hours. What professional men value most about their jobs is their ability to control their working hours so that they can leave early to go to school functions or parents' meetings – and this flexibility was also what other men most wanted.

Why has there been little change in men's overall working patterns?

Source: *HRM Guide UK* (http://www.hrmguide.co.uk), 24 August, 2006.

Discussion on women in the workplace tends to feature family, children and marriage prominently. However, Hamilton, Gordon and Whelan-Berry (2006) found that never-married women without children often experience work–life conflict at similar levels to that experienced by other groups of working women. Work–life benefits typically provided by organizations are frequently regarded as less important and used less often by never-married women without children than by other working women.

Key concept 16.7 The glass ceiling

The term 'glass ceiling' describes the process by which women are barred from promotion by means of an invisible barrier. This involves a number of factors, including attitudes of people in power and the inflexible processes and requirements geared to the cloning process which ensures that 'men of a certain sort' will generally succeed. In the USA, the term is also used to describe the barrier that prevents progress for other disadvantaged groups – for example, ethnic minorities.

Gender and sexual discrimination

A recent review of the top 400 management publications in the world finds that a woman's lot isn't always a happy one – at least not in the workplace (Anon, 2005). Equality has become something of a buzzword but the reality is often quite different. Although many countries have sex or **gender discrimination** and equal pay legislation, organizations merely pay lip service to the equal opportunities policies that it has spawned. Informal psychological and organizational barriers continue to bar the progress of women.

Whereas women's participation in the employment market has increased rapidly, in most countries their share of senior jobs is still low. The first annual FTSE Female Index published in 2000 demonstrated that few women were present on the boards of Britain's biggest businesses. As part of the campaign, FTSE 100 companies were ranked according to the number of women board directors. Although women made up over half of the UK workforce in that year, fewer than 2 per cent of FTSE 100 executive directors and less than 8 per cent of non-executive directors were female. Very nearly half (49 per cent) of these companies had no women on their boards; 54 per cent had no women non-executives; and a staggering 91 per cent had no female executive directors.

The processes of occupational segregation and 'sex-typing' of jobs continue to be prevalent, so that women are concentrated at the base of most organizational hierarchies in jobs that are less prestigious and lower-paid than those favoured by men. As an example De Graft-Johnson, Manley and Greed (2005) reported on 2003 research indicating that while approximately 37 per cent of architectural students are women, and the percentage is increasing, this is not reflected in the architectural profession. Women represent only 13 per cent of the total and are leaving after qualifying. A multiplicity of factors, such as low pay, poor promotion prospects, discriminatory attitudes and sexist behaviour were found to influence departure.

Fuller, Beck and Unwin (2005) argue that gender segregation has been a persistent feature of apprenticeship programmes in countries around the world. In the UK, the Modern Apprenticeship was launched ten years ago as the government's flagship initiative for training new entrants in a range of occupational sectors. One priority was to increase male and female participation in 'non-traditional' occupations normally practised by just one sex. Recent figures indicate that the programme has failed to achieve this aim. Fuller *et al.*'s study explores the attitudes of young people (aged 14 and 15) and employers to non-traditional occupational choices. They also consider factors affecting the decisions of young people to train in non-traditional occupations and recruitment decisions of employers from traditional sectors, such as engineering, construction and childcare. The study finds that none of the institutions and organizations which act as gatekeepers between young people and employers is currently taking responsibility for challenging their perceptions and decisionmaking processes. Occupational stereotypes are deeply entrenched, creating major psychological and social barriers that have to be overcome if a more evenly balanced workforce is to be achieved.

HRM in reality Glass ceiling still barrier

A study by Accenture shows that, despite improvements in the last 10 years, women executives still face an uphill battle for workplace equality. Factors believed to influence this situation vary in different parts of the world.

The study, entitled 'The Anatomy of the Glass Ceiling: Barriers to Women's Professional Advancement', was conducted as part of Accenture's observance of International Women's Day and is based on a survey of 1200 male and female executives in the United States of America, Canada, Austria, Germany, Switzerland, United Kingdom, Australia and the Philippines.

Respondents were asked to score factors they felt influenced their career success across three 'dimensions':

- *individual*: career planning, professional competence, assertiveness, etc.

- *company*: supportive supervisors, transparent promotion processes, tailored training programmes, etc.
- *society*: equal rights, government support of parental leave, etc.

Differences between male and female respondents' answers were used to calculate the current 'thickness' of the 'glass ceiling' – the term describing behaviours, practices and attitudes that create an unacknowledged barrier preventing the advancement of women and other disadvantaged groups to leadership or management positions.

The study found that in Canada, approximately two-thirds of both male and female executives (67 per cent of men and 64 per cent of women) believe that gender equality in the workplace has improved in the last 10 years. However, only one-third (32 per cent) believe that men and women have equal opportunities in the

▶

workplace, and one-third (34 per cent) of female executives believe that their gender limits their career opportunities.

Jodie Wallis, a senior executive in Accenture's Financial Services practice said: 'Equality in the workplace is still a battle for many women. While there has been improvement, companies need to recognize the contributions women make to their organizations. The glass ceiling is starting to crack, but it has not been shattered.'

Some women executives believe the glass ceiling is a function of societal rather than individual factors. Respondents in the United States of America and the United Kingdom, for instance, are confident of their own business capabilities and are more likely to believe that the greatest barriers to their success come not from this 'individual' dimension, or from the culture of their organization, but from society at large.

At the other end of the spectrum, women executives in Canada and the Philippines believe that societal issues are less of a barrier and that corporate cultures are more to blame for the glass ceiling.

The study suggests that Canadian organizations have room for improvement when it comes to supporting equal opportunity in the workplace. Only 28 per cent of Canadian women acknowledged formal mentoring programmes for women within their organizations. In addition, less than half (45 per cent) felt that promotion processes are transparent, compared with 52 per cent of Canadian men.

'Building and retaining a diverse workforce is a tremendous asset to any Canadian firm. At Accenture, we have found that creating an environment where mentoring, networking and sponsorship thrive advances women and the company' said Jodie Wallis.

Among the most important factors contributing to career development identified by Canadian women are:

- assertiveness (80 per cent)
- personal ambition (78 per cent)
- internal networking (69 per cent)
- willingness to relocate (59 per cent).

'The study reminds us that while there has been progress in shattering the glass ceiling over the past 20 years, organizations – and societies – need to realize how important it is to capitalize and build upon the skills of women,' said Kedrick D. Adkins, Accenture's chief diversity officer. 'Creating a business culture that supports innovation, growth and prosperity requires people with diverse talents, and organizations need to ensure that they value all styles of leadership and work. In other words, global inclusion is the key to the long-term success of companies.'

Why do women in different countries have varying views on the principal barriers to equality?

Source: *HRM Guide Canada* (http://www.hrmguide.net/canada/), 8 March, 2006.

HRM in reality Attracting female telecoms engineers

Openreach today launched Open2all, a major initiative to identify and address barriers to women joining BT as telecoms engineers. The aim of Open2all is to encourage more women to consider joining Openreach in an engineering role, thereby increasing the number of female engineers within the company.

Focus groups of male and female engineers in Openreach have identified recruitment, career progression, flexible working and facilities as some of the chief concerns of female colleagues. These key issues form the basis of a three-point plan that Openreach is implementing to boost the number of female engineers. This will focus on:

- *Recruitment*: tailored adverts and better use of channels and networks to ensure that recruitment advertising appeals to and reaches more women.

- *Role definition*: exploring the potential for increasing flexible working practices, job sharing, child-friendly hours and other work–life balance measures.
- *Culture*: altering the male-dominated environment associated with engineering to make the role more attractive to women.

This will be achieved by the continual promotion of diversity within Openreach and by highlighting the success of existing female engineers.

Andrew Jones, managing director, north, and diversity champion, Openreach, said: 'In many areas, Openreach has a significantly diverse workforce to be proud of – indeed, 40 per cent of our executive committee are women. We are keen to replicate this success in our engineering community. The Open2all initiative demonstrates our strong commitment to finding more ways to encourage more women to consider joining Openreach as an engineer.

'Research shows that there is a huge business case for gender diversity – more women in the workforce can contribute to increased levels of innovation, creativity and productivity. Openreach's primary role is to serve communications providers' customers to the best of our ability, and a more representative workforce will allow us to do that.'

Alison Williams, Openreach engineer, Liverpool, said: 'I love my job with Openreach, but there is still a long way to go to convince women that this career choice is open to them. The work is obviously technical, but full training is provided in your first weeks on the job. The job is full of challenges – working in field service fully utilizes your people and problem solving skills and this is why I find it so rewarding.

'I'm pleased that the company is publicly committing to addressing the barriers to entry so that women can feel they are entering the job on a level playing field with men, in everything from career opportunities and pay to facilities and personal safety.'

How would you promote engineering as a career for women?

Source: *HRM Guide UK* (http://www.hrmguide.co.uk/), 27 June, 2006.

Internationally, the United Nations concludes that women are facing a global **glass ceiling** (Key concept 16.7) and that 'in no society do women enjoy the same opportunities as men' (*Financial Times*, 11 December 1995). In developing countries women represent under one-seventh of administrators and managers. In the most developed country, the USA, the **Glass Ceiling Commission** stated that between 95 and 97 per cent of senior managers in the country's biggest corporations were men. According to Robert Young, director general of the Institute of Management: 'men are the prime barrier to women in management. Despite some progress, old-fashioned sexist attitudes are still common and represent a real, not an imagined, barrier.'

Helena Kennedy, a prominent lawyer and one of Britain's few women QCs at the time commented (*Independent*, 19 December 1992) more than a decade ago:

> What we have to fight is the idea that access to these jobs is based on merit and it will only be a matter of time before women break through. What it is actually based on is men choosing people who are like themselves. It's all about cloning. That's why it's so hard to make the breakthrough and that's why it has to be consciously tackled.

Employer prejudices explain some of the difficulties that women experience. Central to many employers' attitudes is a belief in the Victorian model of the family, where the woman stayed at home looking after the children and the man went out to work. This pattern has become uncommon in much of the developed world. Dual-career and one-parent families, equal parenting and the dismantling of life-long career structures have eroded the distinction between male and female roles. Misra and Panigrahi (1996) looked at attitudes among people of different ages regarding female labour force participation. Using National Opinion Research Centre Social Survey data they found that younger people are more favourable towards women working outside the home than older people. Women had more positive attitudes towards this than men. But both women and men disapprove of women working if pre-school children might suffer as a result. A positive attitude towards women working outside the home was also associated with higher education, higher family income, residence in urban areas and generally liberal viewpoints.

Can the human resource function steer employers towards an equality perspective? Woodhams and Lupton (2006) found that the presence of an HR professional in small to medium-sized enterprises is associated with greater take-up of gender-based equality policies but not with greater implementation of associated practices.

Hossain and Tisdell (2005) describe an improvement in the status of women in Bangladesh. They found evidence of growing commercialization of women's work. Most women are self-employed or employed in low-skill jobs, but participation is increasing in high-skill and entrepreneurial jobs as well as policy-making bodies. Gender wage differentials have been considerably reduced in many industries but women tend to be paid less than men.

Remarkable improvements in women's educational attainments are positively correlated with workforce participation.

Gender differences

A further contributor to the problem is our perception of **gender** differences, real or imagined (see Key concept 16.8). There are differences between men and women, other than the physical, but little agreement as to what they are. For example, Bevan and Thompson (1992) found evidence that men and women rated working behaviour differently:

Key concept 16.8 Gender

All human societies divide themselves into two social categories called 'female' and 'male'. Each category is defined on the basis of varying cultural assumptions about the attributes, beliefs and behaviours expected from males and females. The gender of any individual depends on a complex combination of genetic, body, psychological and social elements, none of which are free from possible ambiguity or anomaly (Helman, 1990). Traditionally, sexual differences have been used to justify male-dominated societies in which women have been given inferior and secondary roles in their working lives.

HRM in reality Gender stereotypes

A study by Elizabeth Gorman, assistant professor of sociology at the University of Virginia analyzed hiring decisions of 700 law firms in the USA in the mid-1990s. She found that stereotypes of men as decisive and aggressive and of women as indecisive and gentle are 'alive and well' and influencing personnel decisions at large, private law firms.

Elizabeth Gorman said: 'Women have gained a foothold in the legal profession over the past quarter century. But even among law firms, which should be more than usually attuned to discrimination in employment, the power of stereotypes shapes hiring to a statistically significant degree.'

The study entitled 'Gender Stereotypes, Same-Gender Preferences, and Organizational Variation in the Hiring of Women: Evidence from Law Firms,' published in the *American Sociological Review* (2005) is believed to present the first evidence from the workplace for employer discrimination according to gender stereotypes. In recent years, expert testimony in courts along these lines has been discounted because it relied on controlled laboratory experiments. The study also found that when women are in charge of hiring, organizations hire more women.

Other findings of the study included:

● A majority of the law firms (55 per cent) had a lower proportion of women among their entry level

hires than the proportion of women enrolled in law schools, suggesting a hiring disadvantage for women.

● In 1994–95, on average, only 39 per cent of associates and 13 per cent of partners were women.

● The presence of a female hiring partner increased the odds that a woman would be hired by 13 per cent.

Gorman argues that these results underline the importance of ensuring awareness among hiring officials that gender stereotypes can influence their decisions. Training and sensitization to the issues are important to battling discrimination. She also calls for the establishment of institutional safeguards, such as restricting the discretion of decisionmakers and requiring written records of all hiring decisions. The study suggests that the legal understanding of discrimination should be broadened beyond a deliberate decision not to hire a woman, to encompass the subtle impact of stereotypes on decisionmaking.

Where do gender stereotypes come from?

Source: *HRM Guide USA* (http://www.hrmguide.com), 1 October, 2005.

- Males tended to favour and aspire towards qualities that were essentially individualistic and competitive, such as intelligence, dynamism, energy and assertiveness.
- Women stressed qualities of a more cooperative and consensual nature: thoughtfulness, flexibility, perceptiveness and honesty.

They concluded that since male managers are prevalent, females are disadvantaged by being evaluated against male standards of behaviour. This has been described as the 'male-as-norm syndrome' (Wilson, 1995, p.3). Given similar jobs and appraisal ratings, men are more likely to be offered training or promotion. Kramer and Lambert (2001) examined a large, random sample of female and male employees using a survival analysis technique to investigate the time taken from being hired to being promoted to supervisor. They found evidence for significant pro-male bias in promotion decisions that could not be attributed to differences in time on the job, education, or parenting responsibilities. Brynin (2006) argues that men have traditionally gained more than women from access to technologies at work that bring prestige, job security, more satisfaction and higher pay. Where female jobs have centred on technologies, they tend towards routine and possibly deskilled work.

Wilson (2005) examined how women academics in two British universities perceive the assumption that they are receiving different and unequal treatment in appraisal. It has been argued that men and women appear to have learned that women are different and not equal in organizations. Wilson's study found that, while the women did not necessarily perceive themselves as being seen to be different, men saw them as having different and inferior qualities. Women were seen as 'other' when measured against standards and norms set by men.

Hakim (2006) argues that high levels of female employment and family-friendly policies actually reduce gender equality in the workforce and reinforce the glass ceiling. The emphasis placed on equal opportunities by policymakers and feminists assumes that discrimination is the primary source of sex differentials in labour market outcomes – notably the pay gap between men and women. However, some careers and occupations cannot be domesticated and this also poses limits to social engineering.

Fortin (2005) used data from three World Value Surveys in the 1990s to investigate the impact of gender role attitudes and work values on women's labour-market outcomes across 25 OECD countries. Consistent with Hakim's views, Fortin concluded that anti-egalitarian opinions were weakening but were still negatively associated with female employment rates and the gender pay gap. The persistent perceptions of women's role as homemakers could help to explain the recent slowdown of gender convergence in pay. It seems that a clash between family values and egalitarian views is another obstacle in achieving greater gender equality in the job market.

Also, women are more likely to underestimate their own skill levels and, therefore, inhibit their own progress. However, not all women meekly accept the male order. Some deal with the situation by playing the game according to male rules. In a study of Greek organizations employing both female and male managers, Bourantas and Papalexandris (1990) found no difference between leadership styles. Their explanation was that women were imitating male patterns of behaviour in order to achieve success. This approach attracts mixed, and complex reactions, particularly from other women. For instance, Margaret Thatcher, former UK Prime Minister, sometimes regarded as being a better man than most men, was an object of some fascination. According to Webster (1990, p.2):

> Mrs Thatcher has acted out a role which is forbidden to women within conventional notions of femininity, revelling in power, dominating, 'handbagging' and humiliating men, a role which can be incorporated and allowed within the 'nanny' image, under the cover of rectitude. A common reaction from women is often mixed, a combination of a recognition that Mrs Thatcher has done little or nothing for her own sex, and of an admiration, sometimes unreserved, for the way in which she has shown rather conspicuously and publicly that women are not weak and indecisive, nor deficient in stamina and guts.

Margaret Thatcher saw toughness, practicality and the ability to cope as being particularly female qualities (Webster, 1990, p.51). Nevertheless, she surrounded herself with a cabinet of men and did little to benefit other women politicians. Thatcher appears to have been an exception in trying to assert her views over others. In general, women are more likely to regard themselves as 'enablers' of other people, seeing themselves as opening up information to employees, building up the confidence of their staff and encouraging them to develop and use their skills. In a study of 176 women managers from a number of industries across Australia, Downey, Papageorgiou and Stough (2006) found that female managers displaying transformational leadership behaviours tended to show higher levels of emotional intelligence and intuition than women managers displaying less transformational leadership behaviours.

There is no denying, of course, that not only are men and women sometimes different in their approach but that this may sometimes lead to conflict.

It is clear that much of the debate about male and female behaviour revolves around sexual stereotyping, which has a significant cultural basis. Hofstede (1994, p.16) argues that, within any society, there is a men's culture that is different from women's culture. This difference may explain why traditional gender roles are so difficult to change. Stereotyping can also influence career aspirations. Harper and Haq (2001) examined British cohort data and found that 16-year-old boys and girls showed significant differences in their occupational aspirations, appearing to follow a traditional pattern. They argue that these occupational preferences influence the decisions of young people to apply for certain types of job. Harper and Haq used a conditional hiring model in order to separate the effects of such preferences from the hiring decision of employers. They found no evidence of hiring bias against women except in manual and craft occupations and that the effect of sex discrimination could be exaggerated if occupational aspirations were not taken into account.

Kraus and Yonay (2000) compared the way in which women and men attained workplace authority in female-dominated, mixed, and male-dominated occupations. They found that women have the greatest chances of being given authority when they work in 'male' occupations, arguing that the competition between men and women is weaker in such occupations so that men have less reason to discriminate against women. They observed that men have

---

HRM in reality Pink collar CEOs

A new study shows that twice as many women hold the top executive position in the Fortune 500 compared with five years ago. The number has increased from five in August 2001 and will be 11 in October 2006 when PepsiCo chief finance officer Indra Nooyi is scheduled to take over as CEO.

The study conducted by executive search firm Christian & Timbers found that six out of the 11 female CEOs are working in the 'pink collar' sectors producing or selling food and personal products. In 2001 only one Fortune 500 female CEO was in retail.

Further study findings include:

- Of the six female CEOs in the pink collar sectors, three came from operations, one is moving from CFO to CEO and two came up through marketing.

- In 2006 only three out of 11 female CEOs are in the IT/computer equipment sector compared with two out of five in 2001.

- Five out of 10 female CEOs in the Fortune 501–1000 are in pink collar sectors.

Brendan Burnett Stohner, leader of diversity practice and a vice-chairman of Christian & Timbers said: 'From PepsiCo to Avon to Sara Lee, women are driving big change at some of the biggest companies in the country. Boards are beginning to see that women CEOs can drive bottom-line results and protect the reputation of billion dollar brands. The problem is that women are for the most part, still left out of the corner office of major technology companies, financials and the big industrials. We have a long way to go before we see real equity. The talent is there. At Christian & Timbers our commitment is to get the top women in the country in front of the right boards to move diversity forward.'

Why are so many of the (admittedly small number) of women CEOs in the 'pink collar' sector?

Source: *HRM Guide USA* (http://www.hrmguide.com), 14 September, 2006.

similar chances regardless of the type of occupation in which they are employed. By contrast, in a meta-analytic study, Davison and Burke (2000) found that female and male applicants received lower ratings when being considered for an opposite-sex-type job.

Sexual harassment

Some aspects of male culture are distinctly unattractive – even to many men. From school to shopfloor, locker room to office, the culture of masculinity expresses itself in 'jokes' revolving around three stereotypes of sexuality (Mills and Murgatroyd, 1991, p.78):

HRM in reality Study shows women do negotiate

Recent business texts, including a popular book *Women Don't Ask* (Babcock and Laschever, 2003) suggest that businesswomen are hesitant to negotiate for what it would take to be successful at work. But a survey by the Simmons School of Management and HP of nearly 500 middle and senior-level businesswomen revealed that they are highly likely to negotiate when they take on a challenging new project or job. The vast majority of those who did so reported higher performance reviews, significantly more job satisfaction, ongoing opportunities for new leadership roles, and less likelihood of leaving their companies than those who didn't negotiate.

The survey also showed that women with the most experience in leadership situations tend to carefully diagnose any new position before accepting it; first checking with a broad network of informal 'career advisors' inside and outside the company about what should be negotiated.

Deborah Kolb, professor at the Simmons School of Management, said: 'Many studies of women and negotiating are based on role-playing and games. But when you look at negotiating in the real world, around leadership opportunities and challenges, we see that the successful women do, indeed, negotiate. And it pays off for everyone.

'That's a powerful message to companies as well as to women who want to get ahead. Companies should encourage women to negotiate. If they say, "Let's sit down and figure out what you need up front to be successful in this new job," it pays off in higher motivation and lower turnover.'

The survey found that of the businesswomen who reported taking on a new leadership role:

- 84 per cent said they negotiated with their superiors for additional financial or human resources.
- 62 per cent negotiated for support for their agenda, and for a strategic introduction that made the case why they were right for the job.

- 52 per cent negotiated over job title, job descriptions, key reporting relationships, and mutual expectations with the boss.

Outcomes for women who said they negotiated included:

- 75 per cent reported they were significantly satisfied with their jobs, compared with 27 per cent who did not negotiate.
- 70 per cent said they were not likely to consider employment elsewhere, compared with 30 per cent who did not negotiate.
- 81 per cent said they were offered additional opportunities for leadership roles.
- 86 per cent reported that their last performance review 'exceeded or far exceeded' their expectations.

Deborah Kolb said women should not think the choice is simply to accept or decline a challenging new assignment. She commented: 'No job that's a challenge and a stretch is a perfect fit. Some aspects build on your strengths, others represent a steep learning curve. Ask yourself, "What would it take to make me say yes to this offer? How can I make the job fit who I am, where I am?"

'Access your strengths and weaknesses, and negotiate for whatever you need in the way of job title, resources, a safety net, and senior level support for any difficult actions you may have to take. Dig deep to gather good intelligence and then enlist people to help. That's what successful women do.

'Women who don't negotiate, who just take the job offered to them, are creating problems for themselves down the road.'

What inhibits some women from negotiating improved rewards?

Source: *HRM Guide USA* (http://www.hrmguide.com), 1 February, 2006.

- the ideal, or 'real man' syndrome – toughness, football and so on
- definitions of males as 'not-females'
- the normality of heterosexuality.

Ford (2000) found experimental evidence to suggest that when people who are high in hostile sexism are exposed to sexist jokes they become increasingly tolerant of sex discrimination. The process appears to involve the activation of a non-critical mindset. In traditionally all-male factories, workshops and warehouses, joking is reinforced by sexually explicit, homophobic or racist language, swearing, pictures of nude women (where they have not been banned), sexual bragging and suggestive horseplay. This serves to create an immensely threatening atmosphere for women and others, discouraging any attempt to enter this 'man's world'.

In office and managerial environments these elements are less evident but **sexual harassment** – ranging from unwelcome comments on appearance to physical advances – remains common although surveys give conflicting evidence. Canadian surveys show that as many as 70 per cent of women have been sexually harassed at some time during their working lives (Moynahan, 1993). A survey by the Employment Law Alliance (www.employmentlawalliance.com, 6 February 2002) shows that 21 per cent of US women polled said that they had suffered sexual harassment at work, compared with 7 per cent of men.

Sexual harassment is a difficult topic for managers to deal with, since it involves personal relationships and the individual interpretations of those involved (see Key concept 16.9). The issue has often been trivialized or ignored in a 'conspiracy of silence'. In a survey of top British companies, Davidson and Earnshaw (1991) found that only 64.8 per cent of respondents regarded it as a serious management issue. Given that this was based on a response rate of only 22 per cent from their sample, this finding probably overestimates management concern.

Few cases develop into formal complaints or tribunal cases but the consequences for morale are severe, with victims frequently leaving to escape harassment. The effects on victims can include nervousness and depression. In the work context, this affects concentration and productivity and increases the likelihood of absenteeism (Wright and Bean, 1993). The effects can spill over into the home, possibly leading to the breaking-up of relationships.

Key concept 16.9 Sexual harassment

Definitions vary considerably but most are agreed that it is sexual attention which is unwanted, repeated, and affects a person's work performance or expectations. However, it is possible for one incident to be sufficiently severe to be regarded as harassment. It differs from sexual banter or flirting since it is one-way; it does not have the involvement and acceptance of both parties. In the USA, the Equal Employment Opportunity Commission has extended the definition of sexual harassment to include a range of actions that lead to a 'hostile work environment'. This definition includes unwelcome touching, joking, teasing, innuendos, slurs, and the display of sexually explicit materials.

Employers have a moral duty to protect staff from sexual harassment. In general, if employers tolerate sexual harassment they convey the impression that one gender does not deserve respect; they are prepared to sacrifice motivation and commitment; they must accept the consequences for efficiency. Organizations can deal with sexual harassment by (Moynahan, 1993):

- Surveying the organization to determine the extent of sexual harassment.
- Writing and circulating a strongly worded policy indicating possible disciplinary action.

- Providing an effective reporting mechanism, protecting the rights of accusers and the accused.

- Packaged workshops, which help to define harassment and prevent 'misunderstandings'.

- Assertiveness training, perhaps particularly appropriate for women working in jobs which have traditionally been regarded as male, which encourages the confidence to provide verbal or even written feedback to unwanted behaviour. The ability to say 'no' firmly and at an early stage is particularly effective.

- Gender-awareness training to emphasize different perceptions of teasing and 'harmless fun' between men and women.

HRM in reality Sexual harassment is no joke

New guidelines released by the Equal Opportunities Commission (EOC) are designed to help employers combat the ongoing problem of sexual harassment in the workplace. On the eve of the 20th anniversary of Jean Porcelli's landmark case that established sexual harassment as a form of harassment under the Sex Discrimination Act (SDA) it remains all too common, says the EOC.

Jean Porcelli, a school science technician working for Strathclyde Regional Council in Scotland, brought her case after experiencing a sustained campaign of harassment from two male colleagues, some of which was sexual in nature. At the time she had no remedy under employment protection legislation, which was narrower than the current Employment Rights Act. Supported by the EOC, she used the SDA to challenge her treatment and ensure that her employer took action to address the workplace culture. She was awarded £3000 compensation in 1986 but continued to experience repercussions from her stand.

The EOC defines sexual harassment as ranging from questions or comments about an individual's sex life, to the display of pornography, to rape and sexual assault. This creates a potentially intimidating, hostile or humiliating working environment, which will have an impact on performance. Employers are legally responsible for preventing their staff from being subject to sexual harassment.

EOC research shows that there have been 260 successful sexual harassment cases brought in the last five years, and harassment cases comprise 22 per cent of all successful sex discrimination cases. In addition, it is one of the top five reasons for calls to the EOC helpline.

The EOC is currently working with organizations like the armed forces which have experienced widespread problems of sexual harassment and are taking action to address the problems. Research conducted for the Ministry of Defence and published in 2006 found that sexualized behaviours (jokes, stories, language and material) were widespread in all three armed services. Almost all (99 per cent) of the service women who responded had been in situations in the previous twelve months where such behaviours had taken place, with two-thirds (67 per cent) having had the behaviours directed at them personally and 15 per cent having had a 'particularly upsetting' experience.

Early findings from the EOC's current research, carried out by a team from the Centre for Diversity and Work Psychology, Manchester Business School, suggest that sexual harassment is most common where:

- there is a major gender imbalance in the workplace
- one sex, typically men, hold positions of power and junior roles are held by the other, usually women
- there is job insecurity or a new supervisor or manager has been appointed
- the leadership style is either too authoritarian or too laissez faire.

Unlike Jean Porcelli, many of those who experience harassment leave their jobs, resulting in recruitment costs for employers ranging between £1000 for a manual worker, to £10 000 for a senior manager or director. The EOC guidelines 'Sexual Harassment: Managers' Questions Answered' are intended to help employers prevent sexual harassment happening in the first place and to deal more effectively with it when it does. Among the issues addressed is the need for well-communicated policies, an effective complaints procedure and training to help staff investigate complaints confidentially and compassionately.

Jenny Watson, chair of the Equal Opportunities Commission, said: 'Twenty years on from Jean Porcelli's landmark case, sexual harassment is still an issue causing women stress, health problems and financial penalties when they leave their jobs to avoid it. We suspect that the cases that come to our attention

▶

▶

are the tip of the iceberg. It's important for women to know what they can do to tackle harassment – and for employers to know how they can help stamp it out in the workplace.

'As our new guidelines show, strong leadership and a few simple steps taken by employers can make all the difference, something that the best employers already recognize. Creating a workplace in which everyone is valued and in which there is no place for bullying or harassment helps to boost morale and productivity, and of course helps to avoid the high costs of tribunal claims.'

Jean Porcelli said: 'It disheartens me that sexual harassment still happens – sadly my own daughter has experienced it. And I can certainly understand why so many women are reluctant to come forward. I know I

paid a great price, both personally and professionally. Despite changing jobs, I was labelled a "troublemaker" until the resulting stress and ill health eventually prompted me to take early retirement. In my day, there was no shortage of managers – and even my union officials – who told me to sit down, keep quiet and get on with my job, a response some women still experience today. I hope employers, prompted by the new EOC guidelines, will take a strong leadership role, and in another twenty years time we'll be telling a very different story.'

What are the most effective ways of reducing the occurrence of sexual harassment at work?

Source: *HRM Guide UK* (http://www.hrmguide.co.uk), 10 June, 2006.

Increasingly, employing organizations are liable to legal action for sexual harassment by one employee against another.

Legal definitions of sexual harassment fall into one of two types:

Quid pro quo. A narrow, traditional definition of sexual harassment as a demand by a person in power, for example a supervisor, for sexual favours from a subordinate in return for a job, pay increase, promotion, transfer or other benefit.

Hostile environment. A wider definition, including unwelcome sexual advances that have the effect of creating a hostile, intimidating, abusive or offensive working environment.

Clarke (2006a) examines concerns raised by employers about consensual sexual relationships occurring at work. The study suggests that the link between sexual relationships and sexual harassment is sometimes used as a justification for regulating relationships, particularly hierarchical ones. There also can be a problem of harassment when relationships end. Clarke comments that the willingness of employers, particularly in the USA, to prohibit or regulate relationships might not be motivated by concern for women's equality at work. Recent changes to the law on sexual harassment in the UK might encourage British employers to consider prohibiting or regulating sexual relationships, but there are countervailing legal principles to be considered, such as anti-discrimination law and privacy rights. The study concludes that sex discrimination law should be directed to ensuring that unacceptable behaviour is not tolerated rather than prohibiting consensual relationships.

Summary

Equality of opportunity is both a matter of social justice and sound economic sense. Voluntary approaches to minimize discrimination have been largely ineffective and most developed countries have introduced some form of anti-discrimination legislation. There has been a tendency towards all-embracing laws in recent years, increasingly linked to human rights legislation. Granting opportunity is beneficial to organizational effectiveness as well as personal success. The strategic management of diversity leads to a wider range of ideas and abilities, offering greater scope for innovation and competitive performance in the future.

Further reading

Promoting Equality: Challenging Discrimination and Oppression by Audrey Mullender (Palgrave Macmillan, 2003) provides a comprehensive review of the topic. *The Diversity Training Handbook: A Practical Guide to Understanding and Changing Attitudes* by Phil Clements and John Jones (Kogan Page, 2005) is another useful book as is *Dynamics of Managing Diversity* by Gill Kirton and Anne-Marie Greene (Butterworth-Heinemann, 2004). *Discrimination Law* edited by Malcolm Sargeant (Longman, 2004) is a comprehensive, practical and accessible guide to anti-discrimination law in the UK. *Breaking Through the Glass Ceiling* by Linda Wirth (International Labour Office, 2001) is a revised account of her study on the status of women's employment in a number of countries.

Review questions

1 Distinguish between equal opportunities and the management of diversity. How is it possible to justify either in a commercial organization?

2 Is positive discrimination an effective method of ensuring equal opportunities?

3 Are there any circumstances in which jobs should be reserved for specific individuals or groups without being unfair?

4 Is it true to say that anti-discrimination legislation has had a major effect on equal opportunities in the workplace?

5 Why have different countries chosen to take their own distinctive approaches to anti-discrimination legislation? Compare and contrast the approaches taken by the countries we have discussed.

6 Why are women and members of minority groups placed in unfavourable occupational categories?

7 What are the advantages and disadvantages of using separate laws for each form of discrimination?

8 What is occupational segregation and what part does it play in the process of discrimination?

9 How important is 'cloning' in discriminatory behaviour?

10 In Western countries romantic relationships commonly start in the workplace. What distinguishes such a relationship from sexual harassment?

Case studies for discussion and analysis

Frank and Margaret

Most people think Frank is a nice guy. He is a good networker, knows everyone in the company and is always the first to buy a round of drinks at any social event. He is married, has three children and an attractive house in a very expensive area. He is the senior accounts controller in the purchasing contracts department and is thought to run a very efficient department. For several years he had a relationship with Margaret from government sales. This broke up in a somewhat emotional fashion last December when he finally told her that he had no intention of leaving his wife.

Audrey, the government sales coordinator has come to see you regarding some stories that are being told in her department. It seems that Margaret has been telling people that Frank is not entirely honest. She has claimed that he has been taking bribes from contractors, accepting cash, holidays and improvements for his house in return for signing contracts. Margaret has not said this in Audrey's presence because Audrey is a rather straightlaced person who has always made it clear that she disapproved of the relationship. Audrey and Margaret do not get on very well as a result.

You are the general manager responsible for these departments. How would you proceed?

White male culture and disadvantage

In the September 2001 edition of *HRMagazine*, Michael Welp, a principal at EqualVoice is quoted as saying that white men need to view themselves as part of a culture and a group. He says that:

> Many organizations define diversity as simply respecting everyone's different culture. This attitude ignores the fact that there are systemic advantages for the white male culture. For one thing, we never have to leave our own culture and enter someone else's. This allows us to continue to think of ourselves as individuals, not as part of a white male culture. Everyone else, however, must become bi-cultural in order to fit into our culture.

In the same article, Jeff Hitchcock, author of *Unraveling the White Cocoon* (Kendall/Hunt Publishing, 2001) says that:

> I had never thought of myself as needing to be involved in a diversity process. I had evolved to the point where I realized that we, as white males, had all of the privileges, but I still thought that only people of colour had a need for a sense of community. I realized then that white men also have a part to play in diversity.
>
> I'm not sure it's a good idea to make white men too much of an entity and tell them that they have their own culture.

He offered two reasons for concern:

1 There is a lot of collusion between white men and white women regarding who we are as white people. When you place the focus on white men, it is sometimes difficult to get to the elements of privilege and culture for white men and white women. That is, when you remove white women from the discussion, you lose something. You give white women a 'break' on issues of racism that they don't always deserve.

2 Just as there is a lot of collusion between white men and white women on the issue of race, there is also a lot of collusion between white men and men of color on sexism.

Again he argues that a focus on white males 'gives black men a "break" on the question of how they think about and treat women.'

A study for British think-tank CIVITAS concluded that men are now at a disadvantage in the workplace. In the study, *Women or Men: Who Are The Victims?* (Pizzey, Shackleton and Unwin, 2000), the authors argue that, in many ways, the modern work environment favours women rather than men:

- Male jobs are less secure. Male unemployment is higher than female unemployment. Redundancy rates are higher for men.

- Male jobs are more dangerous. Men are more likely to suffer injuries, including fatal injuries, at work.

- Jobs have been falling in manufacturing, where men predominate, and rising in female-dominated service industries.

- Women are more likely to receive in-work training than men.

- Workplace legislation usually favours women workers, including the right to take time off work for family emergencies. Meanwhile, the trade unions, most of whose members are men, have had their powers reduced.

- Women have more time off work for sickness than men.

- The state pension and most occupational pensions are actuarially unfair to men.

- Women live longer, which means that 'a man and a woman with similar characteristics, retiring at the same age and on the same salary, can expect different benefits from the same contributions'.

Pizzey, Shackleton and Unwin (2000) point out that the often-quoted comparison between the average earnings of men and women – the rate for women is 75 per cent of that for men – does not take into account the difference made by the personal choice to marry. Married men earn more than single men, presumably because they are motivated by their family responsibilities, argue the researchers. But marriage has the opposite effect for women. They may drop out of the employment market completely or change from full-time to part-time working to allow for the demands of childrearing. In fact, the gap in pay between single men and single women is small, and often insignificant.

Decisions about marriage and childbearing are freely taken, they argue, so it is difficult to see how government action could narrow the gap in average earnings without unacceptable interference in people's private lives. The authors warn that 'the labour market is a very complicated place' (2000, p.22), and that attempts to even out differences between broad groups like men and women can lead to laws and regulations which endanger jobs by imposing a burden on employers, rather than achieving their stated aims.

Are men or women the most disadvantaged gender in the employment market?

Source: *HRM Guide USA* (http://www.hrmguide.net/usa/), 6 October, 2001.

Chapter 17
Dealing with discrimination

Learning objectives

The purpose of this chapter is to:

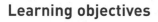

- Evaluate the causes and extent of racial discrimination in the employment market.

- Analyse the basis and effects of institutional racism.

- Assess the effectiveness of legislation in the reduction of disability discrimination.

- Consider the increasing significance of anti-age discrimination initiatives.

Ethnic diversity

For historical reasons, most countries have populations of different ethnic origins. Typically these are highlighted by colour or religious differences. Few countries have true equality between these groups. Stelcner (2000) reviews considerable disparities between incomes earned by 'visible minorities' and aboriginals in Canada in comparison with the white population. Carmichael and Woods (2000) confirm that black, Indian, Pakistani and Bangladeshi workers in the UK are disadvantaged relative to Whites, experiencing higher rates of unemployment and tending to be under-represented in higher-paid, non-manual occupations. Elvira and Zatzick (2002) found that Whites are less likely to be laid off in the USA than non-Whites and that Asians are less likely to be laid off than African-Americans or Hispanics. We could mention numerous other examples.

Racism is usually equated with hostility and prejudice. The media encourages this simplistic picture by linking it to the racial abuse and violent behaviour of neo-fascist parties. Their members' antics are a product of frustration with their own inadequacies – projected onto a visible minority. In general, however, fascists have little power and influence, and the perception of racism as obvious prejudicial opinions and attitudes obscures subtler, more insidious forms of discrimination (Sivanandan, 1991). Racism cannot be reduced to 'human nature and individual fallibility' which leave the state, politics, and 'major structural aspects of contemporary life out of focus' (Husband, 1991, p.50). The complexity of the phenomenon is illustrated by Augoustinos, Tuffin and Rapley (1999) who analysed the way in which two groups of students discussed Aboriginal people in Australia. They found four modes of discourse:

- An imperialist narrative of Australian history that denied any blame for colonialism.

- Economic-rationalist or neo-liberal talk of 'productivity' and entitlement to distance themselves from the contemporary Aboriginal 'plight'.

- A superficially balanced and even-handed account that discounted the seriousness of discrimination and racism in Australia.

- A nationalist belief in the necessity for everyone in the country to identify themselves as 'Australian'.

In the same vein, Howitt and Owusu-Bempah (1990, p.397) point to a 'new racism' characterized as 'being a far more complex and subtle form of racism which, superficially, lacks the traditional emotive denigration of black people'. They conclude that 'seeing racism solely as a form of interpersonal antagonism not only sanitizes it, but prevents us from defining ourselves as racist if we do not *feel* racial hatred'. Hence stereotypes appear that are not seen as 'prejudiced': '. . . Asian women are seen as "passive" or "hysterical" or subject to oppressive practices within the family; there is the stereotype of the strong dominant Afro-Caribbean woman as the head of the household; and the description of the over-aggressive African woman' (Sayal, 1990, p.24).

Subeliani and Tsogas (2005) studied the diversity management practices of Rabobank, a major bank in the Netherlands. They found that these were primarily directed at attracting ethnic customers rather than improving the quality of working life and career prospects of ethnic minority employees who remained segregated in lower positions and not allowed openly to express their culture and religion.

Foster and Harris (2005) examined the way in which managing diversity was understood and applied in one large, long-established British retailing company. They found that business benefits attributed to diversity management are appealing to employers. However, the concept lacks clarity for line managers both in terms of what it is and how it should be implemented within the framework of anti-discrimination legislation. They suggest that line managers are familiar with the value of demonstrating a common approach in decision-making as the key defence against claims of discriminatory treatment. Consequently they tend to regard a diversity management agenda concerned with recognizing and responding to individual differences as more likely to lead to claims of unequal treatment. They argue that, in addition to the operational context, employers need to take account of the tensions facing line managers, their interpretation of diversity management and perceptions of fair treatment.

Stewart and Perlow (2001) looked at applicant race, job status and interviewers' racial attitudes in relation to unfair selection decisions. They found that interviewers with more negative attitudes toward black people showed greater confidence in their decision to hire a black applicant rather than a white applicant for a low-status job and to give a high-status job to a white candidate rather than a black candidate. Frazer and Wiersma (2001) conducted an experiment with 88 white US undergraduates who were asked to look at paper credentials and then interview a high or low-quality black or white applicant. Black and white applicants were 'hired' in equal proportion. But when the interviewers were asked to recall the experience one week later, they rated the answers from black applicants as being significantly less intelligent than the answers given by Whites. Frazer and Wiersma explain this by postulating that the undergraduates had negative schemas towards black people which they suppressed in the public situation of making a hiring decision, but these negative stereotypes were revealed when unobtrusive measures were used.

Murji (2006) examines the use of stereotyped images in a series of advertisements that formed part of the 'personal responsibility' campaign by the Commission for Racial Equality (CRE). The aim was to raise awareness of racial stereotyping and, in one case, to provoke members of the public into complaining about the images presented. The CRE has been the main body charged with implementing and monitoring anti-racism in the UK and the use of racial stereotypes has been controversial, though not always in anticipated ways. It has been argued that the CRE's use of stereotypes is based on questionable evidence, on a problematic conception of positive and negative images, and that it fails to consider how the images can be read in diverse ways. Murji argues that the CRE seems to rely on a quasi-essentialist view of race and racism and consequently appears unable to engage with racism in its diverse manifestations.

Another significant aspect of the problem is not so much **racial discrimination** as racial disadvantage. This arises from the inability of the liberal-minded middle classes to perceive the

---

HRM in reality   Whites' racial identity

What Whites think about their own race is the focus of an innovative national survey by Doug Hartmann, associate professor, and Paul Croll, graduate student, in the University of Minnesota's department of sociology. Analysis of responses from more than 2000 households nationwide showed that there is more recognition among white people of their own racial identity and the social privileges that come with it than was previously thought.

Doug Hartmann said that a previous common assumption was that Whites overlooked their own race: 'It's sort of like having an accent. For some white Americans, racial identity is so fixed, so taken for granted, that "race" becomes something other people have.'

In fact, the researchers found that a majority of Whites (74 per cent) felt that their own racial identity was important to them, and that a similar majority perceived prejudice and discrimination as important factors in explaining white advantage. Minorities were more likely to see their racial identities as important and to see structural reasons for racial disparities.

The research also suggests that awareness of identity and privilege do not always co-exist. 'The fact of the matter is that people claim white identity for defensive as well as progressive reasons,' said Paul Croll.

The researchers found that age and income had little impact on the outcome of the study. Southerners and social conservatives placed more emphasis on their racial identity than other white Americans, while those with more education placed less. Republican and male respondents most strongly resisted the concept that discrimination in legal and financial systems can explain white advantage. Regardless of racial identity, respondents believed strongly in the importance of individual effort, hard work and family upbringing in achieving success.

Is it best to be aware of one's own race?

Source: *HRM Guide USA* (http://www.hrmguide.com), 6 September, 2006.

structural advantages that contribute to their own success. Dominelli (1992, p.165) argues that:

> It is the subtle presence of racism in our normal activities, coupled with our failure to make the connections between the personal, institutional and cultural levels of racism which make it so hard for white people to recognise its existence in their particular behaviour and combat it effectively.

Mason (2000) evaluates the concept of 'pre-labour market inequality' – essentially, the class and cultural background of individuals – and concludes that it has an undoubted impact on individual wellbeing and intergenerational mobility. But the manner in which class background has its effects is not clear. A higher class position may create an advantage in skill acquisition. Alternatively, higher social status may increase access to people in positions of power and authority. Stelcner (2000) also speculates that the shortfall in earnings experienced by aboriginal people in Canada may be due to the apparent lack of certain work-related characteristics more commonly found as part of the culture of white Canadians.

In a British study, Shiner and Modood (2002) observe that young people from ethnic minority backgrounds are admitted into university in large numbers but class or culturally-based institutional biases cause ethnic minority candidates to be filtered into the new university sector. The new universities are grossly under-funded in comparison with institutions with more long-standing university status and are also less favoured by 'blue chip' recruiters.

HRM in reality Accounting industry fails to inspire black accountants

Members of the National Association of Black Accountants cite race and employer loyalty as accounting industry shortcomings, a Howard University survey shows.

Why do so few African-Americans succeed in the accounting profession? A preliminary analysis of results from a survey conducted among members of the National Association of Black Accountants shows that race continues to impact the careers of people of colour in the accounting profession.

Key findings include:

- 59 per cent of respondents believed that because of their race, they had not always received unbiased and objective evaluations from their supervisors.

- 55 per cent felt that mistakes they might make in the workplace directly impacted on the perception and evaluation of other members of their race.

- Almost 50 per cent believed that non-minority counterparts with less technical competence or experience are given more high profile and challenging job assignments.

- 63 per cent felt no obligation to remain with their current employer.

The survey, 'The Professional Experience – The NABA Survey', was conducted by Howard University's Center for Accounting Education (CAE) in December 2005. To date, 427 NABA members have responded: 42 per cent work in public accounting; 38 per cent are employed by corporations; and 20 per cent work in the government or nonprofit sectors.

'In spite of diversity programs initiated by many of the nation's top employers, there is still disparity amongst people of colour in the accounting and finance areas with regard to their ability to advance with their employers,' said Frank Ross, founding member and past NABA president and director of the CAE. 'We hope to provide recommendations for making positive changes to lower attrition and improve advancement for the African-American accounting professional.'

'It has been proven time and again that a diverse company is a stronger, better-performing company,' Norman K. Jenkins, CPA, NABA national president, said. 'The days when companies viewed diversity as a nice thing to do are over. Diversity in the workplace is a business imperative, and those employers who are successful in attracting and retaining diverse financial talent will have a desirable competitive edge.'

'It is important to tap into our membership to assess their experiences,' added Darryl R. Matthews, Sr., NABA's executive director and COO. 'We are hopeful that the CAE's findings will lead to improved work environments so that people of color can blaze career paths with their employers.'

Are there any unique features of the accounting profession that impact on racial diversity?

Source: *HRM Guide USA* (http://www.hrmguide.com/), 21 February, 2006.

Ben-Tovim *et al.* (1992) criticize the ideology of 'colour blindness' which:

● fails to appreciate the pervasiveness of racism

● confuses racism with urban deprivation and class inequality

● is conveniently compatible with a range of political opinions

● accommodates the 'universalistic ideologies and practices of public administration'

● denies racism purely as overt and deliberate discrimination.

They note some rationalizations for ignoring other forms of racism: that raising the question of racism is divisive; that the problems of the ethnic minorities are the same as those of the white population, or the working-class, the inner cities, and so on. Awad, Cokley and Ravitch (2005) investigated the relationship between colour-blind attitudes, modern racist attitudes, and attitudes toward affirmative action. Detractors of affirmative maintain that use of race-conscious policies to remedy past discrimination is contra-indicative of a colour-blind society. Supporters maintain that while a colour-blind society may be desirable, acts of past discrimination and current institutional racism make it necessary to use race-conscious policies. The study found that after controlling for race and sex, colour-blind attitudes emerged as the strongest predictor of attitudes toward affirmative action, followed by modern racism.

The financial impact of race discrimination

According to the TUC (2002) unemployment is up to three times higher among black and Asian workers than it is among white workers in some parts of the UK (Table 17.1). Nationally, unemployment among black and Asian workers is at 11 per cent in comparison with 5 per cent for white counterparts.

Blackaby *et al.* (1999) examined the employment prospects of different ethnic groups using a sample of over 100 000 males from the UK Labour Force Survey. They found significant differences across groups, particularly Indian and Pakistani/Bangladeshi groups. They argue that the differences do not result from different levels of discrimination by the white majority. Instead they propose that this is due to the predominantly Muslim Pakistani/Bangladeshi community being less assimilated in comparison with other ethnic minority groups.

Being a woman from an ethnic minority is doubly disadvantageous. In a US study, Lapidus and Figart (1998) show that if measures of equal worth were applied to jobs, 50 per cent of women of colour and 40 per cent of white women earning less than the federal poverty threshold for a family of three would be lifted out of poverty. Overall, they conclude that being a woman, an African-American, or a worker of Hispanic origin negatively and significantly affected pay levels. In another US study, using a large sample of recent college graduates, Weinberger (1998) found that white male and Hispanic male graduates earn 10 to 15 per cent more per hour than comparable female, black male, or Asian male graduates.

Stoll (2005) found that, in relation to less-educated Whites, comparable Blacks tend to look for work in areas with higher levels of job skill requirements. Racial residential segregation and lower levels of access to car transport account for most of black jobseekers relatively

Region	White workers (%)	Black and Asian workers (%)
London	5	12
North-west	5	12
South-east	3	6
Yorkshire and Humberside	5	11
West Midlands	5	15

Table 17.1

Unemployment in selected English regions

Source: TUC, based on Labour Force Survey September–November 2001. (Other UK regions did not include sufficiently large samples for reliable figures.)

greater geographical skills mismatch. This accounts for a significant share of the racial differences in employment.

Race and performance

As we have already observed, the problems of discrimination and job market disadvantage have complex causes. One aspect is the judgement of performance. A report from the Institute for Employment Studies – 'The Problem of Minority Performance in Organizations' (Tackey, Tamkin and Sheppard, 2001) – concludes that apparent 'underperformance' of minority ethnic employees is due more to the perceptions of white managers than to true measures of their performance or abilities.

According to IES Director Richard Pearson:

> Blanket claims of institutional racism are notoriously imprecise, inevitably emotive, and not particularly helpful for finding answers to the challenges of managing diversity in the workplace. Over time, organizational cultures and systems evolve their own subjectivities, and these only emerge as people become more aware of potential side effects. By actively looking for unconscious or indirect bias in systems, processes and attitudes at work, the real problems of workplace discrimination can begin to be eliminated.

The report reviewed published literature to help answer a key question: are the observed differences in performance between individuals from minority ethnic groups and their white counterparts due to real differences in performance, or biased perceptions by appraisers in

---

HRM in reality   Black and Asian workers suffer wage discrimination

A TUC report, 'Black and Excluded', reveals that black and Asian male workers earn on average £97 per week less than their white counterparts. The report highlights alarming differences in pay within black and Asian communities. On average:

- Pakistani and Bangladeshi men earn £150 per week less than white men.

- Caribbean men earn £115 and Africans £116 per week less than white men.

- Black and Asian women earn £7 per week more than white women – mainly because they are more likely to be in full-time jobs.

- Pakistani and Bangladeshi women earn £34 per week less than white women.

Average weekly earnings in Britain (£)

Origin	Men	Women
White	332	180
All Black	235	187
Caribbean	217	210
African	216	199
Indian	327	194
Pakistani/Bangladeshi	182	146

The TUC is asking for all employers to be legally required to promote good race relations in their organizations. This is a legal duty in the public sector at present – but not in the private and voluntary sectors. The TUC also wants a further change in the law so that trade unions and the Commission for Racial Equality can take collective cases on behalf of individuals or groups of members. The government should also encourage employers to regularly monitor pay data to ensure equality. Apart from direct racial discrimination, factors affecting pay include black and Asian workers being trapped in low-paid jobs and economic sectors such as textiles; language problems, despite high educational achievement; and being concentrated in deprived areas of the country with a dependence on public transport.

John Monks, then TUC general secretary, said:

> New laws in the public sector will make a difference – these must now be extended to end the unfairness in pay for black and Asian workers. These workers already suffer twice the levels of unemployment, lack of promotion opportunities and racial harassment. Unions are seeking to work in partnership with employers and the government to end this disadvantage.

Why do average earnings vary between racial groups?

Source: *HRM Guide UK* (http://www.hrmguide.co.uk), 12 April, 2002.

the organizations in which they work? IES research fellow and co-author, NiiDjan Tackey observes:

> While some studies have found real differences in performance, the weight of evidence suggests that many of the observed differences are due to bias on the part of those making performance judgements. In other words, some white managers assess their minority ethnic subordinates on criteria other than their ability alone.

There are two theories that attempt to explain why this difference in perception occurs:

1 Managers who assess employees' performance subconsciously look for evidence to confirm broader stereotypes – for example, those based on gender or race. When a particular group has negative attributes associated with it, all members of that group are seen in the same light. People who stand out as clear exceptions to the 'rule' are explained by luck or extraordinary effort, rather than genuine ability.

2 Within an organization, people are allocated to one of two kinds of groups: (a) those identified primarily by the physical characteristics of their members (such as race, ethnicity, gender or disability); and (b) those identified by the roles and functions of their members.

It is argued that managers have a tendency to assign people to groups based on a combination of these characteristics, treating them differently according to whether they are in an 'in-group' (i.e. share the same group membership), or an 'out-group'. In-group people get more favourable treatment; out-group people are managed in a more authoritarian, contractual style.

The ways in which individuals are treated form part of organizational culture. Self-limiting patterns are then set up as minority ethnic individuals hold themselves back because of previous lost opportunities, or become demotivated because they feel less valued or are being overlooked.

The report provides advice to organizations that are seeking to understand if they unwittingly discriminate against minority ethnic groups, and what they might do to address any identified problems. It recommends the kinds of information and analysis that are needed to establish and locate any problems. Penny Tamkin, IES principal research fellow, offers the following advice:

- Review your workforce thoroughly to identify any areas of concern.
- Is the issue in recruitment or in treatment of people once employed?
- Where are differences focused: e.g. shortlisting, promotion, assessment?
- Where might the causes lie: systems, processes, attitudes or behaviours?
- How might you challenge written and unwritten rules of how things are done?
- What needs to be changed if behaviour is the problem? How much is possible?
- Review the impact of all your actions and revisit the solutions.

Institutional racism

Braham, Rattansi and Skellington (1992, p.106) suggest that widening our definition of discrimination to include indirect or **'institutional' racism** gives a much better understanding of the barriers faced by ethnic minorities (see Key concept 17.1). Institutional racism is virtually unrecognized in commercial organizations but it is an extremely contentious issue in the public sector – for instance the police service, social work and housing. At one extreme, there are those obsessed with race issues, ignoring other forms of disadvantage. At the other, are those who consider that 'there is no such thing as institutional racism and those who say there is are totalitarian monsters, running amok, reducing nice white people to tears' (Alibhai-Brown, *The Independent,* 11 August 1993).

Braham, Rattansi and Skellington (1992) caution that it is important to acknowledge the wide range of practices involved – some much more obvious than others. Rejecting the proposition that all institutions are uniformly racist, they argue that 'the kind of procedures . . . that

Key concept 17.1 Institutionalized racism

Institutionalized racism is an indirect and largely invisible process. It is a term encompassing the often unintentional barriers that serve to disadvantage members of ethnic minority groups in all aspects of organizational structure, for example selection and promotion procedures. It can be compared with concepts such as cloning and the glass ceiling.

disadvantage black people *also* disadvantage other groups'. We noted in Chapter 14 that the process of cloning is focused on replicating the people in power rather than discriminating against any particular group.

The British civil service is a good illustration of the existence and strength of institutionalized disadvantage. A Cabinet Office report in 1995 concluded that it was a bastion of the white, male middle classes, making it difficult for ethnic minorities to progress into its upper reaches. The report concluded that the main barriers to career development were:

HRM in reality Diversity training doesn't work

A new study shows that diversity training programmes have failed to eliminate bias and increase the number of minorities in management, despite the fact that many corporations have spent increasing amounts of money on this area.

In a paper to be published in the *American Sociological Review*, Alexandra Kalev of the University of California, Berkeley, Frank Dobbin, professor of sociology in Harvard University's Faculty of Arts and Sciences, and Erin Kelly of the University of Minnesota, conclude that such efforts to mitigate managerial bias ultimately fail. In contrast, programmes that establish responsibility for diversity, such as equal opportunity staff positions or diversity task forces, have proved more effective.

Frank Dobbin said:

For the past 40 years companies have tried to increase diversity, spending millions of dollars a year on any number of programs without actually stopping to determine whether or not their efforts have been worth it. Certainly in the case of diversity training, the answer is no. The only truly effective way to increase the presence of minorities and women in managerial positions is through programs that create organizational responsibility. If no one is specifically charged with the task of increasing diversity, then the buck inevitably gets passed *ad infinitum*. To increase diversity, executives must treat it like any other business goal.

This study is described as the first to examine the efficacy of diversity programmes based on the actual change in minority representation in management positions. The authors examined reports submitted to the Equal Employment Opportunity Commission by private sector establishments and conducted a sample survey on the history of diversity programmes within the companies concerned.

These were categorized into three groups: organizational responsibility programmes such as task forces or staff positions; managerial bias programmes such as diversity training; and programmes that created networking or mentoring opportunities. The data showed that organizational responsibility programmes were the most effective. Diversity task forces yielded the greatest results, increasing the proportion of white women in management positions by 14 per cent, black women by 30 per cent, and black men by 10 per cent.

The study found that diversity training aimed at reducing managerial bias may actually increase it. Programmes in this group were followed by a 6 per cent decline in the proportion of black women in management. White women benefited modestly with a 6 per cent increase. Social networking improved representation of white women, but lowered that of black men. Mentoring programmes showed a strong positive effect for black women. Across the board, diversity programmes benefited white women the most, followed by black women, with black men benefiting the least.

Frank Dobbin commented: 'Although the likelihood of minorities holding management positions has increased, the raw percentages of minorities in management remain quite low.'

Why doesn't diversity training work?

Source: *HRM Guide USA* (http://www.hrmguide.com/), 14 September, 2006.

prejudice and/or ignorance among line managers; and a lack of confidence in themselves among ethnic minority staff. These barriers were derived from attitudinal or cultural stereotypes that limited expectations and opportunities on both sides.

The Parekh report

The Parekh report (report of the Commission on the Future of Multi-Ethnic Britain) published in 2000 had a significant impact on the future of race relations in Britain. Set up by the Runnymede Trust in 1998 the Commission consisted of 23 distinguished individuals chaired by Bikhu Parekh. The Runnymede Trust is an independent think-tank that aims to promote racial justice in Britain. The Commission was asked to:

- Analyse the present state of Britain as a multi-ethnic country.
- Suggest ways in which racial discrimination and disadvantage can be countered.
- Suggest how Britain can become 'a confident and vibrant multi-cultural society at ease with its rich diversity'.

Commission members came from a wide range of community backgrounds and professions and had extensive experience of academic or practical involvement with race issues. Two years of deliberation and discussion resulted in the consensus represented by this report.
According to Bikhu Parekh:

Given the fluidity of social life and the constant emergence of new ideas and insights, no report can claim to be the last word on its subject, and this one most certainly advances no such claim. However, as a carefully researched and thought-out document, hammered out in searching discussions conducted in a spirit of intellectual and moral responsibility, it represents, we hope, a major contribution to the national debate.

Recognizing the moral equality of worth of individuals from each of Britain's many communities, Parekh advocates the recognition of differences while stressing the need to combat racism. Racism is seen as 'a subtle and complex phenomenon' that:

May be based on colour and physical features or on culture, nationality and way of life; it may affirm equality of human worth but implicitly deny this by insisting on the superiority of a particular culture; it may admit equality up to a point but impose a glass ceiling higher up.

Method of working

The Commission visited many of Britain's regions, asked a wide range of relevant organizations for their views, conducted interviews and focus group discussions and read hundreds of written submissions. Activists and experts in race-related issues were invited to day-long seminars in which specific issues were debated in detail. Papers were commissioned from experts in particular areas for parts two and three of the report and these were commented on by other experts and debated in meetings of the full Commission.

Overview

The nations of Britain (England, Scotland and Wales in this instance) are viewed as being 'at a turning point in their history'. Two scenarios are presented:

1 Narrow, inward-looking countries unable to forge agreement between themselves or between the regions and communities from which they are composed.
2 Alternatively, they could become a 'community of citizens and communities' at the level of Britain as a whole and also within every region, city, town or neighbourhood.

If the latter is the preferred choice, it will be necessary to:

- rethink both 'the national story and national identity'
- understand the transitional nature of all identities

- achieve a balance between cohesion, difference and equality
- address and eliminate all kinds of racism
- reduce the inequalities in material benefits
- build a 'human rights culture'.

The report looks at a number of areas including: police and policing; education; cultural policy; health and welfare; employment; immigration and asylum policy; responsibilities of politicians; religious motivations and affiliations; and strategies for change at governmental, organizational and other levels.

Employment issues

The report makes the following specific recommendations on employment:

1 The government should 'place a statutory duty on all employers to create and implement equity employment plans' and do so as a matter of priority.

2 The award of 'Investors in People' status should be made conditional on an organization having formulated and implemented an employment equity plan. Also issues of equity should be ' explicitly and comprehensively covered in the Business Excellence Model's guidance materials'.

3 The importance of employment equity should be stressed in such matters as guidance on public procurement and investment subsidies (eg Regional Selective Assistance).

4 Organizations involved in delivering New Deal programmes should be asked to demonstrate a positive contribution to employment equity. Failure to do so should lead to responsibilities being transferred to others.

HRM in reality T&G claims first religious discrimination victory

The Transport and General Workers' Union has claimed its first victory in a case of religious discrimination under new legislation that came into effect in December 2003. According to the T&G press release:

> A Leeds tribunal has ruled in favour of T&G member Mohammed Sajwal Khan, who was sacked after he took extended leave to make a once-in-a-lifetime religious pilgrimage (hajj) to Mecca.

Mr Khan had worked for NIC Hygiene as a bus cleaner for more than seven years when he decided to make the pilgrimage, and applied to use all his annual leave allowance. When he did not get a response his union, the T&G, advised him to submit a written request. As Mr Khan still did not receive a response, his manager said he could assume the leave had been granted. However on his return to the UK from the six-week trip, Mr Khan was suspended without pay and later sacked.

The tribunal found in Mr Khan's favour and awarded him £10 000 in compensation, however he is unlikely to receive the full sum due to the company's financial problems. Mr Khan has said that he and the union fought on the principle rather than the money.

Phil Bown, T&G regional industrial organizer who represented Mr Khan said: 'Mr Khan was treated appallingly by his employer and this case should serve as a warning to other employers who ignore or flout new anti-discrimination laws. Islam requires those Muslims who can make the pilgrimage to Mecca to do so once in their lives and we warned the employers that they risked losing a discrimination case. The T&G has worked with a number of companies to review the issue of extended leave and has produced guidance on the subject.

'The T&G is proud to have backed Mr Khan all the way through the case and this success is a tribute to the benefits of an organized union.'

The T&G has produced a T&G negotiators' guide on Race Equality which includes guidance on religious discrimination and highlights the issue of extended leave.

Is there a straightforward distinction between racial and religious discrimination?

Source: *HRM Guide UK* (http://www.hrmguide.co.uk), 19 January, 2005.

5 Organizations responsible for provision of personal adviser services should be asked to make sure that people from black or Asian backgrounds are 'equitably involved in their programmes, both as managers and as advisers'.

6 The government should commission research on the contributions made by black and Asian-owned businesses to the UK Gross National Product or UK trade balances.

7 The Department of Trade and Industry and the Small Business Service (SBS) should sponsor research on black and Asian business start-ups and their survival patterns. Local targets and SBS national strategies should be based on the findings of this research.

8 Targets should be set at SBS national council and local council levels for increasing the take-up of support by Asian and black small businesses.

9 Undertakings of non-discrimination should be included in the Banking Code and the Mortgage Code.

10 Providers of financial services should be required to monitor and improve procedures, ensuring that their key employees are given race and diversity training.

11 Lending decisions by financial institutions should be monitored by ethnicity.

12 Targets should be set for British Trade International and Business Links partnerships to work more closely with black and Asian business sectors, and to highlight the 'possibility of international trade as a mechanism for encouraging growth'.

13 Business support agencies should be required to develop expertise in helping and advising independent retailers, and each agency involved in urban regeneration or business development should be made aware of the value of the independent retail sector.

Race and ethnicity legislation

Legislation against discrimination has an important bearing on human resource management in countries such as the USA, UK, Canada, New Zealand and South Africa but virtually none in others. The British Race Relations Act 1976 defined two forms of racial discrimination:

Direct discrimination. This occurs when someone is treated less favourably than another because of his or her colour, race, nationality (including citizenship), or ethnic or national origins.

Indirect discrimination. When a requirement or condition that applies equally to everyone has unequal and detrimental impact on a particular racial group, and cannot be justified irrespective of colour, race, nationality or ethnic or national origins.

Among the predominantly Anglo-Celtic countries, the UK was virtually alone in not having an affirmative action policy until recently. In Canada and New Zealand, for example, it is theoretically possible to enforce targets for the recruitment of particular groups. Within the UK, the Commission for Racial Equality (CRE) is able to:

- Give advice to people who feel they have been discriminated against, attempt to reach a settlement between parties such as employers and employees, and also provide legal representation in a court or industrial tribunal.

- Take action against discriminatory advertisements and in situations where people have been instructed or pressurized to discriminate on racial grounds.

- Investigate organizations that have been accused of racial discrimination. If it is shown that discrimination has occurred, the CRE is empowered to issue a non-discrimination notice that the organization is required to observe.

The CRE provides employers with guidance on their responsibilities under the Act and offers advice on equal opportunities and fair employment. This includes an employment code that has been approved by parliament. The code does not have the force of law but failure to follow its recommendations can be used in an industrial tribunal.

Neumark and Stock (2006) studied the effects of state sex and race discrimination laws passed prior to federal anti-discrimination legislation in the USA. State sex discrimination laws targeted pay. The authors found that state equal pay laws raised the relative cost of female labour and reduced relative employment of both black and white women. They found

---

HRM in reality 'Hidden discrimination' prevents visible minorities and aboriginal people gaining equal access to jobs, study finds

A study released by the Canadian Race Relations Foundation shows that visible minorities and aboriginal people miss out on promotions and the best jobs. Written by Jean Lock Kunz, Anne Milan and Sylvain Schetagne from the Canadian Council on Social Development (CCSD) the study, 'Unequal Access: A Canadian Profile of Racial Differences in Education, Employment and Income', was based on quantitative statistics and focus group discussions with visible minorities and aboriginal peoples in cities throughout Canada.

The authors found that:

- Even though visible minorities typically have higher levels of education than their white compatriots, they have lower levels of both employment and income.

- The greatest difficulty in finding suitable jobs is experienced by foreign-born visible minorities. Just half of those with university education have found high-skill jobs.

- University-educated visible minorities and aboriginal people are less likely to be in managerial and professional jobs than white Canadians. In fact, a half of visible minorities who do have managerial jobs are self-employed. This compares with a third of white Canadians.

- There is a greater representation of foreign-born visible minorities and aboriginal peoples within the bottom 20 per cent of income earners than would be expected from their numbers in the population. They are also under-represented in the top 20 per cent of income earners.

- Comparing people with the same level of education, white Canadians (both foreign-born and Canadian-born) are three times as likely as aboriginal peoples and about twice as likely as foreign-born visible minorities to be in the top 20 per cent of income earners. Even when born in Canada, visible minorities continue to be less likely than white Canadians to be in the top 20 per cent of income earners.

- Some 38 per cent of university-educated Canadian-born Whites were within the top 20 per cent of the income scale. This compares with just 29 per cent of Canadian-born visible minorities and 21 per cent of foreign-born visible minorities.

- On average, foreign-born visible minorities earn 78 cents for every dollar earned by foreign-born white Canadians.

'Our findings confirm that the higher you go in the workplace, the whiter it becomes,' says Dr Kunz, senior research associate at the CCSD. 'Racial discrimination is still present in the workplace, mostly in covert forms. Diversity is generally seen at the bottom and middle level of the labour force pyramid.'

While most focus group participants agreed that labour market outcomes are dependent on the right skill sets, education, and the economic conditions, they observed that racial discrimination existed in employment. Participants found that racism is a 'hidden thing' in the workplace. Examples of 'subtle discrimination' include being passed over for promotion, being assigned unpleasant tasks at work, being stereotyped, and being excluded from the 'inner circle' of their workplace.

'This report should be required reading for employers in both the public and private sectors,' says the Honourable Lincoln Alexander, chair of the Canadian Race Relations Foundation. 'The results demonstrate that we need to make greater efforts to eliminate systemic discrimination in Canada.'

Moy Tam, chief operating officer of the Foundation, says that although employment equity laws can play an important role in reducing employment and income disparities, a more sophisticated range of solutions is needed. 'Employment equity alone is not a panacea for eliminating racial discrimination in the workplace,' says Tam. 'We also need to eliminate the barriers faced by immigrants in accessing professions and trades and put more effort into raising public awareness about the existence of systemic discrimination in the workplace.'

Why is employment equity alone not a panacea for eliminating racial discrimination in the workplace?

Source: *HRM Guide Canada* (http://www.hrmguide.net/canada/), 12 December, 2000.

some evidence of positive effects of race discrimination laws on earnings of Blacks relative to Whites, although no evidence of effects on employment.

Disability

Disabled people are among the most disadvantaged because barriers to work are not only social and psychological but also physical. Quota systems for the employment of disabled people have largely been ineffective because of inadequate supervision by governments. Also, where social legislation for the disabled is weak, companies have found it comparatively easy to argue that they cannot provide suitable access or facilities to meet their needs.

Some individual countries outside the EU, including Canada and the USA, have instigated their own legislation. After decades of ineffectual quotas, the UK was the first country in the European Union to introduce a **Disability Discrimination Act** in 1995. This made it illegal for businesses to discriminate against disabled people as employees or customers. In 1995, there were 3.8 million people of working age in the UK alone with some form of **disability**. Less than 30 per cent of disabled adults in the UK are in full-time jobs. The disabled have also been targeted disproportionately for voluntary redundancies.

The Act requires all businesses employing more than 20 people to make 'reasonable adjustments' to shops, offices and factories where administrative or physical barriers have led to

---

HRM in reality Race relations legislation takes effect

The Race Relations (Amendment) Act 2000 came into force in April 2001. It strengthens but does not replace the Act of 1976. Among other effects, it fulfils the recommendation of the Stephen Lawrence inquiry report that advocated that the 'full force' of race relations legislation should apply to the police. Chief officers of police are now liable for acts of discrimination by officers under their direction or control. People who feel they have suffered racial discrimination by the police can take their case to court.

Members of the public can also take a variety of other race discrimination issues to court, including decisions to detain under the Mental Health Act and use of regulatory powers by local authorities in environmental health.

Public bodies now have to assess where and how racial equality can be relevant to the manner in which they carry out their work and deal with any problems they become aware of. More widely, the new Act requires public bodies to take positive steps towards racial equality in both their employment practices and the services they give to the public. The Commission for Racial Equality can enforce this requirement if public bodies fail in their responsibilities.

According to Gurbux Singh, then chairman of the CRE:

> Britain today moves into a new gear on racial equality. All public bodies have new responsibilities and members of the public have new rights. Areas of discrimination that

were immune from the Race Relations Act but which could have a devastating impact on people's lives have now been brought within its scope and individuals will be able to take cases to the courts.

The public sector has not lived up to the justified expectation that it should deliver racial equality. It now has no option but to do so.

> Parliament, united with the agreement of all parties on this historic step, has put racial equality at the heart of the responsibilities of public bodies. They will now need to look at what they do, who they serve and who they employ, and make sure that they provide equality of opportunity across all their activities. This will end the waste of talent that discrimination imposes, improve the quality of individual lives and lay the basis for a new and positive relationship between public authorities such as the police and all members of Britain's diverse communities.

The CRE has published a guidance document on the general duty that public bodies have to promote racial equality and a handbook detailing assistance the CRE can provide for members of the public in pursuit of complaints of racial discrimination.

What are the advantages and disadvantages of commissions focused on particular forms of discriminations (such as the CRE) compared with those encompassing all aspects of equality?

Source: *HRM Guide UK* (http://www.hrmguide.co.uk), 2 April, 2001.

discrimination against disabled people. The government estimated that, on average, this would cost less than £200 per employee.

Introduction of the Act did not take place without criticism. Many disability groups and businesses have argued that it is too vague and does not give clear guidelines. For example, whereas it makes direct discrimination against the disabled illegal, this does not apply to people with 'substantial impairments'. The legislation was initially policed by a weak but complex system of monitoring bodies including the National Disability Council and the National Advisory Council on the Employment of People with Disabilities. In 1999 the Disability Rights Commission Act paved the way for a new Disability Rights Commission to start functioning in 2000. The Commission has the following specific tasks:

Assistance. Assisting disabled people to secure their rights, and arranging for legal advice and help where appropriate.

Information and advice. Providing information and advice to disabled people and to employers and service providers about their rights and duties under the DDA.

Codes of practice. Preparing and reviewing statutory codes of practice, which provide practical guidance to employers and service providers on meeting their obligations under the DDA and on good practice.

Conciliation. Providing an independent conciliation service in the event of disputes between disabled people and service providers over access to goods and services, and monitoring the performance of the conciliation service.

HRM in reality — Unemployment rates for workers with disabilities remain unacceptably high

Canadians with disabilities have a right to work and use their skills and knowledge to earn a living, says Marie Clarke Walker, executive vice-president of the Canadian Labour Congress. She has urged the federal government to use the opportunity of its upcoming review of Canada's labour laws to make the changes necessary to ensure equal and productive participation of Canadians with disabilities in the workplace.

'The unemployment rates for workers with disabilities remain unacceptably high, which is why so many people with disabilities live in poverty. It isn't because there are no jobs available and certainly isn't because people with disabilities can't do the jobs. It's because too many workplaces remain inaccessible and too few see any reason to change,' she says.

Clarke Walker says that the review of Canada's labour code provides a chance to make the country's workplaces open and available to all workers with the ability to get the job done, adding the duty to accommodate must go beyond physical accessibility. She believes that workplace practices – ranging from hiring and promotion to evaluation and individual accommodation (often costing very little, in comparison to the value of the work itself) – need to be brought into the 21st century.

'It wasn't so long ago that women were denied work because employers didn't want to build a different washroom or have to deal with pregnancy or childcare. Discrimination on the basis of mental or physical disability is no less unconstitutional than discrimination on the basis of gender. There's no place for this in Canada any more,' says Clarke Walker.

Sharon Hambleton, Canadian Labour Congress vice-president representing workers with disabilities, says that Canada's unions already make a difference in people's lives. She argues that governments and employers should follow the unions' lead. The unions launched a campaign three years ago to raise awareness of the barriers blocking full participation as union members to persons with disabilities.

'Opportunities are opening up for workers with disabilities to participate at all levels of union activity, which means issues of accommodation and accessibility are finding their way to the bargaining table. Workplaces are being changed for the better, but unions cannot do this by themselves. Modernizing our labour code would certainly help,' says Hambleton.

Is accessibility the greatest barrier to employment for people with disabilities?

Source: *HRM Guide Canada* (http://www.hrmguide.net/canada/), 6 December, 2004.

HRM in reality   Disability Rights Commission handles 500 000 enquiries in 5 years

---

The Disability Rights Commission (DRC) Helpline has received more than half a million enquiries since it was established in 2000. Enquiries have surged since new disability legislation came into force in October 2004. This year alone, the Helpline has handled 124 368 enquiries with 70 per cent coming from disabled individuals, their representatives, relatives or friends.

Bert Massie, chairman of the Disability Rights Commission said:

> We are seeing real and positive changes in the way that disabled people are treated throughout Britain as new legislation strengthens disabled people's rights and government, employers and other organizations are beginning to take disability seriously. This last year saw the introduction of new duties that require every business, large or small to become more user-friendly to Britain's 10 million disabled people.

Employment rights for disabled people were significantly improved from 1 October 2004 when the Disability Discrimination Act (DDA) was extended to cover all employers with the exception of the armed forces. The DRC consider that two landmark employment cases – Archibald vs Fife Council and Miekle vs Nottingham County Council – taken by the DRC were successful in cementing disabled people's rights at work and providing convincing proof that the DDA has teeth.

Bert Massie said:

> The DRC will leave a strong legacy but Britain still has a long way to go before disabled people can take up their place as full and active citizens. In employment disabled people remain twice as likely to be out of work and more likely to earn less; in education they have fewer qualifications; transport remains a barrier for many; and the right to independent living is still a dream rather than a reality. Our Disability Debate is the first wide-ranging debate aimed at breaking down the remaining barriers to disabled people's full involvement and participation in society. Its findings will act as the blueprint for delivering to disabled people in the new Commission for Equalities and Human Rights.

The DRC annual report states that 10 986 enquiries of potential disability discrimination were received in the past year. Almost half of these (49%) were employment-related, highlighting the discrimination that disabled people continue to face in the workplace. A further 35 per cent of potential discrimination enquiries related to services, 12 per cent to education and 4 per cent to premises.

Does the surge of enquiries to the helpline indicate that the Disability Discrimination Act is effective?

Source: *HRM Guide UK* (http://www.hrmguide.co.uk), 24 August, 2005.

HRM in reality   Work a major source of self-esteem for people with disabilities

---

Welcoming federal government's intention to encourage people with disabilities to join the workforce, the Australian Psychological Society (APS) warned that long-term support is needed to ensure this change does not become a repeat of deinstitutionalization.

'Work offers a number of important benefits to those who do it, apart from the financial benefits,' said Dr Bob Montgomery, director of communications for the Australian Psychological Society.

'Work can be a major source of self-esteem, and it gives us a sense of worth as a valuable member of society. It fosters independence and provides adult company and structure to life. Many of these things can be difficult for a person with a disability to enjoy, so the principle of helping this group to find work is admirable.

'If the government is sincere in its intention of helping people with disabilities to find work then it will also have to work to overcome employers' prejudices and help to create positive, inclusive workplaces. The policy

of deinstitutionalization of those with mental illness removed support from people in institutions and left them to fend for themselves. The APS urges the government to provide support for people with disabilities so that they can take their place in the workforce,' said Dr Montgomery.

The APS acknowledged government funding for a further 41 700 rehabilitation places for people with disabilities and extra funding for employers of disabled people for workplace modifications and wage subsidies:

> This support must be adequate and long term, otherwise these changes will only create more stress for people with disabilities and their carers, people who already face the daily task of coping with disability.

What practical measures could be taken to encourage disabled people to find work?

Source: *HRM Guide Australia* (http://www.hrmguide.net/australia/), 17 May, 2005.

Investigation. Undertaking formal investigations into how disabled people are treated in a particular organization or sector, and into unlawful acts by particular organizations.

Research. Carrying out research to inform discussion and policymaking and to ascertain how well the law affecting the rights of disabled people is working.

Pope and Bambra (2005) investigated employment rates of people with a limiting long-term illness or disability and those without since implementation of the UK Disability Discrimination Act in 1996. They found that rates remained relatively stable from 1990 to 2001 for people defined as 'not disabled'. However, rates for people defined as 'disabled' have decreased since 1990, and were at their lowest following implementation of the employment aspects of the DDA. They conclude that legislation may not have been effective in closing the employment gap.

Ageism

Discrimination on the grounds of age is prevalent but often unrecognized. Some countries such as Canada, Australia, New Zealand, and the USA have legislated against **ageism** and a European Union Directive compelled all member states to introduce legislation against ageism by the year 2006. Prior to the introduction of age discrimination legislation, blatant ageism was common in job advertisements. For example, in the UK Heasman (1993, p.28) found that 30 per cent of advertisements carried discriminatory references against older workers. Half of these advertisements specified a maximum age limit of 35. Other advertisements used terminology such as 'youthful' and 'dynamic' which carry an implicit message that older workers were not welcome to apply. Newton (2006) found a clear association between age and the amount of training offered to and received by workers. Employees aged over 55 were less likely than other workers to participate in training, or to have it offered. Older employees were less likely than younger or mid-life workers to take up opportunities for training that were made available and were more likely only to have received on-the-job training.

A report on older workers by the Industrial Society (2000) (now the Work Foundation) argues that while internet start-ups have become synonymous with youth, the new economy actually depends on the over-50s. Falling birth rates are leading to reduced numbers of young people coming into the job market. This means that employers elsewhere are beginning to look more enthusiastically for older employees – especially as over-50s are much fitter and more flexible than ever before. Previously ignored, employers are starting to appreciate the unique skills possessed by older workers.

The report states that there is emerging evidence from the dot.com sector to suggest that firms are increasingly using over-50s in the transition from start-up to long-term success. There is a new demand for 'new elders' possessing health, wealth, wisdom and strategic know-how. These indispensable older workers come in several types:

Warhorses. Seasoned campaigners who have gone through economic downturns in the past and are not afraid of economic cycles.

Trusted guides. Consumers (for example, those looking for mortgage advice) prefer older employees with age and experience over the youthful and enthusiastic but inexperienced employees.

Networkers. Able to develop good business relationships, particularly with partner companies for example in Asia, where to quote one employer: 'veneration and respect for age is important, and counterparts find it more comfortable to build relationships with older business people rather than with young dot.com entrepreneurs'.

Strategists. According to Ronald Cohen, from a venture capitalist firm cited in the report that has invested around US$3 billion in the new economy: 'young entrepreneurs are coming in and asking for experienced people; increasingly they're realizing that they need this to get the business to the stock markets.'

Connectors. Older workers with team-building skills can provide a balance in the 'lean economy' of new organizations.

Statistics presented in the report show that:

- People over 50 are returning to work at a faster rate than the rest of the population as demand increases for their skills. For example, in the year preceding the study, the employment rate for women aged 50 and over increased at nearly three times the rate for the workforce as a whole. By the year 2020, one-in-four of the employed population will be aged 50 and over.
- In the USA older people make up a tenth of the workforce but have been responsible for 22 per cent of the country's job growth.
- The Australian economy created 360 000 full-time jobs between 1996 and 2000, with three-quarters going to employees aged 45 and over.
- Start-ups by entrepreneurs in their early 50s have double the likelihood of survival than those started by people in their early 20s.

On the downside, many employers have been slow to see the value of older workers – the proportion of people between 50 and 65 who are not working has doubled in the last 20 years. A third of those in this age group do not work.

The report argues for flexibility over the retirement age and the adaptation of the rules governing occupational pensions so that people can be partly retired and partly working. The government should also 'temper its enthusiasm for youth with a recognition of the values in age'. In conclusion, the report states that:

> We must look to business to set about sweeping away misconceptions about age. The business case for wisdom is compelling, the demographic pressure for change inescapable. Once employers have recognized the value in age, the work of reassessing the meaning of ageing will begin.

HRM in reality   Living longer, working longer in the USA

People in developed countries are living longer and many are working well past traditional retirement age. Some are even returning to work after 'retiring' and/or opting for 'portfolios' of paid and volunteer positions, according to a recent MetLife Mature Market Institute® study, 'Living Longer, Working Longer: The Changing Landscape of the Aging Workforce', conducted by David DeLong & Associates, Inc. and Zogby International.

'Today, older workers view retirement as a desirable state, not a particular date,' said Dr David DeLong, author of 'Lost Knowledge: Confronting the Threat of an Aging Workforce' and a research fellow at the MIT AgeLab. 'When we conducted the study, we found that mature workers are struggling to balance the conflicting pressures of income security, post-retirement-age employment and, often, age discrimination – perceived or real – as they look for a sense of security and meaning during their "retirement" years.'

This study is unusual in that it examines the actual work experiences of 2719 employees aged 55–70 whereas most other studies offer predictions of ageing baby boomers' retirement expectations. The MetLife study shows that the following percentages of respondents are working or looking for work:

- 78 per cent of respondents age 55–59
- 60 per cent of 60–65 year-olds, and
- 37 per cent of 66–70 year-olds.

Around 15 per cent of employees across all three age groups have accepted retirement benefits from previous employers, but have chosen to return to work (or are looking for work). These 'working retired,' represent:

- 11 per cent of 55–59 year-olds
- 16 per cent of 60–65 year-olds
- 19 per cent of 66–70 year-olds.

Motivations to work

There are significant differences between age groups when it comes to the motivation to work. Employees aged 55–59 cited economic incentives as the major motive, with 72 per cent of this group saying that 'need income to live on' was their primary reason for working. Sixty per cent of 60–65 year-olds also cited this as their main motivation, followed by a desire to 'stay active and engaged' (54 per cent) and 'do meaningful work' (43 per cent). However, 72 per cent of 66–70 year-olds cited the desire to 'stay active and engaged'

▶

as their primary reason to work, followed by 'the opportunity to do meaningful work' (47 per cent) and 'social interaction with colleagues' (42 per cent).

What does 'retirement' mean?
Respondents in the MetLife study cited the following definitions of retirement:

- freedom from the demands of work (26 per cent)
- more control over one's personal time (24 per cent)
- limited financial concerns (21 per cent)
- the ability to pursue other opportunities.

'As organizations seek to attract and retain older workers, they must be careful not to lump all "older workers" into the same category – it's important to differentiate the work experiences and motivations of these employees. While some may be working for financial reasons, others place a special premium on feeling engaged and doing work that means something,' says Sandra Timmermann, EdD, gerontologist and director of the MetLife Mature Market Institute. 'Recruiting and retaining older workers requires careful consideration of job design, work environment, and creating new and challenging opportunities.'

What motivates the 'working retired'?
Twenty per cent of working retireds age 60–65 said they 'wanted to try something new and different'. However, this option was cited by only 12 per cent of 55–59 year-olds and 7 per cent of 66–70 year-olds. Nineteen per cent of 66–70 year-olds cited 'becoming self-employed or starting a business' compared with 7 per cent of 60–65 year-olds and 8 per cent of 55–59 year-olds. Twenty-eight per cent of respondents aged 55–59 said they were 'self-employed or business owner'. This increased to 36 per cent of 60–65 year-olds and 42 per cent of 66–70 year-olds.

'Clearly, these findings suggest there are conditions in the job market and in older workers' desire for autonomy and flexibility that make self-employment an attractive option for those in their late sixties,' said Dr DeLong. 'As the oldest boomers turn 60 in 2006, their desire for autonomy and trying new things could portend a significant wave of departures in the next five years. Employers will need to identify ways to retain the valuable knowledge of these workers.'

Financial reality
Financial necessity underlies the need to work for many older employees. Eighteen per cent of baby boom workers aged 55–59 said that they expected to have no access to retirement benefits (eg pension, 401(k), SEP) and are likely to feel compelled to work beyond traditional retirement age. Fourteen per cent of those aged 60–65 and 10 per cent aged 66–70 expected to receive nothing but Social Security when they finally cease working.

'Retirement experts have been predicting for years the serious repercussions that will arise as baby boomers' lack of retirement assets collides with their increased longevity to create widespread economic hardship. The rational solution – to continue working full-time beyond traditional retirement age – is at odds with many boomers' interests, values and priorities for their retirement,' notes Dr Timmermann.

Some other survey findings

- *Age discrimination.* Older workers frequently cited 'age bias' as a reason for unsuccessful job searches, including:
  - 39 per cent of 55–59 year-olds
  - 42 per cent of 60–65 year-olds
  - 60 per cent of 66–70 year-olds.

- *Preference for part-time work.* Of those still in employment, 76 per cent of 55–59 year-olds worked more than 35 hours a week, compared with only 39 per cent of 66–70 year-olds.

- *Portfolio work.* Interviews were also conducted for the study, in which some older employees said their lives had taken on a 'portfolio quality' – mixing part-time paid work, volunteer work, and travel, together with more time for hobbies and family. In fact, 25 per cent of survey respondents across all age groups had more than one paid job with about 20 per cent of those working having two jobs, and another 4 per cent having three jobs.

What criteria determine whether or not older workers continue to work?

Source: *HRM Guide USA* (http://www.hrmguide.com/), 16 April, 2006.

There is a common view among employers that people over 45 are not worth recruiting, promoting or training. This is against a demographic trend where, in developed countries, a third of the workforce may be in this grouping. The proportion will continue to increase in the 21st century. Common stereotypes about older workers include being slow to learn, unwilling to accept and adapt to new technology, and lacking enthusiasm for training.

However, research shows that older workers:

- are more reliable and conscientious
- are more loyal and committed to stay with their organization
- have greater interpersonal skills
- work harder and more effectively
- show equal levels of productivity to younger staff.

In a survey of Hong Kong and UK workers, Chiu *et al.* (2001) found that stereotyping was linked to respondents' own age although supervisors also took account of perceived work effectiveness. Stereotypical beliefs significantly affected respondents' attitudes towards training, promotion and retention of older workers and their willingness to work with older workers.

HRM in reality Age discrimination regulations

March 9 2006 – Trade and Industry Secretary Alan Johnson has published the final measures to outlaw age discrimination in the workplace. The regulations are the final major stage of implementing the European Employment Directive adopted in November 2000. They will come into effect in October, subject to parliamentary approval, and cover Great Britain – separate legislation will cover Northern Ireland.

The Employment Equality (Age) Regulations 2006 do not affect the age at which people can claim a state pension but will:

- ban age discrimination in terms of recruitment, promotion and training
- ban unjustified retirement ages of below 65
- remove the current age limit for unfair dismissal and redundancy rights
- introduce a right for employees to request working beyond retirement age and a duty on employers to consider that request
- introduce a new requirement for employers to give at least six months notice to employees about their intended retirement date so that individuals can plan better for retirement, and be confident that 'retirement' is not being used as cover for unfair dismissal.

The regulations apply to individuals in work, seeking work or wanting access to training, to all employers, and to all providers of vocational training (including further and higher education institutions) and vocational guidance.

Alan Johnson said: 'Ageism will affect more people, at some stage in their lives, than any other form of discrimination. But until now the law of the land has allowed it to continue. With these new regulations it will become illegal for workers to miss out on recruitment, promotion or training because of prejudice about their age.

'As we are living longer and healthier lives, It is essential that the talents of older workers are not wasted. We must have the opportunity to carry on working where that is what we want. So we will scrap unjustified retirement ages below 65 and introduce a new right to request working beyond 65. In five years we will review all retirement ages to see whether the time is right to abolish them altogether. It's all about choice – not work till you drop but choose when you stop.

'Ageism hits younger people too, who can find themselves discriminated against in the job market. For business to thrive in an increasingly competitive market they must not ignore the skills of any worker, whatever their age. The regulations give younger workers new protection too.

'Considering talent and not age will help employers reap the benefits of an age-diverse workforce in reducing recruitment and training costs and retaining key skills and knowledge.'

The regulations include transitional provisions which will ensure that employers can effectively manage the process of retirement during the first six months of the regulations coming into force. The regulations allow for a retirement age at 65, but the government will review this in five years' time.

Should normal retirement at age 65 be scrapped?

Source: *HRM Guide UK* (http://www.hrmguide.net/australia/), 9 March, 2006.

Older workers are less effective at work that requires heavy physical activity or the continuous, rapid processing of information. Conversely, they are better than younger people at jobs requiring accuracy and reliability, and the use of knowledge.

Older workers often do not portray the kind of image that many younger managers subscribe to. To appear smart and modern, a youthful customer-facing workforce is preferred. Extensive downsizing in organizations throughout the Western world has concentrated on early retirements. The result is that many companies are entirely staffed by people under 50 (with the exception of senior managers).

Summary

This chapter focused on three areas of workplace discrimination: race, disability and age. We observed that all societies appear to favour certain groups more than others and that most developed societies have attempted to combat prejudice, favouritism and discrimination by introducing relevant laws. Each of the forms of discrimination that we have covered has complex causes that are not easily countered by legislation.

Further reading

Much of the available material on race discrimination at work is to be found in more general books on racism and ethnicity. *Stereotypes and Prejudice* edited by Charles Stangor (Psychology Press, 2000) is a collection of readings on stereotypes, prejudice and discrimination. *Theories of Race and Racism* edited by John Solomos and Les Back (Routledge, 1999) is another useful collection of readings. *Racism without Racists: Color-Blind Racism and the Persistence of Racial Inequality in the United States* by Eduardo Bonilla-Silva (2nd edn, Rowman & Littlefield Publishers, 2006) discusses an interesting aspect of racism. *Discrimination and Human Rights* by Sandra Fredman (Oxford University Press, 2001) focuses on the role of human rights law in combating race discrimination. For ageism issues see *Age Discrimination in the American Workplace: Old at a Young Age* by Raymond F. Gregory (Rutgers University Press, 2001); *Older People and Work* by Ali Taqi (International Labour Organisation, 2003); and *Age Discrimination* by Shaman Kapoor (Law Society, 2006). Texts on disability issues include *Blackstone's Guide to the Disability Discrimination Legislation* by Karon Monaghan (Blackstone Press, 2005) in the UK and *Disability, Society, and the Individual* by Julie Smart (Pro-Ed, 2005) with a US perspective.

Review questions

1 Outline the differences between racial prejudice and institutional racism. Do other groups experience institutional barriers?

2 Review the evidence for racial discrimination being a more subtle process than overt prejudice.

3 Why does racial discrimination affect some minority groups more than others?

4 How does workplace culture affect the perception of an individual's performance?

5 Why have some governments showed an apparent reluctance to introduce age discrimination legislation?

6 Discuss the attitudes of young people towards older workers. At what age should people cease paid employment?

7 Given the reducing proportion of younger people in most developed countries, what could be done to encourage the employment of older workers?

8 What are the limitations on the employment of the disabled? What can be done to improve the situation?

9 Are there any aspects of disability discrimination that are fundamentally different from any other form of discrimination in the employment market?

10 What are the arguments for and against the introduction of quotas for the employment of certain groups?

Case study for discussion and analysis

The Black Workers' Support Group

The borough of Kenwood is situated on the outskirts of a large city. It is predominantly populated by white, middle-class people and is considered reasonably affluent by comparison with its inner city neighbours. Just under 20 per cent of residents are over pensionable age, of whom 7 per cent are over 75 years. The vast majority continue to live in their own homes, an increasing proportion living alone. The ageing population has significant resource implications for the local authority.

The Social Services department is responsible for the home care service that comprises three full-time managers and a team of 40 part-time women workers. In addition to providing practical help and social support to their elderly clients, they are often the first people to be alerted to a deterioration in a person's situation. They are a crucial element in enabling people to stay in their own homes, saving the local authority enormous sums of money. However, their status does not reflect their true importance to the community and the section is regularly scrutinized for potential budget cuts.

The local authority has an equal opportunities policy which 'strives towards elimination of discrimination within the workplace'. The Social Services department had noted that the few black staff recruited were in low-paid or insecure posts and tended not to stay long. To try to prevent the policy remaining no more than a piece of paper, it was decided to set up an equal opportunities monitoring committee. This has met quarterly for the last three years and comprises staff representing all grades within Social Services, plus representatives from the main human resources department and two co-opted councillors. It is seen as undesirable to have such a group entirely made up of white representatives so the few black staff available are under constant pressure to volunteer for membership.

One exception to the tendency of black staff to stay no more than a few months is Mary, a middle-aged black woman who has worked for the local authority for 17 years, always as a home carer. She is a tolerant person who likes the flexibility of the work. She has regularly encountered clients whose questions and comments are inadvertently offensive and insensitive but has said little to her managers. However, having been allocated to a couple whose racism is overt and sustained, Mary made a complaint to her harassed line manager, who sympathized and reallocated a white worker to the couple concerned. Mary got on with her job without further comment. Over the next few weeks the manager thought about her own response, felt it had been inadequate, and referred the incident to the equal opportunities monitoring committee.

The reaction of group members was diverse:

- What do you expect? Old people are always unreasonable about everything.
- They may well be suffering from dementia; if so, they can't be held responsible.
- Living in this area, they're probably not used to black people and don't know how to react.
- Would Mary like any further action?
- We did all we could in practical terms – we can't withdraw the service from them.
- The line manager should have visited and confronted them.
- Oh dear, how awful.
- Has this sort of thing happened before, do we know?
- Black staff are particularly discriminated against and should receive appropriate support.

The final response came from one of two black members. He proposed a Black Workers' Support Group, open to anybody working for the local authority who defined themselves as black. The group would meet every two months within paid working time. The existence and purpose of the group would be made known to other colleagues who would be asked to demonstrate support by enabling participants to attend. Benefits to the local authority might accrue from being seen to be implementing its own equal opportunities policy and potentially retaining staff who would feel less isolated and marginalized.

The majority of group members had considerable reservations about this proposal although most did not say so openly. While most doubts centred on the impact on over-stretched departments and the possible adverse reaction of colleagues asked to cover extra duties, one of the councillors was more direct: 'Where exactly will this end? In no time at all we'll be expected to pay for part-time workers' support groups, Irish workers support groups, etc, etc.'

The proposal was referred to the senior managers' meeting for further consideration. There was more support within this forum, but it was felt that the Black Workers' Support Group should be chaired by a senior

▶

manager. Black staff pointed out that the group would not operate on such hierarchical terms and, in any event, all managers of the grade proposed were white. Managers' expectation that they would receive copies of the minutes of each meeting met with a similar response. While uneasy with their lack of control, senior managers felt it would be more controversial to refuse permission. The Black Workers' Support Group went ahead and the local authority began to receive enquiries about the scheme from outside the organization and praise for its initiative. With significant cuts proposed to the home help service in the next financial year, and with school-age children to care for, Mary has felt too busy to attend.

1 How effective is the equal opportunities policy in Kenwood?

2 Did Mary's supervisor make the right decision?

3 What is the value of the Black Workers' Support Group?

Part seven
Performance and compensation

Performance management is important because it plays a pivotal role in any organization's human resource framework. There are clear benefits from managing individual and team performance to achieve organizational objectives. Similarly, compensation in the form of pay, bonuses, stock options and other benefits can be linked to the achievement of particular goals. But such links do not necessarily produce expected results. This is a problematic and complex area in which commonsense solutions do not work.

The chapters in Part seven address a number of specific issues, including:

- How have legislative, technological and organizational changes affected the process of performance assessment?

- Why do organizations favour certain stereotypes of good performance?

- What decisions underpin the adoption of performance assessment strategies?

- What are the theoretical and practical problems associated with performance appraisal and counselling?

- How are the HR and payroll functions related?

- How can pay levels be evaluated fairly?

- Does performance-related pay produce the desired results?

- What roles do bonuses, stock options and other forms of non-monetary compensations play in reward management?

Chapter 18

Performance management

Learning objectives

The purpose of this chapter is to:

- Determine the criteria that distinguish 'good' from less acceptable performance.

- Evaluate the most common techniques for measuring performance.

- Investigate how performance management can be used to reinforce an organization's human resource strategies.

- Consider whether or not performance management really encourages desirable work behaviour.

Performance assessment

In Part five we looked at how the performance of potential recruits can be predicted from evidence collected during selection procedures. This was followed by an examination of the difficulties encountered in any attempt to ensure equal opportunities and to overcome the powerful socio-cultural mechanisms that promote the interests of privileged in-groups. In this chapter we extend our debate to the evaluation of current employee performance.

Performance assessment has a long history based on comparative judgements of human worth. In the early part of the 19th century, for example, Robert Owen used coloured wooden cubes, hung above workstations, to indicate the performance of individual employees at his New Lanark cotton mills in Scotland. Various merit ratings were represented by different coloured cubes, which were changed to indicate improvement or decline in employee performance (Heilbroner, 1953, cited in Murphy and Cleveland, 1995, p.3).

As with the employee selection techniques described in Chapter 15, modern performance assessment developed from sophisticated rating systems designed by work psychologists for military use during the two world wars. By the 1950s, such methods had been adopted by most large US business organizations, spreading worldwide thereafter. Initially, performance assessment was used to provide information for promotions, salary increases and discipline. More recently, performance measurement has had wider purposes:

- To identify and enhance desirable or effective work behaviour.
- Reinforcing this behaviour by linking rewards to measured performance.
- Developing desired competencies and building human capital within organizations.

Enthusiasts for performance assessment argue that it serves a key integrating role within an organization's human resource processes. First, it provides a checking mechanism for resourcing policies and procedures, evaluating the quality of recruits and hence the underlying decisionmaking process. Secondly, it monitors employee commitment and the relevance of their working behaviour to business objectives. Thirdly, it provides a rationale for an organization's pay policies. Taken at face value, these intentions seem entirely compatible with an integrated and strategic approach to human resource management. In reality, however, the definition and measurement of good performance is a controversial matter, involving fundamental issues of motivation, assessment and reward.

Key concept 18.1 Performance management

'A strategic and integrated approach to increasing the effectiveness of organizations by improving the performance of the people who work in them and by developing the capabilities of teams and individual contributors.' (Armstrong and Baron, 1998)

All aspects of **performance management** (see Key concept 18.1) arouse controversy, especially appraisals and **performance-related pay**. Critics point to weaknesses in their methodology and basic philosophy. Employees are often dissatisfied with the methods of performance management systems and managers are frequently reluctant to engage in the process because of its confrontational nature. At a deeper level, it can be argued that if true commitment exists, performance management is superfluous. In too many organizations it enforces the compliance of an unhappy workforce. However, Pettijohn *et al.* (2001) demonstrated that a positive attitude towards appraisal – from employees and managers – is possible if managers are provided with information designed to increase the benefits of engaging in the evaluation process and more thought is given to the appropriateness of measurement criteria.

Despite its problematic reputation, the use of performance assessment has been reinforced through the increasing prevalence of performance-related pay (PRP). As we will see in

Chapter 19 this is based frequently on an oversimplified view of work motivation. Employers, consultants and neo-liberal politicians remain wedded to PRP schemes despite considerable evidence against their effectiveness as motivators. Fletcher (2001) argues that performance assessment has widened both as a concept and as a set of practices, becoming more obviously a part of HRM's strategic integration of human resource activities and business policies. Consequently, research and discussion of the topic has moved beyond measurement issues and criticisms of the accuracy of performance ratings to encompass the social and motivational aspects of assessment. Fletcher divides current concerns into two thematic groups:

- The content of appraisal: contextual performance, goal orientation and self-awareness.
- The process of appraisal: appraiser–appraisee interaction, and multi-source feedback that have cross-cultural implications and are open to technological change.

We begin with a discussion of the environmental factors that have led to to the widespread use of performance assessment techniques. These include legislation, the demands of technological change, increasing flexibility and diversification, and changes in workforce composition. We proceed to look at the way in which organizations favour certain stereotypes of good performance. The next section evaluates decisionmaking underlying the adoption of performance assessment strategies. Finally we discuss the activities involved in assessment such as appraisal and counselling.

The environmental context

'The effects of context variables on appraisal processes and outcomes have been the object of speculation but have not been empirically examined in the detail that these effects warrant. We believe that context is the key to understanding appraisal in organizations' (Murphy and Cleveland, 1995, p.407).

The business environment exercises both a direct and an indirect influence on the conduct of performance assessment. Whereas legislation has specific consequences, particularly in the USA, most environmental factors have a diffuse and often unrealized effect on assessment and pay structures. It is likely that different individuals – and organizations – will respond in varying ways to these factors. Some will be highly sensitive to possible legal implications, practice elsewhere, and the state of the job market; others will be virtually immune to these influences. The main environmental factors identified as having a contextual influence on performance management are examined in the following sub-sections.

Business culture

At a national level, culture affects performance management through socio-political traditions and attitudes that determine whether assessment is acceptable, and to what degree. Cultural norms dictate 'acceptable' standards of performance and the management methods by which they are assured. For example, in a number of Asian societies, the employment relationship is a matter of honour, and obligations are regarded as morally, rather than contractually, binding between the two parties. In a situation where people are automatically expected to do the job as agreed, the role of performance assessment is questionable. Entrekin and Chung (2001) and Hempel (2001) conducted studies of Hong Kong Chinese and Western managers in Hong Kong. Both studies found considerable differences in attitudes towards appraisal and the attribution of good performance between Hong Kong Chinese managers and their counterparts from the UK or the USA. Entrekin and Chung (2001) concluded that Western managers and Chinese managers in Western-owned firms regarded performance assessment more highly than Hong Kong Chinese managers in Hong Kong-owned firms. And, given a choice, supervisory (top-down) appraisal was preferred by Chinese managers over other approaches such as subordinate or peer evaluation. However, Paik, Vance and Stage (2000) examined the characteristics of performance assessment systems in four South-East Asian countries – Indonesia,

Malaysia, the Philippines, and Thailand – and found significant differences in managerial practices and behaviours relevant to the design and conduct of performance appraisal. They suggest that the cultural context of performance assessment is complex and that the familiar clustering of cultures is too simplistic to explain the differences that exist.

Legislation

In free market economies, the employment relationship between workers and employing organizations is seen as a contractual matter. This relationship is expressed in formal or legalistic statements of obligation between the two, such as written employment contracts, job descriptions and performance objectives. Performance measurement has the purpose of ensuring that the employee fulfils the contract. Commitment in Western organizations is rarely a 'hearts and minds' phenomenon and this is exemplified in the policing nature of performance management. It is a modern version of scientific management in which the detail of work is supervised in a sometimes overbearing way. Within English-speaking countries, performance-related pay encapsulates a fusion of the work ethic (Key concept 18.2) and free market ideology: work is virtuous and virtue should be rewarded generously.

Key concept 18.2 The work ethic

The belief that work is virtuous in itself. Work can be defined as 'an activity directed to valued goals beyond enjoyment of the activity itself' (Warr, 1987). Hard work is to be admired and leisure is equated with laziness. Spare time is perceived as evil: 'the devil makes work for idle hands'. In some societies the work ethic became a fundamental religious principle, the Puritans and Calvinists holding it to be such a virtue that Max Weber termed it 'the Protestant work ethic'. Nineteenth-century factory owners used the principle to justify 11 and 12-hour days. The concept is sometimes extended to include the virtue of frugality as against waste. It justifies regarding the poor as sinful, since success and ambition are virtuous and wealth is a sign of God's favour.

Personnel evaluation in Latin America and Spain

A study by Bumeran, a HR technology company owned by Terra Lycos, focused on personnel evaluation in Latin American and Spanish companies. The study looked at the issue from both company and employee perspectives. The online survey received a total of 3500 responses from all countries combined. This represented 450 companies.

Results from the employee perspective included: 35 per cent of respondents stated that they never receive evaluations from their employers; 53 per cent of Brazilian respondents said they were never evaluated; and 49 per cent of Spanish respondents said that they received annual evaluations.

From the company side: 50 per cent of Brazilian companies stated that they never evaluate their employees; 50 per cent of the companies from Spain said that they conduct annual evaluations of their personnel; and in Brazil, Mexico and Spain a similar percentage of both employers and employees indicated that they know the internal procedures and evaluation methods, and when evaluations are done, they are clear and understandable.

Results varied considerably in Argentina, Chile and Venezuela but this may be due to the high level of unemployed respondents. Obviously the unemployed group does not receive any kind of evaluations.

Source: *HRM Guide.com* (http://www.hrmguide.com), 20 June, 2002.

Performance measurement has become a sensitive legal issue in the USA because of possible consequences for equal opportunities (Murphy and Cleveland, 1995, p.11). Since the 1970s, assessments have been regarded as tests and are subject to guidelines enforced by the Equal Employment Opportunities Commission. Employers taking personnel decisions on the basis of performance assessment have to be mindful of possible legal action on one of two grounds: (a) the validity or accuracy of assessment ratings as predictors of future performance and promotion potential; or (b) the validity or accuracy of ratings as measures of past behaviour. This legislation is specific to the USA, but all human resource managers have to be mindful of possible breaches of equal opportunities legislation in their own countries.

General economic conditions

Prevailing attitudes towards employees and, in turn, their response to performance assessment are considerably affected by issues such as unemployment. In line with our discussion in Chapter 6, growth and shrinkage in the job market is conventionally believed to be followed by changes in the behaviour of workers and employers. At times of high unemployment, workers are thought to be concerned about losing their jobs and hence are more conscientious and tolerant of strict management. When suitable employees are scarce, managers must be cautious – unflattering assessments can trigger an employee's move to another organization.

The relationship between the economy and assessment is circular and complex. Performance management is justified by organizational efficiency, and the overall efficiency of organizations in a country is crucial for its economic wellbeing. Income generated by effective, as opposed to inefficient, performance encourages economic wealth. Performance management has become the chosen Western instrument to drive out ineffective activity. It incorporates both stick and carrot: the first in terms of sanction, criticism or discipline; the second in the form of praise or cash.

Industry sector

Methods of performance management vary considerably between different industrial sectors, partly as a function of the nature of the work involved, tradition and fashion. Sales-dominated industries, such as financial services, tend to have clear individual or team objectives that can be translated readily into performance targets. Performance-related pay is common in this sector and commission-only contracts are not unusual. In other sectors, objectives are more diffuse and difficult to measure so that PRP is not easily justified.

Technological change

Computer networking is likely to have a dramatic effect on the nature of supervision, and hence performance assessment (Murphy and Cleveland, 1995, p.408). In Chapter 7 we observed that modern organizations can extend beyond their formal physical boundaries by means of networked systems. Work can be done at a distance by travelling executives, overseas affiliates or telecommuters working from home. This raises intriguing issues for performance management. For instance, how does a manager assess the performance of a homeworker when there is little or no personal contact between the two?

Technology has the power to provide extensive statistics such as the the time an individual spends logged on to a system, number of key strokes and volume of output; but does this information provide a meaningful measure of job performance? If the employee's task involves elements of creativity, accuracy and thoroughness, how can these be assessed? If managers become dependent on 'objective' measures of work, they may be forced to bring their personal assessments into line, 'even if they know that the workers who spend the most time at their desks may not be the best performers' (Murphy and Cleveland, *ibid.*, p.408). Being there, and even being busy, is not the same as being effective. Performance management hinges inevitably on results.

Advanced technology requires expert users. It is common for managers not to possess the same level of expertise as their subordinates. Such managers are not qualified to assess their performance and, moreover, subordinates are well aware of the fact. In these cases, supervisors have neither the competence nor the credibility necessary for effective performance management.

Flexibility and diversification

As we have already seen, in the 1980s and early 1990s, the traditional nature of the employment relationship in free market countries changed, moving the balance of power firmly in favour of employers. We noted that job descriptions have disappeared or, at least, have been diluted, so that employees can be asked to do virtually anything required by the organization. Conversely, performance criteria have been more tightly defined, typically expressed in the form of demanding objectives: forever-moving goalposts. Performance assessment has become the crucial means of monitoring this relationship.

Employee relations

Performance management is a means of enhancing managerial control, particularly through individual performance-related pay schemes. In Chapter 22 we will see that the individualization of pay diminishes or neutralizes the role of collective bargaining. The purpose and influence of trade unions is undermined, reducing both their effectiveness and attractiveness as an alternative focus for employee commitment. Brown and Heywood (2005) used data from the Australian Workplace Industrial Relations Survey to estimate the determinants of performance appraisal systems. As we might expect, complementary human resource management practices, such as formal training and incentive pay, are associated with an increased likelihood of performance appraisal, but union density is associated with a reduced likelihood of performance appraisal.

Workforce composition

Largely forgotten in the controversy over PRP, the other main function of performance assessment is the identification of individual strengths and weaknesses. As we will see in Chapter 20, the latter can be targeted for improvement through training and development. Strengths may indicate a potential star performer, worthy of a management career route and promotion. Assessment employed to determine development needs ultimately serves to increase a nation's human capital.

Less positively, demographics and a history of unequal opportunities affect the conduct of assessment, since they largely determine who assesses whom. For example, in countries such as the UK, it is likely that performance assessments are largely carried out by white male managers, whereas the people they assess are probably of mixed gender and ethnic origin. This is one of a series of organizational issues which we consider further in the next section.

The organization and effective performance

How do organizations decide which performance criteria should be measured? How do they differentiate between a good, average or indifferent employee? On the basis of empirical evidence, Armstrong and Baron (1998) highlight two central propositions used to justify performance assessment:

1 People, either as individuals or teams, put the greatest effort into performing well if they know and understand what is expected of them and have had an involvement in specifying those expectations.

2 Employees' ability to meet performance expectations is based on:
  - individual levels of capability
  - the degree of support provided by management
  - the processes, systems and resources made available to them by the organization.

Noblet *et al.* (2005) suggest that wide-ranging changes that have occurred in the public sector over recent years have placed increasing demands on employees. They found that the presence of support at work, the amount of control employees had over their job, perceptions of pay and the perception of a lack of human resources were found to predict employee outcome variables. They emphasize the impact that middle managers and HR managers can have in reducing detrimental effects caused by introduction of new public management. Public sector managers can use design of jobs and development of social support mechanisms, such as employee assistance programmes, to sustain the quality of working life for their employees.

In practice, according to Armstrong and Barron (1998), performance management has the following aims:

- Assisting in achieving sustainable improvements in an organization's overall performance.

- Serving as a lever for change in developing a more performance-oriented culture.

- Increasing employee motivation and commitment.

- Giving individual employees the means to develop competencies, improve job satisfaction and reach their full potential to their own benefit and that of the organization.

- Improving team spirit and performance.

- Offering a mechanism for regular dialogue and improved communication between individual employees and their managers.

- Providing an outlet for employees to express their aspirations and concerns.

What is the reality? DeNisi and Pritchard (2006) argue that almost a century of research on performance appraisal has resulted in very few specific recommendations about designing and implementing appraisal and performance management systems whose goal is performance improvement. They suggest that there has been too great a focus on measurement issues and not enough attention has been paid to the outcome of the performance management exercise.

In our discussion of organizational HRM in Part three we observed that organizations take many forms. No matter how an organization is structured, its output is the product of an interaction between different employees, departments, divisions and so on. Frequently, it is difficult to determine whose performance has been critical, or most significant, to the completion of a particular task. Current trends towards networking and team-based projects make individual performance even harder to gauge. Claus Offe once stated that identifying an individual's contribution to meeting an organization's goals is like listening to the sound of one hand clapping. Yet some people are singled out as key performers. On what basis? It is arguable that they may not be outstandingly good performers in an absolute sense but, simply, the people who conform most closely to the organization's norms.

Each organization defines effective performance in its own terms: being a 'good' manager in one organization is not the same as being good in another (Gunz, 1990). Company cultures and management styles vary and effective performance often translates as conformity to the house-style. According to Gunz, organizations differ greatly so that:

1 The contexts in which managers operate vary considerably.

2 This leads to different ideas about effective management so that some companies, for example, emphasize engineering quality, others financial performance or market dominance.

3 In each case people find it comparatively easy to recognize good management but may find it hard to say why. This leads to certain types of people being promoted. As these people are seen to succeed everyone else draws their own conclusions about what it takes to get ahead.

4 This closes the loop, reinforcing the dominant image of effectiveness.

As Gunz concludes:

. . . promotion patterns in a firm will be resistant to change because of the model's closed loop. The system is remaking itself in its own image, something organizational managers are usually aware of even if they do not always admit it openly.

This is consistent with evidence from a large number of studies reviewed by Campbell *et al.* (1970) who found that judgements of managerial effectiveness or *good*ness are actually measures of personal success. When people are asked to identify a good manager, they do so on the basis of an individual's promotion record, salary, global ranking of success and so on. Often the identification of promotable staff is devolved to individual managers. They tend to favour subordinates who are reliable – that is, they do things in the way the managers would – or who have skills the manager does not possess.

Most of all, as we have noted already in previous discussions of the cloning process, they favour employees who are similar to themselves. Bates (2002) investigated 'liking' and two types of rater–ratee similarity to predict ratings of managerial competencies. The study showed that technical proficiency, rater–ratee liking, demographic and attitudinal similarity about work were all significant predictors of proficiency ratings. Technical proficiency was the strongest predictor of ratings, followed by attitudinal similarity. A combination of liking, attitudinal and demographic similarity seemed to have a significant influence on ratings, over and above technical performance.

Morgan (1986, p.144) draws parallels between organizations and political systems in that both vary from autocracy to the democratic decisionmaking seen in some voluntary organizations. He attributes a major role in determining successful performance to political processes such as conflict, power-play and intrigue.

Following this line of logic, it is clear that any performance assessment system is vulnerable to the cloning process. Without thought, performance management can drive out diversity. It is also open to manipulation by employees who can identify the qualities necessary to 'get on' in a particular organization.

Behaviour can be fine-tuned to meet the organization's expectations. The latter can be termed '**impression management**' (see Key concept 18.3).

Key concept 18.3 Impression management

Image is created as part of one's self-identity. It is a product of individual and social elements, constantly shaped and reshaped to fit the expected behaviours of the current role. In other words, people act. An image can be learned or acquired through training – a deliberate process called impression management.

Impression management

Every organization has its cultural symbols and rites: standards of dress and personal appearance, time-keeping, participating in semi-social activities, etc. We choose to conform or not. We may pretend to be enthusiastic, agree with management opinions, or even take up golf for networking rather than sporting reasons. Such behaviour can be described as 'manipulating the impression others gain about us' (Hinton, 1993, p.23). The archetypal example is the selection or promotion interview where most of us make a special effort with appearance and manner to achieve a favourable impression. This is easy to sustain for 20–40 minutes, but not necessarily convincing. Long-term success requires a consistent and believable image sustained over a considerable period.

The most significant quality required for selection to top jobs is the ability to create a good impression (Miller and Hanson, 1991). The key feature of a well-honed image is that it gives the impression that applicants have qualities they do not possess: a false portrayal of abilities, disguising the lack of true competencies behind socially valued characteristics.

Control of one's public image depends on self-awareness. Degrees of self-awareness vary. Some people are invariably 'themselves' whereas others are acutely sensitive to the impression they convey and modify their behaviour constantly. For example, salespeople are much more likely to succeed if they can 'fine-tune' the impression made on customers. Snyder (1974) attributed this to 'self-monitoring'. Good salespeople are high self-monitors, responding quickly to customers' reactions. Low self-monitors make little effort to modify their behaviour, even in an employment interview. Day and Schleicher (2006) reviewed empirical and theoretical evidence on the importance of self-monitoring and concluded that high self-monitors are particularly good at 'getting along', for example in meeting others' social expectations, and 'getting ahead', instancing job performance and leadership emergence. Hinton (1993) points to skilled politicians who change their message depending on the audience, and are thereby perceived as being 'in-touch with the people'. They may make contradictory statements to different audiences and portray themselves as liberal or conservative as required.

Some images derive from the role models around us: successful people in the company or media stars. In the UK – particularly in England – the class structure, education system and institutions such as the civil service and the City serve to create and promote specific images. In Part five of this book we noted the condition described by Smith as 'organizational dry rot'. Picking people like ourselves to join our in-group is symptomatic of this condition at a national or institutional level. Too many organizations are dominated by identikit clones with similar images and ideas, whose concept of talent-spotting is finding more of the same.

Influencers

Miller and Hanson (1991) note that our ability to recognize real ability 'is contaminated by what we have come to call *the smile factor*' – closely related to the halo effect described in Chapter 15. The one-to-one interview is the most susceptible but at assessment centres 'the fish-bowl setting gives influencers/impressers space to perform'. A classic example is the excellent salesman who fails to perform well after promotion to sales manager. Time and time again the different requirements of the two jobs are ignored. Miller and Hanson studied four groups of widely different US executives and people deemed to have 'high potential' by their organizations. They describe their results as: '... to put it mildly, alarming. These organizations seeking leaders for major responsibilities were apparently confusing demonstrated leadership with some of the behavioural characteristics which some leaders exhibit.'

They found that all the people studied were particularly good at influencing others. They communicated well and were able to get other people to accept their ideas. They were generally sensitive and articulate, able to listen as well as talk. However, few had the motivation and the ability to manage or exercise leadership. They termed the majority 'influencers', people who wanted 'to have an impact on others but who did not want continuing or complete responsibility for the performance of others'. They were natural coachers and facilitators but reluctant to confront staff over missed deadlines or other forms of poor performance.

Admitting that influencers are likely to be bright and analytical, Miller and Hanson consider them to be too aware of the complexities inherent in any situation. They lack the confidence to take one direction as opposed to any other and, therefore, cannot be proactive or take risks. Further, because they are not aware in detail of the activities of their staff, they are unable to monitor changes effectively. Leaders are able to take tough decisions, can handle ambiguity and give direction. Miller and Hanson concluded that 'as many as eight out of ten people promoted into executive positions are influencers rather than leaders: most of the people running these organizations are not leaders; they only look as though they are.'

Mount, Ilies and Johnson (2006) explored the hypothesis that personality traits will differentially predict counterproductive work behaviours. They found that direct relationships between traits such as 'agreeableness' and interpersonal behaviour, and 'conscientiousness' and organizational behaviour at work are partly explained by an employee's level of job satisfaction.

Key concept 18.4   Charisma

Weber (1947) regarded charisma as one of three sources of authority (the other two being 'rational–legal' and 'traditional'), portraying it as a magical and hypnotic force based on direct personal contact. In modern life charisma is often fake – a product of carefully orchestrated mass communications.

There is nothing new in saying that 'real self' and 'outward image' are different constructions and that success is probably more dependent on the latter than the former. However, it is worth stressing that organizations do not benefit from this process. **Images** are distracting and misleading. Promotion on the basis of image does not produce employees capable of doing the job to an internationally competitive standard. Performance assessments tend to value image qualities: apparent self-confidence, the ability to talk charismatically, etc. Indeed, 'charisma' – the essential characteristic of the successful double-glazing salesman – is much admired and respected in a leader (see Key concept 18.4). According to Bryman (1992, p.22):

> In business and management periodicals the term is employed a great deal in the context of discussions of certain prominent figures. In such discussions, the term is often employed to describe someone who is flamboyant, who is a powerful speaker, and who can persuade others of the importance of his or her message. The non-charismatic leader, by contrast, is often depicted as a lacklustre, ineffectual individual.

Charismatics are perceived as having the power to transform organizations; as having a mission; able to inspire awe and obedience. They can also be lethal: a poison-pill for the ultimate wellbeing of any organization. Yet, like particularly dim lemmings, people managers – from personnel officers to boards of directors – will opt for the charismatic in preference to the non-charismatic.

It can be argued that at senior levels managers need to be figureheads and spokespersons for their organizations. For these roles, the required fluency, credibility and general communicating skills are those of a charismatic person. Indeed there may be a case for such a role to be entirely that of figurehead, not requiring any substantive abilities beyond those required for that role. A monarch or president, for example, can serve as a figurehead without executive power, allowing a prime minister to administer and direct. However, the tendency to overvalue charismatic skills has repeatedly led to foolish choices for 'number one' in large and small organizations. A further danger for performance assessment lies in the tendency to use cloning criteria at junior levels that are only relevant for people at the top of the organization.

Image can be construed as a decorative edifice built on the foundation of **substance**. An image which satisfies an audience does not necessarily preclude ability. Curiously, failure does not seem to dent common belief in the value of charisma. Similarly, the success of people with image and substance is commonly attributed to charisma – reinforcing belief in its necessity. Countering this process is difficult. It requires a recognition by senior managers that they may have succeeded by cultivating successful images rather than being the best available. Their organizations need assessment methods that are immune to this process: techniques to identify substance or necessary competencies, rather than the obscuring irrelevances of a polished image (Key concept 18.5).

Key concept 18.5 Substance versus image

'Substance' can be defined as that body of competencies, knowledge and experience required to fulfil a particular function. 'Image' is the *apparent* totality of such knowledge and abilities as outwardly presented by an individual or group.

Langtry and Langtry (1991) compare two extreme management types which are over-simplified but identifiable within most organizations. 'I' stands for image or 'me', 'O' equals objective or 'others':

- *I* managers maintain a high profile, speak well at meetings and are particularly effective at interviews. They are good networkers and make a point of getting to know the right people. They develop a good 'veneer', deliberately projecting a positive and confident image. Effective self-publicists, they make sure that everyone knows how hard they work and how successful they are. They are skilled careerists, and with sufficient emphasis and repetition they ensure that myth becomes reality.

- *O* managers do not indulge in such elaborate charades. Innovative and supportive, they are quietly hard-working, getting on with the job as efficiently as possible. They only come to the attention of senior management when they challenge simplistic ideas which the *I* manager enthusiastically adopts. The tendency is for their work to be ignored in favour of the *I* manager's claims and their criticism to be interpreted as negative. Their fatal mistake is to assume that recognition will follow a job well done. Usually, however, the *I* manager goes streaking past them up the career ladder.

Obviously, this delightful typology divides managers too sharply into two simple categories but it captures the essence of the problem.

Assessment and organizational change

The conduct of performance management is affected also by the success of the organization. Assessors and assessed may vary their standards depending on their perception of the organization's overall performance, career prospects and, consequently, their feelings of security and optimism. The emotional background to assessment can be directly affected by the prevailing culture of the organization. Attempts to develop a strong, cohesive culture encourage closer agreement between raters on the standards they expect.

As we observed in the early chapters of this book, de-layering and downsizing have had the effect of increasing the ratio of staff to managers throughout the Western business world. As a consequence, managers have a greater number of assessments to conduct on people they know less about. Widespread structural changes in large organizations also bring new combinations of people together with little knowledge of each other – but, perhaps, fewer long-standing prejudices.

Intriguingly, managers' routes to power appear to have a direct effect on the way they assess subordinates (Murphy and Cleveland, 1995, p.415):

> Attribution theory suggests that raters who have risen through the ranks will have a distorted perception of how well they performed in the job (they will readily recall good performance and will discount poor performance), which may lead to unrealistically high standards.

On the other hand, managers look after their own and assess their own staff generously. It is well known that performance ratings tend to the positive, with more people being judged as good performers than one would expect from a normal population. This is termed 'rater inflation'. It happens generally, but is particularly evident when assessors rate employees they have themselves previously promoted or selected. Rater inflation is common also when the process involves an element of self-assessment. Dunning, Heath and Suls (2004) argue that several psychological processes conspire to produce inaccurate self-assessments. People's self-views hold only a 'tenuous to modest' relationship with actual behaviour and performance.

The correlation between self-ratings of skill and actual performance in many domains is only 'moderate to meagre'. At times, other people's predictions prove more accurate.

Dunning *et al.* suggest that there is a tendency for individuals to overrate themselves:

> People say that they are 'above average' in skill (a conclusion that defies statistical possibility), overestimate the likelihood that they will engage in desirable behaviors and achieve favorable outcomes, furnish overly optimistic estimates of when they will complete future projects, and reach judgments with too much confidence.

In the workplace, flawed self-assessments occur at all levels. Employees tend to overestimate their skill, making it difficult to give meaningful feedback. CEOs can be overconfident in their judgements, particularly when developing new markets or projects. Dunning *et al.* suggest that possible solutions include training in routine correction for bias in self-assessments and requiring people to justify decisions in front of their peers. They conclude that self-assessment of skill, expertise and knowledge is intrinsically difficult, and should be approached with caution.

Most explanations of rater inflation are couched in terms of organizational politics:

Preserving morale. A positive performance assessment – whether or not it is deserved – is an act of praise. It offers an opportunity for a manager to say 'thank you' and 'well done', boosting morale and commitment. It engenders good working relationships between managers and subordinates. It maintains a cosy atmosphere.

Avoiding confrontation. Conversely, a critical assessment is likely to have the opposite effects.

Management image. If managers rate staff poorly there is an implication that they make bad selection decisions and run poor-quality departments. This can have unfortunate consequences on their own performance ratings.

From a psychological perspective, it can be argued that managers develop a bonding, or personal working relationship with their favoured staff that inevitably leads to biased assessments of their performance. The organization's human resource strategies should be focused, in part at least, on overcoming this problem. In the next section we consider the strategic choices that are open to us.

Performance strategies

'Organizations face a critical paradox. No other management tool is more critical to productivity than effective performance appraisals, yet they can actually impair employees' performance' (English, 1991, p.56).

As we observed at the beginning of this chapter, performance assessment or appraisal has been in use for a considerable period, particularly for management and sub-management grades in large corporations. The range of jobs covered by performance assessment is steadily increasing but there remain areas of employment where performance measurement does not yet feature and there is a great deal of conflict over its introduction.

From a strategic perspective, the process of assessment is an exercise in management power and control. It is a method by which an enterprise can evaluate its employees and feed back the organization's views to them. Furthermore, evaluation can be linked to 'stick and carrot' measures in the form of critical comment indicating the firm's disapproval, and incentives to reward and encourage 'good' performance in the form of enhanced pay and promotion prospects.

We saw in Part one of this book that 'behavioural consistency' is a major focus for models of HRM which hold that business competitiveness is improved by enhancing employee attitudes, behaviour and commitment. To do so, it is imperative that the organization has effective methods of communicating its standards or norms of behaviour. Assessors and assessed may have entirely different perceptions of both the reasons for performance appraisal and the criteria for judgement. Proponents argue that performance management should be: 'a process or set of processes for establishing shared understanding about what *is* to be achieved, and of managing and developing people in a way which increases the probability that it *will* be achieved in the short and longer term' (Armstrong, 1992, p.163).

Performance management strategies are particularly concerned with workforce motivation or, more accurately, management belief in the factors that lead to employee effort and commitment.

Motivation and performance

A considerable body of literature exists on the relationship between motivation and work performance. Theories range from the simplistic rational 'economic man' concepts underlying scientific management – implying that workers are only interested in money – to complex 'expectancy ' theories which explain motivation in terms of a calculus of conflicting needs. Morgan (1986, p.149) points to the diverse range of interests that people bring to the workplace:

- *Task interests*: focused on the job being performed so that, for example, someone in sales is committed to selling, enjoys dealing with customers and takes pride in being able to clinch a sale.
- *Career interests*: aspirations and visions of one's future – which may or may not include the current job.

These are complemented by extramural interests which incorporate leisure pursuits and domestic relationships. They cannot be divorced from work, since they compete for an individual's time and psychological or physical effort. Performance management strategies must take account of people as whole beings, with work forming just a part of their lives.

Gazioglu and Tansel (2006) analyzed job satisfaction with respect to a variety of personal and job characteristics using data from 28 240 British employees in the 1997 Workplace Employee Relations Survey. Four measures of job satisfaction were considered: influence over job; amount of pay; sense of achievement; and respect from supervisors. They found that those in education and health were less satisfied with their pay but more satisfied with their sense of achievement. Employees who received job training were more satisfied than those who had not. Women are more satisfied than men, and there is a U-shaped relationship between satisfaction and age. Unlike previous studies, they found that married individuals have lower job satisfaction levels than the unmarried.

Achievers and non-achievers

A number of researchers have attempted to identify the important factors leading to successful performance by comparing recognized high achievers with average performers. This method focuses on distinguishing key psychological differences between people in the two groups. However, as Furnham (1990, p.30) notes: 'it cannot be assumed that these factors *caused* the success, indeed they may have been a *consequence* of success.' Factors such as confidence and knowledge of a particular area may have been present at an early stage in a person's career or, alternatively, developed as that career became successful. For example, Charles Handy uses the term 'helicopter view' to describe the broad strategic grasp of business expected from senior managers. They are unlikely to have achieved this perspective without wide experience at lower levels.

Reviewing some of the vast selection of books on the rich and famous, Furnham finds consistent themes such as:

- *Perseverance*: tenacity, single-minded determination and concentration.
- *Ability*: especially in creating and exploiting opportunities.
- *Contacts*: knowing the right people.
- *Self-reliance*: striving for independence.

- *Thinking big*: but taking modest risks.
- *Time management*: making the best use of time and planning progress.

The weakness in these studies lies in their essentially retrospective and descriptive nature. They do not set out to test the hypothesis that individuals setting out on a career with a particular set of personality characteristics will be more successful than average. Nevertheless, Furnham (*ibid.*, p.31) finds that certain values that he describes as PWE (the Protestant work ethic) recur, providing: 'some evidence for the fact that specific PWE values – namely tenacity, perseverance, autonomy, independence, and hard work – are to be found in financially successful individuals and companies alike.'

HRM in reality Overachieving executives

Business executives are showing a dramatic boost in their achievement drives, according to a new study by Hay Group's McClelland Center for Research and Innovation. In fact, they are overachieving to the point of harming not only their own careers, but also the organizations they lead.

The study, 'Leadership Run Amok: The Destructive Potential of Overachievers' by Scott W. Spreier, Mary H. Fontaine and Ruth L. Malloy in the *Harvard Business Review* (June, 2006), shows that executives' achievement motives – defined as 'an innate drive to continually improve performance or meet or exceed a standard of excellence' – have risen sharply in the last 10 years. This has happened at a time of innovation and rapid business growth, but also in a period of business scandals and public loss of confidence in senior managers.

The authors of the study argue that this is not a coincidence. Overachievement often leads to ineffective and sometimes unethical leadership. They cite Enron's Jeff Skilling as an extreme but classic example of an organizational overachiever driven to continually improve results – without regard to the ways in which they were achieved. They also note that the desire to continually do better and to be the best remains a growing problem in other organizations.

According to Scott Spreier, one of the study's authors: 'Achievement has long been an important ingredient in the recipe for individual, organizational, even national success. And in today's uber-competitive environment, it is fast becoming the performance enhancer of choice as more organizations hire, promote, and reward achievement-driven leaders.'

Spreier observes that, like most stimulants, it's easy to overdose on achievement. 'Be careful what you ask for,' cautions Spreier. 'It can backfire big-time. We've seen highly ethical, well-meaning executives transformed into vicious louts who behave very badly. They focus on the end to the exclusion of the means and become coercive and demanding, destroying morale and motivation. The really hard cases cut corners, lie, even cheat, all in the name of outstanding results.'

The dark side of achievement

The authors say that the key to avoiding this is to become aware of how easily our achievement drive can become aroused, and then learning how to better manage it.

'The most effective executives acknowledge their strong need for achievement and its importance in driving organizational performance,' says co-author Mary Fontaine, who directs the McClelland Center. She argues that they also recognize their own drive can often diminish their impact as leaders. So they adopt styles of leadership that more effectively drive performance through others.

'The best leaders aren't out there blindly setting a blistering pace themselves and demanding the same from others,' Fontaine says. 'Instead they take a step back, create the vision, set the direction and standards, and then coach and engage others. In the process, they create energizing work climates in which people feel they have the flexibility, autonomy and clarity they need to continually perform at the top of their game.'

However, even savvy and self-aware executives find it hard to take such an approach in today's competitive climate. They may realize that channeling their achievement drive through others by collaborating and coaching is the best approach but they can lose control in the heat of battle and resort to coercion and control.

Balance is the key, says Ruth Malloy, also a co-author of the study. 'Good leaders know when to draw from their achievement drive and when to control it so that it doesn't get in the way of their effectiveness.'

What are the likely consequences of having overachieving managers assessing employee performance?

Source: *HRM Guide.USA* (http://www.hrmguide.com), 20 June, 2006.

Locus of control

Performance management is based on the underlying belief that managers can influence behaviour and, therefore, that rationality is the basis of human action. Unfortunately, the available psychological evidence suggests that this is not the case. Research shows that people vary significantly in their reactions to the persuasion or coercion of others, depending on their perception of the ability they have to control their own lives. At one extreme, some individuals will believe that what happens in their lives is the consequence of their own decisions, abilities and behaviour. These people are judged to have an 'expectancy of internal control'. There is evidence that individuals who have an expectancy of internal control ('internals') are better performers and tend to occupy most of the higher level jobs (Andrisani and Nestel, 1976). Internals take more notice of the feedback provided by performance mangement but do so according to their own agenda. If good performance produces appropriate rewards, they will deliver more of the same. If it does not, they are likely to devote their internal strengths to finding another job.

At the other extreme are individuals who attribute events to fate, to God, luck or to more powerful people. They consider life to be outside their personal remit and are permanent victims of chance or the wishes of others. They are said to have an 'expectancy of external control' (Furnham, 1990, p.42). People with an expectancy of external control ('externals') will be more compliant at the surface level, following instructions from supervisors and fitting social expectations. 'Following orders' they will fit neatly into bureaucratic structures but will demonstrate little initiative. Externals see little connection between their own performance and eventual success. When criticized for below-average work they will attribute their failure to causes outside themselves and the disapproval of the appraiser to personal dislike.

Are you in charge of life, or is life in charge of you? Most people have times when the former is true, and other times when the progress of life is firmly out of their hands. Some are permanently in one camp or the other. It is clear that being in charge of one's own life, career and circumstances leads to feelings of wellbeing and confidence and equates with successful and happy times. This is true 'empowerment'. However, it is doubtful whether performance management is entirely compatible with this state. In the next section we elaborate on how organizations can place performance assessment within a wider framework of human resource management.

Performance management systems

Among the 10-Cs checklist criteria for HRM discussed in Chapter 3 and elsewhere we placed consistency, coordination and control. These strategic aspects of performance assessment are exemplified in the integration of appraisal and performance-related pay processes within performance management systems. Armstrong (1992, p.162) sees the functions of such systems as:

- Reinforcement of the organization's values and norms.
- Integration of individual objectives with those of the organization.
- Allowing individuals to express their views on the job.
- Providing the means for managers and staff to share their expectations of performance.

A major British survey of public and private sector organizations showed that: 20 per cent claimed to have such a system; 65 per cent had some kind of performance management process; whereas 15 per cent stated that they had no policy (Bevan and Thompson, 1992). The survey showed no consistency in approach or understanding of the concept of performance management. Bevan and Thompson found two contradictory strategic themes for performance management:

Reward-driven integration. Emphasizing performance-related pay based on short-term targets with a consequent undervaluing of any other human resource activities.

Development-driven integration. Using appraisals to provide information for developing an organization's people geared for long-term objectives (in line with our discussion in the next section). When in existence, PRP is complementary to this.

They concluded that the first theme was dominant in the UK, serving to reinforce the prevalent cash-flow driven, short-termism of British managers.

Management by objectives

The origins of strategic performance management can be traced to the concept of management by objectives (Raia, 1974). This is a technique to establish individual performance objectives that are tangible, measurable and verifiable. Individual objectives are derived or cascaded from organizational goals. Top managers agree their own specific objectives compatible with the organization's goals but restricted to their own areas of responsibility. Subordinates do the same at each lower level, forming an interlocked and coherent hierarchy of performance targets. Hence management by objectives lies within the strategic way of thinking that forms a key element in HRM (see Table 18.1). Management by objectives (MBO) encompasses four main stages as detailed in the following sub-sections.

Goal-setting This is the heart of the MBO process. Goals are specific and desired results are to be achieved within an agreed period of time. They must represent real progress. They should be:

- *Challenging*: stretching the individual beyond comfortable performance.
- *Attainable*: realistic within cost and resource constraints.
- *Measurable*: specific, quantifiable and verifiable. Objectives are best set in numerical terms such as 'increased sales by x thousand', 'reduced staff by y per cent'.
- *Relevant*: directly related to the person's job and consistent with overall organizational objectives.

Alternatively, goals are sometimes set against the acronym SMART, linked to: Specific or stretching; Measurable; Agreed or Achievable; Realistic; Time-bounded.

Essential elements	Key stages
Goal-setting	**1** Establish long-range strategic objectives
	2 Formulate specific overall organizational goals
	3 Agree departmental objectives
	4 Set individual performance targets
Action planning	**5** Draw up action plans
Self-control	**6** Implement and take corrective action
Periodic reviews	**7** Review performance against objectives
	8 Appraise overall performance, reinforce appropriate behaviour and strengthen motivation through:
	management development
	reward
	career and HR planning

Table 18.1

The management by objectives process

Source: Adapted from Raia (1974).

Action planning Goals or performance targets are the 'ends' of the MBO process, action plans are the 'means'. They require individual employees to ask themselves what, who, when, where, and how an objective can be achieved.

Self-control MBO is a self-driven process with each person participating in setting their own goals and action plans. This results in greater commitment to their own objectives and an improved understanding of the process. They are expected to control their own behaviour in order to achieve performance targets. In return it is essential that they are given sufficient information and feedback to gauge their progress.

Periodic reviews It is not sufficient to review progress at the end of the MBO process. Individuals must be provided with an opportunity to check their performance at regular intervals so that obstacles can be identified. Reviews should take a positive, coaching approach rather than a critical approach.

MBO pre-dates human resource management and derives from a period when strategic thinking and the integration of organizational objectives were being emphasized by management writers. Since then, the development of HRM has preserved the focus on strategy and integration. This has been reinforced by the fashion for performance-related pay, fostered by the prevalent belief that reward should be firmly tied to results. Whereas MBO concentrated on individual management of one's own performance, the spread of PRP is underpinned by the use of assessment systems to manage the individual. MBO has gone out of fashion to a considerable extent although its basic techniques have been absorbed into newer approaches. It has been criticized for the paperwork involved, the administrative burden it creates and the realization that goals set for individuals are actually dependent on a team, a department or even a substantial part of the organization (Armstrong and Baron, 1998).

Prescriptions for performance management systems

Bevan and Thompson (1992) describe a model performance management system:

- The organization has a shared vision of its objectives or a mission statement that is communicated to its employees.
- There are individual performance management targets, related to unit and wider organizational objectives.
- There is a regular formal review of progress towards achieving the targets.
- There is a review process that identifies training, development and reward outcomes.
- The whole process is itself evaluated – feeding back through changes and improvements.

Rather similar to the MBO approach, the central features of such a system are an objective-setting process and a formal appraisal system. Typically, the performance management system is owned and implemented by line managers. The role of human resource specialists is to aid and advise line managers on the development of the system. In a slightly different approach, English (1991) argues for a 'rational' system of performance management which should have the following characteristics:

- A clear statement of what is to be achieved by the organization.
- Individual and group responsibilities support the organization's goals.
- All performance is measured and assessed in terms of those responsibilities and goals.
- All rewards are based on employee performance.
- Organizational structure, processes, resources, and authority systems are designed to optimize the performance of all employees.
- There is an ongoing effort to create and guide appropriate organizational goals and to seek newer, more appropriate goals.

Many organizations consider that they have a performance management system along these lines. Often they do not because one or more of the following conditions are missing:

- Agreement among all critical parties on what is to be performed.
- An effective way to measure desired performance.
- A reward system tied directly to performance.
- An environment conducive to successful performance.
- A communication programme to gain understanding, acceptance and commitment to the system.
- A performance-based organizational culture.

Key concept 18.6 Appraisals

Performance assessment is one of the many people management techniques that 'classify and order individuals hierarchically' (Townley, 1994, p.33). Appraisals rate individuals on quasi-objective criteria or standards deemed to be relevant to performance. Traditional appraisals rated individuals on a list of qualities – primarily work-related attitudes and personality traits. Modern assessment is often focused on competencies.

The assessment process

'Appraisal is seen as essentially an exercise in personal power. It elevates the role of the supervisor by emphasizing individualism and obscuring the social nature of work' (Storey, 1989, p.14).

In this section we consider performance assessment as an activity. Traditionally, performance assessment uses a rating system known as **appraisal** (Key concept 18.6). In most companies it is a matter of something being done to the employee rather than a process in which the employee plays a valued and important part. Assessments are generally an annual exercise, although some organizations may undertake them more frequently, perhaps every six months, especially with new entrants or recent promotees. For lower-grade employees, some companies are content with an assessment every two years.

Appraisal and conformity

Appraisals tend to be formalized. In many organizations they take the shape of pre-printed forms and typed instructions prepared for the appraising manager or supervisor. Dates of completion and return are fixed and the whole process monitored and administered by the personnel or HR department. Theoretically, appraisals can be completed in a number of ways:

- *Self-assessment.* Individuals assess themselves against rating criteria, or targeted objectives.
- *Peer assessment.* Fellow team members, departmental colleagues, or selected individuals with whom an employee has working interaction, provide assessments.
- *Line management.* The employee's immediate supervisor(s) provide the assessment. Alternatively, other line managers may be involved.
- *Upward appraisal.* Managers are appraised by their staff.
- *360-degree or multi-rater feedback.* Raters may include anyone with a direct knowledge of an individual's performance, including colleagues, direct reports, managers and internal customers.

The traditional performance appraisal was completed by the immediate supervisor or line manager with, usually, further comments or countersignature provided by the supervisor's own manager. This has been described as the 'father and grandfather' system – appropriate terms, given the essentially paternalistic nature of the process.

Appraisal normally requires rating on a series of categories. Management and lower-level appraisals are commonly conducted in different ways. Management assessments tend to feature results-oriented criteria, typically against objectives agreed at the beginning of the year. Non-managerial appraisals are more likely to be 'trait-ratings' – no matter what the questions may ask overtly, they are actually rating the employee on behavioural or personality criteria. In essence, they are no more than crude personality questionnaires. This remains the case if the criteria are couched in terms of job-related qualities. According to Townley (1994, p.43):

> Received wisdom is now that the appraiser judges the work not the person, with trait-rating being replaced by appraisals which identify and measure some aspect of performance. This, however,

HRM in reality Performance management systems fail to motivate

'Most organizations have lost sight of the fact that performance management systems should aim to enhance performance by motivating staff.' This is the conclusion of recent research by The Work Foundation in six case study organizations. The report suggests that 'HR professionals are too concerned with "tweaking" PM forms and software rather than focusing on what should result from the process – improved performance.'

The report, 'What Makes for Effective Performance Management', by Kathy Armstrong and Adrian Ward, identifies 'profound confusion' about what PM is for. It is treated as a reward mechanism, a learning and development experience, or an exercise in control. Motivation appears to be less of a priority. The report argues that while the task of managing performance was universally held to be a 'good thing' by the organizations concerned, they were unable to identify any concrete organizational benefits to justify this opinion.

Marianne Huggett, a consultant with The Work Foundation, said:

> An awful lot of organizations appear to be perpetually tweaking the process of performance management while ignoring the bigger picture of what it is supposed to be about in the first place – improving an organization's performance. In too many organizations, performance management is a matter of elegant bureaucracy – a tiresome form-filling exercise staff and managers could cheerfully live without. Meanwhile, there is a reluctance to ask hard questions about what really comes out of it. In some cases, organizations might be well advised not to worry so much about the forms and bureaucracy, and simply try and encourage ongoing dialogue and quality conversations between line managers and employees instead.

Armstrong and Ward say that 'process can take up the most time and resources, but add only a small amount of value. This can be particularly dangerous where there is little or no attention paid to improving management's skills in managing performance – where the system itself is hoped to solve all the performance management issues, rather than the managers.'

The report cautions against crude use of measurement in PM. The case study organizations use various techniques including 360-degree feedback to 'vast amounts' of quantitative data. Often, this data is synthesized into a single rating that is intended to represent an individual's net contribution and determine their remuneration. This frequently describes an individual's performance as 'satisfactory' or 'average' – which the authors suggest is 'not an overly motivating message'. Furthermore, some managers use performance-related pay mechanisms to compensate staff they regard as being poorly paid.

'The real danger of becoming embroiled in the technical debates about rating, ranking and quotas is that it can drain the capacity of performance management to be a powerful vehicle for feedback, motivation and, yes, performance improvement' the authors say.

The report identifies seven critical issues of process and people management capability that organizations should debate when setting the parameters of performance management:

Process: the means by which individual performance is directed, assessed and rewarded.

People management capability: the skills, attitudes, behaviours and knowledge that line managers need in order to raise performance.

Armstrong and Ward argue that successful PM depends on the interplay of all of these factors.

Why is a rating of 'satisfactory' unlikely to motivate an employee?

Source: *HRM Guide UK* (http://www.hrmguide.co.uk/), 10 June, 2006.

introduces the problem of defining and measuring performance, whether this should include, for example, skill, knowledge, potential and overall 'worth', etc, and the relative weight which should be attached to behaviour or results.

According to Philp (1990):

The disadvantages of this approach are numerous. For instance, the terms themselves are extremely ambiguous and it is unlikely that any group of managers would share exactly the same interpretation of any of them. Any appraisal using such words would be extremely subjective and, as a result, totally unfair. Also, because assessment in these terms deals with the individual rather than with the results they produce for the organization, it is very difficult to communicate with the individual involved. The person being appraised is likely to see any critical assessment of this type as a personal attack. The factors deal with the emotive areas closely concerned with personality, and the majority of people will tend to react defensively.

Nurse (2005) studied workers' perceptions of performance appraisal to determine whether they experienced fair outcomes, and whether it was seen to contribute towards career advancement. Non-union respondents expressed fewer unfavourable perceptions about the interaction than did their trade union counterparts. Workers who believed that performers were not treated fairly as a result of performance appraisal similarly agreed that their expectations regarding development and advancement were not being met. The study found moderate relationships between perceptions about treatment of performers and their expectations about career advancement, as expressed through opportunities for training and development, pay for performance and promotions.

HRM in reality Annual performance appraisals still the norm

A 2002 survey showed that two-thirds (66 per cent) of executives polled scheduled formal employee appraisals annually, with just 29 per cent conducting them more frequently. The survey was conducted by an independent research firm for OfficeTeam, a leading staffing service specializing in highly skilled administrative professionals.

A total of 150 executives were sampled from the USA's 1000 largest companies. Executives were asked, 'How often, if ever, do you conduct formal performance appraisals of your staff?' Responses were: quarterly 10 per cent; twice a year 19 per cent; once a year 66 per cent; as necessary 2 per cent; never/don't conduct formal appraisals 3 per cent.

'Annual performance appraisals are common among companies that tie formal reviews to yearly raises and bonuses,' said Liz Hughes, executive director of OfficeTeam. 'But it's important for managers to provide ongoing feedback to their staff to foster greater productivity and reduce the potential for miscommunication.'

'Don't wait until the formal review to recognize excellent work or raise concerns about weak performance,' advised Hughes. 'Instead, address these situations when they arise and use the review to discuss an employee's overall progress toward established goals.'

She offers these tips for conducting an effective meeting:

Stick to a schedule. Decide on a standard review schedule and adhere to it. Consider holding more frequent meetings for new or less experienced employees.

Consult the experts. Your legal and human resources departments may have guidelines and materials to help you plan the review. Ask if there are policies for discussing compensation, documenting the meetings and for following up.

Be fair and consistent. Meet with each staff member privately for the review, ideally in a place where you can focus without interruption. Evaluate all employees according to the same criteria.

Request participation. Ask the employee to prepare a list of accomplishments, obstacles and goals. Review this document prior to the meeting and use it as the basis for discussion.

Develop an action plan. Even the best employees can improve in some ways. Set objectives with each staff member and plan a course for progress checks prior to the next formal review.

Would it be better to have a shorter or longer assessment period?

Source: *HRM Guide USA* (http://www.hrmguide.net/usa/), 26 February, 2002.

Appraisals are generally disliked by employees and employers alike (Armstrong and Baron, 1998). Human resource practitioners are often made responsible for the paper-distribution and then for policing the process, coercing unwilling participants into completing the paperwork and holding one-to-one confrontations with appraisees.

Despite the fact that most assessors are completely unqualified to make judgements on anyone's personality, even in the most general of terms, the traditional appraisal form asks for a numerical rating on a scale of 1–4 or 1–7 (from excellent to appalling, see Figure 18.1). More detail is asked for as supplementary verbal comments, which could range from one word such as 'good' to a paragraph or more of detailed criticism and/or praise. Moreover, there is usually an overall rating that may be tied to promotability and a section to indicate areas for development or training. Finally, there are normally sections for comments by the person being appraised, possibly in the form of notes of a counselling interview and comments by the appraising manager's own supervisor.

The document is usually signed by all the contributors and forms part of the company's HR records. It can be used for promotion boards, training and management development programmes. What happens if an employee disagrees with the assessment? Despite its critical consequences for promotion prospects and, perhaps, remuneration, only one half of all organizations allow any form of appeal.

Upward feedback

The emphasis of performance management has been on top-down assessments open to a degree of power play by managers and senior executives. Over the last decade or so there has been a trend towards constructive, developmental approaches and moving away from a fixation with ratings. It has also become increasingly acceptable to take views of individual performance from a wide range of perspectives. Upward feedback is a process whereby managers receive comments and criticisms from their subordinates. This may be facilitated by an intermediary to organize the process and maintain a positive and non-acrimonious climate.

Upward feedback is not an appraisal as such and is not linked to standardized competencies. Instead (Forbes, 1996):

- It is intended to deliver candid, accurate feedback from a team to its manager.
- The basis lies in the team's perception of the actions of its manager.
- Upward feedback is not a system of judgement 'but only asks him or her for more, less, or the same of a broad series of behaviours'.
- Leadership, management, task and people factors are given equal weight.
- The facilitator gives confidential feedback, initially to the manager, then between the team and its manager.
- Team members and the manager – and that person's manager – can compare their views on what is required, bringing areas of misunderstanding or disagreement out into the open.

Because upward feedback is not formal appraisal, managers do not need to fear being judged. Conventionally, upward feedback begins with the most senior executive and cascades downwards, with each level in turn receiving feedback.

Based on Forbes (*ibid.*), the benefits of upward feedback can be summarized as follows:

1 Individual/team action plans can improve cooperation between team and manager.
2 Supervisors are encouraged to vary their management style and emphasis.
3 Ideas, problems and suggestions can be collected across a range of individuals or teams. In turn these can be used to set up new cross-functional teams or aid in the management of change.
4 Training requirements can be pinpointed and linked to specific outcomes for the team.
5 It facilitates empowerment and self-management.

Figure 18.1

Traditional appraisal
form – 1980s style

J. SMITH & CO. ANNUAL PERFORMANCE ASSESSMENT

This document should be completed by the responsible line manager and returned to the Human
Resource Department by _____

Name of appraisee:

Job title:

Department:

Name of manager completing assessment:

1 **KNOWLEDGE & EXPERTISE**   A   B   C   D   E   F

   Comments:

2 **ATTITUDE TO WORK**   A   B   C   D   E   F

   Comments:

Figure 18.1

Traditional appraisal
form – 1980s style
continued

3   **RESULTS**   A   B   C   D   E   F

Comments:

4   **INTERPERSONAL SKILLS**   A   B   C   D   E   F

Comments:

5   **WRITTEN AND VERBAL COMMUNICATION**

WRITTEN   A   B   C   D   E   F

Comments:

VERBAL   A   B   C   D   E   F

Comments:

6   **NUMERICAL AND DATA SKILLS** A   B   C   D   E   F

Comments:

7 OVERALL RATING   A B C D E F

Comments:

NOTES ON COUNSELLING INTERVIEW

Manager's signature _____

Date _____

APPRAISEE'S COMMENTS

Appraisee's signature _____

Date _____

SENIOR MANAGER'S COMMENTS

Senior manager's signature _____

Date _____

Figure 18.1

Traditional appraisal
form – 1980s style
continued

6 A benchmark is gradually developed taking the form of an organizational map and data on how employees, managers, and senior executives view requirements in 20 defined behavioural areas in up to 100 practices. An annual comparison can be made from this.

7 It opens up a more communicative culture where different forms of performance assessment can be introduced.

Upward feedback also has its disadvantages. Managers may receive negative comments from assertive and ambitious employees intent on undermining their confidence and authority. No one likes to be rated as a poor performer and some managers may be less firm or directive, even when appropriate, in order to avoid criticism. Similarly, managers may be less critical or demanding of their subordinates in order to reduce the probability of unfavourable feedback.

Waldman and Atwater (2001), in a study of upward feedback in a large telecommunications firm, found that managers who receive poor formal appraisal scores from their bosses are more likely to value the usefulness of upward feedback. Managers who receive lower subordinate ratings are more likely to ask for additional feedback. In general, subordinates are more likely than managers to believe that upward feedback scores should be incorporated into formal performance assessments. Waldman and Atwater also found that subordinate ratings were correlated with formal appraisal scores.

360-degree or multi-rater assessments

Multi-rater assessments have been used by large US corporations for some time and have gradually become more common in other countries. The evolution of business organizations into flatter, team-based structures has led to multiple reporting lines and wider spans of command for managers, so that assessments by single line managers are not as appropriate as they were in the past (Kettley, 1996). A multi-source rating system such as 360-degree performance profiling typically involves information collected from the people working with the person being appraised, managers, staff reporting to that individual and internal (or, exceptionally) external customers. The process follows a sequence such as the following:

1 A skill model or competence framework is devised that lists essential job skills and behaviours.

2 A performance management survey is defined on the basis of the skill model.

3 Individual employees are each asked to recommend 8–12 raters for their personal reviews. Immediate supervisors choose 6–10 of these to complete performance surveys, rating the employee on each skill area, typically on a scale of 1–10. Raters need to have direct knowledge of the employee's performance but supervisors need to ensure that they are not all friends of the appraisee.

4 The reports are collected together and a summary is given to the appraisee, highlighting both strengths and development needs.

This method of performance assessment has its advantages and disadvantages over more traditional methods. It is clear that the number of people involved, and the amount of form-filling required, can lead to a considerable expenditure of time and effort, even when online forms, data-scanning and report-producing software are used. The anonymity of the process may also allow malicious and undefended negative ratings to be given.

Morgan, Cannan and Cullinane (2005) examined the introduction of 360-degree feedback in the civil service as it underwent modernization. They found that at an organizational level it failed to develop the self-awareness anticipated. It was not aligned with other development plans or the organization's core competencies. At an individual level some participants believed that they achieved little from the process overall. The authors suggest this may be related to an expectation that the HRM system would be more proactive in planning development action on their behalf.

Limitations of performance management

Performance appraisal has become one of the most widely used management tools despite widespread criticism of its effectiveness. To add to the controversy, Strebler, Robinson and Bevan (2001) from the UK's Institute of Employment Studies (IES) argue from research on over 1000 British managers that many performance appraisal systems have a limited impact on overall business performance and fail both employees and organizations.

Many organizations try to use performance appraisal and review as a 'strategic lever', not just for the performance of individuals, but also the performance of the whole business. However, according to Strebler and her colleagues:

> This assumes that managers have the ability and motivation to make performance review work, by translating strategic goals into operational practice. Ideally, they should use the appraisal to help the employee see how their contribution adds value to the business as a whole. Too often, however, they are rushed discussions where performance ratings are handed out, where petty lapses in performances are picked upon, or where performance-related pay is awarded.

Additionally, Strebler *et al.* (*ibid.*) contend that performance review is rapidly becoming an 'over-burdened management tool'. Along with its appraisal and objective-setting aspects, line managers are expected to pinpoint staff training requirements, provide career counselling, identify future star performers and do something about poor performers. These are all important elements of people management but the attempt to do so much at the same time often leads to poor results from appraisal schemes.

Performance review systems are frequently rooted in the hierarchical organizations of the past, and often still drive pay or promotion decisions. Organizations are flatter today and there may be limited opportunities for upward progression. Rewards can also take forms other than pay increases. So, according to Strebler *et al.* (*ibid.*), new systems are needed that meet the requirements of individual organizations: textbook models might not be suitable for particular strategies or structures.

They advise a transformation of the performance review 'from a beast of burden into a thoroughbred', starting with business strategy, then being clear about the roles, skills and behaviours required for delivering that strategy. There are some simple rules:

- Clear aims and measurable criteria for success.
- Involving employees in design and implementation of the system.
- Keeping it simple to understand and operate.
- Making its effective use one of managers' core performance goals.
- Ensuring that employees are always able to see the link between their performance goals and those of the organization.
- Using it to keep roles clear and focus on performance improvement.
- Backing up the system with adequate training and development.
- Making any direct link with reward crystal clear, and providing proper safeguards to guarantee equity.
- Reviewing the system regularly and openly to make sure it's working.

Strebler *et al.* (*ibid.*) conclude that human resources functions that can deliver this will be making a real and visible strategic contribution to their organizations.

Counselling interviews

Having tested the manager's talents as untrained psychologist, the next part of the process expects the manager to be a qualified counsellor! This **counselling interview** takes the form of a face-to-face dialogue between (normally) the appraising manager and the appraisee, although it is sometimes done by the countersigning manager. The whole process is designed to focus the power of the organization on a direct and individual basis. However, it is also clear that the scope for conflict and its avoidance are considerable.

Many, perhaps most, managers are reluctant to engage in the appraisal process. First, because it is difficult to criticize someone's performance honestly, knowing that the appraisee will read the comments. Potentially, the whole exercise is confrontational and many counselling interviews have turned sour because of carelessly worded appraisals. Most people find criticism difficult to accept and registering a point with an employee without causing offence requires diplomatic skills.

The process is dependent on the personality and management style of the appraising manager. Some managers will be blunt and, perhaps, brutal in their approach. As a consequence, they may not produce any improvement in behaviour but, rather, sullen resentment and a reduction in quality of performance. Others will regard the whole exercise as something to be avoided. As we noted earlier, the result will be rater-inflation: an assessment that is over-generous or, at best, neutral in order to avoid conflict. The process also depends to a great extent on the quality of the appraising manager. If that individual is not particularly capable, the evaluation of the subordinate may well be inaccurate or misleading and may blight the person's career.

HRM in reality Performance and productivity boosted by regular reviews

Nearly 4 in 5 (79 per cent) of businesses who use performance assessment say that regular employee performance reviews benefit overall business performance, and almost as many (76 per cent) feel that they improve employee productivity, according to a survey released by the *New York Times* Job Market.

250 hiring managers and 200 jobseekers in the New York metropolitan area were interviewed on the telephone by Beta Research Corporation, on behalf of the *New York Times* Job Market.(Jobseekers are defined as those who are currently looking or plan to look for a new job in the next six months). Just over two-thirds (67 per cent) of hiring managers surveyed said their companies currently conduct performance reviews, with even more (74 per cent) saying they planned to do so next year.

Respondents from organizations that do not conduct performance reviews at present, or do not plan to in the coming year, cited the small size of their company (47 per cent) and limited resources (24 per cent) as the main reasons for their decision.

88 per cent of the managers felt regular performance reviews were very important with 75 per cent believing them to be very accurate in assessing employee performance. Intriguingly, 57 per cent felt that regular performance reviews had a significant effect on employee morale. Hiring managers gave the following reasons why they thought it very important to conduct performance reviews:

	%
Identify areas for employee improvement	82
Improve employee productivity	76
Recognize outstanding employee performance	73
Set employee expectations	70
Establish goals for bonuses and salary increases	58
Evaluate potential terminations	54

85 per cent of hiring managers thought that performance reviews were taken very seriously by their organization but jobseekers did not necessarily feel that managers were sufficiently aware of their employees' accomplishments. Whereas almost three-quarters (74 per cent) believed their companies to be very aware of employees' accomplishments, fewer than half (49 per cent) of jobseekers agreed. This mismatch of perceptions may explain why disputes arise. Many managers (59 per cent) and jobseekers (65 per cent) said that disputes over the outcome of performance reviews rarely or never occurred. But when they do, 31 per cent of hiring managers and 23 per cent of jobseekers highlighted different views over job performance as the most common reason.

Why is there a mismatch of perceptions between managers and staff?

Source: *HRM Guide USA* (http://www.hrmguide.net/usa/), 16 October, 2002.

It can be argued that there is an increasing tendency to focus on marginal performers in the light of harsh economic conditions. Companies consider that they are unable to carry inefficient employees and the assessment procedure offers a source of data that will support dismissals. In theory, performance appraisal provides documentary evidence of inefficiency that would be hard to refute. In practice, rater-inflation often undermines the process, providing generous appraisals for questionable performances.

Objectivity and subjectivity in assessment

As we have seen, some of the key issues of performance management revolve around questions of fairness, judgement and interpretation of both results and behaviour. Serious attempts have been made to address these areas. Performance assessment focuses on one or more of the following criteria:

Results. In line with MBO and similar objectives-based systems, employees are rated on their achievements, expressed as well-defined, personal or organizational targets. For example, a salesperson may be given the objective of US$x thousand worth of sales in the year. How this is achieved is not the subject of assessment. As we have already observed, objectives are easier to define for some jobs than others. This approach can be complicated by the use of a 'moving target'.

Processes. In this case the emphasis is not on measurable results but on *how* the outcomes are achieved. It can be argued that compliance with quality procedures or, alternatively, provision of a particular level of service are examples of process assessments. However, if these are measurable in some way, they can be translated into results – for example, proportion of defective items or number of complaints.

Behaviour. Weaker and less objective assessments – but probably the most common – focus on employee behaviour which is only tangentially connected with either achieved results or work processes. A favourite approach for managers incapable of seeing the 'wood from the trees', they allow ample opportunity to dwell on personal prejudices over appearance, dress and manner. Such assessments provide a direct feeder mechanism into culture-bound and organizationally unhealthy practices designed to increase conformity and eliminate diversity. A number of large organizations have countered this tendency by using behaviourally anchored scales.

Behaviourally anchored scales (BARS). These are relatively expensive techniques to maintain, requiring 'experts' to develop rating scales anchored to real-life behaviour through critical incidents. However, they force appraisers to make comparatively objective judgements, placing individual behaviour in the context of the organization as a whole, rather than on inadequate personality categorizations. They are less usable in situations where new technology or procedural changes require frequent updating of scales.

Behavioural observation scales (BOS). These are constructed in a similar way to BARS but assessors are required to list the frequency of occurrence of particular behaviours within a particular period, rather than make comparative judgements of better or worse performance.

Different behaviourally-oriented rating formats may enhance or inhibit the value of performance appraisal as a development tool. Tziner, Joanis and Murphy (2000) compared the effects of rating scale formats on a number of indices of the usefulness of performance appraisal for employee development. Using simple graphic scales, behaviourally anchored rating scales or behaviour observation scales, ratings were made of the job performance of 96 police officers. The BOS ratings produced both the highest ratee satisfaction with the performance appraisal process and the most favourable perceptions of performance goals. Additionally, experts judged the performance improvement goals for officers appraised with BOS to be the most observable and specific.

Competence ratings

In recent years the trend in performance management has been towards assessing people on 'dimensions' of suitable attributes or 'competencies'. These may be derived from job analyses and describe a limited number of core skills or behaviours necessary to do a certain job. In fact, such competencies aggregate to form a key strategic element of business competitiveness – the overall competencies of the firm. There is some ambiguity about the meaning of the term at the level of the individual – it is sometimes used as an equivalent for a psychological trait (perseverance) and, at other times, as a complex hybrid of learning and skill (ability to use computers).

Armstrong and Baron (1998) suggest that competencies should address the following points:

1 What are the 'elements' of the job – its main tasks or key areas?

2 What is an acceptable standard of performance for each element?

3 Which skills and what knowledge does a jobholder need to have in order to be fully capable in each of these job elements – and at what level?

4 How will employees or their managers know that they have achieved the required levels of competence?

Summary

HRM is associated with sophisticated and intensive performance assessment, typically involving performance-related pay. The assessment of performance can be beneficial to personal development. We considered performance management as an integrated system. Theoretical descriptions of such systems emphasize their value to the link between individual employee performance and the achievement of strategic goals. However, there are philosophical issues of what precisely represents 'good' performance, and further technical problems of measurement. We completed the chapter with a critique of appraisal methods and a discussion of recent attempts to objectify their use.

Further reading

Performance Management: Key Strategies and Practical Guidelines by Michael Armstrong (Kogan Page, 2006) is a wide-ranging text that conveys the full flavour of the subject. *Managing Performance* by Michael Armstrong and Angela Baron (CIPD, 2004) is another example. *The Manager's Guide to Performance Management* by Robert Bacal (McGraw-Hill Education, 2003) is particularly reader-friendly. Clive Fletcher's *Appraisal and Feedback: Making Performance Review Work* (CIPD, 2004) is written by a major researcher in the field of assessment. *Abolishing Performance Appraisals: Why They Backfire and What to Do Instead* by Tom Coens and Mary Jenkins (Berrett-Koehler Publishers, 2000) takes an original but positive approach to the process of assessment.

Review questions

1 Why is performance assessment important? What factors determine individual success in an organization?

2 Summarize the external factors that can affect the process of performance assessment within an organization. Do they help or hinder that process?

3 Do organizations prefer conformists? What are the implications of the personal relationship between manager and employee on performance assessment?

4 Should males and females be assessed differently?

5 Discuss the view that performance appraisals are unnecessary.

6 Explain the following terms: (a) behavioural consistency; and (b) competencies.

7 Compare and contrast Bevan and Thompson's textbook model of performance management with English's rational model.

8 Evaluate a significant business (or political) leader. How much of that person's success is due to charisma or impression management?

9 Discuss the ways in which externals and internals react to performance assessment. Would an objective-setting method such as MBO produce the same effects on performance for a person with an internal locus of control as it would for someone with an external locus of control ?

10 Is management by objectives discredited as a performance management technique?

11 How would you conduct a 360-degree performance assessment? Compare and contrast the processes of upward feedback and 360-degree profiling.

12 Define 'rater-inflation'. What are its causes and implications? Is it possible for appraisals to be objective?

Case studies for discussion and analysis

The consumer relations department/International Holidays

1 As general manager, the consumer relations department has been the source of considerable difficulties for you this year. The manager, Jean Davis, her assistant Lyndon Greaves, and the six staff are involved in a constant battle with the sales department. First, they say that the number of complaints has gone up substantially. Jean says that customers seem far more ready to find fault with deliveries than ever before. She blames the salesforce for errors in order-taking. She has become aggressive in the way she deals with sales and has accused you of ignoring the problem. Lyndon is more reasonable but says that his people are grossly overworked. They have developed a backlog in clearing customers' emails and phone calls and sick leave has increased.

Conversely, the sales department is working better than ever before. They have a new PRP system in place, based on targets for orders taken by each person. The field sales force have embraced PRP enthusiastically with orders 20 per cent up on last year. Most have received generous bonuses. The board are very pleased with this and have asked you to extend PRP to other departments, including consumer relations. However, Jean and Lyndon are very negative about the idea, demanding to know how they are likely to be assessed when they are behind on their targets.

What is your analysis of the situation and how would you deal with it?

2 International Holidays is a travel agency group. The company has 43 shop units, each employing between four and eight front-office staff. Each unit has a manager. The company has been suffering from low trading levels in recent years. The situation has not been helped by the trend towards internet booking which has reduced the number of people coming to the company's retail units and threatens the viability of several locations. The managing director has asked you to set up a performance management system to improve the motivation of the staff.

How would you do this? What difficulties would you expect in ensuring that the system achieves its objectives?

Chapter 19
Reward management

Learning objectives

The purpose of this chapter is to:

- Investigate the relationship between the human resource function and payroll administration.

- Outline the rationale behind different compensation packages.

- Evaluate the link between pay and performance.

Pay and compensation

HR and payroll administration

Technology and the pay unit

Pay evaluation

Motivation, pay and benefits

Pay and performance

Flavour of the (last) month?

Criticisms of PRP

Executive pay

Summary

Further reading

Review questions

Case study for discussion and analysis – Fairness

Pay and compensation

Pay is an important feature of human resource management – after all, it is the main reason why people work. It is a sensitive and controversial area that has been extensively debated at both practical and theoretical levels. In the USA the term 'compensation' is used to encompass everything received by an employed individual in return for work. For example, Milcovich, Newman and Milcovich (2001, p.6) state that: 'Employees may see compensation as a *return in exchange* between their employer and themselves, as an *entitlement* for being an employee of the company, or as a *reward* for a job well done' (original emphases).

The reward or compensation that people receive for their contribution to an organization includes monetary and non-monetary components. Remuneration does not simply compensate employees for their efforts – it also has an impact on the recruitment and retention of talented people.

The term '**reward management**' covers both the strategy and the practice of pay systems. Traditionally, human resource or personnel sections have been concerned with levels and schemes of payment whereas the process of paying employees – the payroll function – has been the responsibility of finance departments. There is a trend towards integrating the two, driven by computerized packages offering a range of facilities. These are described later in this chapter.

There are two basic types of pay schemes, although many organizations have systems that include elements of both:

Fixed levels of pay. Wages or salaries that do not vary from one period to the next except by defined pay increases, generally on an annual basis. There may be scales of payments determined by age, responsibility or seniority. Most 'white-collar' jobs were paid in this way until recently.

Reward linked to performance. The link may be daily, weekly, monthly or annualized. Payment for any one period varies from that for any other period, depending on quantity or quality of work. Sales functions are commonly paid on the basis of turnover; manual and production workers may be paid according to work completed or items produced. Catering staff typically rely on direct payment from satisfied customers in the form of service charges or tips (gratuities).

Both methods work smoothly, provided that scales are easy to understand and the methods of measuring completed work are overt, accurate and fair. However, there has been considerable dissatisfaction with the management of pay on both sides of the employment relationship. In recent years, attempts have been made to remedy the situation through new systems and a greater reliance on performance-related pay.

Key concept 19.1 Reward management

Reward or compensation management is an aspect of HRM that focuses pay and other benefits on the achievement of objectives. Typically, it incorporates other changes in pay administration and policy, including: decentralization of responsibility for setting pay levels; uniform appraisal schemes; flexible working practices; and performance-related pay.

Within HRM literature there is some ambiguity as to whether reward should play a supporting role, a view implicit in the Harvard model of HRM, or, conversely, that it should *drive* organizational performance – an opinion which finds greater favour among exponents of 'hard' HRM (Kessler, 1995, p.10). Milcovich *et al.* (2001, p.5) take a broad perspective, arguing that:

In addition to treating pay as an expense, a manager also uses it to influence employee behaviours and improve organization performance. The way people are paid affects the quality of their work;

their attitude towards customers; their willingness to be flexible or learn new skills or suggest innovations; and even their interest in unions or legal action against their employer. This potential to influence employees' behaviours, and subsequently the productivity and effectiveness of the organization, is another reason it is important to be clear about the meaning of compensation.

Wolf (1999, p.41) argues that compensation programmes have been structured to meet three primary design criteria. They must be:

1 *Internally equitable* and pay people in proportion to the relative value of the job.
2 *Externally competitive* and pay people in proportion to the market price of the job.
3 *Personally motivating* to employees.

Wolf adds a fourth objective, which is often kept from line managers: ease of administration for staff. Wolf comments on these objectives:

> Unfortunately, the first two are almost always at cross purposes with each other, forcing an organization to sacrifice one to achieve the other, and achievement of the third means a high degree of individualization, which complicates the fourth, administration.

Many countries have **minimum wage** rates in place which set the base rate for pay across the job market.

HR and payroll administration

Traditionally, payroll sections and the human resource sections that interface with them have suffered from too much administration. Every transaction triggered 'a paper-intensive, repetitive, and inconsistent process' (Hitzeman, 1997). Today, businesses want their pay functions to do more than just administration. They demand efficient payroll processes together with expertise and service. According to Hitzeman such changes in delivery and expectations are forcing pay-related departments to sharpen their focus on key issues.

HRM in reality Top ten excuses for not paying minimum wage

HM Revenue & Customs has published the top ten excuses used by employers to avoid paying the national minimum wage. These excuses were to its 16 minimum wage enforcement teams around the UK. The enforcement teams identified nearly £3.3 million in underpaid salaries across the UK between August 2005 and July 2006.

The top ten unusual or outlandish excuses for not paying the minimum wage were:

1 He doesn't deserve it – he's a total waste of space
2 But she only wanted £3 an hour
3 I didn't think the workers were worth NMW
4 I didn't think it applied to small employers
5 He's disabled
6 They can't cope on their own and it's more than they would get in their own country
7 She's on benefits – if you add those to her pay, it totals the NMW

8 He's over 65, so the national minimum wage doesn't apply
9 The workers can't speak English
10 I only took him on as a favour.

Commenting on the excuses, Paymaster General, Dawn Primarolo, said: 'By far the majority of employers are honest and scrupulous, so instances of non-payment are very much in the minority. But this list shows that there are still some rogue employers out there willing to flout the law, which is why our enforcement teams are hard at work across the UK to ensure that everyone is getting paid at least the national minimum wage.

'We are publishing this list of excuses today to remind employers and employees of their rights and responsibilities in relation to the national minimum wage.'

Do these excuses have any justification?

Source: *HRM Guide UK* (http://www.hrmguide.co.uk), 22 August, 2006.

Hitzeman argues that the pay function is becoming increasingly complex because:

- legal aspects have become more involved
- staff expect higher standards of service
- pay staffing levels have been kept steady or even reduced.

To provide the desired level of service to staff and other 'customers', pay departments need to reorganize both tasks and resources around two central themes: transactions and consulting.

Payroll sections typically deal with issues which go beyond simple pay calculations. They can include:

- health benefit schemes
- pension contributions
- savings
- company share option purchases
- sickness and other forms of paid time off
- expenses.

As a result, payroll staff are involved with the following transactions:

- dealing with routine queries
- filling in forms
- issuing forms for staff to complete
- explaining company policies and procedures.

Consequently, payroll departments handle a great deal of repetitive work and generate mountains of paper. At the same time they are inconsistent in the responses they provide – similar queries often receiving different answers, depending on the staff member involved. In part, this is a function of experience, but also a consequence of how busy they may be. Basically, traditional pay sections are too clerical in focus. The information they use and collect may be of doubtful quality.

The solution may be to split information away from administrative functions into specialist areas. This allows consolidation and standardization of transaction-handling, leading to a degree of efficiency not possible in a traditional, unspecialized department. In large organizations, such a function can become a centre of excellence, taking advantage of professional techniques and up-to-date information technology. This offers the possibility of: more efficient processes and better customer service; consistent handling of queries and situations; better information; and a recognized 'one-stop shop' for pay-related queries.

Technology and the pay unit

Concentration of clerical and transactional tasks into a single unit gives greater opportunity for cross-training. It also exposes staff to wider organizational issues, providing enhanced awareness of the purpose and effects of reward management. A centralized unit can benefit from new technology such as: interactive voice response (IVR) systems, routing basic enquiries and messages to voicemail boxes and recorded standard answers; corporate intranets which give internet-type access to staff within the organization, including message boards, data gathering and online access to company information.

According to Hitzeman (1997), the other important element of the pay function that deserves attention is the provision of an internal consultancy for staff. This is more than using expertise to provide advice and information. The transaction-handling function is operational, emphasizing cost-effectiveness, efficiency and accuracy. By contrast, consulting services are regarded as strategic and value-added, perhaps offering: benefit package design; the ability to handle unusual (exceptional) pay or taxation problems; and strategic remuneration programmes, aimed at recruiting and retaining talented staff.

To distinguish between transaction-handling and consulting, as many administrative tasks as possible can be removed from 'consultant' staff and transferred to the operations unit. Consultants are then able to concentrate on strategic issues. As a further spin-off from setting up data collecting and information presentation systems for the transaction-handling unit, consultants are provided with more accessible and accurate information. This allows situations to be analysed more quickly and easily because useful data is readily available.

As another step in this process, organizations may choose to outsource some of the more routine 'number-crunching' functions to specialist companies. Pension administration is a long-standing example. The most obvious justification for outsourcing is to cut costs by:

- benefiting from the economies of scale open to a specialist provider
- reducing the number of internal pay administrators
- minimizing capital investment in equipment
- reducing overhead costs such as accommodation, heating and lighting.

Separate operations, consulting and outsourced providers can be difficult to manage for a large organization. One solution is to create a Pay and Benefit Service Centre. Typically, this is contacted through the internal telephone system or an external freefone (toll-free) number. Some 80 per cent of calls are dealt with at the first point of contact. These are the most routine questions that can be answered through an interactive keypad system: pressing a combination of keys provides a recorded response to the most common queries. The other 20 per cent require human contact with a customer service representative (CSR). The CSR has access

HRM in reality Pension scheme websites

Awareness of pension scheme websites is considerably higher among employees than the self-employed, according to a report funded by the Economic and Social Research Council e-Society programme.

In a survey of 1337 individuals, Dr Tina Harrison and Kathryn Waite found that less than a quarter of self-employed knew that their pension scheme had a website, and only around half of these had actually used it. Findings show that pension scheme members who had used their website were benefiting from an increased understanding of pensions and, in some cases, an enhanced decisionmaking capacity.

Many large occupational pension schemes now provide a website. The authors found that about three-quarters of occupational scheme members surveyed were aware of their pension website and similarly high proportions had used it. Facilities and features range from purely informational sites, such as web-based scheme booklets, to fully functional integrated sites that allow scheme members to switch funds, change contribution levels and update personal details online. The most popular features are those that allow members to obtain projections of their benefits and to model 'what if' scenarios.

The survey found that the vast majority of pension website users reported increased access to pension information, and half of these said they are better informed as a result. Similar proportions experienced greater confidence when making pension enquiries and decisions as a result of using the website. More than half of website users said they are taking more interest in their pension as a result, and around a third said they have saved more towards their retirement.

Tina Harrison said:

The need for better communication and information provision via the web is important within the broader context of the general move from defined benefit/final salary (DB) to defined contribution (DC) pensions. Defined contribution pensions transfer the investment risk from the employer to the individual. This means there is a greater need for communication, education and ideally consumer involvement in the progress of an individual's pension pot. If the individual can become more engaged in the process, through using a pension website, they will have more heightened awareness of financial issues.

Why is it important to publicize company pension schemes?

Source: *HRM Guide UK* (http://www.hrmguide.co.uk), 2 September, 2006.

to information sources such as scripted answers, a corporate intranet, pay manual, etc. Just 5 per cent will be referred to the payroll experts who will deal with policy and exceptional circumstances.

Pay evaluation

What criteria should be used to determine levels of pay? Dickinson (2006) found evidence for widespread social norms about the most appropriate bases for pay differentials with 'responsibility', 'qualifications' and 'performance' being the most commonly cited by employees. However, large organizations have traditionally resorted to job evaluation to provide the justification for different levels of pay. According to the International Labour Organization, 'job evaluation is directed towards rating the job, not the person'. Job evaluation is particularly concerned with:

● tasks involved in fulfilling a job

● duties that have to be completed

● responsibilities attached.

It is not concerned with elements of job analysis required for the recruitment process such as qualifications, experience, proficiency, or the key considerations of performance management – job behaviour, proficiency and attendance.

The outcome of a traditional job evaluation process is a set of job classifications, perhaps expressed as a formal hierarchy of jobs. The next stage, job pricing, results in a pay scale. Therefore, job pricing determines the remuneration or compensation for each job.

Traditional job evaluation involves the comparison of jobs in a formal, systematic way to identify their relative value to an organization. It has an underlying premise: that some jobs are worth more than others. Job evaluation has its roots in the scientific management movement (Taylorism) of the early 20th century. The methodology has had a particularly strong influence in the USA, where it has focused on position-based job evaluation systems. These systems define the scope and value of jobs by using comparatively narrow job classification grades.

The end of the 20th century saw some radical changes in the nature of work. Increasingly, the concept of flexibility has displaced the notion that work should be composed of a rigid set of pre-defined tasks. The job description seems increasingly inappropriate for the way work is organized today since the content of many jobs varies from one day to the next. This makes job rating and pay evaluation more difficult. Traditional job evaluation is focused on unchanging job descriptions and requirements, encouraging staff to take a rigid attitude to their work. If performance assessment and pay are linked to the completion of specific tasks, the need for change and a flexible approach to customers is ignored. Modern organizations have turned to competency profiles instead.

Over the last few decades, pay evaluation systems have swung from having an individual focus to being job-based and, more recently, back again to a stress on the individual. Risher (1998, p.7, cited in Wolf, 1999, p.45) states that:

> . . . the new work paradigm, in which jobs are more flexible and duties change as required, undermines the traditional focus on jobs ...The newer concepts for managing base pay, pay banding, competency-based pay and skill-based pay shift the focus to the value of the individual. Value is now determined by what the individual can do, not on what he or she actually does from day to day. A new definition of equity, one that will need to be understood by employees, supports paying the most competent people higher salaries. As organizations move to team-pay environments, it will lead to differences in pay for people in similar jobs.

Market-driven criteria

New skills and occupations are characterized by a greater demand for the right people than the job market can supply. The natural response is to increase pay and benefits on offer to

HRM in reality The grass is greener . . .

A majority of workers believe they can get better pay elsewhere, according to a Watson Wyatt survey of nearly 13 000 employees in the USA. The Watson Wyatt WorkUSA® 2002 study shows that just 41 per cent of employees think they are paid as much as people in equivalent positions at other companies. And fewer than half (48 per cent) believe they are paid fairly in comparison to workers with similar jobs in their own organizations.

'Companies must take a close look at employees' perceptions of pay fairness both within and outside their own organizations, or risk losing people once the economy improves and labour market mobility is restored,' said Ilene Gochman, Watson Wyatt's national practice leader for organizational measurement and author of the 2002 study. 'In fact, other Watson Wyatt research has shown that pay dissatisfaction is a key reason why top performing employees leave their companies.'

Inadequate communication is pinpointed as a significant contributor to employees' dissatisfaction with their pay, according to the survey. Just 43 per cent of workers said their organizations were good at explaining how their pay is determined. This is 13 points down since 2000 and the worst figure for pay communication since 1994. And 20 per cent of employees claimed not to know what their total compensation packages are worth.

The survey's findings on employee benefits demonstrate the value of effective communication: over two-thirds (68 per cent) of employees felt that their organizations are good at providing information on their benefits. This strategy seems to be paying off as shown by a ten-point improvement over the 2000 results in the percentage of employees who believe their benefits packages compare well to packages offered by other companies (42 per cent in 2002).

'The high marks given to companies for benefits communication suggest that improvements in pay communications are possible. Companies clearly know how to communicate – they just need to better apply their communication strategies to their pay-related practices,' said Gochman.

Employees' reactions are mixed on specific benefits strategies. Most workers are satisfied with leave benefits (71 per cent), savings plans (67 per cent), healthcare plans (64 per cent) and pension/retirement plans (60 per cent). But it seems that the economic downturn has affected employee attitudes toward profit sharing and stock programs. Satisfaction with profit-sharing plans fell by 10 points to 45 per cent between 2000 and 2002. Satisfaction with stock programs declined by 7 points to 50 per cent over the same period.

Gochman said that the study results show that companies must do a better job linking employees' pay to their performance. 'Despite evidence that pay differentials between strong performers and weak performers boost firms' financial performance, only one-third (35 per cent) of employees told us there is a clear link between how well they do their jobs and the money that they earn.'

Corporate strategy shifts appear to have left many employees confused about the link between their jobs and company objectives. The study shows that fewer than half of employees (49 per cent) understand the steps their organizations are taking to reach new business goals – a drop of 20 per cent since 2000. The study also found that only 35 per cent see clear links between the quality of their job performance and the money they earn.

'Confusion about corporate goals and uncertainty about the link between pay and performance will complicate economic recovery for many companies,' said Ilene Gochman. 'This is extremely unfortunate because we know that there is tremendous positive impact to the bottom line when employees see strong connections between company goals and their jobs. Many employees aren't seeing that connection.'

The study also reveals that three-year total returns to shareholders (TRS) are three times higher in companies where workers understand corporate objectives and the ways in which their jobs contribute to achieving them. 'Companies cannot develop effective teams and working relationships unless everyone involved clearly understands the connections between their jobs and objectives,' Gochman added. 'Workers and their companies excel when they know why their jobs matter and they understand what's in it for them.'

'In every case, we found that employee attitudes make a difference when it comes to business performance,' Gochman said. 'For example, companies that instil trust, manage business changes effectively and communicate openly with employees have much higher shareholder return rates than companies that don't.'

WorkUSA® is one of the largest and most current statistically representative surveys on the attitudes of US workers. The 2002 survey includes responses from 12 750 workers at all job levels and in all major industries.

Why do relatively few employees perceive a link between pay and performance?

Source: *HRM Guide USA* (http://www.hrmguide.net/usa/), 18 October, 2002.

these people. However, this has consequences for other staff in the organization and also for any job evaluation system. Scarcity of skills distorts evaluation systems and raises concerns about fairness. Short-term solutions produce further problems in the future when appropriately skilled staff become plentiful. This situation is common in information technology where, at first, only a few individuals are able to use new computer programmes and packages. Within a matter of months large numbers of trained people become available. A year or two later the packages may be replaced by a new product and the once-valued skills are redundant.

Broadbanding and skill-based pay

Broadbanding has been implemented in a number of different ways, but the basic principle is the same: large numbers of individually rated jobs or job types are clustered into a few, much wider job classifications or 'bands'. Although broadbanding was trumpeted as a panacea in the 1990s, Wolf (1999, p.45) criticizes the exaggerated claims for its effectiveness, stating that these are made on questionable data. It is clear from a number of surveys that managers are not implementing broadbanding thoroughly – for example, bands often are not broad at all. Many organizations are not measuring the cost or effectiveness of broadbanding in comparison with more traditional methods, and improvements in career management (cited as one of the main benefits by proponents) are not being achieved.

Wolf (*ibid.*, p.48) is equally dismissive of skill or competence-based pay systems:

> Whether one relies on old-fashioned job evaluation and traditional job-pay structures or moves to competencies and broad bands, employers still pay for what you know and what you do. No matter how you get there, these are the key compensable elements! Attempts to dress this up in modern garb abound, but the underlying premise remains as an eternal verity.

Kessler (2001, p.221) also concludes that competence (and team) based pay are superficially attractive, but they are difficult to put into practice as competencies are difficult to identify and measure, as are the standards for judging team performance. Kessler considers that:

> It is difficult to avoid the conclusion that while use of pay to encourage the development of employee competencies and a team-based work environment are readily identifiable as business priorities, driving the formulation of new pay strategies, there is precious little evidence to suggest that such priorities are being translated into practice.

Wolf (1999, p.47) concludes that:

> This brave new world of compensation raises many questions. If there are 'no levels, scales or ranges,' what role does 'market competitive pricing' play? Why is it even a factor? Is it subordinate to 'career development' or 'employees' contribution' or are they subordinate to it? Is 'career development' more or less important than 'employees' contribution'?

Can we be confident that pay evaluations are always objective? Mobius and Rosenblat (2006) conducted an experimental study where participants acting as 'employers' determined wages of other participants ('workers') performing a maze-solving task. The skill required had nothing to do with physical attractiveness but physically attractive 'workers' seemed to get a sizeable premium. Three possible explanations were suggested:

- physically attractive workers are more confident and higher confidence increases wages
- for a given level of confidence, physically attractive workers are wrongly considered more able by employers
- controlling for worker confidence, physically attractive workers have oral skills (such as communication and social skills) that raise their wages when they interact with employers.

Motivation, pay and benefits

How important is pay as a motivator? Rynes, Gerhart and Minette (2004, p.382) observe that 'practitioner journals present claims about pay importance that are inconsistent with research about the actual motivational effects of pay. In general, there appears to be a consistent (but incorrect) message to practitioners that pay is not a very effective motivator – a message that, if believed, could cause practitioners to seriously underestimate the motivational potential of a well-designed compensation system.' They argue that most surveys of motivating factors are misleading because employees tend to give 'socially desirable' responses that place pay well down in the list of motivators. They consider that pay is the most important motivator and cite meta-analytic evidence.

HRM in reality Young workers look for flexibility

Research for BT Business conducted earlier this year indicates that more than a third of British workers (37 per cent of men and 34 per cent of women) would be prepared to forgo a pay increase for more flexible working options.

Interest shows regional variation, with 37 per cent of London workers and 23 per cent of those in the north-west of England, Yorkshire and Humberside willing to consider it. The survey also found that 43 per cent of 18 to 29-year-olds are interested, compared with 31 per cent of the over-50s.

The research, conducted by YouGov, indicates that flexible working policies are valued across the age range, but with an above average response from young people, more than three-quarters of whom agreed that it is an important benefit. Almost two-thirds of those aged 18 to 29 identified a better work–life balance as the main advantage, followed by less stress and fewer travel problems. This trend is supported by a DTI survey that found 70 per cent of graduate jobseekers are actively looking for the chance to work flexibly, and almost half consider it the most important benefit an employer could offer.

Beatriz Butsana-Sita, head of marketing, BT Business, said:

> For young people today the idea of being in the same office, at the same time, with the same people every day, is just completely out of date. Wireless and mobile technologies and the ability to work effectively away from the office come as second nature to today's generation of graduates. It's increasingly something that they expect from an employer.

Directors of smaller businesses also recognize that flexible working policies can benefit their organization with 65 per cent citing staff motivation and 50 per cent increased productivity as key advantages. Some 59 per cent of small businesses believe they are as able to offer flexible working as larger organizations and could attract better candidates as a result.

Butsana-Sita continued:

> Flexible working has previously been considered as a 'large company' issue. However, the adoption of converged technology has seen a surge in flexible working practices and aspirations among smaller businesses.
>
> The workforce of the future has been brought up with technology as part of their daily lives. Flexible working allowing a better work–life balance is prized over straight economic affluence. It's something all SME employers should think about.

This is illustrated by Illusion Factor, an integrated communications agency based in London with 30 permanent and 70 project staff. It implemented a converged IT solution (staff Blackberrys, BT Broadband and virtual private network access at home) which allows it to adapt to fluctuating work demands.

Kelvin James, director, Illusion Factor, said:

> Not only does our converged IT network give us a competitive advantage by being very accessible and cost effective for our clients, it also realizes many personal benefits. Our staff can choose how and where they work and on the occasions a deadline means unsociable hours, they have the option to work from home and take the next day off to compensate. I believe this is important for maintaining a good work–life balance and in turn a happy and productive workforce.

BT believes that with the right combination of secure infrastructure, systems and support, any organization, regardless of size, can ensure its employees work together flexibly and effectively.

Is it realistic to believe that any organization can offer flexible working?

Source: *HRM Guide UK* (http://www.hrmguide.co.uk), 18 August, 2006.

Despite its importance, motivation goes beyond pay. Herpen, Praag and Cools (2005) demonstrated a positive relationship between the perceived characteristics of the complete compensation system and extrinsic motivation. Intrinsic motivation, on the other hand, was not affected by the design of monetary compensation, but by promotion opportunities. They also found that the compensation system significantly affected work satisfaction and turnover intent.

According to Rosenbloom (2001, p.2):

Employee benefits constitute a major part of almost any individual's financial and economic security. Such benefits have gone from being considered 'fringe' to the point where they may constitute about 40 per cent of an employee's compensation, and the plans under which they are provided are a major concern of employers.

Key concept 19.2 Employee benefits

Broadly defined, 'employee benefits are virtually any form of compensation other than direct wages paid to employees' (Rosenbloom, 2001, p.3).

HRM in reality Jobseekers want money and job security

Senior managers believe that pay and job security are the most important factors when workers consider job offers, according to a recent survey developed by Robert Half Finance & Accounting. Twenty-seven per cent of chief financial officers (CFOs) polled believed that salary was the biggest consideration for prospective new hires and 24 per cent highlighted company stability. The results were similar to a 2001 survey asking the same question.

Over 1400 CFOs from a stratified random sample of US companies with 20 or more employees were asked, 'In your opinion, which one of the following is the most important consideration for job candidates today when evaluating employment offers?'

CFOs responded:

	2006 %	2001 %
Salary level	27	23
Stability of the company	24	28
Work environment/corporate culture	22	20
Career advancement opportunities	17	21
Equity incentives/stock options	4	4
Other	3	0
Don't know/no answer	3	4

'Businesses that have a successful track record and offer competitive compensation are at an advantage during the hiring process,' said Max Messmer, chairman and CEO of Robert Half International Inc and author of *Human Resources Kit For Dummies*® (John Wiley & Sons, Inc., 2006). 'Employers should emphasize all the factors that distinguish their firms, such as exceptional pay and benefits, a history of stability and growth, and a supportive corporate culture.'

Max Messmer considers that small and newly emerging businesses that cannot afford premium salaries can highlight their other qualities such as the strength of their leadership team. 'The best candidates tend to base at least part of their employment decisions on how much they can learn on the job. During the recruiting process, hiring managers are selling potential employees as much on their own experience and management style as on the other features that make the firm a great place to work.'

Can smaller companies compete effectively in the job market?

Source: *HRM Guide USA* (http://www.hrmguide.com), 20 August, 2006.

The US Chambers of Commerce survey of employee benefits (cited in Rosenbloom, 2001, p.3) includes the following:

1 Employer's share of legally required payments.
2 Employer's share of retirement and savings plan payments.
3 Employer's share of life insurance and death benefit payments.
4 Employer's share of medical and medically related benefit payments.
5 Payment for time not worked (e.g. paid rest periods, paid sick leave, paid vacations, holidays, parental leave, etc.).
6 Miscellaneous benefit payments (including employee discounts, severance pay, educational expenditure and childcare).

Paid time off is still the most common benefit for employees in US private organizations. According to the Bureau of Labor Statistics, US Department of Labor, paid vacations were available to 80 per cent of employees and paid holidays to 77 per cent of employees in private industry during the year 2000. The data comes from the National Compensation Survey (NCS), which provides comprehensive measures of occupational earnings, compensation cost trends, and details of benefit provisions (*HRM Guide USA* [http://www.hrmguide.net/usa/], 19 July, 2002). In 2000:

- Some 52 per cent of employees in private industry participated in medical care plans. Premiums were fully paid by the employer for 32 per cent of those with single coverage plans and 19 per cent of those with family coverage. The majority of medical plan participants were required to contribute a flat monthly amount, averaging US$54.40 for single coverage and US$179.75 for family coverage.
- Around 48 per cent were covered by retirement benefits of at least one type: a defined benefit plan (19 per cent); or a defined contribution plan (36 per cent). Approximately 7 per cent were covered by both types.
- Life insurance was available to over half of all employees in private industry.
- Short-term disability benefits were available to 34 per cent of employees, while long-term disability benefits were only available to 26 per cent.
- Non-production bonuses were offered to 48 per cent of employees.
- Work-related educational assistance (38 per cent).
- Severance pay (20 per cent).
- Job-related travel accident insurance (15 per cent).
- Long-term care insurance (7 per cent).

Access to most benefits (including availability of fully paid medical care and amount of required contributions to cost of medical care) varied by worker and establishment characteristics.

Worker characteristics

This analysis looked at three categories of employees in detail. Retirement benefits covered 66 per cent of professional, technical and related employees; 50 per cent of clerical and sales employees; and 39 per cent of blue-collar and service employees. Work-related educational assistance was available to 62 per cent of professional, technical, and related workers; 37 per cent of clerical and sales workers; and 28 per cent of blue-collar and service workers.

Payment of premiums for medical care coverage also varied by employee characteristics. Some 38 per cent of blue-collar and service workers covered by medical care benefits had their coverage fully paid for by their employers compared with 25 per cent of professional, technical, and related employees and 28 per cent of clerical and sales employees.

Full-time employees were far more likely to have benefits coverage than were part-time employees: 55 per cent of full-time employees were covered by retirement benefits compared with 18 per cent of part-time employees. The disparity in health care benefits was even greater: 61 per cent of full-time employees were covered by medical care plans compared with 13 per cent of part-time workers.

Establishment characteristics

Benefit incidence varied by the number of employees within an establishment. As an example: 65 per cent of workers in establishments with 100 employees or more (medium and large establishments) were covered by retirement benefits compared with 33 per cent of employees in small establishments (those with fewer than 100 workers). Some 86 per cent of employees in medium and large establishments had paid holiday benefits compared with 70 per cent in small establishments.

Benefit cover also varied by industry. Retirement benefits covered 57 per cent of workers in goods-producing industries compared with 45 per cent in service-producing industries. Long-term disability coverage was also more common in goods-producing industries (31 per cent) compared with 24 per cent of employees in service-producing industries. Short-term disability benefits covered 45 per cent of employees in goods-producing industries and 30 per cent of those in service-producing industries.

Morris, Bakan and Wood (2006) highlight some of the contradictions and limitations of flexible reward systems in a study of employees in a large retail organization in the UK. They found that participation lengthens the reward cycle; employees are encouraged to remain with the firm to maximize their shareholdings. However, workers may have different agendas according to individual choices made regarding the scale of participation in such schemes. Junior employees are less likely to choose to actively buy into profit sharing and share ownership schemes. Workers in lower job bands achieve less reward from participation but the

---

HRM in reality Forget the company car – laptops are the best perk

A survey of 994 outplaced employees and managers by global career services company Lee Hecht Harrison found that far more of today's jobhunters want to receive a laptop rather than a company car from their next employer. Respondents were asked to indicate up to nine perks, programs and discretionary benefits they hoped to get in their next job. Four out of five respondents said 'laptop and/or other technology', putting that option just ahead of 'ongoing training opportunities' (77 per cent). 'Use of company car' came way behind (28 per cent) in popularity.

'A company car is a nice perk, but it really doesn't do anything for one's career,' observes Judy Kneisley, senior vice president and general manager of Lee Hecht Harrison's Woodland Hills office. 'Today's jobseekers are much more interested in programs and benefits that will enhance their professional capabilities and allow them more flexibility in terms of when and how they work. Laptops and other technologies, for instance, enable people to access information and get work done from almost anyplace they might be. Likewise, ongoing training opportunities allow employees to continually develop new skills so that they remain valuable and employable regardless of changes in the world of work.'

Kneisley notes that the trend away from perks and towards more pragmatic benefits had already begun in 2003, when Lee Hecht Harrison last conducted this survey in a comparable population. In 1999, when the company first asked jobseekers what they want from their next employer, health club membership (58 per cent) was the most common response, followed by flextime (57 per cent) and use of a company car (53 per cent).

Jobhunters' preferences have changed but their expectations of what they will actually receive largely have not. 'Even with the booming economy of the late 1990s, few jobseekers thought they were likely to get the high-end perks they desired. The big surprise today is that fewer respondents than in prior years think they will receive such benefits as ongoing training opportunities or flextime,' says Kneisley. She adds that, 'Employers seeking to attract talent as the labour market tightens should emphasize these programs that jobseekers want but don't expect. It's a good way to stand out from competitors.'

What perks would you find attractive?

Source: *HRM Guide USA* (http://www.hrmguide.com), 19 May, 2005.

effects of any undermining of collective solidarities are likely to be particularly pronounced in this group.

Rumpel and Medcof (2006) review research on Total Rewards, an approach to reward management adopted by technology-intensive firms such as IBM, Microsoft, AstraZeneca and Johnson & Johnson. Total Rewards takes a holistic approach, going beyond the traditional emphasis on pay and benefits. It considers all the rewards available in the workplace, including opportunities for learning and development, and quality work environment. These factors were found to be a high priority for technical workers and offer an opportunity to tap an organization's unrealized potential. It is argued that effectively managed rewards will ease the critical attraction, retention and motivation challenges faced by high-technology firms.

Pay and performance

Many commentators severely criticized the apparently chaotic and disorganized nature of pay management between the 1950s and 1980s. Subsequently there has been an attempt to remedy this situation. The fashion has been towards the development of performance-related pay schemes that are related to assessments of performance through individual employee appraisal. Wolf (1999, p.48) sums up a common view:

> Pay for performance is the holy grail of modern compensation administration – widely sought but hard to actually achieve. Pay for performance is the flag, motherhood and apple pie, but it is easier said than done. One primary problem is defining performance properly, so that the organization pays for results and not for effort. Once over that hurdle, there remains the large impediment of finding enough money to make the reward for top performance meaningful.

Pay is a sensitive issue. Most employers have been cautious with the introduction of PRP. Often it is applied to senior managers first, then extended to other employees. Usually, it has been an 'add-on' to normal pay. Rarely does it replace the existing pay scheme completely. More commonly, PRP has:

- formed part or (rarely) all of the general pay increase
- been used to extend pay above scale maxima for employees with high levels of performance
- replaced increases previously paid on the basis of age, or length of service.

Such caution is due to the complexity and sensitivity of performance-related pay in the context of employee relations. People take pay scales seriously. Negotiating and justifying radical changes to a pay structure can be difficult and time-consuming. It is sensible to do so in a gradual way, commencing with senior managers who are more likely to be committed to demanding performance objectives. Even if they are not, it gives experience of the advantages and disadvantages of performance-related pay. It also gives pay administrators experience of pay schemes that are more complicated to operate than traditional methods.

The basis of performance-related pay systems

Simplistically, it seems only fair that people should be paid according to their contribution and a number of studies indicate that most people in business agree with this. In a classic experiment, Fossum and Fitch (1985) asked three groups of subjects – students, line managers and compensation managers – to make decisions on pay increases for hypothetical people, taking into account factors such as seniority, budget constraints and cost of living. All three groups gave far more importance to performance and contribution than other factors. Research into the attitudes of corporate boards and chief executive officers, among others, have all produced similar findings.

Theoretically, performance-related pay schemes can benefit both employers and employees. By emphasizing the importance of efficiency and effective job performance, employers can benefit from higher productivity. Higher pay can be targeted at the 'better' performers, encouraging them to stay with the company and continue to perform to a high standard. Good employees benefit from extra pay in return for extra quality of performance. According to this view, properly directed pay can reinforce appropriate behaviour, focusing effort on organizational targets and encouraging a results-based culture. However, these links must be justified and real if they are not to demoralize other members of the workforce. This is particularly important in relation to senior management. Accusations of 'fat cat' behaviour can also seriously affect stock market views of a company's organization.

PRP can be related to the performance assessment of the individual, group (team), department or company. There are several systems in common use.

Appraisal-related pay schemes

Merit pay This is paid as part of a person's annual increase on the basis of an overall performance appraisal. The method has a long track record and is commonly regarded as an effective motivator. However, it is frequently undermined by budget restrictions, when the merit element often is set too low to motivate.

There are also instances when the payment is used as a 'market supplement' to retain individuals who have skills for which there is demand but whose performance is not particularly meritorious. However, it is known that breaking the clear link between appraised

---

British Gas

In 1994 the remuneration committee of British Gas recommended pay increases from 11 to 75 per cent for directors earning £200 000 or more. A new structure replaced a complex system that overemphasized share options and bonuses. This included a pay package worth £475 000 for the chief executive, Cedric Brown, and placed Mr Brown on about 20 times the earnings of the average British Gas employee – a ratio typical of British companies. This compared with differentials of five to eight in Japanese companies.

Facing a House of Commons committee Cedric Brown argued that he was paid much less than many other chief executives of large British companies. In the USA a smaller utility company paid its CEO ten times as much. Indeed it could be regarded as modest when compared with a total payout of US$203 million to Michael Eisner, chairman of Walt Disney in 1993. Mr Brown's remuneration was justified on the grounds that it was 'the rate for the job' and that it would take this kind of salary to attract top international managers. However, Cedric Brown had never worked for any company other than British Gas, had apparently been happy on lower pay in the past, and there was no indication that he was about to be headhunted by anyone else.

Public criticism was fuelled by the fact that 25 000 British Gas workers were in the process of losing their jobs. Redundancies and relocations were making their mark on employee morale and commitment. The changes also included the closure of half its showrooms. The remaining retail outlets would concentrate on appliance sales, and would no longer accept payment for gas bills, offer advice or accept service complaints. The Gas Consumer Council complained about this reduction in customer service, especially given an increase of 19 per cent in complaints over the previous year.

As part of this process, another executive was reported as being offered a bonus of £36 000 on top of his salary of £120 000 for pushing through changes in the work and payscales of retail workers. The 2600 workers were being asked to take pay cuts from their average £13 000 a year salaries along with reductions in holiday entitlements.

The attendant publicity about 'fat cats' dogged Mr Brown for the next two years. Symbolically, angry shareholders brought a pig named Cedric into the annual general meeting and fed it from a trough. Mr Brown suffered further criticism when it was revealed that British Gas had tied itself to a number of supply deals at inflated prices. In 1996 the continued existence of British Gas as an independent entity seemed uncertain. Mr Brown announced his retirement – with a pension of £250 000 a year.

performance and payment of PRP reduces the overall effectiveness of PRP as a motivator for other employees.

Individual incentives Given as unconsolidated (one-off) payments or gifts such as holidays, golf sets or vouchers.

Collective performance schemes

Bonuses These are paid to all staff in an organization, department or team. In common with all collective performance rewards, they are designed to reinforce corporate identity and performance. The John Lewis retail group paid out a total of £57 million in 2002 to its

---

HRM in reality Money isn't everything . . . but it helps

A study by American Express shows that affluent Canadians have a great lifestyle but don't define themselves by their income or believe that their wealth gives them a meaningful life.

Almost all (96 per cent) the 1000 affluent Canadians, with an annual household income of CDN$200 000 or more in the survey, said that the money allowed them to enjoy some of the finer things in life. But they also said they were more interested in collecting experiences and memories than possessions.

The survey also showed that these wealthy Canadians have the following characteristics:

- Almost two-fifths (39 per cent) own two properties.
- They take an average of three vacations a year, where they expect to pay about CDN$2000 per person. Just over a fifth (21 per cent) take four or more vacations a year.
- Dine out seven times a month (on average) and think nothing of spending CDN$100 on a meal.
- Take in a movie, sporting event or concert about once every two weeks.
- One-quarter pay for their children to attend private schools.
- Just over two-fifths (43 per cent) have a home theatre system.
- One-quarter are members of a private golf club or other type of private club.

Degrees of affluence

Seventy-five per cent of affluent Canadians surveyed consider that you're comfortable if you earn CDN$150 000 a year but you cannot consider yourself to be wealthy unless you are pulling in more than half-a-million.

Moreover, most respondents would not retire if they won a million dollars in the national lottery. And only half would definitely retire if they won two million. One in 10 would continue working even if they won CDN$5 million.

Money and success

Almost all respondents believed they had to work hard to get where they are today, but consider the rewards of financial security to be worth the sacrifices. They also felt that having a healthy income and bank balance allowed them to take care of their family and sleep easier at night.

Almost all respondents (98 per cent) considered that they were generally happy, with only 5 per cent saying they still had a lot of money worries. But only one in 10 truly believed that money was the measure of success.

American Express first introduced the icon of affluence – the American Express Platinum Card – 20 years ago, but Rob McClean, vice president of marketing at American Express says, 'Attitudes are very different today compared to when we first launched the Platinum Card. The Platinum crowd today is less driven by status and image than they were during the mid-80s. They're very self-aware and want the best in terms of quality and service. But they don't see themselves as being extravagant and few think of themselves as being rich.'

'We know that these Canadians are a discerning and sophisticated group of consumers who like to enjoy life and aren't shy about spending money,' adds Amex's McClean. 'They're willing to pay for the best if they feel they are getting the best, but they understand the value of their dollar and refuse to spend their money if they don't see the quality and service behind an item.'

Does this article suggest that affluent people do not work for money?

Source: *HRM Guide Canada* (http://www.hrmguide.net/canada/), 1 September, 2004.

58 000 partner employees in the form of bonuses equivalent to 9 per cent of each person's salary. In 1996 the jeans manufacturer Levi Strauss proposed a payout of a year's salary to each permanent employee at the end of 2001, provided they had worked at least three years and the company reached its objective of a US$7.6 billion a year cash-flow. But the plan failed as the company's sales dropped: US$343.9 million from the proposed incentive plan went back into the company in 2000, instead of being paid to staff.

The reward system in Japan is unusual. According to Hart and Kawasaki (1999, p.4):

> Most Japanese workers receive the major part of their direct remuneration via two channels. First, and familiar to workers in other countries, they are paid in the form of regular (usually monthly) wages. Secondly, they receive bonus payments which, typically, are paid twice a year. The bonus constitutes around one-fifth to one-quarter of total cash earnings.

Bonuses paid in other countries are much smaller, so why are Japanese bonuses paid at such a level? Hart and Kawasaki offer a range of alternative explanations, including the possibility that bonuses:

> ... represent a form of efficiency wage by providing a reward for greater effort. By contrast, and at a general level, wages may reflect more systematic and structural elements of remuneration, such as seniority-based pay scales (the *Nenko* system), while bonuses are used to adjust total compensation to fluctuations in firms' economic experience. In this event, we might expect that the bonus should display more flexibility than the wage. One school of thought in this respect regards bonuses as a form of profit-sharing between the firm and its workforce. Another holds that bonuses reflect shared returns to investments in firm-specific skills and know-how.

Profit-related pay　These are schemes in which employees are allocated a payment equivalent to an agreed proportion of the organization's profits. Profit-related pay has been encouraged in the UK through tax incentives.

Option schemes　Executive share **option schemes** are particularly prevalent in the USA but have also become common elsewhere. They allow senior managers to benefit from the continued success of the organization through the purchase of shares at designated dates in the future at a fixed price. The more successful the company, and therefore the greater the likely

---

HRM in reality　£22m share bonus for British Telecom staff

More than 90 000 British Telecom (BT) employees are benefiting from one of Britain's broadest bonus schemes by each receiving shares in the company worth around £250. BT has recently awarded eligible employees shares with an overall value of about £22 million in recognition of their contribution to the company's transformation and growth. On 11 September 2006 these shares qualified for the final dividend of 7.6p per share.

BT's allshare plan gives employees in 41 countries the opportunity to receive free shares once a year if the company achieves preset profitability and customer satisfaction targets. Full and part-time employees who have been with BT for more than a year are eligible. Over the past five years, employees participating in the scheme could have accumulated shares worth more than £1400.

For many years BT has also operated a savings-related share option plan (saveshare) and a monthly purchase plan (directshare) for employees, which enables those in the UK to buy BT shares on a tax advantageous basis. A similar share option plan operates for employees in some 20 other countries.

Hanif Lalani, BT group finance director, said:

> We support employee share ownership through a number of schemes. The share awards under allshare are linked to performance targets and, like any other shareholder, if BT performs successfully then employees also benefit. By encouraging our people to meet these targets, including quarterly updates on progress during the year, we help to secure BT's future as a growing business.

How would you rate share options as a motivating benefit?

Source: *HRM Guide UK* (http://www.hrmguide.co.uk/), 21 August, 2006.

increase in share value, the higher the reward to the executive. This is seen as an important incentive to motivate people who can dramatically affect the prosperity and even survival of the business.

Employee share option schemes apply to less senior staff and tend to be considerably less generous than executive schemes. Generally, a sum is allocated from company profits and used for share purchase for employees. There may also be save as you earn (SAYE) option schemes registered with the taxation authorities. These allow staff to save a proportion of their salary via the pay administration process and have it accumulated for a fixed period. This may be paid to them at the end of that time, with a bonus equivalent to the interest that could have been earned in a savings account. Alternatively, and more beneficially, the sum plus bonus can be used to purchase shares at the price prevailing at the start of the scheme. Preferential tax arrangements have been made for shares held in trust for a fixed period.

Flavour of the (last) month?

Kanter (1989, p.233) observes that whenever any US organization comes up with a 'new' pay scheme a merit element is involved. PRP has also been a prominent feature of the attempt to commercialize practices in the public services, intended as a key factor in encouraging businesslike behaviour amongst managers.

In the UK, the earliest use of PRP in the British civil service dates back to an experiment in 1985 affecting a range of senior grades (principal to under-secretary). The scheme involved payment of a minimum £500 unconsolidated bonus paid as a one-off lump sum to no more than a fifth of eligible staff. The exercise drew a range of comments but it was decided to extend the scheme to most other grades including non-management staff. Ironically, the Review Body on Top Salaries that covered judges, permanent secretaries, senior military officers and diplomats, felt that PRP was unsuitable for politically sensitive posts.

Performance-related pay was introduced for the 800 UK National Health Service general managers in 1986 based on annual objectives, individual performance reviews and financial rewards where the achievement of objectives could be clearly demonstrated (Murlis, 1987). For general managers, the process relied on an appraisal procedure called the 'individual performance review' (IPR). The system had the following characteristics:

- The method was objectives-based, stated wherever possible in quantifiable terms.
- Appraisals were conducted on the 'parent–grandparent' system. Unit general managers would be assessed by the district general manager, with the chair of the regional health authority acting as 'grandparent'.
- Managers were rated on one of five bands. 'Grandparents' had final responsibility and were required to ensure that no more than 20 per cent received the highest rating level and 40 per cent the next highest.
- An individual at the highest level 'consistently exceeds short-term levels of performance and makes excellent progress towards long-term goals' justifying a salary increase of 3–4 per cent a year, up to a maximum of 20 per cent over five years.
- At the lowest level, an individual 'meets few short-term objectives and makes little or no progress towards long-term goals' receiving no increase at all.

Kauhanen and Piekkola (2006) analyzed how features of performance-related pay schemes affect their perceived motivational effects using a Finnish survey for white-collar employees from 1999. They found that the following features are important for a successful PRP scheme:

1 Employees have to feel they are able to affect the outcomes.
2 The organizational level of performance measurement should be close to the employee – individual and team level performance measurement increase the probability that the scheme is perceived to be motivating.
3 Employees should be familiar with the performance measures.

4 The level of payments should be high enough and rewards frequent enough – levels below the median do not generate positive effects.

5 Employees should participate in the design of the PRP scheme.

Long and Shields (2005) studied the incidence of 13 forms of performance pay in 315 Canadian and Australian firms. Overall, firms in both countries showed similar incidences of most forms of performance pay, with employee profit sharing the notable exception. Firm size and unionization were among the most important predictors of individual and organizational performance pay, but neither factor predicted group performance pay. High involvement firms in both Canada and Australia used more organizational performance pay than other firms, but not more group or individual performance pay.

Criticisms of PRP

There is a widespread opinion among senior managers that PRP must be a good thing – but the evidence for its effectiveness is not overwhelming. Indeed, the search for a positive relationship between PRP and good performance has been described as being like 'looking for the Holy Grail' (Fletcher and Williams, 1992). As one variable in a complex situation, it is not surprising that a connection is difficult to prove. A number of major issues can be considered.

Fairness

The concept of 'fairness' is problematic and open to interpretation, with some people seeing pay as a measure of justice (Milcovich, Newman and Milcovich, 2001, p.2). What pay differentials do people consider to be fair? This may vary from country to country. Osberg and Smeeding (2006) compared attitudes in the USA with other countries towards what individuals in specific occupations 'do earn' and what they 'should earn'. Americans showed less awareness of the extent of inequality at the top of income distribution; more polarized attitudes; similar preferences for 'levelling down' at the top of the earnings distribution; but also less concern for reducing differentials at the bottom.

Some employers have gone to elaborate lengths in an attempt to make their system appear fair. This may involve sampling the work of lower-level workers, listening in on phone calls, examining files, or checking through a proportion of completed work. For example, the Bank of America has been cited as spending over a million dollars a year and employing 20 people to monitor 3500 credit card workers for their merit scheme. Not surprisingly, such attempts at 'fairness' have not been entirely popular among employees. The system seems to be distinctly Orwellian: 'big brother is watching you'.

Managerial judgement

The process is dependent on skilled line managers. As we have observed, for various reasons managers feel under pressure to rate their staff as above average. As Kanter (1989) says, 'far from freeing the energies of employees to seek ways to improve their performance, subjectively based merit pay systems throw them back on the merit of their bosses.' Typically such systems are cynically regarded by employees and attacked by unions as being open to abuse and favouritism. They can also result in a rash of high marks by supervisors who feel exposed to the wrath of their employees. Relationships between managers and employees are often uncomfortable, and this process tends to charge that relationship with even more emotion. But line or middle managers are often obliged to implement performance-related systems that they personally do not believe in (Harris, 2000).

Value of reward

Many senior managers seem more concerned with managing the pay bill than motivating staff, so that PRP is often budget-led, not performance-led. A frequent complaint is that the merit element is too small as a percentage of the whole – commonly from 3 to 10 per cent. This is not enough to be a motivator for improved performance. The solution is obvious at one level: increase the merit element to a significantly motivating level such as 15–25 per cent. But this only serves to highlight the difficulty in making a judgement on who gets an increase and being seen to be fair about it (Isaac, 2001). Most employers have not felt confident enough about the process to go beyond a token percentage level.

A demotivator

There may be evidence that people who are rewarded well by PRP are duly motivated, but they are usually a minority in an organization and the effect is outweighed by the demotivation of the majority (Marsden, French and Kobi, 2000). McCausland, Pouliakas and Theodossiou (2005) found that while the predicted job satisfaction of workers receiving PRP is lower on average compared with those on other pay schemes, it has a positive effect on the mean job satisfaction of very highly-paid workers. They suggest that lower-paid employees may perceive PRP to be controlling, whereas higher-paid workers derive a utility benefit from what they view as supportive reward schemes.

PRP and unions

PRP increases the likelihood of flexibility and management power. Not surprisingly, PRP has attracted hostility from many unions as collective bargaining is side-stepped. Hanley and Nguyen (2005) investigated the impact of performance-related pay at the lower end of the remuneration spectrum in Australia. Their study was based on interviews with union officials and analysis of performance appraisal and performance-related pay clauses in union enterprise bargaining agreements. These clauses ranged from minimal stipulation of existence to detailed processes and principles of design and implementation. Specific clauses in white-collar agreements suggest that they are not totally opposed. However, in blue-collar agreements the lack of such clauses is indicative of their propensity to restrict pay increases to a job classification structure. Clauses that aimed to ensure a performance-oriented culture seemed to be viewed as mere sentiment. Overall, only one union supported the notion of performance-related pay.

Conflict with the team philosophy

The obsession with individually based, performance pay conflicts with HRM's emphasis on teams. Employee dissatisfaction was highlighted in an internal review of a performance assessment and payment system covering 68 000 Inland Revenue employees (*Independent*, 5 April 1994). The enquiry surveyed 800 staff and found considerable dissatisfaction, concluding that the performance system was acting as a demotivator for most staff. As well as the familiar complaint that merit payments were too low to provide any incentive, a number of further criticisms of the operation of the system were listed:

- Upward movement of targets: employees found themselves on a treadmill that was continually being speeded up.
- Employees were assessed by managers who did not know them.
- Performance pay for junior employees was restricted by 'budgetary constraints' but this limitation did not seem to apply to senior officials.
- Objectives were often imposed rather than negotiated.
- Subjective criteria led to disagreements on the quality of performance, leading to a perception of unfairness.
- Individual targets were not compatible with team performance.

Similarly Kellough and Nigro (2002) investigated GeorgiaGain, a compensation system developed for the state of Georgia (USA). Performance-related pay was the centrepiece of the initiative that was intended to include a state-of-the-art performance management system, providing performance measurement and evaluation procedures trusted by supervisors and subordinates. But Kellough and Nigro's survey of state employees found them highly critical of the reform and complaining that it had not produced the intended outcomes in most areas.

The reduction of the inflation rate to low single figures has further reduced the perceived effectiveness of incentives. Merit payments of 2–3 per cent are not seen as much reward for exceptional performance. Indeed such payments may be viewed as insulting. Performance systems established in a high inflation period have proven to be a financial embarrassment to some companies. British Telecom scrapped a system for junior and middle managers on the grounds that managers were being overpaid in comparison with equivalents in other firms. Consolidated performance pay was restricted to the top 10 per cent in 1994, with one-off bonuses being paid to most.

Performance and diversity

Fang and Heywood (2006) used the Workplace and Employee Survey to examine the association between payment method and ethnic wage differentials in Canada. Non-Europeans receive lower earnings than Europeans when paid by time rates. However, non-Europeans receive virtually identical earnings to their European counterparts when paid by output. They suggested that tying earnings to productivity made it more difficult for employers to discriminate. Similarly, Heywood and O'Halloran (2005) found no racial wage differential among male workers receiving output-based pay but a significant differential among those paid time rates. The racial wage differential among those receiving bonus pay, usually based on supervisory evaluation, tended to be larger than for those not receiving such bonuses.

Executive pay

Nowhere has the issue of performance-related pay been more controversial than in the compensation arrangements for senior executives. Bender (2004) found that many companies adopted performance-related pay despite believing that the money did not motivate executives. Instead, the reasons were due to 'best practice' in human resource management. The pay structures were designed to attract and retain executives with the potential of large earnings, focus their efforts in the direction agreed by the board and to demonstrate fairness. Variable pay was seen as a symbol of the director's success, both within and outside the organization. Bender's study suggests that companies may use performance-related pay because their competitors do, and because that legitimizes them in the eyes of the establishment.

Bebchuk and Fried (2005) studied executive pay practices in the USA and the corporate governance processes that produce them. They suggest that managerial power and influence have come to play a major role in shaping executive pay, and in ways that end up imposing significant costs on investors and the economy. Their main concerns are the distortion of incentives caused by compensation practices that fail to link pay to performance, limit executives' freedom to sell their shares, or restrict benefits paid to departing executives. They call for greater transparency, improvements in pay practices, and improvements in board accountability to shareholders.

Gordon (2005) acknowledges the strengths of Bebchuk and Fried's case for managerial power in setting executive pay but expresses three major reservations:

1 Concern about apparent lack of pay for performance does not provide sufficient explanation of the controversy over CEO pay and largely ignores popular disquiet about pay levels.

2 Many of the compensation practices identified as indicative of managerial power may have broader explanations. For example, the vast majority of employee stock options are awarded to people well below executive rank.

3 The best way of improving corporate governance may be not a wholesale expansion of shareholder power, but rather measures to increase the independence of the compensation committee.

Guy (2005) investigated the relationship between earnings differentials and CEO pay in 190 British companies between 1970 and 1990. The study concluded that top executive pay prior to 1984 was a stable function of both firm size and earnings differentials lower on the administrative ladder. The use of share options from 1984 onwards represents a change in the mode of top executive compensation and a de-linking of the pay of top executives and that of lower management. Similarly, Erturk *et al.* (2005) found that CEO pay in the UK and USA in the 1980s and 1990s increased at rates that resulted in ever widening gaps between executive and average pay. These increases, they argue, have significantly outrun any sustained increase in value attributable to management effort.

Girma, Thompson and Wright (2006) examined the impact of mergers and acquisitions on the remuneration of CEOs in the UK from 1981 to 1996. They found that CEO pay was not strongly related to company performance but, as in Guy's (2005) study, increased with firm size. CEOs involved in 'wealth-reducing' acquisitions received significantly lower remuneration than those whose deals met with market approval, suggesting that shareholder–principals had some success in penalizing managers for unwarranted empire-building mergers.

However, Stathopoulos, Espenlaub and Walker (2005) analyzed level and composition of the pay of the top executives of a sample of UK public listed companies and found that remuneration reflected organizational performance. Executives of firms that performed badly experienced cuts in salaries, bonuses and equity-based compensation. The study also revealed increased participation and value in the equity-based schemes provided to CEOs and other executives of poorly performing firms in the longer term. CEOs of poorly performing firms were significantly more likely to be dismissed but emoluments were not directly affected during the year of departure. In the same vein, Merhebi *et al.* (2006) reversed earlier Australian studies that found no link between CEO pay and corporate performance. Merhebi

---

HRM in reality Top executives losing out?

Watson Wyatt's 2005 Executive Reward Survey shows that, on average, FTSE 100 executives have seen falls in overall pay packages for the year. The consultancy firm attribute this to increasingly demanding performance conditions imposed on their long-term incentive plans.

The survey found that while average basic salaries and bonuses for FTSE 100 chief executives have continued to rise – by 9.1 per cent and 29 per cent respectively – their total remuneration has fallen on average by 7 per cent to £2.1m. (Yes, that's a mere £2 100 000). Whereas increased bonuses reflect average increases of 20 per cent in profits for the previous year, the value of their long-term incentives has fallen in many cases.

Basic salaries and bonuses for other FTSE 100 executive directors have also risen – by 7.8 per cent and 22 per cent respectively – while their average total remuneration has fallen by 18 per cent to £980 000. According to Watson Wyatt, the value of long-term incentive plans, such as share option plans, has also been undermined by the relatively low volatility in the stock market. Lower volatility has the effect of reducing the potential upside of share options.

'There is a risk that institutional investors may have been too tough in their attempts to ensure executive pay is aligned to shareholder interests,' said Damien Knight, an executive reward consultant at Watson Wyatt. 'Shareholders have understandably been keen to use performance conditions to ensure that the long-term incentives offered to executives are paid out on their actual performance rather than fortunate market conditions. But the performance measures they have imposed have in some cases reduced the real value of the incentives to the executives. The question is: does this leave executives suitably motivated and aligned to shareholders' interests?'

What are your views on Damien Knight's question: 'Does this leave executives suitably motivated and aligned to shareholders' interests?'

Source: *HRM Guide UK* (http://www.hrmguide.co.uk), 30 November, 2005.

et al.'s study suggests that Australian experience is consistent with that of firms from the USA, UK and Canada.

Perkins and Hendry (2005) highlighted the important role of non-executive directors in determining executive pay. They studied the nuances of executive pay decisionmaking, including remuneration committee members' reactions to corporate governance reforms. Such initiatives place non-executive directors in the role of intermediaries, explicitly assigned to resolve the conflict of interest inherent in boardroom remuneration systems, while simultaneously expected to play a team role as board members responsible for the overall strategy and operation of the company.

Summary

Pay is a key element in the management of people. The importance of pay begins with pay administration that deals accurately and swiftly with payroll-related matters. Much of the information used by pay administrators is shared with the human resource function. Pay evaluation systems also impinge on human resource territory. Free market organizations are particularly concerned with performance-related pay as a motivating factor. However, this trend appears to be ideological rather than rational since practical PRP schemes that deliver the results intended are extremely difficult to construct. Current evidence shows that performance pay is likely to demotivate more people than it motivates.

Further reading

Ian Kessler's article on 'Reward system choices', in J. Storey (ed.) *Human Resource Management: A Critical Text*, 2nd edn (Thomson Learning, 2001) provides an in-depth theoretical analysis of research and practice on rewards. *Strategic Reward: Making It Happen* by Michael Armstrong and Duncan Brown (Kogan Page, 2006), *A Handbook of Employee Reward Management and Practice* by Michael Armstrong and Tina Stephens (Kogan Page, 2005) and *Reward Management: A Handbook of Remuneration Strategy and Practice* by Michael Armstrong and Helen Murlis (Kogan Page, 2004) all cover this topic area well.

Review questions

1 What is pay for? What effect does the minimum wage have on employer and employee attitudes to rates of pay?

2 What functions should a payroll department fulfil? Is it appropriate to merge the HR function with a payroll department?

3 What are the implications of paying different salaries for the same job?

4 Does job evaluation have a function in a modern pay system?

5 'A fair day's work for a fair day's pay'. How can a company's pay system be designed to meet this criterion?

6 Outline the arguments for and against the use of performance-related pay.

7 Should executive directors be paid on a different basis from other employees?

8 What advantages do flexible benefits offer for individual employees and their employers?

9 How large does a merit payment or bonus have to be in order to provide an incentive for effective performance?

10 What are the practical consequences of using employee stock options as a motivator?

Case study for discussion and analysis

Fairness

Scenario 1

A photocopying shop has one employee who has worked in the shop for six months and earns US$9 per hour. Business continues to be satisfactory, but a factory in the area has closed and unemployment has increased.

Other small firms have now hired reliable workers working at US$7 an hour to perform jobs similar to those done by the photocopy shop employee. The owner of the shop reduces the employee's wage to US$7.

Is it fair to cut the worker's wage from US$9 to US$7 an hour? Compare your decision with the second scenario.

Scenario 2

A house painter employs two assistants and pays them US$9 per hour. The painter decides to change his business and go into lawn-mowing, where the going wage is lower. He tells the current workers that he will keep them on if they want to work, but will only pay them US$7 per hour.

Is this employer being fair?

Part eight
Learning and development

This part examines human resource development (HRD) at a number of levels. If people are truly 'our greatest asset' and are the key to 'competitive advantage' we must have mechanisms in place to enhance their capabilities and provide opportunities for learning and development. The nature and range of HRD delivery methods has changed considerably in recent years as new technology has come onstream.

The chapters in Part eight encompass a number of key issues such as:

- What is human resource development?

- How and why does vocational learning vary between different countries?

- What is the role of self-development?

- What are the major differences between training and learning?

- Is the 'learning organization' a meaningful concept?

- Do trainers have a role in the context of strategic HRD?

- Is e-learning useful and cost-effective?

- How can we evaluate learning experiences?

Chapter 20
Human resource development

Learning objectives

The purpose of this chapter is to:

- Outline the concept of human resource development.

- Investigate and evaluate HRD initiatives at national level.

- Debate the need for distinctive management and gender-focused HRD programmes.

- Introduce the concept of mentoring.

HRD strategies

HRD at the national level

The meritocratic ideal

Education and training

Vocational education and training

Development programmes

Management development

Developing women

Coaching and mentoring

Summary

Further reading

Review questions

Case study for discussion and analysis – managers more likely to get training than workers

HRD strategies

Business page pundits argue that industrialized states must move away from low technology products with poor margins which can be produced more cheaply in low-wage countries. Similarly, developing countries aiming to join the ranks of the advanced nations must acquire a capacity for producing sophisticated products and services. High technology products require long-term research, expensive and sophisticated production equipment and precise quality procedures. Above all, they require skilled human resources capable of performing effectively in this environment.

At the organizational level, enterprises need people with appropriate skills, abilities and experience. These qualities can be bought from outside the organization through recruitment, consultancy and subcontracting, or grown by training and developing existing employees. This chapter focuses on the second approach. The strategic choice between buying and growing is made on the basis of cost-effectiveness, urgency of requirement, and the need to motivate staff.

Political, cultural and historical elements also influence the decision. Organizations with an internal job market orientation, for example most large German and Japanese companies, have made a practice of growing their own talent.

Key concept 20.1 Human resource development

Human resource development (HRD) is a strategic approach to investing in human capital. It draws on other human resource processes, including resourcing and performance assessment, to identify actual and potential talent. HRD provides a framework for self-development, training programmes and career progression to meet an organization's future skill requirements.

Throughout this book we have distinguished HRM from previous models of people management by its emphasis on the integration of an organization's people policies and activities. Investment in employee skills to support the needs of advanced technology is a prime example of this approach. Financially obsessed managers in free market countries have preferred cost-cutting to investment in people or new technology. Moreover, there has been a chronic failure to understand the link between the two: investment in new equipment has been viewed as worthwhile only if it leads to a cut in employee costs. Managers in Australia and the UK, for example, have been wedded to a penny-pinching mentality, avoiding the kind of high technology that requires expensive, skilled workers. Their counterparts in Singapore and Korea have invested more readily in new machine tools in order to increase output and profitability, frequently taking on extra staff to meet demand.

Learning in the workplace also enhances employee engagement and motivation. For example, Rowden and Conine (2005) found a statistically significant relationship between workplace learning and job satisfaction in small US banks. They highlight the importance of informal and incidental learning and emphasize the need for managers to make learning opportunities available to enhance overall job satisfaction.

The following list (adapted from Thomson and Mabey, 1994, p.7) highlights the principal elements of human resource development:

- Effective resourcing, induction and deployment of high-quality people.
- Identification and improvement of skills and motivation among existing and longer serving employees.
- Regular job analysis in relation to organizational objectives and individual skills.
- Reviewing the use of technology, in particular in replacing routine tasks.
- Performance management and assessment through identification of key tasks.
- A focus on skills and general abilities rather than paper qualifications.

- Training needs identification.
- Provision of training programmes to improve current performance and support career development.
- Provision of opportunities for personal growth and self-development.
- Helping people to manage their own careers.
- Encouraging the acceptance of change as normal and an opportunity.

Systematic **human resource development** (see Key concept 20.1) maximizes the human capital of an organization, devoting time, money and thought to improving the pool of essential competencies among its staff. It has a general impact on business performance by enhancing product knowledge and service expertise. HRD emphasizes people as people rather than numbers, and it motivates staff, drawing on their talents and demonstrating that they are valued by the organization. It is also claimed to empower staff, allowing individuals to take a measure of control over their own careers and develop life patterns that offer increased opportunity and satisfaction.

How 'real' is HRD? Gibb (2002, p.138) takes the view that:

> The idea of HRD promises a great deal, and is seductive; but whether there is evidence of organizational examples of this being delivered is questionable. Indeed the 'rhetoric' involved is arguably being used to cover changes which are far removed from the espoused aims; instead of better valuing the human resource, such re-inventions can mask the greater exploitation of people.

According to Sambrook (2001) HRD has its roots in the early organization development interventions of the 1940s, but the term was first used by Nadler in 1972. Nadler (cited in Nadler and Nadler, 1989, p.4) described HRD as 'organized learning experiences provided by employers, within a specified period of time, to bring about the possibility of performance improvement and/or personal growth.'

What is the relationship between HRD and training? The two terms are sometimes used to mean the same. However, Goss (1994, p.62) observes that they are regarded often as mutually exclusive activities. He attributes this to the hierarchical nature of most organizations in which training is something done to lower-level workers, whereas development is a process experienced by managers – hence 'management development'. As Goss rightly points out, this approach is incompatible with the central principles of HRM, which hold that all employees are assets whose competencies need to be developed. According to Hendry (1995, p.366): 'Increasingly, we are getting away from the divisive notion that managers are "developed" while the shopfloor are merely "trained". The principles of adult learning apply to each.'

It is appropriate, therefore, to regard training as an integral aspect of HRD. Gibb (2002, p.7) argues that:

> . . . past definitions of education, training and development, with their essentially sequential divisions of learning, are no longer useful or acceptable. They would be deemed to draw the boundaries around the subject, in theory and practice, too narrowly, and also inaccurately; they would not capture and deal with the practice and theory of contemporary work and organizations.

Sambrook (2001) argues that HRD can be thought of as a construct, like 'love' or 'quality'. It is intangible in itself since it cannot be found, touched or seen but it may be investigated through features associated with the concept that might distinguish it from training and development. She argues that training and development was focused on operational issues and took a short-term or reactive approach in which specialists 'did training', delivered it to passive trainees and usually conducted it in classrooms.

Sambrook describes this as the 'tell' approach as opposed to 'sell' or 'competent' HRD. Competent HRD focuses on competencies and takes a wider approach, encompassing self-development, employee development, management development and organization development. Probably delivered by facilitators, there is two-way communication and some consultation together with far more diverse training methods. There is an attempt to link HRD to other HR processes and take a wider organizational perspective. Finally, Sambrook identifies strategic HRD or 'gel'. Here the HRD function and the organization are strategically and totally interlinked and there is an emphasis on learning. Individuals are encouraged to take responsibility, to share learning and to be participative and collaborative.

Gibb (2002) prefers the term 'learning and development', considering that it addresses a combination of cognitive capacities, capabilities and behaviours that have to be established or changed in the process. He employs 'cognitive capacities' as a more comprehensive concept than 'knowledge' stating that (Gibb, 2002, p.8):

> . . . accumulating 'knowledge' is just one specific kind of cognitive capacity, and it is indeed only the most basic kind. It cannot be treated as being synonymous with what [learning and development] work involves, where a whole set of cognitive capacities are significant and relevant if people are to be 'thoughtful performers'. The brain is capable of far more than memorizing knowledge, and performance at work involves aspects of cognition other than the use of memorized knowledge.

Similarly, Gibb wraps the older concepts of skill and competence within the term 'capabilities', arguing that 'skill' has too many connotations of physical performance and also that 'competence' is increasingly questioned as a valid and useful concept. His third dimension, behaviours, is favoured over abilities since it draws in the influence of emotions, attitudes and values that mediate actual performance.

HRM in reality Teens are too ambitious

The goals of many teens exceed their likely achievements, leading to wasted time and resources, not to mention anxiety and distress, according to a new study in the journal *Social Problems* by John Reynolds, professor of sociology at Florida State University.

Co-authored by graduate students Michael Stewart, Ryan MacDonald and Lacey Sischo, the study analyzed data from several national surveys to compare changes in high school senior students' educational and occupational plans between 1976 and 2000 and found a widening gap between goals and actual achievements.

Reynolds said: 'Today's teens are both highly ambitious and increasingly unrealistic. While some youth clearly benefit from heightened ambition, it can lead to disappointment and discouragement rather than optimism and success.'

The study found that high school senior students in 2000 were much more ambitious than their 1976 counterparts. In 2000 50 per cent planned to continue their education after college to get an advanced degree, compared with 26 per cent in 1976. In 2000 63 per cent planned to work in a professional job – such as doctor, lawyer, college professor, accountant or engineer – by the age of 30, compared with 41 per cent in 1976. Other categories were labourer, farmer or homemaker; service, sales or clerical; operative or crafts; military or protective services; entrepreneur; and administrator or manager.

The percentage of high school graduates between 25 and 30 who actually earned advanced degrees remained fairly consistent. The gap between expectations of achieving such a degree and what is realistic grew from 22 percentage points in 1976 to 41 percentage points in 2000.

The researchers attribute the senior students' unrealistic expectations to 'the declining influence of grades and high school curricula and the increasing number who plan to go to community college as an educational stepping-stone to a first degree and beyond.' Evidence suggests that such students are much less likely to complete even a first degree, compared with those beginning their college careers at four-year institutions.

John Reynolds commented: 'Unrealistic plans may lead to a misuse of human potential and economic resources. For example, planning to become a medical doctor while making poor grades in high school means that preparation for other more probable vocations is likely to be postponed.

'Like many cultural shifts in today's society, money may be at the root of the "college-for-all" attitude. Parents, high school counsellors and others are giving students the message that a college degree is the only way to get a good job when, in fact, a skilled electrician or plumber can earn as much as say, a college professor.

'Also, other researchers have found that although we are making more money than in the past, what counts for happiness is making more than your peers. This might also fuel irrational plans to work in top occupations.'

Why are today's teens apparently 'both highly ambitious and increasingly unrealistic'?

Source: *HRM Guide USA* (http://www.hrmguide.com), 29 August, 2006.

HRD at the national level

Education plays a key role in causing and, potentially, curing institutionalized discrimination in advanced countries. As early as the 19th century, the sociologist Weber held that people should be promoted solely on the basis of relevant qualifications. He proposed this condition in order to overcome the nepotism and patronage that prevailed in the public and private sectors at that time. Since then qualifications have become significant, if not essential, requirements for a successful career.

The importance of education for personal advancement is best illustrated in France, where a clear and simple equation traditionally existed between management success and intellect. Intellect was taken to be the possession of the right qualifications from the right educational institutions. In France, not only was admission to one's first job dependent on educational attainment but attendance at a *grande école* eased (and still eases) the path right to the top. According to *The Times* (16 January, 1992):

> *L'Expansion* surveyed how the French business community viewed graduates of every one of the top *grandes écoles*. Among the shortcomings cited, graduates of Polytechnique were considered to be too elitist, those of Centrale unimaginative, those of HEC over-ambitious and those of l'ENA too theoretical. This educational typecasting tendency is reinforced by a fairly rigid pecking order in salaries. The market value of new graduates is closely tied to the intellectual reputation of their alma mater.

The right qualification admitted a recruit to a much higher entry level than would otherwise be the case. Thereafter, *grandes écoles* diplomas did not compensate for lack of effort but they made promotion considerably easier (Barsoux and Lawrence, 1990, p.58). As an employee rose in the organization, technical ability became less important than 'social' skills required to delegate, resolve conflicts and motivate staff. At the higher levels (Barsoux and Lawrence, *ibid.*):

> . . . the effects of attending the 'right' school comes to fruition, as some individuals move from line jobs into positions of power that put a premium on such qualities as distinguished appearance, good manners, tact and good taste. Emphasis on social competence tends to favour the products of the *grandes écoles* who possess the necessary self-confidence and social wherewithal. So while companies ostensibly drop educational credentials as a means of selection, they replace them with credentials which elevate members of the same population.

Whereas in some countries – Germany, for example – training was seen as the key to effective performance, the French were inclined to view intellectual quality as the most important factor. Accordingly, French education was highly selective, emphasizing the production of 'high-fliers' who would be given early responsibility in their business careers. They produced managers with an analytical perspective in which every business issue was seen as an intellectual problem as shown in Table 20.1. People rejected by this process had poor prospects compared with the USA, for instance, where – in theory – anyone could get to the top.

But there are *cadres* . . . and *cadres*. As business schools developed and higher education extended in France, junior executive and middle management jobs were increasingly filled by non-*grandes écoles* graduates – and women. Potentially, French education offers a route to the top on grounds of merit. In practice, there is a strong bias towards the children of existing *cadres* and government employees who understand the system and its requirements.

In this respect, it is not unlike the British educational system. A survey reported in *The Economist* (19 December, 1992), found that two-thirds of top jobs surveyed were occupied by 'public school' men, with over 50 per cent having graduated at Oxford or Cambridge Universities. Without going into a detailed historical explanation it should be pointed out that British public schools are actually fee-paying institutions outside the state system. Of the others, 27 per cent came from the most prestigious institutions such as top Scottish universities, leaving only 11 per cent without higher education.

Ten years later, Conlon and Chevalier (2002) found that:

For individuals graduating in 1985 and 1990 (interviewed in 1996), there was a 46 percentage point difference in average returns between graduates from the best and worst institutions. The range of estimates decreased by approximately 10 percentage points for individuals graduating in 1995 (interviewed in 1998). For the 1985 and 1990 cohorts, Oxbridge graduates achieved a 7.9 per cent earnings premium over graduates from 'old' universities, while those attending polytechnics suffered a 3.8 per cent wage penalty compared to those attending 'old' universities. For the 1995 cohort, degree holders from former polytechnics suffered a 7.7 per cent earnings penalty compared to degree holders from 'old' universities.'

This represents virtually no change over two decades. We can attribute this partly to clone-seeking selection and promotion procedures. For example, major companies tend to visit the same narrow range of universities for annual recruitment and headhunters tend to assume their clients have conservative requirements.

Education fails to deliver true meritocracy for a number of reasons, for example:

- Life chances are not taken into account. People from privileged backgrounds have a greater opportunity to achieve acceptable qualifications. They have parents who understand the system and, if necessary, can purchase private education. It is infinitely

Competencies	Characteristics
Intellectual	*Logical thought*: being able to think in a logical and organized manner. *Conceptualization*: an ability to relate apparently unconnected events into a meaningful pattern. *Diagnostic use of concepts*: being able to use theories or models, or develop new ones if required.
Entrepreneurial	*Effective use of resources*: planning and organizing, with an image of efficiency and achievement. *Proactive initiation*: a successful manager takes effective action rather than merely responding to events.
Socio-emotional	*Self-control*: an ability to suppress impulses and control personal reactions. This requires self-discipline and a capacity to place organizational requirements above individual needs. *Spontaneity*: free, unconstrained self-expression. *Conceptual objectivity*: impartiality and the preservation of emotional distance. Being able to balance opposing points of view. *Accurate self-assessment*: a realistic appraisal of one's own strengths and weaknesses. *Stamina and adaptability*: the 'stickability' or resilience required to cope with long hours and flexibility to deal with the unexpected.
Interpersonal	*Self-confidence*: showing that as 'natural leaders' they know what they are doing. *Developing others*: coaching, counselling, mentoring and being part of a team. *Impact*: able to influence others. *Use of unilateral power*: the ability to take the leadership role. *Use of socialized power*: negotiating and alliance-building, team roles. *Use of oral communications*: clear and persuasive communication. *Positive regard*: valuing other people, able to delegate and allowing employees to perform. *Managing group processes*: fostering and developing commitment and team-spirit.

Table 20.1

Generic management competences

Source: Adapted from Vickerstaff (1992), pp.122–24.

easier for a student with affluent, supportive parents to obtain good grades than it is for those having to work to support themselves and, perhaps, children or relatives. In a Norwegian study, Hansen and Mastekaasa (2006) looked at how social class origin affects academic performance at university. They argue that selection procedures for higher education are strong enough to make it unlikely that lower-class students are less talented than students from higher-class backgrounds. However, in an examination of performance at Norwegian universities they found that there was a clear association between grades and class with students from classes that scored highly in respect of cultural capital doing best. This distinction was true for first-year and higher-level studies across a majority of the 36 fields they studied.

- Second chances are discouraged or have reduced effectiveness. Educators, particularly university academics, have achieved their status by passing exams and acquiring degrees. Their personal status and function is legitimized by the belief that clearing these hurdles is indicative of underlying intellect and personal worth. They offer limited sympathy and understanding for people who fail examinations at any stage – unless there are overt causes such as illness. In fact, failure can occur because of a whole range of non-intellectual reasons: domestic, financial or motivational. The critical timespan for education leading to paper qualifications (14–21) coincides with the transition from childhood to adult life – a traumatic maturational period for many. However, people who attempt to recover the situation at a later (more stable) age find the way littered with innumerable obstacles.

- Snobbery: Regardless of the consequences of social circumstances and maturational crises, as we have seen possession of a 'good' degree from a 'good' university is viewed generally as evidence of intrinsic virtue, allowing entry to a range of powerful in-groups. However, in-groups have an unpleasant side to them: prejudice against outsiders. For example, the development of mass higher education in the UK has produced a great deal of snobbish disquiet in certain circles. Worse, a number of major employers now confine their recruitment to a restricted number of older universities where they can continue to find really worthy candidates – people just like themselves. In line with our discussion in previous chapters, this is a low-risk selection strategy from the employer's perspective.

The meritocratic ideal

People in developed – and many developing – countries no longer 'know their place' in society. Those who have a vested interest in preserving plum jobs for a select elite are facing overwhelming opposition from a generation whose career aspirations and expectation of equitable treatment by employers would have been unthinkable a few decades ago. However, there is some way to go before a universal **meritocracy** prevails (see Key concept 20.2).

Key concept 20.2 Meritocracy

Meritocratic procedures aim to make judgements on the basis of evidence of competence such as examination results or the achievement of targets. We have noted already that educational achievement is not simply a matter of merit. Evidence of merit is invariably contaminated by social factors and life chances. A meritocratic but socially fair system should:

- Take aggregate outcomes into account. In other words, if the process does not produce a balanced proportion of gender, ethnic origin and so on, then it is unfair.
- Take life chances into account.
- Require organizations to institutionalize the representation of specific groups within their key decision processes – including selection and promotion.

Education and training

In Chapter 5 we introduced the idea of human capital – investing in people as national or organizational assets. Human capital development in the form of education and skills training can be an effective response to constraints imposed on the employment market. Specific skills may be in short supply – even during periods of considerable unemployment – and technological developments outdate some skills and require entirely different competencies.

There is a considerable variation between education and training levels in different countries. For example, technology and production have long been regarded as high-status activities in Germany. Success in these areas demands a high level of technical training among the workforce. As a consequence, German businesses place a higher value on technical merit than, say, those in the UK. Ironically, training systems in the two countries are similar, depending on a mixture of academic education and vocational courses – unlike France, Japan and the USA where there is a greater concentration on full-time education. Significantly, however, there is a markedly greater commitment to training in Germany with levels of participation and achievement that have no comparison in the UK.

Whereas the British apprentice system had been more or less dismantled by the 1980s, it remained intact in Germany. Some 50 per cent of German school-leavers (compared with a mere 17 per cent in the UK) participate in apprenticeship schemes covering over 300 occupations. Reluctance to train apprentices is not confined to the UK. There appears to be a distinction between the benefits of having an existing apprenticeship system and the additional costs of starting a new apprenticeship programme. Wolter, Mühlemann and Schweri (2006) looked at why so many Swiss firms choose not to train apprentices when cost–benefit studies of apprenticeship have shown that training costs are offset by the productive work most apprentices contribute during the course of their apprenticeship. Using maximum-likelihood selection models, they estimated the net cost of training for firms without an apprenticeship programme. They showed that switching to a training policy would lead to a significantly higher net cost during the apprenticeship period. This less favourable cost–benefit ratio was determined not so much by cost than by insufficient benefit.

Apprenticeships growing in popularity

Statistics from the Australian National Centre for Vocational Education Research (NCVER) show a growing number of people starting an apprenticeship or traineeship.

Seasonally adjusted, the number of new starters on apprenticeships or traineeships has grown for six quarters in a row. In the year to 30 September, 2005, the number of starters (267 600) increased by 5 per cent over the previous year.

Uptake by older people – those aged 45 years and over – showed a relatively high (13 per cent) rate of growth, exceeded only by traditional apprenticeships, which recorded an increase of 14 per cent over the previous year. However, across the country, newly commencing apprentices and trainees were predominantly male and 19 years of age or under.

Higher-level qualifications continued to show a trend of increased commencements in the year to 30 September, 2005 with 8 per cent more people starting training contracts at Australian Qualifications Framework qualification level three or higher.

The total number of apprentices and trainees in-training is relatively stable at 397 800, unchanged from the previous quarter, but down by a single percentage point from the previous year's total of 400 900. 139 600 people completed an apprenticeship or traineeship over the 12 months to 30 September, 2005 – an increase of 5 per cent over the previous year.

Source: *HRM Guide Australia* (http://www.hrmguide.net/australia/), 3 March, 2006.

In the 1990s German companies had a staggering 60 per cent higher rate of productivity than their UK counterparts. Underlying this was a dramatic contrast in levels of participation in training and managerial expectation. In Germany, 90 per cent of employees had completed a minimum of three years' craft training; in the UK the equivalent figure was only 10 per cent. Even more worrying was the fact that British managers surveyed seemed unconcerned. Supported by their higher technical skills, it was scarcely surprising that German companies dominated the high-value, quality end of the market while British companies concentrated on cheaper, low-profit products.

HRM in reality Basic skills need improvement

A CBI report claims that one in three UK employers is forced to send staff for remedial training in basic English and maths skills to make up for the shortcomings of the educational system. The report, 'Working On The Three Rs', commissioned by the Department for Education and Skills, also shows that about one-fifth of employers often find that non-graduate recruits of all ages have literacy or numeracy problems. 140 private sector organizations of different sizes contributed to the report, with two-thirds of the survey questionnaires being completed by HR-related managers.

A response from a catering company highlighted a 'total lack of knowledge of times tables' among staff, meaning that many were unable to carry out basic calculations such as adding VAT or adjusting sale prices. A car company training manager said: 'Some people with GCSEs in maths and English can't get through our basic skills tests, which is worrying ... people who fail have difficulties with basic reading and writing, fractions, multiplication and division.'

Detailed definitions are provided of what it means to be numerate and literate. Top expectations are:

- Numeracy:
  - simple mental arithmetic without a calculator
  - ability to interpret data
  - competence in percentages
  - ability to calculate proportions.

- Literacy:
  - written communication including legible handwriting
  - communicating information orally
  - understanding written instructions
  - correct grammar and spelling.

While these skills should be produced by the education system business says that the current GCSE curriculum is not delivering. UK businesses have to pay for remedial training and suffer from low productivity, compared with competitors overseas where new recruits have higher functional skills. A manager from one of the UK's largest food retailers summed up a common view: 'We don't feel that the current GCSEs, especially in maths, equip young adults with day-to-day skills in using numbers and problem-solving.'

Last year only 54 per cent of GCSE students achieved a Grade C or above in mathematics while 60 per cent did so in English. A mere 45 per cent achieved both. As job opportunities for unskilled workers shrink from the present 3.4 million to a predicted 600 000 by 2020, this is particularly worrying.

Commenting on the report, CBI director-general Richard Lambert said: 'We must raise our game on basic skills in this country. The UK simply can't match the low labour costs of China and India. We have to compete on the basis of quality, and that means improving our skills base, starting with the very basics.

'Employers' views on numeracy and literacy are crystal clear: people need to be able to read and write fluently and to carry out basic mental arithmetic. Far too many school-leavers struggle with these essential life skills.

'The fact that one in three employers ran remedial courses for their staff in the last year is a sad indictment of how the education system has let young people down. Acknowledging the problem and commissioning this report are first steps but the government must show a far greater sense of urgency and purpose if it is to deliver on its promise to sort this out.'

The manufacturing and construction sectors reported the greatest numeracy and literacy problems. A construction firm's personnel manager said: 'The standard of literacy shown by people filling in the double-sided application form for a trainee position is often very poor. Many applicants can't construct a sentence and their grammar, handwriting and spelling are awful.' He added: 'It's a delight when an application form is good.'

Similarly, a building company HR manager highlighted problems with foremen who were unable to calculate how much material was needed for a particular task: 'Many don't have the skills to work out the areas of squares and rectangles, let alone other shapes.'

Employees are often reluctant to ask for help with their literacy and numeracy problems. A personnel development manager at a business consultancy said: 'People become very adept at hiding their lack of literacy and numeracy. For instance one employee used to ask his wife to write his reports for him in the evenings.

'Another very capable employee hid his dyslexia very effectively but it came to light when he refused to apply for promotion. After two hours' discussion he finally said he could not write – the same individual now has a masters degree and is a champion for the "skills for you" training.'

The manager had been head teacher at two secondary schools and said: 'A degree of creativity has been lost in secondary education, and with it the relevancy of learning that should prepare pupils for life. Schools should take into account the breadth of skills needed by school-leavers and make learning practical and relevant to their everyday situation.

'For example, pupils should be taught functional literacy and numeracy skills so that they can book a holiday, calculate 10 per cent off a sale item, or work out their pension contribution as a percentage of their salary.'

The report also indicates that problems are not confined to school-leavers. The CBI's 'Employment Trends Survey 2006', published in September, shows that 23 per cent of employers were not satisfied with graduates' basic literacy and use of English, and 16 per cent were concerned about graduates' numeracy skills.

How critical are basic numeracy and literacy skills to modern organizations?

Source: *HRM Guide UK* (http://www.hrmguide.co.uk/), 21 August, 2006.

Again and again, British firms report 'skill shortages', even in periods of high unemployment, leading to a reliance on overtime, subcontracting (often overseas) or a containment of growth – instead of creating jobs as in the USA. Significant blame is attached to the inadequacies of the British education system with its focus on cultivating an academic elite, as opposed to developing numeracy and communication skills throughout the population. We noted earlier that the recent explosion in higher education and the establishment of vocational qualification targets may eventually lead to improvements.

British companies are not alone in devoting considerable resources towards 'remedial' programmes. The Australian Association of Graduate Employers surveyed 150 of the largest public and private sector employers in the country, asking them about 5000 graduates recruited in the previous three years (*Times Higher*, 25 February, 1994). Their criticisms of new graduates echoed those of British school-leavers, including:

- lack of basic knowledge of grammar, sentence structure and spelling
- inability to explain ideas clearly in writing or speech
- inability of many to write or speak clearly 'in a business sense'.

Employers stated that their deficiencies had been noted during the selection process but these faults were so common that they had to be accepted in order to fill vacancies. Academics were criticized for setting a standard for students based on their own use of jargon and inability to express themselves lucidly in simple English. Employers had to compensate by providing communication courses.

Vocational education and training

However, bad though the British and Australian training performances may be, it has been argued that the real situation is not quite so dire. Whereas, for example, the level of technical qualification in the UK appears to be very low, the reported training activities of organizations are much higher. This discrepancy can be explained by the historical absence of recognized basic and intermediate level vocational certification. It may be that the employment market contains many individuals with usable skills but they have no means of proving their worth to employers.

In fact, the reluctance of many employers to engage in training can probably be pinned down to two issues: (a) the short-term, cost-based approach to all management activities (in this case, demand for a quick and obvious benefit from training expenditure); and (b) the difficulty of proving the connection between training and improved efficiency.

Hendry (1995, p.364) argues that the connection has never been proven:

> One of the things which gets in the way is the fallacy, promoted by the Employment Department among others, that the benefits of training can somehow be demonstrated on the bottom-line. As a rhetorical device, it may encourage employers to train by saying 'training pays', but no one has ever satisfactorily demonstrated this.

In 1993 the UK government introduced the 'Modern Apprenticeship' scheme to provide 16 and 17-year-olds with the opportunity to train for NVQs and SVQs up to level 3 (equivalent to 2 'A' levels). However, progress in gaining the interest of employers was slow. In particular there was considerable reluctance among smaller companies to participate in the scheme or recognize the value of the qualifications.

A further initiative sponsored by the British government is the 'Investor in People' award, given when an assessor is satisfied on four national standards:

1 Public commitment from the top of the organization to develop all employees to achieve business objectives.

2 The organization regularly reviews the training and development needs of all employees.

HRM in reality Aussie bosses support learning

Australian employers show up well in a global comparison of support for employees' further education and training, according to a Robert Half Finance & Accounting Workplace survey.

Eighty-four per cent of Australian finance and HR managers in the survey stated that their organization paid all (or part of) the cost of additional education programmes for their employees. This compares with a global average of 77 per cent. Six per cent of respondents also said that their organization supported employees who were engaged in further training with flexible working hours.

According to Nigel Barcham, managing director of Robert Half Finance & Accounting, supporting employees through continued education is becoming a very important part of Australian companies' employment and HR policies.

'It is the offer of benefits such as payment or reimbursement for additional education programmes that can make or break an employee's decision to work for a company,' he said. 'Over the past decade, Australia has truly become a global player, attracting workers from all over the globe. Training on intercultural behaviour should be incorporated into every workplace to ensure staff coming into the organization are able to integrate seamlessly with those already working there.'

Sixty-five per cent of Australian survey respondents, and 50 per cent globally, said that with increasing globalization of business, training on intercultural behaviour would help employees understand cultural differences.

When hiring new managers, 60 per cent of Australian and UK respondents, and 57 per cent of New Zealand finance and HR managers in the survey, believed that a higher level of work experience was equally important to outstanding graduation results. However, 36 per cent of Australians surveyed thought that work experience was more important than academic results while an additional 3 per cent believed that outstanding graduation results should be mandatory for management recruits.

Nigel Barcham considers that employers should not discount the benefits of a candidate's experience in the workplace.

'Outstanding academic results may show a candidate satisfies the role technically. However, work experience will often provide those higher level skills important to managers, such as problem-solving skills, the ability to adapt to difficult situations and most importantly, people skills.

'Those invaluable qualities make for a more "rounded" manager, something a candidate with a degree alone will not necessarily possess,' Nigel Barcham concluded.

Do you agree that work experience is more important than qualifications?

Source: *HRM Guide Australia* (http://www.hrmguide.net/australia/), 23 August, 2006.

3 The organization takes action to train and develop individuals on recruitment throughout their employment.

4 The organization evaluates the investment in training and development to assess achievement and improve effectiveness.

This particular scheme is aimed at tying training and development to business strategy (Goss, 1994, p.70). Achieving the award requires substantial commitment from an organization. It involves a considerable degree of planning, assessment and documentation in support of an application. Again, however, progress has been slow.

The **Adult Learning** Inspectorate published its first report in 2002 on standards of education and training received by adults and young people in England (*Training Journal*, October 2002, p.5). David Sherlock, the chief inspector, was quoted as saying that while his inspectors:

found some examples of world-class provision, too few young people are receiving the quality of training that will prepare them for employment or address the country's skills shortages. Sixty per

---

HRM in reality UK facing skills crisis

A report from the TUC says that Britain's workplaces are facing a skills crisis with more than one in three employers refusing to train their workers despite government incentives to do so. This leaves nearly 8.5 million workers without training. Further, only 11.5 per cent of those who do receive training receive a nationally recognized qualification. The report entitled '2020 vision for skills' is a response to the review of skills needs for 2020, called for by Chancellor of Exchequer, Gordon Brown, in his 2004 budget.

The report finds that the West Midlands has the worst record in the country with nearly 1 million (44 per cent) of the region's workforce not being trained. The North East has the best record but still has 30 per cent going without training. The improved position in the North East is attributed to high trade union membership in the region and the consequently higher number of union/employer training agreements.

According to the TUC, Britain's workplace skills crisis can be solved if employers and the government invest more in adult skills, provide statutory paid time off for workers to train, and give unions and workers a stronger voice in workplace skills bargaining. The report argues that tackling the skills crisis in this way will not only improve Britain's productivity and competitiveness, but also address associated factors such as poverty and social mobility. To promote these social justice issues, the TUC calls on the government to work with partners through the sector skills councils to tackle skills discrimination among women, black workers, disabled and older workers.

The report suggests that more attention must be given to improving the skills of Britain's current workers, because 70 per cent of the country's 2020

workforce has already completed compulsory education. The report highlights research indicating that six million working age people have severe problems with literacy. Many more have similar problems with numeracy. In the next 15 years some 20 million people will need higher skills levels than at present. Improvement in skills levels is essential if Britain is to close its productivity gap with France and Germany.

The TUC argues that unions are in a unique position to tackle the workplace skills shortage and have already made progress in encouraging and supporting workers back into training and education. The TUC's learning and skills project, unionlearn, together with trade union support, helped over 100 000 people to access courses in 2005 by recruiting over 14 000 union learning representatives. The aim is to increase that figure to 22 000 by the end of the decade supporting over a quarter of a million learners.

Brendan Barber, TUC secretary general, said:

Employers should stop complaining so much about the skills levels of their staff and spend more on training them. Despite many government incentives one in three employers are denying training to millions of workers who need it most. And the government must legislate to make sure that workers get paid time off to train. Britain's unions are already working in partnership with large numbers of employers, through their army of 14 000 union learning representatives, to re-skill their workforces. Government investment has helped this process and it must be increased.

Do employers have any alternative to remedial training?

Source: *HRM Guide UK* (http://www.hrmguide.co.uk), 5 September, 2006.

cent of work-based learning provision was found inadequate. On average, only a third of young people embarking on a modern apprenticeship achieved their qualification.

In particular, inadequacies in the key skills of communication, numeracy and IT use were identified as the biggest cause of young people's failure to succeed with a modern apprenticeship. Key skills were unpopular with both learners and employers, often being left to the end of the programme or omitted entirely.

HRM in reality Employee expectations

A survey by Ross Human Directions (RHD), a recruitment, technology and human resource management firm, shows that organizations are ill-prepared for Generation Y employees.

Who are Generation Y employees? According to RHD, they are the 4.5 million Australians born between 1978 and 1994. RHD's survey, 'Thriving (and surviving) with Generation Y in the workforce', is intended to provide insights into how organizations are acknowledging, understanding and managing the expectations of the youngest generation in their workforces.

The survey indicates that over 58 per cent of Australian organizations have experienced a shift in employer/employee expectations among the younger workforce. But only 21 per cent of those organizations that identified a shift in the expectations of employers and their Generation Y employees believe they are managing this shift successfully.

The survey involved senior HR and operational executives from some 65 organizations across a range of industries. Thirty-two per cent of respondents believed that there was tension between managers and Generation Y employees. Twelve per cent of people in the survey considered that their leaders did not understand the work ethic of the younger generation while another 20 per cent believed the expectations of managers and younger employees did not reconcile, leading to frustration for both groups.

Diane Moynihan, director of marketing, Ross Human Directions said, 'This survey demonstrates that organizations are beginning to acknowledge the values, beliefs and expectations of Generation Y employees. However, it also brings to light the fact that many organizations are not quite sure how to attract, retain and manage Generation Y or what the impact might be on their business.

'With a large number of Generation Y yet to enter the workforce, organizations need to address how they manage Generation Y while harnessing the potential of this creative, innovative and inspired generation,' concluded Moynihan.

Peter Sheahan, a talent specialist and Generation Y expert said, 'Generation Y employees are fast becoming the ambassadors of organizations' brands and reputation. With soaring attrition rates, and Australia's aging workforce, there has never been a more crucial time to engage this generation. "Thriving (and surviving) with Generation Y in the workforce" reveals that while some organizations are beginning to adapt to meet the needs of Generation Y, many have a long way to go.'

Other findings

- Of the 58 per cent of respondents acknowledging a shift in employer/employee expectations amongst the younger workforce, 50 per cent said that they had noticed a shift which may be affecting them but are yet to understand its impact.

- Twenty-nine per cent felt there had been a significant shift in people's expectations which needed to be seriously addressed.

- Generation Y employees rated personal development (80 per cent), career progression (79 per cent) and remuneration and benefits (81 per cent) above things such as stability and security (49 per cent) in their jobs, according to the survey's respondents.

- This contrasts with baby boomers (born between 1950–1964) who ranked stability and security at 87 per cent in importance, while career progression and personal development floundered at 36 and 37 per cent respectively.

- Just over half of respondents said they had modified their recruitment and selection processes (51 per cent) as well as their reward and recognition programmes (51 per cent) to better cater for Generation Y, while 49 per cent stated they had made changes in employee training.

Why are the expectations of 'Generation Y' different from their predecessors?

Source: *HRM Guide Australia* (http://www.hrmguide.net/australia/), 5 April, 2005

Discussion of training and development in the media and management literature tends to become idealistic and evangelical. In reality, many employers take an extremely hard-nosed attitude towards the topic, particularly, as we have seen, in countries such as the UK with a notoriously short-termist view of business. Employer reluctance to embark on training young recruits can be attributed to various factors (Stevens and Walsh, 1991, p.37).

Poaching   Some employers train while others do not. The non-trainers are likely to poach trained workers from those who train. Development requires trainees to acquire general skills as well as skills specific to the training company. Employers are reluctant to offer general skills training for fear of poaching. According to Stevens and Walsh:

> . . . firms may be unwilling to invest in the development of their employees because they are unable to be sure that they, rather than some other employer, may enjoy the benefits of such investment ... investment in training, once completed, is embodied in the individual, and as such is not under the direct control of the firm undertaking the investment.

Whereas Australian and UK firms are afraid of 'free-riders', their German counterparts see themselves as having a responsibility to contribute to the common good. Along with the activities and support of government this attitude maintains a high level of training in Germany. Elsewhere – in France, Japan and the USA, for instance – the poaching problem is less evident since the training of young people takes place largely within the formal education system. Most of the burden and costs are placed upon the trainees.

Cost   Young trainees anticipate higher wages in comparison to recruits for semi-skilled jobs. The reduction in numbers of young people coming onto the employment market has increased competition and wages for higher calibre trainees. Also, people are paid when training but do not produce anything and occupy trainers who are not managing or supervising during this period.

Individual disinterest   Human capital theory predicts that the young are more likely to choose training than the old because their indirect costs are lower than those of older workers. It also predicts that there should be a direct relationship between additional training and increased income. But the perception of young workers may be that there is no direct link: the skill differential may be small or non-existent. They also see that promotions are not based on qualifications. It is known that qualifications are mainly used as filters in the recruitment process. Their value comes a long way behind previous job performance and the selectors' perceptions of their potential. Hence young workers may not see vocational training as being worthwhile. In Australia, an attempt has been made to tie vocational qualifications directly to pay, resulting in a stimulation of training levels.

Weak links between training and performance   Training does not have strategic importance for many companies, partly as we have noted, because of the difficulty of proving the connection between training and improved performance. The problem may be compounded by the delegation of training to personnel specialists or line managers without strategic direction at board level. Lower-level employees are even less likely to be aware of competitor practices than their senior managers.

Development programmes

The fundamental principle of human resource development is that it goes further than piecemeal training. Beginning in this section we examine the organizational and personal decisionmaking processes that lead to systematic, planned HRD programmes. We focus on key aspects such as induction, fostering star performers and management development. We discuss the part played by individuals in their own development, examine the role of mentors and question whether women and men should be offered separate development programmes.

Where does HRD fit into the human resource strategy of an organization? It should be part of a planned and systematic process in which:

- Competencies or capabilities are identified by a performance management system.
- These are matched with needs specified by the human resource strategy.
- Gaps are addressed by the development programme.

Within a HRD programme, training is geared towards planned development rather than being an isolated activity unconnected to the organization's objectives. In fact, HRD programmes can use a combination of organized patterns of experience as well as formal training. It can be an empowering process (Armstrong, 1992, p.152) that provides:

1 A signal that the organization believes its employees are important.

2 The motivation to achieve the skills required by the organization and the consequent reward.

3 Commitment to the organization from an understanding of its values and learning how to uphold them.

4 Identification with the company through a clearer understanding of its aims and policies.

5 Two-way communication between managers and staff as a by-product of workshops and other training activities.

6 Need satisfaction: being selected for training fulfils a need for achievement and recognition in itself.

7 Job enrichment coming from the additional skills obtained from training programmes that can be applied to other aspects of work.

8 Change management: education and training provide people with the understanding and confidence to cope with change.

Dechawatanapaisal and Siengthai (2006) studied factors that shape learning behaviour in the workplace and found that psychological discomfort blocks people from acquiring and learning new knowledge during periods of change. However, effective HR practices can help to moderate individuals' inconsistent attitudes, avoid dissonance and facilitate their learning work behaviour.

Development programmes that fail to treat employees as individuals may be counter-productive. McDermott, Mangan and O'Connor (2006) examined the perceived progress of graduate recruits and assessed their expectations and corresponding satisfaction levels. Surprisingly, they found that graduates recruited by organizations offering a graduate development programme were less satisfied than their counterparts in organizations with no such programme.

Management development

The main focus of HRD for many organizations lies in management development. In principle, anyone can become a manager and many do so without any formal training or development. However, graduates typically aim for formally designated management trainee positions that promise a structured development programme and steady progression through the management ranks.

The trend has been away from long induction ('onboarding') or orientation periods and work shadowing towards immediate 'real' jobs in which trainees perform useful activities, often with management responsibilities. Traditionally, trainees remain in particular functions for fixed periods of time – perhaps six months, a year, or longer. Of late, competence-driven development programmes have required trainees to achieve a certain standard before moving on.

Storey (2001) justifiably observes that 'the panoply of HRM technology is seen in its fullest form in the management of managers'. General management capabilities are developed in various ways. Companies such as Mars, Proctor & Gamble and Unilever have highly structured programmes. Others are more individually based or informal. Training may also involve academic study. At this point it is useful to consider the role of management education.

Management and professional education

Many development programmes involve formal business education, including diplomas, business degrees and, above all, the Masters in Business Administration (MBA). MBA programmes have emphasized rational decisionmaking and a top-down strategic approach to business. It is worth noting, as we observed in Chapter 1, that introduction onto the Harvard MBA was seminal in the growth of HRM. By 1990, American business schools alone awarded 75 000 MBAs of widely varying quality each year.

In the 1980s, MBA graduates could guarantee substantial salary increases and the likelihood of 'fast-track' careers. More recently, their prospects have become less assured. Employers have questioned the quality of the product they receive for premium salaries. Harold Leavitt expresses the opinion that 'business schools transform well-proportioned young men and women . . . into critters with lopsided brains, icy hearts and shrunken souls' (quoted in *The Economist*, 2 March 1991). Such criticisms have encouraged a number of business schools to revise the content and the way in which MBAs are taught, focusing on programmes that are custom-designed to meet the requirements of individual companies.

Nevertheless, academic courses can stretch the boundaries of managers' experience, exposing them to a wide range of concepts, theories and ideas they would never come across otherwise. They also provide students with the means to understand and communicate with people in different business specialisms. McKenna (1994, p.210) argues that academic and experiential learning should 'coexist and complement each other for the betterment of the provision of management education and learning'. Between them, formal education and experiential learning can be used to build a combination of skills, knowledge and abilities – the management competencies necessary for effective managerial performance.

Best companies for executive development

General Electric (GE) has been ranked as the best company for developing executive talent in a survey by Executive Development Associates, a global executive development firm.

Chief learning officers and human resources executives in businesses around the globe were given a list of more than 75 companies in December 2004. They were asked to vote for companies with exceptional executive development strategy, systems and programmes.

'GE received 67.7 per cent of the votes. The survey results certainly reinforce the company's reputation for leadership development. GE's peers view this company as the one to watch for developing executive talent,' says James Bolt, chairman of Executive Development Associates, Inc. The firm pioneered creating custom-designed executive development strategies, systems and programmes, and has worked with more than half of the Fortune 100 and other leading companies around the world. It also sponsors workshops, executive networks, and research to support the success of companies and their leaders.

The 10 companies with the most votes in the survey were:

1	GE	**6**	Bank of America
2	Johnson & Johnson	**7**	Pepsi Co.
3	Dell Inc.	**8**	UBS
4	IBM	**9**	Procter & Gamble
5	Weyerhaeuser	**10**	Cisco Systems

▶

Executive Development Associates intends to conduct the survey annually. 'Research shows us that leading companies around the world lack the quality and depth of executive talent needed to grow and compete in the future, and many companies face increasingly complex strategic and managerial challenges even as their current executive teams are approaching the traditional retirement age,' says Bolt.

The annual survey will serve as a vehicle to showcase firms that consider increasing executive bench strength a top objective of their companies' development programmes and processes in the years to come.

In addition to its '2005 Top 10 Executive Development Companies Peer Voting Survey', every two years the firm conducts a Trends Survey to allow senior executives and leadership development practitioners to compare their experience with others in the field and to anticipate the changes most important to the future. For its surveys, EDA polls senior-level learning and executive development professionals in the Global 500 corporations, as well as members of its Executive Leadership Development Networks groups of leading corporate practitioners who meet regularly to share ideas and best practices.

'The need to invest in the next generation of business leaders is crystal clear,' says Bolt. 'Leadership – creating vision, enrolling and empowering others – has always ranked as the number one topic in executive development programmes around the world. The increasing complexity of the challenges facing organizations means we need to invest equally in building business acumen. Also, if companies are going to have the talent needed to grow and to win in the marketplace, they will have to invest heavily in integrated talent management systems that build deep bench strength, and create metrics to assess their effectiveness.'

Source: *HRM Guide USA* (http://www.hrmguide.com), 24 January, 2005.

Developing management competencies

What are management competencies? There are two main perspectives on skills necessary for management:

1 *One best way*. The generic approach assumes that there is a range of competencies or portable techniques that can be learned and used in a variety of organizational settings.

2 *It depends*. The **contingency** view holds that running an organization efficiently requires competencies or methods unique to that enterprise. This approach emphasizes commonsense, experience, rule-of-thumb techniques and wisdom. It acknowledges the complexity of the business environment. It also recognizes that what has worked once in a particular situation is likely to work again.

Taking the former approach, in the 1970s the American Management Associations initiated a major study of management competencies, whereby 2000 successful managers were studied over a five-year period with the intention of identifying generic (common) competencies from actual job performance. The research identified 30 statistically significant competencies of which 18 were generic and could be regarded as essential for all successful managers (Boyatzis, 1982). The remainder were related to organizational requirements or individual management styles. The generic competencies could be placed in four groups: intellectual, entrepreneurial, socio-emotional and interpersonal (the largest group). These are elaborated in Table 20.1.

Developing women

The low level of women in management has produced a case for special consideration to be given to the development needs of female managers. For example, the provision of career breaks, refresher training, job-sharing and extended childcare facilities can make a considerable difference in career progress. Hammond (1993) identifies three critical stages in women managers' careers:

- joining organizations
- establishing competence in management jobs
- strategies to progress up the management ladder into more senior jobs.

According to Hammond, in comparison to men, women learn more from others and from facing up to hardships. Conversely, men say they gain more from assignments, but it seems that men tend to be given more challenging assignments.

Specific HRD programmes can be set for women focusing on greater self-awareness, appreciation of career opportunities and encouragement to manage their own careers. This kind of programme boosts confidence. It is equally valuable to young trainees and mature returners. Hammond considers that women make outstanding developers. They appear to have more 'attending' skills than men – the ability to work on and care about several tasks simultaneously. However, there are few senior women managers to act as role models.

Development programmes involving seminars or attendance on women-only courses allow many female managers to compare notes, discuss issues in common and make sense of

---

HRM in reality Australians more ambitious than most

Results from a Robert Half Finance & Accounting International Workplace Survey show that 38 per cent of Australian finance managers aspire to lead their company.

More Australian respondents had CEO aspirations than colleagues overseas, topping those in New Zealand (30 per cent), the UK (24 per cent) and globally (23 per cent). Male finance managers are keener on the top job than their female counterparts: 44 per cent of male respondents said they aspired to be CEO – almost double the 23 per cent of female finance managers who had company leadership ambitions.

Around a half of CEOs in Australia are promoted to the role internally. The main obstacles to securing the top job cited by survey respondents were:

- size of the organization (21 per cent)
- too much internal competition (15 per cent)
- having a CEO who would not leave (12 per cent)
- lack of training opportunities (9 per cent).

Despite the finding that 46 per cent of CEOs were recruited externally, a mere 5 per cent of Australian respondents said that a culture of bringing in people from outside the company was thwarting their ambition to make it to the top. Thirty-eight per cent of respondents felt that a financial background was important but the key success factors for CEOs were seen as:

- management capacity (54 per cent)
- good communication skills (49 per cent)
- vision (39 per cent).

Nigel Barcham, managing director, Robert Half Finance & Accounting, said the results underlined the need for companies to continue to develop the 'soft' skills of their finance managers to equip them for senior management positions.

'The results of this survey show that Australia is a stand-out in terms of its ambitious finance managers,' Nigel Barcham said. 'However, organizations should address any issues their employees have surrounding promotion. This ensures talent and ambition is nurtured and those determined employees are able to visualize a clear career path straight to the top.'

What reasons can you think of to explain differing levels of ambition between countries?

Source: *HRM Guide Australia* (http://www.hrmguide.net/australia/), 4 July, 2006.

advancement in what is primarily a male world. Sharing experiences openly and honestly appears to be easier for women than men. Men tend to find it difficult to avoid competing and this leads to exaggeration, denial and an unwillingness to open themselves to criticism. Accordingly, women can gain more from the sharing experience than men. Hammond stresses that they may also bring in life issues outside the immediate work scenario that men tend to ignore.

Coaching and mentoring

Demand is intense for people with the right combination of skills for a particular industry. The market for talented staff, or 'gold-collar workers', is becoming international and the ability to recruit, develop and keep them 'provides a significant and sustainable competitive advantage . . . chief executives ignore this at their peril' (Sadler and Milner, 1993).

Mentor relationships have been found to be highly effective (Key concept 20.3). Kram (1983) found that mentors offered specific benefits in two main areas:

HRM in reality Coaching survey

A 2004 CIPD study shows that coaching is increasingly popular as a means of promoting learning and development. The training and development survey also indicates that coaching is almost universally accepted as a method that delivers tangible business benefits.

Whereas a mere 16 per cent of respondents thought that training courses were the most effective way for people to learn in the workplace, 96 per cent valued coaching as an effective way to promote learning in organizations. Coaching was also viewed as an important way of reducing 'leakage' from training courses and therefore improved their effectiveness.

The survey also shows that coaching is not viewed entirely through rose-tinted glasses. HR professionals are concerned about lack of accreditation and regulation of external providers with only a third of respondents believing that there was sufficient regulation and accreditation of the coaching industry.

More than three-quarters of organizations use coaching but a mere 6 per cent have written strategies for coaching all of their employees. The study shows that most coaches are line managers but just 14 per cent of organizations provide compulsory coaching skills for those who manage staff.

Jessica Rolph, CIPD learning, training and development adviser, says: 'Organizations need to get strategies in place to maximize the impact of coaching for their organization. This will ensure they get the desired business benefits and that employees receive the best learning available.'

Main findings of the survey:

- More than three-quarters of surveyed organizations used coaching as a training method.
- Ninety per cent of respondents considered that coaching was a key mechanism for transferring training skills into the workplace.
- Virtually all respondents (99 per cent) thought that coaching delivered tangible benefits.
- More than 90 per cent of respondents believed that coaching applied appropriately could positively influence the bottom line.
- Line managers were most likely to deliver coaching, but fewer than 20 per cent of organizations had 'all' or 'a majority' of their line managers trained to carry it out.

Rolph says: 'Businesses and coaching professionals must join together to push for greater professionalism across the industry. If pressure is exerted to secure minimum expected standards, qualifications and results, the "cowboy" operators will have no option but to conform. If coaching is taken seriously and is properly managed, it can increase business competitiveness as well as helping individuals attain their potential. However, a number of issues currently exist that may prevent coaching fulfilling its potential: few organizations are training their managers, there is still confusion about standards and terminology, and little evaluation is taking place.'

Can line managers be effective coaches without training for the role?

Source: *HRM Guide UK* (http://www.hrmguide.co.uk), 8 May, 2004

Career support. Sponsoring individuals for high-profile, challenging or stretching tasks; coaching in appropriate techniques; protecting the trainee from unfair treatment.

Psycho-social support. Offering acceptance of anxieties and concerns, counselling from the basis of dealing with similar experiences, providing a role model and friendship within the organization.

Thomson and Mabey (1994, p.60) consider that successful mentors should be 7 to 10 years (or, perhaps, more) older than the individuals they are mentoring. The age gap should allow the mentor to reflect on their own careers and work experience and be able to give considered responses. Key points (*ibid*., p.61) are:

- Meeting with a mentor, typically on a monthly basis, encourages an individual to collect his or her thoughts and structure the learning experience by talking those thoughts through with the mentor.
- Mentors can help to clarify an individual's thinking by questioning and challenging.
- In order to do so, mentors must have the ability to listen well and to probe into shallow thinking.
- The primary role of a mentor is not to advise – although this can occur – but to provide feedback and information on recent developments in the organization.

Key concept 20.3 Mentoring

Mentors are established managers who can provide support, help and advice to more junior members of staff. A mentor should not be a direct line manager, but should have an understanding of the employee's job. Ideally, mentor and junior should have the same gender and ethnic background, so that advice is based on similar life experiences.

Mentors can help build the individual's self-confidence in what may initially seem an unfriendly and perplexing environment. Coetzer (2006) investigated the role of managers as formal and informal learning facilitators in the workplace environment. Key factors included: providing access to a range of workplace activities; promoting communication; facilitating access to direct guidance from workplace models; and designating other learning facilitators. Management practices could also have unintended positive effects on informal workplace learning.

Coaches take a more active role than mentors, appearing in a number of forms, including:

Career coaching. According to Chung, Coleman and Gfroerer (2003, p.141) career coaches act as 'personal consultants for any work-related concerns such as balancing home and work, learning interviewing skills, developing better managerial skills, executive personal and career development, and even managerial training to help managers become career coaches to their employees.'

Executive coaching. Coaches are matched with senior executives, providing 'much of the support that more junior employees expect from their managers. Executive coaches may talk through work problems, facilitating decisions, or advise on the executive's own motivation and developing his or her managerial skills' (Price 2005a, p.281).

Summary

Competitiveness demands a diverse workforce and up-to-date skills. The free market belief in 'buying-in' skill has proven inadequate, even in times of high unemployment. HRD allows people managers to be proactive, focusing on employees as investments for the organization. One of the great strategic contributions of HRM lies in the planning of skill availability in advance of need. Development programmes involve more than training and may be focused on competencies, gender and role. They require constant accurate assessment, counselling and personal challenge. Development also involves socialization of employees to fit the cultural requirements of the company.

Further reading

Swart, Mann, Brown and Price, *Human Resource Development: Strategy and Tactics* (Butterworth-Heinemann, 2005) provides a wide-ranging discussion of HRD and its methods. Stephen Gibb's *Learning and Development* (Palgrave/Macmillan, 2002) provides a good overview accompanied by a number of case study examples. *Employee Training and Development*, 4th edn, by Raymond A. Noe (McGraw-Hill/Irwin, 2006) has become something of a classic. *Human Resource Development: Learning and Training for Individuals and Organizations* by John P. Wilson (2nd edn, Kogan Page) is also comprehensive.

Review questions

1 What are the limitations of the following concepts in describing learning in the workplace: training, education, human resource development, 'knowledge, skills and abilities'?

2 Is a truly meritocratic society an impossible ideal? Does it matter in the workplace?

3 Consider an organization of your choice: (a) Does this organization offer systematic development? (b) Does it aim to develop employee skills as a long-term strategy?

4 Why should businesses compensate for deficiencies in the education of young people?

5 How is human resource development distinguished from training?

6 What are the benefits of apprenticeship systems to a country's human capital base? Should 'new' or 'modern' apprenticeship schemes be restricted to practical skills learning?

7 What additional pressures or incentives could be placed on businesses to take vocational education and training seriously?

8 What are the arguments for and against separate development programmes for women and men?

9 Define the term 'mentoring' and explain its benefits.

10 Why has there been such a strong focus on management development?

11 Why are organizations reluctant to train lower-level employees?

Case study for discussion and analysis

Read the following article. How can we rebalance HRD practices so that all employees receive the learning opportunities they need? Answer this question at the national, organizational and individual levels.

Managers more likely to get training than workers

The CIPD's third annual training survey shows that managers and professionals are far more likely to receive training in the workplace than manual workers. The survey was commissioned from the Centre for Labour Market Studies, Leicester University, who telephone-interviewed over 500 people in December 2000 and January 2001.

Mike Cannell, author of the report and CIPD adviser on training and development says:

> The findings show an alarming gap between the 'haves' and the 'have-nots'. Only 8.4 per cent of our respondents said that managers and professionals in their organizations had received no on-the-job training in the past year, whereas 47 per cent said that their manual workers had received no on-the-job training during the same period. Similarly, although less surprisingly, manual workers are less likely to have a formal coach or mentor than managers and professionals. It is surprising that the main beneficiaries appear to be managerial and white-collar employees given that on-the job-training has historically been a case of manual workers 'sitting with Nelly'. This shift may be due to the widespread use of computers, which has forced every manager to learn about information technology which lends itself to on-the-job training.

Nearly half the training managers interviewed said that they found it difficult to obtain adequate assistance from senior line managers or directors to develop an adequate training strategy. And 16.5 per cent believed that their senior managers and directors had a poor understanding of training and development.

Cannell concludes,

> One of the weaknesses of the UK economy is that we have too many people with low skills and low incomes. It is therefore very disappointing to see that the training needs of some of the very people we should be targeting to get out of this circle, manual workers, are being ignored. The UK economy should be moving towards a high performance/high skilled economy but it can only be achieved if more investment in training, particularly through workplace learning, is undertaken. Maybe one of the reasons for this, as our survey suggests, is that a minority of senior managers and directors are insufficiently committed to developing their employees.

Source: *HRM Guide UK* (http://www.hrmguide.co.uk), 3 April, 2001.

Chapter 21
Learning in organizations

Learning objectives

The purpose of this chapter is to:

● Distinguish between learning in organizations and the 'learning organization'.

● Discuss the relationship between empowerment, self-development and learning.

● Debate the role of the trainer in the context of proactive learning methods.

● Evaluate the use of new learning technologies.

HRD and the organization

From training to development

The learning organization

Empowerment and HRD

Self-development

HRD as an activity

Induction and orientation

Learning methods

E-learning

Leadership development

Evaluating and costing training

Summary

Further reading

Review questions

Case study for discussion and analysis – Lisa

HRD and the organization

Organizational priorities have changed in recent years as the focus has moved from piecemeal training activities to more systematic human resource development. Many businesses have re-oriented themselves away from training individual employees towards becoming 'learning organizations' with the emphasis on continuous learning through a range of delivery methods.

Employees learn continuously but this may take place on an *ad hoc* basis, focused on their own short-term needs rather than long-term development to increase their skills and value to the organization. The aim of HRD is to direct learning and development towards objectives that are compatible with business strategy. **Competitive advantage** can come from the development of an organization's human capital: a learning experience for employees and the organization as a whole (see Key concept 21.1). For some time, this learning experience was encapsulated within a particular model of training: a comparatively straightforward, organized function which depended heavily on planning.

Key concept 21.1 Learning

A relatively permanent change of behaviour as a result of past experience. Learning is taken to mean more than acquiring knowledge. It encompasses the way in which outmoded values and techniques are shed in favour of new ones. At an organizational level this requires a collective process of change in its shared worldview, including perceptions of the company and its market.

The systematic training model, or textbook approach, tended to be somewhat prescriptive, laying down stages and techniques to be followed. Depending on a series of logical steps it normally involved (Sloman, 1994):

- a training policy
- a method for identifying training needs
- formulation of training objectives
- development of a training plan
- implementation of a planned training programme
- validation, evaluation and review of training.

The systematic training model assumed an organizational environment based on slow change, hierarchical lines of authority and clear requirements. It was a logical series of steps centred on the use of an objective training-needs analysis. Normally, this would take the shape of an empirical exercise to identify current needs but bringing in the organization's objectives for consideration. It provided a framework within which the trainer could ensure a thorough and 'professional' job. However, it required a methodical and time-consuming series of activities that do not fit so well with modern organizations.

Today's organizations are constantly changing and have much looser systems of control than the companies of the 1960s. The systematic training model does not incorporate a link with development and other human resource initiatives and, consequently, offers an inadequate framework for modern HRD. For example, structural changes may require the movement of people from activities that are shrinking, or even outsourced, to those which are growing. The skills required are those appropriate to the new work area. It is wasteful in both human and budgetary terms to have to dismiss people in one function while simultaneously hiring new people in another.

Learning in organizations can be approached from either a business or educational perspective. Tight (2000) argues that this is an area in which a variety of 'academic tribes' are operating with only limited contacts with each other, including:

- adult/continuing/lifelong education
- organizational behaviour/occupational psychology, and
- management development/learning/studies.

Each of these 'tribes' has a valuable contribution to make to our understanding. There is a conceptual gap between academic literature on the learning organization and that of organizational learning. Huysman (2000) argues that the two streams of theory and research have operated highly independently of each other. The learning organization stream tends to be mainly prescriptive, linking learning to improvement, while the organizational learning stream analyses learning processes without real interest in the outcome.

Whether or not an organization is growing, there is a need to develop skilled people for the future to replace those who are promoted or leave the company. Consistent with human

---

HRM in reality The new learning executive

Study profiles chief learning officers

A study by the American Society for Training & Development (ASTD) and the University of Pennsylvania has produced a picture of a new breed of learning executive – the chief learning officer (CLO) – that has emerged in the past decade. The challenge of running learning like a business and also making learning a critical contributor to organizational success requires a complex skill set. CLOs must run efficient learning functions that are both strategically aligned with and responsive to the needs of their organizations.

'Profiling a New Breed of Learning Executive', an article in the February 2006 issue of *Training + Development (T+D)* magazine published by ASTD, gives results of the survey of 92 CLOs and identifies the job demands and competencies that are critical for success in this position.

Main findings

- *Time*. CLOs spend most of their time on strategy development and communicating with corporate executives.

- *Biggest challenges*. Communicating and measuring the value of learning, and resource constraints.

- *Greatest accomplishments*. Expanding the scope and reach of the learning function and gaining the respect of executives and business unit leaders with whom they partner to improve productivity and performance.

Brenda Sugrue, one of the authors of the study and senior director of research for ASTD says:

The competencies to which these senior learning executives attribute their success emphasize general business skills (leadership, strategic planning and relationship management) rather than specific and deep knowledge of the field of workplace learning and performance. Additionally, these CLOs recognize the importance of a deeper understanding of the science, technology and measurement of learning and performance.

According to co-author Doug Lynch, vice dean of the Graduate School of Education at the University of Pennsylvania:

The study results confirm that there are many paths to becoming a CLO and the role requires a combination of business savvy and knowledge of key areas of the learning field. Many CLOs are strong in one but not both of those areas, so the Graduate School of Education and the Wharton School of the University of Pennsylvania is preparing to launch a new curriculum that will prepare professionals specifically for this role.

Daniel Blair, director of ASTD's Learning Executives Network (LXN), added: 'The University of Pennsylvania's initiative to create a targeted curriculum and credential for senior learning executives will help current and aspiring CLOs better prepare to be business partners within their organizations.'

How does the chief learning officer's role differ from that of a traditional senior trainer?

Source: *HRM Guide USA* (http://www.hrmguide.com), 28 February, 2006.

resource strategy, succession planning links development to career structures and promotion policies. It must also take individual career plans and intentions into account. Typically, such a programme is linked to the human resource plans of the company, reflecting its anticipated needs in the relatively long term. Good employers take this seriously.

From training to development

With its incorporation into HRD, training has become a complex topic with a significant shift in both emphasis and importance from the systematic training model. Trainers experience a conflict between, on the one hand, the demand for higher levels of learning to meet the skill needs of new strategic initiatives and an increasingly decentralized approach to the delivery of learning on the other. There have been changes in responsibility in line with the growth of HRM, new forms of organization and outsourcing. Training may be the province of line managers using specialist trainers as an internal or external consultancy resource or, alternatively, responsibility may lie with a centralized learning delivery mechanism that may come from an external supplier.

New approaches require effective communication between strategic decisionmakers, line managers, specialist trainers and learning providers. Together, such changes have made the traditional model of training management obsolete. Over a decade ago, Sloman (1994) posed some questions that vexed training managers:

- It is accepted that training should be closely linked with business strategy. But what does this mean in practice? How should this be done?
- How should training relate to corporate culture?
- How important a breakthrough are competencies?
- Should the training manager be operating as an internal consultant? If so, what does this mean in practice?
- Should the company be attempting to become a learning organization, and if so, how?

The strategic link with competitiveness means that HRD has become more important, but there have been pressures on HRD budgets. Critical eyes have looked at development specialists in search of firm evidence of their ability to deliver, in comparison to external providers and new methods of delivering learning. Typically, they are seen more as facilitators and designers of learning programmes than as instructors. Gilley and Gilley (2002, p.5) argue that HRD may be sabotaged by trainers who seem more interested in the process of organizing workshops, seminars, meetings and conferences than the organizational purpose of those events. Today's trainers are more involved with strategic decisionmakers but often have an unclear career path ahead of them. In many cases they have become managers of externally sourced learning materials, providing advice and acting as internal consultants. The idea of regarding a HRD function as an internal consultancy has attracted considerable support. It has an obvious appeal for organizations that divide functions into 'buyers' and 'sellers' and provide an internal accounting system which allocates development costs to budget holders. Separate learning centres can be accurately costed and their value established. The role of 'chief learning officer' has emerged at a strategic level.

There are some debatable aspects to this approach. If an organization employs external providers for learning delivery, it can do so on the basis of single transactions. Should these prove to be unsatisfactory, the purchaser has the option of changing to a different supplier. In other than the largest organizations, the buyer of an internal consultancy's services does not have this freedom. Additionally, the emphasis on 'independence' sits uncomfortably alongside current management thought which places responsibility for all human resource activities with line managers. Some businesses have rationalized these conflicts by regarding themselves as 'learning organizations'.

The learning organization

The learning organization 'captured the imagination of trainers and others' in the 1990s (McKenna, 1994, p.210). As we can see from Key concept 21.2, it is a view that organizations have to go beyond sporadic training into a permanent state of learning in order to survive in today's business environment. Adapted from Pedler, Boydell and Burgoyne (1989), key characteristics for a learning organization are as follows:

1 The formation of organizational policy and strategy, along with its implementation, evaluation and improvement, is consciously structured as a learning process.

2 There is wide participation and identification in the debate over policy and strategy. Differences are recognized, disagreements aired and conflicts tolerated and worked with in order to reach decisions.

3 Management systems for accounting, budgeting and reporting are organized to assist learning from the consequences of decisions.

4 Information systems should 'informate' as well as automate. They should allow staff to question operating assumptions and seek information for individual and collective learning about the organization's goals, norms and processes.

5 Information on expectations, and feedback on satisfaction, should be exchanged by individuals and work units at all levels to assist learning.

6 Employees with external links – such as sales representatives and delivery agents – act as environmental scanners, feeding information back to other staff.

7 There is a deliberate attempt to share information and learn jointly with significant others outside the organization such as key customers and suppliers.

8 The organization's culture and management style encourage experimentation, and learning and development from successes and failures.

9 Everyone has access to resources and facilities for self-development.

Garvin (1993) highlights three important areas:

Meaning. A learning organization has the ability to create, acquire and transfer knowledge. It can modify behaviour to accommodate new knowledge and insights.

Management. The organization shows evidence of learning from others, systematic problem-solving, experimentation and internal transfer of information, for example by job rotation.

Measurement. The organization possesses mechanisms that assess the rate and level of learning. By taking practical aspects of its key functions, such as quality and innovation, managers can ensure that gains are made from the learning process within an acceptable timescale.

Key concept 21.2 Learning organization

Not simply an organization which carries out extensive training but rather an organization 'which facilitates the learning of all its members and continuously transforms itself' (Pedler, Boydell and Burgoyne, 1989). A learning organization is one that lives and breathes knowledge acquisition and skill development – the ultimate extension of 'learning on the job'.

The concept of the learning organization remains fairly abstract and, as a senior consultant engagingly described it, 'quite fluffy' (Prothero, 1997, quoted in Walton, 1999). The seminal ideas of the concept come from two main sources: Pedler *et al.*'s (1989) ideas on the 'learning company' and Senge's 'five disciplines'. According to Senge (1990, cited in Price, 2000) learning organizations are organizations in which:

- the capacity of people to create results they truly desire is continually expanding
- new and open-minded ways of thinking are fostered
- people are given freedom to develop their collective aspirations
- individuals continually learn how to learn together.

This set of goals may seem somewhat ambitious but Senge contends that they can be achieved through the gradual convergence of five 'component technologies', the essential disciplines of which are (Price, 2000):

Systems thinking. People in an organization are part of a system. Systems thinking is a discipline which integrates the other disciplines in a business. It allows the 'whole' (organization) to be greater than the 'parts' (people, departments, teams, equipment and so on).

Personal mastery. This discipline allows people to clarify and focus their personal visions, focus energy, develop patience and see the world as it really is. Employees who possess a high level of personal mastery can consistently generate results that are important to them through their commitment to lifelong learning.

Mental models. These are internalized frameworks that support our views of the world, beliefs in why and how events happen, and our understanding of how things, people and events are related. Senge advocates bringing these to the surface, discussing them with others in a 'learningful' way and unlearning ways of thinking that are not productive.

Building shared vision. Developing 'shared pictures of the future' together so that people are genuinely committed and engaged rather than compliant.

Team learning. Senge sees teams as a vital element of a learning organization. Hence there is a great significance in the ability of teams to learn.

It is evident that many of the virtuous aspects of 'learning organizations', such as extensive job rotation, mirror practices commonly found in large Japanese corporations. The concept has been much trumpeted but one can justifiably ask if such idealistic objectives can be met in a harsh, competitive business environment. Critics argue that the concept may be unrealistic and, sometimes, counter-productive. Elkjaer (2001) describes a Danish learning organization that did not last very long and suggests that its short life had been due to the emphasis placed on changing individual employees while the organization itself – its management structures and work practices – had remained fairly constant. This emphasis on individual learning may have arisen because of the general and abstract terms in which learning is discussed in prescriptive accounts of learning organizations.

Sloman (1994, p.27) contends that the goals of the learning organization model are so remote from most trainers' reality that:

> Bluntly, it asks from most managers too great a leap of faith and does not describe situations they can recognize. Indeed, the very phrase 'learning organization' could be regarded as unhelpful; it is firmly 'trainer-speak' and does not carry a high likelihood of achieving resonance with a hard-bitten manager who is struggling to achieve short-term financial targets.

Perhaps the most striking proof that most companies are *not* learning organizations comes from the very existence of training courses. Firms may decide that they require particular sets of behaviours to retain their competitiveness. They may choose to achieve those behaviours by means of training courses. Doing so indicates that the processes which should create and support those behaviours are missing within those organizations.

On the other hand, managers and others learn a great deal on the job – whether or not they are in a 'learning organization'. They learn how their organization works, how to survive within it, and how to get things done. This informal education within the organization may conflict with learning from formal courses:

> The problem thus is not that managers won't learn, or that they resist learning but that they have learnt too much and too well. They have 'learnt the ropes' and these lessons about how their organization works may obstruct their openness to further learning (Salaman and Butler, 1994, p.38).

Organizational learning and its offshoot the 'learning organization' have been criticized as a rhetorical device designed to offer senior managers new mechanisms of control over employees. Huzzard (2001) agrees that the learning organization can be criticized on this basis but considers that it should not be dismissed without an adequate alternative. Ellinger *et al.* (2002) investigated the relationship between firms' financial performance and the learning organization concept. This is one of the few empirical investigations conducted on the practice and effectiveness of learning organizations. They found a positive correlation between seven action imperatives for a learning organization and four objective measures of financial performance.

Empowerment and HRD

The notion of empowerment has a particular relevance in the context of human resource development. There is nothing new in the notion that decisionmaking should be delegated as low down the organization as possible, and that individuals should take responsibility over their own work, but it has significant implications for the career structures and work behaviour of employees. Empowerment is often presented as something provided for the benefit of employees. In fact, its use is often driven by financial considerations deriving from:

Downsizing. Slimmer companies typically have fewer management layers. The consequence is that the remaining managers are not available for day-to-day decisions – they *must* be taken by lower-level employees.

Speed of response. In an increasingly competitive market, customers expect fast, authoritative decisions on price availability. There is no time for staff to refer to 'the manager'.

In this environment there is a need for confident, speedy decisionmaking based on a high degree of product expertise. Moreover, in return for empowerment, employees must accept that career opportunities have diminished. Much of the ladder has disappeared and vertical promotion is only available to the few star performers. HRD in this case is focused on building resilient people, able to gain rewards from existing jobs. Their future lies in 'horizontal promotion', regular moves between different jobs on a similar level.

Specifically, development programmes require an emphasis on decisionmaking and customer-handling skills together with in-depth product and service knowledge. In the absence of managerial backup it is necessary that empowered staff have a wide understanding of the organization's functions and goals. They must be able to function well in unclear circumstances, without detailed prescriptive rules and be flexible and proactive enough to make events happen. Ironically, however, Moye and Henkin (2006) found that employees who feel empowered in their work environment tend to have higher levels of trust in their managers.

It is evident, therefore, that empowered businesses cannot work with the same personalities – including management – as those found in hierarchical organizations. Neither is there scope for rigid specialists in narrow fields of work. Not surprisingly, workers in these organizations must resemble those in Japanese companies where supervisors have typically managed as many as a hundred individuals. They must be generalists with a broad perspective of their role in the organization. Empowerment is especially significant in fostering an individual employee's self-development.

Self-development

Development is the responsibility of the individual as well as the organization. Career success requires self-control, self-knowledge, systematic career evaluation and frequent role change. Selecting a career path depends on factors such as:

- *Self-awareness*: being able to accurately assess one's own skills, abilities and interests.

- *Ambition*: self-esteem, confidence and motivation.
- *Opportunity*: education, experience and social contacts.

People develop their lives and become distinctive persons through an interaction of three processes: genetic inheritance, life events and self-creation (Glover, 1988). They are so intertwined that we may be unable to attribute a particular event to any one of them. Genetic inheritance determines much of our physical and mental capabilities. Hence the opportunity to succeed in education or business is constrained, to some extent, by inherited factors outside our control. Even health and the duration of our lives are subject in part to genetic determination.

Our lives also depend heavily on accident or chance since the process of living is predominantly an unsystematic series of incidents. We choose to apply for specific jobs, or particular universities, because they meet our needs at a specific point in time. These decisions produce unanticipated side-effects. For example, later we might find ourselves living in a specific location and engaged in projects we would never have contemplated if we had not taken the job or gone to that university.

However, there are major components of life that are controlled by our own actions, leaving scope for intention and direction. The more we plan and take action, the greater the control we have over our lives. To a degree, we shape our own selves by imagining the kind of person we want to be: perhaps being more successful, being respected, or being seen as kind or helpful. When we take actions that contribute to the achievement of these goals we are involved in a process of self-creation. Few of us have a systematic life plan, but rather a loosely organized collection of sometimes minor aims. Viitala (2005) found that many Finnish managers surveyed had no specific development intentions for themselves. In organizations where management development was well-organized and connected to strategic management, managers were more consciously aware of development needs at a personal as well as at a general level. The study revealed that the managers' development intentions differed from those predicted in studies on management competencies. Technical and business skills were emphasized at the expense of social and intrapersonal skills.

Most people have restricted opportunities, so that self-creation is a matter of taking account of reality and adjusting to what is possible. The following independent development checklist (based on Margerison,1991, p.63) can be useful for this purpose:

- What is the best way to spend my time?
- Who else could do my work?
- What am I improving and why?
- What do I feel strongly about?
- What are my special strengths and weaknesses?
- What am I doing to increase my effectiveness?
- What are the likely benefits and risks of achieving my objectives?
- What have I learned in the last month?
- What motivates me most?
- How many of my objectives do I achieve on time?
- What is my action plan for: one month, one year, five years?

Work is a major area in which self-creation can take place. According to Glover (1988), the search for an imagined self explains much of our working behaviour. Self-creation is not necessarily a fully conscious activity, and people are inevitably constrained in achieving their goals. Some jobs crush any opportunity for advancement, forcing people into behaviour that gives a false impression of the personalities they are, or want to be. The apparently unsympathetic Social Security clerk, for instance, may be a creation of the framework of rules within which that individual must operate. The rules of the job mask any warmth or caring.

Organizations may use customer care programmes to train people in a form of impression management, producing staff who are groomed and dressed in a certain way and use approved body language and facial expressions. This veneer of humanity may be beneficial to some and certainly improves the organization's image, but the end-result is a constraint on true self-expression. We have to be careful that the organization does not take over our true selves. In fact, developing one's self is a learning and a recognition process. Work may teach us about a lifestyle that we do not want (Glover, 1988, p.136):

> We are lucky if work brings out in us things we did not know we had. But we can also discover things about ourselves in a less satisfying way. We take a job because it is well paid, or because others find it interesting, and then find we are stifled by it. Parts of us are denied expression. ('It was not really me', we say afterwards.) Relationships lead to the same kind of self-discovery: in some we flourish and in some we are stifled.

HRD as an activity

There is a considerable variation in the way in which HRD is organized and conducted. The difference is greatest between large and small businessses. HRD in small organizations is likely to be unsystematic while large companies may offer sophisticated, highly-structured and

---

HRM in reality Learning survey

A quarter of British office workers blame their 'David Brent'-style bosses for holding back their development, according to recent research conducted for the online learning specialist, SkillSoft. Sixty-three per cent of the 3000 employees surveyed feel they could be doing better in their career. But many workers say they get no support when it comes to training and career development and bosses fail to recognize and nurture their potential.

The survey also found that public service employees get the most encouragement from their managers with 66 per cent saying their employers are happy for them to develop their skills compared with 56 per cent of people working for private companies. Public sector workers also get more opportunities for on-the-job training – 40 per cent say they get formal training and mentoring. This compares with 31 per cent in private firms who receive the same level of support.

According to Kevin Young, managing director of SkillSoft: 'It's evident from this study that a large number of people are not being given the opportunity to live up to their potential at work; particularly in the private sector. Just consider the productivity gains that could be achieved if UK businesses stepped up their commitment to developing their employees' skills.'

Sixty-four per cent of those surveyed said their employer allowed them no time in the working day for their professional development. Eighty-nine per cent of employees said they would prefer to be in control of their own learning.

Kevin Young commented: 'This is in line with some research we did last year amongst employees already using e-learning, the majority of whom were taking control of their own professional development by accessing online learning in the office before or after work, or at home in the evenings and at weekends. The effect on their jobs was evident; nearly everyone interviewed could give practical examples of how they had applied their new knowledge at work.'

Other key findings:

- 53 per cent already willingly spend their own free time on professional development. But many more employees said they would spend their spare time studying if bosses allowed them time to learn in the office as well.

- 43 per cent of employees felt that they needed to spend only 2 to 4 hours a week on training to achieve their full potential.

- Asked about the kind of training they needed, 45 per cent said they would like more training in communications and customer relations skills and 50 per cent wanted more management and leadership skills training.

- 67.5 per cent said they deserved higher pay.

- Most employees enjoy their work – 43 per cent saying that they got some pleasure from their work and 40 per cent go as far as to say they enjoy their jobs 'a lot'. A mere 10 per cent said they don't enjoy their job at all.

Is it possible for self-development to occur without management support?

Source: *HRM Guide UK* (http://www.hrmguide.co.uk), 10 June, 2005.

expensive development programmes. What should be the aim of HRD activities? Vickerstaff (1992, p.132) argues that:

> . . . well-trained employees make better products, serve the customer more effectively, and are likely to have more ideas about how to change the process and the product to improve quality and efficiency. However, the benefits of a well-trained workforce can only be realized if the training effort is properly managed.

Organizations can be described as 'upskillers' or 'de-skillers' (Ashton and Felstead, 1995, p.242). The latter use a scientific management approach to simplify job requirements, remove the opportunity for initiative and reduce employees to a near-robotic state. Training (if it exists) in such cases becomes no more than rote learning of procedures. In many instances, increased skill demands are linked to flexibility, increasing the importance of training attached to multi-skilling and job enlargement. Training and development activities are reaching sophisticated levels in many countries.

The role of the trainer – how to begin

Maresh (1999) argues that trainers should capitalize on the innate nature of the brain to:

- seek and perceive patterns
- create meanings
- integrate sensory experience
- make connections.

The trainer should aim to:

- become proficient at designing and delivering a dynamic curriculum
- assess learning
- effectively administer *true* education.

HRM in reality Toyota's 'train the trainer' centre opens

Toyota has officially opened its European Global Production Centre (E-GPC) in the grounds of its UK production facility at Burnaston, Derbyshire. The E-GPC is a 'train the trainer' centre where future trainers from Toyota's European plants will be taught production and maintenance skills.

With 18 employees, and an investment cost of 16.3 million euros, the new centre is the European branch of Toyota Motor Corporation's Global Production Centre (GPC) in Toyota City, Aichi Prefecture, Japan, established in July 2003. Like the Japanese parent facility, the E-GPC delivers production know-how by means of a series of 'best method' practices for each required skill. The centre delivers a range of courses in its 11 training 'shops' focused on enhancing and developing key vehicle production skills and equipment maintenance knowledge intended to support the Toyota production system with its renowned emphasis on superior quality.

Training methods include lectures, 'visual manual' videos and other techniques to promote easy understanding, as well as through practical training.

Trainees use specially developed workstations, simulated production environments and the latest maintenance technology to develop their skills. Courses will also contribute to improved safety, focused on enhanced ergonomics, and greater efficiency as employees' skills are honed to perform tasks within specific timeframes. This results in improved skills and higher quality 'built in' to the production process.

Trainees spend about two weeks on average at the E-GPC before taking their new knowledge and skills back to their home plants to pass on to other team members.

The GPC was established following Toyota's rapid expansion in overseas production and the need for speedy introduction of Toyota's basic approach toward 'making things' and its 'best method' practices to the company's overseas production affiliates.

How could small companies make use of Toyota's GPC concept?

Source: *HRM Guide UK* (http://www.hrmguide.co.uk), 25 March, 2006.

Maresh argues that 'in the process trainers will release learners' intrinsic drive to acquire knowledge, an admirable outcome from any training.'

People come to learn with a variety of previous experiences, needs and skills, so Maresh advises us to create common ground as a first step in the training process – and every subsequent learning segment. By this she means entering into a dialogue with the members of the training group, acknowledging their experience and speaking directly to 'the familiar frustrations, joys, and challenges that link up to the learning task at hand.'

This is done through a series of questions that highlight the backgrounds of individual members, identify their concerns and gain commitment to the learning process. Maresh suggests 'enrolment' questions beginning with 'How many people have ever . . .' but not relying on just a show of hands. It is essential to elicit information and comments. Moreover, the trainer should repeat what members have said so that everyone hears and to validate the members who made those statements.

For example, a training session on selection interviewing could begin with enrolment questions such as:

- How many people here have been trained as interviewers?
- How many of you have a lot of experience as interviewers, whether or not you have been trained?
- And how many have very little experience of interviewing?
- Any with none at all?
- But surely you all been interviewed by someone else?

Questions such as these should involve everyone in the room and also bring out comments, questions and friendly banter – as well as telling the trainer what level of training will be needed for the group. The common ground acts as a basis for group awareness. When the audience begin to see themselves as a group, they begin to relax and feel comfortable entering into the learning process together. The stage is now set for the trainer to address what Maresh calls the 'big why' in the trainees' minds. Remember that we are building connections and relating to previous experiences. So the purpose, method and intended results of the training need to be explained in relation to the answers given to the enrolment questions. The importance of the subject – especially in relation to trainees' own experience – and what can be done with the learned skills when trainees get back to work should be explored.

Then, Maresh advises, the trainer should say something about his or her own background, ideally using a personal story involving the subject of the training session. According to Maresh:

> This connects the leader to the participants in an esssential way. People's experiences are dramatic. They include emotions, mystery, tension, climaxes and humor. When personal stories are recounted, learners emotionally identify with the parts that have meaning to them, and this confirms their commitment to participate. Personal stories bond the audience to the instructor, the course content, and other participants.

She also addresses the logical component of the adult learner's mind by stressing the need to provide an agenda or list of learning objectives at this point. The team members need to know what the outcomes of the course will be.

Gibb (2002, p.86) summarizes the characteristics of good instructors:

- Being consistent in their ability to manage repeated delivery of the same learning and development (L&D) event.
- Being meticulous and obsessively organized in order to ensure that all aspects of instruction are effective.
- Being sympathetic to learners of different abilities.
- Being patient with the process of showing and telling, trial and error.
- Being objective in assessing others' knowledge, capabilities and behaviour.

Training needs

Customer demands are driving training for service and product quality but this is generally focused on 'core' staff with career structures rather than part-time and temporary employees. However, the latter tend to be highly visible to customers, particularly in retailing. Studies in this sector and in the hotel and catering industry indicate that, in contrast with the management trainees, most staff receive induction training, some customer care instruction and little else (Rainbird and Maguire, 1993).

In addition we need to distinguish the training needs of the individual and those of the organization. Personal and corporate objectives must be reconciled. Individual employees frequently look for wide-ranging courses that will help them in promotion. They will look to develop transferable skills which are seen as valuable by other employers. In contrast, local management are more interested in training which improves performance on their present jobs, leading to improved output quality and productivity. In other words, employees seek training which will make them more marketable whereas organizations prefer training that makes employees more productive.

Taking the organizational viewpoint, Nowack (1991) distinguished these as:

Training needs: for tasks or behaviours that the business considers important and for which the employee's proficiency is inadequate.

Training wants: when employees desire training for tasks and behaviours in which they are not proficient but which the organization considers unimportant.

Nowack considers the first purpose of a training-needs analysis is to 'weed out' the latter. Rainbird and Maguire found evidence for the balance lying predominantly with the management agenda, with training focused more on organizational rather than individual development. Whereas increasing thought is being given to management and professional development this does not seem to be the case with sub-management grades. Their training appears to be heavily biased towards job and company-specific skills.

A decision must also be taken on whether or not to conduct training in-house or employ outside means. If the choice is made for in-house training, should it be by means of a course or on-the-job? We need to ask (Fowler, 1991):

1 What knowledge do employees need to perform their jobs well? This includes detailed job-specific knowledge, such as product information, and broader knowledge, for example about who is responsible for marketing literature in the organization.

2 What skills or competencies are needed, and to what level? Employees must be able to turn basic knowledge into good performance. Skills can be developed through direct tuition, coaching, planned experience or work simulations.

3 What attitude characteristics do we need? Interest, commitment and enthusiasm are always important but there may be a need for employees to develop a particular type or set of attitudes focused on customer service, for example.

The starting point for any development programme is a clear measure of individual aptitudes and experience. Ideally, individual employees should be developed from where they are now with their own particular requirements being addressed. Different people will benefit from different kinds of training even when performing the same job. If the organization is clear on the level of knowledge, skill or attitude required, development can be geared towards correcting individual shortfalls in meeting these standards. The measure will normally be provided:

• Through the performance appraisal process, which should identify each employee's personal training needs as agreed by the individual's supervisor. Sloman (1993) found this to be the primary source of information among his surveyed companies.

• If there is no formal appraisal system, from an examination of each individual's productivity and quality of output. This method is commonly used in production and manual work.

- Assessment centres can be employed for development purposes. Normally used for employees seen to have potential for advancement, workers are assessed in similar ways to the centres used for selection. Information is obtained from group exercises, job simulations and psychometric tests.
- Checklists or questionnaires given to individual employees and their supervisors with training requirements in mind.
- Succession plans indicating the likely next generation of managers and their training shortfall.
- Various methods can be integrated into a skills audit of the company.

The assessment should be considered in terms of immediate training and long-range development and a balanced plan produced. Ironically, employees who have the most extensive education and higher qualification levels appear to have the greatest access to and participation in continuing training (Rainbird and Maguire, 1993). There is also evidence to show that part-time and manual workers are particularly disadvantaged along with employees in small private firms.

A training needs model

Nowack (1991) proposes a nine-step model for a training needs exercise.

1 Prepare a job profile Jobs for which training is required need to be identified clearly. The job profile is based on 12–15 dimensions, or job requirements, within which groups of behaviours can be classified. The number of dimensions depends on factors such as what the job involves, its complexity and required skills for effective performance.

Information is obtained from subject matter experts: people who have detailed knowledge of the job(s) being considered. This includes workers currently performing that work, their supervisors and others involved with the input or output to and from those jobs. Information comes from individual interviews, focus groups and survey techniques. Focus groups, for example, discuss the skills deemed important to each job and list them in dimensional categories within broad areas of:

- necessary technical knowledge and experience
- communication skills
- decisionmaking or problem-solving
- administrative skills
- management skills.

Each group indicates how important they feel each dimension is to a particular job – from 'very' to 'not' important. They are also asked to estimate the likely frequency of occurrence of each dimension in terms of 'several times a day/week/month/year'. The lists are compared and integrated to form a definitive job profile.

2 Preparing a learning or training needs questionnaire This is a critical part of the process. Targeted towards particular jobs or job levels in the organization, it is addressed to the people performing the jobs and their immediate supervisors. It includes questions aimed at obtaining three categories of information:

- *Attitudinal*: describing employees' feelings about their work, their perception of organizational procedures and policies, pay, career, management and environment.
- *Dimensional*: summarizing views on the job dimensions in terms of their importance and employees' proficiency (expressed on a 1–5 scale).
- *Demographic*: relevant questions on employees' time within the organization.

3 Administering the questionnaire A decision must be taken on the size of sample required to complete the questionnaire. This will depend on the resources available and the number of people involved in target jobs. In a relatively small organization the questionnaire can be directed to all relevant employees; in larger organizations where hundreds of people may be performing similar tasks, a sample will be more appropriate. The target audience should offer alternative perspectives of specific jobs, for example by asking workers and their immediate supervisors to evaluate the workers' jobs.

The questionnaire should be accompanied by a covering letter describing: the purpose of the exercise; details on how and when to return the questionnaire; and its voluntary, anonymous and confidential nature. Standard methods can be adopted to increase the percentage of questionnaires returned, such as offering incentives (prize draw, restaurant vouchers, etc.).

4 Analyzing responses Returned questionnaires are statistically analysed, preferably by means of a computerized package. A simple mathematical method can indicate the most crucial training needs: each respondent's measure of importance (I) is multiplied by the equivalent rating for proficiency (P) for every dimension. The resulting ($I{\times}P$) scores can be utilized in a variety of ways. For example, mean scores can be compared across dimensions for a specific group or between groups. Alternatively, supervisors' ratings can be compared with employees' judgements of themselves. It is useful also to compare different departments and to check for differences between new and experienced employees.

5 Interpreting the results Nowack suggests that three follow-up questions should be addressed:

- Is there some commonality between the highest-ranked training needs?
- What is the explanation for any differences between supervisor and employee assessments?
- Is there a reason for differences between groups of employees – e.g. senior and junior workers?

Different levels of employee will inevitably have different perceptions of the importance of particular development needs. Workers on the shopfloor may be particularly concerned with day-to-day matters such as dealing with complaining customers effectively, or working a particular machine. Managers may be more interested in longer-term, strategic requirements, such as filling in stock returns accurately and understanding the fine differences between product categories in order to identify trends. These differences have to be evaluated logically.

6 Follow-up focus groups Interpretation of questionnaire results will identify a need for further clarification. This is best provided by small focus groups which can consist of workers, managers or a mix. They can review $I{\times}P$ scores and offer further explanation. Groups should provide a final executive summary that will be useful for managers and trainees.

7 Feedback A feedback of results to managers and respondents is an essential part of the exercise. Planning and presentation of results is crucial for further progress and as a record of the process for future use.

8 Development objectives The goal is to produce an objective for each dimension identified from the questionnaire and follow-up exercises. They should be tied to an explicit statement of the competencies required for effective performance of the jobs in question. Each training need must be categorized as:

- imparting knowledge
- changing attitudes
- modifying behaviour.

Having done this, the criteria for successful training can be established. For example, if delegation skills are a training need, what behaviour needs to be established by the trainee?

9 A pilot training programme This is a prototype used to test the conclusions of the training needs exercise and provide further information for the final employee development programme.

Induction and orientation

Starting a new job ('onboarding') has been compared with one's first day at school. The newcomer is bound to be: a little nervous, but hopefully enthusiastic; keen to impress, but not wanting to attract too much attention; anxious to learn quickly, but not wanting to be deluged with names, facts and figures; hoping to fit in, but not look too 'new' and inexperienced.

The reception from the employer should ideally anticipate these feelings. After all, the organization has spent good money hiring the newcomer and should treat that person as an investment to be nurtured and encouraged. In reality, however, new recruits are likely to receive an induction or orientation which can be anywhere between two extremes:

In at the deep end: expecting the recruit to get on with the job without any real welcome or information.

Overwhelming: providing the newcomer with an avalanche of introductions, site tours, information packs, etc.

Most large organizations inflict at least some of the following on new hires:

- Handing out the employee handbook – the HR department may be proud of it but it is not going to be an easy read.
- Introducing the new recruit to everybody in the business – embarrassing at best, and likely to be off-putting to a new hire who wants to slide into the job quietly. Besides, no one will remember what they have been told or the names of the people to whom they have been introduced.
- Dishing out even more facts and figures on day one.
- Doing so in the form of a lecture or presentation – with slides.
- Doing it again on day two.
- Not giving the employee their own 'home' – workspace, desk, phone, computer.
- Having the immediate supervisor away on holiday, in a continuous series of meetings, or just too busy to be involved.

These activities run the risk of boring and confusing, rather than helping, the new employee. Obviously, there is information that new recruits need and administration (payroll details, social security, etc) that has to be done. Also, there is a degree of ritual – a 'rite of passage' – expected by the new hire, colleagues and the organization. But the process needs to be thought through, especially in relation to timing, quantity and intensity.

The simple truth is that most people responsible for orienting new employees do not put themselves in the new hire's shoes – i.e. do not take account of just what it is like to start a new job – or think of **induction** as an adult learning process that has to be designed to take account of the ways in which people learn. Unfortunately, joiners are commonly 'thrown in at the deep end'. Finding themselves in a strange environment and told to get on with it, they are easily forgotten. Raw recruits are left feeling anxious and vulnerable, forced to make sense of new surroundings and learn correct procedures the hard way. Many managers regard this approach with favour: after all, this was how they learned to cope and get to grips with the business. It is regarded as a test of competence, of machismo, of ability to survive in a demanding environment. This can be a valuable 'growth' experience but there is a considerable risk of individuals becoming disillusioned, leaving or developing bad habits.

As we noted in earlier chapters, there is a well-known 'induction crisis' in which a proportion of new recruits leave within the first few weeks. Effective recruitment and selection takes time and costs money. Careless handling of new recruits can render this easily into waste. It is a questionable way of dealing with a significant investment. In the same way as young seedlings and transplanted cuttings are the most vulnerable plants a gardener has to look after, newcomers and promotees are the employees at greatest risk of disillusion and failure. They will worry about their ability to fit in, their competence to do the job, and the impression they are creating in the eyes of their bosses and colleagues.

Learning methods

HRD managers are presented with an ever-increasing range of learning methods. Traditionally, they have been divided into:

- *On-the-job training*, including demonstrations of equipment and procedures, instruction manuals, and PC-based training packages.
- *Off-the-job training*, such as group briefings, projects and formal courses.

Off-the-job training can be in-house, taking place within the organization, or external, for example at a local college or university. Methods of learning can include (Price, 2005a):

- Traditional lectures – good for imparting factual material and relatively cheap for large numbers of trainees.
- Case studies – good for problem-solving and simulated experiential learning.
- Brainstorming – a total contrast to the passivity of the lecture.
- Critical incident technique – can be more focused and directly relevant than a case study.
- Discussion and debate – encourages critical thinking.
- Role plays – another simulated experiential form of learning.
- Exercises and games – useful for developing team cohesion and skills.

Induction: getting it right

1 Treat each new employee as an individual – i.e. induction must be tailored to orient individual recruits according to their needs. A school-leaver or fresh graduate will require a different approach to a seasoned professional or experienced worker who can 'hit the ground running'. Don't insult the latter – and waste valuable working time – by putting them through the official HR department induction programme! It is not advisable to have an orientation procedure that is applied to everyone regardless.

2 The immediate line manager should be closely involved, even if arrangements are made by the HR department.

3 It is often useful to allocate a 'buddy' or sponsor on the same working level as the new hire. This allows informal learning to take place about unwritten rules of behaviour, location of important services, and all kinds of 'how to's' that are obvious to an experienced employee, but not to a newcomer. Pick a positive person for this role.

4 Pace the induction process. It is not necessary to do everything on the first morning. The newcomer will still be learning in six months' time.

5 Give the new recruit a real job to do as soon as possible. There is nothing more demoralizing than feeling oneself to be a 'spare part' or a nuisance in a busy department.

Simulation is a key element in several of these methods. For example, Cowey (2005) describes how simulations can be used to overcome the perception of finance training as being dry, difficult and irrelevant. Adobor and Daneshfar (2006) investigated factors that promote

HRM in reality Financial services get the most from e-learning

Businesses in the financial services sector have been more successful in the implementation of e-learning than firms in any other industry, according to research by e-learning provider SkillSoft.

SkillSoft's qualitative study involved employees in 16 global organisations: AT&T; Deloitte; FedEx; Hilton Group; Intelligent Finance; Lloyds TSB; Nestlé; Norwich Union; Price Waterhouse Coopers; Prudential; Royal Mail; Siemens; Schlumberger; Telewest; Wolters Kluwer and Xerox. The researchers found that 94 per cent of staff in the financial services sector (10 per cent more than employees working in other industries) are getting the most from the e-learning opportunities offered to them by actually applying the new skills they have learnt online in the workplace.

Asked about the extent to which they were putting their new knowledge into practice:

- 49 per cent (almost one half) of respondents said that they were drawing on what they had learnt online on a daily basis. Improved communications with customers and colleagues were cited as major benefits.

- 28 per cent stated that they had applied their new skills to specific presentations and projects.

- 11 per cent felt that they had significantly improved their database creation techniques (predominantly Access and Excel).

- 6 per cent considered that they were better at coaching and mentoring.

Additionally:

- 55 per cent of respondents had also passed on their new knowledge to colleagues, and

- 98 per cent would recommend e-learning to friends and fellow workers.

Praising both businesses and employees within the financial sector for their proactive approach to e-learning, Kevin Young, managing director of SkillSoft EMEA said:

When we asked employees in other industries what they felt the barriers were to e-learning many talked in terms of lack of company support, lack of awareness, unavailability of equipment and the inevitable workload and lack of time. Although workload and lack of time was cited as a barrier by 11 per cent of employees working in

the financial sector, more than half of those surveyed (51 per cent) didn't perceive any barriers to online learning at all – suggesting that their organizations had already successfully addressed many of the issues being experienced elsewhere.

The commitment to training is also more pronounced within the financial services industry. Companies operating in the sector are much more likely than those in other industries to have invested in the creation of a dedicated training area for their employees to use (32 per cent as opposed to 10 per cent).

Other findings from the survey were that employees in the financial services industry are:

- More likely to have trained online in the last three months (98 per cent against 92 per cent).

- Prepared to learn in their own time if necessary. 26 per cent learn before work, during their lunch breaks or at the end of the working day – 10 per cent higher than in other industries – and 5 per cent regularly learn at home (as opposed to 1 per cent of those working in other sectors).

- Able to select which courses they do themselves (100 per cent against 94 per cent in other industries).

- Adept at accessing the learning they need as and when they need it. 62 per cent typically spend just 30 minutes online in any one learning session – in contrast to 33 per cent in other industries.

Kevin Young went on to say:

In view of the sporadic nature of these training patterns we asked employees whether, when learning online, they completed a course in one go. 78 per cent said no but, despite this, 98 per cent of these employees said that they still learned what they needed to – 6 per cent more than employees from other sectors. This proves categorically that organizations which insist on measuring the effectiveness of e-learning against the number of actual course completions are missing the point. Employees don't need to complete a whole course to learn what they need in order to be effective.

Why does the financial sector appear to gain more from e-learning than other business sectors?

Source: *HRM Guide UK* (http://www.hrmguide.co.uk), 30 April, 2004.

Key concept 21.3 E-learning

Pantazis (2002) defines e-learning as '. . . instructional content or learning experiences delivered or enabled by electronic technology.'

---

the effective use of simulations in management education. They found that the nature of the simulation and team dynamics affected learning and performance. Positive effects were associated with: the extent to which users perceived the simulation as reflective of real life situations; the ease of use of the simulation; and task conflict, measured by the degree of exchange of ideas. Emotional conflict in the team had a negative association with learning.

E-learning

'E-learning has followed the pattern of the internet – a journey from unrealistic "hype" to a more modest but increasingly important reality. In the late 1990s and early 2000s e-learning was discussed in dramatic terms as a revolution in learning technology that would become a massive industry in a few years. But uptake was slow and largely confined to organizations with a strong focus on information technology. Today, e-learning is increasingly seen as one among many possible elements of open learning and workplace training programmes' (Price, 2005b).

E-learning is computer-based learning, often using internet technology, to deliver interactive learning materials to any location. It has become a major feature in the delivery of learning in recent years. Some of the main reasons for using e-learning include Driscoll (2002: p.8):

Reducing travel and related costs. Trainees do not need to travel away from the workplace.

Enabling learning any time and any place. Training can be accessed from work, home or anywhere in between.

Providing just-in-time learning.

Leveraging existing infrastructure. Existing equipment, networks and facilities can be used.

Enabling delivery independent of a platform. Accessible from any computer system.

Providing tools for tracking and record-keeping. Can be integrated with human resource information systems.

Making updates easy.

Waight and Stewart (2005) studied factors influencing companies' efforts to value the adult learner in e-learning. They describe an interdependence between:

1 Championing factors – leadership, learning culture, technology infrastructure, finance.
2 Antecedents – needs assessment, learning analysis, work setting analysis, work analysis, content analysis, task analysis.
3 Moderators – return on investment, learning theory application, technology and creativity.

They argue that engagement, learning and transfer can be achieved via e-learning if desirable championing factors, antecedents, and moderators are adhered to.

Servage (2005) suggests that the vagueness of e-learning terminology reflects uncritical approaches to e-learning. Servage's review finds North American practitioner literature dominated by concerns about cost and technology in strategizing and implementation to the near exclusion of workers' learning and affective needs. Servage argues that organizational decisionmakers should seek the input and perspective of multiple stakeholders to ensure that e-learning strategies are appropriate not only in terms of financial and technological feasibility but also in the interests of lasting positive effects on employees and organizational culture.

Action learning

Many years before the concept of e-learning was thought of, Revans (1972) argued that classroom-based management education is not adequate (see Table 21.1). He devised a systematic, experiential or 'action learning' programme based on job exchanges that placed managers in unfamiliar situations and asked them to take on challenging tasks. These tasks should have the following characteristics:

1 Based on real work projects.
2 Projects must be owned and defined by senior managers and be important to the future of the organization.
3 The process is an investment requiring a real return on cost.

HRM in reality E-learning reinforces staff loyalty at Hilton

Global hotel group, Hilton, part of Hilton Hotels Corporation, has found a link between employee development and reduced staff turnover for the second year running.

In a worldwide survey of 1500 'team members' conducted anonymously in May 2006, 40 per cent said that the opportunity for development through Hilton University, the group's online learning platform, was the main reason why they intended to continue their careers with Hilton. A further 49 per cent said it was not the main factor but being given the chance to develop professionally was very important to them. Hilton employees around the world can access a wide range of learning activities through Hilton University, including:

- 550 SkillSoft e-learning courses – covering business, professional and IT skills.
- Books24×7 Referenceware – featuring best-selling management, business and technology books and reference materials.
- Online mentoring.
- Virtual classrooms.

The survey also highlighted how learning is being applied in the workplace with over 70 per cent of respondents saying that what they learned yesterday during a learning activity can be used in their work today.

Kevin Young, general manager of SkillSoft EMEA, commented:

> The fact that such a significant number of people are so quickly putting into practice what they've learned is a

good example of the value of just-in-time learning. Being able to use new skills and knowledge immediately means that they are more likely to be retained and used again.

Maarten Staps, international learning and development manager at Hilton who had responsibility for the study, said:

> After conducting this study for the second year, it is encouraging to see that an even greater proportion of team members are remaining loyal to Hilton due to the development opportunities offered through Hilton University. This will have an inevitable impact on the business, both in terms of increased productivity as well as in reduced recruitment costs.

Other findings:

- Over 85 per cent of survey respondents rated Hilton University as 'very good' or 'good'.
- Virtually all (99 per cent) said that they would recommend it to colleagues.
- 90 per cent were convinced that the resources offered to them through Hilton University helped them with their professional development.
- Asked where they liked to learn, team members overwhelmingly said they preferred to learn at their desks or at home. However, an increasing number of respondents are using dedicated Learning Zones within Hilton hotels and offices.

Is the Hilton model applicable to any company?

Source: *HRM Guide USA* (http://www.hrmguide.com), 5 August, 2006.

4 Managers must work in groups, learning from each other and crossing boundaries between functions and departments.

5 Projects must go beyond analysis – they should require real action and change.

6 Content (programmed knowledge) and process (questions/methods) of change should be studied.

7 There must be public commitment from participants to action/report.

Revans' ideas are consistent with the principles of the learning organization discussed earlier in this chapter. The emphasis lies with learning rather than training and with meeting the changing needs of an organization in a competitive world. His approach is also mirrored in many current programmes aimed at developing leaders. Margerison (2002), a keen exponent of action learning, comments:

> Management courses should not be separated from the reality of work. Indeed, a management programme should be based on the issues identified by those attending, and the tutor needs to have the consulting skills to respond to the demands. Courses should be integral to both work and careers and based on what the participants are doing. By focusing on real issues, they can learn with and from others how to tackle them.

But, he also notes that although this is a nice idea, it is hard to do:

> After all, who is running the management development show – the trainers (and that term says it), or the people who do the line management job? Too often, it is the trainers for they insist on running their role-plays, exercises, case studies and giving their standard talks. They are input led. My view is that we should be output led, and follow the needs of the participants in a more mentoring, coaching and facilitating role.

Action learning can be integrated with e-learning. Waddill (2006) investigated the impact of the action learning process on the effectiveness of management level web-based instruction (WBI) or e-learning. Converting a leader-led course proved challenging to facilitate, but the action learning online method was found to be effective.

Leadership development

'I would argue that more leaders have been made by accident, circumstance, sheer grit, or will than have been made by all the leadership courses put together' (Bennis, 1990).

Traditional	Action learning
Individual-based	Group-based
Knowledge emphasis	Skills emphasis
Input-orientated	Output-orientated
Classroom-based	Work-based
Passive	Active
Memory tested	Competence tested
Focus on past	Focus on present and future
Standard cases	Real cases
One way	Interactive
Teacher-led	Student-led

Table 21.1

Comparison of training and 'action learning'

Source: Based on Margerison (1991).

The skills of leadership have attracted management theorists and trainers alike. Whereas good leaders are comparatively easy to recognize when they are in positions of authority, developing people to achieve the necessary qualities is not so easy. Just as the nature of leadership is not fully understood, the appropriate methods of training and leadership are a matter of controversy. At the same time leadership training is a lucrative area for training consultants, and management gurus have been ready to produce packaged methods. According to Crofts (1991), elective as opposed to despotic leadership 'is all about influence, persuasion and motivation – about making people *want* to do things your way.'

It is arguable that many supposed 'leadership' courses are actually teaching management skills rather than those of leadership. A typical leadership course concentrates on:

- Identifying the nature of leadership and the form which the individual trainee wishes to adopt. This incorporates a range of options from being able to give orders (to 'boss') to a more inspirational form.

- Self-awareness – the identification of those leadership skills which individuals feel themselves to be lacking.

- A general boost in self-confidence.

The focus in each case depends on factors such as:

- Participants' level of seniority. It would be counter-productive to encourage a junior manager to adopt the manner and style appropriate to a managing director.

- The organizational culture in which trainees have to operate. Authoritarian forms of leadership would be disastrous in a participative business.

HRM in reality Business-driven action learning

Business, in the past, was not particularly interested in fostering learning and the self-development of its people, says Dr Yury Boshyk, author and international expert on business-driven action learning.

But, he argues, the situation is changing with more companies worldwide – such as General Electric, Siemens, Boeing, Baxter Healthcare, DuPont, Fujitsu, Johnson & Johnson, and Volvo Car Corporation – adopting business-driven action learning as a way to explore new business opportunities and develop their best people.

Dr Boshyk, chairman of the Global Executive Learning Network, addressed the 7th Annual Global Forum on Business-Driven Action Learning and Executive Development held at the Gordon Institute of Business Science (GIBS) in South Africa. The forum was sponsored by Standard Bank. Dr Boshyk said:

As a philosophy, business-driven action learning is based on the belief and practice that learning should be tied to business realities, and that some of the best business solutions can and should come from fellow executives and employees. Many of the companies that utilize business-driven action learning are those who also have a high respect for their people and who appreciate that learning often comes from the sharing of experiences in

an open exchange, which in turn encourages reflection and practical application.

Boshyk's Global Executive Learning Network and Victoria Marsick, co-director of the J.M. Huber Institute for Learning in Organizations at the Columbia University, New York, USA, claim from survey results that between 60 and 65 per cent of 45 top multinational companies are using action learning.

According to Boshyk:

Product life cycles, globalization, and indeed, the entire pace of business life and decisionmaking took on a new meaning in the 1990s. The new business mantra included the key words: speed, flexibility, shareholder value and customer focus, and therefore, the need for change. Many senior executives realized the need to align their organizations to these new objectives.

Changing corporate culture was perceived as a top priority with companies' cultural 'baggage' and old ways of thinking as the greatest obstacles to success. Education and hence the learning organization were 'discovered' by chief executives and it became important in their eyes to learn quickly, and faster than competitors. Reg Revans, one of the founders of action learning, used to say that for competitive reasons, 'learning must be equal to or greater than the rate of change.' But, at the turn of the 21st century it seems clear that individuals and organizations who learn faster than the rate of change gain competitive advantage.

Boshyk argues that as traditional executive education provided to companies was seen not to be translated into business results, chief executives began looking to action learning as a more relevant approach to their new emerging educational needs:

> Companies began to realize that knowledge, with an emphasis on 'actionable knowledge', was a corporate asset and therefore had to be developed for competitive advantage. The past emphasis on individual development and learning was replaced with a view that individual learning should be tied more directly and clearly to organizational objectives as well.

Business-driven action learning (as practised in some of the world's best companies) involves five key elements:

- The active involvement and support of senior executives.
- Participants working in teams on real business issues and exploring new strategic business opportunities.
- Action research and learning focused on internal and external company experiences and thinking that can help resolve business issues.

- Leadership development through teamwork and coaching.
- Follow-up on the business issues and leadership development, thus enhancing positive business results and ensuring that learning is greater than the rate of change.

According to Professor Peter Pribilla, head of corporate human resources at Siemens AG:

> The speed at which a corporation can learn and employ new knowledge is a decisive factor in competition. It is not enough to learn and work. Learning and working must be integrated. Only then can a corporation be a learning organization. Action learning addresses this challenge very efficiently.

Gerard van Schaik, president of the European Foundation for Management Development and former chairman of the executive board of Heineken, says:

> Real progress in business is only achieved by corporations and individuals trying out creative ideas and making them work, running into problems and solving them, by pooling talent and scoring with it, and most of all . . . by having fun and learning while doing. Business-driven action learning is a superb vehicle for achieving this.

Why might action learning be more fun than some other learning methods?

Source: *HRM Guide* (http://www.hrmguide.com), 27 May, 2002.

- Trainees' personalities. People vary in their degrees of assertiveness and sensitivity and need to develop a leadership style that fits naturally with their personality characteristics. It is easier to develop abilities that already exist in an embryonic form than to attempt to change an individual's whole character. The latter is likely to be impossible.

Part of the programme would involve a team exercise requiring the solution of a hypothetical problem.

Many courses have taken on 'outward bound' elements. These use sport or other outdoor physical activities that require skill as a vehicle for experiential learning. Such programmes claim to develop management skills such as leadership, teamwork, communication, problem solving, managing change and coping with stress. However, much of this learning does not translate naturally to the office. There have also been lasting physical and psychological effects of a negative kind – particularly with older, unfit participants.

Blended learning

Recently, it has been argued that effective learning needs a combination of methods, an approach described as 'blended learning'. For example, Collis *et al.* (2005) describe 'putting learning to work', a form of blended learning used at Shell International EP that focuses on learning while in the workplace through work-based activities within technology-supported courses. This has been evolving since 2000.

Graham (2005) looked at IT training of existing employees and argues that it should form an ongoing part of an organization's operations, rather than be reliant on external specialist recruitment and panic reactions to immediate skill shortages. Graham states that a combination of a training needs analysis, psychological, skill-based tests to identify an employee's current ability and willingness to embrace the training, and blended learning, have advantages over other training methods.

Ausburn (2004) investigated course design elements most valued by adult learners in blended learning environments that combine face-to-face contact with web-based learning. Most valued were course designs containing options, personalization, self-direction, variety and a learning community.

Evaluating and costing training

According to Rosania (2000):

> The fact is that trainers do not inherently lack power; what they lack is the ability to use their power in a way that consistently demonstrates the value of their service to their stakeholders. Trainers do not need fancy titles or affiliation with certain departments to demonstrate their value. What trainers need to change is their thinking about how they can contribute to the success of their organizations.

Of course, one basic issue affecting the credibility of trainers is the need to demonstrate the value of training to the organization. In a review of evaluation methods, Rowden (2001) states: 'The "beancounters" in the organization are likely to know exactly how much training "costs" but they may have little idea of its value. HR must be able to supply that information if it is to truly become a strategic part of the organization.'

Kirkpatrick (1994) split evaluation into four levels:

Reaction: is the 'customer' satisfied? If the trainee does not like the programme he or she is unlikely to be motivated to learn.

Learning: Brown and Seidner (1998) state that this 'can be described as the extent to which participants change attitudes, improve knowledge, and/or increase skill as a result of attending the programme.'

Behaviour change: how is actual behaviour changed by training?

Results: the return on investment (ROI) or effect of the training on the organization's bottom-line.

Rowden (2001) examines the last two levels in detail. He proposes the following as the most significant for measuring behaviour change: a 360-degree appraisal feedback process and, secondly, a performance-learning-satisfaction evaluation system. In practice, evaluation is seen as a weak link in the learning process. 'It is the step most likely to be neglected or underdone' (Gibb, 2002, p.107).

Sloman (1993) found that organizations were placing increasing importance on training effectiveness and value for money. More than half of his surveyed companies evaluated every training event and many others were examining ways of doing so. Virtually all respondents had training budgets but practice on decentralizing these varied widely. Many training budgets were held by line managers with a charging mechanism for training activities organized by training departments. One respondent (Sony Manufacturing) abandoned this practice because 'training was not high on people's agenda' and departmental budget spends were not being analysed properly. Other sources indicate a wider problem. For example, of 200 organizations which were 'committed to training', attending conferences held by the UK Work Foundation, only 10 per cent had an evaluation system in place (van de Vliet, 1993). However, by 1999 an IPD survey found that at least 75 per cent of organizations were using some form of evaluation.

What methods are used in practice? The most obvious are 'happy-sheets' or questionnaires handed out to participants on completion of a training course. These are forms that ask trainees to rate the presentation and usefulness of the course and invite comments. The inherent flaws of this approach are well-known (Lewis, 1991):

- They are usually completed in the euphoric period at the end of the course when trainees are relieved to have survived, when they are looking forward to going home, and pressure and stress have lifted. At this point in time the world has taken on a comfortable, rosy glow.

- A personal relationship has been developed with the trainers, so criticism is toned down to avoid upsetting them.

- Most of all, the evaluation concentrates on the wrong issues. Often there is cursory attention to the value of the training experience to the trainees, their future job performance and hence the organization. Instead, forms are likely to concentrate on the overall enjoyability of the course and the quality of the environment in which it took place. According to McKenna (1994, p.212): 'It is known for trainees to be throughly satisfied with a programme merely because the instructor or trainer did a good job entertaining them.' Happy-sheets are excellent for comments on the comfort of hotel accommodation, speed and service in the restaurant and the stuffiness of seminar rooms. Usually they tell us little about the cost-effectiveness of the programme.

HRM in reality Blended learning produces maximum business benefit

A recent survey of 35 major learning organizations shows that multi-pronged learning initiatives – an approach commonly known as blended learning – produces the greatest business benefit. The 2004 e-Learning Trends survey was conducted by THINQ Learning Solutions, Inc.

Ninety-two per cent of respondents rated e-learning programmes as the most effective element in their learning activities, followed by instructor-led training courses at 86 per cent. Most organizations surveyed also included programmes such as virtual classrooms and on-the-job training within their blended learning initiatives – far more frequently than face-to-face tutoring and mentoring.

Along with a range of delivery methods, organizations surveyed were also making the most of varied content offerings. This included commercial off-the-shelf content (COTS) from major vendors such as Thomson NETg and SkillSoft. Virtually all respondents said that their organizations had more than 100 e-learning course titles in circulation or available to their trainees.

But COTS is not adequate for most organizations – 80 per cent of respondents said that they used custom content created specifically for their own needs. Over 90 per cent of the organizations using custom content designed it in-house using authoring tools such as Macromedia's Flash and Dreamweaver technologies.

'There is no one size fits all in a progressive learning organization,' said Ray Maskell, CEO of THINQ

Learning Solutions. 'To optimize the return on investment in training initiatives, organizations are integrating a variety of programmes thereby catering to a broader portion of their workforce. E-learning may be beneficial to one group of employees whereas live instructor-led sessions may be more conducive to the learning habits of others. Blended learning allows industry-leading learning organizations to accommodate individual learning styles while ensuring that critical content is delivered and understood.'

Other significant findings included:

- *Standards.* 75 per cent of respondents said they were SCORM (Sharable Object Reference Model) 1.2 compliant and 66 per cent complied with AICC HACP (Aviation Industry CBT Committee HTTP AICC Communications Protocol).

- *Mobility.* This is a hot topic in the learning industry but fewer than 15 per cent of surveyed organizations were currently using wireless technology in the training environment.

- *Learning Content Management Systems (LCMS).* 34 per cent of respondents were currently using a Learning Content Management System. A further 28 per cent expected to adopt or implement an LCMS in the next two years.

Does blended learning offer the best learning approach?

Source: *HRM Guide USA* (http://www.hrmguide.com), 29 April, 2004.

The evaluation of training has attracted considerable attention (Crittan, 1993). A number of models exist of which Hamblin's (1974) is, perhaps, the best known. Hamblin stratified training into five levels, which could be evaluated independently:

Level 1. The reactions of trainees during training to the trainer, other trainees and external factors.

Level 2. Learning achieved during training, assuming basic aptitude and receptiveness on the part of the trainee.

Level 3. Job behaviour in the work environment at the end of the training period.

Level 4. The overall effects on the organization.

Level 5. Ultimate values: factors such as business survival, profit, welfare of interested parties and social/political welfare.

However, the fact that such models exist has not led many organizations to use them! Hendry (1995, p.366) echoes some astute criticisms of evaluation:

> The whole notion of evaluation is based on training as a discrete event – namely the training course – and justifying the substantial visible costs associated with off-the-job courses and full-time training staff. Take these away, as Hamblin (1974) and Crittan (1993) have observed, and the rationale and pressure for evaluation largely collapses. Evaluation of training events was always a fallacy as long as it ignored the equally important process of practice back on the job which ensures that training transfers.

In practice, Hendry (1995, p.364) argues that the most progressive firms use a mixture of:

'Hard' evaluation criteria. Short-term improvements in measurable performance, such as individual productivity and quality adherence.

'Soft' criteria. Indirect benefits from intermediate human resource goals, including reduction in staff turnover, promotability and flexibility.

Tamkin, Yarnall and Kerrin (2002) and Gibb (2002) concur that although evaluation has grown in priority in recent years, most evaluation activity is unsophisticated. According to Gibb (*ibid.*, p.120):

> So while L&D evaluation is at least now done more widely than ever before it is stuck at the most basic level possible, with the prevalence and preference in L&D for using the basic recipes of levels of evaluation . . . In the end the formulas and techniques for evaluation of L&D have to balance the demands of scientific rigour with those of professional practice, and the theoretical goals of 'truth seeking' with the practical goals of 'pragmatic management'.

Summary

A much-publicized modern approach places development within the learning organization, which contrasts with older notions of learning within organizations. HRD focuses strongly on management development. Career plans, performance objective-setting and training programmes are more often directed at managers than lower-level employees.

With the integration of training activities into human resource development programmes trainers are particularly concerned with cost-effectiveness, quality and the merits of formal as opposed to experiential training. A widening range of learning methods allows employees to acquire information and skills in an active, self-directed manner.

Further reading

Telling Ain't Training by Harold D. Stolovitch and Erica J. Keeps (ASTD, 2002) is an engaging book written by two training professionals but useful for a wider audience. *New Directions in Career Planning and the Workplace: Practical*

Strategies for Career Management Professionals edited by Jean M. Kummerow (Davies-Black Publishing, 2000) includes exercises and examples. *The Action Learning Guidebook* by William J. Rothwell (Jossey-Bass, 1999) covers the action learning process. See also *Beyond E-Learning: Approaches and Technologies to Enhance Organizational Knowledge, Learning, and Performance*, by Marc J. Rosenberg (Pfeiffer, 2005). *Evaluating Training Programs: The Four Levels*, by Donald L. Kirkpatrick, 4th edn (Berrett-Koehler, 2005). *How to Measure Training Success* by Jack Phillips and Ron D. Stone (McGraw-Hill, 2002) extends Kirkpatrick's methodology to include return on investment (ROI).

Review questions

1 What are the main forces driving change in the work of professional trainers?

2 How would you distinguish between learning organizations and learning in organizations? Evaluate the view that 'learning organizations are just hype'.

3 What are the most significant links between performance management and learning and development?

4 There has been a trend towards proactive learning and away from passive training. Should the 'training needs analysis' be modified to become more of a 'learning needs analysis'? If so, how?

5 How has the concept of career development changed in recent years? What are the implications of the reduction in management layers in many large organizations on individual career aspirations?

6 Can anyone be a good trainer? Do we still need training specialists if people can learn for themselves?

7 Outline the essential differences between action learning and formal training.

8 What are the most important features of induction?

9 Is it possible to prove that training is a worthwhile business investment?

10 What are 'e-learning' and 'blended learning'?

Case study for discussion and analysis

Lisa

Lisa was a recent recruit. The personnel manager was very pleased to have taken her on as her assessment centre results were outstanding. She was a graduate in chemical engineering, apparently keen to apply her university training within the organization, a medium-sized manufacturer of aluminium products.

Previous female graduate recruits had received a brief induction period involving visits to all departments, and then been placed in marketing or personnel jobs. None had risen beyond the junior management grades: higher posts seemed to be reserved for men promoted from production and finance. The board had decided that the company's attitude towards women was old-fashioned and was preventing them from making the best use of their human resources. Lisa was the opportunity to do something positive about the problem. With the support of the MD, the personnel manager set out to offer Lisa a development programme that would give her the opportunity to achieve a senior management post within a reasonable period.

Situation

Tina Johnson was a determined and thorough personnel manager. In her late 40s and without much in the way of academic qualifications herself, she was aware that many bright young recruits were going to university before taking their first job. She was also in touch with the greater expectations of young people qualified to this level. She found that they were unhappy with the idea of several years at a junior level before being offered a seriously demanding job.

Lisa did not seem to be any different to the other graduates taken on by the company. Outside the male-dominated production and service areas, there were many female graduates at the lower management levels. Lisa had been with the company for three months and had completed the 'grand tour' which was the company's induction programme.

Tina decided to conduct a development interview with Lisa. She began by asking her how she felt about the company so far.

'It isn't quite what I expected,' said Lisa. She seemed ill-at-ease and nervous.

'Oh, in what way?' asked Tina in a friendly but quizzical tone.

'Well, I suppose I was expecting to use my university training from the beginning ... rather than being shown around places like Marketing and Distribution,' Lisa answered in a very apologetic way.

Tina decided to persist: 'Yes, but we think it's important for you to have a proper induction programme so that you get a basic understanding of the way the company operates. We invest a lot of time and money in our new recruits ... three months is a long time to spend just on induction, you know.'

Lisa continued to look doubtful, and clearly wasn't convinced: 'I just don't think I learned very much, that's all.'

'Why was that?' said Tina, sensing that she had a problem she had not anticipated.

Lisa took some time composing her answer. It was clear that she was fumbling for words that would allow her to express her opinion without upsetting the personnel manager. 'I really wanted to show people that I know a lot about chemical engineering but nobody seems interested. Besides, several people told me that I would probably end up in marketing anyway. Most women do, don't they? Or personnel, and I'm definitely not interested in that.' She emphasized 'personnel' with a grimace.

After the development interview Lisa wrote a letter to Tina Johnson couched in hostile terms, accusing the company of misleading her and having no idea of how to use graduates. She had been offered a scholarship to study for a PhD at an American university and had accepted it. She would be leaving the company in a month's time.

1 How would you have designed Lisa's development programme?

2 What resistance would you have reasonably expected and how would you have overcome it?

Part nine
Employee relations

In this part of the book we examine the mechanisms by which organizations and workers communicate and resolve conflict within the employment relationship. Why 'employee' rather than 'industrial' relations? The latter has acquired a negative connotation, associated with conflict between trade unions and employers and conveys a picture of acrimonious strikes and lock-outs (Blyton and Turnbull, 1994, p.7). 'Employee relations' avoids such preconceptions and also serves to widen the topic to encompass flexible and cooperative relationships between individuals and organizations. As with much of the terminology associated with HRM, the newer term is broader in perspective and indicates a more proactive approach.

The chapters in Part nine address a number of specific issues:

- What is the historical and current status of trade unionism?

- How do different cultural and legislative contexts affect the practice of employee relations?

- What formal and informal mechanisms are used for individual and collective workplace bargaining?

- How does negotiation take place?

- What is the role of arbitration?

- How is 'employee involvement' defined and implemented?

- Is work–life balance a feasible objective?

- Why are health and safety matters often neglected in comparison to other organizational priorities?

Chapter 22
Unions and collective bargaining

Learning objectives

The purpose of this chapter is to:

- Debate the concept of collective employee relations.

- Provide an overview of formal employee relations, including the role of trade unions.

- Evaluate comparative employee relations in a range of developed countries.

- Draw lessons from comparative employee relations.

Introduction

In earlier chapters we observed that HRM is generally associated with a move from collectivist employee relations – stressing union–employer bargaining arrangements – towards individual-based negotiation, reinforced by personal contracts and performance-based pay systems. The change has not been total in those countries where HRM has been influential and is certainly not universal. In reality, collective negotiation and representation remain common.

The common perception also relates to an outmoded picture – a Thatcherite or Reaganite world – which in many countries is being replaced by more formalized models such as that of the European Union. In the UK and Ireland, for example, EU legislation is steadily bringing companies into line with the attitudes of the social market, differentiating them from their US cousins. This is exemplified by the requirement that all large multinational companies operating in more than one EU country must have Europe-wide works councils, ensuring an enhanced role for collective representation in the 21st century. Ironically, of course, this also means that US multinationals must observe what may be a comparatively alien process of compulsory union consultation within their European operations.

> **Key concept 22.1** Employee relations
>
> Employee relations is not confined to unionized collective bargaining but encompasses all employment relationships. It goes beyond the negotiation of pay and benefits to include the conduct of the power relationship between individual employees and their employers.

The **employment relationship** also encapsulates different cultural assumptions about the roles, entitlements and obligations of these stakeholders. Accordingly, national employment systems are heavily influenced by their ideological and cultural traditions. We noted in Part two that businesses operate within varied legal frameworks, reflecting underlying ideological beliefs in the rights of employers and employees. As an example, we shall see later in this chapter that German companies operate within a social market that places great importance on a balanced relationship between employee and employer. German business culture also emphasizes regulation. Hence the German job market is based on detailed legislation, formalized consultation procedures and protected employee rights. Conversely, legislation in free market countries tends to leave employee consultation to local arrangements and provides little employee protection. Paradoxically, countries such as Canada, the UK and the USA have a history of more advanced equal opportunity legislation than Germany, specifically for ethnicity and reflecting their multi-cultural nature.

We begin this chapter at the environmental level with an evaluation of the role of collective bargaining in different business cultures, ranging from the free market in the USA and UK, through the social market represented by Germany, to Japan as an example of Asia–Pacific approaches. We move on to consider the organizational context and discuss both management and employee strategies.

Collectivization and confrontation

This section considers the problematic concept of the employment relationship. Regarded by neo-classical economists (see Part three) as an exchange of labour for pay, it is also a power relationship in which the employer has the formal authority to direct effort towards specific goals, whereas the employee can – informally – frustrate the achievements of those objectives. The employment relationship goes beyond money to include a number of secondary issues, such as working conditions, the length of the working day, holiday time, freedom to arrange one's work and measures of participation.

Through **collectivization**, workers could band together to protect their mutual interests. From the late 19th century, trade unions have fought for improved conditions for their members. The first unions were formed for defensive purposes, often in response to cuts in wages, denying change without payment and setting the scene for future accusations of intransigence.

Trade unions can be categorized as follows (adapted from McIlwee and Roberts, 1991, p.386) :

1 *Craft unions*: recruiting members from distinct trades or occupations, historically linked to an apprenticeship system. Originally such unions aimed to preserve jobs within the craft exclusively for their members. Technological change has blurred and, sometimes, eliminated the craft skills and unions have survived by changing their membership boundaries to incorporate other areas.

2 *Industrial unions*: for example the National Union of Mineworkers in Britain, I G Metall in Germany. The dominant form in Germany but slow to develop in the UK. They aim to represent all employees in a particular industry regardless of their type of work.

3 *General unions*: broad-ranging unions representing a variety of industries and job types with little restriction on potential membership. Some are so extensive that they have been termed 'super-unions'.

4 *Occupational unions*: recruit members within a particular occupation or group such as teachers, police or fire-fighters.

5 *White-collar unions*: concentrating on non-manual occupations such as banking.

Unions have been described as a mixture of movement and organization (Flanders, 1970). On the one hand, they met workers' individual needs: protecting them from exploitation; negotiating improved wages and conditions; developing career prospects. On the other, unions had a wider, collective purpose which often extended into a political role. Workers were expected to subordinate personal advantage to the greater interests of the membership as a whole. In this respect, trade unions offered an alternative focus for employee commitment and a power base which clashed with the prerogatives of management. The Australian Bureau of Statistics has a neat definition of a trade union as: 'an organization, consisting predominantly of employees, the principal activities of which include the negotiation of pay and conditions of employment for its members' (cited in Visser, 2006, p.40).

The history of trade unionism varies from one country to another in terms of:

Business sector. Focusing on job conditions within an industry or specific company. Initially, unions in most countries were organized around specific crafts such as boilermakers; this pattern remained dominant in the UK until the late 20th century. In contrast, since 1945 German trade unions have represented all the workers in a specific industry.

Ideology. Extending their role beyond the workplace and influencing social and political change to the advantage of their members. Many unions were instrumental in the creation of political parties, such as Labo(u)r in Australia and Britain. Employee relations have been a battleground for ideology, local disputes being played out as skirmishes in a much larger war.

Employee relations in North America

In the USA the prevailing business culture of scientific management and Fordism created a particular trade union response and an irreconcilable conflict between the interests of 'capital' and 'labour'.

Remarkably, the view from the 1920s (expressed in the box text, opposite) remains typical of many US organizations today. In fact, most American management writers ignore trade unionism, taking a **unitarist** (see Key concept 22.2) rather than a **pluralist** or collective viewpoint

(Guest, 1992). Beaumont (1992) argues that this perspective is reflected in a considerable reduction in US union membership and collective bargaining in recent decades. American HRM literature also emphasizes individual relationships and marginalizes trade unions (Blyton and Turnbull, 1994). Unions have been viewed as restricting the nation's competitive position and protecting insiders (those with jobs) at the expense of those without. However, Van Ruysseveldt, Huiskamp and van Hoof (1995, p.2) contend that '. . . no modern society has ever accepted a purely individualistic determination of the employment relationship.'

Geare, Edgar and McAndrew (2006) suggest that HRM theorists appear to believe that unitarism is the norm in employment relationships. At the same time, theorists see HRM as the means to achieving unitarism through the introduction of systems of high commitment management in the workplace. But they point out that a number of authors have questioned these assumptions. Geare *et al.*'s study attempted to identify current employment values and beliefs of workers and management and examined the extent to which these influence, or are influenced by, the adoption of high commitment practices in the workplace. They found a curious dichotomy of belief in that managers considered employment relationships in general to be pluralist, but thought they were unitarist in their own organizations.

Kanter (1989, p.117) describes the tradition of American management as being firmly rooted in paranoia:

> One of the lessons America's mythologized cowboys supposedly learned in the rough-and-tumble days of the American frontier was that paranoia was smart psychology. You couldn't trust anybody. They were all out to get you, and they would steal from you as soon as your back was turned.

Key concept 22.2   Unitarism versus pluralism

The unitarist view is implicit in American models of HRM. It holds that the interests of employees and the firm should be the same. Pluralism, on the other hand, recognizes that every organization is composed of different interests that are not balanced. Pluralists accept that conflict is natural and are concerned with the means by which it can be managed.

Assumptions of confrontational industrial relations

1 Workers' and employers' interests are generally opposed. Employers: want highest output at least cost; try to lower wages, increase hours, speed up workers; try to remove least efficient workers; maintain worst possible working conditions; discharge workers when possible; replace expensive, skilled workers with cheaper, low-skilled employees; and reduce numbers through automation. Conversely, unions: attempt to obtain continuous employment; seek highest wage rates; and look for the best working conditions.

2 Effort and increased output produce lower wages. Employers prefer reducing prices to increase market share, rather than pass on productivity benefits to workers as higher wages.

3 Wages depend on the relative bargaining strengths of employers and workers.

4 Employers' bargaining strength is always greater than the workers'.

5 Employers' full bargaining strength will be exerted against individuals.

6 Individual bargaining produces competition between workers. This tends to lower wages to the level accepted by the weakest bargaining worker.

7 This applies during employment as well as recruitment. If workers speed up in response to bonuses, there is competition between workers.

Source: Hoxie (1923).

'Self-reliance' became the motto of the country. Everything outside one's own control was treated as an adversary and a potential enemy and had to be dominated. This applied as much to trade unions as it did to competitors. Elsewhere in the democratic world, such an extreme position was unusual. Nevertheless, it cannot be assumed (by benign unitarists, for example) that there is a common agenda between employers and the employed that can be 'managed'. There is an inevitable, if latent, tension between the two (Blyton and Turnbull, 1994, p.4).

Historically, unions attempted to replace all individual bargaining with collective bargaining (see Key concept 22.3) in order to increase employee bargaining power and counter employers' attempts to create competition between workers. This required solidarity between union members. Union goals were to obtain standardized wages and conditions at the best possible level. In contrast, employers have preferred to deal with employees on an individual basis.

Key concept 22.3 Collective bargaining

Collective bargaining takes place between employers and trade unions when: employees are members of trade unions that undertake to negotiate on their behalf in matters such as pay, working conditions, other benefits, and work allocation; and employers recognize trade unions and their officials as legitimate bargaining agents.

Braverman (1974) regarded the weakness of workers in the employment relationship as an inevitable consequence of the role of management. He concluded that managers owed a responsibility to the market, over and above their duties to shareholders and employees. If managers did not deliver continually increasing levels of productivity and efficiency then their businesses would not survive. The workforce held the key to survival through their creativity, imagination and problem-solving abilities. However, these same qualities could be used to resist managers' aspirations for change.

Employees were human beings with their own objectives that frequently differed from management goals. Under the 19th century craft-based system of production, individual employees held a considerable degree of power through their possession of knowledge. Very often managers had no idea what workers were doing. The value of scientific management and Fordism lay in their ability to de-skill jobs and remove knowledge, and hence bargaining power, from the workforce. Braverman's original analysis has been criticized for oversimplifying the nature of skill since most workers were unskilled or semi-skilled at best. Fordism led to a relative standardization of the employment relationship throughout the developed world until around 1980, with the following characteristics (Van Ruysseveldt et al., 1995, p.2):

- Permanent, full-time jobs.
- Wage increases on the basis of experience and training.
- Extra payments for inconvenient or anti-social arrangements, such as weekend working.
- Regular working hours and a clearly defined working week.
- Paid holidays.
- The right to collective representation and a degree of consultation on changes of working practices.

Trade unions conducted negotiations with employers within this framework. This form of employee relations was associated with vertical and horizontal division of labour, hierarchical management and close supervision of work. However, in the last two decades – as has been made evident in this book – this pattern of working life has disintegrated under the pressures of competition from newly-developing countries and the arrival of flexibility. In consequence, the 'traditional' role of trade unions has been undermined.

Union activity was focused on people within the internal employment market. New working practices, on the other hand, may reduce the core workforce within the internal market to small and sometimes insignificant numbers. Companies such as Wal-Mart made a practice of actively discouraging unionization. Moreover, in line with our discussion in earlier parts of this book, jobs may be on relatively short-term, or part-time contracts. Variable working hours have become a valuable source of flexibility. Extended opening hours have offered employers the opportunity to generate more money from the same equipment and accommodation.

There are significant differences in union density (proportion of the workforce who are trade union members) between Canada and the USA, and also between and within industry sectors in the United States of America. In the period 1950–2003 union density in Canada fluctuated in the range around 28–35 per cent, with a marked drop between the top and bottom of this range between 1995 and 2003. By contrast, there was a consistent drop in US union density between 1960 and 2003, down from comparable levels to those in Canada to a mere 12.4 per cent (15.8 million workers) in 2003. In that year the union density in Canada was 28.4 per cent (Visser, 2006, pp.44–5).

Why is there such a difference? The prevailing view (see Johnson, 2002) is that mandatory voting has discouraged unionization in the USA whereas card-checking (counting the number of existing union members) has encouraged unionization in Canada. In fact, there was a marked change in the proportion of the Canadian workforce covered by mandatory voting between 1993 (18 per cent) and 2000 (62 per cent). Individual provinces have introduced these changes with Ontario being the most significant (because of its population) in 1995.

HRM in reality Unions still rated negatively

Labour unions are still rated negatively by most American adults, according to a recent Harris poll. But the US public also rated corporate America similarly, although less negatively. Americans give credit to labour unions for improving wages and working conditions for workers but they are viewed unfavourably for having too much involvement in politics and too much concern with fighting change. These attitudes are very similar to those found in a Harris Poll conducted in 1993.

A Harris Poll of 1217 US adults surveyed by telephone by Harris Interactive® between 9 and 16 August, 2005 found that negative ratings of the job being done by labour unions were given by majorities of:

- all US adults (68 per cent)
- all working adults (69 per cent), and even
- adults in union households (61 per cent).

However, 61 per cent also rated corporate America negatively, compared with 54 per cent in 1993.

More positively, respondents (particularly those in union households) gave unions credit for:

- Improving wages and working conditions – 75 per cent of all adults and 84 per cent of those in union households.

- Working to get legislation that helped all working people whether they were union members or not – 50 per cent of adults and 58 per cent of those in union households.

But other significant criticisms included:

- 67 per cent of all adults felt that unions were too involved in politics. 65 per cent of those in union households agreed.

- 60 per cent of respondents (and also 60 per cent of those in union households) felt that unions were more concerned with fighting change than with trying to bring about change.

- 55 per cent of adults said that unions stifled individual initiative, a slight decrease from 1993 when 59 per cent agreed. Even in union households 47 per cent agreed, compared with 51 per cent in 1993.

Why do adults in the USA hold comparatively negative views about unions?

Source: *HRM Guide USA* (http://www.hrmguide.com), 1 September, 2005.

According to the US Department of Labor:

- Men are more likely to be union members than women.
- African-Americans are more likely to be union members than either Whites or Hispanics.
- Nearly four in ten government workers were union members in 2002, compared with fewer than one in ten employees in private sector industries.
- Almost two-fifths of workers in protective service occupations (including fire-fighters and police officers) were union members in 2002. Protective service occupations have had the highest union membership rate of any broad occupation group in every year since 1983.

Van Ruysseveldt *et al.*, (1995, p.7) argue that the 'classic' analytical and theoretical frameworks for studing employee relations reflect the times in which they were conceived and do not provide a satisfactory perspective for today. The shift in the nature of the employment relationship, introduction of flexible working practices and elimination of large, homogeneous workforces have been so significant that any pre-1980s perspective becomes simply a historical curiosity.

Employee relations in the UK

The British were once notorious for industrial disputes and walkouts. In fact, they were daily occurrences in the 1960s and 1970s, such that industrial relations was perceived as a 'problem' which brought down governments. Weak management and intransigent unions produced industrial chaos, manifested by low productivity, hostility towards change and highly publicized disputes, fundamentally weakening the UK as an economic power.

The reputation of British personnel managers was not enhanced during this period. When HRM came onto the scene in the 1980s, personnel management had become bogged down in a form of industrial relations characterized by 'fire-fighting' – undermining any claim to being strategic or proactive (Hendry, 1995, p.12). By this time, personnel management had moved away from its neutral balancing role between employees and management. It had

---

HRM in reality Wal-Mart hits back

Wal-Mart has launched a nationwide campaign to 'set the record straight'. The company has placed a full-page ad in more than 100 newspapers across the USA in which Wal-Mart chief executive officer, H. Lee Scott, said it was time for the public to hear the 'unfiltered truth' about Wal-Mart, and time for the company to stand up on behalf of a workforce that includes 1.2 million Americans.

'There are a lot of "urban legends" going around these days about Wal-Mart, but facts are facts,' Scott said. 'Wal-Mart is good for consumers, good for communities and good for the US economy.'

Scott acknowledges the 'unusual approach' by Wal-Mart to place ads in newspapers including *USA Today*, *The Wall Street Journal* and the *New York Times*. The ad is a direct letter from Scott.

'For too long, others have had free rein to say things about our company that just aren't true,' Scott

continued. 'Our associates are tired of it and we've decided it's time to draw our own line in the sand.

'We understand that, as one of the most visible corporations in the world, we will be a target for criticism. When it is valid, we try to learn from it and become a better company,' Scott said. 'But we have made a commitment to our associates, customers and suppliers that when false allegations are made about Wal-Mart, we will actively correct the record. That's what this day is all about.'

Why would Wal-Mart prefer to engage in a defensive publicity campaign rather than allow union representation for its staff?

Source: *HRM Guide USA* (http://www.hrmguide.com), 15 January, 2005.

become a front-line activity in defence of the organization. Strikes, pay deals and overtime needs were largely dealt with in an *ad hoc*, piecemeal fashion with little sign of any strategy. In a context of industrial warfare, long-term thinking was displaced by short-term coping.

Hendry (*ibid.*, p.13) also attributes the lack of strategy to personnel managers' preference for dealing with industrial relations in an informal and personal manner. Their knowledge of the personalities involved on the management and union sides and their willingness to engage in 'off-the-record' discussions and make compromise deals fostered a quick-witted ability to clinch agreement on the spur of the moment. There was no place for long-term strategy – 'manpower tactics' were the prevailing practice (Atkinson, 1984).

The situation changed dramatically during the 1980s and 1990s. Recessions, 'New Right' politics, restrictive legislation on industrial action (see Part three) and massive restructuring in many organizations considerably reduced the power and role of unions. They also led to the downfall of the industrial relations 'industry'. Instead:

- Detailed obligations between employer and employee were replaced by informal commitments.
- Job descriptions became flexible.
- Job demarcations have diminished in the face of flexible working practices.

Consequently, the new employee relations extends beyond collective bargaining – or rather, two-sided warfare – to include non-unionized organizations where dialogue may be between employers and individual employees and alternative negotiating structures exist. Hendry (1995, p.49) reflects on the perspectives of people in the 'industrial relations orthodoxy' who see a 'persistent weakening of employee power within organizations through the substitution of individualized systems for collective ones'. The development of corporate cultures also offends their confrontational instincts and is perceived virtually as a top management plot. HRM is implicated as an anti-union philosophy (Guest, 1989, p.44) which:

1 Can be aggressively anti-union, advocating the withdrawal of recognition from existing unions.

2 Can produce more generous rewards through individual pay deals, making unions seem unnecessary.

3 Neutralizing or controlling unions through close attention to their activities by means of single-union agreements, no-strike clauses and pendulum arbitration. These can be reinforced with careful recruitment, socialization, communications, teamworking and so on.

Such tactics are theoretically plausible. However, it is difficult to find instances of HRM being responsible for these developments. Rather, HRM tends to coincide with such actions. If anything, it comes into play when dealing with subsequent mending of fences (Hendry, 1995, p.51).

Employees and managers frequently have different goals. Governments have also taken sides. For example, prime minister Margaret Thatcher crippled British trade unions in the 1980s. Recent management literature assumes that the worldwide balance of power has swung to employers. This is described by some as a 'new realism' among both managers and employees. Strikes virtually disappeared from the scene in countries such as Britain. In the UK nearly 13 million days a year were lost through industrial action, but in the 1980s this dropped to an average of just over 7 million days a year. In 1995 the comparable figure was just 440 000, and fewer than 150 000 in 2005. The private sector has contained industrial action by tactics such as:

- elaborate communications techniques
- career development
- quality circles
- performance-related pay
- non-union status.

Further restriction of the union role has come in the form of single-union agreements – limiting negotiating rights to one union rather than several – and no-strike deals. We will see later in this section that single-union arrangements are normal in Germany and that German unions regard them as beneficial. In the UK, however, such developments have led to deep philosophical disagreements and some acrimony among trade unions. Unions such as the mainly electrical EEPTU were accused of 'selling out' to employers and 'poaching' members by actively negotiating for single-union agreements; and, despite the rhetoric, it is clear that realism has driven most major unions into similar deals (Goss, 1994, p.142).

Intriguingly, Brown (1994) finds that during the 1980s average pay rises were higher in non-unionized than unionized businesses. Moreover, this was not due to single-union agreements. He finds no evidence that non-unionism in this period was associated with 'progressive' management developments such as HRM. Non-unionism is linked to the absence of a bargaining structure, but Brown argues that removing trade unions leads to worse people management. This is reflected in inferior training, health and safety, and dismissal practices. By their very existence, unions force managers to manage.

For whatever reason, strikes and other cases of reported industrial action are considerably more common in larger organizations. This is not necessarily due to the atmosphere being better in small companies; an obvious corollary is that far fewer people in small firms are members of unions. This is because employers in small companies actively discourage union organization, while unions are not particularly interested in small groups of staff who would need far more attention and provide relatively little extra benefit in either monetary or political terms.

Matlay (2002) observes that although small and medium-size enterprises (SMEs) are becoming increasingly significant, most of the research on employee relations has been conducted in large organizations. In Matlay's opinion, the few studies that have focused on small firms tend to be prescriptive, categorizing workplaces into simplistic 'small is beautiful' or 'bleak house' alternatives. Matlay's own survey of 6000 organizations finds that small business owners or managers tend to use a personalized and informal management style, and that employee relations are widely varied.

The Employment Relations Act 1999

The Employment Relations Act 1999 introduced:

- A statutory procedure for trade unions to be recognized (or derecognized) for collective bargaining purposes in organizations employing more than 20 workers. The Act provides for recognition to be awarded by an independent public body (the Central Arbitration Committee) where: (a) either a majority of the relevant workforce are union members (so-called 'automatic recognition'); or (b) following a ballot where a majority of those voting, and at least 40 per cent of those entitled to vote, support recognition.

- The right for a worker to be accompanied by a trade union official at disciplinary and grievance hearings.

- New protections against dismissal for employees taking official, lawfully organized industrial action, making it unfair to dismiss in the eight weeks following the commencement of action and thereafter if the employer has not taken all reasonable procedural steps to resolve the dispute.

- Strengthened rights to belong to a union.

- Measures to promote family-friendly working.

- Reform of tribunal awards for unfair dismissal (for example, by raising the maximum limit of compensatory awards from £12 000 to £50 000).

A DTI review of the Act early in 2003 indicated that it is succeeding in delivering better working standards and promoting a new climate of cooperation between workers and employers. Key findings of the review suggest that the recognition procedure has operated smoothly with cases now decided in less than half the time, and that inter-union disputes and legal challenges are rare. Also, the Act has encouraged voluntary settlement of recognition claims since 1998.

Moore (2006) focused on employer perspectives of the bargaining process and found evidence of dynamic relationships following voluntary trade union recognition. In the majority of 213 cases examined, there had been collective bargaining on core issues of pay, hours and holiday. There was less likely to have been negotiation over pensions, equal opportunities and training. A proportion of voluntary agreements have been formally limited to core issues, reflecting the influence of The Employment Relations Act 1999 in shaping the nature of voluntary recognition.

The DTI considered modifying aspects of trade union law, including the law on political fund ballots and union elections to lighten the administrative burdens on unions. But the review finds no evidence to support changing the central pillars of the Act, such as:

- The rules governing automatic recognition, where the majority are union members.
- The 40 per cent threshold for statutory recognition ballots.
- The exclusion of workplaces with less than 21 employees from statutory recognition.
- The eight-week period of protection for striking workers against dismissal – though the review suggests that days on which workers are locked out might be disregarded.

The European Union

Since the signing of the Treaty of Rome in 1958, there have been several attempts to develop community-wide initiatives on employee participation and corporate industrial relations. Progress in harmonizing this area has been slow but there has been a considerable convergence of employment conditions. The resistance of British Conservative governments towards

---

HRM in reality Union recognition deals tougher to secure

Today's annual TUC Trade Union Trends 'Focus on Recognition' survey shows that the number of agreements signed with employers has fallen despite a trebling of the number of trade union campaigns for recognition deals.

A total of 61 deals were recorded between November 2004 and October 2005, covering 12 000 employees compared with 179 (covering 20 000 workers) in the previous year, and 166 in the year to October 2003. Meanwhile, the latest survey shows that 13 unions were running a total of 46 campaigns for recognition compared with 7 unions running 16 campaigns in the previous year. Workers covered by new recognition agreements in this year's survey included 7000 employees at NCH – Action for Children and staff at MUTV, AOL, online discount store Bargain Crazy and the Cathay Dim Sum Chinese restaurant in Manchester.

More than 1100 deals, covering over 310 000 employees have been signed since the right to recognition came into force in 2000 (Employment Relations Act 1999).

According to TUC general secretary Brendan Barber:

It was always expected that following an initial surge in deals, unblocked by the new legal right to recognition, unions were going to face a tough task in securing new agreements. The dramatic increase in campaigns for recognition, many in areas where few employees have ever had the benefit of union representation, shows that unions are taking on this challenge.

But unions are facing an increasingly uphill battle. Employers are becoming more and more resistant, though welcome new protection against the worst kind of union busting will now limit this.

A further boost would come if the law gave unions negotiating rights over pensions where they are recognized. The employer retreat from pensions provision is a key cause of the looming pensions crisis. Too many employees do not have the protection of a union when they face pensions cuts.

Why are employers becoming more resistant to union recognition agreements?

Source: *HRM Guide UK*, (http://www.hrmguide.co.uk/), 28 April, 2006.

any control of social policy at a European level is well known. However, the delay can be attributed to deeper philosophical differences within the EU as a whole. There are two perspectives (Cressey, 1993):

- Free market enthusiasts – particularly in the UK – seek deregulation and decentralization of employee relations. They emphasize voluntary, non-statutory arrangements.

- Regulatory-minded people in the Commission, European Parliament and Council of Ministers see a need for a harmonized system of employee relations.

The EU already recognizes employees and their representatives as a 'social partner' in its own institutions. It allows representation, consultation and participation within a number of the EU's tripartite bodies. The argument revolves around an extension of this representation to situations beyond the EU's own institutions.

Brewster (1994) describes Europe as a 'heavily unionized continent'. Membership of trade unions varies from 87.5 per cent in Denmark to a mere 9.1 per cent in France (see Table 22.1). Membership is concentrated in organizations employing over 200 staff. In part, this variation reflects the differing traditions of member states, from the free market capitalist model in the UK, to the social market concepts prevalent in Germany. Brewster concludes that, unlike the UK, unions 'tend to be more involved and to have more positive and less antagonistic relations with employers'.

Table 22.1	Country	Union density
	Denmark	87.5
Trade union membership in the European Community compared with the USA and Japan (trade union density %, 2000)	Finland	79.0
	Sweden	79.0
	Belgium	69.2
	Luxembourg **	50.0
	Ireland	44.5
Source: EIRO and national figures.	Unweighted EU average	43.8
	Austria	39.8
	Italy**	35.4
	Greece	32.5
	Weighted EU average	30.4
	Portugal*	30.0
	Germany**	29.7
	UK	29.0
	Netherlands	27.0
	Japan	21.5
	Spain	15.0
	USA	13.5
	France	9.1

Note: * 1999 figure; ** 1998 figure

During the mid-1990s, government attempts to meet the requirements of the single currency agreement led to extensive industrial action in several European countries, France being a notable instance. Reductions in public spending and cuts in government borrowing hit state sector – or state-subsidized – industries hard, producing wage cuts and job losses. In these cases, efforts to forge pacts with trade unions were generally unsuccessful because governments had nothing to offer in return. Throughout Europe, unions have lost political influence. Ironically, in Belgium and Spain, their allies in government have been instrumental in the imposition of some of the toughest economic measures.

Works councils are required in all companies employing a minimum of 1000 workers in two or more countries in the EU, provided there are at least 150 workers at two sites or more. The councils are to be informed of the state of business and consulted on changes to production or working methods, restructuring and planned closures. Whereas French and German companies have modelled their 'Europe-wide councils' on pre-existing national formats, other organizations are obtaining agreements on widely different bases.

Interpretation and application of EU law by the Commission and the European Court is shaped by their understanding of the 'European social model' which views trade unions as social partners (Bercusson, 2002). The EU Framework Directive on information and consultation further extends the role of employee representatives for companies employing at least 150 employees, or workplace establishments with at least 100 employees. This had to be implemented by national governments by 23 March, 2005. The directive requires a nine-stage process of information and consultation (Bercusson, 2002):

1 Transmission of information/data.

2 Acquaintance with and examination of data.

3 Conduct of an adequate study.

4 Preparation for consultation.

5 Formulation of an opinion.

6 Meeting.

7 Employer's reasoned response to opinion.

8 'Exchange of views and establishment of dialogue', 'discussion', 'with a view to reaching an agreement on decisions'.

9 'The employer and the employees' representatives shall work in a spirit of cooperation and with due regard for their reciprocal rights and obligations, taking into account the interests both of the undertaking or establishment and of the employees.'

German employee relations

By comparison with many other countries, the management of people in Germany is tightly controlled by legal processes. Indeed many aspects of people management dealt with in an *ad hoc* way elsewhere are strictly regulated in the Federal Republic. As a result of the various co-determination laws in the period since the end of World War II, Germany has evolved a system that focuses on **industrial democracy** and harmony. Abandoning the pre-war tradition of small craft-based unions, 15 single-industry unions were organized largely for blue-collar workers. Together with the Police Trade Union, these unions formed the Deutscher Gewerkschaftsbund (DGB) – the Confederation of German Trade Unions – in 1949.

At the time of German unification in 1990 the unions affiliated to the DGB had almost 8 million members, including I G Metall (Metal-Workers' Union) which, with 3.6 million members in West and East Germany, was the largest trade union in the world (Randlesome, 1994, p.109). There are also separate associations representing white-collar workers, civil servants and Christian trade unionists.

Unlike craft and general unions, or professional associations, German unions are industrial: anyone employed in the industry represented by a particular union may be a member. This includes blue-collar and white-collar, skilled and unskilled, manual or supervisory workers. Consequently, demarcation disputes between different grades in a company cannot occur since all are represented by the same union. Some 90 per cent of German employers belong to federations which require them to recognize trade unions (Brewster 1994, p.64). In practical terms, the main instruments of **co-determination** are the supervisory boards and works councils that characterize large companies.

Supervisory boards

Companies employing more than 2000 workers are obliged to have a supervisory board. This is in addition to the management board, which continues to have final authority. The supervisory board consists of 50 per cent shareholder representatives, with the other 50 per cent being worker representatives elected by the workforce – including both basic and executive staff. Elections take place every four years.

The supervisory board oversees management action and monitors and evaluates performance and change. German employers were reluctant to go along with this procedure but most now believe that it functions well, despite the occasional problem. In fact, the number of occasions when the supervisory and management boards fail to agree is limited – largely by means of informal discussions to make sure that they achieve consensus in the official forum. If they fail to agree, the chairperson of the supervisory board (a shareholder representative) has the casting vote. The major drawback of the system is that it slows down the process of decisionmaking.

Works councils

We noted earlier that works councils have been extended to all large companies operating in more than one European country. In Germany, three sets of rights have been given to works councils (Lawrence, 1993, p.34). First there is the co-determination right (*Mitbestimmingsrecht*) – the ability to give consent on a number of issues: the appointment of an employee to a new position; transfers within the organization; transfers from one wage group to another; determining starting and finishing times for the working day; and the introduction of shift working, overtime, etc. According to Lawrence (*ibid.*, p.36):

> A German company that has a bursting order book cannot just institute overtime by its own authority. It needs the agreement of the works council to do this and even then it cannot engage in unlimited overtime working. ... quite small issues between management and workforce can only be said to be 'settled' when they have been formally agreed with the works council and written down.

Secondly there is the consultation right (*Mitwirkungsrecht*) over planning issues, including plant closure, new factories, investment decisions and business policy matters. Finally there is the information right (*Informationsrecht*) to receive information about company performance and prospects.

Legislation on the works council system was significantly amended in 2001 (Weiss, 2002). The amendment was intended to improve the conditions for applying the law in SMEs, increase the powers and resources available to works councils in some areas and adapt the traditional organizational structure to better fit modern situations.

Pay negotiations take place between an appropriate employers' federation and the matching union for that industry. Negotiations take place at the state level, with some variation in settlement levels between rich and less affluent states. Bargaining takes place to a predetermined schedule and in a specific order of states (Lawrence, 1993, p.30). Some smaller companies are not members of employers' federations but tend to follow agreements although they are not obliged to do so. A few large organizations, such as Siemens, conduct negotiations directly with their unions.

Until recently, co-determination brought stability into the German employee relations scene. According to Jacobi and Muller-Jentsch (1990, p.134):

> From the point of view of organization policy, the trade unions have proved to be extremely stable. Their status as a party to collective bargaining has up to now remained unchallenged because of the high degree of juridification and centralization and their monopoly-like legal privileges in collective

bargaining and in calling strikes. Whereas the 'institutionalization of class struggle' could be seen as a fetter on the unions' development of power in the years of sustained high employment, institutional protection now constitutes a bulwark against labour-exclusion strategies.

However, in 1996 some cracks began to appear in these apparently sacrosanct arrangements (*Financial Times*, 21 October, 1996). Viessmann, a mid-sized producer of heating systems, was sued by the IG Metall engineering union on the grounds that it had negotiated new working hours with its employees without involving the union. Faced with the loss of work to a new (and cheaper) factory in the Czech Republic, Viessmann's workers agreed to work 38 rather than 35 hours a week without increased pay. This improved efficiency by 8.6 per cent, matching the savings that would have been gained by the company had it transferred its work to the Czech Republic. I G Metall objected because the German system accords negotiating rights for pay and working hours to the trade unions. In this case, the union action failed because only some 10 per cent of Viessmann's employees were members of IG Metall.

Other companies have negotiated informal agreements and 'opt-out' clauses which have allowed them to reduce employee costs. There have also been murmurings about the structure of supervisory boards. In fact, the cosy consensus between management and employees is under strain. As we have noted already the economic pressures, firstly of additional taxation to support the unification of East and West Germany and, latterly, of government spending cuts to meet single-currency convergence requirements have caused considerable tensions. Unemployment has climbed rapidly since unification and the combination of high rates of pay and generous social security payments has led to the export of jobs on a significant scale.

Addison, Schnabel and Wagner (2001) analysed a large-scale database to investigate the effects of the works council system on a number of variables. They found that works councils were associated with reduced labour fluctuation, higher productivity (but only in larger establishments), and no reduction in innovative activity. At the same time they were also associated with lower profitability and higher wages. Flecker and Schulten (1999) contend that the German employee relations system has never been as uniform as it has been presented in comparative literature and that the strains of unification and other social changes are having a considerable impact. Similar points are made by Hassel (1999). Klikauer (2002), on the other hand, argues that the basic system of German employee relations remains intact despite major changes in the public sector and the consequences of unification.

Raess (2006) focused on the 2003 campaign for equalization of conditions in the German metal industry, and found that globalization affected the bargaining outcome much more than anticipated. Raess argues that the eastern EU enlargement created a 'now or never' atmosphere that helped to spark the union's initiative. Employers' vehement opposition was frequently clothed in concerns about labour costs, emphasizing losses in international competitiveness and/or jobs to low-wage countries. Frequent exit threats were instrumental in splitting workforces by inducing fears and encouraging an anti-union mood. The bargaining round inspired large firms to question the central bargaining institution, thereby subordinating social peace to the goal of defeating I G Metall. Raess concludes that this and subsequent developments in West Germany point to a transformation of German industrial relations as a partial consequence of economic globalization.

Employee relations in Australia and New Zealand

Throughout much of the 20th century, employee relations in Australia and New Zealand were characterized by industrial conciliation and arbitration (Harbridge and Walsh, 2002). In New Zealand, especially, they were criticized for being highly legalistic and interventionist (Vranken, 1999). But the global pressure for greater flexibility has led to radically different approaches. The old industrial relations system, essentially multi-employer bargaining, was effectively dismantled in New Zealand and replaced with a system that favoured individual contracts. The Australian constitution protected conciliation and arbitration but new legislation considerably weakened the system in the 1990s and again in 2006.

Despite the different approaches, the outcome has been similar in both countries: a drop in collective bargaining and union density, reductions in benefits, and major changes in working time arrangements (Harbridge and Walsh, 2002). Union density in Australia fell from 50.2 per cent in 1970 to 22.9 per cent in 2003; similarly, in New Zealand it fell from 55.2 per cent in 1970 to 22.1 per cent in 2002 (Visser, 2006). A study by Allan, Brosnan and Walsh (1999) found that New Zealand's decentralized system had encouraged greater employer experimentation (albeit with both positive and negative outcomes), particularly in the private sector. Vranken (1999) found a growing tension between the specialist labour court and the ordinary courts of law, especially the court of appeal.

Rasmussen and Lind (2003) describe the change in outlook following the 1999 elections when there was 'a marked shift in New Zealand employment relationships with state interventionism, collective bargaining and employee influence being back in favour.' Rasmussen and Lind highlight the 'good faith' bargaining and behaviour codes at the heart of changes to the Employment Relations Act, influenced by Canadian practice. Barry and May (2004) observe that another aspect of the Employment Relations Act, increased protection for trade unions, had led only to the registration of a plethora of small unions with limited interests.

Briggs (2001) observes that globalization and employers are normally regarded as key agents of change, with unions reduced to a reactive or impotent role. Paradoxically, however, Briggs argues that unions were responsible for the shift to enterprise bargaining in Australia in the early 1990s as a consequence of two industrial campaigns. The **Australian Industrial Relations Commission (AIRC)** had been reluctant to introduce enterprise bargaining but a loss of union solidarity behind centralized wage negotiations and a power struggle between the AIRC and the **Australian Council of Trade Unions (ACTU)** created a policy vacuum that had to be filled. As a result the Business Council of Australia (BCA), the employers' organization, was allowed to take the lead in the process of decentralizing pay bargaining in Australia. Similarly, Phillimore (2000) attributes some of the changes to union misjudgements and weak workplace bargaining structures. Wooden and Bora (1999) found that following the changes of the 1990s, workplace-specific factors were responsible for 39 per cent of hourly wage differences.

Deery, Walsh and Knox (2001) looked at employee relations practices and outcomes in non-union and unionized workplaces using the 1995 Australian Workplace Industrial Relations Survey. They found non-union workplaces to be distinctly less innovative in their employee relations practices and had higher dismissal and turnover rates. They also observed that non-union workplaces were notable for the individualistic nature of their contractual, remunerative and bargaining arrangements. However, the federal government considered that existing workplace legislation was too restrictive for business.

In March 2006, most of the provisions of the Howard government's WorkChoices Act came into effect. An examination of some of the rhetoric employed by the government and the trade unions at the time is instructive. According to Kevin Andrews, minister for employment and workplace relations, in a speech in February of that year (www.hrmguide.net/australia/relations/workchoices-andrews.htm, 23 February, 2006) there were a number of 'roadblocks' in the previous industrial relations (IR) system:

- the paternalistic influence of the AIRC and other third parties
- difficulties with bargaining and industrial action that resulted in significant economic loss
- the time and red tape involved in agreement making
- the absence of a genuine award safety net
- the inflexibility of the award system
- a confusing and complex web of competing federal and state employment regulation.

According to the minister, 'WorkChoices will remove these problems by introducing changes including:

- more rational arrangements for setting minimum wages and conditions
- a more streamlined process for the making of **workplace agreements**

- greater award simplification and a more focused role for the Australian Industrial Relations Commission
- better balance in unfair dismissal laws which have held back job growth in Australia
- introduction of a single national industrial relations system.'

WorkChoices featured a new body called the Australian Fair Pay Commission (AFPC) charged with setting and adjusting minimum and classification-based wages. Minister Andrews said that: 'Under WorkChoices key minimum conditions of employment will be set in legislation and, with the decisions of the AFPC, will form the new Australian Fair Pay and Conditions Standard. All new agreements must meet this new standard.

'These key minimum conditions are annual leave, personal/carer's leave, parental leave and maximum ordinary hours of work. To encourage agreement making, all agreements will be lodged with the Office of Employment Advocate, overcoming the previous complex and sometimes adversarial agreement certification and approval process.'

The minister argued that WorkChoices would reduce the complexity of awards and simplify Australia's industrial relations. '. . . it is in Australia's national interest to move towards a single national workplace relations system. Currently, we have six separate workplace relations systems in Australia – one in each state, except Victoria, and a federal system.

'Australia has a workforce of around 10 million, and with thousands of different state and federal awards and pieces of legislation, six similar but not identical workplace relations systems creates costs and complexity for all businesses.'

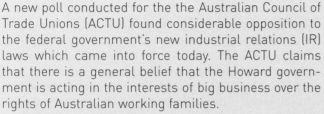

HRM in reality ACTU claims most Australians against new IR laws

A new poll conducted for the the Australian Council of Trade Unions (ACTU) found considerable opposition to the federal government's new industrial relations (IR) laws which came into force today. The ACTU claims that there is a general belief that the Howard government is acting in the interests of big business over the rights of Australian working families.

The survey of a thousand voters was conducted in 24 key coalition-held marginal seats during late February and early March as part of the ACTU's ongoing campaign against the new industrial relations laws.

The survey results indicated that fewer than one in four Australians support the laws, with nearly seven out of ten believing the new IR laws will benefit big corporations and their CEOs while damaging the interests of ordinary families.

The main findings of the survey were:

- 72 per cent of respondents supported unfair dismissal laws that protect workers.
- 59 per cent believed that 'the government's new IR laws alone are a strong reason to vote against the government' at the next federal election.
- 70 per cent believed that individual contracts give too much power to employers.
- 68 per cent thought that the new laws were strong evidence that John Howard governs more for

corporate Australia than for ordinary working families.

- 60 per cent felt that collective bargaining provided better job security for employees.
- 66 per cent believed that the IR laws were a threat to working families.

ACTU president Sharan Burrow said:

Today, Australian working families lose unfair dismissal laws, the strong award system, the safety net, the right to a minimum wage, laws that protect the right to collectively bargain, and laws that have ensured fair representation by unions at the workplace.

The public are asking why the government would introduce laws that are so obviously designed to take working families' wages and conditions backwards, and to remove basic rights for workers at the workplace.

Despite AUS$50 million of government advertising and a year of spin, the public is aware that the government is introducing these laws to benefit big business at the expense of ordinary working families.

What power does a modern trade union movement have to influence government policy?

Source: *HRM Guide Australia* (http://www.hrmguide.net/australia), 27 March, 2006.

The new system would cover around 85 per cent of employees across Australia. In the government's view, WorkChoices would reduce the burden of unfair dismissal provisions on Australian businesses, exempting organizations with up to and including 100 employees from the federal unfair dismissal laws.

According to Kevin Andrews: 'For businesses with more than 100 employees, an employee must have been employed for six months before they can pursue an unfair dismissal claim. In addition, where the employment has been terminated because the employer genuinely no longer requires the job to be done, that is, where the employee's employment has been terminated because of operational requirements, the AIRC will be able to refuse any application for unfair dismissal.

'Having a better balance in the unfair dismissal laws will free small and medium-sized businesses in the WorkChoices system from the fear that a stressful unfair dismissal claim may eventuate whenever they try to resolve workplace issues with their staff. Removing this fear is vital in achieving a better and more productive working environment.'

The government considered that WorkChoices would continue to protect the right to lawful industrial action when negotiating a new collective agreement but would improve the remedies for unprotected industrial action. Kevin Andrews argued that rights come with responsibilities and that unprotected industrial action removed 'impediments to accessing common law tort remedies in relation to unprotected industrial action.' The new Act required a secret ballot before protected industrial action could be taken.

Not surprisingly, Australian unions attacked the details of regulations relating to the WorkChoices Act describing them as harsh and designed to crack down on union activity in the workplace.

Union critics pointed to federal government fines of between AUS\$6000 and AUS\$33 000 for seeking commitments from employers around job security or fair treatment processes and claimed that many basic union activities in the workplace have been effectively outlawed.

ACTU Secretary Greg Combet said (http://www.hrmguide.net/australia/relations/actu-fines.htm, 22 March, 2006):

> These laws are an affront to basic Australian democratic rights. They impose harsh fines on Australian workers and unions simply for standing up for fundamental values like job security and fair treatment for employees.
>
> Under the regulations workers or unions who even ask to have certain matters contained in a workplace agreement will be fined by the government. For example, an individual or union that seeks to have some protection from harsh or unfair dismissal for workers written into a workplace agreement will be fined \$6000 and \$33 000 respectively by the government – even where their employer also wants or agrees to such a provision.
>
> The question that the federal government and Kevin Andrews need to answer is why should a worker or a union be fined by the government for trying to make jobs more secure or asking for fair treatment for workers?
>
> These are things of fundamental importance to workers and working families – job security and fair treatment – but the government is saying it will now be illegal for workers or unions to even ask for these things.
>
> The laws also provide for fines for workers or unions who seek commitments in agreements that union or OH&S representatives will have access to training or that union members be allowed to meet to discuss workplace issues. Clauses regulating the use of independent contractors or labour hire employees have also been banned.

Greg Combet argued that the new laws infringed the basic rights of every Australian employee and that they would increase pressure on people at work and their incomes and lifestyles He concluded that the federal government had not produced a 'valid argument, evidence or justification as to why such laws are necessary.'

Japanese and East Asian employee relations

Kuruvilla and Erickson (2002) argue that employee relations systems change because of the constraints facing those systems. Until the 1980s East Asian employee relations focused on maintaining labour peace and stability during the early stages of industrialization. Since then the major isssues have been numerical and functional flexibility in the face of economic turbulence. Todd and Peetz (2001) observe that employee relations in Malaysia have been characterized by extensive state control, which has guaranteed high levels of managerial prerogative within the workplace, minimal overt conflict and very little bargaining power for workers. They found no evidence of major change and employees remain excluded from the decisionmaking process. But it is possible for particularly strong unions to make an impact (Peetz and Todd, 2001). In Hong Kong, on the other hand, unions are weak (Chan and Snape, 2000) and in Singapore they have a 'special relationship' with the government with a modest amount of influence (Barr, 2000).

Japanese employee relations methods are particularly relevant in two contexts: Japan itself and transplant factories in the Pacific area, North America and Europe. Nissan, for example, has been particularly active in overseas expansion and – in common with many other Japanese corporations – has a specific attitude towards trade unions (Garrahan and Stewart, 1992, p.9). It established a factory in Tennessee, USA, where state laws on the 'right to work' effectively neutralized the power of established unions by allowing the freedom not to belong to unions. Nissan campaigned against the Auto Union with the result that they failed to establish themselves.

In the UK, Nissan took a site in Washington in the north-east of England. The company contracted a single-union deal with the Amalgamated Union of Engineering Workers. This gave the union negligible negotiating powers. In fact, the company staff council had more power.

In Japan itself, Nissan destroyed union power in 1953 after a four-month lock-out of employees, coupled with the use of strong-arm tactics. After the capitulation of the independent national Auto Union, employees were taken back by the company on condition that they joined a company union: the All Nissan Motor Workers Union. After this episode, employee relations were described by the company in the following way: 'Nissan prides itself on 30 years of smooth labour-management relations' (*ibid.*, 1992, p.9).

Critics said that Nissan controlled the union, pointing to the history of employee relations since the 1950s. Employee pay was reduced for six years after 1953. It took until 1964 for that level to be achieved again. Thereafter wage claims were always 100 per cent agreed, but this was not too surprising, given that the claims were always modest and restrained. The company gained a massive increase in productivity as a result.

During 1980 union elections, 99 per cent of employees voted with the elected officials receiving 98 per cent of the total votes cast. The voting process was closely surveyed by company officials. Strangest of all to Western eyes is the part played by union membership in career progression. A period as a union officer – on secondment from the personnel department – is an expected part of the career route. Pressure is put on staff to belong to the company union and they can be dismissed for belonging to other unions, or unacceptable political groups.

Organizations and employee relations

Earlier in this chapter we observed that traditional industrial relations assumed a formal structure in which management and staff negotiated pay levels and working conditions such as hours of work, grade demarcation, holiday entitlement and sick pay arrangements. In some organizations the same structure was used for grievance and disciplinary matters, agreeing levels of performance, attendance requirements – such as shift hours – and work procedures. Within this mechanism, staff were represented by one or more trade unions or staff associations.

In recent years large organizations in free market countries have attempted to move away from traditional mechanisms. The focus has switched to individual rather than collective bargaining. This may take place through:

- Introduction of personal contracts, allowing employers to offer pay increases to staff willing to accept such contracts but not to workers wishing to remain as union members.
- Organizational change methods such as team briefings, where managers cascade information throughout the organization by means of a series of meetings (usually on a monthly basis) and also collect ideas and criticisms at the same meetings to be funnelled upwards.
- Quality circles have also served to circumvent the traditional union role by emphasizing direct dialogue between staff and line management on the subject of improving procedures.

It is not surprising that unions have often resisted the introduction of change methods of this nature because they depend on staff and management talking directly to each other, thereby removing a main source of union power – the filter or gatekeeper of information and innovation. In such situations, collective bargaining has often been reduced to the primary subjects of pay, holidays and discipline, removing the unions from the discussion of procedures.

Individualized systems stress commitment from employees, yet the fashion for downsizing and restructuring imposes a 'fear of commitment' among managers and employees alike (Rousseau, 1995, p.xii). HR policies that emphasize the individual contribute to this fear since they do away with any collective employee defence against the employer. 'Divide and rule.' Hendry (1995, p.57) acknowledges a 'more sophisticated pluralist technique which sees the unitary organization as "bad" because the denial of individual and group interests actually makes for a less effective organization.' In other words, there is a valid criticism that the integrating activities of HRM can rub out the healthy diversity that is essential for future development: 'Such paradoxes, discrepancies, and ambiguities highlight the fact that organizational life is beset by paradoxes, and that (mercifully) managers and organizations cannot get a handle completely on human behaviour.'

Peters (1987) distinguishes two contradictory philosophies operating in modern business organizations:

> *Minimize human resources.* Workers are pure costs. New methods and equipment are now available globally. Businesses in the developed world can: cut employee costs to match those of poorer countries; or switch to industries that are not labour intensive. This involves actual and threatened redundancies, transferring operations to lower-wage countries and automation.
>
> *Increase the value of the people element.* Employees are assets. This approach emphasizes flexibility and creativity and aims to eliminate unnecessary routine by: the intelligent use of technology; and retraining workers for more complex or varied tasks. According to Peters it should be tied to profit-linked bonuses to ensure commitment.

The first approach leads to industrial conflict. Managers must make cuts and be aggressive towards staff. Workers defend their position and oppose change. It is the view which predominated in New Right thinking and predominated in the UK under Conservative rule. The second approach is collaborative. It seeks partnership between workers and employers for mutual benefit. It fits the 'social market' philosophy held by many governments in the European Union. Peters argues that both approaches deliver short-term profits but only the second can maintain competitiveness in the long term.

Other management writers advocate a new form of employee relationship based on co-operation. For example, Kanter (1989, p.127) argues that 'the adversarial mode with its paranoid world view' is unsuitable for the modern world. 'Teaming up' is the route to growth and survival. Corporations need to seek strategic alliances – cooperative arrangements to achieve business goals. Such alliances should be made with unions as well as other businesses. Kanter defines these as 'stakeholder alliances' or 'complementary' coalitions. In 1996, the British Labour Party adopted a similar concept as their 'big idea' for the UK's future. Stuart and Lucio (2002) found that while some unions, such as the MSF (Manufacturing, Science and Finance Union – now part of Amicus) were extremely enthusiastic, most companies did not reciprocate. Oxenbridge and Brown (2002) found a dichotomy between production sector firms that nurtured collective bargaining through informal partnership relationships, and service sector businesses that contained collective bargaining tightly through formalized partnership agreements. Haynes and Allen (2001), meanwhile, found equally distinct polarization among unions – some saw partnership as a potentially effective strategy for restoring union influence, others viewed the concept as fatally flawed.

Participation is also a matter of delegation – involving everyone downwards within the organization as well as the stakeholder partners. It requires a change in behaviour from managers who have previously exercised power in a clear-cut, overtly decisive fashion. A consensus style requires patience; willingness to discuss ideas at an early stage; and ability to listen. Not all managers can make the transition. Partnerships require managers with team leadership skills.

Management strategies towards employee relations have been classified to demonstrate the variety of ways in which managers regard employee relations, ranging from authoritarian and anti-unionist to more sophisticated and inclusive strategies (see Table 22.2). In the same way, employees may take various approaches as we shall see in the next section.

Employee relations strategies

Trade unions in different countries have varying interpretations of their roles and aim for different goals. McIlwee and Roberts (1991, p.390), for example, have outlined the major objectives of British trade unions in the last century:

- *Preventing legal interference in the collective bargaining process.* Trade unions in the UK have favoured voluntary collective bargaining and have resisted government attempts to restrict this process – albeit unsuccessfully in the Thatcher era. Unions have been favourably inclined towards (essentially pre-1979) legislation which aimed to protect employees, but have opposed income policies and limitations on industrial action.

- *Improving monetary rewards for members.* Pressing for higher wages, especially in periods of high inflation. This is the principal concern of most union members: unions that are successful in this respect are likely to benefit from additional recruitment and retention of existing members.

- *Improving other terms and conditions.* As the nature of work and its rewards change, non-monetary benefits become increasingly important. These include reduction of working hours, earlier retirement, longer holidays, improved pension and sick pay schemes.

- *Involvement in determining national economic and industrial objectives.* Accustomed to 'beer and sandwiches' at 10 Downing Street in pre-Thatcher days, these stakeholders have found themselves virtually ignored by neo-liberal governments – both Conservative and Labour.. However, their (reduced) influence continues through ACAS and industrial tribunals.

- *Health and safety at work.*

- *Protection of job opportunities.* Traditionally, unions have fought job cuts in any circumstances, leading to accusations of massive over-staffing in many organizations until the 1980s. Of late, union opposition has been more selective and the 'new realism' has produced a longer-term perspective. Unions have focused increasingly on jobs with a future and have been prepared to negotiate flexible terms with employers in order to preserve work in Britain or to attract jobs from other parts of the EU and elsewhere.

- *Improving public and social services.* The essential purpose of trade unions is the representation of members at work. But workers also have other roles: parents, consumers, tenants, pensioners, the sick, the unemployed. Awareness of this wider context has led to union pressure for changes in society as a whole.

- *A voice in government.* British unions have had a direct relationship with the Labour Party since 1900 – initially it was organized to reflect their views. Many unions contributed funds to the Labour Party and, as the largest source of income, strongly influenced its policies and organization. Conservative legislation in the 1980s allowed members to opt out of their union's political fund, reducing this flow by around 20 per cent.

Table 22.2	Basic	Purcell and Sissons (1983)	Gunnigle *et al.* (1994)
Strategic management styles towards employee relations	**1 Authoritarian.** Typical small company style. Boss rules absolutely – staff have simple 'take it or leave it' choice. Works if employees accept situation – e.g. where there is little or no opportunity to change jobs. Seen in some large organizations. **2 Individual.** Negotiation between management and individuals. Possible for staff teams to discuss common interests jointly. Non-authoritarian. Emphasis on commitment to company goals. Managers reasonable and approachable. No collective body representing staff. **3 Collective.** Dominant method in western world from 1945 until approx. 1980. Since then, social and free market economies have taken different paths. Social market economies, e.g Germany, have industry or company-wide trade unions (or staff associations) negotiating with management on behalf of the staff. Free market economies continue to make extensive use of this approach but management literature and HRM emphasize individual bargaining. Many companies utilize both strategies	**1 Traditional.** Fire-fighting – managers pay little attention to employee relations until trouble arises. Low pay levels. Hostile to unions. Prevails in authoritarian small businesses but seen in larger companies when workers have little choice in their employment. **2 Paternalist.** More benevolent, humanistic style; close parallels with HRM approach. Employers consider unions unnecessary because conditions are so generous. Employee relations concentrate on getting employees to identify with the objectives of the business. **3 Consultative.** Ideal form of employee relations in some eyes. Emphasis is on informal rather than formal systems of bargaining with continuous dialogue. Unions are fully recognized. **4 Constitutional.** Similar to consultative approach but emphasis on formal regulatory agreements to control the relationship between powerful parties on either side. Found in social market economies and strongly encouraged by European Union social policy. **5 Opportunistic.** Responsibility for employee relations left to individual divisions/subsidiaries, leaving no common approach and an emphasis on unit profitability.	**1 Anti-union.** Little or no consideration of employee relations. No collective arrangements such as union representation. Low concern for employee needs. Aggressive opposition to collective bargaining and union recognition. **2 Paternalist.** Concern for employee needs but rejects union recognition and collective bargaining. Little sophistication in human resource policies. **3 Sophisticated paternalist.** Emphasizes welfare and wellbeing of individual staff. Sophisticated HR policies for resourcing, development, reward and communication. Rejects unions and collective bargaining. Equates to 'traditional HRM' – values employees because this is seen to benefit organization. **4 Sophisticated unionized.** Recognizes trade unions but carefully prescribed union role (e.g. single union agreement). Mixed collective and individual arrangements, incorporating HR policies. Neo-pluralist model with HRM-type policies designed to foster consensualism and employee commitment. **5 Traditional unionized.** Pluralist approach typified by adversarial industrial relations. Collective bargaining but multiple unions complicate matters.

The Labour Party itself concluded that identifying too closely with the trade union movement was counter-productive at the end of the 20th century. The proportion of British voters identifying themselves as 'working class' fell dramatically due to government initiatives such as council house sales to tenants and a general improvement in prosperity. The new middle-class ('Thatcher's children') were portrayed as being scared of overtly socialist policies that might reduce their economic wellbeing, and are seen to have lost interest in the underprivileged. The Blair Labour government was scarcely any more receptive to trade union influence.

● *Industrial democracy.* The Conservative government opted out of those sections of the Social Charter that required works councils to be formed in all large companies. The Labour government signed up when they achieved office and EU Directives are pushing them in the direction of recognizable continental forms of employee consultation.

The pattern in other countries varies because of prevailing cultural, historical and legislative factors. These issues are reflected in the nature of employee relations as an activity undertaken by managers, employees and unions.

Summary

'Employee relations' broadens the study of industrial relations to include wider aspects of the employment relationship, including non-unionized workplaces, personal contracts and socio-emotional, rather than contractual, arrangements. This is an area with diverse ideological underpinnings and political ramifications.

Governments have taken an active part in determining its conduct. In Europe, harmonization is leading to the establishment of works councils across the EU, giving a new role for collective representation. Australia and New Zealand have seen some of the most significant changes in employee relations legislation in recent years.

Further reading

Contemporary Employment Relations: A Critical Introduction by Steve Williams and Derek Adam-Smith (Oxford University Press, 2005) and *Employment Relations* by Ed Rose (FT-Prentice Hall, 2004) provide good overviews of the field. *International and Comparative Industrial Relations* edited by Greg Bamber, Russell Lansbury and Nick Wailes (Sage Publications, 2004) compares different developed countries. *Trade Unions* by Sue Fernie and David Metcalf (Routledge, 2005) looks at the future of unions in Britain.

Review questions

1 What are the key differences between unitarist and pluralist views of employee relations?

2 What is meant by the employment relationship? To what extent is it reasonable to say that employee relations should encompass all employment relationships?

3 Do trade unions have a role to play in the modern workplace? Discuss the view that employee relations is an outmoded concept that has no place in organizations managed according to the principles of HRM.

4 What are the principal factors responsible for the changes in union power over the last few decades?

5 How central is the German system of employee relations to the European Unions's 'social partnership' model?

6 Are works councils a handicap or a benefit to business efficiency?

7 Is it wise for governments to suppress independent trade unions?

8 What should trade unions do to be 'new realists' in employee relations?

Case studies for discussion and analysis

Middleton Council/Euro Vehicles

Middleton Council

Middleton Council covers a large urban area bordered by open country. Most of its 300 staff work in the main office complex, Delta House, located in the old town centre. A new shopping mall has opened immediately between the council offices and the old market, transforming a derelict area into a fashionable district. The staff are delighted since they now work in a pleasant and prestigious locality with a massive choice of shops and eating places nearby.

The council has been re-elected after promising a considerable improvement in services. However, all available funds have been devoted to maintaining things as they are. After much debate it has been decided that costs could be cut dramatically by renting out Delta House to a commercial firm and transferring the staff to much cheaper accommodation at the edge of town. The savings could be used to pay for new services promised in the election.

The staff are unionized and have a reputation for resisting changes, no matter how small.

How would you advise the council to proceed?

Euro Vehicles

Euro Vehicles manufactures vans and other light commercial vehicles. Because of severe competition and a declining market, the workforce has been reduced from 11 300 to 2800 in the last three years and the remaining employees are fearful of further redundancy. There are three unions in the two remaining plants, representing clerical, engineering and supervisory staff. Partly as a result of the recent cuts they are all suspicious of management intentions. Management is authoritarian, based on a rigid departmental structure and values technical competence and seniority over anything else. Most of the managers have been promoted from the engineering and production side of the company and are in their 40s and 50s.

The company's production is largely devoted to basic van models built to a 15-year-old design and sold to large utility companies at a very keen price. Marketing is almost non-existent and the Research and Development department was closed as a cost-cutting measure three years ago. The company is currently owned by a large conglomerate that left the management alone until recently but with strict, detailed financial controls. Consequently, the company has been consistently profitable but with a shrinking level of production and increasingly outdated manufacturing equipment. The conglomerate has decided that this 'hands-off' approach is no longer satisfactory. They are prepared to make a major investment but only if they can be convinced that this will be effectively managed.

You have been brought in as a consultant to look at the current organization and to recommend changes that would improve the situation. How would you go about this? What are the implications for employee relations?

Chapter 23

Conflict, bargaining, involvement and wellbeing

Learning objectives

The purpose of this chapter is to:

- Discuss the role of conflict in the workplace.

- Provide an overview of mediation and tribunal systems.

- Evaluate the relationship between employee involvement and workplace productivity.

- Discuss the role of HR practitioners in matters such as work–life balance, health and safety and stress reduction.

Employee relations as an activity

Conflict

Tribunals and arbitration systems

The negotiating process

Models of bargaining

Employee involvement

Work–life balance

Health and safety

Stress

Summary

Further reading

Review questions

Case studies for discussion and analysis –
    Nurses experience abuse/Stress measurement
    questionnaires

Employee relations as an activity

In many developed countries the industrial relations of the 1950s to the 1970s depended on the existence of company rules and regulations that served the purpose of clarifying what was expected of both employees and employers. Since then, the move towards flexibility and empowerment of staff has resulted in 'fuzzier' boundaries between required behaviour and that which is regarded as inappropriate. Employees – particularly managers – have been given greater discretion on decisionmaking in free market economies. This has been encouraged by 'neo-liberal' governments throughout the world. Within the European Union, however, there has been a countervailing emphasis on formal rules because of the predominance of social market economies at the heart of the EU. Typically, most large organizations continue to have formal rules on:

1 *Timekeeping*
   - Normally expected times of attendance, often with monitoring ('clocking-in').
   - Sanctions for lateness.

2 *Absence*
   - An approval mechanism for absence.
   - Authorization for taking annual leave.
   - A reporting procedure when people are absent from the workplace.
   - The need for medical self-certification or a doctor's certificate.

3 *Health and safety*
   - Requirements for appearance or cleanliness – e.g. protective clothing, wearing jewellery.
   - Special hazards such as chemicals and dangerous machinery.
   - Prohibition of smoking, alcohol or drugs.

4 *Gross misconduct*
   - Offences regarded as being serious enough to lead to dismissal without notice.
   - Theft, fraud, deliberate falsification of records.
   - Fighting, assault on another person.
   - Deliberate damage to company property.
   - Serious incapability through alcohol or being under the influence of illegal drugs.
   - Serious negligence that causes unacceptable loss, damage or injury.
   - Serious acts of insubordination.
   - Unauthorized entry to computer records.

5 *Use of company facilities*
   - Use of telephone for private calls.
   - Admission to company premises outside working hours.
   - Use of company equipment – e.g. computers, photocopiers – for personal reasons.
   - Abuse of e-mails and the internet.

6 *Discrimination*
   - Overt discrimination but also sexual harassment and racial abuse.

The enforcement of such rules is a sensitive issue, requiring some kind of formal or informal disciplinary system. Butterfield *et al.* (2005) see disciplinary punishment as an inevitable element of a manager's job. Reviewing literature on the subject, they conclude that although managers typically regard punishment as being justified by deterrence or 'just desserts' (commensurate with the level of offence), the latter is the normal motive for any disciplinary sanction. Impression management plays a significant role: managers are concerned about their reputations to be fair but effective disciplinarians. Actions that are perceived to be unfair will elicit bad reactions from employees, ranging from sullen lack of cooperation to outright hostility or subversion. Butterfield *et al.* argue that there are specific elements of discipline that are important such as: the timeliness of the punishment; the perceived justice of the punishment; the use of constructive criticism; and keeping the punishment private.

Discipline is not only negative, in the sense of being punitive or preventative, it also makes a positive contribution to organizational performance. An effective organization cannot survive if its members behave in an anarchic way. Order within an organization depends on an appropriate mixture of each of these forms of discipline. Within the context of HRM, however, the emphasis has moved away from managerial discipline towards self and, especially, team discipline. Nevertheless, most organizations continue to have institutionalized disciplinary procedures, largely determined by management. Internet use at work is an interesting and growing disciplinary problem at work.

A study conducted in August 2006 (http://www.hrmguide.co.uk/relations/web-use.htm, 21 September, 2006) found that more than one in 50 web pages requested by employees

HRM in reality Businesses failing to control internet use

Employees are ignoring their organizations' internet acceptable usage policies (AUPs) according to a survey by network security provider SmoothWall. Seven out of 10 companies recognize that an AUP is crucial to the security of their IT systems, but 38 per cent of employees governed by such policies claim not to know the rules.

Three hundred business users were polled during November 2005 on their internet usage at work. 85 per cent said they regularly visited news sites and 40 per cent shopped online from work while 37 per cent used eBay and other auction sites. 61 per cent of those surveyed used personal email systems such as GMail or Hotmail at work and 41 per cent admitted to using instant messaging applications such as Microsoft Messenger and Yahoo! Messenger to contact friends and family. Skype is rapidly gaining popularity with 23 per cent using it at work – presumably having loaded the Skype client on to their employers' computers.

'Employees are failing to take notice of the high profile incidents of employees being dismissed for accessing pornography at work, as more than a third of respondents said that they were aware of pornography being downloaded within their organization,' said George Lungley, managing director, SmoothWall.

Most organizations are prepared to allow some nonwork-related web browsing, but the survey indicates far more than incidental usage. Over a third of individuals surveyed admitted to spending more than 30 minutes of each working day accessing nonwork-related websites – and 22 per cent spent over an hour per day. A mere 15 per cent said they only accessed nonwork-related websites during their lunch break or outside core working hours.

Astonishingly, almost a third (31 per cent) of respondents said they occasionally downloaded music or videos at work, and 8 per cent confessed to doing so regularly. Downloading such large files uses large amounts of internet bandwidth and, according to

SmoothWall, employers could be considered to be complicit to any violation of copyright law.

'Companies are obviously still not enforcing internet usage policies. We recommend locking down corporate networks to all but essential business applications and strictly controlling access to nonwork-related websites during working hours,' George Lungley said.

In businesses where an AUP is enforced, the survey found that:

- 19 per cent said the policy was enforced by software control
- 13 per cent said the policy was enforced by management checks
- 28 per cent said the policy was enforced by a combination of software and management controls.
- 40 per cent of respondents said that an AUP was in place but was not enforced.

SmoothWall's recommendation is that businesses prevent the use of nonwork-related applications at work to:

- ensure legal compliance
- avoid time-wasting web-browsing of nonwork-related sites
- prevent the risk of malicious websites infecting PCs with spyware and viruses.

They say that organizations should develop a clear AUP and communicate it to all employees. Critically, the policy should be enforced using centralized software control, to protect the employers' reputation, productivity and computer systems.

Has internet misuse become the greatest discipline problem in modern organizations?

Source: *HRM Guide UK* (http://www.hrmguide.co.uk/), 28 February, 2006.

while at work were from house hunting or job search websites. The study also showed that approximately 26 per cent of companies blocked access to job sites and 20 per cent restricted access to property and house hunting sites. In both the UK and the USA, visits to house hunting related sites outnumbered visits to job search sites. Another study, conducted in conjunction with the CIPD in 2004 showed that 70 per cent of UK businesses have had to discipline employees viewing pornographic images on company computers (http://www.hrmguide.co.uk/relations/computer-use.htm, 14 December, 2004).

Adams *et al.* (2005) studied factors underlying personal online shopping at the workplace. A survey of 852 employees from the USA and Canada found that 72 per cent had shopped online at work, with Americans more likely than Canadians to do so. The most popular reason was the availability of a high-speed internet connection. The degree of 'permissibility' of company policy was positively correlated to the percentage of online shopping that people conducted at work. Corporate monitoring had no impact on an employee's likelihood to shop online at work; although job satisfaction was less, on average, for employees where monitoring was reported.

Dismissal is the ultimate expression of such procedures and also one of the most unpleasant aspects of human resource management. It may arise because of disciplinary issues such as persistent absenteeism, failure of an employee to perform adequately despite support and training, or as a strategic requirement arising from a change in direction by the organization. Most managers regard the 'exiting' process with distaste – often it is more stressful for the sacking manager than the victims. Dismissal inevitably follows some form of conflict.

Career exits

According to the first survey on employee exits by career publisher Vault.com, 61 per cent of respondents have exited a job on bad terms with their employer.

Based on 706 responses from American employees in a variety of industries, the survey found the main reasons for leaving were disagreements with management (73 per cent), disagreements with co-workers (12 per cent), or to start employment with a new company immediately (14 per cent).

One respondent commented, 'Owners of the company were liars, cheaters, and didn't treat their employees well'. Another said, 'My manager wanted me to do something that violated FDA regulations, and then he got HR to begin disciplinary steps because I was disobedient'.

Almost half (47 per cent) did not give notice in person, but instead called or emailed their manager. One respondent explained, 'After having it out with my boss's boss, I called my boss and told him I quit. The funny thing was, at the same time I was in his voicemail, his boss paged him and told him to fire me.'

Types of bad exits included:

- screaming matches (42 per cent)
- negative mass emails (24 per cent)
- negative speeches at company meetings (18 per cent)
- vandalized or stolen company property (12 per cent)
- physical scuffles (4 per cent).

About half of respondents (52 per cent) witnessed or took part in a domino effect in which one person's exit caused others to leave the company soon afterwards.

Source: *HRM Guide USA* (http://www.hrmguide.com), 21 September, 2006.

Conflict

Where does conflict come from? Conflict has both positive and negative aspects as we can see in Table 23.1. A number of basic psychological causes are apparent, regardless of the overt justification for a dispute (McKenna, 1994, p.418):

Frustration and aggression. Disagreement often reflects frustration – feelings of being ignored, of being pressurized or of blocked promotion. Any point of difference, no matter how irrelevant, may spark a reaction to frustration. This may appear in the form of verbal aggression, seemingly out of proportion to the importance of the supposed dispute. Clearly, the dispute masks problems that are attributable to poor communication, lack of empowerment and mistrust.

Different objectives. The rhetoric of HRM states that organizations should aim for shared goals between management and staff. However, in practice, managers and employees have different priorities. Managers may focus on efficiency and cost-effectiveness, whereas employees want higher pay and longer holidays. Unless there are mechanisms, such as team briefings or quality circles, by which mutual understanding of these goals can be improved, differences are likely to be brought to a head at some stage.

Different values. These could be political – a difference in belief about the purpose of business for example – or a disagreement about the manager's right to manage. Many managers believe that they have the authority to issue instructions without being challenged by their staff. On the other hand, some employees consider that managers have this right only if they are prepared to explain their decisions, account for the consequences of their actions, and are prepared to accept questions and criticisms.

Jealousy. Individual employees can be sensitive to other members of staff being paid more than them, or getting extra perks. The conflict arises from jealousy or loss of status.

Positive	Negative	**Table 23.1**
Clearing the air. Allowing people to air their grievances can sometimes lead to an improved atmosphere after the disagreement has finished. This serves to bring 'hidden agendas' out into the open.	**Wasting time and energy**. A simple decision can be quick to implement, but negotiation can take an inordinate amount of time. Often participants forget original purpose of negotiation and get caught up with fighting a war.	Consequences of conflict
Understanding each other's position. When both sides of an agenda are brought out into the open, people must think through their own case in order to express it clearly; and grasp the other point of view in order to challenge it.	**Stress**. Conflicts can become quite personal, abusive and threatening. The postures taken by the two sides can lead to further stress. Mental exhaustion may come from prolonged debate.	
Modification of goal. One side may realize how unpopular or impractical the consequences of their argument may be.	**Worsening the situation**. Conflict may highlight problems, dislikes and grievances better left unstated. Tension may escalate debate into action: strikes, lock-outs, work-to-rule, threatened or implied redundancies. Consequences may be unpleasantness with worse morale and industrial relations after negotiations than before.	

Culture. The tradition of 'us and them' (employees versus management) continues to exist in many organizations, particularly those using an authoritarian style of people management. New staff and management are quickly encouraged to accept the 'normality' of this perspective. In other cases, a change in the management approach disturbs the prevailing employee relations culture.

Conflict is an inevitable feature of negotiating and bargaining. Trained negotiators are taught to deal with conflict, expecting both negative and positive aspects to appear during the process. This will be easier to understand when we consider specific models of negotiation later in this chapter.

Issues of conflict and discipline may not be resolved at local level. Many countries have mechanisms by which disputes may be taken to an outside body, usually in the form of industrial tribunals or arbitration bodies.

Tribunals and arbitration systems

To what extent can differences between employers and workers be resolved through **arbitration** or legal tribunals? It is the view in many countries that an impartial, legally based process has a significant role to play in a number of circumstances. Industrial tribunals take many forms: in Germany the labour courts make legally binding judgements; in the UK tribunal decisions do not set a precedent in law and cannot establish criminal behaviour. Even in the latter case, however, they have a long-term effect since they establish a set of values and

---

FedEx driver illegally denied unemployment benefits

The Massachusetts Department of Workforce Development has ruled that a former FedEx home delivery driver was illegally denied unemployment benefits after finding that he was actually an employee of FedEx, not an independent contractor as the company claimed.

The state examiner found that the driver was entitled to unemployment benefits because his services 'must be considered to have been under the direction and control' of FedEx. The decision noted a number of reasons why the driver should be considered an employee, including the fact that he was required to:

- Work to a schedule dictated by the company and without the flexibility typically afforded a truly independent contractor.

- Rent the company electronic package scanner, required by the company to monitor driver output.

- Buy the company uniform and delivery vehicle from the dealer specified by the company.

FedEx Ground, a subsidiary of FedEx Corporation, is presently the subject of numerous legal proceedings, including class action lawsuits brought by present and former drivers on the basis that they had been misclassified as independent contractors. Since December 2005, FedEx Ground has been assessed liable for nearly US$100 million by courts and/or government agencies regarding employment practices in respect of its drivers.

Lynn Rossman Faris, lead attorney, said: 'State after state, and federal agencies, have been rejecting the company's position and exposing its so-called independent contractor business model as a sham to avoid paying huge amounts in business expenses it – not drivers – should be shouldering.'

Source: *HRM Guide USA* (http://www.hrmguide.com), 23 August, 2006.

influence the behaviour of others. If there is a judgement on a case of significant racial discrimination, for example, the resulting publicity may lead to a moderation of racist behaviour as people fear the possibility of similar action against themselves.

Chelliah and D'Netto (2006) analyzed 342 decisions in 17 industries by arbitrators in the Australian Industrial Relations Commission to assess whether employees benefited from arbitration. They found that 50.6 per cent of arbitration decisions were in favour of employees but only 10.8 per cent of complainants were reinstated. They suggest that employers need to look at ways of creating a more harmonious workplace. Employees do not benefit much from arbitration and reaching a settlement through mediation may be a better option.

In the UK, the **Advisory, Conciliation, and Arbitration Service (ACAS)** plays a similar role to the Australian Industrial Relations Commission in relation to collective disputes. It provides the following services:

Binding arbitration. ACAS can appoint an arbitrator provided that the two parties agree to accept the arbitrator's decision.

Voluntary conciliation. ACAS provides a calm environment and help on defining the important issues. ACAS conciliation staff act as facilitators and do not make judgements or attempt to impose solutions.

Mediation. Intermediate between arbitration and conciliation. ACAS mediators make advisory recommendations that are aimed at preventing disputes from degenerating into industrial action. These recommendations are not binding on the parties involved.

ACAS also plays a major role in promoting agreed settlements in disputes taken to industrial tribunals. Of these, only about one-third go to a full hearing by the tribunal – most are settled with ACAS assistance or withdrawn – and less than half of these are judged in favour of the complainant.

HRM in reality ACAS 2005/2006 report reveals big rise in tribunal cases

In 2005/2006 the Advisory, Conciliation, and Arbitration Service (ACAS) had its busiest year ever:

- 908 553 people rang ACAS's national helpline calls compared with 880 787 last year. The top three enquiry topics were:
  - discipline and grievance
  - redundancies and layoffs
  - contract issues.
- There were 1.3 million visits to the ACAS website.
- 2964 good practice training sessions were held for over 40 000 organizational delegates.
- 109 712 applications were made to tribunals – compared with 81 833 last year. Unfair dismissal remains the largest complaint category with 35 944 applications.
- There was a slight fall – from 1123 last year to 952 this year – in the number of requests for ACAS to intervene in employment disputes and conciliate between the two sides. Pay continues to be the single biggest category.

According to Rita Donaghy, ACAS chair:

We have had another busy and challenging year. Our commitment to improving organizations through better employment relations continues to drive the development of new ACAS services. Last year, we introduced the ACAS model workplace to help organizations identify the features of an effective workplace, developed key partnerships, prepared new guidance for the age regulations and continued to help small businesses develop good employment practices.

She added:

ACAS's integrity, impartiality and fair dealing means more and more people are using our invaluable helpline and website services to access good practice guidance. The challenge for us now is to continue to develop and maintain our high standards and help more organizations realize the benefits of good employment relations.

Why would a service such as ACAS receive increasing numbers of enquiries and referrals?

Source: *HRM Guide UK* (http://www.hrmguide.co.uk), 15 August, 2006.

Tribunals are composed of a qualified lawyer as chair and two lay members – one employer and one trade unionist. The tribunals are informal by legal standards but continue to be intimidating for applicants.

The negotiating process

Negotiation is an ancient art. It is important in fields as diverse as diplomacy, buying and selling, arranging relationships (marriages, business partnerships), as well as employee relations. Negotiation is a form of decisionmaking where two or more parties approach a problem or situation wanting to achieve their own objectives – which may or may not turn out to be the same. In the employee relations arena, negotiation usually takes place within the collective bargaining environment.

Participants enter the process with widely different views: some, typically on the employee side, will view it as being fundamental to industrial democracy, fairness and good business conduct; others see it as a barrier to efficiency, a view more prevalent on the management side. The latter view sees negotiation as compromise and second-best to winning: possibly worse than giving in! As can be seen from Table 23.2, the process also has its own jargon.

Negotiation is not simply a matter of 'splitting the difference' so that neither side achieves what it wants. It can produce an outcome that meets both sets of goals. In negotiating, both sides must have some goals in common and some that conflict. For example, employers and employees will all want the business to survive and expand. However, employers might resist high pay rises to keep costs down, whereas the staff will want increases to boost employee morale. Usually, bargaining takes place because neither side has the power or the authority to force a decision on the other and preserve a harmonious working atmosphere.

Therefore, both sides will open negotiations knowing that they will have to move from the opening position and that there will have to be sacrifices on one item to achieve advantages on another. Even in those ideal circumstances, such as the German model, where deliberate confrontation is not acceptable, there will be an element of conflict between the two sides.

There is also an implicit assumption that the two parties have the same amount of power in the bargaining situation. This is almost certainly not the case and the degree of power will change during the process of negotiation; the location of greatest power may well switch backwards and forwards between the two sides as they achieve positions of advantage. Whatever the actual degree of power, advantages will come from both sides preserving the appearance or illusion of power. There is value, therefore, in playing a game of bluff.

Many texts imply that the methods of bargaining can only be learned through experience and may well suggest that negotiation, like most interpersonal skills, is instinctive rather than learned. Perhaps, the basic requirement is a combination of a competitive, assertive style with a devious and resilient personality. In fact, study of the bargaining process indicates regular patterns and processes that people tend to go through. Gates (2006) provides an overview of skills needed for successful negotiations and seeks to identify the benefits of training key staff

Table 23.2	Statement	Translation
	We explored all options	Everybody talked a lot
Communication in collective bargaining	A great deal of additional work will be necessary	Nobody understood it
	The results were inconclusive	Nothing happened
Source: Adapted from *Toctanic* (undated, circa 1989), unofficial staff publication, British Telecom International.	While no agreement was reached, definite progress was made	Nobody budged an inch
	It is hoped that this report will stimulate interest in the problem	Let somebody else do it next time

in negotiations skills. The study finds that only 5 per cent of the UK's training budget is spent on negotiations skills development. However, it makes a significant difference to the performance of all staff, both in internal and external negotiations.

Studies of industrial negotiations have indicated·that many disputes worsen because of the following factors:

- lack of clarity of aims or goals by one or both sides
- poor understanding of the detailed situation
- the apparent dispute is not the real problem.

These points are well-illustrated in the 'HRM in reality' case of Timex in which poor communication, cultural differences and a complete incompatibility of goals led to the closure of a factory.

HRM in reality Timex

In 1992 Timex was a multinational company with world headquarters in Connecticut, USA. It was controlled by Fred Olsen, a Norwegian entrepreneur and owner of the Olsen shipping line. An electronics components factory in Dundee on the north-east coast of Scotland formed part of the group. Faced with falling orders and short-time working, negotiations began at the end of that year between local management and unions.

On Christmas Eve 1992, management informed its 343 largely female, hourly-paid, workers that their numbers would have to be halved, at least until the latter part of 1993. Notwithstanding the holiday period, negotiations began immediately between officials of the Amalgamated Engineering and Electrical Union (AEEU) and managers from the plant. The management side was led by Timex UK president Peter Hall, described in one report as 'the Englishman from Surrey with the executive haircut and the tartan tie'. He had worked for the company for two years, having been headhunted for the Dundee post after his own electronics business had gone into receivership in the south-east of England.

The unions suggested that lay-offs should be organized on a rotating basis with the company supplementing state benefits. Timex managers did not support the concept of all staff working alternate weeks. They felt that the company should decide who should be laid off. A ballot of members indicated 92 per cent support for a strike that began on 29 January.

In mid-February, two corporate bosses travelled to the plant with a compromise formula. Among new 'fringe benefits' proposed were reductions in contributions to employee pension plans and an in-house savings scheme. The AEEU claimed there was a hidden agenda of more significant measures under consideration, including a pay freeze, cuts in holidays and

overtime payments, and an increase in working arrangements from 37 hours to 40 hours each week.

On 14 February, union members voted to return to work 'under protest', accepting the revised plan for negotiating lay-offs but resisting any erosion of pay and conditions. On 15 February they found factory gates locked. Two days later they received redundancy notices delivered by taxi. The first of an alternative workforce was bussed in the following day. The following months saw numerous violent clashes and arrests in the vicinity of the factory. The company unsuccessfully sought legal redress to limit the activities of pickets, who were supported by a number of high-profile politicians and unionists.

As positions polarized, cultural differences between the protagonists became increasingly evident. Timex was an elusive multinational foe with a reputation as a 'slash and burn' employer ready to redeploy in the interests of profit. Olsen was said to keep up-to-date with the smallest detail of his extensive business empire while remaining unimpressed by consensus or prevailing business fashion. Timex had been based in Dundee for 46 years, entering the globally competitive electronics subcontracting field after watch production ceased in 1983. Dundee was a city in which the demise of traditional industries based on jute and jam-making had contributed to rising unemployment.

The majority of Timex employees had worked for the company for a long time – ranging from ten to 40 years. There was a strong sense of community solidarity extending back over many generations and a tradition of labour activism among women. Non-unionized replacement workers were considered to be 'without dignity or conscience'. Workers were also critical of the AEEU president, Bill Jordan. 'Not for the first time, the focused fervour of a self-sufficient group of workers contrasts sharply with the inevitably distanced pragmatism of their union's top brass.' Within this emotional arena, Timex UK president Peter Hall's tone was described as 'studied, strategic blandness: as far as he is concerned, there is no industrial dispute; he is simply running a business'.

Any hope that Peter Hall was the main obstacle to a negotiated settlement received a major setback in June 1993 when he suddenly resigned. By the next meeting between the two sides Timex management had grown weary of trying to deal with a workforce it did not understand. Senior managers from the United States of America and union officials could find no common ground. The possible exception was the problem at the heart of the original dispute: a loss of £10 million between 1987–1992, coupled with a £2 million shortfall in the first six months of 1993. Timex threatened to close the Dundee factory by Christmas unless there was agreement to wage cuts and retraining to introduce conditions similar to those in Japanese companies operating in Britain.

The proposed deal was unanimously rejected and Timex announced 'an orderly withdrawal' from Dundee. Mohammed Saleh, corporate director of human resources, was reported as telling a press conference: 'I defy anybody to say we are not reasonable . . . It became clear that union members definitely did not want to work under conditions where they would have less wages, or less benefits, than what they had before the strike.' Gavin Laird, general secretary of AEEU blamed the situation on the company's exploitation of 'brutal anti-union legislation', while the Scottish Trades Union Congress said responsibility lay with Timex 'management madness'.

The end could not have been more acrimonious. On Sunday evening, 29 August, 1993, the Dundee factory was abruptly closed leaving John Monks, then general secretary-elect of the Trades Union Congress to comment: 'It is typical of Timex that they, in this very sorry and squalid affair, should have pulled out and in a sense done a moonlight flit.' In October, 1993, a narrow majority voted to accept a pay-off from Timex as recommended by the AEEU union. This provided one week's pay for every year worked, in return for a promise not to use union funds to pursue claims for unfair dismissal and an end to the boycott of Timex products. Jimmy Airlie, the AEEU union leader 'fled Dundee amid accusations of blackmail and betrayal'. He commented that while he understood the bitterness of workers 'the factory has closed, that was the reality'.

In *Scotland on Sunday* (20 June, 1993) Kamal Ahmed reflected:

> At its simplest the most bitter dispute to hit Britain since the 1980s was over 150 jobs and £30 a week. But at deeper, harsher levels, it became a battle for hearts and minds, a fight to the death between a management's right to manage and a worker's right to earn a decent wage . . . and to strike.

1 **What is the main problem underlying this case?**

2 **List the main parties/individuals involved and evaluate their: (a) objectives; (b) degree of flexibility; (c) effectiveness as negotiators.**

3 **What options were open to the negotiators?**

4 **Who made the final decision?**

5 **Was there a better way of dealing with the situation?**

Sources: *The Guardian*, 15–19 June, 1993; *Scotland on Sunday*, 20 June, 1993; *The Scotsman*, 15 October, 1993.

Models of bargaining

There are several models of the bargaining process, the clearest of which identifies four main stages (Lyons, 1988, p.110):

1 *Initial positioning.* Both parties set out their positions and requirements in an emphatic, firm way aimed at giving the impression that there is no possibility of budging from those positions. The situation can appear hopeless at this stage.

2 *Testing.* The next stage is a less formal probing of the other side's demands, testing out which are really unmovable and which might bend in the right circumstances.

3 *Concession.* Some tentative proposals and concessions are exchanged on which detailed negotiations can take place.

4 *Settlement.* Finally, agreement is reached and the package of new terms is settled and actioned.

Obviously, the model does not apply in every case – the Timex negotiations went awry from the beginning and came to an end somewhere in the middle of the sequence. Lyons argues that successful negotiation requires specific skills, examined in the following subsections. These skills were visibly missing at Timex, particularly on the management side.

Analysis

This may be defined as the ability to analyse a situation not only in terms of one's own position and goals but also those of the other side. There should be a long-term perspective – rarely is it clear that one should begin to consider the consequences of the whole process at this basic stage. The analysis must include a decision on which elements can be agreed on an 'I win/you win' basis, as opposed to those which are 'I win/you lose'. It is not worthwhile winning one of the latter if the advantage is trivial in comparison with the longer-term bad feelings that may arise as a consequence.

This phase is frequently glossed over but in fact is possibly the most important. It is the stage at which one should work out what the highest and lowest gains you and your opponent are likely to accept. Additionally, there must be a clear understanding of what the other side really want as opposed to what you think they might want. Clearly, in the Timex case we see little understanding of the opposing perspective and no evidence from the management side of a willingness to accept an 'I win/you win' position.

Effective argument

This has to be carefully balanced between being forceful and being reasonable. The whole point of negotiation is to convince the other side of the merits of your argument as against their own. It is a change process. It is important to avoid cheap point-scoring and abuse in order to preserve mutual respect and avoid distraction from irrelevant side issues. Again, the Timex managers were unable to convince the employees of the merits of their argument and seemingly incapable of understanding the employees' point of view.

Signals of cooperation

The skill of sensing and giving signals of cooperation and possible compromise. Again, virtually absent in the Timex case. Kanter (1989, p.156) found that the participants in successful 'business partnerships' were 'very adept at "reading" signals that indicated whether partner representatives can be trusted'. On the 'tit-for-tat' principle, maximum opportunity comes from rewarding cooperation or compromise with a compromise of your own. On the other hand, one does not reward the opposition for sticking to an unmovable position: every offer one makes has to be conditional on cooperation in return. It may be necessary to keep communication going in order for this process to happen. In the case of a complete deadlock, it may even be necessary to have 'talks about talks'. All offers and threats must have credibility, remembering that it is not real power that matters but the appearance of it.

Attention to detail

Lastly, the final conclusion of negotiations requires the ability to attend to detail, making sure that all aspects are taken care of and there is no way for the other side to avoid its agreed obligations.

Bacon and Blyton (2006) explored the 'mutual gains' argument that employees benefit when teamworking is introduced alongside employee involvement in problem-solving within a cooperative industrial relations climate. They reported the outcome of negotiations to introduce teamworking at two steelworks in the north of England. Moderate union branches and employees at one site cooperated with managers in joint problem-solving teams to redesign work. However, greater job insecurity coerced unions to accept teamworking agreements involving extensive de-manning and a pay increase for fewer employees. Employees perceived greater job security at the other works and, by rejecting joint problem-solving with managers, militant unions protected more jobs and extracted higher payment for teamworking.

Employee involvement

Employee involvement is a wide-ranging topic that hinges on the notion that managers may have a prerogative to manage but this prerogative should not be exercised without considering the opinions of their employees. The concept of employee involvement has a moral, practical and legal basis. The moral dimension is difficult to resolve since it involves an ethical debate on the 'right' of managers to manage and the 'right' of employees to have a say in the way the organization is managed. Fundamentally, it is a matter of personal opinion. The practical and legal aspects are more easily explained and justified.

There are sound practical reasons for taking account of employee views before making significant decisions. They include an acknowledgement of the greater and more detailed knowledge that experienced employees may have of specific processes when compared with a manager who may be relatively new or who has never been involved at a working level with those processes. Changes may seem perfectly reasonable and desirable to the manager, operating at a distance from the activity to be changed. But skilled workers may be aware of implications that are invisible to the manager. In fact, as we observed in Part one, the concept of knowledge management is based on the value of individual expertise and experience that need to be harnessed and used for the benefit of the organization – rather than being ignored by overconfident and unwise managers.

The authority of managers may be constrained by an organization's own rules in the form of company handbooks, job definitions, reporting paths and consultation procedures so that the involvement of employees in decisionmaking cannot be avoided. We noted in previous chapters that legislation can also impose requirements for consultation, for example in the form of works councils required under European legislation. In practice, most countries have employment legislation in place that sets the rights of employees within a legal context. Their rights are usually prescribed both individually and collectively so that (theoretically, at least) it is impossible for an organization and its managers to have total discretion over consultation and, to a lesser extent, involvement.

Key concept 23.1 Employee involvement

An umbrella term that is inconsistently and imprecisely used to embrace a diverse range of management processes involving participation, communication, decisionmaking, industrial democracy and employee motivation.

According to Holden (2001):

> There is an enormous range of employee involvement schemes, varying from those which are informational mechanisms to full-blown democratic systems where employees have as much say in the decisionmaking as does management. This makes an all-encompassing definition problematic. In addition, different labels have been attached to these processes, such as employee or worker participation, industrial democracy, organizational communications, co-determination, employee influence, etc., each of which have their own definitions.

Marchington (2001) considers that employee involvement became prominent in the 1980s as an attempt by employers to find participative ways in which to manage staff. The trend in recent decades towards individual rather than collective employee relations may have encouraged interest in employee involvement. The UK 1998 Workplace Employee Relations Survey (Cully *et al.*, 1999) showed that even in firms that recognized trade unions, managers consulted individual employees (57 per cent) in preference to union representatives (36 per cent).

In fact, 41 per cent of the companies surveyed did not have any union involvement but a mere 8 per cent stated that they never involved individual employees.

The nature of the relationship between employer and employee is described as the 'psychological contract' (see Key concept 23.2). Townley (1994) sees an inevitable gap between what is promised and what is realized: 'the naturally occurring space between expectation and deliverance of work'. The psychological contract implies some kind of exchange within the employment relationship but this is obscured by the power of the economic relationship between employer and employee.

Key concept 23.2 The psychological contract

An informal understanding between the employer and employee. Unlike the formal employment contract, this has no physical existence. It is a set of expectations held by both employers and employees in terms of what they wish to give and receive from their working relationship (Rousseau and Parks, 1993).

Perhaps anticipating employer branding and its implications, Monks (1996) suggests that management of the psychological contract could be a suitable job for the human resource manager. In order for this to be possible, Townley (1994) points to three areas where knowledge is required:

Knowledge of the workforce as a population: where human resource information systems, employee surveys and staff feedback are as important as traditional personnel records.

Knowledge of the activity or work to be performed: detailed information obtainable through job analyses, quality circles and, more recently, the techniques elaborated for knowledge management.

Knowledge of individual workers: through performance assessments and feedback interviews.

She sees the employment relationship becoming a 'calculable arena' – a transformation of 'soft' HR based on indeterminate and sometimes unspecified understanding into a 'harder' form based on detailed information. In her view human resource practices are technologies through which 'activities and individuals become knowable and governable'. From this perspective, HRM becomes a powerful methodology that can turn the apparently imprecise and subjective topic that was once 'personnel' into a technology of people.

In an Australian study, Winter and Jackson (2006) examined perceptions of the state of the psychological contract between managers and employees (including work environment and factors such as salary, recognition and rewards, trust and fairness, open/honest communication). Assessments of the state of the contract were similar. However, managers tended to construct rational explanations and emphasize resource constraints and financial considerations, while employees constructed emotional explanations and attributed the situation to unfair, uncaring or distant management. Winter and Jackson's findings suggest that managers need more effective communication strategies placing them in a better position to explain to employees how the organization can meet (or not) specific contract expectations and obligations.

Employee involvement in practice

Unlike Townley, Marchington (2001) sees employee involvement as a feature of 'soft' rather than 'hard' HRM. In firms with a hard orientation, Marchington considers that the 'numbers-driven', cost-cutting mentality reduces involvement to a one-way communication channel aimed at transmitting management decisions and propaganda to staff. This contrasts with organizations that are true believers in employees as their 'greatest asset' where there is a strategic commitment to sharing information and opinions and achieving a workplace culture that meets business needs.

Peccei and Rosenthal (2001) examined attempts to engender desirable customer-oriented behaviours among employees in the context of a major change initiative in a retail company. The change programme followed (by now) orthodox management theory which assumed that management behaviour, job design and values-based training would produce a feeling of empowerment among employees, and that this sense of empowerment would lead to pro-social customer-oriented behaviour. A large-scale employee survey showed that staff who took a positive view of management behaviour and who had also participated in values-based training were more likely to feel empowered. In turn, Peccei and Rosenthal found a positive relationship between psychological empowerment and customer-oriented behaviour.

Key concept 23.3 Empowerment and empowering

Murrell and Meredith (2000, p.1) define empowering as: '... mutual influence; it is the creation of power; it is shared responsibility; it is vital and energetic, and it is inclusive, democratic and long-lasting.' They argue that 'empowerment' implies a finished process, a state of constancy. Whereas: 'Empowering ... suggests action – enabling the growth of individuals and organizations as they add value to the products or services the organization delivers to its customers, and the promotion of continuous discovery and learning.'

Marchington (2001) identifies the following characteristics in employee involvement schemes:

1 Employee involvement is a process primarily instigated by management.
2 Employees are assumed to want greater involvement, regardless of its form.
3 A unity of purpose is thought to be achievable between employees and their managers.
4 There is an expectation that employee involvement will lead to greater commitment and productivity.

Marchington (*ibid.*) also states that:

For many observers, notions of employee involvement (EI) and participation are central to any consideration of human resource management. Terms such as 'empowerment', 'team working', 'autonomy' and 'communications' are peppered throughout the management literature which publicizes and celebrates the latest initiatives in HRM. Similarly, the concepts of involvement form part of many academic discussions of HRM. Either as explicit elements of its policy and practice, or implicitly as a potential contributor to the achievement of higher levels of employee commitment.

He notes that belief in the link between direct employee involvement and high levels of commitment and performance is based on some questionable assumptions:

1 That line managers will be committed to employee involvement and will ensure that it happens in the workplace.
2 That employee involvement positively influences staff attitudes, causing them to change their working behaviour which, in turn, leads to greater effectiveness and productivity.
3 That trade union officials and other employee representatives will allow themselves to be marginalized or led into acceptance of the management agenda.

Schuster (1998) asks why managers have been so slow in adopting employee-centred management. He postulates five main reasons:

1 Complacency and inertia. He argues that, until recently, many executives had never questioned or considered changing the fairly comfortable status quo.

2 The short-term focus of 'management systems in general, and reward systems in particular'. Executive performance bonuses and incentive plans are tied to one year – and certainly not aimed at building a committed workforce over the long term.

3 Inability to measure the impact of HR practices. Schuster contends that: 'Until recently, little attention has been paid to executive performance regarding effective utilization of human resources, in part because standards for comparison did not exist. Our lack of *control* [original emphasis] over the efficient utilization of the most expensive single cost of operation in many organizations is indeed remarkable.'

4 Reluctance to give up their special status, executive privileges and managerial power.

5 Perhaps the most significant explanation of all – that many managers would like to introduce high-involvement practices 'but are unsure how to begin or exactly how to proceed'.

Pun, Chin and Gill (2001) investigated the characteristics of successful employee involvement initiatives in Hong Kong. They found the most critical factors to be: management commitment; rewards and motivation with a clear corporate mission; continuous improvement; and both extrinsic and intrinsic rewards. Contrary to the view that line managers are obstacles to employee involvement, Fenton-O'Creevy (2001) found that middle managers' attitudes were no more negative than those of senior managers. But there was a complex relationship between perceptions of their own degree of empowerment and attitudes towards employee involvement. Managers with experience of employee involvement were more likely to be supportive, but not if they had recently lost a job. Intriguingly, however, managers who had been through de-layering were more likely to support the involvement of employees. In a UK study, Cox, Zagelmeyer and Marchington (2006) concluded that involvement is not simply there or not: there are degrees of 'embeddedness', a combination of depth and breadth of involvement. The greater the breadth and depth, the higher the resulting commitment and job satisfaction.

According to Fisher (1999, p.3):

> Empowerment has clearly become the latest in a long litany of vogue practices that have ebbed and flowed over corporations like the changing of the tide. Today it is estimated that virtually every corporation in North America and Western Europe is using various forms of empowerment somewhere in their organization. Many even utilize an advanced form of empowerment called *self-directed work teams* (SDWTs) – now more commonly called *high-performance work systems*.

In fact, SDWTs are in a direct line of descent from the 'socio-technical systems' of the 1950s. Fisher argues that companies that take the concept seriously consider empowerment to be more than a passing fad. He also sees the team leader as a key role in the empowerment process. In the past the equivalent would have been supervisor, 'foreman', or manager. Now their titles may include terms such as 'facilitator' or 'adviser' and 'lead', 'coach' or 'train' rather than 'plan', 'organize', 'direct' or 'control'. Under the traditional form of management, supervisors would control subordinates by telling them what to do. In other words, the supervisor was the boss. Fisher contends that all traditional managers are supervisors but, for empowerment to take effect, they must become team leaders. Fisher (*ibid.*, p.11) justifies this by saying that: 'Competitive advantage comes from fully utilizing the *discretionary* effort of the workforce, not from buying the latest gadget or using the latest management fad. Voluntary effort comes from employee commitment, and commitment comes from empowerment.'

Ramaswamy and Schiphorst (2000) found that employee empowerment was increasingly viewed as a serious strategic option by Indian companies whose profitability was being squeezed in a competitive market. On the face of it, power-sharing which resulted in workers taking responsibility for shop-floor decisions on quality, safety, productivity and material seemed attractive to both managers and employees. But trade unions might choose to obstruct or subvert the process. Gill and Krieger (1999) surveyed workplaces in 10 European Union countries and found a considerable gap between the rhetoric and reality of direct participation. Different forms of direct participation were widespread in the 10 countries but the scope was relatively limited. The survey also showed that works councils and union representatives were more likely to be 'agents of change' rather than barriers to achieving employee involvement.

For Murrell and Meredith (2000) managers in an empowering organization:

- Believe that leadership belongs to all employees – and not just a few.
- Know that the company is most likely to succeed when employees have the tools, training and authority to do their best work.
- Understand that information is power – and share it with all employees.
- Value employees enough to build a culture that values and supports individuals.
- Create opportunities for finding solutions and for designing what-can-be, not searching for problems and what-should-have-been.
- Understand that fostering empowerment is a continuous effort – not an end-point to be checked off a list of objectives.

Lee and Koh (2001) argue that although empowerment has been actively practised, the exact meaning of the terms 'empowerment' and 'psychological empowerment' have not been thought through. They contend that empowerment is quite distinct from related concepts such as authority delegation, motivation, self-efficacy, job enrichment, employee ownership, autonomy, self-determination, self-management, self-control, self-influence, self-leadership, high-involvement and participative management. They conclude that empowerment is not just a fad, but a unique concept reflecting a new managerial approach. Conversely, Harley (1999), using data from the 1995 Australian Workplace Industrial Relations Survey could find no meaningful relationship between empowerment and employee autonomy.

Ichniowski *et al.* (2000) review a number of theories as to why high skill, high-involvement workplaces are believed to be more effective than traditional 'top-down' management regimes. They divide these theories into two basic groups:

1 Those that focus on the effort and motivation of workers and work groups and suggest that people work harder.

2 Those that focus on changes in the structure of organizations that produce improvements in efficiency.

In the first group, the emphasis may be on 'working harder' and 'working smarter'. People may work harder if they find elements of a job to be interesting or enjoyable, and this may come from rewards or feedback. They are also less likely to resent aspects of the job if they have contributed to its design.

As regards working smarter, innovative work practices can lead to improved efficiency. Workers can suggest improved work practices because they have a more intimate knowledge of the job than managers or external consultants. Moreover, open discussion allows employees to modify their own work processes to fit more effectively with others as they become aware of the 'bigger picture'. Ichniowski *et al.* point to the need to change work culture from 'rate-busting' – discouraging high levels of performance – to one that values greater efficiency. This process can be encouraged by specifically rewarding high performance through collective bonuses. Helper, Levine and Bendoly (2002) surveyed the benefits of employee involvement practices for blue-collar workers in the auto-supply industry and found wages to be 3–5 per cent higher than would otherwise be the case. They attribute the cause to improved efficiency.

Theories in the second group may emphasize innovative work practices that can also lead to improvements in organizational structure that are independent of motivational effects. Ichniowski *et al.* (2000) give the following as examples:

- Cross-training and flexible job assignment may reduce the costs of absenteeism.
- Delegating decisionmaking to self-directed teams can reduce the number of supervisors or middle managers and improve communication.

- Training in problem-solving, statistical process control and computer skills may enhance the benefits of information technology.
- Involving workers and unions in decisionmaking can reduce grievances and other sources of conflict.

It is clear that such changes associated with employee involvement are complex and make it 'difficult to isolate any single causal mechanism that produces their effects on economic performance'. Nevertheless, Ichniowski *et al.* conclude that the companies which adopt such practices 'should enjoy higher productivity and quality ... , leading to lower costs and higher product demand, all else equal'. But this comes at a cost because employee involvement programmes can be expensive due to extra meetings and related activities.

Silvestro (2002) reports empirical findings from one of the UK's largest supermarket companies that seem to challenge the notion that employee satisfaction and loyalty are key drivers of productivity, efficiency and profit. The study shows an inverse correlation between employee satisfaction and the measures of productivity, efficiency and profitability. In fact, the most profitable stores were those in which employees were least satisfied and length of service tended to be lowest. One possible explanation is that managers at ground level were being pressurized to maximize store efficiency, leading to 'dysfunctional managerial behaviour at store level'.

HRM in reality Controlling absence levels

A survey of top Irish organizations has found that almost 65 per cent of companies do not calculate the annual cost of absence to their business and have no idea what impact it has on their direct or indirect costs.

The report by Mercer Human Resource Consulting argues that in the current economic environment the cost of employee sick days can have an impact on overall competitiveness so it is important that organizations review and manage their absence procedures. Effective reporting and measurement can drive behavioural change, particularly when supported by senior management.

Kevin Kinsella, consultant with Mercer Human Resource Consulting said:

Our experience in this area and indeed our research demonstrates that reporting and measurement of absence plays a very effective role in reducing absence levels. However, many companies take a casual and sporadic approach to absence management and fail to actively manage a major cost driver.

Key survey findings include:

- About a quarter of respondents (26 per cent) estimate the cost of absence to be in excess of €500 000 per annum.
- Minor illness is cited as the most common cause of lost days (33.2 per cent).
- Musculoskeletal illnesses and back pain account for almost 20 per cent of absences.

- Recording of absence is the number one tool in combating absence levels (identified by 90 per cent of companies).
- A fifth of organizations (20 per cent) reported absence levels of over 6 per cent per annum.
- The majority of organizations (65 per cent) do not calculate the cost of absence to their business.
- Some 45 per cent of managers with responsibility for managing absence receive no training in the area.
- Similarly, 41 per cent of managers with responsibility in the area have no formal targets.

Kevin Kinsella added:

Our survey clearly reveals that while senior managers are highly aware that 'absence management' is an issue for their business, very few companies are taking an appropriate, strategic approach to reducing absenteeism in their businesses. There will always be short-term absence in organizations. Mercer's experience and research suggests that there is no one 'magic cure' to manage sickness absence. The introduction of a range of simple measures such as absence reporting; early interventions on health issues; the provision of health insurance; and the provision of support and training for line managers, can however, dramatically reduce absenteeism levels.

Why might organizations fail to control absence levels?

Source: *HRM Guide* (http://www.hrmguide.co.uk/), 14 September, 2006.

Work–life balance

The 'Work–life Balance 2000' baseline study was conducted jointly by the Institute for Employment Research, University of Warwick and IFF Research. It was commissioned by the UK Department of Education and Employment (DfEE) to give baseline information for the department's work–life balance campaign (*HRMGuide.co.uk*, 20 November, 2000). It is representative of national provision of work–life balance arrangements in places of work that have five or more employees. The study consists of two surveys: (a) a survey of employers responsible for 2500 workplaces in Great Britain; and (b) a further survey of around 7500 employees.

The study concludes that there is a widespread demand from employees for the right to balance work and home life. It also reveals that businesses prefer to offer stress counselling for the personal consequences of long working hours (49 per cent) rather than provide assistance for childcare (9 per cent).

One in nine of full-time employees (including men with children) work more than 60 hours every week. Two-thirds of male employees believe that part-time working would damage their career prospects. At the same time there is a clear demand for greater flexibility – especially from fathers. In general, men seem to have a greater enthusiasm for working from home than do women. Virtually all the respondents to both surveys – employees and employers alike – agreed with the concept of work–life balance. But one in eight of employees still worked Saturdays and Sundays and around 20 per cent of employees worked for 24-hour/seven-day-week businesses.

Other conclusions of the study were:

- 80 per cent of workplaces had employees who worked more than their standard hours with 39 per cent doing so without extra pay.

- Just 20 per cent of employers were fully aware of increased maternity leave rights and 24 per cent fully aware of new paternal leave rights.

- 25 per cent of entitled female employees took less than 18 weeks maternity leave.

- 55 per cent of employers consider it acceptable to allow staff to move from full-time to part-time work in some cases.

- 24 per cent of employees now work flexitime with 12 per cent working only during school terms.

- 56 per cent of women preferred flexible working after a pregnancy – for example, part-time or home-based – to having a longer maternity leave period.

Health and safety

According to Naidoo and Wills (2000, p.270):

> The relationship between work and health may appear substantial but it is viewed in different ways by different groups of people. One of the defining characteristics of the workplace setting is that it brings together a variety of groups who have different agendas with regard to work and health. The key parties are workers or employees and their trade unions or staff associations, employers and managers, occupational health staff, health and safety officers, environmental health officers and specialist health promoters.

Sickness absence in the UK due to workplace injury and illness amounts to 19 million days a year or 40 times the amount lost because of industrial action. According to the TUC, sickness absence as a whole costs the British economy somewhere between £4 billion and £9 billion annually. Moreover, 27 000 people leave the employment market each year because of a workplace injury or illness.

An Australian Bureau of Statistics (ABS, 2000) report shows that 477 800 people experienced a work-related injury or illness in the year ending September 2000. This amounts to about 5 per cent of the 9 687 300 Australians aged 15 and over who worked at some time during that period. Broken down into major categories: 60 per 1000 males; 36 per 1000 females; 70 per 1000 males aged 35–44 years; and 41 per 1000 females aged 35–44 years.

The report indicates that, of people who had experienced a work-related injury or illness in the 12 months ending September 2000: 6 per cent were not working at September 2000, and 89 per cent were employees in the job where they experienced a work-related injury or illness. More than twice as many males (323 900) experienced a work-related injury or illness as female workers (154 000). Some 40 per cent of the 477 800 people who experienced a

---

HRM in reality Managers enjoy their work

Stress levels among senior managers are declining, their work–life balance is improving and more people are working long hours because they enjoy their jobs, according to Roffey Park's Management Agenda 2006 survey.

With heavy workloads and the longest working hours in Europe (although it is no secret that this is due to heavy workloads), it also seems that a majority (6 out of 10) of British senior managers work long hours simply because they enjoy their jobs. The survey of 967 middle and senior managers also reports lower stress levels and a more satisfactory work–life balance.

A staggering 85 per cent of respondents said they worked consistently longer than their contracted working week. Of these, nearly a quarter (24 per cent) of men – compared with 8 per cent of women – said they worked an extra 15 hours per week.

Apart from enjoying their work, the reasons given for working longer hours than contracted included:

- having a heavy workload (65 per cent)
- needing to work long hours to be successful (26 per cent)
- being expected to by senior managers (12 per cent)
- doing so simply because others do (6 per cent).

Stress

The survey also found a reduction in reported work stress for the first time in recent years. Two-thirds (67 per cent) claimed to have experienced stress in 2006 compared with 78 per cent in 2005, 74 per cent in 2004 and 70 per cent in 2003. However, public sector managers had a higher level of reported work stress (72 per cent) than those in other sectors.

Commitment

In the 2006 report, for the first time, a majority (57 per cent) of respondents said that their senior managers were committed to achieving a work–life balance, compared with a mere 33 per cent in 2005. Additionally, the number of senior managers and leaders practising a work–life balance has increased from 22 per cent in

2005 to 32 per cent in 2006. Women were the most likely to have different perceptions of work–life balance – 69 per cent of women felt that senior managers were more committed to achieving a work–life balance compared with only 48 per cent of men.

Loyalty

The research showed evidence of organizational loyalty from managers with 82 per cent of respondents feeling quite committed or very committed to their organization and 57 per cent saying they are prepared to go the extra mile to get things done. Over two-thirds (69 per cent) also believed that their organizations are committed to them in return.

Motivation

The report also looked at major motivators and demotivators in the workplace. The most significant motivators include:

- Making a difference (88 per cent)
- Job enjoyment (79 per cent)
- Personal achievement (75 per cent).

Demotivators include:

- Lack of recognition (43 per cent)
- Lack of time to achieve workload (41 per cent)
- Bureaucracy (40 per cent).

Dr Valerie Garrow, principal researcher at Roffey Park and co-author of 'The Management Agenda', commented: 'Managers continue to work long hours, but many say they do so because, as well as dealing with heavy workloads, they enjoy their job. People are clearly motivated by making a difference and having a sense of achievement in the workplace and they are prepared to go the extra mile to get the job done.'

Why are managers' reported stress levels declining?

Source: *HRM Guide UK* (http://www.hrmguide.co.uk), 7 February, 2006.

work-related injury or illness received workers' compensation for their most recent work-related injury or illness.

Around 259 900 did not apply for workers' compensation. Very nearly a half (49 per cent) of these said the main reason for not applying was that they considered the injury or illness to be minor. More than half (54 per cent) of those who did not apply for workers' compensation received no financial assistance for that injury or illness. Of the 46 per cent receiving financial assistance, the most common sources were Medicare and employer-provided sick leave.

Health and safety are workplace issues with considerable organizational and legal implications for HR and other managers. Naidoo and Wills (2000) identify a number of benefits to organizations from the promotion of health in the workplace as (a) 'hard' benefits, such as improvements in productivity as a result of reduced sickness, absence and staff turnover; and (b) 'soft' benefits, including enhanced corporate image.

Organizations may introduce specialist occupational health staff tasked with the following (Naidoo and Wills, *ibid.*):

- surveillance of the work environment, such as monitoring the effects of new technology
- introducing initiatives and providing advice on the control of hazards
- surveillance of employee health including assessing fitness to work and analysing sickness/absence reports
- organizing first aid and emergency responses
- involvement with adaptation of work and working environment to the worker.

Changes away from large, labour-intensive manufacturing organizations towards more fragmented, technology-based industries have dramatically altered the nature of occupational health over the last few decades – in developed countries, at least. Boyd (2001) argues that health and safety (as a topic) occupies a somewhat rhetorical role in HRM literature. Boyd looked at HRM and the management of health and safety in the airline industry and found that airlines have adopted a short-term cost-cutting approach to both in response to increasingly competitive trading conditions. The focus has been on reducing operating costs, achieving immediate productivity gains and prioritizing profit over employee health and safety.

HRM in reality TUC responds to report on UK's poor health and safety record

TUC general secretary, Brendan Barber, welcomed a report from the Crime and Society Foundation which concludes that unions are key to tackling the UK's poor health and safety record. He said:

> With around ten thousand people dying every year as a result of injuries sustained or diseases contracted whilst at work, the government needs to do more to take irresponsible employers to task for their lax approach to health and safety.
>
> In recent years the number of health and safety inspections has fallen and many workplace accidents go unreported. And even when a safety crime is uncovered, few ever result in successful prosecutions. Massive fines like the ones recently incurred by Network Rail and Balfour Beatty for their failings over the Hatfield rail crash may hit the headlines but many negligent employers are quite simply getting away with murder.
>
> Only when the UK has a new law of corporate killing combined with a law change making directors responsible for the health and safety of their employees and customers, will employers start to take their safety responsibilities seriously. Bosses would do well to pay more attention to the warnings coming from unions and their workplace safety reps. It's no accident that workplaces with the best safety records are the ones with employers sensible enough to work hand in hand with unions.

What role can unions play in reducing health and safety problems?

Source: *HRM Guide UK* (http://www.hrmguide.co.uk/), 17 October, 2005.

HRM in reality　Teen work injuries

A survey of 6810 teens shows that of the 50 per cent that were in employment, 514 had been injured at work. In 150 cases the injury was severe enough to affect activities at home, work, or school for more than three days, and 97 filed for workers' compensation.

'The findings from this study clearly indicate that work-related injuries among youth are a significant health problem. Developing programs and strategies to reduce injury must be made a priority,' say the report's authors Kristina M. Zierold, assistant professor of family and community medicine at Wake Forest University School of Medicine, and Henry A. Anderson, chief medical officer of the Wisconsin Division of Public Health.

Training on the job where safety could be stressed is often given by another employee and 'usually consists of explaining how to do the work and how to work the equipment, without emphasis on safety issues. In other instances, no training is given at all. . . . There are no standards governing the safety training' said Zierold. 'Because so many high school students are working during the school year, we advocate introducing a safety training course within the school health curriculum. Training would emphasize how to identify work-related hazards, how to protect themselves from hazards, and how to address their supervisors with their safety concerns. With the safety training, teens could feel empowered at the workplace by knowing their rights and how to protect themselves.'

The researchers note that nationally each year, 'approximately 70 children die from injuries inflicted at work; hundreds are hospitalized and tens of thousands require treatment in hospital emergency rooms. The National Pediatric Trauma Registry and the National Center for Health Statistics report that occupational injuries are the fourth-leading cause of death among youth ages 10–19.'

The new survey showed that some of the jobs and tasks required of teens are illegal. The most dangerous jobs were in:

● lumber mills (51 per cent were injured)
● lumber yards (40 per cent)
● manufacturing (37 per cent)
● gas stations (36 per cent)
● someone else's farm (36 per cent)
● construction (30 per cent).

Why are teenagers more prone to injuries at work than older employees?

Source: *HRM Guide USA* (http://www.hrmguide.com/), 24 August, 2006.

HRM in reality　Stress is a taboo subject

A study released earlier this year shows that stress is still regarded as a taboo subject in today's workplace. Despite the huge costs and high risks associated with work-related stress, many working environments are still chiefly characterized by high pressure and heavy workloads. Moreover, susceptibility to stress is very much considered to be a weakness that employees cannot afford to highlight without fear of repercussions.

These findings come from 'Hot Under the Collar: How Stress is Impacting on the 21st Century Business Environment' completed by Cubiks, a specialist HR consultancy. Specific findings include:

● Complaining of stress will damage your career prospects – 76 per cent of survey respondents thought that their career prospects would be damaged if they complained of stress, and managers confirmed that they are right to think this. 79 per cent of managers said they would be less likely to employ a candidate if they suspected that they were prone to stress and 87 per cent would be less likely to promote an existing employee if they had doubts over their ability to handle stress.

● Stress levels are rising and will get higher – one in four said that their average stress levels at work were either high or very high and almost half expect these levels to increase in the next 12 months.

● The economic downturn is influencing stress levels – only 9 per cent considered poor compensation and benefits to be a major concern, which indicates that those who have not been affected by redundancy or restructuring are grateful to be in employment. Job insecurity was stated as being a cause of stress for almost half of all respondents.

● It's not just emotive tasks such as dismissing staff or announcing redundancies that cause stress for

▶

managers – a large proportion of managers said that core people management tasks such as handling performance appraisals or conducting the recruitment interview were a significant source of stress for them. This suggests that managers are not receiving the training needed to perform in their role.

● Few organizations provide facilities for stressed employees – only one third (34 per cent) of respondents said that stress was recognized as an issue in their workplace and just 31 per cent of respondents said that personal counselling services were available to them. Fewer still (27 per cent) said that their organization has any formal process for handling grievances or concerns relating to stress.

Commenting on the report, Barry Spence, CEO of Cubiks, said: 'It has been well established for some time now that high employee stress levels can have a major negative impact on both individual and organizational performance. Given that this is the case, I'm surprised that so many employers seem to be taking such a cavalier attitude to the way stress is perceived and handled in their workplace.

'Some pressure can, of course, play an important motivational role and actually serve to enhance productivity. However, when it isn't managed carefully it can quickly spiral out of control leading to increased absenteeism, higher rates of staff turnover, early retirements and, in the worst cases, expensive litigation. Stress can affect all of us so employees shouldn't be made to feel as if they should suffer in silence.

'I can only conclude from these findings that employers either don't yet fully appreciate the risks associated with stress or are taking a calculated gamble that stress won't affect them. Whatever the case, the situation needs to be remedied. Today, management needs to know where stress exists in an organization and how it is manifesting itself. They should be open to what a stress audit might find as this could turn out to be surprisingly positive.'

Although 49 per cent of respondents did think that their line-manager would be concerned or sympathetic if they complained of stress, a quarter (24 per cent) believed that their line managers would become irritated or annoyed if they raised stress as an issue. Almost half said that their relationship with their superiors was a considerable or major cause of concern for them and one in four (23 per cent) complained that they were suffering from harassment or bullying.

Barry Spence went on to comment: 'There is a lot of evidence in this survey to suggest that people across industry are being asked to take on responsibility for managing restructuring projects, but are not being equipped to handle this aspect of their role. Perhaps they are not being given the training to make this important step-up, or maybe they are having difficulty in pin-pointing what they need to do and how they should adapt to manage change. Whatever the case, it is worrying to see so many people becoming anxious over the more basic tasks such as interviewing or managing development needs. These are core managerial skills, and without them both they and their teams will suffer.'

According to Matt Dean, employment lawyer and head of Employment Law Training (ELT) at international law firm Simmons & Simmons: 'Providing counselling for employees is an important tool in managing stress. Employers have a duty to provide a safe working environment. The Court of Appeal last year indicated that employers offering a confidential counselling service with appropriate referrals are "unlikely to be in breach of duty". Even with counselling, employers cannot afford to ignore warning signs that an employee is suffering stress. Training for managers in how to recognize warning signs and how to manage this issue is key to limit legal liability and improve morale.'

Why is stress not accepted as a 'legitimate' health problem?

Source: *HRM Guide UK* (http://www.hrmguide.co.uk/), 1 July, 2003.

Stress

Stress is a commonly used word. It has been taken from physics where mechanical stress has been a long-standing concept. In its physical context it describes a strain leading to distortion of an object. For example, a steel girder may bend as the result of temporary forces such as strong winds acting against a bridge. Eventually, however, if the strain is long-lasting or excessive, the girder breaks. Psychological stress draws on the physical analogy but the strain on human beings is seen as coming from life's pressures, boredom, overwork, threat and ambiguity. In essence, pressure overcomes the ability to cope. The social readjustment rating scale shown in Table 23.3 gives an indication of the life events that individuals find most stressful.

Stress is a subjective experience: it is not necessarily easy to identify stress in another person. Neither is it clear that the experience is the same for different people. Indeed, it is apparent that similar situations will produce entirely different reactions in different individuals. Table 23.4 shows the wide range of symptoms that have been linked with stress. Burnout is a related concept (see Key concept 23.4).

Key concept 23.4 Burnout

This refers to a condition in which individuals are completely negative about themselves and their lives. It is associated with physical and mental fatigue. Sufferers feel worthless, disregarded, pessimistic about the future and lacking in control of their lives. This state has been described particularly in professionals such as nurses.

Rank	Life event	Mean value
1	Death of partner	100
2	Divorce	73
3	Marital separation	65
4	Jail term	63
5	Death of close family member	63
6	Personal injury/illness	53
7	Marriage	50
8	Fired at work	47
9	Marital reconciliation	45
10	Retirement	45
11	Illness of family member	44
12	Pregnancy	40
13	Sex difficulties	39
14	Gain new family member	39
15	Business readjustment	39
16	Change in financial state	38
17	Death of close friend	37
21	Foreclosure of mortgage	30
27	Begin/end school	26
32	Change in residence	20
41	Holiday	13

Table 23.3

Social readjustment rating scale (excerpt items)

Source: Adapted from Holmes and Rahe (1967).

Table 23.4	Physical	Mental	Illnesses
	Appetite loss	Irritability	Hypertension
Symptoms of stress	Craving under pressure	Lack of interest in life	Coronary thrombosis
Source: Adapted from Arnold, Robertson and Cooper (1991).	Indigestion	Unable to cope	Hay fever
	Fatigue	Feeling a failure	Migraine
	Insomnia	Self-dislike	Asthma
	Sweating	Decisions hard	Colitis
	Headaches	Hiding feelings	Dyspepsia
	Cramps	Loss of humour	Skin disorders
	Nausea	Dread of future	Diabetes
	Fainting	Feeling ugly	Tuberculosis
	Frequent crying/wanting to cry	Unable to finish one task before going on to next	Menstrual difficulties
	Impotence	Fear of open or enclosed spaces	Hyperthyroidism
	High blood pressure		Depression

HRM in reality Playing hooky

An absenteeism survey conducted for Hudson showed that nearly a third (30 per cent) of US workers admitted to taking a 'sick' day when they were not ill.

Almost half (49 per cent) of the employees who played hooky said they did so because they needed a break, while 22 per cent said they took the time off to care for an ill family member. Younger workers (aged 18–29) and those earning less than US$20 000 a year were the most likely to pretend to be sick at 43 per cent and 37 per cent, respectively.

But feigning sickness is not prevalent – most (77 per cent) of all employees who fake being sick do so only on rare occasions. A mere 6 per cent admit to doing it more than three times a year.

It is interesting to note that a surprising 41 per cent of those who have played hooky thought that their bosses knew they were not actually sick. Women (53 per cent) were more confident of getting away with the practice than men (46 per cent), with 55 per cent of single workers also more confident than married employees (45 per cent).

'With the busy pace of today's working environment, employees are taking matters into their own hands to combat stress and take care of their families, often with the tacit approval of their manager,' says Alicia Barker, vice-president of human resources, Hudson North America. 'While this practice may reduce employees' concerns about breaking the rules, managers can also help by advocating a healthy work–life balance, time management training and stronger personal time policies.'

Intriguingly, nearly twice as many women (25 per cent) as men (13 per cent) under the age of 40 falsely called in sick due to a family member's illness. There was less of a difference between genders among people over 40, with 27 per cent of women and 22 per cent of men admitting to the practice. Altogether, the 40–49 age group had the highest incidence for family care at 30 per cent, probably reflecting the dual challenge of caring for children and ageing parents.

What are the ethical implications of playing hooky?

Source: *HRM Guide USA* (http://www.hrmguide.com), 28 July, 2005.

Stressors include a long list of factors. Too much or too little work may both be stressful. De-layering, downsizing, rightsizing: changes in organization and job structure are rife in modern industry and are perceived as stressful by those who are made to change.

Where job numbers are slashed, the remaining workforce may be pressurized and also be concerned about the future of their own jobs. The 2:3:2 formula – half the people doing three times the work for twice the money – brings its own pressures.

The UK Health and Safety Executive (HSE) has published research showing that occupational groups reporting highest levels of work-related stress were teaching, nursing, management, professionals, other education and welfare (including social workers), road transport and security (including police and prison officers). In each of these groups at least one in five reported high stress (two in five among teachers). Full-time workers were more likely to report high stress than part-time employees .

High levels of stress were reported most frequently by people in managerial and technical occupations, those educated to degree level and those earning more than £20 000. Non-white employees reported comparatively higher levels of stress than white workers but it is pointed out that the numbers involved were small. Little difference was reported in stress levels between male and female workers.

Alker and McHugh (2000) looked at the rationale used for introducing employee assistance or advisory programmes (EAPs) in UK organizations. They found that support was more likely to be given for organizational change than for more humanistic reasons. They offer the explanation that this is consistent with managers' work roles.

Summary

This chapter has focused on employee relations as an activity extending through negotiation and bargaining, discipline and employee involvement. These activities involve a number of skills crucial to human resource managers. HR specialists are also involved in issues that are regulated by extensive legislation and touch on home life and health as well as more familiar workplace topics such as discipline and conflict. Competitive pressure has placed extra burdens on employees, especially those with career aspirations. These burdens can cause health problems, particularly those that are stress-related. HR practitioners have at least a moral responsibility to deal with such matters and encourage the setting up of supportive mechanisms such as employee assistance programmes.

Further reading

How to Reduce Workplace Conflict and Stress: How Leaders and Their Employees Can Protect Their Sanity and Productivity from Tension and Turf Wars by Anna Maravelas (Career Press, 2005) takes a practical but unconventional approach to workplace conflict. *Employee Research: How to Increase Employee Involvement Through Consultation* by Peter Goudge (Kogan Page, 2006) uses a market research approach to make the most of employee involvement. *Tolley's Health and Safety at Work Handbook*, 18th edn (Tolley Publishing, 2005) discusses health and safety in the UK legal context. *The Mind and Heart of the Negotiator* by Leigh L. Thomson (Prentice Hall, 2004) looks at the skills of negotiation and bargaining.

Review questions

1 What are the key skills of negotiation?

2 Should all disputes be resolved by arbitration?

3 Review the positive and negative aspects of conflict in the workplace. Is conflict healthy?

4 How might employee involvement increase the power of managers over employees?

5 Evaluate the proposition that empowerment is a unique and meaningful concept.

6 What is the relationship between employee involvement and productivity?

7 What is 'work–life balance' and how can it be achieved? Is total work–life balance an impossible goal?

8 Should human resource practitioners be involved with health and safety at work?

9 What is stress?

10 What can HR practitioners do to support stressed employees?

Case studies for discussion and analysis

Read the following article. What roles should HR and line managers take in dealing with physical and verbal abuse?

Almost a third of nurses experience abuse

Almost one-third of nurses who took part in a large-scale Tasmanian study reported that they had been subjected to both physical and verbal abuse in the previous four working weeks and a quarter had considered resigning as a result, according to research published in the UK-based *Journal of Advanced Nursing* (Farrell, Bobrowski and Bobrowski, 2006).

The survey was conducted by researchers from the University of Tasmania and was supported by the Australian Nursing Federation. Questionnaires were sent to the 6326 nurses registered with the Nursing Board of Tasmania in late 2002. Some 38 per cent completed the survey, but when this was adjusted for the number of registered nurses actually working during this period, the figure was nearer 55 per cent.

Some form of abuse in the previous four working weeks was reported by two-thirds of the 2407 nurses who took part. This ranged from being sworn at, slapped and spat upon, to being bitten, choked and stabbed. The abused nurses described an average of four verbal incidents and between two to three physical incidents during the period covered.

Of nurses who had been physically abused, 69 per cent had been struck with a hand, fist or elbow and 34 per cent had been bitten. A further 49 per cent said they had been pushed or shoved, 48 per cent had been scratched and 38 per cent spat at. In addition, 6 per cent reported that they had been choked and just less than 1 per cent stabbed.

Verbal abuse was most likely to take the form of rudeness, shouting, sarcasm and swearing. However, 2 per cent said that their home or family had also been threatened. Patients and visitors were the most likely people to abuse nurses, but 4 per cent who reported physical abuse said that it was carried out by another nurse and 3 per cent by a doctor. Of those reporting verbal abuse, 29 per cent said that the perpetrator was a nurse colleague and 27 per cent a doctor.

Lead author Professor Gerald Farrell, now based at La Trobe University School of Nursing and Midwifery in Victoria, Australia said:

> The present findings point to a work environment that is both distressing and dangerous for staff. Eleven per cent of nurses told us that they had left a post because of aggression and 2 per cent had left nursing completely. Two-thirds of those who experienced aggression said that it affected their productivity or led to errors in their work. Ten per cent said it was the most distressing aspect of their work, after the 51 per cent who cited workload as the biggest problem.
>
> Another key finding of this research was that although verbal and physical abuse spreads across every branch of healthcare from paediatrics to psychiatry and community services to critical care few staff made their complaints official.

The researchers believe that the restricted time frame of the study and the fact that aggression was carefully defined, with clear distinctions between verbal and physical abuse, may have captured a greater range of incidents than previous studies. The study concludes that workplace aggression is a worldwide problem and further research is needed to discover why levels are so high in modern healthcare settings.

Gerald Farrell continued:

Our research shows that many nurses are working in environments in which they cannot provide the care that they think is best for patients. At the same time they have to contend with high levels of verbal and physical abuse. It's not surprising that some nurses have left the profession altogether and many more are thinking about it.

We live in an era when employers are constantly being told that they have a duty of care for employees. It's a sad reality that nurses who spend their lives caring for others and providing such a valuable service continue to feel so vulnerable in the workplace.

Source: *HRM Guide Australia* (http://www.hrmguide.net/australia/), 14 September, 2006.

Read the following article and answer the questions at the end.

Evaluating stress measurement questionnaires

In a paper presented at the British Psychological Society Occupational Psychology Conference, researchers are revealing the findings from the first-ever large-scale review of stress measures. The strengths and weaknesses of different approaches to measuring stress are highlighted in their report, which also discusses implications for organizations trying to measure and tackle stress at work.

The report was commissioned by the Health and Safety Executive (HSE) with a remit to review measures of workplace 'stressors' – measures of those aspects or characteristics of jobs, such as workload or lack of control, which, when present at excessive levels, are believed to lead to poor psychological or physical health.

A team of independent organizational psychologists led by Dr Jo Rick from the Institute for Employment Studies (IES) and Dr Rob Briner from Birkbeck College, University of London conducted the research. They used a set of rigorous standards to evaluate over 25 different stress measures that are widely used in the UK. The researchers came up with a number of surprising findings:

1 The amount and quality of evidence they could find about different measures was quite limited. In fact there was only sufficient evidence to allow a detailed analysis of five measures. The lack of evidence suggests that many stress measures have not been adequately developed. In many cases it seems that we do not know if these instruments are accurately measuring stress at all!

2 Even where particular stress measures are supported by evidence, results are inconsistent and mixed in a number of ways. This suggests that these stress measures are not very reliable tools for assessing workplace stress.

3 Most surprisingly, there was an almost complete absence of evidence about the predictive power of these stress measures. This is a worrying finding because the main reason for measuring stress is to assess aspects of work that are likely to lead to health problems so that these harmful aspects can be changed. But it seems that virtually all the available evidence comes from one-off 'snap-shot' studies and these cannot show if the stressful aspects of work tapped by these measures actually lead to ill-health.

Dr Rick (principal research fellow, Institute for Employment Studies) said: 'I was very surprised by the lack of evidence linking the workplace stress measured by these scales to possible ill-health outcomes. This has serious implications for organizations using these measures help . . . tackle stress at work.'

Dr Briner (senior lecturer in organizational psychology, Birkbeck College) added: 'This report shows the need for a fundamental rethink of the way in which stress is measured at work and how more valid and reliable tools for assessing stress can be developed.'

What are the implications of the research? Organizations are required to assess stress but this research indicates that the tools by which they can make an assessment have severe limitations. In fact, organizations that are using commonly available stress measures may not be accurately measuring aspects of the work environment that might lead to ill-health. So they could be focusing on relatively

▶

harmless issues and missing real stress problems in the workplace.

The researchers argue that 'it is not clear, therefore, that using these measures either on their own or as part of a broader stress assessment process fulfils the requirements of health and safety legislation to identify and control those aspects of work that are likely to lead to ill-health or harm.'

They conclude that we need more information about the reliability and validity of existing stress measures but it may be that the existing approach to stress measurement is questionable and new methods and techniques should be considered.

1 Do stress measurement questionnaires really measure stress in a reliable and valid way?

2 Do they actually provide the information that organizations need to tackle workplace stress?

Source: *HRM Guide UK* (http://www.hrmguide.co.uk), 3 January, 2002.

Conclusion

Learning objectives

The purpose of this chapter is to:

- Evaluate whether or not HRM has been meaningfully implemented and, if so, to what extent.

- Investigate the form it may take.

- Determine the principal driving forces for the implementation of HRM.

- Summarize evidence for its effectiveness.

- Consider trends and future developments for the human resource function.

The status and significance of HRM

We began this volume with an analysis of the concept of HRM. We found that interpretations of human resource management range from formal models to comparatively loose portrayals of the territory with which HRM should be concerned. There is general agreement on its underlying philosophy, linking people management to business objectives in a strategic, integrated and coherent way. Beyond that, however, commentators and practitioners interpret HRM in different ways, depending on personal agendas and vested interests. As a result HRM ranges from 'soft', humanistic attempts to win over staff and achieve heart-felt commitment, to 'hard'-nosed extraction of maximum effort at minimum cost.

Regardless of the rationale or the nature of its practice, HRM has become a common label for various forms and functions of people management. In English-speaking countries, the term has replaced 'personnel management' in many contexts. For example, academic courses, journals and textbooks formerly labelled as 'personnel management' are now described as 'human resource management'. However, and particularly at practitioner level, relabeling does not mean necessarily that either the approach or the content have changed (Sisson, 1995, p.87). The diverse interpretations of HRM are apparent when we compare practices in different countries and organizations. We noted earlier that 'personnel' and 'human resources' can co-exist and many organizations throughout the developed world follow North American practice, using the terms interchangeably.

Following a South African study by Wood and Els (*ibid.*) we can identify four distinct patterns of practice:

1 A simple change in nomenclature of relevant personnel sections where, in a number of cases, staff were not seen as managers but instead were viewed as a distinct, relatively junior category of employee.

2 A broadened personnel function encompassing clearly delineated areas such as training and development.

3 HRM practitioners play an important strategic role as facilitators in the adoption of progressive industrial relations policies, rather than developing a vision for managing human resources across the organization.

4 True strategic HRM.

In the South African instance, Wood and Els (2000) found that, whatever the pattern of practice, all the HR practitioners they studied deviated from the 'conventional wisdom' definition of HRM. They attribute this partly to the persistence of effective and militant trade unions, requiring the use of hybrid HR-industrial relations practices. But they also point to the fact that HRM is a complex package of concepts and practices which are adopted and adjusted flexibly to fit the prevailing economic situation and managerial traditions. In the UK its introduction has been a slow process, often introduced as a cosmetic exercise, changing the nameplate on the 'Personnel' office door to 'Human Resources'. Some 15 years ago, Blyton and Turnbull (1992, p.1) wrote that:

> ... in the UK, there is widespread agreement that, in one way or another, the adoption of HRM has so far been limited: limited to a small number of (largely foreign-owned) 'exemplar' companies; limited in the sense of organizations adopting HRM in a very partial and piecemeal way; and limited in many cases to a mere relabeling of existing activity and positions.

To what extent has the situation changed? Since the nature of human resource management still remains a matter of debate, it is scarcely surprising that practitioners interpret it in a variety of ways. Some organizations have taken pragmatic, local initiatives based on specific problems and solutions developed by their own managers, whereas others, particularly in foreign-owned workplaces, have been heavily influenced by managerial practices from elsewhere.

HRM and globalization

Faulkner, Pitkethly and Child (2002) investigated HR practices adopted by companies from the USA, Japan, Germany and France in UK acquisitions, compared with British companies acquired by other UK firms. They found some convergence in HR practices. For example, businesses from all the countries surveyed used performance-related pay and increased the level of training in their new subsidiaries. But HRM practices varied considerably between each nationality and these were strongly influential in changing practices within acquisitions. Walsh (2001) drew on the 1995 Australian Workplace Industrial Relations Survey to investigate the characteristics of HRM in multinational companies operating in Australia. The study suggests that investments in the human resource function and the use of HR practices were generally more prevalent in foreign-owned than Australian organizations. Walsh observes that this was particularly the case for workplaces belonging to US and British-owned firms. Geary and Roche (2001), reviewing evidence in an Irish context, point to the predominance of 'country-of-origin effects' over 'host country effects', particularly in countries with weak industrial relations systems. They found employment relations practices in foreign-owned (especially US-owned) workplaces to be very different from those in Irish-owned establishments. In a European study Poutsma, Ligthart and Veersma (2006) also found that foreign-owned multinational companies moderated national HR practices.

To an extent, the penetration of HRM reflects a complex interaction between globalization (primarily driven by transnational companies), the distinctiveness of local culture and awareness of management literature through education or contact with external agencies. Selmer and de Leon (2001), for example, found that the style of human resource practices in the Philippines is distinctively Pinoy (Filipino). Pinoy HRM has its basis in a system of indigenous core values that emphasize social acceptance. Globalization has had a limited impact since subtle and intricate (but also powerful) local cultural imperatives have strongly influenced HR practices in foreign-owned companies. In an African context, Harvey (2002) states that Western managers can view human resource management on the continent as a dream-like experience because of the sheer complexity and diversity found there. The 'rules, regulations and laws' of many African nations, and the degree to which many African organizations and employees ignore or bend the rules can seem surreal. In Portugal, Cabral-Cardoso (2004) found a reluctance to delegate HRM to line managers.

Taylor and Walley (2002) argue that central and eastern European countries have been a kind of test-bed for HRM since 1989 as communism has been replaced with market economies. Gurkov (2002) reports on a survey of over 700 Russian chief executive officers (CEOs) conducted in 1998, with a similar number surveyed in 2000, on HR practices in Russian industrial companies. There was a significant move towards modern HR practices but most were being implemented on a trial and error basis, without any reference to international practices. Taylor and Walley (2002), in a review of 21 Croatian companies, suggest that subsidiaries of multinational companies are leading the way towards HRM, with industry sector and size of company being other significant factors. They found evidence of a 'hijacking' of HRM by reactionary managers trying to maintain the status quo in some Croatian companies. But younger Croatian managers had a positive attitude towards progressive HR practices and generally identified with HRM except for some lingering suspicions about 'mindset control' which they saw underpinning HRM and also associated with the previous regime.

Hetrick (2002) explored the ways in which HRM emerged as a set of concepts, policies and practices within multinational subsidiaries in Poland between 1996 and 1999. HRM was clearly viewed as an imported 'Anglo-American concept' bearing no resemblance to people management as practised in Polish organizations. Hetrick comments that multinational firms are increasingly viewing HRM as one of the main control mechanisms by which employees can be integrated across national boundaries. Expatriate managers are important in this process as:

- *Role models*: displaying appropriate company behaviours, values and ways of doing things.
- *Fixers*: adapting corporate values and mission statements to local circumstances.
- *Key actors*: enacting the HRM practices.
- *Networkers or boundary spanners*: making connections between local managers and other parts of the business.
- *Agents of the owners*: overseeing the new subsidiary company.
- *Coaches or mentors*: transferring knowledge to local managers.

HRM is not necessarily strong in all Western countries. Wächter and Muller-Camen (2002), noting the importance of German businesses to the European economy, suggest that a well-functioning HR system would be expected. But a number of comparative studies have found HRM in German companies to be less strategically integrated and proactive than that of similar businesses in other countries. They attribute these findings, at least partly, to the co-determination structure of German employee relations where the *Betriebsrat* (works council) has an important strategic role. Hence HRM has to be integrated with a pre-existing local system which, according to Wächter and Muller-Camen, might even be a strategic resource. However, more recently, Ottenbacher, Gnoth and Jones (2006) found that of the seven significant factors in the outcomes of new service developments in the German hospitality industry, four were HR-related: strategic human resource management, empowerment, training of employees and employee commitment.

Papalexandris and Chalikias (2002) compared the practice of HRM in Greek organizations, using Cranet survey results from 1992 to 1999, with a focus on specific core functions such as performance management, employee communications and training and development. It was clear that Greece was following a general European trend towards a more strategic role for human resource management. But the rate of change differed with more improvement in training and development and performance management compared to employee communications. Also Greek companies were generally slower in following the trend than organizations from many other EU countries.

HRM and 'best practice'

It is relevant to ask if HRM is a prescriptive, ideal model of people management or simply a description of 'best practices' in competitive organizations. As we saw in Part one of this book, Jeffrey Pfeffer has inspired a considerable interest in the concept of 'best practice' in HRM. Marchington and Grugulis (2000) question whether the practices typically assumed to be 'good' are actually beneficial to workers. They argue that the literature is underpinned by unitarist thinking and also that the notion of 'best practice' is problematic despite its superficial attractiveness. In particular, they point to weaknesses in relation to the meaning of specific practices, their consistency with each other, and the supposed universal applicability of this version of HRM. Truss (2001) found that the informal organization played a significant role in the process and implementation of HR policies and that successful organizations do not always implement 'best practice' HRM even if intended. Conversely, Hughes (2002) argues that empirical support for universal HRM is growing.

Boxall and Purcell (2000) argue that there is a complex relationship between HRM and the achievement of organizational outcomes and that HR strategies are strongly influenced by national, sectoral and organizational factors. But this conclusion does not necessarily invalidate the concept of 'best practice' because basic principles of people management underpin practice and are essential to the competitiveness of business organizations.

However, there is increasing evidence supporting the notion that HR practices are more effective when combined. For example, Laursen (2002) studied 726 Danish firms with more than 50 employees and found that HR practices influence innovation performance more when applied together than as individual practices. Additionally, application of complementary HR practices is most effective for firms in knowledge-intensive industries. In a study of Pacific Rim countries, Bae *et al.* (2003) found that high performance work practices were at least marginally more effective in local companies than in the multinationals that originally brought in such ideas.

Using data from the 1998 Workplace Employee Relations Survey, Lucas (2002) searched for 'fragments of HRM' within the hospitality industry as compared with all industries and services in Great Britain. Lucas found that HRM in the hospitality industry shared little of the 'soft' aspects of HRM found elsewhere. On the contrary, power and cost-control were emphasized in an industry that exemplified 'hard' HRM in action. Paradoxically, employees in the hospitality industry were generally more content than their counterparts in the broad stream of industries, despite indicators of dissatisfaction.

Guest (2001) argues that attempts to relate HRM to specific outcomes such as business performance suffer from a number of significant practical difficulties. However, he acknowledges that progress has been made, particularly in the area of measuring HRM, but there remains a need for more clearly specified theory, particularly about the nature of HRM itself. Part of the confusion comes from the indistinct boundaries between HRM and a plethora of other fashionable management programmes. Often HRM is used as a label for a collection of different people management techniques, described by Legge (1995, p.34) as 'symbiotic buzzwords'. A specific people management initiative may be regarded as HRM – or, alternatively, bundled up with total quality management, customer care, business process re-engineering and so on.

Recent years have seen an increasing momentum in the implementation of radical management developments. Managers may use a number of simultaneous initiatives without any real awareness or understanding that they are part of 'HRM'. Indeed, a small study of major organizations (Armstrong, 1994) produced evidence of 'strategic HRM' being applied but none of them used the term!

According to Storey (1989, p.1):

> One cannot help but be impressed by the widespread awareness among practitioners of such experimentation; meetings with managers at all levels even in conventional mainstream organizations soon reveal the fact that current 'flavours' have permeated the managerial consciousness and imagination in a way that was never the case with, for example, OD, job enrichment, QWL and other much-vaunted 'movements' of previous decades which some critics cite as equivalents.

Many of these concepts are presented as 'quick fixes' that are found to be attractive by senior managers with little time before objectives have to be achieved, or contracts run out.

Driving forces of HRM

Whether as a label or a variable combination of specific initiatives, we can justifiably ask if the uptake of HRM has been driven by practitioners – people involved in practical people management – and then attracted wider attention; or if it is a creation of academics and consultants with some (and only some) practitioners following on? What is apparent is that the practitioners involved in the introduction of HRM are often line or general managers rather than personnel managers. Clearly, there are many 'stakeholders' in HRM.

Managerialists

Management power increased significantly in the 1980s, especially in English-speaking countries with 'New Right' governments. Keenoy (1990, p.371) calls HRM 'a deliberate and brilliant ambiguity', suspecting a hidden political agenda arising from right-wing government policies. This perspective sees HRM as a reflection of Thatcherite and Reaganite policies which were translated into a wave of managerialism, first in industry and then the public sector.

Certainly, it is evident that politicians take a particular interest in people management when its development affects their view of society. Managerialism's new legitimacy is most clearly seen in the public sector, where government has imposed 'market conditions' and new management structures. Ironically, business concepts such as HRM have been adopted most widely in organizations that are not true 'businesses' at all. These issues are particularly evident when such organizations are privatized. Van der Zwaan, von Eije and de Witte (2002) looked at the organizational and HR changes accompanying the transformation from public to private in a sample of 28 Dutch organizations. They found growth in the culture of efficiency and accountability, together with increased relationship between financial participation and performance, suggesting a link between the adoption of HRM and privatization. Ross (2006) identified similar processes between Western and Eastern Europe in the privatization of a Czech telecoms company, although the weakness of Eastern European institutions tempered the effects.

HRM in reality Hairdressers and managers – today's working icons

A recent report from the Work Foundation identifies the occupations of hairdresser, management consultant, celebrity and manager as offering the best insight into current trends and the nature of working life. In 'Paradigm Trades: The Iconic Jobs of the Early 21st Century' Stephen Overell argues that personalizing the debate in this way represents an alternative approach to considering the future of work.

Stephen Overell said:

> In the early twentieth century, it was obvious what we meant by the word 'worker' – most of us would point to the factory worker, the unionized, male proletarian who was the key figure of his time. Today, it is no longer so obvious. Modern work is contradictory and complex. The idea behind a paradigm trade is that a few workers, doing very different types of work, act as representatives for the entire modern world of work. It is these workers more than any other that offer us spokespeople what is going on at work and within our culture as a whole.

Stephen Overell argues that characteristics of each paradigm occupation offer different insights:

1 Hairdressers (and other personal services)

- much work remains manual, physical and craft-related
- demonstrate the importance of social skills in work
- prove how work has become 'personal' and 'aesthetic'
- show that 'the rhetoric of globalization has been overplayed'.

2 Management consultants

- show the power of the outsider
- are the archetypal knowledge worker
- stand for the current 'pronounced love of change'.

3 Celebrities

- demonstrate how people are becoming their work
- 'showcase the aesthetic turn of modern work and modern life'
- defy the notion of 'productivity'.

4 Managers

- are the biggest and fastest rising group
- demonstrate the growing obsession with hierarchy and status
- their character is central to most fundamental dilemmas relating to morality and the market.

Stephen Overell argues that debate about the future of work has traditionally focused on themes, for example 'portfolio workers' or 'the hourglass economy'. The concept of a paradigm trade personalizes the subject. He adds:

> There are two impulses that our economy believes in more than any other – the power of presentation and the power of organization. The paradigm trades offer the closest thing we can find to spokespeople for the modern world of work.

To what extent would you agree that 'paradigm trades' portray modern work?

Source: *HRM Guide UK* (http://www.hrmguide.co.uk), 23 August, 2006.

Senior managers

The strategic nature of HRM, conventionally owned and driven from the top, has been of great interest to senior managers. It is compatible with the power needs of top managers who want the reins in their own hands. In effect, HRM is part of the fashionable 'ideas industry' which fuels modern management.

In our discussion on the management of change we saw that HRM has been associated with programmes such as TQM, culture change, downsizing and business process re-engineering. Ideas for increasing the effectiveness of business management come and go in a constant stream. Management education and the writings of management gurus alike provide ideas and legitimize their adoption. The concepts they spawn flow in tidal waves across the face of industry. Managerial behaviour follows current fads, conforming to each change in fashion as if they were skirt lengths or hairstyles.

Caldwell (2001) observes that the HR professional has often been viewed as a change agent and that there is evidence for the increased significance of that role. Hailey (2001) describes how HRM interventions and the structure of the HR function itself have been used as change levers to support a shift in business strategy from cost-cutting and acquisition to innovation. Khatri and Budhwar (2002) found that the role and status of the HR function depend on a combination of top management 'enlightenment' and the level of HR competencies. They noted that the businesses they studied pursued four types of HR strategies: informal and not communicated; informal and communicated; formal but not communicated; and formal and communicated. There is also evidence that HR strategies can potentially lower staff turnover by increasing organizational commitment (Buck and Watson, 2002). An intriguing comparison of practices in South Africa and Singapore (Horwitz et al., 2006) showed that practices for motivating and retaining staff were converging but HR strategies for attracting knowledge workers were divergent.

Patrickson and Hartmann (2001) argue that in Australia, as an instance, the workforce is currently more qualified, casualized and diverse than at any previous point in history. HR practitioners have responded to the situation with an increased emphasis on aligning HR strategy with corporate strategy (Sheehan, Holland and Cieri, 2006), giving performance management a higher priority, exploring alternative forms of flexible work arrangements, making greater use of legal expertise, and increasingly adopting human resource information systems.

Senior executives do not have a consistent view of HRM – any more than they have a shared understanding of management. Many do not perceive any distinction between general management and managing people. Even less do they wish to be involved with fine academic distinctions between different models of HRM: 'As chief executive I have to have the organization I want, and if it doesn't marry up with any particular model that the world of HRM has thrown up, well, too bad' (quoted in Armstrong, 1994).

The actual 'doing' of HRM is passed to middle managers who are responsible for its implementation and can be held (conveniently) accountable for any failures. People policies and practices must be integrated and coherent for HRM to be effective but this division of labour leads to a significant weakness: it offers scope for a dislocation between strategic intentions and the conduct of people management at ground level.

Maxwell and Watson (2006) studied line managers and HR specialists in Hilton International's UK hotels. Despite their overlapping responsibilities for people management they found different opinions prevailing in the two groups. Specifically they found significant differences in their perspectives on: understanding/ownership of Hilton's service and HR strategy; line manager involvement in and rankings of HR activities; support of line managers by HR specialists; barriers to line managers' involvement in HR activities; and competence of line managers in HR activities. The business performances of individual hotels improved when the two perspectives converged.

Teo (2002) examined the effectiveness of strategic HRM in an Australian public sector entity, before and after corporatization, and found that the rating of strategic HRM role effectiveness remained low despite overall improvement in the integration of HRM and strategic management. Results showed that the corporate strategic HRM function was more effective in an administrative role than as a value-adding, strategic business partner to line managers. On the other hand, Björkman and Xiucheng (2002) found positive relationships between business performance and the use of 'high performance' HRM systems and integrated HR and business strategies in a number of Chinese–Western joint ventures and subsidiaries. Khilji and Wang (2006) point to the failure of many researchers to distinguish between 'intended' and 'implemented' HR practices, leading to ambiguous conclusions on the effectiveness of strategic HRM.

Nankervis, Compton and Savery (2002) observe that while recent Australian research studies report a gradual but apparently growing convergence between the theory and practice of strategic HRM in large organizations, there is little empirical evidence on HR strategies and practices in small and medium enterprises (SMEs), or on the opinions of their chief executive officers (CEOs). They sampled CEOs in Australian SMEs and found some limited evidence that SMEs may eventually adopt recognizable strategic HRM.

What is clear is that the central tenet of 'soft' HRM – the belief that HRM regards employees as valuable assets and not just costs – is rarely translated into action. The practices associated with HRM are often introduced for reasons of expediency rather than any serious belief in its principles. Indeed, it is arguable that the practice of HRM is rife with hypocrisy and rhetoric. Many organizations in free market countries feel that competitive forces make it impossible to commit themselves to their employees. People management in these firms is firmly focused on cost-cutting. A conflict arises from the inherent contradiction between typical HRM themes such as encouraging long-term employee commitment and short-term cost-effectiveness. According to Gratton (*Financial Times: Mastering Management*, 1995), employees are left:

> . . . to make sense of the paradoxes and mixed messages with which they are faced, who try to understand the underlying message of customer delight when no attempt is made to provide them with the skills necessary to deliver it, who are rewarded and promoted for delivering short-term financial targets and who see the people who try hardest to understand customers' needs penalized for the time they take to do so.

This leads to the question of whether HRM is no more than a matter of fine words. Employees quickly learn to mistrust official rhetoric and instead practise the art of 'sense-making': looking for cues that indicate the route for success or, at least, survival. Informal messages are transmitted through the choice of people who are rewarded and those whose skills are developed. For example, large-scale redundancies – determined at short notice by senior managers – have followed soothing statements about the importance of human resources to an organization's future.

Academics

Market forces have given academics an added interest in HRM (Townley, 1994, p.22; Legge, 1995, p.48). With the reduction in the perceived importance of industrial relations due to government action in a number of countries, academics have had to look elsewhere for research funding and new courses to teach. HRM offers an opportunity for people with expertise in work psychology and industrial sociology to continue with the subjects that interest them – but under a more marketable label.

Townley, for example, regards academics as 'participant constructors' rather than neutral observers. In her view HRM has been 'constructed' as a discipline in order to attract (often private) finance to investigate a new phenomenon – HRM itself – which appears to meet the requirements of flexibility and the free market. HRM has become an academic cottage industry, churning out degree courses, collected papers, journals, texts, and professorial chairs. Paradoxically, some of the most successful products of this industry have been attempts to 'deconstruct' the contradictions and rhetoric of HRM itself! (Legge, 1995, p.49)

Muller (1999) reviewed the German HRM debate and showed it to be dominated by business administration academics specializing in the topic. In the past, these academics – together with practitioners – had generally embraced the techniques and ideology of HRM somewhat uncritically. Muller attributes this to a comparatively low emphasis on empirical research, neglect of industrial relations aspects, and the strong impact of US-developed theories and concepts. More recently, the US approach to HRM has been viewed more critically, along with a more positive assessment of the German HRM model.

The personnel profession

Personnel practitioners have long held ambiguous views on the subject of HRM. Opinion in the profession has swung between various extremes:

- *Ignore it*. It will go away. It is just another fad that will be replaced by another soon enough.
- *Embrace it*. It will give us prestige. We can repackage personnel management as a marketing exercise. Lots more money.
- *Believe in it*. Always a minority position. People are *really* the most valuable resources? So how come I'm not paid as much as the finance manager?
- *Live with it*. OK, so it's an American import, a fad, and something economists will never understand. But it gives me a bit more clout right now.

Hoque and Noon (2001) examined data from the 1998 UK Workplace Employee Relations Survey to establish differences between the characteristics and job-related activities of specialists who used the title 'human resources' and those using the title 'personnel'. They found that practitioners using the HR title were better qualified than their counterparts who used the personnel title and were more involved with strategic planning. Human resource development was more likely to be included in strategic plans in such cases. Additionally, a number of specific practices commonly associated with HRM – for example personality tests, attitude surveys and off-the-job training – were more likely to have been adopted in workplaces with HR specialists than in those with personnel specialists.

Armstrong (2000) contends that many so-called 'HRM' practices were in widespread use before HRM came on the scene in the 1980s. He argues that there has been no great revolution as a result of HRM theory. Instead there has been a process of evolution. The rate of change may have increased but, according to Armstrong, this is not attributable to the arrival of HRM as a philosophy. Rather, rapid changes in the business, political, economic and social environment have forced organizations to respond. Armstrong also points to increasing professionalism among personnel practitioners encouraged by bodies such as the UK's Chartered Institute of Personnel and Development and the dissemination of ideas about HRM by academics publishing in an increasing range of publications.

Rynes, Colbert and Brown (2002) tested such claims on responses obtained from 959 US human resource professionals, specifically focused on their agreement with various HR research findings. They found large discrepancies between research findings and practitioners' beliefs in a number of areas. This was particularly so in the case of employee selection where practitioners seemed to have considerably less faith in the use of intelligence and personality tests than HR research would recommend. Practitioners at higher levels, with SPHR certification and those who read the academic literature, were more likely to agree with research findings. Shepherd and Mathews (2000) examined academic research on employee commitment, a central part of HR models, in relation to the views of practitioners. They surveyed 300 HRM managers and found wide recognition of commitment in terms of its desirability and benefits. But academics and practitioners conceptualized and measured commitment in entirely different ways. Practitioners adopted a subjective and *ad hoc* approach, generally ignoring the formal measuring tools and structured, 'objective' approaches developed by academics.

Moreover, change initiatives, particularly business process re-engineering, frequently lead to a questioning of the need for any personnel or human resource specialists. Storey (1995, p.384) finds this to be a common theme at consultant-organized conferences. Of course, this is consistent with HRM models that place the responsibility for people management in the hands of line managers. Together with marketing and research, it is difficult to measure the effect that HR specialists have on the wellbeing of a company. Paperwork-obsessed personnel administrators, ignorant of wider business issues do not help. They make ripe targets for short-termists working to 'zero-based budgeting' and City analysts with no industrial experience.

An analysis of 1372 responses to an online survey by the Australian Human Resource Institute (AHRI) (Sheehan *et al.*, 2006) identified some recent trends in practitioners' views about the role of HR in Australia. Two-thirds (66 per cent) of respondents felt that the transition to HRM made their job more rewarding but 73 per cent considered that HRM demanded a new set of skills. A mere 10 per cent thought that an increased business focus has resulted in negative effects on traditional personnel functions. Poor understanding of the value of HRM to the bottom line and lack of support from senior managers were identified as the most common limiting factors on the strategic integration of HR. Overall there was an increasing involvement by senior HR managers in organizational strategy with almost half the senior respondents claiming an active role in decisionmaking.

HR at Prudential

Prudential is a financial services company that has recently undertaken radical restructuring. The UK and Europe workforce was cut by about 4500 staff and the HR function centralized. Most of the 8000 staff are based in the UK, with 1000 in Europe and a processing and customer services operation in Mumbai.

The HR function is responsible for core HR activities and learning and development. It also covers corporate and social responsibility, fleet management, payroll and HR systems, pensions and internal communications. It serves its own employees, including those in Mumbai, group headquarters and other services.

There are about 200 people in the HR function compared with over 550 in 2000. There is an 'Ask HR' shared service centre (SSC) with about 50 people, of whom 45 are in the learning and development function in various locations, and smaller specialist teams.

The first point of contact for HR support for all staff is the 'self-service' intranet system. The SSC offers telephone support and gives basic advice, for example, on disciplinary matters. Those needing specialist advice are referred to one of the 'single provision centres' (SPCs) that also coordinate and implement HR policy. SPCs cover employee relations, reward, learning and development, resourcing and internal communications. They are 'virtual' teams, with individuals working from various locations.

In addition to centralized services, there are sixteen business partners, senior appointments who sit on the management board of each major function, such as customer services. They do not generally have teams or separate budgets in order to avoid 'rebuilding local HR empires'.

Flexible working is having a significant impact in HR. 'Hot-desking' is the norm. This has the advantage of allowing people to pursue a career without necessarily having to relocate when they change jobs. However, a degree of social fragmentation also results, making it potentially difficult for new staff or business partners to keep in touch with different areas of responsibility.

Career development
People working in HR see the function as having increasing influence in the organization. The SSC is an entry point for people with a customer service or relationship management background. Administrative or support roles also offer career access for recent entrants with relevant degrees in business, psychology, etc.

Some parts of HR tend to recruit externally for specific expertise, reinforcing the SPC structure. Specialists in SPCs work with managers out in the business. Hiring good people in the reward field proves especially difficult as pragmatic judgements and prompt decisions are needed.

Some business partners interviewed found the role attractive for its variety, closeness to senior management, wide range of relationships, and because they feel they can have an impact. Business partners need relationship building, influencing and negotiating experience, as well as professional skills for benchmarking and 'understanding the business'. Career development for business partners is a challenge, partly because these roles are relatively new in the HR labour market.

Career progression within Prudential takes various routes, for example from the 'Ask HR' helpdesk to employee relations adviser in the SPC, to employee relations consultant. People from the SSC can move into junior training roles; the senior role of development consultant requires specialist knowledge. With specialist experience, an individual might move into a junior business partner role. A senior business partner would be likely to have managed an SPC.

The HR management team reviews staff careers twice a year. Managed moves, especially between generalist and specialist roles often result. This process has to occur regularly to maintain a positive climate of career development in a function that is dispersed organizationally and geographically. The company also recognizes the need for some to move between corporate and consultancy employment in HR.

Current trends place more value on professional qualifications, although some felt these are less important than having the right mindset and learning 'on the job'. Some felt an HR director need not necessarily be an HR professional. Experience is seen as more relevant than formal development, especially in relation to gaining credibility and confidence. 'Hot-desking' affects informal learning in the workplace. Training and development that helps people network externally is seen as important and under-used. HR leaders see the need for both 'hard' HR skills and ethical perspectives on the employment relationship. Creativity is needed to find fresh solutions to tensions between the needs of the business and its employees. The OD skill set is becoming more important.

People performance is now seen as a business differentiator with old-style employee relations becoming less important. Broad reward issues and the 'capability' agenda of learning and development are growing in importance. As the workforce becomes more demanding, the issue of managing opportunities becomes a key issue.

The HR profession

HR staff at all levels were ambivalent about the concept of HR as a profession. People accepted that it had a distinctive influencing role, but felt it did not have a 'fixed' knowledge base. It was felt that HR should take more of a lead on the human capital debate. Some felt that HR is trying too hard to justify itself and should be more positive about its role in dealing with issues which all organizations need to address.

The impact of HRM

Is there any evidence that the implementation of HRM has a significant effect on national or organizational economic performance? After all, this is the justification implicit in HRM models for valuing the human resource above all others. When the first edition of this book was written in the mid-1990s the conclusion was that we simply did not know. The following were given as possible explanations:

- *Insufficient research.* Not because of lack of effort but due to the absence of clear, agreed frameworks within which to conduct comparative research. The root cause of this was perceived as HRM's own ambiguity. How were we to look for evidence of HRM and its effects if we had no agreement on what HRM was?
- *Intangibility.* If people are an 'intangible resource' we have an insurmountable problem – by definition intangibles are unmeasurable!

Since then, progress has been made in conceptualizing the problem and measuring results (see the 'HRM in reality' on HRM and shareholder value). For example, Huang (2000) looked at 315 firms in Taiwan and related their human resource practices to their organizational performance. Huang's study shows a significant relationship between performance and the effectiveness of their HR functions, including planning, staffing, appraisal, compensation, and training and development. Michie and Sheehan-Quinn (2001) surveyed over 200 manufacturing firms in the UK to investigate the relationship between corporate performance and the use of flexible work practices, human resource systems and industrial relations. They found that 'low-road' practices – including short-term contracts, lack of employer commitment to job security, low levels of training and unsophisticated human resource practices – were negatively correlated with corporate performance. In contrast, they established a positive correlation between good corporate performance and 'high-road' work practices – 'high-commitment' organizations or 'transformed' workplaces. They also found that HR practices are more likely to make a contribution to competitive success when introduced as a comprehensive package, or 'bundle' of practices. In a French study, Guerrero and Barraud-Didier (2004) found evidence for synergy between four HR practices (empowerment, compensation, communication and training) had a stronger impact on performance when implemented together. However, testing the related hypothesis of 'complementarity', which also proposes that sets of HR practices deliver better results together than when implemented individually, Horgan and Mühlau (2006) found positive evidence for this in Irish firms but not in companies they surveyed in the Netherlands.

Kelliher and Riley (2002), highlighting evidence to support the view that the impact of HRM is greatest when it involves a set of coherent policies and practices, also consider that HR initiatives should be implemented as part of an integrated package. They instance functional flexibility, which leads to an intensification of work, but in the cases they studied this was less of an issue when supported by higher levels of remuneration. Green *et al.* (2006) sampled 269 human resource professionals in large manufacturing firms across the USA and found a direct, positive and significant impact of strategic HRM on organizational performance. Moreover, they found that SHRM directly and positively influenced individual performance, organizational commitment and job satisfaction.

Michie and Sheehan (1999) used evidence from the UK 1990 Workplace Industrial Relations Survey to show that 'low-road' HRM practices also appeared to be negatively correlated with investment in R&D and new technology. By contrast, 'high-road' work practices were positively correlated with investment in R&D and new technology. Cooke (2001) reviewed a number of British studies on the use of 'high-road' and 'low-road' HRM strategies and concludes that high-road HRM may lead to better organizational performance. But firms do not necessarily opt for this because of the historical, social and institutional context of employment relationships in Britain.

Rondeau and Wager (2001) focused on the ability of certain 'progressive' or 'high-performance' human resource management practices to enhance organizational effectiveness, noting growing evidence that the impact of various HRM practices on performance is contingent on a number of contextual factors, including workplace climate. They conducted a postal survey of 283 Canadian nursing homes which included questions about human resource practices, programmes and policies impacting on workplace climate. The survey also included a variety of performance indicators. Their results indicated that nursing homes with more 'progressive' HRM practices and which also reported a workplace climate valuing employee participation, empowerment and accountability tended to be viewed as better performers. The best performers overall were those nursing homes that had implemented more HRM practices and also reported workplace climates reflecting a strong commitment to their human resources.

Capital investment is another important moderator of HRM's effectiveness. Richard and Johnson (2001) found that strategic HRM significantly reduces employee turnover and increases overall market performance assessment. But the effect of SHRM on firm productivity and return on equity depends on the level of capital investment.

HRM in reality HRM delivers shareholder value

Call it human resource management, personnel or high-performance management, the evidence for the financial benefit from good people management continues to grow. Companies using the best people management practices deliver nearly twice as much value to shareholders as their average competitors, according to a study by consultants Watson Wyatt.

This study is the fourth iteration of Watson Wyatt's respected Human Capital Index (HCI) research. It covers HR practices in more than 600 companies from 16 countries across Europe, combined with independent financial data. The study demonstrates a clear link between specific HR practices and financial performance. Watson Wyatt's North American and Asia-Pacific HCI studies showed similar results.

The new study showed that: good people management was linked to a 90 per cent increase in shareholder value; companies with weak people management practices produced negative returns on equity over the past two years; and the best companies are pulling ahead from the rest. Companies with the best people management practices gain tremendous value while the difference between average and poor performers in HR is negligible in terms of creating shareholder value.

'The perception that HR is a non-strategic business overhead still persists,' says Steven Dicker, a partner at Watson Wyatt and co-author of the HCI report. 'But this is wrong. Our HCI research has again demonstrated the strong link between effective human capital management and shareholder value.'

Commenting on the finding that companies with the best people management deliver nearly twice as much value to their shareholders as their average competitors, Steven Dicker said: 'Great people management is linked with a 90 per cent increase in shareholder value. It is an amazing figure at first sight. As well as highlighting the gulf between the best and the rest, we believe it reflects the growing emphasis on people management within businesses as other sources of competitive advantage prove increasingly difficult to sustain.

'With the return to real-world economics after the bursting of the "tech" bubble and unwinding of the 1990s creative accounting, most businesses are fundamentally "people businesses". Increasingly, it is the quality of a company's people management that determines its real success or failure.'

'However, it is not surprising that many business leaders are sceptical about the value of human resources departments when there is so much poor practice around,' said Doug Ross, also a partner at Watson Wyatt and co-author of the report. 'Human resources has a key role in facilitating good people management throughout the business, and our study shows this can have great value. But in too many cases human resources activity becomes an end in itself, failing to align with the business needs, failing to control costs, failing to manage risks effectively or failing to focus on its contribution to growing revenues.'

Doug Ross highlights three practices in the Watson Wyatt study that stand out as undermining financial performance: using contract workers to provide 'a disposable workforce'; developmental training; and excessive paternalism.

The disposable workforce

'The approach to using temporary workers to provide a cushion of "disposable workers" in case of an economic slowdown or cancellation of non-core projects seems reasonable in principle,' says Doug Ross. 'However, our experience suggests that the temporary workers cause tensions and jealousies with permanent employees in good times because of the different terms and lack of commitment to the company, and now the "disposals" are being implemented the permanent employees feel just as exposed as if permanent employees were being cut.' According to the HCI study, companies that have avoided the 'disposable worker' approach delivered up to 5.6 per cent more shareholder value than average performing companies.

Developmental training

'Developmental training appears to increase the value of the individual but not necessarily the value of the company,' says Doug Ross. 'This is either because the training is not well timed or good enough, or the costs of employment rise as the employee either demands more pay or moves to another employer to realize their newly enhanced value.' According to the HCI study, companies that limit their use of developmental training deliver up to 5.2 per cent more shareholder value than average companies.

Excessive paternalism

'Providing a secure working environment, coupled with effective performance management can create a high value workplace,' says Doug Ross. 'However, some people management practices are excessively

▶

paternalistic, such as maintaining training regardless of economic circumstances and avoiding at almost all costs the termination of employees; these undermine shareholder value.' According to the HCI study, companies that were overly paternalistic lost up to 5.2 per cent of shareholder value compared with average companies.

Watson Wyatt's global HCI is in its fourth year and has undoubtedly become the leading measure of the financial effectiveness of human capital management. The new study, the second time it has been carried out in Europe, confirms the findings of the previous European HCI, carried out when stock markets were at their heights in 2000. This year's study demonstrates that the key HR practices associated with higher value continue to show up in bear as well as bull markets. The same applies to people management practices that are linked with a reduction in shareholder value.

'The Human Capital Index brings up evidence supporting our belief that enhanced people management leads to better financial performance, rather than the other way around,' said Steven Dicker. 'In other words, HCI can be a leading indicator of financial performance.'

Watson Wyatt examined return on equity over the past two years for the companies that participated in both 2000 and 2002 European HCI studies. High scoring companies (top quartile) in the 2000 Human Capital Index study produced returns of over 20 per cent. Conversely, companies that scored low on HCI in 2000 showed a negative return on equity during the same period.

'For many companies, business is now tougher than ever. With no let up in sight, the need to focus on maximizing real, sustainable value from their human capital has never been greater,' said Steven Dicker. 'The good news is that Watson Wyatt's Human Capital Index now provides a clearer, more global route map to maximizing the value of human capital than ever before.'

Are you convinced that HRM practices lead to improved performance and shareholder value?

Source: *HRM Guide UK* (http://www.hrmguide.co.uk), 24 September, 2002.

Further explanations given in the mid-1990s for not being able to assess the impact of HRM were:

> *Confusion with other management initiatives.* We have observed already that it is difficult to untangle the effects of true 'HRM' from other strategic initiatives. HRM is accompanied almost invariably by other packaged programmes such as total quality management (TQM). A US study by Buch and Rivers (2001) looked at the effects of a TQM initiative on a department in a mid-sized utility company. Immediately after the intervention, there appeared to be a culture change that was characterized by empowerment, employee development and teamwork. But eventually there was a shift back to the culture that prevailed before the intervention, accompanied by a significant decline in employee job satisfaction.

> *Situational effects.* HRM is not – and, arguably, cannot be – implemented uniformly. It is found mainly in specific areas. In private industry it has been adopted by large, sophisticated and often non-unionized organizations. These businesses have particular characteristics that are appropriate for HRM. The classic examples of success come from greenfield sites that provide a 'clean slate' with no previous practices or cultural history to prevent management action. HRM may not be appropriate in firms that have strong unions or depend on a low-skilled workforce (Hollinsead and Leat, 1995, p.319). Tansley, Newell and Williams (2001) argue that the term 'greenfield' helps to conceptualize a break with prevailing employee relations practices but it can be a philosophical break with the past rather than a physical change of location. They suggest that the implementation of a human resource information system (HRIS) offers an opportunity to break with the past.

Flexibility and the introduction of managerialism into non-profits and the public sector also test the applicability of HRM. For example, human resource practitioners face dilemmas in preparing HR strategies in situations where the workforce is largely seasonal or made up of volunteers as is the case in the Scottish heritage industry (Graham and Lennon, 2002). In fact, employer–employee relationships are blurred in project-based or virtual organizations where self-employed, contract and salaried employees work together. Rubery *et al.* (2002) contend that complex organizational forms – they instance cross-organization networking, partnerships, alliances, the use of external providers for core as well as peripheral activities, multi-employer sites and blurring of the public/private sector divide – have major implications for the employment relationship.

Greenwood (2002) reviewed the ethical position of HRM and concluded that even when judged by minimum standards, HRM is seriously lacking, not least because of a general disregard of stakeholder theory. Foote (2001) investigated the ethical behaviour of HR managers working in a sample of UK and Irish charities. The study highlights the ethical inconsistency between the application of strong, explicit organizational values to external clients and the limited influence of those values on HR strategies and practices within organizations. HR professionals no longer thought that the HRM function should be the conscience of the organization, but felt that they had a significant role in the provision of advice on ethical action to senior management.

What do people 'at the coal face' feel about the prevalence and effectiveness of human resource management? Gibb (2001) describes a survey of the views of 2632 employees on HRM in the 73 organizations for which they worked. In this study employees were found to be positive about some elements of HRM, including training and development, rewards and levels of personal motivation. They also gave high ratings for the performance of HR staff across a range of services. But the survey found negative employee views on the management of staffing levels, aspects of recruitment and retention, communication and overall levels of morale in their organizations.

What next?

In the past, new management concepts have generally come from North America. Fashionable concepts such as 'knowledge management', 'human capital management' and 'talent management' overlap with many features of human resource management and are often delivered as part of the same 'bundle' of management initiatives. The worldwide economy is changing, with ever-stronger regional groupings challenging individual nation states in importance. East Asia and the European Union appear destined to be major influences at the beginning of the 21st century and neither is entirely dominated by US-style free market ideas. Whereas American concepts reign in business schools, people are being managed increasingly through methods forged within different cultural ideologies. The collectivist traditions of the East and the 'social partner' philosophy of the EU may foster philosophies of people management that eventually value employees more than the 'hard HRM' of the free market. At present, however, the rising power of China appears to place little value on employment rights.

Every two years, the Society for Human Resource Management (SHRM) surveys senior HR professionals in the USA to find their views on the top trends for human resource management (Schramm, 2006). In November 2005, three themes were identified as most significant for US human resource practitioners:

1 The rising cost of health care – a significant element of employee compensation in the USA.
2 Implications of increased global competitiveness.
3 Demographic changes – specifically, an ageing population and impending retirement of the 'baby boomer' generation.

The three trends are related since health and pension costs in the USA increase the cost of American workers in comparison with those in developing countries such as China and India. Combined with an impending shortage of skilled workers, there is a pressure towards offshoring people-intensive jobs overseas and making more imaginative use of an ageing workforce at home. These views represent an American perspective, but practitioners in other countries would probably identify with a number of these trends.

The SHRM symposium on the future of Strategic HR (SHRM, 2005) concluded that formidable barriers continue to exist to the development of human resource management – some of which are created by the profession itself. According to the participants:

- HR people must become more analytical and strategic.
- HR needs to be more closely aligned with the business.
- There should be a focus on key drivers of success such as talent and a minimization of time spent on administration.
- HR practitioners need to be 'more proactive, risk-taking and courageous'.

These are familiar issues that have been problematic for the profession for decades. They are associated with a negative view of HRM held by many senior managers in other business disciplines. To overcome barriers and negativity, HR people need to be: willing to change; understand, and preferably have experience of, other business functions; prepared to align their activities more closely to business strategy; become strategic practitioners; and be accountable for the consequences of human resource initiatives.

Summary

In this chapter we reviewed the present state of HRM and its likely development in the near future. The adoption of human resource management has been driven by a range of stakeholders with different interests and expectations. It has been interpreted differently around the world but globalization has encouraged an increasing convergence. In recent years, improvements in HR metrics have resulted in clear evidence for the effectiveness of HRM initiatives, especially when they are delivered in strategic 'bundles'. HRM also overlaps with other management approaches such as human capital management, talent management and knowledge management and this trend is likely to continue. HR specialists are no longer able to focus solely on their own local employment markets as global competition and outsourcing become dominant factors in the allocation of human resources.

Further reading

For advanced students, two classic texts remain essential reading: *Human Resource Management: A Critical Text*, 2nd edn, edited by John Storey (Thomson Learning, 2001) and *Human Resource Management: Rhetorics and Realities*, 2nd edn, by Karen Legge (Palgrave Macmillan, 2004). *The Future of Human Resource Management: 64 Thought Leaders Explore the Critical HR Issues of Today and Tomorrow*, edited by Mike Losey, Dave Ulrich and Sue Meisinger (Wiley, 2005) presents the views of an international panel of experts on the future of the human resource profession.

Review questions

1 Why is HRM considered to be a complex and diverse concept?

2 Review the evidence for the effectiveness of human resource management. What would make HRM more effective?

3 To what degree is the adoption of HRM driven by globalization?

4 Why is HRM not practised in exactly the same way in all countries?

5 What are the advantages and disadvantages of using 'best practices'?

6 Discuss the view that the concepts of 'fit' and 'best practice' are modern versions of 'hard' and 'soft' HRM.

7 Does HRM represent a totally managerialist philosophy?

8 Why do practitioners and academic researchers have different views on HRM?

9 What impact does 'bundling' have on the success of human resource initiatives?

10 What is the likelihood of the HR profession becoming 'more proactive, risk-taking and courageous'?

Case study for discussion and analysis

Creating a human resource function

Jenny is the new human resource manager at a medium-sized catering supplies company. Prior to her arrival all HR activities were dealt with by the general manager (hiring, training and personnel administration) and the finance manager (pay and benefits, annual leave monitoring, sickness, etc.). Jenny has to create her own HR function and absorb the responsibilities previously handled by these managers. She has a capital budget for IT and a staff budget for the equivalent of three employees. Jenny is free to create an in-house HR function or outsource the activities.

How would you advise Jenny to proceed and what should be her priorities for the new HR function?

Glossary

Action learning Reg Revans argued that classroom-based management education is not adequate. He devised a systematic, experiential or action learning programme based on job exchanges which place managers in unfamiliar situations and ask them to take on challenging tasks.

Action research Organizational development – particularly in its 1960s and 70s form – relied on a methodology described as action research. This was an undramatic but effective long-term change process based on incremental improvements, effectively on a continuous flow of emergent strategies. Action research has become unfashionable with the advent of 'packaged' techniques such as business process re-engineering.

Added-worker hypothesis A hypothesis that predicts an increase in employment participation rates during periods of high unemployment. The premise is that partners go to work to compensate for the lost income of main wage-earners who are made redundant.

Adult learning It has been argued that adult learning is qualitatively different from learning in childhood. The 'andragogy' approach emphasizes the importance of self-directed learning for adults, integrating new material and ideas with current and previous experience.

Advisory, Conciliation, and Arbitration Service (ACAS) Founded in 1975, this is a UK public body with the ambition to 'improve organizations and working life through better employment relations'. It is run by a council with representatives from business, unions, and the independent sector and has approximately 750 staff in England, Scotland and Wales. There are 11 main regional centres plus a head office in London. ACAS defines its services as follows: *Conciliating*: the act of reconciling or bringing together the parties in a dispute with the aim of moving forward to a settlement acceptable to all sides. *Arbitrating*: an independent arbitrator or arbiter (in Scotland) deciding the outcome of a dispute. The decision may well be binding in law. *Mediating*: acting as an intermediary in talking to both sides. The aim is for the parties to resolve the problem between themselves but the mediator will make suggestions along the way.

Affective identification A real intellectual and emotional identification with the organization.

Affirmative action (or positive discrimination). A longstanding approach in the USA, designed to advantage the disadvantaged, including women, African-Americans and Hispanics. Laws only applied to the public sector and its suppliers.

Ageism Discrimination on the grounds of age is prevalent but often unrecognized. Legislation against ageism is becoming common in developed countries.

Alienation A state of estrangement, or a feeling of being an outsider from society. Dull, boring and repetitive work induces a feeling of alienation. Assembly-line workers are involved with a small part of the final product, have little control over the rhythm of their work and may have no idea of the significance of their contribution. Their work can appear to be alien with no relationship or meaning to their lives other than to produce income. As a consequence they may feel little enthusiasm and, often, active hostility towards what seems like forced-labour.

Alternative dispute resolution (ADR) The term has been in use for decades but the various forms of ADR have become increasingly used in recent years. The US Federal *Administrative Dispute Resolution Act 1995* states that 'alternative means of dispute resolution' means any procedure that is used to resolve issues in controversy, including, but not limited to, conciliation, facilitation, mediation, factfinding, minitrials, arbitration, and use of ombuds, or any combination thereof.

American Arbitration Association The American Arbitration Association makes itself available to resolve a wide range of disputes (including labour/employment issues) through mediation, arbitration, elections and other out-of-court settlement procedures. A not-for-profit organization, it claims to be the largest provider of ADR (alternative dispute resolution) procedures in the USA. Also provides panels, education and training services.

Americans with Disabilities Act (ADA) The Americans with Disabilities Act prohibits discrimination against people with disabilities in employment, transportation, public accommodation, communications, and activities of state and local government. The act was signed into law in 1990 but its various elements came into force on different dates including: state and local government activities, 26 January, 1992; employers with 25 or more workers, 26 July, 1992; employers with 15 or more workers, 26 July, 1994. The Act requires that employers, employment agencies, labour organizations and joint labour-management committees must have non-discriminatory application procedures, qualification standards, and selection criteria and in all other terms and conditions of employment and make reasonable accommodation to the known limitations of a qualified applicant or employee unless to do so would cause an undue hardship. The bill makes exceptions regarding the employment of a person with a contagious disease, a person who illegally uses drugs or alcohol, employment of someone by a religious entity, and private membership clubs. (*Source: US Department of Labor*)

Application forms (blanks) Usually sent out to jobseekers who respond to some kind of job advertising. The form or blank is a template for the presentation of personal information that should be relevant to the job applied for. This ensures that all candidates provide the desired range of information in the same order of presentation to facilitate comparison and preparation of a short-list for further selection procedures.

Application letters Traditionally used for job applications they have tended to become little more than cover letters in English-speaking countries, generally being discounted in the selection process. However, in a number of continental European countries, especially France and Switzerland, they are requested to be handwritten and may be subject to graphological analysis as one (sometimes the main) selection procedure.

Appraisals Appraisals rate individuals on quasi-objective criteria or standards deemed to be relevant to performance. Traditional appraisals rated individuals on a list of qualities, primarily work-related attitudes and personality traits. *See also* 'Performance assessment'.

Arbitration Arbitration is a long-standing alternative to court-based litigation. For example, the first institute for arbitration in Denmark was set up in Copenhagen in 1894. The process has a number of variant forms but, in essence, nominated third-parties (arbitrators) can make decisions which are binding on the parties to a dispute. Arbitration procedures can range between the informal and more rule-based systems and are similar to court procedures. Generally, arbitration is seen as providing such benefits as confidentiality, flexibility, speed and relative cheapness.

Assessment *See* 'Appraisals', 'Assessment centre', 'Performance assessment'.

Assessment centre A concept and not necessarily a place. Normally used for selection or employee development, participants are given a variety of exercises, tests, role plays, interviews, etc. over a period of days. Several rates contribute to the assessment.

Attitudes Attitudes are dispositions held by people – towards or against – people, things and ideas. They have individual components based on factors such as personality and understanding, and social elements derived from shared experiences and cultural history. Attitudes are complex systems of belief, evaluation, emotion and behaviour.

Australian Council of Trade Unions (ACTU) Formed in 1927, the Australian Council of Trade Unions is the peak council and national centre representing the unionized Australian workforce. The ACTU holds a Congress every three years that sets out a clear set of policies and objectives for unions. The core activity of unions remains the improvement and representation of workers through workplace and industry activity and collective bargaining. The ACTU also has policies on a range of other issues which affect workers, their families and their communities.

Australian Industrial Relations Commission (AIRC) The AIRC is a national tribunal dealing with employment issues including dispute settlement, unfair dismissal and the setting of wages and conditions.

Australian Workplace Agreement (AWA) An AWA is an individual written agreement between an employer and employee about the employee's terms and conditions of employment, such as pay, hours of work, annual leave and sick leave. Once an Australian workplace agreement starts to operate, it replaces any award or workplace agreement that would otherwise apply to the employee. An Australian workplace agreement overrides employment conditions in state or territory laws, if the Australian workplace agreement mentions those conditions. However, an Australian workplace agreement cannot override state or territory laws which cover occupational health and safety, workers' compensation or training arrangements. (*Source*: *Office of the Employment Advocate*).

Balanced scorecard A conceptual framework used to translate an organization's vision into a set of performance indicators, including measures of: financial performance, customer satisfaction, internal business processes, and learning and growth. Both current performance and efforts to learn and improve can be monitored using these measures.

Bargaining *See also* 'Collective bargaining'.

Behavioural compliance Simply presenting an appearance of the attitudes and behaviours expected by senior managers. Not a true commitment.

Behavioural consistency Maintaining a set of desired behaviours consistently in the workplace. Desired behaviours may be agreed ways of behaving towards customers, team behaviour, etc.

Benchmarking Direct comparisons of different measures between an organization and 'best practice' competitors in the same business sector. This indicates the gap in performance, costs, morale, etc., between that organization and industry best practice.

Best practice Strategies, activities or techniques that are viewed as being highly effective. Note that what is best practice in one context may not work in another.

Biodata Roberts (1997, p.10) describes biodata as a 'set of questions framed around "coincidences" in the lives of good performers.' People who are good at a particular job are likely to be more similar to each other than to individuals selected at random from the general population. Such similarities extend beyond work-related factors into hobbies, sports and social activities.

Business culture *See* 'Corporate culture'.

Business environment Everything outside a business organization which interacts with that organization. Traditionally, human resource managers have been closely involved with employment legislation, industrial tribunals, and trade unions at a functional level. HRM's strategic emphasis requires a focus on other environmental variables. Government economic, social security, education and training policies affect the availability, cost and quality of available employees. International competition, strategic alliances and supranational organizations such as the European Union are exercising increasing influence on people management.

Business goals The strategic objectives of a business.

Business process re-engineering (BPR) A 'fundamental rethinking and radical redesign of business processes to achieve dramatic improvements in critical contemporary measures of performance, such as cost, quality, service and speed' (Hammer and Champy, 1993).

Centralization An organizational process in which an activity or function (including control) is concentrated in one place.

Change Businesses must change to survive. However, change is a difficult management task. Effective change requires sure-footed, considerate people managers who can take employees through the process with minimum anxiety and maximum enthusiasm. It requires the recognition that an organization's people should not be the pawns of strategy but active participants in change.

Change strategy An organizational or HR strategy aimed at implementing planned change.

Charisma Weber regarded charisma as one of three sources of authority (the other two being 'rational', and 'traditional'), portraying it as a magical and hypnotic force based on direct personal contact. In modern life charisma is often fake – a product of carefully orchestrated mass communications.

Childcare In the HR context, a facility that looks after a child during a parent's working hours (including travelling time). Childcare may be provided by an employer as a benefit.

Cloning Cloning, or 'elective homogeneity' is the tendency for selectors to pick people like themselves, thereby reducing the breadth of skills and personalities in an organization. Simply matching the set of characteristics possessed by previous successful post holders, it is a safe, conservative way to fill jobs. As a low risk, but backward-looking approach, it is unlikely to meet the future needs of the organization.

Co-determination Cooperation between employees and management in policymaking.

Coherence HR strategies and actions must be consistent with each other. For example, if a business has a strategy of increasing sales of high-profit-margin products, rewards in the sales department should be focused on these products rather than less profitable items.

Collaborative entrepreneurship Cooperation between two or more individuals in order to found or acquire a business. The degree and nature of collaboration may vary from one company to another in terms of financial input, time devoted, skills and knowledge.

Collective bargaining Collective bargaining takes place between employers and trade unions when: employees are members of trade unions which undertake to negotiate on their behalf in matters such as pay, working conditions, other benefits, and work allocation; and employers recognize trade unions and their officials as legitimate bargaining agents.

Collectivism The opposite of individualism – a preference for being part of a group. In employment relations, a process of combining into unions or staff associations for the purpose of negotiation with management.

Collectivization As individuals, most employees have a limited amount of power in comparison to their employers. But employees can pool the power they have. Through collectivization, workers are able to band together to protect their mutual interests. From the late 19th century onwards, trade unions have fought to improve pay and conditions for their members

Commission for Racial Equality (CRE) The Commission for Racial Equality is a publicly funded, non-governmental body set up under the UK Race Relations Act (1976) to tackle racial discrimination and promote racial equality. It works in both the public and private sectors to encourage fair treatment and to promote equal opportunities for everyone, regardless of their race, colour, nationality, or national or ethnic origin.

Commitment Commitment is defined as the degree of identification and involvement which individuals have with their organization's mission, values and goals. This translates into: their desire to stay with the organization; belief in its objectives and values; and the strength of employee effort in the pursuit of business objectives.

Communication Good communication is essential to the smooth running of the people management system. It must be a two-way process. This can involve a cascaded flow of information from the top and also feedback from lower levels through surveys, performance measures and open meetings.

Competence Organizations must have the capability to meet changing needs. In current parlance this is often expressed in terms of competences – skills, knowledge and abilities. These are qualities possessed by the people who work for those organizations. Competences can be brought into businesses through the recruitment of skilled individuals. They can also be developed within existing people by investing in training, education and experiential programmes.

Competitive advantage A concept popularized by Michael Porter. A condition which enables an organization to operate in a more efficient or otherwise higher-quality manner than the organizations it competes with.

Comprehensiveness All people management activities should be part of a single, comprehensive system. This implies that the attitudes, behaviour and culture of every individual in an organization – especially those with people management responsibilities – should be integrated within a deliberate framework.

Conflict Disagreement that may result in withdrawal of cooperation or, in an employee relations context, may result in some form of industrial action.

Conformity Opposite of creativity. A tendency to obey rules and stick to procedures or conventional ways of doing things.

Confucian dynamism Acceptance of the legitimacy of hierarchy and valuing of perseverance and thrift, without undue emphasis on tradition and social obligations that could impede business initiative.

Congruence One of the '4 Cs' of the Harvard model. An organization should be regarded as a system whose elements and activities have to fit together.

Contingency theory A theory that takes account of the circumstances in one situation at one point in time. Allows for multiple ways of doing things to fit different circumstances.

Contingent employees Temporary, intermittent or seasonal workers. The US Bureau of Labor Statistics' definition of contingent worker includes all salary and wage workers who do not expect their employment to last.

Continuous improvement Operational philosophy based on the view that performance improvement is the ongoing responsibility of everyone in an organization in order to achieve higher levels of performance, profitability and customer satisfaction.

Control HRM is aimed at directing and coordinating employees to meet an organization's objectives and cannot be anarchic nor totally democratic in its approach. Human resource literature mostly advocates a participative approach with a high degree of empowerment and delegation. An autocratic approach is unlikely to encourage good communication and employee commitment.

Cooperatives A cooperative is an autonomous association of persons united voluntarily to meet their common economic, social, and cultural needs and aspirations through a jointly-owned and democratically-controlled enterprise. (*Source: ICA*).

Coordination Tasks divided amongst a group of individuals must be synchronized and integrated in some way so as to achieve the overall objectives of the group. Jobs must fit into a coherent flow of work. Coordination involves the distribution of decisionmaking. This can be formal, with rigid rules and regulations, or informal, giving freedom for local decisions. Coordination may be routine, because of structure and control mechanisms, including a performance management system or direct, by management action.

Core and peripheral staff Core staff are those employees regarded as essential to the organization; peripheral staff are there to meet operational needs but are not regarded as indispensable. Core staff have greater security and may also have better terms and conditions of employment.

Corporate culture Defined by Bower (1966) as 'the way we do things around here'. Trice and Beyer (1984) elaborated this as: 'the system of ... publicly and collectively accepted meanings operating for a given group at a given time'. Hofstede (1994) describes corporate culture as 'the psychological assets of an organization, which can be used to predict what will happen to its financial assets in five years time'. *See also* 'Culture'.

Cost-effectiveness Expressed in terms of profitability, cost-effectiveness has been used extensively as the justification for large-scale job cuts. But as a reflection of the value of its human assets, an organization has a duty to use its people wisely. In itself, there is nothing wrong with an attention to cost – provided that it does not become the one and only management criterion.

Counselling interview In the context of performance and employee development, an interview in which strengths and weaknesses and development actions are discussed. Typically, it follows a performance assessment.

Creativity Creativity can lead to new products and services, novel applications and cost savings. A creative environment develops from a trusting, open culture with good communication and a blame-free atmosphere. Conversely, creativity is inhibited by lack of trust or commitment and fear of the consequences of change.

Credibility Managers and the organizations they represent must have credibility in the eyes of their employees if they are to expect the best performance. A degree of healthy cynicism is unavoidable, but in today's downsized workplaces this frequently extends into mistrust of and contempt for senior management. This feeling reflects the way many staff feel they are themselves regarded by management. Regaining trust depends on personal credibility which, in turn, can only come from honesty and sincerity.

Critical incidents technique A set of procedures for systematically identifying behaviours which contribute to success or failure of individuals or organizations in specific situations.

Culture An all-pervasive system of beliefs and behaviours transmitted socially. Specifically it consists of the set of values – abstract ideals – and norms or rules held by a society, together with its material expressions. *See also* 'Corporate culture'.

Data Hard, factual information often in numerical form – it can tell you when, and how often something happened, how much it cost and so on but it does not say why it happened. *See also* 'Knowledge'.

De-layering Removing one or more levels in a management hierarchy, thereby creating a flatter organization.

Demographic trends Long-term changes in a country's population density, age profile, etc.

Direct discrimination Treating an individual or group less favourably on grounds such as disability, race, religion, age, gender or sexual orientation. Direct discrimination is fairly obvious because of its explicit nature. The use of different criteria for promoting or paying male or female employees is an example of direct discrimination.

Disability The Americans with Disabilities Act (1990) defines disability as follows: 'Anyone with a physical or mental impairment substantially limiting one or more major life activities; has a record of such impairment; or is regarded as having such an impairment, is considered a person with a disability.' In terms of employment, the law defines a 'qualified individual with a disability' as a person with a disability who can perform the essential functions of the job with or without reasonable accommodation. (*Source: US Department of Labor*).

Disability Discrimination Act – Australia The Australian Federal Disability Discrimination Act (DDA) 1992 provides protection for everyone in Australia against discrimination based on disability. It encourages everyone to be involved in implementing the act and to share in the overall benefits to the community and the economy that flow from participation by the widest range of people. According to the Australian Human Rights and Equal Opportunities Commission, disability discrimination happens when people with a disability are treated less fairly than people without a disability. Disability discrimination also occurs when people are treated less fairly because they are relatives, friends, carers, co-workers or associates of a person with a disability. (*Source: Human Rights and Equal Opportunities Commission*).

Disability Discrimination Act – UK The Disability Discrimination Act (DDA) 1995 aims to end the discrimination which many disabled people face. This Act gives disabled people rights in the areas of: employment; access to goods, facilities and services; buying or renting land or property. The employment rights and first rights of access came into force on 2 December, 1996; further rights of access came into force on 1 October, 1999; and the final rights of access came into force in October 2004. An additional Disability Discrimination Act 2005 builds on and extends earlier disability discrimination legislation (*Source: http://www.disability.gov.uk/dda/*).

Discouraged worker hypothesis More people would work if jobs were easy to find – but they do not search when work is scarce. Workers calculate the probability of finding a job in relation to the wage they are likely to get and conclude that the effort is not worthwhile.

Discrimination *See* 'Direct discrimination', 'Indirect discrimination'.

Diversity 'Diversity is the variation of social and cultural identities among people existing together in defined employment or marketing systems' (Cox, O'Neill and Quinn, 2001).

Divisional structure Organizational structure based on semi-autonomous units operating outside the centre.

Division of labour The sub-division of work so that specific tasks or jobs are allocated to individuals deemed most suitable on the basis of skill, experience or cultural tradition.

Downsizing Term used to describe sacking, dismissing or otherwise making redundant a substantial proportion of an organization's workforce.

Economically active Includes the employed – those in paid work – and the unemployed – those who are looking for paid work but are unable to find it.

Economic turbulence Cyclical and non-cyclical changes in the economy that cause periods of high or low demand for goods, services and employees.

Education Formal learning outside (and often before entering) the workplace.

Employee analysis Modern computer packages offer extensive possibilities for modelling the total profile of an organization's human resources. Employees can be classified in a variety of ways, such as function, department or grade.

Employee demand Need for staff.

Employee involvement An umbrella term that is inconsistently and imprecisely used to embrace a diverse range of management processes involving participation, communication, decisionmaking, industrial democracy and employee motivation.

Employee relations Employee relations is an alternative label for 'industrial relations'. It is not confined to unionized collective bargaining but encompasses all employment relationships. It goes beyond the negotiation of pay and benefits to include the conduct of the power relationship between employee and employer.

Employee resourcing Resourcing is the process by which people are identified and allocated to perform necessary work. Resourcing has two strategic imperatives: first, minimizing employee costs and maximizing employee value to the organization; secondly, obtaining the correct behavioural mix of attitude and commitment in the workforce

Employee self-service Employees can view company information, change selected personal details, make benefit enquiries (pension plans, sick pay entitlement), book leave and apply for training programmes through a company's HR portal or intranet. *See also* 'Manager self-service'.

Employee supply Available staff in the employment market.

Employee turnover Measurable incidence of people joining and leaving the organization.

Employer branding The practice of developing, differentiating and leveraging an organization's brand message to its current and future workforce in a manner meaningful to them. Using the methodology of corporate brand-building strategy to attract and keep quality employees. Employer branding is aimed at motivating and securing employees' alignment with the vision and the values of the company.

Employment market The employment market comprises all those people who are available for work. Neo-classical economics views this potential workforce as forming a labour market. The market is affected by national or regional supply and demand for appropriately skilled employees. It is constrained by demographic factors such as the number of young people leaving schools and universities and by cultural variables such as expectations for mothers to stay at home looking after children.

Employment relationship A formal and informal relationship between the employing organization and an employee. The informal element is sometimes referred to as the psychological contract – an undocumented understanding about the nature of employment within the organization. Regarded by neo-classical economists as an exchange of labour for pay, The employment relationship is also a power relationship in which the employer has the formal authority to direct effort towards specific goals, whereas the employee can – informally – frustrate the achievements of those objectives.

Empowerment Being in control of one's own destiny. Enabling someone to take decisions, think, behave and control work in one's own way.

Entrepreneurship A classic definition of entrepreneurship is provided by Timmons (1994, p.7): 'Entrepreneurship is the process of creating or seizing an opportunity and pursuing it regardless of the resources currently controlled.'

Equal access A situation where disadvantaged groups are not barred from entry into organizations but may be confined to lower levels of work.

Equal chance A situation where everyone has the same right, for example, to apply for a vacancy or be considered for promotion.

Equal opportunity policy A written statement of commitment to fair, non-discriminatory human resource management.

Equal Opportunities Commission (UK) The Equal Opportunities Commission (EOC) was established under the Sex Discrimination Act in 1975. It is an independent public body charged with the following tasks: (a) to work towards the elimination of discrimination on the grounds of sex or marriage; (b) to promote equality of opportunity for women and men; (c) to keep under review the Sex Discrimination Act and the Equal Pay Act; and (d) to provide legal advice and assistance to individuals who have been discriminated against. (*Source*: EOC)

Equal Pay Act 1970 Applies to England, Scotland and Wales. Gives an individual a right to the same contractual pay and benefits as a person of the opposite sex in the same employment, where the man and the woman are doing: like work; or work rated as equivalent under an analytical job evaluation study; or work that is proved to be of equal value. The employer will not be required to provide the same pay and benefits if it can be proved that the difference in pay or benefits is genuinely due to a reason other than one related to gender. (*Source*: EOC)

Equal share Access is free to any position within an organization and all groups are represented at all levels. May require a quota systems or 'Affirmative action' to achieve this situation.

Ethnic discrimination *See* 'Race discrimination'.

Explicit knowledge The obvious knowledge found in manuals, documentation, files and other accessible sources. *See also* 'Tacit knowledge'.

Federation A loosely-connected arrangement of businesses with a single holding company or separate firms in alliance.

Flexibility The concept covers a combination of practices which enable organizations to react quickly and cheaply to environmental changes. In essence, flexibility is demanded from the workforce in terms of pay, contractual rights, hours and conditions, and working practices. This extends to the employment market, requiring jobseekers to show a willingness to move location, change occupation and accept radically different terms of employment. *See also* 'Numerical flexibility', 'Functional flexibility', 'Flexible firm', 'Flexible pay', 'Flexible specialization'.

Flexible firm Atkinson's model combining flexibility with Japanese concepts of 'core' and 'peripheral' workforces.

Flexible pay Offering different rates of pay for the same work – depending on geographical location and skills availability.

Flexible specialization Allocation of time and labour according to consumer demand. Staff receive extra training and resources to widen their specialist skills.

Fordism Named after the mass production, assembly-line methods used by Henry Ford for automobile manufacturing.

Functional flexibility Abolishing demarcation rules and skill barriers so that workers can take on a variety of jobs.

Functional structure Form of organization divided into relatively simple parts with defined areas of activity such as production, marketing or personnel.

Gender All human societies divide themselves into two social categories called 'female' and 'male' (this does not exclude other categories). Each category is defined on the basis of varying cultural assumptions about the attributes, beliefs and behaviours expected from males and females. The gender of any individual depends on a complex combination of genetic, body, social, psychological and social elements, none of which is free from possible ambiguity or anomaly. Traditionally, sexual differences have been used to justify male-dominated societies in which women have been given inferior and secondary roles in their working lives.

Gender discrimination Many countries, including all members of the EU, have sex discrimination and equal pay legislation. However, informal psychological and organizational barriers continue to bar the progress of women. The processes of occupational segregation and sex-typing of jobs continue so that women tend to be concentrated at the base of most organizational hierarchies in jobs which are less prestigious and lower paid than those favoured by men.

Gender legislation In December 1975, South Australia became the first state in Australia to have sex discrimination laws.

Glass ceiling The term glass ceiling describes the process which bars women from promotion by means of an invisible barrier. This involves a number of factors, including attitudes of people in power and the inflexible processes and requirements geared to the cloning process which ensures that 'men of a certain type' will generally succeed. In the USA the term is also used to describe the barrier that prevents progress for other disadvantaged groups, for example ethnic minorities.

Glass Ceiling Commission (USA) Created under the Civil Rights Act of 1991 and chaired by the Secretary of State for Labor. According to the mission statement the Glass Ceiling Commission was formed in order to: (1) build public awareness of the specific behaviours, practices, and attitudes that either cause or prevent advancement by minorities and women to leadership and management positions; (2) develop concrete policy recommendations for improving and expanding employment opportunities for minorities and women; and (3) provide leadership in developing and communicating the commission's equal employment opportunity agenda. The Glass Ceiling Commission produced a number of reports between 1991 and 1995.

Globalization A systematic trend towards integration of production and marketing with brand-named goods and virtually identical 'badge-engineered' products such as cars being made available throughout the world. This process has been fostered by 'transnational' or 'multinational' companies operating in more than one country.

Graphology Handwriting analysis to identify features of personality – popular as a selection technique in continental Europe.

Hard HRM Storey (1989) distinguished between hard and soft forms of HRM, typified by the Michigan and Harvard models, respectively. 'Hard' HRM focuses on the resource side of human resources. It emphasizes costs in the form of 'headcounts' and places control firmly in the hands of management. Their role is to manage numbers effectively, keeping the workforce closely matched with requirements in terms of both bodies and behaviour. *See also* 'Soft HRM'.

Harvard model The Harvard Business School generated one of the most influential models of HRM. The Harvard view provides a strategic map of HRM territory which guides all managers in their relations with employees. Beer *et al.* (1984) who devised this approach recognized an element of mutuality in all businesses – that employees are significant stakeholders in an organization.

Headhunting Recruitment method aimed at identifying star performers.

Heroes Personifications of the organization's values according to a number of management theorists: achievers who provide role models for success within the company.

Hierarchy Pattern of responsibility and authority, usually represented by a tree-and-branch organization chart.

High performance work system 'A comprehensive customer-driven system that aligns all of the activities in an organization with the common focus of customer satisfaction through continuous improvement in the quality of goods and services.' (*Source: US Department of Labor*)

HR service centres One of the most widely-used solutions to re-engineered HR in large organizations. Such centres centralize a number of HR processes and may deal with geographically widespread users. Enquiries can be taken by voice, e-mail or internet forms.

Human capital Economic growth creates employment, but economic growth partly depends on skilled human resources – a country's human capital. The concept encompasses investment in the skills of the labour force, including education and vocational training to develop specific skills.

Human relations A humanistic approach to management popularized by Elton Mayo and based on the Hawthorne experiments.

Human resource development (HRD) A strategic approach to investing in human capital. It draws on other human resource processes, including resourcing and performance assessment to identify actual and potential talent. HRD provides a framework for self-development, training programmes and career progression to meet an organization's future skill requirements.

Human resource flow Movement of people through an organization commencing with recruitment.

Human resource information systems (HRIS) 'The HRIS system is the primary transaction processor, editor, record-keeper, and functional application system which lies at the heart of all computerized HR work. It maintains employee, organizational and HR plan data sufficient to support most, if not all, of the HR functions depending on the modules installed.' (Walker, 2001)

Human resource management A philosophy of people management based on the belief that human resources are uniquely important to sustained business success. An organization gains competitive advantage by using its people effectively, drawing on their expertise and ingenuity to meet clearly defined objectives. HRM is aimed at recruiting capable, flexible and committed people, managing and rewarding their performance and developing key competencies. *See also* 'Hard HRM', 'Soft HRM'.

Human resource planning (HRP) A process which anticipates and maps out the consequences of business strategy on an organization's human resource requirements. This is reflected in planning of skill and competence needs as well as total headcounts.

Human resource strategy Overall plan for staffing, developing and rewarding employees and outsourced human resources tied to business objectives.

Human Rights and Equal Opportunity Commission (HREOC), Australia The HREOC is a national independent statutory government body, established in 1986 by an Act of the federal parliament, the Human Rights and Equal Opportunity Commission Act. Under the legislation administered by the Commission, it has responsibilities for inquiring into alleged infringements under three anti-discrimination laws: the Racial Discrimination Act 1975; the Sex Discrimination Act 1984; and the Disability Discrimination Act 1992. It also investigates alleged infringements of human rights under the Human Rights and Equal Opportunity Act 1986. In addition, the Aboriginal and Torres Strait Islander Social Justice Commissioner has specific functions under the HREOC Act and the Native Title Act, 1993. These functions relate to the monitoring of the enjoyment or otherwise by indigenous people of their rights under the law. The Sex Discrimination Commissioner also has responsibilities in relation to federal awards and equal pay under the Workplace Relations Act 1996. Matters which can be investigated by the Commission include discrimination on the grounds of race, colour or ethnic origin, racial vilification, sex, sexual harassment, marital status, pregnancy or disability. (*Source: HREOC*).

Image The apparent totality of knowledge and abilities as outwardly presented by an individual or group. Can be false. See also 'Impression management'.

Implicit knowledge *See* 'Tacit knowledge'.

Implicit theory An internal or mental model of how and why a set of events or behaviours takes place. A belief system developed by individuals to explain part of their world or organization based on their own interpretations and experiences.

Impression management A deliberate process in which a personal image is learned or acquired through training. *See also* 'Image'.

Indirect discrimination A less obvious form of discrimination than direct discrimination. This may take the form of applying certain conditions or requirements that are more easily satisfied by one group than another. One example would be to specify a fixed minimum height requirement for entry into a police force. This is a requirement that would be more easily met by male than female applicants. Another example would be a requirement for an unnecessarily high standard of spoken or written English which would favour people with a particular educational background. *See also* 'Direct discrimination'.

Individualism Opposite of collectivism. Preference to work individually rather than as part of a group.

Induction Initial orientation and training of a new recruit.

Industrial democracy Egalitarian notion of worker involvement in decisionmaking.

Informal organization An organization is both a formal and informal entity. The formal aspect of an organization is its official structure and public image visible in organization charts and annual reports. The informal organization is a more elusive concept, describing the complex network of psychological and social relationships between its people. The informal organization is an unrecognized world of cliques and politics, friendships and enmities, gossip and affairs.

In-group Favoured and usually long-standing members of a society, department or organization.

Insecurity thesis Heery and Salmon (2000) identify a connection between globalization and the 'insecurity thesis', a belief that: 'Employment in the developed economies has become more insecure or unstable in the sense that both continued employment and the level of remuneration have become less predictable and contingent on factors which lie beyond the employee's control.'

Institutionalized racism An indirect and largely invisible process which can be compared with cloning and the glass ceiling. It is a term encompassing the often unintentional barriers and selection/promotion procedures which serve to disadvantage members of ethnic minority groups.

Japanization A term that first came into vogue in the mid-1980s. It is used as a label for the attempts of Western firms to make practical use of 'Japanese' ideas and practices and as a description of the presence and impact of Japanese subsidiaries overseas.

Job analysis The process of job analysis is that of gathering and analysing job-related information. This includes details about tasks to be performed as part of a job and the personal qualities required to do so. Job analysis can provide information for a variety of purposes including: determining training needs, development criteria, appropriate pay and productivity improvements. For resourcing purposes, job analysis can generate job and personnel specifications.

Job description List of essential tasks involved in a particular job.

Job market *See* 'Employment market', 'Labour market'.

Knowledge 'Knowledge is a fluid mix of framed expertise, values, contextual information and expert insight that provides a framework for evaluating and incorporating new experiences and information. It originates from and is applied in the minds of knowers. In organizations it often becomes embedded not only in documents or repositories but also in organizational routines, processes, practices and norms.' (Davenport and Prusack, 2000).

Knowledge management 'Knowledge management caters to the critical issues of organizational adaption, survival and competence in face of increasingly discontinuous environmental change. ... Essentially, it embodies organizational processes that seek synergistic combination of data and information processing capacity of information technologies, and the creative and innovative capacity of human beings.' (Malhotra, 1998)

Labour market The setting in which people who can provide labour meet those who need labour. Labour markets can be: internal, within an organization, or external, outside the organization. Labour market is a somewhat old-fashioned term which implies physical labour as opposed to the time, knowledge and intellectual effort required in many modern jobs. 'Job market' or 'employment market' are more meaningful in today's context. *See* 'Employment market'.

Learning organization Organization that 'lives and breathes' learning and knowledge acquisition.

Management by objectives (MBO) A technique to establish individual performance objectives which are tangible, measurable and verifiable. Individual objectives are derived or cascaded from organizational goals. Top managers agree their own specific objectives compatible with the organization's goals but restricted to their own areas of responsibility. Subordinates do the same at each lower level, forming an interlocked and coherent hierarchy of performance targets.

Manager self-service Managers can have access to 'front-end' applications on their desktops in the form of HR portals. Typically, they are able to view a range of personal details and aggregate information. They are also allowed to change and input certain details and model the consequences on their budgets of salary increases or bonus payments. *See also* 'Employee self-service'.

Managing diversity The management of diversity goes beyond equal opportunity and embodies the belief that people should be valued for their differences and variety. Diversity is perceived to enrich an organization's human capital. Whereas equal opportunity focuses on various disadvantaged groups, the management of diversity is about individuals.

Manpower planning (obsolete) 'A strategy for the acquisition, utilization, improvement and retention of an enterprise's human resources' (anonymous government publication cited in Pratt and Bennett (1989, p.101). *See also* 'Human resource planning'.

Matching model *See* 'Michigan model'.

Matrix structures Organizational structures focused on project teams, bringing skilled individuals together from different parts of the organization. Individuals are responsible to their line manager and to the project manager for different aspects of their jobs.

Mentoring Individual–individual support in an organization providing guidance on career development, learning and performance.

Meritocracy Meritocratic procedures aim to make judgements on the basis of evidence of competence such as examination results or the achievement of targets.

Meta-analysis Statistical technique in which results from a large number of (comparatively) small studies are combined.

Michigan model of HRM The Michigan model is strongly influenced by strategic management literature. HRM is seen as a strategic process, making the most effective use of an organization's human resources. Hence there must be coherent human resource policies that 'fit' closely with overall business strategies.

Minimum wage Lowest allowable level of pay within a state or country.

Mission statement A mission statement should convey the essence of what an organization is about: why it exists, what kind of business it intends to be, and who its intended customers are. The mission is translated into objectives or goals within the strategic management process.

Numerical flexibility Matching employee numbers to fluctuating production levels or service requirements.

Occupational segregation Disproportionate representation of particular groups in specific sectors, job-types or levels of responsibility. Horizontal segregation places men and women, for example, in different jobs, such as chambermaids (women) and porters (men). Vertical segregation places one group in better-paid positions than another group, so that men are better represented at managerial levels while women are concentrated in lower, administrative jobs.

Offshoring Transfer of work and/or employment to another country, typically where employment costs and benefits are lower.

Option scheme Right to buy shares in an employing organization, often at a favourable price.

Organizational design The design of an organization patterns its formal structure and culture. It allocates purpose and power to departments and individuals. It lays down guidelines for authoritarian or participative management by its rigidity or flexibility, its hierarchical or non-hierarchical structure.

Organizational development (OD) Methodology of change characterized by an ongoing series of relatively small improvements.

Organizational goals The logical starting point for human resource management lies in an organization's goals – the reasons for its existence. Most modern businesses express these goals in the form of a mission statement. The allocation and control of human resources serves to assist or constrain the achievement of these objectives.

Organizations The means by which human and other resources are deployed so that work gets done. They are social entities with purposes expressed in the form of common goals and boundaries between themselves and the rest of the world.

Outsourcing Contracting work or an operational function to an external provider.

Particularism A form of discrimination favouring particular groups and individuals over others. It derives from a reliance on personal relationships such as ethnic origin, religion or tribal community. It contrasts with universalism in which personal relationships are ignored and emphasis is on other criteria such as qualifications, expertise and ability to do the job.

Performance assessment One of the many people management techniques which 'classify and order individuals hierarchically' (Townley, 1994, p.33). Modern assessment is often focused on competences. *See also* 'Appraisals'.

Performance management 'A strategic and integrated approach to increasing the effectiveness of organizations by improving the performance of the people who work in them and by developing the capabilities of teams and individual contributors.' (Armstrong and Baron, 1998)

Performance-related pay (PRP) Pay based on merit as assessed by a performance management process.

Personality Generally expressed in terms of types or traits, the latter form the basis of most personality tests used for resourcing and the documentation employed for many performance appraisal systems. An alternative approach is to regard personality as an artefact of a particular set of circumstances. In other words, apparent personality depends on the meaning individuals give to a particular situation.

Personnel specification 'The demands of the job translated into human terms' (Arnold, Robertson and Cooper, 1991, p.95). Personnel specifications list 'essential' criteria which must be satisfied, and other criteria which rule out certain people from being able to do the job.

Person perception The perception of other people. Cues such as facial expression, posture, gesture, body movement, tone of voice, etc., are used to evaluate their current mood and overall personalities (McKenna, 1994, p.144). Each one of us has an implicit personality theory based on our experience, assumptions about people, beliefs and prejudices. The evidence of our senses is used to collect data about the perceived person and attribute characteristics to them according to our implicit theory.

Pluralism The acceptance of several alternative approaches, interests or goals within the same organization or society. A view which recognizes that every organization is composed of different interests which are not balanced. Pluralists accept that conflict is natural and are concerned with the means by which it can be managed.

Positive action Measures to prevent discrimination by insisting, for example, on non-discriminatory recruitment procedures, training programmes and pay rates. This does not include any preferential treatment for disadvantaged groups.

Positive discrimination *See* 'Affirmative action'.

Power distance The perceived status differences between people with high and low degrees of power.

Productivity The amount of output (what is produced) per unit of input used. Labour is one input amongst many. Total productivity is dependent upon a variety of diverse and hard to measure inputs. One simple measure of productivity is the Gross Domestic Product (GDP) per person-hour worked. But it is also a simplistic measure of productivity because it neglects a number of factors such as capital investment.

Psychological contract An informal understanding between the employer and employee. Unlike the formal employment contract, this has no physical existence. It is a set of expectations held by both employers and employees in terms of what they wish to give and receive from their working relationship (Rousseau and Parks, 1993).

Psychometric model The dominant approach to selection in British and US textbooks. In its traditional form, it grounds the 'best-person' model in psychological theory and testing. It embodies the use of refined techniques to achieve the best 'match' between job characteristics identified by formal job analysis and individual characteristics measured by psychological tests, structured interviews and other assessment methods.

Race discrimination Unfavourable treatment on the grounds of race or ethnic origin.

Recruitment Attracting candidates prior to selection.

Reorganization A move from one form of organization to another. For example, a business may change from a divisional to a network structure.

Resourcing *See* 'Employee resourcing'.

Restructuring Breaking up and recombining organizational structures in order to reduce costs, eliminate duplication and achieve greater efficiency.

Retrenchment Downsizing or reducing number of staff on payroll.

Reward management Management of pay, benefits and other forms of compensation.

Scientific management F.W. Taylor devised 'scientific management' as a systematic but controversial programme based on rudimentary time and motion studies, selection of 'first-class men' for the job and premium pay for a 'fair day's work'.

Sexual discrimination *See* 'Gender discrimination'.

Sexual harassment Definitions vary considerably but most are agreed that it is sexual attention which is unwanted, repeated, and affects an employee's work performance or expectations from her/his job. However, it is possible for one incident to be sufficiently severe to be regarded as harassment. It differs from sexual banter or flirting since it is one-way; it does not have the involvement and acceptance of both parties. In the USA, the Equal Employment Opportunity Commission has extended the definition of sexual harassment to include a range of actions which lead to a 'hostile work environment'. This definition includes unwelcome touching, joking, teasing, innuendos, slurs, and the display of sexually explicit materials.

Social dumping The concept of social dumping describes the practice of switching production from countries with relatively high employee costs to those with cheap labour. It is an accusation made against large multinational corporations. Social dumping has led to long-term structural changes including the closure of older heavy manufacturing industries such as steel and shipbuilding in established industrial countries.

Social market A term coined by Alfred Müller-Armack, Secretary of State at the Economics Ministry in Bonn, Federal Republic of Germany between 1958 and 1963. He defined the social market as an economic system that combined market freedom with social equilibrium. In this kind of economic system the government plays a regulating role and creates the framework for market processes, going beyond securing competition to ensure social equity.

Social protection According to the World Bank, social protection measures improve or protect human capital, ranging from labour market interventions, unemployment or old-age insurance, to income support, for individuals, households, and communities.

Soft HRM Storey (1989) distinguished between hard and soft forms of HRM, typified by the Michigan and Harvard models, respectively. 'Soft' HRM stresses the 'human' aspects of HRM. Its concerns are with communication and motivation. People are led rather than managed. They are involved in determining and realizing strategic objectives.

Soft planning Human resource planning based on factors other than numbers of employees.

Specialization The division of work between individuals or departments, allocating responsibilities for specific activities or functions to people who can achieve a high standard of work in a relatively narrow range of activities. They may require specific training or expertise. For example, HR managers are concerned with organization of the HR function and resourcing of all other functions.

Stakeholders Recognizably separate groups or institutions with a special interest in an organization. These include shareholders, employees, managers, customers, suppliers, lenders and government. Each group has its own priorities and demands and fits into the power structure controlling the organization.

Strategic HRM Directing people, processes and HR systems to achieve strategic objectives so that individual goals are tied to the business needs of the whole organization.

Strategy A strategy is the means by which an organization seeks to meet its objectives. It is a deliberate choice, a decision to take a course of action rather than reacting to circumstances. It focuses on significant, long-term goals rather than day-to-day operating matters.

Substance The body of competences, knowledge and experience required to fulfil a particular function.

Synergy Making the new whole worth more than its old parts, sometimes described as 2 + 2 = 5. Synergies involve economies from integrating activities, horizontally or vertically; but also unrealized potential for new ideas, products or processes by melding expertise from the different sources into centres of excellence.

Tacit or implicit knowledge This is found in the heads of an organization's employees. Difficult to access and use – for obvious reasons. Typically, an organization does not even know what this knowledge is. Worse, the knee-jerk reaction of top managers who fire employees at the first sign of any downturn means that the knowledge is often lost.

Talent management A strategic and integrated approach to developing a skilled and competent workforce, involving targeted recruitment, development and retention.

Targeting Quotas for the employment of particular groups have been enforced in the USA. In Europe quota systems have commonly apply to the disabled and, in a few countries, other groups such as ex-servicemen but enforcement is not usually strict. *See also* 'Affirmative action'.

Taylorism An approach to management based on the theories of F.W. Taylor. *See also* 'Scientific management'.

Tokenism The employment or promotion of isolated individuals to represent their gender or colour. For example, a 12-member board of directors with one token woman and one token ethnic minority person.

Total quality management (TQM) A methodology focused on continuous improvement, quality assurance and zero faults. TQM programmes are geared to organizational processes such as production. HR involvement includes the selection of flexible people who are amenable to increasingly demanding levels of quality.

Turnover *See* 'Employee turnover'.

Uncertainty avoidance How people deal with conflict, particularly aggression and the expression of feelings. High uncertainty avoidance favours precise rules, teachers who are always right and superiors who should be obeyed without question. Low uncertainty avoidance favours flexibility, discussion and delegation of decisionmaking.

Unitarism A managerialist stance which assumes that everyone in an organization is a member of a team with a common purpose. The unitarist view is implicit in American models of HRM. It embodies a central concern of HRM, that an organization's people, whether managers or lower-level employees, should share the same objectives and work together harmoniously. From this perspective, conflicting objectives are seen as negative and dysfunctional.

Values Values are at the heart of corporate culture. They are made up of the key beliefs and concepts shared by an organization's employees. Successful companies are clear about these values and their managers publicly reinforce them. Often values are unwritten and operate at a subconscious level.

Virtual organizations Advancing technology allows firms to extend the network concept to form enterprises with no permanent structures. They bring people together for specific projects. Teams dissolve on completion, to reappear in new combinations for other tasks.

Work ethic The belief that work is virtuous in itself. Hard work is to be admired and leisure is equated with laziness. In some societies the work ethic became a fundamental religious principle, the Puritans and Calvinists holding it to be such a virtue that Max Weber termed it the protestant work ethic. The concept is sometimes extended to include the virtue of frugality as against waste. It justifies regarding the poor as sinful, since success and ambition are virtuous and wealth is a sign of God's favour.

World view A set of values and beliefs held by members of a particular culture. This is meaningful to its members but alien to others.

References

Aarons, G.A. and Sawitzky, A.C. (2006) 'Organizational climate partially mediates the effect of culture on work attitudes and staff turnover in mental health services', *Administration and Policy in Mental Health* 33(3): 289–301.

Abrahart, A. and Verme, P. (2001) 'Labor market policies: theoretical background', in I.D. Ortiz (ed.) *Social Protection in Asia and the Pacific*, Asian Development Bank.

Abrashoff, D.M. (2002) *It's Your Ship: Management Techniques from the Best Damn Ship in the Navy*, Warner Books.

ABS (2000) *Work-Related Injuries, Australia, September 2000* (Cat. No. 6324.0), Australian Bureau of Statistics.

Adams, K. (1991) 'Externalisation vs specialisation: what is happening to personnel?', *Human Resource Management Journal* 1(4): 40–54.

Adams, S.M., Weinberg, B.D., Masztal, J.J. and Surette, D.M. (2005) 'This time it is personal: employee online shopping at work', *Interactive Marketing* 6(4): 326–36.

Addison, J.T., Schnabel, C. and Wagner, J. (2001) 'Works councils in Germany: their effects on establishment performance', *Oxford Economic Papers* 53(4): 659–94.

Adler, N.J. (1997) Preface to Lane, H.W., Distefano, J.J. and Maznevski, M.L. *International Management Behavior*, Blackwell.

Adobor, H. and Daneshfar, A. (2006) 'Management simulations: determining their effectiveness', *The Journal of Management Development* 25(2): 151–68.

Aguinis, H., Michaelis, S.E. and Jones, N.M. (2005) 'Demand for certified human resources professionals in internet-based job announcements', *International Journal of Selection and Assessment* 13(2): 160–71.

Ahlrichs, N. (2000) *Competing for Talent: Key Recruitment and Retention Strategies for Becoming an Employer of Choice*, Davies-Black Publishing.

Ajuwon, J. (2002) 'Gatekeepers or innovators', Forum, *Conspectus*, January 2002, Prime Marketing Publications Ltd.

Akinnusi, D. (1991) 'Personnel management in Africa', in C. Brewster and S. Tyson (eds) *International Comparisons in Human Resource Management*, Pitman.

Aldrich, H.E. (1999) *Organizations Evolving*, Sage.

Aldrich, H.E. (2000) 'Learning together: national differences in entrepreneurship research', in D.L. Sexton and H. Landstrom (eds) *The Blackwell Handbook of Entrepreneurship* (Blackwell Handbooks in Management), Blackwell.

Alker, L. and McHugh, D. (2000) 'Human resource maintenance? Organisational rationales for the introduction of employee assistance programmes', *Journal of Managerial Psychology* 15(4): 303–23.

Allan, C., Bamber, G.J. and Timo, N. (2006) 'Fast-food work: are McJobs satisfying?', *Employee Relations* 28(5): 402–20.

Allan, C., Brosnan, P. and Walsh, P. (1999) 'Human resource strategies, workplace reform and industrial restructuring in Australia and New Zealand', *International Journal of Human Resource Management* 10(5): 828–41.

Allen, N.J. and Meyer, M.P. (1990) 'The measurement of antecedents of affective, continuance and normative commitment to the organisation', *Journal of Occupational Psychology* 63: 1–8.

American Management Association (2000) *Auditing Your Human Resources Department*, AMACOM.

Andrisani, P. and Nestel, G. (1976) 'Internal-external control as contributor to and outcome of work experience', *Journal of Applied Psychology* 61: 156–65.

Anon (2005) 'How positive action training can help women managers: an end to jobs for the boys?', *Development and Learning in Organizations: An International Journal* 19(3): 29–31.

Ansoff, H.I. (1968) *Corporate Strategy*, Penguin.

Antila, E. (2006) ' The role of HR managers in international mergers and acquisitions: a multiple case study', *International Journal of Human Resource Management* 17(6): 999–1020.

Appelbaum, S.H. and Shapiro, B.T. (2006) 'Diagnosis and remedies for deviant workplace behaviors', *Journal of American Academy of Business* 9(2): 14–21.

Argyle, M. (1991) *Cooperation: The Basis of Sociability*, Routledge.

Argyris, C. (1957) *Personality and Organization*, Harper and Row.

Armstrong, M. (1987) 'Human resource management: a case of the emperor's new clothes?', *Personnel Management* (August): 31–4.

Armstrong, M. (1992) *Human Resource Management: Strategy and Action*, Kogan Page.

Armstrong, M. (1994) *The Reality of Strategic HRM*, paper presented at the Strategic Direction of Human Resource Management Conference, Nottingham Trent University, 14–15 December.

Armstrong, M. (2000) 'The name has changed but has the game remained the same?', *Employee Relations* 22(6): 576–93.

Armstrong, M. and Baron, A. (1998) *Performance Management: The New Realities*, Chartered Institute of Personnel and Development (CIPD).

Armstrong, P. (1989) 'Limits and possibilities for HRM in an age of management accounting', in J. Storey (ed.) *New Perspectives on Human Resource Management*, Routledge.

Armstrong, P. (1995) 'Accountancy and HRM', in J. Storey (ed.) *Human Resource Management: A Critical Text*, Routledge.

Arnold, J., Robertson, I.T. and Cooper, C.L. (1991) *Work Psychology*, Pitman.

Ashton, D. and Felstead, A. (1995) 'Training and development', in J. Storey (ed.) *Human Resource Management: A Critical Text*, Routledge.

Atkinson, J. (1984) 'Manpower strategies for flexible organizations', *Personnel Management* (August): 28–31.

Augoustinos, M., Tuffin, K. and Rapley, M. (1999) 'Genocide or a failure to gel? Racism, history and nationalism in Australian talk', *Discourse and Society* 10(3): 351–78.

Ausburn, L. (2004) 'Course design elements most valued by adult learners in blended online education environments: an American perspective', *Educational Media International* 41(4): 327–37.

Awad, G.H., Cokley, K. and Ravitch, J. (2005) 'Attitudes toward affirmative action: a comparison of color-blind versus modern racist attitudes', *Journal of Applied Social Psychology* 35(7): 1384–99.

Babcock, L. and Laschever, S. (2003) *Women Don't Ask: Negotiation and the Gender Divide*, Princeton University Press.

Bacon, N. and Blyton, P. (2006) 'Union co-operation in a context of job insecurity: negotiated outcomes from teamworking', *British Journal of Industrial Relations* 44(2): 215–37.

Bae, J., Chen, S.-j., Wan, T.W.D., Lawler, J.J. and Walumbwa, F.O. (2003) 'Human resource strategy and firm performance in Pacific Rim countries', *International Journal of Human Resource Management* 14(8): 1308–32.

Bakke, E.W. (1950) *Bonds of Organization*, Harper and Row.

Barclay, J.M. (2001) 'Improving selection interviews with structure: organisations' use of "behavioural" interviews', *Personnel Review* 30(1): 81–101.

Barnard, C., Deakin, S. and Kilpatrick, C. (2002) 'Equality, non-discrimination and the labour market in the UK', *International Journal of Comparative Labour Law and Industrial Relations* 18(2): 129–47.

Barr, M.D. (2000) 'Trade unions in an elitist society: the Singapore story', *Australian Journal of Politics and History* 46(4): 480–96.

Barry, M. and May, R. (2004) 'New employee representation: legal developments and New Zealand unions', *Employee Relations* 26(2): 203–23.

Barsoux, J.-L. and Lawrence, P. (1990) *Management in France*, Cassell.

Bartram, D. (1991) 'Addressing the abuse of psychological tests', *Personnel Management* (April): 34–9.

Bassett-Jones, N. (2005) 'The paradox of diversity management, creativity and innovation', *Creativity and Innovation Management* 14(2): 169–75.

Bates, R. (2002) 'Liking and similarity as predictors of multi-source ratings', *Personnel Review* 31(5): 540–52.

Beal, B. (2004) 'Psychological search for Hilton hotel managers', *Human Resource Management International Digest* 12(1): 30.

Beardwell, I. (2001) 'An introduction to human resource management: strategy, style or outcome', in I. Beardwell and L. Holden, *Human Resource Management: A Contemporary Perspective*, 3rd edn, Financial Times/Prentice-Hall.

Beardwell, I. and Holden, L. (eds) (1994) *Human Resource Management: A Contemporary Perspective*, Pitman.

Beaumont, P.B. (1992) 'The US human resource management literature: a review', in G. Salaman (ed.) *Human Resource Strategies*, Sage.

Bebchuk, L.A. and Fried, J.M. (2005) 'Pay without performance: overview of the issues', *Journal of Applied Corporate Finance* 17(4): 8–23.

Beer, M., Spector, B.A., Lawrence, P.R., Mills, Q. and Walton, R.E. (1984) *Managing Human Assets*, Harvard Business Press.

Bender, R. (2004) 'Why do companies use performance-related pay for their executive directors?', *Corporate Governance* 12(4): 521–33.

Bennis, W. (1990) 'Managing the dream: leadership in the 21st century', *Training: The Magazine of Human Resource Development* 27(5): 44–6.

Ben-Tovim, G., Gabriel, J., Law, I. and Stredder, K. (1992) 'A political analysis of local struggles for racial equality', in P. Braham, A. Rattansi and R. Skellington (eds) *Racism and Antiracism*, Sage.

Bercusson, B. (2002) 'The European social model comes to Britain', *Industrial Law Journal* 31(3): 209–44.

Bertozzi, F. and Bonoli, G. (2002) 'Europeanisation and the convergence of national social and employment policies: what can the open method of co-ordination achieve?' First draft of paper prepared for the workshop 'Europeanisation of national political institutions', ECPR joint-session, Turin, 22–27 March, 2002.

Bertsch, B. and Williams, R. (1994) 'How multinational CEOs make change programmes stick', *Long Range Planning* 27(5): 12–24.

Bertua, C., Anderson, N. and Salgado, J.F. (2005) 'The predictive validity of cognitive ability tests: a UK meta-analysis', *Journal of Occupational and Organizational Psychology* 78(3): 387–409.

Bevan, S. and Thompson, M. (1992) *Merit Pay, Performance Appraisals and Attitudes to Women's Work*, IMS Publications.

Beynon, H. (1973) *Working for Ford*, Pelican Paperback, Penguin.

Biech, E. (2001) *The Consultant's Quick Start Guide: An Action Plan for Your First Year in Business*, John Wiley & Sons.

Biggs, D. (2006) 'The decline of the temporary worker: a regional perspective', *Local Economy* 21(3): 249–63.

Björkman, I. and Xiucheng, F. (2002) 'Human resource management and the performance of Western firms in China', *International Journal of Human Resource Management* 13(6): 853–64.

Black, S. and Gregersen, H.B. (2002) *Leading Strategic Change*, Financial Times/Prentice-Hall.

Blackaby, D., Leslie, D., Murphy, P. and O'Leary, N. (1999) 'Unemployment among Britain's ethnic minorities', *The Manchester School* 67(1): 1–20.

Blackman, M.C. (2002a) 'The employment interview via the telephone: are we sacrificing accurate personality judgments for cost efficiency?', *Journal of Research in Personality* 36(3): 208–23.

Blackman, M.C. (2002b) 'Personality judgment and the utility of the unstructured employment interview', *Basic and Applied Social Psychology* 24(3): 241–50.

Blake, R. and Mouton, J. (1964) *The Managerial Grid*, Gulf Publishing.

Blanksby, M. and Iles, P. (1990) 'Recent developments in assessment centre theory, practice and operation', *Personnel Review* 19(6): 33–42.

Blanton, H., George, G. and Crocker, J. (2001) 'Contexts of system justification and system evaluation: exploring the social comparison strategies of the (not yet) contented female worker', *Group Processes and Intergroup Relations* 4(2): 126–37.

Blau, P.M. and Schoenherr, R.A. (1971) *The Structure of Organizations*, Basic Books.

Blinkhorn, S. and Johnson, C. (1990) 'The insignificance of personality testing', *Nature* 348(6303): 671–2.

Blumenthal, D. (2001) *Internal Branding: Does it Improve Employees' Quality of Life?* Institute for Brand Leadership.

Blyton, P. and Turnbull, P. (1992) *Reassessing Human Resource Management*, Sage.

Blyton, P. and Turnbull, P. (1994) *The Dynamics of Employee Relations*, Macmillan.

Bolkestein, F. (2000) *The Future of the Social Market Economy*, speech by Commissioner Frits Bolkestein, Brussels, 5 December 2000.

Bourantas, D. and Papalexandris, N. (1990) 'Sex differences in leadership: leadership styles and subordinate satisfaction', *Journal of Managerial Psychology* 5: 7–10.

Boxall, P. (1996) 'The strategic HRM debate and the resource-based view of the firm', *Human Resource Management Journal* 6(3): 59–75.

Boxall, P. and Purcell, J. (2000) 'Strategic human resource management: where have we come from and where should we be going?', *International Journal of Management Reviews* 2(2): 183–203.

Bower, M. (1966) *The Will to Manage*, McGraw-Hill.

Boyatzis, R.E. (1982) *The Competent Manager*, John Wiley & Sons.

Boyd, C. (2001) 'HRM in the airline industry: strategies and outcomes', *Personnel Review* 30(4): 438–53.

Braham, P., Rattansi, A. and Skellington, R. (eds) (1992) *Racism and Antiracism*, Sage.

Braverman, H. (1974) *Labor and Monopoly Capital: The Degradation of Work in the Twentieth Century*, Monthly Review Press.

Breakwell, G.M. (1990) *Interviewing*, BPS/Routledge.

Brewster, C. (1994) 'European HRM: reflection of, or challenge to, the American concept?', in P.S. Kirkbride (ed.) *Human Resource Management in Europe: Perspectives for the 1990s*, Routledge.

Brewster, C. (2002) *Transfer of HRM Practices around the World*, paper presented at Human Resource Management across Countries: the Cultural Dimension Conference, Athens University of Economics and Business, 17 October 2002.

Brewster, C. and Tyson, S. (eds) (1991) *International Comparisons in Human Resource Management*, Pitman.

Brewster, C., Sparrow, P. and Harris, H. (2005) 'Towards a new model of globalizing HRM', *International Journal of Human Resource Management* 16(6): 949–70.

Briggs, C. (2001) 'Australian exceptionalism: the role of trade unions in the emergence of enterprise bargaining', *The Journal of Industrial Relations* 43(1): 27–43.

Briggs, P. (1991) 'Organizational commitment: the key to Japanese success', in C. Brewster and S. Tyson (eds) *International Comparisons in Human Resource Management*, Pitman.

Brown, M. and Heywood, J.S. (2005) 'Performance appraisal systems: determinants and change', *British Journal of Industrial Relations* 43(4): 659–79.

Brown, S. and Seidner, C. (1998) *Evaluating Corporate Training: Models and Issues*, Kluwer Academic Publishers.

Brown, W. (1994) *Bargaining for Full Employment*, Employment Policy Institute.

Bruine de Bruin, W. (2005) 'Save the last dance for me: unwanted serial position effects on jury evaluations', *Acta Psychologica* 118: 245–60.

Brunsson, N. (1989) *The Organization of Hypocrisy: Talk, Decisions and Action in Organizations*, Wiley.

Bryman, A. (1992) *Charisma and Leadership in Organizations*, Sage.

Brynin, M. (2006) 'Gender, technology and jobs', *The British Journal of Sociology* 57(3): 437–53.

Buch, K. and Rivers, E. (2001) 'TQM: the role of leadership and culture', *Leadership and Organization Development Journal* 22(8): 365–71.

Buchanan, D. and Boddy, D. (1992) *The Expertise of the Change Agent*, Prentice-Hall.

Buck, J.M. and Watson, J.L. (2002) 'Retaining staff employees: the relationship between human resources management strategies and organizational commitment', *Innovative Higher Education* 26(3): 175–93.

Bunge, M. and Ardila, R. (1987) *Philosophy of Psychology*, Springer-Verlag.

Buono, A.F. (1991) 'Managing strategic alliances: organizational and human resource considerations', *Business and the Contemporary World* 3(4): 92–101.

Burke, G. and Peppard, J. (eds) (1995) *Examining Business Process Re-engineering: Current Perspectives and Research Directions*, Kogan Page.

Burns, T. and Stalker, G.M. (1961) *The Management of Innovation*, Tavistock Publications.

Butler, R. (1991) *Designing Organizations: A Decision-Making Perspective*, Routledge.

Butterfield, K.D., Treviño, L.K., Wade, K.J. and Ball, G.A. (2005) 'Organizational punishment from the manager's perspective: an exploratory study', *Journal of Managerial Issues* 17(3): 363–82.

Byham, W. (1984) 'Assessing employees without resorting to a "centre"', *Personnel Management* (October): 55.

Cabral-Cardoso, C. (2004) 'The evolving Portuguese model of HRM', *International Journal of Human Resource Management* 15(6): 959–77.

Cakar, F. and Bititci, U.S. (2001) *Human Resource Management as a Strategic Input to Manufacturing*, paper presented at the International Working Conference on Strategic Manufacturing, 26–29 August, 2001, Aalborg, Denmark.

Caldwell, R. (2001) 'Champions, adapters, consultants and synergists: the new change agents in HRM', *Human Resource Management Journal* 11(3): 39–52.

Callaghan, G. and Thompson, P. (2002) '"We recruit attitude": the selection and shaping of routine call centre labour', *Journal of Management Studies* 39(2): 233–54.

Campbell, J.P., Dunnette, M., Lawler, E. and Weick, K. (1970) *Managerial Behavior, Performance and Effectiveness*, McGraw-Hill.

Cannadine, D. (1992) 'The present and the past in the English industrial revolution', in L.R. Berlanstein (ed.) *The Industrial Revolution and Work in Nineteenth-Century Europe*, Routledge.

Carmichael, F. and Woods, R. (2000) 'Ethnic penalties in unemployment and occupational attainment: evidence for Britain', *International Review of Applied Economics* 14(1): 71–98.

Cascio, W.F. (1998) *Applied Psychology in Human Resource Management*, Prentice-Hall.

Catlin, K. and Matthews, J. (2001) *Leading at the Speed of Growth: Journey from Entrepreneur to CEO*, John Wiley & Sons.

Chaffee, E. (1985) 'Three models of strategy', *Academy of Management Review* 10(1): 89–98.

Challiol, H. and Mignonac, K. (2005) 'Relocation decision-making and couple relationships: a quantitative and qualitative study of dual-earner couples', *Journal of Organizational Behavior* 26: 247–74.

Chan, A.W. and Snape, E. (2000) 'Union weakness in Hong Kong: workplace industrial relations and the federation of trade unions', *Economic and Industrial Democracy* 21(2): 117–46.

Chandler, A. (1962) *Strategy and Structure*, MIT Press.

Chapman, D. and Webster, J. (2006) 'Toward an integrated model of applicant reactions and job choice', *International Journal of Human Resource Management* 17(6): 1032–57.

Checkland, P.B. (1981) *Systems Thinking, Systems Practice*, John Wiley & Sons.

Chelliah, J. and D'Netto, B. (2006) 'Unfair dismissals in Australia: does arbitration help employees?', *Employee Relations* 28(5): 483–95.

Chiu, W.C.K., Chan, A.W., Snape, E. and Redman, T. (2001) 'Age stereotypes and discriminatory attitudes towards older workers: an East–West comparison', *Human Relations* 54(5): 629–61.

Chung, T.Z. (1991) 'Culture: a key to management communication between the Asian-Pacific area and Europe', *European Management Journal* 9(4): 419–24.

Chung, Y.B., Coleman, M. and Gfroerer, A. (2003) 'Career coaching: practice, training, professional, and ethical issues', *The Career Development Quarterly* 52(2): 141.

CIPD (2000) *Recruitment Survey Report 14*, June, Chartered Institute of Personnel and Development.

CIPD (2006) *Recruitment, Retention and Turnover, Annual Report*, Chartered Institute of Personnel and Development.

Clarke, A.C. (1973) *Profiles of the Future: An Inquiry into the Limits of the Possible*, HarperCollins.

Clarke, L. (2006a) 'Sexual relationships and sexual conduct in the workplace', *Legal Studies* 26(3): 347–68.

Clarke, L. (2006b) 'Valuing labour', *Building Research and Information* 34(3): 246–56.

Claydon, T. (2001) 'Human resource management and the labour market', in I. Beardwell and L. Holden, *Human Resource Management: A Contemporary Approach*, Pearson.

Clemente, M.N. and Greenspan, D.S. (1999) *Empowering Human Resources in the Merger and Acquisition Process: Guidance for HR Professionals in the Key Areas of M&A Planning and Integration*, Clemente, Greenspan and Co.

Coetzer, A. (2006) 'Managers as learning facilitators in small manufacturing firms', *Journal of Small Business and Enterprise Development* 13(3): 351–62.

Coggburn, J.D. (2005) 'The benefits of human resource centralization: insights from a survey of human resource directors in a decentralized state', *Public Administration Review* 65(4): 424–35.

Collis, B., Bianco, M., Margaryan, A. and Waring, B. (2005) 'Putting blended learning to work: a case study from a multinational oil company', *Education, Communication and Information* 5(3): 233–50.

Conlon, G. and Chevalier, A. (2002) *Rates of Return to Qualifications: A Summary of Recent Evidence*, Council for Industry and Higher Education.

Constant, A. and Shachmurove, Y. (2006) 'Entrepreneurial ventures and wage differentials between Germans and immigrants', *International Journal of Manpower* 27(3): 208–29.

Cooke, F.L. (2001) 'Human resource strategy to improve organizational performance: a route for firms in Britain?', *International Journal of Management Reviews* 3(4): 321–39.

Corbridge, M. and Pilbeam, S. (1998) *Employment Resourcing*, Financial Times/Pitman Publishing.

Corrall, S. (1999) 'Knowledge Management: Are We in the Knowledge Management Business?', *Ariadne*, (http://www.ariadne.ac.uk/issue18/knowledge-mgt/).

Cowey, A. (2005) 'Finance training can be fun and effective', *Industrial and Commercial Training* 37(7): 355–60.

Cox, A., Zagelmeyer, S. and Marchington, M. (2006) 'Embedding employee involvement and participation at work', *Human Resource Management Journal* 16(3): 250–67.

Cox, J. and Tapsell, J. (1991) *The Writing on the Wall: Graphology and Its Validity in Personality Assessments*, paper presented at the British Psychological Society Conference, Cardiff.

Cox, T. Jr., O'Neill, P.H. and Quinn, R.E. (2001) *Creating the Multicultural Organization: A Strategy for Capturing the Power of Diversity*, John Wiley & Sons.

Cressey, P. (1993) 'Employee participation', in M. Gold (ed.) *The Social Dimension: Employment Policy in the European Community*, Macmillan.

Crittan, P. (1993) *Investing in People: Towards Corporate Capability*, Butterworth-Heinemann.

Crofts, A. (1991) 'Learning to lead', *Management Today* (June): 68.

Crouch, C. (2000) 'The snakes and ladders of 21st-century trade unionism', *Oxford Review of Economic Policy* 16(1): 70–83.

Cully, M., Woodland, S., O'Reilly, A. and Dix, G. (1999) *Britain at Work*, Routledge.

Curran, J. and Stanworth, J. (1988) 'The small firm: a neglected area of management', in A.G. Cowling, M.J.K. Stanworth, R.D. Bennett, J. Curran and P. Lyons (eds) *Behavioural Science for Managers*, 2nd edn, Edward Arnold.

D'Annunzio-Green, N. and Francis, H. (2005) 'Tuning into tensions at times of change: the experiences of line and HR managers in a contract catering firm', *International Journal of Contemporary Hospitality Management* 17(4): 345–58.

Dar, A. and Tzannatos, Z. (1999) 'Active Labor Market Programs: A Review of the Evidence Based on Evaluations', *Social Protection Discussion Paper 9901*, World Bank.

Davenport, T.H. and Prusak, L. (2000) *Working Knowledge*, Harvard Business School Press.

Davidson, M.J. and Earnshaw, J. (1991) 'Policies, practices and attitudes towards sexual harassment in UK organizations', *Women in Management Review and Abstracts* 6(6): 15–21.

Davison, H.K. and Burke, M.J. (2000) 'Sex discrimination in simulated employment contexts: a meta-analytic investigation', *Journal of Vocational Behavior* 56(2): 225–48.

Day, D.V. and Schleicher, D.J. (2006) 'Self-monitoring at work: a motive-based perspective', *Journal of Personality* 74(3): 685–714.

De Graft-Johnson, A., Manley, S. and Greed, C. (2005) 'Diversity or the lack of it in the architectural profession', *Construction Management and Economics* 23(10): 1035–43.

Deal, T. and Kennedy, A. (1982) *Corporate Cultures: The Rites and Rituals of Corporate Life*, Addison-Wesley.

Dean, P. (1998) 'Editorial – Action Learning and Performance Improvement', *Performance Improvement Quarterly* 11(1): 3.

Dechawatanapaisal, D. and Siengthai, S. (2006) 'The impact of cognitive dissonance on learning work behavior', *The Journal of Workplace Learning* 18(1): 42–54.

Deery, S., Walsh, J. and Knox, A. (2001) 'The non-union workplace in Australia: bleak house or human resource innovator?', *International Journal of Human Resource Management* 12(4): 669–83.

Delery, J.E. and Doty, D.H. (1996) 'Modes of theorizing in strategic human resource management: tests of universalistic, contingency, and configurational performance predictions', *Academy of Management Journal* 39(4): 802–35.

DeNisi, A.S. and Pritchard, R.D. (2006) 'Performance appraisal, performance management and improving individual performance: a motivational framework', *Management and Organization Review* 2(2): 253–77.

Dibble, S. (1999) *Keeping Your Valuable Employees: Retention Strategies for Your Organization's Most Important Resource*, John Wiley & Sons.

Dick, P. and Nadin, S. (2006) 'Reproducing gender inequalities? A critique of realist assumptions underpinning personnel selection research and practice', *Journal of Occupational and Organizational Psychology* 79(3): 481–98.

Dicken, P. (1998) *Global Shift: Transforming the World Economy*, 3rd edn, The Guilford Press.

Dickinson, J. (2006) 'Employees' preferences for the bases of pay differentials', *Employee Relations* 28(2): 164–83.

Dipboye, R.L., Gaugler, B.B., Hayes, T.L. and Parker, D. (2001) 'The validity of unstructured panel interviews: more than meets the eye?', *Journal of Business and Psychology* 16(1): 35–49.

Dominelli, L. (1992) 'An uncaring profession: an examination of racism in social work', in P. Braham, A. Rattansi and R. Skellington (eds) *Racism and Antiracism*, Sage.

Donaldson, T. and Preston, L.E. (1995) 'The stakeholder theory of the corporation', *Academy of Management Review* 20: 65–91.

Downey, L.A., Papageorgiou, V. and Stough, C. (2006) 'Examining the relationship between leadership, emotional intelligence and intuition in senior female managers', *Leadership and Organizational Development Journal* 27(4): 250–64.

Drenth, P. (1978) 'Personnel selection', in P.B. Warr (ed.) *Psychology at Work*, 2nd edn, Penguin.

Drenth, P.J.D. and Algera, J. (1987) 'Personnel Selection', in P.B. Warr (ed.) *Psychology at Work*, Penguin.

Driscoll, M. (2002) *Web-Based Training: Designing e-Learning Experiences*, Jossey-Bass/Pfeiffer.

Drucker, P. (1998) 'The coming of the new organization', in *The Harvard Business Review on Knowledge Management* (Harvard Business Review Series), Harvard University Press.

Druker, J. and Stanworth, C. (2004) 'Mutual expectations: a study of the threeway relationship between employment agencies, their client organisations and white-collar agency temps', *Industrial Relations Journal* 35(1): 58–75.

Due, J., Madsen, J.S. and Jense, C.S. (1991) 'The social dimension: convergence or diversification of industrial relations in the single European market?', *Industrial Relations Journal* 22(2): 85–102.

Dulewicz, V. (1991) 'Improving assessment centres', *Personnel Management* (June): 50–5.

Duncan, C. (2001) 'The impact of two decades of reform of British public sector industrial relations', *Public Money and Management* 21(1): 27–34.

Dunning, D., Heath, C. and Suls, J.M. (2004) 'Flawed self-assessment: implications for health, education and the workplace', *Psychological Science and the Public Interest* 5(3): 69–106.

Economic Research Forum (2000) *MENA Trends 2000*, Economic Research Forum.

Eder, R. and Harris, M. (1999) 'Employment interview research: historical update and introduction', in R. Eder and M. Harris (eds) *The Employment Interview Handbook*, Sage Publications.

Eiser, J.R. (1994) *Attitudes, Chaos and the Connectivist Mind*, Blackwell.

Elkjaer, B. (2001) 'The learning organization: an undelivered promise', *Management Learning* 32(4): 437–52.

Ellin, A. (2004) 'What your handwriting says about your career', *New York Times* (late edition (East Coast) New York, N.Y.), 18 July: 10.1.

Ellinger, A.D., Ellinger, A.E., Yang, B. and Howton, S.W. (2002) 'The relationship between the learning organization concept and firms' financial performance: an empirical assessment', *Human Resource Development Quarterly* 13(1): 5–21.

Elliott, G.C. (2006) 'International outsourcing: values vs. economics', *Quality Progress* 39(8): 20–25.

Elvira, M.M. and Zatzick, C.D. (2002) 'Who's displaced first? The role of race in layoff decisions', *Industrial Relations* 41(2): 329–61.

English, G. (1991) 'Tuning up for performance management', *Training and Development Journal* (April): 56–60.

Entrekin, L. and Chung, Y.W. (2001) 'Attitudes towards different sources of executive appraisal: a comparison of Hong Kong Chinese and American managers in Hong Kong', *International Journal of Human Resource Management* 12(6): 965–87.

Erturk, I., Froud, J., Johal, S. and Williams, K. (2005) 'Pay for corporate performance or pay as social division? Rethinking the problem of top management pay in giant corporations', *Competition and Change* 9(1): 49–74.

Fang, T. and Heywood, J.S. (2006) 'Output pay and ethnic wage differentials: Canadian evidence', *Industrial Relations* 45(2): 173–94.

Farrell, G.A., Bobrowski, C. and Bobrowski, P. (2006) 'Scoping workplace aggression in nursing: findings from an Australian study', *Journal of Advanced Nursing* 55(6): 778–87.

Faulkner, D., Pitkethly, R. and Child, J. (2002) 'International mergers and acquisitions in the UK 1985–94: a comparison of national HRM practices', *International Journal of Human Resource Management* 13(1): 106–22.

Fayol, H. (1949) *General and Industrial Management*, Pitman.

Fenton-O'Creevy, M. (2001) 'Employee involvement and the middle manager: saboteur or scapegoat?', *Human Resource Management Journal* 11(1): 24–40.

Fisher, K. (1999) *Leading Self-Directed Work Teams*, McGraw-Hill.

Fishlow, A. and Parker, K. (eds.) (1999) *Growing Apart: The Causes and Consequences of Global Wage Inequality*, Council on Foreign Relations.

Fitz-Enz, J. (1994) *How To Measure Human Resource Management*, 2nd edn (McGraw-Hill Training Series), McGraw-Hill.

Flamholtz, E.G. and Randle, Y. (2000) *Growing Pains: Transitioning from an Entrepreneurship to a Professionally Managed Firm*, Jossey-Bass.

Flanders, A. (1970) *Management and Unions*, Faber & Faber.

Flecker, J. and Schulten, T. (1999) 'The end of institutional stability: what future for the "German model"?', *Economic and Industrial Democracy* 20(1): 81–115.

Fletcher, C. (2001) 'Performance appraisal and management: the developing research agenda', *Journal of Occupational and Organizational Psychology* 74(4): 473–87.

Fletcher, C. and Williams, R. (1992) 'The route to performance management', *Personnel Management* (October): 42–7.

Foote, D. (2001) 'The question of ethical hypocrisy in human resource management in the U.K. and Irish charity sectors', *Journal of Business Ethics* 34(1): 25–38.

Forbes, R. (1996) 'Performance management', *HR Monthly*, November 1996, Australian Human Resource Institute.

Ford, T.E. (2000) 'Effects of sexist humor on tolerance of sexist events', *Personality and Social Psychology Bulletin* 26(9): 1094–107.

Forde, C. and Slater, G. (2006) 'The nature and experience of agency working in Britain: what are the challenges for human resource management?', *Personnel Review* 35(2): 141–57.

Fortin, N.M. (2005) 'Gender role attitudes and the labour-market outcomes of women across OECD countries', *Oxford Review of Economic Policy* 21(3): 416–38.

Fossum, J. and Fitch, M. (1985) 'The effects of individual and contextual attributes on the sizes of recommended salary increases', *Personnel Psychology* 38(autumn): 587–602.

Foster, C. and Harris, L. (2005) 'Easy to say, difficult to do: diversity management in retail', *Human Resource Management Journal* 15(3): 4–17.

Foucault, M. (1977) *Discipline and Punish*, Allen Lane.

Fowler, A. (1987) 'When chief executives discover HRM', *Personnel Management* (January): 3.

Fowler, A. (1991) 'How to identify training needs', *Personnel Management Plus* (November): 22.

Fowler, A. (1993) 'How to manage cultural change', *Personnel Management Plus* (November): 25–6.

Frazer, R.A. and Wiersma, J.J. (2001) 'Prejudice versus discrimination in the employment interview: we may hire equally, but our memories harbour prejudice', *Human Relations* 54(2): 173–91.

Fredman, S. (2001) 'Equality: a new generation?', *Industrial Law Journal* 30(2): 145–68.

French, W.L. and Bell, C.H. (1990) *Organization Development: Behavioral Science Interventions for Organization Improvement*, 4th edn, Prentice-Hall.

Friedrich, C., Glaub, M., Gramberg, K. and Frese, M. (2006) 'Does training improve the business performance of small-scale entrepreneurs? An evaluative study', *Industry and Higher Education* 20(2): 75–84.

Frijters, P., Shields, M.A. and Price, S.W. (2005) 'Job search methods and their success: a comparison of immigrants and natives in the UK', *The Economic Journal* 115(507): F359–F376.

Fritz, R. (1996) *Corporate Tides: The Inescapable Laws of Organizational Structure*, Berrett-Koehler.

Fullan, M. (2001) *Leading in a Culture of Change*, Jossey-Bass.

Fuller, A., Beck, V. and Unwin, L. (2005) 'The gendered nature of apprenticeship: employers' and young people's perspectives', *Education + Training* 47(4–5): 298–311.

Furnham, A. (1990) *The Protestant Work Ethic: The Psychology of Work-related Beliefs and Behaviours*, Routledge.

Furnham, A. (1992) *Personality at Work*, Routledge.

Galbraith, J.K. (1967) *The New Industrial State*, H. Hamilton.

Gardiner, G.A. (1923) *Life of George Cadbury*, Cassell.

Gardner, T.M., Wright, P.M. and Gerhart, B.A. (2000) 'The HR–firm relationship. Can it be in the mind of the beholder?', *CAHRS Working Paper 00–20*, Cornell University.

Garrahan, P. and Stewart, P. (1992) *The Nissan Enigma: Flexibility at Work in the Local Economy*, Mansell.

Garvin, D. (1993) 'Building a learning organization', *Harvard Business Review* (July–August): 78–91.

Gates, S. (2006) 'Time to take negotiation seriously', *Industrial and Commercial Training* 38(5): 238–41.

Gazioglu, S. and Tansel, A. (2006) 'Job satisfaction in Britain: individual and job related factors', *Applied Economics* 38(10): 1163–71.

Geare, A., Edgar, F. and McAndrew, I. (2006) 'Employment relationships: ideology and HRM practice', *International Journal of Human Resource Management* 17(7): 1190–208.

Geary, J.F. and Roche, W.K. (2001) 'Multinationals and human resource practices in Ireland: a rejection of the "new conformance thesis"', *International Journal of Human Resource Management* 12(1): 109–27.

Geerlings, W.S.J. and van Veen, K. (2006) 'The future qualities of workforces: a simulation study of the long-term consequences of minor selection decisions', *International Journal of Human Resource Management* 17(7): 1254–66.

Gibb, S. (2001) 'The state of human resource management: evidence from employees' views of HRM systems and staff', *Library Review* 23(4): 318–36.

Gibb, S. (2002) *Learning and Development: Processes, Practices and Perspectives at Work*, Palgrave/Macmillan.

Giddens, A. (1989) *Sociology*, Polity Press.

Giles, E. and Williams, R. (1991) 'Can the personnel department survive quality management?', *Personnel Management* (April).

Gill, C. and Krieger, H. (1999) 'Direct and representative participation in Europe: recent survey evidence', *International Journal of Human Resource Management* 10(4): 572–91.

Gilley, J.W. and Gilley, A.M. (2002) *Strategically Integrated HRD*, Perseus Books Group.

Girma, S., Thompson, S. and Wright, P.W. (2006) 'The impact of merger activity on executive pay in the United Kingdom', *Economica* 73(290): 321–39.

Glover, J. (1988) *I: The Philosophy and Psychology of Personal Identity*, Penguin.

Gold, M. (1993) 'Overview of the social dimension', in M. Gold (ed.) *The Social Dimension: Employment Policy in the European Community*, Macmillan.

Goltz, J. (1998) *The Street Smart Entrepreneur: 133 Tough Lessons I Learned the Hard Way*, LPC.

Gordon, J.N. (2005) 'A remedy for the executive pay problem: the case for "compensation discussion and analysis"', *Journal of Applied Corporate Finance* 17(4): 24–35.

Gorman, E.H. (2005) 'Gender stereotypes, same-gender preferences, and organizational variation in the hiring of women: evidence from law firms', *American Sociological Review* 70: 702–28.

Goss, D. (1994) *Principles of Human Resource Management*, Routledge.

Gotsi, M. and Wilson, A. (2001) 'Corporate reputation management: "living the brand"', *Management Decision* 39(2): 99–104.

Graham, H.T. and Bennett, R. (1992) *Human Resources Management*, 7th edn, M&E Handbook Series, Pitman.

Graham, M. and Lennon, J.J. (2002) 'The dilemma of operating a strategic approach to human resource management in the Scottish visitor attraction sector', *International Journal of Contemporary Hospitality Management* 14(5): 213–20.

Graham, M. (2005) 'How to maximize your investment in IT training', *Human Resource Management International Digest* 13(2): 3–4.

Grant, R.M. (1997) 'The knowledge-based view of the firm: implications for management practice', *Long Range Planning* 30(3): 450–4.

Green, K.W., Wu, C., Whitten, D. and Medlin, B. (2006) 'The impact of strategic human resource management on firm performance and HR professionals' work attitude and work performance', *International Journal of Human Resource Management* 17(4): 559–79.

Greenbank, P. (2006) 'Starting up in business: an examination of the decision-making process', *The International Journal of Entrepreneurship and Innovation* 7(3): 149–69.

Greenwood, M.R. (2002) 'Ethics and HRM: a review and conceptual analysis', *Journal of Business Ethics* 36(3): 261–78.

Griffin, R.W. and Bateman, T.S. (1986) 'Job satisfaction and organizational commitment', in C.L. Cooper and I.T. Robertson (eds) *International Review of Industrial and Organizational Psychology*, John Wiley.

Grint, K. (1995) *Management: A Sociological Introduction*, Polity Press.

Gubman, E. (2004) 'HR strategy and planning: from birth to business results', *HR. Human Resource Planning* 27(1): 13–24.

Guerrero, S. and Barraud-Didier, V. (2004) 'High-involvement practices and performance of French firms', *International Journal of Human Resource Management* 15(8): 1408–23.

Guest, D. (1987) 'Human resource management and industrial relations', *Journal of Management Studies* 24(5): 503–21.

Guest, D. (1989) 'Personnel and HRM: can you tell the difference?', *Personnel Management* (January): 48–51.

Guest, D. (1992) 'Right enough to be dangerously wrong: an analysis of the In Search of Excellence phenomenon', in G. Salaman (ed.) *Human Resource Strategies*, Sage.

Guest, D. (1993) 'Current perspectives on human resource management in the United Kingdom', in J. Storey (ed.) *Human Resource Management: A Critical Text*, Routledge.

Guest, D.E. (1997) 'Human resource management and performance: a review and research agenda', *International Journal of Human Resource Management* 8(3): 263–76.

Guest, D.E. (2001) 'Human resource management: when research confronts theory', *International Journal of Human Resource Management* 12(7): 1092–106.

Gunnigle, P., Flood, P., Morley, M. and Turner, T. (1994) *Continuity and Change in Irish Employee Relations*, Oak Tree Press.

Gunz, H. (1990) 'The dual meaning of managerial careers: organizational and individual levels of analysis', *Journal of Management Studies* 26(May): 3.

Gurkov, I. (2002) 'Innovations and legacies in Russian human resource management practices: surveys of 700 chief executive officers', *Post-Communist Economies* 14(1): 137–44.

Guy, F. (2005) 'Earnings distribution, corporate governance and CEO pay', *International Review of Applied Economics* 19(1): 51–65.

Hailey, V.H. (2001) 'Breaking the mould? Innovation as a strategy for corporate renewal', *International Journal of Human Resource Management* 12(7): 1126–40.

Haire, M. (1959) 'Psychological problems relevant to business and industry', *Psychological Bulletin* 56: 169–94.

Haire, M., Ghiselli, E.E. and Porter, L.W. (1966) *Managerial Thinking: An International Study*, John Wiley.

Hakim, C. (2006) 'Women, careers, and work-life preferences', *British Journal of Guidance and Counselling* 34(3): 279–94.

Hall, L. and Atkinson, C. (2006) 'Improving working lives: flexible working and the role of employee control', *Employee Relations* 28(4): 374–86.

Hall, R. (2006) 'Temporary agency work and HRM in Australia: "cooperation, specialisation and satisfaction for the good of all?"', *Personnel Review* 35(2): 158–74.

Hamblin, A.C. (1974) *Evaluation and Control of Training*, McGraw-Hill.

Hamilton, E.A., Gordon, J.R. and Whelan-Berry, K.S. (2006) 'Understanding the work-life conflict of never-married women without children', *Women in Management Review* 21(5): 393–415.

Hammer, M. (1990) 'Reengineering work: don't automate, obliterate', *Harvard Business Review* (November–December): 119–31.

Hammer, M. (2001) *The Agenda: What Every Business Must Do to Dominate the Decade*, Crown Publications.

Hammer, M. and Champy, J. (1993) *Reengineering the Corporation: A Manifesto for Business Revolution*, Harper Business.

Hammond, K.H. (2001) 'Michael Porter's big ideas', *Fast Company* 44(March): 150.

Hammond, V. (1993) 'Women and development', *Training and Development* (December): 10–11.

Hammonds, K.H. (2005) 'Why we hate HR', *Fast Company* 97(August): 40.

Handy, C. (1989) *The Age of Unreason*, Business Books.

Handy, C. (1993) *Understanding Organizations*, 4th edn, Penguin Books.

Hanley, G. and Nguyen, L. (2005) 'Right on the money: what do Australian unions think of performance-related pay?', *Employee Relations* 27(2): 141–59.

Hansen, M.N. and Mastekaasa, A. (2006) 'Social origins and academic performance at university', *European Sociological Review* 22(3): 277–91.

Hanson, P. (2001) *The M&A Transition Guide: A 10-Step Roadmap for Workforce Integration*, John Wiley & Sons.

Harbridge, R. and Walsh, P. (2002) 'Globalisation and labour market deregulation in Australia and New Zealand: different approaches, similar outcomes', *Employee Relations* 24(4): 423–36.

Harfield, T. (1998) 'Strategic management and Michael Porter: a postmodern reading', *Management at Waikato*, Waikato University.

Harley, B. (1999) 'The myth of empowerment: work organisation, hierarchy and employee autonomy in contemporary Australian workplaces', *Work, Employment and Society* 13(1): 41–66.

Harper, B. (2000) 'Beauty, stature and the labour market: a British cohort study', *Oxford Bulletin of Economics and Statistics* 62(1): 771–800.

Harper, B. and Haq, M. (2001) 'Ambition, discrimination, and occupational attainment: a study of a British cohort', *Oxford Economic Papers* 53(4): 695–720.

Harris, L. (2000) 'Rewarding employee performance: line managers' values, beliefs and perspectives', *International Journal of Human Resource Management* 12(7): 1182–92.

Hart, R.A. and Kawasaki, S. (1999) *Work and Pay in Japan*, Cambridge University Press.

Hartmann, A. (2006) 'The role of organizational culture in motivating innovative behaviour in construction firms', *Construction Innovation* 6(3): 159.

Harvey, M. (2002) 'Human resource management in Africa: Alice's Adventures in Wonderland', *International Journal of Human Resource Management* 13(7): 1119–45.

Haslam, N. and Baron, J. (1994) 'Intelligence, personality, and prudence', in R.J. Sternberg and P. Ruzgis (eds) *Personality and Intelligence*, Cambridge University Press.

Hassel, A. (1999) 'The erosion of the German system of industrial relations', *British Journal of Industrial Relations* 37(3): 483–505.

Haynes, P. and Allen, M. (2001) 'Partnership as union strategy: a preliminary evaluation', *Employee Relations* 23(2): 164–93.

Heasman, K. (1993) 'The case against ageism', *NATFHE Journal* (autumn): 28.

Hebl, M.R. and Skorinko, J.L. (2005) 'Acknowledging one's physical disability in the interview: does "when" make a difference?', *Journal of Applied Social Psychology* 35(12): 2477–92.

Heeks, R. (1996) 'Global software outsourcing to India by multinational corporations', in P. Palvia, S.C. Palvia and E.M. Roche (eds) *Global Information Technology and Systems Management: Key Issues and Trends*, Ivy League Publishing.

Heery, E. and Salmon, J. (2000) 'The insecurity thesis', in E. Heery and J. Salmon *The Insecure Workforce*, Routledge.

Hegewisch, A. and Brewster, C. (1993) *European Developments in Human Resource Management*, Kogan Page.

Helman, C.G. (1990) *Culture, Health and Illness*, 2nd edn, Butterworth-Heinemann.

Helper, S., Levine, D.I. and Bendoly, E. (2002) 'Employee involvement and pay at US and Canadian auto suppliers', *Journal of Economics and Management Strategy* 11(2): 329–77.

Hempel, P.S. (2001) 'Differences between Chinese and Western managerial views of performance', *Personnel Review* 30(2): 203–26.

Hendry, C. (1994) 'The Single European Market and the HRM response', in P.S. Kirkbride (ed.) *Human Resource Management: Perspectives for the 1990s*, Routledge.

Hendry, C. (1995) *Human Resource Management: A Strategic Approach to Employment*, Butterworth-Heinemann.

Heneman, R.L., Tansky, J.W. and Camp, S.M. (2000) 'Human resource management practices in small and medium-sized enterprises: unanswered questions and future research perspectives', *Entrepreneurship Theory and Practice* 25(1): 11–26.

Herpen, M., Praag, M. and Cools, K. (2005) 'The effects of performance measurement and compensation on motivation: an empirical study', *De Economist* 153(3): 303–29.

Herriot, P. and Fletcher, C. (1990) 'Candidate-friendly selection for the 1990s', *Personnel Management* (February): 32–5.

Hetrick, S. (2002) 'Transferring HR ideas and practices: globalization and convergence in Poland', *Human Resource Development International* 5(3): 333–51.

Heywood, J.S. and O'Halloran, P.L. (2005) 'Racial earnings differentials and performance pay', *Journal of Human Resources* 40(2): 435–52.

Hinton, P.R. (1993) *The Psychology of Interpersonal Perception*, Routledge.

Hitzeman, S.E. (1997) *The Strategic Positioning of Today's Benefit Department*, IAHRM.

Hodgkinson, G.P. and Sparrow, P.R. (2002) *Re-framing Strategic Competence: A Psychological Perspective on the Strategic Management Process*, paper presented at the Strategy World Congress, Said Business School, University of Oxford, 18th–19th March, 2002.

Hofstede, G. (1980) *Culture's Consequences: International Differences in Work-related Values*, Sage.

Hofstede, G. (1994) *Cultures and Organizations*, HarperCollins (amended paperback edition of the 1991 McGraw-Hill publication).

Hofstede, G. and Bond, M.H. (1988) 'The Confucius connection: from cultural roots to economic growth', *Organizational Dynamics* 16(4): 4–21.

Hogenesch, K. (2004) 'A new science for finding the right employee?', *NZ Business* 18(2): 10.

Holden, L. (2001) 'Employee involvement and empowerment', in I. Beardwell and L. Holden (eds) *Human Resource Management: A Contemporary Approach*, 3rd edn, Financial Times/Prentice-Hall.

Hollinsead, G. and Leat, M. (1995) *Human Resource Management: An International and Comparative Perspective*, Pitman.

Holloway, W. (1991) *Work Psychology and Organizational Behaviour: Managing the Individual at Work*, Sage Publications.

Holmes, T.H. and Rahe, R.H. (1967) 'The social readjustment rating scale', *Journal of Psychosomatic Research* 11: 213–8.

Hoque, K. and Noon, M. (2001) 'Counting angels: a comparison of personnel and HR specialists', *Human Resource Management Journal* 11(3): 5–22.

Horgan, J. and Mühlau, P. (2006) 'Human resource systems and employee performance in Ireland and the Netherlands: a test of the complementarity hypothesis', *International Journal of Human Resource Management* 17(3): 414–39.

Hornaday, R.W. (1990) 'Dropping the E-word from small business research', *Journal of Small Business Research* (October): 22–33.

Horwitz, F.M. and Smith, D.A. (1998) 'Flexible work practices and human resource management: a comparison of South African and foreign-owned companies,' *International Journal of Human Resource Management* 9: 4.

Horwitz, F.M., Bravington, D. and Silvis, U. (2006) 'The promise of virtual teams: identifying key factors in effectiveness and failure', *Journal of European Industrial Training* 30(6): 472–94.

Horwitz, F.M., Browning, V., Jain, H. and Steenkamp, A.J. (2002) 'Human resource practices and discrimination in South Africa: overcoming the apartheid legacy', *International Journal of Human Resource Management* 13(7): 1105–18.

Horwitz, F.M., Heng, C.T., Quazi, H.A., Nonkwelo, C., Roditi, D. and van Eck, P. (2006) 'Human resource strategies for managing knowledge workers: an Afro-Asian comparative analysis', *International Journal of Human Resource Management* 17(5): 775–811.

Hossain, M.A. and Tisdell, C.A. (2005) 'Closing the gender gap in Bangladesh: inequality in education, employment and earnings', *International Journal of Social Economics* 32(5): 439–53.

Howitt, D. and Owusu-Bempah, J. (1990) 'Racism in a British journal', *Psychologist* (September): 396–9.

Hoxie, R.F. (1923) *Trade Unionism in the United States*, 2nd edn, Appleton-Century Crofts; reproduced in W.E.J. McCarthy (ed.) (1972) *Trade Unions*, Penguin.

Huang, T-C. (2000) 'Are the human resource practices of effective firms distinctly different from those of poorly performing ones? Evidence from Taiwanese enterprises', *International Journal of Human Resource Management* 11(2): 436–51.

Huczynski, A. and Buchanan, D. (2000) *Organizational Behaviour: An Introductory Text*, 4th edn, FT Prentice-Hall.

Hughes, J.M.C. (2002) 'HRM and universalism: is there one best way?', *International Journal of Contemporary Hospitality Management* 14(5): 221–28.

Hui, C.H. (1990) 'Work attitudes, leadership styles, and managerial behaviours in different cultures', in R.W. Brislin (ed.) *Applied Cross-Cultural Psychology*, Sage.

Husband, C. (1991) *Race, Conflictual Politics and Anti-racist Social Work: Lessons from the Past for Action in the 90s*, Northern Curriculum Development Project Setting the Context for Change, Central Council for Education and Training in Social Work, Leeds.

Huysman, M. (2000) 'An organizational learning approach to the learning organization', *European Journal of Work and Organizational Psychology* 9(2): 133–45.

Huzzard, T. (2001) 'Discourse for normalizing what? – The learning organization and the workplace trade union response', *Economic and Industrial Democracy* 22(3): 407–31.

Hyman, R. (1988) 'Flexible specialization: miracle or myth?', in R. Hyman and W. Streek (eds) *New Technology and Industrial Relations*, Blackwell.

Ichniowski, C., Kochan, T.A., Levine, D.I., Olson, C. and Strauss, G. (2000) 'What works at work: overview and assessment', in C. Ichniowski, T.A. Kochan, D.I. Levine, C. Olson and G. Strauss (eds) *The American Workplace: Skills, Compensation, and Employee Involvement*, Cambridge University Press.

Iles, P. (2001) 'Employee resourcing', in J. Storey (ed.) *Human Resource Management: A Critical Text*, 2nd edn, Thomson Learning.

Iles, P. and Maby, C. (1992) 'Personnel strategies', in G. Salaman (ed.) *Human Resource Strategies*, Sage.

Iles, P. and Salaman, G. (1995) 'Recruitment, selection and assessment', in J. Storey (ed.) *Human Resource Management: A Critical Text*, Routledge.

ILO (2004) *World Employment Report 2004–2005*, International Labour Organization.

Industrial Society (2000) *Experience Necessary – The Business Case for Wisdom*, The Industrial Society.

Institute of Work Psychology (2001) *What is a High Performance Work System?*, University of Sheffield.

International Labour Organization (2000) *Decent Work and Poverty Reduction in the Global Economy*, paper submitted by the International Labour Office to the Second Session of the Preparatory Committee for the Special Session of the General Assembly on the Implementation of the Outcome of the World Summit for Social Development and Further Initiatives, April 2000.

IRS (1997) 'The state of selection: an IRS survey', *Employee Development Bulletin*, 85, Industrial Relations Services.

Isaac, J.E. (2001) 'Performance related pay: the importance of fairness', *The Journal of Industrial Relations* 43(2): 111–23.

Jackson, G. (1998) 'Globalization, wages, jobs and myths', *The New Australian* 60: 6–12.

Jacobi, O. and Muller-Jentsch (1990) 'West Germany: continuity and structural change', in G. Baglioni and C. Crouch (eds) *European Industrial Relations: The Challenge of Flexibility*, Sage.

Jacques, R. (1997) 'Review of *Early Management Thought*, D.A. Wren (ed.), Dartmouth', *Electronic Journal of Radical Organisation Theory* III(2) August, Waikato Management School (WMS), University of Waikato, New Zealand.

Jamroq, J.J. and Overhot, M.H. (2004) 'Building a strategic HR function: continuing the evolution', *HR. Human Resource Planning* 7(1): 51–63.

Jenkins, A. (2001) *Companies' Use of Psychometric Testing and the Changing Demand for Skills: A Review of the Literature*, Centre for the Economics of Education, London School of Economics and Political Science.

Johnson, S. (2002) 'Card check or mandatory representation vote? How the type of union recognition procedure affects union certification success', *Economic Journal* (April):344–61.

Johnson, G. and Scholes, K. (1984) *Exploring Corporate Strategy*, Prentice-Hall.

Jones, A. (2006) 'Culture, identity, and motivation: the historical anthropology of a family firm', *Culture and Organization* 12(2): 169–83.

Kahn, H. (1979) *World Economic Development: 1979 and Beyond*, Westview.

Kalev, A., Dobbin, F. and Kelly, E. (forthcoming) 'Best practices or best guesses? Diversity management and the remediation of inequality', *American Sociological Review*.

Kanter, R.M. (1989) *When Giants Learn to Dance*, Simon and Schuster.

Karamanlis, K. (2006) 'Reforms for growth and prosperity', *OECD Observer*, Online Edition, May.

Kauhanen, A. and Piekkola, H. (2006) 'What makes performance-related pay schemes work? Finnish evidence', *Journal of Management and Governance* 10(2): 149–77.

Kavanagh, M.H. and Ashkanasy, N.M. (2006) 'Acceptance of change during a merger', *British Journal of Management* 17(1): S81–S103.

Kearns, P. (2003) *HR Strategy: Business Focused Individually Centred*, Butterworth-Heinemann.

Keenoy, T. (1990) 'HRM: a case of the wolf in sheep's clothing', *Personnel Review* 19(2): 3–9.

Keenoy, T. (1999) 'HRM as hologram: a polemic', *Journal of Management Studies* 36(1): 1–23.

Keenoy, T. and Anthony, P.D. (1992) 'HRM: metaphor, meaning and morality', in P. Blyton and P. Turnbull (eds) *Reassessing Human Resource Management*, Sage.

Kellaway, L. (2001) 'INSIDE TRACK: A prelude to platitudes: handing out staff guidelines to good and bad "behaviours" is surely a sign that an organisation is in deep trouble', *Financial Times* (December): 17.

Kelliher, C. and Riley, M. (2002) 'Making functional flexibility stick: an assessment of the outcomes for stakeholders', *International Journal of Contemporary Hospitality Management* 14(5): 237–42.

Kellough, J.E. and Nigro, L.G. (2002) 'Pay for performance in Georgia state government: employee perspectives on GeorgiaGain after 5 years', *Review of Public Personnel Administration* 22(2): 146–66.

Kessler, I. (1995) 'Reward systems', in J. Storey (ed.) *Human Resource Management: A Critical Text*, Routledge.

Kessler, I. (2001) 'Reward system choices', in J. Storey (ed.) *Human Resource Management: A Critical Text*, 2nd edn, Thomson Learning.

Ketola, T. (2006) 'From CR-psychopaths to responsible corporations: waking up the inner sleeping beauty of companies', *Corporate Social Responsibility and Environmental Management* 13(2): 113.

Kettley, P. (1996) *Personal Feedback: Cases in Point*, IES Report 326, Institute of Employment Studies.

Khatri, N. and Budhwar, P.S. (2002) 'A study of strategic HR issues in an Asian context', *Personnel Review* 31(2): 166–88.

Khilji, S.E. and Wang, X. (2006) '"Intended" and "implemented" HRM: the missing linchpin in strategic human resource management research', *International Journal of Human Resource Management* 17(7): 1171–89.

Kidder, J. (2006) '"It's the job that I love": bike messengers and edgework', *Sociological Forum* 21(1): 31–54.

Kirkpatrick, D. (1994) *Evaluating Training Programs: The Four Levels*, Berrett-Koehler Publishers, Inc.

Klikauer, T. (2002) 'Stability in Germany's industrial relations: a critique on Hassel's erosion thesis', *British Journal of Industrial Relations* 40(2): 295–308.

Kline, B. (1993) *The Handbook of Psychological Testing*, Routledge.

Kobayashi, N. (1992) 'Japan's global and regional roles', *Business and the Contemporary World* 4(4): 18–24.

Kochan, T. and Dyer, L. (2001) 'HRM: an American view', in J. Storey (ed.) *Human Resource Management: A Critical Text*, 2nd edn, Thomson Learning.

Kotey, B. and Slade, P. (2005) 'Formal human resource management practices in small growing firms', *Journal of Small Business Management* 43(1): 16–40.

Krajewski, H.T., Goffin, R.D., McCarthy, J.M., Rothstein, M.G. and Johnston, N. (2006) 'Comparing the validity of structured interviews for managerial-level employees: should we look to the past or focus on the future?', *Journal of Occupational and Organizational Psychology* 79(3): 411–32.

Kram, K.E. (1983) 'Phases of the mentor relationship', *Academy of Management Journal* 26(4): 608–25.

Kramer, L.A. and Lambert, S. (2001) 'Sex-linked bias in chances of being promoted to supervisor', *Sociological Perspectives* 44(1): 111–27.

Kramer, S.N. (1963) *The Sumerians*, University of Chicago Press.

Kraus, V. and Yonay, Y.P. (2000) 'The effect of occupational sex composition on the gender gap in workplace authority', *Social Science Research* 29(4): 583–605.

Kuhn, T.S. (1962) *The Structure of Scientific Revolutions*, University of Chicago Press.

Kuruscu, B. (2006) 'Training and Lifetime Income', *The American Economic Review* 96(3): 832–46.

Kuruvilla, S. and Erickson, C.L. (2002) 'Change and transformation in Asian industrial relations', *Industrial Relations* 41(2): 171–227.

Kutcher, E.J. and Bragger, J.D. (2004) 'Selection interviews of overweight job applicants: can structure reduce the bias?', *Journal of Applied Social Psychology* 34(10): 1993–2022.

Labovitz, G. and Rosansky, V. (1997) *The Power of Alignment: How Great Companies Stay Centered and Accomplish Extraordinary Things*, John Wiley & Sons.

Lane, H.W., Distefano, J.J. and Maznevski, M.L. (1997) *International Management Behavior*, Blackwell.

Langtry, R. and Langtry, B. (1991) 'Why managers keep an eye on their image', *The Independent Business News*, 3 November.

Lapidus, J. and Figart, D.M. (1998) 'Remedying "unfair acts": U.S. pay equity by race and gender', *Feminist Economics* 4(3): 7–28.

Lappalainen, P. (2001) *The Challenges Posed by the EU Anti-Discrimination Directives*, paper presented at the Sixth International Metropolis Conference, Workshop on Anti-discrimination legislation, 27 November, 2001, Rotterdam, the Netherlands.

Lasserre, P. and Schutte, H. (1999) *Strategies for Asia Pacific: Beyond the Crisis*, Macmillan Business.

Laursen, K. (2002) 'The importance of sectoral differences in the application of complementary HRM practices for innovation performance', *International Journal of the Economics of Business* 9(1): 139–56.

Lautenschlager, G.J. (1994) 'Accuracy and faking of background data', in G.A. Stokes, M.D. Mumford and W.A. Owens (eds) *Biodata Handbook*, Consulting Psychologists Press.

Lawler, Edward E. III (1991) *High-Involvement Management: Participative Strategies for Improving Organizational Performance*, Jossey-Bass.

Lawrence, P. (1993) 'Human resource management in Germany', in S. Tyson, P. Lawrence, P. Poirson, L. Manzolini and C.F. Vincente (eds) *Human Resource Management in Europe: Strategic Issues and Cases*, Kogan Page.

Lee, H.W. (2006) 'International human resource management can be achieved through cultural studies and relevant training', *The Business Review* 5(2): 95–100.

Lee, K. and Gao, T. (2005) 'Studying organizational commitment with the OCQ in the Korean retail context: its dimensionality and relationships with satisfaction and work outcomes', *The International Review of Retail, Distribution and Consumer Research* 15(4): 375–99.

Lee, M. and Koh, J. (2001) 'Is empowerment really a new concept?', *International Journal of Human Resource Management* 12(4): 684–95.

Lee, S. (2004) 'Seniority as an employment norm: the case of layoffs and promotion in the US employment relationship', *Socio-Economic Review* 2(1): 65–86.

Leeds, C., Kirkbride, P.S. and Duncan, J. (1994) 'The cultural context of Europe: a tentative mapping', in P.S. Kirkbride (ed.) *Human Resource Management in Europe: Perspectives for the 1990s*, Routledge.

Legge, K. (1989) 'Human resource management: a critical analysis', in J. Storey (ed.) *New Perspectives in Human Resource Management*, Routledge.

Legge, K. (1995) *Human Resource Management: Rhetorics and Realities*, Macmillan Business.

Legge, K. (2001) 'Silver bullet or spent round? Assessing the meaning of the high commitment management/performance relationship', in J. Storey (ed.) *Human Resource Management: A Critical Text*, 2nd edn, Thomson Learning.

Legge, K. (2004) *Human Resource Management: Rhetorics and Realities*, Palgrave Macmillan.

Leibfried, S. and Pierson, P. (2000) 'Social policy: left to courts and markets?', in H. Wallace and W. Wallace (eds) *Policy-Making in the European Union*, Oxford University Press.

Lengnick-Hall, C.A. and Lengnick-Hall, M.L. (1988) 'Strategic HRM – a review of the literature and a proposed typology', *Academy of Management Review* 13(3): 454–70.

Lesonsky, R. (2001) *Start Your Own Business: The Only Start-up Book You'll Ever Need*, 2nd edn, Entrepreneur Media Inc.

Lewis, C. (1985) *Employee Selection*, Hutchinson.

Lewis, P. (1991) 'Eight steps to the successful appointment of a training consultant', *Journal of European Industrial Training* 15(6): 25–9.

Li, A. and Bagger, J. (2006) 'Using the BIDR to distinguish the effects of impression management and self-deception on the criterion validity of personality measures: a meta-analysis', *International Journal of Selection and Assessment* 14(2): 131–41.

Lievens, F., Highhouse, S. and De Corte, W. (2005) 'The importance of traits and abilities in supervisors' hirability decisions as a function of method of assessment', *Journal of Occupational and Organizational Psychology* 78(3): 453–70.

Lindbeck, A. and Snower, D. (1988) *The Insider-Outsider Theory of Unemployment and Employment*, MIT Press.

Long, R.J. and Shields, J.L. (2005) 'Performance pay in Canadian and Australian firms: a comparative study', *International Journal of Human Resource Management* 16(10): 1783–811.

Lu, L.-T. (2006) 'The influence of cultural factors on international human resource issues and international joint venture performance', *Journal of American Academy of Business* 10(1): 192–97.

Lucas, R. (2002) 'Fragments of HRM in hospitality? Evidence from the 1998 workplace employee relations survey', *International Journal of Contemporary Hospitality Management* 14(5): 207–12.

Luce, E. (1995) 'SE Asia: singularly different', *Financial Times*, 4 December.

Lustgarten, L. and Edwards, J. (1992) 'Racial inequality and the limits of law', in P. Braham, A. Rattansi and R. Skellington (eds) *Racism and Antiracism*, Sage.

Lyons, P. (1988) 'Social interaction', in A.G. Cowling, M.J.K. Stanworth, R.D. Bennett, J. Curran and P. Lyons (eds) *Behavioural Sciences for Managers*, 2nd edn, Edward Arnold.

Mabey, C., Salaman, G. and Storey, J. (eds.) (1998) *Strategic Human Resource Management: A Reader*, The Open University/Sage.

Machin, S. and Manning, A. (2004) 'A test of competitive labor market theory: the wage structure among elder care assistants in the South of England', *Industrial and Labor Relations Review* 57(3): 371–85.

Mackay, J. (1992) 'Tying the knot: the human side of acquisitions', *Human Resources* (autumn): 10–14.

Malhotra, Y. (1998) 'TOOLS@WORK: deciphering the knowledge management hype', *Journal for Quality and Participation*, special issue on Learning and Information Management 21(4): 58–60.

Marchington, M. (2001) 'Employee involvement at work', in J. Storey (ed.) *Human Resource Management: A Critical Text*, 2nd edn, Thomson Learning.

Marchington, M. and Grugulis, I. (2000) '"Best practice" human resource management: perfect opportunity or dangerous illusion?', *International Journal of Human Resource Management* 11(6): 1104–24.

Marcoux, A.M. (2000) 'Business ethics gone wrong', *CATO Policy Report*, CATO Institute, 24 July.

Maresh, N. (1999) *ASTD Handbook of Training Design and Delivery*, 2nd edn, American Society for Training and Development.

Margerison, C. (1991) *Making Management Development Work*, McGraw-Hill.

Margerison, C. (2002) 'Careering ahead via work-based learning', *Training Journal* (October): 24.

Marginson, P., Edwards, P.K., Armstrong, P. and Purcell, J. (1993a) Executive Summary of Findings. *Second Company Level Industrial Relations Survey*, Industrial Relations Research Unit (mimeo).

Marginson, P., Edwards, P., Martin, R., Purcell, J. and Sisson, K. (1988) *Beyond the Workplace: Managing Industrial Relations in the Multi-establishment Enterprise*, Blackwell.

Marginson, P., Edwards, P.K., Armstrong, P., Purcell, J. and Hubbard, N. (1993b) *Report of the Initial Findings from the Second Company Level Industrial Relations Survey*. Warwick Papers in Industrial Relations, no.45, University of Warwick.

Marquardt, M.J. and Revans, R. (1999) *Action Learning in Action: Transforming Problems and People for World-Class Organizational Learning*, Davies-Black Publishing.

Marsden, D., French, S. and Kobi, K. (2000) *Why Does Performance Pay Demotivate? Financial Incentives Versus*

Performance Appraisal, Centre for Economic Performance, London School of Economics and Political Science.

Marti, M., Bobier, D. and Baron, R.S. (2000) 'Right before our eyes: the failure to recognize non-prototypical forms of prejudice', *Group Processes and Intergroup Relations* 3(4): 403–18.

Martin, J.P. and Stancanelli, E. (2002) 'Tackling some myths about temporary jobs', *OECD Observer*, 26 June.

Mason, P.L. (2000) 'Understanding recent empirical evidence on race and labor market outcomes in the USA', *Review of Social Economy* 58(3): 319–38.

Matlay, H. (2002) 'Industrial relations in the SME sector of the British economy: an empirical perspective', *Journal of Small Business and Enterprise Development* 9(3): 307–18.

Maurer, R. (1996) *Beyond the Wall of Resistance: Unconventional Strategies That Build Support for Change*, Bard Press.

Maxwell, G.A. and Watson, S. (2006) 'Perspectives on line managers in human resource management: Hilton International's UK hotels', *International Journal of Human Resource Management* 17(6): 1152–70.

McCausland, W.D., Pouliakas, K. and Theodossiou, I. (2005) 'Some are punished and some are rewarded: a study of the impact of performance pay on job satisfaction', *International Journal of Manpower* 26(7–8): 636–59.

McCormick, E.J. and Ilgen, D. (1987) *Industrial and Organizational Psychology*, 8th edn, Unwin Hyman.

McDermott, E., Mangan, J. and O'Connor, M. (2006) 'Graduate development programmes and satisfaction levels', *Journal of European Industrial Training* 30(6): 456–71.

McDonald, P.K., Bradley, L.M. and Guthrie, D. (2006) 'Challenging the rhetoric of choice in maternal labour-force participation: preferred versus contracted work hours', *Gender, Work and Organization* 13(5): 470–91.

McGregor, D. (1960) *The Human Side of Enterprise*, McGraw-Hill.

McIlwee, T. and Roberts, I. (1991) *Human Resource Management*, Elm Publications.

McIntyre, S.L. (2000) 'The failure of Fordism', *Technology and Culture* 41(2): 269–99.

McKenna, E. (1994) *Business Psychology and Organizational Behaviour*, Lawrence Erlbaum Associates.

McKenna, E. (2000) *Business Psychology and Organisational Behaviour: a student's handbook*, Psychology Press.

Meek, V.L. (1988) 'Organizational culture: origins and weaknesses', *Organization Studies* 9(4): 453–73.

Melé, D. (2005) 'Exploring the principle of subsidiarity in organisational forms', *Journal of Business Ethics* 60(3): 293–305.

Merhebi, R., Pattenden, K., Swan, P.L. and Zhou, X. (2006) 'Australian chief executive officer remuneration: pay and performance', *Accounting and Finance* 46(3): 481–97.

Messmer, H. (2006) *Human Resources Kit for Dummies*, 2nd edn, John Wiley & Sons.

Metcalf, D., Hansen, K. and Charlwood, A. (2001) 'Unions and the sword of justice: unions and pay systems, pay inequality, pay discrimination and low pay', *National Institute Economic Review* 176(1): 61–75.

Michelson, G. and Mouly, S. (2000) 'Rumour and gossip in organisations: a conceptual study', *Management Decision* 38(5): 339–46.

Michie, J. and Sheehan, M. (1999) 'HRM practices, R&D expenditure and innovative investment: evidence from the UK's 1990 workplace industrial relations survey (WIRS)', *Industrial and Corporate Change* 8(2): 211–34.

Michie, J. and Sheehan-Quinn, M. (2001) 'Labour market flexibility, human resource management and corporate performance', *British Journal of Management* 12(4): 287–306.

Milcovich, G.T., Newman, J.M. and Milcovich, C. (2001) *Compensation*, 7th edn, McGraw-Hill.

Miles, R. and Snow, C. (1978) *Organizational Strategy, Structure and Process*, McGraw-Hill.

Miles, R.E. and Snow, C.C. (1984) 'Designing strategic human resource systems', *Organizational Dynamics* (summer): 36–52.

Miller, A.F., Jnr and Hanson, M. (1991) 'The smile on the face of the leadership tiger', *Personnel Management* (October): 54–7.

Miller, P. (1989) 'Managing corporate identity in the diversified business', *Personnel Management* (March): 36–9.

Mills, A.J. and Murgatroyd, S.J. (1991) *Organizational Rules: A Framework for Understanding Organizational Action*, Open University.

Millward, N., Forth, J. and Bryson, A. (2000) *All Change at Work*, Routledge.

Ming Chia, Y. (2005) 'Job offers of multi-national accounting firms: the effects of emotional intelligence, extra-curricular activities, and academic performance', *Accounting Education* 14(1): 75–93.

Mintzberg, H. (1983) *Structure in Fives: Designing Effective Organizations*, Prentice-Hall.

Mintzberg, H. (1994) *The Rise and Fall of Strategic Planning*, Prentice-Hall.

Mintzberg, H. and Waters, J.A. (1985) 'Of strategies deliberate and emergent', *Strategic Management Journal* 6: 257–72.

Mintzberg, H., Ahlstrand, B. and Lampel, J. (1998) *Strategy Safari: A Guided Tour Through the Wilds of Strategic Management*, The Free Press.

Misra, R. and Panigrahi, B. (1996) 'Effects of age on attitudes towards working women', *International Journal of Manpower* 17(2): 3–17.

Mobius, M.M. and Rosenblat, T.S. (2006) 'Why beauty matters', *The American Economic Review* 96(1): 222–35.

Molander, C. and Winterton, J. (1994) *Managing Human Resources*, Routledge.

Monks, K. (1996) *Roles in Personnel Management from Welfarism to Modernism: Fast Track or Back Track?* DCU Research Paper No.17, Dublin City University Business School.

Moore, K., Cruickshank, M. and Haas, M. (2006) 'The influence of managers on job satisfaction in occupational therapy', *The British Journal of Occupational Therapy* 69(7): 312–18.

Moore, S. (2006) 'The relationship between legislation and industrial practice: a study of the outcome of trade union recognition', *Employee Relations* 28(4): 363–73.

Morgan, A., Cannan, K. and Cullinane, J. (2005) '360° feedback: a critical enquiry', *Personnel Review* 34(6): 663–80.

Morgan, G. (1986) *Images of Organization*, Sage.

Morris, D., Bakan, I. and Wood, G. (2006) 'Employee financial participation: evidence from a major UK retailer', *Employee Relations* 28(4): 326–41.

Morris, L. (1987) 'The household in the labour market', in C.C. Harris (ed.) *Redundancy and Recession*, Blackwell.

Moscoso, S. (2000) 'Selection interview: a review of validity evidence, adverse impact and applicant reactions', *International Journal of Selection and Assessment* 8(4): 237–47.

Moscoso, S. and Salgado, J.F. (2004) 'Fairness reactions to personnel selection techniques in Spain and Portugal', *International Journal of Selection and Assessment* 12(1–2): 187–96.

Mosel, J.N. and Goheen, H.W. (1958) 'The validity of the employment recommendation questionnaire in personnel selection', *Personnel Psychology* 2: 487–90.

Mount, M., Ilies, R. and Johnson, E. (2006) 'Relationship of personality traits and counterproductive work behaviors: the mediating effects of job satisfaction', *Personnel Psychology* 59(3): 591–622.

Mowday, R., Steers, R. and Porter, L. (1979) 'The measurement of organizational commitment', *Journal of Vocational Behaviour* 14: 224–47.

Moy, J.W. (2006) 'Are employers assessing the right traits in hiring? Evidence from Hong Kong companies', *International Journal of Human Resource Management* 17(4): 734–54.

Moye, M.J. and Henkin, A.B. (2006) 'Exploring associations between employee empowerment and interpersonal trust in managers', *The Journal of Management Development* 25(2): 101–17.

Moynahan, B. (1993) 'Creating harassment-free work zones', *Training and Development* (May): 67–70.

Muller, M. (1999) 'Enthusiastic embrace or critical reception? the German HRM debate', *Journal of Management Studies* 36(4): 465–82.

Murji, K. (2006) 'Using racial stereotypes in anti-racist campaigns', *Ethnic and Racial Studies* 29(2): 260–80.

Murliss, H. (1987) 'Performance-related pay in the public sector', *Public Money* (March): 29–33.

Murphy, K.R. (1994) 'Meta-analysis and validity generalization', in N. Anderson and P. Herriot (eds) *Assessment and Selection in Organizations: Methods and Practice for Recruitment and Appraisal*, First Update and Supplement 1994, Wiley.

Murphy, K.R. and Cleveland, J.N. (1995) *Understanding Performance Appraisal: Social, Organizational and Goal-based Perspectives*, Sage.

Murrell, K.L. and Meredith, M. (2000) *Empowering Employees*, McGraw-Hill.

Nadler, D.A., Gerstein, M.C., Shaw, R.B. & Associates (1992) *Organizational Architecture: Designs for Changing Organizations*, Jossey-Bass.

Nadler, L. and Nadler, Z. (1989) *Developing Human Resources*, Jossey-Bass.

Naidoo, J. and Wills, J. (2000) *Health Promotion: Foundations for Practice*, 2nd edn, Balliere Tindall/RCN.

Nankervis, A., Compton, R. and Savery, L. (2002) 'Strategic HRM in small and medium enterprises: a CEO's perspective?', *Asia Pacific Journal of Human Resources* 40(2): 260–73.

Needle, D. (1994) *Business in Context: An Introduction to Business and its Environment*, 2nd edn, Chapman and Hall.

Nelkin, D. and Tancredi, L. (1989) *Dangerous Diagnostics*, Basic Books.

Neumark, D. and Stock, W.A. (2006) 'The labor market effects of sex and race discrimination laws', *Economic Inquiry* 44(3): 385–419.

Newton, B. (2006) 'Training an age-diverse workforce', *Industrial and Commercial Training* 38(2): 93–97.

Nickson, D., Warhurst, C. and Dutton, E. (2004) *Aesthetic Labour and the Policy-Making Agenda: Time for a Reappraisal of Skills*, SKOPE Research Paper No.48, Summer 2004.

Noblet, A., Teo, S.T.T., McWilliams, J. and Rodwell, J. (2005) 'Which work characteristics predict employee outcomes for the public-sector employee? An examination of generic and occupation-specific characteristics', *International Journal of Human Resource Management* 16(8): 1415–30.

Nowack, K.M. (1991) 'A true training needs analysis', *Training and Development Journal* (April): 69–73.

Nowicki, M.D. and Rosse, J.G. (2002) 'Managers' views of how to hire: building bridges between science and practice', *Journal of Business and Psychology* 17(2): 157–70.

Nunes, M.B., Annansingh, F., Eaglestone, B. and Wakefield, R. (2006) 'Knowledge management issues in knowledge-intensive SMEs', *Journal of Documentation* 62(1): 101–19.

Nurse, L. (2005) 'Performance appraisal, employee development and organizational justice: exploring the linkages', *International Journal of Human Resource Management* 16(7): 1176–94.

O'Doherty, D. (1997) 'Human resource planning: control to seduction', in I. Beardwell and L. Holden (eds) *Human Resource Management: A Contemporary Perspective*, 2nd edn, Pitman Publishing.

O'Dell, C.S. and Essaides, N. (1998) *If Only We Knew What We Know: The Transfer of Internal Knowledge and Best Practice*, Free Press.

Olie, R. (1990) 'Culture and integration problems in international mergers and acquisitions', *European Management Journal* 8(2) 206–15.

Oliver, S. and Kandadi, K.R. (2006) 'How to develop knowledge culture in organizations? A multiple case study of large distributed organizations', *Journal of Knowledge Management* 10(4): 6–24.

O'Malley, M. (2000) *Creating Commitment: How to Attract and Retain Talented Employees by Building Relationships That Last*, John Wiley.

Osberg, L. and Smeeding, T. (2006) '"Fair" inequality? Attitudes toward pay differentials: the United States in comparative perspective', *American Sociological Review* 71(3): 450–73.

Osborne, R.L. and Cowen, S.S. (2002) 'High-performance companies: the distinguishing profile', *Management Decision* 40(3): 227–31.

Ottenbacher, M., Gnoth, J. and Jones, P. (2006) 'Identifying determinants of success in development of new high-contact services: insights from the hospitality industry', *International Journal of Service Industry Management* 17(4): 344–63.

Ouchi, W. (1981) *Theory Z: How American Business Can Meet the Japanese Challenge*, Addison-Wesley.

Oxenbridge, S. and Brown, W. (2002) 'The two faces of partnership?: an assessment of partnership and co-operative employer/trade union relationships', *Employee Relations* 24(3): 262–76.

Paik, Y., Vance, C.M. and Stage, H.D. (2000) 'A test of assumed cluster homogeneity for performance appraisal management in four Southeast Asian countries', *International Journal of Human Resource Management* 11(4): 736–50.

Pantazis, C. (2002) 'Maximizing e-learning to train the 21st century workforce', *Public Personnel Management* 31(1): 21–7.

Papalexandris, N. (1991) 'A comparative study of human resource management in selected Greek and foreign-owned subsidiaries in Greece', in C. Brewster and S. Tyson (eds) *International Comparisons in Human Resource Management*, Pitman.

Papalexandris, N. and Chalikias, J. (2002) 'Changes in training, performance management and communication issues among Greek firms in the 1990s: intercountry and intracountry comparisons', *Journal of European Industrial Training* 26(7): 342–52.

Pascale, R.T. and Athos, A.G. (1981) *The Art of Japanese Management*, Simon and Schuster.

Patrickson, M. and Hartmann, L. (2001) 'Human resource management in Australia – prospects for the twenty-first century', *International Journal of Manpower* 22(3): 198–206.

Peccei, R. and Rosenthal, P. (2001) 'Delivering customer-oriented behaviour through empowerment: an empirical test of HRM assumptions', *Journal of Management Studies* 38(6): 831–57.

Pedler, M., Boydell, T.H. and Burgoyne, J.G. (1989) 'Towards the learning company', *Management Education and Development* 2(3): 19–41.

Peeters, H. and Lievens, F. (2006) 'Verbal and nonverbal impression management tactics in behavior description and situational interviews', *International Journal of Selection and Assessment* 14(3): 206–22.

Peetz, D. and Todd, P. (2001) '"Otherwise you're on your own": unions and bargaining in Malaysian banking', *International Journal of Manpower* 22(4): 333–48.

Peppas, S.C. (2006) 'Diversity in the workplace: Hispanic perceptions of the hiring decision', *Employee Relations* 28(2): 119–29.

Perkins, S.J. and Hendry, C. (2005) 'Ordering top pay: interpreting the signals', *Journal of Management Studies* 42(7): 1443–68.

Peters, T.J. (1987) *Thriving on Chaos*, Alfred A. Knopf.

Peters, T.J. and Waterman, R.H. (1982) *In Search of Excellence*, Harper and Row.

Pettijohn, L.S., Parker, R.S., Pettijohn, C.E. and Kent, O.L. (2001) 'Performance appraisals: usage, criteria and observation', *The Journal of Management Development* 20(9): 754–71.

Pfeffer, J. (1998) *The Human Equation: Building Profits by Putting People First*, Harvard Business School Press.

Pheng, L.S. and Yuquan, S. (2002) 'An exploratory study of Hofstede's cross-cultural dimensions in construction projects', *Management Decision* 40(1): 7–16.

Phillimore, J. (2000) 'The limits of supply-side social democracy: Australian labor, 1983–96', *Politics and Society* 28(4): 557–87.

Philp, T. (1990) *Appraising Performance for Results*, McGraw-Hill.

Pieper, R. (ed.) (1990) *Human Resource Management: An International Comparison*, de Gruyter.

Pink, D. (2001) 'Who has the next big idea?', *Fast Company* 50(September): 108.

Pizzey, E., Shackleton, J.R. and Unwin, P. (2000) *Women or Men: Who are the Victim?* CIVITAS: The Institute for the Study of Civil Society.

Pollitt, D. (2005a) 'Crédit Suisse pioneers structured recruiting: employee selection process based on latest scientific and practical research', *Human Resource Management International Digest* 13(5): 5–7.

Pollitt, D. (2005b) 'HR transformation lowers costs and boosts efficiency at AstraZeneca: site and functionally based service makes way for "one team" approach', *Human Resource Management International Digest* 13(6): 6–11.

Poole, M. (1990) 'Editorial: human resource management in an international perspective', *The International Journal of Human Resource Management* 1(1): 1–16.

Pope, D. and Bambra, C. (2005) 'Has the disability discrimination act closed the employment gap?', *Disability and Rehabilitation* 27(20): 1261–6.

Porter, M. (1990) *The Competitive Advantage of Nations*, Free Press.

Poutsma, E., Ligthart, P.E.M. and Veersma, U. (2006) 'The diffusion of calculative and collaborative HRM practices in European firms', *Industrial Relations* 45(4): 513–46.

PPRU (1999) *Report for The Office of The Data Protection Registrar (UK)*, Personnel Policy Research Unit.

Pratt, K.J. and Bennett, S.G. (1989) *Elements of Personnel Management*, Chapman and Hall.

Price, A.J. (1997) *Human Resource Management in a Business Context*, Thomson Learning.

Price, A.J. (2000) *Principles of Human Resource Management: An Action-Learning Approach*, Blackwell.

Price, A.J. (2005a) 'Learning and development methods, interventions and practices', in J. Swart, C. Mann, S. Brown and A.J. Price (eds) *Human Resource Development: Strategy and Tactics*, Butterworth-Heinemann.

Price, A.J. (2005b) 'The e-learning revolution', in J. Swart, C. Mann, S. Brown and A.J. Price (eds) *Human Resource Development: Strategy and Tactics*, Butterworth-Heinemann.

Pun, K.F., Chin, K.S. and Gill, R. (2001) 'Determinants of employee involvement practices in manufacturing enterprises', *Total Quality Management* 12(1): 95–109.

Purcell, J. (1989) 'The impact of corporate strategy on human resource management', in J. Storey (ed.) *New Perspectives on Human Resource Management*, Routledge.

Purcell, J. (1995) 'Corporate strategy and its link with human resource strategy', in J. Storey (ed.) *Human Resource Management: A Critical Text*, Routledge.

Purcell, J. (2001) 'The meaning of strategy in human resource management', in J. Storey (ed.) *Human Resource Management: A Critical Text*, 2nd edn, Thomson Learning.

Purcell, J. and Sisson, K. (1983) 'Strategies and practice in the management of industrial relations', in G.S. Bain (ed.) *Industrial Relations in Britain*, Blackwell.

Purcell, K. (2002) *Employers in the New Graduate Labour Market: Recruiting from a Wider Spectrum of Graduates*, Employment Studies Research Unit, University of the West of England.

Quince, T. (2001) *Entrepreneurial Collaboration: Terms of Endearment or Rules of Engagement*, Working Papers, ESRC Centre for Business Research, University of Cambridge.

Raelin, J.A. (1991) *The Clash of Cultures: Managers Managing Professionals*, 2nd edn, Harvard Business School.

Raess, D. (2006) 'Globalization and why the "time is ripe" for the transformation of German industrial relations', *Review of International Political Economy* 13(3): 449–79.

Raia, A.P. (1974) *Managing by Objectives*, Scott, Foresman.

Rainbird, H. and Maguire, M. (1993) 'When corporate need supersedes employee development', *Personnel Management* (February): 34–7.

Ramamoorthy, N., Gupta, A., Sardessai, R.M. and Flood, P.C. (2005) 'Individualism/collectivism and attitudes towards human resource systems: a comparative study of American, Irish and Indian MBA students', *International Journal of Human Resource Management* 16(5): 852–69.

Ramaswamy, E.A. and Schiphorst, F.B. (2000) 'Human resource management, trade unions and empowerment: two cases from India', *International Journal of Human Resource Management* 11(4): 664–80.

Randlesome, C. (1994) *The Business Culture in Germany*, Butterworth-Heinemann.

Ranzijn, R., Carson, E., Winefield, A.H. and Price, D. (2006) 'On the scrap-heap at 45: the human impact of mature-aged unemployment', *Journal of Occupational and Organizational Psychology* 79(3): 467–79.

Rasmussen, E. and Lind, J. (2003) 'Productive employment relationships: European experiences', *New Zealand Journal of Industrial Relations* 28(2): 158–69.

Rebick, M. (2005) *The Japanese Employment System*, Oxford Online Monographs.

Reed, S.F. and Lajoux, A.R. (1998) *The Art of M&A: A Merger, Acquisition, Buyout Guide*, 3rd edn, McGraw-Hill.

Revans, R.W. (1972) 'Action learning – a management development programme', *Personnel Review* (autumn).

Reynolds, P.D. (1994) *Reducing Barriers to New Firm Gestation: Prevalence and Success of Nascent Entrepreneurs*, paper presented at the Academy of Management, Dallas, Texas.

Reynolds, P.D. and White, S.B. (1997) *The Entrepreneurial Process: Economic Growth, Men, Women, and Minorities*, Greenwood Publishing Group.

Rhinesmith, S.H. (1996) *A Manager's Guide to Globalization – Six Skills for Success in a Changing World*, 2nd edn, Irwin.

Rice, A.K., Hull, J.M. and Trist, E.L. (1950) 'The representation of labour turnover as a social process', *Journal of Human Relations* 3.

Richard, O.C. and Johnson, N.B. (2001) 'Strategic human resource management effectiveness and firm performance', *International Journal of Human Resource Management* 12(2): 299–310.

Roberts, G. (1997) *Recruitment and Selection: A Competency Approach*, Chartered Institute of Personnel and Development.

Rodger, A. (1952) *The Seven Point Plan*, National Institute for Industrial Psychology.

Rondeau, K.V. and Wager, T.H. (2001) 'Impact of human resource management practices on nursing home performance', *Health Services Management Research* 14(3): 192–202.

Rosania, R.J. (2000) *The Credible Trainer*, American Society for Training and Development.

Rose, M. (1975) *Industrial Behaviour: Theoretical Developments Since Taylor*, Penguin.

Rosenbloom, J.S. (2001) *The Handbook of Employee Benefits*, 5th edn, McGraw-Hill.

Ross, P. (2006) 'Management strategies in transitional economies: organisational restructuring and employment relations (ER) at CeskÂ² Telecom', *Employee Relations* 28(2): 184–200.

Ross, R. and Schneider, R. (1992) *From Equality to Diversity: A Business Case for Equal Opportunities*, Pitman.

Roth, P.L., Bobko, P. and Mcfarland, L.A. (2005) 'A meta-analysis of work sample test validity: updating and integrating some classic literature', *Personnel Psychology* 58(4): 1009–37.

Rothwell, S. (1992) 'The development of the international manager', *Personnel Management* (January): 33–5.

Rothwell, W.J. (1999) *The Action Learning Guidebook: A Real-Time Strategy for Problem Solving*, Jossey-Bass.

Rothwell, W.J., Prescott, R.K. and Taylor, M.W. (1998) *The Strategic Human Resource Leader: How to Prepare Your Organization for the Six Key Trends Shaping the Future*, Davies-Black Publications.

Rousseau, D.M. (1995) *Psychological Contracts in Organizations: Understanding Written and Unwritten Agreements*, Sage.

Rousseau, D.M. and Parks, J.M. (1993) 'The contracts of individuals and organizations', in L.L. Cummings and B.M. Staw (eds) *Research in Organizational Behavior*, Volume 15, JAI Press.

Rowden, R.W. (2001) 'Exploring methods to evaluate the return from training', *American Business Review* 19(1): 6–12.

Rowden, R.W., Jnr and Conine, C.T. (2005) 'The impact of workplace learning on job satisfaction in small US commercial banks', *The Journal of Workplace Learning* 17(4): 215–30.

Rubery, J., Earnshaw, J., Marchington, M., Cooke, F.L. and Vincent, S. (2002) 'Changing organizational forms and the employment relationship', *Journal of Management Studies* 39(5): 645–72.

Rumpel, S. and Medcof, J.W. (2006) 'Total rewards: good fit for tech workers', *Research-Technology Management* 49(5): 27–35.

Russell, C., Mattson, J., Devlin, S. and Atwater, D. (1990) 'Predictive validity of biodata items generated from retrospective life experience essays', *Journal of Applied Psychology* 75: 569–80.

Rutherford, M.W., Buller, P.F. and McMullen, P.R. (2003) 'Human resource management problems over the life cycle of small to medium-sized firms', *Human Resource Management* 42(4): 321.

Ryan, A.M. and Tippins, N.T. (2004) 'Attracting and selecting: what psychological research tells us', *Human Resource Management* 43(4): 305–18.

Rynes, S.L., Colbert, A.E. and Brown, K.G. (2002) 'HR professionals' beliefs about effective human resource practices: correspondence between research and practice', *Human Resource Management* 41(2): 149–74.

Rynes, S.L., Gerhart, B. and Minette, K.A. (2004) 'The importance of pay in employee motivation: discrepancies between what people say and what they do', *Human Resource Management* 43(4): 381–94.

Saari, L.M. and Judge, T.M. (2004) 'Employee attitudes and job satisfaction', *Human Resource Management* 43(4): 395–407.

Sadler, P. and Milner, K. (1993) *The Talent-Intensive Organization: Optimising Your Company's Human Resource Strategies*, Economist Intelligence Unit.

Salaman, G. and Butler, J. (1994) 'Why managers won't learn', in C. Mabey and P. Iles (eds) *Managing Learning*, Routledge/Open University.

Salancik, G.R. (1977) 'Commitment and control of organizational behavior and beliefs', in B.M. Staw and G.R. Salancik (eds) *New Directions in Organizational Behavior*, St Clair Press.

Salgado, J.F. and Moscoso, S. (2002) 'Comprehensive meta-analysis of the construct validity of the employment interview', *European Journal of Work and Organizational Psychology* 11(3): 299–324.

Sambrook, S. (2001) 'HRD as an emergent and negotiated evolution: an ethnographic case study in the British National Health Service', *Human Resource Development Quarterly* 12(2): 169–93.

Sampson, A. (1995) *Company Man: The Rise and Fall of Corporate Life*, Random House.

Sanz-Valle, R., Sabater-Sanchez, R. and Aragon-Sanchez, A. (1998) 'Human resource management and business strategy links: an empirical study', *International Journal of Human Resource Management* 10(4): 655–71.

Sapsford, D. and Tzannatos, Z. (1993) *The Economics of the Labour Market*, Macmillan.

Sartain, L. and Schumann, M. (2006) *Brand From the Inside: Eight Essentials to Emotionally Connect Your Employees to Your Business*, Jossey-Bass.

Sayal, A. (1990) 'Black women and mental health', *Psychologist* (January): 24–7.

Schack, T. (2004) 'Knowledge and performance in action', *Journal of Knowledge Management* 8(4): 38–53.

Schein, E.H. (1988) *Organizational Psychology*, 3rd edn, Prentice-Hall.

Schinkel, S., van Dierendonck, D. and Anderson, N. (2004) 'The impact of selection encounters on applicants: an experimental study into feedback effects after a negative selection decision', *International Journal of Selection and Assessment* 12(1–2): 197–205.

Schleicher, D.J., Venkatamarani, V., Morgeson, F.P. and Campion, M.A. (2006) 'So you didn't get the job ... now what do you think? Examining opportunity-to-perform fairness perceptions', *Personnel Psychology* 59(3): 559–90.

Scholte, J.A. (2000) *Globalization: A Critical Introduction*, Macmillan.

Schramm, J. (2006) *SHRM Workplace Forecast*, SHRM.

Schuler, R.S. (1990) *Personnel and Human Resource Management*, 4th edn, West Publishing,

Schuler, R.S., Jackson, S.E. and Storey, J. (2001) 'HRM and its link with strategic management', in J. Storey (ed.) *Human Resource Management: A Critical Text*, 2nd edn, Thomson Learning.

Schuster, F.E. (1998) *Employee-Centered Management: A Strategy for High Commitment and Involvement*, Quorum Books.

Selmer, J. and de Leon, C. (2001) 'Pinoy-style HRM: human resource management in the Philippines', *Asia Pacific Business Review* 8(1): 127–44.

Seltzer, A. and Merrett, D.T. (2000) 'Personnel policies at the Union Bank of Australia: evidence from the 1888–1900 entry cohorts,' *Journal of Labor Economics* 18(4): 573–613.

Sen, A. (2002) 'How to judge globalism', *The American Prospect* 13(1): 1–14.

Servage, L. (2005) 'Strategizing for workplace e-learning: some critical considerations', *The Journal of Workplace Learning* 17(5–6): 304–17.

Sheehan, C., Holland, P. and Cieri, D.H. (2006) 'Current developments in HRM in Australian organisations', *Asia Pacific Journal of Human Resources* 44(2): 132–52.

Shen, J. and Darby, R. (2006) 'Training and management development in Chinese multinational enterprises', *Employee Relations* 28(4): 342–62.

Shepherd, J.L. and Mathews, B.P. (2000) 'Employee commitment: academic vs practitioner perspectives', *Employee Relations* 22(6): 555–75.

Shih, H.-A., Chiang, Y.-H. and Kim, I.-S. (2005) 'Expatriate performance management from MNEs of different national origins', *International Journal of Manpower* 26(2): 157–76.

Shiner, M. and Modood, T. (2002) 'Help or hindrance? Higher education and the route to ethnic equality', *British Journal of Sociology of Education* 23(2): 209–32.

SHRM (2005) *The SHRM Symposium on the Future of Strategic HR*, Society for Human Resource Management.

Shugrue, E., Berland, J., Gonzales, R. and Duke, K. (1997) 'How IBM reengineered its benefits center into a national HR service center', *Compensation Benefits and Review* (March–April): 41.

Silvestro, R. (2002) 'Dispelling the modern myth: employee satisfaction and loyalty drive service profitability', *International Journal of Operations and Production Management* 22(1): 30–49.

Simon, H.A. (1955) *Recent Advances in Organization Theory*, Research Frontiers in Politics and Government, Brookings Institution, Washington, D.C.

Simon, H.A. (1960) *The New Science of Management Decision*, Harper and Row.

Sisson, K. (1990) 'Introducing the *Human Resource Management Journal*', *Human Resource Management Journal* 1(1): 1–11.

Sisson, K. (1995) 'Human resource management and the personnel function', in J. Storey (ed.) *Human Resource Management: A Critical Text*, Routledge.

Sisson, K. (2001) 'Human resource management and the personnel function – a case of partial impact?', in J. Storey (ed.) *Human Resource Management: A Critical Text*, 2nd edn, Thomson Learning.

Sivanandan, A. (1991) *Black Struggles Against Racism*, Northern Curriculum Development Project Setting the Context for Change: Anti-Racist Social Work Education, Central Council for Education and Training in Social Work, Leeds.

Sloman, M. (1993) 'Training to play a lead role', *Personnel Management* (July): 40–4.

Sloman, M. (1994) 'Coming in from the cold: a new role for trainers', *Personnel Management* (January): 24–7.

Smircich, L. (1983) 'Concepts of culture and organizational analysis', *Administrative Science Quarterly* 28: 339–385.

Smith, C., Child, J. and Rowlinson, M. (1990) *Reshaping Work: The Cadbury Experience*, Cambridge University Press.

Smith, M. (1948) *An Introduction to Industrial Psychology*, 4th edn, Cassell.

Smith, M. (1991) 'Selection in organizations', in M. Smith (ed.) *Analysing Organizational Behaviour*, Macmillan.

Smith, M. and Robertson, I.T. (1993) *The Theory and Practice of Systematic Personnel Selection*, 2nd edn, Macmillan.

Smith, M., Gregg, M. and Andrews, R. (1989) *Selection and Assessment: A New Appraisal*, Pitman.

Smither, R.D. (1994) *The Psychology of Work and Human Performance*, 2nd edn, HarperCollins,

Snell, A.F., Sydell, E.J. and Lueke, S.B. (1999) 'Towards a theory of applicant faking: integrating studies of deception', *Human Resources Management Review* 9: 219–42.

Snow, C.C., Miles, R.E. and Coleman, H.J. (1992) 'Managing 21st century organizations', *Organizational Dynamics* 20(3): 5–20.

Snyder, M. (1974) 'The self-monitoring of expressive behaviour', *Journal of Personality and Social Psychology* 30: 526–37.

Sonnenfeld, J.A., Peiperl, M.A. and Kotter, J.P. (1988) 'Strategic determinants of managerial labor markets: a career systems view', *Human Resource Management* 27(4): 369–88.

Sparrow, P. (1994) 'Organizational competencies: creating a strategic behavioural framework for selection and assessment', in N. Anderson and P. Herriot (eds) *Assessment and Selection in Organizations: Methods and Practice for Recruitment and Appraisal*, First Update and Supplement 1994, Wiley.

Stacey, R.D. (1993) *Strategic Management and Organizational Dynamics*, Pitman.

Stark, S. (2006) 'Using action learning for professional development', *Educational Action Research* 14(1): 23–43.

Stathopoulos, K., Espenlaub, S. and Walker, M. (2005) 'The compensation of UK executive directors: lots of carrots but are there any sticks?', *Competition and Change* 9(1): 89–105.

Steiner, G.A. (1969) *Top Management Planning*, Macmillan.

Stelcner, M. (2000) 'Earnings differentials among ethnic groups in Canada: a review of the research', *Review of Social Economy* 58(3): 295–317.

Sternberg, R.J. (1994) 'Thinking styles: theory and assessment at the interface between intelligence and personality', in R.J. Sternberg and P. Ruzgis (eds) *Personality and Intelligence*, Cambridge University Press.

Stevens, J. and Walsh, T. (1991) 'Training and competitiveness', in J. Stevens and R. Mackay (eds) *Training and Competitiveness*, NEDO/ Kogan Page.

Stewart, L.D. and Perlow, R. (2001) 'Applicant race, job status, and racial attitude as predictors of employment discrimination', *Journal of Business and Psychology* 16(2): 259–75.

Stewart, R. (1993) *The Reality of Management*, 2nd edn, Heinemann.

Stewart, T.A. (2001) *The Wealth of Knowledge: Intellectual Capital and the Twenty-first Century Organization*, Doubleday.

Stoll, M. (2005) 'Geographical skills mismatch, job search and race', *Urban Studies* 42(4): 695–717.

Stolze, W.J. (1999) *Start Up: An Entrepreneur's Guide to Launching and Managing a New Business*, Career Press.

Stone-Romero, E.F., Stone, D.L. and Hyatt, D. (2003) 'Personnel selection procedures and invasion of privacy', *Journal of Social Issues* 59(2): 343–68.

Storey, J. (ed.) (1989) *New Perspectives on Human Resource Management*, Routledge.

Storey, J. (1992) *Developments in the Management of Human Resources*, Blackwell.

Storey, J. (1994a) 'How new-style management is taking hold', *Personnel Management* (January): 32–5.

Storey, J. (ed.) (1994b) *New Wave Manufacturing Strategies: Organizational and Human Resource Management Dimensions*, Paul Chapman Publishing.

Storey, J. (ed.) (1995) *Human Resource Management: A Critical Text*, Routledge.

Storey, J. (ed.) (2001) *Human Resource Management: A Critical Text*, 2nd edn, Thomson Learning.

Storey, J. and Quintas, P. (2001) 'Knowledge management and HRM', in J. Storey (ed.) *Human Resource Management: A Critical Text*, 2nd edn, Thomson Learning.

Straw, J.M. (1989) *Equal Opportunities: The Way Ahead*, Institute for Personnel Management.

Strebler, M.T., Robinson, D. and Bevan, S. (2001) *Performance Review: Balancing Objectives and Content*, IES Report 370, Institute of Employment Studies.

Stuart, M. and Lucio, M.M. (2002) 'Social partnership and the mutual gains organization: remaking involvement and trust at the British workplace', *Economic and Industrial Democracy* 23(2): 177–200.

Subeliani, D. and Tsogas, G. (2005) 'Managing diversity in the Netherlands: a case study of Rabobank', *International Journal of Human Resource Management* 16(5): 831–51.

Sunoo, B.P. (1999) 'How HR supports knowledge sharing', *Workforce* 78(3): 30–4.

Swain, J.W. (2002) 'Machiavelli and modern management', *Management Decision* 40(3): 281–7.

Tackey, N.D., Tamkin, P. and Sheppard, E. (2001) *The Problem of Minority Performance in Organisations*, IES Report 375, Institute of Employment Studies.

Tamkin, P., Barber, L. and Dench, S. (1997) *From Admin to Strategy: The Changing Face of the HR Function*, IES Report 332, Institute of Employment Studies.

Tamkin, P., Yarnall, J. and Kerrin, M. (2002) *Kirkpatrick and Beyond: A Review of Models of Training Evaluation*, IES Report 392, Institute for Employment Studies.

Tan, H.H. and Chee, D. (2005) 'Understanding interpersonal trust in a Confucian-influenced society', *International Journal of Cross Cultural Management* 5(2): 197–212.

Tansley, C., Newell, S. and Williams, H. (2001) 'Effecting HRM-style practices through an integrated human resource information system: an e-greenfield site?', *Personnel Review* 30(3): 351–71.

Taylor, D. and Walley, E.E. (2002) 'Hijacking the Holy Grail? Emerging HR practices in Croatia', *European Business Review* 14(4): 294–303.

Taylor, F. (1947) *Scientific Management*, Harper and Row.

Taylor, S. (2006) 'Communicating across cultures', *The British Journal of Administrative Management* (June/July): 12–13.

Teagarden, M.B., Butler, M.C. and Von Glinow, M.A. (1992) 'Mexico's maquiladora industry: where strategic human resource management makes a difference', *Organizational Dynamics* 21(3): 34–47.

Tebbel, C. (2000) 'HR just makes the grade', *HRMonthly*, February, Australian Human Resources Institute.

Tennenbaum, B. (2005) 'Hire the write way', *Pest Control* 73(8): 112.

Teo, S.T.T. (2002) 'Effectiveness of a corporate HR department in an Australian public-sector entity during commercialization and corporatization', *International Journal of Human Resource Management* 13(1): 89–105.

Thomas, S.L. and Vaught, S. (2001) 'The write stuff: what the evidence says about using handwriting analysis in hiring', *S.A.M. Advanced Management Journal* Autumn(66): 4.

Thompson, A.A. and Strickland, A.J. (1998) *Crafting and Implementing Strategy*, 10th edn, McGraw-Hill.

Thompson, J.L. (1993) *Strategic Management: Awareness and Change*, 2nd edn, Chapman & Hall.

Thomson, R. (1968) *A Pelican History of Psychology*, Penguin.

Thomson, R. and Mabey, C. (1994) *Developing Human Resources*, Butterworth-Heinemann.

Thurley, K. and Wirdenius, H. (1990) *Towards European Management*, Pitman.

Tichy, N.M., Fombrun, C.J. and Devanna, M.A. (1982) 'Strategic human resource management', *Sloan Management Review* 23(2): 47–61.

Tight, M. (2000) 'Critical perspectives on management learning: a view from adult/continuing/lifelong education', *Management Learning* 31(1): 103–19.

Timmons, J.A. (1994) *New Venture Creation: Entrepreneurship for the 21st Century*, 4th edn, Irwin Press.

Tinaikar, R., Hartman, A. and Nath, R. (1995) 'Rethinking business process re-engineering: a social constructivist perspective', in G. Burke and J. Peppard (eds) *Examining Business Process Re-engineering: Current Perspectives and Research Directions*, Kogan Page.

Tiwana, A. (1999) *The Knowledge Management Toolkit: Practical Techniques for Building a Knowledge Management System*, Prentice-Hall.

Todd, P. and Peetz, D. (2001) 'Malaysian industrial relations at century's turn: vision 2020 or a spectre of the past?', *International Journal of Human Resource Management* 12(8): 1365–82.

Torrington, D. (1994) *International Human Resource Management: Think Globally, Act Locally*, Prentice-Hall.

Torrington, D. and Hall, L. (1991) *Personnel Management: A New Approach*, 2nd edn, Prentice-Hall.

Torrington, D. and Hall, L. (1995) *Personnel Management: HRM in Action*, 3rd edn, Prentice-Hall.

Townley, B. (1989) 'Selection and appraisal: reconstituting "social relations?"', in J. Storey (ed.) *New Perspectives on Human Resource Management*, Routledge.

Townley, B. (1994) *Reframing Human Resource Management*, Sage.

Townsend, R. (1970) *Up the Organization*, Michael Joseph.

Triandis, H.C. (1990) 'Theoretical concepts that are applicable to the analysis of ethnocentrism', in R.W. Brislin (ed.) *Applied Cross-Cultural Psychology*, Sage.

Triandis, H.C. (1995) 'A theoretical framework for the study of diversity', in M.M. Chemers, S. Oskamp and M.A. Costanzo (eds) *Diversity in Organizations: New Perspectives for a Changing Workplace*, Sage.

Trice, H.M. and Beyer, J.M. (1984) 'Studying organizational cultures through rites and rituals', *Academy of Management Review* 9: 653–69.

Trompenaars, F. and Hampden-Turner, C. (1997) *Riding the Waves of Culture*, 2nd edn, McGraw-Hill.

Truss, C. (1999) 'Soft and hard HRM', in L. Gratton (ed.) *Strategic Human Resource Management: Corporate Rhetoric and Human Reality*, Oxford University Press.

Truss, C. (2001) 'Complexities and controversies in linking HRM with organizational outcomes', *Journal of Management Studies* 38(8): 1121–49.

Truxillo, D.M., Bauer, T.N., Campion, M.A. and Paronto, M.E. (2006) 'A field study of the role of big five personality in applicant perceptions of selection fairness, self, and the hiring organization', *International Journal of Selection and Assessment* 14(3): 269–77.

TUC (2002) *Racism at Work*, Trades Union Congress.

Turnasella, T. (1999) 'The salary trap', *Compensation and Benefits Review* 31(6): 2–3.

Tyler, E.B. (1871) *Primitive Culture*, Henry Holt.

Tyson, S. (1989) 'The management of the personnel function', *Journal of Management Studies* 24(September): 523–32.

Tyson, S. (1995) *Human Resource Strategy*, Pitman.

Tyson, S., Lawrence, P., Poirson, P., Manzolini, L. and Vincente, C.F. (1993) *Human Resource Management in Europe: Strategic Issues and Cases*, Kogan Page.

Tziner, A., Joanis, C. and Murphy, K.R. (2000) 'A comparison of three methods of performance appraisal with regard to goal properties, goal perception, and ratee satisfaction', *Group and Organization Management* 25(2): 175–90.

Ulrich, D. (1997) *Human Resource Champions: The Next Agenda for Adding Value and Delivering Results*, Harvard Business School Press.

United Nations (1995) *The Copenhagen Declaration and Programme of Action*, United Nations.

United Nations (2005) *World Economic and Social Survey*, United Nations Publications.

US Department of Labor (1998) *Government as a High-Performance Employer*, SCANS Report for America 2000, US Dept of Labor.

van de Vliet, A. (1993) 'Assess for success', *Management Today* (July): 60–5.

van der Zwaan, A.H., von Eije, J.H. and de Witte, M.C. (2002) 'HRM consequences of going public', *International Journal of Manpower* 23(2): 126–36.

Van Iddekinge, C.H., Sager, C.E., Burnfield, J.L. and Heffner, T.S. (2006) 'The variability of criterion-related validity estimates among interviewers and interview panels', *International Journal of Selection and Assessment* 14(3): 193–205.

Van Ruysseveldt, J., Huiskamp, R. and van Hoof, J. (1995) *Comparative Industrial and Employment Relations*, Sage.

Vandenberghe, C. (1999) 'Organizational culture, person-culture fit, and turnover: a replication in the health care industry', *Journal of Organizational Behavior* 20: 175–84.

Vickerstaff, S. (1992) *Human Resource Management in Europe: Text and Cases*, Chapman and Hall.

Viitala, R. (2005) 'Perceived development needs of managers compared to an integrated management competency model', *The Journal of Workplace Learning* 17(7): 436–51.

Visser, J. (2006) 'Union membership statistics in 24 countries', *Monthly Labor Review* (January): 38–49.

Vranken, M. (1999) 'The role of specialist labour courts in an environment of substantive labour law deregulation: a New Zealand case study', *International Journal of Comparative Labour Law and Industrial Relations* 15(3): 303–28.

Wächter, H. and Muller-Camen, M. (2002) 'Co-determination and strategic integration in German firms', *Human Resource Management Journal* 12(3): 76–87.

Waddill, D.D. (2006) 'Action e-learning: an exploratory case study of action learning applied online', *Human Resource Development International* 9(2): 157–71.

Waight, C.L and Stewart, B.L. (2005) 'Valuing the adult learner in e-learning: part one – a conceptual model for corporate settings', *The Journal of Workplace Learning* 17(5–6): 337–45.

Waldman, D.A. and Atwater, L.E. (2001) 'Attitudinal and behavioral outcomes of an upward feedback process', *Group and Organization Management* 26(2): 189–205.

Walker, A.J. (2001) 'Best practices in HR technology', in A.J. Walker (ed.) *Web-Based Human Resources*, McGraw-Hill.

Walker, S.F. and Marr, J.W. (2001) *Stakeholder Power: A Winning Plan for Building Stakeholder Commitment and Driving Corporate Growth*, Perseus Publishing.

Wall, T.D. and Wood, S.J. (2005) 'The romance of HRM and business performance, and the case for big science', *Human Relations* 58(4): 429–62.

Walsh, J. (2001) 'Human resource management in foreign-owned workplaces: evidence from Australia', *International Journal of Human Resource Management* 12(3): 425–44.

Walton, J. (1999) *Strategic Human Resource Development*, Financial Times/Prentice Hall.

Warr, P. (1987) *Psychology at Work*, 2nd edn, Penguin.

Watkins, L.M. and Johnston, L. (2000) 'Screening job applicants: the impact of physical attractiveness and application quality', *International Journal of Selection and Assessment* 8(2): 76–84.

Watson, T. (2003) *Towards a Grown-Up and Critical Academic HRM and the Need to Grow Out of Infantile 'Hard And Soft HRM', 'Rhetoric and Reality' and Functionalist Habits to Engage Critically with the Adult World of Employment Management*, paper presented at Critical Management Studies 2003, Lancaster University, 7–9 July.

Watson, T.J. (1994) *In Search of Management: Culture, Chaos and Control in Management Work*, Routledge.

Weber, M. (1947) *Max Weber: The Theory of Social and Economic Organization*, translated by A.M. Henderson and Talcott Parsons, The Free Press.

Webster, E.C. (1964) *Decision Making in the Employment Interview*, Industrial Relations Centre, McGill University, Montreal.

Webster, W. (1990) *Not a Man to Match Her: The Marketing of a Prime Minister*, Women's Press.

Weinberger, C.J. (1998) 'Race and gender wage gaps in the market for recent college graduates', *Industrial Relations* 37(1): 67–84.

Weisbrot, M. (2002) 'The mirage of progress', *The American Prospect* 13(1): 1–14.

Weisner, W.H. and Cronshaw, S.F. (1988) 'A meta-analytic investigation of the impact of interview format and degree of structure on the validity of the employment interview', *Journal of Occupational Psychology* 61: 275–90.

Weiss, D.S. (1999) *High Performance HR: Leveraging Human Resources for Competitive Advantage*, John Wiley & Sons Ltd.

Weiss, M. (2002) 'Modernizing the German works council system: a recent amendment', *International Journal of Comparative Labour Law and Industrial Relations* 18(3): 251–64.

Whipp, R. (1992) 'Human resource management, competition and strategy: some productive tensions', in P. Blyton and P. Turnbull (eds) *Reassessing Human Resource Management*, Sage, London.

Whitehill, A.M. (1991) *Japanese Management: Tradition and Transition*, Routledge.

Whittaker, H. (1999) *Entrepreneurs as Co-operative Capitalists: High-tech CEOs in the UK*, ESRC Centre for Business Research, Working Paper Series No.125, University of Cambridge.

Whitley, R. (2003) 'From the search for universal correlations to the institutional structuring of economic organization and change: the development and future of organization studies', *Organization* 10(3): 481–501.

Wilkinson, F. (2000) *Human Resource Management and Business Objectives and Strategies in Small and Medium Sized Business*, Working Papers, ESRC Centre for Business Research, University of Cambridge.

Willmott, H. (1993) 'Strength is ignorance; slavery is freedom: managing culture in modern organizations', *Journal of Management Studies* 30(4): 515–52.

Willmott, H. (1995) 'Will the turkeys vote for Christmas? The re-engineering of human resources', in G. Burke and J. Peppard (eds) *Examining Business Process Re-engineering: Current Perspectives and Research Directions*, Kogan Page.

Wilson, F. (2005) 'Caught between difference and similarity: the case of women academics', *Women in Management Review* 20(4): 234–48.

Wilson, F.M. (1995) *Organizational Behaviour and Gender*, McGraw-Hill.

Wilson, T.D. (2002) 'The nonsense of "knowledge management"', *Information Research* 8(1): paper no. 144 [Available at http://InformationR.net/ir/8–1/paper144.html]

Windsor, D. (1998) *The Definition of Stakeholder Status*, paper presented at the International Association for Business and Society (IABS) annual conference in Kona-Kailua, Hawaii (June, 1998).

Winter, R. and Jackson, B. (2006) 'State of the psychological contract: manager and employee perspectives within an Australian credit union', *Employee Relations* 28(5): 421–34.

Wolf, A. and Jenkins, A: (2006) 'Explaining greater test use for selection: the role of HR professionals in a world of expanding regulation', *Human Resource Management Journal* 16(2): 193–213.

Wolf, M.G. (1999) 'Compensation: an overview', in L.A. Berger and D.R. Berger (eds) *The Compensation Handbook*, 4th edn, McGraw-Hill.

Wolff, E.N. (2005) 'The growth of information workers in the U.S. economy', *Communications of the ACM* 48(10): 37–42.

Wolter, S., Mühlemann, S. and Schweri, J. (2006) 'Why some firms train apprentices and many others do not', *German Economic Review* 7(3): 249–64.

Wood, D. (1983) 'Uses and abuses of personnel consultants', *Personnel Management* (October): 407.

Wood, G. and Els, C. (2000) 'The making and remaking of HRM: the practice of managing people in the Eastern Cape Province, South Africa', *International Journal of Human Resource Management* 11(1): 112–25.

Wood, R. and Baron, H. (1992) 'Psychological testing free from prejudice', *Personnel Management* (December): 34–7.

Wood, S. (ed.) (1989) *The Transformation of Work?* Routledge.

Wooden, M. and Bora, B. (1999) 'Workplace characteristics and their effects on wages: Australian evidence', *Australian Economic Papers* 38(3): 276–89.

Woodhams, C. and Lupton, B. (2006) 'Gender-based equal opportunities policy and practice in small firms: the impact of HR professionals', *Human Resource Management Journal* 16(1): 74–97.

Woodward, J. (1980) *Industrial Organization: Theory and Practice*, 2nd edn, Oxford University Press.

Wright, M. and Storey, J. (1994) 'Recruitment', in I. Beardwell and L. Holden (eds) *Human Resource Management*, Pitman.

Wright, P.C. and Bean, S.A. (1993) 'Sexual harassment: an issue of employee effectiveness', *Journal of Managerial Psychology* 8(2): 306.

Wright, P.M. and Snell, S.A. (1998) 'Toward a unifying framework for exploring fit and flexibility in strategic human resource management', *Academy of Management Review* 23(4): 756–72.

WTO (2006) *Trade Picks up in Mid-2005, but 2006 Picture is Uncertain*, Press Release, 11 April, World Trade Organization.

Yang, I. (2005) 'Group leadership in Korea', *The Business Review* 4(2): 73–9.

Yaniv, E. and Farkas, F. (2005) 'The impact of person–organization fit on the corporate brand perception of employees and of customers', *Journal of Change Management* 5(4): 447–61.

Zablow, R.J. (2006) 'Creating and sustaining an ethical workplace', *Risk Management* 53(9): 26–9.

Zickar, M.J., Gibby, R.E. and Robie, C. (2004) 'Uncovering faking samples in applicant, incumbent and experimental data sets: an application of mixed-model item response theory', *Organizational Research Methods* 7(2): 168.

Index